D0050621

THE NORTON BOOK OF
NATURE WRITING

THE NORTON BOOK OF NATURE WRITING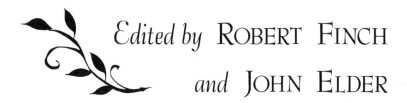

Edited by ROBERT FINCH
and JOHN ELDER

W · W · NORTON & COMPANY · NEW YORK · LONDON

The text of this book is composed in Avanta,
with display type set in Bernhard Modern.
Composition and manufacturing by The Haddon Craftsmen, Inc.
Book design by Antonina Krass.

First Edition

Library of Congress Cataloging-in-Publication Data

The Norton book of nature writing/edited by Robert Finch and John
Elder.—1st ed.
        p. cm.
        1. Natural history. 2. Natural history literature. I. Finch,
Robert, 1943–. II. Elder, John, 1947–.
QH81.N67 1990
508—dc20   89-35531

ISBN 0-393-02799-6

W. W. Norton & Company, Inc., 500 Fifth Avenue, New York, N. Y. 10110
W. W. Norton & Company Ltd., 37 Great Russell Street, London WC1B 3NU
1 2 3 4 5 6 7 8 9 0

810493

CONTENTS

Shall I not have intelligence with the earth? Am I not partly leaves and vegetable mould myself?

—Henry David Thoreau, *Walden*

It is interesting to contemplate a tangled bank, clothed with many plants of many kinds, with birds singing on the bushes, with various insects flitting about, and with worms crawling through the damp earth, and to reflect that these elaborately constructed forms, so different from each other and dependent upon each other in so complex a manner, have all been produced by laws acting around us.

—Charles Darwin, *On the Origin of Species*

ACKNOWLEDGMENTS

Even within the bounds of language and form which we set for this collection, the terrain of nature writing is a vast and only partially mapped one. We feel most grateful to the friends, nature writers, and scholars who offered their guidance as we steered toward a table of contents that would be comprehensive, well balanced, and of high literary quality.

The following individuals suggested authors and selections, read and critiqued our preliminary lists, or shared their bibliographies of nature writing with us: Harriet Chessman, Walter Clark, Annie Dillard, Betsy Hilbert, John Hay, Edward Hoagland, Barry Lopez, Tom Lyon, Kenneth Myers, Aina Niemela, Marge Piercy, Terry Plum, Robert Richardson, George Russell, Scott Sanders, John Tallmadge, Stephen Trimble, Bryan Wolf, and Ann Zwinger. While none of them bears responsibility for any inclusions or omissions here, the book is without doubt a fuller and more interesting one because of their generous help.

Several previous and current anthologies were useful in calling our attention to authors and essays we might otherwise have missed. We want to acknowledge the particular value to us of these editors and collections: William Beebe, *The Book of Naturalists* (New York: Knopf, 1944); Frank Bergon, *The Wilderness Reader* (New York: New American Library, 1980); Daniel Halpern, *On Nature* (San Francisco: North Point, 1987); E.D.H. Johnson, *The Poetry of Earth* (New York: Atheneum, 1974); John Kiernan, *Treasury of Great Nature Writing* (New York: Doubleday, 1957); Joseph Wood Krutch, *Great American Nature Writing* (New York: William Sloane, 1950); Thomas J. Lyon, *This Incomperable Lande* (Boston: Houghton Mifflin, 1988); Scott Russell Sanders, *Audubon Reader: The Best Writings of John James Audubon* (Bloomington: Indiana University Press, 1986); and Odell Shepard, *The Best of W. H. Hudson* (New York: Dutton, 1949).

We owe a special debt to Robert Pack, who recognized in us kindred spirits and first brought us together at the Bread Loaf Writers' Conference. Jim Mairs at Norton initiated and supported this book; we owe much to him and Eve Picower for their editorial enthusiasm and constructive energy on behalf of the project. We were significantly aided in the compilation of such a large body of material by the resources and the patient cooperation of the staff at Middlebury College and the Cape Cod Museum of Natural History. Finally, we want to express our appreciation to Beth Finch and Rita Elder for their discriminating interest throughout.

—R.F.
J.E.

INTRODUCTION

Nature writing, as a recognizable and distinct tradition in English prose, has existed for over two hundred years. During this time it has engaged the imagination and talents of major literary figures on both sides of the Atlantic, produced works of worldwide influence, and achieved a broad and enthusiastic readership. Since World War II the genre has become an increasingly significant and popular one, producing some of the finest nonfiction prose of our time. Yet too often it continues to be identified with or limited to landscape descriptions, accounts of animal behavior, or treatises on "environmental issues," rather than being acknowledged as a literary form in its own right. This anthology is intended to suggest the broad range of nature writing in English and to indicate the rich tradition within which contemporary writers are working.

Nature writers are the children of Linnaeus. Beginning with his *Systema Naturae* (1735) and elaborating on that general system in such volumes as *Species Plantarum* (1753), Linnaeus introduced a framework within which all living things could be classified and identified. Throughout the second half of the eighteenth century and into the nineteenth, parsons, poets, ladies and gentlemen of leisure in England, explorers and collectors in the wilds of America, all carried their copies of Linnaeus.

We open this collection of nature writing with Gilbert White, one of Linnaeus's early English disciples. *A Natural History of Selborne*, first published in 1789, has exerted a profound and lasting influence on nature writers. Darwin may have taken along the first volume of Charles Lyell's *Principles of Geology* when he shipped on the *HMS Beagle*, but he also found space in his luggage for White. Thoreau's shelf of books at Walden was a short one, but there too *A Natural History of Selborne* was included.

While nature has been the subject of imaginative literature in every country and in every age, nature writing in prose has achieved a unique fullness and continuity within the Anglo-American context. Certain historical facts have contributed to this flourishing tradition. When the gospel according to Linnaeus began to be propagated worldwide, there was already a rich English literature of naturalist theology. Writers like John Ray, in such books as *The Wisdom of God manifested in the Works of Creation* (1691), found in nature a confirmation of their faith. The eighteenth century also saw English empire and industry beginning to produce a large class with the education and leisure to pursue their "natural curiosity." Similarly, the early prominence of nature writing in America is associated with the exploration of a diverse, abundant continent. Naturalists were commissioned, first by amateurs and institutions in Britain and then by the fledgling American government, to travel, draw maps, keep lists, and ship specimens. The cultural climate and the natural environment were thus both auspicious for the burgeoning of a genre of nature writing in English. But in this literary form, as in all others, books are also propagated by previous books. And in ways much more characteristic and specific than the broad trends just mentioned, the tradition represented in this anthology grows out of the entrancing letters of Gilbert White.

In his book *Nature's Economy: The Roots of Ecology,* Donald Worster points to one constant element in nature writing from Gilbert White to the present: "The rise of the natural history essay in the latter half of the nineteenth century was an essential legacy of the Selborne Cult. It was more than a scientific-literary genre modeled after White's pioneering achievement. A constant theme of the nature essayists was the search for a lost pastoral haven, for a home in an inhospitable and threatening world." In Worster's view, subsequent writers like John Burroughs, John Muir, W.H. Hudson, and Richard Jefferies all develop, as White did, models of human life integrated into a beloved landscape. They provide their readers with an antidote to industrialism and urbanization and an alternative to "cold science—not by a retreat into unexamined dogmatism, but by restoring to scientific inquiry some of the warmth, breadth and piety which had been infused into it by the departed parson-naturalist."

The word "pastoral" indicates one useful angle to follow into *A Natural History of Selborne,* as it does into nature writing in general. White was the pastor of Selborne, that Southhampton parish of seven hundred souls into which he had been born. When, in his book's "advertisement," he refers to it as a work of "parochial history," he conveys a proprietary tone that often colors nature writers' descriptions of their chosen or ultimate landscapes—from Thoreau's Concord to Muir's Sierra to Abbey's Arches National Monument. Beyond this parochial dimension, however, "pastoral" relates nature writing to the literary tradition stemming from Theocritus's *Idylls* and Virgil's *Eclogues.* White frequently quotes from Virgil, never more charmingly than when, in his Letter XXXVIII to Daines Barrington, he tests an echo with the *Eclogues'* first line: "Tityre, tu patulae recubans . . ." Reclining under a shady tree, piping and singing love songs, the figure of Tityrus defines the pastoral posture of *otium,* or leisure. But the First Eclogue as a whole makes it clear that such an experience of "the golden age" is always individual and momentary, and that it is always ironically enfolded in a world of cities, labor, and war. It is, explicitly, a fortunate, temporary escape.

Nature writing, on the model of *Selborne,* often depicts a sort of golden age. White's book evokes days of hunting for echoes, nights of testing the hoots of owls with pitch-pipes. This English leisure is more active than Roman *otium,* though. White is always walking around looking and poking into things, less like Tityrus under his beech tree than like Winnie the Pooh strolling into the morning: "Well, he was humming this hum to himself, and walking along gaily, wondering what everybody else was doing, and what it felt like being someone else, when suddenly he came to a sandy bank, and in the bank was a large hole. 'Aha!' said Pooh. *(Rum-tum-tiddle-um-tum)."* There is, in fact, an important element of play in much nature writing. One thinks, for instance, of Emerson playing his "ice harp" at Walden Pond or Farley Mowat investigating the diet of wolves by devising his own recipes for Creamed Arctic Mouse. It is as if playing in a landscape were as important as exploring it, or rather, as if the two become one activity in which we rediscover our wholeness as beings in nature.

We enjoy an escapist impulse in certain nature writing, as we do in pastoral poetry and in English children's books by authors like A.A. Milne, Kenneth Grahame, and Beatrix Potter. Escape, first and foremost, from the world of specialized and alienating work. In identifying the period from 1770 to 1880 as "The Golden Age of English Natural History," E.D.H. Johnson emphasized that it was a time when original and important scientific work could be accomplished by classically educated *amateurs.* Gilbert White's letters show us an amateur scientist carrying out original research, in the open air, that is indistinguishable from recreation. We look back at such a life with nostalgia from the divided vantage of C.P. Snow's "two cultures."

If the idyllic flavor of adventures in nature lingers in some writers today, however, the confident and self-contained nature of White's science no longer remains available. Charles Lyell, Darwin, and Alfred Russel Wallace gave a dizzying spin to the static hierarchies of Linnaeus.

The dynamism and vastly magnified time-frame of the new biology and geology left behind the earlier system, with its tidy, fixed categories. A new era of worldwide biological exploration had also begun, inspired by the South American voyages of Alexander von Humboldt from 1799 to 1804. European scientists were especially staggered by the enormous array of species in the tropics, and the Linnaean system began to look increasingly like an antique stamp album, charming but inadequate.

Darwin himself shared White's classical background, as is reflected in his allusive prose style. But the 1859 publication of *Origin of Species* stimulated research in the life-sciences so powerfully that a much higher degree of professionalism and specialization soon developed. As researchers tried to cope with the flood of knowledge, a new protocol of expression developed which was quite different from Darwin's own humane, accessible style. A white-coated, passive, impersonal style became the established voice of "objective science."

In the post-Darwinian world, the older term "natural history" has often been defiantly embraced by nature writers as they respond to the physical creation in ways that, while scientifically informed, are also marked by a personal voice and a concern for literary values. Even if nature writers have often resisted the model of impersonal and specialized science, though, it is also important to note how many of them have been influenced by its concepts, from genetics to molecular biology, from plate tectonics to quantum physics, from population ecology to cognitive theory. No idea has been more influential and inspiring than the grand spectacle of evolution. The selections here by Loren Eiseley, Annie Dillard, and David Rains Wallace, for instance, illustrate how contemporary writers have responded thoughtfully and lyrically to the metaphysical and mythic implications of an evolutionary vision of creation.

Gilbert White established the pastoral dimension of nature writing in the late eighteenth century and remains the patron saint of English nature writing. Henry David Thoreau was an equally crucial figure in mid-nineteenth century America and occupies a similar niche in our country's literary hagiography. The fact that Thoreau is more fully represented in this collection than any other writer reflects our sense that he both touches the genre's roots and anticipates its flowering in this century. In his journals and books he evokes an outwardly quiet life, like White's, of gathered attentiveness to the earth. Walden Pond, no less than Selborne, has been a site of pilgrimage by readers wanting to find an antidote to their own "lives of quiet desperation." Like White, too, Thoreau is deliberately and fiercely parochial and an extraordinarily gifted observer of natural details.

On several important levels, though, this American solitary diverges from his English forerunner. Whereas White conveys a sense of being unconsciously a part of the natural order he beheld, Thoreau brings an ironic awareness to his nature writing, continually recognizing in his wry style that by focusing on nonhuman nature we objectify and abstract it. He acknowledges the advantages of a woodcutter's unlettered response to the woods, and dramatizes the conflicts between his own reverence for "higher laws" and his desire to eat a woodchuck raw. Thoreau's supremely self-conscious style has kept him continuously available to readers who no longer draw a confident distinction between humanity and the rest of the world, and who would find a simpler worship of nature both archaic and incredible.

Another significant way in which Thoreau anticipates contemporary nature writing is in his recognition that the natural environment must be protected. Readers of White have remarked that, though he lived through the American and French Revolutions, as well as the first wave of industrialization in England, none of those events comes into his letters. Moreover, as Mark Daniel noted in his 1983 selection, *The Essential Gilbert White of Selborne*: "White had no sense of responsibility to something called 'nature.'" By contrast Thoreau constantly reflects about such modern incursions into the landscape as the railroad that ran near his cabin at Walden Pond, and in *The Maine Woods* he calls for actions to preserve our great forests from devastation. Because he knows personally and experimentally that "in wildness is the preservation of the world," he searches single-mindedly for ways in which both literature and society might become more integrally "wild."

The second half of the nineteenth century saw the origins of what we today call the environmental movement. Two of its most influential American voices were John Muir and John Burroughs, literary sons of Thoreau, though hardly twins. Muir led the fight to preserve wilderness with his *Century* articles about Yosemite and Hetch Hetchy, as well as with his founding of the Sierra Club. Burroughs popularized the study of local nature with his many volumes of "ramble" essays, and brought political and economic muscle into the conservation movement by befriending such influential figures as Theodore Roosevelt and Harvey Firestone. W.H. Hudson, writing in England, was a major force in the protection of endangered bird populations, and the rural essays of Richard Jefferies helped create an aesthetic foundation for the landscape preservation work of the National Trust.

In the early twentieth century the activist voice and prophetic anger of nature writers who saw, in Muir's words, that "the money changers were in the temple" continued to grow. Building upon the principles of scientific ecology that were being developed in the 1930s and 1940s,

Rachel Carson and Aldo Leopold sought to create a literature in which appreciation of nature's wholeness would lead to ethical principles and social programs.

Today, nature writing in America flourishes as never before. Nonfiction may well be the most vital form of current American literature, and a notable proportion of the best writers of nonfiction practice nature writing. The generous selection of contemporary writers in this anthology reflects not only the impressive flowering of the genre in recent decades, but also its extraordinary range of voice and achievement. It has attracted poets such as John Hay, Wendell Berry, and John Haines, novelists like John Updike, Peter Matthiessen, John Fowles, and Ursula K. Le Guin, as well as such preeminent contemporary essayists as Annie Dillard, Edward Hoagland, John McPhee, and Barry Lopez. On the other hand some of its most notable practitioners have been professional scientists in their own right. Writers like Rachel Carson, Loren Eiseley, Lewis Thomas, Chet Raymo, and E.O. Wilson have, in their literary essays, imbued their respective fields of marine biology, anthropology, cellular biology, astronomy, and sociobiology with humanistic concerns and poetic resonance. Writers from such diverse regions of the humanities and the sciences find common ground in the older and more generalized field of natural history, which, as John Fowles puts it, assumed "that it [was] being presented by an entire human being, with all his complexities, to an audience of other entire human beings."

One common element in so diverse a company of writers is suggested by Thoreau's term "excursions." Contemporary nature writers characteristically take walks through landscapes of associations. Beginning with a closely observed phenomenon, they reflect upon its personal meaning for them. Or, beginning with an argumentative point of view, they venture out into a natural setting that has no vested interest in their opinions and that contradicts or distracts as often as it confirms. In an age that has learned that any theory is subject to almost constant revision, a hallmark of the modern nature essay is its insistent open-endedness.

This process of association often reminds nature writers of other texts as well as other landscapes. Like poets and novelists, they are frequently both inspired by and critical of their predecessors and contemporaries. W.H. Hudson's respectful rebuttal to Melville's "The Whiteness of the Whale" or Henry Beston's homage to "the obstinate and unique genius of Thoreau" or Edward Abbey's remarks on virtually any other writer all provide examples of the ambivalent esteem nature writers have inspired in one another.

To a distinctive degree, nature writing fulfills the essay's purpose of *connection*. It fuses literature's attention to style, form, and the inevitable ironies of expression with a scientific concern for palpable fact. In a time when the natural context of fiction has been attenuated and when much literary theory discovers nothing to read but constructs of self-reflexive language, nature writing asserts both the humane value of literature and the importance to a mature individual's relationship with the world of understanding fundamental physical and biological processes. Alfred North Whitehead called for just such a balance in this eloquent passage from *Science and the Modern World:* "What is wanted is an appreciation of the infinite variety of vivid values achieved by an organism in its proper environment. When you understand all about the sun and all about the atmosphere and all about the rotation of the earth, you may still miss the radiance of the sunset. There is no substitute for the direct perception of the concrete achievement of a thing in its actuality. We want concrete fact with a high light thrown upon what is relevant to its preciousness."

We should include a few remarks about how we chose the selections in this anthology. Our primary aim was to represent, as fully as possible, the range of nature writing in English over the past two centuries. It was particularly important, we felt, to place before American readers the rich and continuing tradition of British nature writing. This tradition often reflects a significantly different sense of landscape and the role of people in it than does its American counterpart, but it also feeds into and enriches the latter.

For the sake of more clearly defining the genre, we have as a rule restricted our selections to nonfiction prose, recognizing, however, that genres do not exist in isolation anymore than writers do. For that matter, in its imaginative cast, nature writing often seems to bear more resemblance to lyric poetry than it does to many other forms of essay writing. It is no accident that the prose works of Coleridge, John Clare, Whitman, Hopkins, and Edward Thomas find a place here.

Landscape and natural settings have also been central elements in the great tradition of both British and American novelists. With writers like Emily Brontë, Thomas Hardy, D.H. Lawrence, Mark Twain, Willa Cather, and William Faulkner, the natural presence often assumes the importance of a major character. Moreover, the work of these and other novelists has strongly influenced many nature writers. Still, the purposes of fiction differ sufficiently from those of nonfiction that, with a few unabashed exceptions, we have chosen to exclude excerpts from novels. The major exception, of course, is *Moby-Dick.* One could argue that much of this archetypal American novel qualifies as nonfiction, and no less a nature writer than Annie Dillard has called it "the best book ever written about nature." But even without arguing its generic status, it seemed clear to us that no representation of nature writing in America would be complete without taking into account Melville and his leviathan.

By restricting our selections to original works in English, we have inevitably excluded such notable literary naturalists as Maurice Maeterlinck, Karl von Frisch, Mikhail Prishvin, and Konrad Lorenz. Here again, however, we have made one important exception: the famous description of the mating habits of the praying mantis by French entomologist Jean Henri Fabre. Not only has Fabre's work, and this essay in particular, had a strong influence on contemporary American nature writers, but the English translation by Alexander Teixeira de Mattos has achieved a classic status of its own.

One thing that struck us in gathering readings for this book was that, although the figure and experience of the Native American come into much early American nature writing, examples of nature writing by Indians in English have not often been available until our day. This is obviously in part a linguistic matter: we have mainly the Victorian translations of a few formal speeches. But it may also reflect the fact that a certain kind of intense and self-conscious awareness of nature follows from a loss of integration between society and nature. Today, through Native American writers like Scott Momaday and Leslie Marmon Silko, as well as through non-Indian writers like Richard Nelson and Gary Nabhan who are seeking to understand the Indian way of knowing the earth, this voice flows into and amplifies the tradition.

The personal element—that is, the filtering of experience through an individual sensibility—is central to what we view as the nature writing tradition. For this reason we have not included selections from a whole line of fine scientific essayists from Thomas Huxley to Stephen Jay Gould, though the ties between the two traditions are strong and significant. On the other hand, we have tried to convey a broader notion of what constitutes "nature" and nature writing by bringing in such nonmainstream examples as Thomas Merton's essay on the teleological connotations of an autumn rainstorm, a chapter from Vicki Hearne's book on the philosophical implications of training animals, and Richard Selzer's treatment of the human body as a landscape.

Though we hope to illuminate a tradition and showcase a genre, we have included no selection simply because it is representative of a particular current or period of nature writing. What finally matters is the vitality of the material itself. Is it a good read? Does each piece, whether old or new, convey a literary power and a character of its own for the contemporary reader? Reflecting our belief that our own time is seeing a remarkable richness in this field, nearly half of the selections are from works published after 1945.

Despite the generous space afforded us by our publisher, we were forced to leave out much we would have liked to include. One unavoidable fact is that some good writers simply do not write, or cannot be adequately represented, in anthologizable dimensions (as Dickens and George Eliot, say, rarely get into English literature anthologies). It also goes without saying that the selections inevitably represent the editors' personal tastes and predilections. But more than that, each age finds its own tastes and needs. Readers will find some familiar names missing; others, once immensely popular, seem to speak to us less strongly today. The anthologist builds in part on previous anthologies, revising, adding, weeding out, recognizing that these new choices, even if right for his or her time, will likewise be revised in turn. To borrow an analogy from the natural sciences: an anthology is somewhat like a landscape at a given moment. It may have a pleasing shape, an authority and a seeming stability. But it remains subject to such processes as erosion and uplift, deposition and depression—even sudden, wholesale shifts of ground. Some new features are brought into being with each new age, only perhaps to disappear in the next. Meanwhile the process as a whole remains vital and dynamic. What is strong endures, what is good shines.

After many months of comparing and sorting our enthusiasms, we sifted through our shopping bags of Xeroxed material to see what we had. What emerged was not so much the prominence of certain recurring ideas and themes, or even patterns of emotions and attitudes evoked by a contemplation of what Thoreau calls "the unhandseled globe." Rather, we were reminded of the English biologist J.S.B. Haldane's remark when asked what he could say about the personality of God on the basis of his evolutionary studies. He replied that the Creator seems to have had "an inordinate fondness for beetles."

Reading this anthology, one might reach the conclusion that nature writers have an inordinate fondness for snakes, turtles, rivers, farm fields, the moon, night, rain, spring, sex, ants, and the nasty habits of insects in general. Birds, on the other hand, though well-represented, are not as prevalent as one might have expected, and fish are virtually ignored. Some geographical areas—the Rocky Mountains, the deserts of the American Southwest, East Africa, the south of England, Cape Cod— receive much attention. Others, such as the Southeastern states (with the important exception of William Bartram's *Travels*) are inexplicably under-represented, and still others, Antarctica for instance, have yet to find their celebrants. Such disparities may, of course, be simply a matter of editorial bias and of historical and cultural circumstance. On the other hand, one is tempted to ask if there may be organisms and locales for which the naturalist imagination has innate affinities. As Barry Lopez speculates when observing the lack of narwhals in Eskimo mythology, are there some animals that are "good to imagine" and others that are not? Or as E.O. Wilson asks in his book *Biophilia*, do human beings instinctively gravitate toward a certain kind of landscape—what he calls "the right place"?

There are certain subjects and ideas which seem to recur persistently, attracting writers of very different temperaments. The ethics of hunting, for instance, are examined in some of the very earliest encounters of Europeans with the enormous herds of mammals on the Great Plains, and the moral implications of taking or exploiting the life of other creatures remains the central topic in many contemporary essays. Evolution has become a nearly universally accepted intellectual principle; yet, as many of these selections illustrate, it contains philosophical, ethical, and social implications with which we have not yet come to terms. Nature's ability to provide relief or solace from human grief has been a constant theme of nature writers. Yet that ability has been called increasingly into question in an age when human activity seems to threaten the planet's basic life-support systems and every landscape is, in Terrence Des Pres's phrase, part of a "nuclear grid." Finally, the recognition of valid alternative conceptions of nature in other cultures has led to a series of provocative inquiries: How does the human mind make sense of nature? How does human meaning in general derive from natural phenomena? And what, ultimately, constitutes the perennial attraction of and need for things natural in our lives?

In the end, however, all of these selections seem to share a larger fundamental intent. In the two centuries since the publication of *A Natural History of Selborne,* nature writers have undertaken excursions away from the dominant literary and scientific models, returning with their testimony about how human beings respond to what is nonhuman, and how individuals and society may achieve more significant and rewarding integration with the earth that sustains them. All literature, by illuminating the full nature of human existence, asks a single question: how shall we live? In our age that question has taken its most urgent form in relation to the natural environment. Because it has never been more necessary, the voice of nature writing has never been stronger than it is today.

John Elder
Robert Finch

THE NORTON BOOK OF
NATURE WRITING

GILBERT WHITE
1720-1793

The Natural History and Antiquities of Selborne *(1789) presents the letters written by a country curate to two fellow-naturalists in other parts of England. Gilbert White's reports, speculations, and queries add up to an engaging self-portrait of a man who delighted in the natural surroundings of the village where he was born, where he served as a priest, and where he eventually died. White's duties in the parish, which his father had served as a priest before him, seem to have left him plenty of time to observe martins, take long daily walks, and correspond with Thomas Pennant and Daines Barrington about "natural curiosities." His remarkable powers of observation and analysis lend vividness to White's letters. As he contemplated the role of earthworms in working the soil, observed the daily habits of his resident tortoise Timothy, or described with precision the aerial mating of swifts, he drew attention to patterns in nature which no one before him had discerned so sharply. He delightfully typified the ideal of amateur science—approaching the physical creation in a playful spirit and making original, substantial contributions to knowledge.*

From The Natural History and Antiquities of Selborne

LETTERS TO THOMAS PENNANT, ESQUIRE

LETTER II

[the Raven-tree]

* * * In the centre of this grove there stood an oak, which, though shapely and tall on the whole, bulged out into a large excrescence about the middle of the stem. On this a pair of ravens had fixed their residence for such a series of years, that the oak was distinguished by the title of the Raven-tree. Many were the attempts of the neighbouring youths to get at this eyry: the difficulty whetted their inclinations, and each was ambitious of surmounting the arduous task. But, when they arrived at the swelling, it jutted out so in their way, and was so far beyond their grasp, that the most daring lads were awed, and acknowledged the undertaking to be too hazardous. So the ravens built on, nest upon nest, in perfect security, till the fatal day arrived in which the wood was to be levelled. It was in the month of February, when those birds usually sit. The saw was applied to the butt, the wedges were inserted into the opening, the woods echoed to the heavy blows of the beetle or mallet, the tree nodded to its fall; but still the dam sat on. At last, when it gave way, the bird was flung from her nest; and, though her parental affection deserved a better fate, was whipped down by the twigs, which brought her dead to the ground.

LETTER VIII

[natural economy]

* * * A circumstance respecting these ponds, though by no means peculiar to them, I cannot pass over in silence; and that is, that instinct by which in summer all the kine, whether oxen, cows, calves, or heifers, retire constantly to the water during the hotter hours; where, being more exempt from flies, and inhaling the coolness of that element, some belly deep, and some only to mid-leg, they ruminate and solace themselves from about ten in the morning till four in the afternoon, and then return to their feeding. During this great proportion of the day they drop much dung, in which insects nestle; and so supply food for the fish, which

The Natural History and Antiquities of Selborne (London: B. White and Son, 1789).

would be poorly subsisted but from this contingency. Thus nature, who is a great economist, converts the recreation of one animal to the support of another!

LETTER XXVII

[hedge-hogs and field-fares]

Selborne, Feb. 22, 1770.

Dear Sir,

Hedge-hogs abound in my gardens and fields. The manner in which they eat their roots of the plantain in my grass-walks is very curious: with their upper mandible, which is much longer than their lower, they bore under the plant, and so eat the root off upwards, leaving the tuft of leaves untouched. In this respect they are serviceable, as they destroy a very troublesome weed; but they deface the walks in some measure by digging little round holes. It appears, by the dung that they drop upon the turf, that beetles are no inconsiderable part of their food. In June last I procured a litter of four or five young hedge-hogs, which appeared to be about five or six days old; they, I find, like puppies, are born blind, and could not see when they came to my hands. No doubt their spines are soft and flexible at the time of their birth, or else the poor dam would have but a bad time of it in the critical moment of parturition: but it is plain that they soon harden; for these little pigs had such stiff prickles on their backs and sides as would easily have fetched blood, had they not been handled with caution. Their spines are quite white at this age; and they have little hanging ears, which I do not remember to be discernible in the old ones. They can, in part, at this age draw their skin down over their faces; but are not able to contract themselves into a ball as they do, for the sake of defence, when full grown. The reason, I suppose, is, because the curious muscle that enables the creature to roll itself up into a ball was not then arrived at its full tone and firmness. Hedge-hogs make a deep and warm *hybernaculum* with leaves and moss, in which they conceal themselves for the winter: but I never could find that they stored in any winter provision, as some quadrupeds certainly do.

I have discovered an anecdote with respect to the field-fare *(turdus pilaris)*, which I think is particular enough: this bird, though it sits on trees in the day-time, and procures the greatest part of its food from white-thorn hedges; yea, moreover, builds on very high trees; as may be seen by the *Fauna Suecica;* yet always appears with us to roost on the ground. They are seen to come in flocks just before it is dark, and to settle and nestle among the heath on our forest. And besides, the larkers, in dragging their nets by night, frequently catch them in the wheat-stubbles; while the bat-fowlers, who take many redwings in the hedges, never entangle any of this species. Why these birds, in the matter of roosting, should differ from all their congeners, and from themselves also with respect to their proceedings by day, is a fact for which I am by no means able to account.

I have somewhat to inform you of concerning the moose-deer; but in general foreign animals fall seldom in my way; my little intelligence is confined to the narrow sphere of my own observations at home.

LETTERS TO THE HONORABLE DAINES BARRINGTON

LETTER VII

[*Timothy the tortoise*]

Ringmer, near Lewes, Oct. 8, 1770.

* * * A land tortoise, which has been kept for thirty years in a little walled court belonging to the house where I now am visiting, retires under ground about the middle of November, and comes forth again about the middle of April. When it first appears in the spring it discovers very little inclination towards food; but in the height of summer grows voracious: and then as the summer declines it's appetite declines; so that for the last six weeks in autumn it hardly eats at all. Milky plants, such as lettuces, dandelions, sowthistles, are it's favourite dish. In a neighbouring village one was kept till by tradition it was supposed to be an hundred years old. An instance of vast longevity in such a poor reptile!

LETTER XIII

[*Timothy digs in*]

April 12, 1772.

Dear Sir,

While I was in Sussex last autumn my residence was at the village near Lewes, from whence I had formerly the pleasure of writing to you. On the first of November I remarked that the old tortoise, formerly mentioned, began first to dig the ground in order to the forming it's hybernaculum, which it had fixed on just beside a great tuft of hepaticas. It scrapes out the ground with it's fore-feet, and throws it up over it's back with it's hind; but the motion of it's legs is ridiculously slow, little exceeding the hour-hand of a clock; and suitable to the composure of an animal said to be a whole month in performing one feat of copulation. Nothing can be more assiduous than this creature night and day in scooping the earth, and forcing it's great body into the cavity; but, as the noons of that season proved unusually warm and sunny, it was continually interrupted, and called forth by the heat in the middle of the day; and though I continued there till the thirteenth of November, yet the work remained unfinished. Harsher weather, and frosty mornings, would have quickened it's operations. No part of it's behaviour ever struck me more than the extreme timidity it always expresses with regard to rain; for though it has a shell that would secure it against the wheel of a loaded cart, yet does it discover as much solicitude about rain as a lady dressed in all her best attire, shuffling away on the first sprinklings, and running its head up in a corner. If attended to, it becomes an excellent weatherglass; for as sure as it walks elate, and as it were on tiptoe, feeding with great earnestness in a morning, so sure will it rain before night. It is totally a diurnal animal, and never pretends to stir after it becomes dark. The tortoise, like other reptiles, has an arbitrary stomach as well as lungs; and can refrain from eating as well as breathing for a great part of the year. When first awakened it eats nothing; nor again in the autumn before it retires: through the height of the summer it feeds voraciously, devouring all the food that comes in it's way. I was much taken with it's sagacity in discerning those that do it kind offices: for, as soon as the good old lady comes in sight who has waited on it for more than thirty years, it hobbles towards it's benefactress with aukward alacrity; but remains inattentive to strangers. Thus not only *"the ox knoweth his owner, and the ass his master's crib,"*[1] but the most abject reptile and torpid of beings distinguishes the hand that feeds it, and is touched with the feelings of gratitude!

I am, &c. &c.

P.S. In about three days after I left Sussex the tortoise retired into the ground under the hepatica.

LETTER XIV

[*parental instincts in birds*]

Selborne, March 26, 1773.

Dear Sir,
    The more I reflect on the στοργη [parental love] of animals, the more I am astonished at it's effects. Nor is the violence of this affection more wonderful than the shortness of it's duration. Thus every hen is in her turn the virago of the yard, in proportion to the helplessness of her

---

[1] *Isaiah i, 3.* [Gilbert White's note]

brood; and will fly in the face of a dog or a sow in defence of those chickens, which in a few weeks she will drive before her with relentless cruelty.

This affection sublimes the passions, quickens the invention, and sharpens the sagacity of the brute creation. Thus an hen, just become a mother, is no longer that placid bird she used to be, but with feathers standing on end, wings hovering, and clocking note, she runs about like one possessed. Dams will throw themselves in the way of the greatest danger in order to avert it from their progeny. Thus a partridge will tumble along before a sportsman in order to draw away the dogs from her helpless covey. In the time of nidification the most feeble birds will assault the most rapacious. All the hirundines of a village are up in arms at the sight of an hawk, whom they will persecute till he leaves that district. A very exact observer has often remarked that a pair of ravens nesting in the rock of Gibraltar would suffer no vulture or eagle to rest near their station, but would drive them from the hill with an amazing fury: even the blue thrush at the season of breeding would dart out from the clefts of the rocks to chase away the kestril, or the sparrow-hawk. If you stand near the nest of a bird that has young, she will not be induced to betray them by an inadvertent fondness, but will wait about at a distance with meat in her mouth for an hour together.

Should I farther corroborate what I have advanced above by some anecdotes which I probably may have mentioned before in conversation, yet you will, I trust, pardon the repetition for the sake of the illustration.

The flycatcher of the *Zoology* (the *stoparola* of Ray) builds every year in the vines that grow on the walls of my house. A pair of these little birds had one year inadvertently placed their nest on a naked bough, perhaps in a shady time, not being aware of the inconvenience that followed. But an hot sunny season coming on before the brood was half fledged, the reflection of the wall became insupportable, and must inevitably have destroyed the tender young, had not affection suggested an expedient, and prompted the parent-birds to hover over the nest all the hotter hours, while with wings expanded, and mouths gaping for breath, they screened off the heat from their suffering offspring.

A farther instance I once saw of notable sagacity in a willowwren, which had built in a bank in my fields. This bird a friend and myself had observed as she sat in her nest; but were particularly careful not to disturb her, though we saw she eyed us with some degree of jealousy. Some days after as we passed that way we were desirous of remarking how this brood went on; but no nest could be found, till I happened to take up a large bundle of long green moss, as it were, carelessly thrown over the nest in order to dodge the eye of any impertinent intruder.

A still more remarkable mixture of sagacity and instinct occurred to me one day as my people were pulling off the lining of an hotbed, in order to add some fresh dung. From out of the side of this bed leaped an animal with great agility that made a most grotesque figure; nor was it without great difficulty that it could be taken; when it proved to be a large white-bellied field-mouse with three or four young clinging to her teats by their mouths and feet. It was amazing that the desultory and rapid motions of this dam should not oblige her litter to quit their hold, especially when it appeared that they were so young as to be both naked and blind!

To these instances of tender attachment, many more of which might be daily discovered by those that are studious of nature, may be opposed that rage of affection, that monstrous perversion of the στοργη [parental love], which induces some females of the brute creation to devour their young because their owners have handled them too freely, or removed them from place to place! Swine, and sometimes the more gentle race of dogs and cats, are guilty of this horrid and preposterous murder. When I hear now and then of an abandoned mother that destroys her offspring, I am not so much amazed; since reason perverted, and the bad passions let loose, are capable of any enormity: but why the parental feelings of brutes, that usually flow in one most uniform tenor, should sometimes be so extravagantly diverted, I leave to abler philosophers than myself to determine.

I am, etc.

LETTER XXI

[*swifts*]

Selborne, Sept. 28, 1774.

Dear Sir,

As the swift or black-martin is the largest of the British *hirundines,* so is it undoubtedly the latest comer. For I remember but one instance of its appearing before the last week in April: and in some of our late frosty, harsh springs, it has not been seen till the beginning of May. This species usually arrives in pairs.

The swift, like the sand-martin, is very defective in architecture, making no crust, or shell, for its nest; but forming it of dry grasses and feathers, very rudely and inartificially put together. With all my attention to these birds, I have never been able once to discover one in the act of collecting or carrying in materials: so that I have suspected (since their nests are exactly the same) that they sometimes usurp upon the house-sparrows, and expel them, as sparrows do the house and sand-martin; well remembering that I have seen them squabbling together at the entrance of their holes; and the sparrows up in arms, and much disconcerted at these intruders. And yet I am assured, by a nice observer in such matters, that they do collect feathers for their nests in Andalusia; and that he has shot them with such materials in their mouths.

Swifts, like sand-martins, carry on the business of nidification quite in the dark, in crannies of castles, and towers, and steeples, and upon the tops of the walls of churches under the roof; and therefore cannot be so narrowly watched as those species that build more openly: but, from what I could ever observe, they begin nesting about the middle of May; and I have remarked, from eggs taken, that they have sat hard by the ninth of June. In general they haunt tall buildings, churches, and steeples, and breed only in such: yet in this village some pairs frequent the lowest and meanest cottages, and educate their young under those thatched roofs. We remember but one instance where they breed out of buildings; and that is in the sides of a deep chalk-pit near the town of Odiham, in this county, where we have seen many pairs entering the crevices, and skimming and squeaking round the precipices.

As I have regarded these amusive birds with no small attention, if I should advance something new and peculiar with respect to them, and different from all other birds, I might perhaps be credited; especially as my assertion is the result of many years' exact observation. The fact that I would advance is, that swifts tread, or copulate, on the wing: and I would wish any nice observer, that is startled at this supposition, to use his own eyes, and I think he will soon be convinced. In another class of animals, viz., the insect, nothing is so common as to see the different species of many genera in conjunction as they fly. The swift is almost continually on the wing; and as it never settles on the ground, on trees, or roofs, would seldom find opportunity for amorous rites, was it not enabled to indulge them in the air. If any person would watch these birds of a fine morning in May, as they are sailing round at a great height from the ground, he would see, every now and then, one drop on the back of another, and both of them sink down together for many fathoms with a loud piercing shriek. This I take to be the juncture when the business of generation is carrying on.

As the swift eats, drinks, collects materials for its nest, and, as it seems, propagates on the wing; it appears to live more in the air than any other bird, and to perform all functions there save those of sleeping and incubation.

This *hirundo* differs widely from its congeners in laying invariably but two eggs at a time, which are milk-white, long, and peaked at the small end; whereas the other species lay at each brood from four to six. It is a most alert bird, rising very early, and retiring to roost very late; and is on the wing in the height of summer at least sixteen hours. In the longest days it does not withdraw to rest till a quarter before nine in the evening, being the latest of all day birds. Just before they retire whole groups of them assemble high in the air, and squeak, and shoot about with wonderful rapidity. But this bird is never so much alive as in sultry thundry weather, when it expresses great alacrity, and calls forth all its powers. In hot mornings several, getting together in little parties, dash round the steeples and churches, squeaking as they go in a very clamorous manner; these, by nice observers, are supposed to be males, serenading their sitting hens; and not without reason, since they seldom squeak till they come close to the walls or eaves, and since those within utter at the same time a little inward note of complacency.

When the hen has sat hard all day, she rushes forth just as it is almost dark, and stretches and relieves her weary limbs, and snatches a scanty meal for a few minutes, and then returns to her duty of incubation. Swifts, when wantonly and cruelly shot while they have young, discover a little lump of insects in their mouths, which they pouch and hold under their tongue. In general they feed in a much higher district than the other species; a proof that gnats and other insects do also abound to a considerable height in the air: they also range to vast distances; since locomotion is no labour to them, who are endowed with such wonderful powers of wing. Their powers seem to be in proportion to their levers; and their wings are longer in proportion than those of almost any other bird. When they mute, or ease themselves in flight, they raise their wings, and make them meet over their backs.

At some certain times in the summer I had remarked that swifts were hawking very low for hours together over pools and streams; and could not help inquiring into the object of their pursuit that induced them to descend so much below their usual range. After some trouble, I found that they were taking *phryganeæ, ephemeræ,* and *libellulæ* (cadew-flies, may-flies, and dragon-flies) that were just emerged out of their aurelia state. I then no longer wondered that they should be so willing to stoop for a prey that afforded them such plentiful and succulent nourishment.

They bring out their young about the middle or latter end of July: but as these never become perchers, nor, that ever I could discern, are fed on the wing by their dams, the coming forth of the young is not so notorious as in the other species.

On the thirtieth of last June I untiled the eaves of an house where many pairs build, and found in each nest only two squab naked *pulli:* on the eighth of July I repeated the same inquiry, and found they had made very little progress towards a fledged state, but were still naked and helpless. From whence we may conclude that birds whose way of life keeps them perpetually on the wing would not be able to quit their nest till the end of the month. Swallows and martins, that have numerous families, are continually feeding them every two or three minutes; while swifts, that have but two young to maintain, are much at their leisure, and do not attend on their nests for hours together.

Sometimes they pursue and strike at hawks that come in their way; but not with that vehemence and fury that swallows express on the same occasion. They are out all day long in wet days, feeding about, and disregarding still rain: from whence two things may be gathered; first, that many insects abide high in the air, even in rain; and next, that the feathers of these birds must be well preened to resist so much wet. Windy, and particularly windy weather with heavy showers, they dislike; and on such days withdraw, and are scarce ever seen.

There is a circumstance respecting the colour of swifts, which seems not to be unworthy our attention. When they arrive in the spring they are all over of a glossy, dark soot-colour, except their chins, which are white; but, by being all day long in the sun and air, they become quite weather-beaten and bleached before they depart, and yet they return glossy again in the spring. Now, if they pursue the sun into lower latitudes, as some suppose, in order to enjoy a perpetual summer, why do they not return bleached? Do they not rather perhaps retire to rest for a season, and at that juncture moult and change their feathers, since all other birds are known to moult soon after the season of breeding?

Swifts are very anomalous in many particulars, dissenting from all their congeners not only in the number of their young, but in breeding but once in a summer; whereas all the other British *hirundines* breed invariably twice. It is past all doubt that swifts can breed but once, since they withdraw in a short time after the flight of their young, and some time before their congeners bring out their second brood. We may here remark, that, as swifts breed but once in a summer, and only two at a time, and the other *hirundines* twice, the latter, who lay from four to six eggs, increase at an average five times as fast as the former.

But in nothing are swifts more singular than in their early retreat. They retire, as to the main body of them, by the tenth of August, and sometimes a few days sooner: and every straggler invariably withdraws by the twentieth, while their congeners, all of them, stay till the beginning of October; many of them all through that month, and some occasionally to the beginning of November. This early retreat is mysterious and wonderful, since that time is often the sweetest season in the year. But, what is more extraordinary, they begin to retire still earlier in the most southerly parts of Andalusia, where they can be no ways influenced by any defect of heat; or, as one might suppose, defect of food. Are they regulated in their motions with us by a failure of food, or by a propensity to moulting, or by a disposition to rest after so rapid a life, or by what? This is one of those incidents in natural history that not only baffles our searches, but almost eludes our guesses!

These *hirundines* never perch on trees or roofs, and so never congregate with their congeners. They are fearless while haunting their nesting places, and are not to be scared with a gun; and are often beaten down with poles and cudgels as they stoop to go under the eaves. Swifts are much infested with those pests to the genus called *hippoboscæ hirundinis;* and often wriggle and scratch themselves, in their flight, to get rid of that clinging annoyance.

Swifts are no songsters, and have only one harsh screaming note; yet there are ears to which it is not displeasing, from an aggreeable association of ideas, since that note never occurs but in the most lovely summer weather.

They never settle on the ground but through accident; and when down can hardly rise, on account of the shortness of their legs and the length of their wings: neither can they walk, but only crawl; but they have a strong grasp with their feet, by which they cling to walls. Their bodies being flat they can enter a very narrow crevice; and where they cannot pass on their bellies they will turn up edgewise.

The particular formation of the foot discriminates the swift from all British *hirundines;* and indeed from all other known birds, the *hirundo melba*, or great white-bellied swift of Gibraltar, excepted; for it is so disposed as to carry '*omnes quatuor digitos anticos*' all its four toes forward; besides, the least toe, which should be the back-toe, consists of one bone alone, and the other three only of two apiece. A construction most rare and peculiar, but nicely adapted to the purposes in which their feet are employed. This, and some peculiarities attending the nostrils and under mandible, have induced a discerning naturalist to suppose that this species might constitute a *genus per se.*

In London a party of swifts frequents the Tower, playing and feeding over the river just below the bridge; others haunt some of the churches of the Borough next the fields; but do not venture, like the house-martin, into the close crowded part of the town.

The Swedes have bestowed a very pertinent name on this swallow, calling it *ring swala*, from the perpetual rings or circles that it takes round the scene of its nidification.

Swifts feed on *coleoptera*, or small beetles with hard cases over their wings, as well as on the softer insects; but it does not appear how they can procure gravel to grind their food, as swallows do, since they never settle on the ground. Young ones, over-run with *hippoboscæ*, are sometimes found, under their nests, fallen to the ground: the number of vermin rendering their abode insupportable any longer. They frequent in this village several abject cottages: yet a succession still haunts the same unlikely roofs: a good proof this that the same birds return to the same spots. As they must stoop very low to get up under these humble eaves, cats lie in wait, and sometimes catch them on the wing.

On the fifth of July, 1775, I again untiled part of a roof over the nest of a swift. The dam sat in the nest; but so strongly was she affected by natural στοργη [parental love] for her brood, which she supposed to be in danger, that, regardless of her own safety, she would not stir, but lay sullenly by them, permitting herself to be taken in hand. The squab young we brought down and placed on the grass-plot, where they tumbled about, and were as helpless as a new-born child. While we contemplated their naked bodies, their unwieldy disproportioned *abdomina*, and their heads, too heavy for their necks to support, we could not but wonder when we reflected that these shiftless beings in a little more than a fortnight would be able to dash through the air almost with the inconceivable swiftness of a meteor; and perhaps, in their emigration must traverse vast continents and oceans as distant as the equator. So soon does nature advance small birds to their ηλικια [full development], or state of perfection; while the progressive growth of men and large quadrupeds is slow and tedious!

I am, etc.

LETTER XXVII

[the bee-boy]

Selborne, Dec. 12, 1775.

Dear Sir,

We had in this village more than twenty years ago an idiot-boy, whom I well remember, who, from a child, shewed a strong propensity to bees; they were his food, his amusement, his sole object. And as people of this cast have seldom more than one point in view, so this lad exerted all his few faculties on this one pursuit. In the winter he dosed away his time, within his father's house, by the fire side, in a kind of torpid state, seldom departing from the chimney-corner; but in the summer he was all alert, and in quest of his game in the fields, and on sunny banks. Honey-bees, humble-bees, and wasps, were his prey wherever he found them: he had no apprehensions from their stings, but would seize them *nudis manibus,* and at once disarm them of their weapons, and suck their bodies for the sake of their honey-bags. Sometimes he would fill his bosom between his shirt and his skin with a number of these captives; and sometimes would confine them in bottles. He was a very *merops apiaster, or beebird;* and very injurious to men that kept bees; for he would slide into their bee-gardens, and, sitting down before the stools, would rap with his fingers on the hives, and so take the bees as they came out. He has been known to overturn hives for the sake of honey, of which he was passionately fond. Where metheglin was making he would linger round the tubs and vessels, begging a draught of what he called *bee-wine.* As he ran about he used to make a humming noise with his lips, resembling the buzzing of bees. This lad was lean and sallow, and of a cadaverous complexion; and, except in his favourite pursuit, in which he was wonderfully adroit, discovered no manner of understanding. Had his capacity been better, and directed to the same object, he had perhaps abated much of our wonder at the feats of a more modern exhibiter of bees: and we may justly say of him now,

> ——————————— Thou,
> Had thy presiding star propitious shone,
> Should'st Wildman[1] be ————.

When a tall youth he was removed from hence to a distant village, where he died, as I understand, before he arrived at manhood.

I am, &c.

LETTER XXXI

[a pregnant viper]

Selborne, April 29, 1776.

Dear Sir,
On August the 4th, 1775, we surprised a large viper, which seemed very heavy and bloated, as it lay in the grass basking in the sun. When we came to cut it up, we found that the abdomen was crowded with young, fifteen in number; the shortest of which measured full seven inches, and were about the size of full-grown earth-worms. This little fry issued into

[1]Author of *A Treatise on the Management of Bees,* 1768.

the world with the true viper-spirit about them, shewing great alertness as soon as disengaged from the belly of the dam: they twisted and wriggled about, and set themselves up, and gaped very wide when touched with a stick, shewing manifest tokens of menace and defiance, though as yet they had no manner of fangs that we could find, even with the help of our glasses.

To a thinking mind nothing is more wonderful than that early instinct which impresses young animals with the notion of the situation of their natural weapons, and of using them properly in their own defence, even before those weapons subsist or are formed. Thus a young cock will spar at his adversary before his spurs are grown; and a calf or a lamb will push with their heads before their horns are sprouted. In the same manner did these young adders attempt to bite before their fangs were in being. The dam however was furnished with very formidable ones, which we lifted up (for they fold down when not used) and cut them off with the point of our scissars.

There was little room to suppose that this brood had ever been in the open air before; and that they were taken in for refuge, at the mouth of the dam, when she perceived that danger was approaching; because then probably we should have found them somewhere in the neck, and not in the abdomen.

LETTER XXXV

[*earthworms*]

Selborne, May 20, 1777.

Dear Sir,

Lands that are subject to frequent inundations are always poor; and probably the reason may be because the worms are drowned. The most insignificant insects and reptiles are of much more consequence, and have much more influence in the economy of nature, than the incurious are aware of; and are mighty in their effect, from their minuteness, which renders them less an object of attention; and from their numbers and fecundity. Earth-worms, though in appearance a small and despicable link in the chain of nature, yet, if lost, would make a lamentable chasm. For, to say nothing of half the birds, and some quadrupeds, which are almost entirely supported by them, worms seem to be the great promoters of vegetation, which would proceed but lamely without them, by boring, perforating, and loosening the soil, and rendering it pervious to rains and the fibres of plants, by drawing straws and stalks of leaves and twigs into it; and, most of all, by throwing up such infinite numbers of lumps of earth called worm-casts, which, being their excrement, is a fine manure for grain and grass. Worms probably provide new soil for hills and slopes where the rain washes the earth away; and they affect slopes, probably to avoid being flooded. Gardeners and farmers express their detestation of worms; the former because they render their walks unsightly, and make them much work: and the latter because, as they think, worms eat their green corn. But these men would find that the earth without worms would soon become cold, hard-bound, and void of fermentation; and consequently sterile: and besides, in favour of worms, it should be hinted that green corn, plants, and flowers, are not so much injured by them as by many species of *coleoptera* (scarabs), and *tipulæ* (long-legs), in their larva, or grub-state; and by unnoticed myriads of small shell-less snails, called slugs, which silently and imperceptibly make amazing havoc in the field and garden.

These hints we think proper to throw out in order to set the inquisitive and discerning to work.

A good monography of worms would afford much entertainment and information at the same time, and would open a large and new field in natural history. Worms work most in the spring; but by no means lie torpid in the dead months; are out every mild night in the winter, as any person may be convinced that will take the pains to examine his grass-plots with a candle; are hermaphrodites, and much addicted to venery, and consequently very prolific.

I am, etc.

LETTER XXXVIII

[*echoes*]

> Fortè puer, comitum seductus ab agmine fido,
> Dixerat, ecquis adest? et, adest, responderat echo.
> Hic stupet; utque aciem partes divisit in omnes;
> Voce, veni, clamat magna. Vocat illa vocantem.
> [Perhaps a youngster, strayed from his friends, had cried,
> "Who's there?" "He's there," the echo had then replied.
> Baffled, he searches round, and with mighty shout,
> "Come out!" he calls, and the voice returns, "Come out!"]
> Ovid, *Metamorphoses*

Selborne, Feb. 12, 1778.

Dear Sir,

In a district so diversified as this, so full of hollow vales and hanging woods, it is no wonder that echoes should abound. Many we have discovered that return the cry of a pack of dogs, the notes of a hunting-horn, a tunable ring of bells, or the melody of birds, very agreeably: but we were still at a loss for a polysyllabical, articulate echo, till a young gentleman, who had parted from his company in a summer evening walk, and was calling after them, stumbled upon a very curious one in a spot where it might least be expected. At first he was much surprised, and could not be persuaded but that he was mocked by some boy; but, repeating his trials in several languages, and finding his respondent to be a very adroit polyglot, he then discerned the deception.

This echo in an evening, before rural noises cease, would repeat ten syllables most articulately and distinctly, especially if quick dactyls were chosen. The last syllables of

> Tityre, tu patulæ recubans . . .
> [Tityrus, under the wide-spreading beech . . .]

were as audibly and intelligibly returned as the first: and there is no doubt, could trial have been made, but that at midnight, when the air is very elastic, and a dead stillness prevails, one or two syllables more might have been obtained; but the distance rendered so late an experiment very inconvenient.

Quick dactyls, we observed, succeeded best; for when we came to try it's powers in slow, heavy, embarrassed spondees of the same number of syllables,

> Monstrum horrendum, informe, ingens . . .
> [Horrible monster, void of form and vast . . .]

we could perceive a return but of four or five.

All echoes have some one place to which they are returned stronger and more distinct than to any other; and that is always the place that lies at right angles with the object of repercussion, and is not too near, nor too far off. Buildings, or naked rocks, re-echo much more articulately than hanging wood or vales; because in the latter the voice is as it were entangled, and embarrassed in the covert, and weakened in the rebound.

The true object of this echo, as we found by various experiments, is the stone-built, tiled hop-kiln in Gally-lane, which measures in front 40 feet, and from the ground to the eaves 12 feet. The true *centrum phonicum,* or just distance, is one particular spot in the King's-field, in the path to Nore-hill, on the very brink of the steep balk above the hollow cart way. In this case there is no choice of distance; but the path, by mere contingency, happens to be the lucky, the identical spot, because the ground rises or falls so immediately, if the speaker either retires or advances, that his mouth would at once be above or below the object.

We measured this polysyllabical echo with great exactness, and found the distance to fall very short of Dr. Plot's rule for distinct articulation: for the Doctor, in his history of Oxfordshire, allows 120 feet for the return of each syllable distinctly: hence this echo, which gives ten distinct syllables, ought to measure 400 yards, or 120 feet to each syllable; whereas our distance is only 258 yards, or near 75 feet, to each syllable. Thus our measure falls short of the Doctor's, as five to eight: but then it must be acknowledged that this candid philosopher was convinced afterwards, that some latitude must be admitted of in the distance of echoes according to time and place.

When experiments of this sort are making, it should always be remembered that weather and the time of day have a vast influence on an echo; for a dull, heavy, moist air deadens and clogs the sound; and hot sunshine renders the air thin and weak, and deprives it of all it's springiness; and a ruffling wind quite defeats the whole. In a still, clear, dewy evening the air is most elastic; and perhaps the later the hour the more so.

Echo has always been so amusing to the imagination, that the poets have personified her; and in their hands she has been the occasion of many a beautiful fiction. Nor need the gravest man be ashamed to appear taken with such a phenomenon, since it may become the subject of philosophical or mathematical inquiries.

One should have imagined that echoes, if not entertaining, must at least have been harmless and inoffensive; yet Virgil advances a strange notion, that they are injurious to bees. After enumerating some probable and reasonable annoyances, such as prudent owners would wish far removed from their bee-gardens, he adds

————— aut ubi concava pulsu
Saxa sonant, vocisque offensa resultat imago.
[. . . or where the smitten hollow rock resounds,
And where the voice's echo strikes and, answering, rebounds.]

This wild and fanciful assertion will hardly be admitted by the philosophers of these days; especially as they all now seem agreed that insects are not furnished with any organs of hearing at all. But if it should be urged, that though they cannot *hear* yet perhaps they may *feel* the repercussions of sounds, I grant it is possible they may. Yet that these impressions are distasteful or hurtful, I deny, because bees, in good summers, thrive well in my outlet, where the echoes are very strong: for this village is another Anathoth, a place of *responses* or *echoes*. Besides, it does not appear from experiment that bees are in any way capable of being affected by sounds: for I have often tried my own with a large speaking-trumpet held close to their hives, and with such an exertion of voice as would have haled a ship at the distance of a mile, and still these insects pursued their various employments undisturbed, and without shewing the least sensibility or resentment.

Some time since it's discovery this echo is become totally silent, though the object, or hop-kiln, remains: nor is there any mystery in this defect; for the field between is planted as an hop-garden, and the voice of the speaker is totally absorbed and lost among the poles and entangled foliage of the hops. And when the poles are removed in autumn the disappointment is the same; because a tall quick-set hedge, nurtured up for the purpose of shelter to the hop ground, entirely interrupts the impulse and repercussion of the voice: so that till those obstructions are removed no more of it's garrulity can be expected.

Should any gentleman of fortune think an echo in his park or outlet a pleasing incident, he might *build* one at little or no expense. For when-ever he had occasion for a new barn, stable, dog-kennel, or the like structure, it would be only needful to erect this building on the gentle declivity of an hill, with a like rising opposite to it, at a few hundred yards distance; and perhaps success might be the easier ensured could some canal, lake, or stream, intervene. From a seat at the *centrum phonicum* he and his friends might amuse themselves sometimes of an evening with the prattle of this loquacious nymph, of whose complacency and decent reserve more may be said than can with truth of every individual of her sex; since she is ————

> ———————— quæ nec *reticere* loquenti,
> Nec *prior* ipsa *loqui* didicit resonabilis echo.
> [. . . answering echo, who has yet to learn
> To *keep her peace* when spoken to, or *speak* the *first* in turn.]

I am, &c.

LETTER XLIII

[bird voices, revenge of the hens]

Selborne, Sept. 9, 1778.

Dear Sir,

From the motion of birds, the transition is natural enough to their notes and language, of which I shall say something. Not that I would pretend to understand their language like the vizer who, by the recital of a conversation which passed between two owls, reclaimed a sultan, before delighting in conquest and devastation; but I would be thought only to mean that many of the winged tribes have various sounds and voices adapted to express their various passions, wants, and feelings; such as anger, fear, love, hatred, hunger and the like. All species are not equally eloquent; some are copious and fluent as it were in their utterance, while others are confined to a few important sounds: no bird, like the fish kind, is quite mute, though some are rather silent. The language of birds is very ancient, and, like other ancient modes of speech, very elliptical: little is said, but much is meant and understood.

The notes of the eagle-kind are shrill and piercing; and about the season of nidification much diversified, as I have been often assured by a curious observer of nature, who long resided at Gibraltar, where eagles abound. The notes of our hawks much resemble those of the king of birds. Owls have very expressive notes; they hoot in a fine vocal sound, much resembling the *vox humana*, and reducible by a pitch-pipe to a musical key. This note seems to express complacency and rivalry among the males; they use also a quick call and an horrible scream; and can snore and hiss when they mean to menace. Ravens, beside their loud croak, can exert a deep and solemn note that makes the woods to echo; the amorous sound of a crow is strange and ridiculous; rooks, in the breeding season, attempt sometimes in the gaiety of their hearts to sing, but with no great success; the parrot-kind have many modulations of voice, as appears by their aptitude to learn human sounds; doves coo in an amorous and mournful manner, and are emblems of despairing lovers; the wood-pecker sets up a sort of loud and hearty laugh; the fern-owl, or goat-sucker, from the dusk till day-break, serenades his mate with the clattering of castanets. All the tuneful *passeres* express their complacency by sweet modulations, and a variety of melody. The swallow, as has been observed in a former letter, by a shrill alarm bespeaks the attention of the other *hirundines,* and bids them be aware that the hawk is at hand. Aquatic and gregarious birds, especially the nocturnal, that shift their quarters in the dark, are very noisy and loquacious; as cranes, wild-geese, wild-ducks, and the like; their perpetual clamour prevents them from dispersing and losing their companions.

In so extensive a subject, sketches and outlines are as much as can be expected; for it would be endless to instance in all the infinite variety of the feathered nation. We shall therefore confine the remainder of this letter to the few domestic fowls of our yards, which are most known, and therefore best understood. At first the peacock, with his gorgeous train, demands our attention; but, like most of the gaudy birds, his notes are grating and shocking to the ear: the yelling of cats, and the braying of an ass, are not more disgustful. The voice of the goose is trumpet-like, and clanking; and once saved the Capitol at Rome, as grave historians assert: the hiss also of the gander is formidable and full of menace, and 'protective of his young.' Among ducks the sexual distinction of voice is remarkable; for, while the quack of the female is loud and sonorous, the voice of the drake is inward and harsh and feeble, and scarce discernible. The cock turkey struts and gobbles to his mistress in a most uncouth manner; he hath also a pert and petulant note when he attacks his adversary. When a hen turkey leads forth her young brood she keeps a watchful eye: and if a bird of prey appear, though ever so high in the air, the careful mother announces the enemy with a little inward moan, and watches him with a steady and attentive look; but if he approach, her note becomes earnest and alarming, and her outcries are redoubled.

No inhabitants of a yard seem possessed of such a variety of expression and so copious a language as common poultry. Take a chicken of four or five days old, and hold it up to a window where there are flies, and it will immediately seize its prey, with little twitterings of complacency; but if you tender it a wasp or a bee, at once its note becomes harsh, and expressive of disapprobation and a sense of danger. When a pullet is ready to lay she intimates the event by a joyous and easy soft note. Of all the occurrences of their life that of laying seems to be the most important; for no sooner has a hen disburdened herself, than she rushes forth with a clamorous kind of joy, which the cock and the rest of his mistresses immediately adopt. The tumult is not confined to the family concerned, but catches from yard to yard, and spreads to every homestead within hearing, till at last the whole village is in an uproar. As soon as a hen becomes a mother her new relation demands a new language; she then runs clocking and screaming about, and seems agitated as if possessed. The father of the flock has also a considerable vocabulary; if he finds food, he calls a favourite concubine to partake; and if a bird of prey passes over, with a warning voice he bids his family beware. The gallant chanticleer has, at command, his amorous phrases, and his terms of defiance. But the sound by which he is best known is his crowing: by this he has been distinguished in all ages as the countryman's clock or larum, as the watchman that proclaims the divisions of the night. Thus the poet elegantly styles him:

> . . . the crested cock, whose clarion sounds
> The silent hours.

A neighbouring gentleman one summer had lost most of his chickens by a sparrow-hawk, that came gliding down between a faggot-pile and the end of his house to the place where the coops stood. The owner, inwardly vexed to see his flock thus diminishing, hung a setting net adroitly between the pile and the house, into which the caitiff dashed and was entangled. Resentment suggested the law of retaliation: he therefore clipped the hawk's wings, cut off his talons, and, fixing a cork on his bill, threw him down among the brood-hens. Imagination cannot paint the scene that ensued; the expressions that fear, rage, and revenge inspired, were new, or at least such as had been unnoticed before: the exasperated matrons upbraided, they execrated, they insulted, they triumphed. In a word, they never desisted from buffeting their adversary till they had torn him in an hundred pieces.

LETTER L

[Timothy observed]

Selborne, April 21, 1780.

Dear Sir,
     The old Sussex tortoise, that I have mentioned to you so often, is become my property. I dug it out of it's winter dormitory in March last, when it was enough awakened to express it's resentments by hissing; and, packing it in a box with earth, carried it eighty miles in post-chaises. The rattle and hurry of the journey so perfectly roused it that, when I turned it out on a border, it walked twice down to the bottom of my garden; however, in the evening, the weather being cold, it buried itself in the loose mould, and continues still concealed.
     As it will be under my eye, I shall now have an opportunity of enlarging my observations on it's mode of life, and propensities; and perceive already that, towards the time of coming forth, it opens a breathing place in the ground near it's head, requiring, I conclude, a freer respiration, as it becomes more alive. This creature not only goes under the earth from the middle of November to the middle of April, but sleeps great part of the summer; for it goes to bed in the longest days at four in the afternoon, and often does not stir in the morning till late. Besides, it retires to rest for every shower; and does not move at all in wet days.
     When one reflects on the state of this strange being, it is a matter of wonder to find that Providence should bestow such a profusion of days, such a seeming waste of longevity, on a reptile that appears to relish it so little as to squander more than two thirds of it's existence in a joyless stupor, and be lost to all sensation for months together in the profoundest of slumbers.

Because we call this creature an abject reptile, we are too apt to undervalue his abilities, and depreciate his powers of instinct. Yet he is, as Mr. Pope says of his lord,

————Much too wise to walk into a well:

and has so much discernment as not to fall down an haha; but to stop and withdraw from the brink with the readiest precaution.

Though he loves warm weather he avoids the hot sun; because his thick shell, when once heated, would, as the poet says of solid armour—"scald with safety." He therefore spends the more sultry hours under the umbrella of a large cabbage-leaf, or amidst the waving forests of an asparagus-bed.

But as he avoids heat in the summer, so, in the decline of the year, he improves the faint autumnal beams, by getting within the reflection of a fruit-wall; and, though he never has read that planes inclining to the horizon receive a greater share of warmth,[1] he inclines his shell, by tilting it against the wall, to collect and admit every feeble ray.

Pitiable seems the condition of this poor embarrassed reptile: to be cased in a suit of ponderous armour, which he cannot lay aside; to be imprisoned, as it were, within his own shell, must preclude, we should suppose, all activity and disposition for enterprise. Yet there is a season of the year (usually the beginning of June) when his exertions are re-markable. He then walks on tiptoe, and is stirring by five in the morning; and, traversing the garden, examines every wicket and interstice in the fences, through which he will escape if possible: and often has eluded the care of the gardener, and wandered to some distant field. The motives that impel him to undertake these rambles seem to be of the amorous kind: his fancy then becomes intent on sexual attachments, which trans-port him beyond his usual gravity, and induce him to forget for a time his ordinary solemn deportment.

While I was writing this letter, a moist and warm afternoon, with the thermometer at 50, brought forth troops of *shell-snails;* and, at the same juncture, the *tortoise* heaved up the mould and put out it's head; and the next morning came forth, as it were raised from the dead; and walked about till four in the afternoon. This was a curious coincidence! a very

[1] *Several years ago a book was written entitled* Fruit-walls improved by inclining them to the horizon: *in which the author has shewn, by calculation, that a much greater number of the rays of the sun will fall on such walls than on those which are perpendicular.* [Gilbert White's note]

amusing occurrence! to see such a similarity of feelings between the two φερεοικοι [house-carriers] for so the Greeks called both the *shell-snail* and the *tortoise.*

Summer birds are, this cold and backward spring, unusually late: I have seen but one swallow yet. This conformity with the weather convinces me more and more that they sleep in the winter.

HECTOR ST. JOHN de CRÈVECOEUR
1735-1813

The "American Farmer" of Crèvecoeur's classic account of early American rural life was in reality a French-born aristocrat who went to school in England, fought with Montcalm in the French and Indian Wars, wandered the frontiers of the Colonies, and was forced out of the young Republic in 1780 because of his Loyalist sympathies. Nevertheless, the idyllic years he and his American wife spent on a farm in New York's Orange County before the Revolution provided the basis for Letters from an American Farmer. *Published in London in 1782, this book became a best-seller in England and Europe and was embraced by the Romantics, along with the works of Bartram and Audubon, as depictions of a wild and unsullied New World paradise.*

Crèvecoeur was an idealist in the best Rousseauian tradition, seeing nature as a system devised by the Creator for humanity's benefit and moral instruction, but as one needing selective interference on occasion. He was also a writer of considerable power, and Letters *represents one of the first genuinely imaginative works of nature writing in America. In addition, it marks the beginning of an agrarian literary tradition that includes writers like Aldo Leopold and Wendell Berry. Crèvecoeur's celebrations of farm life are full of richly-detailed vignettes of the terms of existence in the wild. Though these accounts often have a strong element of embellishment in them, they also possess an emotional veracity, a compassion for animals, and an appreciation of nature's primitive vitality unmatched by any writer until Thoreau.*

From LETTERS FROM AN AMERICAN FARMER

ON THE SITUATION, FEELINGS, AND
PLEASURES OF AN AMERICAN FARMER

* * * Pray do not laugh in thus seeing an artless countryman tracing himself through the simple modifications of his life; remember that you have required it; therefore, with candour, though with diffidence, I endeavour to follow the thread of my feelings, but I cannot tell you all. Often when I plough my low ground, I place my little boy on a chair which screws to the beam of the plough—its motion and that of the horses please him; he is perfectly happy and begins to chat, As I lean over the handle, various are the thoughts which crowd into my mind. I am now doing for him, I say, what my father formerly did for me; may God enable him to live that he may perform the same operations for the same purposes when I am worn out and old! I relieve his mother of some trouble while I have him with me; the odoriferous furrow exhilarates his spirits and seems to do the child a great deal of good, for he looks more blooming since I have adopted that practice; can more pleasure, more dignity, be added to that primary occupation? The father thus ploughing with his child, and to feed his family, is inferior only to the emperor of China ploughing as an example to his kingdom. In the evening, when I return home through my low grounds, I am astonished at the myriads of insects which I perceive dancing in the beams of the setting sun. I was before scarcely acquainted with their existence; they are so small that it is difficult to distinguish them; they are carefully improving this short evening space, not daring to expose themselves to the blaze of our meridian sun. I never see an egg brought on my table but I feel penetrated with the wonderful change it would have undergone but for my gluttony; it might have been a gentle, useful hen leading her chicken with a care and vigilance which speaks shame to many women. A cock perhaps, arrayed with the most majestic plumes, tender to its mate, bold, courageous, endowed with an astonishing instinct, with thoughts, with memory, and every distinguishing characteristic of the reason of man. I never see my trees drop their leaves and their fruit in the autumn, and bud again in the spring, without wonder; the sagacity of those animals which have long been the tenants of my farm astonish me; some of them seem to surpass even men in memory and sagacity. I could tell you singular instances of that kind. What, then, is this instinct which we so debase,

Letters from an American Farmer (London: T. Davies, 1782).

and of which we are taught to entertain so diminutive an idea? My bees, above any other tenants of my farm, attract my attention and respect; I am astonished to see that nothing exists but what has its enemy; one species pursues and lives upon the other: unfortunately, our king-birds are the destroyers of those industrious insects, but on the other hand, these birds preserve our fields from the depredation of crows, which they pursue on the wing with great vigilance and astonishing dexterity.

Thus divided by two interested motives, I have long resisted the desire I had to kill them until last year, when I thought they increased too much, and my indulgence had been carried too far; it was at the time of swarming, when they all came and fixed themselves on the neighbouring trees whence they caught those that returned loaded from the fields. This made me resolve to kill as many as I could, and was just ready to fire when a bunch of bees as big as my fist issued from one of the hives, rushed on one of these birds, and probably stung him, for he instantly screamed and flew, not as before, in an irregular manner, but in a direct line. He was followed by the same bold phalanx, at a considerable distance, which unfortunately, becoming too sure of victory, quitted their military array and disbanded themselves. By this inconsiderate step, they lost all that aggregate of force which had made the bird fly off. Perceiving their disorder, he immediately returned and snapped as many as he wanted; nay, he had even the impudence to alight on the very twig from which the bees had driven him. I killed him and immediately opened his craw, from which I took 171 bees; I laid them all on a blanket in the sun, and to my great surprise, 54 returned to life, licked themselves clean, and joyfully went back to the hive, where they probably informed their companions of such an adventure and escape as I believe had never happened before to American bees! I draw a great fund of pleasure from the quails which inhabit my farm; they abundantly repay me, by their various notes and peculiar tameness, for the inviolable hospitality I constantly show them in the winter. Instead of perfidiously taking advantage of their great and affecting distress when nature offers nothing but a barren universal bed of snow, when irresistible necessity forces them to my barn doors, I permit them to feed unmolested; and it is not the least agreeable spectacle which that dreary season presents, when I see those beautiful birds, tamed by hunger, intermingling with all my cattle and sheep, seeking in security for the poor, scanty grain which but for them would be useless and lost. Often in the angles of the fences where the motion of the wind prevents the snow from settling, I carry them both chaff and grain, the one to feed them, the other to prevent their tender feet from freezing fast to the earth as I have frequently observed them to do.

I do not know an instance in which the singular barbarity of man is so strongly delineated as in the catching and murthering those harmless birds, at that cruel season of the year. Mr. ——, one of the most famous and extraordinary farmers that has ever done honour to the province of Connecticut, by his timely and humane assistance in a hard winter, saved this species from being entirely destroyed. They perished all over the country; none of their delightful whistlings were heard the next spring but upon this gentleman's farm; and to his humanity we owe the continuation of their music. When the severities of that season have dispirited all my cattle, no farmer ever attends them with more pleasure than I do; it is one of those duties which is sweetened with the most rational satisfaction. I amuse myself in beholding their different tempers, actions, and the various effects of their instinct now powerfully impelled by the force of hunger. I trace their various inclinations and the different effects of their passions, which are exactly the same as among men; the law is to us precisely what I am in my barnyard, a bridle and check to prevent the strong and greedy from oppressing the timid and weak. Conscious of superiority, they always strive to encroach on their neighbours; unsatisfied with their portion, they eagerly swallow it in order to have an opportunity of taking what is given to others, except they are prevented. Some I chide; others, unmindful of my admonitions, receive some blows. Could victuals thus be given to men without the assistance of any language, I am sure they would not behave better to one another, nor more philosophically than my cattle do. * * *

ON SNAKES; AND ON THE HUMMING-BIRD

Why would you prescribe this task; you know that what we take up ourselves seems always lighter than what is imposed on us by others. You insist on my saying something about our snakes; and in relating what I know concerning them, were it not for two singularities, the one of which I saw and the other I received from an eyewitness, I should have but very little to observe. The southern provinces are the countries where Nature has formed the greatest variety of alligators, snakes, serpents, and scorpions from the smallest size up to the pine barren, the largest species known here. We have but two, whose stings are mortal, which deserve to be mentioned; as for the black one, it is remarkable for nothing but its industry, agility, beauty, and the art of enticing birds by the power of its eyes. I admire it much and never kill it, though its formidable length and appearance often get the better of the philosophy of some people, particularly Europeans. The most dangerous one is the pilot, or copperhead, for the poison of which no remedy has yet been discovered. It bears the first name because it always precedes the rattle-snake, that is, quits its state of torpidity in the spring a week before the other. It bears the second name on account of its head being adorned with many copper-coloured spots. It lurks in rocks near the water and is extremely active and dangerous. Let man beware of it! I have heard only of one person who was stung by a copperhead in this country. The poor wretch instantly swelled in a most dreadful manner; a multitude of spots of different hues alternately appeared and vanished on different parts of his body; his eyes were filled with madness and rage; he cast them on all present with the most vindictive looks; he thrust out his tongue as the snakes do; he hissed through his teeth with inconceivable strength and became an object of terror to all bystanders. To the lividness of a corpse he united the desperate force of a maniac; they hardly were able to fasten him so as to guard themselves from his attacks, when in the space of two hours death relieved the poor wretch from his struggles and the specta-tors from their apprehensions. The poison of the rattlesnake is not mor-tal in so short a space, and hence there is more time to procure relief; we are acquainted with several antidotes with which almost every family is provided. They are extremely inactive, and if not touched, are perfectly inoffensive. I once saw, as I was travelling, a great cliff which was full of them; I handled several, and they appeared to be dead; they were all entwined together, and thus they remain until the return of the sun. I found them out by following the track of some wild hogs which had fed on them; and even the Indians often regale on them. When they find them asleep, they put a small forked stick over their necks, which they keep immovably fixed on the ground, giving the snake a piece of leather to bite; and this they pull back several times with great force until they observe their two poisonous fangs torn out. Then they cut off the head, skin the body, and cook it as we do eels; and their flesh is extremely sweet and white. I once saw a *tamed one,* as gentle as you can possibly conceive a reptile to be; it took to the water and swam whenever it pleased; and when the boys to whom it belonged called it back, their summons was readily obeyed. It had been deprived of its fangs by the preceding method; they often stroked it with a soft brush, and this friction seemed to cause the most pleasing sensations, for it would turn on its back to enjoy it, as a cat does before the fire. One of this species was the cause, some years ago, of a most deplorable accident, which I shall relate to you as I had it from the widow and mother of the victims. A Dutch farmer of the Minisink went to mowing, with his Negroes, in his boots, a precau-tion used to prevent being stung. Inadvertently he trod on a snake, which immediately flew at his legs; and as it drew back in order to renew its blow, one of his Negroes cut it in two with his scythe. They prosecuted their work and returned home; at night the farmer pulled off his boots and went to bed, and was soon after attacked with a strange sickness at his stomach; he swelled, and before a physician could be sent for, died. The sudden death of this man did not cause much inquiry; the neighbourhood wondered, as is usual in such cases, and without any further examination, the corpse was buried. A few days after, the son put on his father's boots and went to the meadow; at night he pulled them off, went to bed, and was attacked with the same symptoms about the same time, and died in the morning. A little before he expired, the doctor came, but was not able to assign what could be the cause of so singular a disorder; however, rather than appear wholly at a loss before the country people, he pronounced both father and son to have been bewitched. Some weeks after, the widow sold all the movables for the benefit of the younger children, and the farm was leased. One of the neighbours, who bought the boots, presently put them on, and was attacked in the same manner as the other two had been; but this man's wife, being alarmed by what had happened in the former family, despatched one of her Negroes for an eminent physician, who, fortunately having heard something of the dreadful affair, guessed at the cause, applied oil, etc., and recovered the man. The boots which had been so fatal were then carefully examined, and he found that the two fangs of the snake had been left in the leather after being wrenched out of their sockets by the strength with which the snake had drawn back its head. The bladders which contained the poison and several of the small nerves were still fresh and adhered to the boot. The unfortunate father and son had been poisoned by pulling off these boots, in which action they imperceptibly scratched their legs with the points of the fangs, through the hollow of which some of this astonishing poison was conveyed. You have no doubt heard of their rattles if you have not seen them; the only observation I wish to make is that the rattling is loud and distinct when they are angry and, on the contrary, when pleased, it sounds like a distant trepidation, in which nothing distinct is heard. In the thick settlements, they are now become very scarce, for wherever they are met with, open war is declared against them, so that in a few years there will be none left but on our mountains. The black snake, on the contrary, always diverts me because it excites no idea of danger. Their swiftness is astonishing; they will sometimes equal that of a horse; at other times they will climb up trees in quest of our tree toads or glide on the ground at full length. On some occasions they present themselves half in the reptile state, half erect; their eyes and their heads in the erect posture appear to great advantage; the former display a fire which I have often admired, and it is by these they are enabled to fascinate birds and squirrels. When they have fixed their eyes on an animal, they become immovable, only turning their head sometimes to the right and sometimes to the left, but still with their sight invariably directed to the object. The distracted victim, instead of flying its enemy, seems to be arrested by some invincible power; it screams; now approaches and then recedes; and after skipping about with unaccountable agitation, finally rushes into the jaws of the snake and is swallowed, as soon as it is covered with a slime or glue to make it slide easily down the throat of the devourer.

One anecdote I must relate, the circumstances of which are as true as they are singular. One of my constant walks when I am at leisure is in my lowlands, where I have the pleasure of seeing my cattle, horses, and colts. Exuberant grass replenishes all my fields, the best representative of our wealth; in the middle of that track I have cut a ditch eight feet wide, the banks of which Nature adorns every spring with the wild salendine and other flowering weeds, which on these luxuriant grounds shoot up to a great height. Over this ditch I have erected a bridge, capable of bearing a loaded waggon; on each side I carefully sow every year some grains of hemp, which rise to the height of fifteen feet, so strong and so full of limbs as to resemble young trees; I once ascended one of them four feet above the ground. These produce natural arbours, rendered often still more compact by the assistance of an annual creeping plant, which we call a vine, that never fails to entwine itself among their branches and always produces a very desirable shade. From this simple grove I have amused myself a hundred times in observing the great number of humming-birds with which our country abounds: the wild blossoms everywhere attract the attention of these birds, which like bees subsist by suction. From this retreat I distinctly watch them in all their various attitudes, but their flight is so rapid that you cannot distinguish the motion of their wings. On this little bird Nature has profusely lavished her most splendid colours; the most perfect azure, the most beautiful gold, the most dazzling red, are forever in contrast and help to embellish the plumes of his majestic head. The richest palette of the most luxuriant painter could never invent anything to be compared to the variegated tints with which this insect bird is arrayed. Its bill is as long and as sharp as a coarse sewing needle; like the bee, Nature has taught it to find out in the calyx of flowers and blossoms those mellifluous particles that serve it for sufficient food; and yet it seems to leave them untouched, undeprived of anything that our eyes can possibly distinguish. When it feeds, it appears as if immovable, though continually on the wing; and sometimes, from what motives I know not, it will tear and lacerate flowers into a hundred pieces, for, strange to tell, they are the most irascible of the feathered tribe. Where do passions find room in so diminutive a body? They often fight with the fury of lions until one of the combatants falls a sacrifice and dies. When fatigued, it has often perched within a few feet of me, and on such favourable opportunities I have surveyed it with the most minute attention. Its little eyes appear like diamonds, reflecting light on every side; most elegantly finished in all parts, it is a miniature work of our Great Parent, who seems to have formed it the smallest, and at the same time the most beautiful of the winged species.

As I was one day sitting solitary and pensive in my primitive arbour, my attention was engaged by a strange sort of rustling noise at some paces distant. I looked all around without distinguishing anything, until I climbed one of my great hemp stalks, when to my astonishment I beheld two snakes of considerable length, the one pursuing the other with great celerity through a hemp-stubble field. The aggressor was of the black kind, six feet long; the fugitive was a water snake, nearly of equal dimensions. They soon met, and in the fury of their first encounter, they appeared in an instant firmly twisted together; and whilst their united tails beat the ground, they mutually tried with open jaws to lacerate each other. What a fell aspect did they present! Their heads were compressed to a very small size, their eyes flashed fire; and after this conflict had lasted about five minutes, the second found means to disengage itself from the first and hurried toward the ditch. Its antagonist instantly assumed a new posture, and half creeping and half erect, with a majestic mien, overtook and attacked the other again, which placed itself in the same attitude and prepared to resist. The scene was uncommon and beautiful; for thus opposed, they fought with their jaws, biting each other with the utmost rage; but notwithstanding this appearance of mutual courage and fury, the water snake still seemed desirous of retreating toward the ditch, its natural element. This was no sooner perceived by the keen-eyed black one, than twisting its tail twice round a stalk of hemp and seizing its adversary by the throat, not by means of its jaws but by twisting its own neck twice round that of the water snake, pulled it back from the ditch. To prevent a defeat, the latter took hold likewise of a stalk on the bank, and by the acquisition of that point of resistance, became a match for its fierce antagonist. Strange was this to behold; two great snakes strongly adhering to the ground, mutually fastened together by means of the writhings which lashed them to each other, and stretched at their full length, they pulled but pulled in vain; and in the moments of greatest exertions, that part of their bodies which was entwined seemed extremely small, while the rest appeared inflated and now and then convulsed with strong undulations, rapidly following each other. Their eyes seemed on fire and ready to start out of their heads; at one time the conflict seemed decided; the water snake bent itself into two great folds and by that operation rendered the other more than commonly outstretched; the next minute the new struggles of the black one gained an unexpected superiority; it acquired two great folds likewise, which necessarily extended the body of its adversary in proportion as it had contracted its own. These efforts were alternate; victory seemed doubtful, inclining sometimes to the one side and sometimes to the other, until at last the stalk to which the black snake fastened suddenly gave way, and in consequence of this accident they both plunged into the ditch. The water did not extinguish their vindictive rage; for by their agitations I could trace, though not distinguish, their mutual attacks. They soon reappeared on the surface twisted together, as in their first onset; but the black snake seemed to retain its wonted superiority, for its head was exactly fixed above that of the other, which it incessantly pressed down under the water, until it was stifled and sunk. The victor no sooner perceived its enemy incapable of farther resistance than, abandoning it to the current, it returned on shore and disappeared.

From SKETCHES OF EIGHTEENTH CENTURY AMERICA

ENEMIES OF THE FARMER

* * * Nature has placed a certain degree of antipathy between some species of animals and birds. Often one lives on the other; at other times they only attack each other. The king-bird is the most skilful on the wing of any we have here. Every spring he declares war against all the kites, hawks, and crows which pass within the bounds of his precincts. If they build anywhere on your farm, rest assured that none of those great tyrants of the air will fly over it with impunity. Nor is it an unpleasant sight to behold the contest. Like the Indians, they scream aloud when they go to the attack. They fly at first with an apparent trepidation. They err here and there, and then dart with immense impetuosity and with consummate skill, always getting to the windward of their enemy, let it be even the great bald eagle of the Blue Mountains. By repeatedly falling on him and striking him with their bills and sometimes by attacking him under the wings, they will make the largest bird accelerate its motion, and describe the most beautiful curves in those rapid descents which they compel him to delineate. This amuses me much, on two accounts: first, because they are doing my work; second, because I have an excel-

Sketches of Eighteenth century America (New Haven: Yale University Press, 1925).

lent opportunity of viewing the art of flying carried to a great degree of perfection and varied in a multiplicity of appearances. What a pity that I am very often obliged to shoot these little kings of the air! Hunting crows serves only to make them more hungry, nor will they live on grain, but on bees. These precious insects, these daughters of heaven, serve them as food whenever they can catch them.

The blackbird, which you say resembles your starling, visits us every spring in great numbers. They build their nests in our most inaccessible swamps. Their rough notes are delightful enough at a distance. As soon as the corn sprouts, they come to dig it up; nothing but the gun can possibly prevent them. Hanging of their dead companions has no kind of effect. They are birds that show the greatest degree of temerity of any we have. Sometimes we poison corn, which we strew on the ground with the juice of hitch-root. Sometimes, after soaking it, we pass a horsehair through each grain, which we cut about an inch long. These expedients will destroy a few of them, but either by the effect of inspection or by means of some language unknown, like a great many other phenomena, to Man, the rest will become acquainted with the danger, and in two days the survivors will not touch it, but take the utmost pains to eradicate that which lies three inches under the ground. I have often poisoned the very grains I have planted, but in two days it grows as sweet as ever. Thus while our corn is young it requires a great deal of watching. To prevent these depredations, some counties have raised money and given a small bounty of two pence per head. If they are greatly disturbed while they are hatching, they will soon quit that district.

But after all the efforts of our selfishness, are they not the children of the great Creator as well as we? They are entitled to live and to get their food wherever they can get it. We can better afford to lose a little corn than any other grain because it yields above seventy for one. But Man is a huge monster who devours everything and will suffer nothing to live in peace in his neighbourhood. The easiest, best, and the most philanthropic method is to break up either our summer fallow or our buckwheat ground while our corn is young. They will immediately cease to do us mischief and go to prey on the worms and caterpillars which the plough raises. Their depredations proceeded from hunger, not from premeditated malice. As soon as their young ones are able to fly, they bid us farewell. They retire to some other countries which produce what they want, for as they neither sow nor plant, it is necessary that either Man or Nature should feed them. Towards the autumn, they return in astonishing flocks. If our corn-fields are not then well guarded, they will in a few hours make great havoc. They disappear in about a week.

At this season another animal comes out of our woods and demands of Man his portion. It is the squirrel, of which there are three sorts, the grey, the black, both of the same size, and the little ground one, which harbours under rocks and stones. The two former are the most beautiful inhabitants of our forests. They live in hollow trees which they fill with koka toma nuts, chestnuts, and corn when they can get it. Like man they know the approach of the winter and as wisely know how to prepare against its wants. Some years their numbers are very great. They will travel over our fences with the utmost agility, descend into our fields, cut down an ear perhaps eighteen inches long and heavier than themselves. They will strip it of its husk and, properly balancing it in their mouths, return thus loaded to their trees. For my part, I cannot blame them, but I should blame myself were I peaceably to look on and let them carry all. As we pay no tithes in this country, I think we should be a little more generous than we are to the brute creation. If there are but few, a gun and a dog are sufficient. If they openly declare war in great armies, men collect themselves and go to attack them in their native woods. The county assembles and forms itself into companies to which a captain is appointed. Different districts of woods are assigned them; the rendez-vous is agreed on. They march, and that company which kills the most is treated by the rest; thus the day is spent. The meat of these squirrels is an excellent food; they make excellent soup or pies. Their skins are exceed-ingly tough; they are stronger than eels' skins; we use them to tie our flails with.

Mirth, jollity, coarse jokes, the exhilarating cup, and dancing are al-ways the concomitant circumstances which enliven and accompany this kind of meeting, the only festivals that we simple people are acquainted with in this young country. Religion, which in so many parts of the world affords processions and a variety of other exercises and becomes a source of temporal pleasures to the people, here gives us none. What few it yields are all of the spiritual kind. A few years ago I was invited to one of these parties. At my first entrance into the woods, whilst the affrighted echoes were resounding with the noise of the men and dogs, before I had joined the company, I found a bee-tree, which is my favourite talent. But, behold, it contained also the habitation of a squirrel family. The bees were lodged in one of its principal limbs; the others occupied the body of the tree. For the sake of the former I saved the latter. While I was busy in marking it, I perceived a great number of ants (those busy-bodies) travelling up three deep in a continual succession and returning in the same way. Both these columns were perfectly straight in the ascent as well as in the descent and but a small distance apart. I killed a few which I smelled. I found them all replete with honey. I therefore concluded that these were a set of thieves living on the industrious labours of the others. This intrusion gave me a bad opinion of the vigour and vigilance of the latter. However, as the honey season was not come, I resolved to let them alone and to deliver them from the rapacity of an enemy which they could not repel.

Next day, accompanied by my little boy, I brought a kettle, kindled a fire, boiled some water, and scalded the whole host as it ascended and descended. I did not leave one stirring. The lad asked me a great many questions respecting what I was doing, and the answers I made him afforded me the means of conveying to his mind the first moral ideas I had as yet given him. On my return home I composed a little fable on the subject, which I made him learn by heart. God grant that this trifling incident may serve as the basis of a future moral education.

Thus, sir, do we save our corn. But when it is raised on our lowlands, it is subject to transitory frosts, an accident which I have not mentioned to you yet, but as we can foresee them, it is in our power to avoid the mischief they cause. If in any of our summer months the wind blows north-west two days, on the second night the frost is inevitable. The only means we have to preserve our grain from its bad effects on our low grounds—for it seldom reaches the upland—is to kindle a few fires to the windward as soon as the sun goes down. No sooner does that luminary disappear from our sight than the wind ceases. This is the most favourable moment. The smoke will not rise, but, on the contrary, lie on the ground, mixing with the vapours of the evening. The whole will form a body four feet deep which will cover the face of the earth until the power of the sun dissipates it next morning. Whatever is covered with it is perfectly safe. I had once some hops and pole-beans, about twenty feet high. Whatever grew above the body of the smoke was entirely killed; the rest was saved. I had at the same time upwards of three acres of buckwheat which I had sown early for my bees. I lost not a grain. Some of my neighbours have by this simple method saved their tobacco.

These low grounds are exposed, besides, to the ravages of grasshoppers, an intolerable nuisance. While young and deprived of wings, they may be kept off by means of that admirable contrivance which a Negro found out in South Carolina: a few pots filled with brimstone and tar are kindled at nightfall to the windward of the field; the powerful smell of these two ingredients either kills them or drives them away. But when they have wings, they easily avoid it and transport themselves wherever they please. The damage they cause in our hemp grounds as well as in our meadows is inconceivable. They will eat the leaves of the former to the bare stalks and consume the best of our grasses. The only remedy for the latter is to go to mowing as soon as possible. The former devastation is unavoidable. Some years a certain worm, which I cannot describe, insinuates itself into the heart of the corn-stalk while it is young; and if not killed by squeezing the plant, it will eat the embryo of the great stem, which contains the imperceptible rudiments of our future hopes.

Sometimes our rye is attacked by a small animalcula of the worm kind which lodges itself in the stem just below the first joint. There it lives on the sap as it ascends. The ear becomes white and grainless, the perfect symbol of sterility.

I should have never done, were I to recount to you all the inconveniences and accidents which the grains of our fields, the trees of our orchards, as well as those of the woods, are exposed to. If bountiful Nature is kind to us on the one hand, on the other she wills that we shall purchase her kindness not only with sweats and labour but with vigilance and care. These calamities remind us of our precarious situation. The field and meadow-mice come in also for their share, and sometimes take more from Man than he can well spare. The rats are so multiplied that no one can imagine the great quantities of grain they destroy every year. Some farmers, more unfortunate than the others, have lost half of their crops after they were safely lodged in their barns. I'd forgive Nature all the rest if she would rid us of these cunning, devouring thieves which no art can subdue. When the floods rise on our low grounds, the mice quit their burrows and come to our stacks of grain or to our heaps of turnips, which are buried under the earth out of the reach of the frost. There, secured from danger, they find a habitation replenished with all they want. I must not, however, be murmuring and ungrateful. If Nature has formed mice, she has created also the fox and the owl. They both prey on these. Were it not for their kind assistance, the mice would drive us out of our farms.

Thus one species of evil is balanced by another; thus the fury of one element is repressed by the power of the other. In the midst of this great, this astonishing equipoise, Man struggles and lives. * * *

WILLIAM BARTRAM
1739-1823

William Bartram's Travels Through North and South Carolina, Georgia, East and West Florida, the Cherokee Country, the Extensive Territories of the Muscogulges, or Creek Confederacy, and the Country

of the Chactaws *(1791) has entranced readers from its first publication
to the present day. Mangrove swamps and alligators, poisonous snakes
and wolves seem to have been as delightful to Bartram, by the very fact
of their existence, as they would have been terrifying to one more concerned with protecting his own existence. Joy was inseparable from the
study of nature for Bartram, and he frequently weaves Linnaean nomen-
clature into his rhapsodic descriptions in ways that express a litany of
praise. Such a blending of precision with adoration marks his account of
the "crystal bason," which is included here. This passage so impressed
Coleridge that he worked a number of details from it into his description
of the enchanted landscape in "Kubla Khan."*

*As the full title of Bartram's book indicates, he was also interested, in
a particular and discriminating sense, in the native peoples of the Southeast. We can be grateful for the presence in our early literature of nature
of a few writers like Bartram and Thoreau, who combined a vivid and
informed love of the land with respect for the cultures which had
evolved within it before the coming of white settlers.*

From TRAVELS THROUGH NORTH & SOUTH CAROLINA, GEORGIA, EAST & WEST FLORIDA . . .

[Ephemera]

* * * Early in the evening, after a pleasant day's voyage, I made a
convenient and safe harbour, in a little lagoon, under an elevated bank,
on the West shore of the river; where I shall entreat the reader's patience, whilst we behold the closing scene of the short-lived Ephemera,
and communicate to each other the reflections which so singular an
exhibition might rationally suggest to an inquisitive mind. Our place of
observation is happily situated under the protecting shade of majestic
Live Oaks, glorious Magnolias, and the fragrant Orange, open to the
view of the great river and still waters of the lagoon just before us.

At the cool eve's approach, the sweet enchanting melody of the feathered songsters gradually ceases, and they betake themselves to their leafy
coverts for security and repose.

Solemnly and slowly move onward, to the river's shore, the rustling
clouds of the Ephemera. How awful the procession! innumerable mil-

*Travels Through North & South Carolina, Georgia, East & West Florida, the Cherokee
Country, the Extensive Territories of the Muscogulges, or Creek Confederacy, and the
Country of the Chactaws* (Philadelphia: James & Johnson, 1791).

lions of winged beings, voluntarily verging on to destruction, to the brink of the grave, where they behold bands of their enemies with wide open jaws, ready to receive them. But as if insensible of their danger, gay and tranquil each meets his beloved mate in the still air, inimitably bedecked in their new nuptial robes. What eye can trace them, in their varied wanton amorous chaces, bounding and fluttering on the odoriferous air! With what peace, love, and joy, do they end the last moments of their existence!

I think we may assert, without any fear of exaggeration, that there are annually of these beautiful winged beings, which rise into existence, and for a few moments take a transient view of the glory of the Creator's works, a number greater than the whole race of mankind that have ever existed since the creation; and that, only from the shores of this river. How many then must have been produced since the creation, when we consider the number of large rivers in America, in comparison with which, this river is but a brook or rivulet.

The importance of the existence of these beautiful and delicately formed little creatures, whose frame and organization are equally wonderful, more delicate, and perhaps as complicated as those of the most perfect human being, is well worth a few moments contemplation; I mean particularly when they appear in the fly state. And if we consider the very short period of that stage of existence, which we may reasonably suppose to be the only space of their life that admits of pleasure and enjoyment, what a lesson doth it not afford us of the vanity of our own pursuits!

Their whole existence in this world is but one complete year: and at least three hundred and sixty days of that time they are in the form of an ugly grub, buried in mud, eighteen inches under water, and in this condition scarcely locomotive, as each larva or grub has but its own narrow solitary cell, from which it never travels or moves, but in a perpendicular progression of a few inches, up and down, from the bottom to the surface of the mud, in order to intercept the passing atoms for its food, and get a momentary respiration of fresh air; and even here it must be perpetually on its guard, in order to escape the troops of fish and shrimps watching to catch it, and from whom it has no escape, but by instantly retreating back into its cell. One would be apt almost to imagine them created merely for the food of fish and other animals. *   *   *

[encounters with alligators]

*   *   * The evening was temperately cool and calm. The crocodiles began to roar and appear in uncommon numbers along the shores and in the river. I fixed my camp in an open plain, near the utmost projection

of the promontory, under the shelter of a large live oak, which stood on the highest part of the ground, and but a few yards from my boat. From this open, high situation, I had a free prospect of the river, which was a matter of no trivial consideration to me, having good reason to dread the subtle attacks of the alligators, who were crowding about my harbour. Having collected a good quantity of wood for the purpose of keeping up a light and smoke during the night, I began to think of preparing my supper, when, upon examining my stores, I found but a scanty provision. I thereupon determined, as the most expeditious way of supplying my necessities, to take my bob and try for some trout. About one hundred yards above my harbour began a cove or bay of the river, out of which opened a large lagoon. The mouth or entrance from the river to it was narrow, but the waters soon after spread and formed a little lake, extending into the marshes: its entrance and shores within I observed to be verged with floating lawns of the pistia and nymphea and other aquatic plants; these I knew were excellent haunts for trout.

The verges and islets of the lagoon were elegantly embellished with flowering plants and shrubs; the laughing coots with wings half spread were tripping over the little coves, and hiding themselves in the tufts of grass; young broods of the painted summer teal, skimming the still surface of the waters, and following the watchful parent unconscious of danger, were frequently surprised by the voracious trout; and he, in turn, as often by the subtle greedy alligator. Behold him rushing forth from the flags and reeds. His enormous body swells. His plaited tail brandished high, floats upon the lake. The waters like a cataract descend from his opening jaws. Clouds of smoke issue from his dilated nostrils. The earth trembles with his thunder. When immediately from the opposite coast of the lagoon, emerges from the deep his rival champion. They suddenly dart upon each other. The boiling surface of the lake marks their rapid course, and a terrific conflict commences. They now sink to the bottom folded together in horrid wreaths. The water becomes thick and discoloured. Again they rise, their jaws clap together, re-echoing through the deep surrounding forests. Again they sink, when the contest ends at the muddy bottom of the lake, and the vanquished makes a hazardous escape, hiding himself in the muddy turbulent waters and sedge on a distant shore. The proud victor exulting returns to the place of action. The shores and forests resound his dreadful roar, together with the triumphing shouts of the plaited tribes around, witnesses of the horrid combat.

My apprehensions were highly alarmed after being a spectator of so dreadful a battle. It was obvious that every delay would but tend to increase my dangers and difficulties, as the sun was near setting, and the alligators gathered around my harbour from all quarters. From these considerations I concluded to be expeditious in my trip to the lagoon, in order to take some fish. Not thinking it prudent to take my fusee with me, lest I might lose it overboard in case of a battle, which I had every reason to dread before my return, I therefore furnished myself with a club for my defence, went on board, and penetrating the first line of those which surrounded my harbour, they gave way; but being pursued by several very large ones, I kept strictly on the watch, and paddled with all my might towards the entrance of the lagoon, hoping to be sheltered there from the multitude of my assailants; but ere I had half-way reached the place, I was attacked on all sides, several endeavouring to overset the canoe. My situation now became precarious to the last degree: two very large ones attacked me closely, at the same instant, rushing up with their heads and part of their bodies above the water, roaring terribly and belching floods of water over me. They struck their jaws together so close to my ears, as almost to stun me, and I expected every moment to be dragged out of the boat and instantly devoured. But I applied my weapons so effectually about me, though at random, that I was so successful as to beat them off a little; when, finding that they designed to renew the battle, I made for the shore, as the only means left me for my preservation; for, by keeping close to it, I should have my enemies on one side of me only, whereas I was before surrounded by them; and there was a probability, if pushed to the last extremity, of saving myself, by jumping out of the canoe on shore, as it is easy to outwalk them on land, although comparatively as swift as lightning in the water. I found this last expedient alone could fully answer my expectations, for as soon as I gained the shore, they drew off and kept aloof. This was a happy relief, as my confidence was, in some degree, recovered by it. On recollecting myself, I discovered that I had almost reached the entrance of the lagoon, and determined to venture in, if possible, to take a few fish, and then return to my harbour, while day-light continued; for I could now, with caution and resolution, make my way with safety along shore; and indeed there was no other way to regain my camp, without leaving my boat and making my retreat through the marshes and reeds, which, if I could even effect, would have been in a manner throwing myself away, for then there would have been no hopes of ever recovering my bark, and returning in safety to any settlements of men. I accordingly proceeded, and made good my entrance into the lagoon, though not without opposition from the alligators, who formed a line across the entrance, but did not pursue me into it, nor was I molested by any there, though there were some very large ones in a cove at the upper end. I soon caught more trout than I had present occasion for, and the air was too hot and sultry to

admit of their being kept for many hours, even though salted or bar-
becued. I now prepared for my return to camp, which I succeeded in
with but little trouble, by keeping close to the shore; yet I was opposed
upon re-entering the river out of the lagoon, and pursued near to my
landing (though not closely attacked), particularly by an old daring one,
about twelve feet in length, who kept close after me; and when I stepped
on shore and turned about, in order to draw up my canoe, he rushed up
near my feet, and lay there for some time, looking me in the face, his
head and shoulders out of water. I resolved he should pay for his temerity, and having a heavy load in my fusee, I ran to my camp, and returning
with my piece, found him with his foot on the gunwale of the boat, in
search of fish. On my coming up he withdrew sullenly and slowly into
the water, but soon returned and placed himself in his former position,
looking at me, and seeming neither fearful nor any way disturbed. I soon
dispatched him by lodging the contents of my gun in his head, and then
proceeded to cleanse and prepare my fish for supper; and accordingly
took them out of the boat, laid them down on the sand close to the
water, and began to scale them; when, raising my head, I saw before me,
through the clear water, the head and shoulders of a very large alligator,
moving slowly towards me. I instantly stepped back, when, with a sweep
of his tail, he brushed off several of my fish. It was certainly most provi-
dential that I looked up at that instant, as the monster would probably,
in less than a minute, have seized and dragged me into the river. This
incredible boldness of the animal disturbed me greatly, supposing there
could now be no reasonable safety for me during the night, but by
keeping continually on the watch: I therefore, as soon as I had prepared
the fish, proceeded to secure myself and effects in the best manner I
could. In the first place, I hauled my bark upon the shore, almost clear
out of the water, to prevent their oversetting or sinking her; after this,
every moveable was taken out and carried to my camp, which was but a
few yards off; then ranging some dry wood in such order as was the most
convenient, I cleared the ground round about it, that there might be no
impediment in my way, in case of an attack in the night, either from the
water or the land; for I discovered by this time, that this small isthmus,
from its remote situation and fruitfulness, was resorted to by bears and
wolves. Having prepared myself in the best manner I could, I charged
my gun, and proceeded to reconnoitre my camp and the adjacent
grounds; when I discovered that the peninsula and grove, at the distance
of about two hundred yards from my encampment, on the land side,
were invested by a cypress swamp, covered with water, which below was
joined to the shore of the little lake, and above to the marshes surrounding the lagoon; so that I was confined to an islet exceedingly circum-

scribed, and I found there was no other retreat for me, in case of an attack, but by either ascending one of the large oaks, or pushing off with my boat.

It was by this time dusk, and the alligators had nearly ceased their roar, when I was again alarmed by a tumultuous noise that seemed to be in my harbour, and therefore engaged my immediate attention. Returning to my camp, I found it undisturbed, and then continued on to the extreme point of the promontory, where I saw a scene, new and surprising, which at first threw my senses into such a tumult, that it was some time before I could comprehend what was the matter; however, I soon accounted for the prodigious assemblage of crocodiles at this place, which exceeded every thing of the kind I had ever heard of.

How shall I express myself so as to convey an adequate idea of it to the reader, and at the same time avoid raising suspicions of my veracity? Should I say, that the river (in this place) from shore to shore, and perhaps near half a mile above and below me, appeared to be one solid bank of fish, of various kinds, pushing through this narrow pass of St. Juan's into the little lake, on their return down the river, and that the alligators were in such incredible numbers, and so close together from shore to shore, that it would have been easy to have walked across on their heads, had the animals been harmless? What expressions can sufficiently declare the shocking scene that for some minutes continued, whilst this mighty army of fish were forcing the pass? During this attempt, thousands, I may say hundreds of thousands, of them were caught and swallowed by the devouring alligators. I have seen an alligator take up out of the water several great fish at a time, and just squeeze them betwixt his jaws, while the tails of the great trout flapped about his eyes and lips, ere he had swallowed them. The horrid noise of their closing jaws, their plunging amidst the broken banks of fish, and rising with their prey some feet upright above the water, the floods of water and blood rushing out of their mouths, and the clouds of vapour issuing from their wide nostrils, were truly frightful. This scene continued at intervals during the night, as the fish came to the pass. After this sight, shocking and tremendous as it was, I found myself somewhat easier and more reconciled to my situation; being convinced that their extraordinary assemblage here was owing to the annual feast of fish; and that they were so well employed in their own element, that I had little occasion to fear their paying me a visit.

It being now almost night, I returned to my camp, where I had left my fish broiling, and my kettle of rice stewing; and having with me oil, pepper, and salt, and excellent oranges hanging in abundance over my head (a valuable substitute for vinegar) I sat down and regaled myself cheerfully. Having finished my repast, I rekindled my fire for light, and whilst I was revising the notes of my past day's journey, I was suddenly roused with a noise behind me toward the main land. I sprang up on my feet, and listening, I distinctly heard some creature wading the water of the isthmus. I seized my gun and went cautiously from my camp, directing my steps towards the noise: when I had advanced about thirty yards, I halted behind a coppice of orange trees, and soon perceived two very large bears, which had made their way through the water, and had landed in the grove, about one hundred yards distance from me, and were advancing towards me. I waited until they were within thirty yards of me: they there began to snuff and look towards my camp: I snapped my piece, but it flashed, on which they both turned about and galloped off, plunging through the water and swamp, never halting, as I suppose, until they reached fast land, as I could hear them leaping and plunging a long time. They did not presume to return again, nor was I molested by any other creature, except being occasionally awakened by the whooping of owls, screaming of bitterns, or the wood-rats running amongst the leaves.

The wood-rat is a very curious animal. It is not half the size of the domestic rat; of a dark brown or black colour; its tail slender and shorter in proportion, and covered thinly with short hair. It is singular with respect to its ingenuity and great labour in the construction of its habitation, which is a conical pyramid about three or four feet high, constructed with dry branches, which it collects with great labour and perseverance, and piles up without any apparent order; yet they are so interwoven with one another, that it would take a bear or wild-cat some time to pull one of these castles to pieces, and allow the animals sufficient time to secure a retreat with their young.

The noise of the crocodiles kept me awake the greater part of the night; but when I arose in the morning, contrary to my expectations, there was perfect peace; very few of them to be seen, and those were asleep on the shore. Yet I was not able to suppress my fears and apprehensions of being attacked by them in future; and indeed yesterday's combat with them, notwithstanding I came off in a manner victorious, or at least made a safe retreat, had left sufficient impression on my mind to damp my courage; and it seemed too much for one of my strength, being alone in a very small boat, to encounter such collected danger. To pursue my voyage up the river, and be obliged every evening to pass such dangerous defiles, appeared to me as perilous as running the gauntlet betwixt two rows of Indians armed with knives and firebrands. I however resolved to continue my voyage one day longer, if I possibly could with safety, and then return down the river, should I find the like difficulties to oppose. Accordingly I got every thing on board, charged my gun, and set sail, cautiously, along shore. As I passed by Battle lagoon, I began to tremble and keep a good look-out; when suddenly a huge alligator rushed out of the reeds, and with a tremendous roar came up, and darted as swift as an arrow under my boat, emerging upright on my lee quarter, with open jaws, and belching water and smoke that fell upon me like rain in a hurricane. I laid soundly about his head with my club, and beat him off; and after plunging and darting about my boat, he went off on a straight line through the water, seemingly with the rapidity of lightning, and entered the cape of the lagoon. I now employed my time to the very best advantage in paddling close along shore, but could not forbear looking now and then behind me, and presently perceived one of them coming up again. The water of the river hereabouts was shoal and very clear; the monster came up with the usual roar and menaces, and passed close by the side of my boat, when I could distinctly see a young brood of alligators, to the number of one hundred or more, following after her in a long train. They kept close together in a column, without straggling off to the one side or the other; the young appeared to be of an equal size, about fifteen inches in length, almost black, with pale yellow transverse waved clouds or blotches, much like rattlesnakes in colour. I now lost sight of my enemy again.

Still keeping close along shore, on turning a point or projection of the river bank, at once I beheld a great number of hillocks or small pyramids, resembling hay-cocks, ranged like an encampment along the banks. They stood fifteen or twenty yards distant from the water, on a high marsh, about four feet perpendicular above the water. I knew them to be the nests of the crocodile, having had a description of them before; and now expected a furious and general attack, as I saw several large crocodiles swimming abreast of these buildings. These nests being so great a curiosity to me, I was determined at all events immediately to land and examine them. Accordingly, I ran my bark on shore at one of their landing-places, which was a sort of nick or little dock, from which ascended a sloping path or road up to the edge of the meadow, where their nests were; most of them were deserted, and the great thick whitish egg-shells lay broken and scattered upon the ground round about them.

The nests or hillocks are of the form of an obtuse cone, four feet high and four or five feet in diameter at their bases; they are constructed with mud, grass and herbage. At first they lay a floor of this kind of tempered mortar on the ground, upon which they deposit a layer of eggs, and upon this a stratum of mortar, seven or eight inches in thickness, and then another layer of eggs; and in this manner one stratum upon another, nearly to the top. I believe they commonly lay from one to two hundred eggs in a nest: these are hatched, I suppose, by the heat of the sun; and perhaps the vegetable substances mixed with the earth, being acted upon by the sun, may cause a small degree of fermentation, and so increase the heat in those hillocks. The ground for several acres about these nests shewed evident marks of a continual resort of alligators; the grass was every where beaten down, hardly a blade or straw was left standing; whereas, all about, at a distance, it was five or six feet high, and as thick as it could grow together. The female, as I imagine, carefully watches her own nest of eggs until they are all hatched; or perhaps while she is attending her own brood, she takes under her care and protection as many as she can get at one time, either from her own particular nest or others; but certain it is, that the young are not left to shift for themselves; for I have had frequent opportunities of seeing the female alligator leading about the shores her train of young ones, just as a hen does her brood of chickens; and she is equally assiduous and courageous in defending the young, which are under her care, and providing for their subsistence; and when she is basking upon the warm banks, with her brood around her, you may hear the young ones continually whining and barking like young puppies. I believe but few of a brood live to the years of full growth and magnitude, as the old feed on the young as long as they can make prey of them.

The alligator when full grown is a very large and terrible creature, and of prodigious strength, activity and swiftness in the water. I have seen them twenty feet in length, and some are supposed to be twenty-two or twenty-three feet. Their body is as large as that of a horse; their shape exactly resembles that of a lizard, except their tail, which is flat or cuneiform, being compressed on each side, and gradually diminishing from the abdomen to the extremity, which, with the whole body is covered with horny plates or squammæ, impenetrable when on the body of the live animal, even to a rifle ball, except about their head and just behind their fore-legs or arms, where it is said they are only vulnerable. The head of a full grown one is about three feet, and the mouth opens nearly the same length; their eyes are small in proportion, and seem sunk deep in the head, by means of the prominency of the brows; the nostrils are large, inflated and prominent on the top, so that the head in the water resembles, at a distance, a great chunk of wood floating about. Only the upper jaw moves, which they raise almost perpendicular, so as to form a right angle with the lower one. In the fore-part of the upper jaw, on each side, just under the nostrils, are two very large, thick, strong teeth or tusks, not very sharp, but rather the shape of a cone: these are as white as the finest polished ivory, and are not covered by any skin or lips, and always in sight, which gives the creature a frightful appearance: in the lower jaw are holes opposite to these teeth, to receive them: when they clap their jaws together it causes a surprising noise, like that which is made by forcing a heavy plank with violence upon the ground, and may be heard at a great distance.

But what is yet more surprising to a stranger, is the incredible loud and terrifying roar, which they are capable of making, especially in the spring season, their breeding time. It most resembles very heavy distant thunder, not only shaking the air and waters, but causing the earth to tremble; and when hundreds and thousands are roaring at the same time, you can scarcely be persuaded, but that the whole globe is violently and dangerously agitated.

An old champion, who is perhaps absolute sovereign of a little lake or lagoon (when fifty less than himself are obliged to content themselves with swelling and roaring in little coves round about) darts forth from the reedy coverts all at once, on the surface of the waters, in a right line; at first seemingly as rapid as lightning, but gradually more slowly until he arrives at the centre of the lake, when he stops. He now swells himself by drawing in wind and water through his mouth, which causes a loud sonorous rattling in the throat for near a minute, but it is immediately forced out again through his mouth and nostrils, with a loud noise, brandishing his tail in the air, and the vapour ascending from his nostrils like smoke. At other times, when swollen to an extent ready to burst, his head and tail lifted up, he spins or twirls round on the surface of the water. He acts his part like an Indian chief when rehearsing his feats of war; and then retiring, the exhibition is continued by others who dare to step forth, and strive to excel each other, to gain the attention of the favourite female.

Having gratified my curiosity at this general breeding-place and nursery of crocodiles, I continued my voyage up the river without being greatly disturbed by them. In my way I observed islets or floating fields of the bright green Pistia, decorated with other amphibious plants, as Senecio Jacobea, Persicaria amphibia, Coreopsis bidens, Hydrocotyle fluitans, and many others of less note. *   *   *

[*"the crystal bason"*]

*   *   * I now directed my steps towards my encampment, in a different direction. I seated myself upon a swelling green knoll, at the head of the crystal bason. Near me, on the left, was a point or projection of an entire grove of the aromatic Illicium Floridanum; on my right, and all around behind me, was a fruitful Orange grove, with Palms and Magnolias interspersed; in front, just under my feet, was the inchanting

and amazing crystal fountain, which incessantly threw up, from dark, rocky caverns below, tons of water every minute, forming a bason, capacious enough for large shallops to ride in, and a creek of four or five feet depth of water, and near twenty yards over, which meanders six miles through green meadows, pouring its limpid waters into the great Lake George, where they seem to remain pure and unmixed. About twenty yards from the upper edge of the bason, and directly opposite to the mouth or outlet of the creek, is a continual and amazing ebullition, where the waters are thrown up in such abundance and amazing force, as to jet and swell up two or three feet above the common surface: white sand and small particles of shells are thrown up with the waters, near to the top, when they diverge from the centre, subside with the expanding flood, and gently sink again, forming a large rim or funnel round about the aperture or mouth of the fountain, which is a vast perforation through a bed of rocks, the ragged points of which are projected out on every side. Thus far I know to be matter of real fact, and I have related it as near as I could conceive or express myself. But there are yet remaining scenes inexpressibly admirable and pleasing.

Behold, for instance, a vast circular expanse before you, the waters of which are so extremely clear as to be absolutely diaphanous or transparent as the ether; the margin of the bason ornamented with a great variety of fruitful and floriferous trees, shrubs, and plants, the pendant golden Orange dancing on the surface of the pellucid waters, the balmy air vibrating with the melody of the merry birds, tenants of the encircling aromatic grove.

At the same instant innumerable bands of fish are seen, some clothed in the most brilliant colours; the voracious crocodile stretched along at full length, as the great trunk of a tree in size; the devouring garfish, inimical trout, and all the varieties of gilded painted bream; the barbed catfish, dreaded sting-ray, skate, and flounder, spotted bass, sheeps head and ominous drum; all in their separate bands and communities, with free and unsuspicious intercourse performing their evolutions: there are no signs of enmity, no attempt to devour each other; the different bands seem peaceably and complaisantly to move a little aside, as it were to make room for others to pass by.

But behold yet something far more admirable, see whole armies descending into an abyss, into the mouth of the bubbling fountain: they disappear! are they gone for ever? I raise my eyes with terror and astonishment; I look down again to the fountain with anxiety, when behold them as it were emerging from the blue ether of another world, apparently at a vast distance; at their first appearance, no bigger than flies or minnows; now gradually enlarging, their brilliant colours begin to paint the fluid.

Now they come forward rapidly, and instantly emerge, with the elastic expanding column of crystalline waters, into the circular bason or funnel: see now how gently they rise, some upright, others obliquely, or seem to lie as it were on their sides, suffering themselves to be gently lifted or borne up by the expanding fluid towards the surface, sailing or floating like butterflies in the cerulean ether: then again they as gently descend, diverge and move off; when they rally, form again, and rejoin their kindred tribes.

This amazing and delightful scene, though real, appears at first but as a piece of excellent painting; there seems no medium; you imagine the picture to be within a few inches of your eyes, and that you may without the least difficulty touch any one of the fish, or put your finger upon the crocodile's eye, when it really is twenty or thirty feet under water.

And although this paradise of fish may seem to exhibit a just representation of the peaceable and happy state of nature which existed before the fall, yet in reality it is a mere representation; for the nature of the fish is the same as if they were in Lake George or the river; but here the water or element in which they live and move, is so perfectly clear and transparent, it places them all on an equality with regard to their ability to injure or escape from one another; (as all river fish of prey, or such as feed upon each other, as well as the unwieldy crocodile, take their prey by surprise; secreting themselves under covert or in ambush, until an opportunity offers, when they rush suddenly upon them:) but here is no covert, no ambush; here the trout freely passes by the very nose of the alligator, and laughs in his face, and the bream by the trout.

But what is really surprising is, that the consciousness of each other's safety, or some other latent cause, should so absolutely alter their conduct, for here is not the least attempt made to injure or disturb one another. * * *

ALEXANDER WILSON
1766-1813

Emigrating from Scotland as an adult, Wilson fell in love with the wildlife of his adopted country, and was soon roaming the woods of Pennsylvania studying and painting birds. With the publication of his seven-volume American Ornithology *between 1808 and 1814, he gained an authority in the field that caused even Jefferson to write to him with his naturalist questions. Nonetheless, Wilson was often in conflict with other ornithologists of his day and criticized them publicly. The love of nature, like other forms of love, can turn to jealousy. Yet within Wilson's proprietary feelings about American birds there may also have been the more positive element of protective loyalty to old relationships. Joseph Kastner describes an incident, just a few years after Wilson's arrival in America, when he bitterly complained about some birds shot by Charles Willson Peale and his son Rubens in their own naturalist pursuits. "One of the victims was a cardinal he knew well: it would come and sing at his window every morning."*

From AMERICAN ORNITHOLOGY; OR, THE NATURAL HISTORY OF THE BIRDS OF THE UNITED STATES

IVORY-BILLED WOODPECKER

This majestic and formidable species, in strength and magnitude, stands at the head of the whole class of Woodpeckers hitherto discovered. He may be called the king or chief of his tribe; and Nature seems to have designed him a distinguished characteristic, in the superb carmine crest, and bill of polished ivory, with which she has ornamented him. His eye is brilliant and daring; and his whole frame so admirably adapted for his mode of life, and method of procuring subsistence, as to impress on the mind of the examiner the most reverential ideas of the Creator. His manners have also a dignity in them superior to the common herd of Woodpeckers. Trees, shrubbery, orchards, rails, fenceposts, and old prostrate logs, are alike interesting to those, in their humble and indefatigable search for prey; but the royal hunter now before us, scorns the humility of such situations, and seeks the most towering trees of the forest; seeming particularly attached to those prodigious cypress swamps, whose crowded giant sons stretch their bare and blasted, or moss-hung, arms midway to the skies. In these almost inaccessible recesses, amid ruinous piles of impending timber, his trumpet-like note, and loud strokes, resound through the solitary, savage wilds, of which he seems the sole lord and inhabitant. Wherever he frequents, he leaves

American Ornithology; or, The Natural History of the Birds of the United States, 9 vols. (Philadelphia: Bradford & Inskeep, 1808–1814).

numerous monuments of his industry behind him. We there see enormous pine-trees, with cart-loads of bark lying around their roots, and
chips of the trunk itself in such quantities, as to suggest the idea that half
a dozen of axemen had been at work for the whole morning. The body of
the tree is also disfigured with such numerous and so large excavations,
that one can hardly conceive it possible for the whole to be the work of a
Woodpecker. With such strength, and an apparatus so powerful, what
havoc might he not commit, if numerous, on the most useful of our
forest trees; and yet with all these appearances, and much of vulgar
prejudice against him, it may fairly be questioned whether he is at all
injurious; or, at least, whether his exertions do not contribute most powerfully to the protection of our timber. Examine closely the tree where
he has been at work, and you will soon perceive, that it is neither from
motives of mischief nor amusement that he slices off the bark, or digs his
way into the trunk. For the sound and healthy tree is not in the least the
object of his attention. The diseased, infested with insects, and hastening to putrefaction, are *his* favorites; there the deadly crawling enemy
have formed a lodgment, between the bark and tender wood, to drink up
the very vital part of the tree. It is the ravages of these vermin which the
intelligent proprietor of the forest deplores, as the sole perpetrators of
the destruction of his timber. Would it be believed that the larvæ of an
insect, or fly, no larger than a grain of rice, should silently, and in one
season, destroy some thousand acres of pine trees, many of them from
two to three feet in diameter, and a hundred and fifty feet high! Yet
whoever passes along the high road from Georgetown to Charleston, in
South Carolina, about twenty miles from the former place, can have
striking and melancholy proofs of this fact. In some places the whole
woods, as far as you can see around you, are dead, stripped of the bark,
their wintry-looking arms and bare trunks bleaching in the sun, and
tumbling in ruins before every blast, presenting a frightful picture of
desolation. And yet ignorance and prejudice stubbornly persist in directing their indignation against the bird now before us, the constant and
mortal enemy of these very vermin, as if the hand that probed the
wound, to extract its cause, should be equally detested with that which
inflicted it; or as if the thief-catcher should be confounded with the
thief. Until some effectual preventive, or more complete mode of destruction, can be devised against these insects, and their larvæ, I would
humbly suggest the propriety of protecting, and receiving with proper
feelings of gratitude, the services of this and the whole tribe of Woodpeckers, letting the odium of guilt fall to its proper owners.

In looking over the accounts given of the Ivory-billed Woodpecker by
the naturalists of Europe, I find it asserted, that it inhabits from New

Jersey to Mexico. I believe, however, that few of them are ever seen to the north of Virginia, and very few of them even in that state. The first place I observed this bird at, when on my way to the south, was about twelve miles north of Wilmington, in North Carolina. There I found the bird from which the drawing of the figure in the plate was taken. This bird was only wounded slightly in the wing, and on being caught, uttered a loudly-reiterated, and most piteous note, exactly resembling the violent crying of a young child; which terrified my horse so, as nearly to have cost me my life. It was distressing to hear it. I carried it with me in the chair, under cover, to Wilmington. In passing through the streets, its affecting cries surprised every one within hearing, particularly the females, who hurried to the doors and windows, with looks of alarm and anxiety. I drove on, and on arriving at the piazza of the hotel, where I intended to put up, the landlord came forward, and a number of other persons who happened to be there, all equally alarmed at what they heard; this was greatly increased by my asking whether he could furnish me with accommodations for myself and my baby. The man looked blank, and foolish, while the others stared with still greater astonishment. After diverting myself for a minute or two at their expense, I drew my Woodpecker from under the cover, and a general laugh took place. I took him up stairs, and locked him up in my room, while I went to see my horse taken care of. In less than an hour I returned, and on opening the door he set up the same distressing shout, which now appeared to proceed from the grief that he had been discovered in his attempts at escape. He had mounted along the side of the window, nearly as high as the ceiling, a little below which he had begun to break through. The bed was covered with large pieces of plaster; the lath was exposed for at least fifteen inches square, and a hole, large enough to admit the fist, opened to the weather-boards; so that in less than another hour he would certainly have succeeded in making his way through. I now tied a string round his leg, and fastening it to the table, again left him. I wished to preserve his life, and had gone off in search of suitable food for him. As I reascended the stairs, I heard him again hard at work, and on entering had the mortification to perceive that he had almost entirely ruined the mahogany table to which he was fastened, and on which he had wreaked his whole vengeance. While engaged in taking the drawing, he cut me severely in several places, and on the whole, displayed such a noble and unconquerable spirit, that I was frequently tempted to restore him to his native woods. He lived with me nearly three days, but refused all sustenance, and I witnessed his death with regret.

The head and bill of this bird is in great esteem among the southern Indians, who wear them by way of amulet or charm, as well as ornament;

and, it is said, dispose of them to the northern tribes at considerable prices. An Indian believes that the head, skin, or even feathers of certain birds, confer on the wearer all the virtues or excellencies of those birds. Thus I have seen a coat made of the skins, heads and claws of the Raven; caps stuck round with heads of Butcher-birds, Hawks and Eagles; and as the disposition and courage of the Ivory-billed Woodpecker are well known to the savages, no wonder they should attach great value to it, having both beauty, and, in their estimation, distinguished merit to recommend it.

This bird is not migratory, but resident in the countries where it inhabits. In the low counties of the Carolinas, it usually prefers the large-timbered cypress swamps for breeding in. In the trunk of one of these trees, at a considerable height, the male and female alternately, and in conjunction, dig out a large and capacious cavity for their eggs and young. Trees thus dug out have frequently been cut down, with sometimes the eggs and young in them. This hole according to information, for I have never seen one myself, is generally a little winding, the better to keep out the weather, and from two to five feet deep. The eggs are said to be generally four, sometimes five, as large as a pullet's, pure white, and equally thick at both ends; a description that, except in size, very nearly agrees with all the rest of our Woodpeckers. The young begin to be seen abroad about the middle of June. Whether they breed more than once in the same season is uncertain.

So little attention do the people of the countries where these birds inhabit, pay to the minutiæ of natural history, that, generally speaking, they make no distinction between the Ivory-billed and Pileated Woodpecker, represented in the same plate; and it was not till I showed them the two birds together, that they knew of any difference. The more intelligent and observing part of the natives, however, distinguish them by the name of the large and lesser *Logcocks*. They seldom examine them but at a distance, gunpowder being considered too precious to be thrown away on Woodpeckers; nothing less than a Turkey being thought worth the value of a load.

The food of this bird consists, I believe, entirely of insects and their larvæ. The Pileated Woodpecker is suspected of sometimes tasting the Indian corn; the Ivory-billed never. His common note, repeated every three or four seconds, very much resembles the tone of a trumpet, or the high note of a clarionet, and can plainly be distinguished at the distance of more than half a mile; seeming to be immediately at hand, though perhaps more than one hundred yards off. This it utters while mounting along the trunk, or digging into it. At these times it has a stately and novel appearance; and the note instantly attracts the notice of a stranger.

Along the borders of the Savannah river, between Savannah and Augusta, I found them very frequently; but my horse no sooner heard their trumpet-like note, than remembering his former alarm, he became almost ungovernable.

The Ivory-billed Woodpecker is twenty inches long, and thirty inches in extent; the general color is black, with a considerable gloss of green when exposed to a good light; iris of the eye vivid yellow; nostrils covered with recumbent white hairs; fore part of the head black, rest of the crest of a most splendid red, spotted at the bottom with white, which is only seen when the crest is erected, as represented in the plate; this long red plumage being ash-colored at its base, above that white, and ending in brilliant red; a stripe of white proceeds from a point, about half an inch below each eye, passes down each side of the neck, and along the back, where they are about an inch apart, nearly to the rump; the first five primaries are wholly black, on the next five the white spreads from the tip higher and higher to the secondaries, which are wholly white from their coverts downwards: these markings, when the wings are shut, make the bird appear as if his back were white, hence he has been called, by some of our naturalists, the large White-backed Woodpecker; the neck is long; the beak an inch broad at the base, of the color and consistence of ivory, prodigiously strong, and elegantly fluted; the tail is black, tapering from the two exterior feathers, which are three inches shorter than the middle ones, and each feather has the singularity of being greatly concave below; the wing is lined with yellowish white; the legs are about an inch and a quarter long, the exterior toe about the same length, the claws exactly semicircular and remarkably powerful, the whole of a light blue or lead color. The female is about half an inch shorter, the bill rather less, and the whole plumage of the head black, glossed with green; in the other parts of the plumage she exactly resembles the male. In the stomachs of three which I opened, I found large quantities of a species of worm called *borers,* two or three inches long, of a dirty cream-color, with a black head; the stomach was an oblong pouch, not muscular like the gizzards of some others. The tongue was worm-shaped, and for half an inch at the tip as hard as horn, flat, pointed, of the same white color as the bill, and thickly barbed on each side.

JOHN LEONARD KNAPP
1767-1845

When reading Gilbert White as an undergraduate, the young Charles Darwin is supposed to have exclaimed, "Why does not every gentleman become a naturalist?" While Darwin's explorations and researches eventually led him outward to an epochal transformation of the life-sciences, there were also gentlemen who stuck closer to White's own Linnaean model as a way to organize days of rambling and observing out of doors. John Leonard Knapp's Journal of a Naturalist *(1829) acknowledges* The Natural History of Selborne *in the first sentence of its "Preface," but then goes on to say, "The works do not, I apprehend, interfere with each other. The meditations of separate naturalists in fields, in wilds, in woods, may yield a similarity of ideas; yet the different aspects under which the same things are viewed, and characters considered, afford infinite variety of description and narrative...." Much of the charm of this book, written by Knapp on his estate near Bristol, comes from the sense that, despite the systematic, detailed treatment of soils, birds, and other game, and the skillful drawings of details from nature, he is presenting, and means to present, only an aspect: a personal, familiar view of nature such as is available to, and distinct for, every new observer. Writing and nature, in such an approach, renew one another.*

From THE JOURNAL OF A NATURALIST

THE MARTEN

But we must dismiss the vegetable tribes, and enter upon the world of sensitive nature. The quadrupeds naturally present themselves first to our notice, but with us they are few in number; our population scares them, our gamekeepers kill them, and enclosures extirpate their haunts.

The Journal of a Naturalist (London: John Murray, 1829).

Yet the marten *(mustela martes)* lingers with us still, and every winter's snow becomes instrumental to its capture, betraying its footsteps to those who are acquainted with the peculiar trace which it leaves. Its excursions generally terminate at some hollow tree, whence it is driven into a bag; and we are surprised that a predaceous animal, not protected by laws or arbitrary privileges, and of some value too, should still exist. Of all our animals called vermin, we have none more admirably fitted for a predatory life than the marten: it is endowed with strength of body; is remarkably quick and active in all its motions; has an eye so large, clear, perceptive, and moveable in its orbit, that nothing can stir without its observation; and it is supplied, apparently, with a sense of smelling as perfect as its other faculties. Its feet are well adapted to its habits, not treading upright on the balls alone, but with the joint bending, the fleshy parts being imbedded in a very soft and delicate hair, so that the tread of the animal, even upon decayed leaves is scarcely audible; by which means it can steal upon its prey without any noise betraying its approach. The fur is fine, and the skin so thin and flexible, as to impede none of its agile movements. Thus everything combines to render the marten a very destructive creature. It seems to have a great dislike to cold, residing in winter in the hollow of some tree, deeply imbedded in dry foliage, and when in confinement, covering and hiding itself with all the warm materials it can find. In genial seasons it will sleep by day in the abandoned nest of the crow or buzzard, and its dormitory is often discovered by the chattering and mobbing of different birds on the tree. It is certainly not numerous in England, our woods being too small, and too easily penetrated, to afford it adequate quiet and shelter. Its skin is still in some little request, being worth about two shillings and sixpence in the market; but it is used only for inferior purposes, as the furs of colder regions than ours are better, and more easily obtained.

THE HEDGEHOG

Notwithstanding all the persecutions from prejudice and wantonness to which the hedgehog *(erinaceus europæus)* is exposed, it is yet common with us; sleeping by day in a bed of leaves and moss, under the cover of a very thick bramble or furze-bush, and at times in some hollow stump of a tree. It creeps out in the summer evenings; and, running about with more agility than its dull appearance promises, feeds on dew-worms and beetles, which it finds among the herbage, but retires with trepidation at the approach of man. In the autumn, crabs, haws, and the common fruits of the hedge, constitute its diet. In the winter, covering itself deeply in moss and leaves, it sleeps during the severe weather; and, when drawn out from its bed, scarcely anything of the creature is to be observed, it exhibiting only a ball of leaves, which it seems to attach to its spines by repeatedly rolling itself round in its nest. Thus comfortably invested, it suffers little from the season. Some strong smell must proceed from this animal, as we find it frequently, with our sporting dogs, even in this state; and every village boy with his cur detects the haunts of the poor hedgehog, and as assuredly worries and kills him. Killing everything, and cruelty, are the common vices of the ignorant; and unresisting innocence becomes a ready victim to prejudice or power. The snake, the blindworm, and the toad, are all indiscriminately destroyed as venomous animals whenever found; and it is well for the last-mentioned poor animal, which, Boyle says, "lives on poison, and is all venom," if prolonged sufferings do not finish its being: but even we, who should know better, yet give rewards for the wretched urchin's head! that very ancient prejudice of its drawing milk from the udders of resting cows being still entertained, without any consideration of its impracticability from the smallness of the hedgehog's mouth; and so deeply is this character associated with its name, that we believe no argument would persuade to the contrary, or remonstrance avail with our idle boys, to spare the life of this most harmless and least obtrusive creature in existence.

If we were to detail the worst propensities of man, disgusting as they might be, yet the one most eminently offensive would be, cruelty—a compound of tyranny, ingratitude, and pride; tyranny, because there is the power—ingratitude, for the most harmless and serviceable are usually the object—pride, to manifest a contempt of the weakness of humanity. There is no one creature, whose services Providence has assigned to man, that contributes more to his wants, is more conducive to his comforts, than the horse; nor is there one which is subjected to more afflictions than this his faithful servant. The ass, probably and happily, is not a very sensitive animal, but the poor horse no sooner becomes the property of man in the lower walks of life, than he commonly has his ears shorn off; his knees are broken, his wind is broken, his body is starved, and his eyes——!! I fear, in these grades of society, mercy is only known by the name of cowardice, and compassion designated simplicity and effeminacy; and so we become cruel, and consider it as valiance and manliness. Cruelty is a vice repeatedly marked in Scripture as repugnant to the primest attributes of our Maker, "because he delighteth in mercy." One of the three requisites necessary for man to obtain the favour of Heaven, and which was of more avail than sacrifice and oblation, was that of "showing mercy;" and He, who has left us so many examples in a life of compassion and pity, hath most strongly enforced this virtue, by assuring us, that the "merciful are blessed, for they will obtain mercy."

Hedgehogs were formerly an article of food; but this diet was pronounced to be dry, and not nutritive, "because he putteth forth so many prickles." All plants producing thorns, or tending to any roughness, were considered to be of a drying nature; and, upon this foundation, the ashes of the hedgehog were administered as a "great desiccative of fistulas."

The spines of the hedgehog are moveable, not fixed and resisting, but loose in the skin, and when dry, fall backward and forward upon being moved; yet, from the peculiar manner in which they are inserted, it requires more force to draw them out than may be at first sight expected. The hair of most creatures seems to arise from a bulbous root fixed in the skin; but the spines of the hedgehog have their lower ends fined down to a thin neck or thread, which, passing through a small orifice in the skin, is secured on the under side by a round head like that of a pin, or are riveted, as it were, by the termination being enlarged and rounded; and these heads are all visible when the skin becomes dry, as if studded by small pins thrust through. Hence they are moveable in all directions, and, resting upon the muscle of the creature, must be the medium of a very sensible perception to the animal, and more so than hair could be, which does not seem to penetrate so far as the muscular fibre. Now, this little quadruped, upon suspicion of harm, rolls itself up in a ball, hiding his nose and eyes in the hollow of his stomach, and thus the common organs of perception, hearing, seeing, smelling, are precluded from action; but by the sensibility of the spines, he seems fully acquainted with every danger that may threaten him; and upon any attempt to uncoil himself, if these spines be touched, he immediately retracts, assuming his globular form again, awaiting a more secure period for retreat.

THE HARVEST MOUSE

The harvest mouse *(mus messorius)* in some seasons is common with us, but, like other species of mice, varies much in the numbers found. I have seen their nests as late as the middle of September, containing eight young ones, entirely filling the little interior cavity. These nests vary in shape, being round, oval, or pear-shaped, with a long neck, and are to be distinguished from those of any other mouse by being generally suspended on some growing vegetable, a thistle, a bean-stalk, or some adjoining stems of wheat, with which it rocks and waves in the wind; but to prevent the young from being dislodged by any violent agitation of the plant, the parent closes up the entrance so uniformly with the whole fabric, that the real opening is with difficulty found.

They are the most tame and harmless of little creatures; and, taking shelter in the sheaves when in the field, are often brought home with the crop, and found in little shallow burrows on the ground after the removal of a bean-rick. Those that remain in the field form stores for the winter season, and congregate in small societies in holes under some sheltered ditch-bank. An old one, which I weighed, was only one drachm and five grains in weight.

Mankind appear to be progressively increasing. It was an original command of his Creator, and the animals domesticated by him, and fostered for his use, are probably multiplied in proportion to his requirements; but we have no reason to suppose that this annual augmentation proceeds in a proportionate degree with the wild creatures upon the surface of the globe; and we know that many of them are yearly decreasing, and very many that once existed have even become extinct. That there are years of increase and decrease ordained for all the inferior orders of creation, common observation makes manifest. In the years 1819 and 1820, all the country about us was overrun with mice; they harboured under the hassocks of our coarse grasses *(aira cæspitosa)*, perforated the banks of ditches, occasioned much damage by burrowing into our potato heaps, and coursed in our gardens from bed to bed even during daylight. The species were the short-tailed meadow mouse, and the long-tailed garden mouse, and both kinds united in the spring to destroy our early-sown pease and beans. In the ensuing summer, however, they became so greatly reduced, that few were to be seen, and we have not had anything like such an increase since that period. It is probable that some disease afflicted them, and that they perished in their holes, for we never found their bodies, and any emigration of such large companies would certainly have been observed; yet the appearance and disappearance of creatures of this kind lead us to conclude that they do occasionally change their habitations.

A large stagnant piece of water in an inland county, with which I was intimately acquainted, and which I very frequently visited for many years of my life, was one summer suddenly infested with an astonishing number of the short-tailed water rat, none of which had previously existed there. Its vegetation was the common products of such places, excepting that the larger portion of it was densely covered with its usual crop, the smooth horsetail *(equisetum limosum)*. This constituted the food of the creatures, and the noise made by their champing it we could distinctly hear in the evening at many yards' distance. They were shot by dozens daily; yet the survivors seemed quite regardless of the noise, the smoke, the deaths, around them. Before the winter, this great herd disappeared, and so entirely evacuated the place, that a few years after I could not obtain a single specimen. They did not disperse, for the animal is seldom found in the neighbourhood, and no dead bodies were observed. They had certainly made this place a temporary station in their progress from some other; but how such large companies can change their situations unobserved in their transits is astonishing. Birds can move in high regions and in obscurity, and are not commonly objects of notice; but quadrupeds can travel only on the ground, and would be regarded with wonder, when in great numbers, by the rudest peasant.

THE WATER SHREW

That little animal the water shrew *(sorex fodiens)* appears to be but partially known, but is probably more generally diffused than we imagine. The common shrew in particular seasons gambols through our hedgerows, squeaking and rustling about the dry foliage, and is observed by every one; but the water shrew inhabits places that secrete it from general notice, and appears to move only in the evenings, which occasions it being so seldom observed. That this creature was an occasional resident in our neighbourhood, was manifest from the dead bodies of two or three having occurred in my walks; but it was some time before I discovered a little colony of them quietly settled in one of my ponds, overshadowed with bushes and foliage. It is very amusing to observe the actions of these creatures, all life and animation in an element they could not be thought any way calculated for enjoying; but they swim admirably, frolicking over the floating leaves of the pondweed, and up the foliage of the flags, which, bending with their weight, will at times souse them in the pool, and away they scramble to another, searching apparently for the insects that frequent such places, and feeding on drowned moths *(phalæna potamogeta)* and similar insects. They run along the margin of the water, rooting amid the leaves and mud with their long noses for food, like little ducks, with great earnestness and perseverance. Their power of vision seems limited to a confined circumference. The smallness of their eyes, and the growth of the fur about them, are convenient for the habits of the animal, but impediments to extended vision; so that, with caution, we can approach them in their gambols, and observe all their actions. The general blackness of the body, and the triangular spot beneath the tail, as mentioned by Pennant, afford the best ready distinction of this mouse from the common shrew. Both our species of sorex seem to feed by preference on insects and worms; and thus, like the mole, their flesh is rank and offensive to most creatures, which reject them as food. The common shrew, in spring and summer, is ordinarily in motion even during the day, from sexual attachment, which occasions the destruction of numbers by cats, and other prowling animals; and thus we find them strewed in our paths, by gateways, and in our garden walks, dropped by these animals in their progress. It was once thought that some periodical disease occasioned this mortality of the species; but I think we may now conclude that violence alone is the cause of their destruction in these instances. The bite of this creature was considered by the ancients as peculiarly noxious, even to horses and large cattle; and variety of the most extraordinary remedies for the wound, and preventives against it, are mentioned by Pliny and others. The prejudices of antiquity, long as they usually are in keeping possession of the mind, have not been remembered by us; and we only know the hardy shrew now as a perfectly harmless animal, though we still retain a name for it expressive of something malignant and spiteful.

DOROTHY WORDSWORTH
1771-1855

For most of the century after her death, only a few excerpts from Dorothy Wordsworth's journals were widely known. Her place in literary history rested mainly on her relationships with her brother William and with Samuel Taylor Coleridge at the period of their greatest creativity. But since the fuller publication of her Alfoxden Journal, *covering the year 1798, and her* Grasmere Journals, *of 1800–1803, Dorothy Wordsworth has increasingly become valued as an artist in her own right. Her responses to flowers and weather, as well as to the rural poor, are startlingly vivid. It is not hard to understand why William so prized the company of his sister when he was composing his poetry, and why he asked her permission to read and draw from her journals. She achieves a lyrical immediacy that makes a reader see what she has seen, feel what she has felt.*

From JOURNALS OF DOROTHY WORDSWORTH

THE ALFOXDEN JOURNAL 1798

Alfoxden, 20th January 1798.

The green paths down the hillsides are channels for streams. The young wheat is streaked by silver lines of water running between the ridges, the sheep are gathered together on the slopes. After the wet dark days, the country seems more populous. It peoples itself in the sunbeams. The garden, mimic of spring, is gay with flowers. The purple-starred hepatica spreads itself in the sun, and the clustering snow-drops put forth their white heads, at first upright, ribbed with green, and like a rosebud; when completely opened, hanging their heads downwards, but slowly lengthening their slender stems. The slanting woods of an unvarying brown, showing the light through the thin net-work of their upper boughs. Upon the highest ridge of that round hill covered with planted oaks, the shafts of the trees show in the light like the columns of a ruin.

21st. Walked on the hill-tops—a warm day. Sate under the firs in the park. The tops of the beeches of a brown-red, or crimson. Those oaks, fanned by the sea breeze, thick with feathery sea-green moss, as a grove not stripped of its leaves. Moss cups more proper than acorns for fairy goblets.

22nd. Walked through the wood to Holford. The ivy twisting round the oaks like bristled serpents. The day cold—a warm shelter in the hollies, capriciously bearing berries. Query: Are the male and female flowers on separate trees?

23rd. Bright sunshine, went out at 3 o'clock. The sea perfectly calm blue, streaked with deeper colour by the clouds, and tongues or points of sand; on our return of a gloomy red. The sun gone down. The crescent moon, Jupiter, and Venus. The sound of the sea distinctly heard on the tops of the hills, which we could never hear in summer. We attribute this partly to the bareness of the trees, but chiefly to the absence of the singing of birds, the hum of insects, that noiseless noise which lives in the summer air. The villages marked out by beautiful beds of smoke. The turf fading into the mountain road. The scarlet flowers of the moss.

24th. Walked between half-past three and half-past five. The evening cold and clear. The sea of a sober grey, streaked by the deeper grey clouds. The half dead sound of the near sheep-bell, in the hollow of the sloping coombe, exquisitely soothing.

Journals of Dorothy Wordsworth (London: Oxford University Press, 1971).

25th. Went to Poole's after tea. The sky spread over with one continuous cloud, whitened by the light of the moon, which, though her dim
shape was seen, did not throw forth so strong a light as to chequer the
earth with shadows. At once the clouds seemed to cleave asunder, and
left her in the centre of a black-blue vault. She sailed along, followed by
multitudes of stars, small, and bright, and sharp. Their brightness
seemed concentrated, (half-moon).

26th. Walked upon the hill-tops; followed the sheep tracks till we
overlooked the larger coombe. Sat in the sunshine. The distant sheep-
bells, the sound of the stream; the woodman winding along the half-
marked road with his laden pony; locks of wool still spangled with the
dewdrops; the blue-grey sea, shaded with immense masses of cloud, not
streaked; the sheep glittering in the sunshine. Returned through the
wood. The trees skirting the wood, being exposed more directly to the
action of the sea breeze, stripped of the net-work of their upper boughs,
which are stiff and erect, like black skeletons; the ground strewed with
the red berries of the holly. Set forward before two o'clock. Returned a
little after four.

27th. Walked from seven o'clock till half-past eight. Upon the whole
an uninteresting evening. Only once while we were in the wood the
moon burst through the invisible veil which enveloped her, the shadows
of the oaks blackened, and their lines became more strongly marked.
The withered leaves were coloured with a deeper yellow, a brighter gloss
spotted the hollies; again her form became dimmer; the sky flat, un-
marked by distances, a white thin cloud. The manufacturer's dog makes
a strange, uncouth howl, which it continues many minutes after there is
no noise near it but that of the brook. It howls at the murmur of the
village stream.

28th. Walked only to the mill.

29th. A very stormy day. William walked to the top of the hill to see
the sea. Nothing distinguishable but a heavy blackness. An immense
bough riven from one of the fir trees.

30th. William called me into the garden to observe a singular appearance about the moon. A perfect rainbow, within the bow one star, only
of colours more vivid. The semi-circle soon became a complete circle,
and in the course of three or four minutes the whole faded away. Walked
to the blacksmith's and the baker's; an uninteresting evening.

31st. Set forward to Stowey at half-past five. A violent storm in the
wood; sheltered under the hollies. When we left home the moon immensely large, the sky scattered over with clouds. These soon closed in,
contracting the dimensions of the moon without concealing her. The
sound of the pattering shower, and the gusts of wind, very grand. Left

the wood when nothing remained of the storm but the driving wind, and a few scattering drops of rain. Presently all clear, Venus first showing herself between the struggling clouds; afterwards Jupiter appeared. The hawthorn hedges, black and pointed, glittering with millions of diamond drops; the hollies shining with broader patches of light. The road to the village of Holford glittered like another stream. On our return, the wind high—a violent storm of hail and rain at the Castle of Comfort. All the Heavens seemed in one perpetual motion when the rain ceased; the moon appearing, now half veiled, and now retired behind heavy clouds, the stars still moving, the roads very dirty.

1st February. About two hours before dinner, set forward towards Mr Bartholemew's. The wind blew so keen in our faces that we felt ourselves inclined to seek the covert of the wood. There we had a warm shelter, gathered a burthen of large rotten boughs blown down by the wind of the preceding night. The sun shone clear, but all at once a heavy blackness hung over the sea. The trees almost *roared,* and the ground seemed in motion with the multitudes of dancing leaves, which made a rustling sound, distinct from that of the trees. Still the asses pastured in quietness under the hollies, undisturbed by these forerunners of the storm. The wind beat furiously against us as we returned. Full moon. She rose in uncommon majesty over the sea, slowly ascending through the clouds. Sat with the window open an hour in the moonlight.

2nd. Walked through the wood, and on to the Downs before dinner; a warm pleasant air. The sun shone, but was often obscured by straggling clouds. The redbreasts made a ceaseless song in the woods. The wind rose very high in the evening. The room smoked so that we were obliged to quit it. Young lambs in a green pasture in the Coombe, thick legs, large heads, black staring eyes.

3rd. A mild morning, the windows open at breakfast, the redbreasts singing in the garden. Walked with Coleridge over the hills. The sea at first obscured by vapour; that vapour afterwards slid in one mighty mass along the sea-shore; the islands and one point of land clear beyond it. The distant country (which was purple in the clear dull air), overhung by straggling clouds that sailed over it, appeared like the darker clouds, which are often seen at a great distance apparently motionless, while the nearer ones pass quickly over them, driven by the lower winds. I never saw such a union of earth, sky, and sea. The clouds beneath our feet spread themselves to the water, and the clouds of the sky almost joined them. Gathered sticks in the wood; a perfect stillness. The redbreasts sang upon the leafless boughs. Of a great number of sheep in the field, only one standing. Returned to dinner at five o'clock. The moonlight still and warm as a summer's night at nine o'clock.

4th. Walked a great part of the way to Stowey with Coleridge. The morning warm and sunny. The young lasses seen on the hill-tops, in the villages and roads, in their summer holiday clothes—pink petticoats and blue. Mothers with their children in arms, and the little ones that could just walk, tottering by their side. Midges or small flies spinning in the sunshine; the songs of the lark and redbreast; daisies upon the turf; the hazels in blossom; honeysuckles budding. I saw one solitary strawberry flower under a hedge. The furze gay with blossom. The moss rubbed from the pailings by the sheep, that leave locks of wool, and the red marks with which they are spotted, upon the wood.

THE GRASMERE JOURNALS 1800–1803

[April 1802]

Thursday 29th. A beautiful morning. The sun shone and all was pleasant. We sent off our parcel to Coleridge by the waggon. Mr Simpson heard the Cuckow today. Before we went out after I had written down the Tinker (which William finished this morning) Luff called. He was very lame, limped into the kitchen—he came on a little Pony. We then went to John's Grove, sate a while at first. Afterwards William lay, and I lay in the trench under the fence—he with his eyes shut and listening to the waterfalls and the Birds. There was no one waterfall above another— it was a sound of waters in the air—the voice of the air. William heard me breathing and rustling now and then but we both lay still, and unseen by one another. He thought that it would be as sweet thus to lie so in the grave, to hear the *peaceful* sounds of the earth and just to know that our dear friends were near. The Lake was still. There was a Boat out. Silver How reflected with delicate purple and yellowish hues as I have seen Spar. Lambs on the island and running races together by the half dozen in the round field near us. The copses green*ish*, hawthorn green.— Came home to dinner then went to Mr Simpson. We rested a long time under a wall. Sheep and lambs were in the field—cottages smoking. As I lay down on the grass, I observed the glittering silver line on the ridges of the Backs of the sheep, owing to their situation respecting the Sun— which made them look beautiful but with something of strangeness, like animals of another kind—as if belonging to a more splendid world. Met old Mr S. at the door—Mrs S. poorly. I got mullens and pansies. I was sick and ill and obliged to come home soon. We went to bed immediately—I slept up stairs. The air coldish where it was felt somewhat frosty.

Friday April 30th. We came into the orchard directly after Breakfast, and sate there. The lake was calm—the sky cloudy. We saw two fishermen by the lake side. William began to write the poem of the Celandine. I wrote to Mary H. sitting on the fur gown. Walked backwards and

forwards with William—he repeated his poem to me. Then he got to
work again and could not give over—he had not finished his dinner till 5
o'clock. After dinner we took up the fur gown into The Hollins above.
We found a sweet seat and thither we will often go. We spread the gown
put on each a cloak and there we lay. William fell asleep—he had a bad
head ache owing to his having been disturbed the night before with
reading C.'s letter which Fletcher had brought to the door. I did not
sleep but I lay with half shut eyes, looking at the prospect as in a vision
almost I was so resigned to it. Loughrigg Fell was the most distant hill,
then came the Lake slipping in between the copses and above the copse
the round swelling field, nearer to me a wild intermixture of rocks trees,
and slacks of grassy ground.—When we turned the corner of our little
shelter we saw the Church and the whole vale. It is a blessed place. The
Birds were about us on all sides—Skobbys Robins Bullfinches. Crows
now and then flew over our heads as we were warned by the sound of the
beating of the air above. We stayed till the light of day was going and the
little Birds had begun to settle their singing. But there was a thrush not
far off that seemed to sing louder and clearer than the thrushes had sung
when it was quite day. We came in at 8 o'clock, got tea. Wrote to
Coleridge, and I wrote to Mrs Clarkson part of a letter. We went to bed
at 20 minutes past 11 with prayers that Wm might sleep well.

Saturday May 1st. Rose not till ½ past 8. A heavenly morning. As
soon as Breakfast was over we went into the garden and sowed the scarlet
beans about the house. It was a clear sky a heavenly morning. I sowed the
flowers William helped me. We then went and sate in the orchard till
dinner time. It was very hot. William wrote the Celandine. We planned
a shed for the sun was too much for us. After dinner we went again to our
old resting place in the Hollins under the Rock. We first lay under a
holly where we saw nothing but the holly tree and a budding elm mossed
with [?] and the sky above our heads. But that holly tree had a beauty
about it more than its own, knowing as we did where we were. When the
sun had got low enough we went to the Rock shade. Oh the overwhelming beauty of the vale below—greener than green. Two Ravens flew high
high in the sky and the sun shone upon their bellys and their wings long
after there was none of his light to be seen but a little space on the top of
Loughrigg Fell. We went down to tea at 8 o'clock—had lost the poem
and returned after tea. The Landscape was fading, sheep and lambs
quiet among the Rocks. We walked towards Kings and backwards and
forwards. The sky was perfectly cloudless. N.B. Is it often so? 3 solitary
stars in the middle of the blue vault one or two on the points of the high
hills. Wm wrote the Celandine 2nd part tonight. Heard the cuckow
today this first of May.

SAMUEL TAYLOR COLERIDGE
1772-1834

Because of his diverse and restless genius, Coleridge was a figure puzzling to himself as well as to his contemporaries. His ever-growing reputation in our day has been based primarily upon his achievements as a poet, an autobiographical author, and a theologian. Yet, as extensive collections from his journals have continued to appear, the central place of nature in Coleridge's mind and writing has also grown clear. Coleridge found his peace and his focus in the budding revelations of the field, the mystery of moon and water. Both his naturalist's descriptions and his sketches in the notebooks reveal an eye for vivid and numinous details.

From ANIMA POETAE

Observed the great half moon setting behind the mountain ridge, and watched the shapes its various segments presented as it slowly sunk— first the foot of a boot, all but the heel—then a little pyramid △—then a star of the first magnitude, indeed, it was not distinguishable from the evening star at its largest—then rapidly a smaller, a small, a very small star—and, as it diminished in size, so it grew paler in tint. And now where is it? Unseen—but a little fleecy cloud hangs above the mountain ridge, and is rich in amber light.

On the Greta, over the bridge by Mr. Edmundson's father-in-law, the ashes—their leaves of that light yellow which autumn gives them—cast a reflection on the river like a painter's sunshine.

The first sight of green fields with the numberless nodding gold cups, and the winding river with alders on its banks, affected me, coming out

Anima Poetae, ed. Ernest Hartley Coleridge (Boston: Houghton Mifflin, 1895).

of a city confinement, with the sweetness and power of a sudden strain of music.

In natural objects we feel ourselves, or think of ourselves, only by *likenesses;* among men, too often by *differences.* Hence the soothing, love-kindling effect of rural nature—the bad passions of human societies. And why is difference linked with hatred?

On St. Herbert's Island, I saw a large spider with most beautiful legs, floating in the air on his back by a single thread which he was spinning out, and still, as he spun, heaving on the air, as if the air beneath was a pavement elastic to his strokes. From the top of a very high tree he had spun his line; at length reached the bottom, tied his thread round a piece of grass, and reascended to spin another,—a net to hang, as a fisherman's sea-net hangs, in the sun and wind to dry.

After a night of storm and rain, the sky calm and white, by blue vapor thinning into formlessness instead of clouds, the mountains of height covered with snow, the secondary mountains black. The moon descending aslant the ᴀ, through the midst of which the great road winds, set exactly behind Whinlatter Point, marked A. She being an egg, somewhat uncouthly shaped, perhaps, but an ostrich's egg rather than any other (she is two nights more than a half-moon), she set behind the black point, fitted herself on to it like a cap of fire, then became a crescent, then a mountain of fire in the distance, then the peak itself on fire, one steady flame; then stars of the first, second, and third magnitude, and vanishing, upboiled a swell of light, and in the next second the whole sky, which had been *sable blue* around the yellow moon, whitened and brightened for as large a space as would take the moon half an hour to descend through.

What a sky! the not yet orbed moon, the spotted oval, blue at one edge from the deep utter blue of the sky—a MASS of *pearl-*white cloud below, distant, and travelling to the horizon, but all the upper part of the ascent and all the height such *profound* blue, deep as a deep river, and deep in color, and those two depths so entirely *one, as* to give the meaning and explanation of the two different significations of the epithet. Here, so far from *divided,* they were scarcely *distinct,* scattered over with thin pearl-white cloudlets—hands and fingers—the largest not larger than a floating veil! Unconsciously I stretched forth my arms as to embrace the sky, and in a trance I had worshipped God in the moon—the spirit, not the form. I felt in how innocent a feeling Sabeism might have begun. Oh! not only the moon, but the depths of the sky! The moon was the *idea;* but deep sky is, of all visual impressions, the nearest akin to a feeling. It is more a feeling than a sight, or, rather, it is the melting away and entire union of feeling and sight!

I never had a more lovely twig of orange-blossoms, with four old last year's leaves with their steady green well-placed among them, than today, and with a rose-twig of three roses [it] made a very striking nose-gay to an Englishman. The orange twig was so very full of blossoms that one-fourth of the number becoming fruit of the natural size would have broken the twig off. Is there, then, disproportion here? or waste? O no! no! In the first place, here is a prodigality of beauty; and what harm do they do by existing? And is not man a being capable of Beauty even as of Hunger and Thirst? And if the latter be fit objects of a final cause, why not the former? But secondly [Nature] hereby multiplies manifold the chances of a proper number becoming fruit; in this twig, for instance, for one set of accidents that would have been fatal to the year's growth if only as many blossoms had been on it as it was designed to bear fruit, there may now be three sets of accidents—and no harm done. And, thirdly and lastly, for *me* at *least*—or, at least, at present, for in nature doubtless there are many additional reasons, and possibly for *me* at some future hour of reflection, after some new influx of information from books or observance—and, thirdly, these blossoms are Fruit, fruit to the winged insect, fruit to man—yea! and of more solid value, perhaps, than the orange itself! Oh how the Bees be-throng and be-murmur it! O how the honey tells the tale of its birthplace to the sense of sight and odor! and to how many minute and uneyeable insects beside! So, I cannot but think, ought I to be talking to Hartley, and sometimes to detail all the insects that have arts or implements resembling human—the sea-snails, with the nautilus at their head; the wheel-insect, the galvanic eel, etc.

The Pine-Tree blasted at the top was applied by Swift to himself as a prophetic emblem of his own decay. The Chestnut is a fine shady tree, and its wood excellent, were it not that it dies away at the *heart* first. Alas! poor me!

In the first [entrance to the wood] the spots of moonlight of the wildest outlines, not unfrequently approaching so near to the shape of man and the domestic animals most attached to him as to be easily confused with them by fancy and mistaken by terror, moved and started as the wind stirred the branches, so that it almost seemed like a flight of recent spirits, sylphs and sylphids dancing and capering in a world of shadows. Once, when our path was over-canopied by the meeting boughs, as I halloed to those a stone-throw behind me, a sudden flash of light dashed down, as it were, upon the path close before me, with such rapid and indescribable effect that my life seemed snatched away from me, not by terror, but by the whole attention being suddenly and unexpectedly seized hold of. If one could conceive a violent blow given by an unseen hand, yet without pain or local sense of injury, of the weight falling here or there, it might assist in conceiving the feeling. This I found was occasioned by some very large bird, who, scared by my noise, had suddenly flown upward, and by the spring of his feet or body had driven down the branch on which he was aperch.

We understand nature just as if, at a distance, we looked at the image of a person in a looking-glass, plainly and fervently discoursing, yet what he uttered we could decipher only by the motion of the lips or by his mien.

The love of nature is ever returned double to us, not only the delighter in our delight, but by linking our sweetest, but of themselves perishable feelings to distinct and vivid images, which we ourselves, at times, and which a thousand casual recollections, recall to our memory. She is the preserver, the treasurer of our joys. Even in sickness and nervous diseases, she has peopled our imagination with lovely forms which have sometimes overpowered the inward pain and brought with them their old sensations. And even when all men have seemed to desert us, and the friend of our heart has passed on, with one glance from his "cold, disliking eye"—yet even then the blue heaven spreads it out and bends over us, and the little tree still shelters us under its plumage as a second cope, a domestic firmament, and the low-creeping gale will sigh in the heath-plant and soothe us by sound of sympathy till the lulled grief lose itself in fixed gaze on the purple heath-blossom, till the present beauty becomes a vision of memory.

Sometimes when I earnestly look at a beautiful object or landscape, it seems as if I were on the *brink* of a fruition still denied—as if Vision were an *appetite;* even as a man would feel who, having put forth all his muscular strength in an act of prosilience, is at the very moment *held back*—he leaps and yet moves not from his place.

The first man of science was he who looked into a thing, not to learn whether it could furnish him with food, or shelter, or weapons, or tools, or ornaments, or *playwiths,* but who sought to know it for the gratification of *knowing;* while he that first sought to *know* in order to *be* was the first philosopher. I have read of two rivers passing through the same lake, yet all the way preserving their streams visibly distinct—if I mistake not, the Rhone and the Adar, through the Lake of Geneva. In a far finer distinction, yet in a subtler union, such, for the contemplative mind, are the streams of knowing and being. The lake is formed by the two streams in man and nature as it exists in and for man; and up this lake the philosopher sails on the junction-line of the constituent streams, still pushing upward and sounding as he goes, towards the common fountain-head of both, the mysterious source whose being is knowledge, whose knowledge is being—the adorable I AM IN THAT I AM.

The ear-deceiving imitation of a steady soaking rain, while the sky is in full uncurtainment of sprinkled stars and milky stream and dark blue interspace. The rain had held up for two hours or more, but so deep was the silence of the night that the *drip* from the leaves of the garden trees *copied* a steady shower.

The *Libellulidae* fly all ways without needing to turn their bodies— onward, backward, right, and left—with more than swallow-rivalling rapidity of wing, readiness of evolution, and indefatigable continuance.

The merry little gnats *(Tipulidae minimae)* I have myself often watched in an April shower, evidently "dancing the hayes" in and out between the falling drops, unwetted, or, rather, undown-dashed by rocks of water many times larger than their whole bodies.

Spring flowers, I have observed, look best in the day, and by sunshine; but summer and autumnal flower-pots by lamp or candle light. I have now before me a flower-pot of cherry blossoms, polyanthuses, double violets, periwinkles, wall-flowers, but how dim and dusky they look. The scarlet anemone is an exception, and three or four of them with all the rest of the flower-glass sprays of white blossoms, and one or two periwinkles for the sake of the dark green leaves, green stems, and flexible elegant form, make a lovely group both by sun and by candle light.

CHARLES WATERTON
1782-1865

*Scion of an ancient and distinguished Yorkshire family of landed gentry,
Charles Waterton was sent to British Guiana at the age of twenty-two to
manage his family's sugar and coffee plantations. His true avocations,
however, were natural history and exploration, and in 1813 he made the
first of four expeditions into the Amazonian wilderness. Upon returning
to England he published an account of his travels,* Wanderings in South
America *(1825), whose lively style, vivid descriptions, and penchant for
dramatic and somewhat exaggerated adventures made it one of the most
popular nineteenth-century books about that continent. The following
account of his wrestling match with a caiman—a South American
cousin of the alligator—is quintessential Waterton. Its "tall tale" flavor
anticipates the style of such later writers as Mark Twain, Farley Mowat,
and Edward Abbey. Despite the characteristic macho tone of his adventures, Waterton was an early and ardent conservationist, and when he
succeeded to the family seat, Walton Hall, in 1806, he turned its
grounds into the first protected bird sanctuary in the British Isles.*

From Wanderings in South America, the North-West
of the United States, and the Antilles

* * * I had long wished to examine the native haunts of the Cayman; but as the river Demerara did not afford a specimen of the large
kind, I was obliged to go to the river Essequibo to look for one.

I got the canoe ready, and went down in it to George-town; where,
having put in the necessary articles for the expedition, not forgetting a
couple of large shark-hooks, with chains attached to them, and a coil of

Wanderings in South America, the North-West of the United States, and the Antilles
(London: J. Mawman, 1825).

strong new rope, I hoisted a little sail, which I had got made on purpose, and at six o'clock in the morning shaped our course for the river Essequibo. I had put a pair of shoes on to prevent the tar at the bottom of the canoe from sticking to my feet. The sun was flaming hot, and from eleven o'clock till two beat perpendicularly upon the top of my feet, betwixt the shoes and the trowsers. Not feeling it disagreeable, or being in the least aware of painful consequences, as I had been barefoot for months, I neglected to put on a pair of short stockings which I had with me. I did not reflect, that sitting still in one place, with your feet exposed to the sun, was very different from being exposed to the sun while in motion.

We went ashore, in the Essequibo, about three o'clock in the afternoon, to choose a place for the night's residence, to collect firewood, and to set the fish-hooks. It was then that I first began to find my legs very painful: they soon became much inflamed, and red, and blistered; and it required considerable caution not to burst the blisters, otherwise sores would have ensued. I immediately got into the hammock, and there passed a painful and sleepless night, and for two days after, I was disabled from walking.

About midnight, as I was lying awake, and in great pain, I heard the Indian say, 'Massa, massa, you no hear Tiger?' I listened attentively, and heard the softly sounding tread of his feet as he approached us. The moon had gone down; but every now and then we could get a glance of him by the light of our fire; he was the Jaguar, for I could see the spots on his body. Had I wished to have fired at him I was not able to take a sure aim, for I was in such pain that I could not turn myself in my hammock. The Indian would have fired, but I would not allow him to do so, as I wanted to see a little more of our new visitor; for it is not every day or night that the traveller is favoured with an undisturbed sight of the Jaguar in his own forests.

Whenever the fire got low, the Jaguar came a little nearer, and when the Indian renewed it, he retired abruptly; sometimes he would come within twenty yards, and then we had a view of him, sitting on his hind legs like a dog; sometimes he moved slowly to and fro, and at other times we could hear him mend his pace, as if impatient. At last, the Indian not relishing the idea of having such company in the neighbourhood, could contain himself no longer, and set up a most tremendous yell. The Jaguar bounded off like a race-horse, and returned no more; it appeared by the print of his feet the next morning, that he was a full-grown Jaguar.

In two days after this we got to the first falls in the Essequibo. There was a superb barrier of rocks quite across the river. In the rainy season these rocks are for the most part under water; but it being now dry weather, we had a fine view of them, while the water from the river above them rushed through the different openings in majestic grandeur. Here, on a little hill, jutting out into the river, stands the house of Mrs Peterson, the last house of people of colour up this river; I hired a negro from her, and a coloured man, who pretended that they knew the haunts of the Cayman, and understood every thing about taking him. We were a day in passing these falls and rapids, celebrated for the Pacou, the richest and most delicious fish in Guiana. The coloured man was now in his element; he stood in the head of the canoe, and with his bow and arrow shot the Pacou as they were swimming in the stream. The arrow had scarcely left the bow before he had plunged headlong into the river, and seized the fish as it was struggling with it. He dived and swam like an otter, and rarely missed the fish he aimed at.

Did my pen, gentle reader, possess descriptive powers, I would here give thee an idea of the enchanting scenery of the Essequibo; but that not being the case, thou must be contented with a moderate and well-intended attempt.

Nothing could be more lovely than the appearance of the forest on each side of this noble river. Hills rose on hills in fine gradation, all covered with trees of gigantic height and size. Here their leaves were of a lively purple, and there of the deepest green. Sometimes the Carcara extended its scarlet blossoms from branch to branch, and gave the tree the appearance as though it had been hung with garlands.

This delightful scenery of the Essequibo made the soul overflow with joy, and caused you to rove in fancy through fairy-land; till, on turning an angle of the river, you were recalled to more sober reflections on seeing the once grand and towering Mora, now dead and ragged in its topmost branches, while its aged trunk, undermined by the rushing torrent, hung as though in sorrow over the river, which, ere long, would receive it, and sweep it away for ever.

During the day, the trade-wind blew a gentle and refreshing breeze, which died away as the night set in, and then the river was as smooth as glass.

The moon was within three days of being full, so that we did not regret the loss of the sun, which set in all its splendour. Scarce had he sunk behind the western hills, when the goatsuckers sent forth their soft and plaintive cries; some often repeating, 'Who are you—who, who, who are you?' and others, 'Willy, Willy, Willy come go.'

The Indian and Daddy Quashi often shook their head at this, and said they were bringing talk from Yabahou, who is the evil spirit of the Essequibo. It was delightful to sit on the branch of a fallen tree, near the water's edge, and listen to these harmless birds as they repeated their evening song; and watch the owls and vampires as they every now and then passed up and down the river.

The next day, about noon, as we were proceeding onwards, we heard the Campanero tolling in the depth of the forest. Though I should not then have stopped to dissect even a rare bird, having a greater object in view, still I could not resist the opportunity offered of acquiring the Campanero. The place where he was tolling was low and swampy, and my legs not having quite recovered from the effects of the sun, I sent the Indian to shoot the Campanero. He got up to the tree, which he described as very high, with a naked top, and situated in a swamp. He fired at the bird, but either missed it, or did not wound it sufficiently to bring it down. This was the only opportunity I had of getting a Campanero during this expedition. We had never heard one toll before this morning, and never heard one after.

About an hour before sunset, we reached the place which the two men, who had joined us at the falls, pointed out as a proper one to find a Cayman. There was a large creek close by, and a sandbank gently sloping to the water. Just within the forest on this bank, we cleared a place of brushwood, suspended the hammocks from the trees, and then picked up enough of decayed wood for fuel.

The Indian found a large land tortoise, and this, with plenty of fresh fish which we had in the canoe, afforded a supper not to be despised.

The tigers had kept up a continual roaring every night since we had entered the Essequibo. The sound was awfully fine. Sometimes it was in the immediate neighbourhood; at other times it was far off, and echoed amongst the hills like distant thunder.

It may, perhaps, not be amiss to observe here, that when the word tiger is used, it does not mean the Bengal tiger. It means the Jaguar, whose skin is beautifully spotted, and not striped like that of the tiger in the East. It is, in fact, the tiger of the new world, and receiving the name of tiger from the discoverers of South America, it has kept it ever since. It is a cruel, strong, and dangerous beast, but not so courageous as the Bengal tiger.

We now baited a shark-hook with a large fish, and put it upon a board about a yard long, and one foot broad, which we had brought on purpose. This board was carried out in the canoe, about forty yards into the river. By means of a string, long enough to reach the bottom of the river, and at the end of which string was fastened a stone, the board was kept, as it were, at anchor. One end of the new rope I had bought in town, was reeved through the chain of the shark-hook, and the other end fastened to a tree on the sand-bank.

It was now an hour after sunset. The sky was cloudless, and the moon shone beautifully bright. There was not a breath of wind in the heavens, and the river seemed like a large plain of quicksilver. Every now and then a huge fish would strike and plunge in the water; then the owls and goatsuckers would continue their lamentations, and the sound of these was lost in the prowling tiger's growl. Then all was still again and silent as midnight.

The Caymen were now upon the stir, and at intervals their noise could be distinguished amid that of the Jaguar, the owls, the goat-suckers, and frogs. It was a singular and awful sound. It was like a suppressed sigh, bursting forth all of a sudden, and so loud that you might hear it above a mile off. First one emitted this horrible noise, and then another answered him; and on looking at the countenances of the people round me, I could plainly see that they expected to have a Cayman that night.

We were at supper, when the Indian, who seemed to have had one eye on the turtle-pot, and the other on the bait in the river, said he saw the Cayman coming.

Upon looking towards the place, there appeared something on the water like a black log of wood. It was so unlike any thing alive, that I doubted if it were a Cayman; but the Indian smiled, and said he was sure it was one, for he remembered seeing a Cayman, some years ago, when he was in the Essequibo.

At last it gradually approached the bait, and the board began to move. The moon shone so bright, that we could distinctly see him open his huge jaws, and take in the bait. We pulled the rope. He immediately let drop the bait; and then we saw his black head retreating from the board, to the distance of a few yards; and there it remained quite motionless.

He did not seem inclined to advance again; and so we finished our supper. In about an hour's time he again put himself in motion, and took hold of the bait. But, probably, suspecting that he had to deal with knaves and cheats, he held it in his mouth, but did not swallow it. We pulled the rope again, but with no better success than the first time.

He retreated as usual, and came back again in about an hour. We paid him every attention till three o'clock in the morning; when, worn out with disappointment, we went to the hammocks, turned in, and fell asleep.

When day broke, we found that he had contrived to get the bait from the hook, though we had tied it on with string. We had now no more hopes of taking a Cayman, till the return of night. The Indian took off into the woods, and brought back a noble supply of game. The rest of us went into the canoe, and proceeded up the river to shoot fish. We got even more than we could use.

As we approached the shallows, we could see the large Sting-rays moving at the bottom. The coloured man never failed to hit them with his arrow. The weather was delightful. There was scarcely a cloud to intercept the sun's rays.

I saw several scarlet Aras, Anhingas, and ducks, but could not get a shot at them. The parrots crossed the river in innumerable quantities, always flying in pairs. Here, too, I saw the Sun-bird, called Tirana by the Spaniards in the Oroonoque, and shot one of them. The black and white scarlet-headed Finch was very common here. I could never see this bird in the Demerara, nor hear of its being there.

We at last came to a large sand-bank, probably two miles in circumference. As we approached it we could see two or three hundred fresh-water turtle on the edge of the bank. Ere we could get near enough to let fly an arrow at them, they had all sunk into the river and appeared no more.

We went on the sand-bank to look for their nests, as this was the breeding season. The coloured man showed us how to find them. Wherever a portion of the sand seemed smoother than the rest, there was sure to be a turtle's nest. On digging down with our hands, about nine inches deep, we found from twenty to thirty white eggs; in less than an hour we got above two hundred. Those which had a little black spot or two on the shell we ate the same day, as it was a sign that they were not fresh, and of course would not keep: those which had no speck were put into dry sand, and were good some weeks after.

At midnight, two of our people went to this sand-bank, while the rest staid to watch the Cayman. The turtle had advanced on to the sand to lay their eggs, and the men got betwixt them and the water; they brought off half a dozen very fine and well-fed turtle. The eggshell of the fresh-water turtle is not hard like that of the land tortoise, but appears like white parchment, and gives way to the pressure of the fingers; but it is very tough, and does not break. On this sandbank, close to the forest, we found several Guana's nests; but they had never more than fourteen eggs a-piece. Thus passed the day in exercise and knowledge, till the sun's declining orb reminded us it was time to return to the place from whence we had set out.

The second night's attempt upon the Cayman was a repetition of the first, quite unsuccessful. We went a fishing the day after, had excellent sport, and returned to experience a third night's disappointment. On the fourth evening, about four o'clock, we began to erect a stage amongst the trees, close to the water's edge. From this we intended to shoot an arrow into the Cayman: at the end of this arrow was to be attached a string, which would be tied to the rope, and as soon as the Cayman was struck, we were to have the canoe ready, and pursue him in the river.

While we were busy in preparing the stage, a tiger began to roar. We judged by the sound that he was not above a quarter of a mile from us, and that he was close to the side of the river. Unfortunately, the Indian said it was not a Jaguar that was roaring, but a Couguar. The Couguar is of a pale, brownish red colour, and not as large as the Jaguar. As there was nothing particular in this animal, I thought it better to attend to the apparatus for catching the Cayman than to go in quest of the Couguar. The people, however, went in the canoe to the place where the Couguar was roaring. On arriving near the spot, they saw it was not a Couguar but an immense Jaguar, standing on the trunk of an aged Mora-tree, which bended over the river; he growled, and showed his teeth as they approached; the coloured man fired at him with a ball, but probably missed him, and the tiger instantly descended, and took off into the woods. I went to the place before dark, and we searched the forest for about half a mile in the direction he had fled, but we could see no traces of him, or any marks of blood; so I concluded that fear had prevented the man from taking steady aim.

We spent the best part of the fourth night in trying for the Cayman, but all to no purpose. I was now convinced that something was materially wrong. We ought to have been successful, considering our vigilance and attention, and that we had repeatedly seen the Cayman. It was useless to tarry here any longer; moreover, the coloured man began to take airs, and fancied that I could not do without him. I never admit of this in any expedition where I am commander; and so I convinced the man, to his sorrow, that I could do without him; for I paid him what I had agreed to give him, which amounted to eight dollars, and ordered him back in his own curial to Mrs. Peterson's, on the hill at the first falls. I then asked the negro if there were any Indian settlements in the neighbourhood; he said he knew of one, a day and a half off. We went in quest of it, and about one o'clock the next day, the negro showed us the creek where it was.

The entrance was so concealed by thick bushes that a stranger would have passed it without knowing it to be a creek. In going up it we found it dark, winding, and intricate beyond any creek that I had ever seen before. When Orpheus came back with his young wife from Styx, his path must have been similar to this, for Ovid says it was

'Arduus, obliquus, caligine densus opaca,'
['Steep, twisting, and obscured with a dense fog.']

and this creek was exactly so.

When we had got about two-thirds up it, we met the Indians going a fishing. I saw, by the way their things were packed in the curial, that they did not intend to return for some days. However, on telling them what we wanted, and by promising handsome presents of powder, shot, and hooks, they dropped their expedition, and invited us up to the settlement they had just left, and where we laid in a provision of Cassava.

They gave us for dinner boiled ant-bear and red monkey; two dishes unknown even at Beauvilliers in Paris, or at a London city feast. The monkey was very good indeed, but the ant-bear had been kept beyond its time; it stunk like our venison does in England; and so, after tasting it, I preferred dining entirely on monkey. After resting here, we went back to the river. The Indians, three in number, accompanied us in their own curial, and, on entering the river, pointed to a place a little way above, well calculated to harbour a Cayman. The water was deep and still, and flanked by an immense sand-bank; there was also a little shallow creek close by.

On this sand-bank, near the forest, the people made a shelter for the night. My own was already made; for I always take with me a painted sheet, about twelve feet by ten. This, thrown over a pole, supported betwixt two trees, makes you a capital roof with very little trouble.

We showed one of the Indians the shark-hook. He shook his head and laughed at it, and said it would not do. When he was a boy, he had seen his father catch the Caymen, and on the morrow he would make something that would answer.

In the mean time, we set the shark-hook, but it availed us naught; a Cayman came and took it, but would not swallow it.

Seeing it was useless to attend the shark-hook any longer, we left it for the night, and returned to our hammocks.

Ere I fell asleep, a reflection or two broke in upon me. I considered, that as far as the judgment of civilized man went, every thing had been procured and done to ensure success. We had hooks, and lines, and baits, and patience; we had spent nights in watching, had seen the Cayman come and take the bait, and after our expectations had been wound up to the highest pitch, all ended in disappointment. Probably this poor wild man of the woods would succeed by means of a very simple process; and thus prove to his more civilized brother, that notwithstanding books and schools, there is a vast deal of knowledge to be picked up at every step, whichever way we turn ourselves.

In the morning, as usual, we found the bait gone from the shark-hook. The Indians went into the forest to hunt, and we took the canoe to shoot fish, and get another supply of turtle's eggs, which we found in great abundance on this large sand-bank.

We went to the little shallow creek, and shot some young Caymen, about two feet long. It was astonishing to see what spite and rage these little things showed when the arrow struck them; they turned round and bit it, and snapped at us when we went into the water to take them up. Daddy Quashi boiled one of them for his dinner, and found it very sweet and tender. I do not see why it should not be as good as frog or veal.

The day was now declining apace, and the Indian had made his instrument to take the Cayman. It was very simple. There were four pieces of tough hard wood, a foot long, and about as thick as your little finger, and barbed at both ends; they were tied round the end of the rope, in such a manner, that if you conceive the rope to be an arrow, these four sticks would form the arrow's head; so that one end of the four united sticks answered to the point of the arrow-head, while the other end of the sticks expanded at equal distances round the rope, thus—Now it is evident, that if the Cayman swallowed this, (the other end of the rope, which was thirty yards long, being fastened to a tree,) the more he pulled, the faster the barbs would stick into his stomach. This wooden hook, if you may so call it, was well-baited with the flesh of the Acouri, and the entrails were twisted round the rope for about a foot above it.

Nearly a mile from where we had our hammocks, the sand-bank was steep and abrupt, and the river very still and deep; there the Indian pricked a stick into the sand. It was two feet long, and on its extremity was fixed the machine; it hung suspended about a foot from the water, and the end of the rope was made fast to a stake driven well into the sand.

The Indian then took the empty shell of a land tortoise, and gave it some heavy blows with an axe. I asked why he did that. He said, it was to let the Cayman hear that something was going on. In fact, the Indian meant it as the Cayman's dinner-bell.

Having done this, we went back to the hammocks, not intending to visit it again till morning. During the night, the Jaguars roared and grumbled in the forest, as though the world was going wrong with them, and at intervals we could hear the distant Cayman. The roaring of the Jaguars was awful; but it was music to the dismal noise of these hideous and malicious reptiles.

About half past five in the morning, the Indian stole off silently to take a look at the bait. On arriving at the place, he set up a tremendous shout. We all jumped out of our hammocks, and ran to him. The Indians got there before me, for they had no clothes to put on, and I lost two minutes in looking for my trowsers and in slipping into them.

We found a Cayman, ten feet and a half long, fast to the end of the rope. Nothing now remained to do, but to get him out of the water without injuring his scales, 'hoc opus, hic labor' ['this the work, this the labor']. We mustered strong: there were three Indians from the creek, there was my own Indian Yan, Daddy Quashi, the negro from Mrs.

Peterson's, James, Mr. R. Edmonstone's man, whom I was instructing to preserve birds, and, lastly, myself.

I informed the Indians that it was my intention to draw him quietly out of the water, and then secure him. They looked and stared at each other, and said, I might do it myself; but they would have no hand in it; the Cayman would worry some of us. On saying this, 'consedere duces,' [the leaders sat down together,'] they squatted on their hams with the most perfect indifference.

The Indians of these wilds have never been subject to the least restraint; and I knew enough of them to be aware, that if I tried to force them against their will, they would take off, and leave me and my presents unheeded, and never return.

Daddy Quashi was for applying to our guns, as usual, considering them our best and safest friends. I immediately offered to knock him down for his cowardice, and he shrunk back, begging that I would be cautious, and not get myself worried; and apologizing for his own want of resolution. My Indian was now in conversation with the others, and they asked if I would allow them to shoot a dozen arrows into him, and thus disable him. This would have ruined all. I had come above three hundred miles on purpose to get a Cayman uninjured, and not to carry back a mutilated specimen. I rejected their proposition with firmness, and darted a disdainful eye upon the Indians.

Daddy Quashi was again beginning to remonstrate, and I chased him on the sand-bank for a quarter of a mile. He told me afterwards, he thought he should have dropped down dead with fright, for he was firmly persuaded, if I had caught him, I should have bundled him into the Cayman's jaws. Here then we stood, in silence, like a calm before a thunder-storm. 'Hoc res summa loco. Scinditur in contraria vulgus.' ['This is the chief matter in the place. The people is torn in contrary directions.'] They wanted to kill him, and I wanted to take him alive.

I now walked up and down the sand, revolving a dozen projects in my head. The canoe was at a considerable distance, and I ordered the people to bring it round to the place where we were. The mast was eight feet long, and not much thicker than my wrist. I took it out of the canoe, and wrapped the sail round the end of it. Now it appeared clear to me, that if I went down upon one knee, and held the mast in the same position as the soldier holds his bayonet when rushing to the charge, I could force it down the Cayman's throat, should he come open-mouthed at me. When this was told to the Indians, they brightened up, and said they would help me to pull him out of the river.

'Brave squad!' said I to myself, ' "Audax omnia perpeti," ["Bold to endure everything,"] now that you have got me betwixt yourselves and danger.' I then mustered all hands for the last time before the battle. We were, four South American savages, two negroes from Africa, a Creole from Trinidad, and myself a white man from Yorkshire. In fact, a little tower of Babel group, in dress, no dress, address, and language.

Daddy Quashi hung in the rear: I showed him a large Spanish knife, which I always carried in the waistband of my trowsers: it spoke volumes to him, and he shrugged up his shoulders in absolute despair. The sun was just peeping over the high forests on the eastern hills, as if coming to look on, and bid us act with becoming fortitude. I placed all the people at the end of the rope, and ordered them to pull till the Cayman appeared on the surface of the water; and then, should he plunge, to slacken the rope and let him go again into the deep.

I now took the mast of the canoe in my hand (the sail being tied round the end of the mast) and sunk down upon one knee, about four yards from the water's edge, determining to thrust it down his throat, in case he gave me an opportunity. I certainly felt somewhat uncomfortable in this situation, and I thought of Cerberus on the other side of the Styx ferry. The people pulled the Cayman to the surface; he plunged furiously as soon as he arrived in these upper regions, and immediately went below again on their slackening the rope. I saw enough not to fall in love at first sight. I now told them we would run all risks, and have him on land immediately. They pulled again, and out he came,—'monstrum, horrendum, informe,' ['Horrible monster, void of form']. This was an interesting moment. I kept my position firmly, with my eye fixed steadfast on him.

By the time the Cayman was within two yards of me, I saw he was in a state of fear and perturbation; I instantly dropped the mast, sprung up, and jumped on his back, turning half round as I vaulted, so that I gained my seat with my face in a right position. I immediately seized his fore legs, and, by main force, twisted them on his back; thus they served me for a bridle.

He now seemed to have recovered from his surprise, and probably fancying himself in hostile company, he began to plunge furiously, and lashed the sand with his long and powerful tail. I was out of reach of the strokes of it, by being near his head. He continued to plunge and strike, and made my seat very uncomfortable. It must have been a fine sight for an unoccupied spectator.

The people roared out in triumph, and were so vociferous, that it was some time before they heard me tell them to pull me and my beast of burden farther in land. I was apprehensive the rope might break, and then there would have been every chance of going down to the regions under water with the Cayman. That would have been more perilous than Arion's marine morning ride:—

'Delphini insidens vada cærula sulcat Arion.'
['Astride a dolphin Arion ploughed the sky-blue wave.']

The people now dragged us above forty yards on the sand: it was the first and last time I was ever on a Cayman's back. Should it be asked, how I managed to keep my seat, I would answer,—I hunted some years with Lord Darlington's fox hounds.

After repeated attempts to regain his liberty, the Cayman gave in, and became tranquil through exhaustion. I now managed to tie up his jaws, and firmly secured his fore feet in the position I had held them. We had now another severe struggle for superiority, but he was soon overcome, and again remained quiet. While some of the people were pressing upon his head and shoulders, I threw myself on his tail, and by keeping it down to the sand, prevented him from kicking up another dust. He was finally conveyed to the canoe, and then to the place where we had suspended our hammocks. There I cut his throat; and after breakfast was over, commenced the dissection.

Now that the affray had ceased, Daddy Quashi played a good finger and thumb at breakfast; he said he found himself much revived, and became very talkative and useful, as there was no longer any danger. He was a faithful, honest negro. His master, my worthy friend Mr. Edmonstone, had been so obliging as to send out particular orders to the colony, that the Daddy should attend me all the time I was in the forest. He had lived in the wilds of Demerara with Mr. Edmonstone for many years; and often amused me with the account of the frays his master had had in the woods with snakes, wild beasts, and runaway negroes. Old age was now coming fast upon him; he had been an able fellow in his younger days, and a gallant one too, for he had a large scar over his eyebrow, caused by the stroke of a cutlass, from another negro, while the Daddy was engaged in an intrigue.

The back of the Cayman may be said to be almost impenetrable to a musket ball; but his sides are not near so strong, and are easily pierced with an arrow; indeed, were they as strong as the back and the belly, there would be no part of the Cayman's body soft and elastic enough to admit of expansion after taking in a supply of food.

The Cayman has no grinders; his teeth are entirely made for snatch and swallow; there are thirty-two in each jaw. Perhaps no animal in existence bears more decided marks in his countenance of cruelty and malice than the Cayman. He is the scourge and terror of all the large rivers in South America near the line.

One Sunday evening, some years ago, as I was walking with Don Felipe de Ynciarte, governor of Angustura, on the bank of the Oroonoque, 'Stop here a minute or two, Don Carlos,' said he to me, 'while I recount a sad accident. One fine evening last year, as the people of Angustura were sauntering up and down here, in the Alameda, I was within twenty yards of this place, when I saw a large Cayman rush out of the river, seize a man, and carry him down, before any body had it in his power to assist him. The screams of the poor fellow were terrible as the Cayman was running off with him. He plunged into the river with his prey; we instantly lost sight of him, and never saw or heard him more.'

I was a day and a half in dissecting our Cayman, and then we got all ready to return to Demerara. *   *   *

WASHINGTON IRVING
1783-1859

Because of the success of "Rip Van Winkle" and "The Legend of Sleepy Hollow," Washington Irving has often been called America's "first man of letters." This title reflects his ability to support himself largely from his writing, as well as his status as America's literary representative during his long residence in Europe and his friendship with Byron and Scott. In 1832 Irving returned to America and began a series of journeys—along the Ohio and Mississippi Rivers and across the frontier. Among his books describing these adventures were A Tour on the Prairies *(1835) and* Astoria *(1836). Although he often took the role of the civilized, detached observer, his energetic descriptions nevertheless have the power to evoke a continent just being settled and exploited from the East.*

From A Tour on the Prairies

THE GRAND PRAIRIE—A BUFFALO HUNT

After proceeding about two hours in a southerly direction, we emerged toward mid-day from the dreary belt of the Cross Timber, and to our infinite delight beheld "the great Prairie" stretching to the right

A Tour on the Prairies (Norman, Univ. of Oklahoma, 1956). Originally published as part of *The Crayon Miscellany*, 3 vols. (Philadelphia: Carey, Lea & Blanchard, 1835).

and left before us. We could distinctly trace the meandering course of the main Canadian, and various smaller streams, by the strips of green forest that bordered them. The landscape was vast and beautiful. There is always an expansion of feeling in looking upon these boundless and fertile wastes; but I was doubly conscious of it after emerging from our "close dungeon of innumerous boughs."

From a rising ground Beatte pointed out the place where he and his comrades had killed the buffaloes; and we beheld several black objects moving in the distance, which he said were part of the herd. The Captain determined to shape his course to a woody bottom about a mile distant, and to encamp there for a day or two, by way of having a regular buffalo hunt, and getting a supply of provisions. As the troop defiled along the slope of the hill toward the camping ground, Beatte proposed to my messmates and myself, that we should put ourselves under his guidance, promising to take us where we should have plenty of sport. Leaving the line of march, therefore, we diverged toward the prairie; traversing a small valley, and ascending a gentle swell of land. As we reached the summit, we beheld a gang of wild horses about a mile off. Beatte was immediately on the alert, and no longer thought of buffalo hunting. He was mounted on his powerful half-wild horse, with a lariat coiled at the saddle-bow, and set off in pursuit; while we remained on a rising ground watching his maneuvers with great solicitude. Taking advantage of a strip of woodland, he stole quietly along, so as to get close to them before he was perceived. The moment they caught sight of him a grand scamper took place. We watched him skirting along the horizon like a privateer in full chase of a merchantman; at length he passed over the brow of a ridge, and down into a shallow valley; in a few moments he was on the opposite hill, and close upon one of the horses. He was soon head and head, and appeared to be trying to noose his prey; but they both disappeared again below the hill, and we saw no more of them. It turned out afterward that he had noosed a powerful horse, but could not hold him, and had lost his lariat in the attempt.

While we were waiting for his return, we perceived two buffalo bulls descending a slope, toward a stream, which wound through a ravine fringed with trees. The young Count and myself endeavored to get near them under covert of the trees. They discovered us while we were yet three or four hundred yards off, and turning about, retreated up the rising ground. We urged our horses across the ravine, and gave chase. The immense weight of head and shoulders, causes the buffalo to labor heavily up hill; but it accelerates his descent. We had the advantage, therefore, and gained rapidly upon the fugitives, though it was difficult to get our horses to approach them, their very scent inspiring them with terror. The Count, who had a double-barrelled gun loaded with ball, fired, but it missed. The bulls now altered their course, and galloped down hill with headlong rapidity. As they ran in different directions, we each singled one and separated. I was provided with a brace of veteran brass-barrelled pistols, which I had borrowed at Fort Gibson, and which had evidently seen some service. Pistols are very effective in buffalo hunting, as the hunter can ride up close to the animal, and fire at it while at full speed; whereas the long heavy rifles used on the frontier, cannot be easily managed, nor discharged with accurate aim from horseback. My object, therefore, was to get within pistol shot of the buffalo. This was no very easy matter. I was well mounted on a horse of excellent speed and bottom, that seemed eager for the chase, and soon overtook the game; but the moment he came nearly parallel, he would keep sheering off, with ears forked and pricked forward, and every symptom of aversion and alarm. It was no wonder. Of all animals, a buffalo, when close pressed by the hunter, has an aspect the most diabolical. His two short black horns, curve out of a huge frontlet of shaggy hair; his eyes glow like coals; his mouth is open, his tongue parched and drawn up into a half crescent; his tail is erect, and tufted and whisking about in the air, he is a perfect picture of mingled rage and terror.

It was with difficulty I urged my horse sufficiently near, when, taking aim, to my chagrin, both pistols missed fire. Unfortunately the locks of these veteran weapons were so much worn, that in the gallop, the priming had been shaken out of the pans. At the snapping of the last pistol I was close upon the buffalo, when, in his despair, he turned round with a sudden snort and rushed upon me. My horse wheeled about as if on a pivot, made a convulsive spring, and, as I had been leaning on one side with pistol extended, I came near being thrown at the feet of the buffalo.

Three or four bounds of the horse carried us out of the reach of the enemy; who, having merely turned in desperate self-defense, quickly resumed his flight. As soon as I could gather in my panic-stricken horse, and prime the pistols afresh, I again spurred in pursuit of the buffalo, who had slackened his speed to take breath. On my approach he again set off full tilt, heaving himself forward with a heavy rolling gallop, dashing with headlong precipitation through brakes and ravines, while several deer and wolves, startled from their coverts by his thundering career, ran helter-skelter to right and left across the waste.

A gallop across the prairies in pursuit of game is by no means so smooth a career as those may imagine, who have only the idea of an open level plain. It is true, the prairies of the hunting ground are not so much entangled with flowering plants and long herbage as the lower prairies, and are principally covered with short buffalo grass; but they are diversified by hill and dale, and where most level, are apt to be cut up by deep rifts and ravines, made by torrents after rains; and which, yawning from an even surface, are almost like pitfalls in the way of the hunter, checking him suddenly, when in full career, or subjecting him to the risk of limb and life. The plains, too, are beset by burrowing holes of small animals, in which the horse is apt to sink to the fetlock, and throw both himself and his rider. The late rain had covered some parts of the prairie, where the ground was hard, with a thin sheet of water, through which the horse had to splash his way. In other parts there were innumerable shallow hollows, eight or ten feet in diameter, made by the buffaloes, who wallow in sand and mud like swine. These being filled with water, shone like mirrors, so that the horse was continually leaping over them or springing on one side. We had reached, too, a rough part of the prairie, very much broken and cut up; the buffalo, who was running for his life, took no heed of his course, plunging down break-neck ravines, where it was necessary to skirt the borders in search of a safer descent. At length we came to where a winter stream had torn a deep chasm across the whole prairie, leaving open jagged rocks, and forming a long glen bordered by steep crumbling cliffs of mingled stone and clay. Down one of these the buffalo flung himself, half tumbling, half leaping, and then scuttled along the bottom; while I, seeing all further pursuit useless, pulled up, and gazed quietly after him from the border of the cliff, until he disappeared amidst the windings of the ravine.

Nothing now remained but to turn my steed and rejoin my companions. Here at first was some little difficulty. The ardor of the chase had betrayed me into a long, heedless gallop. I now found myself in the midst of a lonely waste, in which the prospect was bounded by undulating swells of land, naked and uniform, where, from the deficiency of landmarks and distinct features, an inexperienced man may become bewildered, and lose his way as readily as in the wastes of the ocean. The day, too, was overcast, so that I could not guide myself by the sun; my only mode was to retrace the track my horse had made in coming, though this I would often lose sight of, where the ground was covered with parched herbage.

To one unaccustomed to it, there is something inexpressibly lonely in the solitude of a prairie. The loneliness of a forest seems nothing to it. There the view is shut in by trees, and the imagination is left free to picture some livelier scene beyond. But here we have an immense extent of landscape without a sign of human existence. We have the consciousness of being far, far beyond the bounds of human habitation; we feel as if moving in the midst of a desert world. As my horse lagged slowly back over the scenes of our late scamper, and the delirium of the chase had passed away, I was peculiarly sensible to these circumstances. The silence of the waste was now and then broken by the cry of a distant flock of pelicans, stalking like spectres about a shallow pool; sometimes by the sinister croaking of a raven in the air, while occasionally a scoundrel wolf would scour off from before me; and, having attained a safe distance, would sit down and howl and whine with tones that gave a dreariness to the surrounding solitude.

After pursuing my way for some time, I descried a horseman on the edge of a distant hill, and soon recognized him to be the Count. He had been equally unsuccessful with myself; we were shortly after rejoined by our worthy comrade, the Virtuoso, who, with spectacles on nose, had made two or three ineffectual shots from horseback.

We determined not to seek the camp until we had made one more effort. Casting our eyes about the surrounding waste, we descried a herd of buffalo about two miles distant, scattered apart, and quietly grazing near a small strip of trees and bushes. It required but little stretch of fancy to picture them so many cattle grazing on the edge of a common, and that the grove might shelter some lowly farm-house.

We now formed our plan to circumvent the herd, and by getting on the other side of them, to hunt them in the direction where we knew our camp to be situated: otherwise, the pursuit might take us to such a distance as to render it impossible to find our way back before nightfall. Taking a wide circuit, therefore, we moved slowly and cautiously, pausing occasionally, when we saw any of the herd desist from grazing. The wind fortunately set from them, otherwise they might have scented us and have taken the alarm. In this way, we succeeded in getting round the herd without disturbing it. It consisted of about forty head, bulls, cows, and calves. Separating to some distance from each other, we now approached slowly in a parallel line, hoping by degrees to steal near without exciting attention. They began, however, to move off quietly, stopping at every step or two to graze, when suddenly a bull that, unobserved by us, had been taking his siesta under a clump of trees to our left, roused himself from his lair, and hastened to join his companions. We were still at a considerable distance, but the game had taken the alarm. We quickened our pace, they broke into a gallop, and now commenced a full chase.

As the ground was level, they shouldered along with great speed, following each other in a line; two or three bulls bringing up the rear, the last of whom, from his enormous size and venerable frontlet, and beard of sunburnt hair, looked like the patriarch of the herd; and as if he might long have reigned the monarch of the prairie.

There is a mixture of the awful and the comic in the look of these huge animals, as they bear their great bulk forward, with an up and down motion of the unwieldy head and shoulders; their tail cocked up like the queue of Pantaloon in a pantomime, the end whisking about in a fierce yet whimsical style, and their eyes glaring venomously with an expression of fright and fury.

For some time I kept parallel with the line, without being able to force my horse within pistol shot, so much had he been alarmed by the assault of the buffalo in the preceding chase. At length I succeeded, but was again balked by my pistols missing fire. My companions, whose horses were less fleet, and more way-worn, could not overtake the herd; at length Mr. L., who was in the rear of the line, and losing ground, levelled his double-barrelled gun, and fired a long raking shot. It struck a buffalo just above the loins, broke its back-bone, and brought it to the ground. He stopped and alighted to dispatch his prey, when borrowing his gun, which had yet a charge remaining in it, I put my horse to his speed, again overtook the herd which was thundering along, pursued by the Count. With my present weapon there was no need of urging my horse to such close quarters; galloping along parallel, therefore, I singled out a buffalo, and by a fortunate shot brought it down on the spot. The ball had struck a vital part; it could not move from the place where it fell, but lay there struggling in mortal agony, while the rest of the herd kept on their headlong career across the prairie.

Dismounting, I now fettered my horse to prevent his straying, and advanced to contemplate my victim. I am nothing of a sportsman; I had been prompted to this unwonted exploit by the magnitude of the game, and the excitement of an adventurous chase. Now that the excitement was over, I could not but look with commiseration upon the poor animal that lay struggling and bleeding at my feet. His very size and importance, which had before inspired me with eagerness, now increased my compunction. It seemed as if I had inflicted pain in proportion to the bulk of my victim, and as if there were a hundred-fold greater waste of life than there would have been in the destruction of an animal of inferior size.

To add to these after-qualms of conscience, the poor animal lingered in his agony. He had evidently received a mortal wound, but death might be long in coming. It would not do to leave him here to be torn piece-meal, while yet alive, by the wolves that had already snuffed his blood, and were skulking and howling at a distance, and waiting for my departure; and by the ravens that were flapping about, croaking dismally in the air. It became now an act of mercy to give him his quietus, and put him out of his misery. I primed one of the pistols, therefore, and advanced close up to the buffalo. To inflict a wound thus in cool blood, I found a totally different thing from firing in the heat of the chase. Taking aim, however, just behind the fore-shoulder, my pistol for once proved true;

the ball must have passed through the heart, for the animal gave one convulsive throe and expired.

While I stood meditating and moralizing over the wreck I had so wantonly produced, with my horse grazing near me, I was rejoined by my fellow sportsman, the Virtuoso; who, being a man of universal adroitness, and withal, more experienced and hardened in the gentle art of "venerie," soon managed to carve out the tongue of the buffalo, and delivered it to me to bear back to the camp as a trophy.

JOHN JAMES AUDUBON
1785-1851

Audubon's elephant folio of The Birds of America *(1827–1838) won him international fame while boosting patriotic pride in America. His compositions emphasized the spectacular drama of wildlife in the New World—showing birds fighting for their lives or hurtling downward toward their prey. In his accompanying text* Ornithological Biography *(5 vols., 1831–39, written in collaboration with the Scottish naturalist William McGillivray) Audubon both told the stories of the birds he had depicted and described his own dangers and triumphs in the wilderness.*

From ORNITHOLOGICAL BIOGRAPHY

PITTING OF THE WOLVES

There seems to be a universal feeling of hostility among men against the Wolf, whose strength, agility, and cunning, which latter is scarcely inferior to that of his relative master Reynard, tend to render him an object of hatred, especially to the husbandman, on whose flocks he is ever apt to commit depredations. In America, where this animal was formerly abundant, and in many parts of which it still occurs in consider-

Ornithological Biography (5 vols., Edinburgh, 1831–1839)

able numbers, it is not more mercifully dealt with than in other parts of the world. Traps and snares of all sorts are set for catching it, while dogs and horses are trained for hunting the Fox. The Wolf, however, unless in some way injured, being more powerful and perhaps better winded than the Fox, is rarely pursued with hounds or any other dogs in the open chase; but as his depredations are at times extensive and highly injurious to the farmer, the greatest exertions have been used to exterminate his race. Few instances have occurred among us of any attack made by Wolves on man, and only one has come under my own notice.

Two young Negroes who resided near the banks of the Ohio, in the lower part of the State of Kentucky, about twenty-three years ago, had sweethearts living on a plantation ten miles distant. After the labours of the day were over, they frequently visited the fair ladies of their choice, the nearest way to whose dwelling lay directly across a great cane brake. As to the lover every moment is precious, they usually took this route, to save time. Winter had commenced, cold, dark, and forbidding, and after sunset scarcely a glimpse of light or glow of warmth, one might imagine, could be found in that dreary swamp, excepting in the eyes and bosoms of the ardent youths, or the hungry Wolves that prowled about. The snow covered the earth, and rendered them more easy to be scented from a distance by the famished beasts. Prudent in a certain degree, the young lovers carried their axes on their shoulders, and walked as briskly as the narrow path would allow. Some transient glimpses of light now and then met their eyes, but so faint were they that they believed them to be caused by their faces coming in contact with the slender reeds covered with snow. Suddenly, however, a long and frightful howl burst upon them, and they instantly knew that it proceeded from a troop of hungry, perhaps desperate Wolves. They stopped, and putting themselves in an attitude of defence, awaited the result. All around was dark, save a few feet of snow, and the silence of night was dismal. Nothing could be done to better their situation, and after standing a few minutes in expectation of an attack, they judged it best to resume their march; but no sooner had they replaced their axes on their shoulders, and begun to move, than the foremost found himself assailed by several foes. His legs were held fast as if pressed by a powerful screw, and the torture inflicted by the fangs of the ravenous animal was for a moment excruciating. Several Wolves in the mean time sprung upon the breast of the other Negro, and dragged him to the ground. Both struggled manfully against their foes; but in a short time one of them ceased to move, and the other, reduced in strength, and perhaps despairing of maintaining his ground, still more of aiding his unfortunate companion, sprung to the branch of a tree, and speedily gained a place of safety near the top. The next morning, the mangled remains of his comrade lay scattered around on the snow, which was stained with blood. Three dead wolves lay around, but the rest of the pack had disappeared, and Scipio, sliding to the ground, took up the axes, and made the best of his way home, to relate the sad adventure.

About two years after this occurrence, as I was travelling between Henderson and Vincennes, I chanced to stop for the night at a farmer's house by the side of a road. After putting up my horse and refreshing myself, I entered into conversation with mine host, who asked if I should like to pay a visit to the wolf-pits, which were about half a mile distant. Glad of the opportunity I accompanied him across the fields to the neighbourhood of a deep wood, and soon saw the engines of destruction. He had three pits, within a few hundred yards of each other. They were about eight feet deep, and broader at bottom, so as to render it impossible for the most active animal to escape from them. The aperture was covered with a revolving platform of twigs, attached to a central axis. On either surface of the platform was fastened a large piece of putrid venison, with other matters by no means pleasant to my olfactory nerves, although no doubt attractive to the wolves. My companion wished to visit them that evening, merely as he was in the habit of doing so daily, for the purpose of seeing that all was right. He said that Wolves were very abundant that autumn, and had killed nearly the whole of his sheep and one of his colts, but that he was now "paying them off in full;" and added that if I would tarry a few hours with him next morning, he would beyond a doubt shew me some sport rarely seen in those parts. We retired to rest in due time, and were up with the dawn.

"I think," said my host, "that all's right, for I see the dogs are anxious to get away to the pits, and although they are nothing but curs, their noses are none the worse for that." As he took up his gun, an axe and a large knife, the dogs began to howl and bark, and whisked around us, as if full of joy. When we reached the first pit, we found the bait all gone, and the platform much injured; but the animal that had been entrapped had scraped a subterranean passage for himself and so scaped. On peeping into the next, he assured me that "three famous fellows were safe enough" in it. I also peeped in and saw the Wolves, two black, and the other brindled, all of goodly size, sure enough. They lay flat on the earth, their ears laid close over the head, their eyes indicating fear more than anger. "But how are we to get them out?"—"How sir," said the farmer, "why by going down to be sure, and ham-stringing them." Being a novice in these matters, I begged to be merely a looker-on. "With all my heart," quoth the farmer, "stand here, and look at me through the brush." Whereupon he glided down, taking with him his axe and knife, and leaving his rifle to my care. I was not a little surprised to see the cowardice of the Wolves. He pulled out successively their hind legs, and with a side stroke of the knife cut the principal tendon above the joint, exhibiting as little fear as if he had been marking lambs.

"Lo!" exclaimed the farmer, when he had got out, "we have forgot the rope; I'll go after it." Off he went accordingly, with as much alacrity as any youngster could shew. In a short time he returned out of breath, and wiping his forehead with the back of his hand— "Now for it." I was desired to raise and hold the platform on its central balance, whilst he, with all the dexterity of an Indian, threw a noose over the neck of one of the Wolves. We hauled it up motionless with fright, as if dead, its disabled legs swinging to and fro, its jaws wide open, and the gurgle in its throat alone indicating that it was alive. Letting him drop on the ground, the farmer loosened the rope by means of a stick, and left him to the dogs, all of which set upon him with great fury and soon worried him to death. The second was dealt with in the same manner; but the third, which was probably the oldest, as it was the blackest, shewed some spirit, the moment it was left loose to the mercy of the curs. This Wolf, which we afterwards found to be a female, scuffled along on its fore legs at a surprising rate, giving a snap every now and then to the nearest dog, which went off howling dismally with a mouthful of skin torn from its side. And so well did the furious beast defend itself, that apprehensive of its escape, the farmer levelled his rifle at it, and shot it through the heart, on which the curs rushed upon it, and satiated their vengeance on the destroyer of their master's flock.

WHITE-HEADED EAGLE

(BALD EAGLE, *HALIAEETUS LEUCOCEPHALUS*)

The figure of this noble bird is well known throughout the civilized world, emblazoned as it is on our national standard, which waves in the breeze of every clime, bearing to distant lands the remembrance of a great people living in a state of peaceful freedom. May that peaceful freedom last forever!

The great strength, daring, and cool courage of the White-headed Eagle, joined to his unequalled power of flight, render him highly conspicuous among his brethren. To these qualities did he add a generous disposition towards others, he might be looked up to as a model of nobility. The ferocious, overbearing, and tyrannical temper which is ever and anon displaying itself in his actions, is, nevertheless, best adapted to his state, and was wisely given him by the Creator to enable him to perform the office assigned to him.

To give you, kind reader, some idea of the nature of this bird, permit me to place you on the Mississippi, on which you may float gently along, while approaching winter brings millions of water-fowl on whistling wings, from the countries of the north, to seek a milder climate in which to sojourn for a season. The Eagle is seen perched, in an erect attitude, on the highest summit of the tallest tree by the margin of the broad stream. His glistening but stern eye looks over the vast expanse. He listens attentively to every sound that comes to his quick ear from afar, glancing now and then on the earth beneath, lest even the light tread of the fawn may pass unheard. His mate is perched on the opposite side, and should all be tranquil and silent, warns him by a cry to continue patient. At this well known call, the male partly opens his broad wings, inclines his body a little downwards, and answers to her voice in tones not unlike the laugh of a maniac. The next moment, he resumes his erect attitude, and again all around is silent. Ducks of many species, the Teal, the Wigeon, the Mallard and others, are seen passing with great rapidity, and following the course of the current; but the Eagle heeds them not: they are at that time beneath his attention. The next moment, however, the wild trumpet-like sound of a yet distant but approaching Swan is heard. A shriek from the female Eagle comes across the stream—for, kind reader, she is fully as alert as her mate. The latter suddenly shakes the whole of his body, and with a few touches of his bill, aided by the action of his cuticular muscles, arranges his plumage in an instant. The snow-white bird is now in sight: her long neck is stretched forward, her eye is on the watch, vigilant as that of her enemy; her large wings seem with difficulty to support the weight of her body, although they flap incessantly. So irksome do her exertions seem, that her very legs are spread beneath her tail, to aid her in her flight. She approaches, however. The Eagle has marked her for his prey. As the Swan is passing the dreaded pair, starts from his perch, in full preparation for the chase, the male bird, with an awful scream, that to the Swan's ear brings more terror than the report of the large duck-gun.

Now is the moment to witness the display of the Eagle's powers. He glides through the air like a falling star; and, like a flash of lightning, comes upon the timorous quarry, which now, in agony and despair, seeks, by various manœuvers, to elude the grasp of his cruel talons. It mounts, doubles, and willingly would plunge into the stream, were it not prevented by the Eagle, which, long possessed of the knowledge that by such a stratagem the Swan might escape him, forces it to remain in the air by attempting to strike it with his talons from beneath. The hope of escape is soon given up by the Swan. It has already become much weakened, and its strength fails at the sight of the courage and swiftness of its antagonist. Its last gasp is about to escape, when the ferocious Eagle strikes with his talons the under side of its wing, and with unresisted power forces the bird to fall in a slanting direction upon the nearest shore.

It is then, reader, that you may see the cruel spirit of this dreaded enemy of the feathered race, whilst, exulting over his prey, he for the first time breathes at ease. He presses down his powerful feet, and drives his sharp claws deeper than ever into the heart of the dying Swan. He shrieks with delight, as he feels the last convulsions of his prey, which has now sunk under his unceasing efforts to render death as painfully felt as it can possibly be. The female has watched every movement of her mate; and if she did not assist him in capturing the Swan, it was not from want of will, but merely that she felt full assurance that the power and courage of her lord were quite sufficient for the deed. She now sails to the spot where he eagerly awaits her, and when she has arrived, they together turn the breast of the luckless Swan upwards, and gorge themselves with gore. * * *

JOHN CLARE
1793-1864

"The Northamptonshire peasant boy" was the son of a farm laborer, and himself began working in the fields and with animals from the age of seven. Like many readers in his day, he was inspired by Thomson's The Seasons, *and produced poetry that applied those literary forms and conventions to his own much more direct experience of rural life. When his* Poems Descriptive of Rural Life and Scenery *was published in 1820, Clare became celebrated in ways that destroyed his own economy and stability without giving him a secure new identity. Poverty and disorientation followed, and from 1837 to the end of his life he was an inmate in a "lunatic asylum." For many readers today Clare's most exciting writing is found in his notebooks—prose descriptions of the life of the fields that are highly emotional and precise, and that are conveyed in a direct, authentic voice.*

THE NATURAL WORLD

I often pulled my hat over my eyes to watch the rising of the lark, or to see the hawk hang in the summer sky and the kite take its circles round the wood. I often lingered a minute on the woodland stile to hear the woodpigeons clapping their wings among the dark oaks. I hunted curious flowers in rapture and muttered thoughts in their praise. I loved the pasture with its rushes and thistles and sheep-tracks. I adored the wild, marshy fen with its solitary heronshaw sweeping along in its melancholy sky. I wandered the heath in raptures among the rabbit burrows and golden-blossomed furze. I dropt down on a thymy molehill or mossy eminence to survey the summer landscape . . . I marked the various colours in flat, spreading fields, checkered into closes of different-tinctured grain like the colours of a map; the copper-tinted clover in blossom; the sun-tanned green of the ripening hay; the lighter hues of wheat and barley intermixed with the sunset glare of yellow charlock and the sunset imitation of the scarlet headaches; the blue corn-bottles crowding their splendid colours in large sheets over the land and troubling the cornfields with destroying beauty; the different greens of the woodland trees, the dark oak, the paler ash, the mellow lime, the white poplars peeping above the rest like leafy steeples, the grey willow shining chilly in the sun, as if the morning mist still lingered on its cool green. I loved the meadow lake with its flags and long purples crowding the water's edge. I listened with delight to hear the wind whisper among the feather-topt reeds, to see the taper bulrush nodding in gentle curves to the rippling water; and I watched with delight on haymaking evenings the setting sun drop behind the Brigs and peep again through the half-circle of the arches as if he longed to stay . . . I observed all this with the same rapture as I have done since. But I knew nothing of poetry. It was felt and not uttered.

The Poet's Eye, ed. Geoffrey Grigson (Frederick Muller Ltd., 1944).

From THE NATURAL HISTORY PROSE WRITINGS OF JOHN CLARE

Feb. 7 [1825]

I always think that this month the prophet of spring brings many beautys to the landscape tho a carless observer woud laugh at me for saying so who believes that it brings nothing because he does not give

The Natural History Prose Writings of John Clare ed. by Margaret Grainger (Clarendon, 1983).

himself the trouble to seek them—I always admire the kindling freshness that the bark of the different sorts of trees & underwood asume in
the forest—the foulroyce twigs kindle into a vivid color at their tops as
red as woodpiegons claws the ash with its grey bark & black swelling
buds the Birch with it 'paper rind' & the darker mottled sorts of hazle &
black alder with the greener hues of sallow willows & the bramble that
still wears its leaves with the privet of a purple hue while the straggling
wood briar shines in a brighter & more beautiful green even then leaves
can boast at this season too odd forward branches in the new laid hedges
of whitethorn begin to freshen into green before the arum dare peep out
of its hood or the primrose & violet shoot up a new leaf thro the warm
moss & ivy that shelters their spring dwellings the furze too on the
common wear a fairer green & here & there an odd branch is covered
with golden flowers & the ling or heath nestling among the long grass
below (covered with the withered flowers of last year) is sprouting up
into fresh hopes of spring the fairey rings on the pastures are getting
deeper dyes & the water weeds with long silver green blades of grass are
mantling the stagnant ponds in their summer liverys I find more beautys
in this month then I can find room to talk about in a letter . . .

I forgot to say in my last that the Nightingale sung as common by day
as night & as often tho its a fact that is not generaly known your London-
ers are very fond of talking about the bird & I believe fancy every bird
they hear after sunset a Nightingale I remember while I was there last
while walking with a friend in the fields of Shacklwell we saw a gentleman & lady listening very attentive by the side of a shrubbery & when
we came up we heard them lavishing praises on the beautiful song of the
nightingale which happened to be a thrush but it did for them & they
listend & repeated their praise with heartfelt satisfaction while the bird
seemed to know the grand distinction that its song had gaind for it &
strove exultingly to keep up the deception by attempting a varied &
more louder song the dews was ready to fall but the lady was heedless of
the wet grass tho the setting sun as a traveller glad to rest was leaning his
enlarged rim on the earth like a table of fire & lessening by degrees out of
sight leaving night & a few gilt clouds behind him such is the ignorance
of Nature in large Citys that are nothing less than overgrown prisons
that shut out the world and all its beautys

The nightingale as I said before is a shoy bird if any one approaches
too near her secret haunts its song ceases till they pass when it is resumd
as loud as before but I must repeat your quotation from Chaucer to
illustrate this

> The new abashèd nightingale
> That stinteth first when she beginneth sing

When that she heareth any herde's tale
Or in the hedges any [wight] stirring
& after siker doth her voice outring

As soon as they have young their song ceases & is heard no more till the
returning may after they cease singing they make a sort of gurring guttural noise as if calling the young to their food I know not what its for
else but they make this noise continually & doubtless before the young
leave the nest I have said all I can say about the Nightingale—In a
thicket of blackthorns near our village called 'bushy close' we have great
numbers of them every year but not so many as we used to have like the
Martins & Swallows & other birds of passage they seem to diminish but
for what cause I know not

As to the cuckoo I can give you no further tidings that what I have
given in my last Artis has one in his collection of stuffed birds (but I have
not sufficient scientific curiosity about me to go & take the exact description of its head rump & wings the length of its tail & the breadth from
the tips of the extended wings these old bookish descriptions you may
find in any natural history if they are of any gratification

for my part I love to look on nature with a poetic feeling which
magnifys the pleasure I love to see the nightingale in its hazel retreat &
the cuckoo hiding in its solitudes of oaken foliage & not to examine their
carcasses in glass cases yet naturalists & botanists seem to have no taste
for this practical feeling they merely make collections of dryd specimens
classing them after Linnaeus into tribes & familys & there they delight
to show them as a sort of ambitious fame with them 'a bird in the hand is
worth two in the bush' well everyone to his hobby

I have none of this curiosity about me tho I feel as happy as they can
about finding a new species of field flower or butterflye which I have not
seen before yet I have no desire further to dry the plant or torture the
butterflye by sticking it on a cork board with a pin—I have no wish to do
this if my feelings woud let me I only crop the blossom of the flower or
take the root from its solitudes if it would grace my garden & wish the
fluttering butterflye to settle till I can come up with it to examine the
powdered colours on its wings & then it may dance off again from fancyd
dangers & welcome) I think your feelings are on the side of Poetry for I
have no specimens to send you so be as it may you must be content with
my descriptions & observations I always feel delighted when an object in
nature brings up in ones mind an image of poetry that describes it from
some favourite author you have a better opportunity of consulting books
than I have therefore I will set down a list of favourite Poems & Poets
who went to nature for their images so that you may consult them &

share the feelings & pleasures which I describe—your favourite Chaucer
is one Passages in Spenser Cowley's grasshopper & Swallow Passages in
Shakespear Milton's Allegro & Penseroso & Parts of Comus the Elizabethan Poets of glorious memory Gay's Shepherds Week Green's Spleen
Thomson's Seasons Collins Ode to Evening Dyer's Grongar Hill &
Fleece Shenstone's Schoolmistress Gray's Ode to Spring T. Warton's
April Summer Hamlet & Ode to a friend Cowper's Task Wordsworth
Logans Ode to the Cuckoo Langhorne's Fables of Flora Jago's Blackbirds Bloomfield Witchwood Forest Shooters hill &c with Hurdis's Eve-
ning Walk in the village Curate & many others that may have slipped
my memory

it might seem impertinent in me to advise you what to read if you
misunderstood my meaning for I dont only do it for your pleasure but I
wish you to make extracts from your readings in your letters to me so that
I may feel some of my old gratifications agen—a clown may say that he
loves the morning but a man of taste feels it in a higher degree by
bringing up in his mind that beautiful line of Thomson's 'The meek eyd
morn appears mother of dews' The rustic sings beneath the evening
moon but it brings no associations he knowns nothing about Miltons
description of it 'Now comes still evening on & twilight grey hath in her
sober livery all things clad' nor of Collins Ode to Evening

the man of taste looks on the little Celandine in Spring & mutters in
his mind some favourite lines from Wordsworths address to that flower
he never sees the daisy without thinking of Burns & who sees the taller
buttercup carpeting the closes in golden fringe without a remembrance
of Chatterton's beautiful mention of it if he knows it 'The kingcup
brasted with the morning dew' other flowers crowd my imagination with
their poetic assosiations but I have no room for them the clown knows
nothing of these pleasures he knows they are flowers & just turns an eye
on them & plods bye therefore as I said before to look on nature with a
poetic eye magnifies the pleasure she herself being the very essence &
soul of Poesy if I had the means to consult & the health to indulge it I
should crowd these letters on Natural History with lucious scraps of
Poesy from my favourite Minstrels & make them less barren of amusement & more profitable of perusal In my catalogue of poets I forgot
Charlotte Smith whose poetry is full of pleasing images from nature—
Does Mr. Whites account of the Cuckoo & Nightingale agree with
mine look & tell me in your next

P.S. I can scarcely believe the account which you mention at the end
of your letter respecting the mans 'puzzling himself with doubts about
the Nightingales singing by day & about the expression of his notes

whether they are grave or gay'—you may well exclaim 'what solemn trifling' it betrays such ignorance that I can scarcely believe it—if the man does but go into any village solitude a few miles from London next may their varied music will soon put away his doubts of its singing by day—nay he may get rid of them now by asking any country clown the question for its such a common fact that all know of it—& as to the 'expression of its notes' if he has any knowledge of nature let him ask himself whether Nature is in the habit of making such happy seeming songs for sorrow as that of the Nightingales—the poets indulgd in fancys but they did not wish that those matter of fact men the Naturalists shoud take them for facts upon their credit—What absurditys for a world that is said to get wiser and wiser every day—

HAWKS

Hawks are beautiful objects when on the wing I have often stood to view a hawk in the sky trembling its wings & then hanging quite still for a moment as if it was as light as a shadow & could find like the clouds a resting place upon the blue air

There are a great many different sorts of hawks about us & several to which I am a stranger too

There is a very large blue one almost as big as a goose they fly in a swooping heavy manner not much unlike the flye of a heron you may see an odd one often in the spring swimming close to the green corn & ranging over an whole field for hours together it hunts leverets & partridges & pheasants I saw one of these which a man had wounded with a gun he had stupified it only for when he got it home it was as fierce & as live as ever the wings when extended was of a great length it was of a blue-grey color hued with deeper tinges of the same its beak was dreadfully hookd & its claws long & of a bright yellow with a yellow ring round each eye which gave a fierce and very severe look at the sight of a cat it put itself in a posture for striking as if it meant to seize it as prey but at a dog it seemd rather scared & sat on its tail end in a defensive posture with its eyes extended & its talons open making at the same time an earpiercing hissing noise which dismayd the dog who woud drop his tail & sneak out as if in fear they tyd a piece of tarmarking & tetherd it in a barn were they kept it 3 or 4 days when it gnawed the string from its leg & effected its liberty by getting thro the barnholes in the wall it ate nothing all that time they offerd it carrion but it woud take no notice of it what its name is I know not they call it the blue hawk

There is a small blue hawk often mistaken for the cuckoo I know nothing of it further then seeing it often on the wing & a rare one about the size of a blackbird of a mottld color & with a white patch of feathers

on the back of the head one of these sort was shot here in the summer by
a field keeper I have never seen anything like it before

Last year I had two tame hawks of what species I cannot tell they were
not quite so large as the sparrow hawk their wings & back feathers was of
a red brown color sheathd wi black their tails was long & barrd with
black & their breasts was of a lighter color & spotted their eyes was large
& of a dark piercing blue their beaks was very much hookd with a sharp
projecting swell in the top mandible not unlike the swell in the middle of
the hookd bill used by hedgers & called by them a tomahawk This made
an incision like a knife in tearing its food the bottom mandible was
curiously shortend as it were for the hook to lap over & seemd as tho
nature had clippd the end off with scissors for that purpose their legs was
short & yellow with a tuft of feathers over each thigh like the bantam
fowl a property belonging to most of the hawk tribe They grew very tame
& woud come at a call or whistle when they were hungry They made a
strange noise that piercd the ear with its shrillness they was very fond of
washing themselves often doing it twice a day in winter after being fed
they woud play in the garden running after each other & seizing bits of
clods or fallen apples in their claws or catching at flies when they rested
they usd always to perch on one leg with the other drawn up among their
feathers they always lovd to perch on the topmost twig of the trees in the
garden were they woud sit in a bold & commanding attitude one was
much larger than the other & the large one was much the tamest When
I went awalking in the fields it woud attempt to flye after me & as I was
fearful of losing it I usd to drive it back but one day it took advantage of
watching & following me & when I got into the fields I was astonishd &
startld to see a hawk settle on my shoulder it was mine who had watchd
me out of the town & took a short cut to flye after me I thought it would
flye away for good so I attempted to catch it but it woud not be made a
prisoner & flew to the trees by the road side I gave it up for lost but as
soon as I got out of sight it set up a noise & flew after me agen & when I
got upon the heath were there were no trees it woud settle upon the
ground before me & if I attempted to catch it it woud run & hide in the
rabbit burrows & when I left it took wing & flew after me & so it kept on
to the other end of my journey when it found home as soon as I did after
this I took no more heed of losing them tho they woud be missing for
days together a boy caught one by suprise & hurt it so that it dyd & the
tamest dyd while I was absent from home 4 days it refusd food & hunted
for me every morning & came to sit in my empty chair as it woud do till
I got up They thought it fretted itself to death in my absence but I think
the meat I gave was too strong for it & I believd it was not well a good
while before I left it I felt heartily sorry for my poor faithful affectionate
hawk

ON ANTS

It has been a commonly believd notion among such naturalists that trusts to books & repeats the old error that ants hurd up & feed on the curnels of grain such as wheat & barley but every common observer knows this to be a falsehood I have noticd them minutely & often & never saw one with such food in its mouth they feed on flyes & caterpillars which I have often seen them tugging home with & for which they climb trees & the stems of flowers—when they first appear in the spring they may be seen carrying out ants in their mouths of a smaller size which they will continue to do a long time transporting them away from home perhaps to form new colonys—they always make a track & keep it & will go for furlongs away from their homes fetching bits of bents & others lugging away with flyes or green maggots which they pick off of flowers & leaves some when overloaded are joind by others till they get a sufficient quantity to master it home—I have often minded that two while passing each other woud pause like old friends longparted see & as if they suddenly reccolected each other they went & put their heads together as if they shook hands or saluted each other when a shower comes on an unusual bustle ensues round their nest some set out & suddenly turn round again without fetching anything home others will hasten to help those that are loaded & when the rain begins to fall the others will leave their loads & make the best of their way as fast as they can their general employment is the gathering of bents &c to cover their habitation which they generally make round an old root which they cut into holes like an honeycomb these holes lead & communicate into each other for a long way in the ground in winter they lye dormant but quickly revive if exposd to the sun there is nothing to be seen of food in their habitations then I have observd stragglers that crawl about the grass seemingly without a purpose & if they accidentally fall into the track of those at labour that quickens their pace & sudden retreat I have fancied these to be the idle & discontented sort of radicals to the government

The smaller ants calld pismires seem to be under a different sort of government at least there is not that regularity observd among them in their labours as there is among the large ones they do not keep one track as the others do but creep about the grass were they please they are uncommonly fond of bread (which the larger ants will not touch) & when the shepherd litters his crumble from his dinner bag on their hill as he often will to observe them it instantly creates a great bustle among the little colony & they hasten away with it as fast as they can till every morsel is cleand up when they pause about as if looking for more—it is

commonly believd by carless observers that every hillock on greens &
commons has been first rooted up & afterwards occupied by these little
tenants but on the contrary most of the hills they occupy are formed by
themselves which they increase every year by bringing up a portion of
mold on the surface finely powdered on which they lay their eggs to
receive the warmth of the sun & the shepherd by observing their wisdom
in this labour judges correctly of the changes of the weather in fact he
finds it an infallible almanack when fine weather sets in their eggs are
brought nearly to the top of the new addition to their hill & as soon as
ever a change is about to take place nay at the approach of a shower they
are observd carrying them deeper down to safer situations & if much wet
is coming they entirely disappear with them into the bottom of the
castle were no rain can reach them for they generally use a composition
of clay in making the hills that forces off the wet & keeps it from
penetrating into their cells if the crown of one of the hills be taken off
with a spade it will appear pierced with holes like a honeycomb—these
little things are armd with stings that blister & torture the skin with a
pain worse than the keen nettle There is a smaller sort still of a deep
black color that like the large ones have no sting I once when sitting at
my dinner hour in the fields seeing a colony of the red pismires near one
of these black ones tryd the experiment to see wether they woud associate with each other & as soon as I put a black one among them they
began to fight with the latter after wounding his antagonist (seeming to
be of inferior strength) curld up & dyd at his feet I then put a red one to
the colony of the blacks which they instantly seized & tho he generaly
contrivd to escape he appeard to be terribly wounded & no doubt was a
cripple for life—these little creatures will raise a large tower of earth as
thick as a mans arm in the form of a sugar loaf to a foot or a foot & a half
high in the grain & long grass for in such places they cannot meet the
sun on the ground so they raise these towers on the top of which they lay
their eggs & as the grass or grain keeps growing they keep raising their
towers till I have met with them as tall as ones knee.

THE BUTTER BUMP*

This is a thing that makes a very odd noise morning & evening among
the flags & large reed shaws in the fens some describe the noise as
something like the bellowing of bulls but I have often heard it & cannot
liken it to that sound at all in fact it is difficult to describe what it is like
its noise has procurd it the above name by the common people the first

*The European Bittern. [Ed. note]

part of its noise is an indistinct muttering sort of sound very like the word butter utterd in a hurried manner & bump comes very quick after & bumps a sound on the ear as if eccho had mockd the bump of a gun just as the mutter ceasd nay this is not like I have often thought the putting ones mouth to the bung hole of an empty large cask & uttering the word 'butter bump' sharply woud imitate the sound exactly after its first call that imitates the word 'butter bump' it repeats the sound bump singly several times in a more determind & louder manner—thus 'butter bump bump bump butter bump it strikes people at first as somthing like the sound of a coopers mallet hitting on empty casks when I was a boy this was one of the fen wonders I usd often to go on a sunday with my mother to see my aunt at peakirk when I often wanderd in the fen with the boys a bird nesting & when I enquird what this strange noise was they described it as coming from a bird larger then an ox that coud kill all the cattle in the fen if it choose & destroy the villager likwise but that it was very harmless & all the harm it did was the drinking so much water as to nearly empty the dykes in summer & spoil the rest so that the stock coud scarcly drink what it left this was not only a story among children but their parents believd the same thing such is the power of superstition over ignorant people who have no desire to go beyond hearsay & enquire for themselves but the 'world gets wiser every day' tis not believd now nor heard as a wonder any longer—they say that it is a small bird that makes the noise not much unlike the quail tho a deal larger & longer on the legs they say it puts its beek in a reed when it makes the noise that gives it that jarring or hollow sound which is heard so far I have no knowledge of its using the reed but I believe they are right in the bird I have startend such a bird my self out of reed shaws my self were I have heard this noise & afterwards the noise has been silent which convinced me that the one was the bird I never saw it but on the wing & it appeard to me larger then a pheasant & not unlike it either in shape or color but it flew different—there is a great many of these birds on whittlesea mere & their noise is easily heard in a morning on the London road which is some miles distant its noise continues all summer & at the latter end of the year it is silent & heard no more till summer

GEORGE CATLIN
1796-1872

Catlin spent decades living among the native peoples of America, paint-ing their portraits and depicting scenes of tribal life. Manners, Customs, and Conditions of the North American Indians (1841) included 300 engravings of his work, as well as many of his observations of the cultures which had developed on the Great Plains. His description of the "buf-falo country" through which he traveled includes one of the earliest recognitions that, with the coming of the white man, the vast herds would soon be destroyed by "profligate waste."

From LETTERS AND NOTES ON THE MANNERS, CUSTOMS, AND CONDITIONS OF THE NORTH AMERICAN INDIANS . . .

LETTER—NO. 31

MOUTH OF TETON RIVER, UPPER MISSOURI

In former Letters I have given some account of the *Bisons,* or (as they are more familiarly denominated in this country) *Buffaloes,* which in-habit these regions in numerous herds; and of which I must say yet a little more.

These noble animals of the ox species, and which have been so well described in our books on Natural History, are a subject of curious inter-est and great importance in this vast wilderness; rendered peculiarly so at this time, like the history of the poor savage; and from the same consid-eration, that they are rapidly wasting away at the approach of civilized man—and like him and his character, in a very few years, to live only in books or on canvass.

Letters and Notes on the Manners, Customs and Conditions of the North American Indi-ans, Written during Eight Years' Travel Amongst the Wildest Tribes of Indians in North America (New York: Wiley and Putnam, 1841).

The word buffalo is undoubtedly most incorrectly applied to these animals, and I can scarcely tell why they have been so called; for they bear just about as much resemblance to the Eastern buffalo, as they do to a zebra or to a common ox. How nearly they may approach to the bison of Europe, which I never have had an opportunity to see, and which, I am inclined to think, is now nearly extinct, I am unable to say; yet if I were to judge from the numerous engravings I have seen of those animals, and descriptions I have read of them, I should be inclined to think, there was yet a wide difference between the bison of the American prairies, and those in the North of Europe and Asia. The American bison, or (as I shall hereafter call it) buffalo, is the largest of the ruminating animals that is now living in America; and seems to have been spread over the plains of this vast country, by the Great Spirit, for the use and subsistence of the red men, who live almost exclusively on their flesh, and clothe themselves with their skins. The reader, by referring back to PLATES 7 and 8, in the beginning of this Work, will see faithful traces of the male and female of this huge animal, in their proud and free state of nature, grazing on the plains of the country to which they appropriately belong. Their colour is a dark brown, but changing very much as the season varies from warm to cold; their hair or fur, from its great length in the winter and spring, and exposure to the weather, turning quite light, and almost to a jet black, when the winter coat is shed off, and a new growth is shooting out.

The buffalo bull often grows to the enormous weight of 2000 pounds, and shakes a long and shaggy black mane, that falls in great profusion and *confusion,* over his head and shoulders; and oftentimes falling down quite to the ground. The horns are short, but very large, and have but one turn, *i.e.* they are a simple arch, without the least approach to a spiral form, like those of the common ox, or of the goat species.

The female is much smaller than the male, and always distinguishable by the peculiar shape of the horns, which are much smaller and more crooked, turning their points more in towards the centre of the forehead.

One of the most remarkable characteristics of the buffalo, is the peculiar formation and expression of the eye, the ball of which is very large and white, and the iris jet black. The lids of the eye seem always to be strained quite open, and the ball rolling forward and down; so that a considerable part of the iris is hidden behind the lower lid, while the pure white of the eyeball glares out over it in an arch, in the shape of a moon at the end of its first quarter.

These animals are, truly speaking, gregarious, but not migratory— they graze in immense and almost incredible numbers at times, and roam about and over vast tracts of country, from East to West, and from West to East, as often as from North to South; which has often been supposed they naturally and habitually did to accommodate themselves to the temperature of the climate in the different latitudes. The limits within which they are found in America, are from the 30th to the 55th degrees of North latitude; and their extent from East to West, which is from the border of our extreme Western frontier limits, to the Western verge of the Rocky Mountains, is defined by quite different causes, than those which the degrees of temperature have prescribed to them on the North and the South. Within these 25 degrees of latitude, the buffaloes seem to flourish, and get their living without the necessity of evading the rigour of the climate, for which Nature seems most wisely to have prepared them by the greater or less profusion of fur, with which she has clothed them.

It is very evident that, as high North as Lake Winnepeg, seven or eight hundred miles North of this, the buffalo subsists itself through the severest winters; getting its food chiefly by browsing amongst the timber, and by pawing through the snow, for a bite at the grass, which in those regions is frozen up very suddenly in the beginning of the winter, with all its juices in it, and consequently furnishes very nutritious and efficient food; and often, if not generally, supporting the animal in better flesh during these difficult seasons of their lives, than they are found to be in, in the 30th degree of latitude, upon the borders of Mexico, where the severity of winter is not known, but during a long and tedious autumn, the herbage, under the influence of a burning sun, is gradually dried away to a mere husk, and its nutriment gone, leaving these poor creatures, even in the dead of winter, to bask in the warmth of a genial sun, without the benefit of a green or juicy thing to bite at.

The place from which I am now writing, may be said to be the very heart or nucleus of the buffalo country, about equi-distant between the two extremes; and of course, the most congenial temperature for them to flourish in. The finest animals that graze on the prairies are to be found in this latitude; and I am sure I never could send from a better source, some further account of the death and destruction that is dealt among these noble animals, and hurrying on their final extinction.

The Sioux are a bold and desperate set of horsemen, and great hunters; and in the heart of their country is one of the most extensive assortments of goods, of whiskey, and other saleable commodities, as well as a party of the most indefatigable men, who are constantly calling for every robe that can be stripped from these animals' backs.

These are the causes which lead so directly to their rapid destruction;

and which open to the view of the traveller so freshly, so vividly, and so familiarly, the scenes of archery—of lancing, and of death-dealing, that belong peculiarly to this wild and shorn country.

The almost countless herds of these animals that are sometimes met with on these prairies, have been often spoken of by other writers, and may yet be seen by any traveller who will take the pains to visit these regions. The *"running season,"* which is in August and September, is the time when they congregate into such masses in some places, as literally to blacken the prairies for miles together. It is no uncommon thing at this season, at these gatherings, to see several thousands in a mass, eddying and wheeling about under a cloud of dust, which is raised by the bulls as they are pawing in the dirt, or engaged in desperate combats, as they constantly are, plunging and butting at each other in the most furious manner. In these scenes, the males are continually following the females, and the whole mass are in constant motion; and all bellowing (or "roaring") in deep and hollow sounds; which, mingled altogether, appear, at the distance of a mile or two, like the sound of distant thunder.

During the season whilst they are congregated together in these dense and confused masses, the remainder of the country around for many miles, becomes entirely vacated; and the traveller may spend many a toilsome day, and many a hungry night, without being cheered by the sight of one; where, if he retraces his steps a few weeks after, he will find them dispersed, and grazing quietly in little families and flocks, and equally stocking the whole country. Of these quiet little herds, a fair representation will be seen in PLATE 106, where some are grazing, others at play, or lying down, and others indulging in their "wallows." "A bull in his wallow" is a frequent saying in this country; and has a very significant meaning with those who have ever seen a buffalo bull performing *ablution,* or rather endeavouring to cool his heated sides, by tumbling about in a mud puddle.

In the heat of summer, these huge animals, which, no doubt, suffer very much with the great profusion of their long and shaggy hair or fur, often graze on the low grounds in the prairies, where there is a little stagnant water lying amongst the grass, and the ground underneath being saturated with it, is soft, into which the enormous bull, lowered down upon one knee, will plunge his horns, and at last his head, driving up the earth, and soon making an excavation in the ground, into which the water filters from amongst the grass, forming for him in a few moments, a cool and comfortable bath, into which he plunges like a hog in his mire.

In this *delectable* laver, he throws himself flat upon his side, and forcing himself violently around, with his horns and his huge hump on his shoulders presented to the sides, he ploughs up the ground by his rotary motion, sinking himself deeper and deeper in the ground, continually enlarging his pool, in which he at length becomes nearly immersed; and the water and mud about him mixed into a complete mortar, which changes his colour, and drips in streams from every part of him as he rises up upon his feet, a hideous monster of mud and ugliness, too frightful and too eccentric to be described!

It is generally the leader of the herd that takes upon him to make this excavation; and if not (but another one opens the ground), the leader (who is conqueror) marches forward, and driving the other from it plunges himself into it; and having cooled his sides, and changed his colour to a walking mass of mud and mortar; he stands in the pool until inclination induces him to step out, and give place to the next in command, who stands ready; and another, and another, who advance forward in their turns, to enjoy the luxury of the wallow; until the whole band (sometimes an hundred or more) will pass through it in turn; each one throwing his body around in a similar manner; and each one adding a little to the dimensions of the pool, while he carries away in his hair an equal share of the clay, which dries to a grey or whitish colour, and gradually falls off. By this operation, which is done, perhaps, in the space of half an hour, a circular excavation of fifteen or twenty feet in diameter, and two feet in depth, is completed, and left for the water to run into, which soon fills it to the level of the ground.

To these sinks, the waters lying on the surface of the prairies, are continually draining, and in them lodging their vegetable deposits; which, after a lapse of years, fill them up to the surface with a rich soil, which throws up an unusual growth of grass and herbage; forming conspicuous circles which arrest the eye of the traveller, and are calculated to excite his surprise for ages to come.

Many travellers who have penetrated not quite far enough into the Western country to see the habits of these animals, and the manner in which these *mysterious* circles are made; but who have seen the prairies strewed with their bleached bones, and have beheld these strange circles, which often occur in groups, and of different sizes—have come home with beautiful and ingenious theories (which *must needs be made*), for the origin of these singular and unaccountable appearances, which, for want of a rational theory, have generally been attributed to *fairy feet,* and gained the appellation of *"fairy circles."*

Many travellers, again, have supposed that these rings were produced by the dances of the Indians, which are oftentimes (and in fact most generally) performed in a circle; yet a moment's consideration disproves such a probability, inasmuch as the Indians always select the ground for their dancing near the sites of their villages, and that always on a dry and hard foundation; when these "fairy circles" are uniformly found to be on low and wet ground.

*   *   *

The poor buffaloes have their enemy *man*, besetting and beseiging them at all times of the year, and in all the modes that man in his superior wisdom has been able to devise for their destruction. They struggle in vain to evade his deadly shafts, when he dashes amongst them over the plains on his wild horse—they plunge into the snow-drifts where they yield themselves an easy prey to their destroyers, and they also stand unwittingly and behold him, unsuspected under the skin of a white wolf, insinuating himself and his fatal weapons into close company, when they are peaceably grazing on the level prairies, and shot down before they are aware of their danger.

There are several varieties of the wolf species in this country, the most formidable and most numerous of which are white, often sneaking about in gangs or families of fifty or sixty in numbers, appearing in distance, on the green prairies like nothing but a flock of sheep. Many of these animals grow to a very great size, being I should think, quite a match for the largest Newfoundland dog. At present, whilst the buffaloes are so abundant, and these ferocious animals are glutted with the buffalo's flesh, they are harmless, and everywhere sneak away from man's presence; which I scarcely think will be the case after the buffaloes are all gone, and they are left, as they must be, with scarcely anything to eat. They always are seen following about in the vicinity of herds of buffaloes and stand ready to pick the bones of those that the hunters leave on the ground, or to overtake and devour those that are wounded, which fall an easy prey to them. While the herd of buffaloes are together, they seem to have little dread of the wolf, and allow them to come in close company with them. The Indian then has taken advantage of this fact, and often places himself under the skin of this animal, and crawls for half a mile or more on his hands and knees, until he approaches within a few rods of the unsuspecting group, and easily shoots down the fattest of the throng.

The buffalo is a very timid animal, and shuns the vicinity of man with the keenest sagacity; yet, when overtaken, and harassed or wounded, turns upon its assailants with the utmost fury, who have only to seek safety in flight. In their desperate resistance the finest horses are often destroyed; but the Indian, with his superior sagacity and dexterity, generally finds some effective mode of escape.

During the season of the year whilst the calves are young, the male seems to stroll about by the side of the dam, as if for the purpose of protecting the young, at which time it is exceedingly hazardous to attack them, as they are sure to turn upon their pursuers, who have often to fly to each others assistance. The buffalo calf, during the first six months is red, and has so much the appearance of a red calf in cultivated fields, that it could easily be mingled and mistaken amongst them. In the fall, when it changes its hair it takes a brown coat for the winter, which it always retains. In pursuing a large herd of buffaloes at the season when their calves are but a few weeks old, I have often been exceedingly amused with the curious manœuvres of these shy little things. Amidst the thundering confusion of a throng of several hundreds or several thousands of these animals, there will be many of the calves that lose sight of their dams; and being left behind by the throng, and the swift passing hunters, they endeavour to secrete themselves, when they are exceedingly put to it on a level prairie, where nought can be seen but the short grass of six or eight inches in height, save an occasional bunch of wild sage, a few inches higher, to which the poor affrighted things will run, and dropping on their knees, will push their noses under it, and into the grass, where they will stand for hours, with their eyes shut, imagining themselves securely hid, whilst they are standing up quite straight upon their hind feet and can easily be seen at several miles distance. It is a familiar amusement for us accustomed to these scenes, to retreat back over the ground where we have just escorted the herd, and approach these little trembling things, which stubbornly maintain their positions, with their noses pushed under the grass, and their eyes strained upon us, as we dismount from our horses and are passing around them. From this fixed position they are sure not to move, until hands are laid upon them, and then for the shins of a novice, we can extend our sympathy; or if he can preserve the skin on his bones from the furious buttings of its head, we know how to congratulate him on his signal success and good luck. In these desperate struggles, for a moment, the little thing is conquered, and makes no further resistance. And I have often, in concurrence with a known custom of the country, held my hands over the eyes of the calf, and breathed a few strong breaths into its nostrils; after which I have, with my hunting companions, rode several miles into our encampment, with the little prisoner busily following the heels of my horse the whole way, as closely and as affectionately as its instinct would attach it to the company of its dam!

This is one of the most extraordinary things that I have met with in the habits of this wild country, and although I had often heard of it, and felt unable exactly to believe it, I am now willing to bear testimony to the fact, from the numerous instances which I have witnessed since I came into the country. During the time that I resided at this post, in the spring of the year, on my way up the river, I assisted (in numerous hunts of the buffalo, with the Fur Company's men,) in bringing in, in the above manner, several of these little prisoners, which sometimes followed for five or six miles close to our horses' heels, and even into the Fur Company's Fort, and into the stable where our horses were led. In this way, before I left for the head waters of the Missouri, I think we had collected about a dozen, which Mr. Laidlaw was successfully raising with the aid of a good milch cow, and which were to be committed to the care of Mr. Chouteau to be transported by the return of the steamer, to his extensive plantation in the vicinity of St. Louis.[1]

It is truly a melancholy contemplation for the traveller in this country, to anticipate the period which is not far distant, when the last of these noble animals, at the hands of white and red men, will fall victims to their cruel and improvident rapacity; leaving these beautiful green fields, a vast and idle waste, unstocked and unpeopled for ages to come, until the bones of the one and the traditions of the other will have vanished, and left scarce an intelligible trace behind.

That the reader should not think me visionary in these contemplations, or romancing in making such assertions, I will hand him the following item of the extravagancies which are practiced in these regions, and rapidly leading to the results which I have just named.

When I first arrived at this place, on my way up the river, which was in the month of May, in 1832, and had taken up my lodgings in the Fur Company's Fort, Mr. Laidlaw, of whom I have before spoken, and also his chief clerk, Mr. Halsey, and many of their men, as well as the chiefs of the Sioux, told me, that only a few days before I arrived, (when an immense herd of buffaloes had showed themselves on the opposite side of the river, almost blackening the plains for a great distance,) a party of five or six hundred Sioux Indians on horseback, forded the river about mid-day, and spending a few hours amongst them, recrossed the river at sun-down and came into the Fort with *fourteen hundred fresh buffalo tongues,* which were thrown down in a mass, and for which they required but a few gallons of whiskey, which was soon demolished, indulging them in a little, and harmless carouse.

This profligate waste of the lives of these noble and useful animals, when, from all that I could learn, not a skin or a pound of the meat (except the tongues), was brought in, fully supports me in the seemingly

[1]The fate of these poor little prisoners, I was informed on my return to St. Louis a year afterwards, was a very disastrous one. The steamer having a distance of 1600 miles to perform, and lying a week or two on sand bars, in a country where milk could not be procured, they all perished but one, which is now flourishing in the extensive fields of this gentleman. [Catlin's note]

extravagant predictions that I have made as to their extinction, which I am certain is near at hand. In the above extravagant instance, at a season when their skins were without fur and not worth taking off, and their camp was so well stocked with fresh and dried meat, that they had no occasion for using the flesh, there is a fair exhibition of the improvident character of the savage, and also of his recklessness in catering for his appetite, so long as the present inducements are held out to him in his country, for its gratification.

In this singular country, where the poor Indians have no laws or regulations of society, making it a vice or an impropriety to drink to excess, they think it no harm to indulge in the delicious beverage, as long as they are able to buy whiskey to drink. They look to white men as wiser than themselves, and able to set them examples—they see none of these in their country but sellers of whiskey, who are constantly tendering it to them, and most of them setting the example by using it themselves; and they easily acquire a taste, that to be catered for, where whiskey is sold at sixteen dollars per gallon, soon impoverishes them, and must soon strip the skin from the last buffalo's back that lives in their country, to "be dressed by their squaws" and vended to the Traders for a pint of diluted alcohol.

From the above remarks it will be seen, that not only the red men, but red men and white, have aimed destruction at the race of these animals; and with them, *beasts* have turned hunters of buffaloes in this country, slaying them, however, in less numbers, and for far more laudable purpose than that of selling their skins. The white wolves, of which I have spoken in a former epistle, follow the herds of buffaloes as I have said, from one season to another, glutting themselves on the carcasses of those that fall by the deadly shafts of their enemies, or linger with disease or old age to be dispatched by these sneaking cormorants, who are ready at all times kindly to relieve them from the pangs of a lingering death.

Whilst the herd is together, the wolves never attack them, as they instantly gather for combined resistance, which they effectually make. But when the herds are travelling, it often happens that an aged or wounded one, lingers at a distance behind, and when fairly out of sight of the herd, is set upon by these voracious hunters, which often gather to the number of fifty or more, and are sure at last to torture him to death, and use him up at a meal. The buffalo, however, is a huge and furious animal, and when his retreat is cut off, makes desperate and deadly resistance, contending to the last moment for the right of life—and oftentimes deals death by wholesale, to his canine assailants, which he is tossing into the air or stamping to death under his feet.

During my travels in these regions, I have several times come across such a gang of these animals surrounding an old or a wounded bull, where it would seem, from appearances, that they had been for several days in attendance, and at intervals desperately engaged in the effort to take his life. But a short time since, as one of my hunting companions and myself were returning to our encampment with our horses loaded with meat, we discovered at a distance, a huge bull, encircled with a gang of white wolves; we rode up as near as we could without driving them away, and being within pistol shot, we had a remarkably good view, where I sat for a few moments and made a sketch in my note-book; after which, we rode up and gave the signal for them to disperse, which they instantly did, withdrawing themselves to the distance of fifty or sixty rods, when we found, to our great surprise, that the animal had made desperate resistance, until his eyes were entirely eaten out of his head— the grizzle of his nose was mostly gone—his tongue was half eaten off, and the skin and flesh of his legs torn almost literally into strings. In this tattered and torn condition, the poor old veteran stood bracing up in the midst of his devourers, who had ceased hostilities for a few minutes, to enjoy a sort of parley, recovering strength and preparing to resume the attack in a few moments again. In this group, some were reclining, to gain breath, whilst others were sneaking about and licking their chaps in anxiety for a renewal of the attack; and others, less lucky, had been crushed to death by the feet or the horns of the bull. I rode nearer to the pitiable object as he stood bleeding and trembling before me, and said to him, "Now is your time, old fellow, and you had better be off." Though blind and nearly destroyed, there seemed evidently to be a recognition of a friend in me, as he straightened up, and, trembling with excitement, dashed off at full speed upon the prairie, in a straight line. We turned our horses and resumed our march, and when we had advanced a mile or more, we looked back, and on our left, where we saw again the ill-fated animal surrounded by his tormentors, to whose insatiable voracity he unquestionably soon fell a victim.

Thus much I wrote of the buffaloes, and of the accidents that befall them, as well as of the fate that awaits them; and before I closed my book, I strolled out one day to the shade of a plum-tree, where I laid in the grass on a favourite bluff, and wrote thus:—

"It is generally supposed, and familiarly said, that a man '*falls*' into a rêverie; but I seated myself in the shade a few minutes since, resolved to *force* myself into one; and for this purpose I laid open a small pocket-map of North America, and excluding my thoughts from every other object in the world, I soon succeeded in producing the desired illusion. This little chart, over which I bent, was seen in all its parts, as nothing but the green and vivid reality. I was lifted up upon an imaginary pair of wings, which easily raised and held me floating in the open air, from whence I could behold beneath me the Pacific and the Atlantic Oceans—the great cities of the East, and the mighty rivers. I could see the blue chain of the great lakes at the North—the Rocky Mountains, and beneath them and near their base, the vast, and almost boundless plains of grass, which were speckled with the bands of grazing buffaloes!

"The world turned gently around, and I examined its surface; continent after continent passed under my eye, and yet amidst them all, I saw not the vast and vivid green, that is spread like a carpet over the Western wilds of my own country. I saw not elsewhere in the world, the myriad herds of buffaloes—my eyes scanned in vain, for they were not. And when I turned again to the wilds of my native land, I beheld them all in motion! For the distance of several hundreds of miles from North to South, they were wheeling about in vast columns and herds—some were scattered, and ran with furious wildness—some lay dead, and others were pawing the earth for a hiding-place—some were sinking down and dying, gushing out their life's blood in deep-drawn sighs—and others were contending in furious battle for the life they possessed, and the ground that they stood upon. They had long since assembled from the thickets, and secret haunts of the deep forest, into the midst of the treeless and bushless plains, as the place for their safety. I could see in an hundred places, amid the wheeling bands, and on their skirts and flanks, the leaping wild horse darting among them. I saw not the arrows, nor heard the twang of the sinewy bows that sent them; but I saw their victims fall!—on other steeds that rushed along their sides, I saw the glistening lances, which seemed to lay across them; their blades were blazing in the sun, till dipped in blood, and then I lost them! In other parts (and there were many), the vivid flash of *fire-arms* was seen—*their* victims fell too, and over their dead bodies hung suspended in air, little clouds of whitened smoke, from under which the flying horsemen had darted forward to mingle again with, and deal death to, the trampling throng.

"So strange were men mixed (both red and white) with the countless herds that wheeled and eddyed about, that all below seemed one vast extended field of battle—whole armies, in some places, seemed to blacken the earth's surface;—in other parts, regiments, battalions, wings, platoons, rank and file, and *"Indian-file"*—all were in motion; and death and destruction seemed to be the watch-word amongst them. In their turmoil, they sent up great clouds of dust, and with them came the mingled din of groans and trampling hoofs, that seemed like the rumbling of a dreadful cataract, or the roaring of distant thunder. Alternate pity and admiration harrowed up in my bosom and my brain, many a hidden thought; and amongst them a few of the beautiful notes that were once sung, and exactly in point: *'Quadrupedante putrem sonitu quatit ungula campum.'* Even such was the din amidst the quadrupeds of these vast plains. And from the craggy cliffs of the Rocky Mountains also were seen descending into the valley, the myriad Tartars, who had not horses to ride, but before their well-drawn bows the fattest of the herds were falling. Hundreds and thousands were strewed upon the plains— they were flayed, and their reddened carcasses left; and about them bands of wolves, and dogs, and buzzards were seen devouring them. Contiguous, and in sight, were the distant and feeble smokes of wigwams and villages, where the skins were dragged, and dressed for white man's luxury! where they were all sold for *whiskey,* and the poor Indians laid drunk, and were crying. I cast my eyes into the towns and cities of the East, and there I beheld buffalo robes hanging at almost every door for traffic; and I saw also the curling smokes of a thousand *Stills*—and I said, 'Oh insatiable man, is thy avarice such! wouldst thou tear the skin from the back of the last animal of this noble race, *and rob thy fellow-man of his meat, and for it give him poison!'* "   *   *   *

RALPH WALDO EMERSON
1803-1882

In the development of American nature writing, Emerson is generally given credit for having inspired such major figures as Thoreau, Melville, Burroughs, Whitman, and Muir. There is no question that his first book, Nature, *published in 1835, had enormous influence on the course of the genre, and the opening sections remain powerful statements of the American imperative to "enjoy an original relation to the universe." The prevailing notion of Emerson, though, is that he was primarily an abstract philosopher and armchair naturalist who preferred his nature warmed-over, and except for some of his poems he is rarely anthologized as a nature writer. In his extensive* Journals, *however, he reveals himself as an original observer and vivid recorder of local natural phenomena. His frequent, affectionate visits to Walden Pond remind us that Emer-*

son was no mere absentee landlord of that famous piece of waterfront property.

From NATURE

"Nature is but an image or imitation of wisdom,
the last thing of the soul; nature being a thing
which doth only do, but not know."—PLOTINUS
(Motto of 1836)

A subtle chain of countless rings
The next unto the farthest brings;
The eye reads omens where it goes,
And speaks all languages the rose;
And, striving to be man, the worm
Mounts through all the spires of form.
(Motto of 1849)

INTRODUCTION

Our age is retrospective. It builds the sepulchres of the fathers. It writes biographies, histories, and criticism. The foregoing generations beheld God and nature face to face; we, through their eyes. Why should not we also enjoy an original relation to the universe? Why should not we have a poetry and philosophy of insight and not of tradition, and a religion by revelation to us, and not the history of theirs? Embosomed for a season in nature, whose floods of life stream around and through us, and invite us, by the powers they supply, to action proportioned to nature, why should we grope among the dry bones of the past, or put the living generation into masquerade out of its faded wardrobe? The sun shines today also. There is more wool and flax in the fields. There are new lands, new men, new thoughts. Let us demand our own works and laws and worship.

Undoubtedly we have no questions to ask which are unanswerable. We must trust the perfection of the creation so far as to believe that whatever curiosity the order of things has awakened in our minds, the order of things can satisfy. Every man's condition is a solution in hieroglyphic to those inquiries he would put. He acts it as life, before he apprehends it as truth. In like manner, nature is already, in its forms and tendencies, describing its own design. Let us interrogate the great appa-

Nature (Boston: J. Monroe, 1836).

rition that shines so peacefully around us. Let us inquire, to what end is nature?

All science has one aim, namely, to find a theory of nature. We have theories of races and of functions, but scarcely yet a remote approach to an idea of creation. We are now so far from the road to truth, that religious teachers dispute and hate each other, and speculative men are esteemed unsound and frivolous. But to a sound judgment, the most abstract truth is the most practical. Whenever a true theory appears, it will be its own evidence. Its test is, that it will explain all phenomena. Now many are thought not only unexplained but inexplicable; as language, sleep, madness, dreams, beasts, sex.

Philosophically considered, the universe is composed of Nature and the Soul. Strictly speaking, therefore, all that is separate from us, all which Philosophy distinguishes as the NOT ME, that is, both nature and art, all other men and my own body, must be ranked under this name, NATURE. In enumerating the values of nature and casting up their sum, I shall use the word in both senses;—in its common and in its philosophical import. In inquiries so general as our present one, the inaccuracy is not material; no confusion of thought will occur. *Nature,* in the common sense, refers to essences unchanged by man; space, the air, the river, the leaf. *Art* is applied to the mixture of his will with the same things, as in a house, a canal, a statue, a picture. But his operations taken together are so insignificant, a little chipping, baking, patching, and washing, that in an impression so grand as that of the world on the human mind, they do not vary the result.

I. NATURE

To go into solitude, a man needs to retire as much from his chamber as from society. I am not solitary whilst I read and write, though nobody is with me. But if a man would be alone, let him look at the stars. The rays that come from those heavenly worlds will separate between him and what he touches. One might think the atmosphere was made transparent with this design, to give man, in the heavenly bodies, the perpetual presence of the sublime. Seen in the streets of cities, how great they are! If the stars should appear one night in a thousand years, how would men believe and adore; and preserve for many generations the remembrance of the city of God which had been shown! But every night come out these envoys of beauty, and light the universe with the admonishing smile.

The stars awaken a certain reverence, because though always present, they are inaccessible; but all natural objects make a kindred impression, when the mind is open to their influence. Nature never wears a mean appearance. Neither does the wisest man extort her secret, and lose his curiosity by finding out all her perfection. Nature never became a toy to a wise spirit. The flowers, the animals, the mountains, reflected the wisdom of his best hour, as much as they had delighted the simplicity of his childhood.

When we speak of nature in this manner, we have a distinct but most poetical sense in the mind. We mean the integrity of impression made by manifold natural objects. It is this which distinguishes the stick of timber of the wood-cutter from the tree of the poet. The charming landscape which I saw this morning is indubitably made up of some twenty or thirty farms. Miller owns this field, Locke that, and Manning the woodland beyond. But none of them owns the landscape. There is a property in the horizon which no man has but he whose eye can integrate all the parts, that is, the poet. This is the best part of these men's farms, yet to this their warranty-deeds give no title.

To speak truly, few adult persons can see nature. Most persons do not see the sun. At least they have a very superficial seeing. The sun illuminates only the eye of the man, but shines into the eye and the heart of the child. The lover of nature is he whose inward and outward senses are still truly adjusted to each other; who has retained the spirit of infancy even into the era of manhood. His intercourse with heaven and earth becomes part of his daily food. In the presence of nature a wild delight runs through the man, in spite of real sorrows. Nature says,—he is my creature, and maugre all his impertinent griefs, he shall be glad with me. Not the sun or the summer alone, but every hour and season yields its tribute of delight; for every hour and change corresponds to and authorizes a different state of the mind, from breathless noon to grimmest midnight. Nature is a setting that fits equally well a comic or a mourning piece. In good health, the air is a cordial of incredible virtue. Crossing a bare common, in snow puddles, at twilight, under a clouded sky, without having in my thoughts any occurrence of special good fortune, I have enjoyed a perfect exhilaration. I am glad to the brink of fear. In the woods, too, a man casts off his years, as the snake his slough, and at what period soever of life is always a child. In the woods is perpetual youth. Within these plantations of God, a decorum and sanctity reign, a perennial festival is dressed, and the guest sees not how he should tire of them in a thousand years. In the woods, we return to reason and faith. There I feel that nothing can befall me in life,—no disgrace, no calamity (leaving me my eyes), which nature cannot repair. Standing on the bare ground,—my head bathed by the blithe air and uplifted into infinite space,—all mean egotism vanishes. I become a transparent eyeball; I am nothing; I see all; the currents of the Universal Being circulate through me; I am part or parcel of God. The name of the nearest friend sounds then foreign and accidental: to be brothers, to be acquaintances, master or servant, is then a trifle and a disturbance. I am the lover of uncontained and immortal beauty. In the wilderness, I find something more dear and connate than in streets or villages. In the tranquil landscape, and especially in the distant line of the horizon, man beholds somewhat as beautiful as his own nature.

The greatest delight which the fields and woods minister is the suggestion of an occult relation between man and the vegetable. I am not alone and unacknowledged. They nod to me, and I to them. The waving of the boughs in the storm is new to me and old. It takes me by surprise, and yet is not unknown. Its effect is like that of a higher thought or a better emotion coming over me, when I deemed I was thinking justly or doing right.

Yet it is certain that the power to produce this delight does not reside in nature, but in man, or in a harmony of both. It is necessary to use these pleasures with great temperance. For nature is not always tricked in holiday attire, but the same scene which yesterday breathed perfume and glittered as for the frolic of the nymphs is overspread with melancholy today. Nature always wears the colors of the spirit. To a man laboring under calamity, the heat of his own fire hath sadness in it. Then there is a kind of contempt of the landscape felt by him who has just lost by death a dear friend. The sky is less grand as it shuts down over less worth in the population. *   *   *

From The Journals of
Ralph Waldo Emerson

July 13. [1833]

I carried my ticket from Mr. Warden to the Cabinet of Natural History in the Garden of Plants. How much finer things are in composition than alone. 'Tis wise in man to make cabinets. When I was come into the Ornithological Chambers I wished I had come only there. The fancy-coloured vests of these elegant beings make me as pensive as the hues and forms of a cabinet of shells, formerly. It is a beautiful collection and makes the visitor as calm and genial as a bridegroom. The limits of the possible are enlarged, and the real is stranger than the imaginary. Some of the birds have a fabulous beauty. One parrot of a fellow called

The Journals of Ralph Waldo Emerson, 10 vols. (Boston: Houghton Mifflin, 1909–1914).

Psittacus erythropterus from New Holland deserves as special mention as a picture of Raphael in a gallery. He is the beau of all birds. Then the humming birds, little and gay. Least of all is the *Trochilus Niger.* I have seen beetles larger. The *Trochilus pella* hath such a neck of gold and silver and fire! *Trochilus Delalandi* from Brazil is a glorious little tot, *la mouche magnifique.* Among the birds of Paradise I remarked the *Manucode* or *Paradisea regia* from New Guinea, the *Paradisea Apoda,* and *Paradisea rubra.* Forget not the *Veuve à epaulettes,* or *Emberiza longicauda,* black with fine shoulder-knots; nor the *Ampelis cotinga;* nor the *Phasianus Argus,* a peacock-looking pheasant; nor the *Trogon pavoninus,* called also *Couroncou pavonin.*

I saw black swans and white peacocks; the ibis, the sacred and the rosy; the flamingo, with a neck like a snake; the toucan rightly called *rhinoceros;* and a vulture whom to meet in the wilderness would make your flesh quiver, so like an executioner he looked.

In the other rooms I saw amber containing perfect musquitoes, grand blocks of quartz, native gold in all its forms of crystallization,—threads, plates, crystals, dust; and silver, black as from fire. Ah! said I, this is philanthropy, wisdom, taste,—to form a cabinet of natural history. Many students were there with grammar and note-book, and a class of boys with their tutor from some school.

Here we are impressed with the inexhaustible riches of nature. The universe is a more amazing puzzle than ever, as you glance along this bewildering series of animated forms,—the hazy butterflies, the carved shells, the birds, beasts, fishes, insects, snakes, and the upheaving principle of life everywhere incipient, in the very rock aping organized forms. Not a form so grotesque, so savage, nor so beautiful but is an expression of some property inherent in man the observer,—an occult relation between the very scorpions and man. I feel the centipede in me,— cayman, carp, eagle, and fox. I am moved by strange sympathies; I say continually "I will be a naturalist."

November 2. [1833]

Nature is a language, and every new fact that we learn is a new word; but rightly seen, taken all together, it is not merely a language, but the language put together into a most significant and universal book. I wish to learn the language, not that I may learn a new set of nouns and verbs, but that I may read the great book which is written in that tongue.

April 11. [1834]

Went yesterday to Cambridge and spent most of the day at Mount Auburn; got my luncheon at Fresh Pond, and went back again to the woods. After much wandering and seeing many things, four snakes glid-

ing up and down a hollow for no purpose that I could see—not to eat,
not for love, but only gliding; then a whole bed of *Hepatica triloba,*
cousins of the Anemone, all blue and beautiful, but constrained by nig-
gard nature to wear their last year's faded jacket of leaves; then a black-
capped titmouse, who came upon a tree, and when I would know his
name, sang *chick-a-dee-dee;* then a far-off tree full of clamorous birds, I
know not what, but you might hear them half a mile; I forsook the
tombs, and found a sunny hollow where the east wind would not blow,
and lay down against the side of a tree to most happy beholdings. At least
I opened my eyes and let what would pass through them into the soul. I
saw no more my relation, how near and petty, to Cambridge or Boston; I
heeded no more what minute or hour our Massachusetts clocks might
indicate—I saw only the noble earth on which I was born, with the great
Star which warms and enlightens it. I saw the clouds that hang their
significant drapery over us. It was Day—that was all Heaven said. The
pines glittered with their innumerable green needles in the light, and
seemed to challenge me to read their riddle. The drab oak-leaves of the
last year turned their little somersets and lay still again. And the wind
bustled high overhead in the forest top. This gay and grand architecture,
from the vault to the moss and lichen on which I lay,—who shall explain
to me the laws of its proportions and adornments?

November 10. [1836]

For form's sake, or for wantonness, I sometimes chaffer with the
farmer on the price of a cord of wood, but if he said twenty dollars
instead of five, I should think it cheap when I remember the beautiful
botanical wonder—the bough of an oak—which he brings me so freely
out of the enchanted forest where the sun and water, air and earth and
God formed it. In like manner I go joyfully through the mire in a wet day
and admire the inconvenience, delighted with the chemistry of a
shower. Live in the fields, and God will give you lectures on natural
philosophy every day. You shall have the snow-bunting, the chickadee,
the jay, the partridge, the chrysalis and wasp for your neighbors.

Language clothes Nature, as the air clothes the earth, taking the exact
form and pressure of every object. Only words that are new fit exactly the
thing, those that are old, like old *scoriæ* that have been long exposed to
the air and sunshine, have lost the sharpness of their mould and fit
loosely. But in new objects and new names one is delighted with the
plastic nature of man as much as in picture or sculpture. Thus Humboldt's "volcanic paps," and "magnetic storms," are the very mnemon-
ics of science, and so in general in books of modern science the vocabulary yields this poetic pleasure. "Veins inosculate."

December 10. [1836]

Pleasant walk yesterday, the most pleasant of days. At Walden Pond I found a new musical instrument which I call the ice-harp. A thin coat of ice covered a part of the pond, but melted around the edge of the shore. I threw a stone upon the ice which rebounded with a shrill sound, and falling again and again, repeated the note with pleasing modulation. I thought at first it was the "peep, peep" of a bird I had scared. I was so taken with the music that I threw down my stick and spent twenty minutes in throwing stones single or in handfuls on this crystal drum.

August 2. [1837]

An enchanting night of south wind and clouds; mercury at 73°; all the trees are wind-harps; blessed be light and darkness; ebb and flow, cold and heat; these restless pulsations of nature which by and by will throb no more.

August 4. [1837]

The grass is mown; the corn is ripe; autumnal stars arise. After raffling all day in Plutarch's *Morals,* or shall I say angling there for such fish as I might find, I sallied out this fine afternoon through the woods to Walden Water. The woods were too full of mosquitoes to offer any hospitality to the muse, and when I came to the blackberry vines, the plucking the crude berries at the risk of splintering my hand and with a mosquito mounting guard over every particular berry seemed a little too emblematical of general life whose shining and glossy fruits are very hard beset with thorns and very sour and good for nothing when gathered. But the pond was all blue and beautiful in the bosom of the woods and under the amber sky—like a sapphire lying in the moss. I sat down a long time on the shore to see the show. The variety and density of the foliage at the eastern end of the pond is worth seeing, then the extreme softness and holiday beauty of the summer clouds floating feathery overhead, enjoying, as I fancied, their height and privilege of motion and yet not seeming so much the drapery of this place and hour as forelooking to some pavilions and gardens of festivity beyond. I rejected this fancy with a becoming spirit and insisted that clouds, woods and waters were all there for me. The waterflies were full of happiness. The frogs that shoot from the land as fast as you walk along, a yard ahead of you, are a meritorious beastie. For their cowardice is only greater than their curiosity and desire of acquaintance with you. Three strokes from the shore the little swimmer turns short round, spreads his webbed paddles, and hangs at the surface, looks you in the face and so continues as long as you do not assault him.

August 12. [1837]

If you gather apples in the sunshine or make hay or hoe corn and then retire within doors and strain your body or squeeze your eyes *six hours after,* you shall still see apples hanging in the bright light with leaves and boughs thereto. There lie the impressions still on the retentive organ though I knew it not. So lies the whole series of natural images with which my life has made me acquainted in my memory, though I know it not, and a thrill of passion, a sudden emotion flashes light upon their dark chamber and the Active power seizes instantly the fit image as the word of his momentary thought. So lies all the life I have lived as my dictionary from which to extract the word which I want to dress the new perception of this moment. This is the way to learn Grammar. God never meant that we should learn Language by Colleges or Books. That only can we say which we have lived.

April 26. [1838]

Yesterday afternoon I went to the Cliff with Henry Thoreau. Warm, pleasant, misty weather, which the great mountain amphitheatre seemed to drink in with gladness. A crow's voice filled all the miles of air with sound. A bird's voice, even a piping frog, enlivens a solitude and makes world enough for us. At night I went out into the dark and saw a glimmering star and heard a frog, and Nature seemed to say, Well do not these suffice? Here is a new scene, a new experience. Ponder it, Emerson, and not like the foolish world, hanker after thunders and multitudes and vast landscapes, the sea or Niagara.

May 11. [1838]

Last night the moon rose behind four distinct pine-tree tops in the distant woods and the night at ten was so bright that I walked abroad. But the sublime light of night is unsatisfying, provoking; it astonishes but explains not. Its charm floats, dances, disappears, comes and goes, but palls in five minutes after you have left the house. Come out of your warm, angular house, resounding with few voices, into the chill, grand, instantaneous night, with such a Presence as a full moon in the clouds, and you are struck with poetic wonder. In the instant you leave far behind all human relations, wife, mother and child, and live only with the savages—water, air, light, carbon, lime, and granite. I think of Kuhleborn. I become a moist, cold element. "Nature grows over me." Frogs pipe; waters far off tinkle; dry leaves hiss; grass bends and rustles, and I have died out of the human world and come to feel a strange, cold, aqueous, terraqueous, aerial, ethereal sympathy and existence. I sow the sun and moon for seeds.

May 14. [1838]

A Bird-while. In a natural chronometer, a Bird-while may be admitted as one of the metres, since the space most of the wild birds will allow you to make your observations on them when they alight near you in the woods, is a pretty equal and familiar measure.

June 28. [1838]

The moon and Jupiter side by side last night stemmed the sea of clouds and plied their voyage in convoy through the sublime Deep as I walked the old and dusty road. The snow and the enchantment of the moonlight make all landscapes alike, and the road that is so tedious and homely that I never take it by day,—by night is Italy or Palmyra. In these divine pleasures permitted to me of walks in the June night under moon and stars, I can put my life as a fact before me and stand aloof from its honor and shame.

April 9. [1840]

We walked this afternoon to Edmund Hosmer's and Walden Pond. The South wind blew and filled with bland and warm light the dry sunny woods. The last year's leaves flew like birds through the air. As I sat on the bank of the Drop, or God's Pond, and saw the amplitude of the little water, what space, what verge, the little scudding fleets of ripples found to scatter and spread from side to side and take so much time to cross the pond, and saw how the water seemed made for the wind, and the wind for the water, dear playfellows for each other,—I said to my companion, I declare this world is so beautiful that I can hardly believe it exists. At Walden Pond the waves were larger and the whole lake in pretty uproar. Jones Very said, 'See how each wave rises from the midst with an original force, at the same time that it partakes the general movement!'

September 8. [1840]

I went into the woods. I found myself not wholly present there. If I looked at a pine-tree or an aster, *that* did not seem to be Nature. Nature was still elsewhere: this, or this was but outskirt and far-off reflection and echo of the triumph that had passed by and was now at its glancing splendor and heyday,—perchance in the neighboring fields, or, if I stood in the field, then in the adjacent woods. Always the present object gave me this sense of the stillness that follows a pageant that has just gone by.

November 20. [1840]

Ah, Nature! the very look of the woods is heroical and stimulating. This afternoon in a very thick grove where Henry Thoreau showed me the bush of mountain laurel, the first I have seen in Concord, the stems of pine and hemlock and oak almost gleamed like steel upon the excited eye.

[December? 1840]

Nature ever flows; stands never still. Motion or change is her mode of existence. The poetic eye sees in Man the Brother of the River, and in Woman the Sister of the River. Their life is always transition. Hard blockheads only drive nails all the time; forever remember; which is fixing. Heroes do not fix, but flow, bend forward ever and invent a resource for every moment. A man is a compendium of nature, an indomitable savage; . . . as long as he has a temperament of his own, and a hair growing on his skin, a pulse beating in his veins, he has a physique which disdains all intrusion, all despotism; it lives, wakes, alters, by omnipotent modes, and is directly related there, amid essences and *billets doux*, to Himmaleh mountain chains, wild cedar swamps, and the interior fires, the molten core of the globe.

[April 13?, 1841]

I read alternately in Doctor Nichol and in Saint-Simon, that is, in the Heavens and in the Earth, and the effect is grotesque enough. When we have spent our wonder in computing this wasteful hospitality with which boon Nature turns off new firmaments without end into her wide common, as fast as the madrepores make coral,—suns and planets hospitable to souls,—and then shorten the sight to look into this court of Louis Quatorze, and see the game that is played there,—duke and marshal, abbé and madame,—a gambling table where each is laying traps for the other, where the end is ever by some lie or fetch to outwit your rival and ruin him with this solemn fop in wig and stars,—the king;—one can hardly help asking if this planet is a fair specimen of the so generous astronomy, and if so, whether the experiment have not failed, and whether it be quite worth while to make more, and glut the innocent space with so poor an article.

But there are many answers at hand to the poor cavil. And all doubt is ribald. An answer,—certainly not the highest,—the astronomy itself may furnish, namely, that all grows, all is nascent, infant. When we are dizzied with the arithmetic of the savant toiling to compute the length of her line, the return of her curve, we are steadied by the perception that a great deal is doing; that all seems just begun; remote aims are in active accomplishment. We can point nowhere to anything final; but tendency appears on all hands: planet, system, constellation, total nature is growing like a field of maize in July; is becoming somewhat else; is in rapid metamorphosis. The embryo does not more strive to be man, than yonder burr of light we call a nebula tends to be a ring, a comet, a globe, and parent of new stars. Why should not then these messieurs of Versailles strut and plot for tabourets and ribbons, for a season, without prejudice to their faculty to run on better errands by and by?

Yet the whole code of nature's laws may be written on the thumbnail, or the signet of a ring. The whirling bubble on the surface of a brook admits us to the secret of the mechanics of the sky. Every shell on the beach is a key to it. A little water made to rotate in a cup explains the formation of the simpler shells; the addition of matter from year to year arrives at last at the most complex forms; and yet so poor is nature with all her craft, that from the beginning to the end of the universe she has but one stuff,—but one stuff with its two ends, to serve up all her dream-like variety. Compound it how she will, star, sand, fire, water, tree, man, it is still one stuff, and betrays the same properties to the anointed eye; and every marshal that bristles, every valet that grimaces in the French Court is related bodily to that heaven which Lagrange has been searching and works every moment by the same laws we thought so grand up there.

But the true answer to the cavil . . . is of course that the cavil only reaches the ear; it does never sink into the heart. I am of the Maker not of the Made. The vastness of the Universe, the portentous year of Mizar and Alcor are no vastness, no longevity to me. In the eternity of truth, in the almightiness of love, I slight these monsters. Through all the running sea of forms, I am truth, I am love, and immutable I transcend form as I do time and space.

June 6. [1841]

I am sometimes discontented with my house because it lies on a dusty road, and with its sills and cellar almost in the water of the meadow. But when I creep out of it into the Night or the Morning and see what majestic and what tender beauties daily wrap me in their bosom, how near to me is every transcendent secret of Nature's love and religion, I see how indifferent it is where I eat and sleep. This very street of hucksters and taverns the moon will transform to a Palmyra, for she is the apologist of all apologists, and will kiss the elm trees alone and hides every meanness in a silver-edged darkness.

Summer, 1841

The metamorphosis of Nature shows itself in nothing more than this, that there is no word in our language that cannot become typical to us of Nature by giving it emphasis. The world is a Dancer; it is a Rosary; it is a Torrent; it is a Boat; a Mist; a Spider's Snare; it is what you will; and the metaphor will hold, and it will give the imagination keen pleasure. Swifter than light the world converts itself into that thing you name, and all things find their right place under this new and capricious classification. There is nothing small or mean to the soul. It derives as grand a joy from symbolizing the Godhead or his universe under the form of a moth or a gnat as of a Lord of Hosts. Must I call the heaven and the earth a maypole and country fair with booths, or an anthill, or an old coat, in order to give you the shock of pleasure which the imagination loves and the sense of spiritual greatness? Call it a blossom, a rod, a wreath of parsley, a tamarisk-crown, a cock, a sparrow, the ear instantly hears and the spirit leaps to the trope. . . .

September, undated. [1843]

The only straight line in Nature that I remember is the spider swinging down from a twig.

February ?, 1844

That bread which we ask of Nature is that she should entrance us, but amidst her beautiful or her grandest pictures I cannot escape the *second thought.* I walked this P.M. in the woods, but there too the snowbanks were sprinkled with tobacco-juice. We have the wish to forget night and day, father and mother, food and ambition, but we never lose our dualism. Blessed, wonderful Nature, nevertheless! without depth, but with immeasurable lateral spaces. If we look before us, if we compute our path, it is very short. Nature has only the thickness of a shingle or a slate: we come straight to the extremes; but sidewise, and at unawares, the present moment opens into other moods and moments, rich, prolific, leading onward without end. . . .

[July, 1844]

Geology has initiated us into the secularity of Nature, and taught us to disuse our dame-school measures, and exchange our Mosaic and Ptolemaic schemes for her large style. We knew nothing rightly, for want of perspective. Now we learn what patient periods must round themselves before the rock is formed; then before the rock is broken, and the first lichen race has disintegrated the thinnest external plate into soil, and opened the door for the remote Flora, Fauna, Ceres, and Pomona to come in. How far off yet is the trilobite! how far the quadruped! how inconceivably remote is man! All duly arrive, and then race after race of men. It is a long way from granite to the oyster; farther yet to Plato and the preaching of the immortality of the soul. Yet all must come, as surely as the first atom has two sides.

August, undated. [1848]

Henry Thoreau is like the wood-god who solicits the wandering poet and draws him into antres vast and desarts idle, and bereaves him of his memory, and leaves him naked, plaiting vines and with twigs in his hand. . . .

I spoke of friendship, but my friends and I are fishes in our habit. As for taking Thoreau's arm, I should as soon take the arm of an elm tree.

[Last days of September.] [1848]

I go twice a week over Concord with Ellery, and, as we sit on the steep park at Conantum, we still have the same regret as oft before. Is all this beauty to perish? Shall none remake this sun and wind, the sky-blue river, the river-blue sky; the yellow meadow spotted with sacks and sheets of cranberry-pickers; the red bushes; the iron-gray house with just the color of the granite rock; the paths of the thicket, in which the only engineers are the cattle grazing on yonder hill; the wide, straggling wild orchard in which Nature has deposited every possible flavor in the apples of different trees? Whole zones and climates she has concentrated into apples. We think of the old benefactors who have conquered these fields; of the old man Moore, who is just dying in these days, who has absorbed such volumes of sunshine like a huge melon or pumpkin in the sun,—who has owned in every part of Concord a woodlot, until he could not find the boundaries of these, and never saw their interiors. But we say, where is he who is to save the present moment, and cause that this beauty be not lost? Shakespeare saw no better heaven or earth, but had the power and need to sing, and seized the dull ugly England, ugly to this, and made it amicable and enviable to all reading men, and now we are fooled into likening this to that; whilst, if one of us had the chanting constitution, that land would no more be heard of.

September 5. [1855]

All the thoughts of a turtle are turtle.

August. *[1862]*

How shallow seemed to me yesterday in the woods the speech one often hears from tired citizens who have spent their brief enthusiasm for the country, that Nature is tedious, and they have had enough of green leaves. Nature and the green leaves are a million fathoms deep, and it is these eyes that are superficial.

CHARLES DARWIN
1809-1882

The Origin of Species *(1859) introduced a comprehensive new paradigm for the life-sciences, and in doing so stimulated an enormous increase in research and in the accumulation of data. Darwin's work laid the foundation for the professional and specialized sciences we know today, but his own career was shaped by very different forces. He found his formal schooling uninspiring. His naturalist collections as a boy, his long walks with the botanist James Henslow during his days at Cambridge, and, above all, his great adventure on H.M.S. Beagle's voyage of exploration contributed much more to his eventual vision of life's evolutionary pattern.*

The Beagle's mission was to map the South American coastline, which necessitated lengthy shore-visits and exposed Darwin to a wide variety of spectacular landscapes, from the Brazilian rain forest to the Argentine pampas to the fjords of Tierra del Fuego. When the ship touched at the Galapagos Islands, off the coast of Ecuador, he entered a laboratory of natural selection. Although Darwin did not publish his theory of evolution for almost three decades, he was keenly aware as a young naturalist that the Galapagos finches, tortoises, and iguanas differed from corresponding species on the mainland, and that they varied intriguingly from island to island of the group.

The transitional character of Darwin, as at once a scientist in the modern sense and a more old-fashioned naturalist, might be illustrated by the fact that in setting out to sea he packed along both the initial volume of Charles Lyell's ground-breaking Principles of Geology *and* Gilbert White's Natural History and Antiquities of Selborne. *The first opened his imagination to science's vast new temporal perspective, while the second grounded his sensibility and his style in an amateur tradition of English natural history.*

From VOYAGE OF H.M.S. BEAGLE

[*Galapagos tortoises*]

* * * I will first describe the habits of the tortoise (Testudo nigra, formerly called Indica), which has been so frequently alluded to. These animals are found, I believe, on all the islands of the Archipelago; certainly on the greater number. They frequent in preference the high damp parts, but they likewise live in the lower and arid districts. I have already shown, from the numbers which have been caught in a single day, how very numerous they must be. Some grow to an immense size: Mr. Lawson, an Englishman, and vice-governor of the colony, told us that he had seen several so large, that it required six or eight men to lift them from the ground; and that some had afforded as much as two hundred pounds of meat. The old males are the largest, the females rarely growing to so great a size: the male can readily be distinguished from the female by the greater length of its tail. The tortoises which live on those islands where there is no water, or in the lower and arid parts of the others, feed chiefly on the succulent cactus. Those which frequent the higher and damp regions, eat the leaves of various trees, a kind of berry (called guayavita) which is acid and austere, and likewise a pale green filamentous lichen (Usnera plicata), that hangs in tresses from the boughs of the trees.

The tortoise is very fond of water, drinking large quantities, and wallowing in the mud. The larger islands alone possess springs, and these are always situated towards the central parts, and at a considerable height. The tortoises, therefore, which frequent the lower districts, when thirsty, are obliged to travel from a long distance. Hence broad and well-beaten paths branch off in every direction from the wells down to the sea-coast; and the Spaniards by following them up, first discovered the watering-places. When I landed at Chatham Island, I could not imagine what animal travelled so methodically along well-chosen tracks.

Journal of Researches into the Geology and Natural History of Various Countries Visited by H.M.S. Beagle (London: H. Colburn, 1836).

Near the springs it was a curious spectacle to behold many of these huge creatures, one set eagerly travelling onwards with outstretched necks, and another set returning, after having drunk their fill. When the tortoise arrives at the spring, quite regardless of any spectator, he buries his head in the water above his eyes, and greedily swallows great mouthfuls, at the rate of about ten in a minute. The inhabitants say each animal stays three or four days in the neighbourhood of the water, and then returns to the lower country; but they differed respecting the frequency of these visits. The animal probably regulates them according to the nature of the food on which it has lived. It is, however, certain, that tortoises can subsist even on those islands, where there is no other water than what falls during a few rainy days in the year.

I believe it is well ascertained, that the bladder of the frog acts as a reservoir for the moisture necessary to its existence: such seems to be the case with the tortoise. For some time after a visit to the springs, their urinary bladders are distended with fluid, which is said gradually to decrease in volume, and to become less pure. The inhabitants, when walking in the lower district, and overcome with thirst, often take advantage of this circumstance, and drink the contents of the bladder if full: in one I saw killed, the fluid was quite limpid, and had only a very slightly bitter taste. The inhabitants, however, always first drink the water in the pericardium, which is described as being best.

The tortoises, when purposely moving towards any point, travel by night and day, and arrive at their journey's end much sooner than would be expected. The inhabitants, from observing marked individuals, consider that they travel a distance of about eight miles in two or three days. One large tortoise, which I watched, walked at the rate of sixty yards in ten minutes, that is 360 yards in the hour, or four miles a day,—allowing a little time for it to eat on the road. During the breeding season, when the male and female are together, the male utters a hoarse roar or bellowing, which, it is said, can be heard at the distance of more than a hundred yards. The female never uses her voice, and the male only at these times; so that when the people hear this noise, they know that the two are together. They were at this time (October) laying their eggs. The female, where the soil is sandy, deposits them together, and covers them up with sand; but where the ground is rocky she drops them indiscriminately in any hole: Mr. Bynoe found seven placed in a fissure. The egg is white and spherical; one which I measured was seven inches and three-eighths in circumference, and therefore larger than a hen's egg. The young tortoises, as soon as they are hatched, fall a prey in great numbers to the carrion-feeding buzzard. The old ones seem generally to die from accidents, as from falling down precipices: at least, several of the inhabitants told me, that they had never found one dead without some evident cause.

The inhabitants believe that these animals are absolutely deaf; certainly they do not overhear a person walking close behind them. I was always amused when overtaking one of these great monsters, as it was quietly pacing along, to see how suddenly, the instant I passed, it would draw in its head and legs, and uttering a deep hiss fall to the ground with a heavy sound, as if struck dead. I frequently got on their backs, and then giving a few raps on the hinder part of their shells, they would rise up and walk away;—but I found it very difficult to keep my balance. The flesh of this animal is largely employed, both fresh and salted; and a beautifully clear oil is prepared from the fat. When a tortoise is caught, the man makes a slit in the skin near its tail, so as to see inside its body, whether the fat under the dorsal plate is thick. If it is not, the animal is liberated; and it is said to recover soon from this strange operation. In order to secure the tortoises, it is not sufficient to turn them like turtle, for they are often able to get on their legs again.

There can be little doubt that this tortoise is an aboriginal inhabitant of the Galapagos; for it is found on all, or nearly all, the islands, even on some of the smaller ones where there is no water; had it been an imported species, this would hardly have been the case in a group which has been so little frequented. Moreover, the old Bucaniers found this tortoise in greater numbers even than at present: Wood and Rogers also, in 1708, say that it is the opinion of the Spaniards, that it is found nowhere else in this quarter of the world. It is now widely distributed; but it may be questioned whether it is in any other place an aboriginal. The bones of a tortoise at Mauritius, associated with those of the extinct Dodo, have generally been considered as belonging to this tortoise: if this had been so, undoubtedly it must have been there indigenous; but M. Bibron informs me that he believes that it was distinct, as the species now living there certainly is. * * *

[retrospect on our voyage]

* * * Our Voyage having come to an end, I will take a short retrospect of the advantages and disadvantages, the pains and pleasures, of our circumnavigation of the world. If a person asked my advice, before undertaking a long voyage, my answer would depend upon his possessing a decided taste for some branch of knowledge, which could by this means be advanced. No doubt it is a high satisfaction to behold various countries and the many races of mankind, but the pleasures gained at the time do not counterbalance the evils. It is necessary to look forward

to a harvest, however distant that may be, when some fruit will be reaped, some good effected.

Many of the losses which must be experienced are obvious; such as that of the society of every old friend, and of the sight of those places with which every dearest remembrance is so intimately connected. These losses, however, are at the time partly relieved by the exhaustless delight of anticipating the long wished-for day of return. If, as poets say, life is a dream, I am sure in a voyage these are the visions which best serve to pass away the long night. Other losses, although not at first felt, tell heavily after a period: these are the want of room, of seclusion, of rest; the jading feeling of constant hurry; the privation of small luxuries, the loss of domestic society, and even of music and the other pleasures of imagination. When such trifles are mentioned, it is evident that the real grievances, excepting from accidents, of a sea-life are at an end. The short space of sixty years has made an astonishing difference in the facility of distant navigation. Even in the time of Cook, a man who left his fireside for such expeditions underwent severe privations. A yacht now, with every luxury of life, can circumnavigate the globe. Besides the vast improvements in ships and naval resources, the whole western shores of America are thrown open, and Australia has become the capital of a rising continent. How different are the circumstances to a man ship-wrecked at the present day in the Pacific, to what they were in the time of Cook! Since his voyage a hemisphere has been added to the civilized world.

If a person suffer much from sea-sickness, let him weigh it heavily in the balance. I speak from experience: it is no trifling evil, cured in a week. If, on the other hand, he take pleasure in naval tactics, he will assuredly have full scope for his taste. But it must be borne in mind, how large a proportion of the time, during a long voyage, is spent on the water, as compared with the days in harbour. And what are the boasted glories of the illimitable ocean? A tedious waste, a desert of water, as the Arabian calls it. No doubt there are some delightful scenes. A moonlight night, with the clear heavens and the dark glittering sea, and the white sails filled by the soft air of a gently-blowing trade-wind; a dead calm, with the heaving surface polished like a mirror, and all still except the occasional flapping of the canvas. It is well once to behold a squall with its rising arch and coming fury, or the heavy gale of wind and mountainous waves. I confess, however, my imagination had painted something more grand, more terrific in the full-grown storm. It is an incomparably finer spectacle when beheld on shore, where the waving trees, the wild flight of the birds, the dark shadows and bright lights, the rushing of the torrents, all proclaim the strife of the unloosed elements. At sea the albatross and little petrel fly as if the storm were their proper sphere, the water rises and sinks as if fulfilling its usual task, the ship alone and its inhabitants seem the objects of wrath. On a forlorn and weather-beaten coast, the scene is indeed different, but the feelings partake more of horror than of wild delight.

Let us now look at the brighter side of the past time. The pleasure derived from beholding the scenery and the general aspect of the various countries we have visited, has decidedly been the most constant and highest source of enjoyment. It is probable that the picturesque beauty of many parts of Europe exceeds anything which we beheld. But there is a growing pleasure in comparing the character of the scenery in different countries, which to a certain degree is distinct from merely admiring its beauty. It depends chiefly on an acquaintance with the individual parts of each view: I am strongly induced to believe that, as in music, the person who understands every note will, if he also possesses a proper taste, more thoroughly enjoy the whole, so he who examines each part of a fine view, may also thoroughly comprehend the full and combined effect. Hence, a traveller should be a botanist, for in all views plants form the chief embellishment. Group masses of naked rock even in the wildest forms, and they may for a time afford a sublime spectacle, but they will soon grow monotonous. Paint them with bright and varied colours, as in Northern Chile, they will become fantastic; clothe them with vegetation, they must form a decent, if not a beautiful picture.

When I say that the scenery of parts of Europe is probably superior to anything which we beheld, I except, as a class by itself, that of the intertropical zones. The two classes cannot be compared together; but I have already often enlarged on the grandeur of those regions. As the force of impressions generally depends on preconceived ideas, I may add, that mine were taken from the vivid descriptions in the Personal Narrative of Humboldt, which far exceed in merit anything else which I have read. Yet with these high-wrought ideas, my feelings were far from partaking of a tinge of disappointment on my first and final landing on the shores of Brazil.

Among the scenes which are deeply impressed on my mind, none exceed in sublimity the primeval forests undefaced by the hand of man; whether those of Brazil, where the powers of Life are predominant, or those of Tierra del Fuego, where Death and Decay prevail. Both are temples filled with the varied productions of the God of Nature:—no one can stand in these solitudes unmoved, and not feel that there is more in man than the mere breath of his body. In calling up images of the past, I find that the plains of Patagonia frequently cross before my eyes; yet these plains are pronounced by all wretched and useless. They can be described only by negative characters; without habitations, without water, without trees, without mountains, they support merely a few dwarf plants. Why then, and the case is not peculiar to myself, have these arid wastes taken so firm a hold on my memory? Why have not the still more level, the greener and more fertile Pampas, which are serviceable to mankind, produced an equal impression? I can scarcely analyze these feelings: but it must be partly owing to the free scope given to the imagination. The plains of Patagonia are boundless, for they are scarcely passable, and hence unknown: they bear the stamp of having lasted, as they are now, for ages, and there appears no limit to their duration through future time. If, as the ancients supposed, the flat earth was surrounded by an impassable breadth of water, or by deserts heated to an intolerable excess, who would not look at these last boundaries to man's knowledge with deep but ill-defined sensations?

Lastly, of natural scenery, the views from lofty mountains, though certainly in one sense not beautiful, are very memorable. When looking down from the highest crest of the Cordillera, the mind, undisturbed by minute details, was filled with the stupendous dimensions of the surrounding masses.

Of individual objects, perhaps nothing is more certain to create astonishment than the first sight in his native haunt of a barbarian,—of man in his lowest and most savage state. One's mind hurries back over past centuries, and then asks, could our progenitors have been men like these?—men, whose very signs and expressions are less intelligible to us than those of the domesticated animals; men, who do not possess the instinct of those animals, nor yet appear to boast of human reason, or at least of arts consequent on that reason. I do not believe it is possible to describe or paint the difference between a wild and tame animal: and part of the interest in beholding a savage, is the same which would lead every one to desire to see the lion in his desert, the tiger tearing his prey in the jungle, or the rhinoceros wandering over the wild plains of Africa.

Among the other most remarkable spectacles which we have beheld, may be ranked the Southern Cross, the cloud of Magellan, and the other constellations of the southern hemisphere—the water-spout—the glacier leading its blue stream of ice, overhanging the sea in a bold precipice—a lagoon-island raised by the reef-building corals—an active volcano—and the overwhelming effects of a violent earthquake. These latter phenomena, perhaps, possess for me a peculiar interest, from their intimate connexion with the geological structure of the world. The earthquake, however, must be to every one a most impressive event: the earth, considered from our earliest childhood as the type of solidity, has oscillated like a thin crust beneath our feet; and in seeing the laboured works of man in a moment overthrown, we feel the insignificance of his boasted power.

It has been said, that the love of the chase is an inherent delight in man—a relic of an instinctive passion. If so, I am sure the pleasure of living in the open air, with the sky for a roof and the ground for a table, is part of the same feeling; it is the savage returning to his wild and native habits. I always look back to our boat cruises, and my land journeys, when through unfrequented countries, with an extreme delight, which no scenes of civilization could have created. I do not doubt that every traveller must remember the glowing sense of happiness which he experienced, when he first breathed in a foreign clime, where the civilized man had seldom or never trod.

There are several other sources of enjoyment in a long voyage, which are of a more reasonable nature. The map of the world ceases to be a blank; it becomes a picture full of the most varied and animated figures. Each part assumes its proper dimensions: continents are not looked at in the light of islands, or islands considered as mere specks, which are, in truth, larger than many kingdoms of Europe. Africa, or North and South America, are well-sounding names, and easily pronounced; but it is not until having sailed for weeks along small portions of their shores, that one is thoroughly convinced what vast spaces on our immense world these names imply.

From seeing the present state, it is impossible not to look forward with high expectations to the future progress of nearly an entire hemisphere. The march of improvement, consequent on the introduction of Christianity throughout the South Sea, probably stands by itself in the records of history. It is the more striking when we remember that only sixty years since, Cook, whose excellent judgment none will dispute, could foresee no prospect of a change. Yet these changes have now been effected by the philanthropic spirit of the British nation.

In the same quarter of the globe Australia is rising, or indeed may be said to have risen, into a grand centre of civilization, which, at some not very remote period, will rule as empress over the southern hemisphere. It is impossible for an Englishman to behold these distant colonies, without a high pride and satisfaction. To hoist the British flag, seems to draw with it as a certain consequence, wealth, prosperity, and civilization.

In conclusion, it appears to me that nothing can be more improving to a young naturalist, than a journey in distant countries. It both sharpens, and partly allays that want and craving, which, as Sir J. Herschel remarks, a man experiences although every corporeal sense be fully satisfied. The excitement from the novelty of objects, and the chance of success, stimulate him to increased activity. Moreover, as a number of isolated facts soon become uninteresting, the habit of comparison leads to generalization. On the other hand, as the traveller stays but a short time in each place, his descriptions must generally consist of mere sketches, instead of detailed observations. Hence arises, as I have found to my cost, a constant tendency to fill up the wide gaps of knowledge, by inaccurate and superficial hypotheses.

But I have too deeply enjoyed the voyage, not to recommend any naturalist, although he must not expect to be so fortunate in his companions as I have been, to take all chances, and to start, on travels by land if possible, if otherwise on a long voyage. He may feel assured, he will meet with no difficulties or dangers, excepting in rare cases, nearly so bad as he beforehand anticipates. In a moral point of view, the effect ought to be, to teach him good-humored patience, freedom from selfishness, the habit of acting for himself, and of making the best of every occurence. In short, he ought to partake of the characteristic qualities of most sailors. Travelling ought also to teach him distrust; but at the same time he will discover, how many truly kind-hearted people there are, with whom he never before had, or ever again will have any further communication, who yet are ready to offer him the most disinterested assistance.

From ON THE ORIGIN OF SPECIES
BY MEANS OF NATURAL SELECTION

[*Conclusion—"the tangled bank"*]

*   *   * Authors of the highest eminence seem to be fully satisfied with the view that each species has been independently created. To my mind it accords better with what we know of the laws impressed on matter by the Creator, that the production and extinction of the past and present inhabitants of the world should have been due to secondary causes, like those determining the birth and death of the individual. When I view all beings not as special creations, but as the lineal descendants of some few beings which lived long before the first bed of the Cambrian system was deposited, they seem to me to become ennobled. Judging from the past, we may safely infer that not one living species will transmit its unaltered likeness to a distant futurity. And of the species now living very few will transmit progeny of any kind to a far distant futurity; for the manner in which all organic beings are grouped, shows that the greater number of species in each genus, and all the species in many genera, have left no

On the Origin of Species by Means of Natural Selection (London: J. Murray, 1859).

descendants, but have become utterly extinct. We can so far take a prophetic glance into futurity as to foretell that it will be the common and widely-spread species, belonging to the larger and dominant groups within each class, which will ultimately prevail and procreate new and dominant species. As all the living forms of life are the lineal descendants of those which lived long before the Cambrian epoch, we may feel certain that the ordinary succession by generation has never once been broken, and that no cataclysm has desolated the whole world. Hence we may look with some confidence to a secure future of great length. And as natural selection works solely by and for the good of each being, all corporeal and mental endowments will tend to progress towards perfection.

It is interesting to contemplate a tangled bank, clothed with many plants of many kinds, with birds singing on the bushes, with various insects flitting about, and with worms crawling through the damp earth, and to reflect that these elaborately constructed forms, so different from each other, and dependent upon each other in so complex a manner, have all been produced by laws acting around us. These laws, taken in the largest sense, being Growth with Reproduction; Inheritance which is almost implied by reproduction; Variability from the indirect and direct action of the conditions of life, and from use and disuse: a Ratio of Increase so high as to lead to a Struggle for Life, and as a consequence to Natural Selection, entailing Divergence of Character and the Extinction of less-improved forms. Thus, from the war of nature, from famine and death, the most exalted object which we are capable of conceiving, namely, the production of the higher animals, directly follows. There is grandeur in this view of life, with its several powers, having been originally breathed by the Creator into a few forms or into one; and that, whilst this planet has gone cycling on according to the fixed law of gravity, from so simple a beginning endless forms most beautiful and most wonderful have been, and are being evolved.

From THE DESCENT OF MAN, AND SELECTION IN RELATION TO SEX

[*Conclusion*—"*the indelible stamp of his lowly origin*"]

*   *   * Man scans with scrupulous care the character and pedigree of his horses, cattle, and dogs before he matches them; but when he comes to his own marriage he rarely, or never, takes any such care. He is im-

The Descent of Man, and Selection in Relation to Sex (London: J. Murray, 1871).

pelled by nearly the same motives as the lower animals, when they are left to their own free choice, though he is in so far superior to them that he highly values mental charms and virtues. On the other hand he is strongly attracted by mere wealth or rank. Yet he might by selection do something not only for the bodily constitution and frame of his off-spring, but for their intellectual and moral qualities. Both sexes ought to refrain from marriage if they are in any marked degree inferior in body or mind; but such hopes are Utopian and will never be even partially real-ised until the laws of inheritance are thoroughly known. Everyone does good service, who aids toward this end. When the principles of breeding and inheritance are better understood, we shall not hear ignorant mem-bers of our legislature rejecting with scorn a plan for ascertaining whether or not consanguineous marriages are injurious to man.

The advancement of the welfare of mankind is a most intricate prob-lem: all ought to refrain from marriage who cannot avoid abject poverty for their children; for poverty is not only a great evil, but tends to its own increase by leading to recklessness in marriage. On the other hand, as Mr. Galton has remarked, if the prudent avoid marriage, whilst the reckless marry, the inferior members tend to supplant the better mem-bers of society. Man, like every other animal, has no doubt advanced to his present high condition through a struggle for existence consequent on his rapid multiplication; and if he is to advance still higher, it is to be feared that he must remain subject to a severe struggle. Otherwise he would sink into indolence, and the more gifted men would not be more successful in the battle of life than the less gifted. Hence our natural rate of increase, though leading to many and obvious evils, must not be greatly diminished by any means. There should be open competition for all men; and the most able should not be prevented by laws or customs from succeeding best and rearing the largest number of offspring. Impor-tant as the struggle for existence has been and even still is, yet as far as the highest part of man's nature is concerned there are other agencies more important. For the moral qualities are advanced, either directly or indirectly, much more through the effects of habit, the reasoning pow-ers, instruction, religion, &c., than through natural selection; though to this latter agency may be safely attributed the social instincts, which afforded the basis for the development of the moral sense.

The main conclusion arrived at in this work, namely, that man is descended from some lowly organised form, will, I regret to think, be highly distasteful to many. But there can hardly be a doubt that we are descended from barbarians. The astonishment which I felt on first see-ing a party of Fuegians on a wild and broken shore will never be forgot-ten by me, for the reflection at once rushed into my mind—such were our ancestors. These men were absolutely naked and bedaubed with paint, their long hair was tangled, their mouths, frothed with excitement, and their expression was wild, startled, and distrustful. They possessed hardly any arts, and like wild animals lived on what they could catch; they had no government, and were merciless to every one not of their own small tribe. He who has seen a savage in his native land will not feel much shame, if forced to acknowledge that the blood of some more humble creature flows in his veins. For my own part I would as soon be descended from that heroic little monkey, who braved his dreaded enemy in order to save the life of his keeper, or from that old baboon, who descending from the mountains, carried away in triumph his young comrade from a crowd of astonished dogs—as from a savage who delights to torture his enemies, offers up bloody sacrifices, practises infanticide without remorse, treats his wives like slaves, knows no decency, and is haunted by the grossest superstitions.

Man may be excused for feeling some pride at having risen, though not through his own exertions, to the very summit of the organic scale; and the fact of his having thus risen, instead of having been aboriginally placed there, may give him hope for a still higher destiny in the distant future. But we are not here concerned with hopes or fears, only with the truth as far as our reason permits us to discover it; and I have given the evidence to the best of my ability. We must, however, acknowledge, as it seems to me, that man with all his noble qualities, with sympathy which feels for the most debased, with benevolence which extends not only to other men but to the humblest living creature, with his god-like intellect which has penetrated into the movements and constitution of the solar system—with all these exalted powers—Man still bears in his bodily frame the indelible stamp of his lowly origin.

HENRY DAVID THOREAU
1817-1862

Thoreau not only traveled a good deal in Concord, Massachusetts, he also lived many lives in it. As schoolteacher, pencil-maker, botanist, editor, surveyor, gardener, poet, lecturer, essayist, moral philosopher, political protester, travel writer, devoted brother and son, woodland hermit and village character, vegetarian and luster-after-raw-woodchuck—

this most cocksure of American writers consistently refuses to be pigeon-holed. The attempts of so many readers to do so spring from his propensity "to make an extreme statement, if so I may make an emphatic one." Thoreau's seeming paradoxes and contradictions are a result, not of any conscious attempt at iconoclasm, but from the inherent complexity of his perceptions coupled with a passion to "drive life into a corner, and reduce it to its lowest terms." The result, among other things, is one of the most condensed and energetic styles in English. Though his books sold little in his lifetime, Walden *has long been recognized as one of the classics of American literature, and Thoreau's ideas and writings have had worldwide influence.*

The primary purpose of the following selections is to suggest the range of Thoreau's personality in all its complex and ambivalent guises. His first book, A Week on the Concord and Merrimack Rivers *(1849), was based on a rowboat voyage he took with his older brother John in 1839 and was written largely during his stay at Walden Pond. One of the first in a long tradition of American river journey books, it contains superb sketches of the early New England landscape and some of Thoreau's most graceful and congenial writing. Contemplating the rivers' "healthy natural tumult" in the company of his beloved brother, he was never happier. From his masterpiece,* Walden: or Life in the Woods *(1854), we have included the chapter on "Brute Neighbors." Its descriptions of wild animals (including the famous battle of the ants) remain among the finest of their kind, ground-breaking in their consciously metaphoric overtones and Thoreau's deliberate exploration of the role of the self-aware narrator as both observer and participant. The section from his long essay, "Walking" (1862), with its ringing defense and celebration of "wildness," has become one of the gospels of the conservation movement. The passage from* The Maine Woods *(1864), on the other hand, describing Thoreau's ascent to the summit of Mt. Katahdin, presents a startlingly different view of nature from that afforded by the domesticated fields and ponds of Concord. Here, actual rather than metaphoric wilderness shakes the very foundations of self and of human pretensions to understanding nature. In "the presence of a force not bound to be kind to man," the very structures of language seem to break down. Finally, we have chosen some selections from the* Journals *(1906), begun when Thoreau was twenty and not published in his lifetime. The* Journals *are not a finished literary work by any means, but they contain some of his most brilliant passages. Intended as "a meteorological journal of the mind," they served, not only as a reservoir of material for his lectures and books, but also as a kind of literary laboratory. In these journal entries Thoreau is less studiedly candid and more genuinely per-*

sonal—revealing, for instance, a poignant attachment to his native town, or taking delight in the antics of a kitten a few months before his own death at the age of forty-four. He is also less attitudinizing and more experimental towards his material, exploring radically different approaches to the same subject—sometimes on the same page. Thoreau was a keen observer of natural process, and many of the journal selections seem to intuit modern ecological principles. Of special relevance to contemporary nature writing are his lively discussions of the relative virtues of poetic and scientific approaches in natural history.

From A WEEK ON THE CONCORD AND MERRIMACK RIVERS

CONCORD RIVER

"Beneath low hills, in the broad interval
Through which at will our Indian rivulet
Winds mindful still of sannup and of squaw,
Whose pipe and arrow oft the plough unburies,
Here, in pine houses, built of new-fallen trees,
Supplanters of the tribe, the farmers dwell."

Emerson

The Musketaquid, or Grass-ground River, though probably as old as the Nile or Euphrates, did not begin to have a place in civilized history, until the fame of its grassy meadows and its fish attracted settlers out of England in 1635, when it received the other but kindred name of CON-CORD from the first plantation on its banks, which appears to have been commenced in a spirit of peace and harmony. It will be Grass-ground River as long as grass grows and water runs here; it will be Concord River only while men lead peaceable lives on its banks. To an extinct race it was grass-ground, where they hunted and fished, and it is still perennial grass-ground to Concord farmers, who own the Great Meadows, and get the hay from year to year. "One branch of it," according to the historian of Concord, for I love to quote so good authority, "rises in the south part of Hopkinton, and another from a pond and a large cedar-swamp in Westborough," and flowing between Hopkinton and Southborough, through Framingham, and between Sudbury and Wayland, where it is sometimes called Sudbury River, it enters Concord at the south part of

A Week on the Concord and Merrimack Rivers (Boston: Ticknor and Fields, 1849).

the town, and after receiving the North or Assabeth River, which has its source a little farther to the north and west, goes out at the northeast angle, and flowing between Bedford and Carlisle, and through Billerica, empties into the Merrimack at Lowell. In Concord it is, in summer, from four to fifteen feet deep, and from one hundred to three hundred feet wide, but in the spring freshets, when it overflows its banks, it is in some places nearly a mile wide. Between Sudbury and Wayland the meadows acquire their greatest breadth, and when covered with water, they form a handsome chain of shallow vernal lakes, resorted to by numerous gulls and ducks. Just above Sherman's Bridge, between these towns, is the largest expanse, and when the wind blows freshly in a raw March day, heaving up the surface into dark and sober billows or regular swells, skirted as it is in the distance with alder-swamps and smoke-like maples, it looks like a smaller Lake Huron, and is very pleasant and exciting for a landsman to row or sail over. The farm-houses along the Sudbury shore, which rises gently to a considerable height, command fine water prospects at this season. The shore is more flat on the Wayland side, and this town is the greatest loser by the flood. Its farmers tell me that thousands of acres are flooded now, since the dams have been erected, where they remember to have seen the white honeysuckle or clover growing once, and they could go dry with shoes only in summer. Now there is nothing but blue-joint and sedge and cut-grass there, standing in water all the year round. For a long time, they made the most of the driest season to get their hay, working sometimes till nine o'clock at night, sedulously paring with their scythes in the twilight round the hummocks left by the ice; but now it is not worth the getting when they can come at it, and they look sadly round to their wood-lots and upland as a last resource.

It is worth the while to make a voyage up this stream, if you go no farther than Sudbury, only to see how much country there is in the rear of us; great hills, and a hundred brooks, and farm-houses, and barns, and haystacks, you never saw before, and men everywhere, Sudbury, that is *Southborough* men, and Wayland, and Nine-Acre-Corner men, and Bound Rock, where four towns bound on a rock in the river, Lincoln, Wayland, Sudbury, Concord. Many waves are there agitated by the wind, keeping nature fresh, the spray blowing in your face, reeds and rushes waving; ducks by the hundred, all uneasy in the surf, in the raw wind, just ready to rise, and now going off with a clatter and a whistling like riggers straight for Labrador, flying against the stiff gale with reefed wings, or else circling round first, with all their paddles briskly moving, just over the surf, to reconnoitre you before they leave these parts; gulls wheeling overhead, muskrats swimming for dear life, wet and cold, with no fire to warm them by that you know of; their labored homes rising here and there like haystacks; and countless mice and moles and winged titmice along the sunny windy shore; cranberries tossed on the waves and heaving up on the beach, their little red skiffs beating about among the alders;—such healthy natural tumult as proves the last day is not yet at hand. And there stand all around the alders, and birches, and oaks, and maples full of glee and sap, holding in their buds until the waters subside. You shall perhaps run aground on Cranberry Island, only some spires of last year's pipe-grass above water, to show where the danger is, and get as good a freezing there as anywhere on the Northwest Coast. I never voyaged so far in all my life. You shall see men you never heard of before, whose names you don't know, going away down through the meadows with long ducking-guns, with water-tight boots wading through the fowl-meadow grass, on bleak, wintry, distant shores, with guns at half-cock, and they shall see teal, blue-winged, green-winged, shelldrakes, whistlers, black ducks, ospreys, and many other wild and noble sights before night, such as they who sit in parlors never dream of. You shall see rude and sturdy, experienced and wise men, keeping their castles, or teaming up their summer's wood, or chopping alone in the woods, men fuller of talk and rare adventure in the sun and wind and rain, than a chestnut is of meat; who were out not only in '75 and 1812, but have been out every day of their lives; greater men than Homer, or Chaucer, or Shakespeare, only they never got time to say so; they never took to the way of writing. Look at their fields, and imagine what they might write, if ever they should put pen to paper. Or what have they not written on the face of the earth already, clearing, and burning, and scratching, and harrowing, and ploughing, and subsoiling, in and in, and out and out, and over and over, again and again, erasing what they had already written for want of parchment. * * *

From WALDEN: OR, LIFE IN THE WOODS

BRUTE NEIGHBORS

* * * Why do precisely these objects which we behold make a world? Why has man just these species of animals for his neighbors; as if nothing but a mouse could have filled this crevice? I suspect that Pilpay & Co. have put animals to their best use, for they are all beasts of burden, in a sense, made to carry some portion of our thoughts.

Walden: or, Life in the Woods (Boston: Ticknor and Fields, 1854).

The mice which haunted my house were not the common ones, which are said to have been introduced into the country, but a wild native kind not found in the village. I sent one to a distinguished naturalist, and it interested him much. When I was building, one of these had its nest underneath the house, and before I had laid the second floor, and swept out the shavings, would come out regularly at lunch time and pick up the crumbs at my feet. It probably had never seen a man before; and it soon became quite familiar, and would run over my shoes and up my clothes. It could readily ascend the sides of the room by short impulses, like a squirrel, which it resembled in its motions. At length, as I leaned with my elbow on the bench one day, it ran up my clothes, and along my sleeve, and round and round the paper which held my dinner, while I kept the latter close, and dodged and played at bopeep with it; and when at last I held still a piece of cheese between my thumb and finger, it came and nibbled it, sitting in my hand, and afterward cleaned its face and paws, like a fly, and walked away.

A phœbe soon built in my shed, and a robin for protection in a pine which grew against the house. In June the partridge *(Tetrao umbellus)*, which is so shy a bird, led her brood past my windows, from the woods in the rear to the front of my house, clucking and calling to them like a hen, and in all her behavior proving herself the hen of the woods. The young suddenly disperse on your approach, at a signal from the mother, as if a whirlwind had swept them away, and they so exactly resemble the dried leaves and twigs that many a traveller has placed his foot in the midst of a brood, and heard the whir of the old bird as she flew off, and her anxious calls and mewing, or seen her trail her wings to attract his attention, without suspecting their neighborhood. The parent will sometimes roll and spin round before you in such a dishabille, that you cannot, for a few moments, detect what kind of creature it is. The young squat still and flat, often running their heads under a leaf, and mind only their mother's directions given from a distance, nor will your approach make them run again and betray themselves. You may even tread on them, or have your eyes on them for a minute, without discovering them. I have held them in my open hand at such a time, and still their only care, obedient to their mother and their instinct, was to squat there without fear or trembling. So perfect is this instinct, that once, when I had laid them on the leaves again, and one accidentally fell on its side, it was found with the rest in exactly the same position ten minutes afterward. They are not callow like the young of most birds, but more perfectly developed and precocious even than chickens. The remarkably adult yet innocent expression of their open and serene eyes is very memorable. All intelligence seems reflected in them. They suggest not merely the purity of infancy, but a wisdom clarified by experience. Such an eye was not born when the bird was, but is coeval with the sky it reflects. The woods do not yield another such a gem. The traveller does not often look into such a limpid well. The ignorant or reckless sportsman often shoots the parent at such a time, and leaves these innocents to fall a prey to some prowling beast or bird, or gradually mingle with the decaying leaves which they so much resemble. It is said that when hatched by a hen they will directly disperse on some alarm, and so are lost, for they never hear the mother's call which gathers them again. These were my hens and chickens.

It is remarkable how many creatures live wild and free though secret in the woods, and still sustain themselves in the neighborhood of towns, suspected by hunters only. How retired the otter manages to live here! He grows to be four feet long, as big as a small boy, perhaps without any human being getting a glimpse of him. I formerly saw the raccoon in the woods behind where my house is built, and probably still heard their whinnering at night. Commonly I rested an hour or two in the shade at noon, after planting, and ate my lunch, and read a little by a spring which was the source of a swamp and of a brook, oozing from under Brister's Hill, half a mile from my field. The approach to this was through a succession of descending grassy hollows, full of young pitch pines, into a larger wood about the swamp. There, in a very secluded and shaded spot, under a spreading white pine, there was yet a clean, firm sward to sit on. I had dug out the spring and made a well of clear gray water, where I could dip up a pailful without roiling it, and thither I went for this purpose almost every day in midsummer, when the pond was warmest. Thither, too, the woodcock led her brood, to probe the mud for worms, flying but a foot above them down the bank, while they ran in a troop beneath; but at last, spying me, she would leave her young and circle round and round me, nearer and nearer till within four or five feet, pretending broken wings and legs, to attract my attention, and get off her young, who would already have taken up their march, with faint, wiry peep, single file through the swamp, as she directed. Or I heard the peep of the young when I could not see the parent bird. There too the turtle doves sat over the spring, or fluttered from bough to bough of the soft white pines over my head; or the red squirrel, coursing down the nearest bough, was particularly familiar and inquisitive. You only need sit still long enough in some attractive spot in the woods that all its inhabitants may exhibit themselves to you by turns.

I was witness to events of a less peaceful character. One day when I went out to my wood-pile, or rather my pile of stumps, I observed two large ants, the one red, the other much larger, nearly half an inch long, and black, fiercely contending with one another. Having once got hold they never let go, but struggled and wrestled and rolled on the chips incesssantly. Looking farther, I was surprised to find that the chips were covered with such combatants, that it was not a *duellum*, but a *bellum*, a war between two races of ants, the red always pitted against the black, and frequently two red ones to one black. The legions of these Myrmidons covered all the hills and vales in my wood-yard, and the ground was already strewn with the dead and dying, both red and black. It was the only battle which I have ever witnessed, the only battle-field I ever trod while the battle was raging; internecine war; the red republicans on the one hand, and the black imperialists on the other. On every side they were engaged in deadly combat, yet without any noise that I could hear, and human soldiers never fought so resolutely. I watched a couple that were fast locked in each other's embraces, in a little sunny valley amid the chips, now at noonday prepared to fight till the sun went down, or life went out. The smaller red champion had fastened himself like a vice to his adversary's front, and through all the tumblings on that field never for an instant ceased to gnaw at one of his feelers near the root, having already caused the other to go by the board; while the stronger black one dashed him from side to side, and, as I saw on looking nearer, had already divested him of several of his members. They fought with more pertinacity than bulldogs. Neither manifested the least disposition to retreat. It was evident that their battle-cry was "Conquer or die." In the meanwhile there came along a single red ant on the hillside of this valley, evidently full of excitement, who either had despatched his foe, or had not yet taken part in the battle; probably the latter, for he had lost none of his limbs; whose mother had charged him to return with his shield or upon it. Or perchance he was some Achilles, who had nourished his wrath apart, and had now come to avenge or rescue his Patroclus. He saw this unequal combat from afar,—for the blacks were nearly twice the size of the red,—he drew near with rapid pace till he stood on his guard within half an inch of the combatants; then, watching his opportunity, he sprang upon the black warrior, and commenced his operations near the root of his right fore leg, leaving the foe to select among his own members; and so there were three united for life, as if a new kind of attraction had been invented which put all other locks and cements to shame. I should not have wondered by this time to find that they had their respective musical bands stationed on some eminent chip, and playing their national airs the while, to excite the slow and cheer the dying combatants. I was myself excited somewhat even as if they had been men. The more you think of it, the less the difference. And certainly there is not the fight recorded in Concord history, at least, if in the history of America, that will bear a moment's comparison with this, whether for the numbers engaged in it, or for the patriotism and heroism displayed. For numbers and for carnage it was an Austerlitz or Dresden. Concord Fight! Two killed on the patriots' side, and Luther Blanchard wounded! Why here every ant was a Buttrick,—"Fire! for God's sake fire!"—and thousands shared the fate of Davis and Hosmer. There was not one hireling there. I have no doubt that it was a principle they fought for, as much as our ancestors, and not to avoid a three-penny tax on their tea; and the results of this battle will be as important and memorable to those whom it concerns as those of the battle of Bunker Hill, at least.

I took up the chip on which the three I have particularly described were struggling, carried into my house, and placed it under a tumbler on my window-sill, in order to see the issue. Holding a microscope to the first-mentioned red ant, I saw that, though he was assiduously gnawing at the near fore leg of his enemy, having severed his remaining feeler, his own breast was all torn away, exposing what vitals he had there to the jaws of the black warrior, whose breastplate was apparently too thick for him to pierce; and the dark carbuncles of the sufferer's eyes shone with ferocity such as war only could excite. They struggled half an hour longer under the tumbler, and when I looked again the black soldier had severed the heads of his foes from their bodies, and the still living heads were hanging on either side of him like ghastly trophies at his saddle-bow, still apparently as firmly fastened as ever, and he was endeavoring with feeble struggles, being without feelers and with only the remnant of a leg, and I know not how many other wounds, to divest himself of them; which at length, after half an hour more, he accomplished. I raised the glass, and he went off over the window-sill in that crippled state. Whether he finally survived that combat, and spent the remainder of his days in some Hôtel des Invalides, I do not know; but I thought that his industry would not be worth much thereafter. I never learned which party was victorious, nor the cause of the war; but I felt for the rest of that day as if I had had my feelings excited and harrowed by witnessing the struggle, the ferocity and carnage, of a human battle before my door.

Kirby and Spence tell us that the battles of ants have long been celebrated and the date of them recorded, though they say that Huber is the only modern author who appears to have witnessed them. "Æneas Sylvius," say they, "after giving a very circumstantial account of one contested with great obstinacy by a great and small species on the trunk of a pear tree," adds that " 'this action was fought in the pontificate of Eugenius the Fourth, in the presence of Nicholas Pistoriensis, an eminent lawyer, who related the whole history of the battle with the greatest fidelity.' A similar engagement between great and small ants is recorded by Olaus Magnus, in which the small ones, being victorious, are said to have buried the bodies of their own soldiers, but left those of their giant enemies a prey to the birds. This event happened previous to the expulsion of the tyrant Christiern the Second from Sweden." The battle which I witnessed took place in the Presidency of Polk, five years before the passage of Webster's Fugitive-Slave Bill.

Many a village Bose, fit only to course a mud-turtle in a victualling cellar, sported his heavy quarters in the woods, without the knowledge of his master, and ineffectually smelled at old fox burrows and woodchucks' holes; led perchance by some slight cur which nimbly threaded the wood, and might still inspire a natural terror in its denizens;—now far behind his guide, barking like a canine bull toward some small squirrel which had treed itself for scrutiny, then, cantering off, bending the bushes with his weight, imagining that he is on the track of some stray member of the jerbilla family. Once I was surprised to see a cat walking along the stony shore of the pond, for they rarely wander so far from home. The surprise was mutual. Nevertheless the most domestic cat, which has lain on a rug all her days, appears quite at home in the woods, and, by her sly and stealthy behavior, proves herself more native there than the regular inhabitants. Once, when berrying, I met with a cat with young kittens in the woods, quite wild, and they all, like their mother, had their backs up and were fiercely spitting at me. A few years before I lived in the woods there was what was called a "winged cat" in one of the farm-houses in Lincoln nearest the pond, Mr. Gilian Baker's. When I called to see her in June, 1842, she was gone a-hunting in the woods, as was her wont (I am not sure whether it was a male or female, and so use the more common pronoun), but her mistress told me that she came into the neighborhood a little more than a year before, in April, and was finally taken into their house; that she was of a dark brownish-gray color, with a white spot on her throat, and white feet, and had a large bushy tail like a fox; that in the winter the fur grew thick and flatted out along her sides, forming strips ten or twelve inches long by two and a half wide, and under her chin like a muff, the upper side loose, the under matted like felt, and in the spring these appendages dropped off. They gave me a pair of her "wings," which I keep still. There is no appearance of a membrane about them. Some thought it was part flying squirrel or some other wild animal, which is not impossible, for, according to naturalists, prolific hybrids have been produced by the union of the marten and domestic cat. This would have been the right kind of cat for me to keep, if I had kept any; for why should not a poet's cat be winged as well as his horse?

In the fall the loon *(Colymbus glacialis)* came, as usual, to moult and bathe in the pond, making the woods ring with his wild laughter before I had risen. At rumor of his arrival all the Mill-dam sportsmen are on the alert, in gigs and on foot, two by two and three by three, with patent rifles and conical balls and spy-glasses. They come rustling through the woods like autumn leaves, at least ten men to one loon. Some station themselves on this side of the pond, some on that, for the poor bird cannot be omnipresent; if he dive here he must come up there. But now the kind October wind rises, rustling the leaves and rippling the surface of the water, so that no loon can be heard or seen, though his foes sweep the pond with spy-glasses, and make the woods resound with their discharges. The waves generously rise and dash angrily, taking sides with all water-fowl, and our sportsmen must beat a retreat to town and shop and unfinished jobs. But they were too often successful. When I went to get a pail of water early in the morning I frequently saw this stately bird sailing out of my cove within a few rods. If I endeavored to overtake him in a boat, in order to see how he would manœuvre, he would dive and be completely lost, so that I did not discover him again, sometimes, till the latter part of the day. But I was more than a match for him on the surface. He commonly went off in a rain.

As I was paddling along the north shore one very calm afternoon, for such days especially they settle on to the lakes, like the milkweed down, having looked in vain over the pond for a loon, suddenly one, sailing out from the shore toward the middle a few rods in front of me, set up his wild laugh and betrayed himself. I pursued with a paddle and he dived, but when he came up I was nearer than before. He dived again, but I miscalculated the direction he would take, and we were fifty rods apart when he came to the surface this time, for I had helped to widen the interval; and again he laughed long and loud, and with more reason than before. He manœuvred so cunningly that I could not get within half a dozen rods of him. Each time, when he came to the surface, turning his head this way and that, he coolly surveyed the water and the land, and apparently chose his course so that he might come up where there was the widest expanse of water and at the greatest distance from the boat. It was surprising how quickly he made up his mind and put his resolve into execution. He led me at once to the widest part of the pond, and could not be driven from it. While he was thinking one thing in his brain, I was endeavoring to divine his thought in mine. It was a pretty game, played on the smooth surface of the pond, a man against a loon. Suddenly your adversary's checker disappears beneath the board, and the problem is to place yours nearest to where his will appear again. Sometimes he would come up unexpectedly on the opposite side of me, having apparently passed directly under the boat. So long-winded was he and so unweariable, that when he had swum farthest he would immediately plunge again, nevertheless; and then no wit could divine where in the deep pond, beneath the smooth surface, he might be speeding his way like a fish, for he had time and ability to visit the bottom of the pond in its deepest part. It is said that loons have been caught in the New York lakes eighty feet beneath the surface, with hooks set for trout,—though Walden is deeper than that. How surprised must the fishes be to see this ungainly visitor from another sphere speeding his way amid their schools! Yet he appeared to know his course as surely under water as on the surface, and swam much faster there. Once or twice I saw a ripple where he approached the surface, just put his head out to reconnoitre, and instantly dived again. I found that it was as well for me to rest on my oars and wait his reappearing as to endeavor to calculate where he would rise; for again and again, when I was straining my eyes over the surface one way, I would suddenly be startled by his unearthly laugh behind me. But why, after displaying so much cunning, did he invariably betray himself the moment he came up by that loud laugh? Did not his white breast enough betray him? He was indeed a silly loon, I thought. I could commonly hear the plash of the water when he came up, and so also detected him. But after an hour he seemed as fresh as ever, dived as willingly, and swam yet farther than at first. It was surprising to see how serenely he sailed off with unruffled breast when he came to the surface, doing all the work with his webbed feet beneath. His usual note was this demoniac laughter, yet somewhat like that of a water-fowl; but occasionally, when he had balked me most successfully and come up a long way off, he uttered a long-drawn unearthly howl, probably more like that of a wolf than any bird; as when a beast puts his muzzle to the ground and deliberately howls. This was his looning,—perhaps the wildest sound that is ever heard here, making the woods ring far and wide. I concluded that he laughed in derision of my efforts, confident of his own resources. Though the sky was by this time overcast, the pond was so smooth that I could see where he broke the surface when I did not hear him. His white breast, the stillness of the air, and the smoothness of the water were all against him. At length, having come up fifty rods off, he uttered one of those prolonged howls, as if calling on the god of loons to aid him, and immediately there came a wind from the east and rippled the surface, and filled the whole air with misty rain, and I was impressed as if it were the prayer of the loon answered, and his god was angry with me; and so I left him disappearing far away on the tumultuous surface.

For hours, in fall days, I watched the ducks cunningly tack and veer and hold the middle of the pond, far from the sportsman; tricks which they will have less need to practise in Louisiana bayous. When compelled to rise they would sometimes circle round and round and over the pond at a considerable height, from which they could easily see to other ponds and the river, like black motes in the sky; and, when I thought they had gone off thither long since, they would settle down by a slanting flight of a quarter of a mile on to a distant part which was left free; but what beside safety they got by sailing in the middle of Walden I do not know, unless they love its water for the same reason that I do.

WALKING

* * * The West of which I speak is but another name for the Wild; and what I have been preparing to say is, that in Wildness is the preservation of the World. Every tree sends its fibres forth in search of the Wild. The cities import it at any price. Men plough and sail for it. From the forest and wilderness come the tonics and barks which brace mankind. Our ancestors were savages. The story of Romulus and Remus being suckled by a wolf is not a meaningless fable. The founders of every state which has risen to eminence have drawn their nourishment and vigor from a similar wild source. It was because the children of the Empire were not suckled by the wolf that they were conquered and displaced by the children of the northern forests who were.

I believe in the forest, and in the meadow, and in the night in which the corn grows. We require an infusion of hemlock-spruce or arbor-vitæ in our tea. There is a difference between eating and drinking for strength and from mere gluttony. The Hottentots eagerly devour the marrow of the koodoo and other antelopes raw, as a matter of course. Some of our Northern Indians eat raw the marrow of the Arctic reindeer, as well as the various other parts, including the summits of the antlers, as long as they are soft. And herein, perchance, they have stolen a march on the cooks of Paris. They get what usually goes to feed the fire. This is probably better than stall-fed beef and slaughter-house pork to make a man of. Give me a wildness whose glance no civilization can endure,—as if we lived on the marrow of koodoos devoured raw.

There are some intervals which border the strain of the wood-thrush, to which I would migrate,—wild lands where no settler has squatted; to which, methinks, I am already acclimated.

The African hunter Cummings tells us that the skin of the eland, as

Excursions (Boston: Ticknor and Fields, 1863).

well as that of most other antelopes just killed, emits the most delicious perfume of trees and grass. I would have every man so much like a wild antelope, so much a part and parcel of Nature, that his very person should thus sweetly advertise our senses of his presence, and remind us of those parts of Nature which he most haunts. I feel no disposition to be satirical, when the trapper's coat emits the odor of musquash even; it is a sweeter scent to me than that which commonly exhales from the merchant's or the scholar's garments. When I go into their wardrobes and handle their vestments, I am reminded of no grassy plains and flowery meads which they have frequented, but of dusty merchants' exchanges and libraries rather.

A tanned skin is something more than respectable, and perhaps olive is a fitter color than white for a man,—a denizen of the woods. "The pale white man!" I do not wonder that the African pitied him. Darwin the naturalist says, "A white man bathing by the side of a Tahitian was like a plant bleached by the gardener's art, compared with a fine, dark green one, growing vigorously in the open fields."

Ben Jonson exclaims,—

"How near to good is what is fair!"

So I would say,—

How near to good is what is *wild!*

Life consists with wildness. The most alive is the wildest. Not yet subdued to man, its presence refreshes him. One who pressed forward incessantly and never rested from his labors, who grew fast and made infinite demands on life, would always find himself in a new country or wilderness, and surrounded by the raw material of life. He would be climbing over the prostrate stems of primitive forest-trees.

Hope and the future for me are not in lawns and cultivated fields, not in towns and cities, but in the impervious and quaking swamps. When, formerly, I have analyzed my partiality for some farm which I had contemplated purchasing, I have frequently found that I was attracted solely by a few square rods of impermeable and unfathomable bog,—a natural sink in one corner of it. That was the jewel which dazzled me. I derive more of my subsistence from the swamps which surround my native town than from the cultivated gardens in the village. There are no richer parterres to my eyes than the dense beds of dwarf andromeda *(Cassandra calyculata)* which cover these tender places on the earth's surface.

Botany cannot go farther than tell me the names of the shrubs which grow there,—the high-blueberry, panicled andromeda, lamb-kill, azalea, and rhodora,—all standing in the quaking sphagnum. I often think that I should like to have my house front on this mass of dull red bushes, omitting other flower plots and borders, transplanted spruce and trim box, even graveled walks,—to have this fertile spot under my windows, not a few imported barrow-fulls of soil only to cover the sand which was thrown out in digging the cellar. Why not put my house, my parlor, behind this plot, instead of behind that meagre assemblage of curiosities, that poor apology for a Nature and Art, which I call my front yard? It is an effort to clear up and make a decent appearance when the carpenter and mason have departed, though done as much for the passer-by as the dweller within. The most tasteful front-yard fence was never an agreeable object of study to me; the most elaborate ornaments, acorn-tops, or what not, soon wearied and disgusted me. Bring your sills up to the very edge of the swamp, then (though it may not be the best place for a dry cellar), so that there be no access on that side to citizens. Front yards are not made to walk in, but, at most, through, and you could go in the back way.

Yes, though you may think me perverse, if it were proposed to me to dwell in the neighborhood of the most beautiful garden that ever human art contrived, or else of a Dismal Swamp, I should certainly decide for the swamp. How vain, then, have been all your labors, citizens, for me!

My spirits infallibly rise in proportion to the outward dreariness. Give me the ocean, the desert, or the wilderness! In the desert, pure air and solitude compensate for want of moisture and fertility. The traveler Burton says of it: "Your *morale* improves; you become frank and cordial, hospitable and single-minded. . . . In the desert, spirituous liquors excite only disgust. There is a keen enjoyment in a mere animal existence." They who have been traveling long on the steppes of Tartary say: "On reëntering cultivated lands, the agitation, perplexity, and turmoil of civilization oppressed and suffocated us; the air seemed to fail us, and we felt every moment as if about to die of asphyxia." When I would recreate myself, I seek the darkest wood, the thickest and most interminable and, to the citizen, most dismal swamp. I enter a swamp as a sacred place,—a *sanctum sanctorum.* There is the strength, the marrow of Nature. The wild-wood covers the virgin-mould,—and the same soil is good for men and for trees. A man's health requires as many acres of meadow to his prospect as his farm does loads of muck. There are the strong meats on which he feeds. A town is saved, not more by the righteous men in it than by the woods and swamps that surround it. A township where one primitive forest waves above while another primitive forest rots below,—

such a town is fitted to raise not only corn and potatoes, but poets and philosophers for the coming ages. In such a soil grew Homer and Confucius and the rest, and out of such a wilderness comes the Reformer eating locusts and wild honey.

To preserve wild animals implies generally the creation of a forest for them to dwell in or resort to. So it is with man. A hundred years ago they sold bark in our streets peeled from our own woods. In the very aspect of those primitive and rugged trees there was, methinks, a tanning principle which hardened and consolidated the fibres of men's thoughts. Ah! already I shudder for these comparatively degenerate days of my native village, when you cannot collect a load of bark of good thickness,—and we no longer produce tar and turpentine.

The civilized nations—Greece, Rome, England—have been sustained by the primitive forests which anciently rotted where they stand. They survive as long as the soil is not exhausted. Alas for human culture! little is to be expected of a nation, when the vegetable mould is exhausted, and it is compelled to make manure of the bones of its fathers. There the poet sustains himself merely by his own superfluous fat, and the philosopher comes down on his marrow-bones.

It is said to be the task of the American "to work the virgin soil," and that "agriculture here already assumes proportions unknown everywhere else." I think that the farmer displaces the Indian even because he redeems the meadow, and so makes himself stronger and in some respects more natural. I was surveying for a man the other day a single straight line one hundred and thirty-two rods long, through a swamp, at whose entrance might have been written the words which Dante read over the entrance to the infernal regions,—"Leave all hope, ye that enter,"—that is, of ever getting out again; where at one time I saw my employer actually up to his neck and swimming for his life in his property, though it was still winter. He had another similar swamp which I could not survey at all, because it was completely under water, and nevertheless, with regard to a third swamp, which I did *survey* from a distance, he remarked to me, true to his instincts, that he would not part with it for any consideration, on account of the mud which it contained. And that man intends to put a girdling ditch round the whole in the course of forty months, and so redeem it by the magic of his spade. I refer to him only as the type of a class.

The weapons with which we have gained our most important victories, which should be handed down as heirlooms from father to son, are not the sword and the lance, but the bushwhack, the turf-cutter, the spade, and the boghoe, rusted with the blood of many a meadow, and begrimed with the dust of many a hard-fought field. The very winds blew the Indian's corn-field into the meadow, and pointed out the way which he had not the skill to follow. He had no better implement with which to intrench himself in the land than a clam-shell. But the farmer is armed with plough and spade.

In literature it is only the wild that attracts us. Dullness is but another name for tameness. It is the uncivilized free and wild thinking in "Hamlet" and the "Iliad," in all the Scriptures and Mythologies, not learned in the schools, that delights us. As the wild duck is more swift and beautiful than the tame, so is the wild—the mallard—thought, which 'mid falling dews wings its way above the fens. A truly good book is something as natural, and as unexpectedly and unaccountably fair and perfect, as a wild flower discovered on the prairies of the West or in the jungles of the East. Genius is a light which makes the darkness visible, like the lightning's flash, which perchance shatters the temple of knowledge itself,—and not a taper lighted at the hearthstone of the race, which pales before the light of common day.

English literature, from the days of the minstrels to the Lake Poets,—Chaucer and Spenser and Milton, and even Shakespeare, included,—breathes no quite fresh and, in this sense, wild strain. It is an essentially tame and civilized literature, reflecting Greece and Rome. Her wilderness is a greenwood, her wild man a Robin Hood. There is plenty of genial love of Nature, but not so much of Nature herself. Her chronicles inform us when her wild animals, but not when the wild man in her, became extinct.

The science of Humboldt is one thing, poetry is another thing. The poet to-day, notwithstanding all the discoveries of science, and the accumulated learning of mankind, enjoys no advantage over Homer.

Where is the literature which gives expression to Nature? He would be a poet who could impress the winds and streams into his service, to speak for him; who nailed words to their primitive senses, as farmers drive down stakes in the spring, which the frost has heaved; who derived his words as often as he used them,—transplanted them to his page with earth adhering to their roots; whose words were so true and fresh and natural that they would appear to expand like the buds at the approach of spring, though they lay half-smothered between two musty leaves in a library,—ay, to bloom and bear fruit there, after their kind, annually, for the faithful reader, in sympathy with surrounding Nature.

I do not know of any poetry to quote which adequately expresses this yearning for the Wild. Approached from this side, the best poetry is tame. I do not know where to find in any literature, ancient or modern, any account which contents me of that Nature with which even I am acquainted. You will perceive that I demand something which no

Augustan nor Elizabethan age, which no *culture,* in short, can give. Mythology comes nearer to it than anything. How much more fertile a Nature, at least, has Grecian mythology its root in than English litera- ture! Mythology is the crop which the Old World bore before its soil was exhausted, before the fancy and imagination were affected with blight; and which it still bears, wherever its pristine vigor is unabated. All other literatures endure only as the elms which overshadow our houses; but this is like the great dragon-tree of the Western Isles, as old as mankind, and, whether that does or not, will endure as long; for the decay of other literatures makes the soil in which it thrives.

The West is preparing to add its fables to those of the East. The valleys of the Ganges, the Nile, and the Rhine having yielded their crop, it remains to be seen what the valleys of the Amazon, the Plate, the Orinoco, the St. Lawrence, and the Mississippi will produce. Perchance, when, in the course of ages, American liberty has become a fiction of the past,—as it is to some extent a fiction of the present,—the poets of the world will be inspired by American mythology.

The wildest dreams of wild men, even, are not the less true, though they may not recommend themselves to the sense which is most com- mon among Englishmen and Americans to-day. It is not every truth that recommends itself to the common sense. Nature has a place for the wild clematis as well as for the cabbage. Some expressions of truth are remi- niscent,—others merely *sensible,* as the phrase is,—others prophetic. Some forms of disease, even, may prophesy forms of health. The geolo- gist has discovered that the figures of serpents, griffins, flying dragons, and other fanciful embellishments of heraldry, have their prototypes in the forms of fossil species which were extinct before man was created, and hence "indicate a faint and shadowy knowledge of a previous state of organic existence." The Hindoos dreamed that the earth rested on an elephant, and the elephant on a tortoise, and the tortoise on a serpent; and though it may be an unimportant coincidence, it will not be out of place here to state, that a fossile tortoise has lately been discovered in Asia large enough to support an elephant. I confess that I am partial to these wild fancies, which transcend the order of time and development. They are the sublimest recreation of the intellect. The partridge loves peas, but not those that go with her into the pot.

In short, all good things are wild and free. There is something in a strain of music, whether produced by an instrument or by the human voice,—take the sound of a bugle in a summer night, for instance,— which by its wildness, to speak without satire, reminds me of the cries emitted by wild beasts in their native forests. It is so much of their wildness as I can understand. Give me for my friends and neighbors wild men, not tame ones. The wildness of the savage is but a faint symbol of the awful ferity with which good men and lovers meet.

I love even to see the domestic animals reassert their native rights,— any evidence that they have not wholly lost their original wild habits and vigor; as when my neighbor's cow breaks out of her pasture early in the spring and boldly swims the river, a cold, gray tide, twenty-five or thirty rods wide, swollen by the melted snow. It is the buffalo crossing the Mississippi. This exploit confers some dignity on the herd in my eyes,— already dignified. The seeds of instinct are preserved under the thick hides of cattle and horses, like seeds in the bowels of the earth, an indefinite period.

Any sportiveness in cattle is unexpected. I saw one day a herd of a dozen bullocks and cows running about and frisking in unwieldy sport, like huge rats, even like kittens. They shook their heads, raised their tails, and rushed up and down a hill, and I perceived by their horns, as well as by their activity, their relation to the deer tribe. But, alas! a sudden loud *Whoa!* would have damped their ardor at once, reduced them from venison to beef, and stiffened their sides and sinews like the locomotive. Who but the Evil One has cried, "Whoa!" to mankind? Indeed, the life of cattle, like that of many men, is but a sort of locomotiveness; they move a side at a time, and man, by his machinery, is meeting the horse and the ox half-way. Whatever part the whip has touched is thenceforth palsied. Who would ever think of a *side* of any of the supple cat tribe, as we speak of a *side* of beef?

I rejoice that horses and steers have to be broken before they can be made the slaves of men, and that men themselves have some wild oats still left to sow before they become submissive members of society. Undoubtedly, all men are not equally fit subjects for civilization; and because the majority, like dogs and sheep, are tame by inherited disposition, this is no reason why the others should have their natures broken that they may be reduced to the same level. Men are in the main alike, but they were made several in order that they might be various. If a low use is to be served, one man will do nearly or quite as well as another; if a high one, individual excellence is to be regarded. Any man can stop a hole to keep the wind away, but no other man could serve so rare a use as the author of this illustration did. Confucius says, "The skins of the tiger and the leopard, when they are tanned, are as the skins of the dog and the sheep tanned." But it is not the part of a true culture to tame tigers, any more than it is to make sheep ferocious; and tanning their skins for shoes is not the best use to which they can be put. ＊ ＊ ＊

From THE MAINE WOODS

KTAADN

*   *   * In the morning, after whetting our appetite on some raw pork, a wafer of hard bread, and a dipper of condensed cloud or waterspout, we all together began to make our way up the falls, which I have described; this time choosing the right hand, or highest peak, which was not the one I had approached before. But soon my companions were lost to my sight behind the mountain ridge in my rear, which still seemed ever retreating before me, and I climbed alone over huge rocks, loosely poised, a mile or more, still edging toward the clouds; for though the day was clear elsewhere, the summit was concealed by mist. The mountain seemed a vast aggregation of loose rocks, as if some time it had rained rocks, and they lay as they fell on the mountain sides, nowhere fairly at rest, but leaning on each other, all rocking-stones, with cavities between, but scarcely any soil or smoother shelf. They were the raw materials of a planet dropped from an unseen quarry, which the vast chemistry of nature would anon work up, or work down, into the smiling and verdant plains and valleys of earth. This was an undone extremity of the globe; as in lignite, we see coal in the process of formation.

At length I entered within the skirts of the cloud which seemed forever drifting over the summit, and yet would never be gone, but was generated out of that pure air as fast as it flowed away; and when, a quarter of a mile farther, I reached the summit of the ridge, which those who have seen in clearer weather say is about five miles long, and contains a thousand acres of table-land, I was deep within the hostile ranks of clouds, and all objects were obscured by them. Now the wind would blow me out a yard of clear sunlight, wherein I stood; then a gray, dawning light was all it could accomplish, the cloud-line ever rising and falling with the wind's intensity. Sometimes it seemed as if the summit would be cleared in a few moments, and smile in sunshine; but what was gained on one side was lost on another. It was like sitting in a chimney and waiting for the smoke to blow away. It was, in fact, a cloud factory,—these were the cloud-works, and the wind turned them off done from the cool, bare rocks. Occasionally, when the windy columns broke in to me, I caught sight of a dark, damp crag to the right or left; the mist driving ceaselessly between it and me. It reminded me of the creations of the old epic and dramatic poets, of Atlas, Vulcan, the Cyclops, and

The Maine Woods (Boston: Ticknor and Fields, 1864).

Prometheus. Such was Caucasus and the rock where Prometheus was bound. Æschylus had no doubt visited such scenery as this. It was vast, Titanic, and such as man never inhabits. Some part of the beholder, even some vital part, seems to escape through the loose grating of his ribs as he ascends. He is more lone than you can imagine. There is less of substantial thought and fair understanding in him than in the plains where men inhabit. His reason is dispersed and shadowy, more thin and subtile, like the air. Vast, Titanic, inhuman Nature has got him at disadvantage, caught him alone, and pilfers him of some of his divine faculty. She does not smile on him as in the plains. She seems to say sternly, Why came ye here before your time. This ground is not prepared for you. Is it not enough that I smile in the valleys? I have never made this soil for thy feet, this air for thy breathing, these rocks for thy neighbors. I cannot pity nor fondle thee here, but forever relentlessly drive thee hence to where I *am* kind. Why seek me where I have not called thee, and then complain because you find me but a stepmother? Shouldst thou freeze or starve, or shudder thy life away, here is no shrine, nor altar, nor any access to my ear.

> "Chaos and ancient Night, I come no spy
> With purpose to explore or to disturb
> The secrets of your realm, but . . .
> . . . . . . as my way
> Lies through your spacious empire up to light."

The tops of mountains are among the unfinished parts of the globe, whither it is a slight insult to the gods to climb and pry into their secrets, and try their effect on our humanity. Only daring and insolent men, perchance, go there. Simple races, as savages, do not climb mountains,— their tops are sacred and mysterious tracts never visited by them. Pomola is always angry with those who climb to the summit of Ktaadn.

According to Jackson, who, in his capacity of geological surveyor of the State, has accurately measured it,—the altitude of Ktaadn is 5300 feet, or a little more than one mile above the level of the sea,—and he adds, "It is then evidently the highest point in the State of Maine, and is the most abrupt granite mountain in New England." The peculiarities of that spacious table-land on which I was standing, as well as the remarkable semi-circular precipice or basin on the eastern side, were all concealed by the mist. I had brought my whole pack to the top, not knowing but I should have to make my descent to the river, and possibly to the settled portion of the State alone, and by some other route, and wishing to have a complete outfit with me. But at length, fearing that my companions would be anxious to reach the river before night, and knowing that the clouds might rest on the mountain for days, I was compelled to descend. Occasionally, as I came down, the wind would blow me a vista open, through which I could see the country eastward, boundless forests, and lakes, and streams, gleaming in the sun, some of them emptying into the East Branch. There were also new mountains in sight in that direction. Now and then some small bird of the sparrow family would flit away before me, unable to command its course, like a fragment of the gray rock blown off by the wind.

I found my companions where I had left them, on the side of the peak, gathering the mountain-cranberries, which filled every crevice between the rocks, together with blueberries, which had a spicier flavor the higher up they grew, but were not the less agreeable to our palates. When the country is settled, and roads are made, these cranberries will perhaps become an article of commerce. From this elevation, just on the skirts of the clouds, we could overlook the country, west and south, for a hundred miles. There it was, the State of Maine, which we had seen on the map, but not much like that,—immeasurable forest for the sun to shine on, that eastern *stuff* we hear of in Massachusetts. No clearing, no house. It did not look as if a solitary traveler had cut so much as a walking-stick there. Countless lakes,—Moosehead in the southwest, forty miles long by ten wide, like a gleaming silver platter at the end of the table; Chesuncook, eighteen long by three wide, without an island; Millinocket, on the south, with its hundred islands; and a hundred others without a name; and mountains, also, whose names, for the most part, are known only to the Indians. The forest looked like a firm grass sward, and the effect of these lakes in its midst has been well compared, by one who has since visited this same spot, to that of a "mirror broken into a thousand fragments, and wildly scattered over the grass, reflecting the full blaze of the sun." It was a large farm for somebody, when cleared. According to the Gazetteer, which was printed before the boundary question was settled, this single Penobscot county, in which we were, was larger than the whole State of Vermont, with its fourteen counties; and this was only a part of the wild lands of Maine. We are concerned now, however, about natural, not political limits. We were about eighty miles, as the bird flies, from Bangor, or one hundred and fifteen, as we had ridden, and walked, and paddled. We had to console ourselves with the reflection that this view was probably as good as that from the peak, as far as it went; and what were a mountain without its attendant clouds and mists? Like ourselves, neither Bailey nor Jackson had obtained a clear view from the summit.

Setting out on our return to the river, still at an early hour in the day, we decided to follow the course of the torrent, which we supposed to be Murch Brook, as long as it would not lead us too far out of our way. We thus traveled about four miles in the very torrent itself, continually crossing and recrossing it, leaping from rock to rock, and jumping with the stream down falls of seven or eight feet, or sometimes sliding down on our backs in a thin sheet of water. This ravine had been the scene of an extraordinary freshet in the spring, apparently accompanied by a slide from the mountain. It must have been filled with a stream of stones and water, at least twenty feet above the present level of the torrent. For a rod or two, on either side of its channel, the trees were barked and splintered up to their tops, the birches bent over, twisted, and sometimes finely split, like a stable-broom; some, a foot in diameter, snapped off, and whole clumps of trees bent over with the weight of rocks piled on them. In one place we noticed a rock, two or three feet in diameter, lodged nearly twenty feet high in the crotch of a tree. For the whole four miles, we saw but one rill emptying in, and the volume of water did not seem to be increased from the first. We traveled thus very rapidly with a downward impetus, and grew remarkably expert at leaping from rock to rock, for leap we must, and leap we did, whether there was any rock at the right distance or not. It was a pleasant picture when the foremost turned about and looked up the winding ravine, walled in with rocks and the green forest, to see, at intervals of a rod or two, a red-shirted or green-jacketed mountaineer against the white torrent, leaping down the channel with his pack on his back, or pausing upon a convenient rock in the midst of the torrent to mend a rent in his clothes, or unstrap the dipper at his belt to take a draught of the water. At one place we were startled by seeing, on a little sandy shelf by the side of the stream, the fresh print of a man's foot, and for a moment realized how Robinson Crusoe felt in a similar case; but at last we remembered that we had struck this stream on our way up, though we could not have told where, and one had descended into the ravine for a drink. The cool air above and the continual bathing of our bodies in mountain water, alternate foot, sitz, douche, and plunge baths, made this walk exceedingly refreshing, and we had traveled only a mile or two, after leaving the torrent, before every thread of our clothes was as dry as usual, owing perhaps to a peculiar quality in the atmosphere.

After leaving the torrent, being in doubt about our course, Tom threw down his pack at the foot of the loftiest spruce-tree at hand, and shinned up the bare trunk some twenty feet, and then climbed through the green tower, lost to our sight, until he held the topmost spray in his hand. McCauslin, in his younger days, had marched through the wilderness with a body of troops, under General Somebody, and with one other man did all the scouting and spying service. The General's word was, "Throw down the top of that tree," and there was no tree in the Maine woods so high that it did not lose its top in such a case. I have heard a story of two men being lost once in these woods, nearer to the settlements than this, who climbed the loftiest pine they could find, some six feet in diameter at the ground, from whose top they discovered a solitary clearing and its smoke. When at this height, some two hundred feet from the ground, one of them became dizzy, and fainted in his companion's arms, and the latter had to accomplish the descent with him, alternately fainting and reviving, as best he could. To Tom we cried, Where away does the summit bear? where the burnt lands? The last he could only conjecture; he descried, however, a little meadow and pond, lying probably in our course, which we concluded to steer for. On reaching this secluded meadow, we found fresh tracks of moose on the shore of the pond, and the water was still unsettled as if they had fled before us. A little farther, in a dense thicket, we seemed to be still on their trail. It was a small meadow, of a few acres, on the mountain side, concealed by the forest, and perhaps never seen by a white man before, where one would think that the moose might browse and bathe, and rest in peace. Pursuing this course, we soon reached the open land, which went sloping down some miles toward the Penobscot.

Perhaps I most fully realized that this was primeval, untamed, and forever untamable *Nature,* or whatever else men call it, while coming down this part of the mountain. We were passing over "Burnt Lands," burnt by lightning, perchance, though they showed no recent marks of fire, hardly so much as a charred stump, but looked rather like a natural pasture for the moose and deer, exceedingly wild and desolate, with occasional strips of timber crossing them, and low poplars springing up, and patches of blueberries here and there. I found myself traversing them familiarly, like some pasture run to waste, or partially reclaimed by man; but when I reflected what man, what brother or sister or kinsman of our race made it and claimed it, I expected the proprietor to rise up and dispute my passage. It is difficult to conceive of a region uninhabited by man. We habitually presume his presence and influence everywhere. And yet we have not seen pure Nature, unless we have seen her thus vast and drear and inhuman, though in the midst of cities. Nature was here something savage and awful, though beautiful. I looked with awe at the ground I trod on, to see what the Powers had made there, the form and fashion and material of their work. This was that Earth of which we have heard, made out of Chaos and Old Night. Here was no man's garden, but the unhandseled globe. It was not lawn, nor pasture, nor mead, nor woodland, nor lea, nor arable, nor waste land. It was the fresh and natural surface of the planet Earth, as it was made forever and ever,—to be the dwelling of man, we say,—so Nature made it, and man may use it if he can. Man was not to be associated with it. It was Matter, vast, terrific,—not his Mother Earth that we have heard of, not for him to tread on, or be buried in,—no, it were being too familiar even to let his bones lie there,—the home, this, of Necessity and Fate. There was clearly felt the presence of a force not bound to be kind to man. It was a place for heathenism and superstitious rites,—to be inhabited by men nearer of kin to the rocks and to wild animals than we. We walked over it with a certain awe, stopping, from time to time, to pick the blueberries which grew there, and had a smart and spicy taste. Perchance where *our* wild pines stand, and leaves lie on their forest floor, in Concord, there were once reapers, and husbandmen planted grain; but here not even the surface had been scarred by man, but it was a specimen of what God saw fit to make this world. What is it to be admitted to a museum, to see a myriad of particular things, compared with being shown some star's surface, some hard matter in its home! I stand in awe of my body, this matter to which I am bound has become so strange to me. I fear not spirits, ghosts, of which I am one,—*that* my body might,—but I fear bodies, I tremble to meet them. What is this Titan that has possession of me? Talk of mysteries! Think of our life in nature,—daily to be shown matter, to come in contact with it,—rocks, trees, wind on our cheeks! the *solid* earth! the *actual* world! the *common sense! Contact! Contact! Who* are we? *where* are we?

Erelong we recognized some rocks and other features in the landscape which we had purposely impressed on our memories, and, quickening our pace, by two o'clock we reached the batteau.[1] ＊ ＊ ＊

[1]The bears had not touched things on our possessions. They sometimes tear a batteau to pieces for the sake of the tar with which it is besmeared. [Thoreau's note]

From JOURNALS

OCT. 16, 1856

[*An Offensive Fungus*]

Found amid the sphagnum on the dry bank on the south side of the Turnpike, just below Everett's meadow, a rare and remarkable fungus, such as I have heard of but never seen before. The whole height six and

Journals (Boston: Houghton Mifflin, 1906).

three quarters inches, two thirds of it being buried in the sphagnum. It may be divided into three parts, pileus, stem, and base,—or scrotum, for it is a perfect phallus. One of those fungi named *impudicus*, I think.[1] In all respects a most disgusting object, yet very suggestive. It is hollow from top to bottom, the form of the hollow answering to that of the outside. The color of the outside white excepting the pileus, which is olive-colored and somewhat coarsely corrugated, with an oblong mouth at tip about one eighth of an inch long, or, measuring the white lips, half an inch. This cap is thin and white within, about one and three eighths inches high by one and a half wide. The stem (bare portion) is three inches long (tapering more rapidly than in the drawing), horizontally viewed of an oval form. Longest diameter at base one and a half inches, at top (on edge of pileus) fifteen sixteenths of an inch. Short diameters in both cases about two thirds as much. It is a delicate white cylinder of a finely honeycombed and crispy material about three sixteenths of an inch thick, or more, the whole very straight and regular. The base, or scrotum, is of an irregular bag form, about one inch by two in the extremes, consisting of a thick trembling gelatinous mass surrounding the bottom of the stem and covered with a tough white skin of a darker tint than the stem. The whole plant rather frail and trembling. There was at first a very thin delicate white collar (or *volva?*) about the base of the stem above the scrotum. It was as offensive to the eye as to the scent, the cap rapidly melting and defiling what it touched with a fetid, oliva-ceous, semiliquid matter. In an hour or two the plant scented the whole house wherever placed, so that it could not be endured. I was afraid to sleep in my chamber where it had lain until the room had been well ventilated. It smelled like a dead rat in the ceiling, in all the ceilings of the house. Pray, what was Nature thinking of when she made this? She almost puts herself on a level with those who draw in privies. The cap had at first a smooth and almost dry surface, of a sort of olive slate-color, but the next day this colored surface all melted out, leaving deep corru-gations or gills—rather honeycomb-like cells—with a white bottom.

NOV. 1, 1858

[*Here*]

As the afternoons grow shorter, and the early evening drives us home to complete our chores, we are reminded of the shortness of life, and become more pensive, at least in this twilight of the year. We are

[1]This is very similar to if not the same with that represented in Loudon's *Encyclopædia* and called *"Phallus impudicus*, Stinking Morel, very fetid."

prompted to make haste and finish our work before the night comes. I leaned over a rail in the twilight on the Walden road, waiting for the evening mail to be distributed, when such thoughts visited me. I seemed to recognize the November evening as a familiar thing come round again, and yet I could hardly tell whether I had ever known it or only divined it. The November twilights just begun! It appeared like a part of a panorama at which I sat spectator, a part with which I was perfectly familiar just coming into view, and I foresaw how it would look and roll along, and prepared to be pleased. Just such a piece of art merely, though infinitely sweet and grand, did it appear to me, and just as little were any active duties required of me. We are independent on all that we see. The hangman whom I have *seen* cannot hang me. The earth which I have *seen* cannot bury me. Such doubleness and distance does sight prove. Only the rich and such as are troubled with ennui are implicated in the maze of phenomena. You cannot see anything until you are clear of it. The long railroad causeway through the meadows west of me, the still twilight in which hardly a cricket was heard,[1] the dark bank of clouds in the horizon long after sunset, the villagers crowding to the post-office, and the hastening home to supper by candle-light, had I not seen all this before! What new sweet was I to extract from it? Truly they mean that we shall learn our lesson well. Nature gets thumbed like an old spelling-book. The almshouse and Frederick were still as last November. I was no nearer, methinks, nor further off from my friends. Yet I sat the bench with perfect contentment, unwilling to exchange the familiar vision that was to be unrolled for any treasure or heaven that could be imagined. Sure to keep just so far apart in our orbits still, in obedience to the laws of attraction and repulsion, affording each other only steady but indispensable starlight. It was as if I was promised the greatest novelty the world has ever seen or shall see, though the utmost possible novelty would be the difference between me and myself a year ago. This alone encouraged me, and was my fuel for the approaching winter. That we may behold the panorama with this slight improvement or change, this is what we sustain life for with so much effort from year to year.

And yet there is no more tempting novelty than this new November. No going to Europe or another world is to be named with it. Give me the old familiar walk, post-office and all, with this ever new self, with this infinite expectation and faith, which does not know when it is beaten. We'll go nutting once more. We'll pluck the nut of the world, and crack it in the winter evenings. Theatres and all other sightseeing are puppet-shows in comparison. I will take another walk to the Cliff, another row

---

[1]Probably too cool for any these evenings; only in the afternoon. [Thoreau's note]

on the river, another skate on the meadow, be out in the first snow, and associate with the winter birds. Here I am at home. In the bare and bleached crust of the earth I recognize my friend.

One actual Frederick that you know is worth a million only read of. Pray, am I altogether a bachelor, or am I a widower, that I should go away and leave my bride? This Morrow that is ever knocking with irresistible force at our door, there is no such guest as that. I will stay at home and receive company.

I want nothing new, if I can have but a tithe of the old secured to me. I will spurn all wealth beside. Think of the consummate folly of attempting to go away from *here!* When the constant endeavor should be to get nearer and nearer *here.* Here are all the friends I ever had or shall have, and as friendly as ever. Why, I never had any quarrel with a friend but it was just as sweet as unanimity could be. I do not think we budge an inch forward or backward in relation to our friends. How many things can you go away from? They see the comet from the northwest coast just as plainly as we do, and the same stars through its tail. Take the shortest way round and stay at home. A man dwells in his native valley like a corolla in its calyx, like an acorn in its cup. *Here,* of course, is all that you love, all that you expect, all that you are. Here is your bride elect, as close to you as she can be got. Here is all the best and all the worst you can imagine. What more do you want? Bear here away then! Foolish people imagine that what they imagine is somewhere else. That stuff is not made in any factory but their own.

NOV. 4, 1858

[Seeing]

If, about the last of October, you ascend any hill in the outskirts of the town and look over the forest, you will see, amid the brown of other oaks, which are now withered, and the green of the pines, the bright-red tops or crescents of the scarlet oaks, very equally and thickly distributed on all sides, even to the horizon. Complete trees standing exposed on the edges of the forest, where you have never suspected them, or their tops only in the recesses of the forest surface, or perhaps towering above the surrounding trees, or reflecting a warm rose red from the very edge of the horizon in favorable lights. All this you will see, and much more, if you are prepared to see it,—if you *look* for it. Otherwise, regular and universal as this phenomenon is, you will think for threescore years and ten that all the wood is at this season sere and brown. Objects are concealed from our view not so much because they are out of the course of our visual ray (continued) as because there is no intention of the mind and eye toward them. We do not realize how far and widely, or how near and narrowly, we are to look. The greater part of the phenomena of nature are for this reason concealed to us all our lives. Here, too, as in political economy, the supply answers to the demand. Nature does not cast pearls before swine. There is just as much beauty visible to us in the landscape as we are prepared to appreciate,—not a grain more. The actual objects which one person will see from a particular hilltop are just as different from those which another will see as the persons are different. The scarlet oak must, in a sense, be in your eye when you go forth. We cannot see anything until we are possessed with the idea of it, and then we can hardly see anything else. In my botanical rambles I find that first the idea, or image, of a plant occupies my thoughts, though it may at first seem very foreign to this locality, and for some weeks or months I go thinking of it and expecting it unconsciously, and at length I surely see it, and it is henceforth an actual neighbor of mine. This is the history of my finding a score or more of rare plants which I could name.

Take one of our selectmen and put him on the highest hill in the township, and tell him to look! What probably, would he see? What would he *select* to look at? Sharpening his sight to the utmost, and putting on the glasses that suited him best, aye, using a spy-glass if he liked, straining his optic nerve to its utmost, and making a full report. Of course, he would see a Brocken spectre of himself. Now take Julius Cæsar, or Emanuel Swedenborg, or a Fiji-Islander, and set him up there! Let them compare notes afterward. Would it appear that they had enjoyed the same prospect? For aught we know, as strange a man as any of these is always at our elbows. It does not appear that anybody saw Shakespeare when he was about in England looking off, but only some of his raiment.

Why, it takes a sharpshooter to bring down even such trivial game as snipes and woodcocks; he must take very particular aim, and know what he is aiming at. He would stand a very small chance if he fired at random into the sky, being told that snipes were flying there. And so it is with him that shoots at beauty. Not till the sky falls will he catch larks, unless he is a trained sportsman. He will not bag any if he does not already know its seasons and haunts and the color of its wing,—if he has not dreamed of it, so that he can *anticipate* it; then, indeed, he flushes it at every step, shoots double and on the wing, with both barrels, even in corn-fields. The sportsman trains himself, dresses, and watches unweariedly, and loads and primes for his particular game. He prays for it, and so he gets it. After due and long preparation, schooling his eye and hand, dreaming awake and asleep, with gun and paddle and boat, he goes out after meadow-hens,—which most of his townsmen never saw nor dreamed of,—paddles for miles against a head wind, and therefore he gets them. He had them half-way into his bag when he started, and has only to shove them down. The fisherman, too, dreams of fish, till he can almost catch them in his sink-spout. The hen scratches, and finds her food right under where she stands; but such is not the way with the hawk.

The true sportsman can shoot you almost any of his game from his windows. It comes and perches at last on the barrel of his gun; but the rest of the world never see it, with the feathers on. He will keep himself supplied by firing up his chimney. The geese fly exactly under his zenith, and honk when they get there. Twenty musquash have the refusal of each one of his traps before it is empty.

JAN. 22, 1859

[The Musquash-hunters]

I hear these guns going to-day, and I must confess they are to me a springlike and exhilarating sound, like the cock-crowing, though each one may report the death of a musquash. This, methinks, or the like of this, with whatever mixture of dross, is the real morning or evening hymn that goes up from these vales to-day, and which the stars echo. This is the best sort of glorifying of God and enjoying him that at all prevails here to-day, without any clarified butter or sacred ladles.

As a mother loves to see her child imbibe nourishment and expand, so God loves to see his children thrive on the nutriment he has furnished them. In the musquash-hunters I see the Almouchicois still pushing swiftly over the dark stream in their canoes. These aboriginal men cannot be repressed, but under some guise or other they survive and reappear continually. Just as simply as the crow picks up the worms which all over the fields have been washed out by the thaw, these men pick up the musquash that have been washed out the banks. And to serve such ends men plow and sail, and powder and shot are made, and the grocer exists to retail them, though he may think himself much more the deacon of some church.

The energy and excitement of the musquash-hunter even, not despairing of life, but keeping the same rank and savage hold on it that his predecessors have for so many generations, while so many are sick and despairing, even this is inspiriting to me. Even these deeds of death are interesting as evidences of life, for life will still prevail in spite of all accidents. I have a certain faith that even musquash are immortal and not born to be killed by Melvin's double-B (?) shot.

Methinks the breadth of waves, whether in water or snow or sand or vapor (in the mackerel sky), is determined generally by the force of the wind or other current striking the water, etc. It depends on how much water, etc., the wind has power to displace.

The musquash-hunter (last night), with his increased supply of powder and shot and boat turned up somewhere on the bank, now that the river is rapidly rising, dreaming of his exploits to-day in shooting musquash, of the great pile of dead rats that will weigh down his boat before night, when he will return wet and weary and weather-beaten to his hut with an appetite for his supper and for much sluggish (punky) social intercourse with his fellows,—even he, dark, dull, and battered flint as he is, is an inspired man to his extent now, perhaps the most inspired by this freshet of any, and the Musketaquid Meadows cannot spare him. There are poets of all kinds and degrees, little known to each other. The Lake School is not the only or the principal one. They love various things. Some love beauty, and some love rum. Some go to Rome, and some go a-fishing, and are sent to the house of correction once a month. They keep up their fires by means unknown to me. I know not their comings and goings.

APRIL 8, 1859

[The Fur Trade]

What a pitiful business is the fur trade, which has been pursued now for so many ages, for so many years by famous companies which enjoy a profitable monopoly and control a large portion of the earth's surface, unweariedly pursuing and ferreting out small animals by the aid of all the loafing class tempted by rum and money, that you may rob some little fellow-creature of its coat to adorn or thicken your own, that you may get a fashionable covering in which to hide your head, or a suitable robe in which to dispense justice to your fellow-men! Regarded from the philosopher's point of view, it is precisely on a level with rag and bone picking in the streets of the cities. The Indian led a more respectable life before he was tempted to debase himself so much by the white man. Think how many musquash and weasel skins the Hudson's Bay Company pile up annually in their warehouses, leaving the bare red carcasses on the banks of the streams throughout all British America,—and this it is, chiefly, which makes it *British* America. It is the place where Great Britain goes a-mousing. We have heard much of the wonderful intelligence of the beaver, but that regard for the beaver is all a pretense, and we would give more for a beaver hat than to preserve the intelligence of the whole race of beavers.

When we see men and boys spend their time shooting and trapping musquash and mink, we cannot but have a poorer opinion of them, unless we thought meanly of them before. Yet the world is imposed on by the fame of the Hudson's Bay and Northwest Fur Companies, who are only so many partners more or less in the same sort of business, with thousands of just such loafing men and boys in their service to abet them. On the one side is the Hudson's Bay Company, on the other the company of scavengers who clear the sewers of Paris of their vermin. There is a good excuse for smoking out or poisoning rats which infest the house, but when they are as far off as Hudson's Bay, I think that we had better let them alone. To such an extent do time and distance, and our imaginations, consecrate at last not only the most ordinary, but even vilest pursuits. The efforts of legislation from time to time to stem the torrent are significant as showing that there is some sense and conscience left, but they are insignificant in their effects. We will fine Abner if he shoots a singing bird, but encourage the army of Abners that compose the Hudson's Bay Company.

One of the most remarkable sources of profit opened to the Yankee within a year is the traffic in skunk-skins. I learn from the newspapers—as from other sources (*vide* Journal of Commerce in *Tribune* for April 5, 1859)—that "the traffic in skunk-skins has suddenly become a most important branch of the fur trade, and the skins of an animal which three years ago were deemed of no value whatever, are now in the greatest demand." "The principal markets are Russia and Turkey, though some are sent to Germany, where they are sold at a large profit." Furs to Russia! "The black skins are valued the most, and during the past winter the market price has been as high as one dollar per skin, while mottled skins brought only seventy cents." "Upward of 50,000 of these skins have been shipped from this city [New York] alone within the past two months." Many of them "are designed for the Leipsic sales, Leipsic being next to Novgorod, in Russia, the most important fur *entrepôt* in Europe. The first intimation received in this market of the value of this new description of fur came from the Hudson's Bay Company, which, having shipped a few to London at a venture, found the returns so profitable that they immediately prosecuted the business on an extensive scale." "The heaviest collections are made in the Middle and Eastern States, in some parts of which the mania for capturing these animals seems to have equalled the Western Pike's Peak gold excitement, men, women, and children turning out *en masse* for that purpose." And beside, "our fur dealers also receive a considerable sum for the *fat* of these animals!!"

Almost all smile, or otherwise express their contempt, when they hear of this or the rat-catching of Paris, but what is the difference between catching and skinning the skunk and the mink? It is only in the name. When you pass the palace of one of the managers of the Hudson's Bay Company, you are reminded that so much he got for his rat-skins. In such a snarl and contamination do we live that it is almost impossible to keep one's skirts clean. Our sugar and cotton are stolen from the slave, and if we jump out of the fire, it is wont to be into the frying-pan at least. It will not do to be thoughtless with regard to any of our valuables or property. When you get to Europe you will meet the most tender-hearted and delicately bred lady, perhaps the President of the Antislavery Society, or of that for the encouragement of humanity to animals, marching or presiding with the scales from a tortoise's back—obtained by laying live coals on it to make them curl up—stuck in her hair, rat-skin fitting as close to her fingers as erst to the rat, and, for her cloak, trimmings perchance adorned with the spoils of a hundred skunks,—rendered inodorous, we trust. Poor misguided woman! Could she not wear other armor in the war of humanity?

When a new country like North America is discovered, a few feeble efforts are made to Christianize the natives before they are all exterminated, but they are not found to pay, in any sense. But the energetic traders of the discovering country organize themselves, or rather inevitably crystallize, into a vast rat-catching society, tempt the natives to become mere vermin-hunters and rum-drinkers, reserving half a continent for the field of their labors. Savage meets savage, and the white man's only distinction is that he is the chief.

She says to the turtle basking on the shore of a distant isle, "I want your scales to adorn my head" (though fire be used to raise them); she whispers to the rats in the wall, "I want your skins to cover my delicate fingers;" and, meeting an army of a hundred skunks in her morning walk, she says, "worthless vermin, strip off your cloaks this instant, and let me have them to adorn my robe with;" and she comes home with her hands muffled in the pelt of a gray wolf that ventured abroad to find food for its young that day.

When the question of the protection of birds comes up, the legislatures regard only a low use and never a high use; the best-disposed legislators employ one, perchance, only to examine their crops and see how many grubs or cherries they contain, and never to study their dispositions, or the beauty of their plumage, or listen and report on the sweetness of their song. The legislature will preserve a bird professedly not because it is a beautiful creature, but because it is a good scavenger or the like. This, at least, is the defense set up. It is as if the question were whether some celebrated singer of the human race—some Jenny Lind or another—did more harm or good; should be destroyed, or not, and therefore a committee should be appointed, not to listen to her singing at all, but to examine the contents of her stomach and see if she devoured anything which was injurious to the farmers and gardeners, or which they cannot spare.

FEB 16, 1860

[Topsell's Gesner]

We cannot spare the very lively and lifelike descriptions of some of the old naturalists. They sympathize with the creatures which they describe. Edward Topsell in his translation of Conrad Gesner, in 1607, called "The History of Four-footed Beasts," says of the antelopes that "they are bred in India and Syria, near the river Euphrates," and then—which enables you to realize the living creature and its habitat—he adds, "and delight much to drink of the cold water thereof." The beasts which most modern naturalists describe do not *delight* in anything, and their water is neither hot nor cold. Reading the above makes you want to go and drink of the Euphrates yourself, if it is warm weather. I do not know how much of his spirit he owes to Gesner, but he proceeds in his translation to say that "they have horns growing forth of the crown of their head, which are very long and sharp; so that Alexander affirmed they pierced through the shields of his soldiers, and fought with them very irefully: at which time his company slew as he travelled to India, eight thousand five hundred and fifty, which great slaughter may be the occasion why they are so rare and seldom seen to this day."

Now here *something* is described at any rate; it is a real account, whether of a real animal or not. You can plainly see the horns which "grew forth" from their crowns, and how well that word "irefully" describes a beast's fighting! And then for the number which Alexander's men slew "as he travelled to India,"—and what a travelling was that, my hearers!—eight thousand five hundred and fifty, just the number you would have guessed after the thousands were given, and [an] easy one to remember too. He goes on to say that "their horns are great and made like a saw, and they with them can cut asunder the branches of osier or small trees, whereby it cometh to pass that many times their necks are taken in the twists of the falling boughs, whereat the beast with repining cry, bewrayeth himself to the hunters, and so is taken." The artist too has done his part equally well, for you are presented with a drawing of the beast with serrated horns, the tail of a lion, a cheek tooth (canine?) as big as a boar's, a stout front, and an exceedingly "ireful" look, as if he were facing all Alexander's army.

Though some beasts are described in this book which have no existence as I can learn but in the imagination of the writers, they really have an existence there, which is saying not a little, for most of our modern authors have not imagined the actual beasts which they presume to describe. The very frontispiece is a figure of "the gorgon," which looks sufficiently like a hungry beast covered with scales, which you may have dreamed of, apparently just fallen on the track of you, the reader, and snuffing the odor with greediness.

These men had an adequate idea of a beast, or what a beast should be, a very *bellua* (the translator makes the word *bestia* to be *"a vastando"*); and they will describe and will draw you a cat with four strokes, more beastly or beast-like to look at than Mr. Ruskin's favorite artist draws a tiger. They had an adequate idea of the wildness of beasts and of men, and in their descriptions and drawings they did not always fail when they *surpassed* nature.

I think that the most important requisite in describing an animal, is to be sure and give its character and spirit, for in that you have, without error, the sum and effect of all its parts, known and unknown. You must tell what it is to man. Surely the most important part of an animal is its *anima*, its vital spirit, on which is based its character and all the peculiarities by which it most concerns us. Yet most scientific books which treat of animals leave this out altogether, and what they describe are as it were phenomena of dead matter. What is most interesting in a dog, for example, is his attachment to his master, his intelligence, courage, and the like, and not his anatomical structure or even many habits which affect us less.

If you have undertaken to write the biography of an animal, you will have to present to us the living creature, *i.e.*, a result which no man can understand, but only in his degree report the impression made on him.

Science in many departments of natural history does not pretend to go beyond the shell; *i.e.*, it does not get to animated nature at all. A history of animated nature must itself be animated.

The ancients, one would say, with their gorgons, sphinxes, satyrs, mantichora, etc., could imagine more than existed, while the moderns cannot imagine so much as exists.

In describing brutes, as in describing men, we shall naturally dwell most on those particulars in which they are most like ourselves,—in which we have most sympathy with them.

We are as often injured as benefited by our systems, for, to speak the truth, no human system is a true one, and a name is at most a mere convenience and carries no information with it. As soon as I begin to be aware of the life of any creature, I at once forget its name. To know the names of creatures is only a convenience to us at first, but so soon as we have learned to distinguish them, the sooner we forget their names the better, so far as any true appreciation of them is concerned. I think, therefore, that the best and most harmless names are those which are an imitation of the voice or note of an animal, or the most poetic ones. But the name adheres only to the accepted and conventional bird or quadruped, never an instant to the real one. There is always something ridiculous in the name of a great man,—as if he were named John Smith. The name is convenient in communicating with others, but it is not to be remembered when I communicate with myself.

If you look over a list of medicinal recipes in vogue in the last century, how foolish and useless they are seen to be! And yet we use equally absurd ones with faith to-day.

When the ancients had not found an animal wild and strange enough to suit them, they created one by the mingled [traits] of the most savage already known,—as hyenas, lionesses, pards, panthers, etc., etc.,—one with another. Their beasts were thus of wildness and savageness all compact, and more *ferine* and *terrible* than any of an unmixed breed could be. They allowed nature great license in these directions. The most strange and fearful beasts were by them supposed to be the offspring of two different savage kinds. So fertile were their imaginations, and such fertility did they assign to nature. In the modern account the fabulous part will be omitted, it is true, but the portrait of the real and living creature also.

The old writers have left a more lively and lifelike account of the gorgon than modern writers give us of real animals.

OCT. 9 1860

[Skeletons vs. Golden Eggs]

This haste to kill a bird or quadruped and make a skeleton of it, which many young men and some old ones exhibit, reminds me of the fable of the man who killed the hen that laid golden eggs, and so got no more gold. It is a perfectly parallel case. Such is the knowledge which you may get from the anatomy as compared with the knowledge you get from the living creature. Every fowl lays golden eggs for him who can find them, or can detect alloy and base metal.

OCT. 10 1860

[A Blue Heron Skeleton]

Horace Mann shows me the skeleton of a blue heron. The neck is remarkably strong, and the bill. The latter is 5+ inches long to the feathers above and 6½ to the gape. A stake-driver which he has, freshly killed, has a bill 3 inches long above and 4⅛ to the gape and between ⅝ and ⁶⁄₈ deep vertically at the base. This bird weighs a little over two pounds, being quite large and fat. Its nails are longer and less curved than those of the heron. The sharp bill of the heron, like a stout pick, wielded by that long and stout neck, would be a very dangerous weapon to encounter. He has made a skeleton of the fish hawk which was brought to me within a month. I remark the great eye-sockets, and the claws, and perhaps the deep, sharp breast-bone. Including its strong hooked bill it is clawed at both ends, harpy-like.

OCT. 13 1860

[Poetic vs. Scientific Description]

The scientific differs from the poetic or lively description somewhat as the photographs, which we so weary of viewing, from paintings and sketches, though this comparison is too favorable to science. All science is only a makeshift, a means to an end which is never attained. After all, the truest description, and that by which another living man can most readily recognize a flower, is the unmeasured and eloquent one which the sight of it inspires. No scientific description will supply the want of this, though you should count and measure and analyze every atom that seems to compose it.

Surely poetry and eloquence are a more universal language than that Latin which is confessedly dead. In science, I should say, all description is postponed till we know the whole, but then science itself will be cast aside. But unconsidered expressions of our delight which any natural object draws from us are something complete and final in themselves, since all nature is to be regarded as it concerns man; and who knows how near to absolute truth such unconscious affirmations may come? Which are the truest, the sublime conceptions of Hebrew poets and *seers,* or the guarded statements of modern geologists, which we must modify or unlearn so fast?

As they who were present early at the discovery of gold in California, and observed the sudden fall in its value, have most truly described that state of things, so it is commonly the old naturalists who first received

American plants that describe them best. A scientific description is such as you would get if you should send out the scholars of the polytechnic school with all sorts of metres made and patented to take the measures for you of any natural object. In a sense you have got nothing new thus, for every object that we see mechanically is mechanically daguerreotyped on our eyes, but a true description growing out [of] the perception and appreciation of it is itself a new fact, never to be daguerreotyped, indicating the highest quality of the plant,—its relation to man,—of far more importance than any merely medicinal quality that it may possess, or be thought to-day to possess. There is a certainty and permanence about this kind of observation, too, that does not belong to the other, for every flower and weed has its day in the medical pharmacopœia, but the beauty of flowers is perennial in the taste of men.

MARCH 22, 1861

[*Tenacity of Life*]

When we consider how soon some plants which spread rapidly, by seeds or roots, would cover an area equal to the surface of the globe, how soon some species of trees, as the white willow, for instance, would equal in mass the earth itself, if all their seeds became full-grown trees, how soon some fishes would fill the ocean if all their ova became full-grown fishes, we are tempted to say that every organism, whether animal or vegetable, is contending for the possession of the planet, and, if any one were sufficiently favored, supposing it still possible to grow, as at first, it would at length convert the entire mass of the globe into its own substance. Nature opposes to this many obstacles, as climate, myriads of brute and also human foes, and of competitors which may preoccupy the ground. Each suggests an immense and wonderful greediness and tenacity of life (I speak of the species, not individual), as if bent on taking entire possession of the globe wherever the climate and soil will permit. And each prevails as much as it does, because of the ample preparations it has made for the contest,—it has secured a myriad chances,—because it never depends on spontaneous generation to save it.

1861

[*A Young Kitten*]

The kitten can already spit at a fortnight old, and it can mew from the first, though it often makes the motion of mewing without uttering any sound.

The cat about to bring forth seeks out some dark and secret place for the purpose, not frequented by other cats.

The kittens' ears are at first nearly concealed in the fur, and at a fortnight old they are mere broad-based triangles with a side foremost. But the old cat is ears for them at present, and comes running hastily to their aid when she hears them mew and licks them into contentment again. Even at three weeks the kitten cannot fairly walk, but only creeps feebly with outspread legs. But thenceforth its ears visibly though gradually lift and sharpen themselves.

At three weeks old the kitten begins to walk in a staggering and creeping manner and even to play a little with its mother, and, if you put your ear close, you may hear it purr. It is remarkable that it will not wander far from the dark corner where the cat has left it, but will instinctively find its way back to it, probably by the sense of touch, and will rest nowhere else. Also it is careful not to venture too near the edge of a precipice, and its claws are ever extended to save itself in such places. It washes itself somewhat, and assumes many of the attitudes of an old cat at this age. By the disproportionate size of its feet and head and legs now it reminds you [of] a lion.

I saw it scratch its ear to-day, probably for the first time; yet it lifted one of its hind legs and scratched its ear as effectually as an old cat does. So this is instinctive, and you may say that, when a kitten's ear first itches, Providence comes to the rescue and lifts its hind leg for it. You would say that this little creature was as perfectly protected by its instinct in its infancy as an old man can be by his wisdom. I observed when she first noticed the figures on the carpet, and also put up her paws to touch or play with surfaces a foot off. By the same instinct that they find the mother's teat before they can see they scratch their ears and guard against falling.

CHARLES KINGSLEY
1819-1875

Charles Kingsley was one of those Victorians who achieved distinction in several careers while also writing prodigiously. Among his important positions were those of Chaplain to Queen Victoria and Professor of Modern History at Cambridge. For most of his life, however, Kingsley

*was a parish priest and canon of the Church of England. Natural history
was his recreation, as it was for so many middleclass Englishmen of his
day.* Glaucus; or, The Wonders of the Shore *(1855) reflects the influence of the marine biologist Philip Henry Gosse, as well as Kingsley's
own residence at the Devon seaport of Torquay.* Prose Idylls: New and
Old *(1873) collected his naturalist sketches, a number of which gravi-
tated to the fen country of eastern England where he grew up. Among
his novels,* Westward Ho! *(1855),* Hypatia *(1853),* Two Years *(1857),
and the children's classic* The Water Babies *(1863) were especially
noted for their vivid landscape descriptions, ranging from South America to the Egyptian desert to north Devon.*

From GLAUCUS; OR, THE WONDERS OF THE SHORE

[*a repellent worm*]

*   *   * And now, worshipper of final causes and the mere useful in
nature, answer but one question,—Why this prodigal variety? All these
Nudibranchs live in much the same way: why would not the same mould
have done for them all? And why, again, (for we must push the argument
a little further,) why have not all the butterflies, at least all who feed on
the same plant, the same markings? Of all unfathomable triumphs of
design, (we can only express ourselves thus, for honest induction, as
Paley so well teaches, allows us to ascribe such results only to the design
of some personal will and mind,) what surpasses that by which the scales
on a butterfly's wing are arranged to produce a certain pattern of artistic
beauty beyond all painter's skill? What a waste of power, on any utilitarian theory of nature! And once more, why are those strange microscopic
atomies, the Diatomaceæ and Infusoria, which fill every stagnant pool;
which fringe every branch of sea-weed; which form banks hundreds of
miles long on the Arctic sea-floor, and the strata of whole moorlands;
which pervade in millions the mass of every iceberg, and float aloft in
countless swarms amid the clouds of the volcanic dust;—why are their
tiny shells of flint as fantastically various in their quaint mathematical
symmetry, as they are countless beyond the wildest dreams of the Poet?
Mystery inexplicable on the conceited notion which, making man forsooth the centre of the universe, dares to believe that this variety of
forms has existed for countless ages in abysmal sea-depths and untrod-

Glaucus; or, The Wonders of the Shore (Boston: Ticknor & Fields, 1855).

den forests, only that some few individuals of the Western races might, in these latter days, at last discover and admire a corner here and there of the boundless realms of beauty. Inexplicable, truly, if man be the centre and the object of their existence; explicable enough to him who believes that God has created all things for Himself, and rejoices in His own handiwork, and that the material universe is, as the wise man says, "A platform whereon His Eternal Spirit sports and makes melody." Of all the blessings which the study of nature brings to the patient observer, let none, perhaps, be classed higher than this: that the further he enters into those fairy gardens of life and birth, which Spenser saw and described in his great poem, the more he learns the awful and yet most comfortable truth, that they do not belong to him, but to One greater, wiser, lovelier than he; and as he stands, silent with awe, amid the pomp of Nature's ever-busy rest, hears, as of old, "The Word of the Lord God walking among the trees of the garden in the cool of the day."

One sight more, and we have done. I had something to say, had time permitted, on the ludicrous element which appears here and there in nature. There are animals, like monkeys and crabs, which seem made to be laughed at; by those at least who possess that most indefinable of faculties, the sense of the ridiculous. As long as man possesses muscles especially formed to enable him to laugh, we have no right to suppose (with some) that laughter is an accident of our fallen nature; or to find (with others) the primary cause of the ridiculous in the perception of unfitness or disharmony. And yet we shrink (whether rightly or wrongly, we can hardly tell) from attributing a sense of the ludicrous to the Creator of these forms. It may be a weakness on my part; at least I will hope it is a reverent one: but till we can find something corresponding to what we conceive of the Divine Mind in any class of phenomena, it is perhaps better not to talk about them at all, but observe a stoic "epoché," waiting for more light, and yet confessing that our own laughter is uncontrollable, and therefore we hope not unworthy of us, at many a strange creature and strange doing which we meet, from the highest ape to the lowest polype.

But, in the meanwhile, there are animals in which results so strange, fantastic, even seemingly horrible, are produced, that fallen man may be pardoned if he shrinks from them in disgust. That, at least, must be a consequence of our own wrong state; for everything is beautiful and perfect in its place. It may be answered, 'Yes, in its place; but its place is not yours. You had no business to look at it, and must pay the penalty for intermeddling.' I doubt that answer: for surely, if man have liberty to do anything, he has liberty to search out freely his Heavenly Father's works; and yet every one seems to have his antipathic animal, and I know one

bred from his childhood to zoology by land and sea, and bold in asserting, and honest in feeling, that all without exception is beautiful, who
yet cannot, after handling, and petting, and admiring all day long every
uncouth and venomous beast, avoid a paroxysm of horror at the sight of
the common house-spider. At all events, whether we were intruding or
not, in turning this stone, we must pay a fine for having done so; for
there lies an animal, as foul and monstrous to the eye as 'hydra, gorgon,
or chimera dire,' and yet so wondrously fitted for its work, that we must
needs endure for our own instruction to handle and look at it. Its name I
know not (though it lurks here under every stone), and should be glad to
know. It seems some very 'low' Ascarid or Planarian worm. You see it?
That black, slimy, knotted lump among the gravel, small enough to be
taken up in a dessert-spoon. Look now, as it is raised and its coils drawn
out. Three feet! Six—nine at least, with a capability of seemingly endless
expansion; a slimy tape of living caoutchouc, some eighth of an inch in
diameter, a dark chocolate-black, with paler longitudinal lines. It is alive?
It hangs helpless and motionless, a mere velvet string across the hand.
Ask the neighbouring Annelids and the fry of the rock fishes, or put it
into a vase at home, and see. It lies motionless, trailing itself among the
gravel; you cannot tell where it begins or ends; it may be a strip of dead
sea-weed, *Himanthalia lorea,* perhaps, or *Chorda filum;* or even a tarred
string. So thinks the little fish who plays over and over it, till he touches
at last what is too surely a head. In an instant a bell-shaped sucker mouth
has fastened to its side. In another instant, from one lip, a concave
double proboscis, just like a tapir's (another instance of the repetition of
forms), has clasped him like a finger, and now begins the struggle; but in
vain. He is being 'played,' with such a fishing-rod as the skill of a Wilson
or a Stoddart never could invent; a living line, with elasticity beyond that
of the most delicate fly-rod, which follows every lunge, shortening and
lengthening, slipping and twining round every piece of gravel and stem
of sea-weed, with a tiring drag such as no Highland wrist or step could
ever bring to bear on salmon or trout. The victim is tired now; and
slowly, yet dexterously, his blind assailant is feeling and shifting along his
side, till he reaches one end of him; and then the black lips expand, and
slowly and surely the curved finger begins packing him end foremost
down into the gullet, where he sinks, inch by inch, till the swelling which
marks his place is lost among the coils, and he is probably macerated into
a pulp long before he has reached the opposite extremity of his cave
of doom. Once safe down, the black murderer contracts again into a
knotted heap, and lies like a boa with a stag inside him, motionless and
blest.

HERMAN MELVILLE
1819-1891

It used to be common to publish "condensed" versions of Moby-Dick *by eliminating the book's many chapters on whale biology, whaling techniques and metaphysical speculation. Now, however, these "discursive" chapters are recognized as integral to its greatness. Both Melville and Thoreau used encounters with nature as springboards for cosmic and moral explorations of the nature of reality, though they reached vastly different conclusions. In "The Whiteness of the Whale" Melville tackles head-on that "nameless horror" in nature, embodied by the white whale, which seems so inimical to man's hopes and desires. In two contrasting chapters, a playful taxonomic description of two whale heads provides an example of the book's extraordinary humor. "The Grand Armada" presents a sympathetic glimpse into the secret domestic lives of whales. It is also among the first instances of what has become one of the most common experiences in modern nature writing: a fundamental change in the narrator's point of view through a personal encounter with an animal.*

From MOBY-DICK; OR, THE WHALE

THE WHITENESS OF THE WHALE

What the white whale was to Ahab, has been hinted; what, at times, he was to me, as yet remains unsaid.

Aside from those more obvious considerations touching Moby Dick, which could not but occasionally awaken in any man's soul some alarm, there was another thought, or rather vague, nameless horror concerning him, which at times by its intensity completely overpowered all the rest; and yet so mystical and well nigh ineffable was it, that I almost despair of

Moby-Dick; or, The Whale (New York: Harper and Brothers, 1851).

putting it in a comprehensible form. It was the whiteness of the whale
that above all things appalled me. But how can I hope to explain myself
here; and yet, in some dim, random way, explain myself I must, else all
these chapters might be naught.

Though in many natural objects, whiteness refiningly enhances
beauty, as if imparting some special virtue of its own, as in marbles,
japonicas, and pearls; and though various nations have in some way
recognised a certain royal pre-eminence in this hue; even the barbaric,
grand old kings of Pegu placing the title "Lord of the White Elephants"
above all their other magniloquent ascriptions of dominion; and the
modern kings of Siam unfurling the same snow-white quadruped in the
royal standard; and the Hanoverian flag bearing the one figure of a
snow-white charger; and the great Austrian Empire, Cæsarian heir to
overlording Rome, having for the imperial color the same imperial hue;
and though this pre-eminence in it applies to the human race itself,
giving the white man ideal mastership over every dusky tribe; and
though, besides all this, whiteness has been even made significant of
gladness, for among the Romans a white stone marked a joyful day; and
though in other mortal sympathies and symbolizings, this same hue is
made the emblem of many touching, noble things—the innocence of
brides, the benignity of age; though among the Red Men of America the
giving of the white belt of wampum was the deepest pledge of honor;
though in many climes, whiteness typifies the majesty of Justice in the
ermine of the Judge, and contributes to the daily state of kings and
queens drawn by milk-white steeds; though even in the higher mysteries
of the most august religions it has been made the symbol of the divine
spotlessness and power; by the Persian fire worshippers, the white forked
flame being held the holiest on the altar; and in the Greek mythologies,
Great Jove himself being made incarnate in a snow-white bull; and
though to the noble Iroquois, the mid-winter sacrifice of the sacred
White Dog was by far the holiest festival of their theology, that spotless,
faithful creature being held the purest envoy they could send to the
Great Spirit with the annual tidings of their own fidelity; and though
directly from the Latin word for white, all Christian priests derive the
name of one part of their sacred vesture, the alb or tunic, worn beneath
the cassock; and though among the holy pomps of the Romish faith,
white is specially employed in the celebration of the Passion of our Lord;
though in the Vision of St. John, white robes are given to the redeemed,
and the four-and-twenty elders stand clothed in white before the great
white throne, and the Holy One that sitteth there white like wool; yet
for all these accumulated associations, with whatever is sweet, and honorable, and sublime, there yet lurks an elusive something in the inner-

most idea of this hue, which strikes more of panic to the soul than that redness which affrights in blood.

This elusive quality it is, which causes the thought of whiteness, when divorced from more kindly associations, and coupled with any object terrible in itself, to heighten that terror to the furthest bounds. Witness the white bear of the poles, and the white shark of the tropics; what but their smooth, flaky whiteness makes them the transcendent horrors they are? That ghastly whiteness it is which imparts such an abhorrent mildness, even more loathsome than terrific, to the dumb gloating of their aspect. So that not the fierce-fanged tiger in his heraldic coat can so stagger courage as the white-shrouded bear or shark.[1]

Bethink thee of the albatross: whence come those clouds of spiritual wonderment and pale dread, in which that white phantom sails in all imaginations? Not Coleridge first threw that spell; but God's great, unflattering laureate, Nature.[2]

---

[1]With reference to the Polar bear, it may possibly be urged by him who would fain go still deeper into this matter, that it is not the whiteness, separately regarded, which heightens the intolerable hideousness of that brute; for, analysed, that heightened hideousness, it might be said, only arises from the circumstance, that the irresponsible ferociousness of the creature stands invested in the fleece of celestial innocence and love; and hence, by bringing together two such opposite emotions in our minds, the Polar bear frightens us with so unnatural a contrast. But even assuming all this to be true; yet, were it not for the whiteness, you would not have that intensified terror.

As for the white shark, the white gliding ghostliness of repose in that creature, when beheld in his ordinary moods, strangely tallies with the same quality in the Polar quadruped. This peculiarity is most vividly hit by the French in the name they bestow upon that fish. The Romish mass for the dead begins with "Requiem eternam" (eternal rest), whence *Requiem* denominating the mass itself, and any other funereal music. Now, in allusion to the white, silent stillness of death in this shark, and the mild deadliness of his habits, the French call him *Requin*.

[2]I remember the first albatross I ever saw. It was during a prolonged gale, in waters hard upon the Antarctic seas. From my forenoon watch below, I ascended to the overclouded deck; and there, dashed upon the main hatches, I saw a regal, feathery thing of unspotted whiteness, and with a hooked, Roman bill sublime. At intervals, it arched forth its vast archangel wings, as if to embrace some holy ark. Wondrous flutterings and throbbings shook it. Though bodily unharmed, it uttered cries, as some king's ghost in supernatural distress. Through its inexpressible, strange eyes, methought I peeped to secrets which took hold of God. As Abraham before the angels, I bowed myself; the white thing was so white, its wings so wide, and in those for ever exiled waters, I had lost the miserable warping memories of traditions and of towns. Long I gazed at that prodigy of plumage. I cannot tell, can only hint, the things that darted through me then. But at last I awoke; and turning, asked a sailor what bird was this. A goney, he replied. Goney! I never had heard that name before; is it conceivable that this glorious thing is utterly unknown to men ashore! never! But some time after, I learned that goney was some seaman's name for albatross. So that by no possibility could Coleridge's wild Rhyme have had aught to do with those mystical impressions which were mine, when I saw that bird upon our deck. For

Most famous in our Western annals and Indian traditions is that of the White Steed of the Prairies; a magnificent milk-white charger, large-eyed, small-headed, bluff-chested, and with the dignity of a thousand monarchs in his lofty, over-scorning carriage. He was the elected Xerxes of vast herds of wild horses, whose pastures in those days were only fenced by the Rocky Mountains and the Alleghanies. At their flaming head he westward trooped it like that chosen star which every evening leads on the hosts of light. The flashing cascade of his mane, the curving comet of his tail, invested him with housings more resplendent than gold and silver-beaters could have furnished him. A most imperial and arch-angelical apparition of that unfallen, western world, which to the eyes of the old trappers and hunters revived the glories of those primeval times when Adam walked majestic as a god, bluff-browed and fearless as this mighty steed. Whether marching amid his aides and marshals in the van of countless cohorts that endlessly streamed it over the plains, like an Ohio; or whether with his circumambient subjects browsing all around at the horizon, the White Steed gallopingly reviewed them with warm nostrils reddening through his cool milkiness; in whatever aspect he presented himself, always to the bravest Indians he was the object of trembling reverence and awe. Nor can it be questioned from what stands on legendary record of this noble horse, that it was his spiritual whiteness chiefly, which so clothed him with divineness; and that this divineness had that in it which, though commanding worship, at the same time enforced a certain nameless terror.

But there are other instances where this whiteness loses all that accessory and strange glory which invests it in the White Steed and Albatross.

What is it that in the Albino man so peculiarly repels and often shocks the eye, as that sometimes he is loathed by his own kith and kin? It is that whiteness which invests him, a thing expressed by the name he bears. The Albino is as well made as other men—has no substantive deformity—and yet this mere aspect of all-pervading whiteness makes

---

neither had I then read the Rhyme, nor knew the bird to be an albatross. Yet, in saying this, I do but indirectly burnish a little brighter the noble merit of the poem and the poet.

I assert, then, that in the wondrous bodily whiteness of the bird chiefly lurks the secret of the spell; a truth the more evinced in this, that by a solecism of terms there are birds called grey albatrosses; and these I have frequently seen, but never with such emotions as when I beheld the Antarctic fowl.

But how had the mystic thing been caught? Whisper it not, and I will tell; with a treacherous hook and line, as the fowl floated on the sea. At last the Captain made a postman of it; tying a lettered, leathern tally round its neck, with the ship's time and place; and then letting it escape. But I doubt not, that leathern tally, meant for man, was taken off in Heaven, when the white fowl flew to join the wing-folding, the invoking, and adoring cherubim! [Melville's notes]

him more strangely hideous than the ugliest abortion. Why should this be so?

Nor, in quite other aspects, does Nature in her least palpable but not the less malicious agencies, fail to enlist among her forces this crowning attribute of the terrible. From its snowy aspect, the gauntleted ghost of the Southern Seas has been denominated the White Squall. Nor, in some historic instances, has the art of human malice omitted so potent an auxiliary. How wildly it heightens the effect of that passage in Froissart, when, masked in the snowy symbol of their faction, the desperate White Hoods of Ghent murder their bailiff in the market-place!

Nor, in some things, does the common, hereditary experience of all mankind fail to bear witness to the supernaturalism of this hue. It cannot well be doubted, that the one visible quality in the aspect of the dead which most appals the gazer, is the marble pallor lingering there; as if indeed that pallor were as much the badge of consternation in the other world, as of mortal trepidation here. And from that pallor of the dead, we borrow the expressive hue of the shroud in which we wrap them. Nor even in our superstitions do we fail to throw the same snowy mantle round our phantoms; all ghosts rising in a milk-white fog—Yea, while these terrors seize us, let us add, that even the king of terrors, when personified by the evangelist, rides on his pallid horse.

Therefore, in his other moods, symbolize whatever grand or gracious thing he will by whiteness, no man can deny that in its profoundest idealized significance it calls up a peculiar apparition to the soul.

But though without dissent this point be fixed, how is mortal man to account for it? To analyse it, would seem impossible. Can we, then, by the citation of some of those instances wherein this thing of whiteness— though for the time either wholly or in great part stripped of all direct associations calculated to impart to it aught fearful, but, nevertheless, is found to exert over us the same sorcery, however modified;—can we thus hope to light upon some chance clue to conduct us to the hidden cause we seek?

Let us try. But in a matter like this, subtlety appeals to subtlety, and without imagination no man can follow another into these halls. And though, doubtless, some at least of the imaginative impressions about to be presented may have been shared by most men, yet few perhaps were entirely conscious of them at the time, and therefore may not be able to recall them now.

Why to the man of untutored ideality, who happens to be but loosely acquainted with the peculiar character of the day, does the bare mention of Whitsuntide marshal in the fancy such long, dreary, speechless processions of slow-pacing pilgrims, down-cast and hooded with new-fallen snow? Or, to the unread, unsophisticated Protestant of the Middle American States, why does the passing mention of a White Friar or a White Nun, evoke such an eyeless statue in the soul?

Or what is there apart from the traditions of dungeoned warriors and kings (which will not wholly account for it) that makes the White Tower of London tell so much more strongly on the imagination of an untravelled American, than those other storied structures, its neighbors— the Byward Tower, or even the Bloody? And those sublimer towers, the White Mountains of New Hampshire, whence, in peculiar moods, comes that gigantic ghostliness over the soul at the bare mention of that name, while the thought of Virginia's Blue Ridge is full of a soft, dewy, distant dreaminess? Or why, irrespective of all latitudes and longitudes, does the name of the White Sea exert such a spectralness over the fancy, while that of the Yellow Sea lulls us with mortal thoughts of long lacquered mild afternoons on the waves, followed by the gaudiest and yet sleepiest of sunsets? Or, to choose a wholly unsubstantial instance, purely addressed to the fancy, why, in reading the old fairy tales of Central Europe, does "the tall pale man" of the Hartz forests, whose changeless pallor unrustlingly glides through the green of the groves— why is this phantom more terrible than all the whooping imps of the Blocksburg?

Nor is it, altogether, the remembrance of her cathedral-toppling earthquakes; nor the stampedoes of her frantic seas; nor the tearlessness of arid skies that never rain; nor the sight of her wide field of leaning spires, wrenched cope-stones, and crosses all adroop (like canted yards of anchored fleets); and her suburban avenues of house-walls lying over upon each other, as a tossed pack of cards;—it is not these things alone which make tearless Lima, the strangest, saddest city thou can'st see. For Lima has taken the white veil; and there is a higher horror in this whiteness of her woe. Old as Pizarro, this whiteness keeps her ruins for ever new; admits not the cheerful greenness of complete decay; spreads over her broken ramparts the rigid pallor of an apoplexy that fixes its own distortions.

I know that, to the common apprehension, this phenomenon of whiteness is not confessed to be the prime agent in exaggerating the terror of objects otherwise terrible; nor to the unimaginative mind is there aught of terror in those appearances whose awfulness to another mind almost solely consists in this one phenomenon, especially when exhibited under any form at all approaching to muteness or universality. What I mean by these two statements may perhaps be respectively elucidated by the following examples.

First: The mariner, when drawing nigh the coasts of foreign lands, if by night he hear the roar of breakers, starts to vigilance, and feels just enough of trepidation to sharpen all his faculties; but under precisely similar circumstances, let him be called from his hammock to view his ship sailing through a midnight sea of milky whiteness—as if from encircling headlands shoals of combed white bears were swimming round him, then he feels a silent, superstitious dread; the shrouded phantom of the whitened waters is horrible to him as a real ghost; in vain the lead assures him he is still off soundings; heart and helm they both go down; he never rests till blue water is under him again. Yet where is the mariner who will tell thee, "Sir, it was not so much the fear of striking hidden rocks, as the fear of that hideous whiteness that so stirred me?"

Second: To the native Indian of Peru, the continual sight of the snow-howdahed Andes conveys naught of dread, except, perhaps, in the mere fancying of the eternal frosted desolateness reigning at such vast altitudes, and the natural conceit of what a fearfulness it would be to lose oneself in such inhuman solitudes. Much the same is it with the backwoodsman of the West, who with comparative indifference views an unbounded prairie sheeted with driven snow, no shadow of tree or twig to break the fixed trance of whiteness. Not so the sailor, beholding the scenery of the Antarctic seas; where at times, by some infernal trick of legerdemain in the powers of frost and air, he, shivering and half shipwrecked, instead of rainbows speaking hope and solace to his misery, views what seems a boundless church-yard grinning upon him with its lean ice monuments and splintered crosses.

But thou sayest, methinks this white-lead chapter about whiteness is but a white flag hung out from a craven soul; thou surrenderest to a hypo, Ishmael.

Tell me, why this strong young colt, foaled in some peaceful valley of Vermont, far removed from all beasts of prey—why is it that upon the sunniest day, if you but shake a fresh buffalo robe behind him, so that he cannot even see it, but only smells its wild animal muskiness—why will he start, snort, and with bursting eyes paw the ground in phrensies of affright? There is no remembrance in him of any gorings of wild creatures in his green northern home, so that the strange muskiness he smells cannot recall to him anything associated with the experience of former perils; for what knows he, this New England colt, of the black bisons of distant Oregon?

No: but here thou beholdest even in a dumb brute, the instinct of the knowledge of the demonism in the world. Though thousands of miles from Oregon, still when he smells that savage musk, the rending, goring bison herds are as present as to the deserted wild foal of the prairies, which this instant they may be trampling into dust.

Thus, then; the muffled rollings of a milky sea; the bleak rustlings of the festooned frosts of mountains; the desolate shiftings of the windrowed snows of prairies; all these, to Ishmael, are as the shaking of that buffalo robe to the frightened colt!

Though neither knows where lie the nameless things of which the mystic sign gives forth such hints; yet with me, as with the colt, somewhere those things must exist. Though in many of its aspects this visible world seems formed in love, the invisible spheres were formed in fright.

But not yet have we solved the incantation of this whiteness, and learned why it appeals with such power to the soul; and more strange and far more portentous—why, as we have seen, it is at once the most meaning symbol of spiritual things, nay, the very veil of the Christian's Deity; and yet should be as it is, the intensifying agent in things the most appalling to mankind.

Is it that by its indefiniteness it shadows forth the heartless voids and immensities of the universe, and thus stabs us from behind with the thought of annihilation, when beholding the white depths of the milky way? Or is it, that as in essence whiteness is not so much a color as the visible absence of color, and at the same time the concrete of all colors; is it for these reasons that there is such a dumb blankness, full of meaning, in a wide landscape of snows—a colorless, all-color of atheism from which we shrink? And when we consider that other theory of the natural philosophers, that all other earthly hues—every stately or lovely emblazoning—the sweet tinges of sunset skies and woods; yea, and the gilded velvets of butterflies, and the butterfly cheeks of young girls; all these are but subtile deceits, not actually inherent in substances, but only laid on from without; so that all deified Nature absolutely paints like the harlot, whose allurements cover nothing but the charnel-house within; and when we proceed further, and consider that the mystical cosmetic which produces every one of her hues, the great principle of light, for ever remains white or colorless in itself, and if operating without medium upon matter, would touch all objects, even tulips and roses, with its own blank tinge—pondering all this, the palsied universe lies before us a leper; and like wilful travellers in Lapland, who refuse to wear colored and coloring glasses upon their eyes, so the wretched infidel gazes himself blind at the monumental white shroud that wraps all the prospect around him. And of all these things the Albino whale was the symbol. Wonder ye then at the fiery hunt?

THE SPERM WHALE'S HEAD—CONTRASTED VIEW

Here, now, are two great whales, laying their heads together; let us join them, and lay together our own.

Of the grand order of folio leviathans, the Sperm Whale and the

Right Whale are by far the most noteworthy. They are the only whales regularly hunted by man. To the Nantucketer, they present the two extremes of all the known varieties of the whale. As the external difference between them is mainly observable in their heads; and as a head of each is this moment hanging from the Pequod's side; and as we may freely go from one to the other, by merely stepping across the deck:—where, I should like to know, will you obtain a better chance to study practical cetology than here?

In the first place, you are struck by the general contrast between these heads. Both are massive enough in all conscience; but there is a certain mathematical symmetry in the Sperm Whale's which the Right Whale's sadly lacks. There is more character in the Sperm Whale's head. As you behold it, you involuntarily yield the immense superiority to him, in point of pervading dignity. In the present instance, too, this dignity is heightened by the pepper and salt color of his head at the summit, giving token of advanced age and large experience. In short, he is what the fishermen technically call a "greyheaded whale."

Let us now note what is least dissimilar in these heads—namely, the two most important organs, the eye and the ear. Far back on the side of the head, and low down, near the angle of either whale's jaw, if you narrowly search, you will at last see a lashless eye, which you would fancy to be a young colt's eye; so out of all proportion is it to the magnitude of the head.

Now, from this peculiar sideway position of the whale's eyes, it is plain that he can never see an object which is exactly ahead, no more than he can one exactly astern. In a word, the position of the whale's eyes corresponds to that of a man's ears; and you may fancy, for yourself, how it would fare with you, did you sideways survey objects through your ears. You would find that you could only command some thirty degrees of vision in advance of the straight side-line of sight; and about thirty more behind it. If your bitterest foe were walking straight towards you, with dagger uplifted in broad day, you would not be able to see him, any more than if he were stealing upon you from behind. In a word, you would have two backs, so to speak; but, at the same time, also, two fronts (side fronts): for what is it that makes the front of a man—what, indeed, but his eyes?

Moreover, while in most other animals that I can now think of, the eyes are so planted as imperceptibly to blend their visual power, so as to produce one picture and not two to the brain; the peculiar position of the whale's eyes, effectually divided as they are by many cubic feet of solid head, which towers between them like a great mountain separating two lakes in valleys; this, of course, must wholly separate the impressions which each independent organ imparts. The whale, therefore, must see one distinct picture on this side, and another distinct picture on that side; while all between must be profound darkness and nothingness to him. Man may, in effect, be said to look out on the world from a sentry-box with two joined sashes for his window. But with the whale, these two sashes are separately inserted, making two distinct windows, but sadly impairing the view. This peculiarity of the whale's eyes is a thing always to be borne in mind in the fishery; and to be remembered by the reader in some subsequent scenes.

A curious and most puzzling question might be started concerning this visual matter as touching the Leviathan. But I must be content with a hint. So long as a man's eyes are open in the light, the act of seeing is involuntary; that is, he cannot then help mechanically seeing whatever objects are before him. Nevertheless, any one's experience will teach him, that though he can take in an undiscriminating sweep of things at one glance, it is quite impossible for him, attentively, and completely, to examine any two things—however large or however small—at one and the same instant of time; never mind if they lie side by side and touch each other. But if you now come to separate these two objects, and surround each by a circle of profound darkness; then, in order to see one of them, in such a manner as to bring your mind to bear on it, the other will be utterly excluded from your contemporary consciousness. How is it, then, with the whale? True, both his eyes, in themselves, must simultaneously act; but is his brain so much more comprehensive, combining, and subtle than man's, that he can at the same moment of time attentively examine two distinct prospects, one on one side of him, and the other in an exactly opposite direction? If he can, then is it as marvellous a thing in him, as if a man were able simultaneously to go through the demonstrations of two distinct problems in Euclid. Nor, strictly investigated, is there any incongruity in this comparison.

It may be but an idle whim, but it has always seemed to me, that the extraordinary vacillations of movement displayed by some whales when beset by three or four boats; the timidity and liability to queer frights, so common to such whales; I think that all this indirectly proceeds from the helpless perplexity of volition, in which their divided and diametrically opposite powers of vision must involve them.

But the ear of the whale is full as curious as the eye. If you are an entire stranger to their race, you might hunt over these two heads for hours, and never discover that organ. The ear has no external leaf whatever; and into the hole itself you can hardly insert a quill, so wondrously minute is it. It is lodged a little behind the eye. With respect to their ears, this important difference is to be observed between the sperm

whale and the right. While the ear of the former has an external opening, that of the latter is entirely and evenly covered over with a membrane, so as to be quite imperceptible from without.

Is it not curious, that so vast a being as the whale should see the world
through so small an eye, and hear the thunder through an ear which is
smaller than a hare's? But if his eyes were broad as the lens of Herschel's
great telescope; and his ears capacious as the porches of cathedrals;
would that make him any longer of sight, or sharper of hearing? Not at
all.—Why then do you try to "enlarge" your mind? Subtilize it.

Let us now with whatever levers and steam-engines we have at hand,
cant over the sperm whale's head, so that it may lie bottom up; then,
ascending by a ladder to the summit, have a peep down the mouth; and
were it not that the body is now completely separated from it, with a
lantern we might descend into the great Kentucky Mammoth Cave of
his stomach. But let us hold on here by this tooth, and look about us
where we are. What a really beautiful and chaste-looking mouth! from
floor to ceiling, lined, or rather papered with a glistening white membrane, glossy as bridal satins.

But come out now, and look at this portentous lower jaw, which seems
like the long narrow lid of an immense snuff-box, with the hinge at one
end, instead of one side. If you pry it up, so as to get it overhead, and
expose its rows of teeth, it seems a terrific portcullis; and such, alas! it
proves to many a poor wight in the fishery, upon whom these spikes fall
with impaling force. But far more terrible is it to behold, when fathoms
down in the sea, you see some sulky whale, floating there suspended,
with his prodigious jaw, some fifteen feet long, hanging straight down at
right-angles with his body, for all the world like a ship's jib-boom. This
whale is not dead; he is only dispirited; out of sorts, perhaps; hypochon-
driac; and so supine, that the hinges of his jaw have relaxed, leaving him
there in that ungainly sort of plight, a reproach to all his tribe, who must,
no doubt, imprecate lock-jaws upon him.

In most cases this lower jaw—being easily unhinged by a practised
artist—is disengaged and hoisted on deck for the purpose of extracting
the ivory teeth, and furnishing a supply of that hard white whalebone
with which the fishermen fashion all sorts of curious articles, including
canes, umbrella-stocks, and handles to riding-whips.

With a long, weary hoist the jaw is dragged on board, as if it were an
anchor; and when the proper time comes—some few days after the other
work—Queequeg, Daggoo, and Tashtego, being all accomplished den-
tists, are set to drawing teeth. With a keen cutting-spade, Queequeg
lances the gums; then the jaw is lashed down to ringbolts, and a tackle
being rigged from aloft, they drag out these teeth, as Michigan oxen drag

stumps of old oaks out of wild wood-lands. There are generally forty-two teeth in all; in old whales, much worn down, but undecayed; nor filled after our artificial fashion. The jaw is afterwards sawn into slabs, and piled away like joists for building houses.

THE RIGHT WHALE'S HEAD—CONTRASTED VIEW

Crossing the deck, let us now have a good long look at the Right Whale's head.

As in general shape the noble Sperm Whale's head may be compared to a Roman war-chariot (especially in front, where it is so broadly rounded); so, at a broad view, the Right Whale's head bears a rather inelegant resemblance to a gigantic galliot-toed shoe. Two hundred years ago an old Dutch voyager likened its shape to that of a shoemaker's last. And in this same last or shoe, that old woman of the nursery tale, with the swarming brood, might very comfortably be lodged, she and all her progeny.

But as you come nearer to this great head it begins to assume different aspects, according to your point of view. If you stand on its summit and look at these two *f*-shaped spout-holes, you would take the whole head for an enormous bass-viol, and these spiracles, the apertures in its sounding-board. Then, again, if you fix your eye upon this strange, crested, comb-like incrustation on the top of the mass—this green, barnacled thing, which the Greenlanders call the "crown," and the Southern fishers the "bonnet" of the Right Whale; fixing your eyes solely on this, you would take the head for the trunk of some huge oak, with a bird's nest in its crotch. At any rate, when you watch those live crabs that nestle here on this bonnet, such an idea will be almost sure to occur to you; unless, indeed, your fancy has been fixed by the technical term "crown" also bestowed upon it; in which case you will take great interest in thinking how this mighty monster is actually a diademed king of the sea, whose green crown has been put together for him in this marvellous manner. But if this whale be a king, he is a very sulky looking fellow to grace a diadem. Look at that hanging lower lip! what a huge sulk and pout is there! a sulk and pout, by carpenter's measurement, about twenty feet long and five feet deep; a sulk and pout that will yield you some 500 gallons of oil and more.

A great pity, now, that this unfortunate whale should be hare-lipped. The fissure is about a foot across. Probably the mother during an important interval was sailing down the Peruvian coast, when earthquakes caused the beach to gape. Over this lip, as over a slippery threshold, we now slide into the mouth. Upon my word were I at Mackinaw, I should take this to be the inside of an Indian wigwam. Good Lord! is this the road that Jonah went? The roof is about twelve feet high, and runs to a pretty sharp angle, as if there were a regular ridge-pole there; while these ribbed, arched, hairy sides, present us with those wondrous, half vertical, scimetar-shaped slats of whalebone, say three hundred on a side, which depending from the upper part of the head or crown bone, form those Venetian blinds which have elsewhere been cursorily mentioned. The edges of these bones are fringed with hairy fibres, through which the Right Whale strains the water, and in whose intricacies he retains the small fish, when open-mouthed he goes through the seas of brit in feeding time. In the central blinds of bone, as they stand in their natural order, there are certain curious marks, curves, hollows, and ridges, whereby some whalemen calculate the creature's age, as the age of an oak by its circular rings. Though the certainty of this criterion is far from demonstrable, yet it has the savor of analogical probability. At any rate, if we yield to it, we must grant a far greater age to the Right Whale than at first glance will seem reasonable.

In old times, there seem to have prevailed the most curious fancies concerning these blinds. One voyager in Purchas calls them the wondrous "whiskers" inside of the whale's mouth;[1] another, "hogs' bristles;" a third old gentleman in Hackluyt uses the following elegant language: "There are about two hundred and fifty fins growing on each side of his upper *chop*, which arch over his tongue on each side of his mouth."

As every one knows, these same "hogs' bristles," "fins," "whiskers," "blinds," or whatever you please, furnish to the ladies their busks and other stiffening contrivances. But in this particular, the demand has long been on the decline. It was in Queen Anne's time that the bone was in its glory, the farthingale being then all the fashion. And as those ancient dames moved about gaily, though in the jaws of the whale, as you may say; even so, in a shower, with the like thoughtlessness, do we nowadays fly under the same jaws for protection; the umbrella being a tent spread over the same bone.

But now forget all about blinds and whiskers for a moment, and, standing in the Right Whale's mouth, look around you afresh. Seeing all these colonnades of bone so methodically ranged about, would you not think you were inside of the great Haarlem organ, and gazing upon its thousand pipes? For a carpet to the organ we have a rug of the softest

---

[1]This reminds us that the Right Whale really has a sort of whisker, or rather a moustache, consisting of a few scattered white hairs on the upper part of the outer end of the lower jaw. Sometimes these tufts impart a rather brigandish expression to his otherwise solemn countenance. [Melville's note]

Turkey—the tongue, which is glued, as it were, to the floor of the mouth. It is very fat and tender, and apt to tear in pieces in hoisting it on deck. This particular tongue now before us; at a passing glance I should say it was a six-barreler; that is, it will yield you about that amount of oil.

Ere this, you must have plainly seen the truth of what I started with—that the Sperm Whale and the Right Whale have almost entirely different heads. To sum up, then: in the Right Whale's there is no great well of sperm; no ivory teeth at all; no long, slender mandible of a lower jaw, like the Sperm Whale's. Nor in the Sperm Whale are there any of those blinds of bone; no huge lower lip; and scarcely anything of a tongue. Again, the Right Whale has two external spout-holes, the Sperm Whale only one.

Look your last, now, on these venerable hooded heads, while they yet lie together; for one will soon sink, unrecorded, in the sea; the other will not be very long in following.

Can you catch the expression of the Sperm Whale's there? It is the same he died with, only some of the longer wrinkles in the forehead seem now faded away. I think his broad brow to be full of a prairie-like placidity, born of a speculative indifference as to death. But mark the other head's expression. See that amazing lower lip, pressed by accident against the vessel's side, so as firmly to embrace the jaw. Does not this whole head seem to speak of an enormous practical resolution in facing death? This Right Whale I take to have been a Stoic; the Sperm Whale, a Platonian, who might have taken up Spinoza in his latter years.

THE GRAND ARMADA

*   *   * Broad on both bows, at the distance of some two or three miles, and forming a great semicircle, embracing one half of the level horizon, a continuous chain of whale-jets were upplaying and sparkling in the noon-day air. Unlike the straight perpendicular twin-jets of the Right Whale, which, dividing at top, fall over in two branches, like the cleft drooping boughs of a willow, the single forward-slanting spout of the Sperm Whale presents a thick curled bush of white mist, continually rising and falling away to leeward.

Seen from the Pequod's deck, then, as she would rise on a high hill of the sea, this host of vapory spouts, individually curling up into the air, and beheld through a blending atmosphere of bluish haze, showed like the thousand cheerful chimneys of some dense metropolis, descried of a balmy autumnal morning, by some horseman on a height.

As marching armies approaching an unfriendly defile in the mountains, accelerate their march, all eagerness to place that perilous passage in their rear, and once more expand in comparative security upon the plain; even so did this vast fleet of whales now seem hurrying forward through the straits; gradually contracting the wings of their semicircle, and swimming on, in one solid, but still crescentic centre.

Crowding all sail the Pequod pressed after them; the harpooneers handling their weapons, and loudly cheering from the heads of their yet suspended boats. If the wind only held, little doubt had they, that chased through these Straits of Sunda, the vast host would only deploy into the Oriental seas to witness the capture of not a few of their number. And who could tell whether, in that congregated caravan, Moby Dick himself might not temporarily be swimming, like the worshipped white-elephant in the coronation procession of the Siamese! So with stun-sail piled on stun-sail, we sailed along, driving these leviathans before us; when, of a sudden, the voice of Tashtego was heard, loudly directing attention to something in our wake.

Corresponding to the crescent in our van, we beheld another in our rear. It seemed formed of detached white vapors, rising and falling something like the spouts of the whales; only they did not so completely come and go; for they constantly hovered, without finally disappearing. Levelling his glass at this sight, Ahab quickly revolved in his pivot-hole, crying, "Aloft there, and rig whips and buckets to wet the sails;—Malays, sir, and after us!"

As if too long lurking behind the headlands, till the Pequod should fairly have entered the straits, these rascally Asiatics were now in hot pursuit, to make up for their over-cautious delay. But when the swift Pequod, with a fresh leading wind, was herself in hot chase; how very kind of these tawny philanthropists to assist in speeding her on to her own chosen pursuit,—mere riding-whips and rowels to her, that they were. As with glass under arm, Ahab to-and-fro paced the deck; in his forward turn beholding the monsters he chased, and in the after one the bloodthirsty pirates chasing *him;* some such fancy as the above seemed his. And when he glanced upon the green walls of the watery defile in which the ship was then sailing, and bethought him that through that gate lay the route to his vengeance, and beheld, how that through that same gate he was now both chasing and being chased to his deadly end; and not only that, but a herd of remorseless wild pirates and inhuman atheistical devils were infernally cheering him on with their curses;— when all these conceits had passed through his brain, Ahab's brow was left gaunt and ribbed, like the black sand beach after some stormy tide has been gnawing it, without being able to drag the firm thing from its place.

But thoughts like these troubled very few of the reckless crew; and

when, after steadily dropping and dropping the pirates astern, the Pequod at last shot by the vivid green Cockatoo Point on the Sumatra side,
emerging at last upon the broad waters beyond; then, the harpooneers
seemed more to grieve that the swift whales had been gaining upon the
ship, than to rejoice that the ship had so victoriously gained upon the
Malays. But still driving on in the wake of the whales, at length they
seemed abating their speed; gradually the ship neared them; and the
wind now dying away, word was passed to spring to the boats. But no
sooner did the herd, by some presumed wonderful instinct of the Sperm
Whale, become notified of the three keels that were after them,—
though as yet a mile in their rear,—than they rallied again, and forming
in close ranks and battalions, so that their spouts all looked like flashing
lines of stacked bayonets, moved on with redoubled velocity.

   Stripped to our shirts and drawers, we sprang to the white-ash, and
after several hours' pulling were almost disposed to renounce the chase,
when a general pausing commotion among the whales gave animating
token that they were now at last under the influence of that strange
perplexity of inert irresolution, which when the fishermen perceive it in
the whale, they say he is *gallied.* [1] The compact martial columns in
which they had been hitherto rapidly and steadily swimming, were now
broken up in one measureless rout; and like King Porus' elephants in the
Indian battle with Alexander, they seemed going mad with consternation. In all directions expanding in vast irregular circles, and aimlessly
swimming hither and thither, by their short thick spoutings, they plainly
betrayed their distraction of panic. This was still more strangely evinced
by those of their number, who, completely paralysed as it were, helplessly floated like water-logged dismantled ships on the sea. Had these
leviathans been but a flock of simple sheep, pursued over the pasture by
three fierce wolves, they could not possibly have evinced such excessive

---

[1]To *gally,* or *gallow,* is to frighten excessively,—to confound with fright. It is an old Saxon
word. It occurs once in Shakspere:—

>   "The wrathful skies
> *Gallow* the very wanderers of the dark,
> And make them keep their caves."
>   *Lear,* Act III. sc. ii.

   To common land usages, the word is now completely obsolete. When the polite landsman first hears it from the gaunt Nantucketer, he is apt to set it down as one of the
whaleman's self-derived savageries. Much the same is it with many other sinewy Saxonisms
of this sort, which emigrated to the New-England rocks with the noble brawn of the old
English emigrants in the time of the Commonwealth. Thus, some of the best and furthest-
descended English words—the etymological Howards and Percys—are now democratised,
nay, plebeianised—so to speak—in the New World. [Melville's note]

dismay. But this occasional timidity is characteristic of almost all herd-ing creatures. Though banding together in tens of thousands, the lion-maned buffaloes of the West have fled before a solitary horseman. Wit-ness, too, all human beings, how when herded together in the sheepfold of a theatre's pit, they will, at the slightest alarm of fire, rush helter-skelter for the outlets, crowding, trampling, jamming, and remorselessly dashing each other to death. Best, therefore, withhold any amazement at the strangely gallied whales before us, for there is no folly of the beasts of the earth which is not infinitely outdone by the madness of men.

Though many of the whales, as has been said, were in violent motion, yet it is to be observed that as a whole the herd neither advanced nor retreated, but collectively remained in one place. As is customary in those cases, the boats at once separated, each making for some one lone whale on the outskirts of the shoal. In about three minutes' time, Quee-queg's harpoon was flung; the stricken fish darted blinding spray in our faces, and then running away with us like light, steered straight for the heart of the herd. Though such a movement on the part of the whale struck under such circumstances, is in no wise unprecedented; and in-deed is almost always more or less anticipated; yet does it present one of the more perilous vicissitudes of the fishery. For as the swift monster drags you deeper and deeper into the frantic shoal, you bid adieu to circumspect life and only exist in a delirious throb.

As, blind and deaf, the whale plunged forward, as if by sheer power of speed to rid himself of the iron leech that had fastened to him; as we thus tore a white gash in the sea, on all sides menaced as we flew, by the crazed creatures to and fro rushing about us; our beset boat was like a ship mobbed by ice-isles in a tempest, and striving to steer through their complicated channels and straits, knowing not at what moment it may be locked in and crushed.

But not a bit daunted, Queequeg steered us manfully; now sheering off from this monster directly across our route in advance; now edging away from that, whose colossal flukes were suspended overhead, while all the time, Starbuck stood up in the bows, lance in hand, pricking out of our way whatever whales he could reach by short darts, for there was no time to make long ones. Nor were the oarsmen quite idle, though their wonted duty was now altogether dispensed with. They chiefly attended to the shouting part of the business. "Out of the way, Commodore!" cried one, to a great dromedary that of a sudden rose bodily to the surface, and for an instant threatened to swamp us. "Hard down with your tail, there!" cried a second to another, which, close to our gunwale, seemed calmly cooling himself with his own fan-like extremity.

All whaleboats carry certain curious contrivances, originally invented by the Nantucket Indians, called druggs. Two thick squares of wood of equal size are stoutly clenched together, so that they cross each other's grain at right angles; a line of considerable length is then attached to the middle of this block, and the other end of the line being looped, it can in a moment be fastened to a harpoon. It is chiefly among gallied whales that this drugg is used. For then, more whales are close round you than you can possibly chase at one time. But sperm whales are not every day encountered; while you may, then, you must kill all you can. And if you cannot kill them all at once, you must wing them, so that they can be afterwards killed at your leisure. Hence it is, that at times like these the drugg comes into requisition. Our boat was furnished with three of them. The first and second were successfully darted, and we saw the whales staggeringly running off, fettered by the enormous sidelong resistance of the towing drugg. They were cramped like malefactors with the chain and ball. But upon flinging the third, in the act of tossing overboard the clumsy wooden block, it caught under one of the seats of the boat, and in an instant tore it out and carried it away, dropping the oarsman in the boat's bottom as the seat slid from under him. On both sides the sea came in at the wounded planks, but we stuffed two or three drawers and shirts in, and so stopped the leaks for the time.

It had been next to impossible to dart these drugged-harpoons, were it not that as we advanced into the herd, our whale's way greatly diminished; moreover, that as we went still further and further from the circumference of commotion, the direful disorders seemed waning. So that when at last the jerking harpoon drew out, and the towing whale sideways vanished; then, with the tapering force of his parting momentum, we glided between two whales into the innermost heart of the shoal, as if from some mountain torrent we had slid into a serene valley lake. Here the storms in the roaring glens between the outermost whales, were heard but not felt. In this central expanse the sea presented that smooth satin-like surface, called a sleek, produced by the subtle moisture thrown off by the whale in his more quiet moods. Yes, we were now in that enchanted calm which they say lurks at the heart of every commotion. And still in the distracted distance we beheld the tumults of the outer concentric circles, and saw successive pods of whales, eight or ten in each, swiftly going round and round, like multiplied spans of horses in a ring; and so closely shoulder to shoulder, that a Titanic circus-rider might easily have overarched the middle ones, and so have gone round on their backs. Owing to the density of the crowd of reposing whales, more immediately surrounding the embayed axis of the herd, no possible chance of escape was at present afforded us. We must watch for a breach in the living wall that hemmed us in; the wall that had only admitted us in order to shut us up. Keeping at the centre of the lake, we were occasionally visited by small tame cows and calves; the women and children of this routed host.

Now, inclusive of the occasional wide intervals between the revolving outer circles, and inclusive of the spaces between the various pods in any one of those circles, the entire area at this juncture, embraced by the whole multitude, must have contained at least two or three square miles. At any rate—though indeed such a test at such a time might be deceptive—spoutings might be discovered from our low boat that seemed playing up almost from the rim of the horizon. I mention this circumstance, because, as if the cows and calves had been purposely locked up in this innermost fold; and as if the wide extent of the herd had hitherto prevented them from learning the precise cause of its stopping; or, possibly, being so young, unsophisticated, and every way innocent and inexperienced; however it may have been, these smaller whales—now and then visiting our becalmed boat from the margin of the lake—evinced a wondrous fearlessness and confidence, or else a still, becharmed panic which it was impossible not to marvel at. Like household dogs they came snuffling round us, right up to our gunwales, and touching them; till it almost seemed that some spell had suddenly domesticated them. Queequeg patted their foreheads; Starbuck scratched their backs with his lance; but fearful of the consequences, for the time refrained from darting it.

But far beneath this wondrous world upon the surface, another and still stranger world met our eyes as we gazed over the side. For, suspended in those watery vaults, floated the forms of the nursing mothers of the whales, and those that by their enormous girth seemed shortly to become mothers. The lake, as I have hinted, was to a considerable depth exceedingly transparent; and as human infants while suckling will calmly and fixedly gaze away from the breast, as if leading two different lives at the time; and while yet drawing mortal nourishment, be still spiritually feasting upon some unearthly reminiscence;—even so did the young of these whales seem looking up towards us, but not at us, as if we were but a bit of Gulf-weed in their new-born sight. Floating on their sides, the mothers also seemed quietly eyeing us. One of these little infants, that from certain queer tokens seemed hardly a day old, might have measured some fourteen feet in length, and some six feet in girth. He was a little frisky; though as yet his body seemed scarce yet recovered from that irksome position it had so lately occupied in the maternal reticule; where, tail to head, and all ready for the final spring, the unborn whale lies bent like a Tartar's bow. The delicate side-fins, and the palms of his flukes, still freshly retained the plaited crumpled appearance of a baby's ears newly arrived from foreign parts.

"Line! line!" cried Queequeg, looking over the gunwale; "him fast! him fast!—Who line him! Who struck?—Two whale; one big, one little!"

"What ails ye, man?" cried Starbuck.

"Look-e here," said Queequeg pointing down.

As when the stricken whale, that from the tub has reeled out hundreds of fathoms of rope; as, after deep sounding, he floats up again, and shows the slackened curling line buoyantly rising and spiralling towards the air; so now, Starbuck saw long coils of the umbilical cord of Madame Leviathan, by which the young cub seemed still tethered to its dam. Not seldom in the rapid vicissitudes of the chase, this natural line, with the maternal end loose, becomes entangled with the hempen one, so that the cub is thereby trapped. Some of the subtlest secrets of the seas seemed divulged to us in this enchanted pond. We saw young Leviathan amours in the deep.[2]

And thus, though surrounded by circle upon circle of consternations and affrights, did these inscrutable creatures at the centre freely and fearlessly indulge in all peaceful concernments; yea, serenely revelled in dalliance and delight. But even so, amid the tornadoed Atlantic of my being, do I myself still for ever centrally disport in mute calm; and while ponderous planets of unwaning woe revolve round me, deep down and deep inland there I still bathe me in eternal mildness of joy.

Meanwhile, as we thus lay entranced, the occasional sudden frantic spectacles in the distance evinced the activity of the other boats, still engaged in drugging the whales on the frontier of the host; or possibly carrying on the war within the first circle, where abundance of room and some convenient retreats were afforded them. But the sight of the enraged drugged whales now and then blindly darting to and fro across the circles, was nothing to what at last met our eyes. It is sometimes the custom when fast to a whale more than commonly powerful and alert, to seek to hamstring him, as it were, by sundering or maiming his gigantic tail-tendon. It is done by darting a short-handled cutting-spade, to which

[2]The sperm whale, as with all other species of the Leviathan, but unlike most other fish, breeds indifferently at all seasons; after a gestation which may probably be set down at nine months, producing but one at a time; though in some few known instances giving birth to an Esau and Jacob:—a contingency provided for in suckling by two teats, curiously situated, one on each side of the anus; but the breasts themselves extend upwards from that. When by chance these precious parts in a nursing whale are cut by the hunter's lance, the mother's pouring milk and blood rivallingly discolor the sea for rods. The milk is very sweet and rich; it has been tasted by man; it might do well with strawberries. When overflowing with mutual esteem, the whales salute *more hominum*. [Melville's note]

is attached a rope for hauling it back again. A whale wounded (as we afterwards learned) in this part, but not effectually, as it seemed, had broken away from the boat, carrying along with him half of the harpoon line; and in the extraordinary agony of the wound, he was now dashing among the revolving circles like the lone mounted desperado Arnold, at the battle of Saratoga, carrying dismay wherever he went.

But agonizing as was the wound of this whale, and an appalling spectacle enough, any way; yet the peculiar horror with which he seemed to inspire the rest of the herd, was owing to a cause which at first the intervening distance obscured from us. But at length we perceived that by one of the unimaginable accidents of the fishery, this whale had become entangled in the harpoon-line that he towed; he had also run away with the cutting spade in him; and while the free end of the rope attached to that weapon, had permanently caught in the coils of the harpoon-line round his tail, the cutting-spade itself had worked loose from his flesh. So that tormented to madness, he was now churning through the water, violently flailing with his flexible tail, and tossing the keen spade about him, wounding and murdering his own comrades.

This terrific object seemed to recall the whole herd from their stationary fright. First, the whales forming the margin of our lake began to crowd a little, and tumble against each other, as if lifted by half spent billows from afar; then the lake itself began faintly to heave and swell; the submarine bridal-chambers and nurseries vanished; in more and more contracting orbits the whales in the more central circles began to swim in thickening clusters. Yes, the long calm was departing. A low advancing hum was soon heard; and then like to the tumultuous masses of block-ice when the great river Hudson breaks up in Spring, the entire host of whales came tumbling upon their inner centre, as if to pile themselves up in one common mountain. Instantly Starbuck and Queequeg changed places; Starbuck taking the stern.

"Oars! Oars!" he intensely whispered, seizing the helm—"gripe your oars, and clutch your souls, now! My God, men, stand by! Shove him off, you Queequeg—the whale there!—prick him!—hit him! Stand up—stand up, and stay so! Spring, men—pull, men; never mind their backs—scrape them!—scrape away!"

The boat was now all but jammed between two vast black bulks, leaving a narrow Dardanelles between their long lengths. But by desperate endeavor we at last shot into a temporary opening; then giving way rapidly, and at the same time earnestly watching for another outlet. After many similar hair-breadth escapes, we at last swiftly glided into what had just been one of the outer circles, but now crossed by random whales, all violently making for one centre. This lucky salvation was cheaply purchased by the loss of Queequeg's hat, who, while standing in the bows to prick the fugitive whales, had his hat taken clean from his head by the air-eddy made by the sudden tossing of a pair of broad flukes close by.

Riotous and disordered as the universal commotion now was, it soon resolved itself into what seemed a systematic movement; for having clumped together at last in one dense body, they then renewed their onward flight with augmented fleetness. Further pursuit was useless; but the boats still lingered in their wake to pick up what drugged whales might be dropped astern, and likewise to secure one which Flask had killed and waifed. The waif is a pennoned pole, two or three of which are carried by every boat; and which, when additional game is at hand, are inserted upright into the floating body of a dead whale, both to mark its place on the sea, and also as token of prior possession, should the boats of any other ship draw near.

The result of this lowering was somewhat illustrative of that sagacious saying in the Fishery,—the more whales the less fish. Of all the drugged whales only one was captured. The rest contrived to escape for the time, but only to be taken, as will hereafter be seen, by some other craft than the Pequod.

JOHN RUSKIN
1819-1900

Ruskin's influence on the art and literature of nature was enormous. In his Modern Painters *(published in five volumes between 1843 and 1860) he emphasized that art must be true to nature, illustrating what such truth meant with examples that included the emotional immediacy of landscape in Wordsworth's poetry and the natural forms carved as decorations in Gothic architecture. Because Ruskin loved the Swiss Alps above all other places, his writing about mountainous scenery was particularly vivid. Echoes of the following excerpts from* Modern Painters *are audible in the language American explorer Clarence King used to de-*

scribe the Sierra in 1879. Ruskin was an art critic who intensified his readers' aesthetic response to the earth.

From MODERN PAINTERS

[the supreme beauty of mountains]

* * * Mountains are, to the rest of the body of the earth, what violent muscular action is to the body of man. The muscles and tendons of its anatomy are, in the mountain, brought out with fierce and convulsive energy, full of expression, passion, and strength; the plains and the lower hills are the repose and the effortless motion of the frame, when its muscles lie dormant and concealed beneath the lines of its beauty, yet ruling those lines in their every undulation. This, then, is the first grand principle of the truth of the earth. The spirit of the hills is action; that of the lowlands, repose; and between these there is to be found every variety of motion and of rest; from the inactive plain, sleeping like the firmament, with cities for stars, to the fiery peaks, which, with heaving bosoms and exulting limbs, with the clouds drifting like hair from their bright foreheads, lift up their Titan hands to Heaven, saying, "I live forever!"

But there is this difference between the action of the earth, and that of a living creature, that while the exerted limb marks its bones and tendons through the flesh, the excited earth casts off the flesh altogether, and its bones come out from beneath. Mountains are the bones of the earth, their highest peaks are invariably those parts of its anatomy which in the plains lie buried under five and twenty thousand feet of solid thickness of superincumbent soil, and which spring up in the mountain ranges in vast pyramids or wedges, flinging their garment of earth away from them on each side. The masses of the lower hills are laid over and against their sides, like the masses of lateral masonry against the skeleton arch of an unfinished bridge, except that they slope up to and lean against the central ridge: and finally, upon the slopes of these lower hills are strewed the level beds of sprinkled gravel, sand, and clay, which form the extent of the champaign. Here then is another grand principle of the truth of earth, that the mountains must come from under all, and be the support of all; and that everything also must be laid in their arms, heap above heap, the plains being the uppermost. Opposed to this truth is

Modern Painters of Truth and Theoretic Faculties (London: Smith, Elder and Company, in 5 volumes, 1846–1860).

every appearance of the hills being laid upon the plains, or built upon them. Nor is this a truth only of the earth on a large scale, for every minor rock (in position) comes out from the soil about it as an island out of the sea, lifting the earth near it like waves beating on its sides.

Such being the structure of the framework of the earth, it is next to be remembered that all soil whatsoever, wherever it is accumulated in greater quantity than is sufficient to nourish the moss of the wallflower, has been so, either by the direct transporting agency of water, or under the guiding influence and power of water. All plains capable of cultivation are deposits from some kind of water—some from swift and tremendous currents, leaving their soil in sweeping banks and furrowed ridges—others, and this is in mountain districts almost invariably the case, by slow deposit from a quiet lake in the mountain hollow, which has been gradually filled by the soil carried into it by the streams, which soil is of course finally left spread at the exact level of the surface of the former lake, as level as the quiet water itself. Hence we constantly meet with plains in hill districts, which fill the hollows of the hills with as perfect and faultless a level as water, and out of which the steep rocks rise at the edge with as little-previous disturbance, or indication of their forms beneath, as they do from the margin of a quiet lake. Every delta—and there is one at the head of every lake in every hill-district—supplies an instance of this. The rocks at Altorf plunge beneath the plain, which the lake has left, at as sharp an angle as they do into the lake itself beside the chapel of Tell. The plain of the Arve, at Sallenche, is terminated so sharply by the hills to the south-east, that I have seen a man sleeping with his back supported against the mountain, and his legs stretched on the plain; the slope which supported his back rising 5,000 feet above him, and the couch of his legs stretched for five miles before him. In distant effect these champaigns lie like deep, blue, undisturbed water, while the mighty hills around them burst out from beneath, raging and tossing like a tumultuous sea.

*   *   *

I find the increase in the calculable sum of elements of beauty to be steadily in proportion to the increase of mountainous character; and that the best image which the world can give of Paradise is in the slope of the meadows, orchards, and corn-fields on the sides of a great Alp, with its purple rocks and eternal snows above; this excellence not being in any wise a matter referable to feeling, or individual preferences, but demonstrable by calm enumeration of the number of lovely colours on the rocks, the varied grouping of the trees, and quantity of noble incidents in stream, crag, or cloud, presented to the eye at any given moment.

For consider, first, the difference produced in the whole tone of landscape colour by the introductions of purple, violet, and deep ultramarine blue, which we owe to mountains. In an ordinary lowland landscape we have the blue of the sky; the green of grass, which I will suppose (and this is an unnecessary concession to the lowlands) entirely fresh and bright; the green of trees; and certain elements of purple, far more rich and beautiful than we generally should think, in their bark and shadows (bare hedges and thickets, or tops of trees, in subdued afternoon sunshine, are nearly perfect purple, and of an exquisite tone), as well as in ploughed fields, and dark ground in general. But among mountains, in *addition* to all this, large unbroken spaces of pure violet and purple are introduced in their distances; and even near, by films of cloud passing over the darkness of ravines or forests, blues are produced of the most subtle tenderness; these azures and purples passing into rose-colour of otherwise wholly unattainable delicacy among the upper summits, the blue of the sky being at the same time purer and deeper than in the plains. Nay, in some sense, a person who has never seen the rose-colour of the rays of dawn crossing a blue mountain twelve or fifteen miles away, can hardly be said to know what *tenderness* in colour means at all; *bright* tenderness he may, indeed, see in the sky or in a flower, but this grave tenderness of the far-away hill-purples he cannot conceive.

Together with this great source of pre-eminence in *mass* of colour, we have to estimate the influence of the finished inlaying and enamel-work of the colour-jewelry on every stone; and that of the continual variety in species of flower; most of the mountain flowers being, besides, separately lovelier than the lowland ones. The wood hyacinth and wild rose are, indeed, the only *supreme* flowers that the lowlands can generally show; and the wild rose is also a mountaineer, and more fragrant in the hills, while the wood hyacinth, or grape hyacinth, at its best cannot match even the dark bell-gentian, leaving the light-blue star-gentian in its uncontested queenliness, and the Alpine rose and Highland heather wholly without similitude. The violet, lily of the valley, crocus, and wood anemone are, I suppose, claimable partly by the plains as well as the hills; but the large orange lily and narcissus I have never seen but on hill pastures, and the exquisite oxalis is pre-eminently a mountaineer.

To this supremacy in mosses and flowers we have next to add an inestimable gain in the continual presence and power of water. Neither in its clearness, its colour, its fantasy of motion, its calmness of space, depth, and reflection, or its wrath, can water be conceived by a lowlander, out of sight of sea. A sea wave is far grander than any torrent—but of the sea and its influences we are not now speaking; and the sea itself, though it *can* be clear, is never calm, among our shores, in the sense that a mountain lake can be calm. The sea seems only to pause; the mountain lake to sleep, and to dream. Out of sight of the ocean a lowlander cannot be considered ever to have seen water at all. The mantling of the pools in the rock shadows, with the golden flakes of light sinking down through them like falling leaves, the ringing of the thin currents among the shallows, the flash and the cloud of the cascade, the earthquake and foam-fire of the cataract, the long lines of alternate mirror and mist that lull the imagery of the hills reversed in the blue of morning,—all these things belong to those hills as their undivided inheritance.

To this supremacy in wave and stream is joined a no less manifest pre-eminence in the character of trees. It is possible among plains, in the species of trees which properly belong to them, the poplars of Amiens, for instance, to obtain a serene simplicity of grace, which, as I said, is a better help to the study of gracefulness, as such, than any of the wilder groupings of the hills; so also, there are certain conditions of symmetrical luxuriance developed in the park and avenue, rarely rivalled in their way among mountains; and yet the mountain superiority in foliage is, on the whole, nearly as complete as it is in water; for exactly as there are some expressions in the broad reaches of a navigable lowland river, such as the Loire or Thames, not, in their way, to be matched among the rock rivers, and yet for all that a lowlander cannot be said to have truly seen the element of water at all; so even in his richest parks and avenues he cannot be said to have truly seen trees. For the resources of trees are not developed until they have difficulty to contend with; neither their tenderness of brotherly love and harmony, till they are forced to choose their ways of various life where there is contracted room for them, talking to each other with their restrained branches. The various action of trees rooting themselves in inhospitable rocks, stooping to look into ravines, hiding from the search of glacier winds, reaching forth to the rays of rare sunshine, crowding down together to drink at sweetest streams, climbing hand in hand among the difficult slopes, opening in sudden dances round the mossy knolls, gathering into companies at rest among the fragrant fields, gliding in grave procession over the heavenward ridges,—nothing of this can be conceived among the unvexed and unvaried felicities of the lowland forest: while to all these direct sources of greater beauty are added, first the power of redundance,—the mere quantity of foliage visible in the folds and on the promontories of a single Alp being greater than that of an entire lowland landscape (unless a view from some cathedral tower); and to this charm of redundance, that of clearer *visibility*,—tree after tree being constantly shown in successive height, one behind another, instead of the mere tops and flanks of masses, as in the plains; and the forms of multitudes of them continually defined against the clear sky, near and above, or against white clouds entangled among their branches, instead of being confused in dimness of distance.

Finally, to this supremacy in foliage we have to add the still less questionable supremacy in clouds. There is no effect of sky possible in the lowlands which may not in equal perfection be seen among the hills; but there are effects by tens of thousands, forever invisible and inconceivable to the inhabitant of the plains, manifested among the hills in the course of one day. The mere power of familiarity with the clouds, of walking with them and above them, alters and renders clear our whole conception of the baseless architecture of the sky; and for the beauty of it, there is more in a single wreath of early cloud, pacing its way up an avenue of pines, or pausing among the points of their fringes, than in all the white heaps that fill the arched sky of the plains from one horizon to the other. And of the nobler cloud manifestations,—the breaking of their troublous seas against the crags, their black spray sparkling with lightning; or the going forth of the morning along their pavements of moving marble, level-laid between dome and dome of snow;—of these things there can be as little imagination or understanding in an inhabitant of the plains as of the scenery of another planet than his own.

And, observe, all these superiorities are matters plainly measurable and calculable, not in any wise to be referred to estimate of *sensation.* Of the grandeur or expression of the hills I have not spoken; how far they are great, or strong, or terrible, I do not for the moment consider, because vastness, and strength, and terror, are not to all minds subjects of desired contemplation. It may make no difference to some men whether a natural object be large or small, whether it be strong or feeble. But loveliness of colour, perfectness of form, endlessness of change, wonderfulness of structure, are precious to all undiseased human minds; and the superiority of the mountains in all these things to the lowland is, I repeat, as measurable as the richness of a painted window matched with a white one, or the wealth of a museum compared with that of a simply furnished chamber. They seem to have been built for the human race, as at once their schools and cathedrals; full of treasures of illuminated manuscript for the scholar, kindly in simple lessons to the worker, quiet in pale cloisters for the thinker, glorious in holiness for the worshipper. And of these great cathedrals of the earth, with their gates of rock, pavements of cloud, choirs of stream and stone, altars of snow, and vaults of purple traversed by the continual stars,—of these, as we have seen, it was written, not long ago, by one of the best of the poor human race for whom they were built, wondering in himself for whom their Creator *could* have made them, and thinking to have entirely discerned the Divine intent in them—"They are inhabited by the Beasts." * * *

WALT WHITMAN
1819-1892

In Leaves of Grass *(1855) Whitman threw open the windows of American poetry. His inclusiveness, registered both in an expansive sense of poetic line and in his enthusiastic cataloguing of persons and sensations, also served the nature writers' purpose, by bringing a wider range of life into our literature, into our consciousness. John Burroughs, one of the most influential nature writers of his generation, considered himself Whitman's protégé and disciple during their years together in Washington, D.C. The two often went on bird-watching and flower-viewing walks together. In the collection of Whitman's prose writings called* Specimen Days *(1882), he shows his alertness to the weather and the life of sky and fields, as well as to the varieties of human experience.*

From SPECIMEN DAYS AND COLLECT

THE WHITE HOUSE BY MOONLIGHT

FEBRUARY 24TH, 1863

A spell of fine soft weather. I wander about a good deal, sometimes at night under the moon. Tonight took a long look at the President's house. The white portico—the palacelike, tall, round columns, spotless as snow—the walls also—the tender and soft moonlight, flooding the pale marble, and making peculiar faint languishing shades, not shadows—everywhere a soft, transparent, hazy, thin, blue moon lace, hanging in

Specimen Days and Collect (Philadelphia: Rees Welsh, 1882).

the air—the brilliant and extra-plentiful clusters of gas, on and around the façade, columns, portico, etc.—everything so white, so marbly pure and dazzling, yet soft—the White House of future poems, and of dreams and dramas, there in the soft and copious moon—the gorgeous front, in the trees, under the lustrous flooding moon, full of reality, full of illusion—the forms of the trees, leafless, silent, in trunk and myriad angles of branches, under the stars and sky—the White House of the land, and of beauty and night—sentries at the gates, and by the portico, silent, pacing there in blue overcoats—stopping you not at all, but eyeing you with sharp eyes, whichever way you move.

A SILENT NIGHT RAMBLE

OCTOBER 20TH, 1863

Tonight, after leaving the hospital at 10 o'clock (I had been on self-imposed duty some five hours, pretty closely confined), I wandered a long time around Washington. The night was sweet, very clear, sufficiently cool, a voluptuous half-moon, slightly golden, the space near it of a transparent blue-gray tinge. I walked up Pennsylvania Avenue, and then to Seventh Street, and a long while around the Patent Office. Somehow it looked rebukefully strong, majestic, there in the delicate moonlight. The sky, the planets, the constellations all so bright, so calm, so expressively silent, so soothing, after those hospital scenes. I wandered to and fro till the moist moon set, long after midnight.

BIRDS MIGRATING AT MIDNIGHT

Did you ever chance to hear the midnight flight of birds passing through the air and darkness overhead, in countless armies, changing their early or late summer habitat? It is something not to be forgotten. A friend called me up just after 12 last night to mark the peculiar noise of unusually immense flocks migrating north (rather late this year). In the silence, shadow, and delicious odor of the hour (the natural perfume belonging to the night alone), I thought it rare music. You could *hear* the characteristic motion—once or twice "the rush of mighty wings," but oftener a velvety rustle, long drawn out—sometimes quite near— with continual calls and chirps, and some song notes. It all lasted from 12 till after 3. Once in a while the species was plainly distinguishable; I could make out the bobolink, tanager, Wilson's thrush, white-crowned sparrow, and occasionally from high in the air came the notes of the plover.

BUMBLEBEES

May-month—month of swarming, singing, mating birds—the bumblebee month—month of the flowering lilac (and then my own birth month). As I jot this paragraph, I am out just after sunrise, and down toward the creek. The lights, perfumes, melodies—the bluebirds, grassbirds, and robins, in every direction—the noisy, vocal, natural concert. For undertones, a neighboring woodpecker tapping his tree, and the distant clarion of chanticleer. Then the fresh earth smells—the colors, the delicate drabs and thin blues of the perspective. The bright green of the grass has received an added tinge from the last two days' mildness and moisture. How the sun silently mounts in the broad clear sky, on his day's journey! How the warm beams bathe all, and come streaming kissingly and almost hot on my face. A while since the croaking of the pond frogs and the first white of the dogwood blossoms. Now the golden dandelions in endless profusion, spotting the ground everywhere. The white cherry and pear blows—the wild violets, with their blue eyes looking up and saluting my feet, as I saunter the wood edge—the rosy blush of budding apple trees—the light-clear emerald hue of the wheatfields—the darker green of the rye—a warm elasticity pervading the air—the cedar bushes profusely decked with their little brown apples—the summer fully awakening—the convocation of black birds, garrulous flocks of them, gathering on some tree, and making the hour and place noisy as I sit near.

Later. Nature marches in procession, in sections, like the corps of an army. All have done much for me, and still do. But for the last two days it has been the great wild bee, the humblebee, or "bumble," as the children call him. As I walk, or hobble, from the farmhouse down to the creek, I traverse the before-mentioned lane, fenced by old rails, with many splits, splinters, breaks, holes, etc., the choice habitat of those crooning, hairy insects. Up and down and by and between these rails, they swarm and dart and fly in countless myriads. As I wend slowly along, I am often accompanied with a moving cloud of them. They play a leading part in my morning, mid-day, or sunset rambles, and often dominate the landscape in a way I never before thought of—fill the long lane, not by scores or hundreds only, but by thousands. Large and vivacious and swift, with wonderful momentum and a loud swelling perpetual hum, varied now and then by something almost like a shriek, they dart to and fro, in rapid flashes, chasing each other, and (little things as they are) conveying to me a new and pronounced sense of strength, beauty, vitality, and movement. Are they in their mating season? Or what is the meaning of this plentitude, swiftness, eagerness, display? As I walked, I thought I was followed by a particular swarm, but upon observation I saw that it was a rapid succession of changing swarms, one after another. As I write, I am seated under a big wild cherry tree—the warm day tempered by partial clouds and a fresh breeze, neither too heavy nor light—and here I sit long and long, enveloped in the deep musical drone of these bees, flitting, balancing, darting to and fro about me by hundreds—big fellows with light yellow jackets, great glistening swelling bodies, stumpy heads and gauzy wings—humming their perpetual rich mellow boom. (Is there not a hint in it for a musical composition, of which it should be the background? Some bumblebee symphony?) How it all nourishes, lulls me, in the way most needed; the open air, the rye fields, the apple orchards. The last two days have been faultless in sun, breeze, temperature, and everything; never two more perfect days, and I have enjoyed them wonderfully. My health is somewhat better, and my spirit at peace. (Yet the anniversary of the saddest loss and sorrow of my life is close at hand.) Another jotting, another perfect day: forenoon, from 7 to 9, two hours enveloped in sound of bumblebees and bird music. Down in the apple trees and in a neighboring cedar were three or four russet-backed thrushes, each singing his best, and roulading in ways I never heard surpassed. Two hours I abandon myself to hearing them, and indolently absorbing the scene. Almost every bird I notice has a special time in the year—sometimes limited to a few days—when it sings its best; and now is the period of these russet-backs. Meanwhile, up and down the lane, the darting, droning, musical bumblebees. A great swarm again for my entourage as I return home, moving along with me as before. As I write this, two or three weeks later, I am sitting near the brook under a tulip tree, 70 feet high, thick with the fresh verdure of its young maturity—a beautiful object—every branch, every leaf perfect. From top to bottom, seeking the sweet juice in the blossoms, it swarms with myriads of these wild bees, whose loud and steady humming makes an undertone to the whole, and to my mood and the hour. *   *   *

CEDAR APPLES

As I journeyed today in a light wagon ten or twelve miles through the country, nothing pleased me more, in their homely beauty and novelty (I had either never seen the little things to such advantage, or had never noticed them before) than that peculiar fruit, with its profuse clear-yellow dangles of inch-long silk or yarn, in boundless profusion spotting the dark-green cedar bushes—contrasting well with their bronze tufts—the flossy shreds covering the knobs all over, like a shock of wild hair on elfin pates. On my ramble afterward down by the creek I plucked one from its bush, and shall keep it. These cedar apples last only a little while, however, and soon crumble and fade.

A JULY AFTERNOON BY THE POND

The fervent heat, but so much more endurable in this pure air—the white and pink pond-blossoms, with great heart-shaped leaves; the glassy waters of the creek, the banks, with dense bushery, and the picturesque beeches and shade and turf; the tremulous, reedy call of some bird from recesses, breaking the warm, indolent, half-voluptuous silence; an occasional wasp, hornet, honey-bee or bumble (they hover near my hands or face, yet annoy me not, nor I them, as they appear to examine, find nothing, and away they go)—the vast space of the sky overhead so clear, and the buzzard up there sailing his slow whirl in majestic spirals and discs; just over the surface of the pond, two large slate-colored dragon-flies, with wings of lace, circling and darting and occasionally balancing themselves quite still, their wings quivering all the time (are they not showing off for my amusement?)—the pond itself, with the sword-shaped calamus; the water snakes—occasionally a flitting blackbird, with red dabs on his shoulders, as he darts slantingly by—the sounds that bring out the solitude, warmth, light, and shade—the quawk of some pond duck (the crickets and grasshoppers are mute in the noon heat, but I hear the song of the first cicadas)—then at some distance the rattle and whir of a reaping machine as the horses draw it on a rapid walk through a rye field on the opposite side of the creek (what was the yellow or light-brown bird, large as a young hen, with short neck and long-stretched legs I just saw, in flapping and awkward flight over there through the trees?)—the prevailing delicate, yet palpable, spicy, grassy, clovery perfume to my nostrils; and over all, encircling all, to my sight and soul, the free space of the sky, transparent and blue—and hovering there in the west, a mass of white-gray fleecy clouds the sailors call "shoals of mackerel"—the sky, with silver swirls like locks of tossed hair, spreading, expanding—a vast voiceless, formless simulacrum—yet maybe the most real reality and formulator of everything—who knows?

A WINTER DAY ON THE SEABEACH

One bright December midday lately I spent down on the New Jersey seashore, reaching it by a little more than an hour's railroad trip over the old Camden and Atlantic. I had started betimes, fortified by nice strong coffee and a good breakfast (cooked by the hands I love, my dear sister

Lou's—how much better it makes the victuals taste, and then assimilate, strengthen you, perhaps make the whole day comfortable afterward). Five or six miles at the last, our track entered a broad region of salt grass meadows, intersected by lagoons, and cut up everywhere by watery runs. The sedgy perfume, delightful to my nostrils, reminded me of "the mash" and South Bay of my native island. I could have journeyed contentedly till night through these flat and odorous sea prairies. From half-past 11 till 2 I was nearly all the time along the beach, or in sight of the ocean, listening to its hoarse murmur and inhaling the bracing and welcome breezes. First, a rapid five-mile drive over the hard sand—our carriage wheels hardly made dents in it. Then after dinner (as there was nearly two hours to spare) I walked off in another direction (hardly met or saw a person) and, taking possession of what appeared to have been the reception room of an old bathhouse range, had a broad expanse of view all to myself—quaint, refreshing, unimpeded—a dry area of sedge and Indian grass immediately before and around me—space, simple, unornamented space. Distant vessels, and the far-off, just visible trailing smoke of an inward-bound steamer; more plainly, ships, brigs, schooners, in sight, most of them with every sail set to the firm and steady wind. The attractions, fascinations there are in sea and shore! How one dwells on their simplicity, even vacuity! What is it in us, aroused by those indirections and directions? That spread of waves and gray-white beach, salt, monotonous, senseless—such an entire absence of art, books, talk, elegance—so indescribably comforting, even this winter day—grim, yet so delicate-looking, so spiritual—striking emotional, impalpable depths, subtler than all the poems, paintings, music I have ever read, seen, heard. (Yet let me be fair, perhaps it is because I have read those poems and heard that music.)

SEASHORE FANCIES

Even as a boy, I had the fancy, the wish, to write a piece, perhaps a poem, about the seashore—that suggesting, dividing line, contact, junction, the solid marrying the liquid—that curious, lurking something (as doubtless every objective form finally becomes to the subjective spirit) which means far more than its mere first sight, grand as that is—blending the real and ideal, and each made portion of the other. Hours, days, in my Long Island youth and early manhood, I haunted the shores of Rockaway or Coney Island, or away east to the Hamptons or Montauk. Once, at the latter place (by the old lighthouse, nothing but sea-tossings in sight in every direction as far as the eye could reach), I remember well, I felt that I must one day write a book expressing this liquid, mystic theme. Afterward, I recollect, how it came to me that instead of any special lyrical or epical or literary attempt, the seashore should be an invisible *influence,* a pervading gauge and tally for me, in my composition. (Let me give a hint here to young writers. I am not sure but I have unwittingly followed out the same rule with other powers besides sea and shores—avoiding them, in the way of any dead set at poetizing them, as too big for formal handling—quite satisfied if I could indirectly show that we have met and fused, even if only once, but enough—that we have really absorbed each other and understand each other.) There is a dream, a picture, that for years at intervals (sometimes quite long ones, but surely again, in time) has come noiselessly up before me, and I really believe, fiction as it is, has entered largely into my practical life—certainly into my writings, and shaped and colored them. It is nothing more or less than a stretch of interminable white-brown sand, hard and smooth and broad, with the ocean perpetually, grandly, rolling in upon it, with slow-measured sweep, with rustle and hiss and foam, and many a thump as of low bass drums. This scene, this picture, I say, has risen before me at times for years. Sometimes I wake at night and can hear and see it plainly.

THOUGHTS UNDER AN OAK—A DREAM

JUNE 2, 1878

This is the fourth day of a dark northeast storm, wind and rain. Day before yesterday was my birthday. I have now entered on my 60th year. Every day of the storm, protected by overshoes and a waterproof blanket, I regularly come down to the pond, and ensconce myself under the lee of the great oak; I am here now writing these lines. The dark smoke-colored clouds roll in furious silence athwart the sky; the soft green leaves dangle all round me; the wind steadily keeps up its hoarse, soothing music over my head—Nature's mighty whisper. Seated here in solitude I have been musing over my life—connecting events, dates, as links of a chain, neither sadly nor cheerily, but somehow, today here under the oak, in the rain, in an unusually matter-of-fact spirit. But my great oak—sturdy, vital, green—five feet thick at the butt: I sit a great deal near or under him. Then the tulip tree near by—the Apollo of the woods—tall and graceful, yet robust and sinewy, inimitable in hang of foliage and throwing-out of limb; as if the beauteous, vital, leafy creature could walk, if it only would. (I had a sort of dream-trance the other day, in which I saw my favorite trees step out and promenade up, down and around, very curiously—with a whisper from one, leaning down as he passed me, *"We do all this on the present occasion, exceptionally, just for you."*)

SWALLOWS ON THE RIVER

SEPT. 3, 1879

Cloudy and wet, and wind due east; air without palpable fog, but very heavy with moisture—welcome for a change. Forenoon, crossing the Delaware, I noticed unusual numbers of swallows in flight, circling, darting, graceful beyond description, close to the water. Thick, around the bows of the ferryboat as she lay tied in her slip, they flew; and as we went out I watched beyond the pierheads, and across the broad stream, their swift-winding loop-ribands of motion, down close to it, cutting and intersecting. Though I had seen swallows all my life, seemed as though I never before realized their peculiar beauty and character in the landscape. (Some time ago, for an hour, in a huge old country barn, watching these birds flying, recalled the 22d book of *The Odyssey,* where Ulysses slays the suitors, bringing things to *éclaircissement,* and Minerva, swallow-bodied, darts up through the spaces of the hall, sits high on a beam, looks complacently on the show of slaughter, and feels in her element, exulting, joyous.)

AMERICA'S CHARACTERISTIC LANDSCAPE

Speaking generally as to the capacity and sure future destiny of that plain and prairie area (larger than any European kingdom) it is the inexhaustible land of wheat, maize, wool, flax, coal, iron, beef and pork, butter and cheese, apples and grapes—land of ten million virgin farms— to the eye at present wild and unproductive—yet experts say that upon it when irrigated may easily be grown enough wheat to feed the world. Then as to scenery (giving my own thought and feeling), while I know the standard claim is that Yosemite, Niagara Falls, the upper Yellowstone and the like, afford the greatest natural shows, I am not so sure but the prairies and plains, while less stunning at first sight, last longer, fill the esthetic sense fuller, precede all the rest, and make North America's characteristic landscape. Indeed through the whole of this journey, with all its shows and varieties, what most impressed me, and will longest remain with me, are these same prairies. Day after day, and night after night, to my eyes, to all my senses—the esthetic one most of all—they silently and broadly unfolded. Even their simplest statistics are sublime.

BEETHOVEN'S SEPTET

FEB. 11, 1880

At a good concert tonight in the foyer of the Opera House, Philadelphia—the band a small but first-rate one. Never did music more sink into and soothe and fill me—never so prove its soul-rousing power, its impossibility of statement. Especially in the rendering of one of Beethoven's master septets by the well-chosen and perfectly combined instruments (violins, viola, clarionet, horn, 'cello, and contrabass) was I carried away, seeing, absorbing many wonders. Dainty abandon, sometimes as if Nature laughing on a hillside in the sunshine; serious and firm monotonies, as of winds; a horn sounding through the tangle of the forest, and the dying echoes; soothing floating of waves, but presently rising in surges, angrily lashing, muttering, heavy; piercing peals of laughter, for interstices; now and then weird, as Nature herself is in certain moods—but mainly spontaneous, easy, careless—often the sentiment of the postures of naked children playing or sleeping. It did me good even to watch the violinists drawing their bows so masterly—every motion a study. I allowed myself, as I sometimes do, to wander out of myself. The conceit came to me of a copious grove of singing birds, and in their midst a simple harmonic duo, two human souls, steadily asserting their own pensiveness, joyousness.

BIRDS—AND A CAUTION

MAY 14, 1888

Home again; down temporarily in the Jersey woods. Between 8 and 9 A.M. a full concert of birds, from different quarters, in keeping with the fresh scent, the peace, the naturalness all around me. I am lately noticing the russet-back, size of the robin or a trifle less, light breast and shoulders, with irregular dark stripes—tail long—sits hunched up by the hour these days, top of a tall bush, or some tree, singing blithely. I often get near and listen as he seems tame; I like to watch the working of his bill and throat, the quaint sidle of his body, and flex of his long tail. I hear the woodpecker, and night and early morning the shuttle of the whippoorwill—noons, the gurgle of thrush delicious, and *meo-o-ow* of the catbird. Many I cannot name; but I do not very particularly seek information. (You must not know too much, or be too precise or scientific about birds and trees and flowers and water craft; a certain free margin, and even vagueness—perhaps ignorance, credulity—helps your enjoyment of these things, and of the sentiment of feathered, wooded, river, or marine Nature generally. I repeat it—don't want to know too exactly, or the reasons why. My own notes have been written offhand in the latitude of middle New Jersey. Though they describe what I saw—what appeared to me—I dare say the expert ornithologist, botanist, or entomologist will detect more than one slip in them.)

JEAN HENRI FABRE
1823-1915

Born in St.-Léons, France, J. Henri Fabre was a self-educated entomologist who for many years taught at various lyceums and wrote popular science books. His significant writing, however, was done after 1879, when he retired to the small village of Sérignan in Provence to pursue his passion for insects. There, over the next three decades, he produced his ten-volume Souvenirs entomologiques, *a pioneering study of insect anatomy and behavior. At a time when most naturalists studied insects primarily from mounted specimens, Fabre went directly to nature, observing living subjects in both the field and laboratory. He had a genius for devising simple experiments which revealed basic patterns of behavior, and though he never accepted Darwinian theory, Darwin himself considered Fabre "the incomparable observer."*

What makes Fabre interesting as a writer is his unabashed emotional involvement in the behavior of his subjects. He is no cold, aloof observer, but a man who is at once fascinated and repelled by the gap between human values and reason and the blind, amoral strategies of instinct. His descriptions of how insects conduct their lives read at once as factual natural history and moral parables—but parables modern in their recognition that there are no parallels for human ethics in nature. In the English translations of Alexander Teixeira de Mattos, Fabre's books have enjoyed wide popularity, influencing such writers as Edwin Way Teale and Annie Dillard. In particular, the following description of the "conjugal atrocities" of praying mantises has gained considerable notori-

ety. Though subsequent studies of mantises indicate that such behavior does not occur in the wild, the appeal of this drama of observation remains undiminished.

From THE LIFE OF THE GRASSHOPPER

THE MANTIS: HER LOVE-MAKING

The little that we have seen of the Mantis' habits hardly tallies with what we might have expected from her popular name. To judge by the term *Prègo-Diéu*, we should look to see a placid insect, deep in pious contemplation; and we find ourselves in the presence of a cannibal, of a ferocious spectre munching the brain of a panic-stricken victim. Nor is even this the most tragic part. The Mantis has in store for us, in her relations with her own kith and kin, manners even more atrocious than those prevailing among the Spiders, who have an evil reputation in this respect.

To reduce the number of cages on my big table and give myself a little more space while still retaining a fair-sized menagerie, I install several females, sometimes as many as a dozen, under one cover. So far as accommodation is concerned, no fault can be found with the common lodging. There is room and to spare for the evolutions of my captives, who naturally do not want to move about much with their unwieldy bellies. Hanging to the trelliswork of the dome, motionless they digest their food or else await an unwary passer-by. Even so do they act when at liberty in the thickets.

Cohabitation has its dangers. I know that even Donkeys, those peace-loving animals, quarrel when hay is scarce in the manger. My boarders, who are less complaisant, might well, in a moment of dearth, become sour-tempered and fight among themselves. I guard against this by keeping the cages well supplied with Locusts, renewed twice a day. Should civil war break out, famine cannot be pleaded as the excuse.

At first, things go pretty well. The community lives in peace, each Mantis grabbing and eating whatever comes near her, without seeking strife with her neighbours. But this harmonious period does not last long. The bellies swell, the eggs are ripening in the ovaries, marriage and laying-time are at hand. Then a sort of jealous fury bursts out, though there is an entire absence of males who might be held responsible for

The Life of the Grasshopper (New York: Dodd, Mead, 1917).

feminine rivalry. The working of the ovaries seems to pervert the flock, inspiring its members with a mania for devouring one another. There are threats, personal encounters, cannibal feasts. Once more the spectral pose appears, the hissing of the wings, the fearsome gesture of the grapnels outstretched and uplifted in the air. No hostile demonstration in front of a Grey Locust or White-faced Decticus could be more menacing.

For no reason that I can gather, two neighbours suddenly assume their attitude of war. They turn their heads to right and left, provoking each other, exchanging insulting glances. The "Puff! Puff!" of the wings rubbed by the abdomen sounds the charge. When the duel is to be limited to the first scratch received, without more serious consequences, the lethal fore-arms, which are usually kept folded, open like the leaves of a book and fall back sideways, encircling the long bust. It is a superb pose, but less terrible than that adopted in a fight to the death.

Then one of the grapnels, with a sudden spring, shoots out to its full length and strikes the rival; it is no less abruptly withdrawn and resumes the defensive. The adversary hits back. The fencing is rather like that of two Cats boxing each other's ears. At the first blood drawn from her flabby paunch, or even before receiving the least wound, one of the duellists confesses herself beaten and retires. The other furls her battle-standard and goes off elsewhither to meditate the capture of a Locust, keeping apparently calm, but ever ready to repeat the quarrel.

Very often, events take a more tragic turn. At such times, the full posture of the duels to the death is assumed. The murderous fore-arms are unfolded and raised in the air. Woe to the vanquished! The other seizes her in her vice and then and there proceeds to eat her, beginning at the neck, of course. The loathsome feast takes place as calmly as though it were a matter of crunching up a Grasshopper. The diner enjoys her sister as she would a lawful dish; and those around do not protest, being quite willing to do as much on the first occasion.

Oh, what savagery! Why, even Wolves are said not to eat one another. The Mantis has no such scruples; she banquets off her fellows when there is plenty of her favourite game, the Locust, around her. She practices the equivalent of cannibalism, that hideous peculiarity of man.

These aberrations, these child-bed cravings can reach an even more revolting stage. Let us watch the pairing and, to avoid the disorder of a crowd, let us isolate the couples under different covers. Each pair shall have its own home, where none will come to disturb the wedding. And let us not forget the provisions, with which we will keep them well supplied, so that there may be no excuse of hunger.

It is near the end of August. The male, that slender swain, thinks the moment propitious. He makes eyes at his strapping companion; he turns his head in her direction; he bends his neck and throws out his chest. His little pointed face wears an almost impassioned expression. Motionless, in this posture, for a long time he contemplates the object of his desire. She does not stir, is as though indifferent. The lover, however, has caught a sign of acquiescence, a sign of which I do not know the secret. He goes nearer; suddenly he spreads his wings, which quiver with a convulsive tremor. That is his declaration. He rushes, small as he is, upon the back of his corpulent companion, clings on as best he can, steadies his hold. As a rule, the preliminaries last a long time. At last, coupling takes place and is also long drawn out, lasting sometimes for five or six hours.

Nothing worthy of attention happens between the two motionless partners. They end by separating, but only to unite again in a more intimate fashion. If the poor fellow is loved by his lady as the vivifier of her ovaries, he is also loved as a piece of highly-flavoured game. And, that same day, or at latest on the morrow, he is seized by his spouse, who first gnaws his neck, in accordance with precedent, and then eats him deliberately, by little mouthfuls, leaving only the wings. Here we have no longer a case of jealousy in the harem, but simply a depraved appetite.

I was curious to know what sort of reception a second male might expect from a recently fertilized female. The result of my enquiry was shocking. The Mantis, in many cases, is never sated with conjugal raptures and banquets. After a rest that varies in length, whether the eggs be laid or not, a second male is accepted and then devoured like the first. A third succeeds him, performs his function in life, is eaten and disappears. A fourth undergoes a like fate. In the course of two weeks I thus see one and the same Mantis use up seven males. She takes them all to her bosom and makes them all pay for the nuptial ecstasy with their lives.

Orgies such as this are frequent, in varying degrees, though there are exceptions. On very hot days, highly charged with electricity, they are almost the general rule. At such times the Mantes are in a very irritable mood. In the cages containing a large colony, the females devour one another more than ever; in the cages containing separate pairs, the males, after coupling, are more than ever treated as an ordinary prey.

I should like to be able to say, in mitigation of these conjugal atrocities, that the Mantis does not behave like this in a state of liberty; that the male, after doing his duty, has time to get out of the way, to make off, to escape from his terrible mistress, for in my cages he is given a respite, lasting sometimes until next day. What really occurs in the thickets I do not know, chance, a poor resource, having never instructed me concerning the love-affairs of the Mantis when at large. I can only go by what happens in the cages, where the captives, enjoying plenty of sunshine and food and spacious quarters, do not seem to suffer from homesickness in any way. What they do here they must also do under normal conditions.

Well, what happens there utterly refutes the idea that the males are given time to escape. I find, by themselves, a horrible couple engaged as follows. The male, absorbed in the performance of his vital functions, holds the female in a tight embrace. But the wretch has no head; he has no neck; he has hardly a body. The other, with her muzzle turned over her shoulder continues very placidly to gnaw what remains of the gentle swain. And, all the time, that masculine stump, holding on firmly, goes on with the business!

Love is stronger than death, men say. Taken literally, the aphorism has never received a more brilliant confirmation. A headless creature, an insect amputated down to the middle of the chest, a very corpse persists in endeavouring to give life. It will not let go until the abdomen, the seat of the procreative organs, is attacked.

Eating the lover after consummation of marriage, making a meal of the exhausted dwarf, henceforth good for nothing, can be understood, to some extent, in the insect world, which has no great scruples in matters of sentiment; but gobbling him up during the act goes beyond the wildest dreams of the most horrible imagination. I have seen it done with my own eyes and have not yet recovered from my astonishment.

Was this one able to escape and get out of the way, caught as he was in the midst of his duty? Certainly not. Hence we must infer that the loves of the Mantis are tragic, quite as much as the Spider's and perhaps even more so. I admit that the restricted space inside the cages favours the slaughter of the males; but the cause of these massacres lies elsewhere.

Perhaps it is a relic of the palæozoic ages, when, in the carboniferous period, the insect came into being as the result of monstrous amours. The Orthoptera, to whom the Mantes belong, are the first-born of the entomological world. Rough-hewn, incomplete in their transformation, they roamed among the arborescent ferns and were already flourishing when none of the insects with delicate metamorphoses, Butterflies, Moths, Beetles, Flies and Bees, as yet existed. Manners were not gentle in those days of passion eager to destroy in order to produce; and the Mantes, a faint memory of the ghosts of old, might well continue the amorous methods of a bygone age.

The habit of eating the males is customary among other members of the Mantis family. I am indeed prepared to admit that it is general. The little Grey Mantis, who looks so sweet and so peaceable in my cages, never seeking a quarrel with her neighbours however crowded they may be, bites into her male and feeds on him as fiercely as the Praying Mantis herself. I wear myself out, scouring the country to procure the indispensable complement to my gynæceum. No sooner is my powerfully-winged and nimble prize introduced than, most often, he is clawed and eaten up by one of those who no longer need his aid. Once the ovaries are satisfied, the Mantes of both species abhor the male, or rather look upon him as nothing better than a choice piece of venison.

ALFRED RUSSEL WALLACE
1823-1913

Collecting seems often to have been the starting place for Victorian naturalists, professional and amateur alike. Even the most polished nature writing from the period can sometimes feel like an assortment of "natural curiosities," to be spread out and delighted in, rather than a unified system or narrative. In 1848 Wallace set out to South America as a professional beetle collector. His Travels on the Amazon and Rio Negro *appeared in 1853. The next major expedition was described in his book on* The Malay Archipelago, *which appeared in 1868. In the meantime Wallace's close observation of birds, botany, and insect-populations drew him to conclusions which he expressed in an 1858 letter to Charles Darwin. Their joint paper to the Linnaean Society on July 1, 1858, formulating the theory of evolution, stands as one of the most dramatic and admirable events in the history of science. It also reflects, perhaps, the broad vistas opened up to those willing to pore over humble details of the creation.*

From THE MALAY ARCHIPELAGO, THE LAND OF THE ORANG-UTAN AND THE BIRD OF PARADISE

CELEBES

* * * I have rarely enjoyed myself more than during my residence here. As I sat taking my coffee at six in the morning, rare birds would often be seen on some tree close by, when I would hastily sally out in my

The Malay Archipelago, the Land of the Orang-utan and the Bird of Paradise (London: Macmillan, 1868).

slippers, and perhaps secure a prize I had been seeking after for weeks. The great hornbills of Celebes (Buceros cassidix) would often come with loud-flapping wings, and perch upon a lofty tree just in front of me; and the black baboon monkeys, Cynopithecus nigrescens, often stared down in astonishment at such an intrusion into their domains; while at night herds of wild pigs roamed about the house, devouring refuse, and obliging us to put away everything eatable or breakable from our little cooking-house. A few minutes' search on the fallen trees around my house at sunrise and sunset, would often produce me more beetles than I would meet with in a day's collecting, and odd moments could be made valuable which when living in villages or at a distance from the forest are inevitably wasted. Where the sugar-palms were dripping with sap, flies congregated in immense numbers, and it was by spending half an hour at these when I had the time to spare, that I obtained the finest and most remarkable collection of this group of insects that I have ever made.

Then what delightful hours I passed wandering up and down the dry river-courses, full of water-holes and rocks and fallen trees, and overshadowed by magnificent vegetation! I soon got to know every hole and rock and stump, and came up to each with cautious step and bated breath to see what treasures it would produce. At one place I would find a little crowd of the rare butterfly Tachyris zarinda, which would rise up at my approach, and display their vivid orange and cinnabar-red wings, while among them would flutter a few of the fine blue-banded Papilios. Where leafy branches hung over the gully, I might expect to find a grand Ornithoptera at rest and an easy prey. At certain rotten trunks I was sure to get the curious little tiger beetle, Therates flavilabris. In the denser thickets I would capture the small metallic blue butterflies (Amblypodia) sitting on the leaves, as well as some rare and beautiful leaf-beetles of the families Hispidæ and Chrysomelidæ.

I found that the rotten jack-fruits were very attractive to many beetles, and used to split them partly open and lay them about in the forest near my house to rot. A morning's search at these often produced me a score of species,—Staphylinidæ, Nitidulidæ, Onthophagi, and minute Carabidæ being the most abundant. Now and then the "sagueir" makers brought me a fine rosechafer (Sternoplus schaumii) which they found licking up the sweet sap. Almost the only new birds I met with for some time were a handsome ground thrush (Pitta celebensis), and a beautiful violet-crowned dove (Ptilonopus celebensis), both very similar to birds I had recently obtained at Aru, but of distinct species.

About the latter part of September a heavy shower of rain fell, admonishing us that we might soon expect wet weather, much to the advantage of the baked-up country. I therefore determined to pay a visit to the falls of the Máros river, situated at the point where it issues from the mountains—a spot often visited by travellers and considered very beautiful. Mr. M. lent me a horse, and I obtained a guide from a neighbouring village; and taking one of my men with me, we started at six in the morning, and after a ride of two hours over the flat rice-fields skirting the mountains which rose in grand precipices on our left, we reached the river about half-way between Máros and the falls, and thence had a good bridle-road to our destination, which we reached in another hour. The hills had closed in round us as we advanced; and when we reached a ruinous shed which had been erected for the accommodation of visitors, we found ourselves in a flat-bottomed valley about a quarter of a mile wide, bounded by precipitous and often overhanging limestone rocks. So far the ground had been cultivated, but it now became covered with bushes and large scattered trees.

As soon as my scanty baggage had arrived and was duly deposited in the shed, I started off alone for the fall, which was about a quarter of a mile further on. The river is here about twenty yards wide, and issues from a chasm between two vertical walls of limestone, over a rounded mass of basaltic rock about forty feet high, forming two curves separated by a slight ledge. The water spreads beautifully over this surface in a thin sheet of foam, which curls and eddies in a succession of concentric cones till it falls into a fine deep pool below. Close to the very edge of the fall a narrow and very rugged path leads to the river above, and thence continues close under the precipice along the water's edge, or sometimes in the water, for a few hundred yards, after which the rocks recede a little, and leave a wooded bank on one side, along which the path is continued, till in about half a mile a second and smaller fall is reached. Here the river seems to issue from a cavern, the rocks having fallen from above so as to block up the channel and bar further progress. The fall itself can only be reached by a path which ascends behind a huge slice of rock which has partly fallen away from the mountain, leaving a space two or three feet wide, but disclosing a dark chasm descending into the bowels of the mountain, and which, having visited several such, I had no great curiosity to explore.

Crossing the stream a little below the upper fall, the path ascends a steep slope for about five hundred feet, and passing through a gap enters a narrow valley, shut in by walls of rock absolutely perpendicular and of great height. Half a mile further this valley turns abruptly to the right, and becomes a mere rift in the mountain. This extends another half mile, the walls gradually approaching till they are only two feet apart, and the bottom rising steeply to a pass which leads probably into another valley, but which I had no time to explore. Returning to where this rift had begun, the main path turns up to the left in a sort of gully, and reaches a summit over which a fine natural arch of rock passes at a height of about fifty feet. Thence was a steep descent through thick jungle with glimpses of precipices and distant rocky mountains, probably leading into the main river valley again. This was a most tempting region to explore, but there were several reasons why I could go no further. I had no guide, and no permission to enter the Bugis territories, and as the rains might at any time set in, I might be prevented from returning by the flooding of the river. I therefore devoted myself during the short time of my visit to obtaining what knowledge I could of the natural productions of the place.

The narrow chasms produced several fine insects quite new to me, and one new bird, the curious Phlægenas tristigmata, a large ground pigeon with yellow breast and crown, and purple neck. This rugged path is the highway from Máros to the Bugis country beyond the mountains. During the rainy season it is quite impassable, the river filling its bed and rushing between perpendicular cliffs many hundred feet high. Even at the time of my visit it was most precipitous and fatiguing, yet women and children came over it daily, and men carrying heavy loads of palm sugar of very little value. It was along the path between the lower and the upper falls, and about the margin of the upper pool, that I found most insects. The large semi-transparent butterfly, Idea tondana, flew lazily along by dozens, and it was here that I at length obtained an insect which I had hoped but hardly expected to meet with—the magnificent Papilio androcles, one of the largest and rarest known swallow-tailed butterflies. During my four days' stay at the falls I was so fortunate as to obtain six good specimens. As this beautiful creature flies, the long white tails flicker like streamers, and when settled on the beach it carries them raised upwards, as if to preserve them from injury. It is scarce even here, as I did not see more than a dozen specimens in all, and had to follow many of them up and down the river's bank repeatedly before I succeeded in their capture. When the sun shone hottest about noon, the moist beach of the pool below the upper fall presented a beautiful sight, being dotted with groups of gay butterflies,—orange, yellow, white, blue, and green,—which on being disturbed rose into the air by hundreds, forming clouds of variegated colours.

Such gorges, chasms, and precipices as here abound, I have nowhere seen in the Archipelago. A sloping surface is scarcely anywhere to be found, huge walls and rugged masses of rock terminating all the mountains and inclosing the valleys. In many parts there are vertical or even overhanging precipices five or six hundred feet high, yet completely clothed with a tapestry of vegetation. Ferns, Pandanaceæ, shrubs, creepers, and even forest trees, are mingled in an evergreen network, through the interstices of which appears the white limestone rock or the dark holes and chasms with which it abounds. These precipices are enabled to sustain such an amount of vegetation by their peculiar structure. Their surfaces are very irregular, broken into holes and fissures, with ledges overhanging the mouths of gloomy caverns; but from each projecting part have descended stalactites, often forming a wild gothic tracery over the caves and receding hollows, and affording an admirable support to the roots of the shrubs, trees, and creepers, which luxuriate in the warm pure atmosphere and the gentle moisture which constantly exudes from the rocks. In places where the precipice offers smooth surfaces of solid rock, it remains quite bare, or only stained with lichens and dotted with clumps of ferns that grow on the small ledges and in the minutest crevices.

The reader who is familiar with tropical nature only through the medium of books and botanical gardens, will picture to himself in such a spot many other natural beauties. He will think that I have unaccountably forgotten to mention the brilliant flowers, which, in gorgeous masses of crimson, gold, or azure, must spangle these verdant precipices, hang over the cascade, and adorn the margin of the mountain stream. But what is the reality? In vain did I gaze over these vast walls of verdure, among the pendant creepers and bushy shrubs, all around the cascade, on the river's bank, or in the deep caverns and gloomy fissures,—not one single spot of bright colour could be seen; not one single tree or bush or creeper bore a flower sufficiently conspicuous to form an object in the landscape. In every direction the eye rested on green foliage and mottled rock. There was infinite variety in the colour and aspect of the foliage, there was grandeur in the rocky masses and in the exuberant luxuriance of the vegetation, but there was no brilliancy of colour, none of those bright flowers and gorgeous masses of blossom, so generally considered to be everywhere present in the tropics. I have here given an accurate sketch of a luxuriant tropical scene as noted down on the spot, and its general characteristics as regards colour have been so often repeated, both in South America and over many thousand miles in the Eastern tropics, that I am driven to conclude that it represents the general aspect of nature in the equatorial (that is, the most tropical) parts of the tropical regions. How is it then, that the descriptions of travellers generally give a very different idea? And where, it may be asked, *are* the glorious flowers that we know do exist in the tropics? These questions can be easily answered. The fine tropical flowering-plants cultivated in our hot-houses have been culled from the most varied regions, and therefore give a most erroneous idea of their abundance in any one region. Many of them are very rare, others extremely local, while a considerable number inhabit the more arid regions of Africa and India, in which tropical vegetation does not exhibit itself in its usual luxuriance. Fine and varied foliage, rather than gay flowers, is more characteristic of those parts where tropical vegetation attains its highest development, and in such districts each kind of flower seldom lasts in perfection more than a few weeks, or sometimes a few days. In every locality a lengthened residence will show an abundance of magnificent and gaily-blossomed plants, but they have to be sought for, and are rarely at any one time or place so abundant as to form a perceptible feature in the landscape. But it has been the custom of travellers to describe and group together all the fine plants they have met with during a long journey, and thus produce the effect of a gay and flower-painted landscape. They have rarely studied and described individual scenes where vegetation was most luxuriant and beautiful, and fairly stated what effect was produced in them by flowers. I have done so frequently, and the result of these examinations has convinced me, that the bright colours of flowers have a much greater influence on the general aspect of nature in temperate than in tropical climates. During twelve years spent amid the grandest tropical vegetation, I have seen nothing comparable to the effect produced on our landscapes by gorse, broom, heather, wild hyacinths, hawthorn, purple orchises, and buttercups. ∗ ∗ ∗

JOHN WESLEY POWELL
1834-1902

Like Audubon and Muir, Powell lives in American literature as a character as well as an author. The one-armed Civil War hero, standing in the prow of a boat plunging through the Colorado's rapids, represents the bravery of explorers all along the frontier and the ambition of scientists eager to map and analyze the Republic's new territories. His Exploration of The Colorado River of the West and Its Tributaries *(1875) grew out of a series of articles for* Scribner's Magazine, *in which Powell synthesized his expeditions of 1869 and 1871. These articles both introduced many readers to the marvels of the Grand Canyon and addressed the question of America's destiny, now that the War was past. What coun-*

try was it that had been held together at such cost? As had also occurred after the Revolution, Americans turned to description of our sublime landscape in defining the national pride available to us as a new people in a new place. In addition to becoming Director of the United States Geological Survey, Major Powell was also to serve as America's Director of the Bureau of Ethnology. His sympathetic interest in native peoples of the Colorado region is often apparent in his Exploration.

From Exploration of the Colorado River

FROM THE LITTLE COLORADO TO THE FOOT OF THE GRAND CANYON

AUGUST 13.

We are now ready to start on our way down the Great Unknown. Our boats, tied to a common stake, chafe each other as they are tossed by the fretful river. They ride high and buoyant, for their loads are lighter than we could desire. We have but a month's rations remaining. The flour has been resifted through the mosquito-net sieve; the spoiled bacon has been dried and the worst of it boiled; the few pounds of dried apples have been spread in the sun and reshrunken to their normal bulk. The sugar has all melted and gone on its way down the river. But we have a large sack of coffee. The lightening of the boats has this advantage: they will ride the waves better and we shall have but little to carry when we make a portage.

We are three quarters of a mile in the depths of the earth, and the great river shrinks into insignificance as it dashes its angry waves against the walls and cliffs that rise to the world above; the waves are but puny ripples, and we but pigmies, running up and down the sands or lost among the boulders.

We have an unknown distance yet to run, an unknown river to explore. What falls there are, we know not; what rocks beset the channel, we know not; what walls rise over the river, we know not. Ah, well! we may conjecture many things. The men talk as cheerfully as ever; jests are bandied about freely this morning; but to me the cheer is somber and the jests are ghastly.

With some eagerness and some anxiety and some misgiving we enter

Exploration of the Colorado River of the West and Its Tributaries (Washington: U.S. Government, 1875).

the canyon below and are carried along by the swift water through walls which rise from its very edge. They have the same structure that we noticed yesterday—tiers of irregular shelves below, and, above these, steep slopes to the foot of marble cliffs. We run six miles in a little more than half an hour and emerge into a more open portion of the canyon, where high hills and ledges of rock intervene between the river and the distant walls. Just at the head of this open place the river runs across a dike; that is, a fissure in the rocks, open to depths below, was filled with eruptive matter, and this on cooling was harder than the rocks through which the crevice was made, and when these were washed away the harder volcanic matter remained as a wall, and the river has cut a gateway through it several hundred feet high and as many wide. As it crosses the wall, there is a fall below and a bad rapid, filled with boulders of trap; so we stop to make a portage. Then on we go, gliding by hills and ledges, with distant walls in view; sweeping past sharp angles of rock; stopping at a few points to examine rapids, which we find can be run, until we have made another five miles, when we land for dinner.

Then we let down with lines over a long rapid and start again. Once more the walls close in, and we find ourselves in a narrow gorge, the water again filling the channel and being very swift. With great care and constant watchfulness we proceed, making about four miles this afternoon, and camp in a cave.

AUGUST 14.

At daybreak we walk down the bank of the river, on a little sandy beach, to take a view of a new feature in the canyon. Heretofore hard rocks have given us bad river; soft rocks, smooth water; and a series of rocks harder than any we have experienced sets in. The river enters the gneiss! We can see but a little way into the granite gorge, but it looks threatening.

After breakfast we enter on the waves. At the very introduction it inspires awe. The canyon is narrower than we have ever before seen it; the water is swifter; there are but few broken rocks in the channel; but the walls are set, on either side, with pinnacles and crags; and sharp, angular buttresses, bristling with wind- and wave-polished spires, extend far out into the river.

Ledges of rock jut into the stream, their tops sometimes just below the surface, sometimes rising a few or many feet above; and island ledges and island pinnacles and island towers break the swift course of the stream into chutes and eddies and whirlpools. We soon reach a place where a creek comes in from the left, and, just below, the channel is choked with boulders, which have washed down this lateral canyon and formed a dam, over which there is a fall of 30 or 40 feet; but on the boulders foothold can be had, and we make a portage. Three more such dams are found. Over one we make a portage; at the other two are chutes through which we can run.

As we proceed the granite rises higher, until nearly a thousand feet of the lower part of the walls are composed of this rock.

About eleven o'clock we hear a great roar ahead, and approach it very cautiously. The sound grows louder and louder as we run, and at last we find ourselves above a long, broken fall, with ledges and pinnacles of rock obstructing the river. There is a descent of perhaps 75 or 80 feet in a third of a mile, and the rushing waters break into great waves on the rocks, and lash themselves into a mad, white foam. We can land just above, but there is no foothold on either side by which we can make a portage. It is nearly a thousand feet to the top of the granite; so it will be impossible to carry our boats around, though we can climb to the summit up a side gulch and, passing along a mile or two, descend to the river. This we find on examination; but such a portage would be impracticable for us, and we must run the rapid or abandon the river. There is no hesitation. We step into our boats, push off, and away we go, first on smooth but swift water, then we strike a glassy wave and ride to its top, down again into the trough, up again on a higher wave, and down and up on waves higher and still higher until we strike one just as it curls back, and a breaker rolls over our little boat. Still on we speed, shooting past projecting rocks, till the little boat is caught in a whirlpool and spun round several times. At last we pull out again into the stream. And now the other boats have passed us. The open compartment of the "Emma Dean" is filled with water and every breaker rolls over us. Hurled back from a rock, now on this side, now on that, we are carried into an eddy, in which we struggle for a few minutes, and are then out again, the breakers still rolling over us. Our boat is unmanageable, but she cannot sink, and we drift down another hundred yards through breakers—how, we scarcely know. We find the other boats have turned into an eddy at the foot of the fall and are waiting to catch us as we come, for the men have seen that our boat is swamped. They push out as we come near and pull us in against the wall. Our boat bailed, on we go again.

The walls now are more than a mile in height—a vertical distance difficult to appreciate. Stand on the south steps of the Treasury building in Washington and look down Pennsylvania Avenue to the Capitol; measure this distance overhead, and imagine cliffs to extend to that altitude, and you will understand what is meant; or stand at Canal Street in New York and look up broadway to Grace Church, and you have about the distance; or stand at Lake Street bridge in Chicago and look down to the Central Depot, and you have it again.

A thousand feet of this is up through granite crags; then steep slopes and perpendicular cliffs rise one above another to the summit. The gorge is black and narrow below, red and gray and flaring above, with crags and angular projections on the walls, which, cut in many places by side canyons, seem to be a vast wilderness of rocks. Down in these grand, gloomy depths we glide, ever listening, for the mad waters keep up their roar; ever watching, ever peering ahead, for the narrow canyon is winding and the river is closed in so that we can see but a few hundred yards, and what there may be below we know not; so we listen for falls and watch for rocks, stopping now and then in the bay of a recess to admire the gigantic scenery; and ever as we go there is some new pinnacle or tower, some crag or peak, some distant view of the upper plateau, some strangely shaped rock, or some deep, narrow side canyon.

Then we come to another broken fall, which appears more difficult than the one we ran this morning. A small creek comes in on the right, and the first fall of the water is over boulders, which have been carried down by this lateral stream. We land at its mouth and stop for an hour or two to examine the fall. It seems possible to let down with lines, at least a part of the way, from point to point, along the right-hand wall. So we make a portage over the first rocks and find footing on some boulders below. Then we let down one of the boats to the end of her line, when she reaches a corner of the projecting rock, to which one of the men clings and steadies her while I examine an eddy below. I think we can pass the other boats down by us and catch them in the eddy. This is soon done, and the men in the boats in the eddy pull us to their side. On the shore of this little eddy there is about two feet of gravel beach above the water. Standing on this beach, some of the men take the line of the little boat and let it drift down against another projecting angle. Here is a little shelf, on which a man from my boat climbs, and a shorter line is passed to him, and he fastens the boat to the side of the cliff; then the second one is let down, bringing the line of the third. When the second boat is tied up, the two men standing on the beach above spring into the last boat, which is pulled up alongside of ours; then we let down the boats for 25 or 30 yards by walking along the shelf, landing them again in the mouth of a side canyon. Just below this there is another pile of boulders, over which we make another portage. From the foot of these rocks we can climb to another shelf, 40 or 50 feet above the water.

On this bench we camp for the night. It is raining hard, and we have no shelter, but find a few sticks which have lodged in the rocks, and kindle a fire and have supper. We sit on the rocks all night, wrapped in our *ponchos,* getting what sleep we can.

AUGUST 15.

This morning we find we can let down for 300 or 400 yards, and it is managed in this way: we pass along the wall by climbing from projecting point to point, sometimes near the water's edge, at other places 50 or 60 feet above, and hold the boat with a line while two men remain aboard and prevent her from being dashed against the rocks and keep the line from getting caught on the wall. In two hours we have brought them all down, as far as it is possible, in this way. A few yards below, the river strikes with great violence against a projecting rock and our boats are pulled up in a little bay above. We must now manage to pull out of this and clear the point below. The little boat is held by the bow obliquely up the stream. We jump in and pull out only a few strokes, and sweep clear of the dangerous rock. The other boats follow in the same manner and the rapid is passed.

It is not easy to describe the labor of such navigation. We must prevent the waves from dashing the boats against the cliffs. Sometimes, where the river is swift, we must put a bight of rope about a rock, to prevent the boat from being snatched from us by a wave; but where the plunge is too great or the chute too swift, we must let her leap and catch her below or the undertow will drag her under the falling water and sink her. Where we wish to run her out a little way from shore through a channel between rocks, we first throw in little sticks of driftwood and watch their course, to see where we must steer so that she will pass the channel in safety. And so we hold, and let go, and pull, and lift, and ward—among rocks, around rocks, and over rocks.

And now we go on through this solemn, mysterious way. The river is very deep, the canyon very narrow, and still obstructed, so that there is no steady flow of the stream; but the waters reel and roll and boil, and we are scarcely able to determine where we can go. Now the boat is carried to the right, perhaps close to the wall; again, she is shot into the stream, and perhaps is dragged over to the other side, where, caught in a whirlpool, she spins about. We can neither land nor run as we please. The boats are entirely unmanageable; no order in their running can be preserved; now one, now another, is ahead, each crew laboring for its own preservation. In such a place we come to another rapid. Two of the boats run it perforce. One succeeds in landing, but there is no foothold by which to make a portage and she is pushed out again into the stream.

The next minute a great reflex wave fills the open compartment; she is water-logged, and drifts unmanageable. Breaker after breaker rolls over her and one capsizes her. The men are thrown out; but they cling to the boat, and she drifts down some distance alongside of us and we are able to catch her. She is soon bailed out and the men are aboard once more; but the oars are lost, and so a pair from the "Emma Dean" is spared. Then for two miles we find smooth water.

Clouds are playing in the canyon to-day. Sometimes they roll down in great masses, filling the gorge with gloom; sometimes they hang aloft from wall to wall and cover the canyon with a roof of impending storm, and we can peer long distances up and down this canyon corridor, with its cloud-roof overhead, its walls of black granite, and its river bright with the sheen of broken waters. Then a gust of wind sweeps down a side gulch and, making a rift in the clouds, reveals the blue heavens, and a stream of sunlight pours in. Then the clouds drift away into the distance, and hang around crags and peaks and pinnacles and towers and walls, and cover them with a mantle that lifts from time to time and sets them all in sharp relief. Then baby clouds creep out of side canyons, glide around points, and creep back again into more distant gorges. Then clouds arrange in strata across the canyon, with intervening vista views to cliffs and rocks beyond. The clouds are children of the heavens, and when they play among the rocks they lift them to the region above.

It rains! Rapidly little rills are formed above, and these soon grow into brooks, and the brooks grow into creeks and tumble over the walls in innumerable cascades, adding their wild music to the roar of the river. When the rain ceases the rills, brooks, and creeks run dry. The waters that fall during a rain on these steep rocks are gathered at once into the river; they could scarcely be poured in more suddenly if some vast spout ran from the clouds to the stream itself. When a storm bursts over the canyon a side gulch is dangerous, for a sudden flood may come, and the inpouring waters will raise the river so as to hide the rocks.

Early in the afternoon we discover a stream entering from the north—a clear, beautiful creek, coming down through a gorgeous red canyon. We land and camp on a sand beach above its mouth, under a great, overspreading tree with willow-shaped leaves. *   *   *

SAMUEL CLEMENS
(MARK TWAIN)
1835-1910

The Mississippi flowed through Twain's life, as through his art. When he met the pilot Horace Bixby in 1857 on a trip down to New Orleans, Samuel Clemens decided to sign on under him as a "cub," learning the river. By 1859 he was fully licensed as a pilot himself; he served in this capacity until the outbreak of the Civil War put an end to river-travel between North and South. He also recalled the signals with which the Mississippi's shifting depths were called out to the pilot when he chose Mark Twain as his pen name. Scenes along the Mississippi figure beautifully in Huckleberry Finn, *which was begun in 1876 and finally published in 1883. This same period saw Twain's return to his piloting experiences in another form. In 1875 two articles entitled "Old Times on the Mississippi" appeared in the* Atlantic Monthly. *They became the seed for* Life on the Mississippi, *published in 1883.*

From LIFE ON THE MISSISSIPPI

[*the book of the river*]

* * * The face of the water, in time, became a wonderful book—a book that was a dead language to the uneducated passenger, but which told its mind to me without reserve, delivering its most cherished secrets as clearly as if it uttered them with a voice. And it was not a book to be read once and thrown aside, for it had a new story to tell every day. Throughout the long twelve hundred miles there was never a page that was void of interest, never one that you could leave unread without loss, never one that you would want to skip, thinking you could find higher

Life on the Mississippi (Boston: Osgood & Co., 1883).

enjoyment in some other thing. There never was so wonderful a book written by man; never one whose interest was so absorbing, so unflagging, so sparklingly renewed with every re-perusal. The passenger who could not read it was charmed with a peculiar sort of faint dimple on its surface (on the rare occasions when he did not overlook it altogether); but to the pilot that was an *italicized* passage; indeed, it was more than that, it was a legend of the largest capitals, with a string of shouting exclamation points at the end of it; for it meant that a wreck or a rock was buried there that could tear the life out of the strongest vessel that ever floated. It is the faintest and simplest expression the water ever makes, and the most hideous to a pilot's eye. In truth, the passenger who could not read this book saw nothing but all manner of pretty pictures in it, painted by the sun and shaded by the clouds, whereas to the trained eye these were not pictures at all, but the grimmest and most dead-earnest of reading-matter.

Now when I had mastered the language of this water and had come to know every trifling feature that bordered the great river as familiarly as I knew the letters of the alphabet, I had made a valuable acquisition. But I had lost something, too. I had lost something which could never be restored to me while I lived. All the grace, the beauty, the poetry had gone out of the majestic river! I still keep in mind a certain wonderful sunset which I witnessed when steamboating was new to me. A broad expanse of the river was turned to blood; in the middle distance the red hue brightened into gold, through which a solitary log came floating, black and conspicuous; in one place a long, slanting mark lay sparkling upon the water; in another the surface was broken by boiling, tumbling rings, that were as many-tinted as an opal; where the ruddy flush was faintest, was a smooth spot that was covered with graceful circles and radiating lines, ever so delicately traced; the shore on our left was densely wooded, and the sombre shadow that fell from this forest was broken in one place by a long, ruffled trail that shone like silver; and high above the forest wall a clean-stemmed dead tree waved a single leafy bough that glowed like a flame in the unobstructed splendor that was flowing from the sun. There were graceful curves, reflected images, woody heights, soft distances; and over the whole scene, far and near, the dissolving lights drifted steadily, enriching it, every passing moment, with new marvels of coloring.

I stood like one bewitched. I drank it in, in a speechless rapture. The world was new to me, and I had never seen anything like this at home. But as I have said, a day came when I began to cease from noting the glories and the charms which the moon and the sun and the twilight wrought upon the river's face; another day came when I ceased altogether to note them. Then, if that sunset scene had been repeated, I should have looked upon it without rapture, and should have commented upon it, inwardly, after this fashion: This sun means that we are going to have wind to-morrow; that floating log means that the river is rising, small thanks to it; that slanting mark on the water refers to a bluff reef which is going to kill somebody's steamboat one of these nights, if it keeps on stretching out like that; those tumbling "boils" show a dissolving bar and a changing channel there; the lines and circles in the slick water over yonder are a warning that that troublesome place is shoaling up dangerously; that silver streak in the shadow of the forest is the "break" from a new snag, and he has located himself in the very best place he could have found to fish for steamboats; that tall dead tree, with a single living branch, is not going to last long, and then how is a body ever going to get through this blind place at night without the friendly old landmark?

No, the romance and the beauty were all gone from the river. All the value any feature of it had for me now was the amount of usefulness it could furnish toward compassing the safe piloting of a steamboat. Since those days, I have pitied doctors from my heart. What does the lovely flush in a beauty's cheek mean to a doctor but a "break" that ripples above some deadly disease? Are not all her visible charms sown thick with what are to him the signs and symbols of hidden decay? Does he ever seen her beauty at all, or doesn't he simply view her professionally, and comment upon her unwholesome condition all to himself? And doesn't he sometimes wonder whether he has gained most or lost most by learning his trade?

JOHN BURROUGHS
1837-1921

John Muir and John Burroughs were undoubtedly the two most popular and successful American nature writers of the late nineteenth and early twentieth centuries, yet in their lives and writings they represented strikingly different approaches to nature. Unlike Muir, who left home early and spent much of his adult life wandering in the rugged mountain wildernesses of California and Alaska, Burroughs spent most of his

*eighty-four years living on a small New York farm overlooking the Hud-
son River, not far from the Catskill Mountains where he was born.
Though not a conservation activist like Muir, his quiet, genial "nature
rambles" did much to popularize amateur nature observation and increase the appreciation of local environments.*

*Burroughs worked in Washington D.C. for ten years, where he be-
came friends with Walt Whitman, who served as a nurse in army hospi-
tals during the Civil War. Burroughs's first book,* Notes on Walt Whitman, Poet and Person *(1867), was the first appreciative study of that
major literary figure, whose cosmic optimism and celebration of the
American landscape is reflected, in a quieter vein, in Burroughs' own
writings. In 1873 Burroughs was able to move back to his beloved Catskill region, where he built Riverby, a stone house overlooking the Hudson River, and wrote more than two dozen books that sold over one and
a half million copies. Later he built "Slabsides," a summer retreat which
became in time a pilgrimage for his legions of admirers, and which today
is owned and maintained by the John Burroughs Society.*

*Though Burroughs's geographical locus was small, his intellectual
range was large. He saw Darwinian evolution as a liberating vision and
was one of the first popular writers to embrace the new biological science. At the turn of the century he joined forces with Theodore Roosevelt and others in a war against the "nature fakers"—writers like Ernest
Thompson Seton whose animal stories, Burroughs felt, were full of an-
thropomorphic fictions and unrealistic events. The dispute, which became quite public and often bitter, helped to rid much nature writing of
the time of excessive sentimentality and to ground it more in scientific
observation. Yet, as Burroughs was fond of saying, "Knowledge is only
half the task. The other half is love."*

*Burroughs's earlier books of genial essays on local birds and flowers
tend to hold diminished interest for today's readers. Yet many of his
descriptions of places remain fresh and provocative, and his later essays
tend to confront larger, more philosophical issues raised by modern science which remain central challenges for writers today.*

IN MAMMOTH CAVE

Some idea of the impression which Mammoth Cave makes upon the
senses, irrespective even of sight, may be had from the fact that blind
people go there to see it, and are greatly struck with it. I was assured that

Riverby (Boston: Houghton Mifflin, 1894).

this is a fact. The blind seem as much impressed by it as those who have their sight. When the guide pauses at the more interesting point, or lights the scene up with a great torch or with Bengal lights, and points out the more striking features, the blind exclaim, "How wonderful! how beautiful!" They can feel it, if they cannot see it. They get some idea of the spaciousness when words are uttered. The voice goes forth in these colossal chambers like a bird. When no word is spoken, the silence is of a kind never experienced on the surface of the earth, it is so profound and abysmal. This, and the absolute darkness, to a person with eyes makes him feel as if he were face to face with the primordial nothingness. The objective universe is gone; only the subjective remains; the sense of hearing is inverted, and reports only the murmurs from within. The blind miss much, but much remains to them. The great cave is not merely a spectacle to the eye; it is a wonder to the ear, a strangeness to the smell and to the touch. The body feels the presence of unusual conditions through every pore.

For my part, my thoughts took a decidedly sepulchral turn; I thought of my dead and of all the dead of the earth, and said to myself, the darkness and the silence of their last resting-place is like this; to this we must all come at last. No vicissitudes of earth, no changes of seasons, no sound of storm or thunder penetrate here; winter and summer, day and night, peace or war, it is all one; a world beyond the reach of change, because beyond the reach of life. What peace, what repose, what desolation! The marks and relics of the Indian, which disappear so quickly from the light of day above, are here beyond the reach of natural change. The imprint of his moccasin in the dust might remain undisturbed for a thousand years. At one point the guide reaches his arm beneath the rocks that strew the floor and pulls out the burnt ends of canes, which were used, probably, when filled with oil or grease, by the natives to light their way into the cave doubtless centuries ago.

Here in the loose soil are ruts worn by cartwheels in 1812, when, during the war with Great Britain, the earth was searched to make saltpetre. The guide kicks corn-cobs out of the dust where the oxen were fed at noon, and they look nearly as fresh as ever they did. In those frail corn-cobs and in those wheel-tracks as if the carts had but just gone along, one seemed to come very near to the youth of the century, almost to overtake it.

At a point in one of the great avenues, if you stop and listen, you hear a slow, solemn ticking like a great clock in a deserted hall; you hear the slight echo as it fathoms and sets off the silence. It is called the clock, and is caused by a single large drop of water falling every second into a little pool. A ghostly kind of clock there in the darkness, that is never wound up and that never runs down. It seemed like a mockery where time is not, and change does not come,—the clock of the dead. This sombre and mortuary cast of one's thoughts seems so natural in the great cave, that I could well understand the emotions of a lady who visited the cave with a party a few days before I was there. She went forward very reluctantly from the first; the silence and the darkness of the huge mausoleum evidently impressed her imagination, so that when she got to the spot where the guide points out the "Giant's Coffin," a huge, fallen rock, which in the dim light takes exactly the form of an enormous coffin, her fear quite overcame her, and she begged piteously to be taken back. Timid, highly imaginative people, especially women, are quite sure to have a sense of fear in this strange underground world. The guide told me of a lady in one of the parties he was conducting through, who wanted to linger behind a little all alone; he suffered her to do so, but presently heard a piercing scream. Rushing back, he found her lying prone upon the ground in a dead faint. She had accidentally put out her lamp, and was so appalled by the darkness that instantly closed around her that she swooned at once.

Sometimes it seemed to me as if I were threading the streets of some buried city of the fore-world. With your little lantern in your hand, you follow your guide through those endless and silent avenues, catching glimpses on either hand of what appears to be some strange antique architecture, the hoary and crumbling walls rising high up into the darkness. Now we turn a sharp corner, or turn down a street which crosses our course at right angles; now we come out into a great circle, or spacious court, which the guide lights up with a quick-paper torch, or a colored chemical light. There are streets above you and streets below you. As this was a city where day never entered, no provision for light needed to be made, and it is built one layer above another to the number of four or five, or on the plan of an enormous ant-hill, the lowest avenues being several hundred feet beneath the uppermost. The main avenue leading in from the entrance is called the Broadway, and if Broadway, New York, were arched over and reduced to utter darkness and silence, and its roadway blocked with mounds of earth and fragments of rock, it would, perhaps, only lack that gray, cosmic, elemental look, to make it resemble this. A mile or so from the entrance we pass a couple of rude stone houses, built forty or more years ago by some consumptives, who hoped to prolong their lives by a residence in this pure, antiseptic air. Five months they lived here, poor creatures, a half dozen of them, without ever going forth into the world of light. But the long entombment did not arrest the disease; the mountain did not draw the virus out, but seemed to draw the strength and vitality out, so that when the victims did go forth into the light and air, bleached as white as chalk, they succumbed at once, and nearly all died before they could reach the hotel, a few hundred yards away.

Probably the prettiest thing they have to show you in Mammoth Cave is the Star Chamber. This seems to have made an impression upon Emerson when he visited the cave, for he mentions it in one of his essays, "Illusions." The guide takes your lantern from you and leaves you seated upon a bench by the wayside, in the profound cosmic darkness. He retreats along a side alley that seems to go down to a lower level, and at a certain point shades his lamp with his hat, so that the light falls upon the ceiling over your head. You look up, and the first thought is that there is an opening just there that permits you to look forth upon the midnight skies. You see the darker horizon line where the sky ends and the mountains begin. The sky is blue-black and is thickly studded with stars, rather small stars, but apparently genuine. At one point a long, luminous streak simulates exactly the form and effect of a comet. As you gaze, the guide slowly moves his hat, and a black cloud gradually creeps over the sky, and all is blackness again. Then you hear footsteps retreating and dying away in the distance. Presently all is still, save the ringing in your own ears. Then after a few moments, during which you have sat in silence like that of the interstellar spaces, you hear over your left shoulder a distant flapping of wings, followed by the crowing of a cock. You turn your head in that direction and behold a faint dawn breaking on the horizon. It slowly increases till you hear footsteps approaching, and your dusky companion, playing the part of Apollo, with lamp in hand ushers in the light of day. It is rather theatrical, but a very pleasant diversion nevertheless.

Another surprise was when we paused at a certain point, and the guide asked me to shout or call in a loud voice. I did so without any unusual effect following. Then he spoke in a very deep bass, and instantly the rocks all about and beneath us became like the strings of an Æolian harp. They seemed transformed as if by enchantment. Then I tried, but did not strike the right key; the rocks were dumb; I tried again, but got no response; flat and dead the sounds came back as if in mockery; then I struck a deeper bass, the chord was hit, and the solid walls seemed to become as thin and frail as a drum-head or as the frame of a violin. They fairly seemed to dance about us, and to recede away from us. Such wild, sweet music I had never before heard rocks discourse. Ah, the magic of the right key! "Why leap ye, ye high hills?" why, but that they had been spoken to in the right voice? Is not the whole secret of life to pitch our voices in the right key? Responses come from the very rocks when we do so. I thought of the lines of our poet of Democracy:—

"Surely, whoever speaks to me in the right voice, him or her I shall follow,
As the water follows the moon, silently, with fluid steps, anywhere around the
    globe."

Where we were standing was upon an arch over an avenue which crossed our course beneath us. The reverberations on Echo River, a point I did not reach, can hardly be more surprising, though they are described as wonderful.

There are four or five levels in the cave, and a series of avenues upon each. The lowest is some two hundred and fifty feet below the entrance. Here the stream which has done all this carving and tunneling has got to the end of its tether. It is here on a level with Green River in the valley below, and flows directly into it. I say the end of its tether, though if Green River cuts its valley deeper, the stream will, of course, follow suit. The bed of the river has probably, at successive periods, been on a level with each series of avenues of the cave. The stream is now doubtless but a mere fraction of its former self. Indeed, every feature of the cave attests the greater volume and activity of the forces which carved it, in the earlier geologic ages. The waters have worn the rock as if it were but ice. The domes and pits are carved and fluted in precisely the way dripping water flutes snow or ice. The rainfall must have been enormous in those early days, and it must have had a much stronger and sharper tooth of carbonic acid gas than now. It has carved out enormous pits with perpendicular sides, two or three hundred feet deep. Goring Dome I remember particularly. You put your head through an irregularly shaped window in the wall at the side of one of the avenues, and there is this huge shaft or well, starting from some higher level and going down two hundred feet below you. There must have been such wells in the old glaciers, worn by a rill of water slowly eating its way down. It was probably ten feet across, still moist and dripping. The guide threw down a lighted torch, and it fell and fell, till I had to crane my neck far out to see it finally reach the bottom. Some of these pits are simply appalling, and where the way is narrow, have been covered over to prevent accidents.

No part of Mammoth Cave was to me more impressive than its entrance, probably because here its gigantic proportions are first revealed to you, and can be clearly seen. That strange colossal underworld here looks out into the light of day, and comes in contrast with familiar scenes and objects. When you are fairly in the cave, you cannot see it; that is, with your aboveground eyes; you walk along by the dim light of your lamp as in a huge wood at night; when the guide lights up the more interesting portions with his torches and colored lights, the effect is weird and spectral; it seems like a dream; it is an unfamiliar world; you hardly know whether this is the emotion of grandeur which you experience, or of mere strangeness. If you could have the light of day in there, you would come to your senses, and could test the reality of your impressions. At the entrance you have the light of day, and you look fairly in the face of this underground monster, yea, into his open mouth, which has a span of fifty feet or more, and down into his contracting throat, where a man can barely stand upright, and where the light fades and darkness begins. As you come down the hill through the woods from the hotel, you see no sign of the cave till you emerge into a small opening where the grass grows and the sunshine falls, when you turn slightly to the right, and there at your feet yawns this terrible pit; and you feel indeed as if the mountain had opened its mouth and was lying in wait to swallow you down, as a whale might swallow a shrimp. I never grew tired of sitting or standing here by this entrance and gazing into it. It had for me something of the same fascination that the display of the huge elemental forces of nature have, as seen in thunder-storms, or in a roaring ocean surf. Two phœbe-birds had their nests in little niches of the rocks, and delicate ferns and wild flowers fringed the edges.

Another very interesting feature to me was the behavior of the cool air which welled up out of the mouth of the cave. It simulated exactly a fountain of water. It rose up to a certain level, or until it filled the depression immediately about the mouth of the cave, and then flowing over at the lowest point, ran down the hill toward Green River, along a little water-course, exactly as if it had been a liquid. I amused myself by wading down into it as into a fountain. The air above was muggy and hot, the thermometer standing at about eighty-six degrees, and this cooler air of the cave, which was at a temperature of about fifty-two degrees, was separated in the little pool or lakelet which is formed from the hotter air above it by a perfectly horizontal line. As I stepped down into it I could feel it close over my feet, then it was at my knees, then I was immersed to my hips, then to my waist, then I stood neck-deep in it, my body almost chilled, while my face and head were bathed by a sultry, oppressive air. Where the two bodies of air came in contact, a slight film of vapor was formed by condensation; I waded in till I could look under this as under a ceiling. It was as level and as well defined as a sheet of ice on a pond. A few moments' immersion into this aerial fountain made one turn to the warmer air again. At the depression in the rim of the basin one had but to put his hand down to feel the cold air flowing over like water. Fifty yards below you could still wade into it as into a creek, and at a hundred yards it was still quickly perceptible, but broader and higher; it had begun to lose some of its coldness, and to mingle with the general air; all the plants growing on the margin of the water-course were in motion, as well as the leaves on the low branches of the trees near by. Gradually this cool current was dissipated and lost in the warmth of the day.

THE GOSPEL OF NATURE

The other day a clergyman who described himself as a preacher of the gospel of Christ wrote, asking me to come and talk to his people on the gospel of Nature. The request set me to thinking whether or not Nature has any gospel in the sense the clergyman had in mind, any message that is likely to be especially comforting to the average orthodox religious person. I suppose the parson wished me to tell his flock what I had found in Nature that was a strength or a solace to myself.

What had all my many years of journeyings to Nature yielded me that would supplement or reinforce the gospel he was preaching? Had the birds taught me any valuable lessons? Had the four-footed beasts? Had the insects? Had the flowers, the trees, the soil, the coming and the going of the seasons? Had I really found sermons in stones, books in running brooks and good in everything? Had the lilies of the field, that neither toil nor spin, and yet are more royally clad than Solomon in all his glory, helped me in any way to clothe myself with humility, with justice, with truthfulness?

It is not easy for one to say just what he owes to all these things. Natural influences work indirectly as well as directly; they work upon the subconscious, as well as upon the conscious, self. That I am a saner, healthier, more contented man, with true standards of life for all my loiterings in the fields and woods, I am fully convinced.

That I am less social, less interested in my neighbors and in the body politic, more inclined to shirk civic and social responsibilities and to stop my ears against the brawling of the reformers, is perhaps equally true.

One thing is certain, in a hygienic way I owe much to my excursions to Nature. They have helped to clothe me with health, if not with humility; they have helped sharpen and attune all my senses; they have kept my eyes in such good trim that they have not failed me for one moment during all the seventy-five years I have had them; they have made my sense of smell so keen that I have much pleasure in the wild, open-air perfumes, especially in the spring—the delicate breath of the

Time and Change (Boston: Houghton Mifflin, 1912).

blooming elms and maples and willows, the breath of the woods, of the pasture, of the shore. This keen, healthy sense of smell has made me abhor tobacco and flee from close rooms, and put the stench of cities behind me. I fancy that this whole world of wild, natural perfumes is lost to the tobacco-user and to the city-dweller. Senses trained in the open air are in tune with open-air objects; they are quick, delicate, and discriminating. When I go to town, my ear suffers as well as my nose: the impact of the city upon my senses is hard and dissonant; the ear is stunned, the nose is outraged, and the eye is confused. When I come back, I go to Nature to be soothed and healed, and to have my senses put in tune once more. I know that, as a rule, country or farming folk are not remarkable for the delicacy of their senses, but this is owing mainly to the benumbing and brutalizing effect of continued hard labor. It is their minds more than their bodies that suffer.

When I have dwelt in cities the country was always nearby, and I used to get a bite of country soil at least once a week to keep my system normal.

Emerson says that "The day does not seem wholly profane in which we have given heed to some natural object." If Emerson had stopped to qualify his remark, he would have added, if we give heed to it in the right spirit, if we give heed to it as a nature-lover and truth-seeker. Nature-love as Emerson knew it, and as Wordsworth knew it, and as any of the choicer spirits of our time have known it, has distinctly a religious value. It does not come to a man or a woman who is wholly absorbed in selfish or worldly or material ends. Except ye become in a measure as little children, ye cannot enter the kingdom of Nature—as Audubon entered it, as Thoreau entered it, as Bryant and Amiel entered it, and as all those enter it who make it a resource in their lives and an instrument of their culture. The forms and creeds of religion change, but the sentiment of religion—the wonder and reverence and love we feel in the presence of the inscrutable universe—persist. Indeed, these seem to be renewing their life today in this growing love for all natural objects and in this increasing tenderness toward all forms of life. If we do not go to church as much as did our fathers, we go to the woods much more, and are much more inclined to make a temple of them than they were.

The lesson in running brooks is that motion is a great purifier and health producer. When the brook ceases to run, it soon stagnates. It keeps in touch with the great vital currents when it is in motion, and unites with other brooks to help make the river. In motion it soon leaves all mud and sediment behind. Do not proper work and the exercise of will power have the same effect upon our lives?

The other day in my walk I came upon a sap bucket that had been left standing by the maple tree all the spring and summer. What a bucketful of corruption was that, a mixture of sap and rain-water that had rotted, and smelled to heaven. Mice and birds and insects had been drowned in it, and added to its unsavory character. It was a bit of Nature cut off from the vitalizing and purifying chemistry of the whole. With what satisfaction I emptied it upon the ground while I held my nose and saw it filter into the turf, where I knew it was dying to go and where I knew every particle of the reeking, fetid fluid would soon be made sweet and wholesome again by the chemistry of the soil.

I am not always in sympathy with nature-study as pursued in the schools, as if this kingdom could be carried by assault. Such study is too cold, too special, too mechanical; it is likely to rub the bloom off Nature. It lacks soul and emotion; it misses the accessories of the open air and its exhilarations, the sky, the clouds, the landscape, and the currents of life that pulse everywhere.

I myself have never made a dead set at studying Nature with notebook and fieldglass in hand. I have rather visited with her. We have walked together or sat down together, and our intimacy grows with the seasons. What I have learned about her ways I have learned easily, almost unconsciously, while fishing or camping or idling about. My desultory habits have their disadvantages, no doubt, but they have their advantages also. A too-strenuous pursuit defeats itself. In the fields and woods more than anywhere else all things come to those who wait, because all things are on the move, and are sure sooner or later to come your way.

To absorb a thing is better than to learn it, and we absorb what we enjoy. We learn things at school, we absorb them in the fields and woods and on the farm. When we look upon Nature with fondness and appreciation she meets us halfway and takes a deeper hold upon us than when studiously conned. Hence I say the way of knowledge of Nature is the way of love and enjoyment, and is more surely found in the open air than in the schoolroom or the laboratory. The other day I saw a lot of college girls dissecting cats and making diagrams of the circulation and muscle attachments, and I thought it pretty poor business unless the girls were taking a course in comparative anatomy with a view to some occupation in life. What is the moral and intellectual value of this kind of knowledge to those girls? Biology is, no doubt, a great science in the hands of great men, but it is not for all. I myself have got along very well without it. I am sure I can learn more of what I want to know from a kitten on my knee than from the carcass of a cat in the laboratory. Darwin spent eight years dissecting barnacles; but he was Darwin, and did not stop at barnacles, as these college girls are pretty sure to stop at cats. He dissected and put together again in his mental laboratory the whole system of animal life, and the upshot of his work was a tremendous gain to our understanding of the universe.

I would rather see the girls in the fields and woods studying and enjoying living nature, training their eyes to see correctly and their hearts to respond intelligently. What is knowledge without enjoyment, without love? It is sympathy, appreciation, emotional experience, which refine and elevate and breathe into exact knowledge the breath of life. My own interest is in living nature as it moves and flourishes about me winter and summer.

I know it is one thing to go forth as a nature-lover, and quite another to go forth in a spirit of cold, calculating, exact science. I call myself a nature-lover and not a scientific naturalist. All that science has to tell me is welcome, is, indeed, eagerly sought for. I must know as well as feel. I am not merely contented, like Wordsworth's poet, to enjoy what others understand. I must understand also; but above all things, I must enjoy. How much of my enjoyment springs from my knowledge I do not know. The joy of knowing is very great; the delight of picking up the threads of meaning here and there, and following them through the maze of confusing facts, I know well. When I hear the woodpecker drumming on a dry limb in spring or the grouse drumming in the woods, and know what it is all for, why, that knowledge, I suppose, is part of my enjoyment. The other part is the associations that those sounds call up as voicing the arrival of spring; they are the drums that lead the joyous procession.

To enjoy understandingly, that, I fancy, is the great thing to be desired. When I see the large ichneumon fly, *Thalessa,* making a loop over her back with her long ovipositor and drilling a hole in the trunk of a tree, I do not fully appreciate the spectacle till I know she is feeling for the burrow of a tree borer, *Tremex,* upon the larvae of which her own young feed. She must survey her territory like an oil-digger and calculate where she is likely to strike oil, which in her case is the burrow of her host *Tremex.* There is a vast series of facts in natural history like this that are of little interest until we understand them. They are like the outside of a book which may attract us, but which can mean little to us until we have opened and perused its pages.

I certainly have found "good in everything"—in all natural processes and products—not the "good" of the Sunday-school books, but the good of natural law and order, the good of that system of things out of which we came and which is the source of our health and strength. It is good that fire should burn, even if it consumes your house; it is good that force should crush, even if it crushes you; it is good that rain should fall, even if it destroys your crops or floods your land. Plagues and pestilences attest the constancy of natural law. They set us to cleaning our streets and houses and to readjusting our relations to outward nature. Only in a live universe could disease and death prevail. Death is a phase of life, a redistributing of the type. Decay is another kind of growth.

Yes, good in everything, because law in everything, truth in every-thing, the sequence of cause and effect in everything, and it may all be good to me if on the right principles I relate my life to it. I can make the heat and the cold serve me, the winds and the floods, gravity and all the chemical and dynamical forces, serve me, if I take hold of them by the right handle. The bad in things arises from our abuse or misuse of them or from our wrong relations to them. A thing is good or bad according as it stands related to my constitution. We say the order of nature is ratio-nal; but is it not because our reason is the outcome of that order? Our well-being consists in learning it and in adjusting our lives to it. When we cross it or seek to contravene it, we are destroyed. But Nature in her universal procedures is not rational as I am rational when I weed my garden, prune my trees, select my seed or my stock, or arm myself with tools or weapons. In such matters I take a short cut to that which Nature reaches by a slow, roundabout, and wasteful process. How does she weed her garden? By the survival of the fittest. How does she select her breed-ing-stock? By the law of battle; the strongest rules. Hers, I repeat, is a slow and wasteful process. She fertilizes the soil by plowing in the crop. She cannot take a short cut. She assorts and arranges her goods by the law of the winds and the tides. She builds up with one hand and pulls down with the other. Man changes the conditions to suit the things. Nature changes the things to suit the conditions. She adapts the plant or the animal to its environment. She does not drain her marshes; she fills them up. Hers is the larger reason—the reason of the All. Man's reason introduces a new method; it cuts across, modifies, or abridges the order of Nature.

I do not see design in Nature in the old teleological sense; but I see everything working to its own proper end, and that end is foretold in the means. Things are not designed; things are begotten. It is as if the final plan of a man's house, after he had begun to build it, should be deter-mined by the winds and the rains and the shape of the ground upon which it stands. The eye is begotten by those vibrations in the ether called light; the ear by those vibrations in the air called sound; the sense of smell by those emanations called odors. There are probably other vibrations and emanations that we have no senses for because our well-being does not demand them.

Yet I would not say that the study of Nature did not favor meekness or sobriety or gentleness or forgiveness or charity, because the great Nature students and prophets, like Darwin, would rise up and confound me. Certainly it favors seriousness, truthfulness, and simplicity of life; or, are only the serious and single-minded drawn to the study of Nature? I doubt very much if it favors devoutness or holiness, as those qualities are inculcated by the church, or any form of religious enthusiasm. Devoutness and holiness come of an attitude toward the universe that is in many ways incompatible with that implied by the pursuit of natural science. The joy of the Nature student like Darwin or any great naturalist is to know, to find out the reason of things and the meaning of things, to trace the footsteps of the creative energy; while the religious devotee is intent only upon losing himself in infinite being. True, there have been devout naturalists and men of science; but their devoutness did not date from their Nature studies, but from their training, or from the times in which they lived. Theology and science, it must be said, will not mingle much better than oil and water, and your devout scientist and devout Nature student lives in two separate compartments of his being at different times. Intercourse with Nature—I mean intellectual intercourse, not merely the emotional intercourse of the sailor or explorer or farmer—tends to beget a habit of mind the farthest possible removed from the myth-making, the vision-seeing, the voice-hearing habit and temper. In all matters relating to the visible, concrete universe it substitutes broad daylight for twilight; it supplants fear with curiosity; it overthrows superstition with fact; it blights credulity with the frost of skepticism. I say frost of skepticism advisedly. Skepticism is a much more healthful and robust habit of mind than the limp, pale-blooded, non-resisting habit that we call credulity.

There can be little doubt, I think, but that intercourse with Nature and a knowledge of her ways tends to simplicity of life. We come more and more to see through the follies and vanities of the world and to appreciate the real values. We load ourselves up with so many false burdens, our complex civilization breeds in us so many false or artificial wants, that we become separated from the real sources of our strength and health as by a gulf.

For my part, as I grow older I am more and more inclined to reduce my baggage, to lop off superfluities. I become more and more in love with simple things and simple folk—a small house, a hut in the woods, a tent on the shore. The show and splendor of great houses, elaborate furnishings, stately halls, oppress me, impose upon me. They fix the attention upon false values, they set up a false standard of beauty; they stand between me and the real feeders of character and thought. A man needs a good roof over his head winter and summer, and a good chimney and a big wood-pile in winter. The more open his four walls are, the more fresh air he will get, and the longer he will live.

Nature is not benevolent; Nature is just, gives pound for pound, measure for measure, makes no exceptions, never tempers her decrees with mercy, or winks at any infringement of her laws. And in the end is not this best? Could the universe be run as a charity or a benevolent institution, or as a poorhouse of the most approved pattern? Without this merciless justice, this irrefragable law, where should we have brought up long ago? It is a hard gospel; but rocks are hard too, yet they form the foundations of the hills.

Man introduces benevolence, mercy, altruism, into the world, and he pays the price in his added burdens; and he reaps his reward in the vast social and civic organizations that were impossible without these things.

Man has been man but a little while comparatively, less than one hour of the twenty-four of the vast geologic day; a few hours more and he will be gone; less than another geologic day like the past, and no doubt all life from the earth will be gone. What then? The game will be played over and over again in other worlds, without approaching any nearer the final end than we are now. There is no final end, as there was no absolute beginning, and can be none with the infinite.

JOHN MUIR
1838-1914

Although John Muir has long been famous as an explorer and environmental activist, critical esteem for his writing has only recently caught up with admiration for his adventures. His style could be exuberant, even florid, and Muir once wryly complained about the necessity, in revising his work, of "slaughtering gloriouses." But his mountain narratives also convey the authority of an acute eye and a firm understanding of geological processes. The first man to ascribe a glacial origin to Yosemite Valley, he buttressed his view both with a careful record of the grooves on rocks and with the knowledge of glaciology he learned at the University of Wisconsin, eventually prevailing over the opposing, "cataclysmic" theory of Josiah Whitney and the scientific establishment.

Born in Dunbar, Scotland, and raised as a youth on a Wisconsin homestead, Muir went on to explore wild places from Alaska to South America. But Yosemite Valley, from the moment he strode into it, became his classic landscape. The effort to save Yosemite, and to preserve the nearby valley at Hetch Hetchy, was the focus of his articles for the Century *magazine, and led to his founding of the Sierra Club in 1892. These articles also became the basis for* The Mountains of California *(1894). Muir's writing introduced the prophetic voice that resounds in contemporary authors like Edward Abbey—the fierce advocacy for wilderness that sometimes leads to searing critiques of society. Looking at the commercial interests establishing themselves in the Sierra at century's end, Muir could already proclaim, "The money-changers are in the temple."*

A WIND-STORM IN THE FORESTS

The mountain winds, like the dew and rain, sunshine and snow, are measured and bestowed with love on the forests to develop their strength and beauty. However restricted the scope of other forest influences, that of the winds is universal. The snow bends and trims the upper forests every winter, the lightning strikes a single tree here and there, while avalanches mow down thousands at a swoop as a gardener trims out a bed of flowers. But the winds go to every tree, fingering every leaf and branch and furrowed bole; not one is forgotten; the Mountain Pine towering with outstretched arms on the rugged buttresses of the icy peaks, the lowliest and most retiring tenant of the dells; they seek and find them all, caressing them tenderly, bending them in lusty exercise, stimulating their growth, plucking off a leaf or limb as required, or removing an entire tree or grove, now whispering and cooing through the branches like a sleepy child, now roaring like the ocean; the winds blessing the forests, the forests the winds, with ineffable beauty and harmony as the sure result.

The Mountains of California (New York: Century, 1894).

After one has seen pines six feet in diameter bending like grasses before a mountain gale, and ever and anon some giant falling with a crash that shakes the hills, it seems astonishing that any, save the lowest thickset trees, could ever have found a period sufficiently stormless to establish themselves; or, once established, that they should not, sooner or later, have been blown down. But when the storm is over, and we behold the same forests tranquil again, towering fresh and unscathed in erect majesty, and consider what centuries of storms have fallen upon them since they were first planted,—hail, to break the tender seedlings; lightning, to scorch and shatter; snow, winds, and avalanches, to crush and overwhelm,—while the manifest result of all this wild storm-culture is the glorious perfection we behold; then faith in Nature's forestry is established, and we cease to deplore the violence of her most destructive gales, or of any other storm-implement whatsoever.

There are two trees in the Sierra forests that are never blown down, so long as they continue in sound health. These are the Juniper and the Dwarf Pine of the summit peaks. Their stiff, crooked roots grip the storm-beaten ledges like eagles' claws, while their lithe, cord-like branches bend round compliantly, offering but slight holds for winds, however violent. The other alpine conifers—the Needle Pine, Mountain Pine, Two-leaved Pine, and Hemlock Spruce—are never thinned out by this agent to any destructive extent, on account of their admirable toughness and the closeness of their growth. In general the same is true of the giants of the lower zones. The kingly Sugar Pine, towering aloft to a height of more than 200 feet, offers a fine mark to storm-winds; but it is not densely foliaged, and its long, horizontal arms swing round compliantly in the blast, like tresses of green, fluent algæ in a brook; while the Silver Firs in most places keep their ranks well together in united strength. The Yellow or Silver Pine is more frequently overturned than any other tree on the Sierra, because its leaves and branches form a larger mass in proportion to its height, while in many places it is planted sparsely, leaving open lanes through which storms may enter with full force. Furthermore, because it is distributed along the lower portion of the range, which was the first to be left bare on the breaking up of the ice-sheet at the close of the glacial winter, the soil it is growing upon has been longer exposed to post-glacial weathering, and consequently is in a more crumbling, decayed condition than the fresher soils farther up the range, and therefore offers a less secure anchorage for the roots.

While exploring the forest zones of Mount Shasta, I discovered the path of a hurricane strewn with thousands of pines of this species. Great and small had been uprooted or wrenched off by sheer force, making a clean gap, like that made by a snow avalanche. But hurricanes capable of doing this class of work are rare in the Sierra, and when we have explored the forests from one extremity of the range to the other, we are compelled to believe that they are the most beautiful on the face of the earth, however we may regard the agents that have made them so.

There is always something deeply exciting, not only in the sounds of winds in the woods, which exert more or less influence over every mind, but in their varied waterlike flow as manifested by the movements of the trees, especially those of the conifers. By no other trees are they rendered so extensively and impressively visible, not even by the lordly tropic palms or tree-ferns responsive to the gentlest breeze. The waving of a forest of the giant Sequoias is indescribably impressive and sublime, but the pines seem to me the best interpreters of winds. They are mighty waving goldenrods, ever in tune, singing and writing wind-music all their long century lives. Little, however, of this noble tree-waving and tree-music will you see or hear in the strictly alpine portion of the forests. The burly Juniper, whose girth sometimes more than equals its height, is about as rigid as the rocks on which it grows. The slender lash-like sprays of the Dwarf Pine stream out in wavering ripples, but the tallest and slenderest are far too unyielding to wave even in the heaviest gales. They only shake in quick, short vibrations. The Hemlock Spruce, however, and the Mountain Pine, and some of the tallest thickets of the Two-leaved species bow in storms with considerable scope and gracefulness. But it is only in the lower and middle zones that the meeting of winds and woods is to be seen in all its grandeur.

One of the most beautiful and exhilarating storms I ever enjoyed in the Sierra occurred in December, 1874, when I happened to be exploring one of the tributary valleys of the Yuba River. The sky and the ground and the trees had been thoroughly rain-washed and were dry again. The day was intensely pure, one of those incomparable bits of California winter, warm and balmy and full of white sparkling sunshine, redolent of all the purest influences of the spring, and at the same time enlivened with one of the most bracing wind-storms conceivable. Instead of camping out, as I usually do, I then chanced to be stopping at the house of a friend. But when the storm began to sound, I lost no time in pushing out into the woods to enjoy it. For on such occasions Nature has always something rare to show us, and the danger to life and limb is hardly greater than one would experience crouching deprecatingly beneath a roof.

It was still early morning when I found myself fairly adrift. Delicious sunshine came pouring over the hills, lighting the tops of the pines, and setting free a stream of summery fragrance that contrasted strangely with the wild tones of the storm. The air was mottled with pine-tassels and bright green plumes, that went flashing past in the sunlight like birds pursued. But there was not the slightest dustiness, nothing less pure than leaves, and ripe pollen, and flecks of withered bracken and moss. I heard trees falling for hours at the rate of one every two or three minutes; some uprooted, partly on account of the loose, water-soaked condition of the ground; others broken straight across, where some weakness caused by fire had determined the spot. The gestures of the various trees made a delightful study. Young Sugar Pines, light and feathery as squirrel-tails, were bowing almost to the ground; while the grand old patriarchs, whose massive boles had been tried in a hundred storms, waved solemnly above them, their long, arching branches streaming fluently on the gale, and every needle thrilling and ringing and shedding off keen lances of light like a diamond. The Douglas Spruces, with long sprays drawn out in level tresses, and needles massed in a gray, shimmering glow, presented a most striking appearance as they stood in bold relief along the hilltops. The madroños in the dells, with their red bark and large glossy leaves tilted every way, reflected the sunshine in throbbing spangles like those one so often sees on the rippled surface of a glacier lake. But the Silver Pines were now the most impressively beautiful of all. Colossal spires 200 feet in height waved like supple goldenrods chanting and bowing low as if in worship, while the whole mass of their long, tremulous foliage was kindled into one continuous blaze of white sun-fire. The force of the gale was such that the most steadfast monarch of them all rocked down to its roots with a motion plainly perceptible when one leaned against it. Nature was holding high festival, and every fiber of the most rigid giants thrilled with glad excitement.

I drifted on through the midst of this passionate music and motion, across many a glen, from ridge to ridge; often halting in the lee of a rock for shelter, or to gaze and listen. Even when the grand anthem had swelled to its highest pitch, I could distinctly hear the varying tones of individual trees,—Spruce, and Fir, and Pine, and leafless Oak,—and even the infinitely gentle rustle of the withered grasses at my feet. Each was expressing itself in its own way,—singing its own song, and making its own peculiar gestures,—manifesting a richness of variety to be found in no other forest I have yet seen. The coniferous woods of Canada, and the Carolinas, and Florida, are made up of trees that resemble one another about as nearly as blades of grass, and grow close together in much the same way. Coniferous trees, in general, seldom possess individual character, such as is manifest among Oaks and Elms. But the California forests are made up of a greater number of distinct species than any other in the world. And in them we find, not only a marked differentiation into special groups, but also a marked individuality in almost every tree, giving rise to storm effects indescribably glorious.

Toward midday, after a long, tingling scramble through copses of hazel and ceanothus, I gained the summit of the highest ridge in the neighborhood; and then it occurred to me that it would be a fine thing to climb one of the trees to obtain a wider outlook and get my ear close to the Æolian music of its topmost needles. But under the circumstances the choice of a tree was a serious matter. One whose instep was not very strong seemed in danger of being blown down, or of being struck by others in case they should fall; another was branchless to a considerable height above the ground, and at the same time too large to be grasped with arms and legs in climbing; while others were not favorably situated for clear views. After cautiously casting about, I made choice of the tallest of a group of Douglas Spruces that were growing close together like a tuft of grass, no one of which seemed likely to fall unless all the rest fell with it. Though comparatively young, they were about 100 feet high, and their lithe, brushy tops were rocking and swirling in wild ecstasy. Being accustomed to climb trees in making botanical studies, I experienced no difficulty in reaching the top of this one, and never before did I enjoy so noble an exhilaration of motion. The slender tops fairly flapped and swished in the passionate torrent, bending and swirling backward and forward, round and round, tracing indescribable combinations of vertical and horizontal curves, while I clung with muscles firm braced, like a bobolink on a reed.

In its widest sweeps my tree-top described an arc of from twenty to thirty degrees, but I felt sure of its elastic temper, having seen others of the same species still more severely tried—bent almost to the ground indeed, in heavy snows—without breaking a fiber. I was therefore safe, and free to take the wind into my pulses and enjoy the excited forest from my superb outlook. The view from here must be extremely beautiful in any weather. Now my eye roved over the piny hills and dales as over fields of waving grain, and felt the light running in ripples and broad swelling undulations across the valleys from ridge to ridge, as the shining foliage was stirred by corresponding waves of air. Oftentimes these waves of reflected light would break up suddenly into a kind of beaten foam, and again, after chasing one another in regular order, they would seem to bend forward in concentric curves, and disappear on some hillside, like sea-waves on a shelving shore. The quantity of light reflected from the bent needles was so great as to make whole groves appear as if covered with snow, while the black shadows beneath the trees greatly enhanced the effect of the silvery splendor.

Excepting only the shadows there was nothing somber in all this wild sea of pines. On the contrary, notwithstanding this was the winter season, the colors were remarkably beautiful. The shafts of the pine and libocedrus were brown and purple, and most of the foliage was well tinged with yellow; the laurel groves, with the pale undersides of their leaves turned upward, made masses of gray; and then there was many a dash of chocolate color from clumps of manzanita, and jet of vivid crimson from the bark of the madroños, while the ground on the hillsides, appearing here and there through openings between the groves, displayed masses of pale purple and brown.

The sounds of the storm corresponded gloriously with this wild exuberance of light and motion. The profound bass of the naked branches and boles booming like waterfalls; the quick, tense vibrations of the pine-needles, now rising to a shrill, whistling hiss, now falling to a silky murmur; the rustling of laurel groves in the dells, and the keen metallic click of leaf on leaf—all this was heard in easy analysis when the attention was calmly bent.

The varied gestures of the multitude were seen to fine advantage, so that one could recognize the different species at a distance of several miles by this means alone, as well as by their forms and colors, and the way they reflected the light. All seemed strong and comfortable, as if really enjoying the storm, while responding to its most enthusiastic greetings. We hear much nowadays concerning the universal struggle for existence, but no struggle in the common meaning of the word was manifest here; no recognition of danger by any tree; no deprecation; but rather an invincible gladness as remote from exultation as from fear.

I kept my lofty perch for hours, frequently closing my eyes to enjoy the music by itself, or to feast quietly on the delicious fragrance that was streaming past. The fragrance of the woods was less marked than that produced during warm rain, when so many balsamic buds and leaves are steeped like tea; but, from the chafing of resiny branches against each other, and the incessant attrition of myriads of needles, the gale was spiced to a very tonic degree. And besides the fragrance from these local sources there were traces of scents brought from afar. For this wind came first from the sea, rubbing against its fresh, briny waves, then distilled through the redwoods, threading rich ferny gulches, and spreading itself in broad undulating currents over many a flower-enameled ridge of the coast mountains, then across the golden plains, up the purple foot-hills, and into these piny woods with the varied incense gathered by the way.

Winds are advertisements of all they touch, however much or little we may be able to read them; telling their wanderings even by their scents alone. Mariners detect the flowery perfume of land-winds far at sea, and sea-winds carry the fragrance of dulse and tangle far inland, where it is quickly recognized, though mingled with the scents of a thousand land-flowers. As an illustration of this, I may tell here that I breathed sea-air on the Firth of Forth, in Scotland, while a boy; then was taken to Wisconsin, where I remained nineteen years; then, without in all this time having breathed one breath of the sea, I walked quietly, alone, from the middle of the Mississippi Valley to the Gulf of Mexico, on a botanical excursion, and while in Florida, far from the coast, my attention wholly bent on the splendid tropical vegetation about me, I suddenly recognized a sea-breeze, as it came sifting through the palmettos and blooming vine-tangles, which at once awakened and set free a thousand dormant associations, and made me a boy again in Scotland, as if all the intervening years had been annihilated.

Most people like to look at mountain rivers, and bear them in mind; but few care to look at the winds, though far more beautiful and sublime, and though they become at times about as visible as flowing water. When the north winds in winter are making upward sweeps over the curving summits of the High Sierra, the fact is sometimes published with flying snow-banners a mile long. Those portions of the winds thus embodied can scarce be wholly invisible, even to the darkest imagination. And when we look around over an agitated forest, we may see something of the wind that stirs it, by its effects upon the trees. Yonder it descends in a rush of water-like ripples, and sweeps over the bending pines from hill to hill. Nearer, we see detached plumes and leaves, now speeding by on level currents, now whirling in eddies, or, escaping over the edges of the whirls, soaring aloft on grand, upswelling domes of air, or tossing on flame-like crests. Smooth, deep currents, cascades, falls, and swirling eddies, sing around every tree and leaf, and over all the varied topography of the region with telling changes of form, like mountain rivers conforming to the features of their channels.

After tracing the Sierra streams from their fountains to the plains, marking where they bloom white in falls, glide in crystal plumes, surge gray and foam-filled in boulder-choked gorges, and slip through the woods in long, tranquil reaches—after thus learning their language and forms in detail, we may at length hear them chanting all together in one grand anthem, and comprehend them all in clear inner vision, covering the range like lace. But even this spectacle is far less sublime and not a whit more substantial than what we may behold of these storm-streams of air in the mountain woods.

We all travel the milky way together, trees and men; but it never occurred to me until this stormday, while swinging in the wind, that trees are travelers, in the ordinary sense. They make many journeys, not extensive ones, it is true; but our own little journeys, away and back again, are only little more than tree-wavings—many of them not so much.

When the storm began to abate, I dismounted and sauntered down through the calming woods. The storm-tones died away, and, turning toward the east, I beheld the countless hosts of the forests hushed and tranquil, towering above one another on the slopes of the hills like a devout audience. The setting sun filled them with amber light, and seemed to say, while they listened, "My peace I give unto you."

As I gazed on the impressive scene, all the so-called ruin of the storm was forgotten, and never before did these noble woods appear so fresh, so joyous, so immortal.

THE WATER-OUZEL

The waterfalls of the Sierra are frequented by only one bird,—the Ouzel or Water Thrush (*Cinclus Mexicanus,* Sw.). He is a singularly joyous and lovable little fellow, about the size of a robin, clad in a plain waterproof suit of bluish gray, with a tinge of chocolate on the head and shoulders. In form he is about as smoothly plump and compact as a pebble that has been whirled in a pot-hole, the flowing contour of his body being interrupted only by his strong feet and bill, the crisp wing-tips, and the up-slanted wren-like tail.

Among all the countless waterfalls I have met in the course of ten years' exploration in the Sierra, whether among the icy peaks, or warm foot-hills, or in the profound yosemitic cañons of the middle region, not one was found without its Ouzel. No cañon is too cold for this little bird, none too lonely, provided it be rich in falling water. Find a fall, or cascade, or rushing rapid, anywhere upon a clear stream, and there you will surely find its complementary Ouzel, flitting about in the spray, diving in foaming eddies, whirling like a leaf among beaten foam-bells; ever vigorous and enthusiastic, yet self-contained, and neither seeking nor shunning your company.

If disturbed while dipping about in the margin shallows, he either sets off with a rapid whir to some other feeding-ground up or down the stream, or alights on some half-submerged rock or snag out in the current, and immediately begins to nod and courtesy like a wren, turning his head from side to side with many other odd dainty movements that never fail to fix the attention of the observer.

He is the mountain streams' own darling, the humming-bird of blooming waters, loving rocky ripple-slopes and sheets of foam as a bee loves flowers, as a lark loves sunshine and meadows. Among all the mountain birds, none has cheered me so much in my lonely wanderings,—none so unfailingly. For both in winter and summer he sings, sweetly, cheerily, independent alike of sunshine and of love, requiring no other inspiration than the stream on which he dwells. While water sings, so must he, in heat or cold, calm or storm, ever attuning his voice in sure accord; low in the drought of summer and the drought of winter, but never silent.

During the golden days of Indian summer, after most of the snow has been melted, and the mountain streams have become feeble,—a succession of silent pools, linked together by shallow, transparent currents and strips of silvery lacework,—then the song of the Ouzel is at its lowest ebb. But as soon as the winter clouds have bloomed, and the mountain treasures are once more replenished with snow, the voices of the streams and ouzels increase in strength and richness until the flood season of early summer. Then the torrents chant their noblest anthems, and then is the flood-time of our songster's melody. As for weather, dark days and sun days are the same to him. The voices of most song-birds, however joyous, suffer a long winter eclipse; but the Ouzel sings on through all the seasons and every kind of storm. Indeed no storm can be more violent than those of the waterfalls in the midst of which he delights to dwell. However dark and boisterous the weather, snowing, blowing, or cloudy, all the same he sings, and with never a note of sadness. No need of spring sunshine to thaw *his* song, for it never freezes. Never shall you hear anything wintry from *his* warm breast; no pinched cheeping, no wavering notes between sorrow and joy; his mellow, fluty voice is ever tuned to downright gladness, as free from dejection as cock-crowing.

It is pitiful to see wee frost-pinched sparrows on cold mornings in the mountain groves shaking the snow from their feathers, and hopping about as if anxious to be cheery, then hastening back to their hidings out of the wind, puffing out their breast-feathers over their toes, and subsiding among the leaves, cold and breakfastless, while the snow continues to fall, and there is no sign of clearing. But the Ouzel never calls forth a single touch of pity; not because he is strong to endure, but rather because he seems to live a charmed life beyond the reach of every influence that makes endurance necessary.

One wild winter morning, when Yosemite Valley was swept its length from west to east by a cordial snow-storm, I sallied forth to see what I might learn and enjoy. A sort of gray, gloaming-like darkness filled the valley, the huge walls were out of sight, all ordinary sounds were smothered, and even the loudest booming of the falls was at times buried beneath the roar of the heavy-laden blast. The loose snow was already over five feet deep on the meadows, making extended walks impossible without the aid of snow-shoes. I found no great difficulty, however, in making my way to a certain ripple on the river where one of my ouzels lived. He was at home, busily gleaning his breakfast among the pebbles of a shallow portion of the margin, apparently unaware of anything extraordinary in the weather. Presently he flew out to a stone against which the icy current was beating, and turning his back to the wind, sang as delightfully as a lark in springtime.

After spending an hour or two with my favorite, I made my way across the valley, boring and wallowing through the drifts, to learn as definitely as possible how the other birds were spending their time. The Yosemite birds are easily found during the winter because all of them excepting the Ouzel are restricted to the sunny north side of the valley, the south side being constantly eclipsed by the great frosty shadow of the wall. And because the Indian Cañon groves, from their peculiar exposure, are the warmest, the birds congregate there, more especially in severe weather.

I found most of the robins cowering on the lee side of the larger branches where the snow could not fall upon them, while two or three of the more enterprising were making desperate efforts to reach the mistle-toe berries by clinging nervously to the under side of the snow-crowned masses, back downward, like woodpeckers. Every now and then they would dislodge some of the loose fringes of the snow-crown, which would come sifting down on them and send them screaming back to camp, where they would subside among their companions with a shiver, muttering in low, querulous chatter like hungry children.

Some of the sparrows were busy at the feet of the larger trees gleaning seeds and benumbed insects, joined now and then by a robin weary of his unsuccessful attempts upon the snow-covered berries. The brave wood-peckers were clinging to the snowless sides of the larger boles and over-arching branches of the camp trees, making short flights from side to side of the grove, pecking now and then at the acorns they had stored in the bark, and chattering aimlessly as if unable to keep still, yet evidently putting in the time in a very dull way, like storm-bound travelers at a country tavern. The hardy nut-hatches were threading the open furrows of the trunks in their usual industrious manner, and uttering their quaint notes, evidently less distressed than their neighbors. The Steller jays were of course making more noisy stir than all the other birds combined; ever coming and going with loud bluster, screaming as if each had a lump of melting sludge in his throat, and taking good care to improve the favorable opportunity afforded by the storm to steal from the acorn stores of the woodpeckers. I also noticed one solitary gray eagle braving the storm on the top of a tall pine-stump just outside the main grove. He was standing bolt upright with his back to the wind, a tuft of snow piled on his square shoulders, a monument of passive endurance. Thus every snow-bound bird seemed more or less uncomfortable if not in positive distress. The storm was reflected in every gesture, and not one cheerful note, not to say song, came from a single bill; their cowering, joyless endurance offering a striking contrast to the spontaneous, irrepressible gladness of the Ouzel, who could no more help exhaling sweet song than a rose sweet fragrance. He *must* sing though the heavens fall. I remember noticing the distress of a pair of robins during the violent earthquake of the year 1872, when the pines of the Valley, with strange movements, flapped and waved their branches, and beetling rock-brows came thundering down to the meadows in tremendous avalanches. It did not occur to me in the midst of the excitement of other observations to look for the ouzels, but I doubt not they were singing straight on through it all, regarding the terrible rock-thunder as fearlessly as they do the booming of the waterfalls.

What may be regarded as the separate songs of the Ouzel are exceedingly difficult of description, because they are so variable and at the same time so confluent. Though I have been acquainted with my favorite ten years, and during most of this time have heard him sing nearly every day, I still detect notes and strains that seem new to me. Nearly all of his music is sweet and tender, lapsing from his round breast like water over the smooth lip of a pool, then breaking farther on into a sparkling foam of melodious notes, which glow with subdued enthusiasm, yet without expressing much of the strong, gushing ecstasy of the bobolink or skylark.

The more striking strains are perfect arabesques of melody, composed of a few full, round, mellow notes, embroidered with delicate trills which fade and melt in long slender cadences. In a general way his music is that of the streams refined and spiritualized. The deep booming notes of the falls are in it, the trills of rapids, the gurgling of margin eddies, the low whispering of level reaches, and the sweet tinkle of separate drops oozing from the ends of mosses and falling into tranquil pools.

The Ouzel never sings in chorus with other birds, nor with his kind, but only with the streams. And like flowers that bloom beneath the surface of the ground, some of our favorite's best song-blossoms never rise above the surface of the heavier music of the water. I have often observed him singing in the midst of beaten spray, his music completely buried beneath the water's roar; yet I knew he was surely singing by his gestures and the movements of his bill.

His food, as far as I have noticed, consists of all kinds of water insects, which in summer are chiefly procured along shallow margins. Here he wades about ducking his head under water and deftly turning over pebbles and fallen leaves with his bill, seldom choosing to go into deep water where he has to use his wings in diving.

He seems to be especially fond of the larvæ of mosquitos, found in abundance attached to the bottom of smooth rock channels where the current is shallow. When feeding in such places he wades up-stream, and often while his head is under water the swift current is deflected upward along the glossy curves of his neck and shoulders, in the form of a clear, crystalline shell, which fairly incloses him like a bell-glass, the shell being broken and re-formed as he lifts and dips his head; while ever and anon he sidles out to where the too powerful current carries him off his feet; then he dexterously rises on the wing and goes gleaning again in shallower places.

But during the winter, when the stream-banks are embossed in snow, and the streams themselves are chilled nearly to the freezing-point, so that the snow falling into them in stormy weather is not wholly dissolved, but forms a thin, blue sludge, thus rendering the current opaque—then he seeks the deeper portions of the main rivers, where he may dive to clear water beneath the sludge. Or he repairs to some open lake or millpond, at the bottom of which he feeds in safety.

When thus compelled to betake himself to a lake, he does not plunge into it at once like a duck, but always alights in the first place upon some rock or fallen pine along the shore. Then flying out thirty or forty yards, more or less, according to the character of the bottom, he alights with a dainty glint on the surface, swims about, looks down, finally makes up his mind, and disappears with a sharp stroke of his wings. After feeding for two or three minutes he suddenly reappears, showers the water from his wings with one vigorous shake, and rises abruptly into the air as if pushed up from beneath, comes back to his perch, sings a few minutes, and goes out to dive again; thus coming and going, singing and diving at the same place for hours.

The Ouzel is usually found singly; rarely in pairs, excepting during the breeding season, and *very* rarely in threes or fours. I once observed three thus spending a winter morning in company, upon a small glacier lake, on the Upper Merced, about 7500 feet above the level of the sea. A storm had occurred during the night, but the morning sun shone unclouded, and the shadowy lake, gleaming darkly in its setting of fresh snow, lay smooth and motionless as a mirror. My camp chanced to be within a few feet of the water's edge, opposite a fallen pine, some of the branches of which leaned out over the lake. Here my three dearly welcome visitors took up their station, and at once began to embroider the frosty air with their delicious melody, doubly delightful to me that particular morning, as I had been somewhat apprehensive of danger in breaking my way down through the snow-choked cañons to the low-lands.

The portion of the lake bottom selected for a feeding-ground lies at a depth of fifteen or twenty feet below the surface, and is covered with a short growth of algæ and other aquatic plants,—facts I had previously determined while sailing over it on a raft. After alighting on the glassy surface, they occasionally indulged in a little play, chasing one another round about in small circles; then all three would suddenly dive together, and then come ashore and sing.

The Ouzel seldom swims more than a few yards on the surface, for, not being web-footed, he makes rather slow progress, but by means of his strong, crisp wings he swims, or rather flies, with celerity under the surface, often to considerable distances. But it is in withstanding the force of heavy rapids that his strength of wing in this respect is most strikingly manifested. The following may be regarded as a fair illustration of his power of sub-aquatic flight. One stormy morning in winter when the Merced River was blue and green with unmelted snow, I observed one of my ouzels perched on a snag out in the midst of a swift-rushing rapid, singing cheerily, as if everything was just to his mind; and while I stood on the bank admiring him, he suddenly plunged into the sludgy current, leaving his song abruptly broken off. After feeding a minute or two at the bottom, and when one would suppose that he must inevitably be swept far down-stream, he emerged just where he went down, alighted on the same snag, showered the water-beads from his feathers, and continued his unfinished song, seemingly in tranquil ease as if it had suffered no interruption.

The Ouzel alone of all birds dares to enter a white torrent. And though strictly terrestrial in structure, no other is so inseparably related to water, not even the duck, or the bold ocean albatross, or the stormy-petrel. For ducks go ashore as soon as they finish feeding in undisturbed places, and very often make long flights overland from lake to lake or field to field. The same is true of most other aquatic birds. But the Ouzel, born on the brink of a stream, or on a snag or boulder in the midst of it, seldom leaves it for a single moment. For, notwithstanding he is often on the wing, he never flies overland, but whirs with rapid, quail-like beat above the stream, tracing all its windings. Even when the stream is quite small, say from five to ten feet wide, he seldom shortens his flight by crossing a bend, however abrupt it may be; and even when disturbed by meeting some one on the bank, he prefers to fly over one's head, to dodging out over the ground. When, therefore, his flight along a crooked stream is viewed endwise, it appears most strikingly wavered—a description on the air of every curve with lightning-like rapidity.

The vertical curves and angles of the most precipitous torrents he traces with the same rigid fidelity, swooping down the inclines of cascades, dropping sheer over dizzy falls amid the spray, and ascending with the same fearlessness and ease, seldom seeking to lessen the steepness of the acclivity by beginning to ascend before reaching the base of the fall. No matter though it may be several hundred feet in height he holds straight on, as if about to dash headlong into the throng of booming rockets, then darts abruptly upward, and, after alighting at the top of the precipice to rest a moment, proceeds to feed and sing. His flight is solid and impetuous, without any intermission of wing-beats,—one homogeneous buzz like that of a laden bee on its way home. And while thus buzzing freely from fall to fall, he is frequently heard giving utterance to a long outdrawn train of unmodulated notes, in no way connected with his song, but corresponding closely with his flight in sustained vigor.

Were the flights of all the ouzels in the Sierra traced on a chart, they would indicate the direction of the flow of the entire system of ancient glaciers, from about the period of the breaking up of the ice-sheet until near the close of the glacial winter; because the streams which the ouzels so rigidly follow are, with the unimportant exceptions of a few side tributaries, all flowing in channels eroded for them out of the solid flank of the range by the vanished glaciers,—the streams tracing the ancient glaciers, the ouzels tracing the streams. Nor do we find so complete compliance to glacial conditions in the life of any other mountain bird, or animal of any kind. Bears frequently accept the pathways laid down by glaciers as the easiest to travel; but they often leave them and cross over from cañon to cañon. So also, most of the birds trace the moraines to some extent, because the forests are growing on them. But they wander far, crossing the cañons from grove to grove, and draw exceedingly angular and complicated courses.

The Ouzel's nest is one of the most extraordinary pieces of bird architecture I ever saw, odd and novel in design, perfectly fresh and beautiful, and in every way worthy of the genius of the little builder. It is about a foot in diameter, round and bossy in outline, with a neatly arched opening near the bottom, somewhat like an old-fashioned brick oven, or Hottentot's hut. It is built almost exclusively of green and yellow mosses, chiefly the beautiful fronded hypnum that covers the rocks and old drift-logs in the vicinity of waterfalls. These are deftly interwoven, and felted together into a charming little hut; and so situated that many of the outer mosses continue to flourish as if they had not been plucked. A few fine, silky-stemmed grasses are occasionally found interwoven with the mosses, but, with the exception of a thin layer lining the floor, their presence seems accidental, as they are of a species found growing with the mosses and are probably plucked with them. The site chosen for this curious mansion is usually some little rock-shelf within reach of the lighter particles of the spray of a waterfall, so that its walls are kept green and growing, at least during the time of high water.

No harsh lines are presented by any portion of the nest as seen in place, but when removed from its shelf, the back and bottom, and sometimes a portion of the top, is found quite sharply angular, because it is made to conform to the surface of the rock upon which and against which it is built, the little architect always taking advantage of slight crevices and protuberances that may chance to offer, to render his structure stable by means of a kind of gripping and dovetailing.

In choosing a building-spot, concealment does not seem to be taken into consideration; yet notwithstanding the nest is large and guilelessly exposed to view, it is far from being easily detected, chiefly because it swells forward like any other bulging moss-cushion growing naturally in such situations. This is more especially the case where the nest is kept fresh by being well sprinkled. Sometimes these romantic little huts have their beauty enhanced by rock-ferns and grasses that spring up around the mossy walls, or in front of the door-sill, dripping with crystal beads.

Furthermore, at certain hours of the day, when the sunshine is poured down at the required angle, the whole mass of the spray enveloping the fairy establishment is brilliantly irised; and it is through so glorious a rainbow atmosphere as this that some of our blessed ouzels obtain their first peep at the world.

Ouzels seem so completely part and parcel of the streams they inhabit, they scarce suggest any other origin than the streams themselves; and one might almost be pardoned in fancying they come direct from the living waters, like flowers from the ground. At least, from whatever cause, it never occurred to me to look for their nests until more than a year after I had made the acquaintance of the birds themselves, although I found one the very day on which I began the search. In making my way from Yosemite to the glaciers at the heads of the Merced and Tuolumne rivers, I camped in a particularly wild and romantic portion of the Nevada cañon where in previous excursions I had never failed to enjoy the company of my favorites, who were attracted here, no doubt, by the safe nesting-places in the shelving rocks, and by the abundance of food and falling water. The river, for miles above and below, consists of a succession of small falls from ten to sixty feet in height, connected by flat, plume-like cascades that go flashing from fall to fall, free and almost channelless, over waving folds of glacier-polished granite.

On the south side of one of the falls, that portion of the precipice which is bathed by the spray presents a series of little shelves and tablets caused by the development of planes of cleavage in the granite, and by the consequent fall of masses through the action of the water. "Now here," said I, "of all places, is the most charming spot for an Ouzel's nest." Then carefully scanning the fretted face of the precipice through the spray, I at length noticed a yellowish moss-cushion, growing on the edge of a level tablet within five or six feet of the outer folds of the fall. But apart from the fact of its being situated where one acquainted with the lives of ouzels would fancy an Ouzel's nest ought to be, there was nothing in its appearance visible at first sight, to distinguish it from other bosses of rock-moss similarly situated with reference to perennial spray; and it was not until I had scrutinized it again and again, and had removed my shoes and stockings and crept along the face of the rock within eight or ten feet of it, that I could decide certainly whether it was a nest or a natural growth.

In these moss huts three or four eggs are laid, white like foam-bubbles; and well may the little birds hatched from them sing water songs, for they hear them all their lives, and even before they are born.

I have often observed the young just out of the nest making their odd gestures, and seeming in every way as much at home as their experienced parents, like young bees on their first excursions to the flower fields. No amount of familiarity with people and their ways seems to change them in the least. To all appearance their behavior is just the same on seeing a man for the first time, as when they have seen him frequently.

On the lower reaches of the rivers where mills are built, they sing on through the din of the machinery, and all the noisy confusion of dogs, cattle, and workmen. On one occasion, while a wood-chopper was at work on the river-bank, I observed one cheerily singing within reach of the flying chips. Nor does any kind of unwonted disturbance put him in bad humor, or frighten him out of calm self-possession. In passing through a narrow gorge, I once drove one ahead of me from rapid to rapid, disturbing him four times in quick succession where he could not very well fly past me on account of the narrowness of the channel. Most birds under similar circumstances fancy themselves pursued, and become suspiciously uneasy; but, instead of growing nervous about it, he made his usual dippings, and sang one of his most tranquil strains. When observed within a few yards their eyes are seen to express remarkable gentleness and intelligence; but they seldom allow so near a view unless one wears clothing of about the same color as the rocks and trees, and knows how to sit still. On one occasion, while rambling along the shore of a mountain lake, where the birds, at least those born that season, had never seen a man, I sat down to rest on a large stone close to the water's edge, upon which it seemed the ouzels and sandpipers were in the habit of alighting when they came to feed on that part of the shore, and some of the other birds also, when they came down to wash or drink. In a few minutes, along came a whirring Ouzel and alighted on the stone beside me, within reach of my hand. Then suddenly observing me, he stooped nervously as if about to fly on the instant, but as I remained as motionless as the stone, he gained confidence, and looked me steadily in the face for about a minute, then flew quietly to the outlet and began to sing. Next came a sandpiper and gazed at me with much the same guileless expression of eye as the Ouzel. Lastly, down with a swoop came a Stellar's jay out of a fir-tree, probably with the intention of moistening his noisy throat. But instead of sitting confidingly as my other visitors had done, he rushed off at once, nearly tumbling heels over head into the lake in his suspicious confusion, and with loud screams roused the neighborhood.

Love for song-birds, with their sweet human voices, appears to be more common and unfailing than love for flowers. Every one loves flowers to some extent, at least in life's fresh morning, attracted by them as instinctively as humming-birds and bees. Even the young Digger Indians have sufficient love for the brightest of those found growing on the mountains to gather them and braid them as decorations for the hair. And I was glad to discover, through the few Indians that could be induced to talk on the subject, that they have names for the wild rose and the lily, and other conspicuous flowers, whether available as food or otherwise. Most men, however, whether savage or civilized, become apathetic toward all plants that have no other apparent use than the use of beauty. But fortunately one's first instinctive love of songbirds is never wholly obliterated, no matter what the influences upon our lives may be. I have often been delighted to see a pure, spiritual glow come into the countenances of hard business-men and old miners, when a song-bird chanced to alight near them. Nevertheless, the little mouthful of meat that swells out the breasts of some song-birds is too often the cause of their death. Larks and robins in particular are brought to market in hundreds. But fortunately the Ouzel has no enemy so eager to eat his little body as to follow him into the mountain solitudes. I never knew him to be chased even by hawks.

An acquaintance of mine, a sort of foot-hill mountaineer, had a pet cat, a great, dozy, overgrown creature, about as broad-shouldered as a lynx. During the winter, while the snow lay deep, the mountaineer sat in his lonely cabin among the pines smoking his pipe and wearing the dull time away. Tom was his sole companion, sharing his bed, and sitting beside him on a stool with much the same drowsy expression of eye as his master. The good-natured bachelor was content with his hard fare of soda-bread and bacon, but Tom, the only creature in the world acknowledging dependence on him, must needs be provided with fresh meat. Accordingly he bestirred himself to contrive squirrel-traps, and waded the snowy woods with his gun, making sad havoc among the few winter birds, sparing neither robin, sparrow, nor tiny nut-hatch, and the pleasure of seeing Tom eat and grow fat was his great reward.

One cold afternoon, while hunting along the river-bank, he noticed a plain-feathered little bird skipping about in the shallows, and immediately raised his gun. But just then the confiding songster began to sing, and after listening to his summery melody the charmed hunter turned away, saying, "Bless your little heart, I can't shoot you, not even for Tom."

Even so far north as icy Alaska, I have found my glad singer. When I was exploring the glaciers between Mount Fairweather and the Stikeen River, one cold day in November, after trying in vain to force a way through the innumerable icebergs of Sum Dum Bay to the great glaciers at the head of it, I was weary and baffled and sat resting in my canoe convinced at last that I would have to leave this part of my work for another year. Then I began to plan my escape to open water before the young ice which was beginning to form should shut me in. While I thus lingered drifting with the bergs, in the midst of these gloomy forebodings and all the terrible glacial desolation and grandeur, I suddenly heard the wellknown whir of an Ouzel's wings, and, looking up, saw my little comforter coming straight across the ice from the shore. In a second or two he was with me, flying three times round my head with a happy salute, as if saying, "Cheer up, old friend; you see I'm here, and all's well." Then he flew back to the shore, alighted on the topmost jag of a stranded iceberg, and began to nod and bow as though he were on one of his favorite boulders in the midst of a sunny Sierra cascade.

The species is distributed all along the mountain-ranges of the Pacific Coast from Alaska to Mexico, and east to the Rocky Mountains. Nevertheless, it is as yet comparatively little known. Audubon and Wilson did not meet it. Swainson was, I believe, the first naturalist to describe a specimen from Mexico. Specimens were shortly afterward procured by Drummond near the sources of the Athabasca River, between the fifty-fourth and fifty-sixth parallels; and it has been collected by nearly all of the numerous exploring expeditions undertaken of late through our Western States and Territories; for it never fails to engage the attention of naturalists in a very particular manner.

Such, then, is our little cinclus, beloved of every one who is so fortunate as to know him. Tracing on strong wind every curve of the most precipitous torrents from one extremity of the Sierra to the other; not fearing to follow them through their darkest gorges and coldest snow-tunnels; acquainted with every waterfall, echoing their divine music; and throughout the whole of their beautiful lives interpreting all that we in our unbelief call terrible in the utterances of torrents and storms, as only varied expressions of God's eternal love.

W(ILLIAM) H(ENRY) HUDSON
1841-1922

Born near Buenos Aires, Argentina, of American parents, W.H. Hudson grew up on his family farm and as a young man roamed widely through the South American countryside on horseback. When he was fifteen rheumatic fever curtailed Hudson's activities, and he remained in poor health most of his life. In 1874 he came to London, where he wrote and published over twenty books, many of them reflecting his intense, life-long interest in birds. Though he achieved great popular success with the publication of Green Mansions *(1904)—a romantic fantasy whose heroine, Rima, lives in the trees of the Venezuelan jungles and communicates with birds—recognition as a serious writer came only in his last years. His reputation today rests on such vivid reminiscences of his Argentine boyhood as* Idle Days in Patagonia *(1893), and on his treatments of the English countryside and its people in such works as* Afoot In England *(1909) and* A Shepherd's Life *(1910). He is now regarded, with Richard Jefferies, as one of the most important English nature writers of the late Victorian period.*

Hudson viewed himself as "a naturalist in the old original sense of the word: one who is mainly concerned with the 'life and conversation of animals' and whose work is consequently more like play." If Thoreau could refer affectionately to his "fishy friend" in the Concord River, Hudson could befriend a pig and at the same time face simply and directly the persistent issue of "eating our fellow mortals." There is a Hardyesque, brooding quality to his writings, yet a largeness of outlook that enables him to utter stark pronouncements on the human condition in a strangely comforting voice. Like John Burroughs, he found in Darwinian theory an enriching vision: "For we are no longer isolated, stand-

ing like starry visitors on a mountain-top, surveying life from the outside; but are on a level with and part and parcel of it."

My Friend the Pig

Is there a man among us who on running through a list of his friends is unable to say that there is one among them who is a perfect pig? I think not; and if any reader says that he has no such an one for the simple reason that he would not and could not make a friend of a perfect pig, I shall maintain that he is mistaken, that if he goes over the list a second time and a little more carefully, he will find in it not only a pig, but a sheep, a cow, a fox, a cat, a stoat, and even a perfect toad.

But all this is a question I am not concerned with, seeing that the pig I wish to write about is a real one—a four-footed beast with parted hoofs. I have a friendly feeling towards pigs generally, and consider them the most intelligent of beasts, not excepting the elephant and the anthropoid ape—the dog is not to be mentioned in this connection. I also like his disposition and attitude towards all other creatures, especially man. He is not suspicious, or shrinkingly submissive, like horses, cattle, and sheep; nor an impudent devil-may-care like the goat; nor hostile like the goose; nor condescending like the cat; nor a flattering parasite like the dog. He views us from a totally different, a sort of democratic, standpoint as fellow-citizens and brothers, and takes it for granted, or grunted, that we understand his language, and without servility or insolence he has a natural, pleasant, camerados-all or hail-fellow-well-met air with us.

It may come as a shock to some of my readers when I add that I like him, too, in the form of rashers on the breakfast-table; and this I say with a purpose on account of much wild and idle talk one hears on this question even from one's dearest friends—the insincere horror expressed and denunciation of the revolting custom of eating our fellow-mortals. The other day a lady of my acquaintance told me that she went to call on some people who lived a good distance from her house, and was obliged to stay to luncheon. This consisted mainly of roast pork, and as if that was not enough, her host, when helping her, actually asked if she was fond of a dreadful thing called the crackling!

It is a common pose; but it is also something more, since we find it mostly in persons who are frequently in bad health and are restricted to a

The Book of a Naturalist (New York: George H. Doran, 1919).

low diet; naturally at such times vegetarianism appeals to them. As their health improves they think less of their fellow-mortals. A little chicken broth is found uplifting; then follows the inevitable sole, then calves' brains, then a sweetbread, then a partridge, and so on, progressively, until they are once more able to enjoy their salmon or turbot, veal and lamb cutlets, fat capons, turkeys and geese, sirloins of beef, and, finally, roast pig. That's the limit; we have outgrown cannibalism, and are not keen about haggis, though it is still eaten by the wild tribes inhabiting the northern portion of our island. All this should serve to teach vegetarians not to be in a hurry. Thoreau's "handful of rice" is not sufficient for us, and not good enough yet. It will take long years and centuries of years before the wolf with blood on his iron jaws can be changed into the white innocent lamb that nourishes itself on grass.

Let us now return to my friend the pig. He inhabited a stye at the far end of the back garden of a cottage or small farmhouse in a lonely little village in the Wiltshire downs where I was staying. Close to the stye was a gate opening into a long green field, shut in by high hedges, where two or three horses and four or five cows were usually grazing. These beasts, not knowing my sentiments, looked askance at me and moved away when I first began to visit them, but when they made the discovery that I generally had apples and lumps of sugar in my coat pockets they all at once became excessively friendly and followed me about, and would put their heads in my way to be scratched, and licked my hands with their rough tongues to show that they liked me. Every time I visited the cows and horses I had to pause beside the pig-pen to open the gate into the field; and invariably the pig would get up and coming towards me salute me with a friendly grunt. And I would pretend not to hear or see, for it made me sick to look at his pen in which he stood belly-deep in the fetid mire, and it made me ashamed to think that so intelligent and good-tempered an animal, so profitable to man, should be kept in such abominable conditions. Oh, poor beast, excuse me, but I'm in a hurry and have no time to return your greeting or even to look at you!

In this village, as in most of the villages in all this agricultural and pastoral county of Wiltshire, there is a pig-club, and many of the cottagers keep a pig; they think and talk a great deal about their pigs, and have a grand pig-day gathering and dinner, with singing and even dancing to follow, once a year. And no wonder that this is so, considering what they get out of the pig; yet in any village you will find it kept in this same unspeakable condition. It is not from indolence nor because they take pleasure in seeing their pig unhappy before killing him or sending him away to be killed, but because they cherish the belief that the filthier the state in which they keep their pig the better the pork will be! I have met even large prosperous farmers, many of them, who cling to this delusion. One can imagine a conversation between one of these Wiltshire pig-keepers and a Danish farmer. "Yes," the visitor would say, "we too had the same notion at one time, and thought it right to keep our pigs as you do; but that was a long time back, when English and Danes were practically one people, seeing that Canute was king of both countries. We have since then adopted a different system; we now believe, and the results prove that we are in the right way, that it is best to consider the animal's nature and habits and wants, and to make the artificial conditions imposed on him as little oppressive as may be. It is true that in a state of nature the hog loves to go into pools and wallow in the mire, just as stags, buffaloes, and many other beasts do, especially in the dog-days when the flies are most troublesome. But the swine, like the stag, is a forest animal, and does not love filth for its own sake, nor to be left in a miry pen, and though not as fastidious as a cat about his coat, he is naturally as clean as any other forest creature."

Here I may add that in scores of cases when I have asked a cottager why he didn't keep a pig, his answer has been that he would gladly do so, but for the sanitary inspectors, who would soon order him to get rid of it, or remove it to a distance on account of the offensive smell. It is probable that if it could be got out of the cottager's mind that there must need be an offensive smell, the number of pigs fattened in the villages would be trebled.

I hope now after all these digressions I shall be able to go on with the history of my friend the pig. One morning as I passed the pen he grunted—spoke, I may say—in such a pleasant friendly way that I had to stop and return his greeting; then, taking an apple from my pocket, I placed it in his trough. He turned it over with his snout, then looked up and said something like "Thank-you" in a series of gentle grunts. Then he bit off and ate a small piece, then another small bite, and eventually taking what was left in his mouth he finished eating it. After that he always expected me to stay a minute and speak to him when I went to the field; I knew it from his way of greeting me, and on such occasions I gave him an apple. But he never ate it greedily: he appeared more inclined to talk than to eat, until by degrees I came to understand what he was saying. What he said was that he appreciated my kind intentions in giving him apples. But, he went on, to tell the real truth, it is not a fruit I am particularly fond of. I am familiar with its taste as they sometimes give me apples, usually the small unripe or bad ones that fall from the trees. However, I don't actually dislike them. I get skim milk and am rather fond of it; then a bucket of mash, which is good enough for hunger; but what I enjoy most is a cabbage, only I don't get one very

often now. I sometimes think that if they would let me out of this muddy
pen to ramble like the sheep and other beasts in the field or on the downs
I should be able to pick up a number of morsels which would taste better
than anything they give me. Apart from the subject of food I hope you
won't mind my telling you that I'm rather fond of being scratched on
the back.

So I scratched him vigorously with my stick, and made him wriggle his
body and wink and blink and smile delightedly all over his face. Then I
said to myself: "Now what the juice can I do more to please him?" For
though under sentence of death, he had done no wrong, but was a good,
honest-hearted fellow-mortal, so that I felt bound to do something to
make the miry remnant of his existence a little less miserable.

I think it was the word *juice* I had just used—for that was how I
pronounced it to make it less like a swear-word—that gave me an inspiration. In the garden, a few yards back from the pen, there was a large
clump of old elder-trees, now overloaded with ripening fruit—the biggest clusters I had ever seen. Going to the trees I selected and cut the
finest bunch I could find, as big round as my cap, and weighing over a
pound. This I deposited in his trough and invited him to try it. He
sniffed at it a little doubtfully, and looked at me and made a remark or
two, then nibbled at the edge of the cluster, taking a few berries into his
mouth, and holding them some time before he ventured to crush them.
At length he did venture, then looked at me again and made more
remarks, "Queer fruit this! Never tasted anything quite like it before,
but I really can't say yet whether I like it or not."

Then he took another bite, then more bites, looking up at me and
saying something between the bites, till, little by little, he had consumed
the whole bunch; then turning round, he went back to his bed with a
little grunt to say that I was now at liberty to go on to the cows and
horses.

However, on the following morning he hailed my approach in such a
lively manner, with such a note of expectancy in his voice, that I concluded he had been thinking a great deal about elder-berries, and was
anxious to have another go at them. Accordingly I cut him another
bunch, which he quickly consumed, making little exclamations the
while—"Thank you, thank you, very good—very good indeed!" It was a
new sensation in his life, and made him very happy, and was almost as
good as a day of liberty in the fields and meadows and on the open green
downs.

From that time I visited him two or three times a day to give him huge
clusters of elder-berries. There were plenty for the starlings as well; the
clusters on those trees would have filled a cart.

Then one morning I heard an indignant scream from the garden, and peeping out saw my friend, the pig, bound hand and foot, being lifted by a dealer into his cart with the assistance of the farmer.

"Good-bye, old boy!" said I as the cart drove off; and I thought that by and by, in a month or two, if several persons discovered a peculiar and fascinating flavour in their morning rasher, it would be due to the elder-berries I had supplied to my friend the pig, which had gladdened his heart for a week or two before receiving his quietus.

From IDLE DAYS IN PATAGONIA

[a state of unthinking watchfulness]

* * * I spent the greater part of one winter at a point on the Rio Negro, seventy or eighty miles from the sea, where the valley on my side of the water was about five miles wide. The valley alone was habitable, where there was water for man and beast, and a thin soil producing grass and grain; it is perfectly level, and ends abruptly at the foot of the bank or terrace-like formation of the higher barren plateau. It was my custom to go out every morning on horseback with my gun, and, followed by one dog, to ride away from the valley; and no sooner would I climb the terrace and plunge into the grey universal thicket, than I would find myself as completely alone and cut off from all sight and sound of human occupancy as if five hundred instead of only five miles separated me from the hidden green valley and river. So wild and solitary and remote seemed that grey waste, stretching away into infinitude, a waste untrodden by man, and where the wild animals are so few that they have made no discoverable path in the wilderness of thorns. There I might have dropped down and died, and my flesh been devoured by birds, and my bones bleached white in sun and wind, and no person would have found them, and it would have been forgotten that one had ridden forth in the morning and had not returned. Or if, like the few wild animals there— puma, huanaco, and hare-like *Dolichotis,* or Darwin's rhea and the crested tinamou among the birds—I had been able to exist without water, I might have made myself a hermitage of brushwood or dug-out in the side of a cliff, and dwelt there until I had grown grey as the stones and trees around me, and no human foot would have stumbled on my hiding-place.

Idle Days in Patagonia (London: J.M. Dent, 1893).

Not once, nor twice, nor thrice, but day after day I returned to this solitude, going to it in the morning as if to attend a festival, and leaving it only when hunger and thirst and the westering sun compelled me. And yet I had no object in going—no motive which could be put into words; for although I carried a gun, there was nothing to shoot—the shooting was all left behind in the valley. Sometimes a *Dolichotis*, starting up at my approach, flashed for one moment on my sight, to vanish the next moment in the continuous thicket; or a covey of tinamous sprang rocket-like into the air, and fled away with long wailing notes and loud whur of wings; or on some distant hill-side a bright patch of yellow, of a deer that was watching me, appeared and remained motionless for two or three minutes. But the animals were few, and sometimes I would pass an entire day without seeing one mammal, and perhaps not more than a dozen birds of any size. The weather at that time was cheerless, generally with a grey film of cloud spread over the sky, and a bleak wind, often cold enough to make my bridle hand feel quite numb. Moreover, it was not possible to enjoy a canter; the bushes grew so close together that it was as much as one could do to pass through at a walk without brushing against them; and at this slow pace, which would have seemed intolerable in other circumstances, I would ride about for hours at a stretch. In the scene itself there was nothing to delight the eye. Everywhere through the light, grey mould, grey as ashes and formed by the ashes of myriads of generations of dead trees, where the wind had blown on it, or the rain had washed it away, the underlying yellow sand appeared, and the old ocean-polished pebbles, dull red, and grey, and green, and yellow. On arriving at a hill, I would slowly ride to its summit, and stand there to survey the prospect. On every side it stretched away in great undulations; but the undulations were wild and irregular; the hills were rounded and cone-shaped, they were solitary and in groups and ranges; some sloped gently, others were ridge-like and stretched away in league-long terraces, with other terraces beyond; and all alike were clothed in the grey everlasting thorny vegetation. How grey it all was! hardly less so near at hand than on the haze-wrapped horizon, where the hills were dim and the outline blurred by distance. Sometimes I would see the large eagle-like, white-breasted buzzard, *Buteo erythronotus*, perched on the summit of a bush half a mile away; and so long as it would continue stationed motionless before me my eyes would remain involuntarily fixed on it, just as one keeps his eyes on a bright light shining in the gloom; for the whiteness of this hawk seemed to exercise a fascinating power on the vision, so surpassingly bright was it by contrast in the midst of that universal unrelieved greyness. Descending from my look-out, I would take up my aimless wanderings again, and visit other elevations to gaze on the same landscape from another point; and so on for hours, and at noon I would dismount and sit or lie on my folded poncho for an hour or longer. One day, in these rambles, I discovered a small grove composed of twenty to thirty trees, about eighteen feet high and taller than the surrounding trees. They were growing at a convenient distance apart, and had evidently been resorted to by a herd of deer or other wild animals for a very long time, for the boles were polished to a glassy smoothness with much rubbing, and the ground beneath was trodden to a floor of clean, loose yellow sand. This grove was on a hill differing in shape from other hills in its neighbourhood, so that it was easy for me to find it on other occasions; and after a time I made a point of finding and using it as a resting-place every day at noon. I did not ask myself why I made choice of that one spot, sometimes going miles out of my way to sit there, instead of sitting down under any one of the millions of trees and bushes covering the country, on any other hillside. I thought nothing at all about it, but acted unconsciously; only afterwards, when revolving the subject, it seemed to me that after having rested there once, each time I wished to rest again the wish came associated with the image of that particular clump of trees, with polished stems and clean bed of sand beneath; and in a short time I formed a habit of returning, animal-like, to repose at that same spot.

It was perhaps a mistake to say that I would sit down and rest, since I was never tired: and yet without being tired, that noonday pause, during which I sat for an hour without moving, was strangely grateful. All day the silence seemed grateful, it was very perfect, very profound. There were no insects, and the only bird sound—a feeble chirp of alarm emitted by a small skulking wren-like species—was not heard oftener than two or three times an hour. The only sounds as I rode were the muffled hoof-strokes of my horse, scratching of twigs against my boot or saddle-flap, and the low panting of the dog. And it seemed to be a relief to escape even from these sounds when I dismounted and sat down: for in a few moments the dog would stretch his head out on his paws and go to sleep, and there would be no sound, not even the rustle of a leaf. For unless the wind blows strong there is no fluttering motion and no whisper in the small stiff undeciduous leaves; and the bushes stand unmoving as if carved out of stone. One day while *listening* to the silence, it occurred to my mind to wonder what the effect would be if I were to shout aloud. This seemed at the time a horrible suggestion of fancy, a "lawless and uncertain thought" which almost made me shudder, and I was anxious to dismiss it quickly from my mind. But during those solitary days it was a rare thing for any thought to cross my mind; animal forms did not cross my vision or bird-voices assail my hearing more rarely. In that novel state of mind I was in, thought had become impossible. Else-where I had always been able to think most freely on horseback; and on the pampas, even in the most lonely places, my mind was always most active when I travelled at a swinging gallop. This was doubtless habit; but now, with a horse under me, I had become incapable of reflection: my mind had suddenly transformed itself from a thinking machine into a machine for some other unknown purpose. To think was like setting in motion a noisy engine in my brain; and there was something there which bade me be still, and I was forced to obey. My state was one of *suspense* and *watchfulness;* yet I had no expectation of meeting with an adven-ture, and felt as free from apprehension as I feel now when sitting in a room in London. The change in me was just as great and wonderful as if I had changed my identity for that of another man or animal; but at the time I was powerless to wonder at or speculate about it; the state seemed familiar rather than strange, and although accompanied by a strong feeling of elation, I did not know it—did not know that something had come between me and my intellect—until I lost it and returned to my former self—to thinking, and the old insipid existence. *   *   *

[*desert solitude*]

*   *   * If there be such a thing as historical memory in us, it is not strange that the sweetest moment in any life, pleasant or dreary, should be when Nature draws near to it, and, taking up her neglected instru-ment, plays a fragment of some ancient melody, long unheard on the earth.

It might be asked: If Nature has at times this peculiar effect on us, restoring instantaneously the old vanished harmony between organism and environment, why should it be experienced in a greater degree in the Patagonian desert than in other solitary places—a desert which is water-less, where animal voices are seldom heard, and vegetation is grey instead of green? I can only suggest a reason for the effect being so much greater in my own case. In sub-tropical woods and thickets, and in wild forests in temperate regions, the cheerful verdure and bright colours of flower and insects, if we have acquired a habit of looking closely at these things, and the melody and noises of bird-life, engages the senses; there is movement and brightness; new forms, animal and vegetable, are continually appear-ing, curiosity and expectation are excited, and the mind is so much occupied with novel objects that the effect of wild nature in its entirety is minimised. In Patagonia the monotony of the plains, or expanse of low hills, the universal unrelieved greyness of everything, and the absence of animal forms and objects new to the eye, leave the mind open and free to receive an impression of visible nature as a whole. One gazes on the prospect as on the sea, for it stretches away sea-like, without change, into infinitude; but without the sparkle of water, the changes of hue which shadow and sunlight and nearness and distance give, and motion of waves and white flash of foam. It has a look of antiquity, of desolation, of eternal peace, of a desert that has been a desert from of old and will continue a desert for ever; and we know that its only human inhabitants are a few wandering savages, who live by hunting as their progenitors have done for thousands of years. Again, in fertile savannahs and pampas there may appear no signs of human occupancy, but the traveller knows that eventually the advancing tide of humanity will come with its flocks and herds, and the ancient silence and desolation will be no more; and this thought is like human companionship, and mitigates the effect of nature's wildness on the spirit. In Patagonia no such thought or dream of the approaching changes to be wrought by human agency can affect the mind. There is no water there, the arid soil is sand and gravel—pebbles rounded by the action of ancient seas, before Europe was; and nothing grows except the barren things that nature loves—thorns, and a few woody herbs, and scattered tufts of wiry bitter grass.

Doubtless we are not all affected in solitude by wild nature in the same degree; even in the Patagonian wastes many would probably experience no such mental change as I have described. Others have their instincts nearer to the surface, and are moved deeply by nature in any solitary place; and I imagine that Thoreau was such a one. At all events, although he was without the Darwinian lights which we have, and these feelings were always to him "strange," "mysterious," "unaccountable," he does not conceal them. There is the "something uncanny in Thoreau" which seems inexplicable and startling to such as have never been startled by nature, nor deeply moved; but which, to others, imparts a peculiarly delightful aromatic flavour to his writings. It is his wish towards a more primitive mode of life, his strange abandonment when he scours the wood like a half-starved hound, and no morsel could be too savage for him; the desire to take a ranker hold on life and live more as the animals do: the sympathy with nature so keen that it takes his breath away; the feeling that all the elements were congenial to him, which made the wildest scenes unaccountably familiar, so that he came and went with a strange liberty in nature. Once only he had doubts, and thought that human companionship might be essential to happiness; but he was at the same time conscious of a slight insanity in the mood; and he soon again became sensible of the sweet beneficient society of nature, of an infinite and unaccountable friendliness all at once like an atmosphere sustaining him. * * *

From BIRDS AND MAN

["something beyond and above knowledge"]

* * * We are bound as much as ever to facts; we seek for them more and more diligently, knowing that to break from them is to be carried away by vain imaginations. All the same, facts in themselves are nothing to us; they are important only in their relations to other facts and things—to all things, and the essence of things, material and spiritual. We are not like children gathering painted shells and pebbles on a beach; but, whether we know it or not, are seeking after something beyond and above knowledge. The wilderness in which we are sojourners is not our home; it is enough that its herbs and roots and wild fruits nourish and give us strength to go onward. Intellectual curiosity, with the gratification of the individual for only purpose, has no place in this scheme of things as we conceive it. Heart and soul are with the brain in all investigation—a truth which some know in rare, beautiful intervals, and others never; but we are all meanwhile busy with our work, like myriads of social insects engaged in raising a structure that was never planned. Perhaps we are not so wholly unconscious of our destinies as were the patient gatherers of facts a hundred years ago. Even in one brief century the dawn has come nearer—perhaps a faint whiteness in the east has exhilarated us like wine. Undoubtedly we are more conscious of many things, both within and without—of the length and breadth and depth of nature; of a unity which was hardly dreamed of by the naturalists of past ages, a commensalism on earth from which the meanest organism is not excluded. For we are no longer isolated, standing like starry visitors on a mountain-top, surveying life from the outside; but are on a level with and part and parcel of it; and if the mystery of life daily deepens, it is because we view it more closely and with clearer vision. * * *

Birds and Man (London: J.M. Dent, 1901).

From AFOOT IN ENGLAND

[ancient ground and "heartless voids"]

* * * An afternoon in the late November of 1903. Frost, gales, and abundant rains have more than half stripped the oaks of their yellow leaves. But the rain is over now, the sky once more a pure lucid blue

Afoot in England (London: J.M. Dent, 1908).

above me—all around me, in fact, since I am standing high on the top of
the ancient stupendous earthwork, grown over with oak wood and underwood of holly and thorn and hazel with a tangle of ivy and bramble
and briar. It is marvellously still; no sound from the village reaches me; I
only hear the faint rustle of the dead leaves as they fall, and the robin, for
one spied me here and has come to keep me company. At intervals he
spurts out his brilliant little fountain of sound; and that sudden bright
melody and the bright colour of the sunlit translucent leaves seem like
one thing. Nature is still, and I am still, standing concealed among trees,
or moving cautiously through the dead russet bracken. Not that I am
expecting to get a glimpse of the badger who has his hermitage in this
solitary place, but I am on forbidden ground, in the heart of a sacred
pheasant preserve, where one must do one's prowling warily. Hard by,
almost within a stone's throw of the wood-grown earthwork on which I
stand, are the ruinous walls of Roman Calleva—the Silchester which the
antiquarians have been occupied in uncovering these dozen years or
longer. The stone walls, too, like the more ancient earthwork, are overgrown with trees and brambles and ivy. The trees have grown upon the
wall, sending roots deep down between the stones, through the crumbling cement; and so fast are they anchored that never a tree falls but it
brings down huge masses of masonry with it. This slow levelling process
has been going on for centuries, and it is doubtless in this way that the
buildings within the walls were pulled down long ages ago. Then the
action of the earth-worms began, and floors and foundations, with fallen
stones and tiles, were gradually buried in the soil, and what was once a
city was a dense thicket of oak and holly and thorn. Finally the wood was
cleared, and the city was a walled wheat-field—so far as we know, the
ground has been cultivated since the days of King John. But the entire
history of this green walled space before me—less than twenty centuries
in duration—does not seem so very long compared with that of the huge
earthen wall I am standing on, which dates back to prehistoric times.

Standing here, knee-deep in the dead ruddy bracken, in the "coloured
shade" of the oaks, idly watching the leaves fall fluttering to the ground,
thinking in an aimless way of the remains of the two ancient cities before
me, the British and the Roman, and of their comparative antiquity, I am
struck with the thought that the sweet sensations produced in me by the
scene differ in character from the feeling I have had in other solitary
places. The peculiar sense of satisfaction, of restfulness, of peace, experienced here is very perfect; but in the wilderness, where man has never
been, or has at all events left no trace of his former presence, there is ever
a mysterious sense of loneliness, of desolation, underlying our pleasure in
nature. Here it seems good to know, or to imagine, that the men I

occasionally meet in my solitary rambles, and those I see in the scattered rustic village hard by, are of the same race, and possibly the descendants, of the people who occupied this spot in the remote past—Iberian and Celt, and Roman and Saxon and Dane. If that hard-featured and sour-visaged old gamekeeper, with the cold blue unfriendly eyes, should come upon me here in my hiding-place, and scowl as he is accustomed to do, standing silent before me, gun in hand, to hear my excuses for trespassing in his preserves, I should say (mentally): This man is distinctly English, and his far-off progenitors, somewhere about sixteen hundred years ago, probably assisted at the massacre of the inhabitants of the pleasant little city at my feet. By-and-by, leaving the ruins, I may meet with other villagers of different features and different colour in hair, skin, and eyes, and of a pleasanter expression; and in them I may see the remote descendants of other older races of men, some who were lords here before the Romans came, and of others before them, even back to Neolithic times.

This, I take it, is a satisfaction, a sweetness and peace to the soul in nature, because it carries with it a sense of the continuity of the human race, its undying vigour, its everlastingness. After all the tempests that have overcome it, through all mutations in such immense stretches of time, how stable it is!

I recall the time when I lived on a vast vacant level green plain, an earth which to the eye, and to the mind which sees with the eye, appeared illimitable, like the ocean; where the house I was born in was the oldest in the district—a century old, it was said; where the people were the children's children of emigrants from Europe who had conquered and colonised the country, and had enjoyed but half a century of national life. But the people who had possessed the land before the emigrants—what of them? They were but a memory, a tradition, a story told in books and hardly more to us than a fable; perhaps they had dwelt there for long centuries, or for thousands of years; perhaps they had come, a wandering horde, to pass quickly away like a flight of migrating locusts; for no memorial existed, no work of their hands, not the faintest trace of their occupancy.

Walking one day at the side of a ditch, which had been newly cut through a meadow at the end of our plantation, I caught sight of a small black object protruding from the side of the cutting, which turned out to be a fragment of Indian pottery made of coarse clay, very black, and rudely ornamented on one side. On searching further a few more pieces were found. I took them home and preserved them carefully, experiencing a novel and keen sense of pleasure in their possession; for though worthless, they were man's handiwork, the only real evidence I had come upon of that vanished people who had been before us; and it was as if those bits of baked clay, with a pattern incised on them by a man's finger-nail, had in them some magical property which enabled me to realise the past, and to see that vacant plain repeopled with long dead and forgotten men.

Doubtless we all possess the feeling in some degree—the sense of loneliness and desolation and dismay at the thought of an uninhabited world, and of long periods when man was not. Is it not the absence of human life or remains rather than the illimitable wastes of thick-ribbed ice and snow which daunts us at the thought of Arctic and Antarctic regions? Again, in the story of the earth, as told by geology, do we not also experience the same sense of dismay, and the soul shrinking back on itself, when we come in imagination to those deserts desolate in time when the continuity of the race was broken and the world depeopled? The doctrine of evolution has made us tolerant of the thought of human animals—our progenitors as we must believe—who were of brutish aspect, and whose period on this planet was so long that, compared with it, the historic and prehistoric periods are but as the life of an individual. A quarter of a million years has perhaps elapsed since the beginning of that cold period which, at all events in this part of the earth, killed Palaeolithic man; yet how small a part of his racial life even that time would seem if, as some believe, his remains may be traced as far back as the Eocene! But after this rude man of the Quarternary and Tertiary epochs has passed away there is a void, a period which to the imagination seems measureless, when sun and moon and stars looked on a waste and mindless world. When man once more reappears he seems to have been re-created on somewhat different lines.

It is this break in the history of the human race which amazes and daunts us, which "shadows forth the heartless voids and immensities of the universe, *and thus stabs us from behind with the thought of annihilation.*"

Here, in these words of Herman Melville, we are let all at once into the true meaning of those disquieting and seemingly indefinable emotions so often experienced, even by the most ardent lovers of nature and of solitude, in uninhabited deserts, on great mountains, and on the sea. We find here the origin of that horror of mountains which was so common until recent times. A friend once confessed to me that he was always profoundly unhappy at sea during long voyages, and the reason was that his sustaining belief in a superintending Power and in immortality left him when he was on that waste of waters which have no human associations. The feeling, so intense in his case, is known to most if not all of us; but we feel it faintly as a disquieting element in nature of which we may be but vaguely conscious.

Most travelled Englishmen who have seen much of the world and resided for long or short periods in many widely separated countries would agree that there is a vast difference in the feeling of strangeness, or want of harmony with our surroundings, experienced in old and in new countries. It is a compound feeling and some of its elements are the same in both cases; but in one there is a disquieting element which the other is without. Thus, in Southern Europe, Egypt, Syria, and in many countries of Asia, and some portions of Africa, the wanderer from home might experience dissatisfaction and be ill at ease and wish for old familiar sights and sounds; but in a colony like Tasmania, and in any new country where there were no remains of antiquity, no links with the past, the feeling would be very much more poignant, and in some scenes and moods would be like the sense of desolation which assails us at the thought of the heartless voids and immensities of the universe.

He recognises that he is in a world on which we have but recently entered, and in which our position is not yet assured.

Here, standing on this mound, as on other occasions past counting, I recognise and appreciate the enormous difference which human associations make in the effect produced on us by visible nature. In this silent solitary place, with the walled field which was once Calleva Atrebatum at my feet, I yet have a sense of satisfaction, of security, never felt in a land which had no historic past. The knowledge that my individual life is but a span, a breath; that in a little while I too must wither and mingle like one of those fallen leaves with the mould, does not grieve me. I know it and yet disbelieve it; for am I not here alive, where men have inhabited for thousands of years, feeling what I now feel—their oneness with everlasting nature and the undying human family? The very soil and wet carpet of moss on which their feet were set, the standing trees and leaves, green or yellow, the rain-drops, the air they breathed, the sunshine in their eyes and hearts, was part of them, not a garment, but of their substance and spirit. Feeling this, death becomes an illusion; and the illusion that the continuous life of the species (its immortality) and the individual life are one and the same is the reality and truth. An illusion, but, as Mill says, deprive us of our illusions and life would be intolerable. Happily we are not easily deprived of them, since they are of the nature of instincts and ineradicable. And this very one which our reason can prove to be the most childish, the absurdest of all, is yet the greatest, the most fruitful of good for the race. To those who have discarded supernatural religion, it may be a religion, or at all events the foundation to build one on. For there is no comfort to the healthy natural man in being told that the good he does will not be interred with his bones, since he does not wish to think, and in fact refuses to think, that his bones will ever be interred. Joy in the "choir invisible" is to him a mere poetic fancy, or at best a rarefied transcendentalism, which fails to sustain him. If altruism, or the religion of humanity, is a living vigorous plant, and as some believe flourishes more with the progress of the centuries, it must, like other "soul-growths," have a deeper, tougher woodier root in our soil. *   *   *

From A Traveller
in Little Things

[the solace of the visible world]

*   *   * On a warm, brilliant morning in late April I paid a visit to a shallow lakelet or pond five or six acres in extent which I had discovered some weeks before hidden in a depression in the land, among luxuriant furze, bramble, and blackthorn bushes. Between the thickets the boggy ground was everywhere covered with great tussocks of last year's dead and faded marsh grass—a wet, rough, lonely place where a lover of solitude need have no fear of being intruded on by a being of his own species, or even a wandering moorland donkey. On arriving at the pond I was surprised and delighted to find half the surface covered with a thick growth of bog-bean just coming into flower. The quaint three-lobed leaves, shaped like a grebe's foot, were still small, and the flower-stocks, thick as corn in a field, were crowned with pyramids of buds, cream and rosy-red like the opening dropwort clusters, and at the lower end of the spikes were the full-blown singular, snow-white, cottony flowers—our strange and beautiful water edelweiss.

A group of ancient, gnarled and twisted alder bushes, with trunks like trees, grew just on the margin of the pond, and by-and-by I found a comfortable arm-chair on the lower stout horizontal branches overhanging the water, and on that seat I rested a long time, enjoying the sight of that unexpected loveliness.

The chiff-chaff, the common warbler of this moorland district, was now abundant, more so than anywhere else in England; two or three were flitting about among the alder leaves within a few feet of my head, and a dozen at least were singing within hearing, chiff-chaffing near and

A Traveller in Little Things (New York: Dutton, 1921).

far, their notes sounding strangely loud at that still, sequestered spot. Listening to that insistent sound I was reminded of Warde Fowler's words about the sweet season which brings new life and hope to men, and how a seal and sanction is put on it by that same small bird's clear resonant voice. I endeavoured to recall the passage, saying to myself that in order to enter fully into the feeling expressed it is sometimes essential to know an author's exact words. Failing in this, I listened again to the bird, then let my eyes rest on the expanse of red and cream-coloured spikes before me, then on the masses of flame-yellow furze beyond, then on something else. I was endeavouring to keep my attention on these extraneous things, to shut my mind resolutely against a thought, intolerably sad, which had surprised me in that quiet solitary place. Surely, I said, this springtime verdure and bloom, this fragrance of the furze, the infinite blue of heaven, the bell-like double note of this my little feathered neighbour in the alder tree, flitting hither and thither, light and airy himself as a wind-fluttered alder leaf—surely this is enough to fill and to satisfy any heart, leaving no room for a grief so vain and barren, which nothing in nature suggested! That it should find me out here in this wilderness of all places—the place to which a man might come to divest himself of himself—that second self which he has unconsciously acquired—to be like the trees and animals, outside of the sad atmosphere of human life and its eternal tragedy! A vain effort and a vain thought, since that from which I sought to escape came from nature itself, from every visible thing; every leaf and flower and blade was eloquent of it, and the very sunshine, that gave life and brilliance to all things, was turned to darkness by it.

Overcome and powerless, I continued sitting there with half-closed eyes until those sad images of lost friends, which had risen with so strange a suddenness in my mind, appeared something more than mere memories and mentally-seen faces and forms, seen for a moment, then vanishing. They were with me, standing by me, almost as in life; and I looked from one to another, looking longest at the one who was the last to go; who was with me but yesterday, as it seemed, and stood still in our walk and turned to bid me listen to that same double note, that little spring melody, which had returned to us; and who led me, waist-deep in the flowering meadow-grasses, to look for this same beautiful white flower which I had found here, and called it our "English edelweiss." How beautiful it all was! We thought and felt as one. That bond uniting us, unlike all other bonds, was unbreakable and everlasting. If one had said that life was uncertain it would have seemed a meaningless phrase. Spring's immortality was in us; ever-living earth was better than any home in the stars which eye hath not seen nor heart conceived. Nature was all in all; we worshipped her and her wordless messages in our hearts were sweeter than honey and the honeycomb.

To me, alone on that April day, alone on the earth as it seemed for a while, the sweet was indeed changed to bitter, and the loss of those who were one with me in feeling appeared to my mind as a monstrous betrayal, a thing unnatural, almost incredible. Could I any longer love and worship this dreadful power that made us and filled our hearts with gladness—could I say of it, "Though it slay me yet will I trust it"? . . .

Is there no escape, then, from this intolerable sadness—from the thought of springs that have been, the beautiful multitudinous life that has vanished? Our maker and mother mocks at our efforts—at our philosophic refuges, and sweeps them away with a wave of emotion. And yet there is deliverance, the old way of escape which is ours, whether we want it or not. Nature herself in her own good time heals the wounds she inflicts—even this most grievous in seeming when she takes away from us the faith and hope of reunion with our lost. They may be in a world of light, waiting our coming—we do not know; but in that place they are unimaginable, their state inconceivable. They were like us, beings of flesh and blood, or we should not have loved them. If we cannot grasp their hands their continued existence is nothing to us. Grief at their loss is just as great for those who have kept their faith as for those who have lost it; and on account of its very poignancy it cannot endure in either case. It fades, returning in its old intensity at ever longer intervals until it ceases. The poet of nature was wrong when he said that without his faith in the decay of his senses he would be worse than dead, echoing the apostle who said that if we had hope in this world only we should be of all men the most miserable. So, too, was the later poet wrong when he listened to the waves on Dover beach bringing the eternal notes of sadness in; when he saw in imagination the ebbing of the great sea of faith which had made the world so beautiful, in its withdrawal disclosing the deserts drear and naked shingles of the world. That desolation, as he imagined it, which made him so unutterably sad, was due to the erroneous idea that our earthly happiness comes to us from otherwhere, some region outside our planet, just as one of our modern Philosophers has imagined that the principle of life on earth came originally from the stars.

The "naked shingles of the world" is but a mood of our transitional day; the world is just as beautiful as it ever was, and our dead as much to us as they ever have been, even when faith was at its highest. They are not wholly, irretrievably lost, even when we cease to remember them, when their images come no longer unbidden to our minds. They are present in nature: through ourselves, receiving but what we give, they have become part and parcel of it and give it an expression. As when the rain clouds disperse and the sun shines out once more, heaven and earth are filled with a chastened light, sweet to behold and very wonderful, so because of our lost ones, because of the old grief at their loss, the visible world is touched with a new light, a tenderness and grace and beauty not its own.   *   *   *

CLARENCE KING
1842-1901

Mountaineering in the Sierra Nevada (1872) was a pioneering work of literature about the Sierra. King's own background, temperament, and interests were such that his book represents a virtual anthology of early responses to the mountainous West. Like John Muir, he was a daring climber; the account of his ascent of Mt. Tyndall (named by King) is one of the most thrilling tales in our literature of exploration. Like Mark Twain and Bret Harte, King fills his narrative with "local color" about the miners, settlers—both Anglo and Mexican—and native peoples of the West. Racism is an element in some of these anecdotes, as it often is in writing produced along the American frontier. Finally, as a Yale graduate, a scientist who would become the founding director of the United States Geological Survey, and the intimate friend of such men as John Hay and Henry Adams, King shows us the reaction of a cultivated Easterner to the revelation of Western mountains. He found the Sierra both a confirmation of Ruskin's aesthetics and an escape from books, both a chance to assert the dominance of his sex, race, and caste and an escape from the restrictions of such identity.

From Mountaineering in the Sierra Nevada

THE RANGE

The western margin of this continent is built of a succession of mountain chains folded in broad corrugations, like waves of stone upon whose seaward base beat the mild small breakers of the Pacific.

Mountaineering in the Sierra Nevada (Boston: James R. Osgood, 1872).

By far the grandest of all these ranges is the Sierra Nevada, a long and massive uplift lying between the arid deserts of the Great Basin and the Californian exuberance of grain-field and orchard; its eastern slope, a defiant wall of rock plunging abruptly down to the plain; the western, a long, grand sweep, well watered and overgrown with cool, stately forests; its crest a line of sharp, snowy peaks springing into the sky and catching the *alpenglow* long after the sun has set for all the rest of America.

The Sierras have a structure and a physical character which are individual and unique. To Professor Whitney and his corps of the Geological Survey of California is due the honor of first gaining a scientific knowledge of the form, plan, and physical conditions of the Sierras. How many thousands of miles, how many toilsome climbs, we made, and what measure of patience came to be expended, cannot be told; but the general harvest is gathered in, and already a volume of great interest (the forerunner of others) has been published.

The ancient history of the Sierras goes back to a period when the Atlantic and Pacific were one ocean, in whose depths great accumulations of sand and powdered stone were gathering and being spread out in level strata.

It is not easy to assign the age in which these submarine strata were begun, nor exactly the boundaries of the embryo continents from whose shores the primeval breakers ground away sand and gravel enough to form such incredibly thick deposits.

It appears most likely that the Sierra region was submerged from the earliest Palæozoic, or perhaps even the Azoic, age. Slowly the deep ocean valley filled up, until, in the late Triassic period, the uppermost tables were in water shallow enough to drift the sands and clays into wave and ripple ridges. With what immeasurable patience, what infinite deliberation, has nature amassed the materials for these mountains! Age succeeded age; form after form of animal and plant life perished in the unfolding of the great plan of development, while the suspended sands of that primeval sea sunk slowly down and were stretched in level plains upon the floor of stone.

Early in the Jurassic period an impressive and far-reaching movement of the earth's crust took place, during which the bed of the ocean rose in crumpled waves towering high in the air and forming the mountain framework of the Western United States. This system of upheavals reached as far east as Middle Wyoming and stretched from Mexico probably into Alaska. Its numerous ridges and chains, having a general northeast trend, were crowded together in one broad zone whose western and most lofty member is the Sierra Nevada. During all of the Cretaceous period, and a part of the Tertiary, the Pacific beat upon its seaward foot-hills, tearing to pieces the rocks, crumbling and grinding the shores, and, drifting the powdered stone and pebbles beneath its waves, scattered them again in layers. This submarine tableland fringed the whole base of the range and extended westward an unknown distance under the sea. To this perpetual sea-wearing of the Sierra Nevada base was added the detritus made by the cutting out of cañons, which in great volumes continually poured into the Pacific, and was arranged upon its bottom by currents.

In the late Tertiary period a chapter of very remarkable events occurred. For a second time the evenly laid beds of the sea-bottom were crumpled by the shrinking of the earth. The ocean flowed back into deeper and narrower limits, and, fronting the Sierra Nevada, appeared the present system of Coast Ranges. The intermediate depression, or sea-trough as I like to call it, is the valley of California, and is therefore a more recent continental feature than the Sierra Nevada. At once then from the folded rocks of the Coast Ranges, from the Sierra summits and the inland plateaus, and from numberless vents caused by the fierce dynamical action, there poured out a general deluge of melted rock. From the bottom of the sea sprung up those fountains of lava whose cooled material forms many of the islands of the Pacific, and, all along the coast of America, like a system of answering beacons, blazed up volcanic chimneys. The rent mountains glowed with outpourings of molten stone. Sheets of lava poured down the slopes of the Sierra, covering an immense proportion of its surface, only the high granite and metamorphic peaks reaching above the deluge. Rivers and lakes floated up in a cloud of steam and were gone forever. The misty sky of these volcanic days glowed with innumerable lurid reflections, and, at intervals along the crest of the range, great cones arose, blackening the sky with their plumes of mineral smoke. At length, having exhausted themselves, the volcanoes burned lower and lower, and, at last, by far the greater number went out altogether. With a tendency to extremes which "development" geologists would hesitate to admit, nature passed under the dominion of ice and snow.

The vast amount of ocean water which had been vaporized floated over the land, condensed upon hill-tops, chilled the lavas, and finally buried beneath an icy covering all the higher parts of the mountain system. According to well-known laws, the overburdened summits unloaded themselves by a system of glaciers. The whole Sierra crest was one pile of snow, from whose base crawled out the ice-rivers, wearing their bodies into the rock, sculpturing as they went the forms of valleys, and brightening the surface of their tracks by the friction of stones and sand which were bedded, armor-like, in their nether surface. Having made their way down the slope of the Sierra, they met a lowland temperature of sufficient warmth to arrest and waste them. At last, from causes which are too intricate to be discussed at present, they shrank slowly back into the higher summit fastnesses, and there gradually perished, leaving only a crest of snow. The ice melted, and upon the whole plateau, little by little, a thin layer of soil accumulated, and, replacing the snow; there sprang up a forest of pines, whose shadows fall pleasantly to-day over rocks which were once torrents of lava and across the burnished pathways of ice. Rivers, pure and sparkling, thread the bottom of these gigantic glacier valleys. The volcanoes are extinct, and the whole theatre of this impressive geological drama is now the most glorious and beautiful region of America.

As the characters of the *Zauberflöte* passed safely through the trial of fire and the desperate ordeal of water, so, through the terror of volcanic fires and the chilling empire of ice, had the great Sierra come into the present age of tranquil grandeur.

Five distinct periods divide the history of the range. First, the slow gathering of marine sediment within the early ocean, during which incalculable ages were consumed.

Second, in the early Jurassic period this level sea-floor came suddenly to be lifted into the air and crumpled in folds, through whose yawning fissures and ruptured axes outpoured wide zones of granite. Third, the volcanic age of fire and steam. Fourth, the glacial period, when the Sierras were one broad field of snow, with huge dragons of ice crawling down its slopes, and wearing their armor into the rocks. Fifth, the present condition, which the following chapters will describe, albeit in a desultory and inadequate manner.

From latitude 35° to latitude 39°30' the Sierra lifts a continuous chain, the profile culminating in several groups of peaks separated by deep depressed curves or sharp notches, the summits varying from eight to fifteen thousand feet; seven to twelve thousand being the common range of passes. Near its southern extremity, in San Bernardino County, the range is cleft to the base with magnificent gateways opening through into the desert. From Walker's Pass for two hundred miles northward the sky line is more uniformly elevated; the passes averaging nine thousand feet high, the actual summit a chain of peaks from thirteen to fifteen thousand feet. This serrated snow and granite outline of the Sierra Nevada, projected against the cold clear blue, is the blade of white teeth which suggested its Spanish name.

Northward still the range gradually sinks; high peaks covered with perpetual snow are rarer and rarer. Its summit rolls on in broken forest-covered ridges, now and then overlooked by a solitary pile of metamorphic or irruptive rock. At length, in Northern California, where it breaks down in a compressed medley of ridges, and open, level expanses of plain, the axis is maintained by a line of extinct volcanoes standing above the lowland in isolated positions. The most lofty of these, Mount Shasta, is a cone of lava fourteen thousand four hundred and forty feet high, its broad base girdled with noble forests, which give way at eight thousand feet to a cap of glaciers and snow.

Beyond this to the northward the extension of the range is quite difficult to definitely assign, for, geologically speaking, the Sierra Nevada system occupies a broad area in Oregon, consisting of several prominent mountain groups, while in a physical sense the chain ceases with Shasta; the Cascades, which are the apparent topographical continuation, being a tertiary structure formed chiefly of lavas which have been outpoured long subsequent to the main upheaval of the Sierra.

It is not easy to point out the actual southern limit either, because where the mountain mass descends into the Colorado desert it comes in contact with a number of lesser groups of hills, which ramify in many directions, all losing themselves beneath the tertiary and quartenary beds of the desert.

For four hundred miles the Sierras are a definite ridge, broad and high, and having the form of a sea-wave. Buttresses of sombre-hued rock, jutting at intervals from a steep wall, form the abrupt eastern slopes; irregular forests, in scattered growth, huddle together near the snow. The lower declivities are barren spurs, sinking into the sterile flats of the Great Basin.

Long ridges of comparatively gentle outline characterize the western side, but this sloping table is scored from summit to base by a system of parallel transverse cañons, distant from one another often less than twenty-five miles. They are ordinarily two or three thousand feet deep, falling at times in sheer, smooth-fronted cliffs, again in sweeping curves like the hull of a ship, again in rugged V-shaped gorges, or with irregular, hilly flanks opening at last through gateways of low, rounded foot-hills out upon the horizontal plain of the San Joaquin and Sacramento.

Every cañon carries a river, derived from constant melting of the perpetual snow, which threads its way down the mountain,—a feeble type of those vast ice-streams and torrents that formerly discharged the summit accumulation of ice and snow while carving the cañons out from solid rock. Nowhere on the continent of America is there more positive evidence of the cutting power of rapid streams than in these very cañons. Although much is due to this cause, the most impressive passages of the Sierra valleys are actual ruptures of the rock; either the engulfment of masses of great size, as Professor Whitney supposes in explanation of the peculiar form of the Yosemite, or a splitting asunder in yawning cracks.

From the summits down half the distance to the plains, the cañons are also carved out in broad, round curves by glacial action. The summit gorges themselves are altogether the result of frost and ice. Here, even yet, may be studied the mode of blocking out mountain peaks; the cracks riven by unequal contraction and expansion of the rock; the slow leverage of ice, the storm, the avalanche.

The western descent, facing a moisture-laden, aerial current from the Pacific, condenses on its higher portions a great amount of water, which has piled upon the summits in the form of snow, and is absorbed upon the upper plateau by an exuberant growth of forest. This prevalent wind, which during most undisturbed periods blows continuously from the ocean, strikes first upon the western slope of the Coast Range, and there discharges, both as fog and rain, a very great sum of moisture; but, being ever reinforced, it blows over their crest, and, hurrying eastward, strikes the Sierras at about four thousand feet above sea-level. Below this line the foot-hills are oppressed by an habitual dryness, which produces a rusty olive tone throughout nearly all the large conspicuous vegetation, scorches the red soil, and, during the long summer, overlays the whole region with a cloud of dust.

Dull and monotonous in color, there are, however, certain elements of picturesqueness in this lower zone. Its oak-clad hills wander out into the great plain like coast promontories, enclosing yellow, or in spring-time green, bays of prairie. The hill forms are rounded, or stretch in long longitudinal ridges, broken across by the river cañons. Above this zone of red earth, softly modelled undulations, and dull, grayish groves, with a chain of mining towns, dotted ranches and vineyards, rise the swelling middle heights of the Sierras, a broad billowy plateau cut by sharp sudden cañons, and sweeping up, with its dark, superb growth of coniferous forest to the feet of the summit peaks.

For a breadth of forty miles, all along the chain, is spread this continuous belt of pines. From Walker's Pass to Sitka one may ride through an unbroken forest, and will find its character and aspect vary constantly in strict accordance with the laws of altitude and moisture, each of the several species of coniferous trees taking its position with an almost mathematical precision. Where low gaps in the Coast Range give free access to the western wind, there the forest sweeps downward and encamps upon the foot-hills, and, continuing northward, it advances toward the coast, securing for itself over this whole distance about the same physical conditions; so that a tree which finds itself at home on the shore of Puget's Sound, in the latitude of Middle California has climbed the Sierras to a height of six thousand feet, finding there its normal requirements of damp, cool air. As if to economize the whole surface of the Sierra, the forest is mainly made up of twelve species of coniferæ, each having its own definitely circumscribed limits of temperature, and yet being able successively to occupy the whole middle Sierra up to the foot of the perpetual snow. The average range in altitude of each species is about twenty-five hundred feet, so that you pass imperceptibly from the zone of one species into that of the next. Frequently three or four are commingled, their varied habit, characteristic foliage, and richly colored trunks uniting to make the most stately of forests.

In the centre of the coniferous belt is assembled the most remarkable family of trees. Those which approach the perpetual snow are imperfect, gnarled, storm-bent; full of character and suggestion, but lacking the symmetry, the rich, living green, and the great size of their lower neighbors. In the other extreme of the pine-belt, growing side by side with foot-hill oaks, is an equally imperfect species, which, although attaining a very great size, still has the air of an abnormal tree. The conditions of drought on the one hand, and rigorous storms on the other, injure and blast alike, while the more verdant centre, furnishing the finest conditions, produces a forest whose profusion and grandeur fill the traveller with the liveliest admiration.

Toward the south the growth of the forest is more open and grove-like, the individual trees becoming proportionally larger and reaching their highest development. Northward its density increases, to the injury of individual pines, until the branches finally interlock, and at last on the shores of British Columbia the trunks are so densely assembled that a dead tree is held in its upright position by the arms of its fellows.

At the one extremity are magnificent purple shafts ornamented with an exquisitely delicate drapery of pale golden and dark blue green; at the other the slender spars stand crowded together like the fringe of masts girdling a prosperous port. The one is a great continuous grove, on whose sunny openings are innumerable brilliant parterres; the other is a dismal thicket, a sort of gigantic canebrake, void of beauty, dark, impenetrable, save by the avenues of streams, where one may float for days between sombre walls of forest. From one to the other of these extremes is an imperceptible transition; only in the passage of hundreds of miles does the forest seem to thicken northward, or the majesty of the single trees appear to be impaired by their struggle for room.

Near the centre is the perfection of forest. At the south are the finest specimen trees, at the north the densest accumulations of timber. In riding throughout this whole region and watching the same species from the glorious ideal life of the south gradually dwarfed toward the north, until it becomes a mere wand; or in climbing from the scattered drought-scourged pines of the foot-hills up through the zone of finest vegetation to those summit crags, where, struggling against the power of tempest and frost, only a few of the bravest trees succeed in clinging to the rocks and to life,—one sees with novel effect the inexorable sway which climatic conditions hold over the kingdom of trees.

Looking down from the summit, the forest is a closely woven vesture, which has fallen over the body of the range, clinging closely to its form, sinking into the deep cañons, covering the hill-tops with even velvety folds, and only lost here and there where a bold mass of rock gives it no foothold, or where around the margin of the mountain lakes bits of alpine meadow lie open to the sun.

Along its upper limit the forest zone grows thin and irregular; black shafts of alpine pines and firs clustering on sheltered slopes, or climbing in disordered processions up broken and rocky faces. Higher, the last gnarled forms are passed, and beyond stretches the rank of silent, white peaks, a region of rock and ice lifted above the limit of life.

In the north, domes and cones of volcanic formation are the summit, but for about three hundred miles in the south it is a succession of sharp granite aiguilles and crags. Prevalent among the granitic forms are singularly perfect conoidal domes, whose symmetrical figures, were it not for their immense size, would impress one as having an artificial finish.

The alpine gorges are usually wide and open, leading into amphitheatres, whose walls are either rock or drifts of never-melting snow. The sculpture of the summit is very evidently glacial. Beside the ordinary phenomena of polished rocks and moraines, the larger general forms are clearly the work of frost and ice; and although this ice-period is only feebly represented to-day, yet the frequent avalanches of winter and freshly scored mountain flanks are constant suggestions of the past.

Strikingly contrasted are the two countries bordering the Sierra on either side. Along the western base is the plain of California, an elliptical basin four hundred and fifty miles long by sixty-five broad; level, fertile, well watered, half tropically warmed; checkered with farms of grain, ranches of cattle, orchard, and vineyard, and homes of commonplace opulence, towns of bustling thrift. Rivers flow over it, bordered by lines of oaks which seem characterless or gone to sleep, when compared with the vitality, the spring, and attitude of the same species higher up on the foot-hills. It is a region of great industrial future, within a narrow range, but quite without charms for the student of science. It has a certain impressive breadth when seen from some overlooking eminence, or when in early spring its brilliant carpet of flowers lies as a foreground over which the dark pine-land and white crest of the Sierra loom indistinctly.

From the Mexican frontier up into Oregon, a strip of actual desert lies under the east slope of the great chain, and stretches eastward sometimes as far as five hundred miles, varied by successions of bare white ground, effervescing under the hot sun with alkaline salts, plains covered by the low ashy-hued sage-plant, high, barren, rocky ranges, which are folds of metamorphic rocks, and piled-up lavas of bright red or yellow colors; all over-arched by a sky which is at one time of a hot metallic brilliancy, and again the tenderest of evanescent purple or pearl.

Utterly opposed are the two aspects of the Sierras from these east and west approaches. I remember how stern and strong the chain looked to me when I first saw it from the Colorado desert.

*   *   *

There are but few points in America where such extremes of physical condition meet. What contrasts, what opposed sentiments, the two views awakened! Spread out below us lay the desert, stark and glaring, its rigid hill-chains lying in disordered grouping, in attitudes of the dead. The bare hills are cut out with sharp gorges, and over their stone skeletons scanty earth clings in folds, like shrunken flesh; they are emaciated corses of once noble ranges now lifeless, outstretched as in a long sleep. Ghastly colors define them from the ashen plain in which their feet are buried. Far in the south were a procession of whirlwind columns slowly moving across the desert in spectral dimness. A white light beat down, dispelling the last trace of shadow, and above hung the burnished shield of hard, pitiless sky.

Sinking to the *west* from our feet the gentle golden-green *glacis* sloped away, flanked by rolling hills covered with a fresh vernal carpet of grass, and relieved by scattered groves of dark oak-trees. Upon the distant valley were checkered fields of grass and grain just tinged with the first ripening yellow. The bounding Coast Ranges lay in the cool shadow of a bank of mist which drifted in from the Pacific, covering their heights. Flocks of bright clouds floated across the sky, whose blue was palpitating with light, and seemed to rise with infinite perspective. Tranquility, abundance, the slow, beautiful unfolding of plant life, dark shadowed spots to rest our tired eyes upon, the shade of giant oaks to lie down under, while listening to brooks, contralto larks, and the soft distant lowing of cattle.

I have given the outlines of aspect along our ride across the Chabazon, omitting many amusing incidents and some *genre* pictures of rare interest among the Kaweah Indians, as I wished simply to illustrate the relations of the Sierra with the country bordering its east base,—the barrier looming above a desert.

In Nevada and California, farther north, this wall rises more grandly, but its face rests upon a modified form of desert plains of less extent than the Colorado, and usually covered with sage-plants and other brushy *compositæ* of equally pitiful appearance. Large lakes of complicated saline waters are dotted under the Sierra shadow, the ancient terraces built upon foot-hill and outlying volcanic ranges indicating their former expansion into inland seas; and farther north still, where plains extend east of Mount Shasta, level sheets of lava form the country, and open black, rocky channels, for the numerous branches of the Sacramento and Klamath.

Approaching the Sierras anywhere from the west, you will perceive a totally different topographical and climatic condition. From the Coast Range peaks especially one obtains an extended and impressive prospect. I had fallen behind the party one May evening of our march across Pacheco's Pass, partly because some wind-bent oaks trailing almost horizontally over the wild-oat surface of the hills, and marking, as a living record, the prevalent west wind, had arrested me and called out compass and note-book; and because there had fallen to my lot an incorrigibly deliberate mustang to whom I had abandoned myself to be carried along at his own pace, comforted withal that I should get in too late to have any hand in the cooking of supper. We reached the crest, the mustang coming to a conspicuous and unwarrantable halt; I yielded, however, and sat still in the saddle, looking out to the east.

Brown foot-hills, purple over their lower slopes with "fil-a-ree" blossoms, descended steeply to the plain of California, a great, inland, prairie sea, extending for five hundred miles, mountain-locked, between the Sierras and coast hills, and now a broad arabesque surface of colors. Miles of orange-colored flowers, cloudings of green and white, reaches of violet which looked like the shadow of a passing cloud, wandering in natural patterns over and through each other, sunny and intense along near our range, fading in the distance into pale bluish-pearl tones, and divided by long, dimly seen rivers, whose margins were edged by belts of bright emerald green. Beyond rose three hundred miles of Sierra half lost in light and cloud and mist, the summit in places sharply seen against a pale, beryl sky, and again buried in warm, rolling clouds. It was a mass of strong light, soft, fathomless shadows, and dark regions of forest. However, the three belts upon its front were tolerably clear. Dusky foot-hills rose over the plain with a coppery gold tone, suggesting the line of mining towns planted in its rusty ravines,—a suggestion I was glad to repel, and look higher into that cool, solemn realm where the pines stand, green-roofed, in infinite colonnade. Lifted above the bustling industry of the plains and the melodramatic mining theatre of the foot-hills, it has a grand, silent life of its own, refreshing to contemplate even from a hundred miles away.

While I looked the sun descended; shadows climbed the Sierras, casting a gloom over foot-hill and pine, until at last only the snow summits, reflecting the evening light, glowed like red lamps along the mountain wall for hundreds of miles. The rest of the Sierra became invisible. The snow burned for a moment in the violet sky, and at last went out.

HENRY JAMES
1843-1916

Though often thought of as a novelist of English drawing rooms and formal society, Henry James loved the countryside, particularly on wild "motor-trips" through Massachusetts and France with fellow novelist Edith Wharton at the wheel. The New England landscape figures prominently in such novels as The Bostonians *and* The Europeans, *and James also wrote some of the first appreciative reviews of John Burroughs's work. His inclusion in this anthology, however, rests on a late work,* The American Scene *(1907), based on a tour of the United States after an absence of nearly twenty-five years. Though critical of the vulgarity and crudity of* fin-de-siècle *America, the book contains many appreciative descriptions of various natural settings—"the large and noble sanities that I see around me"—and a remarkable sense of the "mystery" of place. The following selection is an account of a visit to the Cape Cod village of Cotuit on Nantucket Sound.*

From THE AMERICAN SCENE

NEW ENGLAND: AN AUTUMN IMPRESSION

["a supreme queerness"]

* * * Clearly, none the less, there were puzzles and puzzles, and I had almost immediately the amusement of waking up to another—this one of a different order altogether. The point was that if the bewilder-

The American Scene (London: Chapman and Hull, 1907).

ments I have just mentioned had dropped, most other things had dropped too: the challenge to curiosity here was in the extreme simplification of the picture, a simplification on original lines. Not that there was not still much to think of—if only because one had to stare at the very wonder of a picture so simplified. The thing now was to catch this note, to keep it in the ear and see, really, how far and how long it would sound. The simplification, for that immediate vision, was to a broad band of deep and clear blue sea, a blue of the deepest and clearest conceivable, limited in one quarter by its far and sharp horizon of sky, and in the other by its near and sharp horizon of yellow sand over-fringed with a low woody shore; the whole seen through the contorted crosspieces of stunted, wind-twisted, far-spreading, quite fantastic old pines and cedars, whose bunched bristles, at the ends of long limbs, produced, against the light, the most vivid of all reminders. Cape Cod, on this showing, was exactly a pendent, pictured Japanese screen or banner; a delightful little triumph of "impressionism," which, during my short visit at least, never departed, under any provocation, from its type. Its type, so easily formulated, so completely filled, was there the last thing at night and the first thing in the morning; there was rest for the mind— for that, certainly, of the restless analyst—in having it so exactly under one's hand. After that one could read into it other meanings without straining or disturbing it. There was a couchant promontory in particular, half bosky with the evergreen boskage of the elegant kakemono, half bare with the bareness of refined, the *most* refined, New England decoration—a low, hospitable headland projected, as by some water-colourist master of the trick, into a mere brave wash of cobalt. It interfered, the sweet promontory, with its generous Boston bungalow, its verandahs still haunted with old summer-times, and so wide that the present could elbow and yet not jostle the past—it interfered no whit, for all its purity of style, with the human, the social question always dogging the steps of the ancient contemplative person and making him, before each scene, wish really to get *into* the picture, to cross, as it were, the threshold of the frame. It never lifts, verily, this obsession of the story-seeker, however often it may flutter its wings, it may bruise its breast, against surfaces either too hard or too blank. "The *manners*, the manners: where and what are they, and what have they to tell?"—that haunting curiosity, essential to the honour of his office, yet making it much of a burden, fairly buzzes about his head the more pressingly in proportion as the social mystery, the lurking human secret, seems more shy.

Then it is that, as he says to himself, the secret must be most queer— and it might therefore well have had, so insidiously sounded, a supreme queerness on Cape Cod. For not the faintest echo of it trembled out of the blankness; there were always the little white houses of the village, there were always the elegant elms, feebler and more feathery here than further inland; but the life of the little community was practically locked up as tight as if it had *all* been a question of painted Japanese silk. And that was doubtless, for the story-seeker, absolutely the little story: the constituted blankness was the whole business, and one's opportunity was all, thereby, for a study of exquisite emptiness. This was stuff, in its own way, of a beautiful quality; that impression came to me with a special sweetness that I have not forgotten. The help in the matter was that I had not forgotten, either, a small pilgrimage or two of far-away earlier years—the sense as of absent things in other summer-times, golden afternoons that referred themselves for their character simply to sandy roads and primitive "farms," crooked inlets of mild sea and, at the richest, large possibilities of worked cranberry-swamp. I remembered, in fine, Mattapoisett, I remembered Marion, as admirable examples of that frequent New England phenomenon, the case the consummate example of which I was soon again to recognize in Newport—the presence of an *unreasoned* appeal, in nature, to the sense of beauty, the appeal on a basis of items that failed somehow, count and recount them as one would, to justify the effect and make up the precious sum. The sum, at Newport above all, as I was soon again to see, is the exquisite, the irresistible; but you falter before beginning to name the parts of the explanation, conscious how short the list may appear. Thus everything, in the whole range of imagery, affirms itself and interposes; you will, you inwardly determine, arrive at some notation of manners even if you perish in the attempt. Thus, as I jogged southward, from Boston, in a train that stopped and stopped again, for my fuller enlightenment, and that insisted, the good old promiscuous American car itself, on having as much of its native character as possible for my benefit, I already knew I must fall back on old props of association, some revival of the process of seeing the land grow mild and vague and interchangeably familiar with the sea, all under the spell of the reported "gulf-stream," those mystic words that breathe a softness wherever they sound.

It was imperative here that they should do what they could for me, and they must have been in full operation when, on my arrival at the small station from which I was to drive across to Cotuit—"across the Cape," as who should say, romantic thought, though I strain a point geographically for the romance—I found initiation awaiting me in the form of minimized horse-and-buggy and minimized man. The man was a little boy in tight knickerbockers, the horse barely an animal at all, a mere ambling spirit in shafts on the scale of a hairpin, the buggy disembodied save for its wheels, the whole thing the barest infraction of the road, of the void: circumstances, altogether, that struck the note, the right, the persistent one—that of my baffled endeavour, while in the neighborhood, to catch life in the fact, and of my then having to recognize it as present *without* facts, or with only the few (the little white houses, the feathery elms, the band of ocean blue, the stripe of sandy yellow, the tufted pines in angular silhouette, the cranberry-swamps stringed across, for the picking, like the ruled pages of ledgers), that fell, incorruptibly silent, into the picture. We were still far from our goal, that first hour, when I had recognized the full pictorial and other "value" of my little boy and his little accessories; had seen, in the amiable waste that we continued to plough till we struck, almost with a shock, the inconsistency of a long stretch of new "stone" road, that, socially, economically, every contributive scrap of this detail was required. I drained my small companion, by gentle pressure, of such side-lights as he could project, consisting almost wholly, as they did, of a prompt and shrill, an oddly-emphasized "Yes, *sir!*" to each interrogative attempt to break ground. The summer people had already departed—with, as it seemed to me, undue precipitation; the very hotel offered, in its many-windowed bulk, the semblance of a mere huge brittle sea-shell that children tired of playing with it have cast again upon the beach; the alignments of white cottages were, once more, as if the children had taken, for a change, to building houses of cards and then had deserted *them.* I remember the sense that something *must* be done for penetration, for discovery; I remember an earnest stroll, undertaken for a view of waterside life, which resulted in the perception of a young man, in a spacius but otherwise unpeopled nook, a clear, straightforward young man to converse with, for a grand opportunity, across the water, waist-high in the quiet tide and prodding the sea-bottom for oysters; also in the discovery of an animated centre of industry of which oysters again were the motive: a mute citizen or two packing them in boxes, on the beach, for the Boston market, the hammer of some vague carpentry hard by, and, filling the air more than anything else, the unabashed discourse of three or four school-children at leisure, visibly "prominent" and apparently in charge of the life of the place. I remember not less a longish walk, and a longer drive, into low extensions of woody, piney, pondy landscape, veined with blue inlets and trimmed, on opportunity, with blond beaches—through all of which I pursued in vain the shy spectre of a revelation. The only revelation seemed really to be that, quite as in New Hampshire, so many people had "left" that the remaining characters, on the sketchy page, were too few to form a word. With this, accordingly, of what, in the bright air, for the charmed visitor, were the softness and sweetness of impression *made?* I had again to take it for a mystery. *   *   *

GERARD MANLEY HOPKINS
1844-1889

Nature writing includes many outstanding contributions by writers primarily associated with other genres. With Hopkins, the pattern of gradual emergence as a nature writer is further complicated by his invisibility as a poet during his life-time. When he entered the Jesuit novitiate in 1868 he burned all his early poetry. The ground-breaking work by which we know him today was not printed until Robert Bridges edited it for publication in 1918. Hopkins's artistic achievement has since drawn readers back to his notebooks and sketches, where his vividness and distinction as a nature writer are impressive. "Inscape," his concept for the integrity of every natural object or landscape, as of every authentic poem, is powerfully conveyed in those entries. Natural experience, for Hopkins, is always individual, a lyrical whole, stressed and startling.

From Notebooks and Papers of
Gerard Manley Hopkins

EXTRACTS FROM EARLY DIARIES

[1863]

Note on water coming through a lock.

There are openings near the bottom of the gates (which allow the water to pass through at all times, I suppose.) Suppose three, as there

Notebooks and Papers of Gerard Manley Hopkins, ed. Humphrey House (London & New York: Oxford University Press, 1937).

often are. The water strikes through these with great force and extends itself into three fans. The direction of the water is a little oblique from the horizontal, but the great force with which it runs keeps it almost uncurved except at the edges. The end of these fans is not seen for they strike them under a mass of yellowish boiling foam which runs down between the fans, and meeting covers the whole space of the lock-entrance. Being heaped up in globes and bosses and round masses the fans disappear under it. This turpid mass smooths itself as the distance increases from the lock. But the current is strong and if the basin into which it runs has curving banks it strikes them and the confusion of the already folded and doubled lines of foam is worse confounded.

[1866]

Drops of rain hanging on rails etc seen with only the lower rim lighted like nails (of fingers). Screws of brooks and twines. Soft chalky look with more shadowy middles of the globes of cloud on a night with a moon faint or concealed. Mealy clouds with a not brilliant moon. Blunt buds of the ash. Pencil buds of the beech. Lobes of the trees. Cups of the eyes, Gathering back the lightly hinged eyelids. Bows of the eyelids. Pencil of eyelashes. Juices of the eyeball. Eyelids like leaves, petals, caps, tufted hats, handkerchiefs, sleeves, gloves. Also of the bones sleeved in flesh. Juices of the sunrise. Joints and veins of the same. Vermilion look of the hand held against a candle with the darker parts as the middles of the fingers and especially the knuckles covered with ash.

[1870]

I have no other word yet for that which takes the eye or mind in a bold hand or effective sketching or in marked features or again in graphic writing, which not being beauty nor true inscape yet gives interest and makes ugliness even better than meaninglessness.—On the Common the snow was channeled all in parallels by the sharp driving wind and upon the tufts of grass (where by the dark colour shewing through it looked greyish) it came to turret-like clusters or like broken shafts of basalt.—In the Park in the afternoon the wind was driving little clouds of snow-dust which caught the sun as they rose and delightfully took the eyes: flying up the slopes they looked like breaks of sunlight fallen through ravelled cloud upon the hills and again like deep flossy velvet blown to the root by breath which passed all along. Nearer at hand along the road it was gliding over the ground in white wisps that between trailing and flying shifted and wimpled like so many silvery worms to and from one another.

The squirrel was about in our trees all the winter. For instance about Jan. 2 I often saw it.

March 12—A fine sunset: the higher sky dead clear blue bridged by a broad slant causeway rising from right to left of wisped or grass cloud, the wisps lying across; the sundown yellow, moist with light but ending at the top in a foam of delicate white pearling and spotted with big tufts of cloud in colour russet between brown and purple but edged with brassy light. But what I note it all for is this: before I had always taken the sunset and the sun as quite out of gauge with each other, as indeed physically they are for the eye after looking at the sun is blunted to everything else and if you look at the rest of the sunset you must cover the sun, but today I inscaped them together and made the sun the true eye and ace of the whole, as it is. It was all active and tossing out light and started as strongly forward from the field as a long stone or a boss in the knop of the chalice-stem: it is indeed by stalling it so that it falls into scape with the sky.

May 12 Wych-elms not out till today.—The chestnuts down by St. Joseph's were a beautiful sight: each spike had its own pitch, yet each followed in its place in the sweep with a deeper and deeper stoop. When the wind tossed them they plunged and crossed one another without losing their inscape. (Observe that motion multiplies inscape only when inscape is discovered, otherwise it disfigures.)

One day when the bluebells were in bloom I wrote the following. I do not think I have ever seen anything more beautiful than the bluebell I have been looking at. I know the beauty of our Lord by it. It[s inscape] is [mixed of] strength and grace, like an ash [tree]. The head is strongly drawn over [backwards] and arched down like a cutwater [drawing itself back from the line of the keel]. The lines of the bells strike and overlie this, rayed but not symmetrically, some lie parallel. They look steely against [the] paper, the shades lying between the bells and behind the cockled petal-ends and nursing up the precision of their distinctness, the petal-ends themselves being delicately lit. Then there is the straightness of the trumpets in the bells softened by the slight entasis and [by] the square splay of the mouth. One bell, the lowest, some way detached and carried on a longer footstalk, touched out with the tips of the petals an oval / not like the rest in a plane perpendicular to the axis of the bell but

a little atilt, and so with [the] square-in-rounding turns of the petals.
. . . There is a little drawing of this detached bell.—It looks square-cut in
the original

Sept. 24—First saw the Northern Lights. My eye was caught by
beams of light and dark very like the crown of horny rays the sun makes
behind a cloud. At first I thought of silvery cloud until I saw that these
were more luminous and did not dim the clearness of the stars in the
Bear. They rose slightly radiating thrown out from the earthline. Then I
saw soft pulses of light one after another rise and pass upwards arched in
shape but waveringly and with the arch broken. They seemed to float,
not following the warp of the sphere as falling stars look to do but free
though concentrical with it. This busy working of nature wholly independent of the earth and seeming to go on in a strain of time not
reckoned by our reckoning of days and years but simpler and as if cor-
recting the preoccupation of the world by being preoccupied with and
appealing to and dated to the day of judgment was like a new witness to
God and filled me with delightful fear

Oct. 20—Laus Deo—the river today and yesterday. Yesterday it was a
sallow glassy gold at Hodder Roughs and by watching hard the banks
began to sail upstream, the scaping unfolded, the river was all in tumult
but not running, only the lateral motions were perceived, and the curls
of froth where the waves overlap shaped and turned easily and idly.—I
meant to have written more.—Today the river was wild, very full, glossy
brown with mud, furrowed in permanent billows through which from
head to head the water swung with a great down and up again. These
heads were scalped with rags of jumping foam. But at the Roughs the
sigh was the burly water-backs which heave after heave kept tumbling up
from the broken foam and their plump heap turning open in ropes of
velvet.

Oct. 25—A little before 7 in the evening a wonderful Aurora, the
same that was seen at Rome (shortly after its seizure by the Italian
government) and taken as a sign of God's anger. It gathered a little
below the zenith, to the S.E. I think—a knot or crown, not a true circle,
of dull blood-coloured horns and dropped long red beams down the sky
on every side, each impaling its lot of stars. An hour or so later its colour
was gone but there was still a pale crown in the same place: the skies were
then clear and ashy and fresh with stars and there were flashes of or like
sheet-lightning. The day had been very bright and clear, distances smart,

herds of towering pillow clouds, one great stack in particular over Pendle was knoppled all over in fine snowy tufts and pencilled with bloom-shadow of the greatest delicacy. In the sunset all was big and there was a world of swollen cloud holding the yellow-rose light like a lamp while a few sad milky blue slips passed below it. At night violent hailstorms and hail again next day, and a solar halo. Worth noticing too perhaps the water-runs were then mulled and less beautiful than usual

[1871]

I have been watching clouds this spring and evaporation, for instance over our Lenten chocolate. It seems as if the heat by *aestus,* throes/ one after another threw films of vapour off as boiling water throws off steam under films of water, that is bubbles. One query then is whether these films contain gas or no. The film seems to be set with tiny bubbles which gives it a grey and grained look. By throes perhaps which represent the moments at which the evener stress of the heat has overcome the resistance of the surface or of the whole liquid. It would be reasonable then to consider the films as the shell of gas-bubbles and the grain on them as a network of bubbles condensed by the air as the gas rises.—Candle smoke goes by just the same laws, the visible film being here of unconsumed substance, not hollow bubbles. The throes can be perceived/ like the thrills of a candle in the socket: this is precisely to *reech,* whence *reek.* They may be a breath of air be laid again and then shew like grey wisps on the surface—which shews their part-solidity. They seem to be drawn off the chocolate as you might take up a napkin between your fingers that covered something, not so much from here or there as from the whole surface at one reach, so that the film is perceived at the edges and makes in fact a collar or ring just within the walls all round the cup; it then draws together in a cowl like a candleflame but not regularly or without a break: the question is why. Perhaps in perfect stillness it would not but the air breathing it aside entangles it with itself. The film seems to rise not quite simultaneously but to peel off as if you were tearing cloth; then giving an end forward like the corner of a handkerchief and beginning to coil it makes a long wavy hose you may sometimes look down, as a ribbon or a carpenter's shaving may be made to do. Higher running into frets and silvering in the sun with the endless coiling, the soft bound of the general motion and yet the side lurches sliding into some particular pitch it makes a baffling and charming sight.—Clouds however solid they may look far off are I think wholly made of film in the sheet or in the tuft. The bright woolpacks that pelt before a gale in a clear sky are in the tuft and you can see the wind unravelling and rending them finer than any sponge till within one easy reach overhead they are morselled to nothing and consumed—it depends of course on their size. Possibly each tuft in forepitch or in origin is quained and a crystal. Rarer and wilder packs have sometimes film in the sheet, which may be caught as it turns on the edge of the cloud like an outlying eyebrow. The one in which I saw this was a north-east wind, solid but not crisp, white like the white of egg, and bloated-looking

What you look hard at seems to look hard at you, hence the true and the false in stress of nature. One day early in March when long streamers were rising from over Kemble End one large flake loop-shaped, not a streamer but belonging to the string, moving too slowly to be seen, seemed to cap and fill the zenith with a white shire of cloud. I looked long up at it till the tall height and the beauty of the scaping—regularly curled knots springing if I remember from fine stems, like foliation in wood or stone—had strongly grown on me. It changed beautiful changes, growing more into ribs and one stretch of running into branching like coral. Unless you refresh the mind from time to time you cannot always remember or believe how deep the inscape in things is

May 6—First summer-feeling day—not to last long
The banks are 'versed' with primroses, partly scattered, partly in plots and squats, and at a little distance shewing milk-white or silver—little split till-fulls of silver. I have seen them reflected in green standing farmyard water.

May 9—A simple behaviour of the cloudscape I have not realized before. Before a N.E. wind great bars or rafters of cloud all the morning and in a manner all the day marching across the sky in regular rank and with equal spaces between. They seem prism-shaped, flat-bottomed and banked up to a ridge: their make is like tufty snow in coats

This day and May 11 the bluebells in the little wood between the College and the highroad and in one of the Hurst Green cloughs. In the little wood/opposite the light/they stood in blackish spreads or sheddings like the spots on a snake. The heads are then like thongs and solemn in grain and grape-colour. But in the clough/through the light/ they came in falls of sky-colour washing the brows and slacks of the ground with vein-blue, thickening at the double, vertical themselves and the young grass and brake fern combed vertical, but the brake struck the upright of all this with light winged transomes. It was a lovely sight.—
The bluebells in your hand baffle you with their inscape, made to every sense: if you draw your fingers through them they are lodged and strug-

gle/with a shock of wet heads; the long stalks rub and click and flatten to a fan on one another like your fingers themselves would when you passed the palms hard across one another, making a brittle rub and jostle like the noise of a hurdle strained by leaning against; then there is the faint honey smell and in the mouth the sweet gum when you bite them. But this is easy, it is the eye they baffle. They give one a fancy of panpipes and of some wind instrument with stops—a trombone perhaps. The overhung necks—for growing they are little more than a staff with a simple crook but in water, where they stiffen, they take stronger turns, in the head like sheep-hooks or, when more waved throughout, like the waves riding through a whip that is being smacked—what with these overhung necks and what with the crisped ruffled bells dropping mostly on one side and the gloss these have at their footstalks they have an air of the knights at chess. Then the knot or 'knoop' of buds some shut, some just gaping, which makes the pencil of the whole spike, should be noticed: the inscape of the flower most finely carried out in the siding of the axes, each striking a greater and greater slant, is finished in these clustered buds, which for the most part are not straightened but rise to the end like a tongue and this and their tapering and a little flattening they have made them look like the heads of snakes

Later—The Horned Violet is a pretty thing, gracefully lashed. Even in withering the flower ran through beautiful inscapes by the screwing up of the petals into straight little barrels or tubes. It is not that inscape does not govern the behavior of things in slack and decay as one can see even in the pining of the skin in the old and even in a skeleton but that horror prepossesses the mind, but in this case there was nothing in itself to show even whether the flower were shutting or opening

The 'pinion' of the blossom in the comfrey is remarkable for the beauty of the coil and its regular lessening to its centre. Perhaps the duller-coloured sorts shew it best

Oct. 5—A goldencrested wren had got into my room at night and circled round dazzled by the gaslight on the white cieling; when caught even and put out it would come in again. Ruffling the crest, which is mounted over the crown and eyes like beetle-brows; I smoothed and fingered the little orange and yellow feathers which are hidden in it. Next morning I found many of these about the room and enclosed them in a letter to Cyril on his wedding day.

Aug. 16—We rose at four, when it was stormy and I saw dun-coloured waves leaving trailing hoods of white breaking on the beach. Before going I took a last look at the breakers, wanting to make out how the comb is morselled so fine into string and tassel, as I have lately noticed it to be. I saw big smooth flinty waves, carved and scuppled in shallow grooves, much swelling when the wind freshened, burst on the rocky spurs of the cliff at the little cove and break into bushes of foam. In an enclosure of rocks the peaks of the water romped and wandered and a light crown of tufty scum standing high on the surface kept slowly turning round: chips of it blew off and gadded about without weight in the air. At eight we sailed for Liverpool in wind and rain. I think it is the salt that makes rain at sea sting so much. There was a good-looking young man on board that got drunk and sung "I want to go home to Mamma." I did not look much at the sea: the crests I saw ravelled up by the wind into the air in arching whips and straps of glassy spray and higher broken into clouds of white and blown away. Under the curl shone a bright juice of beautiful green. The foam exploding and smouldering under water makes a chrysoprase green. From Blackburn I walked: infinite stiles and sloppy fields, for there has been much rain. A few big shining drops hit us aslant as if they were blown off from eaves or leaves. Bright sunset: all the sky hung with tall tossed clouds, in the west with strong printing glass edges, westward lamping with tipsy buff-light, the colour of yellow roses. Parlick ridge like a pale goldish skin without body. The plain about Clitheroe was sponged out by a tall white storm of rain. The sun itself and the spot of "session" dappled with big laps and flowers-in-damask of cloud. But we hurried too fast and it knocked me up. We went to the College, the seminary being wanted for the secular priests' retreat: almost no gas, for the retorts are being mended; therefore candles in bottles, things not ready, darkness and despair. In fact being unwell I was quite downcast: nature in all her parcels and faculties gaped and fell apart, *fatiscebat*, like a clod cleaving and holding only by strings of root. But this must often be

Nov. 8—Walking with Wm. Splaine we saw a vast multitude of starlings making an unspeakable jangle. They would settle in a row of trees; then, one tree after another, rising at a signal they looked like a cloud of specks of black snuff or powder struck up from a brush or broom or shaken from a wig; then they would sweep round in whirlwinds—you could see the nearer and farther bow of the rings by the size and blackness; many would be in one phase at once, all narrow black flakes hurling round, then in another; then they would fall upon a field and so on. Splaine wanted a gun: then 'there it would rain meat' he said. I thought they must be full of enthusiasm and delight hearing their cries and stirring and cheering one another

RICHARD JEFFERIES
1848-1887

Jefferies was an unusually prolific writer, one who pursued journalism for a number of years and whose many books included both novels and political commentary. Today, though, he is remembered mainly for his accounts of rural life in an era when the social and economic bases of English agriculture life were changing rapidly. Books like The Gamekeeper at Home *(1878),* Wild Life in a Southern County *(1879), and* Field and Hedgerow *(1889) looked not only at the traditional farming landscapes of England but also at the human communities they supported and the kinds of individuals they produced. He both celebrated a passing way of life and conveyed to his urban readers the harsher elements of a traditional life "in nature."*

Out of Doors in February

The cawing of the rooks in February shows that the time is coming when their nests will be re-occupied. They resort to the trees, and perch above the old nests to indicate their rights; for in the rookery possession is the law, and not nine-tenths of it only. In the slow dull cold of winter even these noisy birds are quiet, and as the vast flocks pass over, night and morning, to and from the woods in which they roost, there is scarcely a sound. Through the mist their black wings advance in silence, the jackdaws with them are chilled into unwonted quiet, and unless you chance to look up the crowd may go over unnoticed. But so soon as the waters begin to make a sound in February, running in the ditches and splashing over stones, the rooks commence the speeches and conversations which will continue till late into the following autumn.

The general idea is that they pair in February, but there are some reasons for thinking that the rooks, in fact, choose their mates at the end

The Open Air (London: Chatto & Windus, 1885).

of the preceding summer. They are then in large flocks, and if only casually glanced at appear mixed together without any order or arrangement. They move on the ground and fly in the air so close, one beside the other, that at the first glance or so you cannot distinguish them apart. Yet if you should be lingering along the by-ways of the fields as the acorns fall, and the leaves come rustling down in the warm sunny autumn afternoons, and keep an observant eye upon the rooks in the trees, or on the fresh-turned furrows, they will be seen to act in couples. On the ground couples alight near each other, on the trees they perch near each other, and in the air fly side by side. Like soldiers each has his comrade. Wedged in the ranks every man looks like his fellow, and there seems no tie between them but a common discipline. Intimate acquaintance with barrack or camp life would show that every one had his friend. There is also the mess, or companionship of half a dozen, a dozen, or more, and something like this exists part of the year in the armies of the rooks. After the nest time is over they flock together, and each family of three or four flies in concert. Later on they apparently choose their own particular friends, that is the young birds do so. All through the winter after, say October, these pairs keep together, though lost in the general mass to the passing spectator. If you alarm them while feeding on the ground in winter, supposing you have not got a gun, they merely rise up to the nearest tree, and it may then be observed that they do this in pairs. One perches on a branch and a second comes to him. When February arrives, and they resort to the nests to look after or seize on the property there, they are in fact already paired, though the almanacs put down St. Valentine's day as the date of courtship.

There is very often a warm interval in February, sometimes a few days earlier and sometimes later, but as a rule it happens that a week or so of mild sunny weather occurs about this time. Released from the grip of the frost, the streams trickle forth from the fields and pour into the ditches, so that while walking along the footpath there is a murmur all around coming from the rush of water. The murmur of the poets is indeed louder in February than in the more pleasant days of summer, for then the growth of aquatic grasses checks the flow and stills it, whilst in February, every stone, or flint, or lump of chalk divides the current and causes a vibration. With this murmur of water, and mild time, the rooks caw incessantly, and the birds at large essay to utter their welcome of the sun. The wet furrows reflect the rays so that the dark earth gleams, and in the slight mist that stays farther away the light pauses and fills the vapour with radiance. Through this luminous mist the larks race after each other twittering, and as they turn aside, swerving in their swift flight, their white breasts appear for a moment. As while standing by a pool the fishes come into sight, emerging as they swim round from the shadow of the deeper water, so the larks dart over the low hedge, and through the mist, and pass before you, and are gone again. All at once one checks his pursuit, forgets the immediate object, and rises, singing as he soars. The notes fall from the air over the dark wet earth, over the dank grass, and broken withered fern of the hedges, and listening to them it seems for a moment spring. There is sunshine in the song: the lark and the light are one. He gives us a few minutes of summer in February days. In May he rises before as yet the dawn is come, and the sunrise flows down to us under through his notes. On his breast, high above the earth, the first rays fall as the rim of the sun edges up at the eastward hill. The lark and the light are as one, and wherever he glides over the wet furrows the glint of the sun goes with him. Anon alighting he runs between the lines of the green corn. In hot summer, when the open hillside is burned with bright light, the larks are then singing and soaring. Stepping up the hill laboriously, suddenly a lark starts into the light and pours forth a rain of unwearied notes overhead. With bright light, and sunshine, and sunrise, and blue skies the bird is so associated in the mind, that even to see him in the frosty days of winter, at least assures us that summer will certainly return.

Ought not winter, in allegorical designs, the rather to be represented with such things that might suggest hope than such as convey a cold and grim despair? The withered leaf, the snowflake, the hedging bill that cuts and destroys, why these? Why not rather the dear larks for one? They fly in flocks, and amid the white expanse of snow (in the south) their pleasant twitter or call is heard as they sweep along seeking some grassy spot cleared by the wind. The lark, the bird of the light, is there in the bitter short days. Put the lark then for winter, a sign of hope, a certainty of summer. Put, too, the sheathed bud, for if you search the hedge you will find the buds there, on tree and bush, carefully wrapped around with the case which protects them as a cloak. Put, too, the sharp needles of the green corn; let the wind clear it of snow a little way, and show that under cold clod and colder snow the green thing pushes up, knowing that summer must come. Nothing despairs but man. Set the sharp curve of the white new moon in the sky: she is white in true frost, and yellow a little if it is devising change. Set the new moon as something that symbols an increase. Set the shepherd's crook in a corner as a token that the flocks are already enlarged in number. The shepherd is the symbolic man of the hardest winter time. His work is never more important than then. Those that only roam the fields when they are pleasant in May, see the lambs at play in the meadow, and naturally think of lambs and May flowers. But the lamb was born in the adversity of snow. Or you might set the morning star, for it burns and burns and glitters in the winter dawn, and throws forth beams like those of metal consumed in oxygen. There is nought that I know by comparison with which I might indicate the glory of the morning star, while yet the dark night hides in the hollows. The lamb is born in the fold. The morning star glitters in the sky. The bud is alive in its sheath; the green corn under the snow; the lark twitters as he passes. Now these to me are the allegory of winter.

These mild hours in February check the hold which winter has been gaining, and as it were, tear his claws out of the earth, their prey. If it has not been so bitter previously, when this Gulf stream or current of warmer air enters the expanse it may bring forth a butterfly and tenderly woo the first violet into flower. But this depends on its having been only moderately cold before, and also upon the stratum, whether it is backward clay, or forward gravel and sand. Spring dates are quite different according to the locality, and when violets may be found in one district, in another there is hardly a woodbine-leaf out. The border line may be traced, and is occasionally so narrow, one may cross over it almost at a step. It would sometimes seem as if even the nut-tree bushes bore larger and finer nuts on the warmer soil, and that they ripened quicker. Any curious in the first of things, whether it be a leaf, or flower, or a bird, should bear this in mind, and not be discouraged because he hears some one else has already discovered or heard something.

A little note taken now at this bare time of the kind of earth may lead to an understanding of the district. It is plain where the plough has turned it, where the rabbits have burrowed and thrown it out, where a tree has been felled by the gales, by the brook where the bank is worn away, or by the sediment at the shallow places. Before the grass and weeds, and corn and flowers have hidden it, the character of the soil is evident at these natural sections without the aid of a spade. Going slowly along the footpath—indeed you cannot go fast in moist February—it is a good time to select the places and map them out where herbs and flowers will most likely come first. All the autumn lies prone on the ground. Dead dark leaves, some washed to their woody frames, short grey stalks, some few decayed hulls of hedge fruit, and among these the mars or stocks of the plants that do not die away, but lie as it were on the surface waiting. Here the strong teazle will presently stand high; here the ground-ivy will dot the mound with bluish-purple. But it will be necessary to walk slowly to find the ground-ivy flowers under the cover of the briers. These bushes will be a likely place for a blackbird's nest; this thick close hawthorn for a bullfinch; these bramble thickets with remnants of old nettle stalks will be frequented by the whitethroat after a

while. The hedge is now but a lattice-work which will before long be
hung with green. Now it can be seen through, and now is the time to
arrange for future discovery. In May everything will be hidden, and
unless the most promising places are selected beforehand, it will not be
easy to search them out. The broad ditch will be arched over, the plants
rising on the mound will meet the green boughs drooping, and all the
vacancy will be filled. But having observed the spot in winter you can
almost make certain of success in spring.

It is this previous knowledge which invests those who are always on
the spot, those who work much in the fields or have the care of woods,
with their apparent prescience. They lead the new comer to a hedge, or
the corner of a copse, or a bend of the brook, announcing beforehand
that they feel assured something will be found there; and so it is. This,
too, is one reason why a fixed observer usually sees more than one who
rambles a great deal and covers ten times the space. The fixed observer
who hardly goes a mile from home is like the man who sits still by the
edge of a crowd, and by-and-by his lost companion returns to him. To
walk about in search of persons in a crowd is well known to be the worst
way of recovering them. Sit still and they will often come by. In a far
more certain manner this is the case with birds and animals. They all
come back. During a twelvemonth probably every creature would pass
over a given locality: every creature that is not confined to certain places.
The whole army of the woods and hedges marches across a single farm in
twelve months. A single tree—especially an old tree—is visited by four-
fifths of the birds that ever perch in the course of that period. Every year,
too, brings something fresh, and adds new visitors to the list. Even the
wild sea birds are found inland, and some that scarce seem able to fly at
all are cast far ashore by the gales. It is difficult to believe that one would
not see more by extending the journey, but, in fact, experience proves
that the longer a single locality is studied the more is found in it. But you
should know the places in winter as well as in tempting summer, when
song and shade and colour attract every one to the field. You should face
the mire and slippery path. Nature yields nothing to the sybarite. The
meadow glows with buttercups in spring, the hedges are green, the
woods lovely; but these are not to be enjoyed in their full significance
unless you have traversed the same places when bare, and have watched
the slow fulfilment of the flowers.

The moist leaves that remain upon the mounds do not rustle, and the
thrush moves among them unheard. The sunshine may bring out a
rabbit, feeding along the slope of the mound, following the paths or
runs. He picks his way, he does not like wet. Though out at night in the
dewy grass of summer, in the rain-soaked grass of winter, and living all

his life in the earth, often damp nearly to his burrows, no time, and no succession of generations can make him like wet. He endures it, but he picks his way round the dead fern and the decayed leaves. He sits in the bunches of long grass, but he does not like the drops of rain or dew on it to touch him. Water lays his fur close, and mats it, instead of running off and leaving him sleek. As he hops a little way at a time on the mound he chooses his route almost as we pick ours in the mud and pools of February. By the shore of the ditch there still stand a few dry, dead dock stems, with some dry reddish-brown seed adhering. Some dry brown nettle stalks remain; some grey and broken thistles; some teazles leaning on the bushes. The power of winter has reached its upmost now, and can go no farther. These bines which still hang in the bushes are those of the greater bindweed, and will be used in a month or so by many birds as conveniently curved to fit about their nests. The stem of wild clematis, grey and bowed, could scarcely look more dead. Fibres are peeling from it, they come off at the touch of the fingers. The few brown feathers that perhaps still adhere where the flowers once were are stained and discoloured by the beating of the rain. It is not dead: it will flourish again ere long. It is the sturdiest of creepers, facing the ferocious winds of the hills, the tremendous rains that blow up from the sea, and bitter frost, if only it can get its roots into soil that suits it. In some places it takes the place of the hedge proper and becomes itself the hedge. Many of the trunks of the elms are swathed in minute green vegetation which has flourished in the winter, as the clematis will in the summer. Of all, the brambles bear the wild works of winter best. Given only a little shelter, in the corner of the hedges or under trees and copses they retain green leaves till the buds burst again. The frosts tint them in autumn with crimson, but not all turn colour or fall. The brambles are the bowers of the birds; in these still leafy bowers they do the courting of the spring, and under the brambles the earliest arum, and cleaver, or avens, push up. Round about them the first white nettle flowers, not long now; latest too, in the autumn. The white nettle sometimes blooms so soon (always according to locality), and again so late, that there seems but a brief interval between, as if it flowered nearly all the year round. So the berries on the holly if let alone often stay till summer is in, and new berries begin to appear shortly afterwards. The ivy, too, bears its berries far into the summer. Perhaps if the country be taken at large there is never a time when there is not a flower of some kind out, in this or that warm southern nook. The sun never sets, nor do the flowers ever die. There is life always, even in the dry fir-cone that looks so brown and sapless.

The path crosses the uplands where the lapwings stand on the parallel ridges of the ploughed field like a drilled company; if they rise they wheel as one, and in the twilight move across the fields in bands, invisible as they sweep near the ground, but seen against the sky in rising over the trees and the hedges. There is a plantation of fir and ash on the slope, and a narrow waggon-way enters it, and seems to lose itself in the wood. Always approach this spot quietly, for whatever is in the wood is sure at some time or other to come to the open space of the track. Wood-pigeons, pheasants, squirrels, magpies, hares, everything feathered or furred, down to the mole, is sure to seek the open way. Butterflies flutter through the copse by it in summer, just as you or I might use the passage between the trees. Towards the evening the partridges may run through to join their friends before roost-time on the ground. Or you may see a covey there now and then, creeping slowly with humped backs, and at a distance not unlike hedgehogs in their motions. The spot therefore should be approached with care; if it is only a thrush out it is a pleasure to see him at his ease and, as he deems, unobserved. If a bird or animal thinks itself noticed it seldom does much, some will cease singing immediately they are looked at. The day is perceptibly longer already. As the sun goes down, the western sky often takes a lovely green tint in this month, and one stays to look at it, forgetting the dark and miry way homewards. I think the moments when we forget the mire of the world are the most precious. After a while the green corn rises higher out of the rude earth.

Pure colour almost always gives the idea of fire, or rather it is perhaps as if a light shone through as well as colour itself. The fresh green blade of corn is like this, so pellucid, so clear and pure in its green as to seem to shine with colour. It is not brilliant—not a surface gleam or an enamel,—it is stained through. Beside the moist clods the slender flags arise filled with the sweetness of the earth. Out of the darkness under—that darkness which knows no day save when the ploughshare opens its chinks—they have come to the light. To the light they have brought a colour which will attract the sunbeams from now till harvest. They fall more pleasantly on the corn, toned, as if they mingled with it. Seldom do we realize that the world is practically no thicker to us than the print of our footsteps on the path. Upon that surface we walk and act our comedy of life, and what is beneath is nothing to us. But it is out from that under-world, from the dead and the unknown, from the cold moist ground, that these green blades have sprung. Yonder a steam-plough pants up the hill, groaning with its own strength, yet all that strength and might of wheels, and piston, and chains, cannot drag from the earth one single blade like these. Force cannot make it; it must grow—an easy word to speak or write, in fact full of potency. It is this mystery of growth and life, of beauty, and sweetness, and colour, starting forth from the clods that gives the corn its power over me. Somehow I identify myself with it; I live again as I see it. Year by year it is the same, and when I see it I feel that I have once more entered on a new life. And I think the spring, with its green corn, its violets, and hawthorn-leaves, and increasing song, grows yearly dearer and more dear to this our ancient earth. So many centuries have flown! Now it is the manner with all natural things to gather as it were by smallest particles. The merest grain of sand drifts unseen into a crevice, and by-and-by another; after a while there is a heap; a century and it is a mound, and then every one observes and comments on it. Time itself has gone on like this; the years have accumulated, first in drifts, then in heaps, and now a vast mound, to which the mountains are knolls, rises up and overshadows us. Time lies heavy on the world. The old, old earth is glad to turn from the cark and care of drifted centuries to the first sweet blades of green.

There is sunshine today after rain, and every lark is singing. Across the vale a broad cloud-shadow descends the hillside, is lost in the hollow, and presently, without warning, slips over the edge, coming swiftly along the green tips. The sunshine follows—the warmer for its momentary absence. Far, far down in a grassy coomb stands a solitary cornrick, conical roofed, casting a lonely shadow—marked because so solitary, and beyond it on the rising slope is a brown copse. The leafless branches take a brown tint in the sunlight; on the summit above there is furze; then more hill lines drawn against the sky. In the tops of the dark pines at the corner of the copse, could the glance sustain itself to see them, there are finches warming themselves in the sunbeams. The thick needles shelter them from the current of air, and the sky is bluer above the pines. Their hearts are full already of the happy days to come, when the moss yonder by the beech, and the lichen on the fir-trunk, and the loose fibres caught in the fork of an unbending bough, shall furnish forth a sufficient mansion for their young. Another broad cloud-shadow, and another warm embrace of sunlight. All the serried ranks of the green corn bow at the word of command as the wind rushes over them.

There is largeness and freedom here. Broad as the down and free as the wind, the thought can roam high over the narrow roofs in the vale. Nature has affixed no bounds to thought. All the palings, and walls, and crooked fences deep down yonder are artificial. The fetters and traditions, the routine, the dull roundabout which deadens the spirit like the cold moist earth, are the merest nothings. Here it is easy with the physical eye to look over the highest roof. The moment the eye of the mind is filled with the beauty of things natural an equal freedom and width of view come to it. Step aside from the trodden footpath of personal experience, throwing away the petty cynicism born of petty hopes disappointed. Step out upon the broad down beside the green corn, and let its freshness become part of life.

The wind passes, and it bends—let the wind, too, pass over the spirit. From the cloud-shadow it emerges to the sunshine—let the heart come out from the shadow of roofs to the open glow of the sky. High above, the songs of the larks fall as rain—receive it with open hands. Pure is the colour of the green flags, the slender-pointed blades—let the thought be pure as the light that shines through that colour. Broad are the downs and open the aspect—gather the breadth and largness of view. Never can that view be wide enough and large enough, there will always be room to aim higher. As the air of the hills enriches the blood, so let the presence of these beautiful things enrich the inner sense. One memory of the green corn, fresh beneath the sun and wind, will lift up the heart from the clods.

Absence of Design in Nature— The Prodigality of Nature and Niggardliness of Man

In the parlour to which I have retired from the heat there is a chair and a table, and a picture on the wall: the chair was made for an object and a purpose, to sit in; the table for a purpose, to write on; the picture was painted for a purpose, to please the eye. But outside, in the meadow, in the hedge, on the hill, in the water; or, looking still farther, to the sun, the moon, and stars, I see no such chair, or table, or picture.

Pondering deeply and for long upon the plants, the living things (myself, too, as a physical being): upon the elements, on the holy miracle, water; the holy miracle, sunlight; the earth, and the air, I come at last—and not without, for a while, sorrow—to the inevitable conclusion that there is no object, no end, no purpose, no design, and no plan; no anything, that is.

By a strong and continued effort, I compelled myself to see the world mentally: with my mind, as it were, abstracted; hold yourself, as it were, apart from it, and there is no object, and no plan; no law, and no rule.

From childhood we build up for ourselves an encyclopaedia of the world, answering all questions: we turn to Day, and the reply is Light; to Night, and the reply is Darkness. It is difficult to burst through these

The Old House at Coate, ed. Samuel J. Looker (London: Lutterworth Press, 1948).

fetters and to get beyond Day and Night: but, in truth, there is no Day and Night; the sun always shines. It is our minds which supply the purpose, the end, the plan, the law, and the rule. For the practical matters of life, these are sufficient—they are like conventional agreements. But if you wish to really know the truth, there is none. When you first realize this, the whole arch of thought falls in; the structure the brain has reared, or, rather, which so many minds have reared for it, becomes a crumbling ruin, and there seems nothing left. I felt crushed when I first saw that there was no chair, no table, no picture, in nature: I use 'nature' in the widest sense; in the cosmos then. Nothing especially made for man to sit on, to write on, to admire—not even the colour of the buttercups or the beautiful sun-gleam which had me spellbound glowing on the water in my hand in the rocky cell.

The rudest quern ever yet discovered in which the earliest man ground his wheat did not fall from the sky; even that poor instrument, the mere hollowed stone, was not thrown to him prepared for use; he had to make it himself. There neither is, nor has been, nor will be any chair, or table, or picture, or quern in the cosmos. Nor is there any plan even in the buttercups themselves, looked at for themselves: they are not geometrical, or mathematical; nor precisely circular, nor anything regular. A general pattern, as a common colour, may be claimed for them, a pattern, however, liable to modification under cultivation; but, fully admitting this, it is no more than saying that water is water: that one crystal is always an octahedron, another a dodecahedron; that one element is oxygen and another hydrogen; that the earth is the earth; and the sun, the sun. It is only stating in the simplest way the fact that a thing *is:* and, after the most rigid research, that is, in the end, all that can be stated.

To say that there is a general buttercup pattern is only saying that it is not a bluebell or violet. Perhaps the general form of the buttercup is not absolutely necessary to its existence; many birds can fly equally well if their tails be removed, or even a great part of their wings. There are some birds that do not fly at all. Some further illustrations presently will arise; indeed, nothing could be examined without affording some. I had forgotten that the parlour, beside the chair and table, had a carpet. The carpet has a pattern: it is woven; the threads can be discerned, and a little investigation shows beyond doubt that it was designed and made by a man. It is certainly pretty and ingenious. But the grass of my golden meadow has no design, and no purpose: it is beautiful, and more; it is divine.

When at last I had disabused my mind of the enormous imposture of a design, an object, and an end, a purpose or a system, I began to see dimly how much more grandeur, beauty and hope there is in a divine chaos—not chaos in the sense of disorder or confusion but simply the absence of order—than there is in a universe made by pattern. This draught-board universe my mind had laid out: this machine-made world and piece of mechanism; what a petty, despicable, micro-cosmus I had substituted for the reality.

Logically, that which has a design or a purpose has a limit. The very idea of a design or a purpose has since grown repulsive to me, on account of its littleness. I do not venture, for a moment, even to attempt to supply a reason to take the place of the exploded plan. I simply deliberately deny, or, rather, I have now advanced to that stage that to my own mind even the admission of the subject to discussion is impossible. I look at the sunshine and feel that there is no contracted order: there is divine chaos, and, in it, limitless hope and possibilities.

Without number, the buttercups crowd the mead: not one here and there, or sufficient only to tint the sward. There is not just enough for some purpose: there they are without number, in all the extravagance of uselessness and beauty. The apple-bloom—it is falling fast now as the days advance—who can count the myriad blossoms of the orchard? There are leaves upon the hedges which bound that single meadow on three sides (the fourth being enclosed by a brook) enough to occupy the whole summer to count; and before it was half done they would be falling. But that half would be enough for shadow—for use.

Half the rain that falls would be enough. Half the acorns on the oaks in autumn, more than enough. Wheat itself is often thrown into the sty. Famines and droughts occur, but whenever any comes it is in abundance—sow a grain of wheat, and the stalk, one stalk alone, of those that rise from it will yield forty times.

There is no *enough* in nature. It is one vast prodigality. It is a feast. There is no economy: it is all one immense extravagance. It is all giving, giving, giving: no saving, no penury; a golden shower of good things is for ever descending. I love beyond all things to contemplate this indescribable lavishness—I would it could be introduced into our human life. I know, none better, having gone through the personal experience myself, that it is at the present moment impossible to practise it: that each individual is compelled, in order to exist, to labour, to save, and to economize. I know, of course, as all do who have ever read a book, that attempts to distribute possessions, to live in community of goods, have each failed miserably. If I rightly judge, the human race would require a century of training before even an approximation to such a thing were possible. All this, and much more to the same effect, I fully admit. But

still the feeling remains and will not be denied. I dislike the word economy: I detest the word thrift; I hate the thought of saving. Maybe some
scheme in the future may be devised whereby such efforts may be turned
to a general end. This alone I am certain of: there is no economy, thrift,
or saving, in nature; it is one splendid waste. It is that waste which makes
it so beautiful, and so irresistible! Now nature was not made by man, and
is a better exemplar than he can furnish: each thread in this carpet goes
to form the pattern; but go out into my golden mead and gather ten
thousand blades of grass, and it will not destroy it.

Perhaps there never were so many houses upon the face of the earth as
at the present day: so luxuriously appointed, so comfortable, so hand-
somely furnished. Yet, with all this wealth and magnificence, these ap-
pointments and engineering: with all these many courses at dinner and
array of wines, it has ever seemed to me a mean and penurious age. It is
formal and in order; there is no heart in it. Food should be broadcast,
open, free: wine should be in flagons, not in tiny glasses; in a word, there
should be genial waste. Let the crumbs fall: there are birds enough to
pick them up.

The greatest proof of the extreme meanness of the age is the long list
of names appended to a subscription for a famine or a fashionable charity. Worthy as are these objects, the donors write down their own unutterable meanness. There are men in their warehouses, their offices, on
their lands, who have served them honourably for years and have received for their wage just exactly as much as experience has proved can
be made to support life. No cheque with a great flourishing signature has
ever been presented to them.

I say that the entire labouring population—some skilled trades excepted as not really labouring—is miserably underpaid, not because
there is a pressure or scarcity, a trouble, a famine, but from pure selfishness. This selfishness, moreover, is not intentional, but quite unconscious; and individuals are not individually guilty, because they are
within their rights. A man has a hundred thousand pounds: he eats and
drinks and pleases his little whims—likely enough quite innocent little
whims—but he never gives to a friend, or a relation; never assists, does
nothing with it. This is commercially right, but it is not the buttercups in
the golden mead; it is not the grain of wheat that yielded forty times. It
is not according to the exemplar of nature. Therefore I say that although
I admit all attempts to adjust possessions have been and for the age at
least must prove failures, yet my feeling remains the same. Thrift, economy, accumulation of wealth, are inventions; they are not nature. As
there are more than enough buttercups in this single meadow for the

pleasure of all the children in the hamlet, so too it is a fact, a very stubborn fact, that there is more than enough food in the world for all its human children. In the year 1880, it was found, on careful calculation made for strictly commercial purposes, that there was a surplus grain production of[1] bushels. That is to say, if every buttercup in this meadow represented a bushel of wheat, there would be all that over and above what was necessary. This is a very extraordinary fact. That the wheat has to be produced, to be distributed; that there are a thousand social complications to be considered, is, of course, incontrovertible. Still, there was the surplus; bushels of golden grain as numerous as the golden buttercups.

But that does not represent the capacity of the earth for production: it is not possible to gauge that capacity—so practically inexhaustible is it.

Thrift and economy and accumulation, therefore, represent a state of things contrary to the exemplar of nature, and in individual life they destroy its beauty. There is no pleasure without waste: the banquet is a formality; the wine tasteless, unless the viands and the liquor are in prodigal quantities. Give me the lavish extravagance of the golden mead!

[1]There is a blank in the manuscript here.

MARY AUSTIN
1868-1934

Although an extremely prolific author, and a celebrated figure in her own day, Mary Austin's work lapsed into obscurity for almost half a century after her death. Perhaps part of the problem was that she cultivated so many fields that critics didn't know what to do with her. Austin was a novelist, a poet, and an essayist; a student of Indian culture, an advocate of native peoples, and a feminist; a pioneer author in the areas of science fiction and the nature writing of the Southwest. Over the past decade, however, increasing numbers of her works have been re-issued, as readers discover in the range of her interests an integrity responsive to the challenges of our own day. One of her finest works, The Land of Little Rain

(1903), evokes the high desert country of Southern California, and has re-established itself as a classic of Western American nature writing.

From THE LAND OF LITTLE RAIN

THE LAND OF LITTLE RAIN

East away from the Sierras, south from Panamint and Amargosa, east and south many an uncounted mile, is the Country of Lost Borders.

Ute, Paiute, Mojave, and Shoshone inhabit its frontiers, and as far into the heart of it as a man dare go. Not the law, but the land sets the limit. Desert is the name it wears upon the maps, but the Indian's is the better word. Desert is a loose term to indicate land that supports no man; whether the land can be bitted and broken to that purpose is not proven. Void of life it never is, however dry the air and villainous the soil.

This is the nature of that country. There are hills, rounded, blunt, burned, squeezed up out of chaos, chrome and vermilion painted, aspiring to the snow-line. Between the hills lie high level-looking plains full of intolerable sun glare, or narrow valleys drowned in a blue haze. The hill surface is streaked with ash drift and black, unweathered lava flows. After rains water accumulates in the hollows of small closed valleys, and, evaporating, leaves hard dry levels of pure desertness that get the local name of dry lakes. Where the mountains are steep and the rains heavy, the pool is never quite dry, but dark and bitter, rimmed about with the efflorescence of alkaline deposits. A thin crust of it lies along the marsh over the vegetating area, which has neither beauty nor freshness. In the broad wastes open to the wind the sand drifts in hummocks about the stubby shrubs, and between them the soil shows saline traces. The sculpture of the hills here is more wind than water work, though the quick storms do sometimes scar them past many a year's redeeming. In all the Western desert edges there are essays in miniature at the famed, terrible Grand Cañon, to which, if you keep on long enough in this country, you will come at last.

Since this is a hill country one expects to find springs, but not to depend upon them; for when found they are often brackish and unwholesome, or maddening, slow dribbles in a thirsty soil. Here you find the hot sink of Death Valley, or high rolling districts where the air has always a tang of frost. Here are the long heavy winds and breathless

The Land of Little Rain (Boston: Houghton Mifflin, 1903).

calms on the tilted mesas where dust devils dance, whirling up into a wide, pale sky. Here you have no rain when all the earth cries for it, or quick downpours called cloud-bursts for violence. A land of lost rivers, with little in it to love; yet a land that once visited must be come back to inevitably. If it were not so there would be little told of it.

This is the country of three seasons. From June on to November it lies hot, still, and unbearable, sick with violent unrelieving storms; then on until April, chill, quiescent, drinking its scant rain and scanter snows; from April to the hot season again, blossoming, radiant, and seductive. These months are only approximate; later or earlier the rain-laden wind may drift up the water gate of the Colorado from the Gulf, and the land sets its seasons by the rain.

The desert floras shame us with their cheerful adaptations to the seasonal limitations. Their whole duty is to flower and fruit, and they do it hardly, or with tropical luxuriance, as the rain admits. It is recorded in the report of the Death Valley expedition that after a year of abundant rains, on the Colorado desert was found a specimen of Amaranthus ten feet high. A year later the same species in the same place matured in the drought at four inches. One hopes the land may breed like qualities in her human offspring, not tritely to "try," but to do. Seldom does the desert herb attain the full stature of the type. Extreme aridity and extreme altitude have the same dwarfing effect, so that we find in the high Sierras and in Death Valley related species in miniature that reach a comely growth in mean temperatures. Very fertile are the desert plants in expedients to prevent evaporation, turning their foliage edgewise toward the sun, growing silky hairs, exuding viscid gum. The wind, which has a long sweep, harries and helps them. It rolls up dunes about the stocky stems, encompassing and protective, and above the dunes, which may be, as with the mesquite, three times as high as a man, the blossoming twigs flourish and bear fruit.

There are many areas in the desert where drinkable water lies within a few feet of the surface, indicated by the mesquite and the bunch grass *(Sporobolus airoides)*. It is this nearness of unimagined help that makes the tragedy of desert deaths. It is related that the final breakdown of that hapless party that gave Death Valley its forbidding name occurred in a locality where shallow wells would have saved them. But how were they to know that? Properly equipped it is possible to go safely across that ghastly sink, yet every year it takes its toll of death, and yet men find there sun-dried mummies, of whom no trace or recollection is preserved. To underestimate one's thirst, to pass a given landmark to the right or left, to find a dry spring where one looked for running water—there is no help for any of these things.

Along springs and sunken watercourses one is surprised to find such water-loving plants as grow widely in moist ground, but the true desert breeds its own kind, each in its particular habitat. The angle of the slope, the frontage of a hill, the structure of the soil determines the plant. South-looking hills are nearly bare, and the lower tree-line higher here by a thousand feet. Cañons running east and west will have one wall naked and one clothed. Around dry lakes and marshes the herbage preserves a set and orderly arrangement. Most species have well-defined areas of growth, the best index the voiceless land can give the traveler of his whereabouts.

If you have any doubt about it, know that the desert begins with the creosote. This immortal shrub spreads down into Death Valley and up to the lower timberline, odorous and medicinal as you might guess from the name, wandlike, with shining fretted foliage. Its vivid green is grateful to the eye in a wilderness of gray and greenish white shrubs. In the spring it exudes a resinous gum which the Indians of those parts know how to use with pulverized rock for cementing arrow points to shafts. Trust Indians not to miss any virtues of the plant world!

Nothing the desert produces expresses it better than the unhappy growth of the tree yuccas. Tormented, thin forests of it stalk drearily in the high mesas, particularly in that triangular slip that fans out eastward from the meeting of the Sierras and coastwise hills where the first swings across the southern end of the San Joaquin Valley. The yucca bristles with bayonet-pointed leaves, dull green, growing shaggy with age, tipped with panicles of fetid, greenish bloom. After death, which is slow, the ghostly hollow network of its woody skeleton, with hardly power to rot, makes the moonlight fearful. Before the yucca has come to flower, while yet its bloom is a creamy cone-shaped bud of the size of a small cabbage, full of sugary sap, the Indians twist it deftly out of its fence of daggers and roast it for their own delectation. So it is that in those parts where man inhabits one sees young plants of *Yucca arborensis* infrequently. Other yuccas, cacti, low herbs, a thousand sorts, one finds journeying east from the coastwise hills. There is neither poverty of soil nor species to account for the sparseness of desert growth, but simply that each plant requires more room. So much earth must be preëmpted to extract so much moisture. The real struggle for existence, the real brain of the plant, is underground; above there is room for a rounded perfect growth. In Death Valley, reputed the very core of desolation, are nearly two hundred identified species.

Above the lower tree-line, which is also the snow-line, mapped out abruptly by the sun, one finds spreading growth of piñon, juniper, branched nearly to the ground, lilac and sage, and scattering white pines.

There is no special preponderance of self-fertilized or wind-fertilized plants, but everywhere the demand for and evidence of insect life. Now where there are seeds and insects there will be birds and small mammals and where these are, will come the slinking, sharp-toothed kind that prey on them. Go as far as you dare in the heart of a lonely land, you cannot go so far that life and death are not before you. Painted lizards slip in and out of rock crevices, and pant on the white hot sands. Birds, humming-birds even, nest in the cactus scrub; woodpeckers befriend the demoniac yuccas; out of the stark, treeless waste rings the music of the night-singing mockingbird. If it be summer and the sun well down, there will be a burrowing owl to call. Strange, furry, tricksy things dart across the open places, or sit motionless in the conning towers of the creosote. The poet may have "named all the birds without a gun," but not the fairy-footed, ground-inhabiting, furtive, small folk of the rainless regions. They are too many and too swift; how many you would not believe without seeing the footprint tracings in the sand. They are nearly all night workers, finding the days too hot and white. In mid-desert where there are no cattle, there are no birds of carrion, but if you go far in that direction the chances are that you will find yourself shadowed by their tilted wings. Nothing so large as a man can move unspied upon in that country, and they know well how the land deals with strangers. There are hints to be had here of the way in which a land forces new habits on its dwellers. The quick increase of suns at the end of spring sometimes overtakes birds in their nesting and effects a reversal of the ordinary manner of incubation. It becomes necessary to keep eggs cool rather than warm. One hot, stifling spring in the Little Antelope I had occasion to pass and repass frequently the nest of a pair of meadowlarks, located unhappily in the shelter of a very slender weed. I never caught them sitting except near night, but at midday they stood, or drooped above it, half fainting with pitifully parted bills, between their treasure and the sun. Sometimes both of them together with wings spread and half lifted continued a spot of shade in a temperature that constrained me at last in a fellow feeling to spare them a bit of canvas for permanent shelter. There was a fence in that country shutting in a cattle range, and along its fifteen miles of posts one could be sure of finding a bird or two in every strip of shadow; sometimes the sparrow and the hawk, with wings trailed and beaks parted, drooping in the white truce of noon.

If one is inclined to wonder at first how so many dwellers came to be in the loneliest land that ever came out of God's hands, what they do there and why stay, one does not wonder so much after having lived there. None other than this long brown land lays such a hold on the affections. The rainbow hills, the tender bluish mists, the luminous radiance of the spring, have the lotus charm. They trick the sense of time, so that once inhabiting there you always mean to go away without quite realizing that you have not done it. Men who have lived there, miners and cattle-men, will tell you this, not so fluently, but emphatically, cursing the land and going back to it. For one thing there is the divinest, cleanest air to be breathed anywhere in God's world. Some day the world will understand that, and the little oases on the windy tops of hills will harbor for healing its ailing, house-weary broods. There is promise there of great wealth in ores and earths, which is no wealth by reason of being so far removed from water and workable conditions, but men are bewitched by it and tempted to try the impossible.

You should hear Salty Williams tell how he used to drive eighteen and twenty-mule teams from the borax marsh to Mojave, ninety miles, with the trail wagon full of water barrels. Hot days the mules would go so mad for drink that the clank of the water bucket set them into an uproar of hideous, maimed noises, and a tangle of harness chains, while Salty would sit on the high seat with the sun glare heavy in his eyes, dealing out curses of pacification in a level, uninterested voice until the clamor fell off from sheer exhaustion. There was a line of shallow graves along that road; they used to count on dropping a man or two of every new gang of coolies brought out in the hot season. But when he lost his swamper, smitten without warning at the noon halt, Salty quit his job; he said it was "too durn hot." The swamper he buried by the way with stones upon him to keep the coyotes from digging him up, and seven years later I read the penciled lines on the pine headboard, still bright and unweathered.

But before that, driving up on the Mojave stage, I met Salty again crossing Indian Wells, his face from the high seat, tanned and ruddy as a harvest moon, looming through the golden dust above his eighteen mules. The land had called him.

The palpable sense of mystery in the desert air breeds fables, chiefly of lost treasure. Somewhere within its stark borders, if one believes report, is a hill strewn with nuggets; one seamed with virgin silver; an old clayey water-bed where Indians scooped up earth to make cooking pots and shaped them reeking with grains of pure gold. Old miners drifting about the desert edges, weathered into the semblance of the tawny hills, will tell you tales like these convincingly. After a little sojourn in that land you will believe them on their own account. It is a question whether it is not better to be bitten by the little horned snake of the desert that goes sidewise and strikes without coiling, than by the tradition of a lost mine.

And yet—and yet—is it not perhaps to satisfy expectation that one falls into the tragic key in writing of desertness? The more you wish of it the more you get, and in the mean time lose much of pleasantness. In that country which begins at the foot of the east slope of the Sierras and spreads out by less and less lofty hill ranges toward the Great Basin, it is possible to live with great zest, to have red blood and delicate joys, to pass and repass about one's daily performance an area that would make an Atlantic seaboard State, and that with no peril, and, according to our way of thought, no particular difficulty. At any rate, it was not people who went into the desert merely to write it up who invented the fabled Hassaympa, of whose waters, if any drink, they can no more see fact as naked fact, but all radiant with the color of romance. I, who must have drunk of it in my twice seven years' wanderings, am assured that it is worth while.

For all the toll the desert takes of a man it gives compensations, deep breaths, deep sleep, and the communion of the stars. It comes upon one with new force in the pauses of the night that the Chaldeans were a desert-bred people. It is hard to escape the sense of mastery as the stars move in the wide clear heavens to risings and settings unobscured. They look large and near and palpitant; as if they moved on some stately service not needful to declare. Wheeling to their stations in the sky, they make the poor world-fret of no account. Of no account you who lie out there watching, nor the lean coyote that stands off in the scrub from you and howls and howls.

EDWARD THOMAS
1878-1917

Born of Welsh parents in London, Edward Thomas had written numerous volumes of essays, criticism, and natural history before his pivotal meeting in 1914 with Robert Frost, who befriended Thomas and encouraged him to begin writing poetry. Three years later he died at the Battle of Arras as the first edition of his Poems *was going to press.*

Thomas's rich descriptions of the Sussex and Hampshire countryside are in the mainstream of English nature writing as represented by Gilbert White, Richard Jefferies, and W.H. Hudson. Yet beneath Thomas's sonorous prose and often archaic diction there is a distinc-

tively modern sense of the individual's isolation, the invasion of the rural landscape by the industrial revolution, the transience of the human species on earth, and the ambivalent nature of our "incompatible desires." There is also a pervasive melancholic tone that makes much of his writing seem in large degree a preparation for death, yet carried out by one that relishes life to the full even as he prepares to leave it.

From The South Country

HAMPSHIRE

The beeches on the beech-covered hills roar and strain as if they would fly off with the hill, and anon they are as meek as a great horse leaning his head over a gate. If there is a misty day there is one willow in a coombe lifting up a thousand silver catkins like a thousand lamps, when there is no light elsewhere. Another day, a wide and windy day, is the jackdaw's, and he goes straight and swift and high like a joyous rider crying aloud on an endless savannah, and, underneath, the rippled pond is as bright as a peacock, and millions of beech leaves drive across the open glades of the woods, rushing to their Acheron. The bush harrow stripes the moist and shining grass; the plough changes the pale stubble into a ridgy chocolate; they are peeling the young ash sticks for hop poles and dipping them in tar. At the dying of that windy day the wind is still; there is a bright pale half-moon tangled in the pink whirl of after-sunset cloud, a sound of blackbirds from pollard oaks against the silver sky, a sound of bells from hamlets hidden among beeches.

Towards the end of March there are six nights of frost giving birth to still mornings of weak sunlight, of an opaque yet not definitely misty air. The sky is of a milky, uncertain pale blue without one cloud. Eastward the hooded sun is warming the slope fields and melting the sparkling frost. In many trees the woodpeckers laugh so often that their cry is a song. A grassy ancient orchard has taken possession of the visible sunbeams, and the green and gold of the mistletoe glows on the silvered and mossy branches of apple trees. The pale stubble is yellow and tenderly lit, and gives the low hills a hollow light appearance as if they might presently dissolve. In a hundred tiers on the steep hill, the uncounted perpendicular straight stems of beech, and yet not all quite perpendicular or quite straight, are silver-grey in the midst of a haze, here brown, there

The South Country (London: J. M. Dent, 1909).

rosy, of branches and swelling buds. Though but a quarter of a mile away in this faintly clouded air they are very small, aerial in substance, infinitely remote from the road on which I stand, and more like reflections in calm water than real things.

At the lower margin of the wood the overhanging branches form blue caves, and out of these emerge the songs of many hidden birds. I know that there are bland melodious blackbirds of easy musing voices, robins whose earnest song, though full of passion, is but a fragment that has burst through a more passionate silence, hedge-sparrows of liquid confiding monotone, brisk acid wrens, chaffinches and yellowhammers saying always the same thing (a dear but courtly praise of the coming season), larks building spires above spires into the sky, thrushes of infinite variety that talk and talk of a thousand things, never thinking, always talking of the moment, exclaiming, scolding, cheering, flattering, coaxing, challenging, with merry-hearted, bold voices that must have been the same in the morning of the world when the forest trees lay, or leaned, or hung, where they fell. Yet I can distinguish neither blackbird, nor robin, nor hedge-sparrow, nor any one voice. All are blent into one seething stream of song. It is one song, not many. It is one spirit that sings. Mixed with them is the myriad stir of unborn things, of leaf and blade and flower, many silences at heart and root of tree, voices of hope and growth, of love that will be satisfied though it leap upon the swords of life. Yet not during all the day does the earth truly awaken. Even in town and city the dream prevails, and only dimly lighted their chalky towers and spires rise out of the sweet mist and sing together beside the waters.

The earth lies blinking, turning over languidly and talking like a half-wakened child that now and then lies still and sleeps though with eyes wide open. The air is still full of the dreams of a night which this mild sun cannot dispel. The dreams are prophetic as well as reminiscent, and are visiting the woods, and that is why they will not cast aside the veil. Who would rise if he could continue to dream? It is not spring yet. Spring is being dreamed, and the dream is more wonderful and more blessed than ever was spring. What the hour of waking will bring forth is not known. Catch at the dreams as they hover in the warm thick air. Up against the grey tiers of beech stems and the mist of the buds and fallen leaves rise two columns of blue smoke from two white cottages among trees; they rise perfectly straight and then expand into a balanced cloud, and thus make and unmake continually two trees of smoke. No sound comes from the cottages. The dreams are over them, over the brows of the children and the babes, of the men and the women, bringing great gifts, suggestions, shadowy satisfactions, consolations, hopes. With inward voices of persuasion those dreams hover and say that all is to be made new, that all is yet before us, and the lots are not yet drawn out of the urn.

We shall presently set out and sail into the undiscovered seas and find new islands of the free, the beautiful, the young. As is the dimly glimmering changeless brook twittering over the pebbles, so is life. It is but just leaving the fount. All things are possible in the windings between fount and sea.

Never again shall we demand the cuckoo's song from the August silence. Never will July nip the spring and lengthen the lambs' faces and take away their piquancy, or June shut a gate between us and the nightingale, or May deny the promise of April. Hark! before the end of afternoon the owls hoot in their sleep in the ivied beeches. A dream has flitted past them, more silent of wing than themselves. Now it is between the wings of the first white butterfly, and it plants a smile in the face of the infant that cannot speak: and again it is with the brimstone butterfly, and the child who is gathering celandine and cuckoo flower and violet starts back almost in fear at the dream.

The grandmother sitting in her daughter's house, left all alone in silence, her hands clasped upon her knees, forgets the courage without hope that has carried her through eighty years, opens her eyes, unclasps her hands from the knot as of stiff rope, distends them and feels the air, and the dream is between her fingers and she too smiles, she knows not why. A girl of sixteen, ill-dressed, not pretty, has seen it also. She has tied up her black hair in a new crimson ribbon. She laughs aloud with a companion at something they know in common and in secret, and as she does so lifts her neck and is glad from the sole of her foot to the crown of her head. She is lost in her laughter and oblivious of its cause. She walks away, and her step is as firm as that of a ewe defending her lamb. She was a poor and misused child, and I can see her as a woman of fifty, sitting on a London bench grey-complexioned, in old black hat, black clothes, crouching over a paper bag of fragments, in the beautiful August rain after heat. But this is her hour. That future is not among the dreams in the air to-day. She is at one with the world, and a deep music grows between her and the stars. Her smile is one of those magical things, great and small and all divine, that have the power to wield universal harmonies. At sight or sound of them the infinite variety of appearances in the world is made fairer than before, because it is shown to be a many-coloured raiment of the one. The raiment trembles, and under leaf and cloud and air a window is thrown open upon the unfathomable deep, and at the window we are sitting, watching the flight of our souls away, away to where they must be gathered into the music that is being built.

Often upon the vast and silent twilight, as now, is the soul poured out as a rivulet into the sea and lost, not able even to stain the boundless crystal of the air; and the body stands empty, waiting for its return, and, poor thing, knows not what it receives back into itself when the night is dark and it moves away. For we stand ever at the edge of Eternity and fall in many times before we die. Yet even such thoughts live not long this day. All shall be healed, says the dream. All shall be made new. The day is a fairy birth, a foundling not fathered nor mothered by any grey yesterdays. It has inherited nothing. It makes of winter and of the old springs that wrought nothing fair a stale creed, a senseless tale: they are naught: I do not wonder any longer if the lark's song has grown old with the ears that hear it or if it still be unchanged.

What dreams are there for that aged child who goes tottering and reeling up the lane at mid-day? He carries a basket of watercress on his back. He has sold two-pennyworth, and he is tipsy, grinning through the bruises of a tipsy fall, and shifting his cold pipe from one side of his mouth to the other. Though hardly sixty he is very old, worn and thin and wrinkled, and bent sideways and forward at the waist and the shoulders. Yet he is very young. He is just what he was forty years ago when the thatcher found him lying on his back in the sun instead of combing out the straw and sprinkling it with water for his use. He laid no plans as a youth; he had only a few transparent tricks and easy lies. Never has he thought of the day after to-morrow. For a few years in his prime he worked almost regularly for one or two masters, leaving them only now and then upon long errands of his own and known only to himself. It was then perhaps that he earned or received as a gift, along with a broken nose, his one name, which is Jackalone. For years he was the irresponsible jester to a smug townlet which was privately amused and publicly scandalized, and rewarded him in a gaol, where, unlike Tasso, he never complained. Since then he has lived by the sale of a chance rabbit or two, of watercress, of greens gathered when the frost is on them and nobody looking, by gifts of broken victuals, by driving a few bullocks to a fair, by casual shelter in barns, in roofless cottages, or under hedges.

He has never had father or mother or brother or sister or wife or child. No dead leaf in autumn wind or branch in flooded brook seems more helpless. He can deceive nobody. He is in prison two or three times a year for little things: it seems a charity to put a roof over his head and clip his hair. He has no wisdom; by nothing has he soiled what gifts were given to him at his birth. The dreams will not pass him by. They come to give him that confidence by which he lives in spite of men's and children's contumely.

How little do we know of the business of the earth, not to speak of the universe; of time, not to speak of eternity. It was not by taking thought that man survived the mastodon. The acts and thoughts that will serve the race, that will profit this commonwealth of things that live in the sun, the air, the earth, the sea, now and through all time, are not known and never will be known. The rumour of much toil and scheming and triumph may never reach the stars, and what we value not at all, are not conscious of, may break the surface of eternity with endless ripples of good. We know not by what we survive. There is much philosophy in that Irish tale of the poor blind woman who recovered her sight at St. Brigit's well. "Did I say more prayers than the rest? Not a prayer. I was young in those days. I suppose she took a liking to me, maybe because of my name being Brigit the same as her own."[1] Others went unrelieved away that day. We are as ignorant still. Hence the batlike fears about immortality. We wish to prolong what we can see and touch and talk of, and knowing that clothes and flesh and other perishing things may not pass over the borders of death with us, we give up all, as if forsooth the undertaker and the gravedigger had arch-angelic functions. Along with the undertaker and the gravedigger ranks the historian and others who seem to bestow immortality. Each is like a child planting flowers severed from their stalks and roots, expecting them to grow. I never heard that the butterfly loved the chrysalis; but I am sure that the caterpillar looks forward to an endless day of eating green leaves and of continually swelling until it would despise a consummation of the size of a railway train. We can do the work of the universe though we shed friends and country and house and clothes and flesh, and become invisible to mortal eyes and microscopes. We do it now invisibly, and it is not these things which are us at all. That maid walking so proudly is about the business of eternity.

And yet it would be vain to pretend not to care about the visible many-coloured raiment of which our houses, our ships, our gardens, our books are part, since they also have their immortal selves and their ever-lasting place, else should we not love them with more than sight and hearing and touch. For flesh loves flesh and soul loves soul. Yet on this March day the supreme felicity is born of the two loves, so closely inter-woven that it is permitted to forget the boundaries of the two, and for soul to love flesh and flesh to love soul. And this ancient child is rid of his dishonours and flits through the land floating on a thin reed of the immortal laughter. This is "not altogether fool." He is perchance play-ing some large necessary part in the pattern woven by earth that draws the gods to lean forward out of the heavens to watch the play and say of him, as of other men, of birds, of flowers: "They also are of our com-pany." . . .

In the warm rain of the next day the chiffchaff sings among the rosy

[1] *A Book of Saints and Wonders,* by Lady Gregory.

blossoms of the leafless larches, a small voice that yet reaches from the valley to the high hill. It is a double, many times repeated note that foretells the cuckoo's. In the evening the songs are bold and full, but the stems of the beeches are faint as soft columns of smoke and the columns of smoke from the cottages are like them in the still air.

Yet another frost follows, and in the dim golden light just after sunrise the shadows of all the beeches lie on the slopes, dark and more tangible than the trees, as if they were the real and those standing upright were the returned spirits above the dead.

Now rain falls and relents and falls again all day, and the earth is hidden under it, and as from a land submerged the songs mount through the veil. The mists waver out of the beeches like puffs of smoke or hang upon them or in them like fleeces caught in thorns: in the just penetrating sunlight the long boles of the beeches shine, and the chaffinch, the yellowhammer and the cirl bunting sing songs of blissful drowsiness. The Downs, not yet green, rise far off and look, through the rain, like old thatched houses. *   *   *

SURREY

Then I saw a huge silence of meadows, of woods, and beyond these, of hills that raised two breasts of empurpled turf into the sky; and, above the hills, one mountain of cloud that beamed as it reposed in the blue as in a sea. The white cloud buried London with a *requiescat in pace.*

I like to think how easily Nature will absorb London as she absorbed the mastodon, setting her spiders to spin the winding-sheet and her worms to fill in the graves, and her grass to cover it pitifully up, adding flowers—as an unknown hand added them to the grave of Nero. I like to see the preliminaries of this toil where Nature tries her hand at mossing the factory roof, rusting the deserted railway metals, sowing grass over the deserted platforms and flowers of rose-bay on ruinous hearths and walls. It is a real satisfaction to see the long narrowing wedge of irises that runs alongside and between the rails of the South-Eastern and Chatham Railway almost into the heart of London. And there are many kinds of weather when the air is full of voices prophesying desolation. The outer suburbs have almost a moorland fascination when fog lies thick and orange-coloured over their huge flat wastes of grass, expectant of the builder, but does not quite conceal the stark outlines of a traction engine, some procumbent timber, a bonfire and frantic figures darting about it, and aerial scaffolding far away. Other fields, yet unravished but menaced, the fog restores to a primeval state. And what a wild noise the wind makes in the telegraph wires as in wintry heather and gorse! When the waste open spaces give way to dense streets there is a common here and a lawn there, where the poplar leaves, if it be November, lie taintless on the grass, and the starlings talk sweet and shrill and cold in the branches, and nobody cares to deviate from the asphalt path to the dewy grass: the houses beyond the green mass themselves gigantic, remote, dim, and the pulse of London beats low and inaudible, as if she feared the irresistible enemy that is drawing its lines invisibly and silently about her on every side. If a breeze arises it makes that sound of the dry curled leaves chafing along the pavement; at night they seem spies in the unguarded by-ways. But there are also days—and spring and summer days, too—when a quiet horror thicks and stills the air outside London.

The ridges of trees high in the mist are very grim. The isolated trees stand cloaked in conspiracies here and there about the fields. The houses, even whole villages, are translated into terms of unreality as if they were carved in air and could not be touched; they are empty and mournful as skulls or churches. There is no life visible; for the ploughmen and the cattle are figures of light dream. All is soft and grey. The land has drunken the opiate mist and is passing slowly and unreluctantly into perpetual sleep. Trees and houses are drowsed beyond awakening or farewell. The mind also is infected, and gains a sort of ease from the thought that an eternal and universal rest is at hand without any cry or any pain. * * *

SUMMER—SUSSEX

Far up on the Downs the air of day and night is flavoured by honeysuckle and new hay. It is good to walk, it is good to lie still; the rain is good and so is the sun; and whether the windy or the quiet air be the better let us leave to a December judgment to decide. One day the rain falls and there is no wind, and all the movement is in the chaos of the dark sky; and thus is made the celestial fairness of an earth that is brighter than the heavens; for the green and lilac of the grasses and the yellow of the goat's-beard flowers glow, and the ripening corn is airy light. But next day the sun is early hot. The wet hay streams and is sweet. The beams pour into a southward coombe of the hills and the dense yew is warm as a fruit-wall, so that the utmost of fragrance is extracted from the marjoram and thyme and fanned by the coming and going of butterflies; and in contrast with this gold and purple heat on flower and wing, through the blue sky and along the hill-top moist clouds are trooping, of the grey colour of melting snow. The great shadows of the clouds brood long over the hay, and in the darker hallows the wind rustles the dripping thickets until mid-day. On another morning after night rain the blue sky is rippled and crimped with high thin white clouds by several opposing breezes. Vast forces seem but now to have ceased their feud. The battle is over, and there are all the signs of it plain to be seen; but they have laid down their arms, and peace is broad and white in the sky, but of many colours on the earth—for there is blue of harebell and purple of rose-bay among the bracken and popping gorse, and heather and foxglove are purple above the sand, and the mint is hoary lilac, the meadow-sweet is foam, there is rose of willow-herb and yellow of flea-bane at the edge of the water, and purple of gentian and cistus yellow on the Downs, and infinite greens in those little dense Edens which nettle and cow-parsnip and bramble and elder make every summer on the banks of the deep lanes. A thousand swifts wheel as if in a fierce wind over the highest places of the hills, over the great seaward-looking camp and its three graves and antique thorns, down to the chestnuts that stand about the rick-yards in the cornland below.

These are the hours that seem to entice and entrap the airy inhabitants of some land beyond the cloud mountains that rise farther than the farthest of downs. Legend has it that long ago strange children were caught upon the earth, and being asked how they had come there, they said that one day as they were herding their sheep in a far country they chanced on a cave; and within they heard music as of heavenly bells, which lured them on and on through the corridors of that cave until they reached our earth; and here their eyes, used only to a twilight between a sun that had set for ever and a night that had never fallen, were dazed by the August glow, and lying bemused they were caught before they could find the earthly entrance to their cave. Small wonder would this adventure be from a region no matter how blessed, when the earth is wearing the best white wild roses or when August is at its height.

The last hay-wagon has hardly rolled between the elms before the reaper and the reaping-machines begin to work. The oats and wheat are in tents over all the land. Then, then it is hard not to walk over the brown in the green of August grass. There is a roving spirit everywhere. The very tents of the corn suggest a bivouac. The white clouds coming up out of the yellow corn and journeying over the blue have set their faces to some goal. The traveller's-joy is tangled over the hazels and over the faces of the small chalk-pits. The white beam and the poplar and the sycamore fluttering show the silver sides of their leaves and rustle farewells. The perfect road that goes without hedges under elms and through the corn says, "Leave all and follow." How the bridges overleap the streams at one leap, or at three, in arches like those of running hounds! The far-scattered, placid sunsets pave the feet of the spirit with many a road to joy; the huge, vacant halls of dawn give a sense of godlike power.

But it is hard to make anything like a truce between these two incompatible desires, the one for going on and on over the earth, the other that would settle for ever, in one place as in a grave and have nothing to do with change. Suppose a man to receive notice of death, it would be hard to decide whether to walk or sail until the end, seeing no man, or none but strangers; or to sit—alone—and by thinking or not thinking to make the change to come as little as is permitted. The two desires will often painfully alternate. Even on these harvest days there is a temptation to take root for ever in some corner of a field or on some hill from which the world and the clouds can be seen at a distance. For the wheat is as red as the most red sand, and up above it tower the elms, dark prophets persuading to silence and a stillness like their own. Away on the lesser Downs the fields of pale oats are liquid within their border of dark woods; they also propose deep draughts of oblivion and rest. Then, again, there is the field—the many fields—where a regiment of shocks of oats are ranked under the white moon between rows of elms on the level Sussex land not far from the sea. The contrast of the airy matter underfoot and the thin moon over head, with the massy dark trees, as it were suspended between; the numbers and the order of the sheaves; their inviolability, though protected but by the gateway through which they are seen—all satisfy the soul as they can never satisfy the frame. Then there are the mists before heat which make us think of autumn or not, according to our tempers. All night the aspens have been shivering and the owls exulting under a clear full moon and above the silver of a great dew. You climb the steep chalk slope, through the privet and dog-wood coppice; among the scattered junipers—in this thick haze as in darkness they group themselves so as to make fantastic likenesses of mounted men, animals, monsters; over the dead earth in the shade of the broad yews, and thence suddenly under lightsome sprays of guelder-rose and their cherry-coloured berries; over the tufted turf; and then through the massed beeches, cold and dark as a church and silent; and so out to the level waste cornland at the top, to the flints and the clay. There a myriad oriflammes of ragwort are borne up on tall stems of equal height, straight and motionless, and near at hand quite clear, but farther away forming a green mist until, farther yet, all but the flowery surface is invisible, and that is but a glow. The stillness of the green and golden multitudes under the grey mist, perfectly still though a wind flutters the high tops of the beech, has an immortal beauty, and that they should ever change does not enter the mind which is thus for the moment lured happily into a strange confidence and ease. But the sun gains power in the south-east. It changes the mist into a fleeting garment, not of cold or of warm grey, but of diaphanous gold. There is a sea-like moan of wind in the half-visible trees, a wavering of the mist to and fro until it is dispersed far and wide as part of the very light, of the blue shade, of the colour of cloud and wood and down. As the mist is unwoven the ghostly moon is disclosed, and a bank of dead white clouds where the Downs should be. Under the very eye of the veiled sun a golden light and warmth begins to nestle among the mounds of foliage at the surface of the low woods. The beeches close by have got a new voice in their crisp, cool leaves, of which every one is doing something—cool, though the air itself is warm. Wood-pigeons coo. The white cloud-bank gives way to an immeasurable half-moon of Downs, some bare, some saddle-backed with woods, and far away and below, out of the ocean of countless trees in the southern veil, a spire. It is a spire which at this hour is doubtless moving a thousand men with a thousand thoughts and hopes and memories of men and causes, but moves me with the thought alone that just a hundred years ago was buried underneath it a child, a little child whose mother's mother was at the pains to inscribe a tablet saying to all who pass by that he was once "an amiable and most endearing child."

And what nights there are on the hills. The ash-sprays break up the low full moon into a flower of many sparks. The Downs are heaved up into the lighted sky—surely they heave in their tranquillity as with a slowly taken breath. The moon is half-way up the sky and exactly over the centre of the long curve of Downs; just above them lies a long terrace of white cloud, and at their feet gleams a broad pond, the rest of the valley being utterly dark and undistinguishable, save a few scattered lamps and one near meadow that catches the moonlight so as to be transmuted to a lake. But every rainy leaf upon the hill is brighter than any of the few stars above, and from many leaves and blades hang drops as large and bright as the glowworms in their recesses. Larger by a little, but not brighter, are the threes and fours of lights at windows in the valley. The wind has fallen, but a mile of woods unlading the rain from their leaves make a sound of wind, while each separate drop can be heard from the nearest branches, a noise of rapt content, as if they were telling over again the kisses of the shower. The air itself is heavy as mead with the scent of yew and juniper and thyme. *   *   *

THE END OF SUMMER

*   *   * All night—for a week—it rains, and at last there is a still morning of mist. A fire of weeds and hedge-clippings in a little flat field is smouldering. The ashes are crimson, and the bluish-white smoke flows in a divine cloudy garment round the boy who rakes over the ashes. The heat is great, and the boy, straight and well made, wearing close gaiters of leather that reach above the knees, is languid at his task, and often

leans upon his rake to watch the smoke coiling away from him like a monster reluctantly fettered, and sometimes bursting into an anger of sprinkled sparks. He adds some wet hay, and the smoke pours out of it like milky fleeces when the shearer reveals the inmost wool with his shears. Above and beyond him the pale blue sky is dimly white-clouded over beech woods, whose many greens and yellows and yellow-greens are softly touched by the early light which cannot penetrate to the blue caverns of shade underneath. Athwart the woods rises a fount of cottage-smoke from among mellow and dim roofs. Under the smoke and partly scarfed at times by a drift from it is the yellow of sunflower and dahlia, the white of anemone, the tenderest green and palest purple of a thick cluster of autumn crocuses that have broken out of the dark earth and stand surprised, amidst their own weak light as of the underworld from which they have come. Robins sing among the fallen apples, and the cooing of wood-pigeons is attuned to the soft light and the colours of the bowers. The yellow apples gleam. It is the gleam of melting frost. Under all the dulcet warmth of the face of things lurks the bitter spirit of the cold. Stand still for more than a few moments and the cold creeps with a warning, and then a menace into the breast. That is the bitterness that makes this morning of all others in the year so mournful in its beauty. The colour and the grace invite to still contemplation and long draughts of dream; the frost compels to motion. The scent is that of wood-smoke, of fruit and of some fallen leaves. This is the beginning of the pageant of autumn, of that gradual pompous dying which has no parallel in human life, yet draws us to it with sure bonds. It is a dying of the flesh, and we see it pass through a kind of beauty which we can only call spiritual, of so high and inaccessible a strangeness is it. The sight of such perfection as is many times achieved before the end awakens the never more than lightly sleeping human desire of permanence. Now, now is the hour; let things be thus; thus for ever; there is nothing further to be thought of; let these remain. And yet we have a premonition that remain they must not for more than a little while. The motion of the autumn is a fall, a surrender, requiring no effort, and therefore the mind cannot long be blind to the cycle of things as in the spring it can when the effort and delight of ascension veils the goal and the decline beyond. A few frosts now, a storm of wind and rain, a few brooding mists, and the woods that lately hung dark and massive and strong upon the steep hills are transfigured and have become cloudily light and full of change and ghostly fair; the crowing of a cock in the still misty morning echoes up in the many-coloured trees like a challenge to the spirits of them to come out and be seen, but in vain. For months the woods have been homely and kind, companions and backgrounds to our actions and thoughts, the wide walls of a mansion utterly our own. We could have gone on living with them for ever. We had given up the ardours, the extreme ecstasy of our first bridal affection, but we had not forgotten them. We could not become indifferent to the Spanish chestnut trees that grow at the top of the steep rocky banks on either side of the road and mingle their foliage overhead. Of all trees well-grown chestnuts are among the most pleasant to look up at. For the foliage is not dense and it is for the most part close to the large boughs, so that the light comes easily down through all the horizontal leaves, and the shape of each separate one is not lost in the multitude, while at the same time the bold twists of the branches are undraped or easily seen through such translucent green. The trunks are crooked, and the handsome deep furrowing of the bark is often spirally cut. The limbs are few and wide apart so as to frame huge delicately lighted and shadowed chambers of silence or of birds' song. The leaves turn all together to a leathern hue, and when they fall stiffen and display their shape on the ground and long refuse to be merged in the dismal trodden hosts. But when the first one floats past the eye and is blown like a canoe over the pond we recover once more our knowledge and fear of Time. All those ladders of goose-grass that scaled the hedges of spring are dead grey; they are still in their places, but they clamber no longer. The chief flower is the yellow bloom set in the dark ivy round the trunks of the ash trees; and where it climbs over the holly and makes a solid sunny wall, and in the hedges, a whole people of wasps and wasp-like flies are always at the bloom with crystal wings, except when a passing shadow disperses them for a moment with one buzz. But these cannot long detain the eye from the crumbling woods in the haze or under the large white clouds—from the amber and orange bracken about our knees and the blue recesses among the distant golden beeches when the sky is blue but beginning to be laden with loose rain-clouds, from the line of leaf-tipped poplars that bend against the twilight sky; and there is no scent of flowers to hide that of dead leaves and rotting fruit. We must watch it until the end, and gain slowly the philosophy or the memory or the forgetfulness that fits us for accepting winter's boon. Pauses there are, of course, or what seem pauses in the declining of this pomp; afternoons when the rooks waver and caw over their beechen town and the pigeons coo content; dawns when the white mist is packed like snow over the vale and the high woods take the level beams and a hundred globes of dew glitter on every thread of the spiders' hammocks or loose perpendicular nets among the thorns, and through the mist rings the anvil a mile away with a music as merry as that of the daws that soar and dive between the beeches and the spun white cloud; mornings full of the sweetness of mushrooms and blackberries from the short turf among the blue scabious bloom and the gorgeous brier; empurpled evenings before frost when the robin sings passionate and shrill and from the garden earth float the smells of a hundred roots with messages of the dark world; and hours full of the thrush's soft November music. The end should come in heavy and lasting rain. At all times I love rain, the early momentous thunderdrops, the perpendicular cataract shining, or at night the little showers, the spongy mists, the tempestuous mountain rain. I like to see it possessing the whole earth at evening, smothering civilization, taking away from me myself everything except the power to walk under the dark trees and to enjoy as humbly as the hissing grass, while some twinkling house-light or song sung by a lonely man gives a foil to the immense dark force. I like to see the rain making the streets, the railway station, a pure desert, whether bright with lamps or not. It foams off the roofs and trees and bubbles into the water-butts. It gives the grey rivers a demonic majesty. It scours the roads, sets the flints moving, and exposes the glossy chalk in the tracks through the woods. It does work that will last as long as the earth. It is about eternal business. In its noise and myriad aspect I feel the mortal beauty of immortal things. And then after many days the rain ceases at midnight with the wind, and in the silence of dawn and frost the last rose of the world is dropping her petals down to the glistering whiteness, and there they rest blood-red on the winter's desolate coast.

ROCKWELL KENT
1882-1971

Like George Catlin, Rockwell Kent was primarily a visual artist, best known for his woodcut illustrations of such classics as Shakespeare's plays and Moby-Dick. *But he also wrote several books, among them two brief but vivid accounts of wilderness adventures.* Wilderness *(1920) recorded a year of homesteading in an isolated Alaska valley with his young son.* N by E *(1930), from which the following chapters are taken, is an account of a voyage taken by Kent and two friends in a small*

*schooner from New York City to Greenland. The trip ended abruptly
and tragically in a shipwreck along Greenland's west coast, killing one of
the crew. Despite the hardships endured, Kent's descriptions of the sea,
the landscape, and the people he encounters reflect his passionate energy
and, as with his illustrations, a cosmic view of man's nature and destiny.*

From N by E

At four-thirty in the afternoon of June 17th we sailed. The exasperating delay that had put off our sailing until that date, and on that date until that hour, the misgivings I had felt about the mate, all were forgotten in that moment of leave taking. The bright sun shone upon us; the lake was blue under the westerly breeze, and luminous, how luminous! the whole far world of our imagination. How like a colored lens the colored present! through it we see the forward vista of our lives. Here, in the measure that the water widened in our wake and heart strings stretched to almost breaking, the golden future neared us and enfolded us, made us at last—how soon!—oblivious to all things but the glamour of adventure. And while one world diminished, narrowed and then disappeared, before us a new world unrolled and neared us to display itself. Who can deny the human soul its everlasting need to make the unknown known; not for the sake of knowing, not to inform itself or be informed or wise, but for the need to exercise the need to know? What is that need but the imagination's hunger for the new and raw materials of its creative trade? Of things and facts assured to us and known we've got to make the best, and live with it. That humdrum is the price of living. We *live* for those fantastic and unreal moments of beauty which our thoughts may build upon the passing panorama of experience.

Soon all that we had ever seen before was left behind and a new land of fields and farms, pastures and meadows, woods and open lands and rolling hills was streaming by, all in the mellow splendor of late afternoon in June, all green and clean and beautiful. We stripped and plunged ahead into the blue water; and catching hold of a rope as it swept by, trailed in the wake. It was so warm—the water and the early summer air. So we shall live all summer naked, and get brown and magnificent!

N by E (New York: Random House, 1930).

I cooked supper: hot baking-powder biscuit and—I don't remember what. "You're a wonderful cook!" said everyone. So I washed the dishes and put the cabin in order.

"Oh," thought I, "people are nice! the world is grand! I'm happy! God is good!"

* * *

In the half light of the early morning of July the fifth all hands bestirred themselves, got up; we came on deck. It was cold. The silent town lay dark against the eastern sky; the land was black, and stranded bergs glowed pale against it. Clear heavens strewn with stars, and a fair wind S. by W.!

Noiselessly, as if stealing away, we hoisted sail, weighed anchor and bore out. And so, without tumult and the clamor of leave takings, quietly as the coming dawn, we entered the solitude of the ocean.

And if we were not annihilated by the contemplation of such vast adventure it was by grace of that wise providence of man's nature which, to preserve his reason, lets him be thoughtless before immensity.

* * *

But that was centuries ago. In Greenland the environment of nature dominates; and into the sparse settlements along its rim of shore, into men's thoughts and moods and lives has entered something of the eternal peacefulness of the wilderness. It had to be. Man is less entity than consequence and his being is but a derivation of a less subjective world, a synthesis of what he calls the elements. Man's very spirit is a sublimation of cosmic energy and worships it as God; and every faculty to feel, perceive and know serves only to relate him closer to what is. God is the Father, man his connatural progeny; and thus the elements at work become for man the pattern for his conduct, the look and feel and sound of them—sunshine and storm, peace and turmoil, lightning and thunder and the quiet interludes—the formulae for his poor imitative moods and their expression. But in the wilderness invariably peace predominates; and seeing the quiet uneventfulness of lives lived there, their ordered lawlessness, the loveliness and grace of bearing and of look and smile that it so often breeds and fosters we may indeed "lament what man has made of man" and hold those circumstances of congestion which are called civilization to be less friendly to beauty than opposed to it.

More than two hundred years ago there came a Christian militant, Hand Egede, to Greenland, and brought those heathen folk the Gospel law. And Greenland, its wilderness and wilderness's heathen folk, reached out and gently laid its peaceful spirit upon Egede and all who followed him and lived there. Thus came the natives of Greenland to

learn somewhat of the virtues of cleanliness and industry and thrift, and
the Christians to become more godly, decent, quiet, honorable, fair than
any Christians aggregate I've met with elsewhere in the world. Christ,
too, if I remember, sojourned in the wilderness.

*   *   *

So, excursioning and voyaging about, landing to stroll the settlements
or climb the neighboring hills, looking at everything and listening, I
came at last to have been north to Seventy and south to Sixty-thirty. My
lingual limitation served to sharpen the perceptive faculties and shield
me from dependence on such facts as others might have told me. It was,
in consequence, what *seemed* to be that made my Greenland world; and
such conclusions as I ventured on were reached inversely, from effect to
cause. All that *looked* beautiful to me, was good; and if I held the smile
of the Eskimo to be evidence of his serenity of soul, the inter-racial
courtesy of the Danes to show the virtue of their rulership, and both to
prove that life in Greenland's solitudes was good for man my thought at
least began where science stops.

VIRGINIA WOOLF
1882 - 1941

As one of the leading Modernists—author of Mrs. Dalloway *(1925),* To
the Lighthouse *(1927), and* Between the Acts *(1941) among many other
novels—Woolf brought a lyrical focus to the stream of consciousness.
She was also one of the most important essayists and critics of her generation, as reflected in such collections as* The Common Reader *(1925)
and* The Death of the Moth *(1942). But her special gifts as a nature
writer became clearest with the publication of her five volume* Diary
*between 1977 and 1984. As many of her entries show, Woolf was as
attentive to the outer weathers, the outer tides and blossomings, as she
was to the inner. She was alert, too, to the terrifying and redemptive
independence of nature from human rationales and needs. As she wrote
in "Time Passes," from* To the Lighthouse, *"In spring, the garden urns,
casually filled with wind-blown plants, were gay as ever."*

The Death of the Moth

Moths that fly by day are not properly to be called moths; they do not excite that pleasant sense of dark autumn nights and ivy-blossom which the commonest yellow-underwing asleep in the shadow of the curtain never fails to rouse in us. They are hybrid creatures, neither gay like butterflies nor sombre like their own species. Nevertheless the present specimen, with his narrow hay-coloured wings, fringed with a tassel of the same colour, seemed to be content with life. It was a pleasant morning, mid-September, mild, benignant, yet with a keener breath than that of the summer months. The plough was already scoring the field opposite the window, and where the share had been, the earth was pressed flat and gleamed with moisture. Such vigour came rolling in from the fields and the down beyond that it was difficult to keep the eyes strictly turned upon the book. The rooks too were keeping one of their annual festivities; soaring round the tree tops until it looked as if a vast net with thousands of black knots in it had been cast up into the air; which, after a few moments sank slowly down upon the trees until every twig seemed to have a knot at the end of it. Then, suddenly, the net would be thrown into the air again in a wider circle this time, with the utmost clamour and vociferation, as though to be thrown into the air and settle slowly down upon the tree tops were a tremendously exciting experience.

The same energy which inspired the rooks, the ploughmen, the horses, and even, it seemed, the lean bare-backed downs, sent the moth fluttering from side to side of his square of the window-pane. One could not help watching him. One was, indeed, conscious of a queer feeling of pity for him. The possibilities of pleasure seemed that morning so enormous and so various that to have only a moth's part in life, and a day moth's at that, appeared a hard fate, and his zest in enjoying his meagre opportunities to the full, pathetic. He flew vigorously to one corner of his compartment, and, after waiting there a second, flew across to the other. What remained for him but to fly to a third corner and then to a fourth? That was all he could do, in spite of the size of the downs, the width of the sky, the far-off smoke of houses, and the romantic voice, now and then, of a steamer out at sea. What he could do he did. Watching him, it seemed as if a fibre, very thin but pure, of the enormous energy of the world had been thrust into his frail and diminutive body. As often as he crossed the pane, I could fancy that a thread of vital light became visible. He was little or nothing but life.

The Death of the Moth and Other Essays (New York: Harcourt Brace, 1942).

Yet, because he was so small, and so simple a form of the energy that was rolling in at the open window and driving its way through so many narrow and intricate corridors in my own brain and in those of other human beings, there was something marvellous as well as pathetic about him. It was as if someone had taken a tiny bead of pure life and decking it as lightly as possible with down and feathers, had set it dancing and zig-zagging to show us the true nature of life. Thus displayed one could not get over the strangeness of it. One is apt to forget all about life, seeing it humped and bossed and garnished and cumbered so that it has to move with the greatest circumspection and dignity. Again, the thought of all that life might have been had he been born in any other shape caused one to view his simple activities with a kind of pity.

After a time, tired by his dancing apparently, he settled on the window ledge in the sun, and, the queer spectacle being at an end, I forgot about him. Then, looking up, my eye was caught by him. He was trying to resume his dancing, but seemed either so stiff or so awkward that he could only flutter to the bottom of the window-pane; and when he tried to fly across it he failed. Being intent on other matters I watched these futile attempts for a time without thinking, unconsciously waiting for him to resume his flight, as one waits for a machine, that has stopped momentarily, to start again without considering the reason of its failure. After perhaps a seventh attempt he slipped from the wooden ledge and fell, fluttering his wings, on to his back on the window sill. The helplessness of his attitude roused me. It flashed upon me that he was in difficulties; he could no longer raise himself; his legs struggled vainly. But, as I stretched out a pencil, meaning to help him to right himself, it came over me that the failure and awkwardness were the approach of death. I laid the pencil down again.

The legs agitated themselves once more. I looked as if for the enemy against which he struggled. I looked out of doors. What had happened there? Presumably it was midday, and work in the fields had stopped. Stillness and quiet had replaced the previous animation. The birds had taken themselves off to feed in the brooks. The horses stood still. Yet the power was there all the same, massed outside indifferent, impersonal, not attending to anything in particular. Somehow it was opposed to the little hay-coloured moth. It was useless to try to do anything. One could only watch the extraordinary efforts made by those tiny legs against an oncoming doom which could, had it chosen, have submerged an entire city, not merely a city, but masses of human beings; nothing, I knew, had any chance against death. Nevertheless after a pause of exhaustion the legs fluttered again. It was superb this last protest, and so frantic that he succeeded at last in righting himself. One's sympathies, of course, were all on the side of life. Also, when there was nobody to care or to know, this gigantic effort on the part of an insignificant little moth, against a power of such magnitude, to retain what no one else valued or desired to keep, moved one strangely. Again, somehow, one saw life, a pure bead. I lifted the pencil again, useless though I knew it to be. But even as I did so, the unmistakable tokens of death showed themselves. The body relaxed, and instantly grew stiff. The struggle was over. The insignificant little creature now knew death. As I looked at the dead moth, this minute wayside triumph of so great a force over so mean an antagonist filled me with wonder. Just as life had been strange a few minutes before, so death was now as strange. The moth having righted himself now lay most decently and uncomplainingly composed. O yes, he seemed to say, death is stronger than I am.

ISAK DINESEN
1883-1962

For many Europeans in the nineteenth and early twentieth centuries, the African continent was their New World, full of economic opportunity and imaginative possibility. During the years 1913–1930 the Baroness Karen Blixen managed a large coffee plantation in the Kenyan highlands, shot lions, and had a love affair with the English game hunter Denys Finch Hatton. When, after a series of economic reversals, she was forced to sell her farm and leave her beloved adopted homeland, she returned to her native Denmark. There, writing in English under the pen name Isak Dinesen, she published Out of Africa *(1937), which has become the most celebrated European account of colonial Africa. The book is a memoir of her years in Kenya, filtered through a strong narrative sensibility. Its lyrical, incantatory language gives her experiences a mythic stature and the place itself an Edenic quality, where animals "were being created before my eyes and sent out as they were finished."*

From OUT OF AFRICA

THE NGONG FARM

I had a farm in Africa, at the foot of the Ngong Hills. The Equator runs across these highlands, a hundred miles to the North, and the farm lay at an altitude of over six thousand feet. In the day-time you felt that you had got high up, near to the sun, but the early mornings and evenings were limpid and restful, and the nights were cold.

The geographical position, and the height of the land combined to create a landscape that had not its like in all the world. There was no fat on it and no luxuriance anywhere; it was Africa distilled up through six thousand feet, like the strong and refined essence of a continent. The colours were dry and burnt, like the colours in pottery. The trees had a light delicate foliage, the structure of which was different from that of the trees in Europe; it did not grow in bows or cupolas, but in horizontal layers, and the formation gave to the tall solitary trees a likeness to the palms, or a heroic and romantic air like fullrigged ships with their sails clewed up, and to the edge of a wood a strange appearance as if the whole wood were faintly vibrating. Upon the grass of the great plains the crooked bare old thorn-trees were scattered, and the grass was spiced like thyme and bog-myrtle; in some places the scent was so strong, that is smarted in the nostrils. All the flowers that you found on the plains, or upon the creepers and liana in the native forest, were diminutive like flowers of the downs,—only just in the beginning of the long rains a number of big, massive heavy-scented lilies sprang out on the plains. The views were immensely wide. Everything that you saw made for greatness and freedom, and unequalled nobility.

The chief feature of the landscape, and of your life in it, was the air. Looking back on a sojourn in the African highlands, you are struck by your feeling of having lived for a time up in the air. The sky was rarely more than pale blue or violet, with a profusion of mighty, weightless, ever-changing clouds towering up and sailing on it, but it has a blue vigour in it, and at a short distance it painted the ranges of hills and the woods a fresh deep blue. In the middle of the day the air was alive over the land, like a flame burning; it scintillated, waved and shone like running water, mirrored and doubled all objects, and created great Fata Morgana. Up in this high air you breathed easily, drawing in a vital assurance and lightness of heart. In the highlands you woke up in the morning and thought: Here I am, where I ought to be.

Out of Africa (New York: Random House, 1938).

*   *   *

Before I took over the management of the farm, I had been keen on shooting and had been out on many Safaris. But when I became a farmer I put away my rifles.

The Masai, the nomadic, cattle-owning nation, were neighbours of the farm and lived on the other side of the river; from time to time some of them would come to my house to complain about a lion that was taking their cows, and to ask me to go out and shoot it for them, and I did so if I could. Sometimes, on Saturday, I also walked out on the Orungi plains to shoot a Zebra or two as meat for my farm-labourers, with a long tail of optimistic young Kikuyu after me. I shot birds on the farm, spurfowl and guineafowl, that are very good to eat. But for many years I was not out on any shooting expedition.

Still, we often talked on the farm of the Safaris that we had been on. Camping-places fix themselves in your mind as if you had spent long periods of your life in them. You will remember a curve of your waggon track in the grass of the plain, like the features of a friend.

Out on the Safaris, I had seen a herd of Buffalo, one hundred and twenty-nine of them, come out of the morning mist under a copper sky, one by one, as if the dark and massive, iron-like animals with the mighty horizontally swung horns were not approaching, but were being created before my eyes and sent out as they were finished. I had seen a herd of Elephant travelling through dense Native forest, where the sunlight is strewn down between the thick creepers in small spots and patches, pacing along as if they had an appointment at the end of the world. It was, in giant size, the border of a very old, infinitely precious Persian carpet, in the dyes of green, yellow and black-brown. I had time after time watched the progression across the plain of the Giraffe, in their queer, inimitable, vegetative gracefulness, as if it were not a herd of animals but a family of rare, long-stemmed, speckled gigantic flowers slowly advancing. I had followed two Rhinos on their morning promenade, when they were sniffing and snorting in the air of the dawn,—which is so cold that it hurts in the nose,—and looked like two very big angular stones rollicking in the long valley and enjoying life together. I had seen the royal lion, before sunrise, below a waning moon, crossing the grey plain on his way home from the kill, drawing a dark wake in the silvery grass, his face still red up to the ears, or during the midday-siesta, when he reposed contentedly in the midst of his family on the short grass and in the delicate, spring-like shade of the broad Acacia trees of his park of Africa.

All these things were pleasant to think of when times were dull on the farm. And the big game was out there still, in their own country; I could go and look them up once more if I liked. Their nearness gave a shine and play to the atmosphere of the farm. * * *

D(AVID) H(ERBERT) LAWRENCE
1885-1930

In one sense D.H. Lawrence was always writing about nature, whether his setting was the hillsides of Tuscany, the coal mines of the English Midlands, or the drawing rooms of an aristocrat's London town house. In most of his fiction the contrast between the barren, self-conscious, self-willed, and mechanized life of modern civilization and the unconscious and instinctive life of "blood knowledge" and "dark gods" is expressed in images of natural rhythms, vivid landscapes, and untamed animals. Many readers find Lawrence's nature and travel essays among his most congenial work, for in them his vital response to life is generally free of the didactic elements of his novels and more political essays. As a boy Lawrence painted watercolors of his native Nottingham flora, and few if any writers have created such passionately intense portraits of flowers as in the following selection from Phoenix *(1936), a posthumous collection of his writings.*

FLOWERY TUSCANY

I

Each country has its own flowers, that shine out specially there. In England it is daisies and buttercups, hawthorn and cowslips. In America, it is goldenrod, stargrass, June daisies, Mayapple and asters, that we call Michaelmas daisies. In India, hibiscus and dattura and champa flowers, and in Australia mimosa, that they call wattle, and sharp-tongued strange heath-flowers. In Mexico it is cactus flowers, that they call roses of the desert, lovely and crystalline among many thorns; and also the

Phoenix: The Posthumous Papers of D.H. Lawrence (New York: Viking Press, 1936).

dangling yard-long clusters of the cream bells of the yucca, like dropping froth.

But by the Mediterranean, now as in the days of the Argosy, and, we hope, for ever, it is narcissus and anemone, asphodel and myrtle. Narcissus and anemone, asphodel, crocus, myrtle, and parsley, they leave their sheer significance only by the Mediterranean. There are daisies in Italy too: at Pæstum there are white little carpets of daisies, in March, and Tuscany is spangled with celandine. But for all that, the daisy and the celandine are English flowers, their best significance is for us and for the North.

The Mediterranean has narcissus and anemone, myrtle and asphodel and grape hyacinth. These are the flowers that speak and are understood in the sun round the Middle Sea.

Tuscany is especially flowery, being wetter than Sicily and more homely than the Roman hills. Tuscany manages to remain so remote, and secretly smiling to itself in its many sleeves. There are so many hills popping up, and they take no notice of one another. There are so many little deep valleys with streams that seem to go their own little way entirely, regardless of river or sea. There are thousands, millions of utterly secluded little nooks, though the land has been under cultivation these thousands of years. But the intensive culture of vine and olive and wheat, by the ceaseless industry of naked human hands and winter-shod feet, and slow-stepping, soft-eyed oxen does not devastate a country, does not denude it, does not lay it bare, does not uncover its nakedness, does not drive away either Pan or his children. The streams run and rattle over wild rocks of secret places, and murmur through blackthorn thickets where the nightingales sing all together, unruffled and undaunted.

It is queer that a country so perfectly cultivated as Tuscany, where half the produce of five acres of land will have to support ten human mouths, still has so much room for the wild flowers and the nightingale. When little hills heave themselves suddenly up, and shake themselves free of neighbours, man has to build his garden and his vineyard, and sculp his landscape. Talk of hanging gardens of Babylon, all Italy, apart from the plains, is a hanging garden. For centuries upon centuries man has been patiently modelling the surface of the Mediterranean countries, gently rounding the hills, and graduating the big slopes and the little slopes into the almost invisible levels of terraces. Thousands of square miles of Italy have been lifted in human hands, piled and laid back in tiny little flats, held up by the drystone walls, whose stones came from the lifted earth. It is a work of many, many centuries. It is the gentle sensitive sculpture of all the landscape. And it is the achieving of the peculiar Italian beauty which is so exquisitely natural, because man, feeling his way sensitively to the fruitfulness of the earth, has moulded the earth to his necessity without violating it.

Which shows that it *can* be done. Man *can* live on the earth and by the earth without disfiguring the earth. It has been done here, on all these sculptured hills and softly, sensitively terraced slopes.

But, of course, you can't drive a steam plough on terraces four yards wide, terraces that dwindle and broaden and sink and rise a little, all according to the pitch and the breaking outline of the mother hill. Corn has got to grow on these little shelves of earth, where already the grey olive stands semi-invisible, and the grapevine twists upon its own scars. If oxen can step with that lovely pause at every little stride, they can plough the narrow field. But they will have to leave a tiny fringe, a grassy lip over the drystone wall below. And if the terraces are too narrow to plough, the peasant digging them will still leave the grassy lip, because it helps to hold the surface in the rains.

And here the flowers take refuge. Over and over and over and over has this soil been turned, twice a year, sometimes three times a year, for several thousands of years. Yet the flowers have never been driven out. There is a very rigorous digging and sifting, the little bulbs and tubers are flung away into perdition, not a weed shall remain.

Yet spring returns, and on the terrace lips, and in the stony nooks between terraces, up rise the aconites, the crocuses, the narcissus and the asphodel, the inextinguishable wild tulips. There they are, for ever hanging on the precarious brink of an existence, but for ever triumphant, never quite losing their footing. In England, in America, the flowers get rooted out, driven back. They become fugitive. But in the intensive cultivation of ancient Italian terraces, they dance round and hold their own.

Spring begins with the first narcissus, rather cold and shy and wintry. They are the little bunchy, creamy narcissus with the yellow cup like the yolk of the flower. The natives call these flowers *tazzette*, little cups. They grow on the grassy banks rather sparse, or push up among thorns.

To me they are winter flowers, and their scent is winter. Spring starts in February, with the winter aconite. Some icy day, when the wind is down from the snow of the mountains, early in February, you will notice on a bit of fallow land, under the olive trees, tight, pale-gold little balls, clenched tight as nuts, and resting on round ruffs of green near the ground. It is the winter aconite suddenly come.

The winter aconite is one of the most charming flowers. Like all the early blossoms, once her little flower emerges it is quite naked. No shutting a little green sheath over herself, like the daisy or the dandelion. Her bubble of frail, pale, pure gold rests on the round frill of her green collar, with the snowy wind trying to blow it away.

But without success. The *tramontana* ceases, comes a day of wild February sunshine. The clenched little nuggets of the aconite puff out, they become light bubbles, like small balloons, on a green base. The sun blazes on, with February splendour. And by noon, all under the olives are wide-open little suns, the aconites spreading all their rays; and there is an exquisitely sweet scent, honey-sweet, not narcissus-frosty; and there is a February humming of little brown bees.

Till afternoon, when the sun slopes, and the touch of snow comes back into the air.

But at evening, under the lamp on the table, the aconites are wide and excited, and there is a perfume of sweet spring that makes one almost start humming and trying to be a bee.

Aconites don't last very long. But they turn up in all odd places—on clods of dug earth, and in land where the broad-beans are thrusting up, and along the lips of terraces. But they like best land left fallow for one winter. There they throng, showing how quick they are to seize on an opportunity to live and shine forth.

In a fortnight, before February is over, the yellow bubbles of the aconite are crumpling to nothingness. But already in a cosy-nook the violets are dark purple, and there is a new little perfume in the air.

Like the debris of winter stand the hellebores, in all the wild places, and the butcher's broom is flaunting its last bright red berry. Hellebore is Christmas roses, but in Tuscany the flowers never come white. They emerge out of the grass towards the end of December, flowers wintry of winter, and they are delicately pale green, and of a lovely shape, with yellowish stamens. They have a peculiar wintry quality of invisibility, so lonely rising from the sere grass, and pallid green, held up like a little hand-mirror that reflects nothing. At first they are single upon a stem, short and lovely, and very wintry-beautiful, with a will not to be touched, not to be noticed. One instinctively leaves them alone. But as January draws towards February, these hellebores, these greenish Christmas roses become more assertive. Their pallid water-green becomes yellow, pale sulphur-yellow-green, and they rise up, they are in tufts, in throngs, in veritable bushes of greenish open flowers, assertive, bowing their faces with a hellebore assertiveness. In some places they throng among the bushes and above the water of the stream, giving the peculiar pale glimmer almost of primroses, as you walk among them. Almost of primroses, yet with a coarse hellebore leaf and an up-rearing hellebore assertiveness, like snakes in winter.

And as one walks among them, one brushes the last scarlet off the butcher's broom. This low little shrub is the Christmas holly of Tuscany, only a foot or so high, with a vivid red berry stuck on in the middle of its sharp hard leaf. In February the last red ball rolls off the prickly plume, and winter rolls with it. The violets already are emerging from the moisture.

But before the violets make any show, there are the crocuses. If you walk up through the pine-wood, that lifts its umbrellas of pine so high, up till you come to the brow of the hill at the top, you can look south, due south, and see snow on the Apennines, and on a blue afternoon, seven layers of blue-hilled distance.

Then you sit down on that southern slope, out of the wind, and there it is warm, whether it be January or February, *tramontana* or not. There the earth has been baked by innumerable suns, baked and baked again; moistened by many rains, but never wetted for long. Because it is rocky, and full to the south, and sheering steep in the slope.

And there, in February, in the sunny baked desert of that crumbly slope, you will find the first crocuses. On the sheer aridity of crumbled stone you see a queer, alert little star, very sharp and quite small. It has opened out rather flat, and looks like a tiny freesia flower, creamy, with a smear of yellow yolk. It has no stem, seems to have been just lightly dropped on the crumbled, baked rock. It is the first hill-crocus.

II

North of the Alps, the everlasting winter is interrupted by summers that struggle and soon yield; south of the Alps, the everlasting summer is interrupted by spasmodic and spiteful winters that never get a real hold, but that are mean and dogged. North of the Alps, you may have a pure winter's day in June. South of the Alps, you may have a midsummer day in December or January or even February. The in-between, in either case, is just as it may be. But the lands of the sun are south of the Alps, for ever.

Yet things, the flowers especially, that belong to both sides of the Alps, are not much earlier south than north of the mountains. Through all the winter there are roses in the garden, lovely creamy roses, more pure and mysterious than those of summer, leaning perfect from the stem. And the narcissus in the garden are out by the end of January, and the little simple hyacinths early in February.

But out in the fields, the flowers are hardly any sooner than English flowers. It is mid-February before the first violets, the first crocus, the first primrose. And in mid-February one may find a violet, a primrose, a crocus in England, in the hedgerows and the garden corner.

And still there is a difference. There are several kinds of wild crocus in this region of Tuscany: being little spiky mauve ones, and spiky little creamy ones, that grow among the pine-trees of the bare slopes. But the beautiful ones are those of a meadow in the corner of the woods, the low hollow meadow below the steep, shadowy pine-slopes, the secretive grassy dip where the water seeps through the turf all winter, where the stream runs between thick bushes, where the nightingale sings his mightiest in May, and where the wild thyme is rosy and full of bees, in summer.

Here the lavender crocuses are most at home—here sticking out of the deep grass, in a hollow like a cup, a bowl of grass, come the lilac-coloured crocuses, like an innumerable encampment. You may see them at twilight, with all the buds shut, in the mysterious stillness of the grassy underworld, palely glimmering like myriad folded tents. So the apaches still camp, and close their tepees, in the hollows of the great hills of the West, at night.

But in the morning it is quite different. Then the sun shines strong on the horizontal green cloud-puffs of the pines, the sky is clear and full of life, the water runs hastily, still browned by the last juice of crushed olives. And there the earth's bowl of crocuses is amazing. You cannot believe that the flowers are really still. They are open with such delight, and their pistil-thrust is so red-orange, and they are so many, all reaching out wide and marvellous, that it suggests a perfect ecstasy of radiant, thronging movement, lit-up violet and orange, and surging in some invisible rhythm of concerted, delightful movement. You cannot believe they do not move, and make some sort of crystalline sound of delight. If you sit still and watch, you begin to move with them, like moving with the stars, and you feel the sound of their radiance. All the little cells of the flowers must be leaping with flowery life and utterance.

And the small brown honey-bees hop from flower to flower, dive down, try, and off again. The flowers have been already rifled, most of them. Only sometimes a bee stands on his head, kicking slowly inside the flower, for some time. He has found something. And all the bees have little loaves of pollen, bee-bread, in their elbow-joints.

The crocuses last in their beauty for a week or so, and as they begin to lower their tents and abandon camp, the violets begin to thicken. It is already March. The violets have been showing like tiny dark hounds for some weeks. But now the whole pack comes forth, among the grass and the tangle of wild thyme, till the air all sways subtly scented with violets, and the banks above where the crocuses had their tents are now swarming brilliant purple with violets. They are the sweet violets of early spring, but numbers have made them bold, for they flaunt and ruffle till

the slopes are a bright blue-purple blaze of them, full in the sun, with an
odd late crocus still standing wondering and erect amongst them.

And now that it is March, there is a rush of flowers. Down by the
other stream, which turns sideways to the sun, and has tangles of brier
and bramble, down where the hellebore has stood so wan and dignified
all winter, there are now white tufts of primroses, suddenly come.
Among the tangle and near the water-lip, tufts and bunches of primroses, in abundance. Yet they look more wan, more pallid, more flimsy
than English primroses. They lack some of the full wonder of the northern flowers. One tends to overlook them, to turn to the great, solemn-
faced purple violets that rear up from the bank, and above all, to the
wonderful little towers of the grape-hyacinth.

I know no flower that is more fascinating, when it first appears, than
the blue grape-hyacinth. And yet, because it lasts so long, and keeps on
coming so repeatedly, for at least two months, one tends later on to
ignore it, even to despise it a little. Yet that is very unjust.

The first grape-hyacinths are flowers of blue, thick and rich and meaningful, above the unrenewed grass. The upper buds are pure blue, shut
tight; round balls of pure, perfect warm blue, blue, blue; while the lower
bells are darkish blue-purple, with the spark of white at the mouth. As
yet, none of the lower bells has withered, to leave the greenish, separate
sparseness of fruiting that spoils the grape-hyacinth later on, and makes
it seem naked and functional. All hyacinths are like that in the seeding.

But, at first, you have only a compact tower of night-blue clearing to
dawn, and extremely beautiful. If we were tiny as fairies, and lived only a
summer, how lovely these great trees of bells would be to us, towers of
night and dawn-blue globes. They would rise above us thick and succulent, and the purple globes would push the blue ones up, with white
sparks of ripples, and we should see a god in them.

As a matter of fact, someone once told me they were the flowers of the
many-breasted Artemis; and it is true, the Cybele of Ephesus, with her
clustered breasts was like a grape-hyacinth at the bosom.

This is the time, in March, when the sloe is white and misty in the
hedge-tangle by the stream, and on the slope of land the peach tree
stands pink and alone. The almond blossom, silvery pink, is passing, but
the peach, deep-toned, bluey, not at all ethereal, this reveals itself like
flesh, and the trees are like isolated individuals, the peach and the apricot.

A man said this spring: "Oh, I *don't* care for peach blossom! It is such
a vulgar pink!" One wonders what anybody means by a "vulgar" pink. I
think pink flannelette is rather vulgar. But probably it's the flannelette's
fault, not the pink. And peach blossom has a beautiful sensual pink, far

from vulgar, most rare and private. And pink is so beautiful in a land-scape, pink houses, pink almond, pink peach and purply apricot, pink asphodels.

It is so conspicuous and so individual, that pink among the coming green of spring, because the first flowers that emerge from winter seem always white or yellow or purple. Now the celandines are out, and along the edges of the *podere*, the big, sturdy, black-purple anemones, with black hearts.

They are curious, these great, dark-violet anemones. You may pass them on a grey day, or at evening or early morning, and never see them. But as you come along in the full sunshine, they seem to be baying at you with all their throats, baying deep purple into the air. It is because they are hot and wide open now, gulping the sun. Whereas when they are shut, they have a silkiness and a curved head, like the curve of an um-brella handle, and a peculiar outward colourlessness, that makes them quite invisible. They may be under your feet, and you will not see them.

Altogether anemones are odd flowers. On these last hills above the plain, we have only the big black-purple ones, in tufts here and there, not many. But two hills away, the young green corn is blue with the lilac-blue kind, still the broad-petalled sort with the darker heart. But these flowers are smaller than our dark-purple, and frailer, more silky. Ours are sub-stantial, thickly vegetable flowers, and not abundant. The others are lovely and silky-delicate, and the whole corn is blue with them. And they have a sweet, sweet scent, when they are warm.

Then on the priest's *podere* there are the scarlet, Adonis-blood anem-ones: only in one place, in one long fringe under a terrace, and there by a path below. These flowers above all you will never find unless you look for them in the sun. Their silver silk outside makes them quite invisible, when they are shut up.

Yet, if you are passing in the sun, a sudden scarlet faces on to the air, one of the loveliest scarlet apparitions in the world. The inner surface of the Adonis-blood anemone is as fine as velvet, and yet there is no sugges-tion of pile, not as much as on a velvet rose. And from this inner smooth-ness issues the red colour, perfectly pure and unknown of earth, no earthiness, and yet solid, not transparent. How a colour manages to be perfectly strong and impervious, yet of a purity that suggests condensed light, yet not luminous, at least, not transparent, is a problem. The poppy in her radiance is translucent, and the tulip in her utter redness has a touch of opaque earth. But the Adonis-blood anemone is neither translucent nor opaque. It is just pure condensed red, of a velvetiness without velvet, and a scarlet without glow.

This red seems to me the perfect premonition of summer—like the red on the outside of apple blossom—and later, the red of the apple. It is the premonition in redness of summer and of autumn.

The red flowers are coming now. The wild tulips are in bud, hanging their grey leaves like flags. They come up in myriads, wherever they get a chance. But they are holding back their redness till the last days of March, the early days of April.

Still, the year is warming up. By the high ditch the common magenta anemone is hanging its silky tassels, or opening its great magenta daisy-shape to the hot sun. It is much nearer to red than the big-petalled anemones are; except the Adonis-blood. They say these anemones sprang from the tears of Venus, which fell as she went looking for Adonis. At that rate, how the poor lady must have wept, for the anemones by the Mediterranean are common as daisies in England.

The daisies are out here too, in sheets, and they too are red-mouthed. The first ones are big and handsome. But as March goes on, they dwindle to bright little things, like tiny buttons, clouds of them together. That means summer is nearly here.

The red tulips open in the corn like poppies, only with a heavier red. And they pass quickly, without repeating themselves. There is little lingering in a tulip.

In some places there are odd yellow tulips, slender, spiky, and Chinese-looking. They are very lovely, pricking out their dulled yellow in slim spikes. But they too soon lean, expand beyond themselves, and are gone like an illusion.

And when the tulips are gone, there is a moment's pause, before summer. Summer is the next move.

III

In the pause towards the end of April, when the flowers seem to hesitate, the leaves make up their minds to come out. For some time, at the very ends of the bare boughs of fig trees, spurts of pure green have been burning like little cloven tongues of green fire vivid on the tips of the candelabrum. Now these spurts of green spread out, and begin to take the shape of hands, feeling for the air of summer. And tiny green figs are below them, like glands on the throat of a goat.

For some time, the long stiff whips of the vine have had knobby pink buds, like flower buds. Now these pink buds begin to unfold into greenish, half-shut fans of leaves with red in the veins, and tiny spikes of flower, like seed-pearls. Then, in all its down and pinky dawn, the vine-rosette has a frail, delicious scent of a new year.

Now the aspens on the hill are all remarkable with the translucent membranes of blood-veined leaves. They are gold-brown, but not like autumn, rather like the thin wings of bats when like birds—call them birds—they wheel in clouds against the setting sun, and the sun glows through the stretched membrane of their wings, as through thin, brown-red stained glass. This is the red sap of summer, not the red dust of autumn. And in the distance the aspens have the tender panting glow of living membrane just come awake. This is the beauty of the frailty of spring.

The cherry tree is something the same, but more sturdy. Now, in the last week of April, the cherry blossom is still white, but waning and passing away: it is late this year; and the leaves are clustering thick and softly copper in their dark, blood-filled glow. It is queer about fruit trees in this district. The pear and the peach were out together. But now the pear tree is a lovely thick softness of new and glossy green, vivid with a tender fullness of apple-green leaves, gleaming among all the other green of the landscape, the half-high wheat, emerald, and the grey olive, half-invisible, the browning green of the dark cypress, the black of the ever-green oak, the rolling, heavy green puffs of the stone-pines, the flimsy green of small peach and almond trees, the sturdy young green of horse-chestnut. So many greens, all in flakes and shelves and tilted tables and round shoulders and plumes and shaggles and uprisen bushes, of greens and greens, sometimes blindingly brilliant at evening, when the land-scape looks as if it were on fire from inside, with greenness and with gold.

The pear is perhaps the greenest thing in the landscape. The wheat may shine lit-up yellow, or glow bluish, but the pear tree is green in itself. The cherry has white, half-absorbed flowers, so has the apple. But the plum is rough with her new foliage, and inconspicuous, inconspicuous as the almond, the peach, the apricot, which one can no longer find in the landscape, though twenty days ago they were the distinguished pink individuals of the whole countryside. Now they are gone. It is the time of green, pre-eminent green, in ruffles and flakes and slabs.

In the wood, the scrub-oak is only just coming uncrumpled, and the pines keep their hold on winter. They are wintry things, stone-pines. At Christmas, their heavy green clouds are richly beautiful. When the cy-presses raise their tall and naked bodies of dark green, and the osiers are vivid red-orange, on the still blue air, and the land is lavender, then, in mid-winter, the landscape is most beautiful in colour, surging with col-our.

But now, when the nightingale is still drawing out his long, wistful, yearning, teasing plaint-note, and following it up with a rich and joyful burble, the pines and the cypresses seem hard and rusty, and the wood has lost its subtlety and its mysteriousness. It still seems wintry in spite of the yellowing young oaks, and the heath in flower. But hard, dull pines above, and hard, dull, tall heath below, all stiff and resistant, this is out of the mood of spring.

In spite of the fact that the stone-white heath is in full flower, and very lovely when you look at it, it does not, casually, give the impression of blossom. More the impression of having its tips and crests all dipped in hoarfrost; or in a whitish dust. It has a peculiar ghostly colourlessness amid the darkish colourlessness of the wood altogether, which completely takes away the sense of spring.

Yet the tall white heath is very lovely, in its invisibility. It grows sometimes as tall as a man, lifting up its spires and its shadowy-white fingers with a ghostly fullness, amid the dark, rusty green of its lower bushiness; and it gives off a sweet honeyed scent in the sun, and a cloud of fine white stone-dust, if you touch it. Looked at closely, its little bells are most beautiful, delicate and white, with the brown-purple inner eye and the dainty pin-head of the pistil. And out in the sun at the edge of the wood, where the heath grows tall and thrusts up its spires of dim white next a brilliant, yellow-flowering vetch-bush, under a blue sky, the effect has a real magic.

And yet, in spite of all, the dim whiteness of all the flowering heath-fingers only adds to the hoariness and out-of-date quality of the pine-woods, now in the pause between spring and summer. It is the ghost of the interval.

Not that this week is flowerless. But the flowers are little lonely things, here and there: the early purple orchid, ruddy and very much alive, you come across occasionally, then the little groups of bee-orchid, with their ragged concerted indifference to their appearance. Also there are the huge bud-spikes of the stout, thick-flowering pink orchid, huge buds like fat ears of wheat, hard-purple and splendid. But already odd grains of the wheat-ear are open, and out of the purple hangs the delicate pink rag of a floweret. Also there are very lovely and choice cream-coloured orchids with brown spots on the long and delicate lip. These grow in the more moist places, and have exotic tender spikes, very rare-seeming. Another orchid is a little, pretty yellow one.

But orchids, somehow, do not make a summer. They are too aloof and individual. The little slate-blue scabious is out, but not enough to raise an appearance. Later on, under the real hot sun, he will bob into notice. And by the edges of the paths there are odd rosy cushions of wild thyme. Yet these, too, are rather samples than the genuine thing. Wait another month, for wild thyme.

The same with the irises. Here and there, in fringes along the upper edge of terraces, and in odd bunches among the stones, the dark-purple iris sticks up. It is beautiful, but it hardly counts. There is not enough of it, and it is torn and buffeted by too many winds. First the wind blows with all its might from the Mediterranean, not cold, but definitely wearying, with its rude and insistent pushing. Then, after a moment of calm, back comes a hard wind from the Adriatic, cold and disheartening. Between the two of them, the dark-purple iris flutters and tatters and curls as if it were burnt: while the little yellow rock-rose streams at the end of its thin stalk, and wishes it had not been in such a hurry to come out.

There is really no hurry. By May, the great winds will drop, and the great sun will shake off his harassments. Then the nightingale will sing an unbroken song, and the discreet, barely audible Tuscan cuckoo will be a little more audible. Then the lovely pale-lilac irises will come out in all their showering abundance of tender, proud, spiky bloom, till the air will gleam with mauve, and a new crystalline lightness will be everywhere.

The iris is half-wild, half-cultivated. The peasants sometimes dig up the roots, iris root, orris root (orris powder, the perfume that is still used). So, in May, you will find ledges and terraces, fields just lit up with the mauve light of irises, and so much scent in the air, you do not notice it, you do not even know it. It is all the flowers of iris, before the olive invisibly blooms.

There will be tufts of iris everywhere, rising up proud and tender. When the rose-coloured wild gladiolus is mingled in the corn, and the love-in-the-mist opens blue: in May and June, before the corn is cut.

But as yet it is neither May nor June, but end of April, the pause between spring and summer, the nightingale singing interruptedly, the bean-flowers dying in the bean-fields, the bean-perfume passing with spring, the little birds hatching in the nests, the olives pruned, and the vines, the last bit of late ploughing finished, and not much work to hand, now, not until the peas are ready to pick, in another two weeks or so. Then all the peasants will be crouching between the pea-rows, endlessly, endlessly gathering peas, in the long pea-harvest which lasts two months.

So the change, the endless and rapid change. In the sunny countries, the change seems more vivid, and more complete than in the grey countries. In the grey countries, there is a grey or dark permanency, over whose surface passes change ephemeral, leaving no real mark. In England, winters and summers shadowily give place to one another. But underneath lies the grey substratum, the permanency of cold, dark reality where bulbs live, and reality is bulbous, a thing of endurance and stored-up, starchy energy.

But in the sunny countries, change is the reality and permanence is artificial and a condition of imprisonment. In the North, man tends instinctively to imagine, to conceive that the sun is lighted like a candle, in an everlasting darkness, and that one day the candle will go out, the sun will be exhausted, and the everlasting dark will resume uninterrupted sway. Hence, to the northerner, the phenomenal world is essentially tragical, because it is temporal and must cease to exist. Its very existence implies ceasing to exist, and this is the root of the feeling of tragedy.

But to the southerner, the sun is so dominant that, if every phenomenal body disappeared out of the universe, nothing would remain but bright luminousness, sunniness. The absolute is sunniness; and shadow, or dark, is only merely relative: merely the result of something getting between one and the sun.

This is the instinctive feeling of the ordinary southerner. Of course, if you start to *reason,* you may argue that the sun is a phenomenal body. Therefore it came into existence, therefore it will pass out of existence, therefore the very sun is tragic in its nature.

But this is just argument. We think, because we have to light a candle in the dark, therefore some First Cause had to kindle the sun in the infinite darkness of the beginning.

The argument is entirely shortsighted and specious. We do not know in the least whether the sun ever came into existence, and we have not the slightest possible ground for conjecturing that the sun will ever pass out of existence. All that we do know, by actual experience, is that shadow comes into being when some material object intervenes between us and the sun, and that shadow ceases to exist when the intervening object is removed. So that, of all temporal or transitory or bound-to-cease things that haunt our existence, shadow or darkness, is the one which is purely and simply temporal. We can think of death, if we like, as of something permanently intervening between us and the sun: and this is at the root of the southern, under-world idea of death. But this doesn't alter the sun at all. As far as experience goes, in the human race, the one thing that is always there is the shining sun, and dark shadow is an accident of intervention.

Hence, strictly, there is no tragedy. The universe contains no tragedy, and man is only tragical because he is afraid of death. For my part, if the sun always shines, and always will shine, in spite of millions of clouds of words, then death, somehow, does not have many terrors. In the sunshine, even death is sunny. And there is no end to the sunshine.

That is why the rapid change of the Tuscan spring is utterly free, for me, of any sense of tragedy. "Where are the snows of yesteryear?" Why, precisely where they ought to be. Where are the little yellow aconites of eight weeks ago? I neither know nor care. They were sunny and the sun shines, and sunniness means change, and petals passing and coming.

The winter aconites sunnily came, and sunnily went. What more? The sun always shines. It is our fault if we don't think so.

HENRY BESTON
1888-1968

In the fall of 1926 Henry Beston came to live in the Fo'castle, a dune cottage of his own design, on a Massachusetts barrier beach fronting the Atlantic Ocean. The Outermost House (1928), his account of "A Year of Life on the Great Beach of Cape Cod," has become a classic of the "solitary sojourn" form of nature writing, which includes Walden *and* Pilgrim At Tinker Creek. *Unlike Thoreau, however, Beston intended not so much to put into practice certain principles of living already held as to "know this coast and share its mysterious and elemental life." His style has a sensual and rhythmic richness unsurpassed in the genre, expressing his belief that "poetry is as necessary to comprehension as science," and conveying a vivid tactile sense of his surroundings. The book is infused with an extraordinary sense of human and natural drama, all encompassed by what Beston called "the burning ritual of the year." He had a gift for creating memorable utterances, and* The Outermost House *contains some of the most quoted passages of twentieth-century nature writing.*

From THE OUTERMOST HOUSE: A YEAR OF LIFE
ON THE GREAT BEACH OF CAPE COD

AUTUMN, OCEAN, AND BIRDS

There is a new sound on the beach, and a greater sound. Slowly, and day by day, the surf grows heavier, and down the long miles of the beach, at the lonely stations, men hear the coming winter in the roar. Mornings

The Outermost House: A Year of Life on the Great Beach of Cape Cod (Garden City, N.Y.: Doubleday, 1928).

and evenings grow cold, the northwest wind grows cold; the last crescent of the month's moon, discovered by chance in a pale morning sky, stands north of the sun. Autumn ripens faster on the beach than on the marshes and the dunes. Westward and landward there is colour; seaward, bright space and austerity. Lifted to the sky, the dying grasses on the dune tops' rim tremble and lean seaward in the wind, wraiths of sand course flat along the beach, the hiss of sand mingles its thin stridency with the new thunder of the sea.

I have been spending my afternoons gathering driftwood and observing birds. The skies being clear, noonday suns take something of the bite out of the wind, and now and then a warmish west-sou'westerly finds its way back into the world. Into the bright, vast days I go, shouldering home my sticks and broken boards and driving shore birds on ahead of me, putting up sanderlings and sandpipers, ringnecks and knots, plovers and killdeer, coveys of a dozen, little flocks, great flocks, compact assemblies with a regimented air. For a fortnight past, October 9th to October 23d, an enormous population of the migrants has been "stopping over" on my Eastham sands, gathering, resting, feeding, and commingling. They come, they go, they melt away, they gather again; for actual miles the intricate and inter-crisscross pattern of their feet runs unbroken along the tide rim of Cape Cod.

Yet it is no confused and careless horde through which I go, but an army. Some spirit of discipline and unity has passed over these countless little brains, waking in each flock a conscious sense of its collective self and giving each bird a sense of himself as a member of some migrant company. Lone fliers are rare, and when seen have an air of being in pursuit of some flock which has overlooked them and gone on. Swift as the wind they fly, speeding along the breakers with the directness of a runner down a course, and I read fear in their speed. Sometimes I see them find their own and settle down beside them half a mile ahead, sometimes they melt away into a vista of surf and sky, still speeding on, still seeking.

The general multitude, it would seem, consists of birds who have spent the summer somewhere on the outer Cape and of autumn reinforcements from the north.

I see the flocks best when they are feeding on the edge of a tide which rises to its flood on the later afternoon. No summer blur of breaker mist or glassiness of heat now obscures these outer distances, and as on I stride, keeping to the lower beach when returning with a load, I can see birds and more birds and ever more birds ahead. Every last advance of a dissolved breaker, coursing on, flat and seething, has those who run away before it, turning its flank or fluttering up when too closely pursued;

every retreating in-sucked slide has those who follow it back, eagerly dipping and gleaning. Having fed, the birds fly up to the upper beach and sit there for hours in the luke-cold wind, flock by flock, assembly by assembly. The ocean thunders, pale wisps and windy tatters of wintry cloud sail over the dunes, and the sandpipers stand on one leg and dream, their heads tousled deep into their feathers.

I wonder where these thousands spend the night. Waking the other morning just before sunrise, I hurried into my clothes and went down to the beach. North and then south I strolled, along an ebbing tide, and north and south the great beach was as empty of bird life as the sky. Far to the south, I remember now, a frightened pair of semipalmated sandpipers did rise from somewhere on the upper beach and fly toward me swift and voiceless, pass me on the flank, and settle by the water's edge a hundred yards or so behind. They instantly began to run about and feed, and as I watched them an orange sun floated up over the horizon with the speed and solemnity of an Olympian balloon.

The tide being high these days late in the afternoon, the birds begin to muster on the beach about ten o'clock in the morning. Some fly over from the salt meadows, some arrive flying along the beach, some drop from the sky. I startle up a first group on turning from the upper beach to the lower. I walk directly at the birds—a general apprehension, a rally, a scutter ahead, and the birds are gone. Standing on the beach, fresh claw marks at my feet, I watch the lovely sight of the group instantly turned into a constellation of birds, into a fugitive pleiades whose living stars keep their chance positions; I watch the spiralling flight, the momentary tilts of the white bellies, the alternate shows of the clustered, grayish backs. The group next ahead, though wary from the first, continues feeding. I draw nearer; a few run ahead as if to escape me afoot, others stop and prepare to fly; nearer still, the birds can stand no more; another rally, another scutter, and they are following their kin along the surges.

No aspect of nature on this beach is more mysterious to me than the flights of these shorebird constellations. The constellation forms, as I have hinted, in an instant of time, and in that same instant develops its own will. Birds which have been feeding yards away from each other, each one individually busy for his individual body's sake, suddenly fuse into this new volition and, flying, rise as one, coast as one, tilt their dozen bodies as one, and as one wheel off on the course which the new group will has determined. There is no such thing, I may add, as a lead bird or guide. Had I more space I should like nothing better than to discuss this new will and its instant or origin, but I do not want to crowd this part of my chapter, and must therefore leave the problem to all who study the psychic relations between the individual and a surrounding many. My special interest is rather the instant and synchronous obedience of each speeding body to the new volition. By what means, by what methods of communication does this will so suffuse the living constellation that its dozen or more tiny brains know it and obey it in such an instancy of time? Are we to believe that these birds, all of them, are *machina,* as Descartes long ago insisted, mere mechanisms of flesh and bone so exquisitely alike that each cogwheel brain, encountering the same environmental forces, synchronously lets slip the same mechanic ratchet? or is there some psychic relation between these creatures? Does some current flow through them and between them as they fly? Schools of fish, I am told, make similar mass changes of direction. I saw such a thing once, but of that more anon.

We need another and a wiser and perhaps a more mystical concept of animals. Remote from universal nature, and living by complicated artifice, man in civilization surveys the creature through the glass of his knowledge and sees thereby a feather magnified and the whole image in distortion. We patronize them for their incompleteness, for their tragic fate of having taken form so far below ourselves. And therein we err, and greatly err. For the animal shall not be measured by man. In a world older and more complete than ours they move finished and complete, gifted with extensions of the senses we have lost or never attained, living by voices we shall never hear. They are not brethren, they are not underlings; they are other nations, caught with ourselves in the net of life and time, fellow prisoners of the splendour and travail of the earth.

The afternoon sun sinks red as fire; the tide climbs the beach, its foam a strange crimson; miles out, a freighter goes north, emerging from the shoals. *   *   *

NIGHT ON THE GREAT BEACH

Our fantastic civilization has fallen out of touch with many aspects of nature, and with none more completely than with night. Primitive folk, gathered at a cave mouth round a fire, do not fear night; they fear, rather, the energies and creatures to whom night gives power; we of the age of the machines, having delivered ourselves of nocturnal enemies, now have a dislike of night itself. With lights and ever more lights, we drive the holiness and beauty of night back to the forests and the sea; the little villages, the crossroads even, will have none of it. Are modern folk, perhaps, afraid of night? Do they fear that vast serenity, the mystery of infinite space, the austerity of stars? Having made themselves at home in a civilization obsessed with power, which explains its whole world in terms of energy, do they fear at night for their dull acquiescence and the pattern of their beliefs? Be the answer what it will, to-day's civilization is full of people who have not the slightest notion of the character or the poetry of night, who have never even seen night. Yet to live thus, to know only artificial night, is as absurd and evil as to know only artificial day.

Night is very beautiful on this great beach. It is the true other half of the day's tremendous wheel; no lights without meaning stab or trouble it; it is beauty, it is fulfilment, it is rest. Thin clouds float in these heavens, islands of obscurity in a splendour of space and stars: the Milky Way bridges earth and ocean; the beach resolves itself into a unity of form, its summer lagoons, its slopes and uplands merging; against the western sky and the falling bow of sun rise the silent and superb undulations of the dunes.

My nights are at their darkest when a dense fog streams in from the sea under a black, unbroken floor of cloud. Such nights are rare, but are most to be expected when fog gathers off the coast in early summer; this last Wednesday night was the darkest I have known. Between ten o'-clock and two in the morning three vessels stranded on the outer beach—a fisherman, a four-masted schooner, and a beam trawler. The fisherman and the schooner have been towed off, but the trawler, they say, is still ashore.

I went down to the beach that night just after ten o'clock. So utterly black, pitch dark it was, and so thick with moisture and trailing showers, that there was no sign whatever of the beam of Nauset; the sea was only a sound, and when I reached the edge of the surf the dunes themselves had disappeared behind. I stood as isolate in that immensity of rain and night as I might have stood in interplanetary space. The sea was troubled and noisy, and when I opened the darkness with an outlined cone of light from my electric torch I saw that the waves were washing up green coils of sea grass, all coldly wet and bright in the motionless and unnatural radiance. Far off a single ship was groaning its way along the shoals. The fog was compact of the finest moisture; passing by, it spun itself into my lens of light like a kind of strange, aërial, and liquid silk. Effin Chalke, the new coast guard, passed me going north, and told me that he had had news at the halfway house of the schooner at Cahoon's.

It was dark, pitch dark to my eye, yet complete darkness, I imagine, is exceedingly rare, perhaps unknown in outer nature. The nearest natural approximation to it is probably the gloom of forest country buried in night and cloud. Dark as the night was here, there was still light on the surface of the planet. Standing on the shelving beach, with the surf breaking at my feet, I could see the endless wild uprush, slide, and withdrawal of the sea's white rim of foam. The men at Nauset tell me that on such nights they follow along this vague crawl of whiteness, trusting to habit and a sixth sense to warn them of their approach to the halfway house.

Animals descend by starlight to the beach, North, beyond the dunes, muskrats forsake the cliff and nose about in the driftwood and weed, leaving intricate trails and figure eights to be obliterated by the day; the lesser folk—the mice, the occasional small sand-coloured toads, the burrowing moles—keep to the upper beach and leave their tiny footprints under the overhanging wall. In autumn skunks, beset by a shrinking larder, go beach combing early in the night. The animal is by preference a clean feeder and turns up his nose at rankness. I almost stepped on a big fellow one night as I was walking north to meet the first man south from Nauset. There was a scamper, and the creature ran up the beach from under my feet; alarmed he certainly was, yet was he contained and continent. Deer are frequently seen, especially north of the light. I find their tracks upon the summer dunes.

Years ago, while camping on this beach north of Nauset, I went for a stroll along the top of the cliff at break of dawn. Though the path followed close enough along the edge, the beach below was often hidden, and I looked directly from the height to the flush of sunrise at sea. Presently the path, turning, approached the brink of the earth precipice, and on the beach below, in the cool, wet rosiness of dawn, I saw three deer playing. They frolicked, rose on their hind legs, scampered off, and returned again, and were merry. Just before sunrise they trotted off north together down the beach toward a hollow in the cliff and the path that climbs it.

Occasionally a sea creature visits the shore at night. Lone coast guardsmen, trudging the sand at some deserted hour, have been startled by seals. One man fell flat on a creature's back, and it drew away from under him, flippering toward the sea, with a sound "halfway between a squeal and a bark." I myself once had rather a start. It was long after sundown, the light dying and uncertain, and I was walking home on the top level of the beach and close along the slope descending to the ebbing tide. A little more than halfway to the Fo'castle a huge unexpected something suddenly writhed horribly in the darkness under my bare foot. I had stepped on a skate left stranded by some recent crest of surf, and my weight had momentarily annoyed it back to life.

Facing north, the beam of Nauset becomes part of the dune night. As I walk toward it, I see the lantern, now as a star of light which waxes and wanes three mathematical times, now as a lovely pale flare of light behind the rounded summits of the dunes. The changes in the atmosphere change the colour of the beam; it is now whitish, now flame golden, now golden red; it changes its form as well, from a star to a blare of light, from a blare of light to a cone of radiance sweeping a circumference of fog. To the west of Nauset I often see the apocalyptic flash of the great light at the Highland reflected on the clouds or even on the moisture in the starlit air, and, seeing it, I often think of the pleasant hours I have spent there when George and Mary Smith were at the light and I had the good fortune to visit as their guest. Instead of going to sleep in the room under the eaves, I would lie awake, looking out of a window to the great spokes of light revolving as solemnly as a part of the universe.

All night long the lights of coastwise vessels pass at sea, green lights going south, red lights moving north. Fishing schooners and flounder draggers anchor two or three miles out, and keep a bright riding light burning on the mast. I see them come to anchor at sundown, but I rarely see them go, for they are off at dawn. When busy at night, these fishermen illumine their decks with a scatter of oil flares. From shore, the ships might be thought afire. I have watched the scene through a night glass. I could see no smoke, only the waving flares, the reddish radiance on sail and rigging, an edge of reflection overside, and the enormous night and sea beyond.

One July night, as I returned at three o'clock from an expedition north, the whole night, in one strange, burning instant, turned into a phantom day. I stopped and, questioning, stared about. An enormous meteor, the largest I have ever seen, was consuming itself in an effulgence of light west of the zenith. Beach and dune and ocean appeared out of nothing, shadowless and motionless, a landscape whose every tremor and vibration were stilled, a landscape in a dream.

The beach at night has a voice all its own, a sound in fullest harmony with its spirit and mood—with its little, dry noise of sand forever moving, with its solemn, overspilling, rhythmic seas, with its eternity of stars that sometimes seem to hang down like lamps from the high heavens—and that sound the piping of a bird. As I walk the beach in early summer my solitary coming disturbs it on its nest, and it flies away, troubled, invisible, piping its sweet, plaintive cry. The bird I write of is the piping plover, *Charadrius melodus,* sometimes called the beach plover or the mourning bird. Its note is a whistled syllable, the loveliest musical note, I think, sounded by any North Atlantic bird.

Now that summer is here I often cook myself a camp supper on the beach. Beyond the crackling, salt-yellow driftwood flame, over the pyramid of barrel staves, broken boards, and old sticks all atwist with climbing fire, the unseen ocean thunders and booms, the breaker sounding hollow as it falls. The wall of the sand cliff behind, with its rim of grass and withering roots, its sandy crumblings and erosions, stands gilded with flame; wind cries over it; a covey of sandpipers pass between the ocean and the fire. There are stars, and to the south Scorpio hangs curving down the sky with ringed Saturn shining in his claw.

Learn to reverence night and to put away the vulgar fear of it, for, with the banishment of night from the experience of man, there vanishes as well a religious emotion, a poetic mood, which gives depth to the adventure of humanity. By day, space is one with the earth and with man—it is his sun that is shining, his clouds that are floating past; at night, space is his no more. When the great earth, abandoning day, rolls up the deeps of the heavens and the universe, a new door opens for the human spirit, and there are few so clownish that some awareness of the mystery of being does not touch them as they gaze. For a moment of night we have a glimpse of ourselves and of our world islanded in its stream of stars—pilgrims of mortality, voyaging between horizons across eternal seas of space and time. Fugitive though the instant be, the spirit of man is, during it, ennobled by a genuine moment of emotional dignity, and poetry makes its own both the human spirit and experience. ✳   ✳   ✳

ORION RISES ON THE DUNES

So came August to its close, ending its last day with a night so luminous and still that a mood came over me to sleep out on the open beach under the stars. There are nights in summer when darkness and ebbing tide quiet the universal wind, and this August night was full of that quiet of absence, and the sky was clear. South of my house, between the bold fan of a dune and the wall of a plateau, a sheltered hollow opens seaward, and to this nook I went, shouldering my blankets sailorwise. In the star-shine the hollow was darker than the immense and solitary beach, and its floor was still pleasantly warm with the overflow of day.

I fell asleep uneasily, and woke again as one wakes out-of-doors. The vague walls about me breathed a pleasant smell of sand, there was no sound, and the broken circle of grass above was as motionless as something in a house. Waking again, hours afterward, I felt the air grown colder and heard a little advancing noise of waves. It was still night. Sleep gone and past recapture, I drew on my clothes and went to the beach. In the luminous east, two great stars aslant were rising clear of the exhalations of darkness gathered at the rim of night and ocean—Betelgeuse and Bellatrix, the shoulders of Orion. Autumn had come, and the Giant stood again at the horizon of day and the ebbing year, his belt still hidden in the bank of cloud, his feet in the deeps of space and the far surges of the sea.

My year upon the beach had come full circle; it was time to close my door. Seeing the great suns, I thought of the last time I marked them in the spring, in the April west above the moors, dying into the light and sinking. I saw them of old above the iron waves of black December, sparkling afar. Now, once again, the Hunter rose to drive summer south before him, once again autumn followed on his steps. I had seen the ritual of the sun; I had shared the elemental world. Wraiths of memories began to take shape. I saw the sleet of the great storm slanting down again into the grass under the thin seepage of moon, the blue-white spill of an immense billow on the outer bar, the swans in the high October sky, the sunset madness and splendour of the year's terns over the dunes, the clouds of beach birds arriving, the eagle solitary in the blue. And because I had known this outer and secret world, and been able to live as I had lived, reverence and gratitude greater and deeper than ever possessed me, sweeping every emotion else aside, and space and silence an instant closed together over life. Then time gathered again like a cloud, and presently the stars began to pale over an ocean still dark with remembered night.

During the months that have passed since that September morning some have asked me what understanding of Nature one shapes from so strange a year? I would answer that one's first appreciation is a sense that the creation is still going on, that the creative forces are as great and as active to-day as they have ever been, and that to-morrow's morning will be as heroic as any of the world. *Creation is here and now.* So near is man to the creative pageant, so much a part is he of the endless and incredible experiment, that any glimpse he may have will be but the revelation of a moment, a solitary note heard in a symphony thundering through debatable existences of time. Poetry is as necessary to comprehension as science. It is as impossible to live without reverence as it is without joy.

And what of Nature itself, you say—that callous and cruel engine, red in tooth and fang? Well, it is not so much of an engine as you think. As for "red in tooth and fang," whenever I hear the phrase or its intellectual echoes I know that some passer-by has been getting life from books. It is true that there are grim arrangements. Beware of judging them by whatever human values are in style. As well expect Nature to answer to your human values as to come into your house and sit in a chair. The economy of nature, its checks and balances, its measurements of competing life— all this is its great marvel and has an ethic of its own. Live in Nature, and you will soon see that for all its non-human rhythm, it is no cave of pain. As I write I think of my beloved birds of the great beach, and of their beauty and their zest of living. And if there are fears, know also that Nature has its unexpected and unappreciated mercies.

Whatever attitude to human existence you fashion for yourself, know that it is valid only if it be the shadow of an attitude to Nature. A human life, so often likened to a spectacle upon a stage, is more justly a ritual. The ancient values of dignity, beauty, and poetry which sustain it are of Nature's inspiration; they are born of the mystery and beauty of the world. Do no dishonour to the earth lest you dishonour the spirit of man. Hold your hands out over the earth as over a flame. To all who loved her, who open to her the doors of their veins, she gives of her strength, sustaining them with her own measureless tremor of dark life. Touch the earth, love the earth, honour the earth, her plains, her valleys, her hills, and her seas; rest your spirit in her solitary places. For the gifts of life are the earth's and they are given to all, and they are the songs of birds at daybreak, Orion and the Bear, and dawn seen over ocean from the beach.

ALDO LEOPOLD
1888-1948

Leopold was a professional conservationist—a forester who early understood the concept and value of wilderness, a professor of wildlife management at the University of Wisconsin who became a champion of the predators' role within a healthy, stable ecosystem. But his chief importance within the environmental movement and the literature of nature alike is as the author of A Sand County Almanac, *published in 1949, shortly after he had died fighting a fire.*

As Leopold follows the year through its circle, at the rural Wisconsin "shack" where his family spent weekends and vacations, he echoes Thoreau's celebration of a quiet landscape. He gives to chickadees and pine seedlings the same attentiveness other nature writers bring to a sperm whale or a sequoia. At the same time, he is a magnificent teacher about the way the natural environment has been impoverished and about some of his own experiments at restoring fertility and diversity to his "sand farm." The clarity of Aldo Leopold's observations and the "Land Ethic" which emerges from them have made A Sand County Almanac *a major influence on American attitudes towards our natural environment.*

From A Sand County Almanac

MARSHLAND ELEGY

A dawn wind stirs on the great marsh. With almost imperceptible slowness it rolls a bank of fog across the wide morass. Like the white ghost of a glacier the mists advance, riding over phalanxes of tamarack, sliding across bog-meadows heavy with dew. A single silence hangs from horizon to horizon.

Out of some far recess of the sky a tinkling of little bells falls soft upon the listening land. Then again silence. Now comes a baying of some sweet-throated hound, soon the clamor of a responding pack. Then a far clear blast of hunting horns, out of the sky into the fog.

High horns, low horns, silence, and finally a pandemonium of trumpets, rattles, croaks, and cries that almost shakes the bog with its nearness, but without yet disclosing whence it comes. At last a glint of sun reveals the approach of a great echelon of birds. On motionless wing they emerge from the lifting mists, sweep a final arc of sky, and settle in clangorous descending spirals to their feeding grounds. A new day has begun on the crane marsh.

A sense of time lies thick and heavy on such a place. Yearly since the ice age it has awakened each spring to the clangor of cranes. The peat layers that comprise the bog are laid down in the basin of an ancient lake. The cranes stand, as it were, upon the sodden pages of their own history. These peats are the compressed remains of the mosses that clogged the pools, of the tamaracks that spread over the moss, of the cranes that bugled over the tamaracks since the retreat of the ice sheet. An endless caravan of generations has built of its own bones this bridge into the future, this habitat where the oncoming host again may live and breed and die.

To what end? Out on the bog a crane, gulping some luckless frog, springs his ungainly hulk into the air and flails the morning sun with mighty wings. The tamaracks re-echo with his bugled certitude. He seems to know.

Our ability to perceive quality in nature begins, as in art, with the pretty. It expands through successive stages of the beautiful to values as yet uncaptured by language. The quality of cranes lies, I think, in this higher gamut, as yet beyond the reach of words.

A Sand County Almanac (New York: Oxford University Press, 1949).

This much, though, can be said: our appreciation of the crane grows with the slow unraveling of earthly history. His tribe, we now know, stems out of the remote Eocene. The other members of the fauna in which he originated are long since entombed within the hills. When we hear his call we hear no mere bird. We hear the trumpet in the orchestra of evolution. He is the symbol of our untamable past, of that incredible sweep of millennia which underlies and conditions the daily affairs of birds and men.

And so they live and have their being—these cranes—not in the constricted present, but in the wider reaches of evolutionary time. Their annual return is the ticking of the geologic clock. Upon the place of their return they confer a peculiar distinction. Amid the endless mediocrity of the commonplace, a crane marsh holds a palentological patent of nobility, won in the march of aeons, and revocable only by shotgun. The sadness discernible in some marshes arises, perhaps, from their once having harbored cranes. Now they stand humbled, adrift in history.

Some sense of this quality in cranes seems to have been felt by sportsmen and ornithologists of all ages. Upon such quarry as this the Holy Roman Emperor Frederick loosed his gyrfalcons. Upon such quarry as this once swooped the hawks of Kublai Khan. Marco Polo tells us: "He derives the highest amusement from sporting with gyrfalcons and hawks. At Changanor the Khan has a great Palace surrounded by a fine plain where are found cranes in great numbers. He causes millet and other grains to be sown in order that the birds may not want."

The ornithologist Bengt Berg, seeing cranes as a boy upon the Swedish heaths, forthwith made them his life work. He followed them to Africa and discovered their winter retreat on the White Nile. He says of his first encounter: "It was a spectacle which eclipsed the flight of the roc in the Thousand and One Nights."

When the glacier came down out of the north, crunching hills and gouging valleys, some adventuring rampart of the ice climbed the Baraboo Hills and fell back into the outlet gorge of the Wisconsin River. The swollen waters backed up and formed a lake half as long as the state, bordered on the east by cliffs of ice, and fed by the torrents that fell from melting mountains. The shorelines of this old lake are still visible; its bottom is the bottom of the great marsh.

The lake rose through the centuries, finally spilling over east of the Baraboo range. There it cut a new channel for the river, and thus drained itself. To the residual lagoons came the cranes, bugling the defeat of the retreating winter, summoning the on-creeping host of living things to their collective task of marsh-building. Floating bogs of sphagnum moss clogged the lowered waters, filled them. Sedge and leatherleaf, tamarack and spruce successively advanced over the bog, anchoring it by their root fabric, sucking out its water, making peat. The lagoons disappeared, but not the cranes. To the moss-meadows that replaced the ancient waterways they returned each spring to dance and bugle and rear their gangling sorrel-colored young. These, albeit birds, are not properly called chicks, but *colts*. I cannot explain why. On some dewy June morning watch them gambol over their ancestral pastures at the heels of the roan mare, and you will see for yourself.

One year not long ago a French trapper in buckskins pushed his canoe up one of the moss-clogged creeks that thread the great marsh. At this attempt to invade their miry stronghold the cranes gave vent to loud and ribald laughter. A century or two later Englishmen came in covered wagons. They chopped clearings in the timbered moraines that border the marsh, and in them planted corn and buckwheat. They did not intend, like the Great Khan at Changanor, to feed the cranes. But the cranes do not question the intent of glaciers, emperors, or pioneers. They ate the grain, and when some irate farmer failed to concede their usufruct in his corn, they trumpeted a warning and sailed across the marsh to another farm.

There was no alfalfa in those days, and the hill-farms made poor hay land, especially in dry years. One dry year someone set a fire in the tamaracks. The burn grew up quickly to bluejoint grass, which, when cleared of dead trees, made a dependable hay meadow. After that, each August, men appeared to cut hay. In winter, after the cranes had gone South, they drove wagons over the frozen bogs and hauled the hay to their farms in the hills. Yearly they plied the marsh with fire and axe, and in two short decades hay meadows dotted the whole expanse.

Each August when the haymakers came to pitch their camps, singing and drinking and lashing their teams with whip and tongue, the cranes whinnied to their colts and retreated to the far fastnesses. 'Red shite-pokes' the haymakers called them, from the rusty hue which at that season often stains the battleship-gray of crane plumage. After the hay was stacked and the marsh again their own, the cranes returned, to call down out of October skies the migrant flocks from Canada. Together they wheeled over the new-cut stubbles and raided the corn until frosts gave the signal for the winter exodus.

These haymeadow days were the Arcadian age for marsh dwellers. Man and beast, plant and soil lived on and with each other in mutual toleration, to the mutual benefit of all. The marsh might have kept on producing hay and prairie chickens, deer and muskrat, crane-music and cranberries forever.

The new overlords did not understand this. They did not include soil, plants, or birds in their ideas of mutuality. The dividends of such a balanced economy were too modest. They envisaged farms not only around, but *in* the marsh. An epidemic of ditch-digging and land-booming set in. The marsh was gridironed with drainage canals, speckled with new fields and farmsteads.

But crops were poor and beset by frosts, to which the expensive ditches added an aftermath of debt. Farmers moved out. Peat beds dried, shrank, caught fire. Sun-energy out of the Pleistocene shrouded the countryside in acrid smoke. No man raised his voice against the waste, only his nose against the smell. After a dry summer not even the winter snows could extinguish the smoldering marsh. Great pockmarks were burned into field and meadow, the scars reaching down to the sands of the old lake, peat-covered these hundred centuries. Rank weeds sprang out of the ashes, to be followed after a year or two by aspen scrub. The cranes were hard put, their numbers shrinking with the remnants of unburned meadow. For them, the song of the power shovel came near being an elegy. The high priests of progress knew nothing of cranes, and cared less. What is a species more or less among engineers? What good is an undrained marsh anyhow?

For a decade or two crops grew poorer, fires deeper, wood-fields larger, and cranes scarcer, year by year. Only reflooding, it appeared, could keep the peat from burning. Meanwhile cranberry growers had, by plugging drainage ditches, reflooded a few spots and obtained good yields. Distant politicians bugled about marginal land, over-production, unemployment relief, conservation. Economists and planners came to look at the marsh. Surveyors, technicians, CCC's, buzzed about. A counter-epidemic of reflooding set in. Government bought land, resettled farmers, plugged ditches wholesale. Slowly the bogs are re-wetting. The fire-pocks become ponds. Grass fires still burn, but they can no longer burn the wetted soil.

All this, once the CCC camps were gone, was good for cranes, but not so the thickets of scrub popple that spread inexorably over the old burns, and still less the maze of new roads that inevitably follow governmental conservation. To build a road is so much simpler than to think of what the country really needs. A roadless marsh is seemingly as worthless to the alphabetical conservationist as an undrained one was to the empire-builders. Solitude, the one natural resource still undowered of alphabets, is so far recognized as valuable only by ornithologists and cranes.

Thus always does history, whether of marsh or market place, end in paradox. The ultimate value in these marshes is wildness, and the crane is wildness incarnate. But all conservation of wildness is self-defeating, for to cherish we must see and fondle, and when enough have seen and fondled, there is no wilderness left to cherish.

Some day, perhaps in the very process of our benefactions, perhaps in the fullness of geologic time, the last crane will trumpet his farewell and spiral skyward from the great marsh. High out of the clouds will fall the sound of hunting horns, the baying of the phantom pack, the tinkle of little bells, and then a silence never to be broken, unless perchance in some far pasture of the Milky Way.

THINKING LIKE A MOUNTAIN

A deep chesty bawl echoes from rimrock to rimrock, rolls down the mountain, and fades into the far blackness of the night. It is an outburst of wild defiant sorrow, and of contempt for all the adversities of the world.

Every living thing (and perhaps many a dead one as well) pays heed to that call. To the deer it is a reminder of the way of all flesh, to the pine a forecast of midnight scuffles and of blood upon the snow, to the coyote a promise of gleanings to come, to the cowman a threat of red ink at the bank, to the hunter a challenge of fang against bullet. Yet behind these obvious and immediate hopes and fears there lies a deeper meaning, known only to the mountain itself. *Only the mountain has lived long enough to listen objectively to the howl of a wolf.*

Those unable to decipher the hidden meaning know nevertheless that it is there, for it is felt in all wolf country, and distinguishes that country from all other land. It tingles in the spine of all who hear wolves by night, or who scan their tracks by day. Even without sight or sound of wolf, it is implicit in a hundred small events: the midnight whinny of a pack horse, the rattle of rolling rocks, the bound of a fleeing deer, the way shadows lie under the spruces. Only the ineducable tyro can fail to sense the presence or absence of wolves, or the fact that mountains have a secret opinion about them.

My own conviction on this score dates from the day I saw a wolf die. We were eating lunch on a high rimrock, at the foot of which a turbulent river elbowed its way. We saw what we thought was a doe fording the torrent, her breast awash in white water. When she climbed the bank toward us and shook out her tail, we realized our error: it was a wolf. A half-dozen others, evidently grown pups, sprang from the willows and all joined in a welcoming mêlée of wagging tails and playful maulings.

What was literally a pile of wolves writhed and tumbled in the center of an open flat at the foot of our rimrock.

In those days we had never heard of passing up a chance to kill a wolf. In a second we were pumping lead into the pack, but with more excitement than accuracy: how to aim a steep downhill shot is always confusing. When our rifles were empty, the old wolf was down, and a pup was dragging a leg into impassable slide-rocks.

We reached the old wolf in time to watch a fierce green fire dying in her eyes. I realized then, and have known ever since, that there was something new to me in those eyes—something known only to her and to the mountain. I was young then, and full of trigger-itch; I thought that because fewer wolves meant more deer, that no wolves would mean hunters' paradise. But after seeing the green fire die, I sensed that neither the wolf nor the mountain agreed with such a view.

Since then I have lived to see state after state extirpate its wolves. I have watched the face of many a newly wolfless mountain, and seen the south-facing slopes wrinkle with a maze of new deer trails. I have seen every edible bush and seedling browsed, first to anaemic desuetude, and then to death. I have seen every edible tree defoliated to the height of a saddlehorn. Such a mountain looks as if someone had given God a new pruning shears, and forbidden Him all other exercise. In the end the starved bones of the hoped-for deer herd, dead of its own too-much, bleach with the bones of the dead sage, or molder under the high-lined junipers.

I now suspect that just as a deer herd lives in mortal fear of its wolves, so does a mountain live in mortal fear of its deer. And perhaps with better cause, for while a buck pulled down by wolves can be replaced in two or three years, a range pulled down by too many deer may fail of replacement in as many decades.

So also with cows. The cowman who cleans his range of wolves does not realize that he is taking over the wolf's job of trimming the herd to fit the range. He has not learned to think like a mountain. Hence we have dustbowls, and rivers washing the future into the sea.

THE LAND ETHIC

When god-like Odysseus returned from the wars in Troy, he hanged all on one rope a dozen slave-girls of his household whom he suspected of misbehavior during his absence.

This hanging involved no question of propriety. The girls were property. The disposal of property was then, as now, a matter of expediency, not of right and wrong.

Concepts of right and wrong were not lacking from Odysseus' Greece: witness the fidelity of his wife through the long years before at last his black-prowed galleys clove the wine-dark seas for home. The ethical structure of that day covered wives, but had not yet been extended to human chattels. During the three thousand years which have since elapsed, ethical criteria have been extended to many fields of conduct, with corresponding shrinkages in those judged by expediency only.

THE ETHICAL SEQUENCE

This extension of ethics, so far studied only by philosophers, is actually a process in ecological evolution. Its sequences may be described in ecological as well as in philosophical terms. An ethic, ecologically, is a limitation on freedom of action in the struggle for existence. An ethic, philosophically, is a differentiation of social from anti-social conduct. These are two definitions of one thing. The thing has its origin in the tendency of interdependent individuals or groups to evolve modes of co-operation. The ecologist calls these symbioses. Politics and economics are advanced symbioses in which the original free-for-all competition has been replaced, in part, by co-operative mechanisms with an ethical content.

The complexity of co-operative mechanisms has increased with population density, and with the efficiency of tools. It was simpler, for example, to define the anti-social uses of sticks and stones in the days of the mastodons than of bullets and billboards in the age of motors.

The first ethics dealt with the relation between individuals; the Mosaic Decalogue is an example. Later accretions dealt with the relation between the individual and society. The Golden Rule tries to integrate the individual to society; democracy to integrate social organization to the individual.

There is as yet no ethic dealing with man's relation to land and to the animals and plants which grow upon it. Land, like Odysseus' slave-girls, is still property. The land-relation is still strictly economic, entailing privileges but not obligations.

The extension of ethics to this third element in human environment is, if I read the evidence correctly, an evolutionary possibility and an ecological necessity. It is the third step in a sequence. The first two have already been taken. Individual thinkers since the days of Ezekiel and Isaiah have asserted that the despoliation of land is not only inexpedient but wrong. Society, however, has not yet affirmed their belief. I regard the present conservation movement as the embryo of such an affirmation.

An ethic may be regarded as a mode of guidance for meeting ecological situations so new or intricate, or involving such deferred reactions, that the path of social expediency is not discernible to the average individual. Animal instincts are modes of guidance for the individual in meeting such situations. Ethics are possibly a kind of community instinct in-the-making.

THE COMMUNITY CONCEPT

All ethics so far evolved rest upon a single premise: that the individual is a member of a community of interdependent parts. His instincts prompt him to compete for his place in that community, but his ethics prompt him also to co-operate (perhaps in order that there may be a place to compete for).

The land ethic simply enlarges the boundaries of the community to include soils, waters, plants, and animals, or collectively: the land.

This sounds simple: do we not already sing our love for and obligation to the land of the free and the home of the brave? Yes, but just what and whom do we love? Certainly not the soil, which we are sending helter-skelter downriver. Certainly not the waters, which we assume have no function except to turn turbines, float barges, and carry off sewage. Certainly not the plants, of which we exterminate whole communities without batting an eye. Certainly not the animals, of which we have already extirpated many of the largest and most beautiful species. A land ethic of course cannot prevent the alteration, management, and use of these "resources," but it does affirm their right to continued existence, and, at least in spots, their continued existence in a natural state.

In short, a land ethic changes the role of *Homo sapiens* from conqueror of the land-community to plain member and citizen of it. It implies respect for his fellow-members, and also respect for the community as such.

In human history, we have learned (I hope) that the conqueror role is eventually self-defeating. Why? Because it is implicit in such a role that the conqueror knows, *ex cathedra*, just what makes the community clock tick, and just what and who is valuable, and what and who is worthless, in community life. It always turns out that he knows neither, and this is why his conquests eventually defeat themselves.

In the biotic community, a parallel situation exists. Abraham knew exactly what the land was for: it was to drip milk and honey into Abraham's mouth. At the present moment, the assurance with which we regard this assumption is inverse to the degree of our education.

The ordinary citizen today assumes that science knows what makes the community clock tick; the scientist is equally sure that he does not.

He knows that the biotic mechanism is so complex that its workings may never be fully understood.

That man is, in fact, only a member of a biotic team is shown by an ecological interpretation of history. Many historical events, hitherto explained solely in terms of human enterprise, were actually biotic interactions between people and land. The characteristics of the land determined the facts quite as potently as the characteristics of the men who lived on it.

Consider, for example, the settlement of the Mississippi valley. In the years following the Revolution, three groups were contending for its control: the native Indian, the French and English traders, and the American settlers. Historians wonder what would have happened if the English at Detroit had thrown a little more weight into the Indian side of those tipsy scales which decided the outcome of the colonial migration into the cane-lands of Kentucky. It is time now to ponder the fact that the cane-lands, when subjected to the particular mixture of forces represented by the cow, plow, fire, and axe of the pioneer, became bluegrass. What if the plant succession inherent in this dark and bloody ground had, under the impact of these forces, given us some worthless sedge, shrub, or weed? Would Boone and Kenton have held out? Would there have been any overflow into Ohio, Indiana, Illinois, and Missouri? Any Louisiana Purchase? Any transcontinental union of new states? Any Civil War?

Kentucky was one sentence in the drama of history. We are commonly told what the human actors in this drama tried to do, but we are seldom told that their success, or the lack of it, hung in large degree on the reaction of particular soils to the impact of the particular forces exerted by their occupancy. In the case of Kentucky, we do not even know where the bluegrass came from—whether it is a native species, or a stowaway from Europe.

Contrast the cane-lands with what hindsight tells us about the Southwest, where the pioneers were equally brave, resourceful, and persevering. The impact of occupancy here brought no bluegrass, or other plant fitted to withstand the bumps and buffetings of hard use. This region, when grazed by livestock, reverted through a series of more and more worthless grasses, shrubs, and weeds to a condition of unstable equilibrium. Each recession of plant types bred erosion; each increment to erosion bred a further recession of plants. The result today is a progressive and mutual deterioration, not only of plants and soils, but of the animal community subsisting thereon. The early settlers did not expect this: on the ciénegas of New Mexico some even cut ditches to hasten it. So subtle has been its progress that few residents of the region are aware of it. It is quite invisible to the tourist who finds this wrecked landscape colorful and charming (as indeed it is, but it bears scant resemblance to what it was in 1848).

This same landscape was "developed" once before, but with quite different results. The Pueblo Indians settled the Southwest in pre-Columbian times, but they happened *not* to be equipped with range livestock. Their civilization expired, but not because their land expired.

In India, regions devoid of any sod-forming grass have been settled, apparently without wrecking the land, by the simple expedient of carrying the grass to the cow, rather than vice versa. (Was this the result of some deep wisdom, or was it just good luck? I do not know.)

In short, the plant succession steered the course of history; the pioneer simply demonstrated, for good or ill, what successions inhered in the land. Is history taught in this spirit? It will be, once the concept of land as a community really penetrates our intellectual life.

THE ECOLOGICAL CONSCIENCE

Conservation is a state of harmony between men and land. Despite nearly a century of propaganda, conservation still proceeds at a snail's pace; progress still consists largely of letterhead pieties and convention oratory. On the back forty we still slip two steps backward for each forward stride.

The usual answer to this dilemma is "more conservation education." No one will debate this, but is it certain that only the *volume* of education needs stepping up? Is something lacking in the *content* as well?

It is difficult to give a fair summary of its content in brief form, but, as I understand it, the content is substantially this: obey the law, vote right, join some organizations, and practice what conservation is profitable on your own land; the government will do the rest.

Is not this formula too easy to accomplish anything worth-while? It defines no right or wrong, assigns no obligation, calls for no sacrifice, implies no change in the current philosophy of values. In respect of land-use, it urges only enlightened self-interest. Just how far will such education take us? An example will perhaps yield a partial answer.

By 1930 it had become clear to all except the ecologically blind that southwestern Wisconsin's topsoil was slipping seaward. In 1933 the farmers were told that if they would adopt certain remedial practices for five years, the public would donate CCC labor to install them, plus the necessary machinery and materials. The offer was widely accepted, but the practices were widely forgotten when the five-year contract period was up. The farmers continued only those practices that yielded an immediate and visible economic gain for themselves.

This led to the idea that maybe farmers would learn more quickly if they themselves wrote the rules. Accordingly the Wisconsin Legislature in 1937 passed the Soil Conservation District Law. This said to farmers, in effect: *We, the public, will furnish you free technical service and loan you specialized machinery, if you will write your own rules for land-use. Each county may write its own rules, and these will have the force of law.* Nearly all the counties promptly organized to accept the proffered help, but after a decade of operation, *no county has yet written a single rule.* There has been visible progress in such practices as strip-cropping, pasture renovation, and soil liming, but none in fencing woodlots against grazing, and none in excluding plow and cow from steep slopes. The farmers, in short, have selected those remedial practices which were profitable anyhow, and ignored those which were profitable to the community, but not clearly profitable to themselves.

When one asks why no rules have been written, one is told that the community is not yet ready to support them; education must precede rules. But the education actually in progress makes no mention of obligations to land over and above those dictated by self-interest. The net result is that we have more education but less soil, fewer healthy woods, and as many floods as in 1937.

The puzzling aspect of such situations is that the existence of obligations over and above self-interest is taken for granted in such rural community enterprises as the betterment of roads, schools, churches, and baseball teams. Their existence is not taken for granted, nor as yet seriously discussed, in bettering the behavior of the water that falls on the land, or in the preserving of the beauty or diversity of the farm landscape. Land-use ethics are still governed wholly by economic self-interest, just as social ethics were a century ago.

To sum up: we asked the farmer to do what he conveniently could to save his soil, and he has done just that, and only that. The farmer who clears the woods off a 75 per cent slope, turns his cows into the clearing, and dumps its rainfall, rocks, and soil into the community creek, is still (if otherwise decent) a respected member of society. If he puts lime on his fields and plants his crops on contour, he is still entitled to all the privileges and emoluments of his Soil Conservation District. The District is a beautiful piece of social machinery, but it is coughing along on two cylinders because we have been too timid, and too anxious for quick success, to tell the farmer the true magnitude of his obligations. Obligations have no meaning without conscience, and the problem we face is the extension of the social conscience from people to land.

No important change in ethics was ever accomplished without an internal change in our intellectual emphasis, loyalties, affections, and convictions. The proof that conservation has not yet touched these foundations of conduct lies in the fact that philosophy and religion have not yet heard of it. In our attempt to make conservation easy, we have made it trivial.

When the logic of history hungers for bread and we hand out a stone, we are at pains to explain how much the stone resembles bread. I now describe some of the stones which serve in lieu of a land ethic.

One basic weakness in a conservation system based wholly on economic motives is that most members of the land community have no economic value. Wildflowers and songbirds are examples. Of the 22,000 higher plants and animals native to Wisconsin, it is doubtful whether more than 5 per cent can be sold, fed, eaten, or otherwise put to economic use. Yet these creatures are members of the biotic community, and if (as I believe) its stability depends on its integrity, they are entitled to continuance.

When one of these non-economic categories is threatened, and if we happen to love it, we invent subterfuges to give it economic importance. At the beginning of the century songbirds were supposed to be disappearing. Ornithologists jumped to the rescue with some distinctly shaky evidence to the effect that insects would eat us up if birds failed to control them. The evidence had to be economic in order to be valid.

It is painful to read these circumlocutions today. We have no land ethic yet, but we have at least drawn nearer the point of admitting that birds should continue as a matter of biotic right, regardless of the presence or absence of economic advantage to us.

A parallel situation exists in respect of predatory mammals, raptorial birds, and fish-eating birds. Time was when biologists somewhat overworked the evidence that these creatures preserve the health of game by killing weaklings, or that they control rodents for the farmer, or that they prey only on "worthless" species. Here again, the evidence had to be economic in order to be valid. It is only in recent years that we hear the more honest argument that predators are members of the community, and that no special interest has the right to exterminate them for the sake of a benefit, real or fancied, to itself. Unfortunately this enlightened view is still in the talk stage. In the field the extermination of predators goes merrily on: witness the impending erasure of the timber wolf by fiat of Congress, the Conservation Bureaus, and many state legislatures.

Some species of trees have been "read out of the party" by economics-minded foresters because they grow too slowly, or have too low a sale value to pay as timber crops: white cedar, tamarack, cypress, beech, and hemlock are examples. In Europe, where forestry is ecologically more advanced, the non-commercial tree species are recognized as members of the native forest community, to be preserved as such, within reason. Moreover some (like beech) have been found to have a valuable function in building up soil fertility. The interdependence of the forest and its constituent tree species, ground flora, and fauna is taken for granted.

Lack of economic value is sometimes a character not only of species or groups, but of entire biotic communities: marshes, bogs, dunes, and "deserts" are examples. Our formula in such cases is to relegate their conservation to government as refuges, monuments, or parks. The difficulty is that these communities are usually interspersed with more valuable private lands; the government cannot possibly own or control such scattered parcels. The net effect is that we have relegated some of them to ultimate extinction over large areas. If the private owner were ecologically minded, he would be proud to be the custodian of a reasonable proportion of such areas, which add diversity and beauty to his farm and to his community.

In some instances, the assumed lack of profit in these "waste" areas has proved to be wrong, but only after most of them had been done away with. The present scramble to reflood muskrat marshes is a case in point.

There is a clear tendency in American conservation to relegate to government all necessary jobs that private landowners fail to perform. Government ownership, operation, subsidy, or regulation is now widely prevalent in forestry, range management, soil and watershed management, park and wilderness conservation, fisheries management, and migratory bird management, with more to come. Most of this growth in governmental conservation is proper and logical, some of it is inevitable. That I imply no disapproval of it is implicit in the fact that I have spent most of my life working for it. Nevertheless the question arises: What is the ultimate magnitude of the enterprise? Will the tax base carry its eventual ramifications? At what point will governmental conservation, like the mastodon, become handicapped by its own dimensions? The answer, if there is any, seems to be in a land ethic, or some other force which assigns more obligation to the private landowner.

Industrial landowners and users, especially lumbermen and stockmen, are inclined to wail long and loudly about the extension of government ownership and regulation to land, but (with notable exceptions) they show little disposition to develop the only visible alternative: the voluntary practice of conservation on their own lands.

When the private landowner is asked to perform some unprofitable act for the good of the community, he today assents only with outstretched palm. If the act costs him cash this is fair and proper, but when it costs only forethought, open-mindedness, or time, the issue is at least debatable. The overwhelming growth of land-use subsidies in recent years must be ascribed, in large part, to the government's own agencies for conservation education: the land bureaus, the agricultural colleges, and the extension services. As far as I can detect, no ethical obligation toward land is taught in these institutions.

To sum up: a system of conservation based solely on economic self-interest is hopelessly lopsided. It tends to ignore, and thus eventually to eliminate, many elements in the land community that lack commercial value, but that are (as far as we know) essential to its healthy functioning. It assumes, falsely, I think, that the economic parts of the biotic clock will function without the uneconomic parts. It tends to relegate to government many functions eventually too large, too complex, or too widely dispersed to be performed by government.

An ethical obligation on the part of the private owner is the only visible remedy for these situations.

THE LAND PYRAMID

An ethic to supplement and guide the economic relation to land presupposes the existence of some mental image of land as a biotic mechanism. We can be ethical only in relation to something we can see, feel, understand, love, or otherwise have faith in.

The image commonly employed in conservation education is "the balance of nature." For reasons too lengthy to detail here, this figure of speech fails to describe accurately what little we know about the land mechanism. A much truer image is the one employed in ecology: the biotic pyramid. I shall first sketch the pyramid as a symbol of land, and later develop some of its implications in terms of land-use.

Plants absorb energy from the sun. This energy flows through a circuit called the biota, which may be represented by a pyramid consisting of layers. The bottom layer is the soil. A plant layer rests on the soil, an insect layer on the plants, a bird and rodent layer on the insects, and so on up through various animal groups to the apex layer, which consists of the larger carnivores.

The species of a layer are alike not in where they came from, or in what they look like, but rather in what they eat. Each successive layer depends on those below it for food and often for other services, and each in turn furnishes food and services to those above. Proceeding upward, each successive layer decreases in numerical abundance. Thus, for every carnivore there are hundreds of his prey, thousands of their prey, millions of insects, uncountable plants. The pyramidal form of the system reflects this numerical progression from apex to base. Man shares an intermediate layer with the bears, raccoons, and squirrels which eat both meat and vegetables.

The lines of dependency for food and other services are called food chains. Thus soil-oak-deer-Indian is a chain that has now been largely converted to soil-corn-cow-farmer. Each species, including ourselves, is a link in many chains. The deer eats a hundred plants other than oak, and the cow a hundred plants other than corn. Both, then, are links in a hundred chains. The pyramid is a tangle of chains so complex as to seem disorderly, yet the stability of the system proves it to be a highly organized structure. Its functioning depends on the co-operation and competition of its diverse parts.

In the beginning, the pyramid of life was low and squat; the food chains short and simple. Evolution has added layer after layer, link after link. Man is one of thousands of accretions to the height and complexity of the pyramid. Science has given us many doubts, but it has given us at least one certainty: the trend of evolution is to elaborate and diversify the biota.

Land, then, is not merely soil; it is a fountain of energy flowing through a circuit of soils, plants, and animals. Food chains are the living channels which conduct energy upward; death and decay return it to the soil. The circuit is not closed; some energy is dissipated in decay, some is added by absorption from the air, some is stored in soils, peats, and long-lived forests; but it is a sustained circuit, like a slowly augmented revolving fund of life. There is always a net loss by downhill wash, but this is normally small and offset by the decay of rocks. It is deposited in the ocean and, in the course of geological time, raised to form new lands and new pyramids.

The velocity and character of the upward flow of energy depend on the complex structure of the plant and animal community, much as the upward flow of sap in a tree depends on its complex cellular organization. Without this complexity, normal circulation would presumably not occur. Structure means the characteristic numbers, as well as the characteristic kinds and functions, of the component species. This interdependence between the complex structure of the land and its smooth functioning as an energy unit is one of its basic attributes.

When a change occurs in one part of the circuit, many other parts must adjust themselves to it. Change does not necessarily obstruct or divert the flow of energy; evolution is a long series of self-induced changes, the net result of which has been to elaborate the flow mechanism and to lengthen the circuit. Evolutionary changes, however, are usually slow and local. Man's invention of tools has enabled him to make changes of unprecedented violence, rapidity, and scope.

One change is in the composition of floras and faunas. The larger predators are lopped off the apex of the pyramid; food chains, for the first time in history, become shorter rather than longer. Domesticated species from other lands are substituted for wild ones, and wild ones are moved to new habitats. In this world-wide pooling of faunas and floras, some species get out of bounds as pests and diseases, others are extinguished. Such effects are seldom intended or foreseen; they represent unpredicted and often untraceable readjustments in the structure. Agricultural science is largely a race between the emergence of new pests and the emergence of new techniques for their control.

Another change touches the flow of energy through plants and animals and its return to the soil. Fertility is the ability of soil to receive, store, and release energy. Agriculture, by overdrafts on the soil, or by too radical a substitution of domestic for native species in the superstructure, may derange the channels of flow or deplete storage. Soils depleted of their storage, or of the organic matter which anchors it, wash away faster than they form. This is erosion.

Waters, like soil, are part of the energy circuit. Industry, by polluting waters or obstructing them with dams, may exclude the plants and animals necessary to keep energy in circulation.

Transportation brings about another basic change: the plants or animals grown in one region are now consumed and returned to the soil in another. Transportation taps the energy stored in rocks, and in the air, and uses it elsewhere; thus we fertilize the garden with nitrogen gleaned by the guano birds from the fishes of seas on the other side of the Equator. Thus the formerly localized and self-contained circuits are pooled on a world-wide scale.

The process of altering the pyramid for human occupation releases stored energy, and this often gives rise, during the pioneering period, to a deceptive exuberance of plant and animal life, both wild and tame. These releases of biotic capital tend to becloud or postpone the penalties of violence.

This thumbnail sketch of land as an energy circuit conveys three basic ideas:

(1) That land is not merely soil.

(2) That the native plants and animals kept the energy circuit open; others may or may not.

(3) That man-made changes are of a different order than evolutionary

changes, and have effects more comprehensive than is intended or foreseen.

These ideas, collectively, raise two basic issues: Can the land adjust itself to the new order? Can the desired alterations be accomplished with less violence?

Biotas seem to differ in their capacity to sustain violent conversion. Western Europe, for example, carries a far different pyramid than Caesar found there. Some large animals are lost; swampy forests have become meadows or plow-land; many new plants and animals are introduced, some of which escape as pests; the remaining natives are greatly changed in distribution and abundance. Yet the soil is still there and, with the help of imported nutrients, still fertile; the waters flow normally; the new structure seems to function and to persist. There is no visible stoppage or derangement of the circuit.

Western Europe, then, has a resistant biota. Its inner processes are tough, elastic, resistant to strain. No matter how violent the alterations, the pyramid, so far, has developed some new *modus vivendi* which preserves its habitability for man, and for most of the other natives.

Japan seems to present another instance of radical conversion without disorganization.

Most other civilized regions, and some as yet barely touched by civilization, display various stages of disorganization, varying from initial symptoms to advanced wastage. In Asia Minor and North Africa diagnosis is confused by climatic changes, which may have been either the cause or the effect of advanced wastage. In the United States the degree of disorganization varies locally; it is worst in the Southwest, the Ozarks, and parts of the South, and least in New England and the Northwest. Better land-uses may still arrest it in the less advanced regions. In parts of Mexico, South America, South Africa, and Australia a violent and accelerating wastage is in progress, but I cannot assess the prospects.

This almost world-wide display of disorganization in the land seems to be similar to disease in an animal, except that it never culminates in complete disorganization or death. The land recovers, but at some reduced level of complexity, and with a reduced carrying capacity for people, plants, and animals. Many biotas currently regarded as "lands of opportunity" are in fact already subsisting on exploitative agriculture, i.e. they have already exceeded their sustained carrying capacity. Most of South America is overpopulated in this sense.

In arid regions we attempt to offset the process of wastage by reclamation, but it is only too evident that the prospective longevity of reclamation projects is often short. In our own West, the best of them may not last a century.

The combined evidence of history and ecology seems to support one general deduction: the less violent the man-made changes, the greater the probability of successful readjustment in the pyramid. Violence, in turn, varies with human population density; a dense population requires a more violent conversion. In this respect, North America has a better chance for permanence than Europe, if she can contrive to limit her density.

This deduction runs counter to our current philosophy, which assumes that because a small increase in density enriched human life, that an indefinite increase will enrich it indefinitely. Ecology knows of no density relationship that holds for indefinitely wide limits. All gains from density are subject to a law of diminishing returns.

Whatever may be the equation for men and land, it is improbable that we as yet know all its terms. Recent discoveries in mineral and vitamin nutrition reveal unsuspected dependencies in the up-circuit: incredibly minute quantities of certain substances determine the value of soils to plants, of plants to animals. What of the down-circuit? What of the vanishing species, the preservation of which we now regard as an esthetic luxury? They helped build the soil; in what unsuspected ways may they be essential to its maintenance? Professor Weaver proposes that we use prairie flowers to reflocculate the wasting soils of the dust bowl; who knows for what purpose cranes and condors, otters and grizzlies may some day be used?

LAND HEALTH AND THE A-B CLEAVAGE

A land ethic, then, reflects the existence of an ecological conscience, and this in turn reflects a conviction of individual responsibility for the health of the land. Health is the capacity of the land for self-renewal. Conservation is our effort to understand and preserve this capacity.

Conservationists are notorious for their dissensions. Superficially these seem to add up to mere confusion, but a more careful scrutiny reveals a single plane of cleavage common to many specialized fields. In each field one group (A) regards the land as soil, and its function as commodity-production; another group (B) regards the land as a biota, and its function as something broader. How much broader is admittedly in a state of doubt and confusion.

In my own field, forestry, group A is quite content to grow trees like cabbages, with cellulose as the basic forest commodity. It feels no inhibition against violence; its ideology is agronomic. Group B, on the other hand, sees forestry as fundamentally different from agronomy because it employs natural species, and manages a natural environment rather than creating an artificial one. Group B prefers natural reproduction on principle. It worries on biotic as well as economic grounds about the loss of species like chestnut, and the threatened loss of the white pines. It worries about a whole series of secondary forest functions: wildlife, recreation, watersheds, wilderness areas. To my mind, Group B feels the stirrings of an ecological conscience.

In the wildlife field, a parallel cleavage exists. For Group A the basic commodities are sport and meat; the yardsticks of production are ciphers of take in pheasants and trout. Artificial propagation is acceptable as a permanent as well as a temporary recourse—if its unit costs permit. Group B, on the other hand, worries about a whole series of biotic side-issues. What is the cost in predators of producing a game crop? Should we have further recourse to exotics? How can management restore the shrinking species, like prairie grouse, already hopeless as shootable game? How can management restore the threatened rarities, like trumpeter swan and whooping crane? Can management principles be extended to wildflowers? Here again it is clear to me that we have the same A-B cleavage as in forestry.

In the larger field of agriculture I am less competent to speak, but there seem to be somewhat parallel cleavages. Scientific agriculture was actively developing before ecology was born, hence a slower penetration of ecological concepts might be expected. Moreover the farmer, by the very nature of his techniques, must modify the biota more radically than the forester or the wildlife manager. Nevertheless, there are many discontents in agriculture which seem to add up to a new vision of "biotic farming."

Perhaps the most important of these is the new evidence that poundage or tonnage is no measure of the food-value of farm crops; the products of fertile soil may be qualitatively as well as quantitatively superior. We can bolster poundage from depleted soils by pouring on imported fertility, but we are not necessarily bolstering food-value. The possible ultimate ramifications of this idea are so immense that I must leave their exposition to abler pens.

The discontent that labels itself "organic farming," while bearing some of the earmarks of a cult, is nevertheless biotic in its direction, particularly in its insistence on the importance of soil flora and fauna.

The ecological fundamentals of agriculture are just as poorly known to the public as in other fields of land-use. For example, few educated people realize that the marvelous advances in technique made during recent decades are improvements in the pump, rather than the well. Acre for acre, they have barely sufficed to offset the sinking level of fertility.

In all of these cleavages, we see repeated the same basic paradoxes: man the conqueror *versus* man the biotic citizen; science the sharpener of his sword *versus* science the searchlight on his universe; land the slave and servant *versus* land the collective organism. Robinson's injunction to Tristram may well be applied, at this juncture, to *Homo sapiens* as a species in geological time:

> Whether you will or not
> You are a King, Tristram, for you are one
> Of the time-tested few that leave the world,
> When they are gone, not the same place it was.
> Mark what you leave.

THE OUTLOOK

It is inconceivable to me that an ethical relation to land can exist without love, respect, and admiration for land, and a high regard for its value. By value, I of course mean something far broader than mere economic value; I mean value in the philosophical sense.

Perhaps the most serious obstacle impeding the evolution of a land ethic is the fact that our educational and economic system is headed away from, rather than toward, an intense consciousness of land. Your true modern is separated from the land by many middlemen, and by innumerable physical gadgets. He has no vital relation to it; to him it is the space between cities on which crops grow. Turn him loose for a day on the land, and if the spot does not happen to be a golf links or a "scenic" area, he is bored stiff. If crops could be raised by hydroponics instead of farming, it would suit him very well. Synthetic substitutes for wood, leather, wool, and other natural land products suit him better than the originals. In short, land is something he has "outgrown."

Almost equally serious as an obstacle to a land ethic is the attitude of the farmer for whom the land is still an adversary, or a taskmaster that keeps him in slavery. Theoretically, the mechanization of farming ought to cut the farmer's chains, but whether it really does is debatable.

One of the requisites for an ecological comprehension of land is an understanding of ecology, and this is by no means co-extensive with "education"; in fact, much higher education seems deliberately to avoid ecological concepts. An understanding of ecology does not necessarily originate in courses bearing ecological labels; it is quite as likely to be labeled geography, botany, agronomy, history, or economics. This is as it should be, but whatever the label, ecological training is scarce.

The case for a land ethic would appear hopeless but for the minority which is in obvious revolt against these "modern" trends.

The "key-log" which must be moved to release the evolutionary process for an ethic is simply this: quit thinking about decent land-use as solely an economic problem. Examine each question in terms of what is ethically and esthetically right, as well as what is economically expedient. A thing is right when it tends to preserve the integrity, stability, and beauty of the biotic community. It is wrong when it tends otherwise.

It of course goes without saying that economic feasibility limits the tether of what can or cannot be done for land. It always has and it always will. The fallacy the economic determinists have tied around our collective neck, and which we now need to cast off, is the belief that economics determines *all* land-use. This is simply not true. An innumerable host of actions and attitudes, comprising perhaps the bulk of all land relations, is determined by the land-users' tastes and predilections, rather than by his purse. The bulk of all land relations hinges on investments of time, forethought, skill, and faith rather than on investments of cash. As a land-user thinketh, so is he.

I have purposely presented the land ethic as a product of social evolution because nothing so important as an ethic is ever "written." Only the most superficial student of history supposes that Moses "wrote" the Decalogue; it evolved in the minds of a thinking community, and Moses wrote a tentative summary of it for a "seminar." I say tentative because evolution never stops.

The evolution of a land ethic is an intellectual as well as emotional process. Conservation is paved with good intentions which prove to be futile, or even dangerous, because they are devoid of critical understanding either of the land, or of economic land-use. I think it is a truism that as the ethical frontier advances from the individual to the community, its intellectual content increases.

The mechanism of operation is the same for any ethic: social approbation for right actions: social disapproval for wrong actions.

By and large, our present problem is one of attitudes and implements. We are remodeling the Alhambra with a steam-shovel, and we are proud of our yardage. We shall hardly relinquish the shovel, which after all has many good points, but we are in need of gentler and more objective criteria for its successful use.

GUSTAV ECKSTEIN
1890-1981

Gustav Eckstein is one of those writers difficult, if not impossible, to categorize. Unfamiliar to most readers today, his books, especially Lives *(1932), had a wide following in the 1930s and 1940s. Eckstein had a long teaching career in physiology and psychiatry at the University of Cincinnati and did pioneering animal behavior work with Ivan Pavlov. He was also an intimate of the New York literati and is said to have been the model for the scientist in George S. Kaufman's* The Man Who Came to Dinner. *As a scientist whose speculations on human and animal nature arise from his observations of laboratory and urban creatures such as rats, cockroaches, canaries, and cats, he anticipates such later writers as Loren Eiseley and Lewis Thomas. Eckstein's idiosyncratic and anecdotal style is highly effective in disassociating us from our normal responses towards these unexotic animals. His other works include* Everyday Miracles *(1948) and* The Body Has A Head *(1961).*

Two Lives

I had got to be a doctor, a man of science, and took a tiny creature, a thing so small it sat with comfort in the palm of my hand, and cut into its skull and removed a tip of its brain. Science has not got much by that, but possibly a few rats have, for he taught me, that little white rat, and I have changed my mind about many things.

The little white rat survived my cunning. There was no mutilation of any function that is commonly said to lodge in the brain. His thought was clear, his spirit brave, he could guide his body, and his length of life seemed even increased, for he reached what in our terms is a hundred years.

The moon tonight is full and flooding through the window. He runs from his chamber—a box that I have set at one end of my roll-top

Lives (New York: Harper, 1932).

desk—to his granary, a drawer on the other side and below. Back and forth, back and forth. He has been running that way for a month of nights. In the day he sleeps, only with the darkening opens his amber nervous eyes, casts about him, wonders what he missed while away, then yawns, a mighty yawn, and scratches like a mountebank by the side of his ear, and scrubs his face. Scrubs rather his head, the whole of it, uses both hands and the lengths of his arms. And now he cleans his tail, cleans that particularly, knowing that never a healthy rat but has a clean one. Then back and forth, and back and forth, and back and forth again. Suddenly he stops, just in the middle of the top of the desk, and one would say he was porcelain did he not sway and lean far out. It is the moon. He is bathed in the moon's flood. He is struck. He is queer.

She I bring him is a tiny thing. In the half-dark she trembles like a patch of that very moonlight. She rushes, in these first hours, explores all this new, is pleased, is pleased, but vouchsafes him no solitary glance. He is gone to his corner. He watches steadily from there.

I had always said he might have the top of the desk and the upper of the three drawers, and he had always kept to that, but she now lives everywhere, bites through the back of the upper drawer, lets herself hang and drop, and by that strategy coming thus from the rear, is in possession of all, immediately bringing her belongings, really his belongings and my belongings—one leap from the top to where I drive my distracted pen, another leap to the drawer, and thereafter subterranean grumblings and thuds and perturbations.

He cannot understand it—this fine slender woman, that she should be so material. What can she think of doing with it all? What does she dream?

I cannot understand either—his bedding, his food, my pencil, my pens, the cork of my ink bottle, the eraser with the chewable rubber at one end and the chewable tuft of brush at the other. Hour after hour diagonally across my work she goes, head held high to keep what she carries above her flying feet. In human distances it must be twenty miles. Certainly more than the tiny burnings of that tiny body drive that machine. Only late does she cease. She looks where he huddles uncovered in his chamber. She seems to think him over. She comes to a conclusion. She waddles toward him, settles into him, drops her head, is ostensibly asleep. He cannot sleep. He does not even close his eyes, squats there motionless, almost breathless, is afraid he may disturb her. I pick up the few gnawed bits of my belongings, turn out the lights.

Three weeks ago was the wedding. So soon as I arrived this morning she made me comprehend it was newspaper she wanted. I brought her a newspaper. She put her foot on it, as if to establish possession, then looked at me hard.

"A single newspaper?"

I brought her an armful.

All day she stuck to the job, did not eat, did not drink. I placed food and drink before her. She ran round them. When I persisted she ran through them, trailed them. The paper she tore into strips, leaped with the strips to the drawer, there continued the tearing, each strip into squares. By noon an inch of squares bedded the bottom of the drawer. By evening, three inches. By midnight, five. And now, shortly after, she is ready to rest. Still she has not eaten. I ask her again. She only turns her head.

Poor husband now and then has tried to tear a little paper too, but it was not in his character, a big bulging character. This new young wife has made great changes in our ways, his and mine. A hush lies over the establishment. I sit before my desk, but do not work. She sits by my side. She is thinking her thoughts. And so is he. And so am I.

Next morning the mother and father are moving about. Mother is thin. They are thirteen, if I count them right, and they wiggle and worm and topple and tumble. She will not eat even now, and he does not find it easy, either. He is bewildered. How can anything like that have happened? I try to explain to him, but I do not rightly understand, myself, and he climbs heavily out of the drawer, and on my arm, and in my pocket hides his confused head. By evening, however, he has talked it over with her, and she has told him something I could not, and in consequence he is licking her, and she is licking them, and he is so interested in what he is doing that he steps all over them, and they squeak and step over one another, the smallest the most stepped on. No one in the heap seems able to take in the whole of the heap. That is somehow sad.

Three out of the litter I intended to leave little mother, but she would have a big family or none. At least she was indifferent to three. Two I found when I came on the fourth morning, dead. The third I never found, though, fearing it might have got into difficulty, I looked under every square of paper. I regret they are gone. They had the color and somewhat the form of the fingers of the newborn baby. The little pink legs were so weak that they dragged, and the little pink tails dragged symmetrically between them. Boneless they seemed, and sightless they were, and they kept up an aimless motion.

Mother appears unconcerned about what has happened, but I am not sure, for mother is hidden deep under her white hair, and perhaps is hidden deeper even than that. At any rate, father, who knows her better than I, is more solicitous today than usual. He picks her vermin with a more insistent care. She lies there very flat, spreads the maximum of surface to the smooth cool table below, and the maximum of surface to great father above. The exertion makes him pant. As to his feelings about the babies, I believe they were mixed. Thirteen was many, and though they were lovely, it must be admitted they were restless.

Both are asleep. I reach into the chamber to pet the back of mother's heaving neck. She starts. She bites me. It is not much of a bite and she is grieved. She probably thought that I was coming for one of the brood. She glances nervously about, finds it hard to recollect.

On shipboard I met a man from Guernsey. We talked things easy to talk, things near our hearts. I told of my rats. Then he told how the level of the olive oil dropped day after day in the thin tall bottle on the second shelf from the top in his pantry in the house in Guernsey. Oil does not dry at such a rate. So, being a philosopher, he sat himself quietly before the pantry and stayed the afternoon. With dark she came, a great gray one, scaled the highest shelf, waddled to a point directly above the bottle, studiously inserted her tail, studiously drew it forth, and licked it clean, and left by the road she came. The gentleman from Guernsey attempted to meet this ingenuity with a trap, but her interest was in oil and, that gone, she returned no more.

Whereupon I told of the skimming of the milk. I was only a boy, alone in the kitchen, and my poor mother a woman so clean, so clean, that had she known she would in the dark have slipped to some distant apothecary to purchase the shameful poison. This one also was great and gray, also knew where she was going. One spring to the back of the chair. One spring to the middle of the table. And there, set there every afternoon to cool, stood a flat dish of milk. Carefully she swung her stern, carefully fitted it to the rim, and, a single sweep, the job was done.

These tails, that look so rigid and are so skillful, much could be written about them. But no one would read. "If it were not for their tails." How often have I heard a growing interest cut short with that.

To be sure, the two rats of whom I have just been telling were hungry rats, but a rat will steal when not hungry. Mother rat will steal from my very hand, will leap out of a sound sleep to snatch a bit of chocolate from under father's nose, and rush with it to a place of hiding. One morning, finding a loaf of bread where she commonly finds a slice, she tried at once to steal the loaf, but it was ten times her size and she lacked the strength. Visibly all curiosity left her. Not able to steal it and store it, what interest in bread?

Father, on the contrary, never steals and never stores, eats from my hand as a dog eats. For certain foods he will tussle when mother tries to take them out of his very mouth, but it is always as if he had forgotten himself. Banana, however, it is not easy to yield. He has a great partiality for banana, and there is no fairness, she not having eaten her own, having hid it away, and having immediately and confidently ambled after his. Once I saw him make straight into his straw, bore his way in, let the banana mash about his face and, though she pushed him on one side, then pushed him on the other, and sought to drive her thin nose alongside his broad nose, he was stubborn. Only after a long time did he back out, looking very comical and feeling very ashamed.

I divide a peanut, call them, and they come pressed one against the other, he so big, she so slight, settle on their haunches, take the separate halves in their hands, and drive their tiny jaws with a speed that makes one think of their tiny hearts.

Toward ten every evening the two take turns to bathe. I have fitted a board across the basin under the tap where the water drips one drop at a time. To be wet all over makes them very weak and very unhappy, but to catch one drop, and wash vigorously with that, and then catch another, that is different. I myself also look forward to it—to see the way they rise from the board, put out those marvelous hands, and wait for the drop.

Father this morning is lying on his side, his two hands folded just under his nose, as if he had fallen asleep in prayer. Father's sleep is pictured with dreams. I can tell by the way he waves the tip of his tail, and when the dream gets too vivid he turns, settles on his belly, sidles over to where mother is sleeping on her belly. Then he scratches his head. A little later he scratches his head again. This time he wakes sufficiently to realize that though he is scratching his head he feels nothing. Promptly he scratches again, and still feels nothing. It is a condition so peculiar that it breaks through his sleep. He opens one eye, not far, but far enough to make out what has happened, for he is scratching not his head but hers, she having pushed hers under his neck and brought it out just inside his right hand. The discovery does not anger him. It does not even surprise him. Gently he puts her head aside, and scratches his own.

It has come of a sudden, as it does—father's aging. It is all in the last weeks. He is thin and walks cautiously and tries to show in his lettuce a pleasure he no longer feels. He is so shaky it worries me when he leaves his chamber because he cannot sleep, sits at the edge of the desk, the better in that posture to fill his hungry lungs. He has fallen several times in the past, and it might be bad with him if he fell now. The two behave very differently when they fall. Father stays where he lands, knows that if I am out of the room, sooner or later I must return, and when I do he had better be where I shall see him, or where, if I do not see him, he can nudge my ankles to remind me. And when I am reminded he is as pleased as a puppy for the way I sympathize in his misfortune. But when mother falls she hastens at once to the most cornery corner. She wants to be found, there is no question, and when I reach her is most relieved, and yet has let me beg her for hours to come out from next a water-pipe.

Tonight it is father sits in the precarious place. He looks tottering, and he frightens me. I mention his name. He moves his tail that is hanging over the edge of the precipice. I mention his name again. He moves his tail faster. He comes to my side of the desk, stands on his two feet like a diminutive polar bear, his beads of eyes trying ever so helplessly to find where I am.

About two o'clock mother rouses me. Two o'clock in the morning. There is a tempest in her chamber. I must come at once and see, and she mounts high on her toes to be sure that I do see. Her drinking-water, I have put it inside her chamber instead of out. Her drinking-water she does not want inside her chamber. Deliberately she tumbles it over her bedding. And now she is enraged also at the wetness of the bedding. She wants the empty dish out. She wants the wet bedding out. I drudge like a scolded maid.

Father grows older and older. Then one evening he leaves drawers and desk top. He goes to be an eagle. At least he goes to be an eagle if it is true that yearning has its way. His gaze was always at the edges of his universe.

I am filled with the pain of the shortness of everything. That is a common pain. But it is freshened by the shortness of this little life. His great events were a thirtieth the length of my great events, yet they make mine seem not long, but brief. When I saw his death coming, how truly frightful was the feeling that nothing could stop it. And that also is a common feeling. But this life lay right there in my hand and made my helplessness seem so much more helpless. Good care and good food and warmth would save him an uneasy week, perhaps, and were I able to add all the cunning in the world it would save him another week perhaps. How then must I know with a new strong draft of conviction that gentleness and gaiety are the best of life.

He knew that. He knew how to be affectionate to his friends. To mother he yielded not only what she needed but what she wanted, and what she did not want, what the sweet and lavish extravagance of her youth and sex made her wish only to cast to the winds, cast off the precipice into the dark empty spaces of the universe.

Every night the last months he and I used to play a game. He had too heavy a body, and his legs were too short, and where he walked he rubbed the earth, so it was difficult to pretend to flee ahead of my hand, then abruptly in the midst of that flight to rear on his hind legs, give the length of his body an exaggerated shiver, as in some barbaric dance, and then continue to flee. Yet that was the game.

I think of that now. I think as one does of everything, of the night he made it plain he needed a wife, and how she nevertheless confounded him when she came, and of the litters that passed one by one, and the signs of maturity, how they passed, and the signs of age, and all in my hand, he learning every day to be less a rat, excellent though that is, learning to be more and more thoughtful, and then the final sharpness, how he mastered even that, grew gentler and gentler, and one night went to be an eagle.

Poor little mother! Babies gone and father gone. I describe how it is with father this morning, how he is off to the Peruvian mountains, and how, a short distance below the highest peak, where there is a good shelter against the blasts of the south, under great wings, nudging his brothers and sisters, he is beginning again, is waiting, though perhaps he knows it not, for little mother.

I put my hand into the dark of the drawer, and she pretends my fingers are the whilom family. She scrubs them roughly one by one. She crawls under them, crawls over them, goes round the nails and up into the crotches. She scrubs them roughly, and when each is done bites it, bumps it aside. I talk to her. She answers out of the dark. Father never would use his voice. Hers is a kind of cluck, and after she has spoken she is quiet. And I am quiet. Each of us has it in mind to wait on what the other will do. But she never can wait, must at least turn round, shove her little self through a quarter of a circle, then fix me with one great glowing eye. What she sees of me with that eye I have no notion. Nor have I any notion of what she makes of what she sees, more than that it is an embodiment with which in her loneliness she finds it possible to commune.

I have talked of my rats to many a person. Some have entered smilingly into my feeling. Some have bantered. Some have doubted me, have thought I was bantering them. There was one, an oldish fellow, whose seriousness was greater even than my own. But I must hereafter be careful what I say. I was telling a very clever lady about putting my hand into the drawer, about little mother holding the hand for a quarter of an hour, then something made me stop, something penetrating in the lady's face. The lady was reading me. I felt it—the way one feels when one tells certain people one's dreams.

Kind lady, now that I need not at the same time look into your canny face, let me add a note to your picture. Let me say that all the while it was teaching me I also was teaching my family what I imagine may be useful to eagles. I was teaching it how to be fond. You may think that all that that requires is to throw a piece of cheese, as one throws a dog a bone, or a man gold. No, at least that is not the way I did it. I taught fondness by being fond. And, when I consider, I was able to teach father with very little, a touch as I happened near his box, a touch as he passed me on his walk to the quarters below. Only in the last months it got to be more. His breathing then was not always easy, and that brought fears, and we sometimes must talk long talks to get over the fears. With mother the greater intimacy came after he died. She was in such plain need, every night would sit beside me there in her drawer, immersed in a world that seemed so limited till each time I would remember afresh how limited my own. After all, what thoughts might she not be thinking? Not thoughts like mine, not severe logical incrustations like mine, but the quality I was sure was charming. I was sure because, like father, little mother had ceased in such an extraordinary way to want. Exactly as she received affection she could do without things. Father, in fact, was only an ordinary rat with the interests of an ordinary rat, in cheese and vermin and women, and then I came. And when he died I was sorry for little mother, and being sorry proved, as so often, the prod to the backward affections, and she too gave up being merely a rat, and one day soared away.

JOSEPH WOOD KRUTCH
1893-1970

This anthology contains several examples of biologists who, rather late in their career, became well-known as writers of humanistic essays. A contrasting example is provided by the career of Joseph Wood Krutch. A New York drama critic and professor of literature in the 1920s and

1930s, Krutch's urbane and urban viewpoint of human nature was expressed in such books as The Modern Temper: A Study *and* A Confession *(1929)—a largely pessimistic view of modern civilization and its discontents. But in middle age he re-read Thoreau and took his advice to heart, eventually moving to Arizona and concentrating his literary energies on the desert environment with which his name is now most strongly associated. His natural history essays, full of wit, wide-ranging allusions and a compassion for all forms of life, made him one of the most popular and influential nature writers of his time. Yet he retained the intellectual's restless curiosity about ultimate meanings, and his essays characteristically embrace an examination of such questions as the nature of life or mankind's true place in the scheme of existence.*

LOVE IN THE DESERT

The ancients called love "the Mother of all things," but they didn't know the half of it. They did not know, for instance, that plants as well as animals have their love life and they supposed that even some of the simpler animals were generated by sunlight on mud without the intervention of Venus.

Centuries later when Chaucer and the other medieval poets made "the mystic rose" a euphemism for an anatomical structure not commonly mentioned in polite society, they too were choosing a figure of speech more appropriate than they realized, because every flower really is a group of sex organs which the plants have glorified while the animals—surprisingly enough, as many have observed—usually leave the corresponding items of their own anatomy primitive, unadorned and severely functional. The ape, whose behind blooms in purple and red, represents the most any of the higher animals has achieved along this line and even it is not, by human standards, any great aesthetic success. At least no one would be likely to maintain that it rivals either the poppy or the orchid.

In another respect also plants seem to have been more aesthetically sensitive than animals. They have never tolerated that odd arrangement by which the same organs are used for reproduction and excretion. Men, from St. Bernard to William Butler Yeats, have ridiculed or scorned it and recoiled in distaste from the fact that, as Yeats put it, "love has pitched his mansion in / The place of excrement." As a matter of fact,

The Voice of the Desert (New York: William Sloane, 1954).

the reptiles are the only backboned animals who have a special organ used only in mating. Possibly—though improbably, I am afraid—if this fact were better known it might be counted in favor of a generally unpopular group.

All this we now know and, appropriately enough, much of it—especially concerning the sexuality of plants—was first discovered during the eighteenth-century Age of Gallantry. No other age would have been more disposed to hail the facts with delight and it was much inclined to expound the new knowledge in extravagantly gallant terms. One does not usually think of systematizers as given to rhapsody, but Linnaeus, who first popularized the fact that plants can make love, wrote rhapsodically of their nuptials:

> *The petals serve as bridal beds which the Great Creator has so gloriously arranged, adorned with such noble bed curtains and perfumed with so many sweet scents, that the bridegroom there may celebrate his nuptials with all the greater solemnity. When the bed is thus prepared, it is time for the bridegroom to embrace his beloved bride and surrender his gifts to her: I mean, one can see how* testiculi *open and emit* pulverem genitalem, *which falls upon* tubam *and fertilizes* ovarium.

In England, half a century later, Erasmus Darwin, distinguished grandfather of the great Charles, wrote even more exuberantly in his didactic poem, "The Loves of the Plants," where all sorts of gnomes, sylphs and other mythological creatures benevolently foster the vegetable *affaires de coeur*. It is said to have been one of the best-selling poems ever published, no doubt because it combined the newly fashionable interest in natural history with the long standing obsession with "the tender passion" as expressible in terms of cupids, darts, flames and all the other clichés which now survive only in St. Valentine's Day gifts.

Such romantic exuberance is not much favored today when the seamy side is likely to interest us more. We are less likely to abandon ourselves to a participation in the joys of spring than to be on our guard against "the pathetic fallacy" even though, as is usually the case, we don't know exactly what the phrase means or what is "pathetic" about the alleged fallacy. Nevertheless, those who consent, even for a moment, to glance at that agreeable surface of things with which the poets used to be chiefly concerned will find in the desert what they find in every other spring, and they may even be aware that the hare, which here also runs races with itself, is a good deal fleeter than any Wordsworth was privileged to observe in the Lake Country.

In this warm climate, moreover, love puts in his appearance even before "the young sonne hath in the Ram his halfe cours y-ronne" or, in scientific prose, ahead of the spring equinox. Many species of birds, which for months have done little more than chirp, begin to remember their songs. In the canyons where small pools are left from some winter rain, the subaqueous and most mysterious of all spring births begins and seems to recapitulate the first morning of creation. Though I have never noticed that either of the two kinds of doves which spend the whole year with us acquire that "livelier iris" which Tennyson celebrated, the lizard's belly turns turquoise blue, as though to remind his mate that even on their ancient level sex has its aesthetic as well as its biological aspect. Fierce sparrow hawks take to sitting side by side on telegraph wires, and the Arizona cardinal, who has remained all winter long more brilliantly red than his eastern cousin ever is, begins to think romantically of his neat but not gaudy wife. For months before, he had been behaving like an old married man who couldn't remember what he once saw in her. Though she had followed him about, he had sometimes driven her rudely away from the feeding station until he had had his fill. Now gallantry begins to revive and he may even graciously hand her a seed.

A little later the cactus wren and the curved-bill thrasher will build nests in the wicked heart of the cholla cactus and, blessed with some mysterious impunity, dive through its treacherous spines. Somewhere among the creosote bushes, by now yellow with blossoms, the jack rabbit—an unromantic looking creature if there ever was one—will be demonstrating that she is really a hare, not a rabbit at all, by giving birth to young furred babies almost ready to go it alone instead of being naked, helpless creatures like the infant cottontail. The latter will be born underground, in a cozily lined nest; the more rugged jack rabbit on the almost bare surface.

My special charge, the Sonoran spadefoot toad, will remain buried no one knows how many feet down for months still to come. He will not celebrate his spring until mid-July when a soaking rain penetrates deeply enough to assure him that on the surface a few puddles will form. Some of those puddles may just possibly last long enough to give his tadpoles the nine or ten days of submersion necessary, if they are to manage the metamorphosis which will change them into toadlets capable of repeating that conquest of the land which their ancestors accomplished so many millions of years ago. But while the buried spadefoots dally, the buried seeds dropped last year by the little six-week ephemerals of the desert will spring up and proceed with what looks like indecent haste to the business of reproduction, as though—as for them is almost the case—life were not long enough for anything except preparation for the next generation.

Human beings have been sometimes praised and sometimes scorned because they fall so readily into the habit of pinning upon their posterity all hope for a good life, of saying, "At least my children will have that better life which I somehow never managed to achieve." Even plants do that, as I know, because when I have raised some of the desert annuals under the unsuitable conditions of a winter living room, they have managed, stunted and sickly though they seemed, to seed. "At least," they seemed to say, "our species is assured another chance." And if this tendency is already dominant in a morning glory, human beings will probably continue to accept it in themselves also, whether, by human standards, it is wise or not.

As I write this another spring has just come around. With a regularity in which there is something pleasantly comic, all the little romances, dramas and tragedies are acting themselves out once more, and I seize the opportunity to pry benevolently.

Yesterday I watched a pair of hooded orioles—he, brilliant in orange and black; she, modestly yellow green—busy about a newly constructed nest hanging from the swordlike leaves of a yucca, where one would have been less surprised to find the lemon yellow cousin of these birds which builds almost exclusively in the yucca. From this paradise I drove away the serpent—in this case a three-foot diamondback rattler who was getting uncomfortably close to the nesting site—and went on to flush out of the grass at least a dozen tiny Gambel's quail whose male parent, hovering close by, bobbed his head plume anxiously as he tried to rally them again. A quarter of a mile away a red and black Gila monster was sunning himself on the fallen trunk of another yucca, and, for all I know, he too may have been feeling some stirring of the spring, though I can hardly say that he showed it.

From birds as brightly colored as the orioles one expects only gay domesticity and lighthearted solicitude. For that reason I have been more interested to follow the home life of the road runner, that unbird-like bird whom we chose at the beginning as a desert dweller par excellence. One does not expect as much of him as one does of an oriole for two good reasons. In the first place, his normal manner is aggressive, ribald and devil-may-care. In the second place, he is a cuckoo, and the shirking of domestic responsibilities by some of the tribe has been notorious for so long that by some confused logic human husbands who are the victims of unfaithfulness not only wear the horns of the deer but are also said to be cuckolded. The fact remains, nevertheless, that though I have watched the developing domestic life of one road runner couple for weeks, I have observed nothing at which the most critical could cavil.

The nest—a rather coarse affair of largish sticks—was built in the crotch of a thorny cholla cactus some ten feet above the ground, which is rather higher than usual. When first found there were already in it two eggs, and both of the parent birds were already brooding them, turn and turn about. All this I had been led to expect because the road runner, unlike most birds, does not wait until all the eggs have been laid before beginning to incubate. Instead she normally lays them one by one a day or two apart and begins to set as soon as the first has arrived. In other words the wife follows the advice of the Planned Parenthood Association and "spaces" her babies—perhaps because lizards and snakes are harder to come by than insects, and it would be too much to try to feed a whole nest full of nearly grown infants at the same time. Moreover, in the case of my couple "self-restraint" or some other method of birth control had been rigorously practiced and two young ones were all there were.

Sixteen days after I first saw the eggs, both had hatched. Presently both parents were bringing in lizards according to a well-worked-out plan. While one sat on the nest to protect the young from the blazing sun, the other went hunting. When the latter returned with a catch, the brooding bird gave up its place, went foraging in its turn and presently came back to deliver a catch, after which it again took its place on the nest. One day, less than a month after the eggs were first discovered, one baby was standing on the edge of the nest itself, the other on a cactus stem a few feet away. By the next day both had disappeared.

Thus, despite the dubious reputation of the family to which he belongs, the road runner, like the other American cuckoos, seems to have conquered both the hereditary taint and whatever temptations his generally rascally disposition may have exposed him to. In this case at least, both husband and wife seemed quite beyond criticism, though they do say that other individuals sometimes reveal a not-too-serious sign of the hereditary weakness when a female will, on occasion, lay her eggs in the nest of another bird of her own species—which is certainly not so reprehensible as victimizing a totally different bird as the European cuckoo does.

Perhaps the superior moral atmosphere of America has reformed the cuckoo's habit and at least no American representative of the family regularly abandons its eggs to the care of a stranger. Nevertheless, those of us who are inclined to spiritual pride should remember that we do have a native immoralist, abundant in this same desert country and just as reprehensible as any to be found in decadent Europe—namely the cowbird, who is sexually promiscuous, never builds a home of his own and is inveterately given to depositing eggs in the nests of other birds. In his defense it is commonly alleged that his "antisocial conduct" should be excused for the same reason that such conduct is often excused in human beings—because, that is to say, it is actually the result not of original sin but of certain social determinants. It seems that long before he became a cowbird this fellow was a buffalo bird. And because he had to follow the wide ranging herds if he was to profit from the insects they started up from the grass, he could never settle down long enough to raise a family. Like Rousseau and like Walt Whitman, he had to leave his offspring (if any) behind.

However that may be, it still can hardly be denied that love in the desert has its still seamier side. Perhaps the moth, whom we have already seen playing pimp to a flower and profiting shamelessly from the affair, can also be excused on socio-economic grounds. But far more shocking things go on in dry climates as well as in wet, and to excuse them we shall have to dig deeper than the social system right down into the most ancient things-as-they-used-to-be. For an example which seems to come straight out of the most unpleasant fancies of the Marquis de Sade, we might contemplate the atrocious behavior of the so-called tarantula spider of the sandy wastes. Here, unfortunately, is a lover whom all the world will find it difficult to love.

This tarantula is a great hairy fellow much like the kind which sometimes comes north in a bunch of bananas and which most people have seen exhibited under a glass in some fruiterer's window. Most visitors to the desert hate and fear him at sight, even though he is disinclined to trouble human beings and is incapable even upon extreme provocation of giving more than a not-too-serious bite. Yet he does look more dangerous than the scorpion and he is, if possible, even less popular.

He has a leg spread of four or sometimes of as much as six inches, and it is said that he can leap for as much as two feet when pouncing upon his insect prey. Most of the time he spends in rather neat tunnels or burrows excavated in the sand, from which entomologists in search of specimens flush him out with water. And it is chiefly in the hottest months, especially after some rain, that one sees him prowling about, often crossing a road and sometimes waiting at a screen door to be let in. Except for man, his most serious enemy is the "tarantula hawk," a large black-bodied wasp with orange-red wings, who pounces upon his larger antagonist, paralyzes him with a sting and carries his now helpless body to feed the young wasps which will hatch in their own underground burrow.

Just to look at the tarantula's hairy legs and set of gleaming eyes is to suspect him of unconventionality or worse, and the suspicions are justified. He is one of those creatures in whom love seems to bring out the worst. Moreover, because at least one of the several species happens to have been the subject of careful study, the details are public. About the only thing he cannot be accused of is "infantile sexuality," and he can't be accused of that only because the male requires some eleven years to reach sexual maturity or even to develop the special organs necessary for his love making—if you can stretch this euphemistic term far enough to include his activities.

When at last he has come of age, he puts off the necessity of risking contact with a female as long as possible. First he spins a sort of web into which he deposits a few drops of sperm. Then he patiently taps the web for a period of about two hours in order to fill with the sperm the two special palps or mouth parts which he did not acquire until the molt which announced his maturity. Then, and only then, does he go off in search of his "mystic and somber Dolores" who will never exhibit toward him any tender emotions.

If, as is often the case, she shows at first no awareness of his presence, he will give her a few slaps until she rears angrily with her fangs spread for a kill. At this moment he then plays a trick which nature, knowing the disposition of his mate, has taught him and for which nature has provided a special apparatus. He slips two spurs conveniently placed on his forelegs over the fangs of the female, in such a way that the fangs are locked into immobility. Then he transfers the sperm which he has been carrying into an orifice in the female, unlocks her fangs and darts away. If he is successful in making his escape, he may repeat the process with as many as three other females. But by this time he is plainly senile and he slowly dies, presumably satisfied that his life work has been accomplished. Somewhat unfairly, the female may live for a dozen more years and use up several husbands. In general outline the procedure is the same for many spiders, but it seems worse in him, because he is big enough to be conspicuous.

It is said that when indiscreet birdbanders announced their discovery that demure little house wrens commonly swap mates between the first and second of their summer broods, these wrens lost favor with many old ladies who promptly took down their nesting boxes because they refused to countenance such loose behavior.

In the case of the tarantula we have been contemplating mores which are far worse. But there ought, it seems to me, to be some possible attitude less unreasonable than either that of the old ladies who draw away from nature when she seems not to come up to their very exacting standards of behavior, and the seemingly opposite attitude of inverted romantics who are prone either to find all beasts other than man completely beastly, or to argue that since man is biologically a beast, nothing should or can be expected of him that is not found in all his fellow creatures.

Such a more reasonable attitude will, it seems to me, have to be founded on the realization that sex has had a history almost as long as the history of life, that its manifestations are as multifarious as the forms assumed by living things and that their comeliness varies as much as do the organisms themselves. Man did not invent it and he was not the first to exploit either the techniques of love making or the emotional and aesthetic themes which have become associated with them. Everything either beautiful or ugly of which he has found himself capable is somewhere anticipated in the repertory of plant and animal behavior. In some creatures sex seems a bare and mechanical necessity; in others the opportunity for elaboration has been seized upon and developed in many different directions. Far below the human level, love can be a game on the one hand, or a self-destructive passion on the other. It can inspire tenderness or cruelty; it can achieve fulfillment through either violent domination or prolonged solicitation. One is almost tempted to say that to primitive creatures, as to man, it can be sacred or profane, love or lust.

The tarantula's copulation is always violent rape and usually ends in death for the aggressor. But over against that may be set not only the romance of many birds but also of other less engaging creatures in whom nevertheless a romantic courtship is succeeded by an epoch of domestic attachment and parental solicitude. There is no justification for assuming, as some romanticists do, that the one is actually more "natural" than the other. In one sense nature is neither for nor against what have come to be human ideals. She includes both what we call good and what we call evil. We are simply among her experiments, though we are, in some respects, the most successful.

Some desert creatures have come quite a long way from the tarantula—and in our direction, too. Even those who have come only a relatively short way are already no longer repulsive. Watching from a blind two parent deer guarding a fawn while he took the first drink at a water hole, it seemed that the deer at least had come a long way.

To be sure many animals are, if this is possible, more "sex obsessed" than we—intermittently at least. Mating is the supreme moment of their lives and for many, as for the male scorpion and the male tarantula, it is also the beginning of the end. Animals will take more trouble and run more risks than men usually will, and if the Strindbergs are right when they insist that the woman still wants to consume her mate, the biological origin of that grisly impulse is rooted in times which are probably more ancient than the conquest of dry land.

Our currently best-publicized student of human sexual conduct has

argued that some of what are called "perversions" in the human being—
homosexuality, for example—should be regarded as merely "normal variations" because something analogous is sometimes observed in the animal kingdom. But if that argument is valid then nothing in the textbooks
of psychopathology is "abnormal." Once nature had established the fact
of maleness and femaleness, she seems to have experimented with every
possible variation on the theme. By comparison, Dr. Kinsey's most adventurous subjects were hopelessly handicapped by the anatomical and
physiological limitations of the human being.

In the animal kingdom, monogamy, polygamy, polyandry and promis-
cuity are only trivial variations. Nature makes hermaphrodites, as well as
Tiresiases who are alternately of one sex and then the other; also hordes
of neuters among the bees and the ants. She causes some males to attach
themselves permanently to their females and teaches others how to accomplish impregnation without ever touching them. Some embrace for
hours; some, like Onan, scatter their seed. Many males in many different
orders—like the seahorse and the ostrich, for example—brood the eggs,
while others will eat them, if they get a chance, quite as blandly as many
females will eat their mate, once his business is done. Various male
spiders wave variously decorated legs before the eyes of a prospective
spouse in the hope (often vain) that she will not mistake them for a meal
just happening by. But husband-eating is no commoner than child-eat-
ing. Both should be classed as mere "normal variants" in human behavior if nothing except a parallel in the animal kingdom is necessary to
establish that status. To her children nature seems to have said, "Copulate you must. But beyond that there is no rule. Do it in whatever way
and with whatever emotional concomitants you choose. That you should
do it somehow or other is all that I ask."

If one confines one's attention too closely to these seamy sides, one
begins to understand why, according to Gibbon, some early Fathers of
the Church held that sex was the curse pronounced upon Adam and
that, had he not sinned, the human race would have been propagated
"by some harmless process of vegetation." Or perhaps one begins to
repeat with serious emphasis the famous question once asked by the
Messrs. Thurber and White, "Is Sex Necessary?" And the answer is
that, strictly speaking, it isn't. Presumably the very first organisms were
sexless. They reproduced by a "process of vegetation" so harmless that
not even vegetable sexuality was involved. What is even more impressive
is the patent fact that it is not necessary today. Some of the most successful of all plants and animals—if by successful you mean abundantly
surviving—have given it up either entirely or almost entirely. A virgin

birth may require a miracle if the virgin is to belong to the human race, but there is nothing miraculous about it in the case of many of nature's successful children. Parthenogenesis, as the biologist calls it, is a perfectly normal event.

Ask the average man for a serious answer to the question what sex is "for" or why it is "necessary," and he will probably answer without thinking that it is "necessary for reproduction." But the biologist knows that it is not. Actually the function of sex is not to assure reproduction but to prevent it—if you take the word literally and hence to mean "exact duplication." Both animals and plants could "reproduce" or "duplicate" without sex. But without it there would be little or no variation, heredities could not be mixed, unexpected combinations could not arise, and evolution would either never have taken place at all or, at least, taken place so slowly that we might all still be arthropods or worse.

If in both the plant and animal kingdom many organisms are actually abandoning the whole of the sexual process, that is apparently because they have resigned their interest in change and its possibilities. Everyone knows how the ants and the bees have increased the singleminded efficiency of the worker majority by depriving them of a sexual function and then creating a special class of sexual individuals. But their solution is far less radical than that of many of the small creatures, including many insects, some of whom are making sexless rather than sexual reproduction the rule, and some of whom are apparently dispensing with the sexual entirely so that no male has ever been found.

In the plant world one of the most familiar and successful of all weeds produces its seeds without pollination, despite the fact that it still retains the flower which was developed long ago as a mechanism for facilitating that very sexual process which it has now given up. That it is highly "successful" by purely biological standards no one who has ever tried to eliminate dandelions from a lawn is likely to doubt. As I have said before, they not only get along very well in the world, they have also been astonishing colonizers here, since the white man unintentionally brought them from Europe, probably in hay. Sexless though the dandelion is, it is inheriting the earth, and the only penalty which it has to pay for its sexlessness is the penalty of abandoning all hope of ever being anything except a dandelion, even of being a better dandelion than it is. It seems to have said at some point, "This is good enough for me. My tribe flourishes. We have found how to get along in the world. Why risk anything?"

But if, from the strict biological standpoint, sex is "nothing but" a mechanism for encouraging variation, that is a long way from saying that there are not other standpoints. It is perfectly legitimate to say that it is also "for" many other things. Few other mechanisms ever invented or stumbled upon opened so many possibilities, entailed so many unforeseen consequences. Even in the face of those who refuse to entertain the possibility that any kind of purpose or foreknowledge guided evolution, we can still find it permissible to maintain that every invention is "for" whatever uses or good results may come from it, that all things, far from being "nothing but" their origins, are whatever they have become. Grant that and one must grant also that the writing of sonnets is one of the things which sex is "for."

Certainly nature herself discovered a very long time ago that sex was—or at least could be used—"for" many things besides the production of offspring not too monotonously like the parent. Certainly also, these discoveries anticipated pretty nearly everything which man himself has ever found it possible to use sex "for." In fact it becomes somewhat humiliating to realize that we seem to have invented nothing absolutely new.

Marital attachment? Attachment to the home? Devotion to children? Long before us, members of the animal kingdom had associated them all with sex. Before us they also founded social groups on the family unit and in some few cases even established monogamy as the rule! Even more strikingly, perhaps, many of them abandoned *force majeure* as the decisive factor in the formation of a mating pair and substituted for it courtships, which became a game, a ritual and an aesthetic experience. Every device of courtship known to the human being was exploited by his predecessors: colorful costume display, song, dance and the wafted perfume. And like man himself, certain animals have come to find the preliminary ceremonies so engaging that they prolong them far beyond the point where they have any justification outside themselves. The grasshopper, for instance, continues to sing like a troubadour long after the lady is weary with waiting.

Even more humiliating, perhaps, than the fact that we have invented nothing is the further fact that the evolution has not been in a straight line from the lowest animal families up to us. The mammals, who are our immediate ancestors, lost as well as gained in the course of their development. No doubt because they lost the power to see colors (which was not recaptured until the primates emerged), the appeal of the eye plays little part in their courtship. In fact "love" in most of its manifestations tends to play a much lesser part in their lives than in that of many lower creatures—even in some who are distinctly less gifted than the outstandingly emotional and aesthetic birds. On the whole, mammalian sex tends to be direct, unadorned, often brutal, and not even the apes, despite their recovery from color blindness, seem to have got very far beyond the

3

most uncomplicated erotic experiences and practices. Intellectually the mammals may be closer to us than any other order of animals, but emotionally and aesthetically they are more remote than some others— which perhaps explains the odd fact that most comparisons with any of them, and all comparisons with the primates, are derogatory. You may call a woman a "butterfly" or describe her as "birdlike." You may even call a man "leonine." But there is no likening with an ape which is not insulting.

How consciously, how poetically or how nobly each particular kind of creature may have learned to love, Venus only knows. But at this very moment of the desert spring many living creatures, plant as well as animal, are celebrating her rites in accordance with the tradition which happens to be theirs.

Fortunately, it is still too early for the tarantulas to have begun their amatory black mass, which, for all I know, may represent one of the oldest versions of the rituals still practiced in the worship of Mr. Swinburne's "mystic and somber Dolores." But this very evening as twilight falls, hundreds of moths will begin to stir themselves in the dusk and presently start their mysterious operations in the heart of those yucca blossoms which are just now beginning to open on the more precocious plants. Young jack rabbits not yet quite the size of an adult cottontail are proof that their parents went early about their business, and many of the brightly colored birds—orioles, cardinals and tanagers—are either constructing their nests or brooding their eggs. Some creatures seem to be worshiping only Venus Pandemos; some others have begun to have some inkling that the goddess manifests herself also as the atavist which the ancients called Venus Eurania. But it is patent to anyone who will take the trouble to look that they stand now upon different rungs of that Platonic ladder of love which man was certainly not the first to make some effort to climb.

Of this I am so sure that I feel it no betrayal of my humanity when I find myself entering with emotional sympathy into a spectacle which is more than a mere show, absorbing though it would be if it were no more than that. Modern knowledge gives me, I think, ample justification for the sense that I am not outside but a part of it, and if it did not give me that assurance, then I should probably agree that I would rather be "some pagan suckled in a creed outworn" than compelled to give it up.

Those very same biological sciences which have traced back to their lowly origins the emotional as well as the physiological characteristics of the sentient human being inevitably furnish grounds for the assumption that if we share much with the animals, they must at the same time share much with us. To maintain that all the conscious concomitants of our physical activities are without analogues in any creatures other than man is to fly in the face of the very evolutionary principles by which those "hardheaded" scientists set so much store. It is to assume that desire and joy have no origins in simpler forms of the same thing, that everything human has "evolved" except the consciousness which makes us aware of what we do. A Descartes, who held that man was an animal-machine differing from other animal-machines in that he alone possessed a gland into which God had inserted a soul, might consistently make between man and the other animals an absolute distinction. But the evolutionist is the last man who has a right to do anything of the sort.

He may, if he can consent to take the extreme position of the pure behaviorist, maintain that in man and the animals alike consciousness neither is nor can be anything but a phosphorescent illusion on the surface of physiological action and reaction, and without any substantial reality or any real significance whatsoever. But there is no choice between that extreme position and recognition of the fact that animals, even perhaps animals as far down in the scale as any still living or preserved in the ancient rocks, were capable of some awareness and of something which was, potentially at least, an emotion.

Either love as well as sex is something which we share with animals, or it is something which does not really exist in us. Either it is legitimate to feel some involvement in the universal Rites of Spring, or it is not legitimate to take our own emotions seriously. And even if the choice between the two possibilities were no more than an arbitrary one, I know which of the alternatives I should choose to believe in and to live by.

THE COLLOID AND THE CRYSTAL

* * * Over the radio the weatherman talked lengthily about cold masses and warm masses, about what was moving out to sea and what wasn't. Did Benjamin Franklin, I wondered, know what he was starting when it first occurred to him to trace by correspondence the course of storms? From my stationary position the most reasonable explanation seemed to be simply that winter had not quite liked the looks of the landscape as she first made it up. She was changing her sheets.

Another forty-eight hours brought one of those nights ideal for frosting the panes. When I came down to breakfast, two of the windows were

Two Worlds (New York: William Sloane, 1953).

almost opaque and the others were etched with graceful, fernlike sprays of ice which looked rather like the impressions left in rocks by some of the antediluvian plants, and they were almost as beautiful as anything which the living can achieve. Nothing else which has never lived looks so much as though it were actually informed with life.

I resisted, I am proud to say, the almost universal impulse to scratch my initials into one of the surfaces. The effect, I knew, would not be an improvement. But so, of course, do those less virtuous than I. That indeed is precisely why they scratch. The impulse to mar and to destroy is as ancient and almost as nearly universal as the impulse to create. The one is an easier way than the other of demonstrating power. Why else should anyone not hungry prefer a dead rabbit to a live one? Not even those horrible Dutch painters of bloody still—or shall we say stilled?—lifes can have really believed that their subjects were more beautiful dead.

Indoors it so happened that a Christmas cactus had chosen this moment to bloom. Its lush blossoms, fuchsia-shaped but pure red rather than magenta, hung at the drooping ends of strange, thick stems and outlined themselves in blood against the glistening background of the frosty pane—jungle flower against frostflower; the warm beauty that breathes and lives and dies competing with the cold beauty that burgeons, not because it wants to, but merely because it is obeying the laws of physics which require that crystals shall take the shape they have always taken since the world began. The effect of red flower against white tracery was almost too theatrical, not quite in good taste perhaps. My eye recoiled in shock and sought through a clear area of the glass the more normal out-of-doors.

On the snow-capped summit of my bird-feeder a chickadee pecked at the new-fallen snow and swallowed a few of the flakes which serve him in lieu of the water he sometimes sadly lacks when there is nothing except ice too solid to be picked at. A downy woodpecker was hammering at a lump of suet and at the coconut full of peanut butter. One nuthatch was dining while the mate waited his—or was it her?—turn. The woodpecker announces the fact that he is a male by the bright red spot on the back of his neck, but to me, at least, the sexes of the nuthatch are indistinguishable. I shall never know whether it is the male or the female who eats first. And that is a pity. If I knew, I could say, like the Ugly Duchess, "and the moral of that is . . ."

But I soon realized that at the moment the frosted windows were what interested me most—especially the fact that there is no other natural phenomenon in which the lifeless mocks so closely the living.

One might almost think that the frostflower had got the idea from the leaf and the branch if one did not know how inconceivably more ancient the first is. No wonder that enthusiastic biologists in the nineteenth century, anxious to conclude that there was no qualitative difference between life and chemical processes, tried to believe that the crystal furnished the link, that its growth was actually the same as the growth of a living organism. But excusable though the fancy was, no one, I think, believes anything of the sort today. Protoplasm is a colloid and the colloids are fundamentally different from the crystalline substances. Instead of crystallizing they jell, and life in its simplest known form is a shapeless blob of rebellious jelly rather than a crystal eternally obeying the most ancient law.

No man ever saw a dinosaur. The last of these giant reptiles was dead eons before the most dubious half-man surveyed the world about him. Not even the dinosaurs ever cast their dim eyes upon many of the still earlier creatures which preceded them. Life changes so rapidly that its later phases know nothing of those which preceded them. But the frost-flower is older than the dinosaur, older than the protozoan, older no doubt than the enzyme or the ferment. Yet it is precisely what it has always been. Millions of years before there were any eyes to see it, millions of years before any life existed, it grew in its own special way, crystallized along its preordained lines of cleavage, stretched out its pseudo-branches and pseudo-leaves. It was beautiful before beauty itself existed.

We find it difficult to conceive a world except in terms of purpose, of will, or of intention. At the thought of the something without beginning and presumably without end, of something which is, nevertheless, regular though blind, and organized without any end in view, the mind reels. Constituted as we are it is easier to conceive how the slime floating upon the waters might become in time *Homo sapiens* than it is to imagine how so complex a thing as a crystal could have always been and can always remain just what it is—complicated and perfect but without any meaning, even for itself. How can the lifeless even obey a law?

To a mathematical physicist I once confessed somewhat shame-facedly that I had never been able to understand how inanimate nature managed to follow so invariably and so promptly her own laws. If I flip a coin across a table, it will come to rest at a certain point. But before it stops at just that point, many factors must be taken into consideration. There is the question of the strength of the initial impulse, of the exact amount of resistance offered by the friction of that particular table top, and of the density of the air at the moment. It would take a physicist a long time to work out the problem and he could achieve only an approximation at that. Yet presumably the coin will stop exactly where it should. Some very rapid calculations have to be made before it can do so, and they are, presumably, always accurate.

And then, just as I was blushing at what I supposed he must regard as my folly, the mathematician came to my rescue by informing me that Laplace had been puzzled by exactly the same fact. "Nature laughs at the difficulties of integration," he remarked—and by "integration" he meant, of course, the mathematician's word for the process involved when a man solves one of the differential equations to which he has reduced the laws of motion.

When my Christmas cactus blooms so theatrically a few inches in front of the frost-covered pane, it also is obeying laws but obeying them much less rigidly and in a different way. It blooms at about Christmastime because it has got into the habit of doing so, because, one is tempted to say, it wants to. As a matter of fact it was, this year, not a Christmas cactus but a New Year's cactus, and because of this unpredictability I would like to call it "he," not "it." His flowers assume their accustomed shape and take on their accustomed color. But not as the frostflowers follow their predestined pattern. Like me, the cactus has a history which stretches back over a long past full of changes and developments. He has not always been merely obeying fixed laws. He has resisted and rebelled; he has attempted novelties, passed through many phases. Like all living things he has had a will of his own. He has made laws, not merely obeyed them.

"Life," so the platitudinarian is fond of saying, "is strange." But from our standpoint it is not really so strange as those things which have no life and yet nevertheless move in their predestined orbits and "act" though they do not "behave." At the very least one ought to say that if life is strange there is nothing about it more strange than the fact that it has its being in a universe so astonishingly shared on the one hand by "things" and on the other by "creatures," that man himself is both a "thing" which obeys the laws of chemistry or physics and a "creature" who to some extent defies them. No other contrast, certainly not the contrast between the human being and the animal, or the animal and the plant, or even the spirit and the body, is so tremendous as this contrast between what lives and what does not.

To think of the lifeless as merely inert, to make the contrast merely in terms of a negative, is to miss the real strangeness. Not the shapeless stone which seems to be merely waiting to be acted upon but the snowflake or the frostflower is the true representative of the lifeless universe as opposed to ours. They represent plainly, as the stone does not, the fixed and perfect system of organization which includes the sun and its planets, includes therefore this earth itself, but against which life has set up its seemingly puny opposition. Order and obedience are the primary characteristics of that which is not alive. The snowflake eternally obeys its one and only law: "Be thou six pointed"; the planets their one and only: "Travel thou in an ellipse." The astronomer can tell where the North Star will be ten thousand years hence; the botanist cannot tell where the dandelion will bloom tomorrow.

Life is rebellious and anarchial, always testing the supposed immutability of the rules which the nonliving changelessly accepts. Because the snowflake goes on doing as it was told, its story up to the end of time was finished when it first assumed the form which it has kept ever since. But the story of every living thing is still in the telling. It may hope and it may try. Moreover, though it may succeed or fail, it will certainly change. No form of frostflower ever became extinct. Such, if you like, is its glory. But such also is the fact which makes it alien. It may melt but it cannot die.

If I wanted to contemplate what is to me the deepest of all mysteries, I should choose as my object lesson a snowflake under a lens and an amoeba under the microscope. To a detached observer—if one can possibly imagine any observer who *could* be detached when faced with such an ultimate choice—the snowflake would certainly seem the "higher" of the two. Against its intricate glistening perfection one would have to place a shapeless, slightly turbid glob, perpetually oozing out in this direction or that but not suggesting so strongly as the snowflake does, intelligence and plan. Crystal and colloid, the chemist would call them, but what an inconceivable contrast those neutral terms imply! Like the star, the snowflake seems to declare the glory of God, while the promise of the amoeba, given only perhaps to itself, seems only contemptible. But its jelly holds, nevertheless, not only its promise but ours also, while the snowflake represents some achievement which we cannot possibly share. After the passage of billions of years, one can see and be aware of the other, but the relationship can never be reciprocal. Even after these billions of years no aggregate of colloids can be as beautiful as the crystal always was, but it can know, as the crystal cannot, what beauty is.

Even to admire too much or too exclusively the alien kind of beauty is dangerous. Much as I love and am moved by the grand, inanimate forms of nature, I am always shocked and a little frightened by those of her professed lovers to whom landscape is the most important thing, and to whom landscape is merely a matter of forms and colors. If they see or are moved by an animal or flower, it is to them merely a matter of a picturesque completion and their fellow creatures are no more than decorative details. But without some continuous awareness of the two great realms of the inanimate and the animate there can be no love of nature as I understand it, and what is worse, there must be a sort of disloyalty to our cause, to us who are colloid, not crystal. The pantheist who feels the oneness of all living things, I can understand; perhaps indeed he and I are in essential agreement. But the ultimate All is not one thing, but two. And because the alien half is in its way as proud and confident and successful as our half, its fundamental difference may not be disregarded with impunity. Of us and all we stand for, the enemy is not so much death as the not-living, or rather that great system which succeeds without ever having had the need to be alive. The frostflower is not merely a wonder; it is also a threat and a warning. How admirable, it seems to say, not living can be! What triumphs mere immutable law can achieve!

Some of Charles Pierce's strange speculations about the possibility that "natural law" is not law at all but merely a set of habits fixed more firmly than any habits we know anything about in ourselves or in the animals suggest the possibility that the snowflake was not, after all, always inanimate, that it merely surrendered at some time impossibly remote the life which once achieved its perfect organization. Yet even if we can imagine such a thing to be true, it serves only to warn us all the more strongly against the possibility that what we call the living might in the end succumb also to the seduction of the immutably fixed.

No student of the anthill has ever failed to be astonished either into admiration or horror by what is sometimes called the perfection of its society. Though even the anthill can change its ways, though even ant individuals—ridiculous as the conjunction of the two words may seem—can sometimes make choices, the perfection of the techniques, the regularity of the habits almost suggest the possibility that the insect is on its way back to inanition, that, vast as the difference still is, an anthill crystallizes somewhat as a snowflake does. But not even the anthill, nothing else indeed in the whole known universe is so perfectly planned as one of these same snowflakes. Would, then, the ultimately planned society be, like the anthill, one in which no one makes plans, any more than a snowflake does? From the cradle in which it is not really born to the grave where it is only a little deader than it always was, the ant-citizen follows a plan to the making of which he no longer contributes anything.

Perhaps we men represent the ultimate to which the rebellion, begun so long ago in some amoeba-like jelly, can go. And perhaps the inanimate is beginning the slow process of subduing us again. Certainly the psychologist and the philosopher are tending more and more to think of us as creatures who obey laws rather than as creatures of will and responsibility. We are, they say, "conditioned" by this or by that. Even the greatest heroes are studied on the assumption that they can be "accounted for" by something outside themselves. They are, it is explained, "the product of forces." All the emphasis is placed, not upon that power to resist and rebel which we were once supposed to have, but upon the "influences" which "formed us." Men are made by society, not society by men. History as well as character "obeys laws." In their view, we crystallize in obedience to some dictate from without instead of moving in conformity with something within.

And so my eye goes questioning back to the frosted pane. While I slept the graceful pseudo-fronds crept across the glass, assuming, as life itself does, an intricate organization. "Why live," they seem to say, "when we can be beautiful, complicated, and orderly without the uncertainty and effort required of a living thing? Once we were all that was. Perhaps some day we shall be all that is. Why not join us?"

Last summer no clod or no stone would have been heard if it had asked such a question. The hundreds of things which walked and sang, the millions which crawled and twined were all having their day. What was dead seemed to exist only in order that the living might live upon it. The plants were busy turning the inorganic into green life and the animals were busy turning that green into red. When we moved, we walked mostly upon grass. Our pre-eminence was unchallenged.

On this winter day nothing seems so successful as the frostflower. It thrives on the very thing which has driven some of us indoors or underground and which has been fatal to many. It is having now its hour of triumph, as we before had ours. Like the cactus flower itself, I am a hothouse plant. Even my cats gaze dreamily out of the window at a universe which is no longer theirs.

How are we to resist, if resist we can? This house into which I have withdrawn is merely an expedient and it serves only my mere physical existence. What mental or spiritual convictions, what will to maintain to my own kind of existence can I assert? For me it is not enough merely to say, as I do say, that I shall resist the invitation to submerge myself into a crystalline society and to stop planning in order that I may be planned for. Neither is it enough to go further, as I do go, and to insist that the most important thing about a man is not that part of him which is "the product of forces" but that part, however small it may be, which enables him to become something other than what the most accomplished sociologist, working in conjunction with the most accomplished psychologist, could predict that he would be.

I need, so I am told, a faith, something outside myself to which I can be loyal. And with that I agree, in my own way. I am on what I call "our side," and I know, though vaguely, what I think that is. Wordsworth's God had his dwelling in the light of setting suns. But the God who dwells there seems to me most probably the God of the atom, the star, and the crystal. Mine, if I have one, reveals Himself in another class of phenomena. He makes the grass green and the blood red.

DONALD CULROSS PEATTIE
1898-1964

The "moderns" that Donald Culross Peattie wrote for in his An Almanac for Moderns *(1935) were a skeptical generation. They were the descendants of Darwin and Freud and the inheritors of World War I, who had seen "the trees blasted by the great guns and the birds feeding on men's eyes." A government botanist and freelance writer, Peattie went to live with his family in rural Illinois during the Depression. His deliberate choice of the archaic literary form of a daily almanac contrasted the stable natural order of the ancient philosophers and naturalists with the modern existential view of nature as soulless and purposeless. Its 365 short chapters not only pose many of the philosophical questions that have preoccupied contemporary nature writers, but also contain an informal survey of natural science and evocative observations of seasonal life. In his combination of lyrical style and scientific observation Peattie anticipates such writers as Lewis Thomas and Loren Eiseley.*

From AN ALMANAC
FOR MODERNS

MARCH TWENTY-FIRST

On this chill uncertain spring day, toward twilight, I have heard the first frog quaver from the marsh. That is a sound that Pharaoh listened to as it rose from the Nile, and it blended, I suppose, with his discontents

An Almanac for Moderns (New York: Putnam, 1935).

and longings, as it does with ours. There is something lonely in that first shaken and uplifted trilling croak. And more than lonely, for I hear a warning in it, as Pharaoh heard the sound of plague. It speaks of the return of life, animal life, to the earth. It tells of all that is most unutterable in evolution—the terrible continuity and fluidity of protoplasm, the irrepressible forces of reproduction—not mystical human love, but the cold batrachian jelly by which we vertebrates are linked to the things that creep and writhe and are blind yet breed and have being. More than half it seems to threaten that when mankind has quite thoroughly shattered and eaten and debauched himself with his own follies, that voice may still be ringing out in the marshes of the Nile and the Thames and the Potomac, unconscious that Pharaoh wept for his son.

It always seems to me that no sooner do I hear the first frog trill than I find the first cloud of frog's eggs in a wayside pool, so swiftly does the emergent creature pour out the libation of its cool fertility. There is life where before there was none. It is as repulsive as it is beautiful, as silvery-black as it is slimy. Life, in short, raw and exciting, life almost in primordial form, irreducible element.

MARCH TWENTY-SECOND

For the ancients the world was a little place, bounded between Ind and Thule. The sky bent very low over Olympus, and astronomers had not yet taken the friendliness out of the stars. The shepherd kings of the desert called them by the names Job knew, Al-Debaran, Fomalhaut, Mizar, Al-Goth, Al-Tair, Deneb and Achernar. For the Greeks the glittering constellations made pictures of their heroes and heroines, and of beasts and birds. The heavenly truth of their Arcadian mythology blazed nightly in the skies for the simplest clod to read.

Through all this celestial splendor the sun plowed yearly in a broad track that they called the zodiac. As it entered each constellation a new month with fresh significances and consequences was marked down by a symbol. Lo, in the months when the rains descended, when the Nile and the Tigris and Yangtse rose, the sun entered the constellations that were like Fishes, and like Water Carriers! In the hot dry months it was in the constellation that is unmistakably a scorpion, bane of the desert. Who could say that the stars in their orderly procession did not sway a man's destiny?

Best of all, the year began with spring, with the vernal equinox. It was a natural, a pastoral, a homely sort of year, which a man could take to his heart and remember; he could tell the date by the feeling in his bones. It is the year which green things, and the beasts and birds in their migrations, all obey, a year like man's life, from his birth cry to the snows upon the philosopher's head.

MARCH TWENTY-THIRD

The old almanacs have told off their years, and are dead with them. The weather-wisdom and the simple faith that cropped up through them as naturally as grass in an orchard, are withered now, and their flowers of homely philosophy and seasonable prediction and reflection are dry, and only faintly, quaintly fragrant. The significance of the Bull and the Crab and the Lion are not more dead, for the modern mind, than the Nature philosophy of a generation ago. This age has seen the trees blasted to skeletons by the great guns, and the birds feeding on men's eyes. Pippa has passed.

It is not that man alone is vile. Man is a part of Nature. So is the atomic disassociation called high explosive. So are violent death, rape, agony, and rotting. They were all here, and quite natural, before our day, in the sweet sky and the blowing fields.

There is no philosophy with a shadow of realism about it, save a philosophy based upon Nature. It turns a smiling face, a surface easily conquered by the gun, the bridge, the dynamite stick. Yet there is no obedience but to its laws. Hammurabi spoke and Rameses commanded, and the rat gnawed and the sun shone and the hive followed its multiplex and golden order. Flowers pushed up their child faces in the spring, and the bacteria slowly took apart the stuff of life. Today the Kremlin commands, the Vatican speaks. And tomorrow the rat will still be fattening, the sun be a little older, and the bacteria remain lords of creation, whose subtraction would topple the rest of life.

Now how can a man base his way of thought on Nature and wear so happy a face? How can he take comfort from withering grass where he lays his head, from a dying sun to which he turns his face, from a mortal woman's head pressed on his shoulder? To say how that might be, well might he talk the year around.

MARCH TWENTY-FOURTH

Perhaps in Tempe the wild lawns are thick with crocuses, and narcissus blows around Paestum, but here on this eastern shore of a western world, spring is a season of what the embittered call realism, by which they mean the spoiling of joy. Joy will come, as the joy of a child's birth comes—after the pains. So dry cold winds still walk abroad, under gray skies.

It is not that nothing blooms or flies; the honey bees were out for an hour, the one hour of sunlight, and above the pools where the salamander's eggs drift in inky swirls, the early midges danced. Down the runs and rills I can hear the calling of a red-bird entreating me to come and find him, come and find him! There is a black storm of grackles in the tree limbs where the naked maple flowers are bursting out in scarlet tips from their bud scales, and a song-sparrow sits on an alder that dangles out its little gold tails.

We are so used to flowers wrapped up in the pretty envelopes of their corollas and calyces, so softened in our taste for the lovely in Nature, that we scarcely rate an alder catkin as a flower at all. Yet it is nothing else—nothing but the male anthers, sowing the wind with their freight of fertilizing pollen. The small, compact female flowers, like tiny cones, wait in the chill wild air for the golden cargo.

So does our spring begin, in a slow flowering on the leafless wood of the bough of hazel and alder and poplar and willow, a hardy business, a spawning upon the air, like the spawning in the ponds, a flowering so primitive that it carries us back to ancient geologic times, when trees that are now fossils sowed the wind like these, their descendants—an epoch when the world, too, was in its naked springtime.

MARCH TWENTY-FIFTH

The beginnings of spring, the true beginnings, are quite unlike the springtides of which poets and musicians sing. The artists become conscious of spring in late April, or May, when it is not too much to say that the village idiot would observe that birds are singing and nesting, that fields bear up their freight of flowering and ants return to their proverbial industry.

But the first vernal days are younger. Spring steals in shyly, a tall, naked child in her pale gold hair, amidst us the un-innocent, skeptics in wool mufflers, prudes in gumshoes and Grundies with head-colds. Very secretly the old field cedars sow the wind with the freight of their ancient pollen. A grackle in the willow croaks and sings in the uncertain, ragged voice of a boy. The marshes brim, and walking is a muddy business. Oaks still are barren and secretive. On the lilac tree only the twin buds suggest her coming maturity and flowering. But there in the pond float the inky masses of those frog's eggs, visibly life in all its rawness, its elemental shape and purpose. Now is the moment when the secret of life could be discovered, yet no one finds it.

MARCH TWENTY-SIXTH

Out of the stoa, two thousand years ago, strode a giant to lay hold on life and explain it. He went down to the "primordial slime" of the seashore to look for its origin. There if anywhere he would find it, he thought, where the salt water and the earth were met, and the mud quivered like a living thing, and from it emerged strange shapeless primitive beings, themselves scarce more than animate bits of ooze. To Aristotle it seemed plain enough that out of the dead and the inanimate is made the living, and back to death are turned the bodies of all things that have lived, to be used over again. So nothing was wasted; all moved in a perpetual cycle. Out of vinegar, he felt certain, came vinegar eels, out of dung came blow-flies, out of decaying fruit bees were born, and out of the rain pool frogs spawned.

But the eye of even Aristotle was purblind in its nakedness. Of the spore and the sperm he never dreamed; he guessed nothing of bacteria. Now man can peer down through the microscope, up at the revealed stars. And behold, the lens has only multiplied the facts and deepened the mystery.

For now we know that spontaneous generation never takes place. Life comes only from life. Was not the ancient Hindu symbol for it a serpent with a tail in its mouth? Intuitive old fellows, those Aryan brothers of ours, wise in their superstitions, like old women. Life, we discover, is a closed, nay, a charmed circle. Wherever you pick it up, it has already begun; yet as soon as you try to follow it, it is already dying.

MARCH TWENTY-SEVENTH

First to grasp biology as a science, Aristotle thought that he had also captured the secret of life itself. From the vast and original body of his observation, he deduced a cosmology like a pure Greek temple, symmetrical and satisfying. For two millenniums it housed the serene intelligence of the race.

Here was an absolute philosophy; nothing need be added to it; detraction was heretical. It traced the ascent of life from the tidal ooze up to man, the plants placed below the animals, the animals ranged in order of increasing intelligence. Beyond man nothing could be imagined but God, the supreme intelligence. God was all spirit; the lifeless rock was all matter. Living beings on this earth were spirit infusing matter.

Still this conception provides the favorite text of poet or pastor, praising the earth and the fullness thereof. It fits so well with the grandeur of the heavens, the beauty of the flowers at our feet, the rapture of the birds! The Nature lover of today would ask nothing better than that it should be true.

Aristotle was sure of it. He points to marble in a quarry. It is only matter; then the sculptor attacks it with his chisel, with a shape in his mind. With form, soul enters into the marble. So all living things are filled with soul, some with more, some with less. But even a jellyfish is infused with that which the rock possesses not. Thus existence has its origin in supreme intelligence, and everything has an intelligent cause and serves its useful purpose. That purpose is the development of higher planes of existence. Science, thought its Adam, had but to put the pieces of the puzzle together, to expose for praise the cosmic design, all beautiful.

MARCH TWENTY-EIGHTH

The hook-nosed Averroës, the Spanish Arab born in Cordova in 1126, and one time cadi of Seville, shook a slow dissenting head. He did not like this simile of Aristotle's, of the marble brought to life and form by the sculptor. The simile, he keenly perceived, would be applicable at best if the outlines of the statue were already performed in the marble as it lay in the quarry. For that is precisely how we find life. The tree is preformed in the seed; the future animal already exists in the embryo. Wherever we look we find form, structure, adaptation, already present. Never has it been vouchsafed to us to see pure creation out of the lifeless.

And Galileo, also, ventured to shake the pillars of the Schoolmen's Aristotelian temple. Such a confirmed old scrutinizer was not to be drawn toward inscrutable will. The stars, nearest of all to Aristotle's God, should have moved with godlike precision, and Galileo, peering, found them erring strangely all across heaven. He shrugged, but was content. Nature itself was the miracle, Nature with all its imperfections. Futile for science to try to discover what the forces of Nature are; it can only discover how they operate.

MARCH TWENTY-NINTH

Comforting, sustaining, like the teat to the nursling, is Aristotle's beautiful idea that everything serves a useful purpose and is part of the great design. Ask, for instance, of what use is grass. Grass, the pietist assures us, was made in order to nourish cows. Cows are here on earth to nourish men. So all flesh is grass, and grass was put here for man.

But of what use, pray, is man? Would anybody, besides his dog, miss him if he were gone? Would the sun cease to shed its light because there were no human beings here to sing the praises of sunlight? Would there be sorrow among the little hiding creatures of the underwood, or loneliness in the hearts of the proud and noble beasts? Would the other simians feel that their king was gone? Would God, Jehovah, Zeus, Allah, miss the sound of hymns and psalms, the odor of frankincense and flattery?

There is no certainty vouchsafed us in the vast testimony of Nature that the universe was designed for man, nor yet for any purpose, even the bleak purpose of symmetry. The courageous thinker must look the inimical aspects of his environment in the face, and accept the stern fact that the universe is hostile and deathy to him save for a very narrow zone where it permits him, for a few eons, to exist.

MARCH THIRTIETH

Archaic and obsolete sounds the wisdom of the great old Greek. Life, his pronouncement ran, is soul pervading matter. What, soul in a jellyfish, an oyster, a burdock? Then by soul he could not have meant that moral quality which Paul of Tarsus or Augustine of Hippo were to call soul. Aristotle is talking rather about that undefined but essential and precious something that just divides the lowliest microörganism from the dust; that makes the ugly thousand-legged creature flee from death; that makes the bird pour out its heart in morning rapture; that makes the love of man for woman a holy thing sacred to the carrying on of the race.

But what is this but life itself? In every instance Aristotle but affirms that living beings are matter pervaded by a noble, a palpitant and thrilling thing called life. This is the mystery, and his neat cosmology solves nothing of it. But it is not Aristotle's fault that he did not give us the true picture of things. It is Nature herself, as we grow in comprehension of her, who weans us from our early faith.

MARCH THIRTY-FIRST

Aristotle's rooms in the little temple of the Lyceum were the first laboratory, where dissection laid bare the sinews and bones of life. The Lyceum was a world closer to the marine biological station at Wood's Hole, Massachusetts, than it was to its neighbor the Parthenon. Its master did for marine biology what Euclid did for geometry; his work on the embryology of the chick still stands as a nearly perfect monograph of biological investigation. The originality, the scope of his works, the magnificence of his dream for biology as an independent science, have probably never been surpassed by any one who has lived since.

Unlike many of the more timid or less gifted investigators of today, Aristotle could not help coming to conclusions about it all. For his cosmology it should be said that it was the best, perhaps the only possible, philosophy of the origin and nature of life which the times permitted. We can all feel in our bones how agreeable it were to accept the notion of design, symmetry, purpose, an evolution toward a spiritual godhead such as Aristotle assures us exists.

But as it was Aristotle himself who taught us to observe, investigate, deduce what facts compel us to deduce, so we must concede that it is Nature herself, century after century—day after day, indeed, in the whirlwind progress of science—that propels us farther and farther away from Aristotelian beliefs. At every point she fails to confirm the grand old man's cherished picture of things. There are persons so endowed by temperament that they will assert that if Nature has no "soul," purpose, nor symmetry, we needs must put them in the picture, lest the resulting composition be scandalous, intolerable, and maddening. To such the scientist can only say, "Believe as you please."

APRIL FIRST

I say that it touches a man that his blood is sea water and his tears are salt, that the seed of his loins is scarcely different from the same cells in a seaweed, and that of stuff like his bones are coral made. I say that physical and biologic law lies down with him, and wakes when a child stirs in the womb, and that the sap in a tree, uprushing in the spring, and the smell of the loam, where the bacteria bestir themselves in darkness, and the path of the sun in the heaven, these are facts of first importance to his mental conclusions, and that a man who goes in no consciousness of them is a drifter and a dreamer, without a home or any contact with reality.

SIGURD OLSON
1899-1982

Certain writers become the representatives for their chosen landscapes. Just as John Muir is identified with Yosemite and Mary Austin with the Southwestern deserts, Sigurd Olson expresses, and assumes, the character of the northern Midwest. His home for much of his career as a teacher, guide, and writer was in Ely, Minnesota—near the Quetico–Superior wilderness which he helped to protect. In his essays and books Olson told the stories of that region of waters and forests. One of his special accomplishments was to integrate the lives of animals, plants, and changing sky with the tales of voyageurs and present-day homesteaders, to convey both the mystery and the human significance of his beloved North Woods. Olson's books include The Singing Wilderness *(1956),* Listening Point *(1958), and* The Lonely Land *(1961).*

NORTHERN LIGHTS

The lights of the aurora moved and shifted over the horizon. Sometimes there were shafts of yellow tinged with green, then masses of evanescence which moved from east to west and back again. Great streamers of bluish white zigzagged like a tremendous trembling curtain from one end of the sky to the other. Streaks of yellow and orange and red shimmered along the flowing borders. Never for a moment were they still, fading until they were almost completely gone, only to dance forth again in renewed splendor with infinite combinations and startling patterns of design.

The lake lay like a silver mirror before me, and from its frozen surface came subterranean rumblings, pressure groans, sharp reports from the newly forming ice. As far as I could see, the surface was clear and shin-

The Singing Wilderness (New York: Knopf, 1956).

ing. That ice was something to remember here in the north, for most years the snows come quickly and cover the first smooth glaze of freezing almost as soon as it is formed, or else the winds ruffle the surface of the crystallizing water and fill it with ridges and unevenness. But this time there had been no wind or snow to interfere, and the ice everywhere was clear—seven miles of perfect skating, something to dream about in years to come.

Hurriedly I strapped on my skates, tightened the laces, and in a moment was soaring down the path of shifting light which stretched endlessly before me. Out in the open away from shore there were few cracks—stroke—stroke—stroke—long and free, and I knew the joy that skating and skiing can give, freedom of movement beyond myself. But to get the feel of soaring, there must be miles of distance and conditions must be right. As I sped down the lake, I was conscious of no effort, only of the dancing lights in the sky and a sense of lightness and exaltation.

Shafts of light shot up into the heavens above me and concentrated there in a final climactic effort in which the shifting colors seemed drained from the horizons to form one gigantic rosette of flame and yellow and greenish purple. Suddenly I grew conscious of the reflections from the ice itself and that I was skating through a sea of changing color caught between the streamers above and below. At that moment I was part of the aurora, part of its light and of the great curtain that trembled above me.

Those moments of experience are rare. Sometimes I have known them while swimming in the moonlight, again while paddling a canoe when there was no wind and the islands seemed inverted and floating on the surface. I caught it once when the surf was rolling on an ocean coast and I was carried on the crest of a wave that had begun a thousand miles away. Here it was once more—freedom of movement and detachment from the earth.

Down the lake I went straight in to the glistening path, speeding through a maze of changing color—stroke—stroke—stroke—the ringing of steel on ice, the sharp, reverberating rumbles of expansion below. Clear ice for the first time in years, and the aurora blazing away above it.

At the end of the lake I turned and saw the glittering lights of Winton far behind me. I lay down on the ice to rest. The sky was still bright and I watched the shifting lights come and go. I knew what the astronomers and the physicists said, that they were caused by sunspots and areas of gaseous disturbance on the face of the sun that bombarded the earth's stratosphere with hydrogen protons and electrons which in turn exploded atoms of oxygen, nitrogen, helium, and the other elements surrounding us. Here were produced in infinite combinations all the colors of the spectrum. It was all very plausible and scientific, but tonight that explanation left me cold. I was in no mood for practicality, for I had just come skating down the skyways themselves and had seen the aurora from the inside. What did the scientists know about what I had done? How could they explain what had happened to me and the strange sensations I had known?

Much better the poem of Robert Service telling of the great beds of radium emanating shafts of light into the northern darkness of the Yukon and how men went mad trying to find them. How infinitely more satisfying to understand and feel the great painting by Franz Johnson of a lone figure crossing a muskeg at night with the northern lights blazing above it. I stood before that painting in the Toronto Art Gallery one day and caught all the stark loneliness, all the beauty and the cold of that scene, and for a moment forgot the busy city outside.

I like to think of them as the ghost dance of the Chippewas. An Indian once told me that when a warrior died, he gathered with his fellows along the northern horizon and danced the war dances they had known on earth. The shifting streamers and the edgings of color came from the giant headdress they wore. I was very young when I first saw them that way, and there were times during those enchanted years when I thought I could distinguish the movements of individual bodies as they rushed from one part of the sky to another. I knew nothing then of protons or atoms and saw the northern lights as they should be seen. I knew, too, the wonderment that only a child can know and a beauty that is enhanced by mystery.

As I lay there on the ice and thought of these things I wondered if legendry could survive scientific truth, if the dance of the protons would replace the ghost dance of the Chippewas. I wondered as I began to skate toward home if anything—even knowing the physical truth— could ever change the beauty of what I had seen, the sense of unreality. Indian warriors, exploding atoms, beds of radium—what difference did it make? What counted was the sense of the north they gave me, the fact that they typified the loneliness, the stark beauty of frozen muskegs, lakes, and forests. Those northern lights were part of me and I of them.

On the way back I noticed that there was a half-moon over the cluster of lights in the west. I skirted the power dam at the mouth of the Kawishiwi River, avoiding the blaze of its light on the black water below the spillway. Then suddenly the aurora was gone and the moon as well.

Stroke—stroke—stroke—the shores were black now, pinnacled spruce and shadowed birch against the sky. At the landing I looked back. The ice was still grumbling and groaning, still shaping up to the mold of its winter bed.

EDWIN WAY TEALE
1899 - 1980

His many books on nature made Teale one of the most important teachers of his generation. Among the best known of them were The Lost Woods *(1945),* North with the Spring *(1951), and* A Walk Through the Year *(1978). He took excursions, in Thoreau's sense of the word, and, as a fine photographer, frequently focused his explorations with close-up images. Teale was most closely associated with one magazine,* Audubon, *of which he served as a contributing editor from 1942 to 1980. In addition to being an important nature writer, Teale advanced and interpreted the tradition through his popular editions of the works of Audubon, Thoreau, Muir, and Fabre.*

THE LOST WOODS

A back-country road was carrying us south, carrying us through a snow-filled landscape and under the sullen gray of a December sky. Minute by minute, the long chain of the Indiana dunes receded behind us. Ahead, beyond the bobbing ears of the horses, I could catch glimpses of the blue-white, far-away ridges of the Valparaiso moraine.

Our low bob-sled tilted and pitched over the frozen ruts. Beside me, my bearded grandfather clung to the black strips of the taut reins and braced himself with felt-booted feet widespread. At every lurch, my own short, six-year-old legs, dangling below the seat, gyrated wildly like the tail of an off-balance cat.

We had left Lone Oak, my grandfather's dune-country farm, that winter morning, to drive to a distant woods. In the late weeks of autumn, my grandfather had been busy there, felling trees and cutting firewood. He was going after a load of this wood and he was taking me along. At first, we drove through familiar country—past Gunder's big red barn,

The Lost Woods: Adventures of a Naturalist (New York: Dodd, Mead, 1945).

the weed lot and the school house. Then we swung south and crossed the right-of-way of the Pere Marquette railroad. Beyond, we journeyed into a world that was, for me, new and unexplored. The road ran on and on. We seemed traversing vast distances while the smell of coming snow filled the air.

Eventually, I remember, we swung off the road into a kind of lane. The fences soon disappeared and we rode out into open country, onto a wide, undulating sea of whiteness with here and there the island of a bush-clump. As we progressed, a ribbon of runner-tracks and hoof-marks steadily unrolled, lengthened, and followed us across the snow.

Winter trees, gray and silent, began to rise around us. They were old trees, gnarled and twisted. We came to a frozen stream and turned to follow its bank. The bob-sled, from time to time, would rear suddenly and then plunge downward as a front runner rode over a low stump or hidden log. Each time the sled seat soared and dropped away, I clung grimly to my place or clawed wildly at my grandfather's overcoat. He observed with a chuckle:

" 'T takes a good driver t' hit *all* th' stumps."

Then, while the snow slipped backward beneath the runners and the great trees of that somber woods closed around us, we rode on in silence. As we advanced, the trees grew steadily thicker; the woods more dark and lonely. In a small clearing, my grandfather pulled up beside a series of low, snow-covered walls. Around us were great white mounds that looked like igloos. The walls were the corded stovewood; the igloos were the snow-clad piles of discarded branches.

Wisps of steam curled up from the sides of the heated horses and my grandfather threw blankets over their backs before he bent to the work of tossing stovewood into the lumber-wagon bed of the bob-sled. The hollow thump and crash of the frozen sticks reverberated through the still woods.

I soon tired of helping and wandered about, small as an atom, among the great trees—oak and beech, hickory and ash and sycamore. An air of strangeness and mystery enveloped the dark woods. I peered timidly down gloomy aisles between the trees. Branches rubbed together in the breeze with sudden shrieks or mournful wailings and the cawing of a distant crow echoed dismally. I was at once enchanted and fearful. Each time I followed one of the corridors away from the clearing, I hurried back to be reassured by the sight of my bundled-up grandfather stooping and rising as he picked up the cordwood and tossed it into the sled.

He stopped from time to time to point out special trees. In the hollow of one great beech, he had found two quarts of shelled nuts stored away by a squirrel. In another tree, with a gaping rectangular hole chopped in its upper trunk, the owner of the woods had obtained several milk-pails full of dark honey made by a wild swarm of bees. Still another hollow tree had a story to tell. It was an immense sycamore by the stream-bank. Its interior, smoke-blackened and cavernous, was filled with a damp and acrid odor. One autumn night, there, hunters had treed and smoked out a raccoon.

There were other exciting discoveries: the holes of owls and wood-peckers; the massed brown leaves of squirrel-nests high in the bare branches; the tracks of small wild animals that wound about among the trees, that crisscrossed on the ice, that linked together the great mounds of the discarded branches. In one place, the wing-feathers of an owl had left their imprint on the snow; and there, the trail of some small animal had ended and there, on the white surface, were tiny drops of red. From the dark mouth of a burrow, under the far bank of the frozen stream, tracks led away over the ice. I longed to follow them around a distant bend in the stream. But the reaches beyond, forbidding under the still tenseness of the ominous sky, slowed my steps to a standstill. However, my mind and imagination were racing.

Behind and beyond the silence and inactivity of the woods, there was a sense of action stilled by our presence; of standing in a charmed circle where all life paused, enchanted, until we passed on. I had the feeling that animals would appear, their interrupted revels and battles would recommence, with our departure. My imagination invested the woods with a fearful and delicious atmosphere of secrecy and wildness. It left me with an endless curiosity about this lonely tract and all of its inhabitants.

After nearly half an hour had gone by, my grandfather's long sled was full and he called me back to the seat. As we rode away, I looked back as long as I could see the trees, watching to the last this gloomy woods, under its gloomy sky, which had made such a profound impression on me. All the way home, I was silent, busy with my own speculations.

Thirty years later, I spent one whole summer's day driving my car over dirt roads of the region, searching for this old, remembered woods. But I never found it. Perhaps I took the wrong turns. Perhaps the woods had been felled and the land turned into cultivated fields. Perhaps I failed to recognize the wooded tract as seen through the eyes of a small boy. I know that, as I drove about, the great distances of childhood had greatly shrunk. How soon I came to the corners! How much smaller were the trees than I remembered them; how much lower the hills! Time seemed to have dwarfed the towering barns of boyhood and to have reduced the size of cornfields and pastures. At any rate, I never saw the ancient trees of that old woodland a second time. The Lost Woods of childhood remained lost forever.

In talking to others, I have come to believe that most of us have had some such experience—that some lonely spot, some private nook, some glen or streamside-scene impressed us so deeply that even today its memory recalls the mood of a lost enchantment. At the age of eighty, my grandmother used to recall with delight a lonely tract she called "The Beautiful Big South Woods." There, as a girl one spring day, she had seen the whole floor of the woods, acre on acre, carpeted with the blooms of bloodroot and spring beauties and blue and pink hepaticas. She had seen the woods only once but she never forgot it.

When Henry Thoreau was five, his parents, then living in the city of Boston, took him eighteen miles into the country to a woodland scene that he, too, never forgot. It was, he said, one of the earliest scenes stamped on the tablets of his memory. During succeeding years of childhood, that woodland formed the basis of his dreams. The spot to which he had been taken was Walden Pond, near Concord. Twenty-three years later, writing in his cabin on the shores of this same pond, Thoreau noted the unfading impression that "fabulous landscape" had made and how, even at that early age, he had given preference to this recess—"where almost sunshine and shadow were the only inhabitants that varied the scene"—over the tumultuous city in which he lived.

John C. Merriam, at the time he was President of the Carnegie Institution of Washington, D.C., wrote of the profound effect a woodland hilltop, rising beyond the pastures of a valley at his childhood home, had had upon his early life. The margin of this forest seemed like an impenetrable wall beyond which lay a place of continuous night. Often at evening he could hear the howling of wolves among the trees. His imagination peopled the hilltop with strange creatures and, in his mind, the timbered tract became symbolical of all that is mysterious and awaiting solution. As the later years of his life passed, this eminent scientist wrote, the thing that led him on was the endless challenge of the unknown—a challenge that appeared to him first in the form of this dark and distant woods of his boyhood.

Such lasting impressions of life, such moments of far-reaching consequences, almost always arrive unbidden. Rarely can they be planned beforehand. A friend of mine, a writer who lived as a small boy in Mexico, once told me that the pivotal day in his life came when he was six. His mother imagined he was destined to be a great pianist. When she heard that Paderewski was to give a concert in Mexico City, she planned that that event would be the turning point in the child's life. The memory of the master's music was to spur him on to greatness. The evening came. The master played. The boy returned home in disgrace. At the end of the first number, he had fallen fast asleep. Thereafter, he was permitted to follow his own bent.

For me, the Lost Woods became a starting point and a symbol. It was a symbol of all the veiled and fascinating secrets of the out-of-doors. It was the starting point of my absorption in the world of Nature. The image of that somber woods returned a thousand times in memory. It aroused in my mind an interest in the ways and the mysteries of the wild world that a lifetime is not too long to satisfy.

THE SELBORNE NIGHTINGALE

One hundred and seventy-seven years had passed since the publication of *The Natural History of Selborne.* One hundred and seventy-three years had elapsed since the death of Gilbert White. Yet, when we emerged from one of the sunken roads or "hollow lanes" along which White had botanized, and came to the village of Selborne that May morning, we found that it still consisted, as it had in his day, of "one straggling street." Although hardly fifty miles from London, the third largest city in the world, it impressed us—as it had impressed so many others before us—as remote, secluded, part of a simpler, more tranquil past. Television antennas rose from most of the cottage roofs and, a mile or so away, the steel spiderweb of a high-tension line ran uphill and downhill across the countryside. But these recent intrusions appeared to disturb not at all the ancient calm of Selborne.

Ranged along a shelf opposite the fireplace in my study at home, sixteen editions of White's *Natural History* stand side by side. Some are illustrated with woodcuts, others with steel engravings, others with photographs. But whatever the form of the art, its goal is the same—to depict the very scenes we now saw around us. We were arriving at the end of a long procession of pilgrims who—on foot, on bicycles, in horse-drawn vehicles, in automobiles and buses—had journeyed in this Hampshire village that Gilbert White, in the beautiful simplicity of his style, had made famous.

We came to Selborne in the green beauty of the English spring. Sunshine flooded the fields, the new-leaved trees, the sleek, silvery pelts of the old thatched roofs. Soon we were installed in an upstairs room of the annex of the Queen's Hotel, almost opposite The Wakes, the rambling house where Gilbert White had lived. For the next three days and nights, our address might have been given: "Under a thatched roof, Across from The Wakes, in Selborne."

Springtime in Britain (New York: Dodd, Mead, 1970).

The small leaded panes of our windows looked down on the same street where the old hunting mare that ran loose on the common had died after it had taken ill and came "down into the village, as it were, to implore the help of men." Near our building, three of the four lime trees White planted in 1756 to screen a butcher's shop and the slaughtering yard behind it, still clung to life. Although they were now mere maimed and hollow stubs of great trees, they were responding with green sprouts to the sunshine and warmth of yet another spring.

Nothing we had ever heard or read, no picture we had seen, quite prepared us for the size of the ancient yew that stands just outside the Church of Saint Mary where White conducted services. Even on the brightest days, a continual twilight lies in the shade of its dense foliage. This yew is believed to have been a well-grown tree, perhaps a century old, when King Alfred was alive. Its age is estimated at more than twelve centuries. When Nellie and I examined its gigantic trunk, nearly twenty-eight feet in circumference, we noticed a roughened vertical strip, perhaps eighteen or twenty inches high and five inches wide. It appeared scarred by the claws of some animal. Turning away, we saw a large yellow-and-white cat watching us from the top of a neighboring grave-stone. In the ancient yew, no doubt, it was making use of one of the oldest scratching posts in Britain.

As from the entrance of a cave on a summer day, cool air flowed from the open door of the church. Within the dim interior of the building we stood beside the massive font formed of three blocks of white stone and dating back to Saxon times. Here the children of Selborne had been baptized for nearly 800 years. Still in evidence are the remains of locks that, in long-gone days, secured a heavy cover over the font to prevent theft of consecrated baptismal water for use in sorcery. At one time, an official who bore the title of "Wiper of Doges" and was equipped with a whip and long tongs for grasping animals, was charged with the ejection of dogs during services. Wherever we looked, in this Hampshire village, we saw reflected the long span of history, the continuity of village life, the antiquity of customs.

One feature of the church that had special interest for us was of more modern origin. This was the Gilbert White memorial window. It de-picts, in stained glass, St. Francis of Assisi surrounded by many of the birds mentioned in the writings of the Selborne naturalist. Outside, in our search for the modest headstone that marks White's grave, we ob-served what seemed to be rows of nail heads running between the ma-sonry layers of the stone tower. Each "nail head" was a bit of dark, iron-filled rock that had been pushed into the wet mortar. We saw this same form of decoration, known as "garnetting," on several of the houses of the village. They seemed, as White expressed it, "studded with ten-penny nails." Nowhere else did we notice such architectural decoration. It appeared confined to this small portion of England along the Hampshire-Surrey border.

The only inscription appearing on the low white stone marking the naturalist's grave is "G.W. 26th June, 1793." And so small is that stone that its face is covered by even so brief an epitaph. As we stood motionless beside it, a song thrush, an earthworm folded over in its bill, alighted in the sunshine on another marker even older, a tombstone silvery with weathered age and golden with lichens. Among some of these very graves, two centuries before, Gilbert White had paused to enjoy such sights as these.

In the vicinity of Selborne public footpaths abound. One, open to all walkers, cuts from the Plestor, or "play-place"—the village green—directly through the graveyard to a swinging stile that emerges on one of White's favorite walks, the path that leads to the Short Lythe and the Long Lythe. "Lythe," derived from a Saxon word meaning valley, is pronounced to rhyme with "myth." On springy turf Nellie and I followed the path down a long slope, past stumps of immense oaks in the shade of which the naturalist may well have rested during summer walks, to the clear, narrow flow of Oakhanger Stream. The water was only a long step or a short jump across. Looking down, we saw cases of caddis flies waving in the riffles. Held within a curve of the stream, one muddy stretch lay like a half moon, shining with the yellow of the massed flowers of the marsh marigold.

On the hillside beyond, in a place it had occupied for generations, a rookery filled the treetops. Through some condition resulting on that May afternoon from the wind, the topography, or the thermal currents, powerful updrafts ascended from the valley. Half a dozen rooks, sporting in the sky, circled continually, riding upward on this elevator of air. The upsurge carried them far above us. At the summit of their climb, they appeared no larger than sparrows.

Now in the open, where swallows—spreading and closing their forked tails—skimmed above the tilted pastures of valley slopes; now in darkening beech woods with twisted roots around us, we progressed along the trail Gilbert White had so often followed. It extended before us—a path of wildflowers. We stopped, walked a few steps, stopped again as some new, unfamiliar bloom of spring caught our eye.

For weeks now the barren strawberry had been in flower. This cinquefoil, so closely resembling in leaf and flower the wild strawberry that a careful examination is needed to distinguish between the two, is one of the earliest wildflowers to appear in Britain. White, four-petaled blooms of a different kind rose in loose clusters above the broad, heart-shaped, garlic-scented leaves of Jack-by-the-hedge, also known as garlic-mustard and sauce-alone. Here, too, we found the bitter vetch, bearing flowers that fade from bright reddish-purple to blue or greenish-brown.

With delight we paused beside other Selborne blooms. We bent to examine the striking cowled flowers of the yellow archangel—sometimes called by country people the weasel-snout. At the top of squared stems, they bloomed in whorls, their three-lobed lower lips streaked with red. Along the more deeply shaded portions of the Long Lythe trail, we came upon that lover of the leaf mold beneath beech trees, the woodruff. Ivory white, the tiny funnel-shaped blooms clustered at the top of stems encircled by slender leaves that radiated outward like the spokes of a wheel. In older times, this perennial plant was gathered and dried and placed among folded linens to impart a pleasant perfume reminiscent of new-mown hay.

For yards at a time, ramsons, *Allium ursinum,* spread in dense green carpets beside our path, their loose, ball-like clusters of white flowers supported by triangular stems. A member of the lily family, this wild-flower over winters as a bulb. Its leaves, like those of the Jack-by-the-hedge, give off an oniony odor when crushed. The ramsoms is, in fact, a wild relative of the onion. The leek, chive, garlic, and onion—originating in Europe and northern Asia—are all cultivated species of *Allium.*

Somewhere on the Long Lythe path, where the fiddleheads of young ferns were unrolling, we were surprised by the curious unflowerlike flowers of the wood spurge. At the top of fleshy stems, the blooms, which do not appear on these perennials until the second year, suggest small greenish cups. Another odd feature of this plant is its milky and poisonous juice.

The sun disappeared behind the horizon as we were returning to the village and, in impressive sequence, we saw our first sunset, our first twilight, our first star-filled night at Selborne. In the dusk swifts flew over the cottages. In the thirty-ninth letter of his book Gilbert White notes that each year the same number of swifts—eight pairs, about four nesting in the church and the rest in cottages—returned to the village. During the intervening years, at least four counts, the latest by James Fisher, have been made of the Selborne swifts. Each time the number remained the same that White reported in 1778.

When John Burroughs came to Selborne eighty-four years before us, he arrived late in June. He was in the midst of that prolonged and fruitless search that resulted in one of the most appealing chapters of *Fresh Fields*—"A Hunt for the Nightingale." Burroughs arrived too late, when the time of singing was virtually over. We, too, had come to

Selborne hoping to hear the nightingale. But we were early. Singing had hardly begun. That evening, and on the succeeding evening, we drove for hours along dark, deserted country roads, pausing often, listening intently, then driving on again. * * *

More than once, during those nights, we looked from our window over the slumbering village lying silent in the moonlight. Across the street the rays glinted from the chimneys of various shapes and sizes, shone from the steeply pitched, diverging roofs that crowned the dark bulk of The Wakes. It was there—only a few hundred feet from the site of the old Selborne Vicarage where he was born on July 18, 1720—that Gilbert White had died on June 26, 1793. It was there he wrote his Selborne letters to the wealthy Welsh natural-scientist and author of *The British Zoology,* Thomas Pennant, and the lawyer-naturalist, the Recorder of Bristol, Daines Barrington. It was there he produced an English classic without realizing he was even writing a book.

When the naturalist occupied The Wakes, it consisted of eight rooms. Subsequent owners added to it, expanding it into a twenty-room dwelling. However, the middle portion still remains substantially as it was in White's time. The house is set close to the street in front. Behind it extends the wide lawn and spacious gardens where the old Sussex tortoise plodded down the paths in summer and hibernated when each autumn came. The shell of this famous reptile, which outlived its master by one year, is now part of the natural history collection of the British Museum, in London.

Where the garden joins grazing land, a ha-ha, or sunken fence, a specially constructed trench—which the tortoise was careful to avoid—forms a barrier that keeps out livestock without obstructing the view. Beside this barrier, we reached Gilbert White's sundial. It was green with the patina of age. When, a few years ago, a bypass road was proposed that would run through the grounds of The Wakes, it was greeted with such a storm of protest that the plan was soon abandoned. Looking across the ha-ha and over the grazing land beyond, we saw, rising high above us, the most remarkable feature of the Selborne countryside, the Hanger. Here the steep drop at the edge of a 300-foot hill or plateau of chalk is clothed with trees. This hill and hanging wood, half a mile long, shelters the village from westerly gales. The Hanger is now under the protection of the National Trust.

At the foot of this escarpment, only a field away from the garden at The Wakes, we found three paths. One ran along the foot of the Hanger; another, the Bostal, angled upward among the hanging trees; the third, the famous Zigzag laid out by Gilbert White and his brother, mounts straight up in a steep stitchwork ascent comprising more than a score of switchbacks. We turned down the first path. It, like the Long Lythe trail, was a pathway of flowers. Again we met the green blooms of the wood spurge. Dog violets and lesser celandine and wood oxalis and, now and then, a scattering of bluebells ran beside us. The golden disk of one dandelion measured an inch and a half across. The English cowslip, sometimes called St. Peter's keys, rose at the edge of the meadow, the yellow flowers all on one side of the upright stems.

Here we came upon a new bird, one of the 120 on White's Selborne list. With blue-gray black, black cap and tail, white rump, and rose-red breast, it was that striking songbird, the bullfinch. Because of its destruction of fruit blooms, this colorful bird—said to mate for life—is legally trapped and shot in the orchard and berry-raising regions of England. Among the roots of the clinging beech trees, a little farther on, we heard a dry rustling among the fallen leaves. As we came close, we discovered the source. A blackbird, tossing leaves with its yellow bill, was searching for food.

Among other beech trees, where a multitude of new leaves—some as delicately tinted as flowers—were unfolding on the branches, we climbed the gentle ascent of the angling Bostal. Above us, up the slope clouded with the pale green of emerging foliage, we heard the ringing "Peeto! Peto! Peeto!" or the monotonous, metallic "tink—tink—tink" of the great tit. As we ascended, the raspoing clamor of rooks rose about us. Half a dozen years before, a number of these birds had moved from the main rookery by Oakhanger Stream and had established their nests in a group of trees not far from The Wakes.

We had climbed over a fallen beech and had stopped to examine another wildflower with greenish blooms, that relative of the wood spurge, the dog's mercury—a plant that flourishes in beech woods and blooms as early as in February and once was employed in medicine—when we came to a muddy spot in the trail. Its soft earth recorded the passing of previous travelers. Imprinted in the mud we saw the tracks of a horse, a dog, a man, and a deer. In the Selborne region roe deer have been increasing in recent times. More rare, but occasionally seen, are fallow deer.

Along the upper portions of the trail, gaps among the treetops revealed glimpses of the village. What we had so often pictured in our imaginations lay outspread below us. The scene remains much the same as White described it. The village, even now, is five miles from the nearest railroad station. It still contains a blacksmith shop. Since the middle of the thirteenth century, there has always been an ironworker in Selborne. Aside from the unpleasant impression made by a few muti-

lated trees, warped to man's caprice, this Hampshire community epito-
mizes in our minds the charm of the English village at its best. Here
Gilbert White's life had been cast in pleasant paths and amid pleasant
surroundings. Almost his only cause for regret was the lack of any companion in all the region to share his interest in natural history.

At the end of our 300-foot ascent, we came out among great
beeches—those dominant trees of the chalk country—on the edge of
the Selborne Common. This expanse extended away for upwards of a
mile with a width, at its greatest point, of about three-fourths of a mile.
Wood pigeons had congregated among the treetops and all around us
and in the distance we heard the hoarse, hollow sound of their calling. At
times, it suggested the barking of far-away dogs; at other times, the
hooting of distant owls. I remembered reading that to some these birds
seem saying: "Take *two* cows, David."

During the Second World War, when I wrote to inquire how Selborne had fared, L. Sunderland, then the vicar, reported that, during the
early days of hostilities, fire bombs had fallen among the beech trees at
the top of the Hanger. Otherwise the village had escaped damage. The
effect of the incendiary bombs had been slight. Evidence of their fall had
long since disappeared.

Nellie and I decided to save the Zigzag path for the following day, our
last in Selborne. But when that day dawned, it came with cold and misty
rain. Hour after hour, it splashed on the street, flowed down the windowpanes, streamed from the thatching of our roof. Gloomily we stared out
at the deluge. This was our final day in the village. This was the night of
the full May moon. This was our last chance to hear a nightingale at
Selborne. The Curator at The Wakes, Cyril Reginald Nortcliffe, had
told us that a friend had reported hearing the song on Selborne Common not far from the top of the Zigzag. But in pouring rain, the chalk
soil of the switchbacks would be as slippery as though covered with lard.
Climbing a greased pole would be almost as easy as attaining the top of
the ascent.

Not everyone, I found, appreciates the voice of the nightingale. There
are those, in fact, to whom the singing of birds in general has little
appeal. I was assured by one inhabitant of Selborne that the nightingale's song is "really an awful noise." Students sometimes complain that
it prevents them from studying. Near Ringmer, in Sussex, at the very
place where Gilbert White had acquired his tortoise, a later occupant,
coming from London, had all the nightingales killed because they disturbed his sleep.

As that rain-lashed day dragged on, our chances of hearing the nightingale seemed to diminish and disappear. The fate of American natural-

ists—early and late—appeared to be to miss the bird at Selborne. But sometimes after five the rain slackened. Then it ceased. Rifts extended in channels of blue sky between the clouds. The sun came out; the sun went in; but the rain was over.

I wandered about taking pictures in the unusual lighting that streamed from the west and flooded the dripping village. Nellie, her cough grown worse on this day of chill and rain, went early to bed. About nine, I decided to check on the slipperiness of the Zigzag. Alone in the dark, a slip and fall on the upper part of the 300-foot precipitous ascent might be a serious matter. Yet—if I could get up and down again, there was still a chance of hearing a Selborne nightingale.

When I started out, the sky, all along the western horizon, was filled with a fading greenish glow. Even here, in southern England, I was in the longer twilight of the north. As I passed the inn, light from one of the windows shone on an elderly gentleman just outside taking, between thumb and forefinger, a pinch of snuff from a snuffbox and carefully applying it to each nostril in turn. Surrounded by darkness, standing out in the lighted space, the scene resembled a tableau, a fragment of the eighteenth century displaced in time. Between darkened fields, I followed a footpath to the base of the looming black shape of the Hanger. In lighter lines, the staggering switchbacks of the Zigzag ascended above me. I tried the lowest one. Wet leaves added to its slipperiness. My feet slid back at every step. But always they were snubbed by pebbles scattered through the clay.

Slowly, steadily, sweeping the wet path ahead with the beam of a flashlight, walking flat-footed, carefully placing my feet, taking no chances, I mounted switchback by switchback up the slippery ascent. From trunk to limbs to tipmost twigs, I worked my way upward among the black silhouettes of trees imprinted against the sky. The lights of the village sank away. Ending the evening chorus, the voices of a few blackbirds and song thrushes carried through the increasing darkness. From time to time, an intermittent wind shook the trees, scattering drops of water on my path.

About two-thirds of the way to the top, I came to a small, level spot, a miniature plateau. There, in the eighteenth century, Gilbert White had built a modest hermitage where he often sat and where he used to entertain his friends. I lost count of the switchbacks, but the number was nearing thirty when I reached the summit of the staggered ascent. Here I found another memento of the naturalist, the famous wishing stone he and his brothers transported from Farringdon, nearly two miles away, and erected at the top of the Zigzag. Around the Sarsen stone the ground is hard-packed, perhaps from the feet of those who have engaged in an old superstition, circling it three times backward and then making a wish.

From the top of the Hanger I looked down the steep climb of the switchbacks and then gazed out over the darkened scene spreading away below. Automobiles were pushing stubby paths of illumination before them along country roads. Clusters of glimmering pinpoints of light marked the position of distant villages. Below the Hanger, in a double line, lighted windows of cottages followed the main street of Selborne. The same glass, in some instances, that now transmitted the brilliance of electric lamps had, in White's time, glowed with the softer illumination of candles. Like Concord, in Massachusetts, in the New World, Selborne, in Hampshire, in the Old, represents one of the places of the earth that, for us, holds a special fascination.

After the rain, the smell of wet, decaying leaves was strong in the darkness. My footfalls were silent on the yielding forest mold. Around me as I advanced among the ancient beeches, the beam of my electric torch encountered shaggy masses of ivy; the shine of holly leaves, the darker mats of moss, the twisted roots and the immense, smooth-barked columns of the trees. So widespread are some of the lower limbs that their tips sweep the ground. Several times, above me, I heard wood pigeons fluttering, blundering among the treetop twigs, as they changed position in the dark.

The wind had died down completely. No breeze stirred the branches. The intense silence seemed to be pressing on my eardrums. This was the quiet Selborne night, the night that had seemed friendly to Gilbert White and now seemed friendly to me. I listened intently, straining to catch some fragment of the hoped-for song. Pausing thus at frequent intervals, I advanced among the trees and glades of the common. Pale forest moths fluttered by, in and out of the beam of my flashlight.

When I reached the eastern edge of the common, I looked away between the massive boles of trees out over a far-spread stretch of lower land. To the southeast loomed the black bulk of Noar Hill, where White had experimented with echoes, employing Latin phrases to insure that he was not being hoaxed. To the left of the hill, orange and immense, the full moon had lifted free of the black horizon line. For a time, it remained entangled in low-lying clouds, its light transforming the edges of the floating vapor into glowing, wavy margins. Then it gained the clear sky, lost its fiery orange hue, diffused a silver and magical light over the outspread land below. Somewhere there, I heard the faint, far-away bawling of a cow. Closer at hand, a cock pheasant uttered its sudden, rasping call among the moonlit fields. Then, for a long time, no sound broke the silence. This was the full May moon—the nightingale moon. But where was the singer and where was its song?

Perhaps half an hour more had gone by and I had worked farther along the edge of the common when my ear caught the voice of a distant bird. It grew louder as I advanced. Creeping close in the deep shade of a beech tree, I sat on a mossy log and listened to a song my ears had never heard before. With its deep bubbling notes, its rushing crescendos, it was—at last—the song of a nightingale.

The bird, hidden in a tangle of low shrubbery, was invisible. But its voice filled all the shadows and moonlit spaces around. Where many thrushes sing over and over the same melodious notes, the nightingale seemed musing, improvising, filling its song with phrases and runs and repeated notes infinitely varied. In general form, the song resembles somewhat that of the mockingbird of our Southern states. But it held more marvelously varied pitch and tone, more beautiful liquid notes and running passages, greater intensity and passion. The impression was inescapable that here was a virtuoso accomplishing the difficult with ease.

The song ranged from a low, bubbling "chook-chook" or "jug-jug" to liquid warbles, soaring trills, and bursting crescendos of sound. There were sudden dramatic silences. Some notes were almost guttural. Others were rich and mellow, wild and pure. Edward Thomas, in *The South Country,* well describes these swift, repeated notes "as rounded and full of sweetness as a grape." From the time of Aristophanes, four centuries before the birth of Christ, men have been trying, with little success, to translate into syllables the song of nightingale. Cold words are powerless to capture the fire of the singer, the richness of the notes, the purity of the tones, the variety of the phrasing, the rapid repetition of one clear note, the sudden end, succeeded by intense silence and then the song beginning again.

In the first chapter of *The Compleat Angler,* Izaak Walton writes of the nightingale as breathing "such sweet lowd musick out of her little instrumental throat, that it might make mankind to think Miracles are not ceased." The human response to this music depends largely upon the individual hearer. John Keats, best of all, has immortalized the effect of the song on the sensitive listener.

As I sat there motionless, the nightingale ascended from the depths of the tangle, where it had been singing, to an upper branch of one of the bushes. Here it perched, facing the moon across the valley. I saw it silhouetted against the luminous sky, its head lifted, its body quivering with the intensity of its song. In shape and size, the nightingale brings to mind our hermit thrush. Its breast is plain, while the breast of the hermit thrush is spotted; but its tail, like the tail of the American bird, has a reddish cast. This I saw clearly on a later day, at the edge of a wood on the Sussex border of Kent, when I watched a nightingale fly up in brilliant sunshine. Although these birds often sing by day as well as by night, the one I saw in Kent remained mute. The south of England comprises most of the range of the species in Britain. Kent, Sussex, Surrey, and Hampshire are especially famed for their nightingales.

I have no idea how long I listened to the song, surrounded by the moonlit night. There was a dreamlike quality about the passing minutes. It became increasingly difficult to grasp the reality that I was actually here, in Gilbert White's Selborne, under the full May moon, listening to the singing of the nightingale. I had come so far for such an hour as this! The only gall in the honey of that moment was the knowledge that Nellie was missing what she so greatly desired to hear. But Sussex and Kent, with their nightingales, still lay before us.

When I finally stood up, I discovered what, in my preoccupation, I had been unaware of before. Like a wick, my clothes had been absorbing moisture all the time I sat on the moldering rain-soaked log. Several times I started away only to return and listen again. When I reached the top of the Zigzag, the Sarsen stone gleamed wanly in the moonlight and The Wakes, in shadows, lay sleeping below. My elation at my great good fortune went with me as I slowly descended the still slippery Zigzag. It remained with me for a long time as I lay in bed, too moved to sleep, reliving all I had seen and heard.

E(LWYN) B(ROOKS) WHITE
1899 - 1985

White is a writer beloved for his voice—modest and humorous, ironic and forgiving. He honed this masterly, humane style during long years on the staff of The New Yorker. *Among the books for which White is especially remembered are his amusing and helpful* The Elements of Style *(1935, with William Strunk, Jr.) and his children's stories* Stuart Little *(1945),* Charlotte's Web *(1952), and* The Trumpet of the Swan *(1970). Collections of his essays, such as* Points of My Compass *(1962),*

*confirm his pleasure in country things, especially gardening, farmyard
animals, and sailing.*

A Slight Sound at Evening

Allen Cove, Summer, 1954

In his journal for July 10–12, 1841, Thoreau wrote: "A slight sound at
evening lifts me up by the ears, and makes life seem inexpressibly serene
and grand. It may be in Uranus, or it may be in the shutter." The book
into which he later managed to pack both Uranus and the shutter was
published in 1854, and now, a hundred years having gone by, *Walden*,
its serenity and grandeur unimpaired, still lifts us up by the ears, still
translates for us that language we are in danger of forgetting, "which all
things and events speak without metaphor, which alone is copious and
standard."

Walden is an oddity in American letters. It may very well be the
oddest of our distinguished oddities. For many it is a great deal too odd,
and for many it is a particular bore. I have not found it to be a well-liked
book among my acquaintances, although usually spoken of with respect,
and one literary critic for whom I have the highest regard can find no
reason for anyone's giving *Walden* a second thought. To admire the
book is, in fact, something of an embarrassment, for the mass of men
have an indistinct notion that its author was a sort of Nature Boy.

I think it is of some advantage to encounter the book at a period in
one's life when the normal anxieties and enthusiasms and rebellions of
youth closely resemble those of Thoreau in that spring of 1845 when he
borrowed an ax, went out to the woods, and began to whack down some
trees for timber. Received at such a juncture, the book is like an invitation to life's dance, assuring the troubled recipient that no matter what
befalls him in the way of success or failure he will always be welcome at
the party—that the music is played for him, too, if he will but listen and
move his feet. In effect, that is what the book is—an invitation, unen-
graved; and it stirs one as a young girl is stirred by her first big party bid.
Many think it a sermon; many set it down as an attempt to rearrange
society; some think it an exercise in nature-loving; some find it a rather
irritating collection of inspirational puffballs by an eccentric show-off. I
think it none of these. It still seems to me the best youth's companion

The Points of My Compass: Letters from the East, the West, the North, the South (New
York: Harper & Row, 1962).

yet written by an American, for it carries a solemn warning against the loss of one's valuables, it advances a good argument for traveling light and trying new adventures, it rings with the power of positive adoration, it contains religious feeling without religious images, and it steadfastly refuses to record bad news. Even its pantheistic note is so pure as to be noncorrupting—pure as the flute-note blown across the pond on those faraway summer nights. If our colleges and universities were alert, they would present a cheap pocket edition of the book to every senior upon graduating, along with his sheepskin, or instead of it. Even if some senior were to take it literally and start felling trees, there could be worse mishaps: the ax is older than the Dictaphone and it is just as well for a young man to see what kind of chips he leaves before listening to the sound of his own voice. And even if some were to get no farther than the table of contents, they would learn how to name eighteen chapters by the use of only thirty-nine words and would see how sweet are the uses of brevity.

If Thoreau had merely left us an account of a man's life in the woods or if he had simply retreated to the woods and there recorded his complaints about society, or even if he had contrived to include both records in one essay, *Walden* would probably not have lived a hundred years. As things turned out, Thoreau, very likely without knowing quite what he was up to, took man's relation to Nature and man's dilemma in society and man's capacity for elevating his spirit and he beat all these matters together, in a wild free interval of self-justification and delight, and produced an original omelette from which people can draw nourishment in a hungry day. *Walden* is one of the first of the vitamin-enriched American dishes. If it were a little less good than it is, or even a little less queer, it would be an abominable book. Even as it is, it will continue to baffle and annoy the literal mind and all those who are unable to stomach its caprices and imbibe its theme. Certainly the plodding economist will continue to have rough going if he hopes to emerge from the book with a clear system of economic thought. Thoreau's assault on the Concord society of the mid-nineteenth century has the quality of a modern Western: he rides into the subject at top speed, shooting in all directions. Many of his shots ricochet and nick him on the rebound, and throughout the melee there is a horrendous cloud of inconsistencies and contradictions, and when the shooting dies down and the air clears, one is impressed chiefly by the courage of the rider and by how splendid it was that somebody should have ridden in there and raised all that ruckus.

When he went to the pond, Thoreau struck an attitude and did so deliberately, but his posturing was not to draw the attention of others to him but rather to draw his own attention more closely to himself. "I learned this at least by my experiment: that if one advances confidently in the direction of his dreams, and endeavors to live the life which he has imagined, he will meet with a success unexpected in common hours." The sentence has the power to resuscitate the youth drowning in his sea of doubt. I recall my exhilaration upon reading it, many years ago, in a time of hesitation and despair. It restored me to health. And now in 1954 when I salute Henry Thoreau on the hundredth birthday of his book, I am merely paying off an old score—or an installment on it.

In his journal for May 3–4, 1838—Boston to Portland—he wrote: "Midnight—head over the boat's side—between sleeping and waking— with glimpses of one or more lights in the vicinity of Cape Ann. Bright moonlight—the effect heightened by seasickness." The entry illuminates the man, as the moon the sea on that night in May. In Thoreau the natural scene was heightened, not depressed, by a disturbance of the stomach, and nausea met its match at last. There was a steadiness in at least one passenger if there was none in the boat. Such steadiness (which in some would be called intoxication) is at the heart of *Walden*—confidence, faith, the discipline of looking always at what is to be seen, undeviating gratitude for the life-everlasting that he found growing in his front yard. "There is nowhere recorded a simple and irrepressible satisfaction with the gift of life, any memorable praise of God." He worked to correct that deficiency. *Walden* is his acknowledgment of the gift of life. It is the testament of a man in a high state of indignation because (it seemed to him) so few ears heard the uninterrupted poem of creation, the morning wind that forever blows. If the man sometimes wrote as though all his readers were male, unmarried, and well-connected, it is because he gave his testimony during the callow years. For that matter, he never really grew up. To reject the book because of the immaturity of the author and the bugs in the logic is to throw away a bottle of good wine because it contains bits of the cork.

Thoreau said he required of every writer, first and last, a simple and sincere account of his own life. Having delivered himself of this chesty dictum, he proceeded to ignore it. In his books and even in his enormous journal, he withheld or disguised most of the facts from which an understanding of his life could be drawn. *Walden*, subtitled "Life in the Woods," is not a simple and sincere account of a man's life, either in or out of the woods; it is an account of a man's journey into the mind, a toot on the trumpet to alert the neighbors. Thoreau was well aware that no one can alert his neighbors who is not wide-awake himself, and he went to the woods (among other reasons) to make sure that he would stay awake during his broadcast. What actually took place during the years 1845–47 is largely unrecorded, and the reader is excluded from the private life of the author, who supplies almost no gossip about himself, a great deal about his neighbors and about the universe.

As for me, I cannot in this short ramble give a simple and sincere account of my own life, but I think Thoreau might find it instructive to know that this memorial essay is being written in a house that, through no intent on my part, is the same size and shape as his own domicile on the pond—about ten by fifteen, tight, plainly finished, and at a little distance from my Concord. The house in which I sit this morning was built to accommodate a boat, not a man, but by long experience I have learned that in most respects it shelters me better than the larger dwelling where my bed is, and which, by design, is a manhouse not a boathouse. Here in the boathouse I am a wilder and, it would appear, a healthier man, by a safe margin. I have a chair, a bench, a table, and I can walk into the water if I tire of the land. My house fronts a cove. Two fishermen have just arrived to spot fish from the air—an osprey and a man in a small yellow plane who works for the fish company. The man, I have noticed, is less well equipped than the hawk, who can dive directly on his fish and carry it away, without telephoning. A mouse and a squirrel share the house with me. The building is, in fact, a multiple dwelling, a semidetached affair. It is because I am semidetached while here that I find it possible to transact this private business with the fewest obstacles.

There is also a woodchuck here, living forty feet away under the wharf. When the wind is right, he can smell my house; and when the wind is contrary, I can smell his. We both use the wharf for sunning, taking turns, each adjusting his schedule to the other's convenience. Thoreau once ate a woodchuck. I think he felt he owed it to his readers, and that it was little enough, considering the indignities they were suffering at his hands and the dressing-down they were taking. (Parts of *Walden* are pure scold.) Or perhaps he ate the woodchuck because he believed every man should acquire strict business habits, and the woodchuck was destroying his market beans. I do not know. Thoreau had a strong experimental streak in him. It is probably no harder to eat a woodchuck than to construct a sentence that lasts a hundred years. At any rate, Thoreau is the only writer I know who prepared himself for his great ordeal by eating a woodchuck; also the only one who got a hangover from drinking too much water. (He was drunk the whole time, though he seldom touched wine or coffee or tea.)

Here in this compact house where I would spend one day as deliberately as Nature if I were not being pressed by the editor of a magazine, and with a woodchuck (as yet uneaten) for neighbor, I can feel the companionship of the occupant of the pond-side cabin in Walden woods, a mile from the village, near the Fitchburg right of way. Even my immediate business is no barrier between us: Thoreau occasionally batted out a magazine piece, but was always suspicious of any sort of purposeful work that cut into his time. A man, he said, should take care not to be thrown off the track by every nutshell and mosquito's wing that falls on the rails.

There has been much guessing as to why he went to the pond. To set it down to escapism is, of course, to misconstrue what happened. Henry went forth to battle when he took to the woods, and *Walden* is the report of a man torn by two powerful and opposing drives—the desire to enjoy the world (and not be derailed by a mosquito wing) and the urge to set the world straight. One cannot join these two successfully, but sometimes, in rare cases, something good or even great results from the attempt of the tormented spirit to reconcile them. Henry went forth to battle, and if he set the stage himself, if he fought on his own terms and with his own weapons, it was because it was his nature to do things differently from most men, and to act in a cocky fashion. If the pond and the woods seemed a more plausible site for a house than an intown location, it was because a cowbell made for him a sweeter sound than a churchbell. *Walden,* the book, makes the sound of a cowbell, more than a churchbell, and proves the point, although both sounds are in it, and both remarkably clear and sweet. He simply preferred his churchbell at a little distance.

I think one reason he went to the woods was a perfectly simple and commonplace one—and apparently he thought so, too. "At a certain season of our life," he wrote, "we are accustomed to consider every spot as the possible site of a house." There spoke the young man, a few years out of college, who had not yet broken away from home. He hadn't married, and he had found no job that measured up to his rigid standards of employment, and like any young man, or young animal, he felt uneasy and on the defensive until he had fixed himself a den. Most young men, of course, casting about for a site, are content merely to draw apart from their kinfolks. Thoreau, convinced that the greater part of what his neighbors called good was bad, withdrew from a great deal more than family: he pulled out of everything for a while, to serve everybody right for being so stuffy, and to try his own prejudices on the dog.

The house-hunting sentence above, which starts the chapter called "Where I Lived, and What I Lived For," is followed by another passage that is worth quoting here because it so beautifully illustrates the offbeat prose that Thoreau was master of, a prose at once strictly disciplined and wildly abandoned. "I have surveyed the country on every side within a dozen miles of where I live," continued this delirious young man. "In imagination I have bought all the farms in succession, for all were to be bought, and I knew their price. I walked over each farmer's premises, tasted his wild apples, discoursed on husbandry with him, took his farm at his price, at any price, mortgaging it to him in my mind; even put a higher price on it—took everything but a deed of it—took his word for his deed, for I dearly love to talk—cultivated it, and him too to some extent, I trust, and withdrew when I had enjoyed it long enough, leaving him to carry it on." A copy-desk man would get a double hernia trying to clean up that sentence for the management, but the sentence needs no fixing, for it perfectly captures the meaning of the writer and the quality of the ramble.

"Wherever I sat, there I might live, and the landscape radiated from me accordingly." Thoreau, the home-seeker, sitting on his hummock with the entire State of Massachusetts radiating from him, is to me the most humorous of the New England figures, and *Walden* the most humorous of the books, though its humor is almost continuously subsurface and there is nothing deliberately funny anywhere, except a few weak jokes and bad puns that rise to the surface like the perch in the pond that rose to the sound of the maestro's flute. Thoreau tended to write in sentences, a feat not every writer is capable of, and *Walden* is, rhetorically speaking, a collection of certified sentences, some of them, it would now appear, as indestructible as they are errant. The book is distilled from the vast journals, and this accounts for its intensity: he picked out bright particles that pleased his eye, whirled them in the kaleidoscope of his content, and produced the pattern that has endured—the color, the form, the light.

On this its hundredth birthday, Thoreau's *Walden* is pertinent and timely. In our uneasy season, when all men unconsciously seek a retreat from a world that has got almost completely out of hand, his house in the Concord woods is a haven. In our culture of gadgetry and the multiplicity of convenience, his cry "Simplicity, simplicity, simplicity!" has the insistence of a fire alarm. In the brooding atmosphere of war and the gathering radioactive storm, the innocence and serenity of his summer afternoons are enough to burst the remembering heart, and one gazes back upon that pleasing interlude—its confidence, its purity, its deliberateness—with awe and wonder, as one would look upon the face of a child asleep.

"This small lake was of most value as a neighbor in the intervals of a gentle rain-storm in August, when, both air and water being perfectly still, but the sky overcast, midafternoon had all the serenity of evening, and the wood-thrush sang around, and was heard from shore to shore."

Now, in the perpetual overcast in which our days are spent, we hear with extra perception and deep gratitude that song, tying century to century.

I sometimes amuse myself by bringing Henry Thoreau back to life and showing him the sights. I escort him into a phone booth and let him dial Weather. "This is a delicious evening," the girl's voice says, "when the whole body is one sense, and imbibes delight through every pore." I show him the spot in the Pacific where an island used to be, before some magician made it vanish. "We know not where we are," I murmur. "The light which puts out our eyes is darkness to us. Only that day dawns to which we are awake." I thumb through the latest copy of *Vogue* with him. "Of two patterns which differ only by a few threads more or less of a particular color," I read, "the one will be sold readily, the other lie on the shelf, though it frequently happens that, after the lapse of a season, the latter becomes the most fashionable." Together we go outboarding on the Assabet, looking for what we've lost—a hound, a bay horse, a turtledove. I show him a distracted farmer who is trying to repair a hay baler before the thunder shower breaks. "This farmer," I remark, "is endeavoring to solve the problem of a livelihood by a formula more complicated than the problem itself. To get his shoestrings he speculates in herds of cattle."

I take the celebrated author to Twenty-One for lunch, so the waiters may study his shoes. The proprietor welcomes us. "The gross feeder," remarks the proprietor, sweeping the room with his arm, "is a man in the larva stage." After lunch we visit a classroom in one of those schools conducted by big corporations to teach their superannuated executives how to retire from business without serious injury to their health. (The shock to men's systems these days when relieved of the exacting routine of amassing wealth is very great and must be cushioned.) "It is not necessary," says the teacher to his pupils, "that a man should earn his living by the sweat of his brow, unless he sweats easier than I do. We are determined to be starved before we are hungry."

I turn on the radio and let Thoreau hear Winchell beat the red hand around the clock. "Time is but the stream I go a-fishing in," shouts Mr. Winchell, rattling his telegraph key. "Hardly a man takes a half hour's nap after dinner, but when he wakes he holds up his head and asks, 'What's the news?' If we read of one man robbed, or murdered, or killed by accident, or one house burned, or one vessel wrecked, or one steamboat blown up, or one cow run over on the Western Railroad, or one mad dog killed, or one lot of grasshoppers in the winter—we need never read of another. One is enough."

I doubt that Thoreau would be thrown off balance by the fantastic sights and sounds of the twentieth century. "The Concord nights," he once wrote, "are stranger than the Arabian nights." A four-engined airliner would merely serve to confirm his early views on travel. Everywhere he would observe, in new shapes and sizes, the old predicaments and follies of men—the desperation, the impedimenta, the meanness— along with the visible capacity for elevation of the mind and soul. "This curious world which we inhabit is more wonderful than it is convenient; more beautiful than it is useful; it is more to be admired and enjoyed than used." He would see that today ten thousand engineers are busy making sure that the world shall be convenient even if it is destroyed in the process, and others are determined to increase its usefulness even though its beauty is lost somewhere along the way.

At any rate, I'd like to stroll about the countryside in Thoreau's company for a day, observing the modern scene, inspecting today's snowstorm, pointing out the sights, and offering belated apologies for my sins. Thoreau is unique among writers in that those who admire him find him uncomfortable to live with—a regular hairshirt of a man. A little band of dedicated Thoreauvians would be a sorry sight indeed: fellows who hate compromise and have compromised, fellows who love wildness and have lived tamely, and at their side, censuring them and chiding them, the ghostly figure of this upright man, who long ago gave corroboration to impulses they perceived were right and issued warnings against the things they instinctively knew to be their enemies. I should hate to be called a Thoreauvian, yet I wince every time I walk into the barn I'm pushing before me, seventy-five feet by forty, and the author of *Walden* has served as my conscience through the long stretches of my trivial days.

Hairshirt or no, he is a better companion than most, and I would not swap him for a soberer or more reasonable friend even if I could. I can reread his famous invitation with undiminished excitement. The sad thing is that not more acceptances have been received, that so many decline for one reason or another, pleading some previous engagement or ill health. But the invitation stands. It will beckon as long as this remarkable book stays in print—which will be as long as there are August afternoons in the intervals of a gentle rainstorm, as long as there are ears to catch the faint sounds of the orchestra. I find it agreeable to sit here this morning, in a house of correct proportions, and hear across a century of time his flute, his frogs, and his seductive summons to the wildest revels of them all.

MERIDEL LESUEUR
B. 1900

LeSueur has been described as a "radical" writer because of her identifi-cation with the labor movement and association with the Communist Party. But the word is also appropriate because of her attention to the agricultural roots of culture. Her early commitment to feminism, as well as her years of living in Iowa, Kansas, and Minnesota, have led LeSueur to pay special attention to the myths of Demeter and Persephone. Several of the pieces included in Ripening: Selected Work, 1927–1980 *(1982) evoke the continuity of human life in the Americas by focusing on the motif of corn.*

The Ancient People and the Newly Come

Born out of the caul of winter in the north, in the swing and circle of the horizon, I am rocked in the ancient land. As a child I first read the scriptures written on the scroll of frozen moisture by wolf and rabbit, by the ancient people and the newly come. In the beginning of the century the Indian smoke still mingled with ours. The frontier of the whites was violent, already injured by vast seizures and massacres. The winter night-mares of fear poisoned the plains nights with psychic airs of theft and utopia. The stolen wheat in the cathedrallike granaries cried out for vengeance.

Most of all one was born into space, into the great resonance of space, a magnetic midwestern valley through which the winds clashed in lassoes of thunder and lightning at the apex of the sky, the very wrath of God.

The body repeats the landscape. They are the source of each other and create each other. We were marked by the seasonal body of earth, by

Ripening: Selected Work, 1927–1980, ed. Elaine Hedges (Old Westbury, N.Y.: Feminist Press, 1982).

the terrible migrations of people, by the swift turn of a century, verging on change never before experienced on this greening planet. I sensed the mound and swell above the mother breast, and from embryonic eye took sustenance and benediction, and went from mother enclosure to prairie spheres curving into eachother.

I was born in winter, the village snow darkened toward midnight, footsteps on boardwalks, the sound of horses pulling sleighs, and the ring of bells. The square wooden saltbox house held the tall shadows, thrown from kerosene lamps, of my grandmother and my aunt and uncle (missionaries home from India) inquiring at the door.

It was in the old old night of the North Country. The time of wood before metal. Contracted in cold, I lay in the prairie curves of my mother, in the planetary belly, and outside the vast horizon of the plains, swinging dark and thicketed, circle within circle. The round moon sinister reversed upside down in the sign of Neptune, and the twin fishes of Pisces swimming toward Aquarius in the dark.

But the house was New England square, four rooms upstairs and four rooms downstairs, exactly set upon a firm puritan foundation, surveyed on a level, set angles of the old geometry, and thrust up on the plains like an insult, a declamation of the conqueror, a fortress of our God, a shield against excess and sin.

I had been conceived in the riotous summer and fattened on light and stars that fell on my underground roots, and every herb, corn plant, cricket, beaver, red fox leaped in me in the old Indian dark. I saw everything was moving and entering. The rocking of mother and prairie breast curved around me within the square. The field crows flew in my flesh and cawed in my dream.

Crouching together on Indian land in the long winters, we grew in sight and understanding, heard the rumbling of glacial moraines, clung to the edge of holocaust forest fires, below-zero weather, grasshopper plagues, sin, wars, crop failures, drouth, and the mortgage. The severity of the seasons and the strangeness of a new land, with those whose land had been seized looking in our windows, created a tension of guilt and a tightening of sin. We were often snowed in, the villages invisible and inaccessible in cliffs of snow. People froze following the rope to their barns to feed the cattle. But the cyclic renewal and strength of the old prairie earth, held sacred by thousands of years of Indian ritual, the guerrilla soil of the Americas, taught and nourished us.

We flowed through and into the land, often evicted, drouthed out, pushed west. Some were beckoned to regions of gold, space like a mirage throwing up pictures of utopias, wealth, and villages of brotherhood. Thousands passed through the villages, leaving their dead, deposits of sorrow and calcium, leaching the soil, creating and marking with their faces new wheat and corn, producing idiots, mystics, prophets, and inventors. Or, as an old farmer said, we couldn't move; nailed to the barn door by the wind, we have to make a windmill, figure out how to plow without a horse, and invent barbed wire. A Dakota priest said to me, "It will be from here that the prophets come."

Nowhere in the world can spring burst out of the iron bough as in the Northwest. When the plains, rising to the Rockies, swell with heat, and the delicate glow and silence of the melting moisture fills the pure space with delicate winds and the promise of flowers. We all came, like the crocus, out of the winter dark, out of the captive village where along the river one winter the whole population of children died of diphtheria. In the new sun we counted the dead, and at the spring dance the living danced up a storm and drank and ate heartily for the pain of it. They danced their alien feet into the American earth and rolled in the haymow to beget against the wilderness new pioneers.

All opened in the spring. The prairies, like a great fan, opened. The people warmed, came together in quilting bees, Ladies' Aid meetings, house raisings. The plowing and the planting began as soon as the thaw let the farmers into the fields. Neighbors helped each other. As soon as the seed was in, the churches had picnics and baptizings. The ladies donned their calico dresses and spread a great board of food, while the children ran potato races and one-legged races and the men played horseshoes and baseball. Children were born at home with the neighbor woman. Sometimes the doctor got there. When I was twelve, I helped the midwife deliver a baby. I held onto the screaming mother, her lips bitten nearly off, while she delivered in pieces a dead, strangled corpse. Some people who made it through the winter died in the spring, and we all gathered as survivors to sing "The Old Rugged Cross," "Shall We Gather at the River?" and "God Be with You Till We Meet Again."

The Poles and the Irish had the best parties, lasting for two or three days sometimes. But even the Baptist revival meetings were full of singing (dancing prohibited), and hundreds were forgiven, talking in tongues. Once I saw them break the ice to baptize a screaming woman into the water of life for her salvation.

On Saturday nights everybody would shoot the works, except the prohibitionists and the "good" people, mostly Protestant teetolers who would appear at church on Sunday morning. The frontier gamblers, rascals, and speculators filled the taverns—drink, women, and gambling consuming the wealth of the people and the land. There were gaming palaces for the rich, even horse racing in Stillwater. In St. Paul Nina Clifford, a powerful figure, had two whorehouses, one for gentlemen from "the Hill" and the other for lumberjacks coming in from the woods to spend their hard-earned bucks. It was said that three powers had divided St. Paul among them—Bishop Ireland took "the Hill," Jim Hill took the city for his trains, and Nina Clifford took all that was below "the Hill."

When the corn was "knee-high by the Fourth of July," and the rainfall was good and the sun just right, there was rejoicing in the great Fourth of July picnics that specialized in oratory. Without loudspeakers there were speeches that could be heard the length of the grove, delivered by orators who practiced their wind. When farm prices fell because of the speculation of the Grain Exchange in Minneapolis, the threatened farmers met on the prairie and in the park, the town plaza, and the courthouse to speak out against the power of monopoly. They came for miles, before and after the harvest, in farm wagons with the whole family. They passed out manifestos and spoke of organizing the people to protect themselves from the predators.

There is no place in the world with summer's end, fall harvest, and Indian summer as in Minnesota. They used to have husking bees. The wagons went down the corn rows, and the men with metal knives on their fingers cut the ears off the stalks and tossed them into the wagons. Then they husked the ears, dancing afterward, and if a man got a red ear he could kiss his girl. In August there were great fairs, and the farmers came in to show their crops and beasts, and the workers showed their new reapers and mowers.

There was the excitement of the fall, the terror of the winter coming on. In the winter we didn't have what we did not can, preserve, ferment, or bury in sand. We had to hurry to cut the wood and to get the tomatoes, beans, and piccalilli canned before frost in the garden. It was like preparing for a battle. My grandmother wrapped the apples in newspaper and put them cheek by jowl in the barrels. Cabbage was shredded and barreled for sauerkraut. Even the old hens were killed. I was always surprised to see my gentle grandmother put her foot on the neck of her favorite hen and behead her with a single stroke of a long-handled ax.

The days slowly getting shorter, the herbs hung drying as the woods turned golden. Everything changes on the prairies at the end of summer, all coming to ripeness, and the thunderheads charging in the magnetic moisture of the vast skies. The autumnal dances are the best medicine against the threat of winter, isolation again, dangers. The barns were turned into dance halls before the winter hay was cut. The women raised their long skirts and danced toward hell in schottisches, round dances, and square dances. The rafters rang with the music of the old fiddlers and the harmonica players.

When the golden leaves stacked Persian carpets on the ground and the cornfields were bare, we saw again the great hunched land naked, sometimes fall plowed or planted in winter wheat. Slowly the curve seemed to rise out of the glut of summer, and the earth document was visible script, readable in the human tenderness of risk and ruin.

The owl rides the meadow at his hunting hour. The fox clears out the pheasants and the partridges in the cornfield. Jupiter rests above Antares, and the fall moon hooks itself into the prairie sod. A dark wind flows down from Mandan as the Indians slowly move out of the summer campground to go back to the reservation. Aries, buck of the sky, leaps to the outer rim and mates with earth. Root and seed turn into flesh. We turn back to each other in the dark together, in the short days, in the dangerous cold, on the rim of a perpetual wilderness.   *   *   *

RENÉ DUBOS
1901-1982

René Dubos was a microbiologist whose early work led to the commercial development of antibiotics. He was also an internationally known environmentalist and the author of over twenty books, including the Pulitzer Prize–winning So Human an Animal *(1969). Born in St. Brice, France, his concept of mankind's role in nature runs counter to much current American environmental thinking. Reflecting the Catholic-agricultural heritage of his native countryside, Dubos challenges accepted beliefs such as that wilderness is the most desirable and inspiring of landscapes, or that human alterations of nature are necessarily destructive.*

From THE WOOING OF EARTH

A FAMILY OF LANDSCAPES

Some of the landscapes that we most admire are the products of environmental degradation. The denuded islands of the Aegean Sea, the rocky shores of the Mediterranean basin, the semidesertic areas of the

The Wooing of Earth (New York: Scribners, 1980).

American Southwest are regions that appeal to countless people from all social and ethnic groups, as well as professional ecologists. Yet these landscapes derive much of their color and sculptural beauty from deforestation and erosion, the two cardinal sins of ecology. The immense majority of people, furthermore, elect to live in places from which the wilderness has been eradicated and which have been profoundly transformed by human habitation. Orthodox ecological criteria are therefore not adequate to evaluate the quality of a particular environment for human life.

Since the humanization of Earth inevitably results in destruction of the wilderness and of many living species that depend on it, there is a fundamental conflict between ecological doctrine and human cultures, a conflict whose manifestations are most glaring in Greece.

On two occasions during the past few years, I visited the eleventh-century Byzantine monastery of Moni Kaisarianis, located some five miles southeast of Athens. The monastery is nestled on the slopes of Mount Hymettus at 1,100 feet elevation. A trail meanders from it toward the Hymettus mountain through an almost treeless landscape amidst thyme, lavender, sage, mint, and other aromatic plants. The rock formations of the area are denuded, but the luminous sky gives them an architectural quality particularly bewitching under the violet light of sunset.

A short distance from the monastery, the trail reaches an outcrop of rocks that affords a sudden view of the Acropolis, Mount Lycabettus, and the entire city of Athens. As is so often the case in Greece, the buildings—whether pagan or Christian—derive a dramatic quality independent of their architectural merit from their natural setting. But the landscape surrounding the monastery is not natural; it has been transformed by several thousand years of human occupation.

The grounds associated with the Moni Kaisarianis monastery are planted with almond and olive trees, two species that have long been part of the Greek flora but originated in south central or southeastern Asia. The road that leads from Athens to the monastery is shaded with eucalyptus trees introduced from Australia. Beyond the monastery, the Hymettus is stark and luminous but its rock formations were originally masked by earth and trees. Its bold architecture became clearly visible only during historical times as a result of deforestation and erosion.

Ecologists and historians agree that most of the Mediterranean world was wooded before human occupation. What we now regard as the typical Greek landscape, often stark and treeless, is the result of human activities. The rock structures were revealed only after the felling of the trees, which resulted in extensive erosion. The slopes have been kept denuded by rabbits, sheep, and goats that continuously destroy any new growth either of trees or grass. Erosion and overgrazing are the forces, inadvertently set in motion by human activities, that enable light to play its bewitching game on the white framework of Attica.

The humanization of the Greek wilderness has been achieved at great ecological loss. Writers of the classical, Hellenistic, and Roman periods were aware of the transformations brought about by deforestation in the Mediterranean world. In *Critias,* Plato compared the land of Attica to the "bones of a wasted body . . . the richer and softer parts of the soil having fallen away, and the mere skeleton being left." In ancient times, still according to Plato, the buildings had "roofs of timber cut from trees which were of a size sufficient to cover the largest houses." After deforestation, however, "the mountains only afforded sustenance to bees." The famous Hymettus honey is thus linked to deforestation, which permitted the growth of sun-loving aromatic plants.

As long as the mountain slopes were wooded, the land of Greece, as well as of other Mediterranean countries, was enriched by rainfall, but by Plato's time erosion caused the water to "flow off the bare earth into the sea. . . ." The sacred groves and other sanctuaries were originally established near springs and streams, but these progressively dried up as a consequence of deforestation.

The Ilissus River, which has its source on Mount Hymettus and runs through Athens, was still a lively stream in Plato's time. On a hot day in midsummer, Socrates and Phaedrus walked toward a tall plane tree on the banks of the Ilissus a short distance from the Agora. There, as reported in the famous dialogue, they discussed rhetoric, philosophy, and love while cooling their feet in the stream that they found "delightfully clear and bright." Today, the Ilissus is dry much of the year and, covered by a noisy roadway, serves as a sewer. There could not be a more dramatic symbol of the damage done by deforestation, erosion, and urban mismanagement.

The reforestation of Greece would certainly result in climatic and agricultural improvements. As Henry Miller writes in *The Colossus of Maroussi,* "The tree brings water, fodder, cattle, produce . . . shade, leisure, song. . . . Greece does not need archeologists—she needs arboriculturists." But a cover of trees would make the landscape very different from the image that we, and the Greeks themselves, have had of Greece since classical times. In his poem "The Satyr or the Naked Song," the Greek poet Kostes Palamas (1859–1943) sees in the stark eroded structures of the present landscape a symbol of the austerity and purity of the Greek genius; the landscape triumphantly proclaims the "divine nudity" of Greece. Henry Miller himself, a few pages before and after the passage quoted above in which he advocates reforestation, marvels at the quality given to the landscape by the rocks that "have been lying for centuries exposed to this divine illumination . . . nestling amid dancing colored shrubs in a blood-stained soil." In Miller's words, these rocks "are symbols of life eternal." He does not mention that they are visible only because of deforestation and erosion.

While visiting the Moni Kaisarianis monastery, I noticed a dark opaque zone on the slopes of Mount Hymettus; this area had been reforested with pines. To me, it looked like an inkblot on the luminous landscape, especially at sunset, when the subtle violet atmosphere suffuses the bare rocks throughout the mountain range. The "divine illumination" lost much of its magic where it was absorbed by the pine trees.

The mountains of Attica were probably difficult to penetrate and frightening when completely wooded, but they have now acquired some of the qualities of a park. The traveler can move on their open surfaces, and vision can extend into a distance of golden light. I have wondered whether the dark and ferocious divinities of the preclassical Greek period did not become more serene and more playful precisely because they had emerged from the dark forests into the open landscape. Would logic have flourished if Greece had remained covered with an opaque tangle of trees?

There is no doubt that people spoiled the water economy and impoverished the land when they destroyed the forests of the Mediterranean world. But it is true also that deforestation allowed the landscape to express certain of its potentialities that had remained hidden under the dense vegetation. Not only did removal of the trees permit the growth of sun-loving aromatic plants and favor the spread of honeybees, as Plato had recognized; more importantly, it revealed the underlying architecture of the area and perhaps helped the soaring of the human mind.

The full expression of the Mediterranean genius may require both the cool mysterious fountains in the sacred groves and the bright light shining on the sun-loving plants amid the denuded rocks. Ecology becomes a more complex but far more interesting science when human aspirations are regarded as an integral part of the landscape.

The wide range of natural and humanized environments of which we have knowledge calls to mind the collection of photographs that Edward Steichen published a few years ago under the title *The Family of Man*. In his book, Steichen created a panorama of the human species as it can be found today all over the Earth in its richly diversified types—the unloved and miserable as well as the loved and glorious, those conveying a sad resignation as well as those radiating a challenging beauty. Just as

Steichen conceived his collection to be, in his own words, "a mirror of the universal elements and emotions in the everydayness of life," so I shall refer to many different aspects of the Earth, some that evolved under the influence of natural forces and others that have been completely transformed by human activities—whether these were ecologically constructive or destructive.

Many people reject Steichen's view that beauty can be found in all the visages of the family of man, and even more will be disturbed by my statement that deforestation and erosion have produced some of the most admired landscapes. It is obvious, of course, that the Earth and its atmosphere have been spoiled in many places by human carelessness and greed, but I feel nevertheless that almost any kind of scenery, even artificial and desolate, can be a source of interest and pleasure if one knows how to recognize in it patterns of visual organization, aspects of ecological curiosity, and matters of human concern. * * *

NORMAN MACLEAN
B. 1902

It has been remarked that nature writers start later and keep going longer than writers in most other fields. An English professor at the University of Chicago for more than four decades, Norman Maclean published A River Runs Through It and Other Stories *in 1976, when he was 73 years old. This volume is a collection of two novellas and a short story closely based on Maclean's experiences growing up and working as a logger and on a U.S. Forest Service crew in the Idaho and Montana mountains during the 1920s. The title story, from which the following passage was excerpted, is a narrative memoir of his family, in which, as he put it, "there was no clear line between religion and fly fishing." The central relationship is between the narrator and his brother Paul, whose troubled life contrasts sharply with his consummate skill as a fly-fisherman. The book contains stunning descriptions, not only of the canyon river country but of trout-fishing itself, imbued with metaphoric and symbolic resonances reminiscent of Melville's descriptions of whales and whaling. Here, Maclean seems to suggest, in sympathetic contact with nature, we achieve a grace and unity in our lives sadly at odds with our dealings with one another.*

From A River Runs Through It

*   *   * Paul and I fished a good many big rivers, but when one of us referred to "the big river" the other knew it was the Big Blackfoot. It isn't the biggest river we fished, but it is the most powerful, and per pound, so are its fish. It runs straight and hard—on a map or from an airplane it is almost a straight line running due west from its headwaters at Rogers Pass on the Continental Divide to Bonner, Montana, where it empties into the South Fork of the Clark Fork of the Columbia. It runs hard all the way.

Near its headwaters on the Continental Divide there is a mine with a thermometer that stopped at 69.7 degrees below zero, the lowest temperature ever officially recorded in the United States (Alaska omitted). From its headwaters to its mouth it was manufactured by glaciers. The first sixty-five miles of it are smashed against the southern wall of its valley by glaciers that moved in from the north, scarifying the earth; its lower twenty-five miles were made overnight when the great glacial lake covering northwestern Montana and northern Idaho broke its ice dam and spread the remains of Montana and Idaho mountains over hundreds of miles of the plains of eastern Washington. It was the biggest flood in the world for which there is geological evidence; it was so vast a geological event that the mind of man could only conceive of it but could not prove it until photographs could be taken from earth satellites.

The straight line on the map also suggests its glacial origins; it has no meandering valley, and its few farms are mostly on its southern tributaries which were not ripped up by glaciers; instead of opening into a wide flood plain near its mouth, the valley, which was cut overnight by a disappearing lake when the great ice dam melted, gets narrower and narrower until the only way a river, an old logging railroad, and an automobile road can fit into it is for two of them to take to the mountainsides.

It is a tough place for a trout to live—the river roars and the water is too fast to let algae grow on the rocks for feed, so there is no fat on the fish, which must hold most trout records for high jumping.

Besides, it is the river we knew best. My brother and I had fished the

A River Runs Through It and Other Stories (Chicago: University of Chicago Press, 1976).

Big Blackfoot since nearly the beginning of the century—my father before then. We regarded it as a family river, as a part of us, and I surrender it now only with great reluctance to dude ranches, the unselected inhabitants of Great Falls, and the Moorish invaders from California.

Early next morning Paul picked me up in Wolf Creek, and we drove across Rogers Pass where the thermometer is that stuck at three-tenths of a degree short of seventy below. As usual, especially if it were early in the morning, we sat silently respectful until we passed the big Divide, but started talking the moment we thought we were draining into another ocean. Paul nearly always had a story to tell in which he was the leading character but not the hero.

He told his Continental Divide stories in a seemingly light-hearted, slightly poetical mood such as reporters often use in writing "human-interest" stories, but, if the mood were removed, his stories would appear as something about him that would not meet the approval of his family and that I would probably find out about in time anyway. He also must have felt honor-bound to tell me that he lived other lives, even if he presented them to me as puzzles in the form of funny stories. Often I did not know what I had been told about him as we crossed the divide between our two worlds.

"You know," he began, "it's been a couple of weeks since I fished the Blackfoot." At the beginning, his stories sounded like factual reporting. He had fished alone and the fishing had not been much good, so he had to fish until evening to get his limit. Since he was returning directly to Helene he was driving up Nevada Creek along an old dirt road that followed section lines and turned at right angles at section corners. It was moonlight, he was tired and feeling in need of a friend to keep him awake, when suddenly a jackrabbit jumped on to the road and started running with the headlights. "I didn't push him too hard," he said, "because I didn't want to lose a friend." He drove, he said, with his head outside the window so he could feel close to the rabbit. With his head in the moonlight, his account took on poetic touches. The vague world of moonlight was pierced by the intense white triangle from the headlights. In the center of the penetrating isosceles was the jackrabbit, which, except for the length of his jumps, had become a snowshoe rabbit. The phosphorescent jackrabbit was doing his best to keep in the center of the isosceles but was afraid he was losing ground and, when he looked back to check, his eyes shone with whites and blues gathered up from the universe. My brother said, "I don't know how to explain what happened next, but there was a right-angle turn in this section-line road, and the rabbit saw it, and I didn't."

Later, he happened to mention that it cost him $175.00 to have his car fixed, and in 1937 you could almost get a car rebuilt for $175.00. Of course, he never mentioned that, although he did not drink when he fished, he always started drinking when he finished.

I rode part of the way down the Blackfoot wondering whether I had been told a little human-interest story with hard luck turned into humor or whether I had been told he had taken too many drinks and smashed hell out of the front end of his car.

Since it was no great thing either way, I finally decided to forget it, and, as you see, I didn't. I did, though, start thinking about the canyon where we were going to fish.

The canyon above the old Clearwater bridge is where the Blackfoot roars loudest. The backbone of a mountain would not break, so the mountain compresses the already powerful river into sound and spray before letting it pass. Here, of course, the road leaves the river; there was no place in the canyon for an Indian trail; even in 1806 when Lewis left Clark to come up the Blackfoot, he skirted the canyon by a safe margin. It is no place for small fish or small fishermen. Even the roar adds power to the fish or at least intimidates the fisherman.

When we fished the canyon we fished on the same side of it for the simple reason that there is no place in the canyon to wade across. I could hear Paul start to pass me to get to the hole above, and, when I realized I didn't hear him anymore, I knew he had stopped to watch me. Although I have never pretended to be a great fisherman, it was always important to me that I was a fisherman and looked like one, especially when fishing with my brother. Even before the silence continued, I knew that I wasn't looking like much of anything.

Although I have a warm personal feeling for the canyon, it is not an ideal place for me to fish. It puts a premium upon being able to cast for distance, and yet most of the time there are cliffs or trees right behind the fisherman so he has to keep all his line in front of him. It's like a baseball pitcher being deprived of his windup, and it forces the fly fisherman into what is called a "roll cast," a hard cast that I have never mastered. The fisherman has to work enough line into his cast to get distance without throwing any line behind him, and then he has to develop enough power from a short arc to shoot it out across the water.

He starts accumulating the extra amount of line for the long cast by retrieving his last cast so slowly that an unusual amount of line stays in the water and what is out of it forms a slack semiloop. The loop is enlarged by raising the casting arm straight up and cocking the wrist until it points to 1:30. There, then, is a lot of line in front of the fisherman, but it takes about everything he has to get it high in the air and out over the water so that the fly and leader settle ahead of the line—the arm is a piston, the wrist is a revolver that uncocks, and even the body gets behind the punch. Important, too, is the fact that the extra amount of line remaining in the water until the last moment gives a semisolid bottom to the cast. It is a little like a rattlesnake striking, with a good piece of his tail on the ground as something to strike from. All this is easy for a rattlesnake, but has always been hard for me.

Paul knew how I felt about my fishing and was careful not to seem superior by offering advice, but he had watched so long that he couldn't leave now without saying something. Finally he said, "The fish are out farther." Probably fearing he had put a strain on family relations, he quickly added, "Just a little farther."

I reeled in my line slowly, not looking behind so as not to see him. Maybe he was sorry he had spoken, but, having said what he said, he had to say something more. "Instead of retrieving the line straight toward you, bring it in on a diagonal from the downstream side. The diagonal will give you a more resistant base to your loop so you can put more power into your forward cast and get a little more distance."

Then he acted as if he hadn't said anything and I acted as if I hadn't heard it, but as soon as he left, which was immediately, I started retrieving my line on a diagonal, and it helped. The moment I felt I was getting a little more distance I ran for a fresh hole to make a fresh start in life.

It was a beautiful stretch of water, either to a fisherman or a photographer, although each would have focused his equipment on a different point. It was a barely submerged waterfall. The reef of rock was about two feet under the water, so the whole river rose into one wave, shook itself into spray, then fell back on itself and turned blue. After it recovered from the shock, it came back to see how it had fallen.

No fish could live out there where the river exploded into the colors and curves that would attract photographers. The fish were in that slow backwash, right in the dirty foam, with the dirt being one of the chief attractions. Part of the speckles would be pollen from pine trees, but most of the dirt was edible insect life that had not survived the waterfall.

I studied the situation. Although maybe I had just added three feet to my roll cast, I still had to do a lot of thinking before casting to compensate for some of my other shortcomings. But I felt I had already made the right beginning—I had already figured out where the big fish would be and why.

Then an odd thing happened. I saw him. A black back rose and sank in the foam. In fact, I imagined I saw spines on his dorsal fin until I said to myself, "God, he couldn't be so big you could see his fins." I even added, "You wouldn't even have seen the fish in all that foam if you hadn't first thought he would be there." But I couldn't shake the conviction that I had seen the black back of a big fish, because, as someone often forced to think, I know that often I would not see a thing unless I thought of it first.

Seeing the fish that I first thought would be there led me to wondering which way he would be pointing in the river. "Remember, when you make the first cast," I thought, "that you saw him in the backwash where the water is circling upstream, so he will be looking downstream, not upstream, as he would be if he were in the main current."

I was led by association to the question of what fly I would cast, and to the conclusion that it had better be a large fly, a number four or six, if I was going after the big hump in the foam.

From the fly, I went to the other end of the cast, and asked myself where the hell I was going to cast from. There were only gigantic rocks at this waterfall, so I picked one of the biggest, saw how I could crawl up it, and knew from that added height I would get added distance, but then I had to ask myself, "How the hell am I going to land the fish if I hook him while I'm standing up there?" So I had to pick a smaller rock, which would shorten my distance but would let me slide down it with a rod in my hand and a big fish on.

I was gradually approaching the question all river fishermen should ask before they make the first cast, "If I hook a big one, where the hell can I land him?"

One great thing about fly fishing is that after a while nothing exists of the world but thoughts about fly fishing. It is also interesting that thoughts about fishing are often carried on in dialogue form where Hope and Fear—or, many times, two Fears—try to outweigh each other.

One fear looked down the shoreline and said to me (a third person distinct from the two fears), "There is nothing but rocks for thirty yards, but don't get scared and try to land him before you get all the way down to the first sandbar."

The Second Fear said, "It's forty, not thirty, yards to the first sandbar and the weather has been warm and the fish's mouth will be soft and he will work off the hook if you try to fight him forty yards downriver. It's not good but it will be best to try to land him on a rock that is closer."

The First Fear said, "There is a big rock in the river that you will have to take him past before you land him, but, if you hold the line tight enough on him to keep him this side of the rock, you will probably lose him."

The Second Fear said, "But if you let him get on the far side of the rock, the line will get caught under it, and you will be sure to lose him."

That's how you know when you have thought too much—when you

become a dialogue between *You'll probably lose* and *You're sure to lose.* But I didn't entirely quit thinking, although I did switch subjects. It is not in the book, yet it is human enough to spend a moment before casting in trying to imagine what the fish is thinking, even if one of its eggs is as big as its brain and even if, when you swim underwater, it is hard to imagine that a fish has anything to think about. Still, I could never be talked into believing that all a fish knows is hunger and fear. I have tried to feel nothing but hunger and fear and don't see how a fish could ever grow to six inches if that were all he ever felt. In fact, I go so far sometimes as to imagine that a fish thinks pretty thoughts. Before I made the cast, I imagined the fish with the black back lying cool in the carbonated water full of bubbles from the waterfalls. He was looking downriver and watching the foam with food in it backing upstream like a floating cafeteria coming to wait on its customers. And he probably was imagining that the speckled foam was eggnog with nutmeg sprinkled on it, and, when the whites of eggs separated and he saw what was on shore, he probably said to himself, "What a lucky son of a bitch I am that this guy and not his brother is about to fish this hole."

I thought all these thoughts and some besides that proved of no value, and then I cast and I caught him.

I kept cool until I tried to take the hook out of his mouth. He was lying covered with sand on the little bar where I had landed him. His gills opened with his penultimate sighs. Then suddenly he stood up on his head in the sand and hit me with his tail and the sand flew. Slowly at first my hands began to shake, and, although I thought they made a miserable sight, I couldn't stop them. Finally, I managed to open the large blade to my knife which several times slid off his skull before it went through his brain.

Even when I bent him he was way too long for my basket, so his tail stuck out.

There were black spots on him that looked like crustaceans. He seemed oceanic, including barnacles. When I passed my brother at the next hole, I saw him study the tail and slowly remove his hat, and not out of respect to my prowess as a fisherman.

I had a fish, so I sat down to watch a fisherman.

He took his cigarettes and matches from his shirt pocket and put them in his hat and pulled his hat down tight so it wouldn't leak. Then he unstrapped his fish basket and hung it on the edge of his shoulder where he could get rid of it quick should the water get too big for him. If he studied the situation he didn't take any separate time to do it. He jumped off a rock into the swirl and swam for a chunk of cliff that had dropped into the river and parted it. He swam in his clothes with only his

left arm—in his right hand, he held his rod high and sometimes all I
could see was the basket and rod, and when the basket filled with water
sometimes all I could see was the rod.

The current smashed him into the chunk of cliff and it must have
hurt, but he had enough strength remaining in his left fingers to hang to
a crevice or he would have been swept into the blue below. Then he still
had to climb to the top of the rock with his left fingers and his right
elbow which he used like a prospector's pick. When he finally stood on
top, his clothes looked hydraulic, as if they were running off him.

Once he quit wobbling, he shook himself duck-dog fashion, with his
feet spread apart, his body lowered and his head flopping. Then he
steadied himself and began to cast and the whole world turned to water.

Below him was the multitudinous river, and, where the rock had
parted it around him, big-grained vapor rose. The mini-molecules of
water left in the wake of his line made momentary loops of gossamer,
disappearing so rapidly in the rising big-grained vapor that they had to be
retained in memory to be visualized as loops. The spray emanating from
him was finer-grained still and enclosed him in a halo of himself. The
halo of himself was always there and always disappearing, as if he were
candlelight flickering about three inches from himself. The images of
himself and his line kept disappearing into the rising vapors of the river,
which continually circled to the tops of the cliffs where, after becoming a
wreath in the wind, they became rays of the sun.

The river above and below his rock was all big Rainbow water, and he
would cast hard and low upstream, skimming the water with his fly but
never letting it touch. Then he would pivot, reverse his line in a great
oval above his head, and drive his line low and hard downstream, again
skimming the water with his fly. He would complete this grand circle
four or five times, creating an immensity of motion which culminated in
nothing if you did not know, even if you could not see, that now somewhere out there a small fly was washing itself on a wave. Shockingly,
immensity would return as the Big Blackfoot and the air above it became
iridescent with the arched sides of a great Rainbow.

He called this "shadow casting," and frankly I don't know whether to
believe the theory behind it—that the fish are alerted by the shadows of
flies passing over the water by the first casts, so hit the fly the moment it
touches the water. It is more or less the "working up an appetite" theory,
almost too fancy to be true, but then every fine fisherman has a few fancy
stunts that work for him and for almost no one else. Shadow casting
never worked for me, but maybe I never had the strength of arm and
wrist to keep line circling over the water until fish imagined a hatch of
flies was out.

My brother's wet clothes made it easy to see his strength. Most great casters I have known were big men over six feet, the added height certainly making it easier to get more line in the air in a bigger arc. My brother was only five feet ten, but he had fished so many years his body had become partly shaped by his casting. He was thirty-two now, at the height of his power, and he could put all his body and soul into a four-and-a-half-ounce magic totem pole. Long ago, he had gone far beyond my father's wrist casting, although his right wrist was always so important that it had become larger than his left. His right arm, which our father had kept tied to the side to emphasize the wrist, shot out of his shirt as if it were engineered, and it, too, was larger than his left arm. His wet shirt bulged and came unbuttoned with his pivoting shoulders and hips. It was also not hard to see why he was a street fighter, especially since he was committed to getting in the first punch with his right hand.

Rhythm was just as important as color and just as complicated. It was one rhythm superimposed upon another, our father's four-count rhythm of the line and wrist being still the base rhythm. But superimposed upon it was the piston two count of his arm and the long overriding four count of the completed figure eight of his reversed loop.

The canyon was glorified by rhythms and colors. ＊ ＊ ＊

JOHN STEINBECK
1902-1968

Steinbeck's novels are rooted in the landscape of California, particularly in the farming and fishing communities of the Salinas Valley and the Carmel Peninsula. One early novel, To a God Unknown *(1933) is essentially a modern retelling of a pagan fertility myth. Though the depiction of a roadside tortoise included here comes from his novel* The Grapes of Wrath *(1939), it can stand alone as a fine natural portrait. In 1940 Steinbeck undertook a research voyage to the Gulf of Mexico with his close friend, the marine biologist Edward F. Ricketts. Their joint account of that voyage was published in* The Sea of Cortez *(1941). Steinbeck's portion was republished in 1951 as* The Log from the Sea of Cortez; *its introduction is one of the most concise statements ever made on the difference between the scientific and personal approaches to nature writing.*

From THE GRAPES OF WRATH

The concrete highway was edged with a mat of tangled, broken, dry grass, and the grass heads were heavy with oat beards to catch on a dog's coat, and foxtails to tangle in a horse's fetlocks, and clover burrs to fasten in sheep's wool; sleeping life waiting to be spread and dispersed, every seed armed with an appliance of dispersal, twisting darts and parachutes for the wind, little spears and balls of tiny thorns, and all waiting for animals and for the wind, for a man's trouser cuff or the hem of a woman's skirt, all passive but armed with appliances of activity, still, but each possessed of the anlage of movement.

The sun lay on the grass and warmed it, and in the shade under the grass the insects moved, ants and ant lions to set traps for them, grasshoppers to jump into the air and flick their yellow wings for a second, sow bugs like little armadillos, plodding restlessly on many tender feet. And over the grass at the roadside a land turtle crawled, turning aside for nothing, dragging his high-domed shell over the grass. His hard legs and yellow-nailed feet threshed slowly through the grass, not really walking, but boosting and dragging his shell along. The barley beards slid off his shell, and the clover burrs fell on him and rolled to the ground. His horny beak was partly open, and his fierce, humorous eyes, under brows like fingernails, stared straight ahead. He came over the grass leaving a beaten trail behind him, and the hill, which was the highway embankment, reared up ahead of him. For a moment he stopped, his head held high. He blinked and looked up and down. At last he started to climb the embankment. Front clawed feet reached forward but did not touch. The hind feet kicked his shell along, and it scraped on the grass, and on the gravel. As the embankment grew steeper and steeper, the more frantic were the efforts of the land turtle. Pushing hind legs strained and slipped, boosting the shell along, and the horny head protruded as far as the neck could stretch. Little by little the shell slid up the embankment until at last a parapet cut straight across its line of march, the shoulder of the road, a concrete wall four inches high. As though they worked independently the hind legs pushed the shell against the wall. The head upraised and peered over the wall to the broad smooth plain of cement. Now the hands, braced on top of the wall, strained and lifted, and the

The Grapes of Wrath (New York: Viking, 1939).

shell came slowly up and rested its front end on the wall. For a moment the turtle rested. A red ant ran into the shell, into the soft skin inside the shell, and suddenly head and legs snapped in, and the armored tail clamped in sideways. The red ant was crushed between body and legs. And one head of wild oats was clamped into the shell by a front leg. For a long moment the turtle lay still, and then the neck crept out and the old humorous frowning eyes looked about and the legs and tail came out. The back legs went to work, straining like elephant legs, and the shell tipped to an angle so that the front legs could not reach the level cement plain. But higher and higher the hind legs boosted it, until at last the center of balance was reached, the front tipped down, the front legs scratched at the pavement, and it was up. But the head of wild oats was held by its stem around the front legs.

Now the going was easy, and all the legs worked, and the shell boosted along, waggling from side to side. A sedan driven by a forty-year old woman approached. She saw the turtle and swung to the right, off the highway, the wheels screamed and a cloud of dust boiled up. Two wheels lifted for a moment and then settled. The car skidded back onto the road, and went on, but more slowly. The turtle had jerked into its shell, but now it hurried on, for the highway was burning hot.

And now a light truck approached, and as it came near, the driver saw the turtle and swerved to hit it. His front wheel struck the edge of the shell, flipped the turtle like a tiddly-wink, spun it like a coin, and rolled it off the highway. The truck went back to its course along the right side. Lying on its back, the turtle was tight in its shell for a long time. But at last its legs waved in the air, reaching for something to pull it over. Its front foot caught a piece of quartz and little by little the shell pulled over and flopped upright. The wild oat head fell out and three of the spear-head seeds stuck in the ground. And as the turtle crawled on down the embankment, its shell dragged dirt over the seeds. The turtle entered a dust road and jerked itself along, drawing a wavy shallow trench in the dust with its shell. The old humorous eyes looked ahead, and the horny beak opened a little. His yellow toe nails slipped a fraction in the dust.

From THE LOG FROM THE SEA OF CORTEZ

INTRODUCTION

The design of a book is the pattern of a reality controlled and shaped by the mind of the writer. This is completely understood about poetry or fiction, but it is too seldom realized about books of fact. And yet the

The Log from the Sea of Cortez (New York: Viking, 1951).

impulse which drives a man to poetry will send another man into the tide pools and force him to try to report what he finds there. Why is an expedition to Tibet undertaken, or a sea bottom dredged? Why do men, sitting at the microscope, examine the calcareous plates of a sea-cucumber, and, finding a new arrangement and number, feel an exaltation and give the new species a name, and write about it possessively? It would be good to know the impulse truly, not to be confused by the "services to science" platitudes or the other little mazes into which we entice our minds so that they will not know what we are doing.

We have a book to write about the Gulf of California. We could do one of several things about its design. But we have decided to let it form itself: its boundaries a boat and a sea; its duration a six weeks' charter time; its subject everything we could see and think and even imagine; its limits—our own without reservation.

We made a trip into the Gulf; sometimes we dignified it by calling it an expedition. Once it was called the Sea of Cortez, and that is a better-sounding and a more exciting name. We stopped in many little harbors and near barren coasts to collect and preserve the marine invertebrates of the littoral. One of the reasons we gave ourselves for this trip—and when we used this reason, we called the trip an expedition—was to observe the distribution of invertebrates, to see and to record their kinds and numbers, how they lived together, what they ate, and how they reproduced. That plan was simple, straightforward, and only a part of the truth. But we did tell the truth to ourselves. We were curious. Our curiosity was not limited, but was as wide and horizonless as that of Darwin or Agassiz or Linnaeus or Pliny. We wanted to see everything our eyes would accommodate, to think what we could, and, out of our seeing and thinking, to build some kind of structure in modeled imitation of the observed reality. We knew that what we would see and record and construct would be warped, as all knowledge patterns are warped, first, by the collective pressure and stream of our time and race, second by the thrust of our individual personalities. But knowing this, we might not fall into too many holes—we might maintain some balance between our warp and the separate things, the external reality. The oneness of these two might take its contribution from both. For example: the Mexican sierra has "XVII–15–IX" spines in the dorsal fin. These can easily be counted. But if the sierra strikes hard on the line so that our hands are burned, if the fish sounds and nearly escapes and finally comes in over the rail, his colors pulsing and his tail beating the air, a whole new relational externality has come into being—an entity which is more than the sum of the fish plus the fisherman. The only way to count the spines of the sierra unaffected by this second relational reality is to sit in a laboratory, open an evil-smelling jar, remove a stiff colorless fish from formalin solution, count the spines, and write the truth "D. XVII–15–IX." There you have recorded a reality which cannot be assailed—probably the least important reality concerning either the fish or yourself.

It is good to know what you are doing. The man with his pickled fish has set down one truth and has recorded in his experience many lies. The fish is not that color, that texture, that dead, nor does he smell that way.

Such things we had considered in the months of planning our expedition and we were determined not to let a passion for unassailable little truths draw in the horizons and crowd the sky down on us. We knew that what seemed to us true could be only relatively true anyway. There is no other kind of observation. The man with his pickled fish has sacrificed a great observation about himself, the fish, and the focal point, which is his thought on both the sierra and himself.

We suppose this was the mental provisioning of our expedition. We said, "Let's go wide open. Let's see what we see, record what we find, and not fool ourselves with conventional scientific strictures. We could not observe a completely objective Sea of Cortez anyway, for in that lonely and uninhabited Gulf our boat and ourselves would change it the moment we entered. By going there, we would bring a new factor to the Gulf. Let us consider that factor and not be betrayed by this myth of permanent objective reality. If it exists at all, it is only available in pickled tatters or in distorted flashes. Let us go," we said, "into the Sea of Cortez, realizing that we become forever a part of it; that our rubber boots slogging through a flat of eelgrass, that the rocks we turn over in a tide pool, make us truly and permanently a factor in the ecology of the region. We shall take something away from it, but we shall leave something too." And if we seem a small factor in a huge pattern, nevertheless it is of relative importance. We take a tiny colony of soft corals from a rock in a little water world. And that isn't terribly important to the tide pool. Fifty miles away the Japanese shrimp boats are dredging with overlapping scoops, bringing up tons of shrimps, rapidly destroying the species so that it may never come back, and with the species destroying the ecological balance of the whole region. That isn't very important in the world. And thousands of miles away the great bombs are falling and the stars are not moved thereby. None of it is important or all of it is.

We determined to go doubly open so that in the end we could, if we wished, describe the sierra thus: "D. XVII–15–IX; A. II–15–IX," but also we could see the fish alive and swimming, feel it plunge against the lines, drag it threshing over the rail, and even finally eat it. And there is no reason why either approach should be inaccurate. Spine-count description need not suffer because another approach is also used. Perhaps out of the two approaches, we thought, there might emerge a picture more complete and even more accurate than either alone could produce. And so we went.

GEORGE ORWELL
1903-1950

Born in India and educated in England, Eric Blair adopted the pen name George Orwell to write such satirical novels as Animal Farm *(1946), a political fable, and* 1984 *(1949), a vision of a totalitarian future. "Some Thoughts On the Common Toad" comes from his collection of essays,* Shooting an Elephant *(1950), which also contains his famous essay "Politics and the English Language." Though not overtly political, Orwell's celebration of the annual reemergence and mating of toads gathers ideological import as it goes. If Steinbeck's description of the highway tortoise in* Grapes of Wrath *represents, as Joseph Wood Krutch put it, "the sociological turtle," Orwell here gives us the anti-bureaucratic amphibian.*

SOME THOUGHTS ON THE COMMON TOAD

Before the swallow, before the daffodil, and not much later than the snowdrop, the common toad salutes the coming of spring after his own fashion, which is to emerge from a hole in the ground, where he has lain buried since the previous autumn, and crawl as rapidly as possible towards the nearest suitable patch of water. Something—some kind of shudder in the earth, or perhaps merely a rise of a few degrees in the temperature—has told him that it is time to wake up: though a few toads appear to sleep the clock round and miss out a year from time to time— at any rate, I have more than once dug them up, alive and apparently well, in the middle of the summer.

Shooting an Elephant and Other Essays (New York: Harcourt, Brace & World, 1950).

At this period, after his long fast, the toad has a very spiritual look, like a strict Anglo-Catholic towards the end of Lent. His movements are languid but purposeful, his body is shrunken, and by contrast his eyes look abnormally large. This allows one to notice, what one might not at another time, that a toad has about the most beautiful eye of any living creature. It is like gold, or more exactly it is like the golden-colored semi-precious stone which one sometimes sees in signet rings, and which I think is called a chrysoberyl.

For a few days after getting into the water the toad concentrates on building up his strength by eating small insects. Presently he has swollen to his normal size again, and then he goes through a phase of intense sexiness. All he knows, at least if he is a male toad, is that he wants to get his arms round something, and if you offer him a stick, or even your finger, he will cling to it with surprising strength and take a long time to discover that it is not a female toad. Frequently one comes upon shapeless masses of ten or twenty toads rolling over and over in the water, one clinging to another without distinction of sex. By degrees, however, they sort themselves out into couples, with the male duly sitting on the female's back. You can now distinguish males from females, because the male is smaller, darker and sits on top, with his arms tightly clasped round the female's neck. After a day or two the spawn is laid in long strings which wind themselves in and out of the reeds and soon become invisible. A few more weeks, and the water is alive with masses of tiny tadpoles which rapidly grow larger, sprout hind-legs, then fore-legs, then shed their tails: and finally, about the middle of the summer, the new generation of toads, smaller than one's thumb-nail but perfect in every particular, crawl out of the water to begin the game anew.

I mention the spawning of the toads because it is one of the phenomena of spring which most deeply appeal to me, and because the toad, unlike the skylark and the primrose, has never had much of a boost from the poets. But I am aware that many people do not like reptiles or amphibians, and I am not suggesting that in order to enjoy the spring you have to take an interest in toads. There are also the crocus, the missel thrush, the cuckoo, the blackthorn, etc. The point is that the pleasures of spring are available to everybody, and cost nothing. Even in the most sordid street the coming of spring will register itself by some sign or other, if it is only a brighter blue between the chimney pots or the vivid green of an elder sprouting on a blitzed site. Indeed it is remarkable how Nature goes on existing unofficially, as it were, in the very heart of London. I have seen a kestrel flying over the Deptford gasworks, and I have heard a first-rate performance by a black bird in the Euston Road.

There must be some hundreds of thousands, if not millions, of birds living inside the four-mile radius, and it is rather a pleasing thought that none of them pays a halfpenny of rent.

As for spring, not even the narrow and gloomy streets round the Bank of England are quite able to exclude it. It comes seeping in everywhere, like one of those new poison gases which pass through all filters. The spring is commonly referred to as "a miracle," and during the past five or six years this worn-out figure of speech has taken on a new lease of life. After the sort of winters we have had to endure recently, the spring does seem miraculous, because it has become gradually harder and harder to believe that it is actually going to happen. Every February since 1940 I have found myself thinking that this time winter is going to be permanent. But Persephone, like the toads, always rises from the dead at about the same moment. Suddenly, towards the end of March, the miracle happens and the decaying slum in which I live is transfigured. Down in the square the sooty privets have turned bright green, the leaves are thickening on the chestnut trees, the daffodils are out, the wallflowers are budding, the policeman's tunic looks positively a pleasant shade of blue, the fishmonger greets his customers with a smile, and even the sparrows are quite a different color, having felt the balminess of the air and nerved themselves to take a bath, their first since last September.

Is it wicked to take a pleasure in spring, and other seasonal changes? To put it more precisely, is it politically reprehensible, while we are all groaning, under the shackles of the capitalist system, to point out that life is frequently more worth living because of a blackbird's song, a yellow elm tree in October, or some other natural phenomenon which does not cost money and does not have what the editors of the Left-wing newspapers call a class angle? There is no doubt that many people think so. I know by experience that a favorable reference to "Nature" in one of my articles is liable to bring me abusive letters, and though the key-word in these letters is usually "sentimental," two ideas seem to be mixed up in them. One is that any pleasure in the actual process of life encourages a sort of political quietism. People, so the thought runs, ought to be discontented, and it is our job to multiply our wants and not simply to increase our enjoyment of the things we have already. The other idea is that this is the age of machines and that to dislike the machine, or even to want to limit its domination, is backward-looking, reactionary, and slightly ridiculous. This is often backed up by the statement that a love of Nature is a foible of urbanized people who have no notion what Nature is really like. Those who really have to deal with the soil, so it is argued, do not love the soil, and do not take the faintest interest in birds or flowers, except from a strictly utilitarian point of view. To love the country one must live in the town, merely taking an occasional week-end ramble at the warmer times of year.

This last idea is demonstrably false. Medieval literature, for instance, including the popular ballads, is full of an almost Georgian enthusiasm for Nature, and the art of agricultural peoples such as the Chinese and Japanese centres always round trees, birds, flowers, rivers, mountains. The other idea seems to me to be wrong in a subtler way. Certainly we ought to be discontented, we ought not simply to find out ways of making the best of a bad job, and yet if we kill all pleasure in the actual process of life, what sort of future are we preparing for ourselves? If a man cannot enjoy the return of spring, why should he be happy in a labor-saving Utopia? What will he do with the leisure that the machine will give him? I have always suspected that if our economic and political problems are ever really solved, life will become simpler instead of more complex, and that the sort of pleasure one gets from finding the first primrose will loom larger than the sort of pleasure one gets from eating an ice to the tune of a Wurlitzer. I think that by retaining one's childhood love of such things as trees, fishes, butterflies and—to return to my first instance—toads, one makes a peaceful and decent future a little more probable, and that by preaching the doctrine that nothing is to be admired except steel and concrete, one merely makes it a little surer that human beings will have no outlet for their surplus energy except in hatred and leader-worship.

At any rate, spring is here, even in London, N.1, and they can't stop you enjoying it. This is a satisfying reflection. How many a time have I stood watching the toads mating, or a pair of hares having a boxing match in the young corn, and thought of all the important persons who would stop me enjoying this if they could. But luckily they can't. So long as you are not actually ill, hungry, frightened or immured in a prison or a holiday camp, spring is still spring. The atom bombs are piling up in the factories, the police are prowling through the cities, the lies are streaming from the loudspeakers, but the earth is still going round the sun, and neither the dictators nor the bureaucrats, deeply as they disapprove of the process, are able to prevent it.

LAURENS VAN DER POST
B. 1906

The range of Laurens Van Der Post's writing reflects his many careers as farmer, explorer, soldier, anthropologist, and naturalist. Following his childhood and youth in South Africa, he served the British government in various capacities, in such places as North Africa and Java. Van Der Post's voice is that of a seasoned, cosmopolitan writer, but one which is also alert to life's overtones of symbolism and mystery. The Lost World of the Kalahari *(1958) and* The Heart of the Hunter *(1961) are works of sympathetic participation in the vision of the Kalahari Bushmen. Nature for Van Der Post, as for these endangered hunting cultures, is a holy world of quest, sacrifice, and rebirth.*

From THE HEART OF THE HUNTER

A BRAVERY OF BIRDS

From Tsane we travelled fast eastwards towards the great pans of Kukong and Kakia along one of the oldest tracks across the desert. At one place where there was unexpectedly good shade in which we paused to rest at noon, Ben said, "You know, I came by here first as a boy of eight leading the oxen in my father's front wagon. We camped here, and almost at once some Bushmen came to see us. They had their shelters only a hundred yards from here, and came to offer us skins of game in exchange for tobacco. I passed this spot many times afterwards and always they reappeared for the same purpose, friendly, gay and excited. Ten years ago I came by again, but they had vanished. I was afraid they had died in the outbreak of pest which raged just then in the Kalahari, until I met an old Bushman I knew at the well at Kukong. I asked him, because you know it is amazing how they pass on news of one another from end to end of the desert. He seemed astonished that I had not

The Heart of the Hunter (New York: William Morrow, 1961).

heard of so shocking an event. Did I not know, he asked, that they had heard people passing along the track one day and rushed out as they always did to barter their skins? Well, the government was travelling by, and when the police with the government saw that among the skins there was one of a gemsbuck, they took the two best young hunters away with them. The remaining people immediately moved right away from the tracks. They were safe all right, but their hearts were troubled for the two young men who had not come back, as the hearts of all the people had been wide open to the young men. As you see, the Bushmen are not back on their ancient stand and will, I fear, never be again."

"But why did the police do that?" someone asked.

"Because the gemsbuck is royal game here and protected," Ben said, his voice edged with the irony of it, "and the Bushman is not."

"What happened to the two young hunters? Do you know?" I asked.

He shook his head sadly, saying he could only guess they had never returned because once such essentially innocent people had been punished and imprisoned they became so deeply confused that they seldom found the way back.

The same evening, camp made earlier than usual because of good progress that day, Ben and I took our guns to see if we could not shoot a springbuck for our supper and breakfast. We found some in a pan nearby, but they were on the other side, too far for us to stalk effectively before dark. The moment we set foot on the floor of the pan they were aware of us, stopped grazing and stood, heads up, to watch us apprehensively. So we started to climb back on to the ridge overlooking the pan with the idea of sitting down there for a while to enjoy the stillness and beauty of the evening.

The end of the journey was very near now. It is remarkable how a sense of valediction heightens one's awareness of the beauty of the world. I think it is because beauty is a summons to journey, is both a hail and a farewell of the spirit, and since our deepest pattern is a round of departure and return, we never recognize it more clearly than at the beginning and end of our journeys. Indeed all the traffic and the travail in between may be directed just to that end. Besides, when one has lived as close to nature for as long as we had done, one is not tempted to commit the metropolitan error of assuming that the sun rises and sets, the day burns out and the night falls, in a world outside oneself. These are great and reciprocal events, which occur also in ourselves. In this moment of heightened sensibility, there on the lip of the pan, I was convinced that, just as the evening was happening in us, so were we in it, and the music of our participation in a single overwhelming event was flowing through us.

This sense of participation enclosed in one moment of time was increased by the presence of the pan itself. From the ridge where we seated ourselves we had an immense view of the desert. In that light it looked in terms of earth what the sea is in terms of water, without permanent form and without end. Then suddenly there was the pan at our feet, a shape which was definite and real, the ridge describing an almost perfect circle against the sky and presenting the waste around it with a flawless container. It was a geometrical paradigm of life's need for form, a demonstration of the proposition that unless life were contained it could not be. I remembered the excitement I felt on first seeing an Etruscan vase, perceiving why the summons for a renewal of the European spirit had to emerge in men's imagination as a vision of a greater container in the shape of the Holy Grail. But I got no further, for just then Ben interrupted. He asked, in a voice so much affected by the mood of the moment that it was barely more than a whisper, "Do you remember this place?"

"I do, Ben." I recognized it as country we had passed through several times before, but no more. Knowing from his tone he had something particular in mind, I said, "Why did you ask?"

"Because of the ostriches. We saw them first just by those bushes there. Surely you remember them?" He sounded somewhat disappointed at my vague response.

But I had it now! The pan was the scene of one of the loveliest deeds I have ever seen. Nearly ten years ago, Ben and I had come fast over the ridge one evening and without pause slipped down the side silently in our truck. As a result we surprised what looked like a lone couple of ostriches on the edge of the floor of the pan. The birds had panicked; they circled each other wildly until a clear design of action emerged. To our amazement the female broke away from her mate and came resolutely towards us. Ben, who was driving, halted the truck at once and said, "Please, don't move! Just watch this."

Knowing how ostriches hate and fear men, I do not think I have ever seen a braver deed. The bird was desperately afraid. Her heart beating visibly in her throat, she advanced towards us like a soldier against a machine-gun post. With the late afternoon sun making a halo round her feathers, which stood erect with the fearful tension in her, she came on pretending to be mortally hurt, limping badly and trailing one great wing as if it were broken. Then, trying to give the impression that she had only just seen us, she stopped, whisked about and skipped with broken steps sideways into the bush. Before she had gone far, however, she halted. The one great wing sagged more than ever, giving her a list like a ship about to founder. She looked fearfully over her shoulder to see if we were following her. When she saw we had not done so, she appeared baffled and dismayed, and once more came back towards us to repeat the performance, this time so close that the trailing wing nearly touched the bumper of the truck.

Meanwhile the male, in the shining black dress of a bountiful summer, hurried the other way in a zigzag fashion like a ship tacking into the wind. He would rush off in a few giant strides, stop, lower his head, flap his wings, look up to see how the female was getting on, then run off on the other tack again. When his rushes had presently taken him into a bare patch of sand higher up on the ridge, we saw the cause of it all: the male was trying to hustle out of danger nineteen little ostrich chickens, while the female distracted our attention by doing all she could to entice us into capturing her instead. The chickens were so new that the sheen of the yolk of the eggs from which they had been hatched was like silk upon them. All the time they were within sight their mother became increasingly reckless in her efforts to draw us away, and once she looked truly tragic with despair because we would not follow her. Not until her family was out of sight did she desist: even then she did not hasten to join them, but with her wing still trailing drew away from us in the opposite direction. How could I not remember?

I looked at the place where it had all happened, and in the light of the memory it looked like hallowed ground. I think Ben felt something similar, because he began speaking to me with a release of emotion he rarely allowed himself. And I report his words here in full because they helped me greatly later in understanding the imagery of birds in the first spirit of things.

People, he said, often asked him which of all the creatures encountered in his many years as a hunter and dweller, in far-away places of Africa, he found most impressive. Always he answered that it would have to be a bird of some kind. This never failed to surprise them, because people are apt to be dazzled by physical power, size, frightfulness, and they expected him to say an elephant, lion, buffalo or some other imposing animal. But he stuck to his answer; there was nothing more wonderful in Africa than its birds. I asked why precisely. He paused and drew a circle with his finger in the red sand in front of him before saying that it was for many reasons, but in the first place because birds flew. He said it in such a way that I felt I had never before experienced fully the wonder of birds flying.

I waited silently for him to find the next link in his chain of thought. In the second place, he remarked, because birds sang. He himself loved all natural sounds in the bush and the desert, but he had to admit none equalled the sounds of birds. It was as if the sky made music in their throats and one could hear the sun rise and set, the night fall and the first stars come out in their voices. Other animals were condemned to make only such noises as they must, but birds seemed free to utter the sounds they wanted to, to shape them at will and invent new ones to express all the emotions of living matter released on wings from its own dead weight. He knew of nothing so beautiful as the sight of a bird utterly abandoned to its song, every bit of its being surrendered to the music, the tip of the tiniest feather trembling like a tuning fork with sound. Sometimes too, birds danced to their own music. And they not only sang. They also conversed. There appeared to be little they could not convey to one another by sound. He himself had always listened with the greatest care to bird sound and never ceased to marvel at the variety of intelligence it conveyed to him.

Stranger still was their capacity of being aware of things before they happened. This was positively amazing. When the great earth tremor shook the northern Kalahari some years before, Ben was travelling with a herd of cattle along the fringes of the Okovango swamp. One day he was watching some old-fashioned storks, sacred ibis and giant herons along the edges of a stream. Suddenly the birds stopped feeding, looked uneasily about them, and then all at once took to their wings as if obedient to a single command. They rose quickly in the air and began wheeling over the river, making the strangest sounds. The sound had not fallen long on the still air before the ground under his feet started to shake, the cattle to bellow and run, and as far as his eyes could see the banks of the stream began to break away from the bush, as if sliced from it by a knife, and to collapse into the water. He had no doubt the birds knew what was coming, and he made a careful note of their behaviour and the sound they uttered.

Even more wonderful, however, was their beauty. Colour, for instance, lovely as it was in most animals, served the latter only for camouflage. But with birds it was much more. Of all the creatures, none dressed so well as the birds of Africa. They had summer and winter dresses, special silks for making love, coats and skirts for travel, and more practical clothes that did not show the dirt and wear and tear of domestic use. Even the soberest ones among them, which went about the country austere as elders of the Dutch Reformed Church collecting from parsimonious congregations on Sunday mornings—the old-fashioned storks in black and white, or the secretary birds with their stiff starched fronts and frock coats—their dress was always of an impeccable taste.

This beauty and good taste did not stop at dress. It showed in the building of their nests: no animals could rival the diversity and elegance of the home birds made for themselves. The worst builders were the carnivorous ones—the toughy-pants like the lamb-catchers, Batteleurs and white-breasted jackal birds. Just as the warrior races in Africa built the worst huts in the land, so did the fighting birds make the ugliest homes; but on the whole the nests of the birds were things of beauty and joy.

Most wonderful of all was the way this beauty appeared in their eggs—shaped and painted as if by an artist. Had I ever seen a bird's egg that was ugly? Compare these lovely speckled, dappled or sky-blue surfaces, slightly milky as if veiled by a remote cirrhus cloud, to the eggs laid by snakes, turtles and crocodiles. Even the drabbest of eggs laid by a bird was beautiful in comparison. Ben himself was always excited when a mere farmyard hen produced eggs with a gipsy tan and tiny sun-freckles on the shell. Again, birds collaborated, in forethought and purpose, with other living creatures. There was the bird that picked the crocodile's teeth clean for him; the bird that rode the rhinoceros, feeding on the parasites that troubled him and warning him of danger in return for his hospitality; the egret who did the same for cattle and buffalo; and perhaps the greatest of them all, the honey-diviner who, as I had seen for myself, even co-operated with the universally feared and mistrusted man.

Finally there was their quality of courage. I had witnessed an example of it that day years ago in a female ostrich; but all birds had it. When one considered what tender, small, delicate and defenceless things most birds were, they were perhaps the bravest creatures in the world. He had seen far more moving instances of the courage of the birds of Africa than he could possibly relate, but he would mention only one of the most common—birds defending their nests against snakes. On those occasions they had a rallying cry, which was a mixture of faith and courage just keeping ahead of despair and fear. It would draw birds from all around to the point of danger, and the recklessness with which one little feathered body after another would hurl itself at the head of a snake, beating with its wings and shrieking its Valkyrian cry, had to be seen to be believed. Ben once saw a black mamba driven dazed out of a tree by only a score or so of resolute little birds. The mamba, which he killed, measured close on ten feet, and this snake is itself a creature of fiery courage and determination. No, all in all, he had no doubt that birds were the most wonderful of all living things.

Ben paused, and motioned to me to listen. The first of the night plover was calling from the far end of the pan, a long sort of wail like a ship's pipe mustering her crew to take her out to sea. It was nearly dark. I had not noticed the quick flight of time, so absorbed had I been in listening. When the plover's call died away, Ben jumped to his feet with a cat-like ease that never failed to astonish me in so big a man and asked with one of his rare smiles, had I not heard the referee's whistle? Light, he said, had stopped play. The game was over and it was time to get back to camp.

T(ERENCE) H(ANBURY) WHITE
1906-1964

White's novels based on the Arthurian legends were collected in 1958 into The Once and Future King. *During much of the research and writing for this major project he lived as a recluse, first in Ireland and then on the Channel Island of Alderney. While he sometimes preferred to isolate himself from human society, White responded intensely and lovingly to animals. The Goshawk (1951) conveyed his enduring interest in falcons and falconry. The selection here on snakes comes from* England Have My Bones *(1936).*

THE SNAKES ARE ABOUT

The snakes are about again. Last year I used to go out with Hughesdon to catch them, and then turn them loose in the sitting-room. At one time I had about a dozen. There are four in the room just now.

Grass snakes are fascinating pets. It is impossible to impose upon them, or to steal their affections, or to degrade either party in any way. They are always inevitably themselves, and with a separate silurian beauty. The plates of the jaw are fixed in an antediluvian irony. They move with silence, unless in crackling grass or with a scaly rustle over a wooden floor, pouring themselves over obstacles and round them. They are inquisitive. They live loose in the room, except that I lock them up at nights so that the maids can clean in the mornings without being frightened. The big open fireplace is full of moss and ferns, and there is an

England Have My Bones (New York: Macmillan, 1936).

aquarium full of water in which they can soak themselves if they wish. But mostly they prefer to lie under the hot pipes of the radiator, or to burrow inside the sofa. We had to perform a Caesarian operation on the sofa last year, to get out a big male.

It is nice to come into the room and look quickly round it, to see what they are doing. Perhaps there is one behind Aldous Huxley on the bookshelves, and it is always worth moving the left-hand settle away from the wall. One of them has a passion for this place and generally falls out. Another meditates all day in the aquarium, and the fourth lives in the moss.

Or it is nice to be working in the arm-chair, and to look up suddenly at an imagined sound. A female is pouring from behind the sofa. As the floor is of polished wood she gets a poor grip on it (she prefers the sheepskin hearth-rug) and elects to decant herself along the angle between wall and floor. Here she can press sideways as well as downwards, and gets a better grip.

She saw our movement as we looked up, and now stops dead, her head raised in curiosity. Her perfect forked tongue flickers blackly out of its specially armoured hole (like the hole for the starting handle in a motor, but constructed so as to close itself when not in use) and waves itself like lightning in our direction. It is what she feels with in front of her, her testing antennae, and this is her mark of interrogation. An empathic movement: she can't reach us, but she is thinking Who or What? And so the tongue comes out. We sit quite still.

The tongue comes out two or three times (its touch on the hand is as delicate as the touch of a butterfly) and flickers in the air. It is a beautiful movement, with more down in it than up. It can be faintly reproduced by waggling the bent forefinger quickly in a vertical plane. Then she goes on with her pour, satisfied, towards her objective in the moss. We sit as still as a mouse.

I try to handle these creatures as little as possible. I do not want to steal them from themselves by making them pets. The exchange of hearts would degrade both of us. It is only that they are nice. Nice to see the strange wild things loose, living their ancient unpredictable lives with such grace. They are more ancient than the mammoth, and infinitely more beautiful. They are dry, cool and strong. The fitting and variation of the plates, the lovely colouring, the movement, their few thoughts: one could meditate upon them like a jeweller for months.

It is exciting to catch them. You go to a good wood, and look for snaky places in it. It is difficult to define these. There has to be undergrowth, but not overgrowth: a sunny patch, a glade or tiny clearing in the trees: perhaps long grass and a bit of moss, but not too wet. You go into it and there is a rustle. You can see nothing, but dive straight at the sound. You see just a few inches of the back, deceptively fluid for catching hold of, as it flashes from side to side. You must pounce on it at once, for there is no time to think, holding it down or grabbing it by head or tail or anywhere. There is no time to select. This is always exciting to me, because I frighten myself by thinking that it might be an adder. As a matter of fact, there are very few adders in the Shire, and in any case they move differently. An adder would strike back at you, I suppose, but a grass snake does not. It pretends to strike, with mouth wide open and the most formidable-looking fangs; but it stops its head within a millimetre of the threatened spot, a piece of bluff merely.

When you have grabbed your snake, you pick it up. Instantly it curls round your hand and arm, hissing and lunging at you with the almost obtuse angle of its jaw; exuding a white fluid from its vent, which has a metallic stink like acetylene. Take no notice of it at all. Like an efficient governess with a refractory child, you speak sharply to the smelly creature and hold it firmly. You take hold of its tail, unwind it, roll it in a ball (it is wriggling so much that it generally helps in this), tie it up in your handkerchief, put it in your trouser pocket and look for another.

When you loose it in your sitting-room it rushes off along the floor, swishing frantically but making little progress on the polished wood, and conceals itself in the darkest corner. At night, when you come to lock it up, it makes a fuss. It produces the smell again, and the hiss. In the morning it is the same. Next night perhaps the smell is omitted, or fainter. In a few days there is only a dim hiss, a kind of grumble. This goes as well, until there is only a gentle protesting undulation as it is lifted off the ground.

I remember particularly two of last year's snakes. One was a baby male (the yellow markings are brighter in the male) only about eight inches long. He was a confiding snake, and I once took him to church in my pocket, to make him a Christian and to comfort me during the sermon. I hope it was not an undue interference with his life: I never carried him about like that again, he seemed to like the warmth of my pocket, and I believe he did not change his creed.

Talking of Christians, I never christened the snakes. To have called them names would have been ridiculous, as it is with cars. A snake cannot have a name. If it had to be addressed I suppose it would be addressed by its generic title: Snake.

The other one, I regret to say, was nearly a pet. She was a well-grown female with a scar on her neck. I suppose this had been done to her by man. It was the scar that first attracted me to her, or rather made me take special notice of her, because she was easy to distinguish. I soon found that when the time came for putting her to bed she did not undulate. She never troubled to conceal herself at bedtime, nor to slide away from me when I approached. She would crawl right up to me, and pour over my feet while I was working. There was no horrible affection or prostration; only she was not afraid of me. She went over my feet because they were in a direct line with the place she was making for. She trusted, or at least was indifferent.

It was a temptation. One coldish afternoon she was sitting in my chair when I wanted to read. I picked her up and put her in my lap. She was not particularly comfortable, and began to go away. I held her gently by the tail. She decided that it was not worth a scene, and stayed. I put my free hand over her, and she curled up beneath it, the head sticking out between two fingers and the tongue flickering every now and then, when a thought of curiosity entered her slow, free mind.

After that I used sometimes to sit with my two hands cupped, and she would curl between them on cold days. My hands were warm, that was all.

It was not quite all. I am afraid a hideous tinge of possession is creeping into this account. When other people came into the room she used to hiss. I would be dozing with her tight, dry coils between my palms, and there would be a hiss. The door would have opened and somebody would have come in. Or again, if I showed her to people she would hiss at them. If they tried to catch her, she would pour away. But when I gave her to them she was quiet.

I think I succeeded in keeping my distance. At any rate, she had a love affair with one of the males. I remember finding them coiled together on the corner table: a double rope-coil of snake which looked like a single one, except that it had two heads. I did not realise that this was an affair of the heart, at the time.

Later on she began to look ill. She was lumpy and flaccid. I became worried about the commissariat. Snakes rarely eat—seldom more than once a fortnight—but when they do eat they are particular. The staple food is a live frog, swallowed alive and whole. Anybody who has ever kept snakes will know how difficult it is to find a frog. The whole of the Shire seems to be populated by toads: one can scarcely move without treading on a toad: but toads disagree with snakes. They exude something from the skin.

I had been short of frogs lately, and (as I merely kept them loose in the aquarium so that the snakes could help themselves when they wanted) did not know when she had last had a meal. I thought I was starving her and became agitated. I spent hours looking for frogs, and found one eventually, but she wouldn't touch it. I tried a gold-fish, but that was no good either. She got worse. I was afraid she was poisoned, or melancholic from her unnatural surroundings.

Then came the proud day. I got back at half-past twelve, and looked
for her on the hearth-rug, but she was not there. She was in the aquarium, sunlit from the french windows. Not only she. I went closer and
looked. There were twenty-eight eggs.

Poor old lady, she was in a dreadful state. Quite apathetic and powerless, she could scarcely lift her head. Her body had fallen in on itself,
leaving two ridges, as if she were quite a slim snake dressed in clothes too
big for her. When I picked her up she hung limp, as if she were actually
dead; but her tongue flickered. I didn't know what to do.

I got a gold-fish bowl and half-filled it with fresh grass clippings. I put
her in it, with the frog, and tied paper over the top as if it were a jam jar.
I made holes in the paper and took it out on to the lawn, in the full glare
of the summer sun. Snakes are woken up by heat, and the bowl would
concentrate the sun's beams. It was all I could think of or do, before I
went in to lunch.

I came back in half an hour. The bowl was warm with moisture, the
grass clippings were browning, the frog was gone; and inside was Matilda
(she positively deserved a name) as fit as a flea and twice as frisky.

The scarred snake may have been a good mistress, but she was a bad
mother. If she had known anything about maternity, she would not have
laid her eggs in the aquarium. It seems that water is one of the things
that is fatal to the eggs of grass snakes. I picked them out, and put them
in another gold-fish bowl, this time full of grass clippings that were
already rotten. Then I left them in the sun. They only went mouldy.

She was completely tame, and the inevitable happened. The time
came for me to go away for two months, so I gave her her liberty. I took
her out into the fountain court (next time it shall be into the deepest and
most unpopulated forest) and put her on the ground in the strong July
sunlight. She was delighted by it, and pleased to go. I watched her
to-froing away, till she slipped into the angle of a flowerbed, and then
went resolutely indoors. There were plenty of other things in the future
besides grass snakes.

That night I went down to the lake to bathe, and stepped over a dead
snake in the moonlight. I guessed before I looked for the scar. I had kept
my distance successfully, so that there were no regrets at parting, but I
had destroyed a natural balance. She had lost her bitter fear of man: a
thing which it is not wise to lose.

I feel some difficulty in putting this properly. Some bloody-minded
human being had come across her on a path and gone for her with a
stick. She was harmless, useless dead, very beautiful, easy prey. He
slaughtered her with a stick, and grass snakes are not easy to kill. It is easy
to maim them, to bash them on the head until the bones are pulp. The
lower jaw no longer articulates with the upper one, but lies sideways

under the crushed skull, shewing the beautiful colours of its unprotected inner side. The whole reserved face suddenly looks pitiful, because it has been spoilt and ravaged. The black tongue makes a feeble flicker still.

These things had been done, to a creature which was offering confidence, with wanton savagery. Why? Why the waste of beauty and the degradation to the murderer himself? He was not creating a beauty by destroying this one. He cannot even have considered himself clever.

RACHEL CARSON
1907-1964

Trained as a marine biologist, Rachel Carson pursued careers both as a specialist in commercial fisheries and as a writer. The Sea Around Us *(1951) portrayed the ocean as a single complex entity, changing the scale of her readers' perspectives in much the same way Lewis Thomas was to do with his view of earth as a living cell.* The Edge of the Sea *(1955) explored the special richness of "the marginal world." Her most influential book was* Silent Spring *(1962), in which Carson demonstrated the harmful effects of pesticides on the health of the environment. Her ability at once to specify the chemical and biological details of the problem and to evoke the devastation of wildlife in forest and stream gave her book an extraordinary impact on public opinion. Following its publication President Kennedy called for a federal investigation, which resulted in much tighter controls on the use of D.D.T. and other toxic products.*

From THE EDGE OF THE SEA

THE MARGINAL WORLD

The edge of the sea is a strange and beautiful place. All through the long history of Earth it has been an area of unrest where waves have broken heavily against the land, where the tides have pressed forward

The Edge of the Sea (New York: Houghton Mifflin, 1955).

over the continents, receded, and then returned. For no two successive days is the shore line precisely the same. Not only do the tides advance and retreat in their eternal rhythms, but the level of the sea itself is never at rest. It rises or falls as the glaciers melt or grow, as the floor of the deep ocean basins shifts under its increasing load of sediments, or as the earth's crust along the continental margins warps up or down in adjustment to strain and tension. Today a little more land may belong to the sea, tomorrow a little less. Always the edge of the sea remains an elusive and indefinable boundary.

The shore has a dual nature, changing with the swing of the tides, belonging now to the land, now to the sea. On the ebb tide it knows the harsh extremes of the land world, being exposed to heat and cold, to wind, to rain and drying sun. On the flood tide it is a water world, returning briefly to the relative stability of the open sea.

Only the most hardy and adaptable can survive in a region so mutable, yet the area between the tide lines is crowded with plants and animals. In this difficult world of the shore, life displays its enormous toughness and vitality by occupying almost every conceivable niche. Visibly, it carpets the intertidal rocks; or half hidden, it descends into fissures and crevices, or hides under boulders, or lurks in the wet gloom of sea caves. Invisibly, where the casual observer would say there is no life, it lies deep in the sand, in burrows and tubes and passageways. It tunnels into solid rock and bores into peat and clay. It encrusts weeds or drifting spars or the hard, chitinous shell of a lobster. It exists minutely, as the film of bacteria that spreads over a rock surface or a wharf piling; as spheres of protozoa, small as pinpricks, sparkling at the surface of the sea; and as Lilliputian beings swimming through dark pools that lie between the grains of sand.

The shore is an ancient world, for as long as there has been an earth and sea there has been this place of the meeting of land and water. Yet it is a world that keeps alive the sense of continuing creation and of the relentless drive of life. Each time that I enter it, I gain some new awareness of its beauty and its deeper meanings, sensing that intricate fabric of life by which one creature is linked with another, and each with its surroundings.

In my thoughts of the shore, one place stands apart for its revelation of exquisite beauty. It is a pool hidden within a cave that one can visit only rarely and briefly when the lowest of the year's low tides fall below it, and perhaps from that very fact it acquires some of its special beauty. Choosing such a tide, I hoped for a glimpse of the pool. The ebb was to fall early in the morning. I knew that if the wind held from the northwest and no interfering swell ran in from a distant storm the level of the sea should drop below the entrance to the pool. There had been sudden ominous showers in the night, with rain like handfuls of gravel flung on the roof. When I looked out into the early morning the sky was full of a gray dawn light but the sun had not yet risen. Water and air were pallid. Across the bay the moon was a luminous disc in the western sky, suspended above the dim line of distant shore—the full August moon, drawing the tide to the low, low levels of the threshold of the alien sea world. As I watched, a gull flew by, above the spruces. Its breast was rosy with the light of the unrisen sun. The day was, after all, to be fair.

Later, as I stood above the tide near the entrance to the pool, the promise of that rosy light was sustained. From the base of the steep wall of rock on which I stood, a moss-covered ledge jutted seaward into deep water. In the surge at the rim of the ledge the dark fronds of oarweeds swayed, smooth and gleaming as leather. The projecting ledge was the path to the small hidden cave and its pool. Occasionally a swell, stronger than the rest, rolled smoothly over the rim and broke in foam against the cliff. But the intervals between such swells were long enough to admit me to the ledge and long enough for a glimpse of that fairy pool, so seldom and so briefly exposed.

And so I knelt on the wet carpet of sea moss and looked back into the dark cavern that held the pool in a shallow basin. The floor of the cave was only a few inches below the roof, and a mirror had been created in which all that grew on the ceiling was reflected in the still water below.

Under water that was clear as glass the pool was carpeted with green sponge. Gray patches of sea squirts glistened on the ceiling and colonies of soft coral were a pale apricot color. In the moment when I looked into the cave a little elfin starfish hung down, suspended by the merest thread, perhaps by only a single tube foot. It reached down to touch its own reflection, so perfectly delineated that there might have been, not one starfish, but two. The beauty of the reflected images and of the limpid pool itself was the poignant beauty of things that are ephemeral, existing only until the sea should return to fill the little cave.

Whenever I go down into this magical zone of the low water of the spring tides, I look for the most delicately beautiful of all the shore's inhabitants—flowers that are not plant but animal, blooming on the threshold of the deeper sea. In that fairy cave I was not disappointed. Hanging from its roof were the pendent flowers of the hydroid Tubularia, pale pink, fringed and delicate as the wind flower. Here were creatures so exquisitely fashioned that they seemed unreal, their beauty too fragile to exist in a world of crushing force. Yet every detail was functionally useful, every stalk and hydranth and petal-like tentacle fashioned for dealing with the realities of existence. I knew that they were merely waiting, in that moment of the tide's ebbing, for the return of the sea. Then in the rush of water, in the surge of surf and the pressure of the incoming tide, the delicate flower heads would stir with life. They would sway on their slender stalks, and their long tentacles would sweep the returning water, finding in it all that they needed for life.

And so in that enchanted place on the threshold of the sea the realities that possessed my mind were far from those of the land world I had left an hour before. In a different way the same sense of remoteness and of a world apart came to me in a twilight hour on a great beach on the coast of Georgia. I had come down after sunset and walked far out over sands that lay wet and gleaming, to the very edge of the retreating sea. Looking back across that immense flat, crossed by winding, water-filled gullies and here and there holding shallow pools left by the tide, I was filled with awareness that this intertidal area, although abandoned briefly and rhythmically by the sea, is always reclaimed by the rising tide. There at the edge of low water the beach with its reminders of the land seemed far away. The only sounds were those of the wind and the sea and the birds. There was one sound of wind moving over water, and another of water sliding over the sand and tumbling down the faces of its own wave forms. The flats were astir with birds, and the voice of the willet rang insistently. One of them stood at the edge of the water and gave its loud, urgent cry; an answer came from far up the beach and the two birds flew to join each other.

The flats took on a mysterious quality as dusk approached and the last evening light was reflected from the scattered pools and creeks. Then birds became only dark shadows, with no color discernible. Sanderlings scurried across the beach like little ghosts, and here and there the darker forms of the willets stood out. Often I could come very close to them before they would start up in alarm—the sanderlings running, the willets flying up, crying. Black skimmers flew along the ocean's edge silhouetted against the dull, metallic gleam, or they went flitting above the sand like large, dimly seen moths. Sometimes they "skimmed" the winding creeks of tidal water, where little spreading surface ripples marked the presence of small fish.

The shore at night is a different world, in which the very darkness that hides the distractions of daylight brings into sharper focus the elemental realities. Once, exploring the night beach, I surprised a small ghost crab in the searching beam of my torch. He was lying in a pit he had dug just above the surf, as though watching the sea and waiting. The blackness of the night possessed water, air, and beach. It was the darkness of an older world, before Man. There was no sound but the all-enveloping, primeval sounds of wind blowing over water and sand, and of waves crashing on the beach. There was no other visible life—just one small crab near the sea. I have seen hundreds of ghost crabs in other settings, but suddenly I was filled with the odd sensation that for the first time I knew the creature in its own world—that I understood, as never before, the essence of its being. In that moment time was suspended; the world to which I belonged did not exist and I might have been an onlooker from outer space. The little crab alone with the sea became a symbol that stood for life itself—for the delicate, destructible, yet incredibly vital force that somehow holds its place amid the harsh realities of the inorganic world.

The sense of creation comes with memories of a southern coast, where the sea and the mangroves, working together, are building a wilderness of thousands of small islands off the southwestern coast of Florida, separated from each other by a tortuous pattern of bays, lagoons, and narrow waterways. I remember a winter day when the sky was blue and drenched with sunlight; though there was no wind one was conscious of flowing air like cold clear crystal. I had landed on the surf-washed tip of one of those islands, and then worked my way around to the sheltered bay side. There I found the tide far out, exposing the broad mud flat of a cove bordered by the mangroves with their twisted branches, their glossy leaves, and their long prop roots reaching down, grasping and holding the mud, building the land out a little more, then again a little more.

The mud flats were strewn with the shells of that small, exquisitely colored mollusk, the rose tellin, looking like scattered petals of pink roses. There must have been a colony nearby, living buried just under the surface of the mud. At first the only creature visible was a small heron in gray and rusty plumage—a reddish egret that waded across the flat with the stealthy, hesitant movements of its kind. But other land creatures had been there, for a line of fresh tracks wound in and out among the mangrove roots, marking the path of a raccoon feeding on the oysters that gripped the supporting roots with projections from their shells. Soon I found the tracks of a shore bird, probably a sanderling, and followed them a little; then they turned toward the water and were lost, for the tide had erased them and made them as though they had never been.

Looking out over the cove I felt a strong sense of the interchangeability of land and sea in this marginal world of the shore, and of the links between the life of the two. There was also an awareness of the past and of the continuing flow of time, obliterating much that had gone before, as the sea had that morning washed away the tracks of the bird.

The sequence and meaning of the drift of time were quietly summarized in the existence of hundreds of small snails—the mangrove periwinkles—browsing on the branches and roots of the trees. Once their ancestors had been sea dwellers, bound to the salt waters by every tie of their life processes. Little by little over the thousands and millions of years the ties had been broken, the snails had adjusted themselves to life out of water, and now today they were living many feet above the tide to which they only occasionally returned. And perhaps, who could say how many ages hence, there would be in their descendants not even this gesture of remembrance for the sea.

The spiral shells of other snails—these quite minute—left winding tracks on the mud as they moved about in search of food. They were horn shells, and when I saw them I had a nostalgic moment when I wished I might see what Audubon saw, a century and more ago. For such little horn shells were the food of the flamingo, once so numerous on this coast, and when I half closed my eyes I could almost imagine a flock of these magnificent flame birds feeding in that cove, filling it with their color. It was a mere yesterday in the life of the earth that they were there; in nature, time and space are relative matters, perhaps most truly perceived subjectively in occasional flashes of insight, sparked by such a magical hour and place.

There is a common thread that links these scenes and memories—the spectacle of life in all its varied manifestations as it has appeared, evolved, and sometimes died out. Underlying the beauty of the spectacle there is meaning and significance. It is the elusiveness of that meaning that haunts us, that sends us again and again into the natural world where the key to the riddle is hidden. It sends us back to the edge of the sea, where the drama of life played its first scene on earth and perhaps even its prelude; where the forces of evolution are at work today, as they have been since the appearance of what we know as life; and where the spectacle of living creatures faced by the cosmic realities of their world is crystal clear.

LOREN EISELEY
1907-1977

Few writers so effectively fuse personal and professional perspectives in their work as does Eiseley, and his nature essays introduced a strong autobiographical element into contemporary nature writing. Born in the

*bleak Nebraska plains country and raised as a solitary child by a deaf and
mentally unstable mother, he began writing poetry and stories at an early
age. After a circuitous and interrupted academic career, including several years as a drifter through the West during the Depression, he eventually became a professor of anthropology and Curator of Early Man at
the University of Pennsylvania. His first book,* The Immense Journey
*(1957), was an unexpected best-seller and has proved to be one of the
most influential collections of American essays published since mid-cen-
tury. Its evolutionary perspective, emphasizing the long hidden past of
human nature, is colored by a dark and brooding temperament, infusing
ordinary natural events with symbolic resonance. Though Eiseley's outlook is often characterized by loneliness and pessimism, he finds comfort
in our shared condition with other animals and in man's capacity for
"rare and hidden communion with nature."*

THE JUDGMENT OF THE BIRDS

It is a commonplace of all religious thought, even the most primitive,
that the man seeking visions and insight must go apart from his fellows
and live for a time in the wilderness. If he is of the proper sort, he will
return with a message. It may not be a message from the god he set out
to seek, but even if he has failed in that particular, he will have had a
vision or seen a marvel, and these are always worth listening to and
thinking about.

The world, I have come to believe, is a very queer place, but we have
been part of this queerness for so long that we tend to take it for granted.
We rush to and fro like Mad Hatters upon our peculiar errands, all the
time imagining our surroundings to be dull and ourselves quite ordinary
creatures. Actually, there is nothing in the world to encourage this idea,
but such is the mind of man, and this is why he finds it necessary from
time to time to send emissaries into the wilderness in the hope of learning of great events, or plans in store for him, that will resuscitate his
waning taste for life. His great news services, his world-wide radio network, he knows with a last remnant of healthy distrust will be of no use
to him in this matter. No miracle can withstand a radio broadcast, and it
is certain that it would be no miracle if it could. One must seek, then,
what only the solitary approach can give—a natural revelation.

Let it be understood that I am not the sort of man to whom is en-

The Immense Journey (New York: Random House, 1957).

trusted direct knowledge of great events or prophecies. A naturalist, however, spends much of his life alone, and my life is no exception. Even in New York City there are patches of wilderness, and a man by himself is bound to undergo certain experiences falling into the class of which I speak. I set mine down, therefore: a matter of pigeons, a flight of chemicals, and a judgment of birds, in the hope that they will come to the eye of those who have retained a true taste for the marvelous, and who are capable of discerning in the flow of ordinary events the point at which the mundane world gives way to quite another dimension.

New York is not, on the whole, the best place to enjoy the downright miraculous nature of the planet. There are, I do not doubt, many remarkable stories to be heard there and many strange sights to be seen, but to grasp a marvel fully it must be savored from all aspects. This cannot be done while one is being jostled and hustled along a crowded street. Nevertheless, in any city there are true wildernesses where a man can be alone. It can happen in a hotel room, or on the high roofs at dawn.

One night on the twentieth floor of a midtown hotel I awoke in the dark and grew restless. On an impulse I climbed upon the broad old-fashioned window sill, opened the curtains and peered out. It was the hour just before dawn, the hour when men sigh in their sleep, or, if awake, strive to focus their wavering eyesight upon a world emerging from the shadows. I leaned out sleepily through the open window. I had expected depths, but not the sight I saw.

I found I was looking down from that great height into a series of curious cupolas or lofts that I could just barely make out in the darkness. As I looked, the outlines of these lofts became more distinct because the light was being reflected from the wings of pigeons who, in utter silence, were beginning to float outward upon the city. In and out through the open slits in the cupolas passed the white-winged birds on their mysterious errands. At this hour the city was theirs, and quietly, without the brush of a single wing tip against stone in that high, eerie place, they were taking over the spires of Manhattan. They were pouring upward in a light that was not yet perceptible to human eyes, while far down in the black darkness of the alleys it was still midnight.

As I crouched half asleep across the sill, I had a moment's illusion that the world had changed in the night, as in some immense snowfall, and that if I were to leave, it would have to be as these other inhabitants were doing, by the window. I should have to launch out into that great bottomless void with the simple confidence of young birds reared high up there among the familiar chimney pots and interposed horrors of the abyss.

I leaned farther out. To and fro went the white wings, to and fro. There were no sounds from any of them. They knew man was asleep and this light for a little while was theirs. Or perhaps I had only dreamed about man in this city of wings—which he could surely never have built. Perhaps I, myself, was one of these birds dreaming unpleasantly a moment of old dangers far below as I teetered on a window ledge.

Around and around went the wings. It needed only a little courage, only a little shove from the window ledge to enter that city of light. The muscles of my hands were already making little premonitory lunges. I wanted to enter that city and go away over the roofs in the first dawn. I wanted to enter it so badly that I drew back carefully into the room and opened the hall door. I found my coat on the chair, and it slowly became clear to me that there was a way down through the floors, that I was, after all, only a man.

I dressed then and went back to my own kind, and I have been rather more than usually careful ever since not to look into the city of light. I had seen, just once, man's greatest creation from a strange inverted angle, and it was not really his at all. I will never forget how those wings went round and round, and how, by the merest pressure of the fingers and a feeling for air, one might go away over the roofs. It is a knowledge, however, that is better kept to oneself. I think of it sometimes in such a way that the wings, beginning far down in the black depths of the mind, begin to rise and whirl till all the mind is lit by their spinning, and there is a sense of things passing away, but lightly, as a wing might veer over an obstacle.

To see from an inverted angle, however, is not a gift allotted merely to the human imagination. I have come to suspect that within their degree it is sensed by animals, though perhaps as rarely as among men. The time has to be right; one has to be, by chance or intention, upon the border of two worlds. And sometimes these two borders may shift or interpenetrate and one sees the miraculous.

I once saw this happen to a crow.

This crow lives near my house, and though I have never injured him, he takes good care to stay up in the very highest trees and, in general, to avoid humanity. His world begins at about the limit of my eyesight.

On the particular morning when this episode occurred, the whole countryside was buried in one of the thickest fogs in years. The ceiling was absolutely zero. All planes were grounded, and even a pedestrian could hardly see his outstretched hand before him.

I was groping across a field in the general direction of the railroad station, following a dimly outlined path. Suddenly out of the fog, at about the level of my eyes, and so closely that I flinched, there flashed a pair of immense black wings and a huge beak. The whole bird rushed over my head with a frantic cawing outcry of such hideous terror as I have never heard in a crow's voice before, and never expect to hear again.

He was lost and startled, I thought, as I recovered my poise. He ought not to have flown out in this fog. He'd knock his silly brains out.

All afternoon that great awkward cry rang in my head. Merely being lost in a fog seemed scarcely to account for it—especially in a tough, intelligent old bandit such as I knew that particular crow to be. I even looked once in the mirror to see what it might be about me that had so revolted him that he had cried out in protest to the very stones.

Finally, as I worked my way homeward along the path, the solution came to me. It should have been clear before. The borders of our worlds had shifted. It was the fog that had done it. That crow, and I knew him well, never under normal circumstances flew low near men. He had been lost all right, but it was more than that. He had thought he was high up, and when he encountered me looming gigantically through the fog, he had perceived a ghastly and, to the crow mind, unnatural sight. He had seen a man walking on air, desecrating the very heart of the crow king-dom, a harbinger of the most profound evil a crow mind could conceive of—air-walking men. The encounter, he must have thought, had taken place a hundred feet over the roofs.

He caws now when he sees me leaving for the station in the morning, and I fancy that in that note I catch the uncertainty of a mind that has come to know things are not always what they seem. He has seen a marvel in his heights of air and is no longer as other crows. He has experienced the human world from an unlikely perspective. He and I share a viewpoint in common: our worlds have interpenetrated, and we both have faith in the miraculous.

It is a faith that in my own case has been augmented by two remark-able sights. As I have hinted previously, I once saw some very odd chemi-cals fly across a waste so dead it might have been upon the moon, and once, by an even more fantastic piece of luck, I was present when a group of birds passed a judgment upon life.

On the maps of the old voyageurs it is called *Mauvaises Terres*, the evil lands, and, slurred a little with the passage through many minds, it has come down to us anglicized as the Badlands. The soft shuffle of moccasins has passed through its canyons on the grim business of war and flight, but the last of those slight disturbances of immemorial si-lences died out almost a century ago. The land, if one can call it a land, is a waste as lifeless as that valley in which lie the kings of Egypt. Like the Valley of the Kings, it is a mausoleum, a place of dry bones in what once was a place of life. Now it has silences as deep as those in the moon's airless chasms.

Nothing grows among its pinnacles; there is no shade except under great toadstools of sandstone whose bases have been eaten to the shape of wine glasses by the wind. Everything is flaking, cracking, disintegrating, wearing away in the long, imperceptible weather of time. The ash of ancient volcanic outbursts still sterilizes its soil, and its colors in that waste are the colors that flame in the lonely sunsets on dead planets. Men come there but rarely, and for one purpose only, the collection of bones.

It was a late hour on a cold, wind-bitten autumn day when I climbed a great hill spined like a dinosaur's back and tried to take my bearings. The tumbled waste fell away in waves in all directions. Blue air was darkening into purple along the bases of the hills. I shifted my knapsack, heavy with the petrified bones of long-vanished creatures, and studied my compass. I wanted to be out of there by nightfall, and already the sun was going sullenly down in the west.

It was then that I saw the flight coming on. It was moving like a little close-knit body of black specks that danced and darted and closed again. It was pouring from the north and heading toward me with the undeviating relentlessness of a compass needle. It streamed through the shadows rising out of monstrous gorges. It rushed over towering pinnacles in the red light of the sun, or momentarily sank from sight within their shade. Across that desert of eroding clay and wind-worn stone they came with a faint wild twittering that filled all the air about me as those tiny living bullets hurtled past into the night.

It may not strike you as a marvel. It would not, perhaps, unless you stood in the middle of a dead world at sunset, but that was where I stood. Fifty million years lay under my feet, fifty million years of bellowing monsters moving in a green world now gone so utterly that its very light was travelling on the farther edge of space. The chemicals of all that vanished age lay about me in the ground. Around me still lay the shearing molars of dead titanotheres, the delicate sabers of soft-stepping cats, the hollow sockets that had held the eyes of many a strange, outmoded beast. Those eyes had looked out upon a world as real as ours; dark, savage brains had roamed and roared their challenges into the steaming night.

Now they were still here, or, put it as you will, the chemicals that made them were here about me in the ground. The carbon that had driven them ran blackly in the eroding stone. The stain of iron was in the clays. The iron did not remember the blood it had once moved within, the phosphorus had forgot the savage brain. The little individual moment had ebbed from all those strange combinations of chemicals as it would ebb from our living bodies into the sinks and runnels of oncoming time.

I had lifted up a fistful of that ground. I held it while that wild flight of south-bound warblers hurtled over me into the oncoming dark. There went phosphorus, there went iron, there went carbon, there beat the calcium in those hurrying wings. Alone on a dead planet I watched that incredible miracle speeding past. It ran by some true compass over field and waste land. It cried its individual ecstasies into the air until the gullies rang. It swerved like a single body, it knew itself and, lonely, it bunched close in the racing darkness, its individual entities feeling about them the rising night. And so, crying to each other their identity, they passed away out of my view.

I dropped my fistful of earth. I heard it roll inanimate back into the gully at the base of the hill: iron, carbon, the chemicals of life.

Like men from those wild tribes who had haunted these hills before me seeking visions, I made my sign to the great darkness. It was not a mocking sign, and I was not mocked. As I walked into my camp late that night, one man, rousing from his blankets beside the fire, asked sleepily, "What did you see?"

"I think, a miracle," I said softly, but I said it to myself. Behind me that vast waste began to glow under the rising moon.

I have said that I saw a judgment upon life, and that it was not passed by men. Those who stare at birds in cages or who test minds by their closeness to our own may not care for it. It comes from far away out of my past, in a place of pouring waters and green leaves. I shall never see an episode like it again if I live to be a hundred, nor do I think that one man in a million has ever seen it, because man is an intruder into such silences. The light must be right, and the observer must remain unseen. No man sets up such an experiment. What he sees, he sees by chance.

You may put it that I had come over a mountain, that I had slogged through fern and pine needles for half a long day, and that on the edge of a little glade with one long, crooked branch extending across it, I had sat down to rest with my back against a stump. Through accident I was concealed from the glade, although I could see into it perfectly.

The sun was warm there, and the murmurs of forest life blurred softly away into my sleep. When I awoke, dimly aware of some commotion and outcry in the clearing, the light was slanting down through the pines in such a way that the glade was lit like some vast cathedral. I could see the dust motes of wood pollen in the long shaft of light, and there on the extended branch sat an enormous raven with a red and squirming nestling in his beak.

The sound that awoke me was the outraged cries of the nestling's parents, who flew helplessly in circles about the clearing. The sleek black monster was indifferent to them. He gulped, whetted his beak on the dead branch a moment and sat still. Up to that point the little tragedy had followed the usual pattern. But suddenly, out of all that area of woodland, a soft sound of complaint began to rise. Into the glade fluttered small birds of half a dozen varieties drawn by the anguished outcries of the tiny parents.

No one dared to attack the raven. But they cried there in some instinctive common misery, the bereaved and the unbereaved. The glade filled with their soft rustling and their cries. They fluttered as though to point their wings at the murderer. There was a dim intangible ethic he had violated, that they knew. He was a bird of death.

And he, the murderer, the black bird at the heart of life, sat on there, glistening in the common light, formidable, unmoving, unperturbed, untouchable.

The sighing died. It was then I saw the judgment. It was the judgment of life against death. I will never see it again so forcefully presented. I will never hear it again in notes so tragically prolonged. For in the midst of protest, they forgot the violence. There, in that clearing, the crystal note of a song sparrow lifted hesitantly in the hush. And finally, after painful fluttering, another took the song, and then another, the song passing from one bird to another, doubtfully at first, as though some evil thing were being slowly forgotten. Till suddenly they took heart and sang from many throats joyously together as birds are known to sing. They sang because life is sweet and sunlight beautiful. They sang under the brooding shadow of the raven. In simple truth they had forgotten the raven, for they were the singers of life, and not of death.

I was not of that airy company. My limbs were the heavy limbs of an earthbound creature who could climb mountains, even the mountains of the mind, only by a great effort of will. I knew I had seen a marvel and observed a judgment, but the mind which was my human endowment was sure to question it and to be at me day by day with its heresies until I grew to doubt the meaning of what I had seen. Eventually darkness and subtleties would ring me round once more.

And so it proved until, on the top of a stepladder, I made one more observation upon life. It was cold that autumn evening, and, standing under a suburban street light in a spate of leaves and beginning snow, I was suddenly conscious of some huge and hairy shadows dancing over the pavement. They seemed attached to an odd, globular shape that was magnified above me. There was no mistaking it. I was standing under the shadow of an orb-weaving spider. Gigantically projected against the street, she was about her spinning when everything was going underground. Even her cables were magnified upon the sidewalk and already I was half-entangled in their shadows.

"Good Lord," I thought, "she has found herself a kind of minor sun and is going to upset the course of nature."

I procured a ladder from my yard and climbed up to inspect the situation. There she was, the universe running down around her, warmly arranged among her guy ropes attached to the lamp supports—a great black and yellow embodiment of the life force, not giving up to either frost or stepladders. She ignored me and went on tightening and improving her web.

I stood over her on the ladder, a faint snow touching my cheeks, and surveyed her universe. There were a couple of iridescent green beetle cases turning slowly on a loose strand of web, a fragment of luminescent eye from a moth's wing and a large indeterminable object, perhaps a cicada, that had struggled and been wrapped in silk. There were also little bits and slivers, little red and blue flashes from the scales of anonymous wings that had crushed there.

Some days, I thought, they will be dull and gray and the shine will be out of them; then the dew will polish them again and drops hang on the silk until everything is gleaming and turning in the light. It is like a mind, really, where everything changes but remains, and in the end you have these eaten-out bits of experience like beetle wings.

I stood over her a moment longer, comprehending somewhat reluctantly that her adventure against the great blind forces of winter, her seizure of this warming globe of light, would come to nothing and was hopeless. Nevertheless it brought the birds back into my mind, and that faraway song which had traveled with growing strength around a forest clearing years ago—a kind of heroism, a world where even a spider refuses to lie down and die if a rope can still be spun on to a star. Maybe man himself will fight like this in the end, I thought, slowly realizing that the web and its threatening yellow occupant had been added to some luminous store of experience, shining for a moment in the fogbound reaches of my brain.

The mind, it came to me as I slowly descended the ladder, is a very remarkable thing; it has gotten itself a kind of courage by looking at a spider in a street lamp. Here was something that ought to be passed on to those who will fight our final freezing battle with the void. I thought of setting it down carefully as a message to the future: *In the days of the frost seek a minor sun.*

But as I hesitated, it became plain that something was wrong. The marvel was escaping—a sense of bigness beyond man's power to grasp, the essence of life in its great dealings with the universe. It was better, I decided, for the emissaries returning from the wilderness, even if they were merely descending from a stepladder, to record their marvel, not to define its meaning. In that way it would go echoing on through the minds of men, each grasping at that beyond out of which the miracles emerge, and which, once defined, ceases to satisfy the human need for symbols.

In the end I merely made a mental note: One specimen of Epeira observed building a web in a street light. Late autumn and cold for spiders. Cold for men, too. I shivered and left the lamp glowing there in my mind. The last I saw of Epeira she was hauling steadily on a cable. I stepped carefully over her shadow as I walked away.

THE STAR THROWER

I

It has ever been my lot, though formally myself a teacher, to be taught surely by none. There are times when I have thought to read lessons in the sky, or in books, or from the behavior of my fellows, but in the end my perceptions have frequently been inadequate or betrayed. Nevertheless, I venture to say that of what man may be I have caught a fugitive glimpse, not among multitudes of men, but along an endless wave-beaten coast at dawn. As always, there is this apparent break, this rift in nature, before the insight comes. The terrible question has to translate itself into an even more terrifying freedom.

If there is any meaning to this book [*The Unexpected Universe*], it began on the beaches of Costabel with just such a leap across an unknown abyss. It began, if I may borrow the expression from a Buddhist sage, with the skull and the eye. I was the skull. I was the inhumanly stripped skeleton without voice, without hope, wandering alone upon the shores of the world. I was devoid of pity, because pity implies hope. There was, in this desiccated skull, only an eye like a pharos light, a beacon, a search beam revolving endlessly in sunless noonday or black

The Unexpected Universe (New York: Harcourt Brace Jovanovich, Inc., 1964).

night. Ideas like swarms of insects rose to the beam, but the light consumed them. Upon that shore meaning had ceased. There were only the dead skull and the revolving eye. With such an eye, some have said, science looks upon the world. I do not know. I know only that I was the skull of emptiness and the endlessly revolving light without pity.

Once, in a dingy restaurant in the town, I had heard a woman say: "My father reads a goose bone for the weather." A modern primitive, I had thought, a diviner, using a method older than Stonehenge, as old as the arctic forests.

"And where does he do that?" the woman's companion had asked amusedly.

"In Costabel," she answered complacently, "in Costabel." The voice came back and buzzed faintly for a moment in the dark under the revolving eye. It did not make sense, but nothing in Costabel made sense. Perhaps that was why I had finally found myself in Costabel. Perhaps all men are destined at some time to arrive there as I did.

I had come by quite ordinary means, but I was still the skull with the eye. I concealed myself beneath a fisherman's cap and sunglasses, so that I looked like everyone else on the beach. This is the way things are managed in Costabel. It is on the shore that the revolving eye begins its beam and the whispers rise in the empty darkness of the skull.

The beaches of Costabel are littered with the debris of life. Shells are cast up in windrows; a hermit crab, fumbling for a new home in the depths, is tossed naked ashore, where the waiting gulls cut him to pieces. Along the strip of wet sand that marks the ebbing and flowing of the tide, death walks hugely and in many forms. Even the torn fragments of green sponge yield bits of scrambling life striving to return to the great mother that has nourished and protected them.

In the end the sea rejects its offspring. They cannot fight their way home through the surf which casts them repeatedly back upon the shore. The tiny breathing pores of starfish are stuffed with sand. The rising sun shrivels the mucilaginous bodies of the unprotected. The seabeach and its endless war are soundless. Nothing screams but the gulls.

In the night, particularly in the tourist season, or during great storms, one can observe another vulturine activity. One can see, in the hour before dawn on the ebb tide, electric torches bobbing like fireflies along the beach. This is the sign of the professional shellers seeking to outrun and anticipate their less aggressive neighbors. A kind of greedy madness sweeps over the competing collectors. After a storm one can see them hurrying along with bundles of gathered starfish, or, toppling and over-burdened, clutching bags of living shells whose hidden occupants will be slowly cooked and dissolved in the outdoor kettles provided by the resort hotels for the cleaning of specimens. Following one such episode I met the star thrower.

As soon as the ebb was flowing, as soon as I could make out in my sleeplessness the flashlights on the beach, I arose and dressed in the dark. As I came down the steps to the shore I could hear the deeper rumble of the surf. A gaping hole filled with churning sand had cut sharply into the breakwater. Flying sand as light as powder coated every exposed object like snow. I made my way around the altered edges of the cove and proceeded on my morning walk up the shore. Now and then a stooping figure moved in the gloom or a rain squall swept past me with light pattering steps. There was a faint sense of coming light somewhere behind me in the east.

Soon I began to make out objects, up-ended timbers, conch shells, sea wrack wrenched from the far-out kelp forests. A pink-clawed crab encased in a green cup of sponge lay sprawling where the waves had tossed him. Long-limbed starfish were strewn everywhere, as though the night sky had showered down. I paused once briefly. A small octopus, its beautiful dark-lensed eyes bleared with sand, gazed up at me from a ragged bundle of tentacles. I hesitated, and touched it briefly with my foot. It was dead. I paced on once more before the spreading whitecaps of the surf.

The shore grew steeper, the sound of the sea heavier and more menacing, as I rounded a bluff into the full blast of the offshore wind. I was away from the shellers now and strode more rapidly over the wet sand that effaced my footprints. Around the next point there might be a refuge from the wind. The sun behind me was pressing upward at the horizon's rim—an ominous red glare amidst the tumbling blackness of the clouds. Ahead of me, over the projecting point, a gigantic rainbow of incredible perfection had sprung shimmering into existence. Somewhere toward its foot I discerned a human figure standing, as it seemed to me, within the rainbow, though unconscious of his position. He was gazing fixedly at something in the sand.

Eventually he stooped and flung the object beyond the breaking surf. I labored toward him over a half-mile of uncertain footing. By the time I reached him the rainbow had receded ahead of us, but something of its color still ran hastily in many changing lights across his features. He was starting to kneel again.

In a pool of sand and silt a starfish had thrust its arms up stiffly and was holding its body away from the stifling mud.

"It's still alive," I ventured.

"Yes," he said, and with a quick yet gentle movement he picked up the star and spun it over my head and far out into the sea. It sank in a burst of spume, and the waters roared once more.

"It may live," he said, "if the offshore pull is strong enough." He spoke gently, and across his bronzed worn face the light still came and went in subtly altering colors.

"There are not many come this far," I said, groping in a sudden embarrassment for words. "Do you collect?"

"Only like this," he said softly, gesturing amidst the wreckage of the shore. "And only for the living." He stooped again, oblivious of my curiosity, and skipped another star neatly across the water.

"The stars," he said, "throw well. One can help them."

He looked full at me with a faint question kindling in his eyes, which seemed to take on the far depths of the sea.

"I do not collect," I said uncomfortably, the wind beating at my garments. "Neither the living nor the dead. I gave it up a long time ago. Death is the only successful collector." I could feel the full night blackness in my skull and the terrible eye resuming its indifferent journey. I nodded and walked away, leaving him there upon the dune with that great rainbow ranging up the sky behind him.

I turned as I neared a bend in the coast and saw him toss another star, skimming it skillfully far out over the ravening and tumultuous water. For a moment, in the changing light, the sower appeared magnified, as though casting larger stars upon some greater sea. He had, at any rate, the posture of a god.

But again the eye, the cold world-shriveling eye, began its inevitable circling in my skull. He is a man, I considered sharply, bringing my thought to rest. The star thrower is a man, and death is running more fleet than he along every seabeach in the world.

I adjusted the dark lens of my glasses and, thus disguised, I paced slowly back by the starfish gatherers, past the shell collectors, with their vulgar little spades and the stick-length shelling pincers that eased their elderly backs while they snatched at treasures in the sand. I chose to look full at the steaming kettles in which beautiful voiceless things were being boiled alive. Behind my sunglasses a kind of litany began and refused to die down. *"As I came through the desert thus it was, as I came through the desert."*

In the darkness of my room I lay quiet with the sunglasses removed, but the eye turned and turned. In the desert, an old monk had once advised a traveler, the voices of God and the Devil are scarcely distinguishable. Costabel was a desert. I lay quiet, but my restless hand at the bedside fingered the edge of an invisible abyss. "Certain coasts"—the remark of a perceptive writer came back to me—"are set apart for ship-wreck." With unerring persistence I had made my way thither.

II

There is a difference in our human outlook, depending on whether we have been born on level plains, where one step reasonably leads to an-other, or whether, by contrast, we have spent our lives amidst glacial crevasses and precipitous descents. In the case of the mountaineer, one step does not always lead rationally to another save by a desperate leap over a chasm, or by an even more hesitant tiptoeing across precarious snow bridges.

Something about these opposed landscapes has its analogue in the mind of man. Our prehistoric life, one might say, began amidst enfor-ested gloom with the abandonment of the protected instinctive life of nature. We sought, instead, an adventurous existence amidst the crater lands and ice fields of self-generated ideas. Clambering onward, we have slowly made our way out of a maze of isolated peaks into the level plains of science. Here, one step seems definitely to succeed another, the uni-verse appears to take on an imposed order, and the illusions through which mankind has painfully made its way for many centuries have given place to the enormous vistas of past and future time. The encrusted eye in the stone speaks to us of undeviating sunlight; the calculated elliptic of Halley's comet no longer forecasts world disaster. The planet plunges on through a chill void of star years, and there is little or nothing that remains unmeasured.

Nothing, that is, but the mind of man. Since boyhood I had been traveling across the endless coordinated realms of science, just as, in the body, I was a plains dweller, accustomed to plodding through distances unbroken by precipices. Now that I come to look back, there was one contingent aspect of that landscape I inhabited whose significance, at the time, escaped me. "Twisters," we called them locally. They were a species of cyclonic, bouncing air funnel that could suddenly loom out of nowhere, crumpling windmills or slashing with devastating fury through country towns. Sometimes, by modest contrast, more harmless varieties known as dust devils might pursue one in a gentle spinning dance for miles. One could see them hesitantly stalking across the alkali flats on a hot day, debating, perhaps, in their tall, rotating columns, whether to ascend and assume more formidable shapes. They were the trickster part of an otherwise pedestrian landscape.

Infrequent though the visitations of these malign creations of the air might be, all prudent homesteaders in those parts had provided themselves with cyclone cellars. In the careless neighborhood in which I grew up, however, we contented ourselves with the queer yarns of cyclonic folklore and the vagaries of weather prophecy. As a boy, aroused by these tales and cherishing a subterranean fondness for caves, I once attempted to dig a storm cellar. Like most such projects this one was never completed. The trickster element in nature, I realize now, had so buffeted my parents that they stoically rejected planning. Unconsciously, they had arrived at the philosophy that foresight merely invited the attention of some baleful intelligence that despised and persecuted the calculating planner. It was not until many years later that I came to realize that a kind of maleficent primordial power persists in the mind as well as in the wandering dust storms of the exterior world.

A hidden dualism that has haunted man since antiquity runs across his religious conceptions as the conflict between good and evil. It persists in the modern world of science under other guises. It becomes chaos versus form or antichaos. Form, since the rise of the evolutionary philosophy, has itself taken on an illusory quality. Our apparent shapes no longer have the stability of a single divine fiat. Instead, they waver and dissolve into the unexpected. We gaze backward into a contracting cone of life until words leave us and all we know is dissolved into the simple circuits of a reptilian brain. Finally, sentience subsides into an animalcule.

Or we revolt and refuse to look deeper, but the void remains. We are rag dolls made out of many ages and skins, changelings who have slept in wood nests or hissed in the uncouth guise of waddling amphibians. We have played such roles for infinitely longer ages than we have been men. Our identity is a dream. We are process, not reality, for reality is an illusion of the daylight—the light of our particular day. In a fortnight, as aeons are measured, we may lie silent in a bed of stone, or, as has happened in the past, be figured in another guise. Two forces struggle perpetually in our bodies: Yam, the old sea dragon of the original Biblical darkness, and, arrayed against him, some wisp of dancing light that would have us linger, wistful, in our human form. "Tarry thou, till I come again"—an old legend survives among us of the admonition given by Jesus to the Wandering Jew. The words are applicable to all of us. Deep-hidden in the human psyche there is a similar injunction, no longer having to do with the longevity of the body but, rather, a plea to wait upon some transcendent lesson preparing in the mind itself.

Yet the facts we face seem terrifyingly arrayed against us. It is as if at our backs, masked and demonic, moved the trickster as I have seen his role performed among the remnant of a savage people long ago. It was that of the jokester present at the most devout of ceremonies. This creature never laughed; he never made a sound. Painted in black, he followed silently behind the officiating priest, mimicking, with the added flourish of a little whip, the gestures of the devout one. His timed and stylized posturings conveyed a derision infinitely more formidable than actual laughter.

In modern terms, the dance of contingency, of the indeterminable, outwits us all. The approaching fateful whirlwind on the plain had mercifully passed me by in youth. In the moment when I witnessed that fireside performance I knew with surety that primitive man had lived with a dark message. He had acquiesced in the admission into his village of a cosmic messenger. Perhaps the primitives were wiser in the ways of the trickster universe than ourselves; perhaps they knew, as we do not, how to ground or make endurable the lightning.

At all events, I had learned, as I watched that half-understood drama by the leaping fire, why man, even modern man, reads goose bones for the weather of his soul. Afterward I had gone out, a troubled unbeliever, into the night. There was a shadow I could not henceforth shake off, which I knew was posturing and would always posture behind me. That mocking shadow looms over me as I write. It scrawls with a derisive pen and an exaggerated flourish. I know instinctively it will be present to caricature the solemnities of my deathbed. In a quarter of a century it has never spoken.

Black magic, the magic of the primeval chaos, blots out or transmogrifies the true form of things. At the stroke of twelve the princess must flee the banquet or risk discovery in the rags of a kitchen wench; coach reverts to pumpkin. Instability lies at the heart of the world. With uncanny foresight folklore has long toyed symbolically with what the nineteenth century was to proclaim a reality—namely, that form is an illusion of the time dimension, that the magic flight of the pursued hero or heroine through frogskin and wolf coat has been, and will continue to be, the flight of all men.

Goethe's genius sensed, well before the publication of the *Origin of Species*, the thesis and antithesis that epitomize the eternal struggle of the immediate species against its dissolution into something other: in modern terms, fish into reptile, ape into man. The power to change is both creative and destructive—a sinister gift, which, unrestricted, leads onward toward the formless and inchoate void of the possible. This force can only be counterbalanced by an equal impulse toward specificity. Form, once arisen, clings to its identity. Each species and each individual holds tenaciously to its present nature. Each strives to contain the creative and abolishing maelstrom that pours unseen through the generations. The past vanishes; the present momentarily persists; the future is potential only. In this specious present of the real, life struggles to maintain every manifestation, every individuality, that exists. In the end, life always fails, but the amorphous hurrying stream is held and diverted into new organic vessels in which form persists, though the form may not be that of yesterday.

The evolutionists, piercing beneath the show of momentary stability, discovered, hidden in rudimentary organs, the discarded rubbish of the past. They detected the reptile under the lifted feathers of the bird, the lost terrestrial limbs dwindling beneath the blubber of the giant cetaceans. They saw life rushing outward from an unknown center, just as today the astronomer senses the galaxies fleeing into the infinity of darkness. As the spinning galactic clouds hurl stars and worlds across the night, so life, equally impelled by the centrifugal powers lurking in the germ cell, scatters the splintered radiance of consciousness and sends it prowling and contending through the thickets of the world.

All this devious, tattered way was exposed to the ceaselessly turning eye within the skull that lay hidden upon the bed in Costabel. Slowly that eye grew conscious of another eye that searched it with equal penetration from the shadows of the room. It may have been a projection from the mind within the skull, but the eye was, nevertheless, exteriorized and haunting. It began as something glaucous and blind beneath a web of clinging algae. It altered suddenly and became the sand-smeared eye of the dead cephalopod I had encountered upon the beach. The transformations became more rapid with the concentration of my attention, and they became more formidable. There was the beaten, bloodshot eye of an animal from somewhere within my childhood experience. Finally, there was an eye that seemed torn from a photograph, but that looked through me as though it had already raced in vision up to the steep edge of nothingness and absorbed whatever terror lay in that abyss. I sank back again upon my cot and buried my head in the pillow. I knew the eye and the circumstance and the question. It was my mother. She was long dead, and the way backward was lost.

III

Now it may be asked, upon the coasts that invite shipwreck, why the ships should come, just as we may ask the man who pursues knowledge why he should be left with a revolving search beam in the head whose light falls only upon disaster or the flotsam of the shore. There is an answer, but its way is not across the level plains of science, for the science of remote abysses no longer shelters man. Instead, it reveals him in vaporous metamorphic succession as the homeless and unspecified one, the creature of the magic flight.

Long ago, when the future was just a simple tomorrow, men had cast intricately carved game counters to determine its course, or they had traced with a grimy finger the cracks on the burnt shoulder blade of a hare. It was a prophecy of tomorrow's hunt, just as was the old farmer's anachronistic reading of the weather from the signs on the breastbone of a goose. Such quaint almanacs of nature's intent had sufficed mankind since antiquity. They would do so no longer, nor would formal apologies to the souls of the game men hunted. The hunters had come, at last, beyond the satisfying supernatural world that had always surrounded the little village, into a place of homeless frontiers and precipitous edges, the indescribable world of the natural. Here tools increasingly revenged themselves upon their creators and tomorrow became unmanageable. Man had come in his journeying to a region of terrible freedoms.

It was a place of no traditional shelter, save those erected with the aid of tools, which had also begun to achieve a revolutionary independence from their masters. Their ways had grown secretive and incalculable. Science, more powerful than the magical questions that might be addressed by a shaman to a burnt shoulder blade, could create these tools but had not succeeded in controlling their ambivalent nature. Moreover, they responded all too readily to that urge for tampering and dissolution which is part of our primate heritage.

We had been safe in the enchanted forest only because of our weakness. When the powers of that gloomy region were given to us, immediately, as in a witch's house, things began to fly about unbidden. The tools, if not science itself, were linked intangibly to the subconscious poltergeist aspect of man's nature. The closer man and the natural world drew together, the more erratic became the behavior of each. Huge shadows leaped triumphantly after every blinding illumination. It was a magnified but clearly recognizable version of the black trickster's antics behind the solemn backs of the priesthood. Here, there was one difference. The shadows had passed out of all human semblance; no societal ritual safely contained their posturings, as in the warning dance of the trickster. Instead, unseen by many because it was so gigantically real, the multiplied darkness threatened to submerge the carriers of the light.

Darwin, Einstein, and Freud might be said to have released the shadows. Yet man had already entered the perilous domain that henceforth would contain his destiny. Four hundred years ago Francis Bacon had already anticipated its dual nature. The individuals do not matter. If they had not made their discoveries, others would have surely done so. They were good men, and they came as enlighteners of mankind. The tragedy was only that at their backs the ritual figure with the whip was invisible. There was no longer anything to subdue the pride of man. The world had been laid under the heavy spell of the natural; henceforth, it would be ordered by man.

Humanity was suddenly entranced by light and fancied it reflected light. Progress was its watchword, and for a time the shadows seemed to recede. Only a few guessed that the retreat of darkness presaged the emergence of an entirely new and less tangible terror. Things, in the words of G. K. Chesterton, were to grow incalculable by being calculated. Man's powers were finite; the forces he had released in nature recognized no such limitations. They were the irrevocable monsters conjured up by a completely amateur sorcerer.

But what, we may ask, was the nature of the first discoveries that now threaten to induce disaster? Pre-eminent among them was, of course, the perception to which we have already referred: the discovery of the interlinked and evolving web of life. The great Victorian biologists saw, and yet refused to see, the war between form and formlessness, chaos and antichaos, which the poet Goethe had sensed contesting beneath the smiling surface of nature. "The dangerous gift from above," he had termed it, with uneasy foresight.

By contrast, Darwin, the prime student of the struggle for existence, sought to visualize in a tangled bank of leaves the silent and insatiable war of nature. Still, he could imply with a veiled complacency that man might "with some confidence" look forward to a secure future "of inappreciable length." This he could do upon the same page in the *Origin of Species* where he observes that "of the species now living very few will transmit progeny to a far distant futurity." The contradiction escaped him; he did not wish to see it. Darwin, in addition, saw life as a purely selfish struggle, in which nothing is modified for the good of another species without being directly advantageous to its associated form.

If, he contended, one part of any single species had been formed for the exclusive good of another, "it would annihilate my theory." Powerfully documented and enhanced though the statement has become, famine, war, and death are not the sole instruments biologists today would accept as the means toward that perfection of which Darwin spoke. The subject is subtle and intricate; let it suffice to say here that the sign of the dark cave and the club became so firmly fixed in human thinking that in our time it has been invoked as signifying man's true image in books selling in the hundreds of thousands.

From the thesis and antithesis contained in Darwinism we come to Freud. The public knows that, like Darwin, the master of the inner world took the secure, stable, and sunlit province of the mind and revealed it as a place of contending furies. Ghostly transformations, flitting night shadows, misshapen changelings existed there, as real as anything that haunted the natural universe of Darwin. For this reason, appropriately, I had come as the skull and the eye to Costabel—the coast demanding shipwreck. Why else had I remembered the phrase, except for a dark impulse toward destruction lurking somewhere in the subconscious? I lay on the bed while the agonized eye in the remembered photograph persisted at the back of my closed lids.

It had begun when, after years of separation, I had gone dutifully home to a house from which the final occupant had departed. In a musty attic—among old trunks, a broken aquarium, and a dusty heap of fossil shells collected in childhood—I found a satchel. The satchel was already a shabby antique, in whose depths I turned up a jackknife and a "rat" of hair such as women wore at the beginning of the century. Beneath these lay a pile of old photographs and a note—two notes, rather, evidently dropped into the bag at different times. Each, in a thin, ornate hand, reiterated a single message that the writer had believed important. "This satchel belongs to my son, Loren Eiseley." It was the last message. I recognized the trivia. The jackknife I had carried in childhood. The rat of hair had belonged to my mother, and there were also two incredibly pointed slippers that looked as though they had been intended for a formal ball, to which I knew well my mother would never in her life have been invited. I undid the rotted string around the studio portraits.

Mostly they consisted of stiff, upright bearded men and heavily clothed women equally bound to the formalities and ritual that attended upon the photography of an earlier generation. No names identified the pictures, although here and there a reminiscent family trait seemed faintly evident. Finally I came upon a less formal photograph, taken in the eighties of the last century. Again no names identified the people, but a commercial stamp upon the back identified the place: Dyersville, Iowa. I had never been in that country town, but I knew at once it was my mother's birthplace.

Dyersville, the thought flashed through my mind, making the connection now for the first time: the dire place. I recognized at once the two sisters at the edge of the photograph, the younger clinging reluctantly to the older. Six years old, I thought, turning momentarily away from the younger child's face. Here it began, her pain and mine. The eyes in the photograph were already remote and shadowed by some inner turmoil. The poise of the body was already that of one miserably departing the peripheries of the human estate. The gaze was mutely clairvoyant and lonely. It was the gaze of a child who knew unbearable difference and impending isolation.

I dropped the notes and pictures once more into the bag. The last message had come from Dyersville: "my son." The child in the photograph had survived to be an ill-taught prairie artist. She had been deaf. All her life she had walked the precipice of mental breakdown. Here on this faded porch it had begun—the long crucifixion of life. I slipped downstairs and out of the house. I walked for miles through the streets.

Now at Costabel I put on the sunglasses once more, but the face from the torn photograph persisted behind them. It was as though I, as man, was being asked to confront, in all its overbearing weight, the universe itself. "Love not the world," the Biblical injunction runs, "neither the things that are in the world." The revolving beam in my mind had stopped, and the insect whisperings of the intellect. There was, at last, an utter stillness, a waiting as though for a cosmic judgment. The eye, the torn eye, considered me.

"But I *do* love the world," I whispered to a waiting presence in the empty room. "I love its small ones, the things beaten in the strangling surf, the bird, singing, which flies and falls and is not seen again." I choked and said, with the torn eye still upon me, "I love the lost ones, the failures of the world." It was like the renunciation of my scientific heritage. The torn eye surveyed me sadly and was gone. I had come full upon one of the last great rifts in nature, and the merciless beam no longer was in traverse around my skull.

But no, it was not a rift but a joining: the expression of love projected beyond the species boundary by a creature born of Darwinian struggle, in the silent war under the tangled bank. "There is no boon in nature," one of the new philosophers had written harshly in the first years of the industrial cities. Nevertheless, through war and famine and death, a sparse mercy had persisted, like a mutation whose time had not yet come. I had seen the star thrower cross that rift and, in so doing, he had reasserted the human right to define his own frontier. He had moved to the utmost edge of natural being, if not across its boundaries. It was as though at some point the supernatural had touched hesitantly, for an instant, upon the natural.

Out of the depths of a seemingly empty universe had grown an eye, like the eye in my room, but an eye on a vastly larger scale. It looked out upon what I can only call itself. It searched the skies and it searched the depths of being. In the shape of man it had ascended like a vaporous emanation from the depths of night. The nothing had miraculously gazed upon the nothing and was not content. It was an intrusion into, or a projection out of, nature for which no precedent existed. The act was, in short, an assertion of value arisen from the domain of absolute zero. A little whirlwind of commingling molecules had succeeded in confronting its own universe.

Here, at last, was the rift that lay beyond Darwin's tangled bank. For a creature, arisen from that bank and born of its contentions, had stretched out its hand in pity. Some ancient, inexhaustible, and patient intelligence, lying dispersed in the planetary fields of force or amidst the inconceivable cold of interstellar space, had chosen to endow its desolation with an apparition as mysterious as itself. The fate of man is to be the ever-recurrent, reproachful Eye floating upon night and solitude. The world cannot be said to exist save by the interposition of that inward eye—an eye various and not under the restraints to be apprehended from what is vulgarly called the natural.

I had been unbelieving. I had walked away from the star thrower in the hardened indifference of maturity. But thought mediated by the eye is one of nature's infinite disguises. Belatedly, I arose with a solitary mission. I set forth in an effort to find the star thrower.

IV

Man is himself, like the universe he inhabits, like the demoniacal stirrings of the ooze from which he sprang, a tale of desolations. He walks in his mind from birth to death the long resounding shores of endless disillusionment. Finally, the commitment to life departs or turns to bitterness. But out of such desolation emerges the awesome freedom to choose—to choose beyond the narrowly circumscribed circle that delimits the animal being. In that widening ring of human choice, chaos and order renew their symbolic struggle in the role of titans. They contend for the destiny of a world.

Somewhere far up the coast wandered the star thrower beneath his rainbow. Our exchange had been brief because upon that coast I had learned that men who ventured out at dawn resented others in the greediness of their compulsive collecting. I had also been abrupt because I had, in the terms of my profession and experience, nothing to say. The star thrower was mad, and his particular acts were a folly with which I had not chosen to associate myself. I was an observer and a scientist. Nevertheless, I had seen the rainbow attempting to attach itself to earth.

On a point of land, as though projecting into a domain beyond us, I found the star thrower. In the sweet rain-swept morning, that great many-hued rainbow still lurked and wavered tentatively beyond him. Silently I sought and picked up a still-living star, spinning it far out into the waves. I spoke once briefly. "I understand," I said. "Call me another thrower." Only then I allowed myself to think, He is not alone any longer. After us there will be others.

We were part of the rainbow—an unexplained projection into the natural. As I went down the beach I could feel the drawing of a circle in men's minds, like that lowering, shifting realm of color in which the thrower labored. It was a visible model of something toward which man's mind had striven, the circle of perfection.

I picked and flung another star. Perhaps far outward on the rim of space a genuine star was similarly seized and flung. I could feel the movement in my body. It was like a sowing—the sowing of life on an infinitely gigantic scale. I looked back across my shoulder. Small and dark against the receding rainbow, the star thrower stooped and flung once more. I never looked again. The task we had assumed was too immense for gazing. I flung and flung again while all about us roared the insatiable waters of death.

But we, pale and alone and small in that immensity, hurled back the living stars. Somewhere far off, across bottomless abysses, I felt as though another world was flung more joyfully. I could have thrown in a frenzy of joy, but I set my shoulders and cast, as the thrower in the rainbow cast, slowly, deliberately, and well. The task was not to be assumed lightly, for it was men as well as starfish that we sought to save. For a moment, we cast on an infinite beach together beside an unknown hurler of suns. It was, unsought, the destiny of my kind since the rituals of the Ice Age hunters, when life in the Northern Hemisphere had come close to vanishing. We had lost our way, I thought, but we had kept, some of us, the memory of the perfect circle of compassion from life to death and back again to life—the completion of the rainbow of existence. Even the hunters in the snow, making obeisance to the souls of the hunted, had known the cycle. The legend had come down and lingered that he who gained the gratitude of animals gained help in need from the dark wood.

I cast again with an increasingly remembered sowing motion and went my lone way up the beaches. Somewhere, I felt, in a great atavistic surge of feeling, somewhere the Thrower knew. Perhaps he smiled and cast once more into the boundless pit of darkness. Perhaps he, too, was lonely, and the end toward which he labored remained hidden—even as with ourselves.

I picked up a star whose tube feet ventured timidly among my fingers while, like a true star, it cried soundlessly for life. I saw it with an unaccustomed clarity and cast far out. With it, I flung myself as forfeit, for the first time, into some unknown dimension of existence. From Darwin's tangled bank of unceasing struggle, selfishness, and death, had arisen, incomprehensibly, the thrower who loved not man, but life. It was the subtle cleft in nature before which biological thinking had faltered. We had reached the last shore of an invisible island—yet, strangely, also a shore that the primitives had always known. They had sensed intuitively that man cannot exist spiritually without life, his brother, even if he slays. Somewhere, my thought persisted, there is a hurler of stars, and he walks, because he chooses, always in desolation, but not in defeat.

In the night the gas flames under the shelling kettles would continue to glow. I set my clock accordingly. Tomorrow I would walk in the storm. I would walk against the shell collectors and the flames. I would walk remembering Bacon's forgotten words "for the uses of life." I would walk with the knowledge of the discontinuities of the unexpected universe. I would walk knowing of the rift revealed by the thrower, a hint that there looms, inexplicably, in nature something above the role men give her. I knew it from the man at the foot of the rainbow, the starfish thrower on the beaches of Costabel.

ARCHIE CARR
1909-1987

Born in Mobile, Alabama, Archie Carr taught biology at the University of Florida for many years. He conducted pioneering research on the remarkable ocean migrations of sea turtles and became an internationally-known leader of conservation efforts to protect these endangered marine reptiles. His book, So Excellent A Fishe: A Natural History of Sea Turtles *(1967), is considered a classic in the field. Carr's style is witty and full of sharp observations of local cultures. In this chapter from* The Windward Road: Adventures of a Naturalist on Remote Caribbean Shores *(1957), an account of his research on ridley turtles, the author demonstrates two critical requirements of a good nature writer: the ability to turn frustrations into opportunities, and the willingness to be diverted from one's intended pursuits by new and unexpected distractions—in this case, the love life of sloths.*

From THE WINDWARD ROAD

THE LIVELY PETES OF PARQUE VARGAS

It was midday outside, but in Parque Vargas it was twilight. On the hot streets around the plaza the people of Puerto Limón had given up for the day. There were a few bicycles still and an occasional taxi clattered

The Windward Road: Adventures of a Naturalist on Remote Carribean Shores (New York: Knopf, 1967).

by, and the little shoeshine boys still shrieked at intervals. Inside the shady park most of the sloths had given up hours before and hung quietly now, back down, from the high limbs of the Indian laurel trees. A casual observer would have said that *all* the sloths were sleeping; but I knew better, or hoped I did.

There was one sloth up there that I felt sure was, relatively speaking, seething with emotion. It was not the sort of emotion that stirs the surface appreciably, but I was certain it was there all the same. It was this sloth and its supposed emotion, and my suspense over the outcome of it, that held me in the dim interior of the plaza on that fifth day of my stay in Puerto Limón.

To walk into Parque Vargas from the searing sunshine on the streets around it was like diving into a deep spring. The light was the same and the feel of the air on your skin was too. The limbs of the tall trees interlocked so closely that only a stray splash of sunlight reached the ground, and so high that eddies of breeze, geared by the bay wind, swirled and drifted among the trunks. It is hard to imagine the appeal of such a place unless you have waited for time to pass in a Caribbean town. For five days I had been doing a great deal of waiting here in midtown Limón, and I should have been on a low limb indeed if it had not been for the sloths and the shade and the wind-drift in Parque Vargas.

The first day I entered the tiny office of Aerovías Costarricenses, I was struck by the unpretentious scale of the enterprise. There was a counter across the single room and a platform scale in front of it. Behind the counter there was a table, a typewriter, and a girl, and the girl was pretty like any Tica; but she seemed depressed when I asked if I could charter a plane for the next day.

"Our plane is discomposed," she said in Spanish.

"Your plane?" I said. "Do you have only one plane? What is the matter with it?"

"*¿Quién sabe?*" the girl said. "Paco is trying to find out. He flew to San José Wednesday and the trip is high, over the volcano; too high. He flies over 12,500 feet, and this is bad for a plane like ours; and when he got back it was discomposed. All the passengers and freight for Sixaola and la Barra are waiting. *Lástima*—a pity."

"Then you have no idea when I might be able to hire the plane?"

"Where do you want to go?" she said.

"To Tortuguero. Maybe to la Barra."

"But we go to those places. Why hire the plane? Why do you not just go as a passenger? It's all the same, only cheaper."

"But I want to fly low and look for turtles."

"Paco likes to fly low and look for turtles."

"Well—would he circle when I asked him to?"

"That would cost more, I suppose. A little. But if you will fly with the guaro you can go at almost the passenger rate."

"The guaro?" I said. "What guaro?" *Guaro* is a corruption of the Castilian word *aguardiente* and is used in most parts of Central America for locally made sugarcane rum. The girl held a hand out three feet above the floor. She held it knuckles-down, not palm-down as a gringo would.

"It is a big can of guaro for the company laborers," she said. "The Atlantic Trading Company at Tortuguero. The company employs a great many Mosquitos, and they need guaro. If Saturday night comes and the guaro lacks, they are sad; and they sometimes go away."

"All right," I said. "I don't mind riding with the guaro if we can fly low. When do you think the plane might possibly be ready?"

"This is all I can tell you: the first flight will have to be for Sixaola and the second for Barra del Colorado. You should be ready to leave the day after the plane is composed—or if it is finished late, the second day after. Where can I locate you, noontimes?"

I told her. Then I went away and waited five days. Mornings I hired a bicycle or a horse, and once, at prohibitive cost, a taxi, and went up the coast or back into the fecund hinterland catching frogs and lizards and snakes; or swam in the rock pools behind the reef at the point; or visited the turtle crawls and fish-landings across the river.

Every day at noon I came back to the plaza and waited and felt the coolness and watched the sloths in the trees. If you should ever have to do any waiting where there are sloths, I can recommend watching them as a way to pass the time. It is as good as reading *War and Peace*—it never gives out on you. You can while away a whole half-hour finding out whether a given sloth intends to reach for another twigful of leaves, or to scratch himself again. No matter which course he chooses, you can count on spending another half-hour watching him carry it out.

In Parque Vargas there are nine sloths. One man I talked to insisted that there are twenty-five, but I counted them every day for five days and always came out with nine. The consensus among the people I questioned was that this number was probably right and that it had remained about the same ever since they could remember. The nine sloths live in twenty-eight *laurel de la India* trees. The trees, which are a species of *Ficus* (fig), are wound about with philodendrons and their limbs sweep up and interlace to form a closed canopy that is a fine continuous roadway and pasture for the sloths.

The sloths in Parque Vargas are Gray's three-toed sloth, a race confined to Panama and Costa Rica and belonging to a genus that is found in lowland woods from Honduras to Bolivia. Sloths are among the strangest of all mammals. If you work at it you can make out a case for placing them in the order Edentata, along with the anteaters and armadillos. But no anteater or armadillo can begin to match the sloth for eccentricity.

In the first place, sloths *look* strange before they make a move of any kind. The mature animal weighs about twenty-five pounds and has a round, earless head on a long neck, bulging eyes, and long legs that seem to have no joints. Each hand and foot has three permanently flexed claws with which the creature hangs upside down beneath the limbs he lives on. The fur is coarse and bristly, and during the wet season green algae grow among the hairs and give it a greenish color thought to be useful as camouflage.

But nothing in the appearance of this animal is anywhere near as curious as its incredible sloth. I use the term in its original sense of "slowness"—with none of its acquired connotation of *reprehensible* slowness. The sloth of these animals is one of the marvels of nature. It is a mockery of motion, an eerily mechanical, nerve-racking slowness that contractile protoplasm was never meant to support. The cytoplasm of an amœba streams faster than a sloth flees from a hungry boa constrictor. And besides being thus pointlessly, unbearably slow in everything it undertakes, the sloth is hesitant and vacillating in undertaking anything.

For example, a sloth may initiate some simple, straightforward move—like reaching for another handhold, say—and you may find that you must wait many minutes before it is clear whether he is carrying out the act or has stopped to reconsider the whole plan.

In spite of all this it seems to me unfair to brand the sloth as stupid and of "primitive mentality," as writers on the subject are inclined to do. It is quite possible that the animal is not stupid at all, and that its physical slowness is just that and nothing more, or even possibly a useful adaptation that we have not the wit to understand. Apparently no animal psychologist has turned his attention to sloths. They have never been put through a maze, for example, to get really reliable data on their learning ability. Putting a sloth through a maze would be quite a technical feat, I imagine, and very time consuming; but it must be done sooner or later, in fairness to the sloth. Meantime I shall go on wondering if the sloth may not be every bit as bright as its way of life calls for.

The slowness of sloths must be, in some way that I have never heard explained, part of a pattern of adaptation for life in the treetops. Some arboreal vertebrates are not slow, to be sure. Squirrels, for instance, are paragons of agility. But on the other hand there are three very different

groups of backboned animals—sloths, chameleons, and the slow loris—
that do live in treetops and that share the same odd retardation of
motion and locomotion. Since these animals are not closely related, the
loris being a kind of lemur—a primate like ourselves—the chameleon a
lizard, and the sloth a climbing relative of the anteaters, and since their
terrestrial relatives are not in any case notably slothful, the only sensible
conclusion is that slowing down your muscles may be one way of fitting
yourself for life in trees. The Pleistocene relatives of the modern tree
sloths were ground-dwelling creatures, some of which were as big as
oxen. We call them ground "sloths," but this does not mean that they
were any more deliberate in their movements than, say, a bear. They are
sloths only by a kind of reverse inheritance from their arboreal descendants.

Simply talking to people in the park, I was unable to find out either
when the trees there were planted, or when the sloths came to live in
them. Some said both had been there always. This is clearly a mistake,
since the tree, as its Spanish name indicates, is native to Asia. Others
said that a man who liked sloths put a pair there during the 1890's, and
that the trees were already well matured then and formed the continuous canopy requisite to flourishing sloth life. An old woman sitting on a
bench said that she remembered the time when a mayor of the town
decided the sloths were a public nuisance and a menace to the future of
the trees and should be shot. A policeman was detailed to kill them, with
a military rifle that made a great *bulla* here in the center of the city. I
told the woman that I had counted nine sloths only that morning.

"Exactly," she said with emphasis. "Now they are many. *Abundan.* It
is my belief that the soldier missed two of them, or perhaps missed a
pregnant female."

There may be records somewhere that would help establish the date
of founding of the sloth-*laurel* community in Parque Vargas, but this is
not essential. The important thing is that a native animal and an exotic
plant have come together there and have worked out a natural equilibrium, with the sloth population completely dependent on the trees for
food and yet not damaging them beyond the point of tolerance. It would
be interesting to know exactly how the balance is maintained from one
generation to the next. The sloths eat the leaves and fruit of the trees,
and have no other food, and it seems safe to assume that the supply of
food is the dominant factor controlling the size of the colony. Such
uncluttered examples of population balance are easy to arrange among
weevils in a flour bin or among protozoa in a jar of broth; but they are
hard to find in nature, and especially among vertebrates. No zoologist of

my acquaintance would have ventured to predict that two sloths placed in a grove of twenty-eight trees, of a sort untasted by sloths before and surrounded by city streets, would give rise to a population stabilized at nine individuals after thirty or forty years, or whatever the period has been.

It is curious how little this colony of extraordinary creatures intrudes upon the life of the city. Once in a great while a baby sloth, which normally clings spraddle-legged to its mother's upturned belly, falls out of a tree. Very rarely, for no discernible reason, a grown one descends and shuffles painfully across the bare earth among the plants and buttressed tree trunks. At such times a crowd of urchins and idle people gathers about the pitiful form. The boys shout and push one another toward the sloth, and when they try to stir up trouble between it and a jaded bitch more interested in sleep, the policeman strolls over from the sidewalk and tells them to stop molesting animals.

The only real excitement the sloths occasion comes when one of them swings from one handhold to another across the busy street on one of the electric wires that are strung through the trees. These are the times when everybody downtown stops to watch and talk about the sloths. "The lively Pete will be electrocuted," the Latins tell one another. The Castilian word for the sloth is *perezoso,* meaning about the same as ours; but in Central America it is everywhere known as *perico ligero,* "lively Pete," which is a fine example of vernacular irony. A windowful of Latin and creole girls across the street shrieks at the policeman at the corner of the park to stop the sloth before he gets to the insulator nailed to the angle of their building. A growing gang of boys leaning on bicycles howls and whistles with joy and mock lust.

"Yes, mon," one of them says. "I glod-ly walk this wy-ah upside down to get in that room. I do it fas-teah than the *perico!*"

After a while someone phones the power company, a truck comes with a ladder, and the sloth is plucked down and returned to the park. The people wander away or hang around in knots talking about the elections that are coming. The sloths are forgotten by everybody but me.

I was watching them still, as I said, on my fifth day in Limón. It was noon, and I was lying on my back and looking straight up to where two sloths were hanging in the deep shadows. There were several people on neighboring benches, but they had long ago got used to me and were paying me no attention. One of the sloths was scratching, dragging a foot across its shaggy side with the speed and regularity of the pendulum of a grandfather's clock. There was no likelihood that it would do anything else for hours. I had already lost interest in that sloth. But the other one, as I have said, excited me.

For fifteen minutes this second sloth had seemed to me to be moving nearer the first. If this was true, and the approach not just fortuitous, then perhaps the first sloth was a female and the second a male. It could be that I was at last to be allowed to witness what I had hoped for five days to see—the love-making of the lively Pete. Slow as the animal is, and upside down . . . I was intensely, perhaps even morbidly curious, and this approach was the first hint of sex that had crept into the activities of the sloths.

I waited longer. The advancing sloth—the supposed rutting male—had reached a point no more than two feet from what I hoped was his goal and he was still moving. I had every reason to feel that there was purpose in his advance, and to hope that within a few minutes I would learn whether his motive was really sex or just pugnacity or sociability instead. When the gap had narrowed to ten or twelve inches, the sloth stopped dead still, then unhooked one fore foot, moved it slowly to one side, and held it poised there. For a full minute he hung motionless. Then he began turning his head with barely perceptible motion—a slow swoop and swing to the left, then back one hundred and eighty degrees to the right, then forward again, where it stopped. He seemed to be staring fixedly at the sloth in front. I was not able to make out his expression, but I can tell you I was on tenterhooks. Something was bound to happen now.

It did. A little boy touched my shoulder. *"Señor,"* he piped, *"está compuesto el avión*—the airplane is fixed!" His voice trembled with excitement at the news he bore.

"Wait a minute," I said. "Look up there. Look at those lively Petes." I pointed with tense concern, and the boy looked up into the dome of the grove and saw two sloths on a limb, one of them scratching itself rhythmically, the other hanging immobile from three legs.

"Yes, sir," he said. "You can see them any time. They live there."

"Sure, I know that," I said, still excited. "But what are they going to do?"

"Do?" the boy said.

"Yes. What are they going to do now?"

He hovered uncertainly, trying to pin down the joke that must be eluding him. "What are they going to do?" he said timidly.

"Sí, hombre!" I said. "What's the matter with you?"

He shrugged and spread his hands and rolled his eyes up toward the sloths and then back at me with mild reproach.

"They will hang there till it gets too hot. After that they will go to sleep." Then he tried once more to bring order into his world: "But, señor, the lady at the Aerovías says you must come now. Paco is making the Sixaola flight this afternoon and tomorrow you can have the airplane, but he has to see you now before he goes. *Ahorita!*"

With a sigh I rolled off the bench and onto my feet and found a coin for the boy.

"*Bueno. Muy bien,*" I said.

But the boy was tough, really. He was going to try once more to get at the bottom of this thing.

"You are not content?" he said, eyeing me narrowly. "Though the airplane is composed?"

I was not content. I was cheated. Five days' waiting and hardly a foot between two sloths and their sex rites; and suddenly the wretched plane was composed.

"Well, yes and no." I said.

The little boy looked at me with widening eyes. He did not know whether it was being grown up or being a gringo that had warped my soul. But he was sure life was becoming a complex thing here in this city where he was born.

WALLACE STEGNER
B. 1909

As a novelist and short-story writer, Wallace Stegner has explored the experience of pioneers, mountain men, and settlers in the inter-mountain West. His essays, too, collected in The Sound of Mountain Water *(1969), investigate the issue of Western identity. Like Mary Austin, he asks his questions while looking at the landscape, and feels the winds that blow away our easy, familiar answers. During his years as Professor of English and Director of the Writing Program at Stanford, Stegner advocated the work of Western writers like John Wesley Powell and A. B. Guthrie, Jr., while encouraging a new generation of authors working in that always-new terrain.*

GLEN CANYON SUBMERSUS

Glen Canyon, once the most serenely beautiful of all the canyons of the Colorado River, is now Lake Powell, impounded by the Glen Canyon Dam. It is called a great recreational resource. The Bureau of Reclamation promotes its beauty in an attempt to counter continuing criticisms of the dam itself, and the National Park Service, which manages the Recreation Area, is installing or planning facilities for all the boating, water skiing, fishing, camping, swimming, and plain sightseeing that should now ensue.

But I come back to Lake Powell reluctantly and skeptically, for I remember Glen Canyon as it used to be.

Once the river ran through Glen's two hundred miles in a twisting, many-branched stone trough eight hundred to twelve hundred feet deep, just deep enough to be impressive without being overwhelming. Awe was never Glen Canyon's province. That is for the Grand Canyon. Glen Canyon was for delight. The river that used to run here cooperated with the scenery by flowing swift and smooth, without a major rapid. Any ordinary boatman could take anyone through it. Boy Scouts made annual pilgrimages on rubber rafts. In 1947 we went through with a party that contained an old lady of seventy and a girl of ten. There was superlative camping anywhere, on sandbars furred with tamarisk and willow, under cliffs that whispered with the sound of flowing water.

Through many of those two hundred idyllic miles the view was shut in by red walls, but down straight reaches or up side canyons there would be glimpses of noble towers and buttes lifting high beyond the canyon rims, and somewhat more than halfway down there was a major confrontation where the Kaiparowits Plateau, seventy-five hundred feet high, thrust its knife-blade cliff above the north rim to face the dome of Navajo Mountain, more than ten thousand feet high, on the south side. Those two uplifts, as strikingly different as if designed to dominate some gigantic world's fair, added magnificence to the intimate colored trough of the river.

Seen from the air, the Glen Canyon country reveals itself as a barestone, salmon-pink tableland whose surface is a chaos of domes, knobs, beehives, baldheads, hollows, and potholes, dissected by the deep corkscrew channels of streams. Out of the platform north of the main river rise the gray-green peaks of the Henry Mountains, the last-discovered

The Sound of Mountain Water (New York: Doubleday, 1969).

mountains in the contiguous United States. West of them is the bloody welt of the Waterpocket Fold, whose westward creeks flow into the Escalante, the last-discovered river. Northward rise the cliffs of Utah's high plateaus. South of Glen Canyon, like a great period at the foot of the fifty-mile exclamation point of the Kaiparowits, is Navajo Mountain, whose slopes apron off on every side into the stone and sand of the reservation.

When cut by streams, the Navajo sandstone which is the country rock forms monolithic cliffs with rounded rims. In straight stretches the cliffs tend to be sheer, on the curves undercut, especially in the narrow side canyons. I have measured a six-hundred-foot wall that was undercut a good five hundred feet—not a cliff at all but a musical shell for the multiplication of echoes. Into these deep scoured amphitheaters on the outside of bends, the promontories on the inside fit like thighbones into a hip socket. Often, straightening bends, creeks have cut through promontories to form bridges, as at Rainbow Bridge National Monument, Gregory Bridge in Fiftymile Canyon, and dozens of other places. And systematically, when a river cleft has exposed the rock to the lateral thrust of its own weight, fracturing begins to peel great slabs from the cliff faces. The slabs are thinner at top than at bottom, and curve together so that great alcoves form in the walls. If they are near the rim, they may break through to let a window-wink of sky down on a canyon traveler, and always they make panels of fresh pink in weathered and stained and darkened red walls.

Floating down the river one passed, every mile or two on right or left, the mouth of some side canyon, narrow, shadowed, releasing a secret stream into the taffy-colored, whirlpooled Colorado. Between the mouth of the Dirty Devil and the dam, which is a few miles above the actual foot of the Glen Canyon, there are at least three dozen such gulches on the north side, including the major canyon of the Escalante; and on the south nearly that many more, including the major canyon of the San Juan. Every such gulch used to be a little wonder, each with its multiplying branches, each as deep at the mouth as its parent canyon. Hundreds of feet deep, sometimes only a few yards wide, they wove into the rock so sinuously that all sky was shut off. The floors were smooth sand or rounded stone pavement or stone pools linked by stone gutters, and nearly every gulch ran, except in flood season, a thin clear stream. Silt pockets out of reach of flood were gardens of fern and redbud; every talus and rockslide gave footing to cottonwood and willow and single-leafed ash; ponded places were solid with watercress; maidenhair hung from seepage cracks in the cliffs.

Often these canyons, pursued upward, ended in falls, and sometimes the falls came down through a slot or a skylight in the roof of a domed chamber, to trickle down the wall into a plunge pool that made a lyrical dunk bath on a hot day. In such chambers the light was dim, reflected, richly colored. The red rock was stained with the dark manganese exudations called desert varnish, striped black to green to yellow to white along horizontal lines of seepage, patched with the chemical, sunless green of moss. One such grotto was named Music Temple by Major John Wesley Powell on his first exploration, in 1869; another is the so-called Cathedral in the Desert, at the head of Clear Water Canyon off the Escalante.

That was what Glen Canyon was like before the closing of the dam in 1963. What was flooded here was potentially a superb national park. It had its history, too, sparse but significant. Exploring the gulches, one came upon ancient chiseled footholds leading up the slickrock to mortared dwellings or storage cysts of the Basket Makers and Pueblos who once inhabited these canyons. At the mouth of Padre Creek a line of chiseled steps marked where Fathers Escalante and Dominguez, groping back toward Santa Fe in 1776, got their animals down to the fjord that was afterward known as the Crossing of the Fathers. In Music Temple men from Powell's two river expeditions had scratched their names. Here and there on the walls near the river were names and initials of men from Robert Brewster Stanton's party that surveyed a water-level railroad down the canyon in 1889–90, and miners from the abortive goldrush of the 1890's. There were Mormon echoes at Lee's Ferry, below the dam, and at the slot canyon called Hole-in-the Rock, where a Mormon colonizing party got their wagons down the cliffs on their way to the San Juan in 1880.

Some of this is now under Lake Powell. I am interested to know how much is gone, how much left. Because I don't much like the thought of power boats and water skiers in these canyons, I come in March, before the season has properly begun, and at a time when the lake (stabilized they say because of water shortages far downriver at Lake Mead) is as high as it has ever been, but is still more than two hundred feet below its capacity level of thirty-seven hundred feet. Not everything that may eventually be drowned will be drowned yet, and there will be none of the stained walls and exposed mudflats that make a drawdown reservoir ugly at low water.

Our boat is the Park Service patrol boat, a thirty-four-foot diesel workhorse. It has a voice like a bulldozer's. As we back away from the dock and head out deserted Wahweap Bay, conversing at the tops of our lungs with our noses a foot apart, we acknowledge that we needn't have worried about motor noises among the cliffs. We couldn't have heard a Chriscraft if it had passed us with its throttle wide open.

One thing is comfortingly clear from the moment we back away from the dock at Wahweap and start out between the low walls of what used to be Wahweap Creek toward the main channel. Though they have diminished it, they haven't utterly ruined it. Though these walls are lower and tamer than they used to be, and though the whole sensation is a little like looking at a picture of Miss America that doesn't show her legs, Lake Powell *is* beautiful. It isn't Glen Canyon, but it is something in itself. The contact of deep blue water and uncompromising stone is bizarre and somehow exciting. Enough of the canyon feeling is left so that traveling up-lake one watches with a sense of discovery as every bend rotates into view new colors, new forms, new vistas: a great glowing wall with the sun on it, a slot side canyon buried to the eyes in water and inviting exploration, a half-drowned cave on whose roof dance the little flames of reflected ripples.

Moreover, since we float three hundred feet or more above the old river, the views out are much wider, and where the lake broadens, as at Padre Creek, they are superb. From the river, Navajo Mountain used to be seen only in brief, distant glimpses. From the lake it is often visible for minutes, an hour, at a time—gray-green, snow-streaked, a high mysterious bubble rising above the red world, incontrovertibly the holy mountain. And the broken country around the Crossing of the Fathers was always wild and strange as a moon landscape, but you had to climb out to see it. Now, from the bay that covers the crossing and spreads into the mouths of tributary creeks, we see Gunsight Butte, Tower Butte, and the other fantastic pinnacles of the Entrada formation surging up a sheer thousand feet above the rounding platform of the Navajo. The horizon reels with surrealist forms, dark red at the base, gray from there to rimrock, the profiles rigid and angular and carved, as different as possible from the Navajo's filigreed, ripple-marked sandstone.

We find the larger side canyons, as well as the deeper reaches of the main canyon, almost as impressive as they used to be, especially after we get far enough up-lake so that the water is shallower and the cliffs less reduced in height. Navajo Canyon is splendid despite the flooding of its green bottom that used to provide pasture for the stolen horses of raiders. Forbidden Canyon that leads to Rainbow Bridge is lessened, but still marvelous: it is like going by boat to Petra. Rainbow Bridge itself is still the place of magic that it used to be when we walked the six miles up from the river, and turned a corner to see the great arch framing the dome of Navajo Mountain. The canyon of the Escalante, with all its tortuous side canyons, is one of the stunning scenic experiences of a lifetime, and far easier to reach by lake than it used to be by foot or horseback. And all up and down these canyons, big or little, is the constantly changing, nobly repetitive spectacle of the cliffs with their contrasts of rounding and sheer, their great blackboard faces and their amphitheaters. Streaked with desert varnish, weathered and lichened and shadowed, patched with clean pink fresh-broken stone, they are as magically colored as shot silk.

And there is God's plenty of it. This lake is already a hundred and fifty miles long, with scores of tributaries. If it ever fills—which its critics guess it will not—it will have eighteen hundred miles of shoreline. Its fishing is good and apparently getting better, not only catfish and perch but rainbow trout and largemouth black bass that are periodically sown broadcast from planes. At present its supply and access points are few and far apart—at Wahweap, Hall's Crossing, and Hite—but when floating facilities are anchored in the narrows below Rainbow Bridge and when boat ramps and supply stations are developed at Warm Creek, Hole-in-the-Rock, and Bullfrog Basin, this will draw people. The prediction of a million visitors in 1965 is probably enthusiastic, but there is no question that as developed facilities extend the range of boats and multiply places of access, this will become one of the great water playgrounds.

And yet, vast and beautiful as it is, open now to anyone with a boat or the money to rent one, available soon (one supposes) to the quickie tour by float-plane and hydrofoil, democratically accessible and with its most secret beauties captured on color transparencies at infallible exposures, it strikes me, even in my exhilaration, with the consciousness of loss. In gaining the lovely and the usable, we have given up the incomparable.

The river's altitude at the dam was about 3150 feet. At 3490 we ride on 340 feet of water, and that means that much of the archaeology and most of the history, both of which were concentrated at the river's edge or near it, are as drowned as Lyonesse. We chug two hundred feet over the top of the square masonry tower that used to guard the mouth of Forbidden Canyon. The one small ruin that we see up Navajo Canyon must once have been nearly inaccessible, high in the cliff. Somehow (though we do not see them) we think it ought to have a line of footholds leading down into and under the water toward the bottom where the squash and corn gardens used to grow.

The wildlife that used to live comfortably in Glen Canyon is not there on the main lake. Except at the extreme reach of the water up side canyons, and at infrequent places where the platform of the Navajo sandstone dips down so that the lake spreads in among its hollows and baldheads, this reservoir laps vertical cliffs, and leaves no home for beaver or waterbird. The beaver have been driven up the side canyons, and have toppled whole groves of cottonwoods ahead of the rising water. While the water remains stable, they have a home; if it rises, they move upward; if it falls, the Lord knows what they do, for falling water will leave long mud flats between their water and their food. In the side canyons we see a few mergansers and redheads, and up the Escalante Arm the blue herons are now nesting on the cliffs, but as a future habitat Lake Powell is as unpromising for any of them as for the beaver.

And what has made things difficult for the wildlife makes them difficult for tourists as well. The tamarisk and willow bars are gone, and finding a campsite, or even a safe place to land a boat, is not easy. When the stiff afternoon winds sweep up the lake, small boats stay in shelter, for a swamping could leave a man clawing at a vertical cliff, a mile from any crawling-out place.

Worst of all are the places I remember that are now irretrievably gone. Surging up-lake on the second day I look over my shoulder and recognize the swamped and truncated entrance to Hidden Passage Canyon, on whose bar we camped eighteen years ago when we first came down this canyon on one of Norman Nevills' river trips. The old masked entrance is swallowed up, the water rises almost over the shoulder of the inner cliffs. Once that canyon was a pure delight to walk in; now it is only another slot with water in it, a thing to poke a motorboat into for five minutes and then roar out again. And if that is Hidden Passage, and we are this far out in the channel, then Music Temple is straight down.

The magnificent confrontation of the Kaiparowits and Navajo Mountain is still there, possibly even more magnificent because the lake has lifted us into a wider view. The splendid sweep of stained wall just below the mouth of the San Juan is there, only a little diminished. And Hole-in-the-Rock still notches the north rim, though the cove at the bottom where the Mormons camped before rafting the river and starting across the bare rock-chaos of Wilson Mesa is now a bay, with sunfish swimming among the tops of drowned trees. The last time I was here, three years ago, the river ran in a gorge three hundred feet below where our boat ties up for the night, and the descent from rim to water was a longer, harder way. The lake makes the feat of those Mormons look easier than it was, but even now, no one climbing the thousand feet of cliff to the slot will ever understand how they got their wagons down there.

A mixture of losses, diminishments, occasional gains, precariously maintained by the temporary stabilization of the lake. There are plenty of people willing to bet that there will never be enough water in the Colorado to fill both Lake Mead, now drawn far down, and Lake Powell, still 210 feet below its planned top level, much less the two additional dams proposed for Marble and Bridge canyons,[1] between these two. If

---

[1]Since given up, at least temporarily [Stegner's note].

there ever is—even if there is enough to raise Lake Powell fifty or a hundred feet—there will be immediate drastic losses of beauty. Walls now low, but high enough to maintain the canyon feeling, will go under, walls now high will be reduced. The wider the lake spreads, the less character it will have. Another fifty feet of water would submerge the Gregory Natural Bridge and flood the floor of the Cathedral in the Desert; a hundred feet would put both where Music Temple is; two hundred feet would bring water and silt to the very foot of Rainbow Bridge. The promontories that are now the most feasible camping places would go, as the taluses and sandbars have already gone. Then indeed the lake would be a vertical-walled fjord widening in places to a vertical-walled lake, neither as beautiful nor as usable as it still is. And the moment there is even twenty or thirty feet of drawdown, every side canyon is a slimy stinking mudflat and every cliff is defaced at the foot by a band of mud and minerals.

By all odds the best thing that could happen, so far as the recreational charm of Lake Powell is concerned, would be a permanently stabilized lake, but nobody really expects that. People who want to see it in its diminished but still remarkable beauty should go soon. And people who, as we do, remember this country before the canyons were flooded, are driven to dream of ways by which some parts of it may still be saved, or half-saved.

The dream comes on us one evening when we are camped up the Escalante. For three days we have been deafened by the noise of our diesel engines, and even when that has been cut off there has been the steady puttering of the generator that supplies our boat with heat, light, and running water. Though we weakly submit to the comforts, we dislike the smell and noise: we hate to import into this rock-and-water wilderness the very things we have been most eager to escape from. A wilderness that must be approached by power boat is no wilderness any more, it has lost its magic. Now, with the engines cut and the generator broken down, we sit around a campfire's more primitive light and heat and reflect that the best moments of this trip have been those in which the lake and its powerboat necessities were least dominant—eating a quiet lunch on a rock in Navajo Canyon, walking the 1.7 miles of sandy trail to the Rainbow Bridge or the half mile of creek bottom to the Cathedral in the Desert, climbing up the cliff to Hole-in-the-Rock. Sitting on our promontory in the Escalante canyon without sign or sound of the mechanical gadgetry of our civilization, we feel descending on us, as gentle as evening on a blazing day, the remembered canyon silence. It is a stillness like no other I have experienced, for at the very instant of bouncing and echoing every slight noise off cliffs and around bends, the canyons swallow them. It is as if they accentuated them, briefly and with a smile, as if they said, "Wait!" and suddenly all sound has vanished, there is only a hollow ringing in the ears.

We find that whatever others may want, we would hate to come here in the full summer season and be affronted with the constant roar and wake of power boats. We are not, it seems, water-based in our pleasures; we can't get a thrill out of doing in these marvelous canyons what one can do on any resort lake. What we have most liked on this trip has been those times when ears and muscles were involved, when the foot felt sand or stone, when we could talk in low voices, or sit so still that a brilliant collared lizard would come out of a crack to look us over. For us, it is clear, Lake Powell is not a recreational resource, but only a means of access; it is the canyons themselves, or what is left of them, that we respond to.

Six or seven hundred feet above us, spreading grandly from the rim, is the Escalante Desert, a basin of unmitigated stone furrowed by branching canyons as a carving platter is furrowed by gravy channels. It is, as a subsidiary drainage basin, very like the greater basin in whose trough once lay Glen Canyon, now the lake. On the north this desert drains from the Circle Cliffs and the Aquarius Plateau, on the east from the Waterpocket Fold, on the west from the Kaiparowits. In all that waste of stone fifty miles long and twenty to thirty wide there is not a resident human being, not a building except a couple of cowboy shelter shacks, not a road except the washed-out trail that the Mormons of 1880 established from the town of Escalante to Hole-in-the-Rock. The cattle and sheep that used to run on this desert range have ruined it and gone. That ringing stillness around us is a total absence of industrial or civilized decibels.

Why not, we say, sitting in chilly fire-flushed darkness under mica stars, why not throw a boom across the mouth of the Escalante Canyon and hold this one precious arm of Lake Powell for the experiencing of silence? Why not, giving the rest of that enormous water to the motorboats and the waterskiers, keep one limited tributary as a canoe or rowboat wilderness? There is nothing in the way of law or regulation to prevent the National Park Service from managing the Recreation Area in any way it thinks best, nothing that forbids a wilderness or primitive or limited-access area within the larger recreational unit. The Escalante Desert is already federal land, virtually unused. It and its canyons are accessible by packtrain from the town of Escalante, and will be accessible by boat from the facility to be developed at Hole-in-the-Rock. All down the foot of the Kaiparowits, locally called Fiftymile Mountain or Wild Horse Mesa, the old Mormon road offers stupendous views to those who from choice or necessity want only to drive to the edge of the silence and look in.

I have been in most of the side gulches off the Escalante—Coyote Gulch, Hurricane Wash, Davis Canyon, and the rest. All of them have bridges, windows, amphitheaters, grottoes, sudden pockets of green. And some of them, including the superlative Coyote Gulch down which even now it is possible to take a packtrain to the river, will never be drowned even if Lake Powell rises to its planned thirty-seven-hundred-foot level. What might have been done for Glen Canyon as a whole may still be done for the higher tributaries of the Escalante. Why not? In the name of scenery, silence, sanity, why not?

For awe pervades that desert of slashed and channeled stone overlooked by the cliffs of the Kaiparowits and the Aquarius and the distant peaks of the Henrys; and history, effaced through many of the canyons, still shows us its dim marks here: a crude *mano* discarded by an ancient campsite, a mortared wall in a cave, petroglyphs picked into a cliff face, a broken flint point glittering on its tee of sand on some blown mesa, the great rock where the Mormons danced on their way to people Desolation. This is country that does not challenge our identity as creatures, but it lets us shed most of our industrial gadgetry, and it shows us our true size.

Exploring the Escalante basin on a trip in 1961, we probed for the river through a half dozen quicksand gulches and never reached it, and never much cared because the side gulches and the rims gave us all we could hold. We saw not a soul outside our own party, encountered not a vehicle, saw no animals except a handful of cows and one mule that we scared up out of Davis Gulch when we rolled a rock over the rim. From every evening camp, when the sun was gone behind the Kaiparowits rim and the wind hung in suspension like a held breath and the Henrys northeastward and Navajo Mountain southward floated light as bubbles on the distance, we watched the eastern sky flush a pure, cloudless rose, darker at the horizon, paler above; and minute by minute the horizon's darkness defined itself as the blue-domed shadow of the earth cast on the sky, thinning at its upward arc to violet, lavender, pale lilac, but clearly defined, steadily darkening upward until it swallowed all the sky's light and the stars pierced through it. Every night we watched the earth-shadow climb the hollow sky, and every dawn we watched the same blue shadow sink down toward the Kaiparowits, to disappear at the instant when the sun splintered sparks off the rim.

In that country you cannot raise your eyes—unless you're in a canyon—without looking a hundred miles. You can hear coyotes who have somehow escaped the air-dropped poison baits designed to exterminate them. You can see in every sandy pocket the pug tracks of wildcats, and every waterpocket in the rock will give you a look backward into geologic time, for every such hole swarms with triangular crablike creatures locally called tadpoles but actually first cousins to the trilobites who left their fossil skeletons in the Paleozoic.

In the canyons you do not have the sweep of sky, the long views, the freedom of movement on foot, but you do have the protection of cliffs, the secret places, cool water, arches and bridges and caves, and the sunken canyon stillness into which, musical as water falling into a plunge pool, the canyon wrens pour their showers of notes in the mornings.

Set the Escalante Arm aside for the silence, and the boatmen and the water skiers can have the rest of that lake, which on the serene, warm, sun-smitten trip back seems more beautiful than it seemed coming up. Save this tributary and the desert back from it as wilderness, and there will be something at Lake Powell for everybody. Then it may still be possible to make expeditions as rewarding as the old, motorless river trips through Glen Canyon, and a man can make his choice between forking a horse and riding down Coyote Gulch or renting a houseboat and chugging it up somewhere near the mouth of the Escalante to be anchored and used as a base for excursions into beauty, wonder, and the sort of silence in which you can hear the swish of falling stars.

Coda: Wilderness Letter

Los Altos, Calif. Dec. 3, 1960

David E. Pesonen
Wildland Research Center
Agricultural Experiment Station
243 Mulford Hall
University of California
Berkeley 4, Calif.

Dear Mr. Pesonen:

I believe that you are working on the wilderness portion of the Outdoor Recreation Resources Review Commission's report. If I may, I should like to urge some arguments for wilderness preservation that involve recreation, as it is ordinarily conceived, hardly at all. Hunting, fishing, hiking, mountain-climbing, camping, photography, and the enjoyment of natural scenery will all, surely, figure in your report. So will the wilderness as a genetic reserve, a scientific yardstick by which we may measure the world in its natural balance against the world in its man-made imbalance. What I want to speak for is not so much the wilderness uses, valuable as those are, but the wilderness *idea,* which is a resource in itself. Being an intangible and spiritual resource, it will seem mystical to the practical-minded—but then anything that cannot be moved by a bulldozer is likely to seem mystical to them.

I want to speak for the wilderness idea as something that has helped form our character and that has certainly shaped our history as a people. It has no more to do with recreation than churches have to do with recreation, or than the strenuousness and optimism and expansiveness of what historians call the "American Dream" have to do with recreation. Nevertheless, since it is only in this recreation survey that the values of wilderness are being compiled, I hope you will permit me to insert this idea between the leaves, as it were, of the recreation report.

Something will have gone out of us as a people if we ever let the remaining wilderness be destroyed; if we permit the last virgin forests to be turned into comic books and plastic cigarette cases; if we drive the few remaining members of the wild species into zoos or to extinction; if we pollute the last clear air and dirty the last clean streams and push our paved roads through the last of the silence, so that never again will Americans be free in their own country from the noise, the exhausts, the stinks of human and automotive waste. And so that never again can we have the chance to see ourselves single, separate, vertical and individual in the world, part of the environment of trees and rocks and soil, brother to the other animals, part of the natural world and competent to belong in it. Without any remaining wilderness we are committed wholly, without chance for even momentary reflection and rest, to a headlong drive into our technological termite-life, the Brave New World of a completely man-controlled environment. We need wilderness preserved—as much of it as is still left, and as many kinds—because it was the challenge against which our character as a people was formed. The reminder and the reassurance that it is still there is good for our spiritual health even if we never once in ten years set foot in it. It is good for us when we are young, because of the incomparable sanity it can bring briefly, as vacation and rest, into our insane lives. It is important to us when we are old simply because it is there—important, that is, simply as idea.

We are a wild species, as Darwin pointed out. Nobody ever tamed or domesticated or scientifically bred us. But for at least three millennia we have been engaged in a cumulative and ambitious race to modify and gain control of our environment, and in the process we have come close to domesticating ourselves. Not many people are likely, any more, to look upon what we call "progress" as an unmixed blessing. Just as surely as it has brought us increased comfort and more material goods, it has brought us spiritual losses, and it threatens now to become the Frankenstein that will destroy us. One means of sanity is to retain a hold on the natural world, to remain, insofar as we can, good animals. Americans still have that chance, more than many peoples; for while we were demonstrating ourselves the most efficient and ruthless environment-busters in history, and slashing and burning and cutting our way through a wilderness continent, the wilderness was working on us. It remains in us as surely as Indian names remain on the land. If the abstract dream of human liberty and human dignity became, in America, something more than an abstract dream, mark it down at least partially to the fact that we were in subtle ways subdued by what we conquered.

The Connecticut Yankee, sending likely candidates from King Arthur's unjust kingdom to his Man Factory for rehabilitation, was overoptimistic, as he later admitted. These things cannot be forced, they have to grow. To make such a man, such a democrat, such a believer in human individual dignity, as Mark Twain himself, the frontier was necessary, Hannibal and the Mississippi and Virginia City, and reaching out from those the wilderness; the wilderness as opportunity and as idea, the thing that has helped to make an American different from and, until we forget it in the roar of our industrial cities, more fortunate than other men. For an American, insofar as he is new and different at all, is a civilized man who has renewed himself in the wild. The American experience has been the confrontation by old peoples and cultures of a world as new as if it had just risen from the sea. That gave us our hope and our excitement, and the hope and excitement can be passed on to newer Americans, Americans who never saw any phase of the frontier. But only so long as we keep the remainder of our wild as a reserve and a promise—a sort of wilderness bank.

As a novelist, I may perhaps be forgiven for taking literature as a reflection, indirect but profoundly true, of our national consciousness. And our literature, as perhaps you are aware, is sick, embittered, losing its mind, losing its faith. Our novelists are the declared enemies of their society. There has hardly been a serious or important novel in this century that did not repudiate in part or in whole American technological culture for its commercialism, its vulgarity, and the way in which it has dirtied a clean continent and a clean dream. I do not expect that the preservation of our remaining wilderness is going to cure this condition. But the mere example that we can as a nation apply some other criteria than commercial and exploitative considerations would be heartening to many Americans, novelists or otherwise. We need to demonstrate our acceptance of the natural world, including ourselves; we need the spiritual refreshment that being natural can produce. And one of the best places for us to get that is in the wilderness where the fun houses, the bulldozers, and the pavements of our civilization are shut out.

Sherwood Anderson, in a letter to Waldo Frank in the 1920's, said it better than I can. "Is it not likely that when the country was new and men were often alone in the fields and the forest they got a sense of bigness outside themselves that has now in some way been lost . . . Mystery whispered in the grass, played in the branches of trees overhead, was caught up and blown across the American line in clouds of dust at evening on the prairies . . . I am old enough to remember tales that strengthen my belief in a deep semi-religious influence that was formerly at work among our people. The flavor of it hangs over the best work of Mark Twain . . . I can remember old fellows in my home town speaking feelingly of an evening spent on the big empty plains. It had taken the shrillness out of them. They had learned the trick of quiet . . ."

We could learn it too, even yet; even our children and grandchildren could learn it. But only if we save, for just such absolutely non-recreational, impractical, and mystical uses as this, all the wild that still remains to us.

It seems to me significant that the distinct downturn in our literature from hope to bitterness took place almost at the precise time when the frontier officially came to an end, in 1890, and when the American way of life had begun to turn strongly urban and industrial. The more urban it has become, and the more frantic with technological change, the sicker and more embittered our literature, and I believe our people, have become. For myself, I grew up on the empty plains of Saskatchewan and Montana and in the mountains of Utah, and I put a very high valuation on what those places gave me. And if I had not been able periodically to renew myself in the mountains and deserts of western America I would be very nearly bughouse. Even when I can't get to the back country, the thought of the colored deserts of southern Utah, or the reassurance that there are still stretches of prairie where the world can be instantaneously perceived as disk and bowl, and where the little but intensely important human being is exposed to the five directions and the thirty-six winds, is a positive consolation. The idea alone can sustain me. But as the wilderness areas are progressively exploited or "improved," as the jeeps and bulldozers of uranium prospectors scar up the deserts and the roads are cut into the alpine timberlands, and as the remnants of the unspoiled and natural world are progressively eroded, every such loss is a little death in me. In us.

I am not moved by the argument that those wilderness areas which have already been exposed to grazing or mining are already deflowered, and so might as well be "harvested." For mining I cannot say much good except that its operations are generally short-lived. The extractable wealth is taken and the shafts, the tailings, and the ruins left, and in a dry country such as the American West the wounds men make in the earth do not quickly heal. Still, they are only wounds; they aren't absolutely mortal. Better a wounded wilderness than none at all. And as for grazing, if it is strictly controlled so that it does not destroy the ground cover, damage the ecology, or compete with the wildlife it is in itself nothing that need conflict with the wilderness feeling or the validity of the wilderness experience. I have known enough range cattle to recognize them as wild animals; and the people who herd them have, in the wilderness context, the dignity of rareness; they belong on the frontier, moreover, and have a look of rightness. The invasion they make on the virgin country is a sort of invasion that is as old as Neolithic man, and they can, in moderation, even emphasize a man's feeling of belonging to the natural world. Under surveillance, they can belong; under control, they need not deface or mar. I do not believe that in wilderness areas where grazing has never been permitted, it should be permitted; but I do not believe either that an otherwise untouched wilderness should be eliminated from the preservation plan because of limited existing uses such as grazing which are in consonance with the frontier condition and image.

Let me say something on the subject of the kinds of wilderness worth preserving. Most of those areas contemplated are in the national forests and in high mountain country. For all the usual recreational purposes, the alpine and forest wilderness are obviously the most important, both as genetic banks and as beauty spots. But for the spiritual renewal, the recognition of identity, the birth of awe, other kinds will serve every bit as well. Perhaps, because they are less friendly to life, more abstractly non-human, they will serve even better. On our Saskatchewan prairie, the nearest neighbor was four miles away, and at night we saw only two lights on all the dark rounding earth. The earth was full of animals—field mice, ground squirrels, weasels, ferrets, badgers, coyotes, burrowing owls, snakes. I knew them as my little brothers, as fellow creatures, and I have never been able to look upon animals in any other way since. The sky in that country came clear down to the ground on every side, and it was full of great weathers, and clouds, and winds, and hawks. I hope I learned something from knowing intimately the creatures of the earth; I hope I learned something from looking a long way, from looking up, from being much alone. A prairie like that, one big enough to carry the eye clear to the sinking, rounding horizon, can be as lonely and grand and simple in its forms as the sea. It is as good a place as any for the wilderness experience to happen; the vanishing prairie is as worth preserving for the wilderness idea as the alpine forests.

So are great reaches of our western deserts, scarred somewhat by prospectors but otherwise open, beautiful, waiting, close to whatever God you want to see in them. Just as a sample, let me suggest the Robbers' Roost country in Wayne County, Utah, near the Capitol Reef

National Monument. In that desert climate the dozer and jeep tracks will not soon melt back into the earth, but the country has a way of making the scars insignificant. It is a lovely and terrible wilderness, such a wilderness as Christ and the prophets went out into; harshly and beautifully colored, broken and worn until its bones are exposed, its great sky without a smudge or taint from Technocracy, and in hidden corners and pockets under its cliffs the sudden poetry of springs. Save a piece of country like that intact, and it does not matter in the slightest that only a few people every year will go into it. That is precisely its value. Roads would be a desecration, crowds would ruin it. But those who haven't the strength or youth to go into it and live can simply sit and look. They can look two hundred miles, clear into Colorado; and looking down over the cliffs and canyons of the San Rafael Swell and the Robbers' Roost they can also look as deeply into themselves as anywhere I know. And if they can't even get to the places on the Aquarius Plateau where the present roads will carry them, they can simply contemplate the *idea,* take pleasure in the fact that such a timeless and uncontrolled part of earth is still there.

These are some of the things wilderness can do for us. That is the reason we need to put into effect, for its preservation, some other principle than the principles of exploitation or "usefulness" or even recreation. We simply need that wild country available to us, even if we never do more than drive to its edge and look in. For it can be a means of reassuring ourselves of our sanity as creatures, a part of the geography of hope.

Very sincerely yours,

Wallace Stegner

JACQUETTA HAWKES
B. 1910

Daughter of a Cambridge University biochemist and cousin to poet Gerard Manley Hopkins, Jacquetta Hawkes has always considered science and art to be complementary approaches to understanding nature and human culture. A professional archaeologist, she conducted excava-

tions in England, Europe, and the Middle East in the 1930s, served in the War Cabinet Offices during World War II, founded the British Commission for UNESCO and was governor of the British Film Institute. Her many publications include archeological works, poetry, biographies, and novels, as well as plays written in collaboration with her husband, the writer J. B. Priestley.

A Land, *published in 1952 with illustrations by the sculptor Henry Moore, is on one level a fascinating geological and archeological history of the British Isles. But it is also an extended poetic and philosophical meditation on time, the growth of human consciousness, and especially the interplay between landscapes and the cultures that form and are formed by them. No less than geologists and archaeologists, Hawkes asserts, poets, painters, and musicians have helped shape our vision of landscape. Hawkes's gift for story-telling, her intelligent, intimate style and broad knowledge of her subject, combine with the singular insularity and continuity of England's long history to produce a compelling narrative with mythic dimensions.*

From A LAND

TWO THEMES

When I have been working late on a summer night, I like to go out and lie on the patch of grass in our back garden. This garden is a square of about twenty feet, so that to lie in it is like exposing oneself in an open box or tray. Not far below the topsoil is the London Clay which, as Primrose Hill, humps up conspicuously at the end of the road. The humus, formed by the accumulations first of forest and then of meadow land, must once have been fertile enough, but nearly a century in a back garden has exhausted it. After their first season, plants flower no more, and are hard put to it each year even to make a decent show of leaves. The only exceptions are the lilies of the valley, possessors of some virtue that enables them to draw their tremendous scent from the meanest soils. The sunless side of the garden has been abandoned to them, and now even in winter it is impossible to fork the earth there, so densely is it matted with the roots and pale nodes from which their flowers will rise.

Another result of the impoverishment of the soil is that the turf on which I lie is meagre and worn, quite without buoyancy. I would not have it otherwise, for this hard ground presses my flesh against my bones

A Land (New York: Random House, 1952).

and makes me agreeably conscious of my body. In bed I can sleep, here I can rest awake. My eyes stray among the stars, or are netted by the fine silhouettes of the leaves immediately overhead and from them passed on to the black lines of neighbouring chimney pots, misshapen and stolid, yet always inexplicably poignant. Cats rustle in the creeper on the end wall. Sometimes they jump down so softly that I do not hear them alight and yet am aware of their presence in the garden with me. Making their silken journeys through the dark, the cats seem as untamed, as remote, as the creatures that moved here before there were any houses in the Thames valley.

By night I have something of the same feeling about cats that I have always, and far more strongly, about birds: that perfectly formed while men were still brutal, they now represent the continued presence of the past. Once birds sang and flirted among the leaves while men, more helpless and less accomplished, skulked between the trunks below them. Now they linger in the few trees that men have left standing, or fit themselves into the chinks of the human world, into its church towers, lamp-posts and gutters. It is quite illogical that this emotion should be concentrated on birds; insects, for example, look, and are, more ancient. Perhaps it is evoked by the singing, whistling and calling that fell into millions of ancestral ears and there left images that we all inherit. The verses of medieval poets are full of birds as though in them these stored memories had risen to the surface. Once in the spring I stood at the edge of some Norfolk ploughland listening to the mating calls of the plover that were tumbling ecstatically above the fields. The delicious effusions of turtle doves bubbled from a coppice at my back. It seemed to me that I had my ear to a great spiral shell and that these sounds rose from it. The shell was the vortex of time, and as the birds themselves took shape, species after species, so their distinctive songs were formed within them and had been spiralling up ever since. Now, at the very lip of the shell, they reached my present ear.

As I lie looking at the stars with that blend of wonder and familiarity they alone can suggest, a barge turning the bend in Regent's Park Canal hoots, a soft wedge of sound in the darkness that is cut across by the long rumble of a train drawing out from Euston Station. Touched by these sounds, like a snail I retract my thoughts from the stars and banish the picture of the earth and myself hanging among them. Instead I become conscious of the huge city spreading for miles on all sides, of the innumerable fellow creatures stretched horizontally a few feet above the ground in their upstairs bedrooms, and of the railways, roads and canals rayed out towards all the extremities of Britain. The people sitting in those lighted carriages, even the bargee leaning sleepily on his long tiller, are not individuals going to board meetings in Manchester or bringing in coal for London furnaces. For the instant they are figures moved about the map by unknown forces, as helpless as the shapes of history that can be seen behind them, all irresistibly impelled to the achievement of this moment.

The Thames flows widening towards the city it has created; the coast-line of Britain encloses me within a shape as familiar as the constellations of the stars, and as consciously felt as the enclosing walls of this garden. The coast with its free, sweeping lines among the young formations of the east and south, and its intricate, embattled line of headland and bay among the ancient rocks of the west and north. The shape seems constant in its familiarity yet in fact is continuously changing. Even the stern white front that Albion turns to the Continent is withdrawing at the rate of fifteen inches a year. I remember as a small child being terrified by a big fall of cliff at Hunstanton, and I am certain that my terror was not so much due to the thought of being crushed—the fall had happened some days before, as by some inkling of impermanence. It was the same knowledge, though in a sadder and less brutal form, that came stealing in from the submerged forest, also to be seen at Hunstanton, a dreary expanse of blackened tree stumps exposed at low tide.

Always change, and yet at this moment, at every given moment, the outline of Britain, like all outlines, has reality and significance. It is the endless problem of the philosophers; either they give process, energy, its due and neglect its formal limitations, or they look only at forms and forget the irresistible power of change. The answers to all the great secrets are hidden somewhere in this thicket, those of ethics and aesthetics as well as of metaphysics.

I know of no philosophy that can disprove that this land, having achieved this moment, was not always bound to achieve it, or that I, because I exist, was not always inevitably coming into existence. It is therefore as an integral part of the process that I claim to tell the story of the creation of what is at present known as Britain, a land which has its own unmistakable shape at this moment of time.

There are many ways in which this story can be told, just as a day in the life of this house behind me could be described in terms of its intake of food and fuel, and its corresponding output through drains, dustbins and chimneys, or in terms of the movement in space and time of its occupants, or of their emotional relationships. All these forms, even the most material, would be in some sense creations of the storyteller's mind, and for this reason the counterpoint to the theme of the creation of a land shall be the growth of consciousness, its gradual concentration and intensification within the human skull.

That consciousness has now reached a stage in its growth at which it is impelled to turn back to recollect happenings in its own past which it has, as it were, forgotten. In the history of thought, this is the age of history. Some forms of these lost memories lie in the unconscious strata of mind itself, these dark, rarely disturbed layers that have accumulated, as mould accumulates in a forest, through the shedding of innumerable lives since the beginning of life. In its search for these forms consciousness is working, not always I think very sensitively, through its psychologists. I am certainly involved in their findings, but as narrator am not concerned with them. Instead I am concerned with other forms of memory, those recollections of the world and of man that are pursued on behalf of consciousness by geologists and archaeologists.

Unfortunately they have not yet gone far enough to recall the formation of the planet Earth. In my own childhood I drew a crude picture in my mind of a fragment flying off from the side of the sun, much as a piece of clay, carelessly handled, flies from a pot revolving on the potter's wheel. Then there were other, conflicting, pictures of the formation of planets by awe-inspiring cosmic road accidents, immense collisions. It seems that both were fanciful. Yet as we have not yet remembered what did happen, I must begin with a white-hot young earth dropping into its place like a fly into an unseen four-dimensional cobweb, caught up in a delicate tissue of forces where it assumed its own inevitable place, following the only path, the only orbit that was open to it.

At first the new planet was hot enough to shine with its own light, but so small a particle, lacking the nuclear energy that allows the sun to shine gloriously for billions of years at the expense only of some slight change in girth, could not keep its heat for very long. Its rays turned from white to red, then faded till Earth was lit only from without, from the sun round which it swung on an invisible thread. From that time night and day were established, the shadow of the Earth pointing into space like a huge black tent.

Writing in 1949 I say that night and day were established. It is, I know, foolish to use these words for a time before consciousness had grown in men and had formed the image of night and day as the spinning globe sent them from sunlight under the cone of shadow and out again at dawn. I should wait to use these words until this procession of light and darkness had formed one of the most deep-set images in the mind of man. But the concept is now so familiar that I cannot express myself otherwise.

I lie here and feel Earth rustling through space, its rotundity between me and the sun, the shadow above me acting as a searchlight to reveal the stars whose light left them long before there were eyes on this planet to receive it. Now the two little globes of my eyes, unlit in the darkness, look up at their shining globes, and who shall say that we do not gaze at one another, affect one another?

The first pallor of the rising moon dimming the stars over the chimneys reminds me of our modest satellite. I have known her for so long that she is an accepted part of the night, yet were I lying on Jupiter the sky would be radiant with ten moons, while on Saturn the rings would glisten day and night in a glorious bow. Now she has risen into sight, our one familiar moon. A beautiful world to our eyes, but cold and lifeless; without water or atmosphere she is a presage of what Earth might become. I should like to know whether in those icy rocks there are the fossils of former life, organisms that had gone some way in the process in which we are involved before they were cut short by an eternal drought. Do they lie in the rocks beneath the rays of a sun that once gave them life but now beats meaninglessly on a frigid landscape?

I feel them at their employment, the sun, moon, Earth and all the rest, even while more intimately I am aware of Britain moving through the night which, like a candle extinguisher, has put out her ordinary life. But if, which heaven forbid, I were at this moment to leap into a jet aeroplane we could catch up with day in a few hours, or could plunge into winter in a few days. It is difficult to remember for how great a part of history these thoughts and images would have appeared as the wildest delusions of a madman. We felt more secure when we believed ourselves to be standing on a plate under the protective dome of heaven with day and night given for work and sleep. If we were less confident in Athens it was only by intuition and native courage. Now knowledge of material facts imposes humility upon us, willy nilly. Not that I would allow myself to repent the divine curiosity that has led to this knowledge. Like everyone else within the walls of these islands I am a European, and as a European committed utterly to *la volonté de la conscience et la volonté de la découverte.* To enjoy, to create (which is to love) and to try to understand is all that at the moment I can see of duty. As for apparent material facts, I hope that in time we shall have come to know so many, and to have seen through so many, that they will no longer appear as important as they now do.

At present, certainly, they are powerful; we have allowed them to become our masters. Yet, strangely, as I lie here in my ignorance under the stars, I am aware of awe but not of terror, of humility but not of insignificance.

Meanwhile the moon has drawn clear of the chimneys. How ungrateful we have been to call her inconstant when she is the only body in the heavens to have remained faithful to us in spite of our intelligence, the only body that still revolves about us. She is riding high and I must go to bed before first the Isle of Thanet noses out, and then London itself emerges on the other side of night.

LEWIS THOMAS
B. 1913

Born in Flushing, New York, the son of a general practitioner, Dr. Thomas has had a long and distinguished medical career, including the presidency of the Memorial Sloane-Kettering Cancer Center from 1973 to 1980. His essays first appeared in The New England Journal of Medicine *and were collected in* The Lives of a Cell: Notes of a Biology Watcher *(1974), which won the National Book Award. Two other collections have followed:* The Medusa and the Snail: More Notes of a Biology Watcher *(1979), and* Late Night Thoughts on Listening to Mahler's Ninth Symphony *(1983).*

The compassion and concern for the earth and its creatures that pervade Lewis Thomas's writing would be enough to earn him inclusion in the company of nature writers. But it is his novel application of the concepts and language of modern cellular biology to traditional environmental subjects that has significantly enlarged and enriched the genre and earned him a place as one of the most innovative and important writers in the field today. Characterized by wit, tough-minded optimism and an extraordinary ability to make specialized concepts accessible to the general reader, his books take challenging ecological positions. He claims, for instance, that the community of life is not fragile but "the toughest membrane imaginable in the universe, opaque to probability, impermeable to death"—an assertion that demonstrates the importance of metaphor to scientific as well as to artistic thought.

ANTAEUS IN MANHATTAN

Insects again.

When social animals are gathered together in groups, they become qualitatively different creatures from what they were when alone or in

The Lives of a Cell: Notes of a Biology Watcher (New York: Viking, 1974).

pairs. Single locusts are quiet, meditative, sessile things, but when locusts are added to other locusts, they become excited, change color, undergo spectacular endocrine revisions, and intensify their activity until, when there are enough of them packed shoulder to shoulder, they vibrate and hum with the energy of a jet airliner and take off.

Watson, Nel, and Hewitt have collected large numbers of termites in the field and placed them together for observation, in groups and pairs. The grouped termites become increasingly friendly and active, but show no inclination to lay eggs or mate; instead, they cut down on their water intake, watching their weight, and the mitochondria of their flight muscles escalate in metabolic activity. Grouped termites keep touching each other incessantly with their antennae, and this appears to be the central governing mechanism. It is the being touched that counts, rather than the act of touching. Deprived of antennae, any termite can become a group termite if touched frequently enough by the others.

Isolated, paired termites are something else again. As soon as they are removed from the group, and the touching from all sides comes to an end, they become aggressive, standoffish; they begin drinking compulsively, and abstain from touching each other. Sometimes, they even bite off the distal halves of each other's antennae, to eliminate the temptation. Irritably, settling down to make the best of a poor situation, they begin preparations for the laying of eggs and the taking care of the brood. Meanwhile, the mitochondria in their flight muscles go out of business.

The most intensely social animals can only adapt to group behavior. Bees and ants have no option when isolated, except to die. There is really no such creature as a single individual; he has no more life of his own than a cast-off cell marooned from the surface of your skin.

Ants are more like the parts of an animal than entities on their own. They are mobile cells, circulating through a dense connective tissue of other ants in a matrix of twigs. The circuits are so intimately woven that the anthill meets all the essential criteria of an organism.

It would be wonderful to understand how the anthill communication system works. Somehow, by touching each other continually, by exchanging bits of white stuff carried about in their mandibles like money, they manage to inform the whole enterprise about the state of the world outside, the location of food, the nearness of enemies, the maintenance requirements of the Hill, even the direction of the sun; in the Alps, mountaineers are said to use the ameboid configurations of elongated ant nests as pointers to the south. The Hill, for its part, responds by administering the affairs of the institution, coordinating and synchronizing the movements of its crawling parts, aerating and cleaning the nest so that it can last for as long as forty years, fetching food in by long tentacles, rearing broods, taking slaves, raising crops, and, at one time or another, budding off subcolonies in the near vicinity, as progeny.

The social insects, especially ants, have been sources of all kinds of parables, giving lessons in industry, interdependence, altruism, humility, frugality, patience. They have been employed to instruct us in the whole range of our institutional virtues, from the White House to your neighborhood savings bank.

And now, at last, they have become an Art Form. A gallery in New York exhibited a collection of 2 million live army ants, on loan from Central America, in a one-colony show entitled "Patterns and Structures." They were displayed on sand in a huge square bin, walled by plastic sides high enough to prevent them from crawling over and out into Manhattan. The inventor of the work arranged and rearranged the location of food sources in different places, according to his inspiration and their taste, and they formed themselves into long, black, ropy patterns, extended like writhing limbs, hands, fingers, across the sand in crescents, crisscrosses, and long ellipses, from one station to another. Thus deployed, they were watched with intensity by the crowds of winter-carapaced people who lined up in neat rows to gaze down at them. The ants were, together with the New Yorkers, an abstraction, a live mobile, an action painting, a piece of found art, a happening, a parody, depending on the light.

I can imagine the people moving around the edges of the plastic barrier, touching shoulder to shoulder, sometimes touching hands, exchanging bits of information, nodding, smiling sometimes, prepared as New Yorkers always are to take flight at a moment's notice, their mitochondria fully stoked and steaming. They move in orderly lines around the box, crowding one another precisely, without injury, peering down, nodding, and then backing off to let new people in. Seen from a distance, clustered densely around the white plastic box containing the long serpentine lines of army ants, turning to each other and murmuring repetitively, they seem an absolute marvel. They might have dropped here from another planet.

I am sad that I did not see any of this myself. By the time I had received the communication on television and in my morning paper, felt the tugging pull toward Manhattan, and made my preparations to migrate, I learned that the army ants had all died.

The Art Form simply disintegrated, all at once, like one of those exploding, vanishing faces in paintings by the British artist Francis Bacon.

There was no explanation, beyond the rumored, unproved possibility of cold drafts in the gallery over the weekend. Monday morning they were sluggish, moving with less precision, dully. Then, the death began, affecting first one part and then another, and within a day all 2 million were dead, swept away into large plastic bags and put outside for engulfment and digestion by the sanitation truck.

It is a melancholy parable. I am unsure of the meaning, but I do think it has something to do with all that plastic—that, and the distance from the earth. It is a long, long way from the earth of a Central American jungle to the ground floor of a gallery, especially when you consider that Manhattan itself is suspended on a kind of concrete platform, propped up by a meshwork of wires, pipes, and water mains. But I think it was chiefly the plastic, which seems to me the most unearthly of all man's creations so far. I do not believe you can suspend army ants away from the earth, on plastic, for any length of time. They will lose touch, run out of energy, and die for lack of current.

One steps on ants, single ants or small clusters, every day without giving it a thought, but it is impossible to contemplate the death of so vast a beast as these 2 million ants without feeling twinges of sympathy, and something else. Nervously, thinking this way, thinking especially about Manhattan and the plastic platform, I laid down my newspaper and reached for the book on my shelf that contained, I knew, precisely the paragraph of reassurance required by the moment:

> It is not surprising that many analogies have been drawn between the social insects and human societies. Fundamentally, however, these are misleading or meaningless, for the behavior of insects is rigidly stereotyped and determined by innate instructive mechanisms; they show little or no insight or capacity for learning, and they lack the ability to develop a social tradition based on the accumulated experience of many generations.

It is, of course, an incomplete comfort to read this sort of thing to one's self. For full effect, it needs reading aloud by several people at once, moving the lips in synchrony.

DEATH IN THE OPEN

Most of the dead animals you see on highways near the cities are dogs, a few cats. Out in the countryside, the forms and coloring of the dead are strange; these are the wild creatures. Seen from a car window they appear as fragments, evoking memories of woodchucks, badgers, skunks, voles, snakes, sometimes the mysterious wreckage of a deer.

It is always a queer shock, part a sudden upwelling of grief, part unaccountable amazement. It is simply astounding to see an animal dead on a highway. The outrage is more than just the location; it is the impropriety of such visible death, anywhere. You do not expect to see dead animals in the open. It is the nature of animals to die alone, off somewhere, hidden. It is wrong to see them lying out on the highway; it is wrong to see them anywhere.

Everything in the world dies, but we only know about it as a kind of abstraction. If you stand in a meadow, at the edge of a hillside, and look around carefully, almost everything you can catch sight of is in the process of dying, and most things will be dead long before you are. If it were not for the constant renewal and replacement going on before your eyes, the whole place would turn to stone and sand under your feet.

There are some creatures that do not seem to die at all; they simply vanish totally into their own progeny. Single cells do this. The cell becomes two, then four, and so on, and after a while the last trace is gone. It cannot be seen as death; barring mutation, the descendants are simply the first cell, living all over again. The cycles of the slime mold have episodes that seem as conclusive as death, but the withered slug, with its stalk and fruiting body, is plainly the transient tissue of a developing animal; the free-swimming amebocytes use this organ collectively in order to produce more of themselves.

There are said to be a billion billion insects on the earth at any moment, most of them with very short life expectancies by our standards. Someone has estimated that there are 25 million assorted insects hanging in the air over every temperate square mile, in a column extending upward for thousands of feet, drifting through the layers of the atmosphere like plankton. They are dying steadily, some by being eaten, some just dropping in their tracks, tons of them around the earth, disintegrating as they die, invisibly.

Who ever sees dead birds, in anything like the huge numbers stipulated by the certainty of the death of all birds? A dead bird is an incongruity, more startling than an unexpected live bird, sure evidence to the human mind that something has gone wrong. Birds do their dying off somewhere, behind things, under things, never on the wing.

Animals seem to have an instinct for performing death alone, hidden. Even the largest, most conspicuous ones find ways to conceal themselves in time. If an elephant missteps and dies in an open place, the herd will not leave him there; the others will pick him up and carry the body from place to place, finally putting it down in some inexplicably suitable location. When elephants encounter the skeleton of an elephant out in the open, they methodically take up each of the bones and distribute them, in a ponderous ceremony, over neighboring acres.

It is a natural marvel. All of the life of the earth dies, all of the time, in the same volume as the new life that dazzles us each morning, each spring. All we see of this is the odd stump, the fly struggling on the porch floor of the summer house in October, the fragment on the highway. I have lived all my life with an embarrassment of squirrels in my backyard, they are all over the place, all year long, and I have never seen, anywhere, a dead squirrel.

I suppose it is just as well. If the earth were otherwise, and all the dying were done in the open, with the dead there to be looked at, we would never have it out of our minds. We can forget about it much of the time, or think of it as an accident to be avoided, somehow. But it does make the process of dying seem more exceptional than it really is, and harder to engage in at the times when we must ourselves engage.

In our way, we conform as best we can to the rest of nature. The obituary pages tell us of the news that we are dying away, while the birth announcements in finer print, off at the side of the page, inform us of our replacements, but we get no grasp from this of the enormity of scale. There are 3 billion of us on the earth, and all 3 billion must be dead, on a schedule, within this lifetime. The vast mortality, involving something over 50 million of us each year, takes place in relative secrecy. We can only really know of the deaths in our households, or among our friends. These, detached in our minds from all the rest, we take to be unnatural events, anomalies, outrages. We speak of our own dead in low voices; struck down, we say, as though visible death can only occur for cause, by disease or violence, avoidably. We send off for flowers, grieve, make ceremonies, scatter bones, unaware of the rest of the 3 billion on the same schedule. All of that immense mass of flesh and bone and consciousness will disappear by absorption into the earth, without recognition by the transient survivors.

Less than a half century from now, our replacements will have more than doubled the numbers. It is hard to see how we can continue to keep the secret, with such multitudes doing the dying. We will have to give up the notion that death is catastrophe, or detestable, or avoidable, or even strange. We will need to learn more about the cycling of life in the rest of the system, and about our connection to the process. Everything that comes alive seems to be in trade for something that dies, cell for cell. There might be some comfort in the recognition of synchrony, in the formation that we all go down together, in the best of company.

THE WORLD'S BIGGEST MEMBRANE

Viewed from the distance of the moon, the astonishing thing about the earth, catching the breath, is that it is alive. The photographs show the dry, pounded surface of the moon in the foreground, dead as an old bone. Aloft, floating free beneath the moist, gleaming membrane of bright blue sky, is the rising earth, the only exuberant thing in this part of the cosmos. If you could look long enough, you would see the swirling of the great drifts of white cloud, covering and uncovering the half-hidden masses of land. If you had been looking for a very long, geologic time, you could have seen the continents themselves in motion, drifting apart on their crustal plates, held afloat by the fire beneath. It has the organized, self-contained look of a live creature, full of information, marvelously skilled in handling the sun.

It takes a membrane to make sense out of disorder in biology. You have to be able to catch energy and hold it, storing precisely the needed amount and releasing it in measured shares. A cell does this, and so do the organelles inside. Each assemblage is poised in the flow of solar energy, tapping off energy from metabolic surrogates of the sun. To stay alive, you have to be able to hold out against equilibrium, maintain imbalance, bank against entropy, and you can only transact this business with membranes in our kind of world.

When the earth came alive it began constructing its own membrane, for the general purpose of editing the sun. Originally, in the time of prebiotic elaboration of peptides and nucleotides from inorganic ingredients in the water on the earth, there was nothing to shield out ultraviolet radiation except the water itself. The first thin atmosphere came entirely from the degassing of the earth as it cooled, and there was only a vanishingly small trace of oxygen in it. Theoretically, there could have been some production of oxygen by photo-dissociation of water vapor in ultraviolet light, but not much. This process would have been self-limiting, as Urey showed, since the wave lengths needed for photolysis are the very ones screened out selectively by oxygen; the production of oxygen would have been cut off almost as soon as it occurred.

The formation of oxygen had to await the emergence of photosynthetic cells, and these were required to live in an environment with sufficient visible light for photosynthesis but shielded at the same time against lethal ultraviolet. Berkner and Marshall calculate that the green cells must therefore have been about ten meters below the surface of water, probably in pools and ponds shallow enough to lack strong convection currents (the ocean could not have been the starting place).

You could say that the breathing of oxygen into the atmosphere was the result of evolution, or you could turn it around and say that evolution was the result of oxygen. You can have it either way. Once the photosynthetic cells had appeared, very probably counterparts of today's blue-green algae, the future respiratory mechanism of the earth was set in place. Early on, when the level of oxygen had built up to around 1 per cent of today's atmospheric concentration, the anaerobic life of the earth was placed in jeopardy, and the inevitable next stage was the emergence of mutants with oxidative systems and ATP. With this, we were off to an explosive developmental stage in which great varieties of respiring life, including the multicellular forms, became feasible.

Berkner has suggested that there were two such explosions of new life, like vast embryological transformations, both dependent on the threshold levels of oxygen. The first, at 1 per cent of the present level, shielded out enough ultraviolet radiation to permit cells to move into the surface layers of lakes, rivers, and oceans. This happened around 600 million years ago, at the beginning of the Paleozoic era, and accounts for the sudden abundance of marine fossils of all kinds in the record of this period. The second burst occurred when oxygen rose to 10 per cent of the present level. At this time, around 400 million years ago, there was a sufficient canopy to allow life out of the water and onto the land. From here on it was clear going, with nothing to restrain the variety of life except the limits of biologic inventiveness.

It is another illustration of our fantastic luck that oxygen filters out the very bands of ultraviolet light that are most devastating for nucleic acids and proteins, while allowing full penetration of the visible light needed for photosynthesis. If it had not been for this semipermeability, we could never have come along.

The earth breathes, in a certain sense. Berkner suggests that there may have been cycles of oxygen production and carbon dioxide consumption, depending on relative abundances of plant and animal life, with the ice ages representing periods of apnea. An overwhelming richness of vegetation may have caused the level of oxygen to rise above today's concentration, with a corresponding depletion of carbon dioxide. Such a drop in carbon dioxide may have impaired the "greenhouse" property of the atmosphere, which holds in the solar heat otherwise lost by radiation from the earth's surface. The fall in temperature would in turn have shut off much of living, and, in a long sigh, the level of oxygen may have dropped by 90 per cent. Berkner speculates that this is what happened to the great reptiles; their size may have been all right for a richly oxygenated atmosphere, but they had the bad luck to run out of air.

Now we are protected against lethal ultraviolet rays by a narrow rim of ozone, thirty miles out. We are safe, well ventilated, and incubated, provided we can avoid technologies that might fiddle with that ozone, or shift the levels of carbon dioxide. Oxygen is not a major worry for us, unless we let fly with enough nuclear explosives to kill off the green cells in the sea; if we do that, of course, we are in for strangling.

It is hard to feel affection for something as totally impersonal as the atmosphere, and yet there it is, as much a part and product of life as wine or bread. Taken all in all, the sky is a miraculous achievement. It works, and for what it is designed to accomplish it is as infallible as anything in nature. I doubt whether any of us could think of a way to improve on it, beyond maybe shifting a local cloud from here to there on occasion. The word "chance" does not serve to account well for structures of such magnificence. There may have been elements of luck in the emergence of chloroplasts, but once these things were on the scene, the evolution of the sky became absolutely ordained. Chance suggests alternatives, other possibilities, different solutions. This may be true for gills and swim-bladders and forebrains, matters of detail, but not for the sky. There was simply no other way to go.

We should credit it for what it is: for sheer size and perfection of function, it is far and away the grandest product of collaboration in all of nature.

It breathes for us, and it does another thing for our pleasure. Each day, millions of meteorites fall against the outer limits of the membrane and are burned to nothing by the friction. Without this shelter, our surface would long since have become the pounded powder of the moon. Even though our receptors are not sensitive enough to hear it, there is comfort in knowing that the sound is there overhead, like the random noise of rain on the roof at night.

THE TUCSON ZOO

Science gets most of its information by the process of reductionism, exploring the details, then the details of the details, until all the smallest bits of the structure, or the smallest parts of the mechanism, are laid out for counting and scrutiny. Only when this is done can the investigation be extended to encompass the whole organism or the entire system. So we say.

The Medusa and the Snail: More Notes of a Biology Watcher (New York: Viking, 1979).

Sometimes it seems that we take a loss, working this way. Much of today's public anxiety about science is the apprehension that we may forever be overlooking the whole by an endless, obsessive preoccupation with the parts. I had a brief, personal experience of this misgiving one afternoon in Tucson, where I had time on my hands and visited the zoo, just outside the city. The designers there have cut a deep pathway between two small artificial ponds, walled by clear glass, so when you stand in the center of the path you can look into the depths of each pool, and at the same time you can regard the surface. In one pool, on the right side of the path, is a family of otters; on the other side, a family of beavers. Within just a few feet from your face, on either side, beavers and otters are at play, underwater and on the surface, swimming toward your face and then away, more filled with life than any creatures I have ever seen before, in all my days. Except for the glass, you could reach across and touch them.

I was transfixed. As I now recall it, there was only one sensation in my head: pure elation mixed with amazement at such perfection. Swept off my feet, I floated from one side to the other, swiveling my brain, staring astounded at the beavers, then at the otters. I could hear shouts across my corpus callosum, from one hemisphere to the other. I remember thinking, with what was left in charge of my consciousness, that I wanted no part of the science of beavers and otters; I wanted never to know how they performed their marvels; I wished for no news about the physiology of their breathing, the coordination of their muscles, their vision, their endocrine systems, their digestive tracts. I hoped never to have to think of them as collections of cells. All I asked for was the full hairy complexity, then in front of my eyes, of whole, intact beavers and otters in motion.

It lasted, I regret to say, for only a few minutes, and then I was back in the late twentieth century, reductionist as ever, wondering about the details by force of habit, but not, this time, the details of otters and beavers. Instead, me. Something worth remembering had happened in my mind, I was certain of that; I would have put it somewhere in the brain stem; maybe this was my limbic system at work. I became a behavioral scientist, an experimental psychologist, an ethologist, and in the instant I lost all the wonder and the sense of being overwhelmed. I was flattened.

But I came away from the zoo with something, a piece of news about myself: I am coded, somehow, for otters and beavers. I exhibit instinctive behavior in their presence, when they are displayed close at hand behind glass, simultaneously below water and at the surface. I have receptors for this display. Beavers and otters possess a "releaser" for me, in the terminology of ethology, and the releasing was my experience. What was released? Behavior. What behavior? Standing, swiveling flabbergasted, feeling exultation and a rush of friendship. I could not, as the result of the transaction, tell you anything more about beavers and otters than you already know. I learned nothing new about them. Only about me, and I suspect also about you, maybe about human beings at large: we are endowed with genes which code out our reaction to beavers and otters, maybe our reaction to each other as well. We are stamped with stereotyped, unalterable patterns of response, ready to be released. And the behavior released in us, by such confrontations, is, essentially, a surprised affection. It is compulsory behavior and we can avoid it only by straining with the full power of our conscious minds, making up conscious excuses all the way. Left to ourselves, mechanistic and autonomic, we hanker for friends.

Everyone says, stay away from ants. They have no lessons for us; they are crazy little instruments, inhuman, incapable of controlling themselves, lacking manners, lacking souls. When they are massed together, all touching, exchanging bits of information held in their jaws like memoranda, they become a single animal. Look out for that. It is a debasement, a loss of individuality, a violation of human nature, an unnatural act.

Sometimes people argue this point of view seriously and with deep thought. Be individuals, solitary and selfish, is the message. Altruism, a jargon word for what used to be called love, is worse than weakness, it is sin, a violation of nature. Be separate. Do not be a social animal. But this is a hard argument to make convincingly when you have to depend on language to make it. You have to print up leaflets or publish books and get them bought and sent around, you have to turn up on television and catch the attention of millions of other human beings all at once, and then you have to say to all of them, all at once, all collected and paying attention: be solitary; do not depend on each other. You can't do this and keep a straight face.

Maybe altruism is our most primitive attribute, out of reach, beyond our control. Or perhaps it is immediately at hand, waiting to be released, disguised now, in our kind of civilization, as affection or friendship or attachment. I don't see why it should be unreasonable for all human beings to have strands of DNA coiled up in chromosomes, coding out instincts for usefulness and helpfulness. Usefulness may turn out to be the hardest test of fitness for survival, more important than aggression, more effective, in the long run, than grabbiness. If this is the sort of information biological science holds for the future, applying to us as well as to ants, then I am all for science.

One thing I'd like to know most of all: when those ants have made the Hill, and are all there, touching and exchanging, and the whole mass begins to behave like a single huge creature, and *thinks,* what on earth is that thought? And while you're at it, I'd like to know a second thing: when it happens, does any single ant know about it? Does his hair stand on end?

GAVIN MAXWELL
1914-1969

Gavin Maxwell was drawn, as a number of contemporary nature writers have been, to a landscape on the margins of twentieth century industrial society. His own "Sand County" was the western coast and islands of Scotland, where isolation allowed for a new kind of centering, and for a friendship with the earth carried out on more equal terms. In Ring of Bright Water *(1969) he describes how he became a part of the enlivening community along that chilly shore.*

From RING OF BRIGHT WATER

I had been at Camusfeàrna for eight years before I piped water to the house; before that it came from the burn in buckets. During the first years there was a stout stone-piered bridge across the burn, and under it one could draw water that had not been fouled by the cattle at their ford a little lower; then, in 1953, the bridge was swept away by a winter spate, and there was none built again for five years. In the summer there is no more than a foot or so of water among the stones, deepening to three or four feet when it runs amber-coloured and seemingly motionless between the alder banks, but wedged high among the branches are wads of debris that show the level of its torrential winter spates. When the gales blow in from the south-west and the burn comes roaring down in a

Ring of Bright Water (New York: Dutton, 1960).

foaming peaty cataract to meet the invading sea, the alders stand under water for half their height, and in the summer blackened trailers of dry seaweed dangle from branches ten feet and more above the stream.

After the bridge had gone, the winter crossing of the burn to climb the hill to Druimfiaclach was always perilous, sometimes impossible. I stretched a rope between the alders from bank to bank, but it was slender support, for even when the water was no more than thigh deep the pure battering weight of it as it surged down from the waterfall would sweep one's legs from the bottom and leave one clinging to the rope without foothold, feet trailing seaward.

The purely natural changes that have taken place during my ten years at Camusfeàrna are astonishing. One is inclined to think of such a landscape as immutable without the intervention of man, yet in these few years the small alterations to the scene have been continuous and progressive. The burn has swept the soil from under its banks so that the alder roots show white and bare, and some of the trees have fallen; where there are none at the burn side the short green turf has been tunnelled under by the water so that it falls in and the stream's bed becomes ever wider and shallower. Farther down towards the sea, where the burn bends round to encircle Camusfeàrna, the burrowing of a colony of sand martins in the sand cliff that is its landward bank has had the same effect, undermining the turf above so that it gives beneath the sheeps' feet and rolls down to the water's edge. Below the sand martins' burrows is now a steep slope of loose sand where ten years ago it was vertical. The sand dunes between the house and the sea form and re-form, so that their contour is never the same for two years, though the glaucous, rasping marram grass that grows on them imparts an air of static permanency. The whole structure of these dunes that now effectively block much of the beach from the house, and incidentally afford to it some shelter from the southerly gales, is in any case a thing of recent times, for I am told that when the present house was built fifty-odd years ago the field stretched flat to the sea, and the seaward facing wall of the house was left windowless for that reason.

The beach itself, wherever the rock does not shelve straight into the sea, is in constant change too; broad belts of shingle appear in the sand where there was no shingle before; soft stretches of quicksand come and go in a few weeks; sand bars as white as snow-drifts and jewelled with bright shells rise between the islands and vanish as though they had melted under the summer suns.

Even the waterfall, to me perhaps the most enduring symbol of Camusfeàrna, has changed and goes on changing. When I am away from the place and think of it, it is of the waterfall that I think first. Its voice is in one's ears day and night; one falls asleep to it, dreams with it and wakens to it; the note changes with the season, from the dull menacing roar of winter nights to the low crooning of the summer, and if I hold a shell to my ear it is not the sea's murmur that comes to me but the sound of the Camusfeàrna waterfall. Above the bridge where I used to draw my water the burn rushes over stones and between boulders with the alders at its banks, and a wealth of primroses and wild hyacinths among the fern and mosses. In spring it is loud with bird song from the chaffinches that build their lichen nests in the forks of the alders, and abob with wagtails among the stones. This part of the burn is "pretty" rather than beautiful, and it seems to come from nowhere, for the waterfall is hidden round a corner and the stream seems to emerge from a thirty-foot wall of rock hung with honeysuckle and with rowan trees jutting from cracks and fissures. But looking up the burn from the foot of that rock the word "pretty" becomes wholly inapplicable; the waterfall is of a beauty it would be hard to devise. It is not high, for the tall cataracts of eighty feet are some two hundred yards higher up its course; it emerges between boulders and sheer rock walls to drop some fifteen feet, over about the same breadth, from the twilight world of the deep narrow gorge it has carved through the hill face over thousands, perhaps millions, of years. It emerges frothing from that unseen darkness to fall like a tumbling cascade of brilliants into a deep rounded cauldron enclosed by rock walls on three sides, black water in whorled black rock, with the fleecy white spume ringing the blackness of the pool. Up above the black sides of the pot there are dark-green watery mosses growing deep and cushioned wherever there is a finger-hold for soil; the domed nest that the dippers build here every year is distinguishable from the other moss cushions by nothing but its symmetry. The sun reaches the waterfall for only a short time in the afternoon; it forms a rainbow over the leaping spray, and at the top of the fall between the boulders it gives to the smooth-flowing, unbroken water the look of spun green glass.

For most of the year the waterfall has volume enough for a man to stand on a ledge between it and the rock and remain almost dry; between oneself and the sky it forms a rushing, deafening curtain of milky brilliance through which nothing but light is discernible. If one steps forward so that the weight of water batters full on head and shoulders it is of the massiveness only that one is conscious, and it would be impossible to say whether the water were cold or hot. Only when one steps from it again, and the flying icy drops tingle on the skin, does the sensation become one of snow water.

It would seem that the waterfall could never change, yet year by year its form differs as a new boulder is swept down by the spates to lodge above its lip; or a tree falls from its precarious grip on the cliff faces above it and jams the doorway of its emergence; or a massive section of rock breaks away, split by the prising leverage of slow-growing tree roots.

In spring and autumn the natural decoration surrounding the waterfall surpasses anything that artifice could achieve; in spring the green banks above the rock are set so thickly with primroses that blossom almost touches blossom, and the wild blue hyacinths spring from among them seemingly without leaf; in late summer and autumn the scarlet rowanberries flare from the ferned rock walls, bright against the falling white water and the darkness of the rock.

It is the waterfall, rather than the house, that has always seemed to me the soul of Camusfeàrna, and if there is anywhere in the world to which some part of me may return when I am dead it will be there.

If it is the waterfall that seems the soul of Camusfeàrna, it is the burn and the sea that give its essential character, that sparkling silver that rings the green field and makes it almost an island. Below the house the beach is long and shelving, the tide running back at low springs for more than two hundred yards over alternate stone and sand. There is only one thing lacking at Camusfeàrna; within its narrow compass it contains every attraction but an anchorage. To look down from the hill above upon the bay and the scattered, intricate network of islands and skerries it would appear incredible that no one of those bights or niches should afford shelter, yet because of the long ebb of the tide each one of these seemingly tranquil miniature harbours dries out at low water. For years I had no boat at Camusfeàrna, and when at last I did buy a dinghy I was intimidated by the thought of those interminable hauls to and from the water's edge, and I bought a little nine-foot flat-bottomed pram that one could almost pick up. But to have a boat again at all, even that toy, brought a hankering to extend one's range up and down the coast and over to Skye, and now I have two dinghies with outboard motors, one of them a sturdy lifeboat's dinghy of fifteen feet, with decked-in bows. There are moorings laid in the bay where the burn flows out to the sea, and the pram is kept drawn up on the beach as ferry to and from the larger boat, but when the wind blows strong from the south it is always an anxious business. The suddenness and intensity of West Highland squalls, even in summer, has to be experienced to be understood; pale-blue satin water can become in a matter of minutes an iron-grey menace raging in white at the crests of massive waves. But the compensations outweigh the anxiety, for it was frustrating to live at the sea's edge and be unable to voyage upon it, to be unable to visit the distant islands, to fish in summer, to reach the nearest shop without the long climb to Druimfiaclach. The possession of the boats opened a whole new world around Camusfeàrna, a wide extension of its small enclosed paradise, and in summer the hours afloat drift by with work unheeded and the business of life seeming far off and worthless.

There is a perpetual mystery and excitement in living on the seashore, which is in part a return to childhood and in part because for all of us the sea's edge remains the edge of the unknown; the child sees the bright shells, the vivid weeds and red sea-anemones of the rock pools with wonder and with the child's eye for minutiae; the adult who retains wonder brings to his gaze some partial knowledge which can but increase it, and he brings, too, the eye of association and of symbolism, so that at the edge of the ocean he stands at the brink of his own unconscious.

The beaches of Camusfeàrna are a treasure house for any man whose eye finds wealth at the sea's edge. There are more shells than I have seen on any other littoral; a great host of painted bivalves of bewildering variety and hue, from coral pinks and primrose yellows to blues and purples and mother-of-pearl, from jewel-like fan shells no bigger than a little fingernail to the great scallops as big as a side-plate; nutshells and Hebridean ark shells and pearly top-shells and delicate blush-pink cowries. The sandbars and beaches between the islands are formed of the disintegration of these myriad calceous houses, true shell sand that is blindingly white under the sun and crusted in deep layers at the tide's edge with tiny intact empty shells gaudy as multi-coloured china beads. A little above the shells, because they are heavier, lies a filigree of white and purple coral, loose pieces each of which would lie in the palm of a hand, but there are so many of them that they form a dense, brittle layer over the sand. On still summer days when the tide wells up the beaches without so much as a wrinkle or ripple of wavelet at its edge, the coral floats off on the maniscus of the water, so that the sea seems to be growing flowers as an ornamental pond grows water lilies, delicately branched white and purple flowers on the aquamarine of the clear water.

Where shells lie thick it is often those that are broken that have the greatest beauty of form; a whelk is dull until one may see the sculptural perfection of the revealed spiral, the skeletal intricacy of the whorled mantle. Many of the shells at Camusfeàrna, and the stones, too, have been embroidered with the white limy tunnels of the serpulid tube-worm, strange hieroglyphics that even in their simplest forms may appear urgently significant, the symbols of some forgotten alphabet, and when a surface is thickly encrusted it assumes the appearance of Hindoo temple carving, or of Rodin's Gates of Hell, precise in every riotous ramification. Parts of the sculpture appear almost representational; a terrified beast flees before a pursuing predator; a well-meaning saint impales a dragon; the fingers of a hand are raised, like those of a Byzantine Christ, in a gesture that seems one of negation rather than benediction.

But above all it is the fantastic colouring of the beaches that as an image overpowers the minutiae. Above the tide-line the grey rocks are splashed gorse-yellow with close-growing lichen, and with others of blue-green and salmon pink. Beneath them are the vivid orange-browns and siennas of wrack-weeds, the violet of mussel-beds, dead-white sand, and water through which one sees down to the bottom, as through pale green bottle-glass, to where starfish and big spiny sea urchins of pink and purple rest upon the broad leaves of the sea-tangle.

The beaches are rich, too, in edible shellfish. Besides the ubiquitous mussels, limpets and periwinkles, there are cockle beds, razor-shell beds, and even an oyster bed, though this last remains one of the mysteries of Camusfeàrna. The oysters were introduced many years ago by a former owner of the estate, in a little circular bay almost closed from the sea and no more than twenty yards across, where a trickle of fresh water comes down over the sand from an island spring. At the tideline above this bay arrives a constant litter of tantalizingly freshly emptied oyster shells that would not disgrace Wheeler's, and, very occasionally, a live oyster, but for all my searching year by year I have never discovered where the bed lies. This is as well, perhaps, for I suspect that by now the colony would have succumbed to my gluttony.

Below the tide around the islands the white sand alternates with a heavy rubbery jungle of sea-tangle or umbrella weed. The lobsters lurk in this dimness by day, and lobster-pots set in the sand patches between the weed are rarely unsuccessful. A variety of other life besides lobsters enters the pots, creatures couth and uncouth; sometimes the bait is covered with gigantic whelks, and almost always there are big edible crabs. Often there is a curious beast called the velvet swimming crab, with a shield of brown velvet and reproachful red eyes, and once I caught one of the most repulsive creatures I have ever come across, a spider crab. It was not only the enormously long legs and absence of pincers that were nauseating; he was grown over from head to foot, as it were, with a crinkly, purplish-red seaweed, lending him the same air of doubtful reality as a shroud traditionally imparts to a ghost. The weed is, in fact, grafted into position by the crab itself, for camouflage, and this implication of furtive cunning coming on top of the outrageous personal appearance is not reassuring.

I must confess to a slight but perceptible revulsion to all crabs before they are prepared for eating, greatest in the case of the spider crab and in *diminuendo* down to the hermit-crabs that inhabit empty shells, for their unattractive nakedness is decently covered in someone else's discarded finery. Hermit crabs have given rise to some of the few occasions in my adult life on which I have laughed out loud when quite alone. Sometimes when gathering periwinkles to eat, bucket in hand and scooping them several dozen to a swipe, my attention has been caught by some monster winkle at the floor of a pool, one that would at least provide a mouthful for a marmoset rather than a mouse. Even as my fingers have broken the surface of the water, shaping themselves avidly for capture, the shell, its bluff so accidentally called, has suddenly scuttled away with an air of chagrin and embarrassment, as though two of the Marx brothers, detected in the front and rear halves of a stage cow, still made a last hopeless effort to maintain the deception.

JOHN HAY
B. 1915

In his Foreword to The Run *(1959), John Hay states, "This book mirrors an attempt to go farther afield, from one man's center." Hay's "center," for most of his writing career, has been the sandy peninsula of Cape Cod, a fertile ground for many nature writers. Grandson and namesake of Abraham Lincoln's personal secretary and Theodore Roosevelt's secretary of state, Hay was born in Ipswich, Massachusetts. He first came to Cape Cod in 1942 to study with the poet Conrad Aiken. After service in World War II he built a home in the town of Brewster, where he has lived ever since. The Run, a personal account of the life cycle of alewives, or migratory herring, was the first of a distinguished series of nature books which reflect Hay's dual emphasis on locality—identification of and with a known home ground—and a recognition of the global connections in local phenomena: "All landscape contains the potential world." His work has traced a widening gyre of settings over the years, including Maine, New Hampshire, Greenland, and Costa Rica. Hay's quietly suggestive and elegant style masks one of the most innovative and daring of contemporary writers in the genre. His books explore not only various outer environments he has encountered, but also the inner, hidden connections between human and other lives, expressing his belief*

*that the deepest sources of our being lie in a nature we have done our
best to ignore.*

From THE RUN

THE COMMON NIGHT

Did the alewives choose the night or late evening hours to come in by?
So I had been told. By daylight evidence, the fish population increased at
the Herring Run on the mornings following a nightly high tide. I had
also heard that there were more alewives running during the tides of the
full moon, in the farthest monthly reaches of ebb and flood; but this was
a correlation that would be hard for me to make without more years to
judge by. In the middle of May on the days just after the first quarter of
the moon, which came on the sixteenth, the fish seemed to be running
just about as hard as they did during the days preceding the full moon in
April, which had appeared on the twenty-fourth. Judging accordingly, it
seemed as though their migration had its own ebb and flood during those
months. All this was not much better than impression plus hearsay, but
there seemed to be some justice to the night tide theory, so, to begin
with, I went down to the shore late one evening during an incoming tide
to see if there might be any sign of the alewives.

About eight o'clock, an hour before high tide, the tide was running
strongly in at Paine's Creek. The channel in the marshes flooded over its
banks and marsh grasses were floating and stirring as the swaying waters
rose around them. It was near dark. I could see some seaweed flinging by
against the sandy bottom at the mouth of the creek, and a big, ghostly
green eel slithered up at the edge of the bank the waves were licking,
seemed to look up at me, looped back into the water, and disappeared;
but it was too dark to see much more than those black clumps of seaweed
racing by. I saw a group of gulls standing in shoal waters beyond the
beach, where waves were rolling in hard under a steady northwest wind.
The sun's cauldron had dropped down, a raw, glistening orange-red, into
the sea and back of the curved horizon, leaving its horizontal flush behind.

I walked back under the lee of the sand banks bordering the curving
creek. The tide was pulsing and roaring, its waters loping in to the creek
which began to turn a harder, darker blue under the sky. Then I began to

The Run (New York: Doubleday, 1959).

hear the innumerable soft slaps of fish breaking the surface. The alewives were making their entry from the sea.

And the gulls proclaimed their coming. Out in the Bay, they began to gather by the hundreds, clambering up with a scrambled yelping and hollering. The last smoky, red line of sunset was disappearing and they hovered over it in a maddened, high, wide swarm like huge bees. It grew darker, and a black-crowned night heron, or "quawk," sometimes "quok," a name true to the sound it makes, flew by with rounded wings against a star. The gulls began to disappear, streaming faintly like ashes against the last fires on the sea, but still crying vastly and collectively toward a world of distances. And in terrible simplicity, the alewives were swimming toward the inland gauntlet they would have to run, having a title, by their common, wild, and ancient advent, to all great kindled things. Who will see more than that in his short life, with its many meetings and separations?

I by an old and natural right felt a fierce water-deep wonder of the spirit. The beyondness in me went back to its beginnings. I thought of the nights on which children I have known were born, and of the voyages of war, leave-takings at railroad stations and at ports of embarkation, and of dreams in which I struggled toward new meetings and other lives. The wind blew through the arches of the stars, and the surfaces of the dipping earth, water, and sky in their lasting communion made me dizzy. I felt a cold inevitable grandeur, below consciousness, a swim and go in an uttermost wild world, past home or my life's memory.

So by this evidence the alewives came in at night, and, as a further discovery not to be denied, so had I. Perhaps it was the closest I would ever get to the non-human fish in a darkness where all the components of existence ran the same race. That real depth, fish-oriented, nakedly omnipotent, fills men when they recognize it with more awe than their limited worlds can encompass.

As I started back, about a quarter of an hour before the full tide, headlights swept over where the road ended at the shore, and in a minute or two a couple of fishermen lurched down the sand with high rubber waders on, carrying their casting rods. They stood on the beach in the dark, one of them coaching the other in baiting his hook. I came up and spoke to them, hardly able to make out their faces. The older one, he who did the coaching, told me that they had just got a pail of herrin' from the Brewster run to use as bait. They had hopes that there would be some bass here, the famous "stripers" chasing the alewives in. They brought their long rods sideways and back to sling the bait out into the black and silver waves. The older man spoke low words against the wind, and I strained to hear him. Suddenly he thought he felt what must be alewives nosing his line and bumping against it on their way by into the mouth of the inlet. Last year, he told me, he had seen hundreds of them dead on the flats, and the gulls, he said, had slit their sides open as if with knives to get the roe. The waves had begun to slacken off when I left, and the fishermen were still casting, but without much hope of a strike.

From IN DEFENSE OF NATURE

THE DOVEKIE AND THE OCEAN SUNFISH

It was in December and a slight snow had started. Inland of Cape Cod waters there was very little wind, and the flakes were spaced far apart. They seemed to hover. They would lift and dip, then slant down and touch slowly to the ground. The day was gray and quiet, tempered by the even recital of falling flakes, with a dull sky and a strip of gray sea in the distance. I watched the snow flakes acting in the space around me, over and inside and by each other in slow periods, and then I drove down to the Outer Beach.

The surf there was roaring, and hard wet flakes of snow came in heavily, driven by a seaward wind, and made my eyes smart. The curled-over, breaking waves were glassy green in the gray day and pushed in soapy sheets of foam along the sands. The ocean itself seemed full of kingly mountains meeting or withholding, conflicting, pushing each other aside, part of a collective immensity that could express itself in the last little bursting spit of a salt bubble flung out of the foam that seethed into the beach, a kind of statement of articulated aim out of a great language still untamed.

Out on those cold looming and receding waters seabirds rode. There were flocks of dark brown and black-and-white eiders a few hundred yards beyond the shoreline. Gulls beat steadily along the troughs of the waves. Then I caught sight of thirty or forty dovekies, the chunky black and white "little auks" that come down from the far north during the winter to feed off the coast. Their color showed clearly against the green water, white under black heads, black backs and wings, with little up-turned tail feathers. They dipped continually into the water, so quickly as to escape my notice much of the time. They made fish flips into those tumultuous sea surfaces as easily as minnows in a gentle pond.

The dovekie (called little auk in Europe) breeds by the millions in the

In Defense of Nature (Boston: Little, Brown, 1969).

high Arctic, principally in North Greenland, Spitzbergen, northern Novaya Zemlya, and Franz Joseph Land, with scattered colonies in subarctic areas. Drift ice is their principal habitat. They like areas where the ice
is not too densely packed, and they feed in openings or leads between the
ice floes, on small crustaceans in the plankton. They seem to avoid the
warm waters of the Gulf Stream, following the Arctic currents instead.
Especially during periods of great population growth, emigration flights
of the dovekies take them on long journeys which scatter them to many
regions, and occasionally take them inland in dovekie "wrecks" where
they may be killed or injured, and become vulnerable to many kinds of
predators. Their short narrow wings make it difficult, though not impossible, for them to take off from inland areas. One winter I saw many dead
ones scattered down the Cape Cod highway, little "penguin-like" birds
unknown to most car drivers.

These dovekies off Cape Cod waters were flying and diving, casting
their bodies back and forth between air and water like so many balls.
Their speed is not great, but when they fly off over the water their
wingbeat is very quick, and their landing and diving is done with a dash
and play that belies their stumpy appearance. In fact a dovekie in flight,
though it lacks the agility and swinging maneuverability of a swallow, is
at the same time somewhat reminiscent of those birds, with its short
wings alternately beating fast and gliding, like a swift. When they swam
under water these chunky little "pineknots" did so with a quick, supple,
almost fishlike beat, making me think that fins after all were not so far
removed from wings.

Not visible, though they brought it with them in some measure these
vast distances down to New England, was the grandeur of the Arctic,
whose auroras, growling ice and sunsets I could only imagine. Dovekies
breed in bare heaps of rock that cover great screes, hillsides of stone,
sloping down to the sea. They arrive in there in the spring when green
begins to show through frozen ground and rivulets and waterfalls begin
to sound while the dovekies themselves utter a watery, twittering, trilling
call. There they dot the slopes in great numbers "like pepper and salt," it
says in *The Birds of Greenland,* and fly about "in huge flocks which
resemble at a distance swarms of mosquitoes or drifting smoke."

To the Eskimos these little birds are of primary importance. They net
them with long-handled nets as they fly over their breeding cliffs and
store them in the frozen ground for winter food. Eskimo women gather
their eggs, where their nests are found between the rocks and stones,
beginning in June. They also use their skins for a birdskin coat called a
tingmiaq. For one such coat about fifty skins are needed. Admiral Donald B. MacMillan, the Arctic explorer, has described—in a passage
quoted by Forbush—how much the spring arrival of the dovekies has

meant to the Eskimos: "But what is that great, pulsating, musical note which seems to fill all space? Now loud and clear, now diminishing to a low hum, the sound proclaims the arrival of the true representative of bird life in the Arctic, the dovekie, or little auk *(Plautus alle)*. The long dark winter has at last passed away. The larder open to all is empty. The sun is mounting higher into the heavens day by day. Now and then a seal is seen sunning himself at his hole. The Eskimos are living from hand to mouth. And then that glad cry, relieving all anxiety for the future, bringing joy to every heart, '*Ark-pood-e-ark-suit! Ark-pood-e-ark-suit!*' (Little auks! Little auks!)."

Arctic foxes also depend on the dovekies for food, as well as their immaculately bluish white eggs. Dovekies are preyed upon by ravens and gyrfalcons too, but the big, persistent enemy of which they are in mortal fear is the glaucous or burgomaster gull.

The nitrogen-rich guano of the dovekies, filtering down through the massive hillsides of loose bare stone, fertilizes a deep growth of moss in brilliant green bands. This and other plant life supports hare and ptarmigan and is probably good pasturage for what was once an abundant population of caribou. And in the sea this little bird that makes for provision in depth, both good and cruel, is often eaten by white whales, large fish, and seals.

What a major burden for one so small! Millions of dovekies feed their young during the nesting season and a whole Arctic world depends that they be successful, on and on into the future. The little ones are constantly hungry and chirp in a shrill impatient way until: "the old bird feeds them by disgorging into their bills the content of its well-filled pouch. The consoling, soothing murmur of the old bird to the young, and the satisfied chirping of the young shows how solicitous the one and how grateful the other." Sweet domesticity still keeps the terrible world in order. The little auk is also a tough, all-weather bird, capable of survival in extreme circumstances, and so far it has the room it needs and the isolation and a major range.

How can we predators dare count the bodies, human and other than human, of those on whom we prey! How dare we wipe out whole populations in the first place, either by pulling a trigger or spreading our wastes and poisons by the ton. Still, "dare" may not be the right word for a brutal carelessness so widespread that many men do not dare do anything but trade on it. How many tons of waste go into the air every minute? How much sewage goes into the earth's once pure and flowing waters, or oil's dirty devastation is spread on the seas? How much over-killing will it take for us to come face to face with what is left of the vital innocence that has upheld the world without us up to now, like the dovekie and its Arctic pyramid of needs?

As I watched the dovekies, I saw one come in out of the water, letting itself be washed ashore with the broad sheet of foam sent in ahead of the breakers. It staggered and flopped ahead up the slope of sand beyond the water's reach and stood there. I walked up to the little bird and it made only a slight effort to get away. Its thick breast feathers were coated with oil. They were also stained with the red of its blood. Since oil fouling causes birds to lose the natural insulation of their feathers, and poisons them when they preen, I supposed that this one had been weakened and perhaps flung against a rock by the waves. I picked it up, and what a trembling there was in it, what a whirring heart! I carried it back to my car, thinking to clean the oil off later and see if I could bring it back to health, always a precarious job. But after a few minutes in the heated car the bird's blood began to flow from its breast, to my great dismay, and there seemed to be little I could do about it. I began to feel like a terrible meddler and a coward. With that I took it back to calmer waters, on the bay side of the Cape, and let it go without illusions about the cruel mother that might take care of it better than I, but I felt that my fruitless attempts to save it would be worse. I remember the little beak with its pink lining, open and threatening, as the dovekie protested my picking it up, the black eyes blinking and glistening, the feel of its heart. It was more than a small bird in mortal trouble. It had in it the greatness of its northern range. I had, I suppose, with no excuses for what I failed to do, given it back to its own latitude, to the spirit of choking, roaring waters, of skies with smoky clouds where the little auks themselves looked like smoke in the distance, and of swinging winds and draws between the ice floes, and the rivulets of spring. That bird, which had bloodied me and been so close and warm in my hand, left me on the beach to shake with the weight of human ignorance. *   *   *

THOMAS MERTON
1915-1968

From 1941 to the end of his life, Thomas Merton lived as a Catholic monk at the Abbey of Our Lady of Gethsemani near Bardstown, Kentucky. A member of the Trappist order, which strictly observes vows of silence, he nonetheless became a leading writer of his generation, publishing dozens of books of poetry, essays, religious meditations, plays and novels, as well as his well-known autobiography, The Seven Storey Mountain *(1948). Because of its exploratory rather than doctrinaire approach towards religious questions, Merton's work has appealed to a wide audience. Though he led the life of a solitary contemplative, his writing reflects a deep awareness of current political and cultural issues. In the following essay, from* Raids on the Unspeakable *(1964), his description of a rainshower at night in the woods—"this wonderful, unintelligible, perfectly innocent speech"—gradually expands into a meditation on solitude, personal freedom, and the nature of joy. In 1968, while traveling in Thailand, Merton was accidentally electrocuted.*

RAIN AND THE RHINOCEROS

Let me say this before rain becomes a utility that they can plan and distribute for money. By "they" I mean the people who cannot understand that rain is a festival, who do not appreciate its gratuity, who think that what has no price has no value, that what cannot be sold is not real, so that the only way to make something *actual* is to place it on the market. The time will come when they will sell you even your rain. At the moment it is still free, and I am in it. I celebrate its gratuity and its meaninglessness.

The rain I am in is not like the rain of cities. It fills the woods with an immense and confused sound. It covers the flat roof of the cabin and its porch with insistent and controlled rhythms. And I listen, because it reminds me again and again that the whole world runs by rhythms I have not yet learned to recognize, rhythms that are not those of the engineer.

I came up here from the monastery last night, sloshing through the cornfield, said Vespers, and put some oatmeal on the Coleman stove for supper. It boiled over while I was listening to the rain and toasting a piece of bread at the log fire. The night became very dark. The rain surrounded the whole cabin with its enormous virginal myth, a whole world of meaning, of secrecy, of silence, of rumor. Think of it: all that speech pouring down, selling nothing, judging nobody, drenching the thick mulch of dead leaves, soaking the trees, filling the gullies and crannies of the wood with water, washing out the places where men have stripped the hillside! What a thing it is to sit absolutely alone, in the

Raids on the Unspeakable (New York: New Directions, 1964).

forest, at night, cherished by this wonderful, unintelligible, perfectly innocent speech, the most comforting speech in the world, the talk that rain makes by itself all over the ridges, and the talk of the watercourses everywhere in the hollows!

Nobody started it, nobody is going to stop it. It will talk as long as it wants, this rain. As long as it talks I am going to listen.

But I am also going to sleep, because here in this wilderness I have learned how to sleep again. Here I am not alien. The trees I know, the night I know, the rain I know. I close my eyes and instantly sink into the whole rainy world of which I am a part, and the world goes on with me in it, for I am not alien to it. I am alien to the noises of cities, of people, to the greed of machinery that does not sleep, the hum of power that eats up the night. Where rain, sunlight and darkness are contemned, I cannot sleep. I do not trust anything that has been fabricated to replace the climate of woods or prairies. I can have no confidence in places where the air is first fouled and then cleansed, where the water is first made deadly and then made safe with other poisons. There is nothing in the world of buildings that is not fabricated, and if a tree gets in among the apartment houses by mistake it is taught to grow chemically. It is given a precise reason for existing. They put a sign on it saying it is for health, beauty, perspective; that it is for peace, for prosperity; that it was planted by the mayor's daughter. All of this is mystification. The city itself lives on its own myth. Instead of waking up and silently existing, the city people prefer a stubborn and fabricated dream; they do not care to be a part of the night, or to be merely of the world. They have constructed a world outside the world, against the world, a world of mechanical fictions which contemn nature and seek only to use it up, thus preventing it from renewing itself and man.

Of course the festival of rain cannot be stopped, even in the city. The woman from the delicatessen scampers along the sidewalk with a newspaper over her head. The streets, suddenly washed, became transparent and alive, and the noise of traffic becomes a plashing of fountains. One would think that urban man in a rainstorm would *have* to take account of nature in its wetness and freshness, its baptism and its renewal. But the rain brings no renewal to the city, only to tomorrow's weather, and the glint of windows in tall buildings will then have nothing to do with the new sky. All "reality" will remain somewhere inside those walls, counting itself and selling itself with fantastically complex determination. Meanwhile the obsessed citizens plunge through the rain bearing the load of their obsessions, slightly more vulnerable than before, but still only barely aware of external realities. They do not see that the streets shine beautifully, that they themselves are walking on stars and water, that they are running in skies to catch a bus or a taxi, to shelter somewhere in the press of irritated humans, the faces of advertisements and the dim, cretinous sound of unidentified music. But they must know that there is wetness abroad. Perhaps they even *feel* it. I cannot say. Their complaints are mechanical and without spirit.

Naturally no one can believe the things they say about the rain. It all implies one basic lie: *only the city is real.* That weather, not being planned, not being fabricated, is an impertinence, a wen on the visage of progress. (Just a simple little operation, and the whole mess may become relatively tolerable. Let business *make* the rain. This will give it meaning.)

Thoreau sat in *his* cabin and criticized the railways. I sit in mine and wonder about a world that has, well, progressed. I must read *Walden* again, and see if Thoreau already guessed that he was part of what he thought he could escape. But it is not a matter of "escaping." It is not even a matter of protesting very audibly. Technology is here, even in the cabin. True, the utility line is not here yet, and so G.E. is not here yet either. When the utilities and G.E. enter my cabin arm in arm it will be nobody's fault but my own. I admit it. I am not kidding anybody, even myself. I will suffer their bluff and patronizing complacencies in silence. I will let them think they know what I am doing here.

They are convinced that *I am having fun.*

This has already been brought home to me with a wallop by my Coleman lantern. Beautiful lamp: It burns white gas and sings viciously but gives out a splendid green light in which I read Philoxenos, a sixth-century Syrian hermit. Philoxenos fits in with the rain and the festival of night. Of this, more later. Meanwhile: what does my Coleman lantern tell me? (Coleman's philosophy is printed on the cardboard box which I have (guiltily) not shellacked as I was supposed to, and which I have tossed in the woodshed behind the hickory chunks.) Coleman says that the light is good, and has a reason: it *"Stretches days to give more hours of fun."*

Can't I just be in the woods without any special reason? Just being in the woods, at night, in the cabin, is something too excellent to be justified or explained! It just *is.* There are always a few people who are in the woods at night, in the rain (because if there were not the world would have ended), and I am one of them. We are not having fun, we are not "having" anything, we are not *"stretching our days,"* and if we had fun it would not be measured by hours. Though as a matter of fact that is what fun seems to be: a state of diffuse excitation that can be measured by the clock and "stretched" by an appliance.

There is no clock that can measure the speech of this rain that falls all night on the drowned and lonely forest.

Of course at three-thirty A.M. the SAC plane goes over, red light winking low under the clouds, skimming the wooded summits on the south side of the valley, loaded with strong medicine. Very strong. Strong enough to burn up all these woods and stretch our hours of fun into eternities.

And that brings me to Philoxenos, a Syrian who had fun in the sixth century, without benefit of appliances, still less of nuclear deterrents.

Philoxenos in his ninth *memra* (on poverty) to dwellers in solitude, says that there is no explanation and no justification for the solitary life, since it is without a law. To be a contemplative is therefore to be an outlaw. As was Christ. As was Paul.

One who is not "alone," says Philoxenos, has not discovered his identity. He seems to be alone, perhaps, for he experiences himself as "individual." But because he is willingly enclosed and limited by the laws and illusions of collective existence, he has no more identity than an unborn child in the womb. He is not yet conscious. He is alien to his own truth. He has senses, but he cannot use them. He has life, but no identity. To have an identity, he has to be awake, and aware. But to be awake, he has to accept vulnerability and death. Not for their own sake: not out of stoicism or despair—only for the sake of the invulnerable inner reality which we cannot recognize (which we can only *be*) but to which we awaken only when we see the unreality of our vulnerable shell. The discovery of this inner self is an act and affirmation of solitude.

Now if we take our vulnerable shell to be our true identity, if we think our mask is our true face, we will protect it with fabrications even at the cost of violating our own truth. This seems to be the collective endeavor of society: the more busily men dedicate themselves to it, the more certainly it becomes a collective illusion, until in the end we have the enormous, obsessive, uncontrollable dynamic of fabrications designed to protect mere fictitious identities—"selves," that is to say, regarded as objects. Selves that can stand back and see themselves having fun (an illusion which reassures them that they are real).

Such is the ignorance which is taken to be the axiomatic foundation of all knowledge in the human collectivity: in order to experience yourself as real, you have to suppress the awareness of your contingency, your

unreality, your state of radical need. This you do by creating an awareness of yourself as *one who has no needs that he cannot immediately
fulfill.* Basically, this is an illusion of omnipotence: an illusion which the
collectivity arrogates to itself, and consents to share with its individual
members in proportion as they submit to its more central and more rigid
fabrications.

You have needs; but if you behave and conform you can participate in
the collective power. You can then satisfy all your needs. Meanwhile, in
order to increase its power over you, the collectivity increases your needs.
It also tightens its demand for conformity. Thus you can become all the
more committed to the collective illusion in proportion to becoming
more hopelessly mortgaged to collective power.

How does this work? The collectivity informs and shapes your will to
happiness ("have fun") by presenting you with irresistible images of
yourself as you would like to be: having *fun that is so perfectly credible
that it allows no interference of conscious doubt.* In theory such a good
time can be so convincing that you are no longer aware of even a remote
possibility that it might change into something less satisfying. In practice, expensive fun always admits of a doubt, which blossoms out into
another full-blown need, which then calls for a still more credible and
more costly refinement of satisfaction, which again fails you. The end of
the cycle is despair.

Because we live in a womb of collective illusion, our freedom remains
abortive. Our capacities for joy, peace, and truth are never liberated.
They can never be used. We are prisoners of a process, a dialectic of false
promises and real deceptions ending in futility.

"The unborn child," says Philoxenos, "is already perfect and fully
constituted in his nature, with all his senses, and limbs, but he cannot
make use of them in their natural functions, because, in the womb, he
cannot strengthen or develop them for such use."

Now, since all things have their season, there is a time to be unborn.
We must begin, indeed, in the social womb. There is a time for warmth
in the collective myth. But there is also a time to be born. He who is
spiritually "born" as a mature identity is liberated from the enclosing
womb of myth and prejudice. He learns to think for himself, guided no
longer by the dictates of need and by the systems and processes designed
to create artificial needs and then "satisfy" them.

This emancipation can take two forms: first that of the active life,
which liberates itself from enslavement to necessity by considering and
serving the needs of others, without thought of personal interest or
return. And second, the contemplative life, which must not be construed as an escape from time and matter, from social responsibility and

from the life of sense, but rather, as an advance into solitude and the desert, a confrontation with poverty and the void, a renunciation of the empirical self, in the presence of death, and nothingness, in order to overcome the ignorance and error that spring from the fear of "being nothing." The man who dares to be alone can come to see that the "emptiness" and "usefulness" which the collective mind fears and condemns are necessary conditions for the encounter with truth.

It is in the desert of loneliness and emptiness that the fear of death and the need for self-affirmation are seen to be illusory. When this is faced, then anguish is not necessarily overcome, but it can be accepted and understood. Thus, in the heart of anguish are found the gifts of peace and understanding: not simply in personal illumination and liberation, but by commitment and empathy, for the contemplative must assume the universal anguish and the inescapable condition of mortal man. The solitary, far from enclosing himself in himself, becomes every man. He dwells in the solitude, the poverty, the indigence of every man.

It is in this sense that the hermit, according to Philoxenos, imitates Christ. For in Christ, God takes to Himself the solitude and dereliction of man: every man. From the moment Christ went out into the desert to be tempted, the loneliness, the temptation and the hunger of every man became the loneliness, temptation and hunger of Christ. But in return, the gift of truth with which Christ dispelled the three kinds of illusion offered him in his temptation (security, reputation and power) can become also our own truth, if we can only accept it. It is offered to us also in temptation. "You too go out into the desert," said Philoxenos, "having with you nothing of the world, and the Holy Spirit will go with you. See the freedom with which Jesus has gone forth, and go forth like Him—see where he has left the rule of men; leave the rule of the world where he has left the law, and go out with him to fight the power of error."

And where is the power of error? We find it was after all not in the city, but in *ourselves.*

Today the insights of a Philoxenos are to be sought less in the tracts of theologians than in the meditations of the existentialists and in the Theater of the Absurd. The problem of Berenger, in Ionesco's *Rhinoceros,* is the problem of the human person stranded and alone in what threatens to become a society of monsters. In the sixth century Berenger might perhaps have walked off into the desert of Scete, without too much concern over the fact that all his fellow citizens, all his friends, and even his girl Daisy, had turned into rhinoceroses.

The problem today is that there are no deserts, only dude ranches.

The desert islands are places where the wicked little characters in the

Lord of the Flies come face to face with the Lord of the Flies, form a small, tight, ferocious collectivity of painted faces, and arm themselves with spears to hunt down the last member of their group who still remembers with nostalgia the possibilities of rational discourse.

When Berenger finds himself suddenly the last human in a rhinoceros herd he looks into the mirror and says, humbly enough, "After all, man is not as bad as all that, is he?" But his world now shakes mightily with the stampede of his metamorphosed fellow citizens, and he soon becomes aware that the very stampede itself is the most telling and tragic of all arguments. For when he considers going out into the street "to try to convince them," he realizes that he "would have to learn their language." He looks in the mirror and sees that *he no longer resembles anyone*. He searches madly for a photograph of people as they were before the big change. But now humanity itself has become incredible, as well as hideous. To be the last man in the rhinoceros herd is, in fact, to be a monster.

Such is the problem which Ionesco sets us in his tragic irony: solitude and dissent become more and more impossible, more and more absurd. That Berenger finally accepts his absurdity and rushes out to challenge the whole herd only points up the futility of a commitment to rebellion. At the same time in *The New Tenant (Le Nouveau Locataire)* Ionesco portrays the absurdity of a logically consistent individualism which, in fact, is a self-isolation by the pseudo-logic of proliferating needs and possessions.

Ionesco protested that the New York production of *Rhinoceros* as a farce was a complete misunderstanding of his intention. It is a play not merely against *conformism* but about *totalitarianism*. The rhinoceros is not an amiable beast, and with him around the fun ceases and things begin to get serious. Everything has to make sense and be totally useful to the totally obsessive operation. At the same time Ionesco was criticized for not giving the audience "something positive" to take away with them, instead of just "refusing the human adventure." (Presumably "rhinoceritis" is the latest in human adventure!) He replied: "They [the spectators] leave in a void—and that was my intention. It is the business of a free man to pull himself out of this void by his own power and not by the power of other people!" In this Ionesco comes very close to Zen and to Christian eremitism.

"In all the cities of the world, it is the same," says Ionesco. "The universal and modern man is the man in a rush (i.e. a rhinoceros), a man who has no time, who is a prisoner of necessity, who cannot understand that *a thing might perhaps be without usefulness;* nor does he understand that, at bottom, it is the useful that may be a useless and back-breaking burden. If one does not understand the usefulness of the useless and the uselessness of the useful, one cannot understand art. And a country where art is not understood is a country of slaves and robots. . . ." (*Notes et Contre Notes,* p. 129) Rhinoceritis, he adds, is the sickness that lies in wait "for those who *have lost the sense and the taste for solitude.*"

The love of solitude is sometimes condemned as "hatred of our fellow men." But is this true? If we push our analysis of collective thinking a little further we will find that the dialectic of power and need, of submission and satisfaction, ends by being a dialectic of hate. Collectivity needs not only to absorb everyone it can, but also implicitly to hate and destroy whoever cannot be absorbed. Paradoxically, one of the needs of collectivity is to reject certain classes, or races, or groups, in order to strengthen its own self-awareness by hating them instead of absorbing them.

Thus the solitary cannot survive unless he is capable of loving everyone, without concern for the fact that he is likely to be regarded by all of them as a traitor. Only the man who has fully attained his own spiritual identity can live without the need to kill, and without the need of a doctrine that permits him to do so with a good conscience. There will always be a place, says Ionesco, *"for those isolated consciences who have stood up for the universal conscience"* as against the mass mind. But their place is solitude. They have no other. Hence it is the solitary person (whether in the city or in the desert) who does mankind the inestimable favor of reminding it of its true capacity for maturity, liberty and peace.

It sounds very much like Philoxenos to me.

And it sounds like what the rain says. We still carry this burden of illusion because we do not dare to lay it down. We suffer all the needs that society demands we suffer, because if we do not have these needs we lose our "usefulness" in society—the usefulness of suckers. We fear to be alone, and to be ourselves, and so to remind others of the truth that is in them.

"I will not make you such rich men as have need of many things," said Philoxenos (putting the words on the lips of Christ), "but I will make you true rich men who have need of nothing. Since it is not he who has many possessions that is rich, but he who has no needs." Obviously, we shall always have *some* needs. But only he who has the simplest and most natural needs can be considered to be without needs, since the only needs he has are real ones, and the real ones are not hard to fulfill if one is a free man!

The rain has stopped. The afternoon sun slants through the pine trees: and how those useless needles smell in the clear air!

A dandelion, long out of season, has pushed itself into bloom between the smashed leaves of last summer's day lilies. The valley resounds with the totally uninformative talk of creeks and wild water.

Then the quails begin their sweet whistling in the wet bushes. Their noise is absolutely useless, and so is the delight I take in it. There is nothing I would rather hear, not because it is a better noise than other noises, but because it is the voice of the present moment, the present festival.

Yet even here the earth shakes. Over at Fort Knox the Rhinoceros is having fun.

JOHN GRAVES
B. 1920

Rivers are always a kind of intersection. Paddling downstream one glides over the element of waterfowl and fish, while passing a shore that may be marked both by present-day human settlements and by the tumbledown remnants of long gone lives. In 1957 John Graves set out down the Brazos River, which flows southeast across Texas from the New Mexico border to the Gulf of Mexico, because he wanted to record such a community of fluid association before it was destroyed by a dam. Good-bye to a River (1959) is thus, like many works by twentieth-century nature writers, at once a celebration and an elegy. For Graves the river's voice was amplified by the spray of human conversation hanging natu-rally above its current until, with the completion of the dam, that too was stilled.

From GOODBYE TO A RIVER

Elm stinks, wherefore literal farmers give it a grosser name, but it makes fine lasting coals. That morning I was up before dawn to blow away the ashes from the orange-velvet embers underneath, and to build

Goodbye to a River (New York: Knopf, 1960).

more fire on them with twigs and leaves and brittle sticks of dead cotton-wood. I huddled over it in the cold, still, graying darkness and watched coffee water seethe at the edges of a little charred pot licked by flame, and heard the horned owl stop that deceptively gentle five-noted comment he casts on the night. The geese at the island's head began to talk among themselves, then to call as they rose to go to pastures and peanut fields, and night-flushed bobwhites started whistling *where-you? where-you?* to one another somewhere above the steep dirt river bank. Drinking coffee with honey in it and canned milk, smoking a pipe that had the sweetness pipes only have in cold quiet air, I felt good if a little scratchy-eyed, having gone to sleep the night before struck with the romance of stars and firelight, with the flaps open and only the blanket over me, to wake at two thirty chilled through.

On top of the food box alligator-skin corrugations of frost had formed, and with the first touch of the sun the willows began to whisper as frozen leaves loosed their hold and fell side-slipping down through the others that were still green. Titmice called, and flickers and a redbird, and for a moment, on a twig four feet from my face, a chittering kinglet jumped around alternately hiding and flashing the scarlet of its crown. . . . I sat and listened and watched while the world woke up, and drank three cups of the syrupy coffee, better I thought than any I'd ever tasted, and smoked two pipes.

You run a risk of thinking yourself an ascetic when you enjoy, with that intensity, the austere facts of fire and coffee and tobacco and the sound and feel of country places. You aren't, though. In a way you're more of a sensualist than a fat man washing down sauerbraten and dumplings with heavy beer while a German band plays and a plump blonde kneads his thigh. . . . You've shucked off the gross delights, and those you have left are few, sharp, and strong. But they're sensory. Even Thoreau, if I remember right a passage or so on his cornbread, was guilty, though mainly he was a real ascetic.

Real ones shouldn't care. They ought to be able to live on pâté and sweet peaches and roast suckling pig or alternatively on cheese and garlic in a windmill or the scraps that housewives have thrown in begging bowls. Groceries and shelter should matter only as fuel and frame for life, and life as energy for thought or beyond-communion or (Old Man Goodnight has to fit somewhere, and a fraught executive or two I've known, and maybe Davis Birdsong hurling his bulldozer against the tough cedar brush in a torn shirt and denim pants, coughing yellow flu sputum while the December rain pelts him, not caring) for action.

But I hadn't set up as an ascetic, anyhow. I sat for a long time savoring the privilege of being there, and didn't overlay the taste of the coffee with any other food. A big red-brown butterfly sat spread on the cotton-wood log my ax was stuck in, warming itself in the sun. I watched until it flew stiffly away, then got up and followed, for no good reason except that the time seemed to have come to stir and I wanted a closer look at the island than I'd gotten the evening before.

It was shaped like an attenuated teardrop or the cross section of an airplane's wing, maybe three quarters of a mile long and 100 yards or so wide at its upper, thicker end. Its foundation everywhere appeared to be a heavy deposit of the multicolored gravel, and its flat top except for a few high dunes of the padding sand was eight or ten feet above the present level of the river. All around, it dropped off steeply, in spots directly to the water, in others to beaches, and toward the pointed tail the willows and weeds stood rank. I rooted about there and found nothing but coon tracks and a few birds still sleepy and cold on their roosts, but, emerging among cockleburs above a beach by the other channel, scared four ducks off a quiet eddy. I'd left the gun in the tent; shots from here and there under the wide sky's bowl reminded me that busier hunters than I were finding game.

Let them. I considered that maybe in the evening I'd crouch under a bush at the island's upper end and put out sheets of notepaper on the off chance that more geese would come, and the off-off chance that if they did they'd feel brotherly toward notepaper. You can interest them some-times in newspapers.

And maybe I wouldn't.

The shores on either side of the river from the island were dirt and steep, twenty feet high, surmounted by pecans and oaks with the bare sky of fields or pastures beyond. They seemed separate from the island; it was big enough, with a strong enough channel on either side, to seem to have a kind of being of its own distinct from that of the banks—a sand and willow and cottonwood and driftwood biome—though in dry times doubtless there would be only one channel and no island, but just a great bar spreading out below the right bank.

Jays, killdeers, wrens, cardinals, woodpeckers . . . With minute and amateurish interest, I found atop a scoop in the base of a big, drifted, scorched tree trunk five little piles of fox dung, a big owl's puke ball full of hair and rat skulls, and three fresher piles of what had to be coon droppings, brown and small, shaped like a dog's or a human's.

Why, intrigued ignorance asked, did wild things so often choose to stool on rocks, stumps, and other elevations?

Commonsense replied: Maybe for the view.

On the flat beach at the head of the island the night's geese had laid down a texture of crisscrossed toe-prints. Elsewhere, in dry sand, I found little pointed diggings an inch in diameter and four to five inches deep, much like those an armadillo makes in grassland but with no tracks beside them. A bird? A land-foraging crawfish? Another puzzle for my ignorance, underlined now by the clear note of the unknown sad-whistling bird from a willow a few steps from me. He wouldn't show himself, and when I eased closer said irascibly: *Heap, heap!* and fluttered out the other side. . . .

The trouble was, I *was* ignorant. Even in that country where I belonged, my ken of natural things didn't include a little bird that went *heap-heap* and

— — —, — — —,

and a few moronic holes in the sand. Or a million other matters worth the kenning.

I grew up in a city near there—more or less a city, anyhow, a kind of spreading imposition on the prairies—that was waked from a dozing cow-town background by a standard boom after the First World War and is still, civic-souled friends tell me, bowling right along. It was a good enough place, not too big then, and a mile or so away from where I lived, along a few side streets and across a boulevard and a golf course, lay woods and pastures and a blessed river valley where the stagnant Trinity writhed beneath big oaks. In retrospect, it seems we spent more time there than we did on pavements, though maybe it's merely that remembrance of that part is sharper. There were rabbits and squirrels to hunt, and doves and quail and armadillos and foxes and skunks. A few deer ran the woods, and one year, during a drouth to the west, big wolves. Now it's mostly subdivisions, and even then it lay fallow because it was someone's real-estate investment. The fact that caretakers were likely to converge on us blaspheming at the sound of a shot or a shout, scattering us to brush, only made the hunting and the fishing a bit saltier. I knew one fellow who kept a permanent camp there in a sumac thicket, with a log squat-down hut and a fireplace and all kinds of food and utensils hidden in tin-lined holes in the ground, and none of the caretakers ever found it. Probably they worried less than we thought; there weren't many of us.

I had the Brazos, too, and South Texas, where relatives lived, and my adults for the most part were good people who took me along on country expeditions when they could. In terms of the outdoors, I and the others like me weren't badly cheated as such cheatings go nowadays, but we were cheated nevertheless. We learned quite a lot, but not enough.

Instead of learning to move into country, as I think underneath we wanted, we learned mostly how to move onto it in the old crass Anglo-Saxon way, in search of edible or sometimes just mortal quarry. We did a lot of killing, as kids will, and without ever being told that it was our flat duty, if duty exists, to know all there was to know about the creatures we killed.

Hunting and fishing are the old old entry points into nature for men, and not bad ones either, but as standardly practiced these days, for the climactic ejaculation of city tensions, they don't go very deep. They aren't thoughtful; they hold themselves too straitly to their purpose. Even for my quail-hunting uncles in South Texas, good men, good friends to me, all smaller birds of hedge and grass were "chee-chees," vermin, confusers of dogs' noses. . . . And if, with kids' instinctive thrustingness, we picked up a store of knowledge about small things that lived under logs and how the oriole builds its nest, there was no one around to consolidate it for us. Our knowledge, if considerable, remained random.

This age, of course, is unlikely to start breeding people who have the organic kinship to nature that the Comanches had, or even someone like Mr. Charlie Goodnight. For them every bush, every bird's cheep, every cloud bank had not only utilitarian but mystical meaning; it was all an extension of their sensory systems, an antenna as rawly receptive as a snail's. Even if their natural world still existed, which it doesn't, you'd have to snub the whole world of present men to get into it that way.

Nor does it help to be born in the country. As often as not these days, countrymen know as little as we others do about those things. They come principally of the old hardheaded tradition that moved onto the country instead of into it. For every Charles Goodnight there were several dozen Ezra Shermans, a disproportion that has bred itself down through the generations. Your standard country lore about animals—about the nasal love life of the possum, or the fabled hoop snake—is picturesque rather than accurate, anthropocentric rather than understanding.

But Charlie Goodnight and the Ezra Shermans and their children and grandchildren all combined have burned out and chopped out and plowed out and grazed out and killed out a good part of that natural world they knew, or didn't know, and we occupy ourselves mainly, it sometimes seems, in finishing the job. The rosy preindustrial time is past when the humanism of a man like Thoreau (*was* it humanism?) could still theorize in terms of natural harmony. Humanism has to speak in the terms of extant human beings. The terms of today's human beings are air conditioners and suburbs and water impoundments overlaying whole countrysides, and the hell with nature except maybe in a cross-sectional park here and there. In our time quietness and sun and leaves and bird song and all the multitudinous lore of the natural world have to come second or third, because whether we wanted to be born there or not, we were all born into the prickly machine-humming place that man has hung for himself above that natural world.

Where, tell me, is the terror and wonder of an elephant, now that they can be studied placid in every zoo, and any office-dwelling sport with a recent lucky break on the market can buy himself one to shoot through telescopic sights with a cartridge whose ballistics hold a good fileful of recorded science's findings? With a box gushing refrigerated air (or warmed, seasonally depending) into a sealed house and another box flashing loud bright images into jaded heads, who gives a rat's damn for things that go bump in the night? With possible death by blast or radiation staring at us like a buzzard, why should we sweat ourselves over where the Eskimo curlew went?

The wonder is that a few people do still sweat themselves, that the tracks of short varmints on a beach still have an audience. A few among the audience still know something, too. If they didn't, one wouldn't have to feel so cheated, not knowing as much. . . . Really knowing, I mean—from childhood up and continuously, with all of it a flavor in you . . . Not just being able to make a little seem a lot; there is enough of that around. I can give you as much book data about the home life of the yellow-breasted chat as the next man can. Nor do I mean vague mystic feelings of unity with Comanche and Neanderthal as one wanders the depleted land, gun at the ready, a part of the long flow of man's hunting compulsion. I mean *knowing.*

So that what one does in time, arriving a bit late at an awareness of the swindling he got—from no one, from the times—is to make up the shortage as best he may, to try to tie it all together for himself by reading and adult poking. But adult poking is never worth a quarter as much as kid poking, not in those real terms. There's never the time for that whole interest later, or ever quite the pure and subcutaneous receptiveness, either.

I mean, too—obviously—if you care. I know that the whicker of a plover in the September sky doesn't touch all other men in their bowels as it touches me, and that men whom it doesn't touch at all can be good men. But it touches me. And I care about knowing what it is, and—if I can—why. * * *

WILLIAM WARNER
B. 1920

When William Warner wrote Beautiful Swimmers *(1976) he had already achieved distinguished careers in the Foreign Service, the Peace Corps, and the Smithsonian Institution. Like his own professional life, his book covers a broad range: "Watermen, Crabs and the Chesapeake Bay." Much of the best nature writing, rather than treating "nature" in an abstract or exclusive sense, includes human beings in the drama of a place on earth, recognizes the value of non-human life within our history and our spiritual life.* Beautiful Swimmers *celebrates both the Atlantic blue crab and the "watermen" who pursue it in the world's most productive (though now endangered) crabbing grounds. It won the 1976 Pulitzer Prize for nonfiction.*

From BEAUTIFUL SWIMMERS:
WATERMEN, CRABS, AND THE CHESAPEAKE BAY

BEAUTIFUL SWIMMER

The Atlantic blue crab is known to scientists as *Callinectes sapidus* Rathbun. It is very well named. *Callinectes* is Greek for beautiful swimmer. *Sapidus,* of course, means tasty or savory in Latin. Rathbun is the late Dr. Mary J. Rathbun of the Smithsonian Institution, who first gave the crab its specific name.

Dr. Rathbun, known as Mary Jane to her Smithsonian colleagues, has often been called the dean of American carcinologists, as experts in crabs and other crustaceans are properly termed. Before her death in 1943, Mary Jane identified and described over 998 new species of crabs, an absolute record in the annals of carcinology. In only one case did she

Beautiful Swimmers: Watermen, Crabs, and the Chesapeake Bay (Boston: Little, Brown, 1976).

choose to honor culinary qualities. History has borne out the wisdom of her choice. No crab in the world has been as much caught or eagerly consumed as *sapidus.*

Whether or not *Callinectes* may justly be considered beautiful depends on whom you ask. Scientists tend to avoid aesthetic judgments. Many lay observers think the blue crab frightening or even ugly in appearance. They do not understand its popular name and often ask what is blue about a blue crab. The question betrays a basic ignorance of truly adult specimens. Most people see the species in the smaller back bays of the Atlantic coast; crabs never grow very large in these waters, since they are quite salty throughout and lack the brackish middle salinities that assure optimum growth in the Chesapeake and other large estuaries. The barrier beach islands and their back bays may provide our most dramatic seascapes, but they are not the place to see the pleasing hues of well-grown crabs. Large males have a deep lapis lazuli coloration along their arms, more on the undersides than on top, extending almost to the points of the claws. In full summer the walking and swimming legs of both sexes take on a lighter blue, which artists would probably call cerulean. Females, as we have said before, decorate their claws with a bright orange-red, which color is seen only at the extreme tips among males. Since females wave their claws in and out during courtship, it may be that this dimorphism is a sexually advantageous adaptation. If so, it is probably a very important one, since the blue crab is believed to be somewhat color blind.

Those who most appreciate *Callinectes'* beauty, I think, are crabbers and other people who handle crabs professionally. Some years ago in the month of October, I visited a clean and well-managed crab house in Bellhaven, North Carolina, a pleasant town on Pamlico Sound's Pungo River. In the company of the plant owner's wife I watched dock handlers load the cooking crates with good catches of prime sooks. As they should be at that time of year, the sooks were fully hard and fat, although relatively recently moulted. Their abdomens were therefore pure white, with a lustrous alabaster quality. (Later in the intermoult period crab abdomens take on the glazed and slightly stained look of aging horses' teeth; often they are also spotted with "rust.") The carapaces or top shells were similarly clean. Thus, gazing down at the mass of three thousand or more crabs in each crate, we saw a rich and fragmented palette of olive greens, reds, varying shades of blue and marble white.

"Now, tell me, did ever you see such beautiful crabs?" the owner's wife asked, quite spontaneously.

"Prettiest crabs I seen all year," a black dockhand volunteered.

I had to agree. Anyone would.

Still, as is often said, beauty is in the eyes of the beholder. We can but little imagine the sheer terror which the sight of a blue crab must inspire in a fat little killifish or a slow-moving annelid worm. The crab's claw arms will be held out at the ready, waving slowly in the manner of a shadow boxer. Walking legs will be slightly doubled, ready for tigerlike springs, and the outer maxillipeds—literally "jaw feet" or two small limbs in front of the crab's mouth—will flutter distractingly. The effect must be mesmeric, such as the praying mantis is said to possess over its insect victims. Perhaps not quite so hypnotic but of extreme importance to the crab in this situation are its eyes. Like most crustaceans, the blue crab has stalked eyes. When a crab is at peace with the world, they are but two little round beads. On the prowl, they are elevated and look like stubby horns. As with insects, the eyes are compound. This means that they possess thousands of facets—multiple lenses, if you prefer—which catch and register a mosaic of patterns. More importantly, simple laboratory tests seem to indicate that the stalked and compound eyes give the blue crab almost three-hundred-and-sixty-degree vision. Those who with ungloved hand try to seize a crab with raised eyestalks from the rear will have this capability most forcefully impressed on them. If at all, the blue crab may have a forward blind spot at certain ranges in the small space directly between its eyes. Perhaps this accounts for the crab's preference for shifting lateral motion, from which it is easier to correct this deficiency, rather than rigid forward and back movement. Whatever the answer, a blue crab sees very well. Although colors may be blurred, the crab is extremely sensitive to shapes and motions. It has good range, too, at least for a crustacean. I have frequently tried standing still in a boat as far as fifteen feet from cornered individuals and then raising an arm quickly. Instantly the crabs respond, claws flicked up to the combat position.

Beauty, then, to some. Piercing eyes and a fearful symmetry, like William Blake's tiger, to others. But there are no such divided views on *Callinectes'* swimming ability. Specialists and lay observers alike agree that the blue crab has few peers in this respect. Some carcinologists believe that a few larger portunids or members of the swimming crab family—*Portunus pelagicus,* for example, which ranges from the eastern Mediterranean to Tahiti—might be better swimmers. But from what I have seen of the family album, I rather suspect that these crabs would fare best in distance events in any aquatic olympiad, while the Atlantic blue and some of its close relatives might take the sprints.

Certainly the blue crab is superbly designed for speed in the water. Its body is shallow, compressed and fusiform, or tapering at both ends. Although strong, its skeletal frame is very light, as anyone who picks up a cast-off shell readily appreciates. At the lateral extremities are wickedly tapered spines, the Pitot tubes, one might say, of the crab's supersonic airframe. (These spines grow very sharp in large crabs; good-sized specimens falling to a wooden deck occasionally impale themselves on them, quivering like the target knives of a sideshow artist.) This lateral adaptation is as it should be, of course, for an animal given to sideways travel.·

Remarkable as this airframe body structure may be, it is the blue crab's propulsion units that are most responsible for its swimming success. These are the fifth or last pair of appendages, most commonly known as the swimming legs. Beginning at their fourth segments, the swimming legs become progressively thinner and flatter. The seventh or final segment is completely flat and rounded like a paddle, ideally shaped for rapid sculling. Equally remarkable is the articulation of the swimming legs. Even knowledgeable observers are surprised to learn that a blue crab can bend them above and behind its back until the paddles touch. They are unaware of this extreme flexibility, no doubt, because the occasions to observe it are rather rare. One such is to steal up on a pair of courting crabs. Prominent in the male blue crab's repertoire of courtship signals is one involving the swimming legs. A randy Jimmy will wave them sensuously and synchronously from side to side above his back, with the paddle surfaces facing forward, as though tracing little question marks and parentheses in the water. Females show appreciation by rapidly waving their claws or rocking side to side on their walking legs.

But courting gestures are not the principal function of the powerfully muscled and flexible swimming legs. They mainly serve to propel the crab, of course, not only sideways, but also forward or backward, not to mention helicopter-style rotation which permits a crab to hover like a hawk. Most of the time all we see of these actions is a blur. As those who try wading in shallows with a dip net know, a startled blue crab bursts off the bottom in a cloud of mud or sand and darts away with the speed of a fish. Such rapid all-directional movement is of great advantage to swimming crabs. Consider the unfortunate lobster. Its rigid and overlapping abdominal or "tail" segments restrict it to dead ahead or astern. Of the two directions, it seems to prefer swimming backward. Such inclination coupled with dim vision is probably why lobsters are always bumping into things. But again this is probably as it should be. It is to the lobster's advantage to back into corners. Safely positioned in a rocky niche, the lobster is well-nigh invulnerable to frontal attack, thanks to its enormously powerful claws. By contrast, open water speed and burying in soft bottoms are the swimming crabs' main escape tactics.

Less recognized are the blue crab's walking abilities. As befits an arthropod, *Callinectes* has many well-articulated joints. It has no less than seventy, in fact, in its five principal pairs of limbs. Three of these pairs are the walking legs; they permit the crab to scuttle along very nicely both on dry land and on sandy or muddy bottoms. It is true that a blue crab does not like dry land locomotion, yet it does rather well in emergencies. Each year the city of Crisfield, "Seafood Capital of the Nation," sponsors an event known as the National Hard Crab Derby, certainly one of our nation's more bizarre folk celebrations. At the crack of a gun, crabs are unceremoniously dumped from a forty-stall starting gate on to a sixteen-foot board track, very slightly inclined. Thus stimulated, blue crabs that are not stopped by distractions will scurry down the course in eight to twelve seconds. Terrestial species like the nimble ghost crab, for whom running is a principal defense measure, do better, of course. Still, the Derby organizers, who have matched many species over the years, consider the blue crab's time entirely respectable. For those who cannot attend the Derby, a good way to see crabs moving out of water is to visit a loading dock. Crawling is scarcely the word for what happens when lively individuals escape from a barrel. They streak across the dock in rapid bursts, nine times out of ten in the direction of the water. Handlers have to jump to catch them.

With such advantages do blue crabs go about their life, which is an almost continual hunt for food. They will hunt, in fact, at the least opportunity and with great patience. A good place to observe their patience is at the ferry dock at Tylerton on Smith Island. The watermen here have the habit of dumping their worn-out boat engines right off the dock, asking any who criticize the practice what earthly purpose is served in lugging the heavy things any farther. Although their wives may complain about the impression created on visitors, the local marine fauna love the old engine blocks. Minnows and the fry of larger fish swarm through these rusty castles, swimming in and out of their numerous turrets and vaulted chambers. As might be expected, crabs are attracted. They hold themselves poised in the water, hovering perfectly, with arms rigidly extended. If the tide is not strong, it is another excellent opportunity to appreciate swimming leg flexibility; each leg can easily be seen whirling in medium-speed helicopter rotation, with the paddles serving as the variable pitch rotor blades. When choice minnows present themselves, of course, the crabs dart at them. They usually miss. But being mostly juveniles, they happily try again and again. I have watched this phenomenon at length and often, to the point, I am sure, that the Tylertonians think me strange.

Older crabs are said to be too wise to engage in such shenanigans; they prefer to hunt live prey by burying themselves lightly in sand or mud and seizing by surprise. We cannot say, however, what any blue crab may do in a pinch. Dr. Austin Williams of the National Marine Fisheries Service, an expert who has recently published a definitive reappraisal of the genus *Callinectes,* tells of a singular occurrence which involved three-inch or virtually adult crabs, since at this length blue crabs are but one or two moults away from legal catch size.

"I was working down at the University of North Carolina's Marine Laboratory in Morehead City, and we had just built a series of experimental ponds," Dr. Williams recalls. "The ponds were new, with clay liners, and no established fauna to speak of. Not long after introducing the crabs, I was surprised to see them gathering in numbers near the outlets of the pipes supplying water to each pond. The crabs were highly agitated, stabbing away at nothing that I could see. On further investigation we found that our pumped water was not yet saline enough. We were breeding mosquitos, it seems. The crabs were actually snapping at mosquito larvae with their claws."

It was impossible to see if the crabs gained anything from this exercise. Dr. Williams does not rule out the possibility, since the crabs kept at it tirelessly. "Anyway, we decided we were very bad husbandmen to have our crabs doing this," he says. "They must have been nearly starving." Happily, the ponds soon produced more substantial fare, and the crabs were eventually seen to stop snapping at nothing.

How often crabs hunt and kill each other is a matter of considerable debate. Throughout history, the world has viewed crabs as unpleasant and bellicose animals. "Crab" is synonymous with a nasty or complaining disposition in a great many languages. Both *cancer* and *karkinos,* the Latin and Greek forms respectively, have been borrowed to describe the world's most deadly disease. Thus cancer and carcinogens, much to the annoyance of carcinologists who are forever receiving letters from medical libraries asking what stage of the disease they are investigating. From time to time *Crustaceana,* the International Journal of Crustacean Research, suggests a change to "crustaceologist," but nothing has come of this.

Most crabbers believe the crab's bad name is not fully warranted. Opinions vary, however. "Who knows?" asks "Chas" Howard of Crisfield's Maryland Crabmeat Company. "Only thing I know is they can crawl, swim and bite like hell."

"Oh, if they're hungry enough, they fight," Grant Corbin has told me. "Get too many crowded together and that's bad, too. You remember the day we went out in June getting pots half full, with maybe ten to twenty crabs? Well, then you remember there weren't neither dead one. More than that, though, and they start beating on each other."

"Undoubtedly, crowding is a big factor, as in the crab floats," says

Gordon Wheatley, an experienced crab scraper who is also principal of Tangier Island's combined grade and high school. "But sometimes crabs are just plain belligerent for no reason. Nothing within clawshot is safe."

Beyond fighting, cannibalism per se is certainly not thought to be a favored practice among blue crabs. No one has ever seen one healthy hard blue crab purposely set out to eat another in its entirety. But let a fighting crab get a walking leg or other choice morsel from one of his brothers and he will of course eat it, provided other crabs do not first steal it from him. In nature a crab that has lost a limb has an excellent chance to escape. The nearby crab community invariably swarms around the victor, who will be hard put to defend his prize. The loser is thus ignored. He or she is free to wander off and will easily grow another limb by means of a remarkable crustacean attribute known as autogeny. (The opposite, autotomy, or dropping off the limb at the socket in the first place, is done even more easily.) This is not the case, however, within the restrictions of a crab float. Quite the contrary, a floated crab with a missing claw or other disadvantage attracts further attacks. Eventually it may be killed and consumed. Thus it happens, a cannibalism of opportunity.

Also arguing against complete cannibalism—necrophagism, I suppose I should say—is the blue crab's aversion to dead of the same species. Crabbers are unanimous in their opinion that a dead crab repels live individuals, as has been repeatedly demonstrated in crab pots. "No doubt about it," says Captain Ernest Kitching of Ewell. "Crabs has got more sense. I wouldn't want to go crawl into a place with dead people, would you?"

Ask the question often enough and you begin to get a guarded and qualified consensus. Persons who know the blue crab best say that it does not normally eat its own kind or go around spoiling for a fight at every opportunity. But given an emergency or crowded artificial conditions, it will. Crowding, in fact, can even touch off wild and indiscriminate fighting under natural conditions. I had an excellent opportunity to observe such combat late one August while driving down a doubtful road on the lonely peninsula in the Dorchester marshes known as Bishop's Head. In spite of difficulties in keeping to the muddy tracks, my attention was drawn to great numbers of *Uca pugnax,* or the mudbank fiddler crab, scurrying across the road. In an adjoining creek the water continually boiled with sizeable surface explosions. The disturbance, I thought, was nothing less than a school of wayward blues or more probably spawning rockfish. Quickly I began to think of assembling my fishing rod.

But, stopping the car and getting out, I was immediately aware that fish were not the prime cause of the commotion. What had happened was this. An unusually strong spring tide had all but emptied the creek, leaving largely dry its steep five-foot banks, which were riddled with crab burrows. The impression created was of an old fashioned high-walled bathtub with three quarters of the water let out. Conditions were obviously too extreme for the little mud fiddlers, who even less than their cousin *Uca pugilator,* or the sand fiddler, cannot stand too much drying out. Undoubtedly the fiddlers were marching across the road in search of more water and a calmer venue. But more fascinating than the fiddlers' retreat was the scene in the remaining sluiceway of water, which was very clear and not more than four feet wide and a foot or two deep. Too many large blue crabs had come far up this creek, as they commonly do in marsh creeks in August to mate, and now it offered them too little space. Quite simply, the crabs were getting in each other's way. Courtship practices undoubtedly further aggravated the situation, this being the peak mating period. At courting time male blue crabs show some degree of territoriality, mainly by exhibiting a threat posture, or holding their arms out fully extended in a straight line with the claws slightly open. Between bumping into each other and threat postures that failed to convey their message, therefore, the crabs fought hard and frequently. Being generally excited, they also lunged at anything that moved in the water. Small boils punctuated by a spray of tiny silver minnows broke the surface whenever a partially buried crab jumped at live prey. Larger boils came when crabs met head-on. For the most part they sought to avoid each other, backpedaling and sidestepping, claws at the ready, very much as good boxers bob and weave in the ring. But soon, or at least every ten seconds, little volcanos erupted as one or another crab got cornered and elected to fight. Most often when the mud settled and the water cleared, one of the combatants had the limb of another in its claws. Within seconds came larger eruptions as every crab within sight zeroed in to steal the prize.

Just as insects and a glaring sun began to dictate departure, I saw a female with claws folded into the submissive posture moving carefully to avoid all possible encounters. She was of good size, six inches or better, with the clean shell of grayish cast that is a sign of recent moulting, a sook in buckram condition, in other words. Being unsure of her still weak muscles, she wisely avoided the general fray. At one point, however, her caution went too far. She found herself half out of water behind a mudball cemented with weeds. A rusty looking little male—two-thirds her size, but hard and fat—suddenly materialized on the other side of the mudball with thoughts other than courtship obviously on his mind. Both crabs then tested the obstacle with their claws for firmness. Satisfied with its consistency, the male started to crawl up and over it. Immediately the sook climbed backward out of the water a full three feet up the steep bank and settled into a cavity excavated at full tide. There she sat motionless in the broiling sun for a long time, watching me and the little male. I was clearly the lesser of two evils, being close enough to touch her. Only when the male was out of sight did she climb down and re-enter the water. Instantly she buried herself in a quiet corner, until only her eyestalks were visible.

Blue crabs hate direct sunlight and cannot long tolerate it. Loose in a boat, they always run for the shade. The sook's evasive action therefore struck me as remarkable. I do not really know how long it lasted. It seemed like five minutes. I received about six mosquito and two green fly bites, in any event, having remained motionless so as not to scare the crab. As I finally left, the creek water continued to boil unabated. The mysteries of autotomy and autogeny would be sorely tested there, I thought to myself. * * *

FARLEY MOWAT
B. 1921

One of Canada's most popular writers, Farley Mowat is a gifted story-teller whose material comes in large part from his own experiences as an naturalist and anthropologist. His work has included such juvenile books as The Dog That Wouldn't Be *(1957) and* Owls in the Family *(1961), popular histories such as* Westviking: The Ancient Norse in Greenland and North America *(1965), and short stories (*The Snow Walker, *1975). His best-known work,* Never Cry Wolf *(1963), is an account of his misadventures as an Arctic field biologist for the Dominion Wildlife Service and has become a classic in the field. Often unashamedly an-thropomorphic, it sharply satirizes governmental and scientific bureauc-racy and is one of the first books to paint a sympathetic, even affection-ate portrait of the wolf. The chapter excerpted here dramatizes Mowat's process of self-education among these animals, which eventually results in his determination to "know the wolves, not for what they were sup-posed to be but for what they actually were."*

In his work Mowat has focused primarily on the Arctic, specifically on its wildlife and native peoples and their mistreatment at the hands of government and industry. In his later books—A Whale for the Killing *(1972)*, The Great Betrayal: Arctic Canada Now *(1976)*, And No Birds Sang *(1979)—his sympathy for threatened species and cultures has been expressed in an increasingly angry and cynical voice. But in such works as* People of the Deer *(1952)—based upon two years of living among the Ihalmuit caribou hunters—he achieves a balance between admiration and realism, capturing both the beauty and dignity of their way of life and the hardship and suffering inherent in it.*

From Never Cry Wolf

The lack of sustained interest which the big male wolf had displayed toward me was encouraging enough to tempt me to visit the den again the next morning; but this time, instead of the shotgun and the hatchet (I still retained the rifle, pistol and hunting knife) I carried a high-powered periscopic telescope and a tripod on which to mount it.

It was a fine sunny morning with enough breeze to keep the mosquito vanguard down. When I reached the bay where the esker was, I chose a prominent knoll of rock some four hundred yards from the den, behind which I could set up my telescope so that its objective lenses peered over the crest, but left me in hiding. Using consummate fieldcraft, I approached the chosen observation point in such a manner that the wolves could not possibly have seen me and, since the wind was from them to me, I was assured that they would have had no suspicion of my arrival.

When all was in order, I focused the telescope; but to my chagrin I could see no wolves. The magnification of the instrument was such that I could almost distinguish the individual grains of sand in the esker; yet, though I searched every inch of it for a distance of a mile on each side of the den, I could find no indication that wolves were about, or had ever been about. By noon, I had a bad case of eyestrain and a worse one of cramps, and I had almost concluded that my hypothesis of the previous day was grievously at fault and that the "den" was just a fortuitous hole in the sand.

This was discouraging, for it had begun to dawn on me that all of the intricate study plans and schedules which I had drawn up were not going to be of much use without a great deal of co-operation on the part of the wolves. In country as open and as vast as this one was, the prospects of

Never Cry Wolf (Boston: Little, Brown, 1963).

getting within visual range of a wolf except by the luckiest of accidents (and I had already had more than my ration of these) were negligible. I realized that if this was not a wolves' den which I had found, I had about as much chance of locating the actual den in this faceless wilderness as I had of finding a diamond mine.

Glumly I went back to my unproductive survey through the telescope. The esker remained deserted. The hot sand began sending up heat waves which increased my eyestrain. By 2:00 P.M. I had given up hope. There seemed no further point in concealment, so I got stiffly to my feet and prepared to relieve myself.

Now it is a remarkable fact that a man, even though he may be alone in a small boat in mid-ocean, or isolated in the midst of the trackless forest, finds that the very process of unbuttoning causes him to become peculiarly sensitive to the possibility that he may be under observation. At this critical juncture none but the most self-assured of men, no matter how certain he may be of his privacy, can refrain from casting a surreptitious glance around to reassure himself that he really is alone.

To say I was chagrined to discover I was *not* alone would be an understatement; for sitting directly behind me, and not twenty yards away, were the missing wolves.

They appeared to be quite relaxed and comfortable, as if they had been sitting there behind my back for hours. The big male seemed a trifle bored; but the female's gaze was fixed on me with what I took to be an expression of unabashed and even prurient curiosity.

The human psyche is truly an amazing thing. Under almost any other circumstances I would probably have been panic-stricken, and I think few would have blamed me for it. But these were not ordinary circumstances and my reaction was one of violent indignation. Outraged, I turned my back on the watching wolves and with fingers which were shaking with vexation, hurriedly did up my buttons. When decency, if not my dignity, had been restored, I rounded on those wolves with a virulence which surprised even me.

"Shoo!" I screamed at them. "What the hell do you think you're at, you . . . you . . . peeping Toms! Go away, for heaven's sake!"

The wolves were startled. They sprang to their feet, glanced at each other with a wild surmise, and then trotted off, passed down a draw, and disappeared in the direction of the esker. They did not once look back.

With their departure I experienced a reaction of another kind. The realization that they had been sitting almost within jumping distance of my unprotected back for God knows how long set up such a turmoil of the spirit that I had to give up all thought of carrying on where my discovery of the wolves had forced me to leave off. Suffering from both mental and physical strain, therefore, I hurriedly packed my gear and set out for the cabin.

My thoughts that evening were confused. True, my prayer had been answered, and the wolves had certainly co-operated by reappearing; but on the other hand I was becoming prey to a small but nagging doubt as to just *who* was watching *whom*. I felt that I, because of my specific superiority as a member of *Homo sapiens*, together with my intensive technical training, was entitled to pride of place. The sneaking suspicion that this pride had been denied and that, in point of fact, *I* was the one who was under observation, had an unsettling effect upon my ego.

In order to establish my ascendancy once and for all, I determined to visit the wolf esker itself the following morning and make a detailed examination of the presumed den. I decided to go by canoe, since the rivers were now clear and the rafting lake ice was being driven offshore by a stiff northerly breeze.

It was a fine, leisurely trip to Wolf House Bay, as I had now named it. The annual spring caribou migration north from the forested areas of Manitoba toward the distant tundra plains near Dubawnt Lake was under way, and from my canoe I could see countless skeins of caribou crisscrossing the muskegs and the rolling hills in all directions. No wolves were in evidence as I neared the esker, and I assumed they were away hunting a caribou for lunch.

I ran the canoe ashore and, fearfully laden with cameras, guns, binoculars and other gear, laboriously climbed the shifting sands of the esker to the shadowy place where the female wolf had disappeared. En route I found unmistakable proof that this esker was, if not the home, at least one of the favorite promenades of the wolves. It was liberally strewn with scats and covered with wolf tracks which in many places formed well-defined paths.

The den was located in a small wadi in the esker, and was so well concealed that I was on the point of walking past without seeing it, when a series of small squeaks attracted my attention. I stopped and turned to look, and there, not fifteen feet below me, were four small, gray beasties engaged in a free-for-all wrestling match.

At first I did not recognize them for what they were. The fat, fox faces with pinprick ears; the butterball bodies, as round as pumpkins; the short, bowed legs and the tiny upthrust sprigs of tails were so far from my conception of a wolf that my brain refused to make the logical connection.

Suddenly one of the pups caught my scent. He stopped in the midst of attempting to bite off a brother's tail and turned smoky blue eyes up toward me. What he saw evidently intrigued him. Lurching free of the scrimmage, he padded toward me with a rolling, wobbly gait; but a flea bit him unexpectedly before he had gone far, and he had to sit down to scratch it.

At this instant an adult wolf let loose a full-throated howl vibrant with alarm and warning, not more than fifty yards from me.

The idyllic scene exploded into frenzied action.

The pups became gray streaks which vanished into the gaping darkness of the den mouth. I spun around to face the adult wolf, lost my footing, and started to skid down the loose slope toward the den. In trying to regain my balance I thrust the muzzle of the rifle deep into the sand, where it stuck fast until the carrying-strap dragged it free as I slid rapidly away from it. I fumbled wildly at my revolver, but so cluttered was I with cameras and equipment straps that I did not succeed in getting the weapon clear as, accompanied by a growing avalanche of sand, I shot past the den mouth, over the lip of the main ridge and down the full length of the esker slope. Miraculously, I kept my feet; but only by dint of superhuman contortions during which I was alternately bent forward like a skier going over a jump, or leaning backward at such an acute angle I thought my backbone was going to snap.

It must have been quite a show. When I got myself straightened out and glanced back up the esker, it was to see *three* adult wolves ranged side by side like spectators in the Royal Box, all peering down at me with expressions of incredulous delight.

I lost my temper. This is something a scientist seldom does, but I lost mine. My dignity had been too heavily eroded during the past several days and my scientific detachment was no longer equal to the strain. With a snarl of exasperation I raised the rifle but, fortunately, the thing was so clogged with sand that when I pressed the trigger nothing happened.

The wolves did not appear alarmed until they saw me begin to dance up and down in helpless fury, waving the useless rifle and hurling imprecations at their cocked ears; whereupon they exchanged quizzical looks and silently withdrew out of my sight.

I too withdrew, for I was in no fit mental state to carry on with my exacting scientific duties. To tell the truth, I was in no fit mental state to do anything except hurry home to Mike's and seek solace for my tattered nerves and frayed vanity in the bottom of a jar of wolf-juice.

I had a long and salutary session with the stuff that night, and as my spiritual bruises became less painful under its healing influence, I reviewed the incidents of the past few days. Inescapably, the realization was being borne in upon my preconditioned mind that the centuries-old and universally accepted human concept of wolf character was a palpable lie. On three separate occasions in less than a week I had been completely at the mercy of these "savage killers"; but far from attempting to tear me limb from limb, they had displayed a restraint verging on contempt, even when I invaded their home and appeared to be posing a direct threat to the young pups.

This much was obvious, yet I was still strangely reluctant to let the myth go down the drain. Part of this reluctance was no doubt due to the thought that, by discarding the accepted concepts of wolf nature, I would be committing scientific treason; part of it to the knowledge that recognition of the truth would deprive my mission of its fine aura of danger and high adventure; and not the least part of that reluctance was probably due to my unwillingness to accept the fact that I had been made to look like a blithering idiot—not by my fellow man, but by mere brute beasts.

Nevertheless I persevered.

When I emerged from my session with the wolf-juice the following morning I was somewhat the worse for wear in a physical sense; but I was cleansed and purified spiritually. I had wrestled with my devils and I had won. I had made my decision that, from this hour onward, I would go open-minded into the lupine world and learn to see and know the wolves, not for what they were supposed to be, but for what they actually were.

From PEOPLE OF THE DEER

THE LIFEBLOOD OF THE LAND

On the day following the arrival of Hans and the children, I was awakened by the sound of heavy firing. The crash of gunshots intruded itself into my dreams until I thought I was again back in the Italian hills, listening to an exchange of rifle fire between the German outposts and our own. When I came to full consciousness the firing remained, so I hurriedly pulled on my clothes and went out into the June morning.

Franz, Anoteelik and Hans were sitting on the ridge above the cabin and they were steadily firing their rifles across the river. On the sloping southern bank nearly a hundred deer, all does, were milling in stupid

People of the Deer (Boston: Little, Brown, 1952).

anxiety. I could see the gray bursts of dust as bullets sang off the rocks, and I could hear the flat thud of bullets going home in living flesh.

The nearest animals were waist-deep in the fast brown water and could not return to shore, for the press of deer behind cut off retreat. The does that were still on land were running in short, futile starts, first east and then west again, and it was some time before they began to gallop with long awkward strides, along the riverbank. Their ponderous bellies big with fawn swung rhythmically as they fled upstream, for their time was nearly on them.

When the last of the straggling herd had passed out of range beyond the first bend of the river, the firing stopped and the three hunters ran down the bank and hurriedly began to clear the snow away from the green back of a canoe, which lay beside the cabin. I helped them and in a few moments the canoe was free and ready for the water. Franz and I pushed off into the still-flooded river, and we worked with all our power to gain the other bank before the current could sweep us out into the opening bay. It was hard and exciting work, but even in the fury of that struggle I had time to notice that the water was not all brown. Long, tenuous, crimson streamers were flowing down the river, fading and disappearing as they joined the full flow of the current. We grounded on the opposite shore and leaped into the water to beach the canoe, out of the river's grasp.

The excitement of the shooting, and of the river crossing, ebbed as suddenly as it had risen and I stood on the rough rocks along the slope and looked down on the dead and dying deer. There were a dozen of them lying in my sight along the shore. Their blood was still pumping thickly into the foam-flecked eddies at the river's edge, for only two of them were dead. The rest lay quivering on the rocks and lifted heavy heads to watch us blankly or, struggling to their feet, plunged forward only to fall again.

It was a sight of slaughter and of horror, and the knowledge that each of these dying beasts was swollen with young did not make the bloody spectacle easier to bear. I was seeing the blood of the land flow for the first time, but though my eyes were still those of a stranger and I was sickened by the sight, Franz was quite unperturbed. Rapidly, and with the agility of a deer himself, he leapt among the rocks to reach the cripples. He carried a short-bladed knife and as he reached each wounded doe he made one dexterous thrust into the back of her neck and neatly severed the spinal cord running inside the vertebrae. It was efficient and it was mercifully quick. Within ten minutes all the wounded animals lay still and Franz began the task of cutting up the meat.

One long stroke sufficed to open up the bellies. The sharp blade was used with such control that while it split the skin, it did not even mark the soft tissues of the swollen stomachs, distended with the fermenting leaves and lichens that the deer had fed upon. Then, reaching a bare arm into the hot cavities, Franz disemboweled each beast with one strong pull. Carefully he removed the livers and the kidneys and, using his knife as a chopper, he severed the hindquarters from the trunks. Leaving the forelimbs untouched, he sliced through the skin under the chins and cut out the heavy tongues.

I watched with fascination and repulsion, but so sure were all Franz's movements and so deft his touch, that the horror of the scene began to dull. I was filled with admiration for the man's skill. Though I did not know it then, I was watching a man of Tyrrell's deer people do his work, for Franz had learned his knacker's arts at the hands of the Ihalmiut, who are, in truth, a People of the Deer.

In less than twenty minutes all the carcasses were drawn and we were carrying the hindquarters to the shore. Where half an hour ago a herd of living deer had stood, now there were only shapeless, bloody heaps of meat that steamed gently upon the melting snow. The transition was too quick to have its full effect upon me then, and by the time I had lived in the land long enough to understand the truth behind a killing such as this, I too came to view it through Northern eyes, and to recognize the stark utility of death. But now it was my first spring in the Barrens, and the deer had returned. With their coming the long hiatus that life suffers during the interminable winter months was over. Outside the cabin the meat-hungry dogs raised their gaunt faces and howled exuberantly as each new change of breeze brought the strong smell of deer.

Kunee and Anoteelik were in an ecstasy. Anoteelik rushed knee-deep into the swollen river to help us land and eagerly snatched up a piece of still-warm meat and wolfed it down with feverish excitement. I remembered that this was the first fresh meat he had tasted in long months, and Anoteelik had not yet forgotten those starvation days by Ootek's Lake. Kunee was not far behind him, and I cannot describe the emotions that filled me as I watched this girl-child with a knife in one hand and a great chunk of dripping back meat in the other, stuffing her little face and burping like an old clubman after a Gargantuan meal.

For the first time Hans showed some animation. He smiled. I do not know whether it was from the pleasure in the killing or from anticipation of fresh food. His smile was—well, expressionless.

Franz too was smiling as we unloaded the heavy cargo and he shouted at Kunee to get a fire going. A new spirit of enthusiasm and fresh life was in the place, as if new blood flowed through the veins of those about me.

Even I was stung by an emotion I could not analyze, and I felt alive as I have never felt before.

The fire had just been lit and a pot of deer tongues just set to boil when a wild babble from the dogs brought me outside again. This time I looked directly to the crossing, and where the butchery had taken place there was a great new herd of does milling as it came up against the stream.

This time there was no shooting, though Hans could hardly restrain his urge to take up a rifle and empty it again. The deer seemed to ignore the cabin that stood in full view and in a minute they had all taken to the stream. Heavy as they were, they swam buoyantly and powerfully so that they made the crossing without losing ground and landed literally in our own front yard.

The dogs became insane and threatened to tear their tethering posts out of the frozen ground. The deer paid them, and us, but little heed. Splitting into two groups, they flowed past the cabin, enveloping it for a brief instant in their midst. The stink of barnyard was strong in our nostrils as they passed, then they were gone beyond the ridge.

In less than an hour I had seen so many deer that it seemed as if the world was full of them, but I had seen nothing yet. That afternoon Franz took me on his sled and we drove warily along the rotten shore ice of the bay, to the Ghost Hills. The heat was remarkably intense; at noon the thermometer had reached 100; and so we wore nothing but thin trousers and cotton shirts. Water lay deep upon the ice and the sled was really more of a boat than a land conveyance. An hour's travel took us to the north shore of the bay, and here we tied the dogs and climbed a long gentle ridge that faced the south. Below us lay Windy Bay, and beyond it the shattered slopes of the Ghost Hills. It was a scene to be recorded on gray paper, for the growing things had not been able to keep pace with the precipitate transition of the seasons, and the subtle overlay of color that would suffuse the summer plains had not yet begun to flow. The rotting surface of the ice was dark, but framed in ivory drifts, still lingering on the shores and in a thousand gullys and ravines. The hills were dun-colored heights sheathed in rock and long-dead lichens, with startlingly black patches of dwarf spruce spotted along their lower slopes. To the north, the plains sank into white and snow-filled hollows, hiding the muskegs and ponds; then lifted to reveal a hueless and leaden waste that stretched to the horizon.

From our vantage point all of this achromatic world lay somberly below us as we waited for the coming of the deer. We had not long to wait. Franz caught my arm and pointed to the convoluted slopes of the distant southern hills, and I could just discern a line of motion. It seemed to me that the slopes were sliding gently downward to the bay, as if the innumerable boulders that protruded from the hills had suddenly been set adrift to roll, in slow motion, down upon the ice. I watched intently, not certain whether the sun's glare had begun to affect my eyes so that they played fool tricks on me. Then the slow avalanches reached the far shore and debouched over the bay. I tried to count the little dots. Ten, fifty, a hundred, three hundred—and I gave up. In broken twisted lines, in bunched and beaded ropes, the deer streamed out onto the ice until they were moving north across a front of several miles.

From that distance they barely seemed to move, and yet in a few minutes they had reached the center of the bay and had begun to take on shape. I had binoculars, but in my preoccupation with the spectacle below I had not thought to use them. Now I lifted the glasses to my eyes. The long skeins dissolved at once into endless rows of deer, each following upon the footsteps of the animals ahead. Here and there along the lines a yearling kept its place beside a mother who was swollen with the new fawn she carried. There were no bucks. All these animals were does, all pregnant, all driving inexorably towards the north and the flat plains where they would soon give birth.

The leaders reached our shore and began the ascent, but across the bay the avalanche continued and grew heavier. The surface of the bay, for six miles east and west, had become one undulating mass of animals, and still they came.

Without hurry, but without pause, unthinking, but directly driven, they filed down to the ice and, following the tracks of those who had crossed first, made for our shore. Highways began to grow. The black ice was pounded and shattered until it again became white with broken crystals. The broad roads stretched across the bay, multiplied, grew into one another until at length they disappeared and the whole sweep of ice was one great road.

The herds were swelling past our lookout now. Ten paces from us, five, then we were forced to stand and wave our arms to avoid being trampled on. The does gazed briefly and incuriously at us, swung a few feet away and passed on to the north without altering their gait.

Hours passed like minutes. The flow continued at an unbroken level until the sun stood poised on the horizon's rim. And I became slowly conscious of a great apathy. Life, my life and that of Franz, of all living things I knew, seemed to have become meaningless. For here was life on such a scale that it was beyond all comprehension. It numbed my mind and left me feeling as if the inanimate world had been saturated with a reckless prodigality in that sacred and precious thing called life. I thought of the twelve deer slaughtered on the banks of Windy River and

I no longer felt horror or disgust. I felt nothing for the dead who were drowned beyond memory in this living flow of blood that swept across the plains.

It was nearly dusk when we roused ourselves. We walked silently to the sled and I felt a little sick. I began to doubt the reality of the vision I had seen. The ice had begun to freeze as the sun went down and the sled bumped so wickedly over the endless hoofprints that I was forced to run along behind it. A dozen times we passed close to a late herd of deer and each time the dogs, in defiance of Franz, lunged in pursuit and could be halted only when we overturned the sled to hold them back. There was no doubt about it—the vision had been real.

That night I sat for a long time on the ridge behind the cabin, smoking and thinking of that vision. I knew little of the People of the Deer as yet and now that I had seen the herds, I was aware that I knew nothing of the deer themselves. The People and the deer fused in my mind, an entity. I found I could not think of one without the other, and so by accident I stumbled on the secret of the Ihalmiut before I had even met them. I believe it was this vague awareness of the indivisibility of the Barrens People and the caribou that made my later attempts to understand the Eskimos yield fruit.

Since the time of the first arctic explorations, *la Foule*—the Throng—has baffled the curiosity of men. Unlike the immense herds of the prairie buffalo whose habits were open to the eyes of human intruders, the caribou have always remained wrapped in an aura of mystery that has never quite been penetrated. It was known that at certain times of the year, and in certain places, the deer would suddenly appear in herds which blanketed the land. Then, in a few days, they would be gone again. Where had they gone? Well, to the north, the south, or to the east and west, but to what destinations and for what reasons, no one knew.

But as time passed a rough pattern began to emerge from all the conflicting tales told about the deer, and it became known that most of the great herds summered on the plains of the open Barrens and, for the most part, wintered southward inside the protecting timber of the high arctic forests. These two movements were known, but after I had been a year in the Barrens, yet another movement became obvious to me—a migration that I shall discuss in detail later on.

The does, moving up from the forests to cross the mouth of Windy Bay in the first weeks of spring, soon began to disappear and there came a week when only little bands of stragglers, the sterile does, were seen. These did not hurry, for they were not driven by the compulsion of their swollen bellies. Old does, and those that had not been bred, passed gently by but on their heels there came a new upsurge. The bucks arrived. For a few days the hard-packed crossing places were again so thickly carpeted by the brown backs of animals that the ice could not be seen. Then suddenly the bucks too had passed our camp, following the trails of their does who were even then giving birth on the flat lands five hundred miles to the north of us. The bucks passed, and that was the end of the spring migration, though stragglers continued to come our way for many weeks.

The beasts that passed under my eyes that spring were hardly things of beauty. Their rough coats were molting, and in places the passage through the thick forests had rubbed the winter hair away from great patches of black skin. The distended bellies of the does and ugly bovine heads of all the animals, quite without antlers in the spring, bore no resemblance to the graceful shapes that our minds conjure up at the word "deer." Certainly these caribou were not graceful, swift-limbed animals; and yet their long and knobby legs, with huge splayed feet, carried them over the rough land with a deceptive speed and sureness.

Nor did their manners make them more attractive. Does, fawns and bucks, without exception, enlivened the long day's trek with a ceaseless succession of belly noises that made each herd seem like one noisy knot of rampant indigestion. The belly rumblings formed an undertone to the castanet-like clatter of their feet, for the "ankles" of caribou are fitted with a loose cartilage that, when they move, emits a clicking noise not unlike the muted sound of rocks being tapped against each other, under water.

By the end of June the last stragglers, the wounded and the sick, had passed by Windy Bay, leaving the land about our camp to countless flocks of ducks, gulls and sandpipers who kept up a constant cry and movement over the little ponds and the softening muskeg bogs. The snow was gone by then, yet the passage of the deer was still remembered, for the low bogs had been so cut and torn by the pounding hoofs that areas of moss, covering acres in extent, had been churned to chocolate-colored puddings of ancient peat, torn from its frozen sleep and left to melt under the heat of a forgotten sun. The heavy stench of barnyards hung over such spots as these for many weeks.

Even the surfaces of the great ridges, paved with frost-shattered rocks, clearly showed the eternal passage of the deer. Trails crossed and intersected everywhere, so that in all the country it was difficult to find a single square yard of land which did not bear the deep impress of a long-used trail. Even on solid rock the trails were clearly marked and some had been worn into the gray gneiss for a foot in depth.

But while the land at Windy Bay was given over to birds, the anxious does had borne their fawns on the chosen ground of the high flat plains that lie to the south of Baker Lake and Thelon River. The fawns were with the herds, grunting and coughing about their restless mothers. These precocious children can outrun a man within hours of their birth and can give even the great arctic wolf a difficult pursuit. It is well for them that they are so forward, for their dull-eyed mothers are singularly lacking in maternal instinct and it sometimes happens that the does desert their young in the face of danger. So it is not uncommon to meet young fawns roaming alone in the wide spaces of the plains. These lost youngsters will attach themselves to men and follow them for hours, for, like all caribou, the fawns are cursed with a great curiosity about things better left alone.

When the fawning is done with, the restless urge that brought the Throng northward still remains upon it. Now the great herds split into little groups which remain forever on the move. In eddies and milling crowds they circle aimlessly across hundreds of miles of tundra in each few days. The deer have no home. Winter and summer they must always be on the move, for when such numbers gather at any given spot, the lichens and dwarf willow leaves that form their chief foods are speedily exhausted and if the deer remain, they starve.

Thus throughout the hot July days the northern plains are filled with restless little groups of deer which shift about and pass like tumbleweed. But in late July a new compulsion seems to seize them, and this is the movement I referred to earlier as one that still remains quite unexplained. A few of the tiny groups suddenly decide to drift towards the south. As they move, they are like the beginnings of a growing avalanche, for they pick up and carry with them all the herds they meet, and the momentum of the march increases rapidly from day to day. By early August this movement is a flood. The blood of the Barrens flows back the way it came in spring, led by the does and fawns who congregate in immense herds. So the midsummer movement rushed southward at increasing speed until, reaching the forest edge, the wave of deer is halted and flung back in disorder and confusion, as waves are flung back under granite cliffs. The vast summer herds break up, and once again they eddy slowly about with complete aimlessness. Behind the wave of does, and sometimes mingling with them, the bucks, now carrying incredible spreads of velvet-covered antlers, follow along the trail of the stampede. Then, slowly, a recoil begins, and once again the deer drift to the North.

No man can tell the full reason behind this summer flight, for winter is still far away and before it comes, all the deer will have moved north again nearly to the limits reached in spring. Perhaps they make this summer migration because of the flies. Mosquitoes and black flies abound so richly in the Barrens that for weeks on end a wise man does not stir from his dark cabin by day unless driven by urgent need. Summer travel is a constant flight, an endeavor to escape the pursuing haze of winged tormentors. I have seen men remove their shirts after a day in the summer Barrens, and those shirts had to be peeled away from the body, for they were glued to the flesh with the blood of countless bites. The flies are not the least of the Barrens' defenses and they have greatly assisted in protecting the land so long from white men's violation.

If it is difficult for men to escape from the bloodsucking flies, then it is impossible for the deer to escape. At the height of the fly season the deer become emaciated shadows of themselves who hardly dare take time to eat and rest. They flee along the highest and most windswept ridges in a futile effort to escape a plague that has been known to destroy them from sheer loss of blood.

Yet the bloodsucking and the flesh-eating flies are not the most dreaded of the hosts. There are two other flies, both large, gaudy things which look like bumblebees. The arrival of a single one of these flamboyant raiders can inspire terror in a herd of deer that neither man nor wolves can equal. Once, while I was watching a small herd of bucks quietly feeding along a steep riverbank, I saw the animals suddenly go mad. The herd disintegrated and its members fled wildly in all directions, with tossing heads and with high reckless leaps that sometimes plunged them sickeningly on the sharp, shattered rocks. One buck turned to the river, and without a moment's hesitation flung himself over the steep bank and crashed into the shallow water below, to lie dying with a broken neck.

I paddled over to the still-quivering corpse, and there met the murderer: a winged, yellow horror perched on the dead deer with its ovipositor throbbing and swelling as it sought a place to lay its microscopic eggs. These eggs hatch into minute larvae which burrow through the hide, enter the bloodstream and in time emerge from the flesh to lie in little pockets just underneath the skin on the back of the deer. By the next spring these pockets have reached full size, and each contains an aqueous grub as big as the end joint of a man's finger. I have counted two hundred of these white and repulsive parasites under the back hide of a single deer. In June the obese larvae burrow out through the skin, riddling it as if by machine-gun fire, and drop off to pupate on the ground.

The second of the two devil flies is of an even more evil nature, for its larvae live not under the skin, but in a tight and squirming mass the size of a small grapefruit which clogs the cavities of the deer's nose and throat until it seems impossible that the victim can escape death by asphyxiation. I once took a hundred and thirty of these giant maggots, each an inch long, from the throat and nostrils of a single doe.

Now perhaps—though I cannot prove the supposition—it is the threat of these many varieties of winged furies which drives the deer so far north in the early spring, for the farther north, the later is the coming of the fly season. Then—again perhaps—as the flies die off from north to south with the progress of summer, the deer may follow that line of recession in search of undepleted pastures. I do not know if this is true, but I do know that the summer arrival of the deer in the central Barrens during my stay in the land coincided exactly with the final abrupt disappearance of the flies at that point.

While I am speaking of the flies I may as well exhaust the subject of the minute beasts who prey upon the deer. The big fly maggots are well known to all who know the caribou, but fortunately for their peace of mind few Northerners have any idea of the menageries of other unpleasant beasts that exist under the skin of the deer. Parasites are so numerous, I conclude from my own studies, that there comes a time in the life of every deer, if it survives the other perils, when it is so overloaded with parasites that it simply dies of outright starvation though it spends all day eating. All other things being equal, I doubt if a deer can expect to live more than a dozen years before it is so riddled with worms and cysts that death must inevitably ensue. For the record, and for the enlightenment of any reader who may someday be offered a prime roast of caribou, here is a list of the actual parasites I took from one old buck.

In the body muscles there was a concentration of tapeworm cysts that averaged two per cubic inch of meat. No part of the muscle tissues was free of these abhorrent things, and in addition to them, there was a liberal sprinkling of the cysts of nematode worms. The lungs also were very active even after death. I counted and removed 17 nematode worms, most of them over six inches in length. In the liver there were tapeworm cysts of two species, some of them the size of a tennis ball. The intestines yielded one adult tapeworm of great length and antiquity, and even in the heart muscles I found 6 tapeworm cysts. Of minor parasites, there were 190 warble-fly larvae under the hide and about 75 bott-fly larvae cozily ensconced within the throat and nasal passages.

Now this particular deer was no exception. It was simply old and therefore very heavily parasitized. But all deer which I have examined, except fawns and some yearlings, have yielded a corresponding count of parasites in degrees of intensity varying with the beast's age.

The interesting point here is that all the nematodes and tapeworms have at least two-stage life cycles. That is, they need another host, apart from the deer, to complete their lives. Encysted parasites reach maturity only when the flesh they are lurking in is eaten by another animal. That animal is often man.

I do not know what sort of internal shape the native eaters of deer—or I myself—may be in. Nor do I want to know. I'm sorry that I brought up the subject. I can only comfort myself with the reflection that if the parasites to be picked up from eating deer meat were pathogenic, then there would be no Eskimos at all. It is thin comfort when I recall the raw meat dinners I have eaten in the Barrens. * * *

JOHN HAINES
B. 1924

From his early work as a sculptor, to his experience as a homesteader in Alaska between 1954 and 1969, to his poetry, there is a stark integrity to John Haines's work. His desire has been to strip life down to its essential forms and colors. Reviewers of his books of poems—which include Winter News *(1966),* The Stone Harp *(1971), and* News from the Glacier *(1982)—have noticed his ability to evoke a cold, white world that seems in some way absolute. In addition to his poetry, Haines has produced several volumes of essays treating his experiences of homesteading and trapping in Alaska and meditating upon the meaning of place.* Living off the Country: Essays on Poetry and Place *appeared in 1981;* The Stars, The Snow, The Fire: Twenty-Five Years in the Northern Wilderness *came out in 1989.*

MOMENTS AND JOURNEYS

The movement of things on this earth has always impressed me. There is a reassuring vitality in the annual rise of a river, in the return of the Arctic sun, in the poleward flight of spring migrations, in the sea-

Living Off the Country (Ann Arbor: University of Michigan, 1981).

sonal trek of nomadic peoples. A passage from Edwin Muir's autobiography speaks to me of its significance.

> I remember . . . while we were walking one day on the Mönchsberg—a smaller hill on the opposite side of the river—looking down on a green plain that stretched away to the foothills, and watching in the distance people moving along the tiny roads. Why do such things seem enormously important to us? Why, seen from a distance, do the casual journeys of men and women, perhaps going on some trivial errand, take on the appearance of a pilgrimage? I can only explain it by some deep archetypal image in our minds of which we become conscious only at the rare moments when we realize that our own life is a journey. [Edwin Muir, *An Autobiography* (Sommers, Conn.: Seabury, 1968), p. 217].

This seems to me like a good place to begin, not only for its essential truth, but because it awakens in me a whole train of images—images of the journey as I have come to understand it, moments and stages in existence. Many of these go back to the years I lived on my homestead in Alaska. That life itself, part of the soil and weather of the place, seemed to have about it much of the time an aura of deep and lasting significance. I wasn't always aware of this, of course. There were many things to be struggled with from day to day, chores of one sort or another—cabins to be built, crops to be looked after, meat to kill, and wood to cut—all of which took a kind of passionate attention. But often when I was able to pause and look up from what I was doing, I caught brief glimpses of a life much older than mine.

Some of these images stand out with great force from the continual coming and going of which they were part—Fred Campbell, the old hunter and miner I had come to know, that lean, brown man of patches and strange fits. He and I and my first wife, Peg, with seven dogs—five of them carrying packs—all went over Buckeye Dome one day in the late summer of 1954. It was a clear, hot day in mid-August, the whole troop of us strung out on the trail. Campbell and his best dog, a yellow bitch named Granny, were in the lead. We were in a hurry, or seemed to be, the dogs pulling us on, straining at their leashes for the first two or three miles, and then, turned loose, just panting along, anxious not to be left behind. We stopped only briefly that morning, to adjust a dog pack and to catch our wind. Out of the close timber with its hot shadows and swarms of mosquitoes, we came into the open sunlight of the dome. The grass and low shrubs on the treeless slopes moved gently in the warm air that came from somewhere south, out of the Gulf of Alaska.

At midday we halted near the top of the dome to look for water among the rocks and to pick blueberries. The dogs, with their packs removed, lay down in the heat, snapping at flies. Buckeye Dome was the high place nearest to home, though it was nearly seven miles by trail from Richardson. It wasn't very high, either—only 3,000 feet—but it rose clear of the surrounding hills. From its summit you could see in any direction, as far west as Fairbanks when the air was clear enough. We saw other high places, landmarks in the distance, pointed out to us and named by Campbell: Banner Dome, Cockscomb, Bull Dome, and others I've forgotten. In the southeast, a towering dust cloud rose from the Delta River. Campbell talked to us of his trails and camps, of years made of such journeys as ours, an entire history told around the figure of one man. We were new to the North and eager to learn all we could. We listened, sucking blueberries from a tin cup.

And then we were on the move again. I can see Campbell in faded jeans and red felt hat, bending over one of the dogs as he tightened a strap, swearing and saying something about the weather, the distance, and himself getting too old to make such a trip. We went off down the steep north slope of the dome in a great rush, through miles of windfalls, following that twisting, root-grown trail of his. Late in the evening, wading the shallows of a small creek, we came tired and bitten to his small cabin on the shore of a lake he had named for himself.

That range of images is linked with another at a later time. By then I had my own team, and with our four dogs we were bound uphill one afternoon in the cool September sunlight to pick cranberries on the long ridge overlooking Redmond Creek. The tall, yellow grass on the partly cleared ridge bent over in the wind that came easily from the west. I walked behind, and I could see, partly hidden by the grass, the figures of the others as they rounded the shoulder of a little hill and stopped to look back toward me. The single human figure there in the sunlight under moving clouds, the dogs with their fur slightly ruffled, seemed the embodiment of an old story.

And somewhere in the great expanse of time that made life in the wilderness so open and unending, other seasons were stations on the journey. Coming across the Tanana River on the midwinter ice, we had three dogs in harness and one young female running loose beside us. We had been three days visiting a neighbor, a trapper living on the far side of the river, and were returning home. Halfway across the river we stopped to rest; the sled was heavy, the dogs were tired and lay down on the ice.

Standing there, leaning on the back of the sled, I knew a vague sense of remoteness and peril. The river ice always seemed a little dangerous, even when it was thick and solid. There were open stretches of clear, blue water, and sometimes large, deep cracks in the ice where the river could be heard running deep and steady. We were heading downriver into a cloudy December evening. Wind came across the ice, pushing a little dry snow, and no other sound—only the vast presence of snow and ice, scattered islands, and the dark crest of Richardson Hill in the distance.

To live by a large river is to be kept in the heart of things. We become involved in its life, the heavy sound of it in the summer as it wears away silt and gravel from its cutbanks, pushing them into sandbars that will be islands in another far off year. Trees are forever tilting over the water, to fall and be washed away, to lodge in a drift pile somewhere downstream. The heavy gray water drags at the roots of willows, spruce, and cottonwoods; sometimes it brings up the trunk of a tree buried in sand a thousand years before, or farther back than that, in the age of ice. The log comes loose from the fine sand, heavy and dripping, still bearing the tunnel marks made by the long dead insects. Salmon come in midsummer, then whitefish, and salmon again in the fall; they are caught in our nets and carried away to be smoked and eaten, to be dried for winter feed. Summer wears away into fall; the sound of the river changes. The water clears and slowly drops; pan ice forms in the eddies. One morning in early winter we wake to a great and sudden silence: the river is frozen.

We stood alone there on the ice that day, two people, four dogs, and a loaded sled, and nothing before us but land and water into Asia. It was time to move on again. I spoke to the dogs and gave the sled a push.

Other days. On a hard-packed trail home from Cabin Creek, I halted the dogs part way up a long hill in scattered spruce. It was a clear evening, not far below zero. Ahead of us, over an open ridge, a full moon stood clear of the land, enormous and yellow in the deep blue of the Arctic evening. I recalled how Billy Melvin, an old miner from the early days at Richardson, had once described to me a moonrise he had seen, a full moon coming up ahead of him on the trail, "big as a rain barrel." And it was very much like that—an enormous and rusty rain barrel into which I looked, and the far end of the barrel was open. I stood there, thinking it might be possible to go on forever into that snow and yellow light, with no sound but my own breathing, the padding of the dog's feet, and the occasional squeak of the sled runners. The moon whitened and grew smaller; twilight deepened, and we went on to the top of the hill.

What does it take to make a journey? A place to start from, something to leave behind. A road, a trail, or a river. Companions, and something like a destination: a camp, an inn, or another shore. We might imagine a journey with no destination, nothing but the act of going, and with never an arrival. But I think we would always hope to find *something* or *someone,* however unexpected and unprepared for. Seen from a distance or taken part in, all journeys may be the same, and we arrive exactly where we are.

One late summer afternoon, near the road to Denali Park, I watched the figures of three people slowly climb the slope of a mountain in the northeast. The upper part of the mountain was bare of trees, and the small alpine plants there were already red and gold from the early frost. Sunlight came through broken rain clouds and lit up the slope and its three moving figures. They were so far away that I could not tell if they were men or women, but the red jacket worn by one of them stood out brightly in the sun. They climbed higher and higher, bound for a ridge where some large rocks broke through the thin soil. A shadow kept pace with them, slowly darkening the slope below them, as the sun sank behind another mountain in the southwest. I wondered where they were going—perhaps to hunt mountain sheep—or they were climbing to a berry patch they knew. It was late in the day; they would not get back by dark. I watched them as if they were figures in a dream, who bore with them the destiny of the race. They stopped to rest for a while near the skyline, but were soon out of sight beyond the ridge. Sunlight stayed briefly on the high rock summit, and then a rain cloud moved in and hid the mountaintop.

When life is simplified, its essence becomes clearer, and we know our lives as part of some ancient human activity in a time measured not by clocks and calendars but by the turning of a great wheel, the positions of which are not wage-hours, nor days and weeks, but immense stations called Spring, Summer, Autumn, and Winter. I suppose it will seem too obvious to say that this sense of things will be far less apparent to people closed off in the routine of a modern city. I think many people must now and then be aware of such moments as I have described, but do not remember them, or attach no special significance to them. They are images that pass quickly from view because there is no place for them in our lives. We are swept along by events we cannot link together in a significant pattern, like a flood of refugees pushed on by the news of a remote disaster. The rush of conflicting impressions keeps away stillness, and it is in stillness that the images arise, as they will, fluently and naturally, when there is nothing to prevent them.

There is the dream journey and the actual life. The two seem to touch now and then, and perhaps when men lived less complicated and distracted lives the two were not separate at all, but continually one thing. I have read somewhere that this was once true for the Yuma Indians who lived along the Colorado River. They dreamed at will, and moved without effort from waking into dreaming life; life and dream were bound together. And in this must be a kind of radiance, a very old and deep assurance that life has continuity and meaning, that things are somehow in place. It is the journey resolved into one endless present.

And the material is all around us. I retain strong images from treks with my stepchildren: of a night seven years ago when we camped on a mountaintop, a night lighted by snow patches and sparks from a windy fire going out. Sleeping on the frozen ground, we heard the sound of an owl from the cold, bare oak trees above us. And there was a summer evening I spent with a small class of schoolchildren near Painted Rock in central California. We had come to learn about Indians. The voices of the children carried over the burned fields under the red glare of that sky, and the rock gave back heat in the dusk like an immense oven. There are ships and trains that pull away, planes that fly into the night; or the single figure of a man crossing an otherwise empty lot. If such moments are not as easily come by, as clear and as resonant as they once were in the wilderness, it may be because they are not so clearly linked to the life that surrounds them and of which they are part. They are present nonetheless, available to imagination, and of the same character.

One December day a few years ago, while on vacation in California, I went with my daughter and a friend to a place called Pool Rock. We drove for a long time over a mountain road, through meadows touched by the first green of the winter rains, and saw few fences or other signs of people. Leaving our car in a small campground at the end of the road, we hiked four miles up a series of canyons and narrow gorges. We lost our way several times but always found it again. A large covey of quail flew up from the chaparral on a slope above us; the tracks of deer and bobcat showed now and then in the sand under our feet. An extraordinary number of coyote droppings scattered along the trail attracted our attention. I poked one of them with a stick, saw that it contained much rabbit fur and bits of bone. There were patches of ice in the streambed, and a few leaves still yellow on the sycamores.

We came to the rock in mid-afternoon, a great sandstone pile rising out of the foothills like a sanctuary or a shrine to which one comes yearly on a pilgrimage. There are places that take on symbolic value to an individual or a tribe, "soul-resting places," a friend of mine has called them. Pool Rock has become that to me, symbolic of that hidden, original life we have done so much to destroy.

We spent an hour or two exploring the rock, a wind and rain-scoured honeycomb stained yellow and rose by a mineral in the sand. Here groups of the Chumash Indians used to come, in that time of year when water could be found in the canyons. They may have come to gather certain foods in season, or to take part in magic rites whose origin and significance are no longer understood. In a small cave at the base of the rock, the stylized figures of headless reptiles, insects, and strange bird-men are painted on the smoke-blackened walls and ceiling. These and some bear paw impressions gouged in the rock, and a few rock mortars used for grinding seeds, are all that is left of a once-flourishing people.

We climbed to the summit of the rock, using the worn footholds made long ago by the Chumash. We drank water from the pool that gave the rock its name, and ate our lunch, sitting quietly in the cool sunlight. And then the wind came up, whipping our lunchbag over the edge of the rock; a storm was moving in from the coast. We left the rock by the way we had come, and hiked down the gorge in the windy, leaf-blown twilight. In the dark, just before the rain, we came to the campground, laughing, speaking of the things we had seen, and strangely happy.

ANN HAYMOND ZWINGER
B. 1925

Born in Muncie, Indiana, Ann Zwinger studied art history at Wellesley College and Indiana University. Most of her books are illustrated with her own graceful and meticulous drawings of plants, which she considers integral complements to the writing itself. Her first book, Beyond the Aspen Grove *(1970), is an account of learning how to live on a wild tract of land high in the Colorado Rockies. She has also written books about Wyoming, Utah, and the Baja Peninsula, and co-authored* A Conscious Stillness: Two Naturalists on Thoreau's Rivers *(1982) with Edwin Way Teale. The following selection, set in the Sonoran Desert, is from* The Mysterious Lands *(1989), a personal account of the four great desert regions of the American West. Rarely do Zwinger's accounts contain dramatic events or sweeping philosophical statements. But her careful attention to the texture and color of the natural world, combined with an intelligent and amiable voice, have cumulative strength. Her books succeed in what Joseph Conrad described as the most important and most difficult task of the artist: "to make you see."*

From THE MYSTERIOUS LANDS

OF RED-TAILED HAWKS AND BLACK-TAILED GNATCATCHERS

Three concerns haunted me before I came on this bighorn sheep count: that I would be uneasy alone, that time would hang heavy, that I could not endure the heat. Instead I have felt at home, there have not been enough hours in the day, and the heat has become a bearable if not always welcome companion. The words of Joseph Wood Krutch, also writing about the Sonoran Desert, come to mind: "Not to have known—as most men have not—either the mountain or the desert is not to have known one's self. Not to have known one's self is to have known no one."

At noontime I am concentrating so hard on taking notes that when a cicada lets off a five-second burst like a bandsaw going through metal I jump. When there has been no activity at the tank for over an hour I opt for a can of tuna sprinkled with the juice of half a lemon.

No sooner do I open the can and get my fork out than all the birds explode from the rocks on which they've congregated. A red-tailed hawk bullets straight toward me, talons extended, tail spread. No sound, no screaming. It breaks off, rises with no rodent in its talons, wheels, spirals upward, and swoops again. Again no luck. It makes no third try. Its disappearance is followed by a great shocked silence. Half an hour passes before the doves venture, one by one, back to their sentinel rock.

I see only this one hawk stoop. The only time redtails are quiet is on the attack. Otherwise I hear their eerie *KEEEeeeer KEEeeer* that ricochets off the sky itself long before they come in to water. One afternoon a redtail sits on the steep cliff to the right; a couple of feet below it perch some house finches; a black-throated sparrow searches the bush beside it; a pair of ash-throated flycatchers rest above it; and across the tank, a batch of doves roost peacefully on their rock. All birds must be vulnerable to attack at the water hole and many avoid too much exposure by being able to drink very quickly, or coming in early and late when raptors are not hunting. Yet there are also these moments when the lion and the lamb lie down together.

I put aside my field glasses and lift my fork. This time a turkey vulture alights on the big rock. The rock is nearly vertical on the side overlooking the tank and this is where it chooses to descend to water. It gets about a quarter of the way down, contorted in an awkward position, big feet

The Mysterious Lands (New York: Dutton, 1989).

splayed out on the rock, tail pushed up behind at a painful angle, as it looks intently down at the water, a hilarious study in reluctance. Gingerly it inches down (vultures have no claw-grasping capability as birds of prey like eagles and hawks do) until it can hold no longer and crash-lands so ridiculously onto the apron to drink that I laugh out loud. The closeness of the rocks around the pool impedes the bird's maneuvering space because of its broad wingspan, and so it edges as close as it can to ensure dropping upon the only place where it can stand and drink.

Four species of this misanthropic-looking bird existed in the Pleistocene, and this creature looks like one of the originals. On the ground, vultures are hunched and awkward bundles of feathers, but in the air, where I watch them during much of the day, they are magnificent, graceful soarers. They ascend with the updrafts coming off the hot desert floor, floating and lifting to cooler air, where visibility is superb; at five hundred feet the visible horizon is twenty-seven miles away, and at two thousand feet, fifty-five miles. Such big raptors generally get as much water as they need from the carrion they consume.

One more try on the tuna fish. A Harris' antelope squirrel scuttles down the wash to nibble on saguaro seeds. Tail held high over its back for shade, a single white stripe on each flank, it has quick, jerky movements typical of the ever-watchful. It stands slightly hunkered up on its hind legs to eat, but its rear end never touches the hot sand. It spends little time feeding and soon tucks back into the brush near the blind, where it undoubtedly has a burrow. There it spread-eagles on the cool soil and unloads its body heat, before taking on the desert again. Still, it withstands unusually high heat loads because of a lower basal metabolism.

The next day, emboldened, it hops up on the iceless ice chest in the blind and puts its head in my empty plastic cup, which tips over with a clatter, sending the squirrel flying.

I eat lunch at a fashionable three o'clock. By four o'clock, shadows cover the tank and the blind is in sun. A cloud cover that has kept the temperature relatively low all day has disappeared and the sun has an unobstructed shot at my back. Until the sun drops behind the ridge, it is the most miserable time of the day.

The resident robber fly alights in front of me, makes a slapdash attempt at a wandering fly, misses, and returns to watching. Flies are widely dispersed in the desert, more prevalent than any other insect order, and of these, bee flies and robber flies are the most numerous. The huge eyes of robber flies give them peripheral vision; with streamlined stilettolike bodies that allow swift flight, and needlelike beaks, they are efficient predators on the desert wafters and drifters. I've watched this one impale a smaller fly in flight, almost too quickly for the eye to follow, then alight to suck out the juices. Today it seems scarcely to care.

In the evening a caterwauling of Gambel's quail issues from the mesquite trees, where they perch in the branches. Their fussing is interspersed with a short soapsudsy cluck, embellished by a silvery *tink* at the end. The first night I was here they scolded and fumed about the stranger in their midst. The second night they gossiped and fussed, and the third night I awoke to find them within a few feet of the cot.

They visit the big mesquites only in the evening, always after sunset, and they are always noisy. I would think a predator could hear them a mile off. Their drinking patterns have evolved to avoid predators: they commonly come in to water twice a day, one period beginning at dawn, the other ending at dusk. Birds of prey tend to arrive around noon, so the quail's watering time does not overlap.

Quail have been termed "annual" birds because of their variable yearly populations. In the Sonoran Desert, the number of young quail per adult found in the fall correlates to rainfall during the previous December to April; in the Mojave, the same high correlation exists between young and October-to-March precipitation (a relationship that exists in other desert animals, among them bighorn sheep). Their reproductive activity begins before green vegetation becomes a part of their diet, the amount of which would give them clues to the amount of nourishment available, and hence the clutch size that could survive. Although quail do not breed at all in exceptionally dry years, they are one of the most prolific of birds.

They remind me of charming windup toys, painted wooden birds bustling about with staccato movements, officiously giving each other directions as they bustle among the creosote bushes. As I watch them, I remember the Kawaiisu Indian story about the tear marks on Quail's face because her young died, one after the other, when she made her cradles out of sandbar willow—a wood that the Indians therefore do not use for cradles.

The day dims and I stretch out to count the stars framed in a triangle of mesquite branches. Content, I realize I have reached, as Sigurd Olsen wrote, "the point where days are governed by daylight and dark, rather than by schedules, where one eats if hungry and sleeps when tired, and becomes completely immersed in the ancient rhythms, then one begins to live."

Yes.

Early in the morning, and again in the evening, bees create an unholy cantillation around the blind, some working the few mesquite and creosote flowers that remain, but most of them just circling in holding patterns of their own devising.

The number of creosote bushes in the western deserts make it a prime source for pollen and nectar. Several bee species are closely associated pollinators of the creosote bush although it does not depend on any single species for successful pollination. The most numerous pollinator in the summertime is *Perdita larrea,* a tiny bee just an eighth of an inch long. Because of its small size *Perdita* can harvest pollen larger bees cannot, but smallness may also curtail its value as a pollinator. Smallness prevents it from making reliable contact with a stigma, and its foraging range is modest and limited.

While the bees are outside the blind I remain quietly inside, hoping that the shade will discourage them from visiting and, most of all, from stinging at some imagined insult. With great relief each day I watch the bees move toward the water tank as the day heats. A thin black cloud of them is visible through the spotting scope. More than once I see a bighorn sheep make a hurried withdrawal from the tank, shaking its head vigorously from what I assume to be a bee's umbrage.

This morning bighorns remain at the tank, either drinking or standing around, for more than an hour before they leave. I follow them with the field glasses as long as I can. When I begin recording my stopwatch notations on the work sheet, I hear a strong bleating at erratic intervals. Search as I may, I can neither see around the saguaro to identify the activity nor locate the source by sound.

By default, I see a great deal of the old saguaro for the next quarter hour. The cactus is badly riddled about eight feet off the ground, so that daylight shows through the ribs, undoubtedly the work of the resident white-throated wood rat. Wood rats are the only animals that consistently eat cactus; other species may feed on it occasionally but cannot make it a steady diet because of the high content of malic and oxalic acids, created by the cactus's CAM photosynthesis. Oxalic acid is in the form of insoluble calcium oxalate crystals that, in humans, cause severe renal problems. For six months cactus is the wood rat's major source of food, reaching a peak in late May when it may comprise more than 90 percent of its diet.

The saguaro is closely pleated, waiting to expand when the rains come. The bellowslike action, which permits expansion of the stem without tearing the inelastic skin, allows precise adjustment to water storage, an action that starts with even very light rainfall. Water loss during the dry season reduces the volume of storage tissue, shrinking the stem; as the diameter becomes smaller, the ribs draw closer together, hence the pleated look. After a rain the process reverses rapidly, with more intensity on the south side of the stem, probably because water-conducting tissue is more prevalent there; the north side does not begin to swell until a few days later. About three feet off the ground on the north side facing me, an extra rib has been added to the basic number of twelve ribs. This onset of radial growth, or bifurcation, doesn't occur until the trunk grows to at least twelve inches in diameter.

A cactus of this immense size can absorb 95 percent of its total weight in water, sometimes up to a ton, expanding for up to three weeks after rains. Confined to the upper three inches of soil, tough ropelike roots may extend outward fifteen or twenty feet, placed to suck up as much water as possible before it evaporates. Lacking a stabilizing taproot, a saguaro topples if these lateral roots are severed.

The south and north sides of the cactus are measurably different. Ribs on the south side are deeper. Receiving the greater amount of direct sunlight, the deeper furrows provide a modicum of shade, reducing the time that direct sunlight heats the surface. Spine lengths on the south side are longer, and may provide an insulating layer of air. Fruits ripen first on the south side. Branch ends are usually colder than the main stalk during the night, and since single flowers form at the tips only, more rapid development occurs on the warmer side. Dryness promotes the formation of flower buds; plants growing with a favorable water supply make handsome vegetative growth but tend not to bloom.

Flowering is, after all, not an aesthetic contribution, but a survival mechanism.

The variety of birds in the Cabeza Prieta has been a surprise, especially at this hot, dry time of year. A pair of ash-throated flycatchers, tails a bright reddish brown, forage in the mesquite. Only gullies and washes with larger shrubs and trees support enough insects to attract the flycatchers. Three verdins squabble in a saltbush, their yellow caps bright but their bodies blending and disappearing in the fretted background. Feeding on insects (as most migratory birds do) they can exist without free water as long as insects are available. Subject to more water loss because of a less advantageous ratio of surface area to volume than that enjoyed by larger birds, they spend the day closeted in shade and shadow. Females weave ball-like nests in the thorniest of bushes, catclaw and sometimes cholla, and line them with down and feathers for the young, while the male builds a simpler nest for protection against the chill of desert nights. A wreath of spiny twigs around each entrance protects the relatively low-placed and vulnerable nests.

Wings whir close by as a Costa's hummingbird checks out my hanging red nylon stuff sack, then perches on a mesquite twig. This three-gram female loses nearly half of her body weight on hot days, making dependence on surface water and succulent food greater than that of large birds, which lose much less. When nectar from ocotillo and Indian paintbrush, as well as agaves, is available, hummingbirds obtain moisture in their food, but at this dry time of the year, when no flowers bloom, they must have access to free water instead.

At dusk a desert cottontail rollicks down the wash, which is now in partial shade. This cottontail is lighter than the mountain cottontails with which I am familiar, illustrating the tendency of desert mammals to be paler in pelage, somewhat smaller, and with longer ears and legs than their cooler-climate counterparts. It does not hop; its front and back feet move together in a rocking motion like a hobbyhorse canter. It nibbles some fallen saguaro fruit, then beds down on the other side of the sandy strip in a thicket of saltbush. Another one appears. The first returns. They face each other three feet apart, feinting. The first one dashes for the other, who levitates straight up while the first dashes beneath, and then both bucket off. To me it looks like great good fun and I enjoy their silly antics.

My band of bighorn sheep prefer morning watering. They come with some precision to the tank. This morning there is a considerable amount of amatory exercise going on between the young rams and the ewes. Breeding season is not far off and mating behavior patterns briefly interrupt the more unstructured ambles to the tank.

A ram follows a young ewe downslope, nose so close to her tail that he trips for not watching where his feet are going; the scent of a ewe's urine communicates whether or not she is in estrus. The ewe appears to ignore him, stopping to browse along the way or simply look about. I watch three different pairs, and each female, at different times, stops and urinates, a behavior that occurs only when a ram closely follows.

A group of six sheep come in early today, with some I've not seen before. They remain two hours, most of it standing around and mountain watching, before they move back up the hill. Busy recording, I hear the cracking of branches close by, and suddenly there are five right in front of the blind, noisily cracking mesquite pods. Although they prefer grass, there is precious little of that here and so they have become more opportunistic in their feeding. The group includes both a young ram and a big mature ram, two lambs, and a female. They are obviously aware I am here, look at me with less than the curiosity I feel I deserve, but otherwise pay no more attention to me than to the saguaro. I hear them crunching mesquite pods as they move downslope.

Sweeping the slope with binoculars, I spot more sheep on the hillside.

As I switch to the spotting scope to watch them more closely, I hear a jet coming in low. A sonic boom rips the air and reverberates so close the whole blind vibrates, and even though I know it's coming, I still jump when the sound hits.

The bighorns on the hillside never turn a hair. The ten white-winged doves on the sentinel rock never move. The mourning doves never stop calling. I later find this to be generally true, that the frequency of a sonic boom resembles that of a thunderstorm, and that wildlife here generally is not disturbed by either. This observer is.

At midday, when tank activity has closed down and the temperature reads 106 degrees F., the metal of the spotting scope burns my fingers. The water I take from the jerry can to drink is hot enough to brew tea with. I can't complain. Early travelers had it much worse; John Durivage, crossing the same desert in 1849, found

> the water was detestable and at any other time would have proved a power-ful emetic, but now it was *agua dulce*. A tincture of bluelick, iodides of sulfur, Epsom salts, and a strong decoction of decomposed mule flesh were the component parts of this delectable compound.

A western whiptail lizard patters out from behind a water can and prowls the edge of the blind, snuffling the dirt floor as it goes. I puzzle over the dark color, an allover deep smoky brown with a checkered back pattern, a good-size lizard with a long tail, the last three inches of which are almost black—until I realize that the soil under the mesquite tree where it forages is brown from the humus of leaves and pods and twigs built up over the years. Western whiptails are very variable in color, tending to match the ground upon which they travel. When the lizard reaches my bare right foot, to my delight, it tickles right over my toes.

I pour four inches of water into the bucket, put my shirt in, wet it thoroughly, and put it back on wet. Even though the water is hot it chills immediately and sits on my skin like salvation. It refreshes and energizes me enough to take a walk. When I return, hundreds of bees have found the water I unadvisedly left in the bucket. My blue sleeping bag is the dearest object of their desire. They cling to my blue shirt with ecstasy or joyously explore every object in the blind.

I sulk outside in the flimsy shade of a creosote bush for forty-five minutes while they enjoy my grudging hospitality.

Behind me, the next morning, are the subtle sounds in the brush that indicate small-animal movement, but peer as I may, I see nothing. Finally I pick out a dull-brown robin-size bird, which scratches the dirt, pauses, disappears, pops up on a branch and down again, difficult to see and to follow. I finally get a good glimpse of a fierce yellow eye and an almost raptorlike gaze: a curve-billed thrasher. With something in its beak it flies to a nearby cholla and solves a mystery: at last I know who built the large messy nest in the cholla in which I found three fully-feathered, grayish-brown young, eyes tightly closed, beaks like hand-drawn brackets too big for their heads, so nondescript as to be unidentifiable. A high percentage of desert birds nest in inaccessible cavities, spiny trees and shrubs and cacti, symptomatic of the strong predatory pressures on nesting birds here, but only cactus wrens and curve-billed thrashers regularly brave the cholla.

By noon the temperature is 102 degrees F. and climbing. I was going to walk, for there are things I want to check out. I was going to draw, but even with a paper towel beneath my arm I still perspire enough to buckle the paper, and the drawings are out of proportion and awkward. I was going to do a lot of things, but the heat, combined with my usual after-lunch low metabolism, saps my ambition. A white-winged dove calls, repetitive, insistent, annoying. A thankless breeze comes through the blind. The little ground squirrel arrives, unnecessarily spry and lively and perky. I feel listless to the point of stupor.

Actually I may have reached the point where I can live with this heat, this everywhere, this without-respite hot. My skin feels cool so evaporative cooling is working. It would be heaven to pour a pail of cool water over my overheated head, but all the water is hot. Not warm. Hot. And I yearn for every ice cube I ever heedlessly rinsed down a drain.

The silence of noon is palpable, more an onerous, enveloping physical presence than a lack of sound. A female Gila woodpecker lands on a mesquite branch, mouth agape. When a mourning dove coos, it has a lunatic overtone. A fly's drone sounds like a freight train.

The white-winged doves sit on the sentinel boulder above the tank, in full sun. The heat radiating off the rocks must make the cul-de-sac in which the tank sits unbearable, yet the doves appear unperturbed. The thrasher, beak agape, sits on her nest, lit by full sun. In this high-heat time of day she must be there to shield the young, enjoying none of the comforts of a shaded nest but also not vulnerable to attack, a brutal trade-off.

Rather than evaporating water to lower body temperature, most desert birds allow a passive rise in body temperature. Birds ordinarily have a higher body temperature than mammals, well above 100 degrees F., and this higher temperature allows them to dissipate heat by radiation. Birds, with the exception of burrowing owls, cannot utilize burrows for cooling, nor can they sweat. They can sit in the shade and extend their wings to

expose bare patches of skin; they can compress their plumage to reduce
its insulating value; or they can gape, which is a means of evaporative
cooling.

When ambient temperature rises above body temperature, there is
one more option: gular flutter—fluttering the thin floor of the mouth
and the soft skin under the throat. Gular flutter increases evaporation
and is highly developed in several desert bird species, among them doves,
quails, nighthawks, and roadrunners.

But sometimes even that doesn't suffice. On the last afternoon I check
the thermometer at three o'clock, already 108 degrees on its way up to
112 degrees F. Heat rolls down off the surrounding ridges like a *nuée
ardente,* consuming everything in its path.

Hopping up on a bough of the mesquite against which the blind is
built is a tiny black-tailed gnatcatcher, not much bigger than a hummingbird. Illustrations in bird-identification books show such plump,
neatly feathered creatures. This little soul is waiflike and thin, feathers
disheveled and tufting out, the Edith Piaf of the bird world.

She walks up the branch in front of me, less than an arm's length
away. She stands with her body high off the branch, tail quivering. As I
watch her, her head nods forward in that familiar "I can't hold my head
up another minute" droop. As soon as her head drops she jerks it up and
opens her eyes in a gesture so reminiscent of a child fighting sleep I have
to smile. She moves to stand beside my duffel bag, which is wedged up
against the tree trunk and, as I watch, slowly lists until she leans completely against it as if exhausted by the heat. Her head drops forward and
she starts awake several times more. Finally her head remains down. She
sleeps.

In time my head falls forward and I too jerk awake, and finally, very
quietly, scoot down in the chair so that my neck can rest on the back,
and then I doze as well. I awake with a stiff neck just as the little
gnatcatcher stirs. She pulls herself upright, shakes her feathers flat, looks
about perkily for a moment, and in leisurely fashion, hops into the brush.

My last evening here. I walk up to the divide that separates my valley
from the desert flats to the west, winding to the top, flushing a lizard,
climbing over granite boulders, avoiding the barbed and the spurred.
When I reach the top I climb up on a boulder that is set out of the wind
that hollows through the defile. Below, saguaros stalk down a dry wash
and then disappear as the land levels out into a wild, open emptiness.

Looking out over the pure sweep of seamless desert, I am surprised to
realize that the easy landscapes stifle me—closed walls of forests, ceilings
of boughs, neat-trimmed lawns, and ruffled curtains of trees hide the soft
horizons. I prefer the absences and the big empties, where the wind

ricochets from sand grain to mountain. I prefer the crystalline dryness and an unadulterated sky strewn from horizon to horizon with stars. I prefer the raw edges and the unfinished hems of the desert landscape.

Desert is where I want to be when there are no more questions to ask.

J(OHN) A(LEC) BAKER
B. 1926

In 1967 an unknown 41-year-old writer published an extraordinary book chronicling an intense, ten-year exploration of the lives and nature of peregrine falcons along the tidal coastlines of eastern England. The Peregrine, *J.A. Baker's account of these supreme predators, condensed into the diary of a single winter, is a combination of accurate detailed observation and a willed identification with his subject. His style is full of hard, Saxon, richly imagistic language reminiscent of Gerard Manley Hopkins. Like many contemporary nature writers he believes that "honest observation" is not enough, that the "emotions and behavior of the watcher are also facts, and they must be truthfully recorded." In* The Peregrine, *from which the following introductory chapter is taken, and in his subsequent book,* The Hill of Summer *(1969), he evokes his native Essex landscape with the same parochial devotion as Gilbert White and Richard Jefferies. Yet Baker's view of nature is more disturbing than these earlier writers', and his countryside is almost devoid of human figures.*

From THE PEREGRINE

BEGINNINGS

East of my home, the long ridge lies across the skyline like the low hull of a submarine. Above it, the eastern sky is bright with reflections of distant water, and there is a feeling of sails beyond land. Hill trees mass

The Peregrine (New York: Harper and Row, 1967).

together in a dark-spired forest, but when I move towards them they slowly fan apart, the sky descends between, and they are solitary oaks and elms, each with its own wide territory of winter shadow. The calmness, the solitude of horizons lures me towards them, through them, and on to others. They layer the memory like strata.

From the town, the river flows north-east, bends east round the north side of the ridge, turns south to the estuary. The upper valley is a flat open plain, lower down it is narrow and steep-sided, near the estuary it is again flat and open. The plain is like an estuary of land, scattered with island farms. The river flows slowly, meanders; it is too small for the long, wide estuary, which was once the mouth of a much larger river that drained most of middle England.

Detailed descriptions of landscape are tedious. One part of England is superficially so much like another. The differences are subtle, coloured by love. The soil here is clay: boulder clay to the north of the river, London clay to the south. There is gravel on the river terraces, and on the higher ground of the ridge. Once forest, then pasture, the land is now mainly arable. Woods are small, with few large trees; chiefly oak standards with hornbeam or hazel coppice. Many hedges have been cut down. Those that still stand are of hawthorn, blackthorn, and elm. Elms grow tall in the clay; their varying shapes contour the winter sky. Cricket-bat willows mark the river's course, alders line the brook. Hawthorn grows well. It is a country of elm and oak and thorn. People native to the clay are surly and slow to burn, morose and smouldering as alder wood, laconic, heavy as the land itself.

There are four hundred miles of tidal coast, if all the creeks and islands are included; it is the longest and most irregular county coastline. It is the driest county, yet watery-edged, flaking down to marsh and salting and mud-flat. The drying sandy mud of the ebb-tide makes the sky clear above; clouds reflect water and shine it back inland.

Farms are well ordered, prosperous, but a fragrance of neglect still lingers, like a ghost of fallen grass. There is always a sense of loss, a feeling of being forgotten. There is nothing else here; no castles, no ancient monuments, no hills like green clouds. It is just a curve of the earth, a rawness of winter fields. Dim, flat, desolate lands that cauterise all sorrow.

I have always longed to be a part of the outward life, to be out there at the edge of things, to let the human taint wash away in emptiness and silence as the fox sloughs his smell into the cold unworldliness of water; to return to the town as a stranger. Wandering flushes a glory that fades with arrival.

I came late to the love of birds. For years I saw them only as a tremor at the edge of vision. They know suffering and joy in simple states not possible for us. Their lives quicken and warm to a pulse our hearts can never reach. They race to oblivion. They are old before we have finished growing.

The first bird I searched for was the nightjar, which used to nest in the valley. Its song is like the sound of a stream of wine spilling from a height into a deep and booming cask. It is an odorous sound, with a bouquet that rises to the quiet sky. In the glare of day it would seem thinner and drier, but dusk mellows it and gives it vintage. If a song could smell, this song would smell of crushed grapes and almonds and dark wood. The sound spills out, and none of it is lost. The whole wood brims with it. Then it stops. Suddenly, unexpectedly. But the ear hears it still, a prolonged and fading echo, draining and winding out among the surrounding trees. Into the deep stillness, between the early stars and the long afterglow, the nightjar leaps up joyfully. It glides and flutters, dances and bounces, lightly, silently away. In pictures it seems to have a frog-like despondency, a mournful aura, as though it were sepulchred in twilight, ghostly and disturbing. It is never like that in life. Through the dusk, one sees only its shape and its flight, intangibly light and gay, graceful and nimble as a swallow.

Sparrowhawks were always near me in the dusk, like something I meant to say but could never quite remember. Their narrow heads glared blindly through my sleep. I pursued them for many summers, but they were hard to find and harder to see, being so few and so wary. They lived a fugitive, guerrilla life. In all the overgrown neglected places the frail bones of generations of sparrowhawks are sifting down now into the deep humus of the woods. They were a banished race of beautiful barbarians, and when they died they could not be replaced.

I have turned away from the musky opulence of the summer woods, where so many birds are dying. Autumn begins my season of hawk-hunting, spring ends it, winter glitters between like the arch of Orion.

I saw my first peregrine on a December day at the estuary ten years ago. The sun reddened out of the white river mist, fields glittered with rime, boats were encrusted with it; only the gently lapping water moved freely and shone. I went along the high river-wall towards the sea. The stiff crackling white grass became limp and wet as the sun rose through a clear sky into dazzling mist. Frost stayed all day in shaded places, the sun was warm, there was no wind.

I rested at the foot of the wall and watched dunlin feeding at the tide-line. Suddenly they flew upstream, and hundreds of finches fluttered overhead, whirling away with a 'hurr' of desperate wings. Too slowly it came to me that something was happening which I ought not to miss. I scrambled up, and saw that the stunted hawthorns on the inland slope of the wall were full of fieldfares. Their sharp bills pointed to the northeast, and they clacked and spluttered in alarm. I followed their point, and saw a falcon flying towards me. It veered to the right, and passed inland. It was like a kestrel, but bigger and yellower, with a more bullet-shaped head, longer wings, and greater zest and buoyancy of flight. It did not glide till it saw starlings feeding in stubble, then it swept down and was hidden among them as they rose. A minute later it rushed overhead and was gone in a breath into the sunlit mist. It was flying much higher than before, flinging and darting forwards, with its sharp wings angled back and flicking like a snipe's.

This was my first peregrine. I have seen many since then, but none has excelled it for speed and fire of spirit. For ten years I spent all my winters searching for that restless brilliance, for the sudden passion and violence that peregrines flush from the sky. For ten years I have been looking upward for that cloud-biting anchor shape, that crossbow flinging through the air. The eye becomes insatiable for hawks. It clicks towards them with ecstatic fury, just as the hawk's eye swings and dilates to the luring food-shapes of gulls and pigeons.

To be recognised and accepted by a peregrine you must wear the same clothes, travel by the same way, perform actions in the same order. Like all birds, it fears the unpredictable. Enter and leave the same fields at the same time each day, soothe the hawk from its wildness by a ritual of behavior as invariable as its own. Hood the glare of the eyes, hide the white tremor of the hands, shade the stark reflecting face, assume the stillness of a tree. A peregrine fears nothing he can see clearly and far off. Approach him across open ground with a steady unfaltering movement. Let your shape grow in size but do not alter its outline. Never hide yourself unless concealment is complete. Be alone. Shun the furtive oddity of man, cringe from the hostile eyes of farms. Learn to fear. To share fear is the greatest bond of all. The hunter must become the thing he hunts. What is, is now, must have the quivering intensity of an arrow thudding into a tree. Yesterday is dim and monochrome. A week ago you were not born. Persist, endure, follow, watch.

Hawk-hunting sharpens vision. Pouring away behind the moving bird, the land flows out from the eye in deltas of piercing colour. The angled eye strikes through the surface dross as the obliqued axe cuts to the heart of a tree. A vivid sense of place grows like another limb. Direction has colour and meaning. South is a bright, blocked place, opaque and stifling; West is a thickening of the earth into trees, a drawing together, the great beef side of England, the heavenly haunch; North is open, bleak, a way to nothing; East is a quickening in the sky, a beckoning of light, a storming suddenness of sea. Time is measured by a clock of blood. When one is active, close to the hawk, pursuing, the pulse races, time goes faster; when one is still, waiting, the pulse quietens, time is slow. Always, as one hunts for the hawk, one has an oppressive sense of time contracting inwards like a tightening spring. One hates the movement of the sun, the steady alteration of the light, the increase of hunger, the maddening metronome of the heart-beat. When one says 'ten o'clock' or 'three o'clock,' this is not the grey and shrunken time of towns; it is the memory of a certain fulmination or declension of light that was unique to that time and that place on that day, a memory as vivid to the hunter as burning magnesium. As soon as the hawk-hunter steps from his door he knows the way of the wind, he feels the weight of the air. Far within himself he seems to see the hawk's day growing steadily towards the light of their first encounter. Time and the weather hold both hawk and watcher between their turning poles. When the hawk is found, the hunter can look lovingly back at all the tedium and misery of searching and waiting that went before. All is transfigured, as though the broken columns of a ruined temple had suddenly resumed their ancient splendour.

I shall try to make plain the bloodiness of killing. Too often this has been slurred over by those who defend hawks. Flesh-eating man is in no way superior. It is so easy to love the dead. The word 'predator' is baggy with misuse. All birds eat living flesh at some time in their lives. Consider the cold-eyed thrush, that springy carnivore of lawns, worm stabber, basher to death of snails. We should not sentimentalise his song, and forget the killing that sustains it.

In my diary of a single winter I have tried to preserve a unity, binding together the bird, the watcher, and the place that holds them both. Everything I describe took place while I was watching it, but I do not believe that honest observation is enough. The emotions and behavior of the watcher are also facts, and they must be truthfully recorded.

For ten years I followed the peregrine. I was possessed by it. It was a grail to me. Now it has gone. The long pursuit is over. Few peregrines are left, there will be fewer, they may not survive. Many die on their backs, clutching insanely at the sky in their last convulsions, withered and burnt away by the filthy, insidious pollen of farm chemicals. Before it is too late, I have tried to recapture the extraordinary beauty of this bird and to convey the wonder of the land he lived in, a land to me as profuse and glorious as Africa. It is a dying world, like Mars, but glowing still.

JOHN FOWLES
B. 1926

Best known as the author of such novels as The Collector *(1963)* The
Magus *(1966) and* The French Lieutenant's Woman *(1969), Fowles has
also collaborated with landscape photographers in such works as* Islands
(1979), and The Tree *(1979). Myth and local natural history play important roles in much of his fiction. The protagonist of* The French Lieutenant's Woman, *for instance, is a collector of local fossils, and Fowles
himself was a curator of a local natural history museum in Dorset. The
following essay, first included as the central section of* The Tree, *examines the pervasive cultural myth of "the green man" in order to confront
the question of what ultimately constitutes our need for contact with
nature's presence, or "green chaos"—a need that for Fowles seems to
reside in the basic structure of the human psyche.*

From THE TREE

A few years ago I stood in a historic place. It was not a great battle-
field, a house, a square, the site of one famous event; but the site only of
countless very small ones—a neat little eighteenth-century garden, formally divided by gravel walks into parterres, with a small wooden house
in one corner where the garden's owner had once lived. There is only one
other garden to compare with it in human history, and that is the one in
the Book of Genesis, which never existed outside words. The one in
which I stood is very real, and it lies in the old Swedish university town of
Uppsala. Its owner was the great warehouse clerk and indexer of nature,
Carl Linnaeus, who between 1730 and 1760 docketed, or attempted to
docket, most of animate being. Perhaps nothing is more moving at Uppsala than the actual smallness and ordered simplicity of that garden (my

The Tree (Boston: Little, Brown, 1979).

father would have loved it) and the immense consequences that sprung from it in terms of the way we see and think about the external world. It is something more than one more famous shrine for lovers of nature, like Selborne or Coate Farm or Walden Pond. In fact, for all its air of gentle peace, it is closer to a nuclear explosion, whose radiations and mutations inside the human brain were incalculable and continue to be so: the place where an intellectual seed landed, and is now grown to a tree that shadows the entire globe.

I am a heretic about Linnaeus, and find nothing less strange, or more poetically just, than that he should have gone mad at the end of his life. I do not dispute the value of the tool he gave to natural science—which was in itself no more than a shrewd extension of the Aristotelian system and which someone else would soon have elaborated, if he had not; but I have doubts about the lasting change it has effected in ordinary human consciousness.

I sense in my collaborator on this book one likeness with my father. It is not that I don't share some of Frank Horvat's fertile attachment—and my father's—to the single tree, the tree in itself, and the art of cultivating it, literally or artistically. But I must confess my own love is far more of trees, more exactly of the complex internal landscapes they form when left to themselves. In the colonial organism, the green coral, of the wood or forest, experience, adventure, aesthetic pleasure, I think I could even say truth, all lie for me beyond the canopy and exterior wall of leaves, and beyond the individual.

Evolution has turned man into a sharply isolating creature, seeing the world not only anthropocentrically but singly, mirroring the way we like to think of our private selves. Almost all our art before the Impressionist—or their St. John the Baptist, William Turner—betrays our love of clearly defined boundaries, unique identities, of the individual thing released from the confusion of background. This power of detaching an object from its surroundings and making us concentrate on it is an implicit criterion in all our judgements on the more realistic side of visual art; and very similar, if not identical, to what we require of optical instruments like microscopes and telescopes—which is to magnify, to focus sharper, to distinguish better, to single from the ruck. A great deal of science is devoted to this same end: to providing specific labels, explaining specific mechanisms and ecologies, in short for sorting and tidying what seems in the mass indistinguishable one from the other. Even the simplest knowledge of the names and habits of flowers or trees starts this distinguishing or individuating process, and removes us a step from total reality towards anthropocentrism; that is, it acts mentally as an equivalent of the camera view-finder. Already it destroys or curtails certain possibilities of seeing, apprehending and experiencing. And that is the bitter fruit from the tree of Uppsalan knowledge.

It also begs very considerable questions as to the realities of the boundaries we impose on what we see. In a wood the actual visual "frontier" of any one tree is usually impossible to distinguish, at least in summer. We feel, or think we feel, nearest to a tree's "essence" (or that of its species) when it chances to stand like us, in isolation; but evolution did not intend trees to grow singly. Far more than ourselves they are social creatures, and no more natural as isolated specimens than man is as a marooned sailor or a hermit. Their society in turn creates or supports other societies of plants, insects, birds, mammals, micro-organisms; all of which we may choose to isolate and section off, but which remain no less the ideal entity, or whole experience, of the wood—and indeed are still so seen by most of primitive mankind.

Scientists restrict the word symbiotic to those relationships between species that bring some detectable mutual benefit; but the true wood, the true place of any kind, is the sum of all its phenomena. They are all in some sense symbiotic, being together in a togetherness of beings. It is only because such a vast sum of interactions and coincidences in time and place is beyond science's calculation (a scientist might say, beyond useful function, even if calculable) that we so habitually ignore it, and treat the flight of the bird and the branch it flies from, the leaf in the wind and its shadow on the ground, as separate events, or riddles—what bird? which branch? what leaf? which shadow? These question-boundaries (where do I file that?) are ours, not of reality. We are led to them, caged by them not only culturally and intellectually, but quite physically, by the restlessness of our eyes and their limited field and acuity of vision. Long before the glass lens and the movie-camera were invented, they existed in our eyes and minds, both in our mode of perception and in our mode of analysing the perceived: endless short sequence and jump-cut, endless need to edit and range this raw material.

I spent all my younger life as a more or less orthodox amateur naturalist; as a pseudo-scientist, treating nature as some sort of intellectual puzzle, or game, in which being able to name names and explain behaviourisms—to identify and to understand machinery—constituted all the pleasures and the prizes. I became slowly aware of the inadequacy of this approach: that it insidiously cast nature as a kind of opponent, an opposite team to be outwitted and beaten; that in a number of very important ways it distracted from the total experience and the total meaning of nature—and not only of what I personally needed from nature, not only as I had long, if largely unconsciously, begun to feel it (which was neither scientifically nor sentimentally, but in a way for which I had, and still have, no word). I came to believe that this approach represented a major human alienation, affecting all of us, both personally and socially; moreover, that such alienation had much more ancient roots behind the historical accident of its present scientific, or pseudo-scientific, form.

Naming things is always implicitly categorizing and therefore collecting them, attempting to own them; and because man is a highly acquisitive creature, brainwashed by most modern societies into believing that the act of acquisition is more enjoyable than the fact of having acquired, that getting beats having got, mere names and the objects they are tied to soon become stale. There is a constant need, or compulsion, to seek new objects and names—in the context of nature, new species and experiences. Everyday ones grow mute with familiarity, so known they become unknown. And not only in non-human nature: only fools think our attitude to our fellow-men is a thing distinct from our attitude to "lesser" life on this planet.

All this is an unhappy legacy from Victorian science, which was so characteristically obsessed with both the machine and exact taxonomy. I came only the other day on a letter in a forgotten drawer of the little museum of which I am curator. It was from a well-known Victorian fern expert, concerning some twenty or so specimens he had been sent from Dorset—all reducible, to a modern botanist, to three species. But this worthy gentleman felt obliged, in a welter of Latin polysyllables, to grant each specimen some new sub-specific or varietal rank, as if they were unbaptized children and might all go to hell if they were not given individual names. It would be absurd to deny the Victorians their enormous achievements in saner scientific fields, and I am not engaging in some sort of Luddite fantasy, wishing the machine they invented had been different, or even not at all. But we are far better at seeing the immediate advantages of such gains in knowledge of the exterior world than at assessing the costs of them. The particular cost of understanding the mechanism of nature, of having so successfully itemized and pigeon-holed it, lies most of all in the ordinary person's perception of it, in his or her ability to live with and care for it—and not to see it as challenge, defiance, enemy. Selection from total reality is no less necessary in science than it is in art; but outside those domains (in both of which the final test of selection is utility, or yield, to our own species) it seriously distorts and limits any worthwhile relationship.

I caused my hosts at Uppsala, where I went to lecture on the novel, some puzzlement by demanding (the literary business once over) to see Linnaeus's garden rather than the treasures of one of the most famous libraries in Europe. The feeling that I was not behaving as a decent writer should was familiar. Again and again in recent years I have told visiting literary academics that the key to my fiction, for what it is worth, lies in my relationship with nature—I might almost have said, for reasons I will explain, in trees. Again and again I have seen, under varying degrees of politeness, this assertion treated as some sort of irrelevant quirk, eccentricity, devious evasion of what must be the real truth: literary influences and theories of fiction, all the rest of that purely intellectual midden which faculty hens and cocks so like scratching over. Of course such matters are a part of the truth; but they are no more the whole truth than that the tree we see above ground is the whole tree. Even if we do discuss nature, I soon sense that we are talking about two different things: on their side some abstract intellectual concept, and on mine an experience whose deepest value lies in the fact that it cannot be directly described by any art . . . including that of words.

One interrogator even accused me of bad faith: that if I sincerely felt so deeply on the matter, I should write more about it. But what I gain most from nature is beyond words. To try to capture it verbally immediately places me in the same boat as the namers and would-be owners of nature: that is, it exiles me from what I most need to learn. It is a little as it is in atomic physics, where the very act of observation changes what is observed; though here the catch lies in trying to describe the observation. To enter upon such a description is like trying to capture the uncapturable. Its only purpose can be to flatter the vanity of the describer—a function painfully obvious in many of the more sentimental natural history writers.

But I think the most harmful change brought about by Victorian science in our attitude to nature lies in the demand that our relation with it must be purposive, industrious, always seeking greater knowledge. This dreadfully serious and puritanical approach (nowhere better exhibited in the nineteenth century than in the countless penny magazines aimed at young people) has had two very harmful effects. One is that it turned the vast majority of contemporary Western mankind away from what had become altogether too much like a duty, or a school lesson; the second is that the far saner eighteenth-century attitude, which viewed nature as a mirror for philosophers, as an evoker of emotion, as a pleasure, a poem, was forgotten. There are intellectual reasons as well for this. Darwin made sentimental innocence, nature as mainly personal or aesthetic experience, vaguely wicked. Not only did he propose a mechanism seemingly as iron as the steam-engine, but his very method of discovery, and its success in solving a great conundrum, offered an equally iron or one-sided model for the amateur naturalist himself, and made the older and more humanist approach seem childish. A "good" amateur naturalist today merely means one whose work is valued by the professional scientists in his field.

An additional element of alienation has come with the cinema and television, which are selective in another way. They present natural reality not only through other eyes, but a version of it in which the novelty or rarity of the subject plays a preponderant part in choice and treatment. Of course the nature film or programme has an entertainment value; of course there are some social goods in the now ubiquitous availability of copies of other people's images and opinions of actual things and events; but as with the Linnaean system, there is a cost. Being taken by camera into the deepest African jungle, across the Arctic wastes, thirty fathoms deep in the sea, may seem a "miracle of modern technology", but it will no more bring the viewer nearer the reality of nature, or a proper human relationship with the actual nature around him, than merely reading novels is likely to teach the writing of them. The most one can say is that it may help; a much more common result is to be persuaded of the futility of even trying.

Increasingly we live (and not only in terms of nature and novels) by the old tag, *Aut Caesar, aut nullus.* If I can't be Caesar, I'll be no one. If I can't have the knowledge of a scientist, I'll know nothing. If I can't have superb close-ups and rare creatures in the nature around me, to hell with it. Perhaps any representation of nature is better, to those remote from it in their daily lives, than none. Yet a great deal of such representation seems to me to descend straight from the concept of the menagerie, another sadly alienating selection, or reduction, from reality. Poking umbrellas through iron bars did not cease with the transition from the zoo to the screen.

Much of seventeenth- and eighteenth-century science and erudition is obsolete nonsense in modern scientific terms: in its personal interpolations, its diffuse reasoning, its misinterpreted evidence, its frequent blend of the humanities with science proper—its quotations from Horace and Virgil in the middle of a treatise on forestry. But one general, if unconscious, assumption lying behind almost all pre-Victorian science— that it is being presented by an entire human being, with all his complexities, to an audience of other entire human beings—has been much too soon dismissed as a mere historical phenomenon, at best exhibiting an engaging amateurishness, at worst sheer stupidity, from neither of which we have anything to learn. It is not of course the fault of modern scientists that most of their formal discourse is now of so abstruse a nature that only their fellow specialists can hope to understand it; that the discourse itself is increasingly mechanical, with words reduced to cogs and treated as poor substitutes for some more purely scientific formulation; nor is it directly their fault that their vision of empirical knowledge, the all-important value they put upon proven or demonstrable fact, has seeped down to dominate the popular view of nature—and our education about it. Our fallacy lies in supposing that the limiting nature of scientific method corresponds to the nature of ordinary experience.

Ordinary experience, from waking second to second, is in fact highly synthetic (in the sense of combinative or constructive), and made of a complexity of strands, past memories and present perceptions, times and places, private and public history, hopelessly beyond science's powers to analyse. It is quintessentially "wild," in the sense my father disliked so much: unphilosophical, irrational, uncontrollable, incalculable. In fact it corresponds very closely—despite our endless efforts to "garden," to invent disciplining social and intellectual systems—with wild nature. Almost all the richness of our personal existence derives from this synthetic and eternally present "confused" consciousness of both internal and external reality, and not least because we know it is beyond the analytical, or destructive, capacity of science.

Half by its principles, half by its inventions, science now largely dictates and forms our common, or public, perception of and attitudes to external reality. One can say of an attitude that it is generally held by society; but society itself is an abstraction, a Linnaeus-like label we apply to a group of individuals seen in a certain context and for a certain purpose; and before the attitude can be generally held, it must pass through the filter of the individual consciousness, where this irreducible "wild" component lies—the one that may agree with science and society, but can never be wholly plumbed, predicted or commanded by them.

One of the oldest and most diffused bodies of myth and folklore has accreted round the idea of the man in the trees. In all his manifestations, as dryad, as stag-headed Herne, as outlaw, he possesses the characteristic of elusiveness, a power of "melting" into the trees, and I am certain the attraction of the myth is so profound and universal because it is constantly "played" inside every individual consciousness.

This notion of the green man—or green woman, as W. H. Hudson made her—seen as emblem of the close connection between the actuality of present consciousness (not least in its habitual flight into a mental greenwood) and what seems to me lost by science in man's attitude to nature—that is, the "wild" side of his own, his inner feeling as opposed to the outer, fact-bound, conforming face imposed by fashion—helped me question my old pseudo-scientist self. But it also misled me for a time. In the 1950s I grew interested in the Zen theories of "seeing" and of aesthetics: of learning to look beyond names at things-in-themselves. I stopped bothering to identify species new to me, I concentrated more and more on the familiar, daily nature around me, where I then lived. But living without names is impossible, if not downright idiocy, in a writer; and living without explanation or speculation as to causality, little better—for Western man, at least. I discovered, too, that there was less conflict than I had imagined between nature as external assembly of names and facts and nature as internal feeling; that the two modes of seeing or knowing could in fact marry and take place almost simultaneously, and enrich each other.

Achieving a relationship with nature is both a science and an art, beyond mere knowledge or mere feeling alone; and I now think beyond oriental mysticism, transcendentalism, "meditation techniques" and the rest—or at least as we in the West have converted them to our use, which seems increasingly in a narcissistic way: to make ourselves feel more positive, more meaningful, more dynamic. I do not believe nature is to be reached that way either, by turning it into a therapy, a free clinic for admirers of their own sensitivity. The subtlest of our alienations from it, the most difficult to comprehend, is our eternal need to use it in some way, to derive some personal yield. We shall never fully understand nature (or ourselves), and certainly never respect it, until we dissociate the wild from the notion of usability—however innocent and harmless the use. For it is the general uselessness of so much of nature that lies at the root of our ancient hostility and indifference to it.

There is a kind of coldness, I would rather say a stillness, an empty space, at the heart of our forced co-existence with all the other species of the planet. Richard Jefferies coined a word for it: the ultra-humanity of all that is not man . . . not with us or against us, but outside and beyond us, truly alien. It may sound paradoxical, but we shall not cease to be alienated—by our knowledge, by our greed, by our vanity—from nature until we grant it its unconscious alienation from us.

I am not one of those supreme optimists who think all the world's ills, and especially this growing divide between man and nature, can be cured by a return to a quasi-agricultural, ecologically "caring" society. It is not that I doubt it might theoretically be so cured; but the possibility of the return defeats my powers of imagination. The majority of Western man is now urban, and the whole world will soon follow suit. A very significant tilt of balance in human history is expected by the end of the coming decade: over half of all mankind will by then have moved inside towns and cities. Any hope of reversing that trend, short of some universal catastrophe, is as tiny and precarious as the Monarch butterflies I watched, an autumn or two ago, migrating between the Fifth Avenue skyscrapers in central Manhattan. All chance of a close acquaintance with nature, be it through intellect and education, be it in the simplest way of all, by having it near at hand, recedes from the many who already effectively live in a support system in outer space, a creation of science, and without means to escape it, culturally or economically.

But the problem is not, or only minimally, that nature itself is in imminent danger or that we shall lose touch with it simply because we have less access to it. A number of species, environments, unusual ecologies are in danger, there are major pollution problems; but even in our most densely populated countries the ordinary wild remains far from the brink of extinction. We may not exaggerate the future threats and dangers, but we do exaggerate the present and actual state of this global nation—underestimate the degree to which it is still surviving and accessible to those who want to experience it. It is far less nature itself that is yet in true danger than our attitude to it. Already we behave as if we live in a world that holds only a remnant of what there actually is; in a world that may come, but remains a black hypothesis, not a present reality.

I believe the major cause of this more mental than physical rift lies less in the folly or onesidedness of our societies and educational systems, or in the historical evolution of man into a predominantly urban and industrial creature, a thinking termite, than in the way we have, during these last hundred and fifty years, devalued the kind of experience or knowledge we loosely define as art; and especially in the way we have failed to grasp its deepest difference from science. No art is truly teachable in its essence. All the knowledge in the world of its techniques can provide in itself no more than imitations or replicas of previous art. What is irreplaceable in any object of art is never, in the final analysis, its technique or craft, but the personality of the artist, the expression of his or her unique and individual feeling. All major advances in technique have come about to serve this need. Techniques in themselves are always reducible to sciences, that is, to learnability. Once Joyce has written, Picasso painted, Webern composed, it requires only a minimal gift, besides patience and practice, to copy their techniques exactly; yet we all know why this kind of technique-copy, even when it is so painstakingly done—for instance, in painting—that it deceives museum and auction-house experts, is counted worthless beside the work of the original artist. It is not *of* him or her; it is not art, but imitation.

As it is with the true "making" arts, so it is with the other aspects of human life of which we say that full knowledge or experience also requires an art—some inwardly creative or purely personal factor beyond the power of external teaching to instil or science to predict. Attempts to impart recipes or set formulae as to practice and enjoyment are always two-edged, since the question is not so much whether they may or may not enrich the normal experience of that abstract thing, the normal man or woman, but the certainty that they must in some way damage that other essential component of the process, the contribution of the artist in this sense—the individual experiencer, the "green man" hidden in the leaves of his or her unique and once-only being.

Telling people why, how and when they ought to feel this or that— whether it be with regard to the enjoyment of nature, of food, of sex, or anything else—may, undoubtedly sometimes does, have a useful function in dispelling various kinds of socially harmful ignorance. But what this instruction cannot give is the deepest benefit of any art, be it of making, or of knowing, or of experiencing: which is self-expression and self-discovery. The last thing a sex-manual can be is an *ars amoris*—a science of coupling, perhaps, but never an art of love. Exactly the same is true of so many nature-manuals. They may teach you how and what to look for, what to question in external nature; but never in your own nature.

In science greater knowledge is always and indisputably good; it is by no means so throughout all human existence. We know it from art proper, where achievement and great factual knowledge, or taste, or intelligence, are in no way essential companions; if they were, our best artists would also be our most learned academics. We can know it by reducing the matter to the absurd, and imagining that God, or some Protean visitor from outer space, were at one fell sweep to grant us all knowledge. Such omniscience would be worse than the worst natural catastrophe, for our species as a whole; would extinguish its soul, lose it all pleasure and reason for living.

This is not the only area in which, like the rogue computer beloved of science fiction fans, some socially or culturally consecrated proposition—which may be true or good in its social or cultural context— extends itself to the individual; but it is one of the most devitalizing. Most mature artists know that great general knowledge is more a hindrance than a help. It is only innately mechanical, salami-factory novelists who set such great store by research; in nine cases out of ten what natural knowledge and imagination cannot supply is in any case precisely what needs to be left out. The green man in all of us is well aware of this. In practice we spend far more time rejecting knowledge than trying to gain it, and wisely. But it is in the nature of all society, let alone one deeply imbued with a scientific and technological ethos, to bombard us with ever more knowledge—and to make any questioning or rejection of it unpatriotic and immoral.

Art and nature are siblings, branches of the one tree; and nowhere more than in the continuing inexplicability of many of their processes, and above all those of creation and of effect on their respective audiences. Our approach to art, as to nature, has become increasingly scientized (and dreadfully serious) during this last century. It sometimes seems now as if it is principally there not for itself but to provide material for labelling, classifying, analysing—specimens for "setting," as I used to set moths and butterflies. This is of course especially true of—and pernicious in—our schools and universities. I think the first sign that I might one day become a novelist (though I did not then realize it) was the passionate detestation I developed at my own school for all those editions of examination books that began with a long introduction: an anatomy lesson that always reduced the original text to a corpse by the time one got to it, a lifeless demonstration of a pre-established proposition. It took me years to realize that even geniuses, the Shakespeares, the Racines, the Austens, have human faults.

Obscurity, the opportunity a work of art gives for professional explainers to show their skills, has become almost an aesthetic virtue; at another extreme the notion of art as vocation (that is, something to which one is genetically suited) is dismissed as non-scientific and inegalitarian. It is not a gift beyond personal choice, but one that can be acquired, like knowledge of science, by rote, recipe and hard work. Elsewhere we become so patterned and persuaded by the tone of the more serious reviewing of art in our magazines and newspapers that we no longer notice their overwhelmingly scientific tone, or the paradox of this knowing-naming technique being applied to a non-scientific object—one whose production the artist himself cannot fully explain, and one whose effect the vast majority of the non-reviewing audience do not attempt to explain.

The professional critic or academic would no doubt say this is mere ignorance, that both artists and audiences have to be taught to understand themselves and the object that links them, to make the relationship articulate and fully conscious; defoliate the wicked green man, hunt him out of his trees. Of course there is a place for the scientific, or quasi-scientific, analysis of art, as there is (and far greater) for that of nature. But the danger, in both art and nature, is that all emphasis is placed on the created, not the creation.

All artefacts, all bits of scientific knowledge, share one thing in common: that is, they come to us from the past, they are relics of something already observed, deduced, formulated, created, and as such qualify to go through the Linnaean and every other scientific mill. Yet we cannot say that the "green" or creating process does not happen or has no importance just because it is largely private and beyond lucid description and rational analysis. We might as well argue that the young wheat-plant is irrelevant because it can yield nothing to the miller and his stones. We know that in any sane reality the green blade is as much the ripe grain as the child is father to the man. Nor of course does the simile apply to art alone, since we are all in a way creating our future out of our present, our "published" outward behavior out of our inner green being. One main reason we may seldom feel this happening is that society does not want us to. Such random personal creativity is offensive to all machines.

I began this wander through the trees—we shall come to them literally, by the end—in search of that much looser use of the word "art" to describe a way of knowing and experiencing and enjoying outside the major modes of science and art proper . . . a way not concerned with scientific discovery and artefacts, a way that is internally rather than externally creative, that leaves very little public trace; and yet which for those very reasons is almost wholly concentrated in its own creative process. It is really only the qualified scientist or artist who can escape from the interiority and constant nowness, the green chaos of this experience, by making some aspect of it exterior and so fixing it in past time, or known knowledge. Thereby they create new, essentially parasitical orders and categories of phenomena that in turn require both a science and an art of experiencing.

But nature is unlike art in terms of its product—what we in general know it by. The difference is that it is not only created, an external object with a history, and so belonging to a past; but also creating in the present, as we experience it. As we watch, it is so to speak rewriting, reformulating, repainting, rephotographing itself. It refuses to stay fixed and fossilized in the past, as both the scientist and the artist feel it somehow ought to; and both will generally try to impose this fossilization on it.

Verbal tenses can be very misleading here: we stick adamantly in speech to the strict protocol of actual time. Of and in the present we speak in the present, of the past in the past. But our psychological tenses can be very different. Perhaps because I am a writer (and nothing is more fictitious than the past in which the first, intensely alive and present, draft of a novel goes down on the page), I long ago noticed this in my naturalist self: that is, a disproportionately backward element in any present experience of nature, a retreat or running-back to past knowledge and experience, whether it was the definite past of personal memory or the indefinite, the imperfect, of stored "ological" knowledge and proper scientific behaviour. This seemed to me often to cast a mysterious veil of deadness, of having already happened, over the actual and present event or phenomenon.

I had a vivid example of it only a few years ago in France, long after I thought I had grown wise to this self-imposed brainwashing. I came on my first Military Orchid, a species I had long wanted to encounter, but hitherto never seen outside a book. I fell on my knees before it in a way that all botanists will know. I identified, to be quite certain, with Professors Clapham, Tutin and Warburg in hand (the standard British *Flora*), I measured, I photographed, I worked out where I was on the map, for future reference. I was excited, very happy, one always remembers one's "first" of the rarer species. Yet five minutes after my wife had finally (other women are not the only form of adultery) torn me away, I suffered a strange feeling. I realized I had not actually *seen* the three plants in the little colony we had found. Despite all the identifying, measuring, photographing, I had managed to set the experience in a kind of present past, a having-looked, even as I was temporally and physically still looking. If I had had the courage, and my wife the patience, I would have asked her to turn and drive back, because I knew I had just fallen, in the stupidest possible way, into an ancient trap. It is not necessarily too little knowledge that causes ignorance; possessing too much, or wanting to gain too much, can produce the same result.

There is something in the nature of nature, in its presentness, its seeming transcience, its creative ferment and hidden potential, that corresponds very closely with the wild, or green man, in our psyches; and it is a something that disappears as soon as it is relegated to an automatic pastness, a status of merely classifiable *thing*, image taken *then*. "Thing" and "then" attract each other. If it is thing, it was then; if it was then, it is thing. We lack trust in the present, this moment, this actual seeing, because our culture tells us to trust only the reported back, the publicly framed, the edited, the thing set in the clearly artistic or the clearly scientific angle of perspective. One of the deepest lessons we have to learn is that nature, of its nature, resists this. It waits to be seen otherwise, in its individual presentness and from our individual presentness.

I come now near the heart of what seems to me to be the single greatest danger in the rich legacy left us by Linnaeus and the other founding fathers of all our sciences and scientific mores and methods—or more fairly, left us by our leaping evolutionary ingenuity in the invention of tools. All tools, from the simplest word to the most advanced space probe, are disturbers and rearrangers of primordial nature and reality—are, in the dictionary definition, "mechanical implements for working upon something." What they have done, and I suspect in direct proportion to our ever-increasing dependence on them, is to addict us to purpose: both to looking for purpose in everything external to us and to looking internally for purpose in everything we do—to seek explanation of the outside world by purpose, to justify our seeking by purpose. This addiction to finding a reason, a function, a quantifiable yield, has now infiltrated all aspects of our lives—and become effectively synonymous with pleasure. The modern version of hell is purposelessness.

Nature suffers particularly in this, and our indifference and hostility to it is closely connected with the fact that its only purpose appears to be being and surviving. We may think that this comprehends all animate existence, including our own; and so it must, ultimately; but we have long ceased to be content with so abstract a motive. A scientist would rightly say that all form and behaviour in nature is highly purposive, or strictly designed for the end of survival—specific or genetic, according to theory. But most of this functional purpose is hidden to the non-scientist, indecipherable; and the immense variety of nature appears to hide nothing, nothing but a green chaos at the core—which we brilliantly purposive apes can use and exploit as we please, with a free conscience.

A green chaos. Or a wood.

FRANKLIN RUSSELL

B. 1926

Franklin Russell is a native of New Zealand, a Canadian citizen, and a long-time resident of New York City. In the early 1960s Russell found himself "stifled by the synthetic nature of life" in his Manhattan apartment and set off to discover the world of islands—specifically, the seabird colonies of Maine and the Canadian maritimes. The result was The Secret Islands *(1965), a series of adventures and encounters not only with birds but with colorful human figures from remote communities whose way of life had changed little over two centuries. The author's approach is personal and confessional, recording his failures as well as his achievements. Russell is not the first writer to find nature's impersonal fecundity overwhelming and even appalling; but few have described it in such vivid and dramatic detail as in the following account of the birds of Funk Island, an isolated rock fifty miles off the coast of Newfoundland. It is a place where ordinary categories of meaning seem to break down, where "Chaos is order. Order is a mystery. Time is meaningless"—an experience at once disconcerting and strangely vitalizing.*

From THE SECRET ISLANDS

THE ISLAND OF AUKS

Arthur Sturge was caught in an immortal moment, straining back on his oar as he moved the heavy dory toward Funk Island. This was the last lunge of the journey; the longliner heaved behind us; Uncle Jacob had bellowed his final exhortation of good luck.

I saw the island close up as I glanced over Sturge's shoulder, and I knew I was duplicating the experience of a thousand men before me. From the boat it seemed incredible that such a stream of humanity— explorers, Indians, sealers, whalers, codfishermen—had ever reached this lonely place. Yet the island, and its auks, had drawn them as it was drawing me.

The island was a blank wall of rock, thirty feet high, suave and bland, and topped by a thin, fast-moving frieze of murres who, presumably, were anxiously watching our boat. I have read about a moment of truth, even written about it, but not until I was in this dory, in this place, did I really understand what it meant. It was the final throw of the dice. Would we be able to land?

"Hard to say. Them waves is risin' high. . . ."

I looked toward the island and saw the water pitching, silent and ominous, up the blank rock. I had come this far, but now I could think only of being capsized—dashed against the rocks or maimed under the boat's keel. I had already talked to a dozen men who had traveled thousands of miles only to be turned back at this point.

I sat in the back of the dory, carried forward by the momentum of a determination long sustained. In a moment, the boat was rising and falling against the rock face on six-foot waves.

"Get up front," Arthur Sturge said.

He eased the boat toward the rock. Willie hunched in the bows. At the peak of a wave, he jumped, grabbed at the rock face, and clung. I could see that the rock was gouged with handholds into which my fingers must fit as I jumped.

"Arl roight!" Arthur shouted.

Willie now had his back to the rock; he was facing me so that he might try to seize me if I fell. The boat rose and wobbled at its peak; I jumped, hit the rocks, and felt my fingers slip into the grooves. As I clung there, I realized the grooves were man-made. Of course. Other men had

The Secret Islands (New York: Norton, 1965).

met the same problem. Of course they had done something about it. These grooves into which my fingers fitted so neatly might have been cut in Drake's time, or before, when the Beothuk Indians came to plunder the island; or had they been cut by Eskimos, a thousand years before Christ?

Muscles knotted, and I strained upward. The problems of landing on Funk Island have remained unchanged. Rockets to the moon and the splitting of the atom mean nothing when it comes to landing on Funk Island. The equation for success is constant: an open boat with a skillful oarsman and a man willing to jump.

Willie had disappeared over the top of the rock while I was still absorbed in finding hand- and footholds in rock slippery with algae and bird excrement. I mounted the crest of the rock and Funk Island spread out, an explosion of sight, sound, and smell. I saw, but I did not see; I saw dark masses of murres in the distance; I saw curtains of buzzing kittiwakes interposing themselves like thousands of pretty white butterflies; I saw rolling hummocks of bare rock. But it was the sound that came to me first. We walked forward over intransigent, bare granite, and the sound swelled like thunder. A literate biologist has described it as "a rushing of waters," but that description does not satisfy poet or artist. It is orchestral, if a million players can be imagined: rich, sensuous, hypnotic.

When we came to the edge of the first great concourse of birds, perhaps two hundred thousand of them staining the rock densely black and white, the orchestral analogy became even more vivid because I could hear, among those thousands of voices, rippling spasms of pathos and melancholy—Brahmsian. The adult birds cried *ehr-ehr-ehr*, crescendo, diminuendo, gushes of emotion. The cries of the flying birds— and there were thousands in the air—swelled and faded in haunting harmony as they passed low overhead. Buried in this amalgam of voices were the piping screams of the young murres, sounds so piercing they hurt the ear.

We moved around the periphery of the murres. With every step, I was conscious of new expansions in the scope of sound. A sibilant undertone to the massive main theme was faintly discernible, the sound of innumerable wings beating: *flacka-flacka-flacka-flacka*. Wings struck each other—*clack, clack, clack*—as birds, flying in thick layers, collided in mid-air. Then another buried sound, a submelody, a counterpoint: *gaggla-gaggla-gaggla*. The gannets were hidden somewhere among the murre hordes. Other sounds were reduced to minutiae in the uproar: the thin cries of herring gulls, the rasping moans of kittiwakes hovering high overhead.

I had been on the island an hour and only now was I really registering the sound of it.

Next, overwhelmingly, came real vision. The murres were massed so thickly they obscured the ground. The birds stood shoulder to shoulder, eyeball to eyeball. In places, they were so densely packed that if one bird stretched or flapped her wings, she sent a sympathetic spasm rippling away from her on all sides.

All life was in constant, riotous motion. Murre heads wavered and darted; wings beat; birds landed clumsily among the upraised heads of their comrades; birds took off and thrashed passageways through the birds ahead of them, knocking them down. Chicks ran from adult to adult; eggs rolled across bare rock, displaced by kicking feet.

The murres heeded me, yet they did not. I approached them and a rising roar of protest sounded, a concentration of the general uproar, which seemed not directed at me at all but at the outrage of intrusion. I walked away from them and the roar died instantly.

The sun was well up, a brilliant star in an azure sky, and I walked to the quiet shore, away from the main masses of murres. Willie had disappeared into a gully. Perhaps I needed time to assimilate. But there was no time. The multiple dimensions of the sight came pouring in. The air streamed with birds coming at me. I threw up my hands, shouted at them, but the shout was lost, ineffectual, not causing a single bird to swerve or otherwise acknowledge me.

At least a hundred thousand birds were aloft at once. They circled the island endlessly, like fighter bombers making strafing runs on a target, flying the full length of the island, then turning out to sea and sweeping back offshore to begin another run. They came on relentlessly and the sky danced with them.

This was not, I realized, the hostile reaction of individual birds who saw their nests threatened. Instead, the murres were a tribe of animals resisting a threat to their island. Individually, they intimidated nothing. Collectively, they emanated power and strength. I looked into a thousand cold eyes and felt chill, impersonal hostility in the air.

I climbed to the top of a ridge and looked down the length of the island, looked into the masses of birds hurtling toward me, looked down to the grounded hordes, a living, writhing backbone of murres, murres, murres. Then, after the visual shock came the olfactory impact.

The smell of Funk Island is the smell of death. It is probably the source of the island's name, which in various languages means "to steam," "to create a great stench," "to smoke"; it may also mean "fear." The island certainly smells ghastly. No battlefield could ever concentrate such a coalition of dead and dying.

A change of wind brought the smell to us, choking, sickening. As I walked down a slope and out of the force of the wind, the air clotted with the smell. In a hollow at the bottom of the slope, it had collected in such concentration that I gagged and my throat constricted. The fishermen *knew* the smell was poisonous. Uncle Jacob Sturge had told me how one fisherman who tried to run through the concentration of birds was nearly gassed unconscious.

The smell of Funk Island comes from a combination of corruption. There are no scavengers, except bacteria, so dead bodies lie where they have fallen. The debris of a million creatures has nowhere to go. Eggs by the scores of thousands lie everywhere, so that I could not see which were being brooded, which were rotten. In one small gully, unwanted or untended eggs had been kicked together in a one hundred foot driftline by the constantly moving feet of the birds.

The smell of the island came in diminishing waves as the sea breeze died and the heat rose from the rocks. A ripple of explosions fled away among a nearby concentration of birds. I listened; the sound was man-like. It reminded me of a popgun I had used when I was a boy. From a nearby hill packed with murres, another flurry of explosions, then single shots haphazardly firing all around me. If the smell of the island needed an exemplifying sound, this was it. The explosions were the sound of rotten eggs bursting in the growing heat.

I walked, while the smell gathered in my nostrils and took on various identities. It was the thin, sour smell of bird excrement: acidic, astringent, more than a hundred tons of it splashed on the island every day. Underlying that smell was the stench of the rotting fish which lay everywhere after being vomited up by the parent murres but not eaten by the nestlings. The smell was of putrescence, of oil, of fish, and of an indescribable other thing: the stench of a million creatures packed together in a small place.

I walked halfway down the length of the island, a distance of perhaps five hundred feet, but my progress was slow because of the difficulty I had in assimilating everything I saw.

In my mind were scraps of history. I was thinking, for instance, of how Newfoundland's ancient Indians, the Beothuks, camped in a gulch when they were on bird- and egg-hunting expeditions; of how, until recently, the gulch was an archaeological repository of old knives, spoons, belaying pins, and broken pots, testifying to more than two hundred years of exploitation of the island by hunters of meat, oil, eggs, and feathers.

Willie appeared on a far ridge. He was standing at the edge of Indian Gulch. I walked toward him along the rim of a concourse of murres. A feeble spring flowed into the gulch and created a small pond, which was also fed by the sea during heavy swells. Sea water belched up into it through a narrow crack in the rock. Into this pond poured a ceaseless flow of excrement, coughed-up fish, bodies, rotten eggs, and live nestlings. By midsummer, the water was mucid, pea-green, fermenting, almost bubbling with corruption.

The murres were not distressed by this putrid mess; as Willie walked along the top of the gulch, hundreds of them dropped down to the water and floated. Suddenly, the pond was roiled into green foam as a group of birds took off. Their departure triggered another flight, which because murres fly poorly, was a failure. The birds crashed on top of each other or piled into heaps along the steep banks. This drew a sympathetic flight from murres perched precariously on the cliffs and a cloud of birds took off. Their departure sent eggs and nestlings spilling off the cliffs into the water.

But on Funk Island, nothing matters. Death is nothing. Life is nothing. Chaos is order. Order is a mystery. Time is meaningless. The deep-throated roar of the colony cries out to a heedless sky. The human observer, cowed by its primitive energy, by its suggestion of the unnameable, stumbles on blindly.

As I walked, I examined my growing sense of reality and sought a guidepost to what it all meant. I had thought (an hour before? two hours? it was nearer to four hours) that a sweep of Brahmsian rhetoric could describe the island. Already, the image was obsolete. Now, I felt a mechanistic sense, Prokofievian, an imperative monotone, the sound of Mars. The struggling, homuncular forms piled together in such utter, inhuman chaos denied any ordered view of the universe.

I had to wonder whether a poet had preceded me to the island; or did the island have a counterpart elsewhere? De la Mare's disgust at the massacre?

> And silence fell: the rushing sun
> Stood still in paths of heat,
> Gazing in waves of horror on
> The dead about my feet.

It was nearly noon, and sun flames reached for the island and scorched it. I was enervated, but I was also recovering normal sensibility, which brought me *details* of the life of the murre colony. Everywhere I looked now, young murres looked back. In places, they were packed thirty and forty together among the adults. There is only one word to describe them and it is not in any dictionary. They are murrelings: tiny, rotund, dusky balls of fluff with the most piercing voices ever given a young bird.

Their piping screams must be essential for them to assert themselves
above the roar of the adults. How else could they identify themselves to
their parents? Yet, bafflement grew as I watched them. One murreling
in that featureless mass of birds was infinitely smaller than one needle in
a stack of hay. How contact is kept with the parent birds remains a
mystery of biology.

Warned by the scope of destruction in the colony, I was not surprised
to find that the murrelings were expendable. Life moves to and from the
colony at high speed. A murreling fell from a rock, bounced into an evil
puddle, and was trampled by a throng of adults. Hearing screams from a
rock I disengaged a murreling jammed in a crevice, looked down, saw a
mass of fluffy bodies wedged deeper in the crevice. Murrelings fell from
cliffs into the sea, rose and floated in foam, screaming. Murrelings lay
dead among pustular eggs; they lay in heaps and windrows in olivaceous
puddles.

I knew from murre literature that the murrelings often became
shocked by prolonged rain and died by the thousands. That, in the
context of this island, was not surprising. An *individual* death was shocking. Willie had walked back up the other side of the island and we met at
the edge of a group of murres. Willie groaned.

"I don't feel well," he said, rolling his eyes in mock nausea.

As he spoke, I looked over his shoulder in horror. In the middle of the
murre mass, standing on slightly higher ground, was a group of gannets.
These birds, though inferior in number, occupied the best territory.
Though dominant, they seemed to have an amicable relationship with
the murres. In places, murres and gannets were mixed together; murrelings gathered around gannets as though they were murres.

A gannet on a nest had reached down casually for one of these nearby
murrelings, and as I watched, upended it and swallowed the struggling
youngster. It was not the sight of such casual destruction that was shocking; it was the sound of the murreling dying.

It screamed when it was seized by the gannet's beak, which was bigger
than the murreling's entire body. It screamed as it was hoisted into the
air. Horrifyingly, it screamed loudest as it was being swallowed. The
gannet, though a big, powerful bird, had to swallow hard to get the
murreling down. Its neck writhed and its beak gaped and all the time the
awful screams of the murreling came up out of the gannet's throat. The
cries became fainter and fainter.

"Horrible," Willie said. "Oi never gets used to it."

The roar of the birds became a lamentation, a collusion of agony and
sorrow. The flying creatures seemed to be in streaming retreat. Why *that*
murreling and not any of the others still around at the feet of the gan-

net? If gannets really relished murre flesh, surely they would quickly wipe out all the murrelings near them. But they do not.

It was now afternoon and the sun plashed white and pitiless light on rock. For some time, I had been aware of a growing disorientation. I took a picture to the east, seventy thousand birds; to the west, one hundred thousand; in the air, twenty thousand. The noise, the smell, the screams, the corpses, the green puddles, pushed bonily into my chest. I fumbled with film but could not decide how to reload the camera or, indeed, remember what setting to use, or how to release the shutter.

"Oi t'ink oi'll go and sit behind dat rock," Willie said. "Oi goes funny in de head after a while here."

Uncle Jacob had mentioned that the island could drive a man mad. I was being sickened by the pressure of it. Once, in Australia, I watched men systematically kill several hundred thousand rabbits they had penned against a fence. The steady thocking of cudgels hammering rabbit skulls continued hour after hour, eventually dulling the eye and diminishing the hearing. On Funk Island, my observing sense was losing its ability to see and to record.

I sought release in reverie and walked, half-conscious of what I was doing, toward an incongruous green field that lay alone in the middle of the island. Its bareness suggested another place of personal memory, and an association of ideas. My ancestors were Scottish and fought the English at Culloden. When I went to Culloden, two hundred years after the battle, I was overwhelmed by those long, sinister mounds of mass burial of the clans.

This Funk Island field was also a midden of slain creatures. It was a great natural-history site, as significant to an ornithologist as Ashurbanipal's palace would be to an archaeologist. Here, generations of flightless great auks had flocked to breed after eight months of oceanic wandering. Their occupancy built up soil. Here, also, they were slain throughout the eighteenth century until they became extinct, probably early in the nineteenth.

A puffin bolted out of the ground ahead and flipped a bone from her burrow entrance as she left. I knelt and clawed a handful of bones out of the burrow. I saw other burrows, bones spilling out of them as though they were entrances to a disorderly catacomb.

This was not fantasy. These were great-auk bones, still oozing out of the earth nearly a hundred and fifty years after the last bird had gone. The bones permeated the ground under my feet; puffins dug among them and kicked them aside to find graveyard sanctuary. Life in the midst of death.

All at once, walking across bare rock, the murres well distant, I felt a release. Willie was not in sight; the longliner was off fishing somewhere. The granite underfoot changed texture, became a desert I had walked, then a heath, a moor I had tramped, and eventually, all the bare and empty places of earth I had ever known. I felt the presence of friends and heard their voices. But something was wrong. Some were still friends but others had closed, deceitful faces. Inhibition and self-deception fell away; flushes of hate and love passed as the faces moved back and forth. Forgotten incidents came to mind. What was happening?

Uncle Jacob's voice: "A man could go mad on the Funks."

This was enough. I turned toward the shore, to the *Doris and Lydia,* which had appeared from nowhere. Willie leaped eagerly from his place of refuge behind a rock. The roar of the murres receded. I imagined the island empty during much of the long year, naked as a statue against the silent hiss of mist coming out of the Labrador Current, or the thunder of an Atlantic gale piling thirty-foot waves up the sides of the island.

"She be a sight to see in the winter," Uncle Benny had said.

The seasons of millennia switched back and forth. The island suffocated in the original gases of earth: argon, radon, krypton, xenon, neon. The island disappeared in yellow fog, and water slid down its sides. The island was a corpse, dead a million years, its surface liquefied, with rot running into its granite intestines. The island festered, and rivulets of pus coursed down its sides. The island was death. The island was life.

Only in retrospect could the island become real. Later, I was to return to the island and actually live on it in order to turn my disbelief into lasting memory. Willie moved parallel to me, jumping from rock to rock and displacing a fluttering canopy of kittiwakes. He was a different man now as he met me at the landing site, beaming and lighthearted.

"So dat's de Funks, eh?" he said, and he was proud that I had seen it.

In the boat below us, Arthur and Cyril smiled. Arthur was relaxed now, in contrast to his silent, absorbed intensity when he was trying to get me to the island, and on it. Both men, and Willie, poised at the top of the cliff, were caught for a moment by the camera, like toreros who have survived a bloody afternoon and will hear the bugles again tomorrow.

With a final look over my shoulder at the silently fleeing birds, I slid down the cliff to the boat and Funk Island became a part of the history of my life.

EDWARD ABBEY
1927-1989

Over fifteen years as a fire lookout and park ranger in the Southwest, Abbey developed the passions that pervade and enliven much of his writing—deep love of the desert and bitterness about its desecration by the miners, dammers, developers, and tourists. One of his marks as a writer is the fierceness with which he pursues his polemic on behalf of the desert, declaring war against the atrocities he has witnessed. Abbey's novel The Monkey Wrench Gang *(1975) portrays a band of environmental guerillas so vividly that it encouraged the founding of the radical environmental movement Earth First!* Desert Solitaire *(1968), his best known work, describes Abbey's experiences as a ranger at Utah's Arches National Monument. With sardonic honesty Abbey shows, reflects upon, and rails against his own implication in the culture of "industrial tourism." But the central source of his book's power is its evocation of the desert landscape itself, in its overwhelming, threatening presence and its elusive beauty.*

From DESERT SOLITAIRE

THE SERPENTS OF PARADISE

The April mornings are bright, clear and calm. Not until the afternoon does the wind begin to blow, raising dust and sand in funnelshaped twisters that spin across the desert briefly, like dancers, and then collapse—whirlwinds from which issue no voice or word except the forlorn moan of the elements under stress. After the reconnoitering dust-devils comes the real, the serious wind, the voice of the desert rising to a demented howl and blotting out sky and sun behind yellow clouds of dust, sand, confusion, embattled birds, last year's scrub-oak leaves, pollen, the husks of locusts, bark of juniper. . . .

Desert Solitaire (New York: McGraw-Hill, 1968).

Time of the red eye, the sore and bloody nostril, the sand-pitted windshield, if one is foolish enough to drive his car into such a storm. Time to sit indoors and continue that letter which is never finished— while the fine dust forms neat little windows under the edge of the door and on the windowsills. Yet the springtime winds are as much a part of the canyon country as the silence and the glamorous distances; you learn, after a number of years, to love them also.

The mornings therefore, as I started to say and meant to say, are all the sweeter in the knowledge of what the afternoon is likely to bring. Before beginning the morning chores I like to sit on the sill of my doorway, bare feet planted on the bare ground and a mug of hot coffee in hand, facing the sunrise. The air is gelid, not far above freezing, but the butane heater inside the trailer keeps my back warm, the rising sun warms the front, and the coffee warms the interior.

Perhaps this is the loveliest hour of the day, though it's hard to choose. Much depends on the season. In midsummer the sweetest hour begins at sundown, after the awful heat of the afternoon. But now, in April, we'll take the opposite, that hour beginning with the sunrise. The birds, re-turning from wherever they go in winter, seem inclined to agree. The pinyon jays are whirling in garrulous, gregarious flocks from one stunted tree to the next and back again, erratic exuberant games without any apparent practical function. A few big ravens hang around and croak harsh clanking statements of smug satisfaction from the rimrock, lifting their greasy wings now and then to probe for lice. I can hear but seldom see the canyon wrens singing their distinctive song from somewhere up on the cliffs: a flutelike descent—never ascent—of the whole-tone scale. Staking out new nesting claims, I understand. Also invisible but invari-ably present at some indefinable distance are the mourning doves whose plaintive call suggests irresistibly a kind of seeking-out, the attempt by separated souls to restore a lost communion:

Hello . . . they seem to cry, *who* . . . *are* . . . *you?*

And the reply from a different quarter. *Hello* . . . (pause) *where* . . . *are* . . . *you?*

No doubt this line of analogy must be rejected. It's foolish and unfair to impute to the doves, with serious concerns of their own, an interest in questions more appropriate to their human kin. Yet their song, if not a mating call or a warning, must be what it sounds like, a brooding medita-tion on space, on solitude. The game.

Other birds, silent, which I have not yet learned to identify, are also lurking in the vicinity, watching me. What the ornithologist terms l.g.b.'s—little gray birds—they flit about from point to point on noiseless wings, their origins obscure.

As mentioned before, I share the housetrailer with a number of mice. I don't know how many but apparently only a few, perhaps a single family. They don't disturb me and are welcome to my crumbs and leavings. Where they came from, how they got into the trailer, how they survived before my arrival (for the trailer had been locked up for six months), these are puzzling matters I am not prepared to resolve. My only reservation concerning the mice is that they do attract rattlesnakes.

I'm sitting on my doorstep early one morning, facing the sun as usual, drinking coffee, when I happen to look down and see almost between my bare feet, only a couple of inches to the rear of my heels, the very thing I had in mind. No mistaking that wedgelike head, that tip of horny segmented tail peeping out of the coils. He's under the doorstep and in the shade where the ground and air remain very cold. In his sluggish condition he's not likely to strike unless I rouse him by some careless move of my own.

There's a revolver inside the trailer, a huge British Webley .45, loaded, but it's out of reach. Even if I had it in my hands I'd hesitate to blast a fellow creature at such close range, shooting between my own legs at a living target flat on solid rock thirty inches away. It would be like murder; and where would I set my coffee? My cherrywood walking stick leans against the trailerhouse wall only a few feet away but I'm afraid that in leaning over for it I might stir up the rattler or spill some hot coffee on his scales.

Other considerations come to mind. Arches National Monument is meant to be among other things a sanctuary for wildlife—for all forms of wildlife. It is my duty as a park ranger to protect, preserve and defend all living things within the park boundaries, making no exceptions. Even if this were not the case I have personal convictions to uphold. Ideals, you might say. I prefer not to kill animals. I'm a humanist; I'd rather kill a *man* than a snake.

What to do. I drink some more coffee and study the dormant reptile at my heels. It is not after all the mighty diamondback, *Crotalus atrox*, I'm confronted with but a smaller species known locally as the horny rattler or more precisely as the Faded Midget. An insulting name for a rattlesnake, which may explain the Faded Midget's alleged bad temper. But the name is apt: he is small and dustylooking, with a little knob above each eye—the horns. His bite though temporarily disabling would not likely kill a full-grown man in normal health. Even so I don't really want him around. Am I to be compelled to put on boots or shoes every time I wish to step outside? The scorpions, tarantulas, centipedes, and black widows are nuisance enough.

I finish my coffee, lean back and swing my feet up and inside the doorway of the trailer. At once there is a buzzing sound from below and the rattler lifts his head from his coils, eyes brightening, and extends his narrow black tongue to test the air.

After thawing out my boots over the gas flame I pull them on and come back to the doorway. My visitor is still waiting beneath the doorstep, basking in the sun, fully alert. The trailerhouse has two doors. I leave by the other and get a long-handled spade out of the bed of the government pickup. With this tool I scoop the snake into the open. He strikes; I can hear the click of the fangs against steel, see the strain of venom. He wants to stand and fight, but I am patient; I insist on herding him well away from the trailer. On guard, head aloft—that evil slit-eyed weaving head shaped like the ace of spades—tail whirring, the rattler slithers sideways, retreating slowly before me until he reaches the shelter of a sandstone slab. He backs under it.

You better stay there, cousin, I warn him; if I catch you around the trailer again I'll chop your head off.

A week later he comes back. If not him, his twin brother. I spot him one morning under the trailer near the kitchen drain, waiting for a mouse. I have to keep my promise.

This won't do. If there are midget rattlers in the area there may be diamondbacks too—five, six or seven feet long, thick as a man's wrist, dangerous. I don't want *them* camping under my home. It looks as though I'll have to trap the mice.

However, before being forced to take that step I am lucky enough to capture a gopher snake. Burning garbage one morning at the park dump, I see a long slender yellow-brown snake emerge from a mound of old tin cans and plastic picnic plates and take off down the sandy bed of a gulch. There is a burlap sack in the cab of the truck which I carry when plucking Kleenex flowers from the brush and cactus along the road; I grab that and my stick, run after the snake and corner it beneath the exposed roots of a bush. Making sure it's a gopher snake and not something less useful, I open the neck of the sack and with a great deal of coaxing and prodding get the snake into it. The gopher snake, *Drymarchon corais couperi,* or bull snake, has a reputation as the enemy of rattlesnakes, destroying or driving them away whenever encountered.

Hoping to domesticate this sleek, handsome and docile reptile, I release him inside the trailerhouse and keep him there for several days. Should I attempt to feed him? I decide against it—let him eat mice. What little water he may need can also be extracted from the flesh of his prey.

The gopher snake and I get along nicely. During the day he curls up like a cat in the warm corner behind the heater and at night he goes about his business. The mice, singularly quiet for a change, make themselves scarce. The snake is passive, apparently contented, and makes no resistance when I pick him up with my hands and drape him over an arm or around my neck. When I take him outside into the wind and sunshine his favorite place seems to be inside my shirt, where he wraps himself around my waist and rests on my belt. In this position he sometimes sticks his head out between shirt buttons for a survey of the weather, astonishing and delighting any tourists who may happen to be with me at the time. The scales of a snake are dry and smooth, quite pleasant to the touch. Being a cold-blooded creature, of course, he takes his temperature from that of the immediate environment—in this case my body.

We are compatible. From my point of view, friends. After a week of close association I turn him loose on the warm sandstone at my doorstep and leave for patrol of the park. At noon when I return he is gone. I search everywhere beneath, nearby and inside the trailerhouse, but my companion has disappeared. Has he left the area entirely or is he hiding somewhere close by? At any rate I am troubled no more by rattlesnakes under the door.

The snake story is not yet ended.

In the middle of May, about a month after the gopher snake's disappearance, in the evening of a very hot day, with all the rosy desert cooling like a griddle with the fire turned off, he reappears. This time with a mate.

I'm in the stifling heat of the trailer opening a can of beer, barefooted, about to go outside and relax after a hard day watching cloud formations. I happen to glance out the little window near the refrigerator and see two gopher snakes on my verandah engaged in what seems to be a kind of ritual dance. Like a living caduceus they wind and unwind about each other in undulant, graceful, perpetual motion, moving slowly across a dome of sandstone. Invisible but tangible as music is the passion which joins them—sexual? combative? both? A shameless *voyeur,* I stare at the lovers, and then to get a closer view run outside and around the trailer to the back. There I get down on hands and knees and creep toward the dancing snakes, not wanting to frighten or disturb them. I crawl to within six feet of them and stop, flat on my belly, watching from the snake's-eye level. Obsessed with their ballet, the serpents seem unaware of my presence.

The two gopher snakes are nearly identical in length and coloring; I cannot be certain that either is actually my former household pet. I cannot even be sure that they are male and female, though their performance resembles so strongly a *pas de deux* by formal lovers. They intertwine and separate, glide side by side in perfect congruence, turn like mirror images of each other and glide back again, wind and unwind again. This is the basic pattern but there is a variation: at regular intervals the snakes elevate their heads, facing one another, as high as they can go, as if each is trying to outreach or overawe the other. Their heads and bodies rise, higher and higher, than topple together and the rite goes on.

I crawl after them, determined to see the whole thing. Suddenly and simultaneously they discover me, prone on my belly a few feet away. The dance stops. After a moment's pause the two snakes come straight toward me, still in flawless unison, straight toward my face, the forked tongues flickering, their intense wild yellow eyes staring directly into my eyes. For an instant I am paralyzed by wonder; then, stung by a fear too ancient and powerful to overcome I scramble back, rising to my knees. The snakes veer and turn and race away from me in parallel motion, their lean elegant bodies making a soft hissing noise as they slide over the sand and stone. I follow them for a short distance, still plagued by curiosity, before remembering my place and the requirements of common courtesy. For godsake let them go in peace, I tell myself. Wish them luck and (if lovers) innumerable offspring, a life of happily ever after. Not for their sake alone but for your own.

In the long hot days and cool evenings to come I will not see the gopher snakes again. Nevertheless I will feel their presence watching over me like totemic deities, keeping the rattlesnakes far back in the brush where I like them best, cropping off the surplus mouse population, maintaining useful connections with the primeval. Sympathy, mutual aid, symbiosis, continuity.

How can I descend to such anthropomorphism? Easily—but is it, in this case entirely false? Perhaps not. I am not attributing human motives to my snake and bird acquaintances. I recognize that when and where they serve purposes of mine they do so for beautifully selfish reasons of their own. Which is exactly the way it should be, I suggest, however, that it's a foolish, simple-minded rationalism which denies any form of emotion to all animals but man and his dog. This is no more justified that the Moslems are in denying souls to women. It seems to me possible, even probable, that many of the nonhuman undomesticated animals experience emotions unknown to us. What do the coyotes mean when they yodel at the moon? What are the dolphins trying so patiently to tell us? Precisely what did those two enraptured gopher snakes have in mind when they came gliding toward my eyes over the naked sandstone? If I had been as capable of trust as I am susceptible to fear I might have learned something new or some truth so very old we have all forgotten it.

They do not sweat and whine about their condition,
They do not lie awake in the dark and weep for their sins. . . .

All men are brothers, we like to say, half-wishing sometimes in secret it were not true. But perhaps it is true. And is the evolutionary line from protozoan to Spinoza any less certain? That also may be true. We are obliged, therefore, to spread the news, painful and bitter though it may be for some to hear, that all living things on earth are kindred.

THE GREAT AMERICAN DESERT

In my case it was love at first sight. This desert, all deserts, any desert. No matter where my head and feet may go, my heart and my entrails stay behind, here on the clean, true, comfortable rock, under the black sun of God's forsaken country. When I take on my next incarnation, my bones will remain bleaching nicely in a stone gulch under the rim of some faraway plateau, way out there in the back of beyond. An unrequited and excessive love, inhuman no doubt but painful anyhow, especially when I see my desert under attack. "The one death I cannot bear," said the Sonoran-Arizonan poet Richard Shelton. The kind of love that makes a man selfish, possessive, irritable. If you're thinking of a visit, my natural reaction is like a rattlesnake's—to warn you off. What I want to say goes something like this.

Survival Hint #1: Stay out of there. Don't go. Stay home and read a good book, this one for example. The Great American Desert is an awful place. People get hurt, get sick, get lost out there. Even if you survive, which is not certain, you will have a miserable time. The desert is for movies and God-intoxicated mystics, not for family recreation.

Let me enumerate the hazards. First the Walapai tiger, also known as conenose kissing bug. *Triatoma protracta* is a true bug, black as sin, and it flies through the night quiet as an assassin. It does not attack directly like a mosquito or deerfly, but alights at a discreet distance, undetected, and creeps upon you, its hairy little feet making not the slightest noise. The kissing bug is fond of warmth and like Dracula requires mammalian blood for sustenance. When it reaches you the bug crawls onto your skin so gently, so softly that unless your senses are hyperacute you feel nothing. Selecting a tender point, the bug slips its conical proboscis into your

The Journey Home: Some Words in Defense of the American West (New York: Dutton, 1977).

flesh, injecting a poisonous anesthetic. If you are asleep you will feel nothing. If you happen to be awake you may notice the faintest of pinpricks, hardly more than a brief ticklish sensation, which you will probably disregard. But the bug is already at work. Having numbed the nerves near the point of entry the bug proceeds (with a sigh of satisfaction, no doubt) to withdraw blood. When its belly is filled, it pulls out, backs off, and waddles away, so drunk and gorged it cannot fly.

At about this time the victim awakes, scratching at a furious itch. If you recognize the symptoms at once, you can sometimes find the bug in your vicinity and destroy it. But revenge will be your only satisfaction. Your night is ruined. If you are of average sensitivity to a kissing bug's poison, your entire body breaks out in hives, skin aflame from head to toe. Some people become seriously ill, in many cases requiring hospitalization. Others recover fully after five or six hours except for a hard and itchy swelling, which may endure for a week.

After the kissing bug, you should beware of rattlesnakes; we have half a dozen species, all offensive and dangerous, plus centipedes, millipedes, tarantulas, black widows, brown recluses, Gila monsters, the deadly poisonous coral snakes, and giant hairy desert scorpions. Plus an immense variety and near-infinite number of ants, midges, gnats, bloodsucking flies, and blood-guzzling mosquitoes. (You might think the desert would be spared at least mosquitoes? Not so. Peer in any water hole by day: swarming with mosquito larvae. Venture out on a summer's eve: The air vibrates with their mournful keening.) Finally, where the desert meets the sea, as on the coasts of Sonora and Baja California, we have the usual assortment of obnoxious marine life: sandflies, ghost crabs, stingrays, electric jellyfish, spiny sea urchins, maneating sharks, and other creatures so distasteful one prefers not even to name them.

It has been said, and truly, that everything in the desert either stings, stabs, stinks, or sticks. You will find the flora here as venomous, hooked, barbed, thorny, prickly, needled, saw-toothed, hairy, stickered, mean, bitter, sharp, wiry, and fierce as the animals. Something about the desert inclines all living things to harshness and acerbity. The soft evolve out. Except for sleek and oily growths like the poison ivy—oh yes, indeed— that flourish in sinister profusion on the dank walls above the quicksand down in those corridors of gloom and labyrinthine monotony that men call canyons.

We come now to the third major hazard, which is sunshine. Too much of a good thing can be fatal. Sunstroke, heatstroke, and dehydration are common misfortunes in the bright American Southwest. If you can avoid the insects, reptiles, and arachnids, the cactus and the ivy, the smog of the southwestern cities, and the lung fungus of the desert valleys (carried by dust in the air), you cannot escape the desert sun. Too much exposure to it eventually causes, quite literally, not merely sunburn but skin cancer.

Much sun, little rain also means an arid climate. Compared with the high humidity of more hospitable regions, the dry heat of the desert seems at first not terribly uncomfortable—sometimes even pleasant. But that sensation of comfort is false, a deception, and therefore all the more dangerous, for it induces overexertion and an insufficient consumption of water, even when water is available. This leads to various internal complications, some immediate—sunstroke, for example—and some not apparent until much later. Mild but prolonged dehydration, continued over a span of months or years, leads to the crystallization of mineral solutions in the urinary tract, that is, to what urologists call urinary calculi or kidney stones. A disability common in all the world's arid regions. Kidney stones, in case you haven't met one, come in many shapes and sizes, from pellets smooth as BB shot to highly irregular calcifications resembling asteroids. Vietcong shrapnel, and crown-of-thorns starfish. Some of these objects may be "passed" naturally; others can be removed only by means of the Davis stone basket or by surgery. Me—I was lucky; I passed mine with only a groan, my forehead pressed against the wall of a pissoir in the rear of a Tucson bar that I cannot recommend.

You may be getting the impression by now that the desert is not the most suitable of environments for human habitation. Correct. Of all the Earth's climatic zones, excepting only the Antarctic, the deserts are the least inhabited, the least "developed," for reasons that should now be clear.

You may wish to ask, Yes, okay, but among North American deserts which is the *worst?* A good question—and I am happy to attempt to answer.

Geographers generally divide the North American desert—what was once termed "the Great American Desert"—into four distinct regions or subdeserts. These are the Sonoran Desert, which comprises southern Arizona, Baja California, and the state of Sonora in Mexico; the Chihuahuan Desert, which includes west Texas, southern New Mexico, and the states of Chihuahua and Coahuila in Mexico; the Mojave Desert, which includes southeastern California and small portions of Nevada, Utah, and Arizona; and the Great Basin Desert, which includes most of Utah and Nevada, northern Arizona, northwestern New Mexico, and much of Idaho and eastern Oregon.

Privately, I prefer my own categories. Up north in Utah somewhere is the canyon country—places like Zeke's Hole, Death Hollow, Pucker

Pass, Buckskin Gulch, Nausea Crick, Wolf Hole, Mollie's Nipple, Dirty Devil River, Horse Canyon, Horseshoe Canyon, Lost Horse Canyon, Horsethief Canyon, and Horseshit Canyon, to name only the more classic places. Down in Arizona and Sonora there's the cactus country; if you have nothing better to do, you might take a look at High Tanks, Salome Creek, Tortilla Flat, Esperero ("Hoper") Canyon, Holy Joe Peak, Depression Canyon, Painted Cave, Hell Hole Canyon, Hell's Half Acre, Iceberg Canyon, Tiburon (Shark) Island, Pinacate Peak, Infernal Valley, Sykes Crater, Montezuma's Head, Gu Oidak, Kuakatch, Pisinimo, and Baboquivari Mountain, for example.

Then there's The Canyon. *The* Canyon. The Grand. That's one world. And North Rim—that's another. And Death Valley, still another, where I lived one winter near Furnace Creek and climbed the Funeral Mountains, tasted Badwater, looked into the Devil's Hole, hollered up Echo Canyon, searched for and never did find Seldom Seen Slim. Looked for *satori* near Vane, Nevada, and found a ghost town named Bonnie Claire. Never made it to Winnemucca. Drove through the Smoke Creek Desert and down through Big Pine and Lone Pine and home across the Panamints to Death Valley again—home sweet home that winter.

And which of these deserts is the worst? I find it hard to judge. They're all bad—not half bad but all bad. In the Sonoran Desert, Phoenix will get you if the sun, snakes, bugs, and arthropods don't. In the Mojave Desert, it's Las Vegas, more sickening by far than the Glauber's salt in the Death Valley sinkholes. Go to Chihuahua and you're liable to get busted in El Paso and sandbagged in Ciudad Juárez—where all old whores go to die. Up north in the Great Basin Desert, on the Plateau Province, in the canyon country, your heart will break, seeing the strip mines open up and the power plants rise where only cowboys and Indians and J. Wesley Powell ever roamed before.

Nevertheless, all is not lost; much remains, and I welcome the prospect of an army of lug-soled hiker's boots on the desert trails. To save what wilderness is left in the American Southwest—and in the American Southwest only the wilderness is worth saving—we are going to need all the recruits we can get. All the hands, heads, bodies, time, money, effort we can find. Presumably—and the Sierra Club, the Wilderness Society, the Friends of the Earth, the Audubon Society, the Defenders of Wildlife operate on this theory—those who learn to love what is spare, rough, wild, undeveloped, and unbroken will be willing to fight for it, will help resist the strip miners, highway builders, land developers, weapons testers, power producers, tree chainers, clear cutters, oil drillers, dam beavers, subdividers—the list goes on and on—before that zinc-hearted, termite-brained, squint-eyed, nearsighted, greedy crew succeeds in completely californicating what still survives of the Great American Desert.

So much for the Good Cause. Now what about desert hiking itself, you may ask. I'm glad you asked that question. I firmly believe that one should never—I repeat *never*—go out into that formidable wasteland of cactus, heat, serpents, rock, scrub, and thorn without careful planning, thorough and cautious preparation, and complete—never mind the expense!—*complete* equipment. My motto is: Be Prepared.

That is my belief and that is my motto. My practice, however, is a little different. I tend to go off in a more or less random direction myself, half-baked, half-assed, half-cocked, and half-ripped. Why? Well, because I have an indolent and melancholy nature and don't care to be bothered getting all those *things* together—all that bloody *gear*—maps, compass, binoculars, poncho, pup tent, shoes, first-aid kit, rope, flashlight, inspirational poetry, water, food—and because anyhow I approach nature with a certain surly ill-will, daring Her to make trouble. Later when I'm deep into Natural Bridges National Moneymint or Zion National Parkinglot or say General Shithead National Forest Land of Many Abuses why then, of course, when it's a bit late, then I may wish I had packed that something extra: matches perhaps, to mention one useful item, or maybe a spoon to eat my gruel with.

If I hike with another person it's usually the same; most of my friends have indolent and melancholy natures too. A cursed lot, all of them. I think of my comrade John De Puy, for example, sloping along for mile after mile like a goddamned camel—indefatigable—with those J. C. Penny hightops on his feet and that plastic pack on his back he got with five books of Green Stamps and nothing inside it but a sketchbook, some homemade jerky and a few cans of green chiles. Or Douglas Peacock, ex-Green Beret, just the opposite. Built like a buffalo, he loads a ninety-pound canvas pannier on his back at trailhead, loaded with guns, ammunition, bayonet, pitons and carabiners, cameras, field books, a 150-foot rope, geologist's sledge, rock samples, assay kit, field glasses, two gallons of water in steel canteens, jungle boots, a case of C-rations, rope hammock, pharmaceuticals in a pig-iron box, raincoat, overcoat, two-man mountain tent, Dutch oven, hibachi, shovel, ax, inflatable boat, and near the top of the load and distributed through side and back pockets, easily accessible, a case of beer. Not because he enjoys or needs all that weight—he may never get to the bottom of that cargo on a ten-day outing—but simply because Douglas uses his packbag for general storage both at home and on the trail and perfers not to have to rearrange everything from time to time merely for the purposes of a hike. Thus my friends De Puy and Peacock; you may wish to avoid such extremes.

A few tips on desert etiquette:

1. Carry a cooking stove, if you must cook. Do not burn desert wood, which is rare and beautiful and required ages for its creation (an ironwood tree lives for over 1,000 years and juniper almost as long).

2. If you must, out of need, build a fire, then for God's sake allow it to burn itself out before you leave—do not bury it, as Boy Scouts and Campfire Girls do, under a heap of mud or sand. Scatter the ashes; replace any rocks you may have used in constructing a fireplace; do all you can to obliterate the evidence that you camped here. (The Search & Rescue Team may be looking for you.)

3. Do not bury garbage—the wildlife will only dig it up again. Burn what will burn and pack out the rest. The same goes for toilet paper: Don't bury it, *burn it.*

4. Do not bathe in desert pools, natural tanks, *tinajas,* potholes. Drink what water you need, take what you need, and leave the rest for the next hiker and more important for the bees, birds, and animals—bighorn sheep, coyotes, lions, foxes, badgers, deer, wild pigs, wild horses—whose *lives* depend on that water.

5. Always remove and destroy survey stakes, flagging, advertising signboards, mining claim markers, animal traps, poisoned bait, seismic exploration geophones, and other such artifacts of industrialism. The men who put those things there are up to no good and it is our duty to confound them. Keep America Beautiful. Grow a Beard. Take a Bath. Burn a Billboard.

Anyway—why go into the desert? Really, why do it? That sun, roaring at you all day long. The fetid, tepid, vapid little water holes slowly evaporating under a scum of grease, full of cannibal beetles, spotted toads, horsehair worms, liver flukes, and down at the bottom, inevitably, the pale cadaver of a ten-inch centipede. Those pink rattlesnakes down in The Canyon, those diamondback monsters thick as a truck driver's wrist that lurk in shady places along the trail, those unpleasant solpugids and unnecessary Jerusalem crickets that scurry on dirty claws across your face at night. Why? The rain that comes down like lead shot and wrecks the trail, those sudden rockfalls of obscure origin that crash like thunder ten feet behind you in the heart of a dead-still afternoon. The ubiquitous buzzard, so patient—but only so patient. The sullen and hostile Indians, all on welfare. The ragweed, the tumbleweed, the Jimson weed, the snakeweed. The scorpion in your shoe at dawn. The dreary wind that blows all spring, the psychedelic Joshua trees waving their arms at you on moonlight nights. Sand in the soup de jour. Halazone tablets in your canteen. The barren hills that always go up, which is bad, or down, which is worse. Those canyons like catacombs with quicksand lapping at your crotch. Hollow, mummified horses with forelegs casually crossed, dead for ten years, leaning against the corner of a barbed-wire fence. Packhorses at night, iron-shod, clattering over the slickrock through your camp. The last tin of tuna, two flat tires, not enough water and a forty-mile trek to Tule Well. An osprey on a cardón cactus, snatching the head off a living fish—always the best part first. The hawk sailing by at 200 feet, a squirming snake in its talons. Salt in the drinking water. Salt, selenium, arsenic, radon and radium in the water, in the gravel, in your bones. Water so hard it bends light, drills holes in rock and chokes up your radiator. Why go there? Those places with the hardcase names: Starvation Creek, Poverty Knoll, Hungry Valley, Bitter Springs, Last Chance Canyon, Dungeon Canyon, Whipsaw Flat, Dead Horse Point, Scorpion Flat, Dead Man Draw, Stinking Spring, Camino del Diablo, Jornado del Muerto . . . Death Valley.

Well then, why indeed go walking into the desert, that grim ground, that bleak and lonesome land where, as Genghis Khan said of India, "the heat is bad and the water makes men sick"?

Why the desert, when you could be strolling along the golden beaches of California? Camping by a stream of pure Rocky Mountain spring water in colorful Colorado? Loafing through a laurel slick in the misty hills of North Carolina? Or getting your head mashed in the greasy alley behind the Elysium Bar and Grill in Hoboken, New Jersey? Why the desert, given a world of such splendor and variety?

A friend and I took a walk around the base of a mountain up beyond Coconino County, Arizona. This was a mountain we'd been planning to circumambulate for years. Finally we put on our walking shoes and did it. About halfway around this mountain, on the third or fourth day, we paused for a while—two days—by the side of a stream, which the Navajos call Nasja because of the amber color of the water. (Caused perhaps by juniper roots—the water seems safe enough to drink.) On our second day there I walked down the stream, alone, to look at the canyon beyond. I entered the canyon and followed it for half the afternoon, for three or four miles, maybe, until it became a gorge so deep, narrow and dark, full of water and the inevitable quagmires of quicksand, that I turned around and looked for a way out. A route other than the way I'd come, which was crooked and uncomfortable and buried—I wanted to see what was up on top of this world. I found a sort of chimney flue on the east wall, which looked plausible, and sweated and cursed my way up through that until I reached a point where I could walk upright, like a human being. Another 300 feet of scrambling brought me to the rim of the canyon. No one, I felt certain, had ever before departed Nasja Canyon by that route.

But someone had. Near the summit I found an arrow sign, three feet long, formed of stones and pointing off into the north toward those same old purple vistas, so grand, immense, and mysterious, of more canyons, more mesas and plateaus, more mountains, more cloud-dappled sun-spangled leagues of desert sand and desert rock, under the same old wide and aching sky.

The arrow pointed into the north. But what was it pointing *at?* I looked at the sign closely and saw that those dark, desert-varnished stones had been in place for a long, long, time; they rested in compacted dust. They must have been there for a century at least. I followed the direction indicated and came promptly to the rim of another canyon and a drop-off straight down of a good 500 feet. Not that way, surely. Across this canyon was nothing of any unusual interest that I could see—only the familiar sun-blasted sandstone, a few scrubby clumps of blackbrush and prickly pear, a few acres of nothing where only a lizard could graze, surrounded by a few square miles of more nothingness interesting chiefly to horned toads. I returned to the arrow and checked again, this time with field glasses, looking away for as far as my aided eyes could see toward the north, for ten, twenty, forty miles into the distance. I studied the scene with care, looking for an ancient Indian ruin, a significant cairn, perhaps an abandoned mine, a hidden treasure of some inconceivable wealth, the mother of all mother lodes. . . .

But there was nothing out there. Nothing at all. Nothing but the desert. Nothing but the silent world.

That's why.

PETER MATTHIESSEN
B. 1927

Peter Matthiessen has written novels, including At Play in the Fields of the Lord *(1965) and* Far Tortuga *(1975), and works of nonfiction, including* The Tree Where Man Was Born *(1972),* The Wind Birds

(1973), and The Snow Leopard *(1978). Many of his works reflect his own expeditions to wild places around the world, from Kenya to New Guinea, Nepal to the Northwest Territories. Matthiessen bears witness to the damage inflicted on wilderness and on isolated cultures alike by rampant exploitation. But he also celebrates the excellence, and elusiveness, of wildness.*

From THE TREE WHERE MAN WAS BORN

RITES OF PASSAGES

*   *   * One morning the dog pile broke apart before daylight and headed off toward the herds under Naabi Hill. Unlike lions, which often go hungry, the wild dogs rarely fail to make a kill, and this time they were followed from the start by three hyenas that had waited near the den. The three humped along behind the pack, and one of the dogs paused to sniff noses with a hyena by way of greeting. In the distance, zebras yelped like dogs, and the dogs chittered quietly like birds as they loped along. As the sun rose out of the Gol Mountains, they faked an attack on a string of wildebeest and moved on.

A mile and a half east of the den, the pack cut off a herd of zebra and ran it in tight circles. There were foals in this herd, but the dogs had singled out a pregnant mare. When the herd scattered, they closed in, streaming along in the early light, and almost immediately she fell behind and then gave up, standing motionless as one dog seized her nose and others ripped at her pregnant belly and others piled up under her tail to get at her entrails at the anus, surging at her with such force that the flesh of her uplifted quarters quaked in the striped skin. Perhaps in shock, their quarry shares the detachment of the dogs, which attack it peaceably, ears forward, with no slightest sign of snapping or snarling. The mare seemed entirely docile, unafraid, as if she had run as she had been hunted, out of instinct, and without emotion: only rarely will a herd animal attempt to defend itself with the hooves and teeth used so effectively in battles with its own kind, though such resistance might well spare its life. The zebra still stood a full half-minute after her guts had been snatched out, then sagged down dead. Her unborn colt was dragged into the clear and snapped apart off to one side.

The morning was silent but for the wet sound of eating; a Caspian

The Tree Where Man Was Born (New York: Dutton, 1972).

plover and a band of sand grouse picked at the mute prairie. The three hyenas stood in wait, and two others appeared after the kill. One snatched a scrap and ran with it; the meat, black with blood and mud, dragged on the ground. Chased by the rest, the hyena made a shrill sound like a pig squeal. When their spirit is up, hyenas will take on a lion, and if they chose, could bite a wild dog in half, but in daylight, they seem ill at ease; they were scattered by one tawny eagle, which took over the first piece of meat abandoned by the dogs. The last dog to leave, having finished with the fetus, drove the hyenas off the carcass of the mare on its way past, then frisked on home. In a day and a night, when lions and hyenas, vultures and marabous, jackals, eagles, ants, and beetles have all finished, there will be no sign but the stained pressed grass that a death ever took place.

All winter in the Serengeti damp scrawny calves and afterbirths are everywhere, and old or diseased animals fall in the night. Fat hyenas, having slaked their thirst, squat in the rain puddles, and gaping lions lie belly to the sun. On Naabi Hill the requiem birds, digesting carrion, hunch on the canopies of low acacia. Down to the west, a young zebra wanders listlessly by itself. Unlike topi and kongoni, which are often seen alone, the zebra and wildebeest prefer the herd; an animal by itself may be sick or wounded, and draws predators from all over the plain. This mare had a deep gash down her right flank, and a slash of claws across the striping of her quarters; red meat gleamed on right foreleg and left fetlock. It seemed strange that an attacking lion close enough to maul so could have botched the job, but the zebra pattern makes it difficult to see at night, when it is most vulnerable to attack by lions, and zebra are strong animals; a thin lioness that I saw once at Ngorongoro had a broken incisor hanging from her jaw that must have been the work of a flying hoof.

Starvation is the greatest threat to lions, which are inefficient hunters and often fail to make a kill. Unlike wild dog packs, which sometimes overlap in their wide hunting range, lions will attack and even eat another lion that has entered their territory, snapping and snarling in the same antagonistic way with which they join their pride mates on a kill, whereas when hunting, they are silent and impassive. In winter when calves of gazelle and gnu litter the plain, the lions are well fed, but at other seasons they may be so hungry that their own cubs are driven from the kills: ordinarily, however, the lion will permit cubs to feed even when the lioness that made the kill is not permitted to approach. Until it is two, the cub is a dependent, and less than half of those born in the Serengeti survive the first year of life. In hard times, cubs may be eaten by hyenas, or by the leopard, which has a taste for other carnivores, including domestic cats and dogs.

A former warden of the Serengeti who feels that plains game should be killed to feed these starving cubs is opposed by George Schaller on the grounds that such artificial feeding would interfere with the balance of lion numbers as well as with the natural selection that maintains the vitality of the species. Dr. Schaller is correct, I think, and yet my sympathies are with the predator, not with the hunted, perhaps because a lion is perceived as an individual, whereas one member of a herd of thousands seems but a part of a compound organism, with little more identity than one termite in a swarm. Separated from the herd, it gains identity, like the zebra killed by the wild dogs, but even so I felt more pity for an injured lion that I saw near the Seronera River in the hungry months of summer, a walking husk of mane and bone, so weak that the dry weather wind threatened to knock it over.

The death of any predator is disturbing. I was startled one day to see a hawk in the talons of Verreaux's eagle-owl; perhaps it had been killed in the act of killing. Another day, by a korongo, I helped Schaller collect a dying lioness. She had emaciated hindquarters and the staggers, and at our approach, she reeled to her feet, then fell. In the interests of science as well as mercy, for he wished an autopsy, George shot her with an overdose of tranquilizer. Although she twitched when the needle struck, and did not rise, she got up after a few minutes and weaved a few feet more and fell again as if defeated by the obstacle of the korongo, where frogs trilled in oblivion of unfrogly things. I had the strong feeling that the lioness, sensing death, had risen to escape it, like the vultures I had heard of somewhere that flew up from the poisoned meat set out for lions, circling higher and higher into the sky, only to fall like stones as life forsook them. A moment later, her head rose up, then flopped for the last time, but she would not die. Sprinkled with hopping lion flies and the fat ticks that in lions are a sign of poor condition, she lay there in a light rain, her gaunt flanks twitching.

The episode taught me something about George Schaller, who is single-minded, not easy to know. George is a stern pragmatist, unable to muster up much grace in the face of unscientific attitudes; he takes a hard-eyed look at almost everything. Yet at this moment his boyish face was openly upset, more upset than I had ever thought to see him. The death of the lioness was painless, far better than being found by the hyenas, but it was going on too long; twice he returned to the Land Rover for additional dosage. We stood there in a kind of vigil, feeling more and more depressed, and the end, when it came at last, was shocking. The poor beast, her life going, began to twitch and tremble. With a little grunt, she turned onto her back and lifted her hind legs into the air. Still grunting, she licked passionately at the grass, and her haunches shuddered in long spasms, and this last abandon shattered the detachment I had felt until that moment. I was swept by a wave of feeling, then a pang so sharp that, for a moment, I felt sick, as if all the waste and loss in life, the harm one brings to oneself and others, had been drawn to a point in this lonely passage between light and darkness.

Mid-March when the long rains were due was a time of wind and dry days in the Serengeti, with black trees in iron silhouette on the hard sunsets and great birds turning forever on a silver sky. A full moon rose in a night rainbow, but the next day the sun was clear again, flat as a disc in the pale universe.

Two rhino and a herd of buffalo had brought up the rear of the eastward migration. Unlike the antelope, which blow with the wind and grasses, the dark animals stood earthbound on the plain. The antelope, all but a few, had drifted east under the Crater Highlands, whereas the zebra, in expectation of the rains, were turning west again toward the woods. Great herds had gathered at the Seronera River, where the local prides of lion were well fed. Twenty lions together, dozing in the golden grass, could sometimes be located by the wave of a black tail tuft or the black ear tips of a lifted head that gazed through the sun shimmer of the seed heads. Others gorged in uproar near the river crossings, tearing the fat striped flanks on fresh green beds—now daytime kills were common. Yet for all their prosperity, there was an air of doom about the lions. The males, especially, seemed too big, and they walked too slowly between feast and famine, as if in some dim intuition that the time of the great predators was running out.

Pairs of male lions, unattached to any pride, may hunt and live together in great harmony, with something like demonstrative affection. But when two strangers meet, there seems to be a waiting period, while fear settles. One sinks into the grass at a little distance, and for a long time they watch each other, and their sad eyes, unblinking, never move. The gaze is the warning, and it is the same gaze, wary but unwavering, with which lions confront man. The gold cat eyes shimmer with hidden lights, eyes that see everything and betray nothing. When the lion is satisfied that the threat is past, the head is turned, as if ignoring it might speed the departure of an unwelcome and evil-smelling presence. In its torpor and detachment, the lion sometimes seems the dullest beast in Africa, but one has only to watch a file of lions setting off on the evening hunt to be awed anew by the power of this animal.

One late afternoon of March, beyond Maasai Kopjes, eleven lionesses lay on a kill, and the upraised heads, in a setting sun, were red. With their grim visages and flat glazed eyes, these twilight beasts were ominous. Then the gory heads all turned as one, ear tips alert. No animal was in sight, and their bellies were full, yet they glared steadfastly away into the emptiness of plain, as if something that no man could sense was imminent.

Not far off there was a leopard; possibly they scented it. The leopard lay on an open rise, in the shadow of a wind-worn bush, and unlike the lions, it lay gracefully. Even stretched on a tree limb, all four feet hanging, as it is seen sometimes in the fever trees, the leopard has the grace of complete awareness, with all its tensions in its pointed eyes. The lion's gaze is merely baleful; that of the leopard is malevolent, a distillation of the trapped fear that is true savagery.

Under a whistling thorn the leopard lay, gold coat on fire in the sinking sun, as if imagining that so long as it lay still it was unseen. Behind it was a solitary thorn tree, black and bony in the sunset, and from a crotch in a high branch, turning gently, torn hide matted with caked blood, the hollow form of a gazelle hung by the neck. At the insistence of the wind, the delicate black shells of the turning hoofs, on tiptoe, made a dry clicking in the silence of the plain.

ELEPHANT KINGDOMS

One morning a great company of elephants came from the woodlands, moving eastward toward the Togoro Plain. "It's like the old Africa, this," Myles Turner said, coming to fetch me. "It's one of the greatest sights a man can see."

We flew northward over the Orangi River. In the wake of the elephant herds, stinkbark acacia were scattered like sticks, the haze of yellow blossoms bright in the killed trees. Through the center of the destruction, west to east, ran a great muddied thoroughfare of the sort described by Selous in the nineteenth century. Here the center of the herd had passed. The plane turned eastward, coming up on the elephant armies from behind. More than four hundred animals were pushed together in one phalanx; a smaller group of one hundred and another of sixty were nearby. The four hundred moved in one slow-stepping swaying mass, with the largest cows along the outer ranks and big bulls scattered on both sides. "Seventy and eighty pounds, some of those bulls," Myles said. (Trophy elephants are described according to the weight of a single tusk; an eighty-pound elephant would carry about twice that weight in ivory. "Saw an eighty today." *"Did* you!")

Myles said that elephants herded up after heavy rains, but that this was an enormous congregation for the Serengeti. In 1913, when the first safari came here, the abounding lions and wild dogs were shot as vermin, but no elephants were seen at all. Even after 1925, when the plains were hunted regularly by such men as Philip Percival and the American, Martin Johnson, few elephants were reported. Not until after 1937, it is said, when the Serengeti was set aside as a game reserve (it was not made a national park until 1951), did harried elephants from the developing agricultural country of west Kenya move south into this region, but it seems more likely that they were always present in small numbers, and merely increased as a result of human pressures in suitable habitats outside the park.

Elephants, with their path-making and tree-splitting propensities, will alter the character of the densest bush in very short order; probably they rank with man and fire as the greatest force for habitat change in Africa. In the Serengeti, the herds are destroying many of the taller trees which are thought to have risen at the beginning of the century, in a long period without grass fires that followed plague, famine, and an absence of the Maasai. Dry season fires, often set purposely by poachers and pastoral peoples, encourage grassland by suppressing new woody growth; when accompanied by drought, and fed by a woodland tinder of elephant-killed trees, they do lasting damage to the soil and the whole environment. Fires waste the dry grass that is used by certain animals, and the regrowth exhausts the energy in the grass roots that is needed for good growth in the rainy season. In the Serengeti in recent years, fire and elephants together have converted miles and miles of acacia wood to grassland, and damaged the stands of yellowbark acacia or fever tree along the water courses. The range of the plains game has increased, but the much less numerous woodland species such as the roan antelope and oribi become ever more difficult to see.

Beneath the plane, the elephant mass moved like gray lava, leaving behind a ruined bog of mud and twisted trees. An elephant can eat as much as six hundred pounds of grass and browse each day, and it is a destructive feeder, breaking down many trees and shrubs along the way. The Serengeti is immense, and can absorb this damage, but one sees quickly how an elephant invasion might affect more vulnerable areas. Ordinarily the elephant herds are scattered and nomadic, but pressure from settlements, game control, and poachers sometimes confines huge herds to restricted habitats which they may destroy. Already three of Tanzania's new national parks—Serengeti, Manyara, and Ruaha—have more elephants than is good for them. The elephant problem, where and when and how to manage them, is a great controversy in East Africa, and its solution must affect the balance of animals and man throughout the continent.

Anxious to see the great herd from the ground, I picked up George Schaller at Seronera and drove northwest to Banagi, then westward on the Ikoma-Musoma track to the old northwest boundary of the park, where I headed across country. I had taken good bearings from the air, but elephants on the move can go a long way in an hour, and even for a vehicle with four-wheel drive, this rough bush of high grass, potholes, rocks, steep brushy streams, and swampy mud is very different from the hardpan of the plain. The low hot woods lacked rises or landmarks, and for a while it seemed that I had actually misplaced four hundred elephants.

Then six bulls loomed through the trees, lashing the air with their trunks, ears blowing, in a stiff-legged swinging stride; they forded a steep gully as the main herd, ahead of them, appeared on a wooded rise. Ranging up and down the gully, we found a place to lurch across, then took off eastward, hoping to find a point downwind of the herd where the elephants would pass. But their pace had slowed as the sun rose; we worked back to them, upwind. The elephants were destroying a low wood—this is not an exaggeration—with a terrible cracking of trees, but after a while they moved out onto open savanna. In a swampy stream they sprayed one another and rolled in the water and coated their hides with mud, filling the air with a thick sloughing sound like the wet meat sound made by predators on a kill. Even at rest the herd flowed in perpetual motion, the ears like delicate great petals, the ripple of the mud-caked flanks, the coiling trunks—a dream rhythm, a rhythm of wind and trees. "It's a nice life," Schaller said. "Long, and without fear." A young one could be killed by a lion, but only a desperate lion would venture near a herd of elephants, which are among the few creatures that reach old age in the wild.

There has been much testimony to the silence of the elephant, and all of it is true. At one point there came a cracking sound so small that had I not been alert for the stray elephants all around, I might never have seen the mighty bull that bore down on us from behind. A hundred yards away, it came through the scrub and deadwood like a cloud shadow, dwarfing the small trees of the open woodland. I raised binoculars to watch him turn when he got our scent, but the light wind had shifted and instead the bull was coming fast, looming higher and higher, filling the field of the binoculars, forehead, ears, and back agleam with wet mud dredged up from the donga. There was no time to reach the car, nothing to do but stand transfixed. A froggish voice said, "What do you think, George?" and got no answer.

Then the bull scented us—the hot wind was shifting every moment— and the dark wings flared, filling the sky, and the air was split wide by that ultimate scream that the elephant gives in alarm or agitation, that primordial warped horn note out of oldest Africa. It altered course without missing a stride, not in flight but wary, wideeared, passing man by. Where first aware of us, the bull had been less than one hundred feet away—I walked it off—and he was somewhat nearer where he passed. "He was pretty close," I said finally to Schaller. George cleared his throat. "You don't want them any closer than that," he said. "Not when you're on foot." Schaller, who has no taste for exaggeration, had a very respectful look upon his face.

Stalking the elephants, we were soon a half-mile from my Land Rover. What little wind there was continued shifting, and one old cow, getting our scent, flared her ears and lifted her trunk, holding it upraised for a long time like a question mark. There were new calves with the herd, and we went no closer. Then the cow lost the scent, and the sloughing sound resumed, a sound that this same animal has made for four hundred thousand years. Occasionally there came a brief scream of agitation, or the crack of a killed tree back in the wood, and always the *thuck* of mud and water, and a rumbling of elephantine guts, the deepest sound made by any animal on earth except the whale.

Africa. Noon. The hot still waiting air. A hornbill, gnats, the green hills in the distance, wearing away west toward Lake Victoria.

*   *   *

Of all African animals, the elephant is the most difficult for man to live with, yet its passing—if this must come—seems the most tragic of all. I can watch elephants (and elephants alone) for hours at a time, for sooner or later the elephant will do something very strange such as mow grass with its toenails or draw the tusks from the rotted carcass of another elephant and carry them off into the bush. There is mystery behind that masked gray visage, an ancient life force, delicate and mighty, awesome and enchanted, commanding the silence ordinarily reserved for mountain peaks, great fires, and the sea. I remember a remark made by a girl about her father, a businessman of narrow sensibilities who, casting about for a means of self-gratification, traveled to Africa and slew an elephant. Standing there in his new hunting togs in a vast and hostile silence, staring at the huge dead bleeding thing that moments before had borne such life, he was struck for the first time in his headlong passage through his days by his own irrelevance. "Even *he*," his daughter said, "knew he'd done something stupid."

The elephant problem, still unresolved, will eventually affect conservation policies throughout East Africa, where even very honest governments may not be able to withstand political pressure to provide meat for the people. Already there is talk of systematic game-cropping in the parks on a sustained yield basis, especially since park revenues from meat and hides and tusks could be considerable, and this temptation may prove impossible to resist for the new governments. Or an outbreak of political instability might wreck the tourist industry that justifies the existence of the parks, thus removing the last barrier between the animals and a hungry populace. African schoolchildren are now taught to appreciate their wild animals and the land, but public attitudes may not change in time to spare the wildlife in the next decades, when the world must deal with the worst consequences of overpopulation and pollution. And a stubborn fight for animal preservation in disregard of people and their famine-haunted future would only be the culminating failure of the western civilization that, through its blind administration of vaccines and quinine, has upset the ecologies of a whole continent. Thus wildlife must be treated in terms of resource management in this new Africa which includes, besides gazelles, a growing horde of tattered humans who squat for days and weeks and months and years on end, in a seeming trance, awaiting hope. In the grotesque costumes of Africa roadsides— rag-wrapped heads and the wool greatcoats and steel helmets of old white man's wars are worn here in hundred-degree heat—the figures look like survivors of a cataclysm. Once, in Nanyuki, I saw a legless man, lacking all means of locomotion, who had been installed in an old auto tire in a ditch at the end of town. Fiercely, eyes bulging, oblivious of the rush of exhaust fumes spinning up the dust around his ears, he glared at an ancient newspaper, as if deciphering the news of doomsday. *   *   *

RED GOD

*   *   * Sun, heat, stillness were all one. The dying sun in the Ngurumans gave color to the cooking fire, and after dark came a hot wind that fanned night fires all around the horizon, and drove one tongue of flame onto the ridge above the lifeless lake. Though ready to break camp at a moment's notice, I slept poorly—the moon and wind and fire made me restless. But in a red dawn, the wind died again, and the fire sank into the grass, waiting for night.

South of Magadi the road scatters, and wandering tracks cross the white lake bed. There is water where the wading birds are mirrored, and in the liquid shimmer of the heat, a still wildebeest wavers in its own reflection. An hour later, from the west, the ghostly beast was still in sight; it had not moved.

The track winds southwest toward Shombole. Huge termitaria slouch here and there in the dry scrub, and over toward the Nguruman Escarpment, a whirlwind spins a plume of desert dust up the Rift's dark face into the smoky sky of East African summer. Eventually the track descends again, between the dead volcano and the marsh of Uaso Ngiro. In a water gleam that parts the fierce bright reeds, a woman and a man are bathing. The woman squats, her small shoulders demure, but the man stands straight as a gazelle and gazes, body shining, the archetypal man of Africa that I first saw in the Sudan.

The Shombole track comes to an end at three shacks under the volcano, where a duka serves the outlying Maasai with beads and wire for ornament, red cloth, sweet drinks, and cocoa. I gave a ride to a young morani who guided me with brusque motions through the bush to a stony cattle trail that winds between hill and marsh, around Shombole. Farther on, we picked up two Maasai women, and all four of us were squashed into the front when, in the full heat of the desert afternoon, on hot rocky ground at the mud edge of a rotting swamp in this lowest and hottest pit of the Rift Valley floor, my faithful Land Rover, thirty-five miles from Magadi and ninety-five beyond Nairobi, gave a hellish clang and, dragging its guts over the stones, lurched to a halt.

In a bad silence, the Maasai women thanked me and departed. The boy stood by, less out of expectation of reward or even curiosity, I decided, than some sense of duty toward a stranger in Maasai Land. Squatting on my heels and swatting flies, I peered dizzily at the heavy iron shaft, the sand and stone and thorn stuck to raw grease where the shaft had sheared at the universal coupling, cutting off the transmission of power to the rear wheels. In front-wheel drive, the car would move forward weakly, but my limited tools were not able to detach the revolving shaft from the transmission: dragging and clanging in an awful din of steel and rocks, it threatened to shake the car to pieces.

To cool my nerves, I drank a quart of Tusker beer. The Land Rover had picked a poor place to collapse, but at least it had got me to my destination, and the sun if not the heat would soon be gone. Any time now, the airplane of Douglas-Hamilton, coming to meet me, would be landing on the bare mud flats at the north end of Natron. Tomorrow we were to climb Shombole, and after that, if no repairs seemed possible, Iain could fly out to Magadi, and leave word of my straits and whereabouts. But as it happened, Iain and Oria were never to appear: they had sent word to Nairobi that has not reached me to this day. Next morning I rigged a whole series of rope slings, held in place by stay lines from the side, that carried the rotating shaft just off the ground, although they burned through regularly from friction. Setting off at sunrise at three miles an hour, with the frequent stops to repair or replace the sling giving the straining car an opportunity to cool off, I arrived in two hours at the duka. A length of soft iron wire presented me by the proprietor was better than the rope, but not much better, and the last of it wore through as I reached Magadi in mid-afternoon, having made not less than fifteen trips beneath the car, in terrific heat, measuring my length in the fine volcanic ash that a hellish wind impacted in hair, lungs, and fingernails. The kind Asian manager of the Magadi Store and his driver-mechanic replaced the sheared bevel pinion with an ingenious makeshift rig that would see the car safely to Nairobi, but all of this still lay ahead as I stood there looking as stupid as I felt under the gaze of that young herdsman by the shores of Natron.

*   *   *

Since the disabled car was inland from the lake, it seemed best to walk the last mile to the flats, to greet Iain and Oria and to make certain that I was not overlooked; already I was listening for the droning of the motor that would draw to a point the misty distances down toward Lengai. Accompanied by the morani, I followed a cattle trail between the marsh and a thorny rock strangely swollen by thick pink blossoms of the desert rose. Near the mouth of the Uaso Ngiro, green reeds give way to open flats where the Natron leaves a crust crisscrossed by ostrich tracks. Here the young warrior, mounting the rock, made a grand sweeping gesture of his cape toward the horizons of Maasai Land, and sighed with all his being. The red and blue beads swinging from his ears stood for sun and water, but now the sun was out of balance with the rain, and the grass was thin. The Maasai speak of the benevolent Black God who brings rain, and the malevolent Red God who begrudges it, the Black God living in dark thunderheads and the Red in the merciless dry-season sun; Black God and Red are different tempers of Ngai, for God is embodied in the rain and the fierce heat, besides ruling the great pastures of the sky. Looming thunder is feared: the Red God seeks to pierce the Black God's kingdoms, in hope of bringing harm to man. But in distant thunder the Maasai hear the Black God saying, "Let man be. . . ."

From where we stood, awed by the view, white flats extended a half-mile to the water's edge, where the heat waves rose in a pink fire of thousands upon thousands of flamingos. All around the north end of the lake the color shimmered, and for some distance down both shores; on the west shore, under the dark Sonjo escarpments, an upside-down forest was reflected. Southeast, the outline of Gelai was a phantom mountain in an amorphous sky, and in the south, the lake vanished in brown vapors that shrouded Ol Doinyo Lengai.

In this somber kingdom of day shadows and dead smokes, the fresh pinks of flamingos and the desert rose appeared unnatural. What belonged here were those tracks of giant birds, like black crosses in the crystalline white soda, and this petrified white bone dung of hyena, and the hieroglyph of a gazelle in quest of salt that had followed some dim impulse far out onto the flats. I remembered the Grant's gazelles on the Chalbi Desert, and the rhino that had climbed Lengai, and the wildebeest at a dead halt for want of impulse, in the shimmer of the soda lake, at noon. What drives such animals away from life-giving conditions into the wasteland—what happens in those rigid clear-eyed heads? How did the hippopotamus find its way up into the Crater Highlands, to blunder into the waters of Ngorongoro? Today one sees them there with wonder, encircled by steep walls, and the mystery deepens when a fish eagle plummets to the springs east of the lake and rises once more against the sky, in its talons a gleam of unknown life from the volcano.

We walked out into the silence of the flats. Somewhere on the mud, our footprints crossed the border of Tanzania, for Natron lies entirely in that country. I listened for the airplane but there was nothing, only the buzzing of these birds that fed with their queer heads upside down, straining diatoms and algae from the stinking waters even as they squirted it with the guano that kept the algae reproducing—surely one of the shortest and most efficient life chains in all nature, at once exhilarating and oppressive in the mindlessness of such blind triumphal life in a place so poisonous and dead. A string of flamingos rose from the pink gases, restoring sharpness to the sky, then sank again into the oblivion of their millions.

Twilight was coming. The boy pointed to a far en-gang under Shombole. *"Aia,"* he said, by way of parting—So be it—and stalked away in fear of the African night, his red cape darkening against the white. *"Aia,"* I said, watching him go. Soon he vanished under the volcano. This age-set of moran may be the last, for the Maasai of Kenya, upset at being left behind by tribes they once considered worthless, voted this year to discontinue the moran system and send young Maasai to school. But in Maasai Land all change comes slowly, whether in Kenya or Tanzania. The month before, in the region of Ol Alilal, in the Crater Highlands, there was a new age-set of circumcised boys dressed in the traditional black garments bound with broad bead belts and wearing the spectral white paint around the eyes that signifies death and rebirth as a man, and on their shaved heads, arranged on a wood frame that looked from afar like an informal halo, black ostrich plumes danced in the mountain wind. When their hair grew out again, the boys would be young warriors, perhaps the last age-set of moran.

One of the Ol Alilal moran was very sick, and we took him in to the government dispensary at Nainokanoka. This tall boy of seventeen- or eighteen could no longer walk; I carried his light body in my arms to the dark shack where to judge from his face, he thought that he would die. Yet here at least he had a chance that he might not have had at Ol Alilal. Though the Maasai have little faith in witchcraft, they recognize ill provenance and evil spirits, and a person dying is removed outside the fences so that death will not bring the village harm. Eventually the body is taken to the westward toward the setting sun, and laid on its left side with knees drawn up, head to the north and face to the east, right arm crossing the breast and left cushioning the head. There it is left to be dealt with by hyenas. Should someone die inside a hut, then the whole village must be moved, and it is said that the people listen for the howl of the hyena, and establish the new village in that direction. The Maasai are afraid of death, though not afraid to die.

For a long time I stood motionless on the white desert, numbed by these lowering horizons so oblivious of man, understanding at last the stillness of the lone animals that stand transfixed in the distances of Africa. Perhaps because I was alone, and therefore more conscious of my own insignificance under the sky, and aware, too, that the day was dying, and that the airplane would not appear, I felt overwhelmed by the age and might of this old continent, and drained of strength: all seemed pointless in such emptiness, there was nowhere to go. I wanted to lie flat out on my back on this almighty mud, but instead I returned slowly into Kenya, pursued by the mutter of primordial birds. The flamingo sound, rising and falling with the darkening pinks of the gathering birds, was swelling again like an oncoming rush of motley wings—birds, bats, ancient flying things, thick insects.

The galumphing splosh of a pelican, gathering tilapia from the freshwater mouth of the Uaso Ngiro, was the first sound to rise above the wind of the flamingos. Next came a shrill whooping of the herdsmen, hurrying the last cattle across delta creeks to the bomas in the foothills of Shombole. A Maasai came running from the hills to meet me, bearing tidings of two dangerous lions—*"Simba! Simba mbili!"*—that haunted this vicinity. He asked nothing of me except caution, and as soon as his warning was delivered, ran back a mile or more in the near-darkness to the shelter of his en-gang. Perhaps the earliest pioneers were greeted this way almost everywhere by the wild peoples—the thought was saddening, but his act had made me happy.

I built a fire and broiled the fresh beef I had brought for three, to keep it from going bad, and baked a potato in the coals, and fried tomatoes, and drank another beer, all the while keeping an eye out for bad lions. I also made tea and boiled two eggs for breakfast, to dispense with fire-making in the dawn. As yet I had no energy to think about tomorrow, much less attempt makeshift repairs; the cool of first light would be time enough for that. Moving slowly so as not to stir the heat, I brushed my teeth and rigged my bed roll and climbed out on the car roof, staring away over Lake Natron. I was careful to be quiet: the night has ears, as the Maasai say.

From the Crater Highlands rose the Southern Cross; the Pleiades, which the Maasai associate with rains, had waned in early June. July is the time of wind and quarrels, and now, in August, the grass was dry and dead. In August, September, and October, called the Months of Hunger, the people pin grass to their clothes in hope of rain, for grass is sign of prosperity and peace, but not until the Pleiades returned, and the southeast monsoon, would the white clouds come that bring the precious water. (The Mbugwe of the southern flats of Lake Manyara resort to rainmakers, and formerly, in time of drought, so it is said, would sacrifice an unblemished black bull, then an unblemished black man, and finally the rainmaker himself.)

The light in my small camp under Shombole was the one light left in all the world. Staring up at the black cone that filled the night sky to the east, I knew I would never climb it. There was a long hard day ahead with nothing certain at the end of it, and I had no heart for the climb alone, especially here in this sullen realm that had held me at such a distance. The ascent of Lengai and the descent into Embagai Crater had both been failures, and the great volcanoes of the Crater Highlands had remained lost in the clouds. At Natron, my friends had failed to come and my transport had broken down, and tomorrow I would make a slow retreat. And perhaps this came from the pursuit of some fleeting sense of Africa, seeking to fix in time the timeless, to memorize the immemorial, instead of moving gently, in awareness, letting the sign, like the crimson bird, become manifest where it would.

From where I watched, a sentinel in the still summer, there rose and fell the night highlands of two countries, from the Loita down the length of the Ngurumans to the Sonjo scarps that overlook Lake Natron. In the Loita, so the Maasai say, lives Enenauner, a hairy giant, one side flesh, the other stone, who devours mortal men lost in the forests; Enenauner carries a great club, and is heard tokking on trees as it moves along. A far hyena summoned the night feeders, and flamingos in crescent moved north across a crescent moon toward Naivasha and Nakuru. Down out of the heavens came their calls, a remote electric sound, as if in this place, in such immensities of silence, one had heard heat lightning.

Toward midnight, in the Sonjo Hills, there leapt up two sudden fires. Perhaps this was sign of the harvest festival, Mbarimbari, for these were not the grass fires that leap along the night horizons in the dry season; the twin flames shone like leopard's eyes from the black hills. At this time of year God comes to the Sonjo from Ol Doinyo Lengai, and a few of their ancient enemies, the Maasai, bring goats to be slaughtered at Mbarimbari, where they howl to Ngai for rain and children.

The Sonjo, isolated from the world, know that it is coming to an end. Quarrels and warfare will increase, and eventually the sky will be obscured by a horde of birds, then insect clouds, and finally a shroud of dust. Two suns will rise from the horizons, one in the east, one in the west, as a signal to man that the end of the world is near. At the ultimate noon, when the two suns meet at the top of the sky, the earth will shrivel like a leaf, and all will die.

From THE WIND BIRDS

* * * The restlessness of shorebirds, their kinship with the distance and swift seasons, the wistful signal of their voices down the long coastlines of the world make them, for me, the most affecting of wild creatures. I think of them as birds of wind, as "wind birds." To the traveler confounded by exotic birds, not to speak of exotic specimens of his own kind, the voice of the wind birds may be the lone familiar note in a strange land, and I have many times been glad to find them; meeting a whimbrel one fine summer day of February in Tierra del Fuego, I wondered if I had not seen this very bird a half-year earlier, at home. The spotted and white-rumped sandpipers, the black-bellied and golden plovers are birds of Sagaponack, but the spotted sandpiper has cheered me with its jaunty teeter on the Amazon and high up in the Andes (and so has its Eurasian counterpart, the common sandpiper, on the White Nile and in Galway and in the far-off mountains of New Guinea); one bright noon at the Straits of Magellan, the white-rump passed along the shore in flocks. I have seen golden plover on Alaskan tundra and in the canefields of Hawaii, and heard the black-belly's wild call on wind-bright seacoast afternoons from Yucatán to the Great Barrier Reef.

The voice of the black-bellied plover carries far, a fluting, melancholy *toor-a-lee* or *pee-ur-ee* like a sea bluebird's, often heard before the bird is seen. In time of storm, it sometimes seems to be the only bird aloft, for, with its wing span of two feet or more, the black-bellied plover is a strong

The Wind Birds (New York: Viking, 1973).

flier; circumpolar and almost cosmopolitan, it migrates down across the world from breeding grounds within the Arctic Circle. Yet as a wanderer it is rivaled by several shorebirds, not least of all the sanderling of the Sagaponack beach, which ranks with the great skua and the Arctic tern as one of the most far-flung birds on earth.

The sanderling is the white sandpiper or "peep" of summer beaches, the tireless toy bird that runs before the surf. Because of the bold role it plays in its immense surroundings, it is the one sandpiper that most people have noticed. Yet how few notice it at all, and few of the fewer still who recognize it will ever ask themselves why it is there or where it might be going. We stand there heedless of an extraordinary accomplishment: the diminutive creature making way for us along the beaches of July may be returning from an annual spring voyage which took it from central Chile to nesting grounds in northeast Greenland, a distance of eight thousand miles. One has only to consider the life force packed tight into that puff of feathers to lay the mind wide open to the mysteries—the order of things, the why and the beginning. As we contemplate that sanderling, there by the shining sea, one question leads inevitably to another, and all questions come full circle to the questioner, paused momentarily in his own journey under the sun and sky. *   *   *

RICHARD SELZER
B. 1928

Like Lewis Thomas, another physician, Richard Selzer asks us to look at our own bodies as a part of nature in order to see both in new ways. In this essay from Mortal Lessons *(1976), for instance, skin becomes "the organ of recollection." Selzer's writings, based on his extensive experience as a general surgeon, combine a celebratory lyricism with a detailed knowledge of the human anatomy—a recognition that, as with natural landscapes and processes, full understanding requires a synthesis of technical skill and knowledge with sympathetic imagination. To put it another way, the doctor's dilemma reflects the ecologist's conundrum in that both need to observe clearly and accurately the condition of a wounded body without being either alienated from it or overwhelmed by emotion.*

SKIN

I sing of skin, layered fine as baklava, whose colors shame the dawn, at once the scabbard upon which is writ our only signature, and the instrument by which we are thrilled, protected, and kept constant in our natural place. Here is each man bagged and trussed in perfect amiability. See how it upholsters the bone and muscle underneath, now accenting the point of an elbow, now rolling over the pectorals to hollow the grotto of an armpit. Nippled and umbilicated, and perforated by the most diverse and marvelous openings, each with its singular rim and curtain. Thus the carven helix of the ear, the rigid nostrils, the puckered continence of the anus, the moist and sensitive lips of mouth and vagina.

What is it, then, this seamless body-stocking, some two yards square, this our casing, our facade, that flushes, pales, perspires, glistens, glows, furrows, tingles, crawls, itches, pleasures, and pains us all our days, at once keeper of the organs within, and sensitive probe, adventurer into the world outside?

Come, let us explore: there exists the rosy coast, these estuaries of pearl.

Gaze upon the skin as I have, through a microscope brightly, and tremble at the wisdom of God, for here is a magic tissue to suit all seasons. Two layers compose the skin—the superficial epidermis and, deeper, the dermis. Between is a plane of pure energy where the life-force is in full gallop. Identical cells spring full-grown here, each as tall and columnar as its brother, to form an unbroken line over the body. No sooner are these cells formed than they move toward the surface, whether drawn to the open air by some protoplasmic hunger or pushed outward by the birth of still newer cells behind. In migration the skin cells flatten, first to cubes, then plates. Twenty-six days later the plates are no more than attenuated wisps of keratin meshed together to guard against forces that would damage the skin by shearing or compression. Here they lie, having lost all semblance of living cellularity, until they are shed from the body in a continuous dismal rain. Thus into the valley of

Mortal Lessons (New York: Simon and Schuster, 1976).

death this number marches in well-stepped soldiery, gallant, summoned to a sacrifice beyond its ken. But . . . let the skin be cut or burned, and the brigade breaks into a charge, fanning out laterally across the wound, racing to seal off the defect. The margins are shored up; healing earthworks are raised, and guerrilla squads of invading bacteria are isolated and mopped up. The reserves too are called to the colors and the rate of mitosis increases throughout the injured area. Hurrah for stratified squamous epithelium!

Beneath the epidermis lies the dermis, a resilient pad of elastic tissue in which glands, hair follicles, nerves and blood vessels are arranged in infinitely variable mosaic. Within this rich bed three million sweat glands lie; these, in full sluice, can extract from the blood up to three kilograms of fluid in a single hour. Such a warm fall cools the body even as it evaporates from its surface and, incidentally, flushes from us the excess of salt that threatens to make of the body juices a pickling brine. In this, the sweat glands are helpmates to the kidney. Ah, but the skin *harbors* water and heat as well, containing our fluid and blood lest, one sunny day, we leak our way to dusty desiccation on some pavement or, bitten, bleed an hour or two, and die.

These sweat glands are most numerous on the palms and soles, and have their highest density at birth, decreasing steadily thereafter. Only the glans penis, clitoris, labia minora, and the inner surface of the prepuce have no sweat glands, a curiously sexual deficiency that ought to tell us something, but for God's sake what?

Never mind. Exclusiveness, in no matter what context, is not without its charms.

Still other glands of the dermis yield odoriferous oils. In that they attract mates and repel enemies, these musky syrups, called pheromones, engage in a kind of cutaneous communication. One may well deplore the perverse vanity which insists that we spray, roll on, and dab our flesh so as to deny these darling chemicals their true role. To banish our natural stink is to play havoc with no less than the procreative process itself, depriving it of its olfactory joys, at the very least. Such misguided fastidiousness will do us no good in the end. Keep in mind, a single sniff of pheromone can raise expectations to which a whole Pacific of perfume cannot pretend, nor an Atlantic of attar attain.

Besides, some of us need all the help we can get.

Ranking with the earlobes as our most adorable gewgaws are the nails that decorate the fingers and toes. One parts with the nails only under political duress and in great pain. Long since having retired their acquisitive and protective functions, they are more like the sweet hooflets of a yearling than the talons of a hawk. Still, among guitar players, certain Japanese weavers, and women with time on their hands, length is prized. For such specialists as for all who find it impossible to go on without knowing, it must be put abroad that nails grow faster in the dominant hand, grow twenty percent faster in the summer than in the winter, and grow twice as fast during the day as at night. Pregnancy, trauma, and nail-biting (mother's bane) are said to increase the rate of nail growth.

Four living paints, called biochromes, combine to give the skin its color at any given moment. There are brown, yellow, bright red, and purplish red. The bright red is called oxyhemoglobin and is carried by the blood to the skin. In the state of anemia or hemorrhage, there is less blood, thus less bright red, and the skin whitens, turns pale, until the line between pillowcase and patient is as indistinct as any horizon where sea and sky blend. Among those so afflicted were Elizabeth Barrett Browning, Annabel Lee, and The Lady of the Camellias. It is all very nineteenth-century.

Melanin is the brown pigment, which, under the influence of glands afar, gives to the skin what darkness it has. Without it we are albinos—pink, wretched creatures whose oxyhemoglobin is not masked by melanin, and for whom the sun's rays are no solace but ten thousand cruel fires that anger and abrade the tissues to malignancy.

It is differences in the number and size of pigment granules called melanosomes that account for whether your skin is naturally black or white. If your skin is black, you own more and larger of these organelles. But it happens that, for as yet unexplained reasons, a man may turn piebald.

Think, if you will, upon one Henry Moss. In Goochland County, Virginia, sprang he, black as an eggplant, from the loins of his mother and father in the otherwise unremembered year of 1754. Farmers his begetters were, and so did young Henry remain until the Revolutionary War broke out. He was twenty-two, and with many other free blacks, he enlisted in the Colonial Army, where he served for six years. Upon his discharge, Henry moved to Maryland, married, and took up once again his hoe and his plowshare. For ten years he farmed in peaceful anonymity, and would have done so until he died, had not Fate, in the year 1792, given him her most enigmatic smile—for in 1792 Henry Moss began to turn white.

First from his fingertips did the rich blackness fade—to no mere cocoa or tan, but to such a white as matched the fairness of a Dane. Soon the snowy tide had flooded his wrists, his arms, his neck. Next, his chest and abdomen and back undarkened in great irregular patches. He was

Holstein. He was Dalmatian. The blanching spread, coalesced, until four years later Henry Moss was almost totally white. Imagine the dismay of poor Henry Moss as he gazed into his mirror and saw vanishing therefrom the last bits of his dermal heritage. What face was this, what head, where the once kinky wool crisped thick and full, and where now limp white hair hung lank and silky? Was it some dread leprosy? Some awful spot presaging dissolution?

Not for long was Henry Moss to wander his little farm alone and palely loitering, for even as he gazed into that mirror, he felt the first fierce fetch of fame . . . and Philadelphia! To Philadelphia, Athens of America, city of culture and sophistication, came Henry Moss with his new whiteness upon him, and in his bosom the glory that transfigures, for Henry Moss had gazed deep into that mirror and seen reflected there his fortune and his destiny.

It was the practice of the innkeepers and hostelers of that time to maintain upon their premises for the enjoyment of their clients any of a number of oddities of natural history. There was a dead whale which had been caught in the Delaware River; a pygarg, which was a strange Russian beast, part camel, part bear; a learned pig that could tell the time of day and who transmitted this data in cunning little grunts; and Miss Sarah Rogers, who, born without arms or legs, still managed to paint elegant flowers and to thread needles with her lips and tongue and teeth. To these was added Henry Moss, the black man who was turning white! Scrub him hard, and see for yourself.

Overnight Henry Moss became a star. For his appearance at Mr. Leech's tavern on Market Street, The Sign of the Black Horse, handbills were passed out upon the streets. A GREAT CURIOSITY, the handbills proclaimed, a sight to open "a wide field of amusement for the philosophical genius."

But Henry Moss was no mere odd outscouring of the human race, suitable only for gawking. Henry Moss wore a message that rocked the very roofbeams of racial chauvinism so muscularly buttressed by our forefathers. Henry Moss was proof that the races were interchangeable, the skin reversible. As naught now, the vaunted difference. Black was white. Why not white . . . black? Why not, indeed!

In time Henry Moss was brought before a convocation of the leading physicians of Philadelphia, where the matter was discussed. Questions were raised, debates joined. Was the source of blackness to be found in the peculiar climate of Africa? If uprooted for a generation or two, would the black essence recede, to be replaced by the white? Would Henry Moss reblacken if transported to Africa? Would the progeny of a white turn black over there? Or was it indeed some perverse chemistry of the skin?

No answers were given. And the celebrated case of Henry Moss faded as swiftly as had the color of his skin. Still, one is left to wonder. . . . Had the good doctors of Philadelphia been led to believe in the interchangeability of the races, might not the blot of slavery, the Civil War itself, have been overleaped? Do you think Henry's *vitiglio* (a disease in which the pigment cells mysteriously fail to produce melanin) might have changed the course of history? Well, it didn't.

And what of Henry Moss? He surfaced last in rural Georgia where he earned a modest keep showing himself in the saloons of that back country. Like many a fading star, Henry ended playing the boonies.

The skin is the screen upon which the state of the other organs is cast. One can read their health in its condition and hue.

Ails the liver? Then the skin yellows into jaundice as the dislocated bile floods across it.

In the anemic state, the skin turns paper white as the enfeebled blood fails, until it would seem that a mere blush would divert blood enough to send the body into shock.

The first sign of certain cancers hidden deep within the body is itching of the skin or a painful rash.

Trouble in the brain is often heralded by the disappearance of feeling in a part of the skin.

In the poverty of oxygen lack, the skin leadens, is prinked with purple.

So it goes, as the skin reflects the occult mishaps of the marshy interior. It is upon the skin that the calamities of the flesh are made most brutally apparent. Here is all decay realized, all blight and blister exposed.

Awed and hurting, the diabetic watches his feet advance from bevelled grace through sore and ulcer to the blunt black scab of gangrene, extrapolating, as he must, from the part to the sum of his parts, to the whole, and feeling for his sad sweet blood only the most anguished rue.

The youth whose face blazes with rubies and carbuncles would sell his birthright, mortgage his future, to peel his soiled mask from him and don another. But there is no other. Nor any acnesarium where he might hide his pimentoes, eschewing both the pleasures and the risks of new manhood. He is badly touched indeed.

And what heartbroken psoriatic, surveying his embattled skin, would not volunteer for an unanesthetized flaying could it but rid him of his pink sequins, his silver spangles?

I hold no brief for rosy, turgid youth. It does but stir envy and leave compassion unaroused. My sympathies lie with the aging—those, motley with spots, gypsy with plaques and knobs, in whom each misfeatured stain announces with grim certainty the relentless slouching toward . . .

the end. Those in whom the elastica has so "given" that one is hung with dewlaps and is with wrinkled crepe empanoplied, in whom neither surgery, nor paints, nor other borrowed trumpery can anymore dissemble, they are the creatures that my heart and my feelings are tied to—those whose state of grace is marginal, the ragtail and bobtag, those in whom the difference from homely to comely is but a single freckle, one wart, a crease.

Yes, my sympathies lie with *us*.

Imagine God as tailor. His shelves are lined with rolls of skin, each with its subtleties of texture and hue. Six days a week He cuts lengths with which to wrap those small piles of flesh and bone into the clever parcels we call babies. Now engage the irreverence to consider that, either out of the tedium born of infinity, or out of mere sly parsimony, He uses for the occasional handicraft a remnant of yard goods, the last of an otherwise perfect bolt, dusty, soiled, perhaps a bit too small or large, one whose woof is warped or that is cut on the bias. I have received many such people in my examination rooms. Like imperfect postage stamps, they are the collector's items of the human race.

Such were the sorrows of wife Margaret vergh Gryffith, who, in the year 1588, in the month of May, in the town of Llangadfan, in Montgomeryshire, in the country of Wales, awoke one morning, stretched, rubbed her eyes to clear them of sleep, and felt (qual orrore!) a growth upon her forehead. At first a scaly eminence, a small rising at the very center of her brow; soon a horrid excrescence that no amount of dedicated picking, scraping, or nailed excavation could dislodge, so firm were its rootings. Daily it grew longer and larger in its girth, as though all of the young matron's energies were concentrated and refined to this one wicked purpose. Through salve and unguent she passed, through poultice and plaster, through the cook of cautery and the sizzle of scarification to the endless agitation of *concealment.* But there was no way to do it, no cap or snood, net or kerchief, hood or cowl to hide this . . . *horn.* Yes, at last it must be said. Margaret vergh Gryffith had grown a horn which stood priapically from her brow for a height of three inches, then curved downward toward her nose to crook just above her right eye— there, where there is nothing for it but to *see* it or shut forever her eyes and sit blind beneath her antler.

Imagine poor Margaret's shame, her altered sense of herself. See her devising more and more desperate articles and habits of concealment. It was of no use. As well hang a smoking brazier on the thing and walk abroad. The horn could not be hid! Wheresoever she faced, in whatever stance, however deep her crouch, it was the horn stood high and hard before her, rejecting all drapery, a lewd probe that announced to her

Puritan contemporaries as the very cornified concretion of adultery, an adultery she did not commit.

Then were fiery sermons delivered in all the cathedrals of Wales, to which the people came, and listened, and trembled in their pews. As far away as London was Margaret vergh Gryffith "made readie to be seene" and led out upon platforms whilst men thundered and pointed; and alone in their boudoirs, women raised cold fearful fingertips to their foreheads, and shuddered.

Shame on you, London. Where was your bold surgeon in 1588 who would dare thrust to the fore of the lickerish crowd, to lead the horned woman away to his surgery, to amputate the hideous prong of packed and layered keratin from her head?

Ah, he jests at scars who never felt a wound.

How proud and easy we slide in our skin. Extensible, it stretches to fit our farthest reach, contracts to our least flicker, and all in silky silence. How our skin becomes us! Lucky is Man to have his hide.

Moreover, it is not the brain nor the heart that is the organ of recollection. It is the skin! For to gaze upon the skin is to bring to life the past.

Here, in the crook of this arm, where the loose skin lies in transverse folds, in this very place, she rested the back of her head, her hair so black and glossy I could see myself in the mass of it.

And from this lower lip she drew two drops of my blood, that I was glad to give her.

And look, this scar upon my cheek that marked the end of love between two brothers.

It is all here engraved, that which I was, that which I did, all the old stories, but now purified somehow, the commonplace washed away, rinsed of all that is ordinary, and glowing as they never did, even when they happened.

URSULA K. LE GUIN
B. 1929

Daughter of an anthropologist and a writer, Ursula Le Guin is the author of such highly-acclaimed works of science-fiction and fantasy as The Left Hand of Darkness *(1969),* The Lathe of Heaven *(1971) and* The Earthsea Trilogy *(1977)*. *Yet, like much of the best nature writing, her work transcends the traditional genres, using imagined worlds and societies to examine such subjects as the cultural roots of human nature, sexual politics, and the power of myth and dream. In the following essay, which describes the 1980 eruption of Mount St. Helens near her home in Portland, Oregon, she examines how, in an age without communal myth, we try to reduce natural disasters to human scale by creating personal metaphors out of them.*

A Very Warm Mountain

An enormous region extending from north-central Washington to northeastern California and including most of Oregon east of the Cascades is covered by basalt lava flows. . . . The unending cliffs of basalt along the Columbia River . . . 74 volcanoes in the Portland area . . . A blanket of pumice that averages about 50 feet thick . . .

*—Roadside Geology of Oregon
Alt and Hyndman, 1978.*

Everybody takes it personally. Some get mad. Damn stupid mountain went and dumped all that dirty gritty glassy gray ash that flies like flour and lies like cement all over their roofs, roads, and rhododendrons. Now they have to clean it up. And the scientists are a real big help, all they'll say is we don't know, we can't tell, she might dump another load of ash on you just when you've got it all cleaned up. It's an outrage.

Some take it ethically. She lay and watched her forests being cut and her elk being hunted and her lakes being fished and fouled and her ecology being tampered with and the smoky, snarling suburbs creeping closer to her skirts, until she saw it was time to teach the White Man's Children a lesson. And she did. In the process of the lesson, she blew her forests to matchsticks, fried her elk, boiled her fish, wrecked her ecosystem, and did very little damage to the cities: so that the lesson taught to the White Man's Children would seem, at best, equivocal.

But everybody takes it personally. We try to reduce it to human scale. To make a molehill out of the mountain.

Some got very anxious, especially during the dreary white weather that hung around the area after May 18 (the first great eruption, when she blew 1300 feet of her summit all over Washington, Idaho, and points east) and May 25 (the first considerable ashfall in the thickly populated Portland area west of the mountain). Farmers in Washington State who had the real fallout, six inches of ash smothering their crops, answered the reporters' questions with polite stoicism; but in town a lot of people were cross and dull and jumpy. Some erratic behavior, some really weird driving. "Everybody on my bus coming to work these days talks to everybody else, they never used to." "Everybody on my bus coming to work sits there like a stone instead of talking to each other like they used to." Some welcomed the mild sense of urgency and emergency as bringing people together in mutual support. Some—the old, the ill— were terrified beyond reassurance. Psychologists reported that psychotics had promptly incorporated the volcano into their private systems; some thought they were controlling her, and some thought she was controlling them. Businessmen, whom we know from the Dow Jones Reports to be an almost ethereally timid and emotional breed, read the scare stories in Eastern newspapers and cancelled all their conventions here; Portland hotels are having a long cool summer. A Chinese Cultural Attaché, evidently preferring earthquakes, wouldn't come farther north than San Francisco. But many natives were irrationally exhilarated, secretly, heartlessly welcoming every steam-blast and earth-tremor: Go it, mountain!

Everybody read in the newspapers everywhere that the May 18 eruption was "five hundred times greater than the bomb dropped on Hiroshima." Some reflected that we have bombs much more than five hundred times more powerful than the 1945 bombs. But these are never mentioned in the comparisons. Perhaps it would upset people in Moscow, Idaho or Missoula, Montana, who got a lot of volcanic ash dumped on them, and don't want to have to think, what if that stuff had been radioactive? It really isn't nice to talk about, is it. I mean, what if something went off in New Jersey, say, and *was* radioactive—Oh, stop it. That volcano's way out west there somewhere anyhow.

Everybody takes it personally.

I had to go into hospital for some surgery in April, while the mountain was in her early phase—she jumped and rumbled, like the Uncles in *A Child's Christmas in Wales,* but she hadn't done anything spectacular. I was hoping she wouldn't perform while I couldn't watch. She obliged and held off for a month. On May 18 I was home, lying around with the cats, with a ringside view: bedroom and study look straight north about forty-five miles to the mountain.

I kept the radio tuned to a good country western station and listened to the reports as they came in, and wrote down some of the things they said. For the first couple of hours there was a lot of confusion and contradiction, but no panic, then or later. Late in the morning a man who had been about twenty miles from the blast described it: "Pumice-balls and mud-balls began falling for about a quarter of an hour, then the stuff got smaller, and by nine it was completely and totally black dark. You couldn't see ten feet in front of you!" He spoke with energy and admiration. Falling mud-balls, what next? The main West Coast artery, I-5, was soon closed because of the mud and wreckage rushing down the Toutle River towards the highway bridges. Walla Walla, 160 miles east, reported in to say their street lights had come on automatically at about ten in the morning. The Spokane–Seattle highway, far to the north, was closed, said an official expressionless voice, "on account of darkness."

At one-thirty that afternoon, I wrote:

> *It has been warm with a white high haze all morning, since six A.M., when I saw the top of the mountain floating dark against yellow-rose sunrise sky above the haze.*

That was, of course, the last time I saw or will ever see that peak.

> *Now we can see the mountain from the base to near the summit. The mountain itself is whitish in the haze. All morning there has been this long, cobalt-bluish drift to the east from where the summit would be. And about ten o'clock there began to be visible clots, like cottage cheese curds, above the summit. Now the eruption cloud is visible from the summit of the mountain till obscured by a cloud layer at about twice the height of the mountain, i.e., 25–30,000 feet. The eruption cloud is very solid-looking, like sculptured marble, a beautiful blue in the deep relief of baroque curls, sworls, curled-cloud-shapes—darkening towards the top—a wonderful color. One is aware of motion, but (being shaky, and looking through shaky binoculars) I don't actually see the carven-blue-sworl-shapes move. Like the shadow on a sundial. It is* enormous. *Forty-five miles away. It is so much bigger than the mountain itself. It is silent, from this distance. Enormous, silent. It looks not like anything earthy, from the earth, but it does not look like anything atmospheric, a natural cloud, either. The blue of it is storm-cloud blue but the shapes are far more delicate, complex, and immense than stormcloud shapes, and it has this solid look; a weightiness, like the capital of some unimaginable column—which in a way indeed it is, the pillar of fire being underground.*

At four in the afternoon a reporter said cautiously, "Earthquakes are being felt in the metropolitan area," to which I added, with feeling, "I'll say they are!" I had decided not to panic unless the cats did. Animals are supposed to know about earthquakes, aren't they? I don't know what our cats know; they lay asleep in various restful and decorative poses on the swaying floor and the jiggling bed, and paid no attention to anything except dinner time. I was not allowed to panic.

At four-thirty a meteorologist, explaining the height of that massive, storm-blue pillar of cloud, said charmingly, "You must understand that the mountain is very warm. Warm enough to lift the air over it to 75,000 feet."

And a reporter: "Heavy mud flow on Shoestring Glacier, with continuous lightning." I tried to imagine that scene. I went to the television, and there it was. The radio and television coverage, right through, was splendid. One forgets the joyful courage of reporters and cameramen when there is something worth reporting, a real Watergate, a real volcano.

On the 19th, I wrote down from the radio, "A helicopter picked the logger up while he was sitting on a log surrounded by a mud flow." This rescue was filmed and shown on television: the tiny figure crouching hopeless in the huge abomination of ash and mud. I don't know if this man was one of the loggers who later died in the Emanuel Hospital burn center, or if he survived. They were already beginning to talk about the "killer eruption," as if the mountain had murdered with intent. Taking it personally . . . Of course she killed. Or did they kill themselves? Old Harry who wouldn't leave his lodge and his whiskey and his eighteen cats at Spirit Lake, and quite right too, at eighty-three; and the young cameraman and the young geologist, both up there on the north side on the job of their lives; and the loggers who went back to work because logging was their living; and the tourists who thought a volcano is like Channel Six, if you don't like the show you turn it off, and took their RVs and their kids up past the roadblocks and the reasonable warnings and the weary county sheriffs sick of arguing: they were all there to keep the appointment. Who made the appointment?

A firefighter pilot that day said to the radio interviewer, "We do what the mountain says. It's not ready for us to go in."

On the 21st I wrote:

Last night a long, strange, glowing twilight; but no ash has yet fallen west of the mountain. Today, fine, gray, mild, dense Oregon rain. Yesterday afternoon we could see her vaguely through the glasses. Looking appallingly lessened—short, flat—That is painful. She was so beautiful. She hurled her beauty in dust clear to the Atlantic shore, she made sunsets and sunrises of it, she gave it to the western wind. I hope she erupts magma and begins to build herself again. But I guess she is still unbuilding. The Pres. of the U.S.

came today to see her. I wonder if he thinks he is on her level. Of course he
could destroy much more than she has destroyed if he took a mind to.

On June 4 I wrote:

> *Could see her through the glasses for the first time in two weeks or so. It's*
> *been dreary white weather with a couple of hours sun in the afternoons.—*
> *Not the new summit, yet; that's always in the roil of cloud/plume. But both*
> *her long lovely flanks. A good deal of new snow has fallen on her (while we*
> *had rain), and her SW face is white, black, and gray, much seamed, in*
> *unfamiliar patterns.*
> *"As changeless as the hills—"*
> *Part of the glory of it is being included in an event on the geologic scale.*
> *Being enlarged. "I shall lift up mine eyes unto the hills," yes: "whence*
> *cometh my help."*

In all the Indian legends dug out by newspaper writers for the occasion, the mountain is female. Told in the Dick-and-Jane style considered
appropriate for popular reportage of Indian myth, with all the syllables
hyphenated, the stories seem even more naive and trivial than myths out
of context generally do. But the theme of the mountain as woman—first
ugly, then beautiful, but always a woman—is consistent. The mapmak-
ing whites of course named the peak after a man, an Englishman who
took his title, Baron St. Helens, from a town in the North Country: but
the name is obstinately feminine. The Baron is forgotten, Helen remains. The whites who lived on and near the mountain called it The
Lady. Called her The Lady. It seems impossible not to take her personally. In twenty years of living through a window from her I guess I have
never really thought of her as "it."

She made weather, like all single peaks. She put on hats of cloud, and
took them off again, and tried a different shape, and sent them all skimming off across the sky. She wore veils: around the neck, across the
breast: white, silver, silver-gray, gray-blue. Her taste was impeccable. She
knew the weathers that became her, and how to wear the snow.

Dr. William Hamilton of Portland State University wrote a lovely
piece for the college paper about "volcano anxiety," suggesting that the
silver cone of St. Helens had been in human eyes a breast, and saying:

> *St. Helens' real damage to us is not . . . that we have witnessed a denial of*
> *the trustworthiness of God (such denials are our familiar friends). It is the*
> *perfection of the mother that has been spoiled, for part of her breast has been*
> *removed. Our metaphor has had a mastectomy.*
> *At some deep level, the eruption of Mt. St. Helens has become a new*
> *metaphor for the very opposite of stability—for that greatest of twentieth-*

century fears—cancer. Our uneasiness may well rest on more elusive levels than dirty windshields.

This comes far closer to home than anything else I've read about the "meaning" of the eruption, and yet for me it doesn't work. Maybe it would work better for men. The trouble is, I never saw St. Helens as a breast. Some mountains, yes: Twin Peaks in San Francisco, of course, and other round, sweet California hills—breasts, bellies, eggs, anything maternal, bounteous, yielding. But St. Helens in my eyes was never part of a woman; she is a woman. And not a mother but a sister.

These emotional perceptions and responses sound quite foolish when written out in rational prose, but the fact is that, to me, the eruption was all mixed up with the women's movement. It may be silly but there it is; along the same lines, do you know any woman who wasn't rooting for Genuine Risk to take the Triple Crown? Part of my satisfaction and exultation at each eruption was unmistakably feminist solidarity. You men think you're the only ones can make a really nasty mess? You think you got all the firepower, and God's on your side? You think you run things? Watch this, gents. Watch the Lady act like a woman.

For that's what she did. The well-behaved, quiet, pretty, serene, domestic creature peaceably yielding herself to the uses of man all of a sudden said NO. And she spat dirt and smoke and steam. She blackened half her face, in those first March days, like an angry brat. She fouled herself like a mad old harridan. She swore and belched and farted, threatened and shook and swelled, and then she spoke. They heard her voice two hundred miles away. Here I go, she said. I'm doing my thing now. Old Nobodaddy you better JUMP!

Her thing turns out to be more like childbirth than anything else, to my way of thinking. But not on our scale, not in our terms. Why should she speak in our terms or stoop to our scale? Why should she bear any birth that we can recognize? To us it is cataclysm and destruction and deformity. To her—well, for the language for it one must go to the scientists or to the poets. To the geologists. St. Helens is doing exactly what she "ought" to do—playing her part in the great pattern of events perceived by that noble discipline. Geology provides the only time-scale large enough to include the behavior of a volcano without deforming it. Geology, or poetry, which can see a mountain and a cloud as, after all, very similar phenomena. Shelley's cloud can speak for St. Helens:

> I silently laugh
> At my own cenotaph . . .
> And arise, and unbuild it again.

So many mornings waking I have seen her from the window before
any other thing: dark against red daybreak, silvery in summer light, faint
above river-valley fog. So many times I have watched her at evening, the
faintest outline in mist, immense, remote, serene: the center, the central
stone. A self across the air, a sister self, a stone. "The stone is at the
center," I wrote in a poem about her years ago. But the poem is impertinent. All I can say is impertinent.

When I was writing the first draft of this essay in California, on July
23, she erupted again, sending her plume to 60,000 feet. Yesterday,
August 7, as I was typing the words "the 'meaning' of the eruption," I
checked out the study window and there it was, the towering blue cloud
against the quiet northern sky—the fifth major eruption. How long may
her labor be? A year, ten years, ten thousand? We cannot predict what
she may or might or will do, now, or next, or for the rest of our lives, or
ever. A threat: a terror: a fulfillment. This is what serenity is built on.
This unmakes the metaphors. This is beyond us, and we must take it
personally. This is the ground we walk on.

EDWARD O. WILSON
B. 1929

*One of the foremost authorities on social insects, E.O. Wilson gained
notoriety in 1975 with the publication of* Sociobiology: The New Synthesis, *an attempt to give a biological and evolutionary basis to social and
individual behavior, including that of human beings. The controversy
set off by the book and fueled by Wilson's subsequent publications (including* On Human Nature, *which won the Pulitzer Prize in 1978)
remains unabated. His critics accuse him of a reductionist and mechanistic view of culture and morality, with dangerous eugenic and racist overtones, while his admirers claim that his work is Darwinian in scope and
import and that, like his nineteenth-century predecessor, he is the target
of philistines who object to his conclusions on ethical and emotional,
rather than on scientific grounds. By contrast,* Biophilia: The Human
Bond to Other Species *(1984) is a collection of personal humanistic
essays written in elegant, often rapt prose. "Biophilia" is a term coined*

by Wilson which he defines as "the innate tendency to focus on life and lifelike processes." A central concept of the book is that humanistic values are strengthened, not weakened, by understanding their evolutionary origins. Wilson believes that our humanity is rooted in our kinship with other animals and that "the key to saving life is learning to love it more." Several of the essays draw on his boyhood adventures in rural Alabama and his work as a participant in the Critical Size Project of the World Wildlife Fund, an attempt to determine the relationship of size to biological diversity in the world's threatened tropical rain forests. The following selection argues, as does much of nature writing, new and old, that an ongoing synthesis of scientific and imaginative approaches to life is integral to full human understanding.

From BIOPHILIA

THE BIRD OF PARADISE

Come with me now to another part of the living world. The role of science, like that of art, is to blend exact imagery with more distant meaning, the parts we already understand with those given as new into larger patterns that are coherent enough to be acceptable as truth. The biologist knows this relation by intuition during the course of field work, as he struggles to make order out of the infinitely varying patterns of nature.

Picture the Huon Peninsula of New Guinea, about the size and shape of Rhode Island, a weathered horn projecting from the northeastern coast of the main island. When I was twenty-five, with a fresh Ph.D. from Harvard and dreams of physical adventure in far-off places with unpronounceable names, I gathered all the courage I had and made a difficult and uncertain trek directly across the peninsular base. My aim was to collect a sample of ants and a few other kinds of small animals up from the lowlands to the highest part of the mountains. To the best of my knowledge I was the first biologist to take this particular route. I knew that almost everything I found would be worth recording, and all the specimens collected would be welcomed into museums.

Three days' walk from a mission station near the southern Lae coast brought me to the spine of the Sarawaget range, 12,000 feet above sea level. I was above treeline, in a grassland sprinkled with cycads, squat

Biophilia: The Human Bond to Other Species (Cambridge: Harvard University Press, 1984).

gymnospermous plants that resemble stunted palm trees and date from the Mesozoic Era, so that closely similar ancestral forms might have been browsed by dinosaurs 80 million years ago. On a chill morning when the clouds lifted and the sun shone brightly, my Papuan guides stopped hunting alpine wallabies with dogs and arrows, I stopped putting beetles and frogs in bottles of alcohol, and together we scanned the rare panoramic view. To the north we could make out the Bismarck Sea, to the south the Markham Valley and the more distant Herzog Mountains. The primary forest covering most of this mountainous country was broken into bands of different vegetation according to elevation. The zone just below us was the cloud forest, a labyrinth of interlocking trunks and branches blanketed by a thick layer of moss, orchids, and other epiphytes that ran unbroken off the tree trunks and across the ground. To follow game trails across this high country was like crawling through a dimly illuminated cave lined with a spongy green carpet.

A thousand feet below, the vegetation opened up a bit and assumed the appearance of typical lowland rain forest, except that the trees were denser and smaller and only a few flared out into a circle of blade-thin buttresses at the base. This is the zone botanists call the mid-mountain forest. It is an enchanted world of thousands of species of birds, frogs, insects, flowering plants, and other organisms, many found nowhere else. Together they form one of the richest and most nearly pure segments of the Papuan flora and fauna. To visit the mid-mountain forest is to see life as it existed before the coming of man thousands of years ago.

The jewel of the setting is the male Emperor of Germany bird of paradise *(Paradisaea guilielmi)*, arguably the most beautiful bird in the world, certainly one of the twenty or so most striking in appearance. By moving quietly along secondary trails you might glimpse one on a lichen-encrusted branch near the tree tops. Its head is shaped like that of a crow—no surprise because the birds of paradise and crows have a close common lineage—but there the outward resemblance to any ordinary bird ends. The crown and upper breast of the bird are metallic oil-green and shine in the sunlight. The back is glossy yellow, the wings and tail deep reddish maroon. Tufts of ivory-white plumes sprout from the flanks and sides of the breast, turning lacy in texture toward the tips. The plume rectrices continue on as wirelike appendages past the breast and tail for a distance equal to the full length of the bird. The bill is blue-gray, the eyes clear amber, the claws brown and black.

In the mating season the male joins others in leks, common courtship arenas in the upper tree branches, where they display their dazzling ornaments to the more somberly caparisoned females. The male spreads his wings and vibrates them while lifting the gossamer flank plumes. He calls loudly with bubbling and flutelike notes and turns upside down on the perch, spreading the wings and tail and pointing his rectrices skyward. The dance then reaches a climax as he fluffs up the green breast feathers and opens out the flank plumes until they form a brilliant white circle around his body, with only the head, tail, and wings projecting beyond. The male sways gently from side to side, causing the plumes to wave gracefully as if caught in an errant breeze. Seen from a distance his body now resembles a spinning and slightly out-of-focus white disk.

This improbable spectacle in the Huon forest has been fashioned by millions of generations of natural selection in which males competed and females made choices, and the accouterments of display were driven to a visual extreme. But this is only one trait, seen in physiological time and thought about at a single level of causation. Beneath its plumed surface, the Emperor of Germany bird of paradise possesses an architecture culminating an ancient history, with details exceeding those that can be imagined from the naturalist's simple daylight record of color and dance.

Consider one such bird for a moment in the analytic manner, as an object of biological research. Encoded within its chromosomes is the developmental program that led with finality to a male *Paradisaea guilielmi*. The completed nervous system is a structure of fiber tracts more complicated than any existing computer, and as challenging as all the rain forests of New Guinea surveyed on foot. A microscopic study will someday permit us to trace the events that culminate in the electric commands carried by the efferent neurons to the skeletal-muscular system and reproduce, in part, the dance of the courting male. This machinery can be dissected and understood by proceeding to the level of the cell, to enzymatic catalysis, microfilament configuration, and active sodium transport during electric discharge. Because biology sweeps the full range of space and time, there will be more discoveries renewing the sense of wonder at each step of research. By altering the scale of perception to the micrometer and millisecond, the laboratory scientist parallels the trek of the naturalist across the land. He looks out from his own version of the mountain crest. His spirit of adventure, as well as personal history of hardship, misdirection, and triumph, are fundamentally the same.

Described this way, the bird of paradise may seem to have been turned into a metaphor of what humanists dislike most about science: that it reduces nature and is insensitive to art, that scientists are conquistadors who melt down the Inca gold. But bear with me a minute. Science is not just analytic; it is also synthetic. It uses artlike intuition and imagery. In the early stages, individual behavior can be analyzed to the level of genes and neurosensory cells, whereupon the phenomena have indeed been mechanically reduced. In the synthetic phase, though, even the most elementary activity of these biological units creates rich and subtle patterns at the levels of organism and society. The outer qualities of *Paradisaea guilielmi*, its plumes, dance, and daily life, are functional traits open to a deeper understanding through the exact description of their constituent parts. They can be redefined as holistic properties that alter our perception and emotion in surprising and pleasant ways.

There will come a time when the bird of paradise is reconstituted by the synthesis of all the hard-won analytic information. The mind, bearing a newfound power, will journey back to the familiar world of seconds and centimeters. Once again the glittering plumage takes form and is viewed at a distance through a network of leaves and mist. Then we see the bright eye open, the head swivel, the wings extend. But the familiar motions are viewed across a far greater range of cause and effect. The species is understood more completely; misleading illusions have given way to light and wisdom of a greater degree. One turn of the cycle of intellect is then complete. The excitement of the scientist's search for the true material nature of the species recedes, to be replaced in part by the more enduring responses of the hunter and poet.

What are these ancient responses? The full answer can only be given through a combined idiom of science and the humanities, whereby the investigation turns back into itself. The human being, like the bird of paradise, awaits our examination in the analytic-synthetic manner. As always by honored tradition, feeling and myth can be viewed at a distance through physiological time, idiosyncratically, in the manner of traditional art. But they can also be penetrated more deeply than ever was possible in the prescientific age, to their physical basis in the processes of mental development, the brain structure, and indeed the genes themselves. It may even be possible to trace them back through time past cultural history to the evolutionary origins of human nature. With each new phase of synthesis to emerge from biological inquiry, the humanities will expand their reach and capability. In symmetric fashion, with each redirection of the humanities, science will add dimensions to human biology.

JOHN MCPHEE
B. 1931

A pioneer of the "new journalism," John McPhee first published most of his numerous books as essays in The New Yorker. *Though celebrated for the great variety of his subjects—ranging from the history of oranges to profiles of athletes to the development of experimental aircraft—a preponderance of his books focus on natural or environmental topics.* The Pine Barrens *(1968) describes a large, little-known wild area not far from his home in Princeton, New Jersey.* Encounters with the Archdruid *(1971) is an in-depth study of radical conservationist David Brower,* Coming Into the Country *(1977), generally considered his best work, is a study of the Alaskan wilderness and the political issues surrounding it. A recent trio of books,* Basin and Range *(1981),* In Suspect Terrain *(1983), and* Rising from the Plains *(1987), are all based on his experiences with North American geologists. McPhee has been widely praised for his vivid descriptions, evocations of character, and uncanny ability to take difficult or arcane subjects and render them of compelling interest to the general reader. Like a good novelist, McPhee creates a strong point of view not through overtly expressed opinions, but by the careful choice of fact and detail and the sheer possessive energy of his writing.*

From COMING INTO THE COUNTRY

[the grizzly bear]

* * * We passed first through stands of fireweed, and then over ground that was wine-red with the leaves of bearberries. There were curlewberries, too, which put a deep-purple stain on the hand. We kicked at some wolf scat, old as winter. It was woolly and white and filled with the hair of a snowshoe hare. Nearby was a rich inventory of caribou pellets and, in increasing quantity as we moved downhill, blueberries—

Coming into the Country (New York: Farrar, Straus & Giroux, 1977).

an outspreading acreage of blueberries. Fedeler stopped walking. He touched my arm. He had in an instant become even more alert than he usually was, and obviously apprehensive. His gaze followed straight on down our intended course. What he saw there I saw now. It appeared to me to be a hill of fur. "Big boar grizzly," Fedeler said in a near-whisper. The bear was about a hundred steps away, in the blueberries, grazing. The head was down, the hump high. The immensity of muscle seemed to vibrate slowly—to expand and contract, with the grazing. Not berries alone but whole bushes were going into the bear. He was big for a barren-ground grizzly. The brown bears of Arctic Alaska (or grizzlies; they are no longer thought to be different) do not grow to the size they will reach on more ample diets elsewhere. The barren-ground grizzly will rarely grow larger than six hundred pounds.

"What if he got too close?" I said.

Fedeler said, "We'd be in real trouble."

"You can't outrun them," Hession said.

A grizzly, no slower than a racing horse, is about half again as fast as the fastest human being. Watching the great mound of weight in the blueberries, with a fifty-five-inch waist and a neck more than thirty inches around, I had difficulty imagining that he could move with such speed, but I believed it, and was without impulse to test the proposition. Fortunately, a light southerly wind was coming up the Salmon valley. On its way to us, it passed the bear. The wind was relieving, coming into our faces, for had it been moving the other way the bear would not have been placidly grazing. There is an old adage that when a pine needle drops in the forest the eagle will see it fall; the deer will hear it when it hits the ground; the bear will smell it. If the boar grizzly were to catch our scent, he might stand on his hind legs, the better to try to see. Although he could hear well and had an extraordinary sense of smell, his eyesight was not much better than what was required to see a blueberry inches away. For this reason, a grizzly stands and squints, attempting to bring the middle distance into focus, and the gesture is often misunderstood as a sign of anger and forthcoming attack. If the bear were getting ready to attack, he would be on four feet, head low, ears cocked, the hair above his hump muscle standing on end. As if that message were not clear enough, he would also chop his jaws. His teeth would make a sound that would carry like the ringing of an axe.

One could predict, but not with certainty, what a grizzly would do. Odds were very great that one touch of man scent would cause him to stop his activity, pause in a moment of absorbed and alert curiosity, and then move, at a not undignified pace, in a direction other than the one from which the scent was coming. That is what would happen almost every time, but there was, to be sure, no guarantee. The forest Eskimos fear and revere the grizzly. They know that certain individual bears not only will fail to avoid a person who comes into their country but will approach and even stalk the trespasser. It is potentially inaccurate to extrapolate the behavior of any one bear from the behavior of most, since they are both intelligent and independent and will do what they choose to do according to mood, experience, whim. A grizzly that has ever been wounded by a bullet will not forget it, and will probably know that it was a human being who sent the bullet. At sight of a human, such a bear will be likely to charge. Grizzlies hide food sometimes—a caribou calf, say, under a pile of scraped-up moss—and a person the bear might otherwise ignore might suddenly not be ignored if the person were inadvertently to step into the line between the food cache and the bear. A sow grizzly with cubs, of course, will charge anything that suggests danger to the cubs, even if the cubs are nearly as big as she is. They stay with their mother two and a half years.

None of us had a gun. (None of the six of us had brought a gun on the trip.) Among nonhunters who go into the terrain of the grizzly, there are several schools of thought about guns. The preferred one is: Never go without a sufficient weapon—a high-powered rifle or a shotgun and plenty of slug-loaded shells. The option is not without its own inherent peril. A professional hunter, some years ago, spotted a grizzly from the air and—with a client, who happened to be an Anchorage barber—landed on a lake about a mile from the bear. The stalking that followed was evidently conducted not only by the hunters but by the animal as well. The professional hunter was found dead from a broken neck, and had apparently died instantly, unaware of danger, for the cause of death was a single bite, delivered from behind. The barber, noted as clumsy with a rifle, had emptied his magazine, missing the bear with every shot but one, which struck the grizzly in the foot. The damage the bear did to the barber was enough to kill him several times. After the corpses were found, the bear was tracked and killed. To shoot and merely wound is worse than not to shoot at all. A bear that might have turned and gone away will possibly attack if wounded.   *   *   *

UNDER THE SNOW

When my third daughter was an infant, I could place her against my shoulder and she would stick there like velvet. Only her eyes jumped from place to place. In a breeze, her bright-red hair might stir, but she would not. Even then, there was profundity in her repose.

Table of Contents (New York: Farrar, Straus & Giroux, 1985).

When my fourth daughter was an infant, I wondered if her veins were full of ants. Placing her against a shoulder was a risk both to her and to the shoulder. Impulsively, constantly, everything about her moved. Her head seemed about to revolve as it followed the bestirring world.

These memories became very much alive some months ago when—one after another—I had bear cubs under my vest. Weighing three, four, 5.6 pounds, they were wild bears, and for an hour or so had been taken from their dens in Pennsylvania. They were about two months old, with fine short brown hair. When they were made to stand alone, to be photographed in the mouth of a den, they shivered. Instinctively, a person would be moved to hold them. Picked up by the scruff of the neck, they splayed their paws like kittens and screamed like baby bears. The cry of a baby bear is muted, like a human infant's heard from her crib down the hall. The first cub I placed on my shoulder stayed there like a piece of velvet. The shivering stopped. Her bright-blue eyes looked about, not seeing much of anything. My hand, cupped against her back, all but encompassed her rib cage, which was warm and calm. I covered her to the shoulders with a flap of down vest and zipped up my parka to hold her in place.

I was there by invitation, an indirect result of work I had been doing nearby. Would I be busy on March 14th? If there had been a conflict—if, say, I had been invited to lunch on that day with the Queen of Scotland and the King of Spain—I would have gone to the cubs. The first den was a rock cavity in a lichen-covered sandstone outcrop near the top of a slope, a couple of hundred yards from a road in Hawley. It was on posted property of the Scrub Oak Hunting Club—dry hardwood forest underlain by laurel and patches of snow—in the northern Pocono woods. Up in the sky was Buck Alt. Not long ago, he was a dairy farmer, and now he was working for the Keystone State, with directional antennae on his wing struts angled in the direction of bears. Many bears in Pennsylvania have radios around their necks as a result of the summer trapping work of Alt's son Gary, who is a wildlife biologist. In winter, Buck Alt flies the country listening to the radio, crissing and crossing until the bears come on. They come on stronger the closer to them he flies. The transmitters are not omnidirectional. Suddenly, the sound cuts out. Buck looks down, chooses a landmark, approaches it again, on another vector. Gradually, he works his way in, until he is flying in ever tighter circles above the bear. He marks a map. He is accurate within two acres. The plane he flies is a Super Cub.

The den could have served as a set for a Passion play. It was a small chamber, open on one side, with a rock across its entrance. Between the freestanding rock and the back of the cave was room for one large bear, and she was curled in a corner on a bed of leaves, her broad head plainly visible from the outside, her cubs invisible between the rock and a soft place, chuckling, suckling, in the wintertime tropics of their own mammalian heaven. Invisible they were, yes, but by no means inaudible. What biologists call chuckling sounded like starlings in a tree.

People walking in woods sometimes come close enough to a den to cause the mother to get up and run off, unmindful of her reputation as a fearless defender of cubs. The cubs stop chuckling and begin to cry: possibly three, four cubs—a ward of mewling bears. The people hear the crying. They find the den and see the cubs. Sometimes they pick them up and carry them away, reporting to the state that they have saved the lives of bear cubs abandoned by their mother. Wherever and whenever this occurs, Gary Alt collects the cubs. After ten years of bear trapping and biological study, Alt has equipped so many sows with radios that he has been able to conduct a foster-mother program with an amazingly high rate of success. A mother in hibernation will readily accept a foster cub. If the need to place an orphan arises somewhat later, when mothers and their cubs are out and around, a sow will kill an alien cub as soon as she smells it. Alt has overcome this problem by stuffing sows' noses with Vicks VapoRub. One way or another, he has found new families for forty-seven orphaned cubs. Forty-six have survived. The other, which had become accustomed over three weeks to feedings and caresses by human hands, was not content in a foster den, crawled outside, and died in the snow.

With a hypodermic jab stick, Alt now drugged the mother, putting her to sleep for the duration of the visit. From deeps of shining fur, he fished out cubs. One. Two. A third. A fourth. Five! The fifth was a foster daughter brought earlier in the winter from two hundred miles away. Three of the four others were male—a ratio consistent with the heavy preponderance of males that Alt's studies have shown through the years. To various onlookers he handed the cubs for safekeeping while he and several assistants carried the mother into the open and weighed her with block and tackle. To protect her eyes, Alt had blindfolded her with a red bandanna. They carried her upside down, being extremely careful lest they scrape and damage her nipples. She weighed two hundred and nineteen pounds. Alt had caught her and weighed her some months before. In the den, she had lost ninety pounds. When she was four years old, she had had four cubs; two years later, four more cubs; and now, after two more years, four cubs. He knew all that about her, he had caught her so many times. He referred to her as Daisy. Daisy was as nothing compared with Vanessa, who was sleeping off the winter somewhere else. In ten seasons, Vanessa had given birth to twenty-three cubs, and had lost none. The growth and reproductive rates of black bears are greater in Pennsylvania than anywhere else. Black bears in Pennsylvania grow more rapidly than grizzlies in Montana. Eastern black bears are generally much larger than Western ones. A seven-hundred-pound bear is unusual but not rare in Pennsylvania. Alt once caught a big boar like that who had a thirty-seven-inch neck and was a hair under seven feet long.

This bear, nose to tail, measured five feet five. Alt said, "That's a nice long sow." For weighing the cubs, he had a small nylon stuff sack. He stuffed it with bear and hung it on a scale. Two months before, when the cubs were born, each would have weighed approximately half a pound— less than a newborn porcupine. Now the cubs weighed 3.4, 4.1, 4.4, 4.6, 5.6—cute little numbers with soft tan noses and erectile pyramid ears. Bears have sex in June and July, but the mother's system holds the fertilized egg away from the uterus until November, when implantation occurs. Fetal development lasts scarcely six weeks. Therefore, the creatures who live upon the hibernating mother are so small that everyone survives.

The orphan, less winsome than the others, looked like a chocolate-covered possum. I kept her under my vest. She seemed content there and scarcely moved. In time, I exchanged her for 5.6—the big boy in the litter. Lifted by the scruff and held in the air, he bawled, flashed his claws, and curled his lips like a woofing boar. I stuffed him under the vest, where he shut up and nuzzled. His claws were already more than half an inch long. Alt said that the family would come out of the den in a few weeks but that much of the spring would go by before the cubs gained weight. The difference would be that they were no longer malleable and ductile. They would become pugnacious and scratchy, not to say vicious, and would chew up the hand that caressed them. He said, "If you have an enemy, give him a bear cub."

Six men carried the mother back to the den, the red bandanna still tied around her eyes. Alt repacked her into the rock. "We like to return her to the den as close as possible to the way we found her," he said. Someone remarked that one biologist can work a coon, while an army is needed to deal with a bear. An army seemed to be present. Twelve people had followed Alt to the den. Some days, the group around him is four times as large. Alt, who is in his thirties, was wearing a visored khaki cap with a blue-and-gold keystone on the forehead, and a khaki cardigan under a khaki jump suit. A lithe and light-bodied man with tinted glasses and a blond mustache, he looked like a lieutenant in the Ardennes Forest. Included in the retinue were two reporters and a news photographer. Alt encourages media attention, the better to soften the image of the bears. He says, "People fear bears more than they need to, and respect them not enough." Over the next twenty days, he had scheduled four hundred visitors—state senators, representatives, commissioners, television reporters, word processors, biologists, friends—to go along on his rounds of dens. Days before, he and the denned bears had been hosts to the BBC. The Brits wanted snow. God was having none of it. The BBC brought in the snow.

In the course of the day, we made a brief tour of dens that for the time being stood vacant. Most were rock cavities. They had been used before, and in all likelihood would be used again. Bears in winter in the Pocono Plateau are like chocolate chips in a cookie. The bears seldom go back to the same den two years running, and they often change dens in the course of a winter. In a forty-five-hundred-acre housing development called Hemlock Farms are twenty-three dens known to be in current use and countless others awaiting new tenants. Alt showed one that was within fifteen feet of the intersection of East Spur Court and Pommel Drive. He said that when a sow with two cubs was in there he had seen deer browsing by the outcrop and ignorant dogs stopping off to lift a leg. Hemlock Farms is expensive, and full of cantilevered cypress and unencumbered glass. Houses perch on high flat rock. Now and again, there are bears in the rock—in, say, a floor-through cavity just under the porch. The owners are from New York. Alt does not always tell them that their property is zoned for bears. Once, when he did so, a "FOR SALE" sign went up within two weeks.

Not far away is Interstate 84. Flying over it one day, Buck Alt heard an oddly intermittent signal. Instead of breaking off once and cleanly, it broke off many times. Crossing back over, he heard it again. Soon he was in a tight turn, now hearing something, now nothing, in a pattern that did not suggest anything he had heard before. It did, however, suggest the interstate. Where a big green sign says, "MILFORD 11, PORT JERVIS 20," Gary hunted around and found the bear. He took us now to see the den. We went down a steep slope at the side of the highway and, crouching, peered into a culvert. It was about fifty yards long. There was a disc of daylight at the opposite end. Thirty inches in diameter, it was a perfect place to stash a body, and that is what the bear thought, too. On Gary's first visit, the disc of daylight had not been visible. The bear had denned under the eastbound lanes. She had given birth to three cubs. Soon after he found her, heavy rains were predicted. He hauled the family out and off to a vacant den. The cubs weighed less than a pound. Two days later, water a foot deep was racing through the culvert.

Under High Knob, in remote undeveloped forest about six hundred metres above sea level, a slope falling away in an easterly direction contained a classic excavated den: a small entrance leading into an intimate ovate cavern, with a depression in the center for a bed—in all, about twenty-four cubic feet, the size of a refrigerator-freezer. The den had not been occupied in several seasons, but Rob Buss, a district game protector who works regularly with Gary Alt, had been around to check it three days before and had shined his flashlight into a darkness stuffed with fur. Meanwhile, six inches of fresh snow had fallen on High Knob, and now Alt and his team, making preparations a short distance from the den, scooped up snow in their arms and filled a big sack. They had nets of nylon mesh. There was a fifty-fifty likelihood of yearling bears in the den. Mothers keep cubs until their second spring. When a biologist comes along and provokes the occupants to emerge, there is no way to predict how many will appear. Sometimes they keep coming and coming, like clowns from a compact car. As a bear emerges, it walks into the nylon mesh. A drawstring closes. At the same time, the den entrance is stuffed with a bag of snow. That stops the others. After the first bear has been dealt with, Alt removes the sack of snow. Out comes another bear. A yearling weighs about eighty pounds, and may move so fast that it runs over someone on the biological team and stands on top of him sniffing at his ears. Or her ears. Janice Gruttadauria, a research assistant, is a part of the team. Bear after bear, the procedure is repeated until the bag of snow is pulled away and nothing comes out. That is when Alt asks Rob Buss to go inside and see if anything is there.

Now, moving close to the entrance, Alt spread a tarp on the snow, lay down on it, turned on a five-cell flashlight, and put his head inside the den. The beam played over thick black fur and came to rest on a tiny foot. The sack of snow would not be needed. After drugging the mother with a jab stick, he joined her in the den. The entrance was so narrow he had to shrug his shoulders to get in. He shoved the sleeping mother, head first, out of the darkness and into the light.

While she was away, I shrugged my own shoulders and had a look inside. The den smelled of earth but not of bear. The walls were dripping with roots. The water and protein metabolism of hibernating black bears has been explored by the Mayo Clinic as a research model for, among other things, human endurance on long flights through space and medical situations closer to home, such as the maintenance of anephric human beings who are awaiting kidney transplants.

Outside, each in turn, the cubs were put in the stuff sack—a male and a female. The female weighed four pounds. Greedily, I reached for her when Alt took her out of the bag. I planted her on my shoulder while I wrote down facts about her mother: weight, a hundred and ninety-two pounds; length, fifty-eight inches; some toes missing; severe frostbite from a bygone winter evidenced along the edges of the ears.

Eventually, with all weighing and tagging complete, it was time to go. Alt went into the den. Soon he called out that he was ready for the mother. It would be a tight fit. Feet first, she was shoved in, like a safe-deposit box. Inside, Alt tugged at her in close embrace, and the two of them gradually revolved until she was at the back and their positions had reversed. He shaped her like a doughnut—her accustomed den position. The cubs go in the center. The male was handed in to him. Now he was asking for the female. For a moment, I glanced around as if looking to see who had her. The thought crossed my mind that if I bolted and ran far enough and fast enough I could flag a passing car and keep her. Then I pulled her from under the flap of my vest and handed her away.

Alt and others covered the entrance with laurel boughs, and covered the boughs with snow. They camouflaged the den, but that was not the purpose. Practicing wildlife management to a fare-thee-well, Alt wanted the den to be even darker than it had been before; this would cause the family to stay longer inside and improve the cubs' chances when at last they faced the world.

In the evening, I drove down off the Pocono Plateau and over the folded mountains and across the Great Valley and up the New Jersey Highlands and down into the basin and home. No amount of intervening terrain, though—and no amount of distance—could remove from my mind the picture of the covered entrance in the Pennsylvania hillside, or the thought of what was up there under the snow.

JOHN G. MITCHELL
B. 1931

John Mitchell cut his journalistic teeth on his hometown Cincinnati newspaper, then served a seven-year stint on the New York Journal American's *"prowl desk," investigating heroin addiction, slumlords, and racketeering. Since 1974 he has become known to readers of* Audubon *magazine for his balanced yet impassioned reporting on such controver-*

sial environmental subjects as corporate pollution, timber companies, oil drilling, and the development of the Amazon Basin. Nothing he has written, however, stirred as much controversy as a five-part series on hunting which appeared in Audubon in 1979 and in book form in The Hunt *(1980). Hunting inspires emotional partisanship that often far exceeds its actual environmental consequences. It seems to challenge our moral conceptions of ourselves while refusing to submit to logical resolution. Not surprisingly, Mitchell's passionate but balanced exploration of the ethical and ecological ramifications of hunting earned him condemnation from extremists on both sides.*

From THE HUNT

THE GUNS OF GAYLORD

My father shot and killed his first moose in New Brunswick in 1922. It was also his last, anywhere. The animal weighed eight hundred pounds after gutting and the antlers measured fifty inches across the full spread. The old man and his guide were a long portage from their canoe and a dozen miles out from the nearest roadhead when the big bull went down with a hole half the diameter of a man's little finger behind its shoulder. They gutted the moose in the shallow pond where it fell, quartered it, and carried everything edible or mountable to the canoe. The edible parts were long gone before my time. As for the moose's head, when I came of an age to notice such things, I found it mounted above the fireplace of our cottage in northern Michigan. Firelight flashed across the brown marbles of its make-believe eyes. Wherever I moved, the eyes seemed to follow. I spoke to the moose. I said: Moose, why do you watch me? Why do you look so sad when it no longer hurts? The moose did not answer. My father did not answer either, and I had asked him a more reasonable question. I asked him if killing moose is fun.

Perhaps there was no answer from the old man because he could no longer be sure how he felt about such things. Though he would live most of his life in it, he was not of the twentieth century. It seemed to me, for he was old enough to be my grandfather, that he was always back somewhere on the other side of the century, in a time of horses and bugles, among fresh memories of Cheyenne lances at the Little Bighorn and Krupp cannon at the Centennial Exposition in Philadelphia's Fair-

The Hunt (New York: Knopf, 1980).

mount Park. He missed both of those events by three years, but not the great flights of passenger pigeons that still darkened the skies of Kentucky on summer mornings, or the diminishing herds of bison that would linger for a decade in Texas, though the last of that breed in Kansas was dropped in its tracks on the Santa Fe Trail the month he was born.

He was a country boy, and he learned to shoot early and well and possibly with some confusion as to what was or was not decent and right in the slaughter of wild animals; confusion, because he came of shooting age at the interface between traditions, between the extirpative excesses of the western mountain man and the newfangled restraints of the eastern aristocrat-sportsman. The bison were going fast then, and the pigeons would soon be gone forever, but not the old wrathy frontier appetite for killing. It would simply adapt itself to the law of the bag limit, so that in time most of my father's contemporaries would learn to be content slaying five of a species in a single day, instead of five hundred. My father was content with one moose for a lifetime.

I do not remember him especially as a hunter. There were occasional autumn trips after quail; and if you count the pursuit of fish with rod and reel a form of hunting, as I do, then there were summer trips in Michigan after trout and bass and walleyes as well. But he was not a hunter in the classic manner of those who are absorbed in guns and dogs and the vicarious fireside palaver of men impatient for the opening day.

Recognizing the old man's desultory attention to the blood sport, I am at a loss to explain my own early eagerness to taste of it. A country boy I was not, though woods and fields would be plentiful for a while yet in the suburbs where I grew up. I learned to shoot passably with a Daisy air rifle and a bolt-action single-shot .22, and later with shotguns of various gauges and vintages. I was about ten when I first shot a squirrel out of a beech tree in southern Ohio, and I was surprised how much lighter than human blood was the animal's as it splashed on the copper October leaves, and how sticky as it started to dry on the tip of my finger, and later how uncommonly tasty the thighs that came to table from the fat in the frying pan. I think I may have been sorry for the squirrel as I ate it, but only a little.

If I had stayed with it, I might have been more of a hunter. But somehow in the crucial years of post-adolescence there seemed always to be other distractions on autumn weekends, such as chasing footballs. More lasting by far were the later distractions of jobs and children— female children who would acquire their mother's loathing of guns and would stare at their father with ill-concealed contempt as he ineptly explained how he had once enjoyed walking in the woods with a rifle in the crook of his arm. What did he kill with the rifle? they wanted to know. Rabbits and squirrels, he answered. And they were sure good to eat.

My friends of recent years tend to be the kind who object to the killing of anything. They speak of a reverence for life. Rifles and shotguns, not to mention handguns, give them a certain claustrophobic tremor in the viscera. They have lived their lives against the background of a constant gunnery—murder, hijacking, assassination, and war. Their most unpopular war is the one in the woods. They do not understand, or do not want to understand, how anyone could possibly derive joy from shooting at animals. They see the hunter as a bumbling sadist, and they speak sardonically of protecting their constitutional right to arm bears. "If you can't play a sport," the old anti-hunting advisory goes, "then shoot one." But of course they wouldn't. It might entail using a gun.

Not all of my friends frown on hunting. I have sat together with a few for and many against, partaking of the domesticated flesh of an animal killed in a slaughterhouse by a man with a blunt instrument, and listened to the two sides arguing. Pro-hunter says that he, too, has a reverence for life, but no hangups about death. "How can you eat this beef," he demands, "and say it is wrong to hunt deer?"

"But no one shoots cows for sport," says the anti.

"You mean for *fun,*" says her friend. And there's an echo for my ear.

Pro-hunter throws up his hands. "Telling you about hunting," he says, "is like trying to explain sex to a eunuch."

On which analogy the anti pounces like a quick cat. "It's cigars all over again," she says. "The gun is a phallic crutch. Correct?"

(In the matter of hunting or not hunting, everyone is so desperately eager to be considered correct. Yet there is such an overburden of dishonesty on both sides.)

"And what side are you on?" It is my north country friend, the attorney from Bay City. We are standing before the stone fireplace of the cottage in Michigan. It is his place now, gone from my own family's clutches for half a lifetime, a third-party ownership having fallen somewhere between. I do not think the children of the third party had much esteem for my father's moose. They put curlers to its beard and left it festooned with red ribbons. The Bay City family, moving in, restored dignity to the threadbare head.

Whenever I am in northern Michigan, I make it my unofficial business to detour into the old place, take passing advantage of my friend's hospitality when he is around, or trespass a little when he is not. This time I am on my way to Gaylord for opening day of the hunting season and I am not even sure which side I am on. My friend, a man of strong opinions, is waiting for my answer. I look beyond his face and see the birch fire crackling on the undersides of the brown marble eyes. And I wonder: Why is it that the moose still watches me like this? Since it no longer hurts. *   *   *

COUNTRY MATTERS

*   *   * Tom Davis and I arrived at Grousehaven just before dark. Bill Boyer, who has owned the place since 1926, hailed us from the door of his cabin and said there was a crackling good birch fire inside, and we were welcome to it and whatever else of a warming kind we might happen to find, if only we didn't mind putting up with the ornery critter staked out by the hearth. Davis wanted to know what kind of dog it was, and Boyer said, "Don't mean the dog. I mean Fred Bear."

He was there, all right, about as un-ornery a man as you will ever meet—the slow easy hand reaching out and the face almost breaking in half with a grin. We talked about his bow-and-arrow business down in Gainesville, Florida, and how different the labor situation was there as compared with that of Grayling, up here, where Bear Archery used to be; and then we went through some of Bill Boyer's scrapbooks, with the yellow-edged photographs of all the hunts over the years, and the men who came here sometimes Opening Day—Arthur Godfrey and the Air Force generals Twining and LeMay. Which explained why, here at Grousehaven, there was an airstrip long enough to handle the likes of a DC-3. Handled quite a few, I'd heard, back when Opening Day at Grousehaven drew nearly as many gold stars as a meeting of the Joint Chiefs of Staff. But now there just weren't that many of Boyer's old hunting friends coming up any more. The years had been culling them out.

Still, there were enough here this time around to make the dinner table crowded over at the lodge. Boyer's two sons, Alger and Harold, were up (Alger all the way from New York); and Bob Munger, who had hunted all over the world with Fred Bear in expeditionary days when Bear was a star of ABC-TV's "American Sportsman," and who now was a kind of one-man Greek chorus to the master archer's epic storytelling, especially when it seemed to Munger that his friend might be handling the facts as one handles a drawstring; and F. F. Everest, whom everyone deferred to as "the General," because that's what the man was, four stars, now retired but once the commander of all of America's tactical air bases from Prestwick, Scotland, eastward to Turkey. Not to mention a half dozen younger men, mostly from Michigan, and mightily honored, as Davis and I were, to be filling the places of those who would, or could, no longer be with us.

After supper that night; the table talk drifted from epic tales of the hunt to the deplorable qualifications of so many of the hunters who would be out in the woods of Michigan on Opening Day, men with no skill in woodscraft and little respect for a loaded rifle, and less for the game. Someone suggested that it was probably easier in some states to get a hunting license than a certified copy of one's own birth certificate. "That's exactly the point," said the General. "It's too damn easy. We've got to make it necessary in America for every hunter who goes into the woods to know what the hell the score is."

From the end of the table, Fred Bear said he'd go along with a system whereby every aspiring hunter would be exposed to sixteen hours of instruction. But that wasn't good enough for the General. "Oh hell, Bear," he said. "Sixteen hours is like pissing in the sea and expecting the tide to rise. I'd hunted all over the world, but in Germany I still had to study two weeks to pass interrogation by the *Forstmeister* of the *Revier* where I wanted to hunt red stag. That's the way it ought to be." There were a few mild dissents around the table, some saying that in America, unlike Germany, hunting was a democratic right that sort of ran with the land; and maybe if you made the standards *too* high, you'd find yourself on the indefensible side of a discriminatory situation. The argument did not impress the General. "Damnit," he said. "If a man's going to do anything—drive a car, fly a plane, shoot a rifle—he's got to be taught to do it *right.*" From the corner of my eye I could see Tom Davis nodding his head vigorously. He looked like a man who wanted to stand up and cheer.

Later, Fred Bear went back to Bill Boyer's cabin to keep our host company, Munger turned in for the night, some of the others settled down in front of a television set, and the General waved Davis and me toward his own room, where there was a bottle of fine old bourbon and some more talk about the way things ought to be, and, at my insistence, about the General himself. He sat on the edge of his cot, assembling around him all the gear he would need for the morning's hunt—the treasured .30/06 that had been with him around the world, the hand-loaded cartridges, the binoculars in their weathered case, the sturdy cane that would help take some of the pressure off his ailing leg. And there on the cot, too, was the birthday card that we had passed around the supper table for signatures, noting that Opening Day would be the third day of F. F. Everest's seventy-sixth year.

He had come out of Council Bluffs, Iowa, son of a bird-shooting man; had graduated from West Point about the time Bill Boyer was first setting up camp in these Ogemaw woods; studied ordnance, flew all the early planes while the horse soldiers were pooh-poohing air power, fought a war in the Solomon Islands, moved up through the ranks to become top chief of the Tactical Air Command, then retired to South Carolina. And still the General believed in doing things only if one could do them right.

The German hunting system had greatly impressed the General. He spoke of the difficulty of obtaining a license and of how each candidate must undergo the most rigorous course of training. Figures I had come across somewhere in the literature indicated that a candidate for the hunt had to complete the equivalent of a hundred-hour course of instruction in management practices, wildlife biology, hunting traditions and ethics, and use of firearms. And I told the General I had heard that more than a third of those who attempt to qualify as hunters are rejected for failing the required tests. "You'd screen out most of the slobs," said the General, "if we did that here."

In the morning, we were up at five. There was a thin cover of snow on the ground, and small crisp flakes were still coming down out of a black sky. No one had much to say at breakfast. Davis handed me a dozen cartridges for the Mauser, then headed off with a flashlight to his appointed beat on the near side of a spruce swamp. I was directed to another place, the Horseshoe, on the swamp's other side, and the General was to be posted somewhere more or less in between. I went into the Horseshoe off a dirt track, tripping on low brush in the dark, found a tight cluster of oaks, crawled in among them, and waited for the dawn. It took its own sweet time coming. By my watch it was seven before things began to gray up enough to look around—the oaks starkly silhouetted the understory running off close to the ground, almost park-like, a big opening in the woods, upwind, where deer might be crossing on their way to the swamp. I took a handful of cartridges out of my pocket and pressed four into the magazine, and then chambered the top one with the bolt. The safety was set. The scope sight was clear of the tissues I had wedged at either end to prevent the glass from fogging when the rifle came out of the warmth of the camper at five. Now I was ready. Were the deer?

About five minutes later I heard the first faraway shot. Too far away, I figured, to be from any of the Grousehaven guns. With the light spreading out all around, there were more shots, in singles and series, and one very close—Davis?—the General? Then I could see deer moving toward my opening in the woods. Three of them stepping high, white tails slowly a-wag, cautiously looking it all over, sniffing, going for the swamp. The butt of the Mauser was against my shoulder now and my thumb sneaked up along the bolt to flick off the safety as each of the animals moved into and across the lens of the scope. All ears and no horn. So I reset the safety, lowered the rifle, and watched the does mosey along into the swamp. Only after they were gone did I begin to wonder what I might have done, at that range, if one of the three had been a buck.

There were no deer in the afternoon. The sun went down under purpled clouds and it grew suddenly cold in the woods on the way back to camp. When I got there, two deer were hanging from the buck pole behind the lodge, and Alger Boyer was trying to convince a skeptical audience that his was as big as the General's. Then Tom Davis straggled in skunked from the swamp. "Tomorrow's the big one," he said to me later, in the camper as we turned in for the night. "I can just about feel it. Can't you?"

I could feel *something* the next morning, but it wasn't the big day. It was the numbing cold, reaching down through four layers of chamois and wool until I thought I would never stop shaking. Or maybe it wasn't the cold at all. Maybe it was staring through a cross-haired lens into the eyes of a buck at seventy paces.

Day Two had begun a little later than the first—Davis off to a new beat, to Fred Bear's own favored haunt in a part of the woods called Lost Acres; and I, back to the Horseshoe, but with just enough light this time to pick out a spot with a better field of fire across the opening where I had seen the three does the morning before. It was an old blind that hadn't been used, I guessed, for years—six black oaks in a tight ring with thick slabs of bark wedged into the spaces between the tree trunks. A little pillbox in the forest, with lichens and moss for interior decor.

The shaking started a little before eight, right after the herd came out of the brush at the west end of the clearing. I stopped counting after twenty. I had never before seen so many deer at one time in one wild place. All of them were moving slowly in scattered groups toward the swamp. Through the scope I could distinctly see one spikehorn buck, but all of the others—impossibly—appeared to be does. It was hard to tell, even with the scope, for most of them were maybe three hundred yards out. My thumb went up along the bolt, found the safety latch, snapped it down and off. I put my shoulder against the nearest tree and snugged the Mauser's barrel into a crotch between two slabs of the pillbox's bark. I brought the scope back to the spikehorn buck. And waited, shaking.

And waited, thinking, too. For there had been another letter on my desk when I returned from Missouri, a letter from a friend who had come to suspect that I was up to no good. If I was really serious about trying to "defend" hunting for pleasure, he wrote, then I would surely have to deal with the moral arguments of Joseph Wood Krutch, among others, and not be taken in by the "obscurantist mystique" of a "sophistical reactionary" such as Ortega y Gasset. To say that "one does not hunt in order to kill—one kills in order to have hunted" was not an adequate reply, my friend believed, to a clear and simple question like Krutch's "How justify the killing of any living thing for the sake of *pleasure?*" But what, after all, was so clear and simple about Krutch's question? Or was it *too* simple? How justify the killing of a carrot for the sake of holding it in your hand and admiring its color and texture, and then eating it, with pleasure? How justify the use of wood, the felling of a living giant, the saw blade dripping sap, when coal for heat, or steel for structure, would serve just as well, though not so pleasurably? If there was one line to be drawn among living things, and another between the acceptable pleasures and the damnable ones, where did one draw them? I have heard of ethical vegetarians—and I respect them—who eschew all flesh but still devour eggs, and possibly with a good deal of shame rather than pleasure, for what is the cooking of an egg if it is not abortion? Heavy thoughts for so early a morning in the Michigan woods.

I had just emerged from my sophistical reactions to Krutch and my critical friend when I saw the second buck. It was standing about sixty or seventy yards out, in the open, head down and broadside to my blind. I swiveled the rifle a few inches to the left, laid the cross hairs across a point behind and slightly under its shoulder, eased my finger around the trigger. A touch of ice. A pounding in the temples, a sound as of drums inside the heart. Easy now. Easy. Use it right. Do it right. Do it.

The buck's head jerked up and its eyes were on me. The forelegs splayed out as if to brace themselves, the nose brushed the air in an arc. The buck wasn't sure yet. I hadn't moved. The wind was to my advantage. The buck held fast. Then the eyes—the huge glistening eyes that had torn my own away from the cross hairs on the shoulder—turned in the other direction as a foreleg stiffly stamped the ground. Just once. Do it now. But do it *right?* After all these years? After all the contempt felt in the last year for the ones who do *not* do it right? If I missed, if I wounded the animal, if I should have to take more than one shot, if its dying was drawn out—would it be right? Would *I* be right?

I opened the bolt of the Mauser, ejecting the cartridge into the palm of my hand. Another touch of ice. And when I looked out again into the clearing, the buck was gone. I sat there for another hour with an empty chamber in the rifle, and the sun came over the tops of the spruce at the edge of the swamp, and the shaking stopped. Then I went out of the Horseshoe toward camp. Just short of the airstrip, on a dirt track, a car came up behind me and I stepped aside to let it pass. The car stopped, and Bill Boyer, with Fred Bear grinning beside him, leaned out from the driver's seat to inquire if I had had any luck.

"I had plenty," I said.

"You get one?"

"Not this time," I said. "I've got some learning to do first."

They both looked disappointed and I wanted to tell them not to be. But I didn't, because there was better news. Boyer and Bear had just come out from Lost Acres, and they said Tom Davis was back there now, dressing his deer.

EDWARD HOAGLAND
B. 1932

For many years Edward Hoagland spent his winters in New York City, where he was born, and his summers in the small town of Barton in northern Vermont. This city-country rhythm is strongly present in his work, and seems deliberately to dramatize the divided attitude of modern man towards nature. Hoagland is a tough-minded optimist, not about specific environmental issues, but in the belief that life in general "can and ought to be good, and is even meant *to be good." Unlike most writers of his generation who have deplored and fought against the destruction of the natural world, Hoagland assumes, and even accepts, the impending loss of much that he loves, both in civilization and in the wild. By doing so he is able to rejoice in and capture what is vanishing with unfettered relish, keen perception, and a kind of fatalistic good humor. Such collections as* The Courage of Turtles *(1971),* Walking the Dead Diamond River *(1973) and* Red Wolves and Black Bears *(1976) celebrate with equal vitality and admiration the life of circus clowns, turtles, city streets, wilderness canoeing, tugboats, wolves, and other writers.*

HAILING THE ELUSORY MOUNTAIN LION

The swan song sounded by the wilderness grows fainter, ever more constricted, until only sharp ears can catch it at all. It fades to a nearly inaudible level, and yet there never is going to be any one time when we

Walking the Dead Diamond River (New York: Random House, 1973).

can say right *now* it is gone. Wolves meet their maker in wholesale lots, but coyotes infiltrate eastward, northward, southeastward. Woodland caribou and bighorn sheep are vanishing fast, but moose have expanded their range in some areas.

Mountain lions used to have practically the run of the Western Hemisphere, and they still do occur from Cape Horn to the Big Muddy River at the boundary of the Yukon and on the coasts of both oceans, so that they are the most versatile land mammal in the New World, probably taking in more latitudes than any other four-footed wild creature anywhere. There are perhaps only four to six thousand left in the United States, though there is no place that they didn't once go, eating deer, elk, pikas, porcupines, grasshoppers, and dead fish on the beach. They were called mountain lions in the Rockies, pumas (originally an Incan word) in the Southwestern states, cougars (a naturalist's corruption of an Amazonian Indian word) in the Northwest, panthers in the traditionalist East—"painters" in dialect-proud New England—or catamounts. The Dutchmen of New Netherland called them tigers, red tigers, deer tigers, and the Spaniards *leones* or *leopardos*. They liked to eat horses—wolves preferred beef and black bears favored pork—but as adversaries of mankind they were overshadowed at first because bears appeared more formidable and wolves in their howling packs were more flamboyant and more damaging financially. Yet this panoply of names is itself quite a tribute, and somehow the legends about "panthers" have lingered longer than bear or wolf tales, helped by the animal's own limber, far-traveling stealth and as a carry-over from the immense mythic force of the great cats of the Old World. Though only Florida among the Eastern states is known for certain to have any left, no wild knot of mountains or swamp is without rumors of panthers; nowadays people delight in these, keeping their eyes peeled. It's wishful, and the wandering, secretive nature of the beast ensures that even Eastern panthers will not soon be certifiably extinct. An informal census among experts in 1963 indicated that an island of twenty-five or more may have survived in the New Brunswick–Maine–Quebec region, and Louisiana may still have a handful, and perhaps eight live isolated in the Black Hills of South Dakota, and the Oklahoma panhandle may have a small colony—all outside the established range in Florida, Texas, and the Far West. As with the blue whale, who will be able to say when they have been eliminated?

"Mexican lion" is another name for mountain lions in the border states—a name that might imply a meager second-best rating there yet ties to the majestic African beasts. Lions are at least twice as big as mountain lions, measuring by weight, though they are nearly the same in length because of the mountain lion's superb long tail. Both animals sometimes pair up affectionately with mates and hunt in tandem, but mountain lions go winding through life in ones or twos, whereas the lion is a harem-keeper, harem-dweller, the males eventually becoming stay-at-homes, heavy figureheads. Lions enjoy the grassy flatlands, forested along the streams, and they stay put, engrossed in communal events—roaring, grunting, growling with a racket like the noise of gears being stripped—unless the game moves on. They sun themselves, preside over the numerous kibbutz young, sneeze from the dust, and bask in dreams, occasionally waking up to issue reverberating, guttural pronouncements which serve notice that they are now awake.

Mountain lions spirit themselves away in saw-toothed canyons and on escarpments instead, and when conversing with their mates they coo like pigeons, sob like women, emit a flat slight shriek, a popping bubbling growl, or mew, or yowl. They growl and suddenly caterwaul into fal-setto—the famous scarifying, metallic scream functioning as a kind of hunting cry close up, to terrorize and start the game. They ramble as much as twenty-five miles in a night, maintaining a large loop of territory which they cover every week or two. It's a solitary, busy life, involving a survey of several valleys, many deer herds. Like tigers and leopards, mountain lions are not sociably inclined and don't converse at length with the whole waiting world, but they are even less noisy; they seem to speak most eloquently with their feet. Where a tiger would roar, a mountain lion screams like a castrato. Where a mountain lion hisses, a leopard would snarl like a truck stuck in snow.

Leopards are the best counterpart to mountain lions in physique and in the tenor of their lives. Supple, fierce creatures, skilled at concealment but with great self-assurance and drive, leopards are bolder when facing human beings than the American cats. Basically they are hot-land beasts and not such remarkable travelers individually, though as a race they once inhabited the broad Eurasian land mass all the way from Great Britain to Malaysia, as well as Africa. As late as the 1960s, a few were said to be still holding out on the shore of the Mediterranean at Mount Mycale, Turkey. (During a forest fire twenty years ago a yearling swam the narrow straits to the Greek island Samos and holed up in a cave, where he was duly killed—perhaps the last leopard ever to set foot in Europe on his own.) Leopards are thicker and shorter than adult mountain lions and seem to lead an athlete's indolent, incurious life much of the time, testing their perfected bodies by clawing tree trunks, chewing on old skulls, executing acrobatic leaps, and then rousing themselves to the semiweekly antelope kill. Built with supreme hardness and economy, they make little allowance for man—they don't see him as different. They relish the flesh of his dogs, and they run up a tree when hunted and then sometimes spring down, as heavy as a chunk of iron wrapped in a flag. With stunning, gorgeous coats, their tight, dervish faces carved in a snarl, they head for the hereafter as if it were just one more extra-emphatic leap—as impersonal in death as the crack of the rifle was.

The American leopard, the jaguar, is a powerfully built, serious fellow, who, before white men arrived, wandered as far north as the Carolinas, but his best home is the humid basin of the Amazon. Mountain lions penetrate these ultimate jungles too, but rather thinly, thriving better in the cooler, drier climate of the untenanted pampas and on the mountain slopes. They are blessed with a pleasant but undazzling coat, tan except for a white belly, mouth and throat, and some black behind the ears, on the tip of the tail and at the sides of the nose, and so they are hunted as symbols, not for their fur. The cubs are spotted, leopardlike, much as lion cubs are. If all of the big cats developed from a common ancestry, the mountain lions' specialization has been unpresumptuous—away from bulk and savagery to traveling light. Toward deer, their prey, they may be as ferocious as leopards, but not toward chance acquaintances such as man. They sometimes break their necks, their jaws, their teeth, springing against the necks of quarry they have crept close to—a fate in part resulting from the circumstance that they can't ferret out the weaker individuals in a herd by the device of a long chase, the way wolves do; they have to take the luck of the draw. None of the cats possess enough lung capacity for gruelling runs. They depend upon shock tactics, bursts of speed, sledge-hammer leaps, strong collarbones for hitting power, and shearing dentition, whereas wolves employ all the advantages of time in killing their quarry, as well as the numbers and gaiety of the pack, biting the beast's nose and rump—the technique of a thousand cuts—lapping the bloody snow. Wolves sometimes even have a cheering section of flapping ravens accompanying them, eager to scavenge after the brawl.

It's a risky business for the mountain lion, staking the strength and impact of his neck against the strength of the prey animal's neck. Necessarily, he is concentrated and fierce; yet legends exist that mountain lions have irritably defended men and women lost in the wilderness against marauding jaguars, who are no friends of theirs, and (with a good deal more supporting evidence) that they are susceptible to an odd kind of fascination with human beings. Sometimes they will tentatively seek an association, hanging about a campground or following a hiker out of curiosity, perhaps, circling around and bounding up on a ledge above to watch him pass. This mild modesty has helped preserve them from extinction. If they have been unable to make any adjustments to the advent of man, they haven't suicidally opposed him either, as the buffalo, wolves, and grizzlies did. In fact, at close quarters they seem bewildered. When treed, they don't breathe a hundred-proof ferocity but puzzle over what to do. They're too light-bodied to bear down on the hunter and kill him easily, even if they should attack—a course they seem to have no inclination for. In this century in the United States only one person, a child of thirteen, has been killed by a mountain lion; that was in 1924. And they're informal animals. Lolling in an informal sprawl on a high limb, they can't seem to summon any Enobarbus-like front of resistance for long. Daring men occasionally climb up and toss lassos about a cat and haul him down, strangling him by pulling from two directions, while the lion, mortified, appalled, never does muster his fighting aplomb. Although he could fight off a pack of wolves, he hasn't worked out a posture to assume toward man and his dogs. Impotently, he stiffens, as the dinosaurs must have when the atmosphere grew cold.

Someday hunting big game may come to be regarded as a form of vandalism, and the remaining big creatures of the wilderness will skulk through restricted reserves wearing radio transmitters and numbered collars, or bearing stripes of dye, as many elephants already do, to aid the busy biologists who track them from the air. Like a vanishing race of trolls, more report and memory than a reality, they will inhabit children's books and nostalgic articles, a special glamour attaching to those, like mountain lions, that are geographically incalculable and may still be sighted away from the preserves. Already we've become enthusiasts. We want game about us—at least at a summer house; it's part of privileged living. There is a precious privacy about seeing wildlife, too. Like meeting a fantastically dressed mute on the road, the fact that no words are exchanged and that *he's* not going to give an account makes the experience light-hearted; it's wholly ours. Besides, if anything out of the ordinary happened, we know we can't expect to be believed, and since it's rather fun to be disbelieved—fishermen know this—the privacy is even more complete. Deer, otter, foxes are messengers from another condition of life, another mentality, and bring us tidings of places where we don't go.

Ten years ago at Vavenby, a sawmill town on the North Thompson River in British Columbia, a frolicsome mountain lion used to appear at dusk every ten days or so in a bluegrass field alongside the river. Deer congregated there, the river was silky and swift, cooling the summer air, and it was a festive spot for a lion to be. She was thought to be a female, and reputedly left tracks around an enormous territory to the north and west—Raft Mountain, Battle Mountain, the Trophy Range, the Murtle River, and Mahood Lake—territory on an upended, pelagic scale, much of it scarcely accessible to a man by trail, where the tiger lilies grew four feet tall. She would materialize in this field among the deer five minutes before dark, as if checking in again, a habit that may have resulted in her death eventually, though for the present the farmer who observed her visits was keeping his mouth shut about it. This was pioneer country; there were people alive who could remember the time when poisoning the carcass of a cow would net a man a pile of dead predators—a family of mountain lions to bounty, maybe half a dozen wolves, and both black bears and grizzlies. The Indians considered lion meat a delicacy, but they had clans which drew their origins at the Creation from ancestral mountain lions, or wolves or bears, so these massacres amazed them. They thought the outright bounty hunters were crazy men.

Even before Columbus, mountain lions were probably not distributed in saturation numbers anywhere, as wolves may have been. Except for the family unit—a female with her half-grown cubs—each lion seems to occupy its own spread of territory, not as a result of fights with intruders but because the young transient share the same instinct for solitude and soon sheer off to find vacant mountains and valleys. A mature lion kills only one deer every week or two, according to a study by Maurice Hornocker in Idaho, and therefore is not really a notable factor in controlling the local deer population. Rather, it keeps watch contentedly as that population grows, sometimes benefitting the herds by scaring them onto new wintering grounds that are not overbrowsed, and by its very presence warding off other lions.

This thin distribution, coupled with the mountain lion's taciturn habits, make sighting one a matter of luck, even for game officials located in likely country. One warden in Colorado I talked to had indeed seen a pair of them fraternizing during the breeding season. He was driving a jeep over an abandoned mining road, and he passed two brown animals sitting peaceably in the grass, their heads close together. For a moment he thought they were coyotes and kept driving, when all of a sudden the picture registered that they were *cougars!* He braked and backed up, but of course they were gone. He was an old-timer, a man who had crawled inside bear dens to pull out the cubs, and knew where to find clusters of buffalo skulls in the recesses of the Rockies where the last bands had hidden; yet this cryptic instant when he was turning his jeep round a curve was the only glimpse—unprovable—that he ever got of a mountain lion.

Such glimpses usually are cryptic. During a summer I spent in Wyoming in my boyhood, I managed to see two coyotes, but both occasions were so fleeting that it required an act of faith on my part afterward to feel sure I had seen them. One of the animals vanished between rolls of ground; the other, in rougher, stonier, wooded country, cast his startled gray face in my direction and simply was gone. Hunching, he swerved for cover, and the brush closed over him. I used to climb to a vantage point above a high basin at twilight and watch the mule deer steal into the meadows to feed. The grass grew higher than their stomachs, the steep forest was close at hand, and they were as small and fragile-looking as filaments at that distance, quite human in coloring, gait and form. It was possible to visualize them as a naked Indian hunting party a hundred years before—or not to believe in their existence at all, either as Indians or deer. Minute, aphid-sized, they stepped so carefully in emerging, hundreds of feet below, that, straining my eyes, I needed to tell myself constantly that they were deer; my imagination, left to its own devices with the dusk settling down, would have made of them a dozen other creatures.

Recently, walking at night on the woods road that passes my house in Vermont, I heard footsteps in the leaves and windfalls. I waited, listening—they sounded too heavy to be anything less than a man, a large deer or a bear. A man wouldn't have been in the woods so late, my dog stood respectfully silent and still, and they did seem to shuffle portentously. Sure enough, after pausing at the edge of the road, a fully grown bear appeared, visible only in dimmest outline, staring in my direction for four or five seconds. The darkness lent a faintly red tinge to his coat; he was well built. Then, turning, he ambled off, almost immediately lost to view, though I heard the noise of his passage, interrupted by several pauses. It was all as concise as a vision, and since I had wanted to see a bear close to my own house, being a person who likes to live in a melting pot, whether in the city or country, and since it was too dark to pick out his tracks, I was grateful when the dog inquisitively urinated along the bear's path, thereby confirming that at least I had witnessed *something*. The dog seemed unsurprised, however, as if the scent were not all that remarkable, and, sure enough, the next week in the car I encountered a yearling bear in daylight two miles downhill, and a cub a month later. My farmer neighbors were politely skeptical of my accounts, having themselves caught sight of only perhaps a couple of bears in all their lives.

So it's with sympathy as well as an awareness of the tricks that enthusiasm and nightfall may play that I have been going to nearby towns seeking out people who have claimed at one time or another to have seen a mountain lion. The experts of the state—game wardens, taxidermists, the most accomplished hunters—emphatically discount the claims, but the believers are unshaken. They include some summer people who were enjoying a drink on the back terrace when the apparition of a great-tailed cat moved out along the fringe of the woods on a deer path; a boy who was hunting with his .22 years ago near the village dump and saw the animal across a gully and fired blindly, then ran away and brought back a search party, which found a tuft of toast-colored fur; and a state forestry employee, a sober woodsman, who caught the cat in his headlights while driving through Victory Bog in the wildest corner of the Northeast Kingdom. Gordon Hickok, who works for a furniture factory and has shot one or two mountain lions on hunting trips in the West, saw one cross U.S. 5 at a place called Auger Hole near Mount Hor. He tracked it with dogs a short distance, finding a fawn with its head gnawed off. A high-school English teacher reported seeing a mountain lion cross another road, near Runaway Pond, but the hunters who quickly went out decided that the prints were those of a big bobcat, splayed impressively in the mud and snow. Fifteen years ago a watchman in the fire tower on top of Bald Mountain had left grain scattered in the grooves of a flat rock under the tower to feed several deer. One night, looking down just as the dusk turned murky, he saw two slim long-tailed lions creep out of the scrubby border of spruce and inspect the rock, sniffing deer droppings and dried deer saliva. The next night, when he was in his cabin, the dog barked and, looking out the window, again he saw the vague shape of a lion just vanishing.

A dozen loggers and woodsmen told me such stories. In the Adirondacks I've also heard some persuasive avowals—one by an old dog-sled driver and trapper, a French Canadian; another by the owner of a tourist zoo, who was exhibiting a Western cougar. In Vermont perhaps the most eager rumor buffs are some of the farmers. After all, now that packaged semen has replaced the awesome farm bull and so many procedures have been mechanized, who wants to lose *all* the adventure of farming? Until recently the last mountain lion known to have been killed in the Northeast was recorded in 1881 in Barnard, Vermont. However, it has been learned that probably another one was shot from a tree in 1931 in Mundleville, New Brunswick, and still another trapped seven years later in Somerset County in Maine. Bruce S. Wright, director of the Northeastern Wildlife Station (which is operated at the University of New Brunswick with international funding), is convinced that though they are exceedingly rare, mountain lions are still part of the fauna of the region; in fact, he has plaster casts of tracks to prove it, as well as a compilation of hundreds of reported sightings. Some people may have mistaken a golden retriever for a lion, or may have intended to foment a hoax, but all in all the evidence does seem promising. Indeed, after almost twenty years of search and study, Wright himself finally saw one.

The way these sightings crop up in groups has often been poohpoohed as greenhorn fare or as a sympathetic hysteria among neighbors, but it is just as easily explained by the habit mountain lions have of establishing a territory that they scout through at intervals, visiting an auspicious deer-ridden swamp or remote ledgy mountain. Even at such a site a successful hunt could not be mounted without trained dogs, and if the population of the big cats was extremely sparse, requiring of them long journeys during the mating season, and yet with plenty of deer all over, they might not stay for long. One or two hundred miles is no obstacle to a Western cougar. The cat might inhabit a mountain ridge one year, and then never again.

Fifteen years ago, Francis Perry, who is an ebullient muffin of a man, a farmer all his life in Brownington, Vermont, saw a mountain lion "larger and taller than a collie, and grayish yellow" (he had seen them in circuses). Having set a trap for a woodchuck, he was on his way to visit the spot when he came over a rise and, at a distance of fifty yards, saw the beast engaged in eating the dead woodchuck. It bounded off, but Perry set four light fox traps for it around the woodchuck. Apparently, a night or two later the cat returned and got caught in three of these, but they couldn't hold it; it pulled free, leaving the marks of a struggle. Noel Perry, his brother, remembers how scared Francis looked when he came home from the first episode. Noel himself saw the cat (which may have meant that Brownington Swamp was one of its haunts that summer), once when it crossed a cow pasture on another farm the brothers owned, and once when it fled past his rabbit dogs through underbrush while he was training them—he thought for a second that its big streaking form was one of the dogs. A neighbor, Robert Chase, also saw the animal that year. Then again last summer, for the first time in fifteen years, Noel Perry saw a track as big as a bear's but round like a mountain lion's, and Robert's brother, Larry Chase, saw the actual cat several times one summer evening, playing a chummy hide-and-seek with him in the fields.

Elmer and Elizabeth Ambler are in their forties, populists politically, and have bought a farm in Glover to live the good life, though he is a truck driver in Massachusetts on weekdays and must drive hard in order to be home when he can. He's bald, with large eyebrows, handsome teeth and a low forehead, but altogether a strong-looking, clear, humane face. He is an informational kind of man who will give you the history of various breeds of cattle or a talk about taxation in a slow and musical voice, and both he and his wife, a purposeful, self-sufficient redhead, are fascinated by the possibility that they live in the wilderness. Beavers inhabit the river that flows past their house. The Amblers say that on Black Mountain nearby hunters "disappear" from time to time, and bears frequent the berry patches in their back field—they see them, their visitors see them, people on the road see them, their German shepherds meet them and run back drooling with fright. They've stocked their farm with horned Herefords instead of the polled variety so that the creatures can "defend themselves." Ambler is intrigued by the thought that apart from the danger of bears, someday "a cat" might prey on one of his cows. Last year, looking out the back window, his wife saw through binoculars an animal with a flowing tail and "a cat's gallop" following a line of trees where the deer go, several hundred yards uphill behind the house. Later, Ambler went up on snowshoes and found tracks as big as their shepherds'; the dogs obligingly ran alongside. He saw walking tracks, leaping tracks and deer tracks marked with blood going toward higher ground. He wonders whether the cat will ever attack him. There are plenty of bobcats around, but they both say they know the difference. The splendid, nervous *tail* is what people must have identified in order to claim they have seen a mountain lion.

I, too, cherish the notion that I may have seen a lion. Mine was crouched on an overlook above a grass-grown, steeply pitched wash in the Alberta Rockies—a much more likely setting than anywhere in New England. It was late afternoon on my last day at Maligne Lake, where I had been staying with my father at a national-park chalet. I was twenty; I could walk forever or could climb endlessly in a sanguine scramble, going out every day as far as my legs carried me, swinging around for home before the sun went down. Earlier, in the valley of the Athabasca, I had found several winter-starved or wolf-killed deer, well picked and scattered, and an area with many elk antlers strewn on the ground where the herds had wintered safely, dropping their antlers but not their bones. Here, much higher up, in the bright plenitude of the summer, I had watched two wolves and a stately bull moose in one mountain basin, and had been up on the caribou barrens on the ridge west of the lake and brought back the talons of a hawk I'd found dead on the ground. Whenever I was watching game, a sort of stopwatch in me started running. These were moments of intense importance and intimacy, of new intimations and aptitudes. Time had a jam-packed character, as it does during a mile run.

I was good at moving quietly through the woods and at spotting game, and was appropriately exuberant. The finest, longest day of my stay was the last. Going east, climbing through a luxuriant terrain of up-and-down boulders, brief brilliant glades, sudden potholes fifty feet deep—a forest of moss-hung lodgepole pines and firs and spare, gaunt spruce with the black lower branches broken off—I came upon the remains of a young bear, which had been torn up and shredded. Perhaps wolves had cornered it during some imprudent excursion in the early spring. (Bears often wake up while the snow is still deep, dig themselves out and rum-

mage around in the neighborhood sleepily for a day or two before bedding down again under a fallen tree.) I took the skull along so that I could
extract the teeth when I got hold of some tools. Discoveries like this
represent a superfluity of wildlife and show how many beasts there are
scouting about.

I went higher. The marmots whistled familially; the tall trees wilted to
stubs of themselves. A pretty stream led down a defile from a series of
openings in front of the ultimate barrier of a vast mountain wall which I
had been looking at from a distance each day on my outings. It wasn't
too steep to be climbed, but it was a barrier because my energies were
not sufficient to scale it and bring me back the same night. Besides, it
stretched so majestically, surflike above the lesser ridges, that I liked to
think of it as the Continental Divide.

On my left as I went up this wash was an abrupt, grassy slope that
enjoyed a southern exposure and was sunny and windblown all winter,
which kept it fairly free of snow. The ranger at the lake had told me it
served as a wintering ground for a few bighorn sheep and for a band of
mountain goats, three of which were in sight. As I approached laboriously, these white, pointy-horned fellows drifted up over a rise, managing to combine their retreat with some nippy good grazing as they went,
not to give any pursuer the impression that they had been pushed into
flight. I took my time too, climbing to locate the spring in a precipitous
cleft of rock where the band did most of its drinking, and finding the
shallow, high-ceilinged cave where the goats had sheltered from storms,
presumably for generations. The floor was layered with rubbery droppings, tramped down and sprinkled with tufts of shed fur, and the back
wall was checkered with footholds where the goats liked to clamber and
perch. Here and there was a horn lying loose—a memento for me to add
to my collection from an old individual that had died a natural death,
secure in the band's winter stronghold. A bold, thriving family of pack
rats emerged to observe me. They lived mainly on the nutritives in the
droppings, and were used to the goats' tolerance; they seemed astonished when I tossed a stone.

I kept scrabbling along the side of the slope to a section of outcroppings where the going was harder. After perhaps half an hour, crawling
around a corner, I found myself faced with a bighorn ram who was
taking his ease on several square yards of bare earth between large rocks,
a little above the level of my head. Just as surprised as I, he stood up. He
must have construed the sounds of my advance to be those of another
sheep or goat. His horns had made a complete curl and then some; they
were thick, massive and bunched together like a high Roman helmet,

and he himself was muscly and military, with a grave-looking nose. A squared-off, middle-aged, trophy-type ram, full of imposing professionalism, he was at the stage of life when rams sometimes stop herding and live as rogues.

He turned and tried a couple of possible exits from the pocket where I had found him, but the ground was badly pitched and would require a reeling gait and loss of dignity. Since we were within a national park and obviously I was unarmed, he simply was not inclined to put himself to so much trouble. He stood fifteen or twenty feet above me, pushing his tongue out through his teeth, shaking his head slightly and dipping it into charging position as I moved closer by a step or two, raising my hand slowly toward him in what I proposed as a friendly greeting. The day had been a banner one since the beginning, so while I recognized immediately that this meeting would be a valued memory, I felt as natural in his company as if he were a friend of mine reincarnated in a shag suit. I saw also that he was going to knock me for a loop, head over heels down the steep slope, if I sidled nearer, because he did not by any means feel as expansive and exuberant at our encounter as I did. That was the chief difference between us. I was talking to him with easy gladness, and beaming; he was not. He was unsettled and on his mettle, waiting for me to move along, the way a bighorn sheep waits for a predator to move on in wildlife movies when each would be evenly matched in a contest of strength and position. Although his warlike nose and high bone helmet, blocky and beautiful as weaponry, kept me from giving in to my sense that we were brothers, I knew I could stand there for a long while. His coat was a down-to-earth brown, edgy with muscle, his head was that of an unsmiling veteran standing to arms, and despite my reluctance to treat him as some sort of boxed-in prize, I might have stayed on for half the afternoon if I hadn't realized that I had other sights to see. It was not a day to dawdle.

I trudged up the wash and continued until, past tree line, the terrain widened and flattened in front of a preliminary ridge that formed an obstacle before the great roaring, silent, surflike mountain wall that I liked to think of as the Continental Divide, although it wasn't. A cirque separated the preliminary ridge from the ultimate divide, which I still hoped to climb to and look over. The opening into this was roomy enough, except for being littered with enormous boulders, and I began trying to make my way across them. Each was boat-sized and rested upon underboulders; it was like running in place. After tussling with this landscape for an hour or two, I was limp and sweating, pinching my cramped legs. The sun had gone so low that I knew I would be finding my way home by moonlight in any case, and I could see into the cirque, which was big and symmetrical and presented a view of sheer barbarism; everywhere were these cruel boat-sized boulders.

Giving up and descending to the goats' draw again, I had a drink from the stream and bathed before climbing farther downward. The grass was green, sweet-smelling, and I felt safely close to life after that sea of dead boulders. I knew I would never be physically younger or in finer country; even then the wilderness was singing its swan song. I had no other challenges in mind, and though very tired, I liked looking up at the routes where I'd climbed. The trio of goats had not returned, but I could see their wintering cave and the cleft in the rocks where the spring was. Curiously, the bighorn ram had not left; he had only withdrawn upward, shifting away from the outcroppings to an open sweep of space where every avenue of escape was available. He was lying on a carpet of grass and, lonely pirate that he was, had his head turned in my direction.

It was from this same wash that looking up, I spotted the animal I took to be a mountain lion. He was skulking among some outcroppings at a point lower on the mountainside than the ledges where the ram originally had been. A pair of hawks or eagles were swooping at him by turns, as if he were close to a nest. The slant between us was steep, but the light of evening was still more than adequate. I did not really see the wonderful tail—that special medallion—nor was he particularly big for a lion. He was gloriously catlike and slinky, however, and so indifferent to the swooping birds as to seem oblivious of them. There are plenty of creatures he wasn't: he wasn't a marmot, a goat or other grass-eater, a badger, a wolf or coyote or fisher. He *may* have been a big bobcat or a wolverine, although he looked ideally lion-colored. He had a cat's strong collarbone structure for hitting, powerful haunches for vaulting, and the almost mystically small head mountain lions possess, with the gooseberry eyes. Anyway, I believed him to be a mountain lion, and standing quietly I watched him as he inspected in leisurely fashion the ledge that he was on and the one under him savory with every trace of goat—frosty-colored with the white hairs they'd shed. The sight was so dramatic that it seemed to be happening close to me, though in fact he and the hawks or eagles, whatever they were, were miniaturized by distance.

If I'd kept motionless, eventually I could have seen whether he had the proper tail, but such scientific questions had no weight next to my need to essay some kind of communication with him. It had been exactly the same when I'd watched the two wolves playing together a couple of days before. They were above me, absorbed in their game of noses-and-paws. I had recognized that I might never witness such a scene again, yet I couldn't hold myself in. Instead of talking and raising my arm to them, as I had with the ram, I'd shuffled forward impetuously as if to say *Here I am!* Now, with the lion, I tried hard to dampen my impulse and restrained myself as long as I could. Then I stepped toward him, just barely squelching a cry in my throat but lifting my hand—as clumsy as anyone is who is trying to attract attention.

At that, of course, he swerved aside instantly and was gone. Even the two birds vanished. Foolish, triumphant and disappointed, I hiked on down into the lower forests, gargantuanly tangled, another life zone—not one which would exclude a lion but one where he would not be seen. I'd got my second wind and walked lightly and softly, letting the silvery darkness settle around me. The blowdowns were as black as whales; my feet sank in the moss. Clearly this was as crowded a day as I would ever have, and I knew my real problem would not be to make myself believed but rather to make myself understood at all, simply in reporting the story, and that I must at least keep the memory straight for myself. I was so happy that I was unerring in distinguishing the deer trails going my way. The forest's night beauty was supreme in its promise, and I didn't hurry.

THOUGHTS ON RETURNING TO THE CITY AFTER FIVE MONTHS ON A MOUNTAIN WHERE THE WOLVES HOWLED

City people are more supple than country people, and the sanest city people, being more tested and more broadly based in the world of men, are the sanest people on earth. As to honesty, though, or good sense, no clear-cut distinction exists either way.

I like gourmets, even winetasters. In the city they correspond to the old-timers who knew all the berries and herbs, made money collecting the roots of the ginseng plant, and knew the taste of each hill by its springs. Alertness and adaptability in the city are transferable to the country if you feel at home there, and alertness there can quickly be transmuted into alertness here. It is not necessary to choose between being a country man and a city man, as it is to decide, for instance, some time along in one's thirties, whether one is an Easterner or a Westerner. (Middle Westerners, too, make the choice: people in Cleveland consider themselves Easterners, people in Kansas City know they are Western.)

Red Wolves and Black Bears (New York: Random House, 1976).

But one can be both a country man and a city man. Once a big frog in a local pond, now suddenly I'm tiny again, and delighted to be so, kicking my way down through the water, swimming along my anchor chains and finding them fast in the bottom.

Nor must one make a great sacrifice in informational matters. I know more about bears and wolves than anybody in my town or the neighboring towns up there and can lead lifelong residents in the woods, yet the fierce, partisan block associations in my neighborhood in New York apparently know less than I do about the closer drug-peddling operations or they surely would have shut them down. This is not to say that such information is of paramount importance, however. While, lately, I was tasting the October fruit of the jack-in-the-pulpit and watching the club-moss smoke with flying spores as I walked in the woods, my small daughter, who had not seen me for several weeks, missed me so much that when I did return, she threw up her arms in helpless and choked excitement to shield her eyes, as if I were the rising sun. The last thing I wish to be, of course, is the sun—being only a guilty father.

But what a kick it is to be back, seeing newspaperman friends; newspapermen are the best of the city. There are new restaurants down the block, and today I rescued an actual woodcock—New York is nothing if not cosmopolitan. Lost, it had dived for the one patch of green in the street, a basket of avocados in the doorway of Shanvilla's Grocery, and knocked itself out. I'd needed to drag myself back from that mountain where the wolves howl, and yet love is what I feel now; the days are long and my eyes and emotions are fresh.

The city is dying irreversibly as a metropolis. We who love it must recognize this if we wish to live in it intelligently. All programs, all palliatives and revenue-sharing, can only avail to ease what we love into oblivion a little more tenderly (if a tender death is ever possible for a city). But to claim that the city is dying, never to "turn the corner," is not to announce that we should jump for the lifeboats. There are still no better people than New Yorkers. No matter where I have been, I rediscover this every fall. And my mountain is dying too. The real estate ads up in that country put it very succinctly. "Wealth you can walk on," they say. As far as that goes, one cannot live intelligently without realizing that we and our friends and loved ones are all dying. But one's ideals, no: no matter what currently unfashionable ideals a person may harbor in secret, from self-sacrifice and wanting to fall in love to wanting to fight in a war, there will continue to be opportunities to carry them out.

My country neighbor is dying right now, wonderfully fiercely—nothing but stinging gall from his lips. The wolves' mountain bears his name, and at eighty-six he is dying almost on the spot where he was born, in the oneroom schoolhouse in which he attended first grade, to which he moved when his father's house burned. This would not be possible in the city. In the city we live by being supple, bending with the wind. He lived by bending with the wind too, but his were the north and west winds.

You New Yorkers will excuse me for missing my barred owls, ruffed grouse and snowshoe rabbits, my grosbeaks and deer. I love what you love too. In the city and in the country there is a simple, underlying basis to life which we forget almost daily: that life is good. We forget because losing it or wife, children, health, friends is so awfully painful, and because life is hard, but we know from our own experience as well as our expectations that it can and ought to be good, and is even *meant* to be good. Any careful study of living things, whether wolves, bears or man, reminds one of the same direct truth; also of the clarity of the fact that evolution itself is obviously not some process of drowning beings clutching at straws and climbing from suffering and travail and virtual expiration to tenuous, momentary survival. Rather, evolution has been a matter of days well-lived, chameleon strength, energy, zappy sex, sunshine stored up, inventiveness, competitiveness, and the whole fun of busy brain cells. Watch how a rabbit loves to run; watch him set scenting puzzles for the terrier behind him. Or a wolf's amusement at the anatomy of a deer. Tug, tug, he pulls out the long intestines: ah, Yorick, how *long* you are!

An acre of forest will absorb six tons of carbon dioxide in a year.

Wordsworth walked an estimated 186,000 miles in his lifetime.

Robert Rogers' Twenty-first Rule of Ranger warfare was: "If the enemy pursue your rear, take a circle till you come to your own tracks, and there form an ambush to receive them, and give them the first fire."

Rain-in-the-face, a Hunkpapa Sioux, before attacking Fort Totten in the Dakota Territory in 1866: "I prepared for death. I painted as usual like the eclipse of the sun, half black and half red."

JOHN UPDIKE
B. 1932

Prolific author of novels, short stories and poems, Updike is probably best known for his depictions of contemporary small town and suburban life in such books as Rabbit, Run *(1960) and* Couples *(1968). His fiction and poetry, however, contain intense and lyrical evocations of nature, and in his shorter essays, many of them written for* The New Yorker*'s "Talk of the Town" section, he often describes how natural events, such as a solar eclipse or a spring shower, can penetrate consciousness even in suburban backyards and behind the granite facades of big cities.*

SPRING RAIN

April 1962

As the sky is pushed farther and farther away by the stiff-arms of this and that new steel frame, we sometimes wonder if what is reaching us is really weather at all. Whenever we have looked down at the street this spring, the perpetually raincoated figures have appeared to be marching, jerkily foreshortened and steadfastly downstaring, under a kind of sooty fluorescence bearing little relation to the expansive and variable light of outdoors. The other day, as if at the repeated invitation of all those raincoats, it *did* rain, and we ventured outdoors ourself; that is to say, we made our way down several corridors and shafts and into a broader corridor called Forty-fourth Street, whose ceiling, if one bothered to look, consisted of that vaguely tonic, vaporish semi-opacity old-fashionedly termed the Firmament. On this day, the Firmament, which showed as a little, ragged strip wedged between the upper edges of the buildings, seemed in a heavy temper. Water was being silently inserted in the slots between the building tops, and a snappy little secondary rain was dripping from marquees, overhead signs, fire escapes, and ledges. On the street itself, whose asphalt had emerged from the blanket of winter as creased and bumpy as a slept-on sheet, the water was conducting with itself an extravagantly complicated debate of ripple and counter-ripple, flow and anti-flow. It looked black but not dirty, and we thought, in that decisive syntactical way we reserve for such occasions, how all water is in passage from purity to purity. Puddles, gutters, sewers are incidental disguises: the casual avatars of perpetually reincarnated cloud droplets; momentary embarrassments, having nothing to do with the ineluctable poise of H_2O. Throw her on the street, mix her with candy wrappers, splash her with taxi wheels, she remains a virgin and a lady.

The breeze caught its breath, the rain slackened, and the crowds that had been clustered in entranceways and under overhangs shattered and scattered like drying pods. We went over to Fifth Avenue; the buildings

Assorted Prose (New York: Knopf, 1965).

there, steeped in humidity, seemed to be a kind of print of their own images, a slightly too inky impression of an etching entitled "Fifth Avenue, Manhattan, c. 1962."

No matter how long we live among rectangular stones, we still listen, in the pauses of a rain, for the sound of birds chirping as they shake themselves. No birds chirped, but the cars and buses squawked in deeper, openly humorous voices, and a trash can and a mailbox broke into conversation. CAST YOUR BALLOT HERE FOR A CLEANER NEW YORK, the trash can said, and MAIL EARLY IN THE DAY IT'S THE BETTER WAY, the mailbox beside it quickly responded. Both seemed to be rejoicing in the knowledge of their own inner snugness—of all the paper, folded or crumpled, addressed or discarded, that they had kept dry through the shower.

The façades of the buildings darkened in tint, the lights within windows seemed not merely to burn but to blaze, and abruptly the rain was upon us again. In the instant before it fell, the air felt full of soft circular motions and a silent cry of "Hurry!" Pedestrians hustled for shelter. The search converted Fifth Avenue into a romantic and primitive setting for adventure. Pelted, we gained the cave of Finchley's Tudor arcade, with its patio-red floor and plastic orange tree and California sports jackets. The next instant, we ran on into the green glade of the Olivetti entrance, with its typewriter-tipped stalagmite. Finally, we lodged in the narrow but deep shelter of Brentano's leafy *allée* of best-sellers, and from there we observed how the rain, a gusty downpour now, had the effect of exquisitely pressing the city down into itself. Everything—taxi roofs, umbrellas, cellophane-skinned hats, even squinting eyebrows—conveyed a sharp impression of shelter. Just as in a Miró painting the ovals and ellipses and lima beans of color sail across the canvas, so the city seemed a mobile conglomerate of dabs of dryness swimming through a fabric of wet. The rain intensified yet one more notch; the Fred F. French Building developed a positively livid stain along its bricks and the scene seemed squeezed so tight that it yielded the essence of granite, the very idea of a city. In a younger century, we might have wept for joy.

And when the rain stopped at last, a supernaturally well-staged effect was produced in the north. Owing to the arrangement of the slabs of Rockefeller Center, the low, westward-moving sun had laid an exclusive shaft of light upon the face of St. Patrick's Cathedral. Like two elegant conical bottles, the steeples were brimful of a mildly creamy glow. We hastened toward the omen, but by the time we reached the site the sunshine had faded. Yet, looking up through the skeleton globe upheld here by the grimacing Atlas, we saw beyond the metal framework what was, patchy blue and scudding gray, indisputably sky.

ECLIPSE

I went out into the backyard and the usually roundish spots of dappled sunlight underneath the trees were all shaped like feathers, crescent in the same direction, from left to right. Though it was five o'clock on a summer afternoon, the birds were singing good-bye to the day, and their merged song seemed to soak the strange air in an additional strangeness. A kind of silence prevailed. Few cars were moving on the streets of the town. Of my children only the baby dared come into the yard with me. She wore only underpants, and as she stood beneath a tree, bulging her belly toward me in the mood of jolly flirtation she has grown into at the age of two, her bare skin was awash with pale crescents. It crossed my mind that she might be harmed, but I couldn't think how. *Cancer?*

The eclipse was to be over 90 percent in our latitude and the newspapers and television for days had been warning us not to look at it. I looked up, a split-second Prometheus, and looked away. The bitten silhouette of the sun lingered redly on my retinas. The day was half-cloudy, and my impression had been of the sun struggling, amid a furious knotted huddle of black and silver clouds, with an enemy too dreadful to be seen, with an eater as ghostly and hungry as time. Every blade of grass cast a long bluish-brown shadow, as at dawn.

My wife shouted from behind the kitchen screen door that as long as I was out there I might as well burn the wastepaper. She darted from the house, eyes downcast, with the wastebasket, and darted back again, leaving the naked baby and me to wander up through the strained sunlight to the wire trash barrel. After my forbidden peek at the sun, the flames dancing transparently from the blackening paper—yesterday's Boston *Globe,* a milk carton, a Hi-Ho cracker box—seemed dimmer than shadows, and in the teeth of all the warnings I looked up again. The clouds seemed bunched and twirled as if to plug a hole in the sky, and the burning afterimage was the shape of a near-new moon, horns pointed down. It was gigantically unnatural, and I lingered in the yard under the vague apprehension that in some future life I might be called before a cosmic court to testify to this assault. I seemed to be the sole witness. The town around my yard was hushed, all but the singing of the birds, who were invisible. The feathers under the trees had changed direction, and curved from right to left.

Then I saw my neighbor sitting on her porch. My neighbor is a widow, with white hair and brown skin; she has in her yard an aluminum-and-nylon-net chaise longue on which she lies at every opportunity, head back, arms spread, prostrate under the sun. Now she hunched dismally on her porch steps in the shade, which was scarcely darker than the light. I walked toward her and hailed her as a visitor to the moon might salute a survivor of a previous expedition. "How do you like the eclipse?" I called over the fence that distinguished our holdings on this suddenly insubstantial and lunar earth.

"I don't like it," she answered, shading her face with a hand. "They say you shouldn't go out in it."

"I thought it was just you shouldn't look at it."

"There's something in the rays," she explained, in a voice far louder than it needed to be, for silence framed us. "I shut all the windows on that side of the house and had to come out for some air."

"I think it'll pass," I told her.

"Don't let the baby look up," she warned, and turned away from talking to me, as if the open use of her voice exposed her more fatally to the rays.

Superstition, I thought, walking back through my yard, clutching my child's hand as tightly as a good-luck token. There was no question in her touch. Day, night, twilight, noon were all wonders to her, unscheduled, free from all bondage of prediction. The sun was being restored to itself and soon would radiate influence as brazenly as ever—and in this sense my daughter's blind trust was vindicated. Nevertheless, I was glad that the eclipse had passed, as it were, over her head; for in my own life I felt a certain assurance evaporate forever under the reality of the sun's disgrace.

WENDELL BERRY
B. 1934

Our approach to agriculture lays the foundation for our culture as a whole; our attentiveness to our immediate physical environments reflects the clarity of our vision and self-expression. These convictions, developed most systematically in The Unsettling of America *(1977), appear throughout Wendell Berry's life and writing. They are expressed through his decision to reclaim a worn-out hill farm in his native Kentucky; through his novels, such as* The Memory of Old Jack *(1974),*

which celebrate the virtues and struggles of his ancestors in that land;
through his volumes of poetry including Farming: A Handbook (1970)
and Clearing (1977); and through his essays on agriculture, wilderness,
and the need for different attitudes toward the land. Like Aldo Leopold,
Berry understands that respectful, joyful work is a valid and constructive
form of relation to nature. The farm, as well as the wilderness, is precious.

AN ENTRANCE TO THE WOODS

On a fine sunny afternoon at the end of September I leave my work in
Lexington and drive east on I-64 and the Mountain Parkway. When I
leave the Parkway at the little town of Pine Ridge I am in the watershed
of the Red River in the Daniel Boone National Forest. From Pine Ridge
I take Highway 715 out along the narrow ridgetops, a winding tunnel
through the trees. And then I turn off on a Forest Service Road and
follow it to the head of a foot trail that goes down the steep valley wall of
one of the tributary creeks. I pull my car off the road and lock it, and lift
on my pack.

It is nearly five o'clock when I start walking. The afternoon is brilliant
and warm, absolutely still, not enough air stirring to move a leaf. There is
only the steady somnolent trilling of insects, and now and again in the
woods below me the cry of a pileated woodpecker. Those, and my footsteps on the path, are the only sounds.

From the dry oak woods of the ridge I pass down into the rock. The
foot trails of the Red River Gorge all seek these stony notches that little
streams have cut back through the cliffs. I pass a ledge overhanging a
sheer drop of the rock, where in a wetter time there would be a waterfall.
The ledge is dry and mute now, but on the face of the rock below are the
characteristic mosses, ferns, liverwort, meadow rue. And here where the
ravine suddenly steepens and narrows, where the shadows are long-lived
and the dampness stays, the trees are different. Here are beech and
hemlock and poplar, straight and tall, reaching way up into the light.
Under them are evergreen thickets of rhododendron. And wherever the
dampness is there are mosses and ferns. The faces of the rock are intricately scalloped with veins of ironstone, scooped and carved by the wind.

Finally from the crease of the ravine I am following there begins to

Recollected Essays 1965–1980 (San Francisco: North Point Press, 1981).

come the trickling and splashing of water. There is a great restfulness in the sounds these small streams make; they are going down as fast as they can, but their sounds seem leisurely and idle, as if produced like gemstones with the greatest patience and care.

A little later, stopping, I hear not far away the more voluble flowing of the creek. I go on down to where the trail crosses and begin to look for a camping place. The little bottoms along the creek here are thickety and weedy, probably having been kept clear and cropped or pastured not so long ago. In the more open places are little lavender asters, and the even smaller-flowered white ones that some people call beeweed or farewell-summer. And in low wet places are the richly flowered spikes of great lobelia, the blooms an intense startling blue, exquisitely shaped. I choose a place in an open thicket near the stream, and make camp.

It is a simple matter to make camp. I string up a shelter and put my air mattress and sleeping bag in it, and I am ready for the night. And supper is even simpler, for I have brought sandwiches for this first meal. In less than an hour all my chores are done. It will still be light for a good while, and I go over and sit down on a rock at the edge of the stream.

And then a heavy feeling of melancholy and lonesomeness comes over me. This does not surprise me, for I have felt it before when I have been alone at evening in wilderness places that I am not familiar with. But here it has a quality that I recognize as peculiar to the narrow hollows of the Red River Gorge. These are deeply shaded by the trees and by the valley walls, the sun rising on them late and setting early; they are more dark than light. And there will often be little rapids in the stream that will sound, at a certain distance, exactly like people talking. As I sit on my rock by the stream now, I could swear that there is a party of campers coming up the trail toward me, and for several minutes I stay alert, listening for them, their voices seeming to rise and fall, fade out and lift again, in happy conversation. When I finally realize that it is only a sound the creek is making, though I have not come here for company and do not want any, I am inexplicably sad.

These are haunted places, or at least it is easy to feel haunted in them, alone at nightfall. As the air darkens and the cool of the night rises, one feels the immanence of the wraiths of the ancient tribesmen who used to inhabit the rock houses of the cliffs; of the white hunters from east of the mountains; of the farmers who accepted the isolation of these nearly inaccessible valleys to crop the narrow bottoms and ridges and pasture their cattle and hogs in the woods; of the seekers of quick wealth in timber and ore. For though this is a wilderness place, it bears its part of the burden of human history. If one spends much time here and feels much liking for the place, it is hard to escape the sense of one's predecessors. If one has read of the prehistoric Indians whose flint arrowpoints and pottery and hominy holes and petroglyphs have been found here, then every rock shelter and clifty spring will suggest the presence of those dim people who have disappeared into the earth. Walking along the ridges and the stream bottoms, one will come upon the heaped stones of a chimney, or the slowly filling depression of an old cellar, or will find in the spring a japonica bush or periwinkles or a few jonquils blooming in a thicket that used to be a dooryard. Wherever the land is level enough there are abandoned fields and pastures. And nearly always there is the evidence that one follows in the steps of the loggers.

That sense of the past is probably one reason for the melancholy that I feel. But I know that there are other reasons.

One is that, though I am here in body, my mind and my nerves too are not yet altogether here. We seem to grant to our high-speed roads and our airlines the rather thoughtless assumption that people can change places as rapidly as their bodies can be transported. That, as my own experience keeps proving to me, is not true. In the middle of the afternoon I left off being busy at work, and drove through traffic to the freeway, and then for a solid hour or more I drove sixty or seventy miles an hour, hardly aware of the country I was passing through, because on the freeway one does not have to be. The landscape has been subdued so that one may drive over it at seventy miles per hour without any concession whatsoever to one's whereabouts. One might as well be flying. Though one is in Kentucky one is not experiencing Kentucky; one is experiencing the highway, which might be in nearly any hill country east of the Mississippi.

Once off the freeway, my pace gradually slowed, as the roads became progressively more primitive, from seventy miles an hour to a walk. And now, here at my camping place, I have stopped altogether. But my mind is still keyed to seventy miles an hour. And having come here so fast, it is still busy with the work I am usually doing. Having come here by the freeway, my mind is not so fully here as it would have been if I had come by the crookeder, slower state roads; it is incalculably farther away than it would have been if I had come all the way on foot, as my earliest predecessors came. When the Indians and the first white hunters entered this country they were altogether here as soon as they arrived, for they had seen and experienced fully everything between here and their starting place, and so the transition was gradual and articulate in their consciousness. Our senses, after all, were developed to function at foot speeds; and the transition from foot travel to motor travel, in terms of evolutionary time, has been abrupt. The faster one goes, the more strain there is on the senses, the more they fail to take in, the more confusion they must tolerate or gloss over—and the longer it takes to bring the mind to a stop in the presence of anything. Though the freeway passes through the very heart of this forest, the motorist remains several hours' journey by foot from what is living at the edge of the right-of-way.

But I have not only come to this strangely haunted place in a short time and too fast. I have in that move made an enormous change: I have departed from my life as I am used to living it, and have come into the wilderness. It is not fear that I feel; I have learned to fear the everyday events of human history much more than I fear the everyday occurrences of the woods; in general, I would rather trust myself to the woods than to any government that I know of. I feel, instead, an uneasy awareness of severed connections, of being cut off from all familiar places and of being a stranger where I am. What is happening at home? I wonder, and I know I can't find out very easily or very soon.

Even more discomforting is a pervasive sense of unfamiliarity. In the places I am most familiar with—my house, or my garden, or even the woods near home that I have walked in for years—I am surrounded by associations; everywhere I look I am reminded of my history and my hopes; even unconsciously I am comforted by any number of proofs that my life on the earth is an established and a going thing. But I am in this hollow for the first time in my life. I see nothing that I recognize. Everything looks as it did before I came, as it will when I am gone. When I look over at my little camp I see how tentative and insignificant it is. Lying there in my bed in the dark tonight, I will be absorbed in the being of this place, invisible as a squirrel in his nest.

Uneasy as this feeling is, I know it will pass. Its passing will produce a deep pleasure in being there. And I have felt it often enough before that I have begun to understand something of what it means:

Nobody knows where I am. I don't know what is happening to anybody else in the world. While I am here I will not speak, and will have no reason or need for speech. It is only beyond this lonesomeness for the places I have come from that I can reach the vital reality of a place such as this. Turning toward this place, I confront a presence that none of my schooling and none of my usual assumptions have prepared me for: the wilderness, mostly unknowable and mostly alien, that is the universe. Perhaps the most difficult labor for my species is to accept its limits, its weakness and ignorance. But here I am. This wild place where I have camped lies within an enormous cone widening from the center of the earth out across the universe, nearly all of it a mysterious wilderness in which the power and the knowledge of men count for nothing. As long as its instruments are correct and its engines run, the airplane now flying through this great cone is safely within the human freehold; its behavior is as familiar and predictable to those concerned as the inside of a man's living room. But let its instruments or its engines fail, and at once it enters the wilderness where nothing is foreseeable. And these steep narrow hollows, these cliffs and forested ridges that lie below, are the antithesis of flight.

Wilderness is the element in which we live encased in civilization, as a mollusk lives in his shell in the sea. It is a wilderness that is beautiful, dangerous, abundant, oblivious of us, mysterious, never to be conquered or controlled or second-guessed, or known more than a little. It is a wilderness that for most of us most of the time is kept out of sight, camouflaged, by the edifices and the busyness and the bothers of human society.

And so, coming here, what I have done is strip away the human facade that usually stands between me and the universe, and I see more clearly where I am. What I am able to ignore much of the time, but find undeniable here, is that all wildernesses are one: there is a profound joining between this wild stream deep in one of the folds of my native country and the tropical jungles, the tundras of the north, the oceans and the deserts. Alone here, among the rocks and the trees, I see that I am alone also among the stars. A stranger here, unfamiliar with my surroundings, I am aware also that I know only in the most relative terms my whereabouts within the black reaches of the universe. And because the natural processes are here so little qualified by anything human, this fragment of the wilderness is also joined to other times; there flows over it a nonhuman time to be told by the growth and death of the forest and the wearing of the stream. I feel drawing out beyond my comprehension perspectives from which the growth and the death of a large poplar would seem as continuous and sudden as the raising and the lowering of a man's hand, from which men's history in the world, their brief clearing of the ground, will seem no more than the opening and shutting of an eye.

And so I have come here to enact—not because I want to but because, once here, I cannot help it—the loneliness and the humbleness of my kind. I must see in my flimsy shelter, pitched here for two nights, the transience of capitols and cathedrals. In growing used to being in this place, I will have to accept a humbler and a truer view of myself than I usually have.

A man enters and leaves the world naked. And it is only naked—or nearly so—that he can enter and leave the wilderness. If he walks, that is; and if he doesn't walk it can hardly be said that he has entered. He can bring only what he can carry—the little that it takes to replace for a few hours or a few days an animal's fur and teeth and claws and functioning instincts. In comparison to the usual traveler with his dependence on machines and highways and restaurants and motels—on the economy and the government, in short—the man who walks into the wilderness is naked indeed. He leaves behind his work, his household, his duties, his comforts—even, if he comes alone, his words. He immerses himself in what he is not. It is a kind of death.

The dawn comes slow and cold. Only occasionally, somewhere along the creek or on the slopes above, a bird sings. I have not slept well, and I waken without much interest in the day. I set the camp to rights, and fix breakfast, and eat. The day is clear, and high up on the points and ridges to the west of my camp I can see the sun shining on the woods. And suddenly I am full of an ambition: I want to get up where the sun is; I want to sit still in the sun up there among the high rocks until I can feel its warmth in my bones.

I put some lunch into a little canvas bag, and start out, leaving my jacket so as not to have to carry it after the day gets warm. Without my jacket, even climbing, it is cold in the shadow of the hollow, and I have a long way to go to get to the sun. I climb the steep path up the valley wall, walking rapidly, thinking only of the sunlight above me. It is as though I have entered into a deep sympathy with those tulip poplars that grow so straight and tall out of the shady ravines, not growing a branch worth the name until their heads are in the sun. I am so concentrated on the sun that when some grouse flush from the undergrowth ahead of me, I am thunderstruck; they are already planing down into the underbrush again before I can get my wits together and realize what they are.

The path zigzags up the last steepness of the bluff and then slowly levels out. For some distance it follows the backbone of a ridge, and then where the ridge is narrowest there is a great slab of bare rock lying full in the sun. This is what I have been looking for. I walk out into the center of the rock and sit, the clear warm light falling unobstructed all around. As the sun warms me I begin to grow comfortable not only in my clothes, but in the place and the day. And like those light-seeking poplars of the ravines, my mind begins to branch out.

Southward, I can hear the traffic on the Mountain Parkway, a steady continuous roar—the corporate voice of twentieth-century humanity, sustained above the transient voices of its members. Last night, except for an occasional airplane passing over, I camped out of reach of the sounds of engines. For long stretches of time I heard no sounds but the sounds of the woods.

Near where I am sitting there is an inscription cut into the rock:

A · J · SARGENT
fEB · 24 · 1903

Those letters were carved there more than sixty-six years ago. As I look around me I realize that I can see no evidence of the lapse of so much time. In every direction I can see only narrow ridges and narrow deep hollows, all covered with trees. For all that can be told from this height by looking, it might still be 1903—or, for that matter, 1803 or 1703, or 1003. Indians no doubt sat here and looked over the country as I am doing now; the visual impression is so pure and strong that I can almost imagine myself one of them. But the insistent, the overwhelming, evidence of the time of my own arrival is in what I can hear—that roar of the highway off there in the distance. In 1903 the continent was still covered by a great ocean of silence, in which the sounds of machinery were scattered at wide intervals of time and space. Here, in 1903, there were only the natural sounds of the place. On a day like this, at the end of September, there would have been only the sounds of a few faint crickets, a woodpecker now and then, now and then the wind. But today, two-thirds of a century later, the continent is covered by an ocean of engine noise, in which silences occur only sporadically and at wide intervals.

From where I am sitting in the midst of this island of wilderness, it is as though I am listening to the machine of human history—a huge flywheel building speed until finally the force of its whirling will break it in pieces, and the world with it. That is not an attractive thought, and yet I find it impossible to escape, for it has seemed to me for years now that the doings of men no longer occur within nature, but that the natural places which the human economy has so far spared now survive almost accidentally within the doings of men. This wilderness of the Red River now carries on its ancient processes *within* the human climate of war and waste and confusion. And I know that the distant roar of engines, though it may *seem* only to be passing through this wilderness, is really bearing down upon it. The machine is running now with a speed that produces blindness—as to the driver of a speeding automobile the only thing stable, the only thing not a mere blur on the edge of the retina, is the automobile itself—and the blindness of a thing with power promises the destruction of what cannot be seen. That roar of the highway is the voice of the American economy; it is sounding also wherever strip mines are being cut in the steep slopes of Appalachia, and wherever cropland is being destroyed to make roads and suburbs, and wherever rivers and marshes and bays and forests are being destroyed for the sake of industry or commerce.

No. Even here where the economy of life is really an economy—where the creation is yet fully alive and continuous and self-enriching, where whatever dies enters directly into the life of the living—even here one cannot fully escape the sense of an impending human catastrophe. One cannot come here without the awareness that this is an island surrounded by the machinery and the workings of an insane greed, hungering for the world's end—that ours is a "civilization" of which the work of no builder or artist is symbol, nor the life of any good man, but rather the bulldozer, the poison spray, the hugging fire of napalm, the cloud of Hiroshima.

Though from the high vantage point of this stony ridge I see little hope that I will ever live a day as an optimist, still I am not desperate. In fact, with the sun warming me now, and with the whole day before me to wander in this beautiful country, I am happy. A man cannot despair if he can imagine a better life, and if he can enact something of its possibility. It is only when I am ensnarled in the meaningless ordeals and the ordeals of meaninglessness, of which our public and political life is now so productive, that I lose the awareness of something better, and feel the despair of having come to the dead end of possibility.

Today, as always when I am afoot in the woods, I feel the possibility, the reasonableness, the practicability of living in the world in a way that would enlarge rather than diminish the hope of life. I feel the possibility of a frugal and protective love for the creation that would be unimaginably more meaningful and joyful than our present destructive and wasteful economy. The absence of human society, that made me so uneasy last night, now begins to be a comfort to me. I am afoot in the woods. I am alive in the world, this moment, without the help or the interference of any machine. I can move without reference to anything except the lay of the land and the capabilities of my own body. The necessities of foot travel in this steep country have stripped away all superfluities. I simply could not enter into this place and assume its quiet with all the belongings of a family man, property holder, etc. For the time, I am reduced to my irreducible self. I feel the lightness of body that a man must feel who has just lost fifty pounds of fat. As I leave the bare expanse of the rock and go in under the trees again, I am aware that I move in the landscape as one of its details.

Walking through the woods, you can never see far, either ahead or behind, so you move without much of a sense of getting anywhere or of moving at any certain speed. You burrow through the foliage in the air much as a mole burrows through the roots in the ground. The views that open out occasionally from the ridges afford a relief, a recovery of orientation, that they could never give as mere "scenery," looked at from a turnout at the edge of a highway.

The trail leaves the ridge and goes down a ravine into the valley of a creek where the night chill has stayed. I pause only long enough to drink the cold clean water. The trail climbs up onto the next ridge.

It is the ebb of the year. Though the slopes have not yet taken on the bright colors of the autumn maples and oaks, some of the duller trees are already shedding. The foliage has begun to flow down the cliff faces and the slopes like a tide pulling back. The woods is mostly quiet, subdued, as if the pressure of survival has grown heavy upon it, as if above the growing warmth of the day the cold of winter can be felt waiting to descend.

At my approach a big hawk flies off the low branch of an oak and out over the treetops. Now and again a nuthatch hoots, off somewhere in the woods. Twice I stop and watch an ovenbird. A few feet ahead of me there is a sudden movement in the leaves, and then quiet. When I slip up and examine the spot there is nothing to be found. Whatever passed there has disappeared, quicker than the hand that is quicker than the eye, a shadow fallen into a shadow.

In the afternoon I leave the trail. My walk so far has come perhaps three-quarters of the way around a long zig-zagging loop that will eventually bring me back to my starting place. I turn down a small unnamed branch of the creek where I am camped, and I begin the loveliest part of the day. There is nothing here resembling a trail. The best way is nearly always to follow the edge of the stream, stepping from one stone to another. Crossing back and forth over the water, stepping on or over rocks and logs, the way ahead is never clear for more than a few feet. The stream accompanies me down, threading its way under boulders and logs and over little falls and rapids. The rhododendron overhangs it so closely in places that I can go only by stopping. Over the rhododendron are the great dark heads of the hemlocks. The streambanks are ferny and mossy. And through this green tunnel the voice of the stream changes from rock to rock; subdued like all the other autumn voices of the woods, it seems sunk in a deep contented meditation on the sounds of *l*.

The water in the pools is absolutely clear. If it weren't for the shadows and ripples you would hardly notice that it is water; the fish would seem to swim in the air. As it is, where there is no leaf floating, it is impossible to tell exactly where the plane of the surface lies. As I walk up on a pool the little fish dart every which way out of sight. And then after I sit still a while, watching, they come out again. Their shadows flow over the rocks and leaves on the bottom. Now I have come into the heart of the woods.

I am far from the highway and can hear no sound of it. All around there is a grand deep autumn quiet, in which a few insects dream their summer songs. Suddenly a wren sings way off in the underbrush. A redbreasted nuthatch walks, hooting, headfirst down the trunk of a walnut. An ovenbird walks out along the limb of a hemlock and looks at me, curious. The little fish soar in the pool, turning their clean quick angles, their shadows seeming barely to keep up. As I lean and dip my cup in the water, they scatter. I drink, and go on.

When I get back to camp it is only the middle of the afternoon or a little after. Since I left in the morning I have walked something like eight miles. I haven't hurried—have mostly poked along, stopping often and looking around. But I am tired, and coming down the creek I have got both feet wet. I find a sunny place, and take off my shoes and socks and set them to dry. For a long time then, lying propped against the trunk of a tree, I read and rest and watch the evening come.

All day I have moved through the woods, making as little noise as possible. Slowly my mind and my nerves have slowed to a walk. The quiet of the woods has ceased to be something that I observe; now it is something that I am a part of. I have joined it with my own quiet. As the twilight draws on I no longer feel the strangeness and uneasiness of the evening before. The sounds of the creek move through my mind as they move through the valley, unimpeded and clear.

When the time comes I prepare supper and eat, and then wash kettle and cup and spoon and put them away. As far as possible I get things ready for an early start in the morning. Soon after dark I go to bed, and I sleep well.

I wake long before dawn. The air is warm and I feel rested and wide awake. By the light of a small candle lantern I break camp and pack. And then I begin the steep climb back to the car.

The moon is bright and high. The woods stands in deep shadow, the light falling soft through the openings of the foliage. The trees appear immensely tall, and black, gravely looming over the path. It is windless and still; the moonlight pouring over the country seems more potent than the air. All around me there is still that constant low singing of the insects. For days now it has continued without letup or inflection, like ripples on water under a steady breeze. While I slept it went on through the night, a shimmer on my mind. My shoulder brushes a low tree overhanging the path and a bird that was asleep on one of the branches startles awake and flies off into the shadows, and I go on with the sense that I am passing near to the sleep of things.

In a way this is the best part of the trip. Stopping now and again to rest, I linger over it, sorry to be going. It seems to me that if I were to stay on, today would be better than yesterday, and I realize it was to renew the life of that possibility that I came here. What I am leaving is something to look forward to.

N. SCOTT MOMADAY
B. 1934

Momaday manages in his writing both to celebrate and extend his Kiowa heritage and to enrich the traditions of fiction, poetry, and nature writing in English. Among his books are The Way to Rainy Mountain *(1969), retelling Kiowa folktales; a novel,* House Made of Dawn *(1968); and* The Gourd Dancer *(1976), a volume of poems. One of the central challenges he sets for himself as an artist is to convey Native American insights and symbols in new language and forms. The key is to understand the power, and dangers, of naming, rightly understood. Momaday has said in an interview that "I believe that the Indian has an understanding of the physical world and of the earth as a spiritual entity that is his, very much his own. The non-Indian can benefit a good deal by having that perception revealed to him."*

From THE WAY TO RAINY MOUNTAIN

THE WAY TO RAINY MOUNTAIN

A single knoll rises out of the plain in Oklahoma, north and west of the Wichita Range. For my people, the Kiowas, it is an old landmark, and they gave it the name Rainy Mountain. The hardest weather in the world is there. Winter brings blizzards, hot tornadic winds arise in the spring, and in summer the prairie is an anvil's edge. The grass turns

The Way to Rainy Mountain (University of New Mexico Press, 1969).

brittle and brown, and it cracks beneath your feet. There are green belts along the rivers and creeks, linear groves of hickory and pecan, willow and witch hazel. At a distance in July or August the steaming foliage seems almost to writhe in fire. Great green and yellow grasshoppers are everywhere in the tall grass, popping up like corn to sting the flesh, and tortoises crawl about on the red earth, going nowhere in the plenty of time. Loneliness is an aspect of the land. All things in the plain are isolate; there is no confusion of objects in the eye, but *one* hill or *one* tree or *one* man. To look upon that landscape in the early morning, with the sun at your back, is to lose the sense of proportion. Your imagination comes to life, and this, you think, is where Creation was begun.

I returned to Rainy Mountain in July. My grandmother had died in the spring, and I wanted to be at her grave. She had lived to be very old and at last infirm. Her only living daughter was with her when she died, and I was told that in death her face was that of a child.

I like to think of her as a child. When she was born, the Kiowas were living the last great moment of their history. For more than a hundred years they had controlled the open range from the Smoky Hill River to the Red, from the headwaters of the Canadian to the fork of the Arkansas and Cimarron. In alliance with the Comanches, they had ruled the whole of the southern Plains. War was their sacred business, and they were among the finest horsemen the world has ever known. But warfare for the Kiowas was preeminently a matter of disposition rather than of survival, and they never understood the grim, unrelenting advance of the U.S. Cavalry. When at last, divided and ill-provisioned, they were driven onto the Staked Plains in the cold rains of autumn, they fell into panic. In Palo Duro Canyon they abandoned their crucial stores to pillage and had nothing then but their lives. In order to save themselves, they surrendered to the soldiers at Fort Sill and were imprisoned in the old stone corral that now stands as a military museum. My grandmother was spared the humiliation of those high gray walls by eight or ten years, but she must have known from birth the affliction of defeat, the dark brooding of old warriors.

Her name was Aho, and she belonged to the last culture to evolve in North America. Her forebears came down from the high country in western Montana nearly three centuries ago. They were a mountain people, a mysterious tribe of hunters whose language has never been positively classified in any major group. In the late seventeenth century they began a long migration to the south and east. It was a journey toward the dawn, and it led to a golden age. Along the way the Kiowas were befriended by the Crows, who gave them the culture and religion of the Plains. They acquired horses, and their ancient nomadic spirit was suddenly free of the ground. They acquired Tai-me, the sacred Sun Dance doll, from that moment the object and symbol of their worship, and so shared in the divinity of the sun. Not least, they acquired the sense of destiny, therefore courage and pride. When they entered upon the southern Plains they had been transformed. No longer were they slaves to the simple necessity of survival; they were a lordly and dangerous society of fighters and thieves, hunters and priests of the sun. According to their origin myth, they entered the world through a hollow log. From one point of view, their migration was the fruit of an old prophecy, for indeed they emerged from a sunless world.

Although my grandmother lived out her long life in the shadow of Rainy Mountain, the immense landscape of the continental interior lay like memory in her blood. She could tell of the Crows, whom she had never seen, and of the Black Hills, where she had never been. I wanted to see in reality what she had seen more perfectly in the mind's eye, and traveled fifteen hundred miles to begin my pilgrimage.

Yellowstone, it seemed to me, was the top of the world, a region of deep lakes and dark timber, canyons and waterfalls. But, beautiful as it is, one might have the sense of confinement there. The skyline in all directions is close at hand, the high wall of the woods and deep cleavages of shade. There is a perfect freedom in the mountains, but it belongs to the eagle and the elk, the badger and the bear. The Kiowas reckoned their stature by the distance they could see, and they were bent and blind in the wilderness.

Descending eastward, the highland meadows are a stairway to the plain. In July the inland slope of the Rockies is luxuriant with flax and buckwheat, stonecrop and larkspur. The earth unfolds and the limit of the land recedes. Clusters of trees, and animals grazing far in the distance, cause the vision to reach away and wonder to build upon the mind. The sun follows a longer course in the day, and the sky is immense beyond all comparison. The great billowing clouds that sail upon it are the shadows that move upon the grain like water, dividing light. Farther down, in the land of the Crows and Blackfeet, the plain is yellow. Sweet clover takes hold of the hills and bends upon itself to cover and seal the soil. There the Kiowas paused on their way; they had come to the place where they must change their lives. The sun is at home on the plains. Precisely there does it have the certain character of a god. When the Kiowas came to the land of the Crows, they could see the dark lees of the hills at dawn across the Bighorn River, the profusion of light on the grain shelves, the oldest deity ranging after the solstices. Not yet would they veer southward to the caldron of the land that lay below; they must wean their blood from the northern winter and hold the mountains a while longer in their view. They bore Tai-me in procession to the east.

A dark mist lay over the Black Hills, and the land was like iron. At the top of a ridge I caught sight of Devil's Tower upthrust against the gray sky as if in the birth of time the core of the earth had broken through its crust and the motion of the world was begun. There are things in nature that engender an awful quiet in the heart of man; Devil's Tower is one of them. Two centuries ago, because they could not do otherwise, the Kiowas made a legend at the base of the rock. My grandmother said:

> *Eight children were there at play, seven sisters and their brother. Suddenly the boy was struck dumb; he trembled and began to run upon his hands and feet. His fingers became claws, and his body was covered with fur. Directly there was a bear where the boy had been. The sisters were terrified; they ran, and the bear after them. They came to the stump of a great tree, and the tree spoke to them. It bade them climb upon it, and as they did so it began to rise into the air. The bear came to kill them, but they were just beyond its reach. It reared against the tree and scored the bark all around with its claws. The seven sisters were borne into the sky, and they became the stars of the Big Dipper.*

From that moment, and so long as the legend lives, the Kiowas have kinsmen in the night sky. Whatever they were in the mountains, they could be no more. However tenuous their well-being, however much they had suffered and would suffer again, they had found a way out of the wilderness.

My grandmother had a reverence for the sun, a holy regard that now is all but gone out of mankind. There was a wariness in her, and an ancient awe. She was a Christian in her later years, but she had come a long way about, and she never forgot her birthright. As a child she had been to the Sun Dances; she had taken part in those annual rites, and by them she had learned the restoration of her people in the presence of Tai-me. She was about seven when the last Kiowa Sun Dance was held in 1887 on the Washita River above Rainy Mountain Creek. The buffalo were gone. In order to consummate the ancient sacrifice—to impale the head of a buffalo bull upon the medicine tree—a delegation of old men journeyed into Texas, there to beg and barter for an animal from the Goodnight herd. She was ten when the Kiowas came together for the last time as a living Sun Dance culture. They could find no buffalo; they had to hang an old hide from the sacred tree. Before the dance could begin, a company of soldiers rode out from Fort Sill under orders to disperse the tribe.

Forbidden without cause the essential act of their faith, having seen the wild herds slaughtered and left to rot upon the ground, the Kiowas backed away forever from the medicine tree. That was July 20, 1890, at the great bend of the Washita. My grandmother was there. Without bitterness, and for as long as she lived, she bore a vision of deicide.

Now that I can have her only in memory, I see my grandmother in the several postures that were peculiar to her: standing at the wood stove on a winter morning and turning meat in a great iron skillet; sitting at the south window, bent above her beadwork, and afterwards, when her vision failed, looking down for a long time into the fold of her hands; going out upon a cane, very slowly as she did when the weight of age came upon her; praying. I remember her most often at prayer. She made long, rambling prayers out of suffering and hope, having seen many things. I was never sure that I had the right to hear, so exclusive where they of all mere custom and company. The last time I saw her she prayed standing by the side of her bed at night, naked to the waist, the light of a kerosene lamp moving upon her dark skin. Her long, black hair, always drawn and braided in the day, lay upon her shoulders and against her breasts like a shawl. I do not speak Kiowa, and I never understood her prayers, but there was something inherently sad in the sound, some merest hesitation upon the syllables of sorrow. She began in a high and descending pitch, exhausting her breath to silence; then again and again—and always the same intensity of effort, of something that is, and is not, like urgency in the human voice. Transported so in the dancing light among the shadows of her room, she seemed beyond the reach of time. But that was illusion; I think I knew then that I should not see her again.

Houses are like sentinels in the plain, old keepers of the weather watch. There, in a very little while, wood takes on the appearance of great age. All colors wear soon away in the wind and rain, and then the wood is burned gray and the grain appears and the nails turn red with rust. The windowpanes are black and opaque; you imagine there is nothing within, and indeed there are many ghosts, bones given up to the land. They stand here and there against the sky, and you approach them for a longer time than you expect. They belong in the distance; it is their domain.

Once there was a lot of sound in my grandmother's house, a lot of coming and going, feasting and talk. The summers there were full of excitement and reunion. The Kiowas are a summer people; they abide the cold and keep to themselves, but when the season turns and the land becomes warm and vital they cannot hold still; an old love of going returns upon them. The aged visitors who came to my grandmother's house when I was a child were made of lean and leather, and they bore themselves upright. They wore great black hats and bright ample shirts that shook in the wind. They rubbed fat upon their hair and wound their braids with strips of colored cloth. Some of them painted their faces and carried the scars of old and cherished enmities. They were an old council of warlords, come to remind and be reminded of who they were. Their wives and daughters served them well. The women might indulge themselves; gossip was at once the mark and compensation of their servitude. They made loud and elaborate talk among themselves, full of jest and gesture, fright and false alarm. They went abroad in fringed and flowered shawls, bright beadwork and German silver. They were at home in the kitchen, and they prepared meals that were banquets.

There were frequent prayer meetings, and great nocturnal feasts. When I was a child I played with my cousins outside, where the lamplight fell upon the ground and the singing of the old people rose up around us and carried away into the darkness. There were a lot of good things to eat, a lot of laughter and surprise. And afterwards, when the quiet returned, I lay down with my grandmother and could hear the frogs away by the river and feel the motion of the air.

Now there is a funeral silence in the rooms, the endless wake of some final word. The walls have closed in upon my grandmother's house. When I returned to it in mourning, I saw for the first time in my life how small it was. It was late at night, and there was a white moon, nearly full. I sat for a long time on the stone steps by the kitchen door. From there I could see out across the land; I could see the long row of trees by the creek, the low light upon the rolling plains, and the stars of the Big Dipper. Once I looked at the moon and caught sight of a strange thing. A cricket had perched upon the handrail, only a few inches away from me. My line of vision was such that the creature filled the moon like a fossil. It had gone there, I thought, to live and die, for there, of all places, was its small definition made whole and eternal. A warm wind rose up and purled like the longing within me.

The next morning I awoke at dawn and went out on the dirt road to Rainy Mountain. It was already hot, and the grasshoppers began to fill the air. Still, it was early in the morning, and the birds sang out of the shadows. The long yellow grass on the mountain shone in the bright light, and a scissortail hied above the land. There, where it ought to be, at the end of a long and legendary way, was my grandmother's grave. Here and there on the dark stones were ancestral names. Looking back once, I saw the mountain and came away.

SUE HUBBELL
B. 1935

A former librarian, Sue Hubbell earns her living as a bee-keeper in the Ozark Mountains, where she has lived since 1973. A Country Year (1987), her first book, is as much an account of a middle-aged woman coming into her own identity as it is a careful record of natural and human life in rural Missouri. Beginning with the pain of a divorce, the book describes her choice to forge an independent life in the country and her discovery of new enthusiasms: "Wild things and wild places pull me more strongly than they did a few years ago, and domesticity, dusting and cookery not at all." Her viewpoint is both clear-eyed and compassionate, but she deliberately shies away from grand statements and "nobler quests—white whales and Holy Grails—" making a case for small things well-done and clearly seen.

From A COUNTRY YEAR

SPRING

*   *   * I met Paul, the boy who was to become my husband, when he was sixteen and I was fifteen. We were married some years later, and the legal arrangement that is called marriage worked well enough while we were children and while we had a child. But we grew older, and the son went off to school, and marriage did not serve as a structure for our lives as well as it once had. Still, he was the man in my life for all those years. There was no other. So when the legal arrangement was ended, I had a difficult time sifting through the emotional debris that was left after the framework of an intimate, thirty-year association had broken.

I went through all the usual things: I couldn't sleep or eat, talked feverishly to friends, plunged recklessly into a destructive affair with a

A Country Year (New York: Harper & Row, 1987).

man who had more problems than I did but who was convenient, made a series of stupid decisions about my honey business and pretty generally botched up my life for several years running. And for a long, long time, my mind didn't work. I could not listen to the news on the radio with understanding. My attention came unglued when I tried to read anything but the lightest froth. My brain spun in endless, painful loops, and I could neither concentrate nor think with any semblance of order. I had always rather enjoyed having a mind, and I missed mine extravagantly. I was out to lunch for three years.

I mused about structure, framework, schemata, system, classification and order. I discovered a classification Jorge Luis Borges devised, claiming that

> *A certain Chinese encyclopedia divides animals into:*
> *a. Belonging to the Emperor*
> *b. Embalmed*
> *c. Tame*
> *d. Sucking pigs*
> *e. Sirens*
> *f. Fabulous*
> *g. Stray dogs*
> *h. Included in the present classification*
> *i. Frenzied*
> *j. Innumerable*
> *k. Drawn with a very fine camel-hair brush*
> *l. Et cetera*
> *m. Having just broken the water pitcher*
> *n. That from a long way off look like flies.*

Friends and I laughed over the list, and we decided that the fact that we did so tells more about us and our European, Western way of thinking than it does about a supposed Oriental world view. We believe we have a more proper concept of how the natural world should be classified, and when Borges rumples that concept it amuses us. That I could join in the laughter made me realize I must have retained some sense of that order, no matter how disorderly my mind seemed to have become.

My father was a botanist. When I was a child he reserved Saturday afternoons for me, and we spent many of them walking in woods and rough places. He would name the plants we came upon by their Latin binomials and tell me how they grew. The names were too hard for me, but I did understand that plants had names that described their relationships one to another and found this elegant and interesting even when I was six years old.

So after reading the Borges list, I turned to Linnaeus. Whatever faults the man may have had as a scientist, he gave us a beautiful tool for thinking about diversity in the world. The first word in his scheme of Latin binomials tells the genus, grouping diverse plants which nevertheless share a commonality; the second word names the species, plants alike enough to regularly interbreed and produce offspring like themselves. It is a framework for understanding, a way to show how pieces of the world fit together.

I have no Latin, but as I began to botanize, to learn to call the plants around me up here on my hill by their Latin names, I was diverted from my lack of wits by the wit of the system.

Commelina virginica, the common dayflower, is a rangy weed bearing blue flowers with unequal sepals, two of them showy and rounded, the third hardly noticeable. After I identified it as that particular *Commelina,* named from a sample taken in Virginia, I read in one of my handbooks, written before it was considered necessary to be dull to be taken seriously:

> *Delightful Linnaeus, who dearly loved his little joke, himself confesses to have named the day-flowers after three brothers Commelyn, Dutch botanists, because two of them—commemorated in the showy blue petals of the blossom—published their works; the third, lacking application and ambition, amounted to nothing, like the third inconspicuous whitish third petal.*

There is a tree growing in the woodland with shiny, oval leaves that turn brilliant red early in the fall, sometimes even at summer's end. It has small clusters of white flowers in June that bees like, and later blue fruits that are eaten by bluebirds and robins. It is one of the tupelos, and people in this part of the country call it black-gum or sour-gum. When I was growing up in Michigan I knew it as pepperidge. Its botanic name is *Nyssa sylvatica. Nyssa* groups the tupelos, and is derived from the Nyseides—the Greek nymphs of Mount Nysa who cared for the infant Dionysus. *Sylvatica* means "of the woodlands." *Nyssa sylvatica,* a wild, untamed name. The trees, which are often hollow when old, served as beehives for the first American settlers, who cut sections of them, capped them and dumped in the swarms that they found. To this day some people still call beehives "gums," unknowingly acknowledging the common name of the tree. The hollow logs were also used for making pipes that carried salt water to the salt works in Syracuse in colonial days. The ends of the wooden pipes could be fitted together without using iron bands, which would rust.

This gives me a lot to think about when I come across *Nyssa sylvatica* in the woods.

I botanized obsessively during that difficult time. Every day I learned new plants by their Latin names. I wandered about the woods that winter, good for little else, examining the bark of leafless trees. As wildflowers began to bloom in the spring, I carried my guidebooks with me, and filled a fat notebook as I identified the plants, their habitats, habits and dates of blooming. I had to write them down, for my brain, unaccustomed to exercise, was now on overload.

One spring afternoon, I was walking back down my lane after getting the mail. I had two fine new flowers to look up when I got back to the cabin. Warblers were migrating, and I had been watching them with binoculars; I had identified one I had never before seen. The sun was slanting through new leaves, and the air was fragrant with wild cherry (*Prunus serotina: Prunus*—plum, *serotina*—late blooming) blossoms, which my bees were working eagerly. I stopped to watch them, standing in the sunbeam. The world appeared to have been running along quite nicely without my even noticing it. Quietly, gratefully, I discovered that a part of me that had been off somewhere nursing grief and pain had returned. I had come back from lunch.

Once back, I set about doing all the things that one does when one returns from lunch. I cleared the desk and tended to the messages that others had left. I had been gone for a long time, so there was quite a pile to clear away before I could settle down to the work of the afternoon of my life, the work of building a new kind of order, a structure on which a fifty-year-old woman can live her life alone, at peace with herself and the world around her. *   *   *

WINTER

*   *   * A group of people concerned about a proposal to dam the river came over to my place last evening to talk. The first to arrive was my nearest neighbor. He burst excitedly into the cabin, asking me to bring a flashlight and come back to his pickup; he had something to show me. I followed him to his truck, where he took the flashlight and switched it on to reveal a newly killed bobcat stretched out in the bed of his truck. The bobcat was a small one, probably a female. Her broad face was set off by longer hair behind her jaws, and her pointed ears ended in short tufts of fur. Her tawny winter coat, heavy and full, was spotted with black, and her short stubby tail had black bars. Her body was beginning to stiffen in death, and I noticed a small trickle of blood from her nostrils.

"They pay thirty-five dollars a pelt now over at the country seat," my neighbor explained. "That's groceries for next week," he said proudly. None of us back here on the river has much money, and an opportunity to make next week's grocery money was fortunate for him, I knew. "And I guess you'll thank me because that's surely the varmint that's been getting your chickens," he added, for I had said nothing yet.

But I wasn't grateful. I was shocked and sad in a way that my neighbor would not have understood.

I had not heard a shot and didn't see the gun that he usually carries in the rack in his pickup, so I asked him how he had killed her.

"It was just standing there in the headlights when I turned the corner before your place," he said, "so I rammed it with the pickup bumper and knocked it out, and then I got out and finished it off with the tire iron."

His method of killing sounds more savage than it probably was. Animals in slaughterhouses are stunned before they are killed. Once stunned, the important thing was to kill the bobcat quickly, and I am sure my neighbor did so, for he is a practiced hunter.

Others began to arrive at the meeting and took note of the kill. One of them, a trapper, said that the going price of $35 a pelt was a good one. Not many years ago, the pelt price was under $2. Demand for the fur, formerly scorned for its poor quality, was created by a ban on imported cat fur and a continuing market for fur coats and trim.

My neighbor and the trapper are both third-generation Ozarkers. They could have gone away from here after high school, as did many of their classmates, and made easy money in the cities, but they stayed because they love the land. This brings us together in our opposition to damming the river to create a recreational lake, but our sensibilities are different, the product of different personalities and backgrounds. They come from families who have lived off the land from necessity; they have a deep practical knowledge of it and better skills than I have for living here with very little money. The land, the woods and the rivers, and all that are in and on them are resources to be used for those who have the knowledge and skills. They can cut and sell timber, clear the land for pasture, sell the gravel from the river. Ozarkers pick up wild black walnuts and sell them to the food-processing companies that bring hulling machines to town in October. There are fur buyers, too, so they trap animals and sell the pelts. These Ozarkers do not question the happy fact that they are at the top of the food chain, but kill to eat what swims in the river and walks in the woods, and accept as a matter of course that it takes life to maintain life. In this they are more responsible than I am; I buy my meat in neat sanitized packages from the grocery store.

Troubled by this a few years back, I raised a dozen chickens as meat birds, then killed and dressed the lot, but found that killing chicken Number Twelve was no easier than killing chicken Number One. I didn't like taking responsibility for killing my own meat, and went back to buying it at the grocery store. I concluded sourly that righteousness and consistency are not my strong points, since it bothered me not at all to pull a carrot from the garden, an act quite as life-ending as shooting a deer.

I love this land, too, and I was grateful that we could all come together to stop it from being destroyed by an artificial lake. But my aesthetic is a different one, and comes from having lived in places where beauty, plants and animals are gone, so I place a different value on what remains than do my Ozark friends and neighbors. Others at the meeting last night had lived at one time in cities, and shared my prejudices. In our arrogance, we sometimes tell one another that we are taking a longer view. But in the very long run I'm not so sure, and as in most lofty matters, like my failed meat project, I suspect that all our opinions are simply an expression of a personal sense of what is fitting and proper.

Certainly my reaction to seeing the dead bobcat was personal. I knew that bobcat, and she probably knew me somewhat better, for she would have been a more careful observer than I.

Four or five years ago, a man from town told me he had seen a mountain lion on Pigeon Hawk Bluff, the cliffs above the river just to the west of my place. There is a rocky outcropping there, and he had left his car on the road and walked out to it to look at the river two hundred and fifty feet below. He could see a dead turkey lying on a rock shelf, and climbed down to take a closer look. As he reached out to pick up the bird, he was attacked by a mountain lion who came out of a small cave he had not been able to see from above. He showed me the marks along his forearm—scars, he claimed, where the mountain lion had raked him before he could scramble away. There were marks on his arm, to be sure, but I don't know that a mountain lion or any other animal put them there. I suspect that the story was an Ozark stretcher, for the teller, who logs in many hours with the good old boys at the café in town, is a heavy and slow-moving man; it is hard to imagine him climbing nimbly up or down a steep rock face. Nor would I trust his identification of a mountain lion, an animal more talked of at the café than ever seen in this country.

Mountain lions are large, slender, brownish cats with long tails and small rounded ears. This area used to be part of their range, but as men moved in to cut timber and hunt deer, the cats' chief prey, their habitat was destroyed and they retreated to the west and south. Today they are seen regularly in Arkansas, but now and again there are reports of mountain lions in this part of the Ozarks. With the deer population growing, as it has in recent years under the Department of Conservation's supervision, wildlife biologists say that mountain lions will return to rocky and remote places to feed on them.

After the man told me his story, I watched around Pigeon Hawk Bluff on the outside chance that he might really have seen a mountain lion but in the years since I have never spotted one. I did, however, see a bobcat one evening, near the rock outcropping. This part of the Ozarks is still considered a normal part of bobcat range, but they are threatened by the same destruction of habitat that pushed the mountain lion back to wilder places, and they are uncommon.

Bobcats also kill and feed on deer, but for the most part they eat smaller animals: mice, squirrels, opossums, turkey, quail and perhaps some of my chickens. They are night hunters, and seek out caves or other suitable shelters during the day. In breeding season, the females often chose a rocky cliff cave as a den. I never saw the bobcat's den, but it may have been the cave below the lookout point on the road, although that seems a trifle public for a bobcat's taste. The cliff is studded with other caves of many sizes, and most are inaccessible to all but the most sure-footed. I saw the bobcat several times after that, walking silently along the cliff's edge at dusk. Sometimes in the evening I heard the piercing scream of a bobcat from that direction, and once, coming home late at night, I caught her in the road in the pickup's headlight beam. She stood there, blinded, until I switched off the headlights. Then she padded away into the shadows.

That stretch of land along the river, with its thickets, rocky cliffs and no human houses, would make as good a home ground as any for a bobcat. Females are more particular about their five miles or so of territory than are males, who sometimes intrude upon one another's bigger personal ranges, but bobcats all mark their territories and have little contact with other adults during their ten years or so of life.

I don't know for sure that the bobcat I have seen and heard over the past several years was always the same one, but it probably was, and last night probably I saw her dead in the back of my neighbor's pickup truck. *   *   *

CHET RAYMO
B. 1936

Chet Raymo continues a distinguished line of nature writers who have also been teachers of science. He particularly resembles one of his predecessors, Loren Eiseley, in his impulse to convey the grandeur of creation, to stimulate awe. In addition to teaching physics and astronomy at Stonehill College, in Easton, Massachusetts, he writes columns on science for The Boston Globe. *In those columns, as in his best known book* The Soul of the Night *(1985), his characteristics as a writer are descriptive precision, narrative energy, and alertness to the spiritual meanings of the physical universe.*

The Silence

Yesterday on Boston Common I saw a young man on a skateboard collide with a child. The skateboarder was racing down the promenade and smashed into the child with full force. I saw this happen from a considerable distance. It happened without a sound. It happened in dead silence. The cry of the terrified child as she darted to avoid the skateboard and the scream of the child's mother at the moment of impact were absorbed by the gray wool of the November day. The child's body simply lifted up into the air and, in slow motion, as if in a dream, floated above the promenade, bounced twice like a rubber ball, and lay still.

All of this happened in perfect silence. It was as if I were watching the tragedy through a telescope. It was as if the tragedy were happening on another planet. I have seen stars exploding in space, colossal, planet-shattering, distanced by light-years, framed in the cold glass of a telescope, utterly silent. It was like that.

The Soul of the Night (Englewood Cliffs, N.J.: Prentice-Hall, 1985).

During the time the child was in the air, the spinning Earth carried her half a mile to the east. The motion of the Earth about the sun carried her back again forty miles westward. The drift of the solar system among the stars of the Milky Way bore her silently twenty miles toward the star Vega. The turning pinwheel of the Milky Way Galaxy carried her 300 miles in a great circle about the galactic center. After that huge flight through space she hit the ground and bounced like a rubber ball. She lifted up into the air and flew across the Galaxy and bounced on the pavement.

It is a thin membrane that separates us from chaos. The child sent flying by the skateboarder bounced in slow motion and lay still. There was a long pause. Pigeons froze against the gray sky. Promenaders turned to stone. Traffic stopped on Beacon Street. The child's body lay inert on the asphalt like a piece of crumpled newspaper. The mother's cry was lost in the space between the stars.

How are we to understand the silence of the universe? They say that certain meteorites, upon entering the Earth's atmosphere, disintegrate with noticeable sound, but beyond the Earth's skin of air the sky is silent. There are no voices in the burning bush of the Galaxy. The Milky Way flows across the dark shoals of the summer sky without an audible ripple. Stars blow themselves to smithereens; we hear nothing. Millions of solar systems are sucked into black holes at the centers of the galaxies; they fall like feathers. The universe fattens and swells in a Big Bang, a fireball of Creation exploding from a pinprick of infinite energy, the ultimate fire-cracker; there is no soundtrack. The membrane is ruptured, a child flies through the air, and the universe is silent.

In Catholic churches between Good Friday and Easter Eve the bells are stilled. Following a twelfth-century European custom, the place of the bells is taken by *instruments des ténèbres* (instruments of darkness), wooden clackers and other noisemakers that remind the faithful of the terrifying sounds that were presumed to have accompanied the death of Christ. It was unthinkable that a god should die and the heavens remain silent. Lightning crashed about the darkened hill of Calvary. The veil of the temple was loudly rent. The Earth quaked and rocks split. Stars boomed in their courses. This din and thunder, according to medieval custom, are evoked by the wooden instruments.

Yesterday on Boston Common a child flew through the air, and there was no protest from the sky. I listened. I turned the volume of my indignation all the way up, and I heard nothing.

There is a scene in Michelangelo Antonioni's film *Red Desert* in which a woman approaches a construction site where men are building a large linear-array radio telescope. "What is it for?" she asks. One of the work-men replies, "It is for listening to the stars." "Oh," she exclaims with innocent enthusiasm. "Can I listen?"

Let us listen. Let us connect the multimillion-dollar telescopes to our kitchen radios and convert the radiant energy of the stars into sound. What would we hear? The random crackle of the elements. The static of electrons fidgeting between energy levels in the atoms of stellar atmos-pheres. The buzz of hydrogen. The hiss and sputter of matter intent upon obeying the stochastic laws of quantum physics. Random, statisti-cal, indifferent noise. It would be like the hum of a beehive or the clatter of shingle slapped by a wave.

In high school we did an experiment with an electric bell in a glass jar. The bell was suspended inside the jar, and the wires carrying electricity were led in through holes in the rubber stopper that closed the jar's mouth. The bell was set clanging. Then the air was pumped from the jar. Slowly, the sound of the bell was snuffed out. The clapper beat a silent tattoo. We watched the clapper thrashing silently in the vacuum, like a moth flailing its soft wings against the outside of a window pane.

Even by the standard of the vacuum in the bell jar, the space between the stars is empty. The emptiness between the stars is unimaginably vast. If the sun were a golf ball in Boston, the Earth would be a pinpoint twelve feet away, and the nearest star, Alpha Centauri, would be another golf ball (two golf balls, really, two golf balls and a pea; it is a triple star) in Cincinnati. The distances between the stars are huge compared with the sizes of the stars: a golf ball in Boston, two golf balls and a pea in Cincinnati, a marble in Miami, a basketball in San Francisco. The track-less trillions of miles between the stars are a vacuum more perfect than any vacuum that has yet been created on Earth. In our part of the Milky Way Galaxy, interstellar space contains about one atom of matter per cubic centimeter, one atom in every volume of space equal to the size of a sugar cube. The silent vacuum of the bell jar was a million times inferior to the vacuum of space. In the almost perfect vacuum of inter-stellar space, stars detonate, meteors blast craters on moons, and planets split at their seams with no more sound than the pulsing clapper of the bell in the evacuated jar.

Once I saw the Crab Nebula through a powerful telescope. The neb-ula is the expanding debris of an exploded star, a wreath of shredded star-stuff eight light-years wide and 5000 light-years away. What I saw in the telescope was hardly more than a blur of light, more like a smudge of dust on the mirror of the scope than the shards of a dying star. But seeing through a telescope is 50 percent vision and 50 percent imagination. In the blur of light I could easily imagine the outrushing shock wave, the expanding envelope of high-energy radiation, the torn filaments of gas, the crushed and pulsing remnant of the skeletal star. I stood for a quarter of an hour with my eye glued to the eyepiece of the scope. I felt a powerful sensation of energy unleashed, of an old building collapsing onto its foundations in a roar of dust at the precise direction of a demolition expert. As I watched the Crab Nebula, I felt as if I should be wearing earplugs, like an artilleryman or the fellow who operates a jack-hammer. But there was no sound.

The Chinese saw the Crab when it blew up. In A.D. 1054 a new star appeared in Taurus. For weeks it burned more brightly than Venus, bright enough to be seen in broad daylight. Then the star gradually faded from sight. The Chinese recorded the "guest star" in their annals. Nine hundred years later the explosion continues. We point our tele-scopes to the spot in Taurus where the "guest star" appeared in 1054, and we see the bubble of furious gas still rushing outward.

Doris Lessing began her fictional chronicle of space with this dedica-tion: *For my father, who used to sit, hour after hour, night after night, outside our home in Africa, watching the stars. "Well," he would say, "if we blow ourselves up, there's plenty more where we came from."* Yes, there's plenty more, all right, even if one or two blow themselves up now and then. A billion billion stars scattered in the vacuum of space. A star blew up for the Chinese in 1054. A star blew up for Tycho Brahe in 1572, and another for Kepler in 1604. They go in awesome silence.

The physical silence of the universe is matched by its moral silence. A child flies through the air toward injury, and the galaxies continue to whirl on well-oiled axes. But why should I expect anything else? There are no Elysian Fields up there beyond the seventh sphere where gods pause in their revels to glance down aghast at our petty tragedies. What's up there is just one galaxy after another, magnificent in their silent turning, sublime in their huge indifference. The number of galaxies may be infinite. Our indignation is finite. Divide any finite number by infin-ity and you get zero.

Only a few hundred yards from the busy main street of my New England village, the Queset Brook meanders through a marsh as appar-ently remote as any I might wish for. To drift down that stream in November is to enter a primeval silence. The stream is dark and sluggish. It pushes past the willow roots and the thick green leaves of the arrow-head like syrup. The wind hangs dead in the air. The birds have fled south. Trail bikes are stacked away for the winter, and snowmobiles are still buried at the backs of garages. For a few weeks in November the marsh near Queset Brook is as silent as the space between the stars.

How fragile is our hold on silence. The creak of a wagon on a distant highway was sometimes noise enough to interrupt Thoreau's reverie. Thoreau was perceptive enough to know that the whistle of the Fitchburg Railroad (whose track lay close by Walden Pond) heralded something more than the arrival of the train, but he could hardly have imagined the efficiency with which technology has intruded upon our world of natural silence. Thoreau rejoiced in owls; their hoot, he said, was a sound well suited to swamps and twilight woods. The interval between the hoots was a deepened silence suggesting, said Thoreau, "a vast and undeveloped nature which men have not recognized." Thoreau rejoiced in that silent interval, as I rejoice in the silence of the November marsh.

As a student, I came across a book by Max Picard called *The World of Silence*. The book offered an insight that seems more valuable to me now than it did then. Silence, said Picard, is the source from which language springs, and to silence language must constantly return to be recreated. Only in relation to silence does sound have significance. It is for this silence, so treasured by Picard, that I turn to the marsh near Queset Brook in November. It is for this silence that I turn to the stars, to the ponderous inaudible turning of galaxies, to the clanging of God's great bell in the vacuum. The silence of the stars is the silence of creation and re-creation. It is the silence of that which cannot be named. It is a silence to be explored alone. Along the shore of Walden Pond the owl hooted a question whose answer lay hidden in the interval. The interval was narrow but infinitely deep, and in that deep hid the soul of the night.

I drift in my canoe down the Queset Brook and I listen, ears alert, like an animal that sniffs a meal or a threat on the wind. I am not sure what it is that I want to hear out of all this silence, out of this palpable absence of sound. A scrawny cry, perhaps, to use a phrase of the poet Wallace Stevens: "A scrawny cry from outside . . . a chorister whose c preceded the choir . . . still far away." Is that too much to hope for? I don't ask for the full ringing of the bell. I don't ask for a clap of thunder that would rend the veil in the temple. A scrawny cry will do, from far off there among the willows and the cattails, from far off there among the galaxies.

The child sent flying by the young man on the skateboard bounced on the pavement and lay still. The pigeons froze against the gray sky. Promenaders turned to stone. How long was it that the child's body lay there like a piece of crumpled newspaper? How long did my heart thrash silently in my chest like the clapper of a bell in a vacuum? Perhaps it was a minute, perhaps only a fraction of a second. Then the world's old rhythms began again. A crowd gathered. Someone lifted the injured child into his arms and rushed with the mother toward help. Gawkers milled about distractedly and dispersed. The clamor of the city engulfed the Common. Traffic moved again on Beacon Street.

RICHARD K. NELSON
B. 1941

Anthropology, when carried out with the sympathetic and imaginative intensity of a writer like Richard Nelson, expands the English tradition of nature writing. It opens up an Anglo-American worldview to a new possibility of identification with animals, and broadens our definition of culture within the circling of the seasons. Nelson has often lived and studied with Northern peoples over the past twenty years and has, in books such as Make Prayers to the Raven *(1983), connected descriptions of the cycle of water and light in that challenging terrain with the myths and techniques through which the native peoples have both endured and deepened their wisdom in the land. Increasingly, the key for him has been the hunting through which peoples like the Koyukon have confirmed their kinship with all of life. Through hunting Nelson too has learned a sacramental approach to the taking of life. It is a gift from the animal, the transmission of life and beauty in the future of our planet.*

THE GIFTS

Cold, clear, and calm in the pale blue morning. Snow on the high peaks brightening to amber. The bay a sheet of gray glass beneath a faint haze of steam. A November sun rises with the same fierce, chill stare of an owl's eye.

I stand at the window watching the slow dawn, and my mind fixes on the island. Nita comes softly down the stairs as I pack gear and complain

On Nature (San Francisco: North Point Press, 1987).

of having slept too late for these short days. A few minutes later, Ethan trudges out onto the cold kitchen floor, barefoot and half asleep. We do not speak directly about hunting, to avoid acting proud or giving offense to the animals. I say only that I will go to the island and look around; Ethan says only that he would rather stay at home with Nita. I wish he would come along so I could teach him things, but know it will be quieter in the woods with just the dog.

They both wave from the window as I ease the skiff away from shore, crunching through cakes of freshwater ice the tide has carried in from Salmon River. It is a quick run through Windy Channel and out onto the freedom of the Sound, where the slopes of Mt. Sarichef bite cleanly into the frozen sky. The air stings against my face, but the rest of me is warm inside thick layers of clothes. Shungnak whines, paces, and looks over the gunwale toward the still-distant island.

Broad swells looming off the Pacific alternately lift the boat and drop it between smooth-walled canyons of water. Midway across the Sound a dark line of wind descends swiftly from the north, and within minutes we are surrounded by whitecaps. There are two choices: either beat straight up into them or cut an easier angle across the waves and take the spray. I vacillate for a while, then choose the icy spray over the intense pounding. Although I know it is wrong to curse the wind, I do it anyway.

A kittiwake sweeps over the water in great, vaulting arcs, its wings flexed against the touch and billow of the air. As it tilts its head passing over the boat, I think how clumsy and foolish we must look. The island's shore lifts slowly in dark walls of rock and timber that loom above the apron of snow-covered beach. As I approach the shelter of Low Point, the chop fades and the swell is smaller. I turn up along the lee, running between the kelp beds and the surf, straining my eyes for deer that may be feeding at the tide's edge.

Near the end of the point is a narrow gut that opens to a small, shallow anchorage. I ease the boat between the rocks, with lines of surf breaking close on either side. The waves rise and darken, their sharp edges sparkle in the sun, then long manes of spray whirl back as they turn inside out and pitch onto the shallow reef. The anchor slips down through ten feet of crystal water to settle among the kelp fronds and urchin-covered rocks. On a strong ebb the boat would go dry here, but today's tide change is only six feet. Before launching the punt I meticulously glass the broad, rocky shore and the sprawls of brown grass along the timber's edge. A tight bunch of rock sandpipers flashes up from the shingle and an otter loops along the windows of drift logs, but there is no sign of deer. I can't help feeling a little anxious, because the season is drawing short and our year's supply of meat is not yet in. Throughout the fall, deer have been unusually wary, haunting the dense underbrush and slipping away at the least disturbance. I've come near a few, but these were young ones that I stalked only for the luxury of seeing them from close range.

Watching deer is the same pleasure now that it was when I was younger, when I loved animals only with my eyes and judged hunting to be outside the bounds of morality. Later, I tried expressing this love through studies of zoology, but this only seemed to put another kind of barrier between humanity and nature—the detachment of science and abstraction. Then, through anthropology, I encountered the entirely different views of nature found in other cultures. The hunting peoples were most fascinating because they had achieved deepest intimacy with their wild surroundings and had made natural history the focus of their lives. At the age of twenty-two, I went to live with Eskimos on the arctic coast of Alaska. It was my first year away from home, I had scarcely held a rifle in my hands, and the Eskimos—who call themselves the Real People—taught me their hunter's way.

The experience of living with Eskimos made very clear the direct, physical connectedness between all humans and the environments they draw existence from. Some years later, living with Koyukon Indians in Alaska's interior, I encountered a rich new dimension of that connectedness, and it profoundly changed my view of the world. Traditional Koyukon people follow a code of moral and ethical behavior that keeps a hunter in right relationship to the animals. They teach that all of nature is spiritual and aware, that it must be treated with respect, and that humans should approach the living world with restraint and humility. Now I struggle to learn if these same principles can apply in my own life and culture. Can we borrow from an ancient wisdom to structure a new relationship between ourselves and the environment? Or is Western society irreversibly committed to the illusion that humanity is separate from and dominant over the natural world?

A young bald eagle watches nervously from the peak of a tall hemlock as we bob ashore in the punt. Finally the bird lurches out, scoops its wings full of dense, cold air, and soars away beyond the line of trees. While I trudge up the long tide flat with the punt, Shungnak prances excitedly back and forth hunting for smells. The upper reaches are layered and slabbed with ice; slick cobbles shine like steel in the sun; frozen grass crackles underfoot. I lean the punt on a snow-covered log, pick up my rifle and small pack, and slip through the leafless alders into the forest.

My eyes take a moment adjusting to the sudden darkness, the deep green of boughs, and the somber, shadowy trunks. I feel safe and hidden here. The entire forest floor is covered with deep moss that should sponge gently beneath my feet. But today the softness is gone: frozen moss crunches with each step and brittle twigs snap, ringing out in the crisp air like strangers' voices. It takes a while to get used to this harshness in a forest that is usually so velvety and wet and silent. I listen to the clicking of gusts in the high branches and think that winter has come upon us like a fist.

At the base of a large nearby tree is a familiar patch of white—a scatter of deer bones—ribs, legs, vertebrae, two pelvis bones, and two skulls with half-bleached antlers. I put them here last winter, saying they were for the other animals, to make clear that they were not being thoughtlessly wasted. The scavengers soon picked them clean, the deer mice have gnawed them, and eventually they will be absorbed into the forest again. Koyukon elders say it shows respect, putting animal bones back in a clean, wild place instead of throwing them away with trash or scattering them in a garbage dump. The same obligations of etiquette that bind us to our human community also bind us to the natural community we live within.

Shungnak follows closely as we work our way back through a maze of windfalls, across clear disks of frozen ponds, and around patches of snow beneath openings in the forest canopy. I step and wait, trying to make no sound, knowing we could see deer at any moment. Deep snow has driven them down off the slopes and they are sure to be distracted with the business of the mating season.

We pick our way up the face of a high, steep scarp, then clamber atop a fallen log for a better view ahead. I peer into the semi-open understory of twiggy bushes, probing each space with my eyes. A downy woodpecker's call sparks from a nearby tree. Several minutes pass. Then a huckleberry branch moves, barely twitches, without the slightest noise . . . not far ahead.

Amid the scramble of brush where my eyes saw nothing a few minutes ago, a dim shape materializes, as if its own motion had created it. A doe steps into an open space, deep brown in her winter coat, soft and striking and lovely, dwarfed among the great trees, lifting her nose, looking right toward me. For perhaps a minute we are motionless in each other's gaze; then her head jerks to the left, her ears twitch back and forth, her tail flicks up, and she turns away in the stylized gait deer always use when alarmed.

Quick as a breath, quiet as a whisper, the doe glides off into the forest. Sometimes when I see a deer this way I know it is real at the moment, but afterward it seems like a daydream.

As we work our way back into the woods, I keep hoping for another look at her and thinking that a buck might have been following nearby. Any deer is legal game and I could almost certainly have taken her, but I would rather wait for a larger buck and let the doe bring on next year's young. Shungnak savors the ghost of her scent that hangs in the still air, but she has vanished.

Farther on, the snow deepens to a continuous cover beneath smaller trees, and we cross several sets of deer tracks, including some big prints with long toe drags. The snow helps to muffle our steps, but it is hard to see very far because the bushes are heavily loaded with powder. The thicket becomes a latticed maze of white on black, every branch hung and spangled in a thick fur of jeweled snow. We move through it like eagles cleaving between tumbled columns of cloud. New siftings occasionally drift down when the treetops are touched by the breeze.

Slots between the trunks up ahead shiver with blue where a muskeg opens. I angle toward it, feeling no need to hurry, picking every footstep carefully, stopping often to stare into the dizzying crannies, listening for any splinter of sound, keeping my senses tight and concentrated. A raven calls from high above the forest, and as I catch a glimpse of it an old question runs through my mind: Is this only the bird we see, or does it have the power and awareness Koyukon elders speak of? It lifts and plays on the wind far aloft, then folds up and rolls halfway over, a strong sign of luck in hunting. Never mind the issue of knowing; we should assume that power is here and let ourselves be moved by it.

I turn to look at Shungnak, taking advantage of her sharper hearing and magical sense of smell. She lifts her nose to the fresh but nebulous scent of several deer that have moved through here this morning. I watch her little radar ears, waiting for her to focus in one direction and hold it, hoping to see her body tense as it does when something moves nearby. But so far she only hears the twitching of red squirrels on dry bark. Shungnak and I have very different opinions of the squirrels. They excite her more than any other animal because she believes she will catch one someday. But for the hunter they are deceptive spurts of movement and sound, and their sputtering alarm calls alert the deer.

We approach a low, abrupt rise, covered with obscuring brush and curtained with snow. A lift of wind hisses in the high trees, then drops away and leaves us in near-complete silence. I pause to choose a path through a scramble of blueberry bushes and little windfalls ahead, then glance back at Shungnak. She has her eyes and ears fixed off toward our left, almost directly across the current of breeze. She stands very stiff, quivering slightly, leaning forward as if she has already started to run but cannot release her muscles. I shake my finger at her as a warning to stay.

I listen as closely as possible, but hear nothing. I work my eyes into every dark crevice and slot among the snowy branches, but see nothing. I stand perfectly still and wait, then look again at Shungnak. Her head turns so slowly that I can barely detect the movement, until finally she is looking straight ahead. Perhaps it is just another squirrel. . . . I consider taking a few steps for a better view.

Then I see it.

A long, dark body appears among the bushes, moving deliberately upwind, so close I can scarcely believe I didn't see it earlier. Without looking away, I carefully slide the breech closed and lift the rifle to my shoulder, almost certain that a deer this size will be a buck. Shungnak, now forgotten behind me, must be contorted with the suppressed urge to give chase.

The deer walks easily, silently, along the little rise, never looking our way. Then he makes a sharp turn straight toward us. Thick tines of his antlers curve over the place where I have the rifle aimed. Koyukon elders teach that animals will come to those who have shown them respect, and will allow themselves to be taken in what is only a temporary death. At a moment like this, it is easy to sense that despite my abiding doubt there is a shared world beyond the one we know directly, a world the Koyukon people empower with spirits, a world that demands recognition and exacts a price from those who ignore it.

This is a very large buck. It comes so quickly that I have no chance to shoot, and then it is so close that I haven't the heart to do it. Fifty feet away, the deer lowers his head almost to the ground and lifts a slender branch that blocks his path. Snow shakes down onto his neck and clings to the fur of his shoulders as he slips underneath. Then he half-lifts his head and keeps coming. I ease the rifle down to watch, wondering how much closer he will get. Just now he makes a long, soft rutting call, like the bleating of a sheep except lower and more hollow. His hooves tick against dry twigs hidden by the snow.

In the middle of a step he raises his head all the way up, and he sees me standing there—a stain against the pure white of the forest. A sudden spasm runs through his entire body, his front legs jerk apart, and he freezes all akimbo, head high, nostrils flared, coiled and hard. I can only look at him and wait, my mind snarled with irreconcilable emotions. Here is a perfect buck deer. In the Koyukon way, he has come to me; but in my own he has come too close. I am as congealed and transfixed as he is, as devoid of conscious thought. It is as if my mind has ceased to function and I only have eyes.

But the buck has no choice. He suddenly unwinds in a burst of ignited energy, springs straight up from the snow, turns in mid-flight, stabs the frozen earth again, and makes four great bounds off to the left. His thick body seems to float, relieved of its own weight, as if a deer has the power to unbind itself from gravity.

The same deeper impulse that governs the flight of a deer governs the predator's impulse to pursue it. I watch the first leaps without moving a muscle. Then, not pausing for an instant of deliberation, I raise the rifle back to my shoulder, follow the movement of the deer's fleeing form, and wait until it stops to stare back. Almost at that instant, still moving without conscious thought, freed of the ambiguities that held me before, now no less animal than the animal I watch, my hands warm and steady and certain, acting from a more elemental sense than the ones that brought me to this meeting, I carefully align the sights and let go the sudden power.

The gift of the deer falls like a feather in the snow. And the rifle's sound has rolled off through the timber before I hear it.

I walk to the deer, now shaking a bit with swelling emotion. Shungnak is beside it already, whining and smelling, racing from one side to the other, stuffing her nose down in snow full of scent. She looks off into the brush, searching back and forth, as if the deer that ran is somewhere else, still running. She tries to lick at the blood that trickles down, but I stop her out of respect for the animal. Then, I suppose to consummate her own frustrated predatory energy, she takes a hard nip at its shoulder, shuns quickly away, and looks back as if she expects it to leap to its feet again.

As always, I whisper thanks to the animal for giving itself to me. The words are my own, not something I have learned from the Koyukon. Their elders might say that the words we use in prayer to spirits of the natural world do not matter. Nor, perhaps, does it matter what form these spirits take in our own thoughts. What truly matters is only that prayer be made, to affirm our humility in the presence of nurturing power. Most of humanity throughout history has said prayers to the powers of surrounding nature, which they have recognized as their source of life. Surely it is not too late to recover this ancestral wisdom.

It takes a few minutes before I settle down inside and can begin the other work. Then I hang the deer with rope strung over a low branch and back twice through pulley-loops. I cut away the dark, pungent scent glands on its legs, and next make a careful incision along its belly, just large enough to reach the warm insides. The stomach and intestines come easily and cleanly; I cut through the diaphragm, and there is a hollow sound as the lungs pull free. Placing them on the soft snow, I whisper that these parts are left here for the other animals. Shungnak wants to take some for herself but I tell her to keep away. It is said that the life and awareness leaves an animal's remains slowly, and there are rules about what should be eaten by a dog. She will have her share of the scraps later on, when more of the life is gone.

After the blood has drained out, I sew the opening shut with a piece of line to keep the insides clean, and then toggle the deer's forelegs through a slit in the hind leg joint, so it can be carried like a pack. I am barely strong enough to get it up onto my back, but there is plenty of time to work slowly toward the beach, stopping often to rest and cool down. During one of these stops I hear two ravens in an agitated exchange of croaks and gurgles, and I wonder if those black eyes have already spotted the remnants. No pure philanthropist, the raven gives a hunter luck only as a way of creating luck for himself.

Finally, I push through the low boughs of the beachside trees and ease my burden down. Afternoon sun throbs off the water, but a chill north wind takes all warmth from it. Little gusts splay in dark patterns across the anchorage; the boat paces on its mooring line; the Sound is racing with whitecaps. I take a good rest, watching a fox sparrow flit among the drift logs and a bunch of crows hassling over some bit of food at the water's edge.

Though I feel utterly satisfied, grateful, and contented, there is much to do and the day will slope away quickly. We are allowed more than one deer, so I will stay on the island for another look around tomorrow. It takes two trips to get everything out to the skiff, then we head up the shore toward the little cabin and secure anchorage at Bear Creek. By the time the boat is unloaded and tied off, the wind has faded and a late afternoon chill sinks down in the pitched, hard shadow of Sarichef.

Half-dry wood hisses and sputters, giving way reluctantly to flames in the rusted stove. It is nearly dusk when I bring the deer inside and set to work on it. Better to do this now than to wait, in case tomorrow is another day of luck. The animal hangs from a low beam, dim-lit by the kerosene lamp. I feel strange in its presence, as if it still watches, still glows with something of its life, still demands that nothing be done or spoken carelessly. A hunter should never let himself be deluded by pride or a false sense of dominance. It is not through our own power that we take life in nature; it is through the power of nature that life is given to us.

The soft hide peels away slowly from shining muscles, and the inner perfection of the deer's body is revealed. Koyukon and Eskimo hunters teach a refined art of taking an animal into its component parts, easing blades through crisp cartilage where bone joins bone, following the body's own design until it is disarticulated. There is no ugliness in it, only hands moving in concert with the beauty of an animal's making. Perhaps we have been too removed from this to understand, and we have lost touch with the process of one life being passed on to another. As my hands work inside the deer, it is as if something has already begun to flow into me.

When the work is finished, I take two large slices from the hind quarter and put them in a pan atop the now-crackling stove. In a separate pot, I boil scraps of meat and fat for Shungnak, who has waited with as much patience as possible for a husky raised in a hunter's team up north. When the meat is finished cooking I sit on a sawed log and eat straight from the pan.

A meal could not be simpler, more satisfying, or more directly a part of the living process. I wish Ethan was here to share it, and I would explain to him again that when we eat the deer its flesh is then our flesh. The deer changes form and becomes us, and we in turn become creatures made of deer. Each time we eat the deer we should remember it and feel gratitude for what it has given us. And each time, we should carry a thought like a prayer inside: "Thanks to the animal and to all that made it—the island and the forest, the air, and the rain . . ." We should remember that in the course of things, we are all generations of deer and of the earth-life that feeds us.

Warm inside my sleeping bag, I let the fire ebb away to coals. The lamp is out. The cabin roof creaks in the growing cold. I drift toward sleep, feeling pleased that there is no moon, so the deer will wait until dawn to feed. On the floor beside me, Shungnak jerks and whimpers in her dog's dreams.

Next morning we are in the woods with the early light. We follow yesterday's tracks, and just beyond the place of the buck, a pair of does drifts at the edge of sight and disappears. For an hour we angle north, then come slowly back somewhat deeper in the woods, moving crosswise to a growing easterly breeze. In two separate places, deer snort and pound away, invisible beyond a shroud of brush. Otherwise there is nothing.

Sometime after noon we come to a narrow muskeg with scattered lodgepole pines and a ragged edge of bushy, low-growing cedar. I squint against the sharp glare of snow. It has that peculiar look of old powder, a bit settled and touched by wind, very lovely but without the airy magic of a fresh fall. I gaze up the muskeg's easy slope, and above the encroaching wall of timber, seamed against the deep blue sky, is the brilliant peak of Sarichef with a great plume of snow streaming off in what must be a shuddering gale. It has a contradictory look of absoluteness and unreality about it, like a Himalayan summit suspended in mid-air over the saddle of a low ridge.

I move very slowly up the muskeg's east side, away from the breeze and in the sun's full warmth. Deer tracks crisscross the opening, but none of the animals stopped here to feed. Next to the bordering trees, the tracks follow a single, hard-packed trail, showing the deers' preference for cover. Shungnak keeps her nose to the thickly scented snow. We come across a pine sapling that a buck has torn with his antlers, scattering twigs and flakes of bark all around. But his tracks are hardened, frosted, and lack sharpness, so they are at least a day old.

We slip through a narrow point of trees, then follow the open edge again, pausing long moments between each footstep. A mixed tinkle of crossbills and siskins moves through the high timber, and a squirrel rattles from deep in the woods, too far off to be scolding us. Shungnak begins to pick up a strong ribbon of scent, but she hears nothing. I stop for several minutes to study the muskeg's long, raveled fringe, the tangle of shade and thicket, the glaze of mantled boughs.

Then my eye barely catches a fleck of movement up ahead, near the ground and almost hidden behind the trunk of a leaning pine, perhaps a squirrel's tail or a bird. I lift my hand slowly to shade the sun, stand dead still, and wait to see if something is there. Finally it moves again.

At the very edge of the trees, almost out of sight in a little swale, small and furry and bright-tinged, turning one direction and then another, is the funnel of a single ear. Having seen this, I soon make out the other ear and the slope of a doe's forehead. Her neck is behind the leaning pine, but on the other side I can barely see the soft, dark curve of her back above the snow. She is comfortably bedded, gazing placidly into the distance, chewing her cud.

Shungnak has stopped twenty yards behind me in the point of trees and has no idea about the deer. I shake my finger at her until she lays her ears back and sits. Then I watch the doe again. She is fifty yards ahead of me, ten yards beyond the leaning tree, and still looking off at an angle. Her left eye is clearly visible and she refuses to turn her head away, so it might be impossible to get any closer. Perhaps I should just wait here, in case a buck is attending her nearby. But however improbable it might be under these circumstances, a thought is lodged in my mind: I can get near her.

My first step sinks down softly, but the second makes a loud budging sound. She snaps my way, stops chewing, and stares for several minutes. It seems hopeless, especially out here in an open field of crisp snow with only the narrow treetrunk for a screen. But she slowly turns away and starts to chew again. I move just enough so the tree blocks her eye and the rest of her head, but I can still see her ears. Every time she chews they shake just a bit, so I can watch them and step when her hearing is obscured by the sound of her own jaws.

Either this works or the deer has decided to ignore me, because after a short while I am near enough so the noise of my feet has to reach her easily. She should have jumped up and run long ago, but instead she lays there in serene repose. I deliberate on every step, try for the softest snow, wait long minutes before the next move, stalking like a cat toward ambush. I watch beyond her, into the surrounding shadows and across to the muskeg's farther edge, for the shape of a buck deer; but there is nothing. I feel ponderous, clumsy-footed, out-of-place, inimical. I should turn and run away, take fear on the deer's behalf, flee the mirrored image in my mind. But I clutch the cold rifle at my side and creep closer.

The wind refuses to blow and my footsteps seem like thunder in the still sunshine. But the doe only turns once to look my way, without even pointing her ears toward me, then stares off and begins to chew again.

I am ten feet from the leaning tree. My heart pounds so hard, I think those enchanted ears should hear the rush of blood in my temples. Yet a strange certainty has come into me, a quite unmystical confidence. Perhaps she has decided I am another deer, a buck attracted by her musk or a doe feeding gradually toward her. My slow pace and lapses of stillness would not seem human. For myself, I have lost awareness of elapsed time; I have no feeling of patience or impatience. It is as if the deer has moved slowly toward me on a cloud of snow, and I am adrift in the pure motion of experience.

I take the last step to the trunk of the leaning pine. It is bare of branches, scarcely wider than my hand, but perfectly placed to break my odd profile. There is no hope of getting any closer, so I slowly poke my head out to watch. She has an ideal spot: screened from the wind, warmed by the sun, and with a clear view of the muskeg. I can see muscles working beneath the close fur of her jaw, the rise and fall of her side each time she breathes, the shining edge of her ebony eye.

I hold absolutely still, but her body begins to stiffen, she lifts her head higher, and her ears twitch anxiously. Then instead of looking at me she turns her face to the woods, shifting her ears toward a sound I cannot hear. A few seconds later, the unmistakable voice of a buck drifts up, strangely disembodied, as if it comes from an animal somewhere underneath the snow. I huddle as close to the tree as I can, press against the hard, dry bark, and peek out around its edge.

There is a gentle rise behind the doe, scattered with sapling pines and clusters of juniper bushes. A rhythmic crunching of snow comes invisibly from the slope, then a bough shakes . . . and a buck walks easily into the open sunshine.

Focusing his attention completely on the doe, he comes straight toward her and never sees my intrusive shape just beyond. He slips through a patch of small trees, stops a few feet from where she lies, lowers his head and stretches it toward her, then holds this odd pose for a long moment. She reaches her muzzle out to one side, trying to find his scent. When he starts to move up behind her she stands quickly, bends her body into a strange sideways arc, and stares back at him. A moment later she walks off a bit, lifts her tail, and puts droppings in her tracks. The buck moves to the warm ground of her bed and lowers his nose to the place where her female scent is strongest.

Inching like a reptile on a cold rock, I have stepped out from the tree and let my whole menacing profile become visible. The deer are thirty feet away and stand well apart, so they can both see me easily. I am a hunter hovering near his prey and a watcher craving inhuman love, torn between the deepest impulses, hot and shallow-breathed and seething with unreconciled intent, hidden from opened eyes that look into the nimbus of sun and see nothing but the shadow they have chosen for themselves. In this shadow now, the hunter has vanished and only the watcher remains.

Drawn by the honey of the doe's scent, the buck steps quickly toward her. And now the most extraordinary thing happens. The doe turns away from him and walks straight for me. There is no hesitation, only a wild deer coming along the trail of hardened snow where the other deer have passed, the trail in which I stand at this moment. She raises her head, looks at me, and steps without hesitation.

My existence is reduced to a pair of eyes; a rush of unbearable heat flushes through my cheeks; and a sense of absolute certainly fuses in my mind.

The snow blazes so brightly that my head aches. The deer is a dark form growing larger. I look up at the buck, half embarrassed, as if to apologize that she has chosen me over him. He stares at her for a moment, turns to follow, then stops and watches anxiously. I am struck by how gently her narrow hooves touch the trail, how little sound they make as she steps, how thick the fur is on her flank and shoulder, how unfathomable her eyes look. I am consumed with a sense of her perfect elegance in the brilliant light. And then I am lost again in the whirling intensity of experience.

The doe is now ten feet from me. She never pauses or looks away. Her feet punch down mechanically into the snow, coming closer and closer, until they are less than a yard from my own. Then she stops, stretches her neck calmly toward me, and lifts her nose.

There is not the slightest question in my mind, as if this was certain to happen and I have known all along exactly what to do. I slowly raise my hand and reach out . . .

And my fingers touch the soft, dry, gently needling fur on top of the deer's head, and press down to the living warmth of flesh underneath.

She makes no move and shows no fear, but I can feel the flaming strength and tension that flow in her wild body as in no other animal I have ever touched. Time expands and I am suspended in the clear reality of that moment.

Then, by the flawed conditioning of a lifetime among fearless domesticated things, I instinctively drop my hand and let the deer smell it. Her dark nose, wet and shining, touches gently against my skin at the exact instant I realize the absoluteness of my error. And a jolt runs through her entire body as she realizes hers. Her muscles seize and harden; she seems to wrench her eyes away from me but her body remains, rigid and paralyzed. Having been deceived by her other senses, she keeps her nose tight against my hand for one more moment.

Then all the energy inside her triggers in a series of exquisite bounds. She flings out over the hummocks of snow-covered moss, suspended in effortless flight like fog blown over the muskeg in a gale. Her body leaps with such power that the muscles should twang aloud like a bowstring; the earth should shudder and drum; but I hear no sound. In the center of the muskeg she stops to look back, as if to confirm what must seem impossible. The buck follows in more earthbound undulations; they dance away together, and I am left in the meeting-place alone.

There is a blur of rushing feet behind me. No longer able to restrain herself, Shungnak dashes past, buries her nose in the soft tracks, and then looks back to ask if we can run after them. I had completely forgotten her, sitting near enough to watch the whole encounter, somehow resisting what must have been a prodigious urge to explode in chase. When I reach out to hug her, she smells the hand that touched the deer. And it seems as if it happened long ago.

For the past year I have kept a secret dream, that I would someday come close enough to touch a deer on this island. But since the idea came it seemed harder than ever to get near them. Now, totally unexpected and in a strange way, it has happened. Was the deer caught by some reckless twinge of curiosity? Had she never encountered a human on this wild island? Did she yield to some odd amorous confusion? I really do not care. I would rather accept this as pure experience and not give in to the notion that everything must be explained.

Nor do I care to think that I was chosen to see some manifestation of power, because I have little tolerance for such dreams of self-importance. I have never asked that nature open any doors to reveal the truth of spirit or mystery; I aspire to no shaman's path; I expect no visions, no miracles except the ones that fill every instant of ordinary life.

But there are vital lessons in the experience of moments such as these, if we live them in the light of wisdom taken from the earth and shaped by generations of elders. Two deer came and gave the choices to me. One deer I took and we will now share a single body. The other deer I touched and we will now share that moment. These events could be seen as opposites, but they are in fact identical. Both are founded in the same principles, the same relationship, the same reciprocity.

Move slowly, stay quiet, watch carefully . . . and be ever humble. Never show the slightest arrogance or disrespect. Koyukon elders would explain, in words quite different from my own, that I moved into two moments of grace, or what they would call luck. This is the source of success for a hunter or a watcher, not skill, not cleverness, not guile. Something is only given in nature, never taken.

I have heard the elders say that everything in nature has its own spirit and possesses a power beyond ours. There is no way to prove them right or wrong, though the beauty and interrelatedness of things should be evidence enough. We need not ask for shining visions as proof, or for a message from a golden deer glowing in the sky of our dreams. Above all else, we should assume that power moves in the world around us and act accordingly. If it is a myth, then spirit is within the myth and we should live by it. And if there is a commandment to follow, it is to approach all of earth-life, of which we are a part, with humility and respect.

Well soaked and shivering from a rough trip across the Sound, we pull into the dark waters of the bay. Sunset burns on Twin Peaks and the spindled ridge of Antler Mountain. The little house is warm with lights that shimmer on the calm near shore. I see Nita looking from the window and Ethan dashes out to wait by the tide, pitching rocks at the mooring buoy. He strains to see inside the boat, knowing that a hunter who tells his news aloud may offend the animals by sounding boastful. But when he sees the deer his excited voice seems to roll up and down the mountainside.

He runs for the house with Shungnak, carrying a load of gear, and I know he will burst inside with the news. Ethan, joyous and alive, boy made of deer.

ROBERT FINCH
B. 1943

As a Cape Cod nature writer, Robert Finch lives and works at the confluence of powerful currents. Henry Thoreau, Henry Beston, and John Hay have all testified to the revelations of sky and dunes in that sea-surrounded land. Finch's own three books about the Cape, Common Ground *(1981),* The Primal Place *(1983), and* Outlands *(1986), perpetuate this rich tradition. But when he writes about natural processes that have been memorably evoked by his predecessors, Finch imparts his own contemporary slant. Though he has been active as an environmentalist, his books do not draw bitter lines between the older tides of nature and the current boom of tourism and construction. Rather, Finch is a writer who discovers and conveys saving continuities. Pausing amid the bustling tourist commerce of Chatham, just after he has returned from a solitary week on a barrier beach, he can describe himself as "content to be where I am, standing in that place of migrations and appetites."*

WHAT THE STONES SAID

(FOR THE CHATHAM CHORALE)

> I would know my shadow and my light,
> So shall I at last be whole.
> —Sir Michael Tippett,
> A Child of Our Time

On Thursday night, following choir practice, I drove back by way of Nickerson State Park. I was in no rush to get home. "Hill Street Blues" was a repeat, and I was still full of the music and words of Tippett's oratorio, awed by his power to forge such deep beauty out of the world's

Outlands: Journeys to the Outer Edges of Cape Cod (Boston: David R. Godine, 1986).

terror and suffering during those first dark years of World War II in England.

So I turned off into the park and drove down the unlit winding road to the small boat landing on the shores of Cliff Pond. Despite recent rains, the water level in the pond was still down, leaving a wide band of exposed beach around its perimeter. It was a clear, calm night, a few degrees below freezing, the full moon quarter-risen above the surrounding rim of dark, undulating hills. From the southeast, distant but clearly audible, came the sounds of rock music being played loudly on a radio—a car radio, I guessed, parked in one of the campgrounds somewhere beyond the pond. It varied in volume and carried cleanly through the night, though somehow I did not find it obtrusive. It sounded as if the dark hills themselves were singing.

> The world turns on its dark side.
> It is winter.

Though it had dropped below freezing for the past several nights, the broad waters of Cliff Pond remained unfrozen and almost perfectly still. They mirrored, in moonlight, the low, dark hills on the far western shore like a statement of perfect peace and contentment, the fulfilled stillness of a long, hushed, fermataed closing chord.

I walked the perimeter of the pond, something over two and a half miles, in about an hour, and during the entire circuit I neither saw nor heard a single wintering duck on its surface, not out in its center, not in the long southern coves, not even in any of the little cut-off side ponds. It was as though the pond had dismissed them, and all animated life, in order to make this pure statement of itself, unblurred by any moving details.

This is the hardest of all sounds in nature to hear: the silent assertion of a landscape itself. It requires a rare confluence of moods—clarity on nature's part, receptiveness on our own—a suspension of normal expectations and a relaxed extension of our senses, to feel such deep vibrations.

I walked south, clockwise around the pond, along an exposed shore several yards wide. The recent rains seemed to have sunk in, and the water level to have receded again, leaving a hardened, slick path of frozen ground around its rim. In the shallow water along the shore only the reflection of a single star, jiggling slowly up and down as though on an elastic string, betrayed any agitation in the pond.

Looking up, I found the star's original counterpart in the sky above the southern coves: the blinking, ice-blue chip of Sirius. To its right the faint outline of Orion rose late above the hills, as though weary and drained by his nightly climbs through the winter skies. Even Sirius was somewhat paled by the moonlight, though quite near it an even brighter star—Jupiter or Venus—shone in companionable splendor. It was the day after planetary syzygy, the day after the end of the world. Along the crest of the hills the bone-white disk of the moon sliced through the stiff pines.

> Man has measured the heavens with a telescope,
> driven the gods from their thrones.
> But the soul, the soul watching the chaotic mirror,
> knows that the Gods return.

The moonlight, rather than illuminating, seemed to cloak the visible world, reducing everything to vague, generalized outlines. By contrast, the world of sound seemed to sharpen and clarify as I walked. I became more conscious of my feet, especially along the rocky or cobbled shores that characterize the northeastern corners of the coves, their stones driven or plowed up onto the beaches by northwest wind and ice. Beneath my steps, the stones seemed like voices, human voices, struck into sound by my passage. The larger, bread-loaf-sized stones uttered mute complaints and silent groans, as though the compact and compressed history of their existence, normally quelled by day and smothered with water, were released by the dead moonlight.

We all believe as children, and sometimes later, that the earth is quick with unperceived life, released at night. As the sun's warmth quickens that which moves and grows by day, so to human imagination the moon's cold light gives life to inanimate forms, to rocks, stones, and sticks. Now its perfect, passive illumination seemed to release the voice, the implicit eloquence of shape and endless transformation inherent in all unmoving, moved things.

Deep in the long coves there were stretches of smaller stones along the beach, ones only slightly larger than pebbles, that virtually startled me with their panicky excitement as I passed. Farther up on the beach a group of larger rocks, small boulders really, their tops partially hoary with lichen, held aloof counsel together. They made me feel like an eavesdropper, and I could almost hear them pause in their conversation as I passed.

> The dark forces rise like a flood.
> Men's hearts are heavy: they cry for peace.

Strewn here and there along the exposed shore were sections of dead pine trunks I had never noticed before, barkless and supine beneath the moon. Drowned and felled in a time of high water past, they too seemed to cry out in agony, like tortured shapes. One long section, spiked with short broken-off branches, looked like some giant upturned caterpillar. Yet at the same time the sinuous musculature of its silvered grain stood out expressively in the moonlight and gave it the aspect of a human torso, truncate of limbs and arching up from the cold stones, so that I found myself turning away from its naked suffering.

I was amazed at how many times I must have passed these shapes, unremarked, by day. Now I could not bear to look closely at them, so piteously did they cry out.

Along the northeastern point of the westernmost cove someone had lifted some of the rocks and piled them in a line to form a short miniature jetty that protruded a few feet down into the water. It ran out like a short play, but one that used real people for actors, and it was silent. To the north, on the ridge across the pond, the state forestry camp glowed soundlessly like some distant hill city. At the head of the cove I rang the branches of a shrubby swamp maple growing along the shore; they clacked icily, but said nothing.

Then a curious thing happened. As I looked up again at Sirius, I noticed a bright reddish star below it that had not been there earlier. Mars, I thought; but it was much brighter than Mars. After a minute or two I realized that the star was moving perceptibly, though not visibly—like the minute hand of a clock—in relation to Sirius, gradually rising and at last gaining ascendancy over it. A satellite, I thought, probably Communist.

I remembered, twenty years ago, how we went outside to watch the first *Sputniks* and *Telstars,* how fascinated we were to see these new stars moving so swiftly against the grain of the slow-wheeling night. We even danced to songs about them. Now I resented the smooth apparent motion of the satellite as a harbinger of a future sky cross-hatched and gridded over with man-made lights and weapons. It rose several degrees a minute, and was as bright as any star in the sky; yet when I looked again a few minutes later, it was gone.

> The cold deepens.
> The world descends into the icy waters,
> Where lies the jewel of great price.

Along the northwest shore of the pond, perhaps because it is more protected from the wind, the water at the edge was beginning to freeze.

In a ragged band anywhere from a few inches to several feet wide, the ice was extending its teeth out from the edge in Jack Frost window patterns. It was still just the barest film of ice, so thin that when I detached one of the newly formed shards and lifted it toward my mouth, it melted and fell from between my fingers, shattering into a billion bits on the hardened beach.

Earlier, along the open shores, I had played with the moon in the water, making its reflected disk skip along the smooth shore edge like a flat stone. Now I dragged its image through the burgeoning arsenal of ice growing in the water, ripping it through phalanxes of knives, fishbone spines, and jack-o'-lantern teeth.

> The words of wisdom are these:
> Winter cold means inner warmth,
> the secret nursery of the seed.

At last I was nearing the Big Rocks, a pair of enormous glacial erratics situated near the northwest corner of the pond. Normally the lower of the two boulders sits several feet in the water, but now both lay completely beached. I approached them with a growing anticipation mixed with apprehension. I could not conceive what profound cries or utterances such towering forms might make, and was ready to cover my ears, if necessary.

But unexpectedly, they did not speak at all. Rather, they *sang*—softly, with all the reserve of their great masses and strength: a high, falsetto song, arched and drawn out, such as great whales make, unheard by us, beneath their sea. It seemed not only to contain all previous sounds made by the rocks and fallen trees, but to carry the cry of all creation, deteriorating like a cherished face in the rain of time.

Their enormous, ice-rounded bulks moved through the night like the measures of their song. I followed them as far as I dared, and it seemed that if a wind had come up then, I might have been swept away for good.

I think it is only at times of such extraordinary outer calm, and inner fullness, that we hear such voices in nature. Remembered by day, they embarrass us, like disturbing dreams. We tell no one and make consicous efforts to forget them, nailing up lights on wooden crosses along such dark stretches of our thoroughfares, to prevent them from recurring.

We move through our days on a kind of automatic pilot, unaware of how tightly we hold ourselves in and apart from one another, how much stress and resistance are involved in keeping a steady course against the universal winds. But here, for an hour, all winds seemed to cease, the multifarious sounds they muffle were released, and nature's unstrung voices made themselves heard in the dark silence.

The moving waters renew the earth.
It is spring.

As I approached the landing, the spears of ice along the pond's edge gradually drew in and disappeared, and water once more met the shore. Now the slightest wind came up. Its moon-edged ripples were just barely visible out from shore, yet it was enough to cloud the pond surface, to silence the beach, and to keep the hills from answering themselves. From somewhere far off, in an unseen tree, a single crow cawed high and sharp, breaking the night.

PETER STEINHART
B. 1943

Peter Steinhart is a native of San Francisco who "grew up watching California's plum and mustard flowered valleys vanish under smog, concrete, and muttering haste." Nevertheless, he remains a Californian, who has taught at Stanford University and published a book, Tracks in the Sky *(1987), about the wildlife and wetlands of the Pacific Flyway. Author of the "Essay" column in* Audubon *magazine for the past decade, Steinhart has established himself as one of our finest journalistic interpreters of environmental and scientific ideas. What distinguishes his essays is the personal context and grace of language with which he explicates his topics, and his belief that "when we change nature we change our own hearts and minds."*

DREAMING ELANDS

Sometimes I dream about elands. They don't talk to me or leap over rooftops or turn into pretty damsels. They just lope silently along the horizon of a blue-skied plain. They are big, alert, and stately. They move like cows with their ancestral wildness and long-legged grace restored.

Audubon, March 1982.

That is how I saw elands long ago in Africa, and the dreams give me a feeling of satisfaction. But I don't know why I dream of them or what elands mean.

I do know, however, that we all dream and think in terms of animals. Leonardo da Vinci was beset by the dream of a vulture perched over his childhood crib. Modern Brazilians may choose lottery numbers on the basis of the animal seen in a recent dream. Malays believe being snakebit in a dream promises luck in love. Sometimes we dream half-animals, as when Alexander dreamed of a satyr dancing on his shield and so foresaw victory in his siege of Tyre. Or we think men into animals, turn Dr. Jekyll into Mr. Hyde or football players into apes to suggest psychological changes. Animals are far more fundamental to our thinking than we suppose. They are not just a part of the fabric of thought: they are a part of the loom.

Animals are what men use to wrap ideas into visible form. We can see it in the development of our own language. We make abstractions manifest by embodying them in animals, and our language is a vast, shadowy bestiary. We call muscles "muscles" because the Romans thought they resembled mice (Latin: *mus*) running under the skin. Erosion is what happens when rodents nibble on wood, a little at a time, out of sight and mind. An auspicious occasion is one in which the birds (Latin: *avis*) are seen (as in "spectate") to fly in the right direction. A person is said to be chubby because he resembles a fish that swims in the Thames River. A cynic is, in Greek, a surly dog. Sarcasm is the tearing of flesh, as by dogs, and the word transposes the snarl of the dog to the expression on our faces when we say something nasty. We are bullish and bearish, hawkish and dovelike, shrewish and bovine, busy as beavers, timid as rabbits, mad as hornets, sly as foxes.

Animals let us represent feelings that are otherwise undefinable. We can be happy as larks or cross as a bear. Freud noted that when children have family problems that are too threatening to deal with, they typically fantasize about animals. And if something strikes us as out of place, we are apt to mark it with a monster, an amalgam of animal forms which suggests the essential qualities of the conflict. A werewolf is half-human sociability, half-lupine hunger. Dragons are the evil we attribute to snakes, but magnified by wings, claws, and fire.

Once we nail concepts to animals, we arrange them into roadmaps of custom. In traditional societies, animal symbols preserved the rules of conduct. Classless societies kept the rules of marriage, inheritance, and authority in ancestral totems, which were generally wild animals. A man who traced his descent from the ancestral turtle might have a specific kind of relationship to a man who descended from the eagle. By thinking about the ecological and mythological relationships between totems, the people carried about in their minds their Constitutions and Magna Cartas.

Folktales continue this tradition. They contain rules for the use of love, power, and cooperation that we cannot fit into legal or religious documents. A people who celebrate foxes carry in their fables ideas about how the individual may challenge the will of the group. Modern animal stories, such as *Watership Down*, hold similar rules. And C. S. Lewis described the character of Badger in Kenneth Grahame's *Wind in the Willows* as an "extraordinary amalgam of high rank, coarse manners, gruffness, shyness, and goodness . . . The child who has once met Mr. Badger has ever afterwards in his bones a knowledge of humanity and of English social history which he could not get in any other way."

The tradition of keeping rules and ideas in animal form is rich even in modern societies. Our unreasoning fear of snakes hearkens back to an ancient notion that evil spirits live in the earth. We still put bird wings on angels. Athletic teams and military units select bears and bluejays as mascots. The industrial arm of this tradition uses animals to sell us detergents, beer, and the services of bankers. When we sell automobiles, for example, we offer as symbols hawks, mustangs, cougars, skylarks, and impalas. We sell no turkeys or Holsteins because they are not symbols of freedom, and we buy cars, above all, as engines of personal independence.

If advertising animals seems contrived, what children do with animals is not. Children love to name animals and explore the differences between them. My two-year-old daughter shouts with glee when she sees a horse. She delights in pictures of elephants and monkeys and turtles and wants to talk about their eyes, ears, and tails. Animals are part of her capacity for joy.

That joy is not simply a matter of fictitious companions and imaginary adventures. It is the joy of recognizing and understanding life outside of one's own form. It was programed into human childhood long ago. Traditional socieites encourage children to collect names, for as adults they must know many more animals and plants than they use for food and fiber. The Penobscot Indians, for example, classify snakes into genus and species but have no practical or ritual use for them. The Hanunóo of the Philippines know 1,800 plants, 500 more than botanists can find in their neighborhood. And when traditional children aren't looking at nature, they are fed animal images in myth and folklore.

Likewise, in modern life, we feed our children fables, give them teddy bears and rocking horses and embroider duckies and bunnies on their bibs. We encourage them to shout the names of animals as they wander through picture books and zoos. They play games like "Foxes and Geese," assuming alternately the roles of predator and prey, weak and strong.

All children thereby find special qualities in parrots, camels, or frogs, and the qualities become synonymous with the animal. We use such images as substitutes for people in our thoughts. People are too complex and too close to us to yield to such simplification. A wolf may always in our thoughts be a cunning killer. One's father may be a headhunter or a Congolese mercenary, but may nevertheless cry at weddings and be baffled by tax forms. Cunning is much clearer when we think of it as a wolf. And it is safer to talk of such things as greed or aggression in lions or bears than in a brother or a neighbor, for we can focus upon the quality without exposing our human relationships to conflict.

In all societies, animals give our children images of order and diversity. We are teaching them to think, not just about food on the table or fangs in the bushes, but about ourselves. We are teaching them to separate human qualities from human beings, but not from life. Animals thus enable us to add the reach of the eye to the reach of the heart. And that makes us braver and more patient with adversity in our own lives. It makes us better able to get along with one another.

Paul Shepard, professor of natural philosophy at Pitzer College, believes the human mind was shaped by the act of watching animals. In *Thinking Animals,* Shepard writes, "Animals are among the first inhabitants of the mind's eye. They are basic to the development of speech and thought . . . indispensable to our becoming human in the fullest sense."

Shepard believes animals are essential to the act of classification because they are lively and diverse. He notes that children also classify household tools, kinds of automobiles, and parts of things, but "with animals, the categories are all living. And a lively image is more potent." And animal forms tend to grade into one another, so that they test one's perceptions rigorously and require skill in making distinctions. Only animals fit the need, and, concludes Shepard, "From the standpoint of the developing brain, an assembly, say, of horselike animals—donkeys, tarpans, zebras, asses, and other groups of their odd-toed relatives—is as essential as blood."

The process of classifying animals, Shepard believes, is inborn and scheduled for the first twelve years of life. "That part of the young brain combining signals from vision, sound, and touch in the inferior parietal lobule physically matures, or becomes myelinated, with the end of childhood," he writes. "Names pass through a part of it, the Wernicke's area, like beasts entering Noah's Ark, and with the transitional period of puberty, the door closes on the real world, that is on the raw materials from which a cosmos is to be created." Adolescents typically lose their interest in animals.

For the process to work, the animals must exist in real life. Says Shepard, "It wouldn't work unless there were an order [in] which animals really participate, an ecosystem as organic and as whole and as lively as our bodies are. The games of animal imitation are hollow if we never have any external evidence that the things we imitate have a stable and good relationship in the world."

Shepard warns that the trend toward extinction of wild animals is a threat to human thought. If we eliminate animals, we eliminate much of the naming and classifying and reduce the number and quality of ideas we may embody. "Just as you blind a young animal for life by covering its eyes at the time when the final neural connections are being made," he writes, "if you deprive a child of natural diversity, you curb its mental development."

The most important result of "minding animals," Shepard believes, is that the animal images teach us that the separateness of other creatures is not threatening, and so teach us to live with diversity. If, despite the conflict of deer and wolf or plankton and whale, life survives, then we may also hope to survive our conflicts with the strangers who crowd the human world. If we can master our fear of disorder by naming lions and pythons, perhaps we can master our fears of men and live with the difficulties of race, class, and locality.

Shepard suggests that as we lose natural diversity we will suffer a form of insanity. He notes that we see an increasing number of adults who cannot deal with fear, control, dominance, or acceptance, and who seem unable to fit themselves into some kind of order with other people or with their setting. We see, too, many people who oversimplify human diversity in order to make life seem less fearsome, or who hide behind locked doors because life's categories are simply overwhelming.

"The loss of natural diversity probably shapes our whole notion about the world," says Shepard. "Instead of a world that grows, a world in which we deal with mysterious forces we have to feel some humility about, we see it as a machine." We view our brains as computers, our bodies as puzzles for doctors to assemble, and our societies merely as devices made for the distribution of goods.

The solution, Shepard thinks, may be to make environment and animals the setting, rather than the subject, of education. He suggests that we send our children out of the cities, where they can be spared the false sameness, the man-centeredness and the mechanical determinism of modern life. In the countryside, Shepard believes, children may pass through the age of naming with an opportunity to see the true breadth and variety of life.

Some of these thoughts leave me a bit breathless. I have no doubt that a natural world, being the world in which our minds evolved, encourages our minds to be what they have been. I am not sure what evolutionary effects cities may have upon our minds. They may stupefy and simplify, rob us of the common sense of diversity and give us over to fantasy and fear. Then again, they may not. Perhaps we *could* survive without animals. Our minds, like it or not, are still evolving, and we have no way of seeing over the evolutionary horizon.

But I believe with Paul Shepard that animals are a part of our minds, a part of the loom upon which we spin out thoughts. We are drawn to animals, not just because they are lively and pretty, but because we think through them. And a world without an abundance of kinds is bound to be a different world. A humanity without abundant animals is bound to be a different humanity. Despite its flaws, I like the humanity we have. Perhaps that is why I dream about elands.

ANNIE DILLARD
B. 1945

Annie Dillard possesses one of the most recognizable voices in contemporary American prose. Her energetic and eclectic style, ranging from that of the religious mystic to that of the stand-up comedian, reflects her perception that existence embraces both the sublime and the absurd. Born in Pittsburgh and educated at Hollins College in Virginia, Dillard describes herself as "a poet and a walker with a background in theology and a penchant for quirky facts." Her books, she says, are not consciously about nature so much as "about what it feels like to be alive." Yet Pilgrim at Tinker Creek, *which won the Pulitzer Prize for Non-Fiction in 1974, has become one of the most influential and widely imitated works of contemporary nature writing. Its account of a year in the Roanoke Valley of the Blue Ridge Mountains explores the nature of human consciousness as much as local natural history, and gravitates towards mystery rather than conclusions. In contrast to other contemporary writers like Edward Abbey and Wendell Berry, Dillard's intent is not to discover or champion an environmental ethic but to bear witness equally to the unaneled beauty and terror of existence. Her other works include* Tickets for a Prayer Wheel *(1974), a poetry collection;* Teaching a Stone to Talk *(1982); and* An American Childhood *(1987), a memoir. She has taught at Wesleyan University since 1979.*

From PILGRIM AT TINKER CREEK

HEAVEN AND EARTH IN JEST

I used to have a cat, an old fighting tom, who would jump through the open window by my bed in the middle of the night and land on my chest. I'd half-awaken. He'd stick his skull under my nose and purr, stinking of urine and blood. Some nights he kneaded my bare chest with his front paws, powerfully, arching his back, as if sharpening his claws, or pummeling a mother for milk. And some mornings I'd wake in daylight to find my body covered with paw prints in blood; I looked as though I'd been painted with roses.

It was hot, so hot the mirror felt warm. I washed before the mirror in a daze, my twisted summer sleep still hung about me like sea kelp. What blood was this, and what roses? It could have been the rose of union, the blood of murder, or the rose of beauty bare and the blood of some unspeakable sacrifice or birth. The sign on my body could have been an emblem or a stain, the keys to the kingdom or the mark of Cain. I never knew. I never knew as I washed, and the blood streaked, faded, and finally disappeared, whether I'd purified myself or ruined the blood sign of the passover. We wake, if we ever wake at all, to mystery, rumors of death, beauty, violence. . . . "Seem like we're just set down here," a woman said to me recently, "and don't nobody know why."

These are morning matters, pictures you dream as the final wave heaves you up on the sand to the bright light and drying air. You remember pressure, and a curved sleep you rested against, soft, like a scallop in its shell. But the air hardens your skin; you stand; you leave the lighted shore to explore some dim headland, and soon you're lost in the leafy interior, intent, remembering nothing.

I still think of that old tomcat, mornings, when I wake. Things are tamer now; I sleep with the window shut. The cat and our rites are gone

Pilgrim at Tinker Creek (New York: Harper and Row, 1974).

and my life is changed, but the memory remains of something powerful playing over me. I wake expectant, hoping to see a new thing. If I'm lucky I might be jogged awake by a strange birdcall. I dress in a hurry, imagining the yard flapping with auks, or flamingos. This morning it was a wood duck, down at the creek. It flew away.

I live by a creek, Tinker Creek, in a valley in Virginia's Blue Ridge. An anchorite's hermitage is called an anchor-hold; some anchor-holds were simple sheds clamped to the side of a church like a barnacle to a rock. I think of this house clamped to the side of Tinker Creek as an anchor-hold. It holds me at anchor to the rock bottom of the creek itself and it keeps me steadied in the current, as a sea anchor does, facing the stream of light pouring down. It's a good place to live; there's a lot to think about. The creeks—Tinker and Carvin's—are an active mystery, fresh every minute. Theirs is the mystery of the continuous creation and all that providence implies: the uncertainty of vision, the horror of the fixed, the dissolution of the present, the intricacy of beauty, the pressure of fecundity, the elusiveness of the free, and the flawed nature of perfection. The mountains—Tinker and Brushy, McAfee's Knob and Dead Man—are a passive mystery, the oldest of all. Theirs is the one simple mystery of creation from nothing, of matter itself, anything at all, the given. Mountains are giant, restful, absorbent. You can heave your spirit into a mountain and the mountain will keep it, folded, and not throw it back as some creeks will. The creeks are the world with all its stimulus and beauty; I live there. But the mountains are home.

The wood duck flew away. I caught only a glimpse of something like a bright torpedo that blasted the leaves where it flew. Back at the house I ate a bowl of oatmeal; much later in the day came the long slant of light that means good walking.

If the day is fine, any walk will do; it all looks good. Water in particular looks its best, reflecting blue sky in the flat, and chopping it into graveled shallows and white chute and foam in the riffles. On a dark day, or a hazy one, everything's washed-out and lackluster but the water. It carries its own lights. I set out for the railroad tracks, for the hill the flocks fly over, for the woods where the white mare lives. But I go to the water.

Today is one of those excellent January partly cloudies in which light chooses an unexpected part of the landscape to trick out in gilt, and then shadow sweeps it away. You know you're alive. You take huge steps, trying to feel the planet's roundness arc between your feet. Kazantazkis says that when he was young he had a canary and a globe. When he freed the canary, it would perch on the globe and sing. All his life, wandering the earth, he felt as though he had a canary on top of his mind, singing.

West of the house, Tinker Creek makes a sharp loop, so that the creek is both in back of the house, south of me, and also on the other side of the road, north of me. I like to go north. There the afternoon sun hits the creek just right, deepening the reflected blue and lighting the sides of trees on the banks. Steers from the pasture across the creek come down to drink; I always flush a rabbit or two there; I sit on a fallen trunk in the shade and watch the squirrels in the sun. There are two separated wooden fences suspended from cables that cross the creek just upstream from my tree-trunk bench. They keep the steers from escaping up or down the creek when they come to drink. Squirrels, the neighborhood children, and I use the downstream fence as a swaying bridge across the creek. But the steers are there today.

I sit on the downed tree and watch the black steers slip on the creek bottom. They are all bred beef: beef heart, beef hide, beef hocks. They're a human product like rayon. They're like a field of shoes. They have cast-iron shanks and tongues like foam insoles. You can't see through to their brains as you can with other animals; they have beef fat behind their eyes, beef stew.

I cross the fence six feet above the water, walking my hands down the rusty cable and tightroping my feet along the narrow edge of the planks. When I hit the other bank and terra firma, some steers are bunched in a knot between me and the barbed-wire fence I want to cross. So I suddenly rush at them in an enthusiastic sprint, flailing my arms and hollering, "Lightning! Copperhead! Swedish meatballs!" They flee, still in a knot, stumbling across the flat pasture. I stand with the wind on my face.

When I slide under a barbed-wire fence, cross a field, and run over a sycamore trunk felled across the water, I'm on a little island shaped like a tear in the middle of Tinker Creek. On one side of the creek is a steep forested bank; the water is swift and deep on that side of the island. On the other side is the level field I walked through next to the steers' pasture; the water between the field and the island is shallow and sluggish. In summer's low water, flags and bulrushes grow along a series of shallow pools cooled by the lazy current. Water striders patrol the surface film, crayfish hump along the silt bottom eating filth, frogs shout and glare, and shiners and small bream hide among roots from the sulky green heron's eye. I come to this island every month of the year. I walk around it, stopping and staring, or I straddle the sycamore log over the creek, curling my legs out of the water in winter, trying to read. Today I sit on dry grass at the end of the island by the slower side of the creek. I'm drawn to this spot. I come to it as to an oracle; I return to it as a man years later will seek out the battlefield where he lost a leg or an arm.

A couple of summers ago I was walking along the edge of the island to see what I could see in the water, and mainly to scare frogs. Frogs have an inelegant way of taking off from invisible positions on the bank just ahead of your feet, in dire panic, emitting a froggy "Yike!" and splashing into the water. Incredibly, this amused me, and, incredibly, it amuses me still. As I walked along the grassy edge of the island, I got better and better at seeing frogs both in and out of the water. I learned to recognize, slowing down, the difference in texture of the light reflected from mudbank, water, grass, or frog. Frogs were flying all around me. At the end of the island I noticed a small green frog. He was exactly half in and half out of the water, looking like a schematic diagram of an amphibian, and he didn't jump.

He didn't jump; I crept closer. At last I knelt on the island's winter-killed grass, lost, dumbstruck, staring at the frog in the creek just four feet away. He was a very small frog with wide, dull eyes. And just as I looked at him, he slowly crumpled and began to sag. The spirit vanished from his eyes as if snuffed. His skin emptied and drooped; his very skull seemed to collapse and settle like a kicked tent. He was shrinking before my eyes like a deflating football. I watched the taut, glistening skin on his shoulders ruck, and rumple, and fall. Soon, part of his skin, formless as a pricked balloon, lay in floating folds like bright scum on top of the water: it was a monstrous and terrifying thing. I gaped bewildered, appalled. An oval shadow hung in the water behind the drained frog; then the shadow glided away. The frog skin bag started to sink.

I had read about the giant water bug, but never seen one. "Giant water bug" is really the name of the creature, which is an enormous, heavy-bodied brown beetle. It eats insects, tadpoles, fish, and frogs. Its grasping forelegs are mighty and hooked inward. It seizes a victim with these legs, hugs it tight, and paralyzes it with enzymes injected during a vicious bite. That one bite is the only bite it ever takes. Through the puncture shoots the poisons that dissolve the victim's muscles and bones and organs—all but the skin—and through it the giant water bug sucks out the victim's body, reduced to a juice. This event is quite common in warm fresh water. The frog I saw was being sucked by a giant water bug. I had been kneeling on the island grass; when the unrecognizable flap of frog skin settled on the creek bottom, swaying, I stood up and brushed the knees of my pants. I couldn't catch my breath.

Of course, many carnivorous animals devour their prey alive. The usual method seems to be to subdue the victim by downing or grasping it so it can't flee, then eating it whole or in a series of bloody bites. Frogs eat everything whole, stuffing prey into their mouths with their thumbs. People have seen frogs with their wide jaws so full of live dragonflies they couldn't close them. Ants don't even have to catch their prey: in the spring they swarm over newly hatched, featherless birds in the nest and eat them tiny bite by bite.

That it's rough out there and chancy is no surprise. Every live thing is a survivor on a kind of extended emergency bivouac. But at the same time we are also created. In the Koran, Allah asks, "The heaven and the earth and all in between, thinkest thou I made them *in jest?*" It's a good question. What do we think of the created universe, spanning an unthinkable void with an unthinkable profusion of forms? Or what do we think of nothingness, those sickening reaches of time in either direction? If the giant water bug was not made in jest, was it then made in earnest? Pascal uses a nice term to describe the notion of the creator's, once having called forth the universe, turning his back to it: *Deus Absconditus.* Is this what we think happened? Was the sense of it there, and God absconded with it, ate it, like a wolf who disappears round the edge of the house with the Thanksgiving turkey? "God is subtle," Einstein said, "but not malicious." Again, Einstein said that "nature conceals her mystery by means of her essential grandeur, not by her cunning." It could be that God has not absconded but spread, as our vision and understanding of the universe have spread, to a fabric of spirit and sense so grand and subtle, so powerful in a new way, that we can only feel blindly of its hem. In making the thick darkness a swaddling band for the sea, God "set bars and doors" and said, "Hitherto shalt thou come, but no further." But have we come even that far? Have we rowed out to the thick darkness, or are we all playing pinochle in the bottom of the boat?

Cruelty is a mystery, and the waste of pain. But if we describe a world to compass these things, a world that is a long, brute game, then we bump against another mystery: the inrush of power and light, the canary that sings on the skull. Unless all ages and races of men have been deluded by the same mass hypnotist (who?), there seems to be such a thing as beauty, a grace wholly gratuitous. About five years ago I saw a mockingbird make a straight vertical descent from the roof gutter of a four-story building. It was an act as careless and spontaneous as the curl of a stem or the kindling of a star.

The mockingbird took a single step into the air and dropped. His wings were still folded against his sides as though he were singing from a limb and not falling, accelerating thirty-two feet per second per second, through empty air. Just a breath before he would have been dashed to the ground, he unfurled his wings with exact, deliberate care, revealing the broad bars of white, spread his elegant, white-banded tail, and so floated onto the grass. I had just rounded a corner when his insouciant step caught my eye; there was no one else in sight. The fact of his free fall was like the old philosophical conundrum about the tree that falls in the forest. The answer must be, I think, that beauty and grace are performed whether or not we will or sense them. The least we can do is try to be there.

Another time I saw another wonder: sharks off the Atlantic coast of Florida. There is a way a wave rises above the ocean horizon, a triangular wedge against the sky. If you stand where the ocean breaks on a shallow beach, you see the raised water in a wave is translucent, shot with lights. One late afternoon at low tide a hundred big sharks passed the beach near the mouth of a tidal river in a feeding frenzy. As each green wave rose from the churning water, it illuminated within itself the six- or eight-foot-long bodies of twisting sharks. The sharks disappeared as each wave rolled toward me; then a new wave would swell above the horizon, containing in it, like scorpions in amber, sharks that roiled and heaved. The sight held awesome wonders: power and beauty, grace tangled in a rapture with violence.

We don't know what's going on here. If these tremendous events are random combinations of matter run amok, the yield of millions of monkeys at millions of typewriters, then what is it in us, hammered out of those same typewriters, that they ignite? We don't know. Our life is a faint tracing on the surface of mystery, like the idle, curved tunnels of leaf miners on the face of a leaf. We must somehow take a wider view, look at the whole landscape, really see it, and describe what's going on here. Then we can at least wail the right question into the swaddling band of darkness, or, if it comes to that, choir the proper praise.

At the time of Lewis and Clark, setting the prairies on fire was a well-known signal that meant, "Come down to the water." It was an extravagant gesture, but we can't do less. If the landscape reveals one certainty, it is that the extravagant gesture is the very stuff of creation. After the one extravagant gesture of creation in the first place, the universe has continued to deal exclusively in extravagances, flinging intricacies and colossi down aeons of emptiness, heaping profusions on profligacies with ever-fresh vigor. The whole show has been on fire from the word go. I come down to the water to cool my eyes. But everywhere I look I see fire; that which isn't flint is tinder, and the whole world sparks and flames.

I have come to the grassy island late in the day. The creek is up; icy water sweeps under the sycamore log bridge. The frog skin, of course, is utterly gone. I have stared at that one spot on the creek bottom for so long, focusing past the rush of water, that when I stand, the opposite bank seems to stretch before my eyes and flow grassily upstream. When the bank settles down I cross the sycamore log and enter again the big plowed field next to the steers' pasture.

The wind is terrific out of the west; the sun comes and goes. I can see the shadow on the field before me deepen uniformly and spread like a plague. Everything seems so dull I am amazed I can even distinguish objects. And suddenly the light runs across the land like a comber, and up the trees, and goes again in a wink: I think I've gone blind or died. When it comes again, the light, you hold your breath, and if it stays you forget about it until it goes again.

It's the most beautiful day of the year. At four o'clock the eastern sky is a dead stratus black flecked with low white clouds. The sun in the west illuminates the ground, the mountains, and especially the bare branches of trees, so that everywhere silver trees cut into the black sky like a photographer's negative of a landscape. The air and the ground are dry; the mountains are going on and off like neon signs. Clouds slide east as if pulled from the horizon, like a tablecloth whipped off a table. The hemlocks by the barbed-wire fence are flinging themselves east as though their backs would break. Purple shadows are racing east; the wind makes me face east, and again I feel the dizzying, drawn sensation I felt when the creek bank reeled.

At four-thirty the sky in the east is clear; how could that big blackness be blown? Fifteen minutes later another darkness is coming overhead from the northwest; and it's here. Everything is drained of its light as if sucked. Only at the horizon do inky black mountains give way to distant, lighted mountains—lighted not by direct illumination but rather paled by glowing sheets of mist hung before them. Now the blackness is in the east; everything is half in shadow, half in sun, every clod, tree, mountain, and hedge. I can't see Tinker Mountain through the line of hemlock, till it comes on like a streetlight, ping, *ex nihilo*. Its sandstone cliffs pink and swell. Suddenly the light goes; the cliffs recede as if pushed. The sun hits a clump of sycamores between me and the mountains; the sycamore arms light up, and *I can't see the cliffs*. They're gone. The pale network of sycamore arms, which a second ago was transparent as a screen, is suddenly opaque, glowing with light. Now the sycamore arms snuff out, the mountains come on, and there are the cliffs again.

I walk home. By five-thirty the show has pulled out. Nothing is left but an unreal blue and a few banked clouds low in the north. Some sort of carnival magician has been here, some fast-talking worker of wonders who has the act backwards. "Something in this hand," he says, "something in this hand, something up my sleeve, something behind my back . . ." and abracadabra, he snaps his fingers, and it's all gone. Only the bland, blank-faced magician remains, in his unruffled coat, barehanded, acknowledging a smattering of baffled applause. When you look again the whole show has pulled up stakes and moved on down the road. It never stops. New shows roll in from over the mountains and the magician reappears unannounced from a fold in the curtain you never dreamed was an opening. Scarves of clouds, rabbits in plain view, disappear into the black hat forever. Presto chango. The audience, if there is an audience at all, is dizzy from head-turning, dazed.

Like the bear who went over the mountain, I went out to see what I could see. And, I might as well warn you, like the bear, all that I could see was the other side of the mountain: more of same. On a good day I might catch a glimpse of another wooded ridge rolling under the sun like water, another bivouac. I propose to keep here what Thoreau called "a meteorological journal of the mind," telling some tales and describing some of the sights of this rather tamed valley, and exploring, in fear and trembling, some of the unmapped dim reaches and unholy fastnesses to which those tales and sights so dizzyingly lead.

I am no scientist. I explore the neighborhood. An infant who has just learned to hold his head up has a frank and forthright way of gazing about him in bewilderment. He hasn't the faintest clue where he is, and he aims to learn. In a couple of years, what he will have learned instead is how to fake it: he'll have the cocksure air of a squatter who has come to feel he owns the place. Some unwonted, taught pride diverts us from our original intent, which is to explore the neighborhood, view the landscape, to discover at least *where* it is that we have been so startlingly set down, if we can't learn why.

So I think about the valley. It is my leisure as well as my work, a game. It is a fierce game I have joined because it is being played anyway, a game of both skill and chance, played against an unseen adversary—the conditions of time—in which the payoffs, which may suddenly arrive in a blast of light at any moment, might as well come to me as anyone else. I stake the time I'm grateful to have, the energies I'm glad to direct. I risk getting stuck on the board, so to speak, unable to move in any direction, which happens enough, God knows; and I risk the searing, exhausting nightmares that plunder rest and force me face down all night long in some muddy ditch seething with hatching insects and crustaceans.

But if I can bear the nights, the days are a pleasure. I walk out; I see something, some event that would otherwise have been utterly missed and lost; or something sees me, some enormous power brushes me with its clean wing, and I resound like a beaten bell.

I am an explorer, then, and I am also a stalker, or the instrument of the hunt itself. Certain Indians used to carve long grooves along the wooden shafts of their arrows. They called the grooves "lightning marks," because they resembled the curved fissure lightning slices down the trunks of trees. The function of lightning marks is this: if the arrow fails to kill the game, blood from a deep wound will channel along the lightning mark, streak down the arrow shaft, and spatter to the ground, laying a trail dripped on broad-leaves, on stones, that the barefoot and trembling archer can follow into whatever deep or rare wilderness it leads. I am the arrow shaft, carved along my length by unexpected lights and gashes from the very sky, and this book is the straying trail of blood.

Something pummels us, something barely sheathed. Power broods and lights. We're played on like a pipe; our breath is not our own. James Houston describes two young Eskimo girls sitting cross-legged on the ground, mouth on mouth, blowing by turns each other's throat cords, making a low, unearthly music. When I cross again the bridge that is really the steers' fence, the wind has thinned to the delicate air of twilight; it crumples the water's skin. I watch the running sheets of light raised on the creek's surface. The sight has the appeal of the purely passive, like the racing of light under clouds on a field, the beautiful dream at the moment of being dreamed. The breeze is the merest puff, but you yourself sail headlong and breathless under the gale force of the spirit.

THE FIXED

*   *   * Once, when I was ten or eleven years old, my friend Judy brought in a Polyphemus moth cocoon. It was January; there were doily snowflakes taped to the schoolroom panes. The teacher kept the cocoon in her desk all morning and brought it out when we were getting restless before recess. In a book we found what the adult moth would look like; it would be beautiful. With a wingspread of up to six inches, the Polyphemus is one of the few huge American silk moths, much larger than, say, a giant or tiger swallowtail butterfly. The moth's enormous wings are velveted in a rich, warm brown, and edged in bands of blue and pink delicate as a watercolor wash. A startling "eyespot," immense, and deep blue melding to an almost translucent yellow, luxuriates in the center of each hind wing. The effect is one of a masculine splendor foreign to the butterflies, a fragility unfurled to strength. The Polyphemus moth in the picture looked like a mighty wraith, a beating essence of the hardwood forest, alien-skinned and brown, with spread, blind eyes. This was the giant moth packed in the faded cocoon. We closed the book and turned to the cocoon. It was an oak leaf sewn into a plump oval bundle; Judy had found it loose in a pile of frozen leaves.

We passed the cocoon around; it was heavy. As we held it in our hands, the creature within warmed and squirmed. We were delighted, and wrapped it tighter in our fists. The pupa began to jerk violently, in heart-stopping knocks. Who's there? I can still feel those thumps, urgent through a muffling of spun silk and leaf, urgent through the swaddling of many years, against the curve of my palm. We kept passing it around. When it came to me again it was hot as a bun; it jumped half out of my hand. The teacher intervened. She put it, still heaving and banging, in the ubiquitous Mason jar.

It was coming. There was no stopping it now, January or not. One end of the cocoon dampened and gradually frayed in a furious battle. The whole cocoon twisted and slapped around in the bottom of the jar. The teacher fades, the classmates fade, I fade: I don't remember anything but that thing's struggle to be a moth or die trying. It emerged at last, a sodden crumple. It was a male; his long antennae were thickly plumed, as wide as his fat abdomen. His body was very thick, over an inch long, and deeply furred. A gray, furlike plush covered his head; a long, tan furlike hair hung from his wide thorax over his brown-furred, segmented abdomen. His multijointed legs, pale and powerful, were shaggy as a bear's. He stood still, but he breathed.

He couldn't spread his wings. There was no room. The chemical that coated his wings like varnish, stiffening them permanently, dried, and hardened his wings as they were. He was a monster in a Mason jar. Those huge wings stuck on his back in a torture of random pleats and folds, wrinkled as a dirty tissue, rigid as leather. They made a single nightmare clump still wracked with useless, frantic convulsions.

The next thing I remember, it was recess. The school was in Shadyside, a busy residential part of Pittsburgh. Everyone was playing dodgeball in the fenced playground or racing around the concrete schoolyard by the swings. Next to the playground a long delivery drive sloped downhill to the sidewalk and street. Someone—it must have been the teacher—had let the moth out. I was standing in the driveway, alone, stock-still, but shivering. Someone had given the Polyphemus moth his freedom, and he was walking away.

He heaved himself down the asphalt driveway by infinite degrees, unwavering. His hideous crumpled wings lay glued and rucked on his back, perfectly still now, like a collapsed tent. The bell rang twice; I had to go. The moth was receding down the driveway, dragging on. I went; I ran inside. The Polyphemus moth is still crawling down the driveway, crawling down the driveway hunched, crawling down the driveway on six furred feet, forever. *   *   *

THE PRESENT

CATCH IT IF YOU CAN.

It is early March. I am dazed from a long day of interstate driving homeward; I pull in at a gas station in Nowhere, Virginia, north of

Lexington. The young boy in charge ("Chick 'at oll?") is offering a free cup of coffee with every gas purchase. We talk in the glass-walled office while my coffee cools enough to drink. He tells me, among other things, that the rival gas station down the road, whose FREE COFFEE sign is visible from the interstate, charges you fifteen cents if you want your coffee in a Styrofoam cup, as opposed, I guess, to your bare hands.

All the time we talk, the boy's new beagle puppy is skidding around the office, sniffing impartially at my shoes and at the wire rack of folded maps. The cheerful human conversation wakes me, recalls me, not to a normal consciousness, but to a kind of energetic readiness. I step outside, followed by the puppy.

I am absolutely alone. There are no other customers. The road is vacant, the interstate is out of sight and earshot. I have hazarded into a new corner of the world, an unknown spot, a Brigadoon. Before me extends a low hill trembling in yellow brome, and behind the hill; filling the sky, rises an enormous mountain ridge, forested, alive and awesome with brilliant blown lights. I have never seen anything so tremulous and live. Overhead, great strips and chunks of cloud dash to the northwest in a gold rush. At my back the sun is setting—how can I not have noticed before that the sun is setting? My mind has been a blank slab of black asphalt for hours, but that doesn't stop the sun's wild wheel. I set my coffee beside me on the curb; I smell loam on the wind; I pat the puppy; I watch the mountain.

My hand works automatically over the puppy's fur, following the line of hair under his ears, down his neck, inside his forelegs, along his hot-skinned belly.

Shadows lope along the mountain's rumpled flanks; they elongate like root tips, like lobes of spilling water, faster and faster. A warm purple pigment pools in each ruck and tuck of the rock; it deepens and spreads, boring crevasses, canyons. As the purple vaults and slides, it tricks out the unleafed forest and rumpled rock in gilt, in shape-shifting patches of glow. These gold lights veer and retract, shatter and glide in a series of dazzling splashes, shrinking, leaking, exploding. The ridge's bosses and hummocks sprout bulging from its side; the whole mountain looms miles closer; the light warms and reddens; the bare forest folds and pleats itself like living protoplasm before my eyes, like a running chart, a wildly scrawling oscillograph on the present moment. The air cools; the puppy's skin is hot. I am more alive than all the world.

This is it, I think, this is it, right now, the present, this empty gas station, here, this western wind, this tang of coffee on the tongue, and I am patting the puppy, I am watching the mountain. And the second I verbalize this awareness in my brain, I cease to see the mountain or feel the puppy. I am opaque, so much black asphalt. But at the same second, the second I know I've lost it, I also realize that the puppy is still squirming on his back under my hand. Nothing has changed for him. He draws his legs down to stretch the skin taut so he feels every fingertip's stroke along his furred and arching side, his flank, his flung-back throat.

I sip my coffee. I look at the mountain, which is still doing its tricks, as you look at a still-beautiful face belonging to a person who was once your lover in another country years ago: with fond nostalgia, and recognition, but no real feeling save a secret astonishment that you are now strangers. Thanks. For the memories. It is ironic that the one thing that all religions recognize as separating us from our creator—our very self-consciousness—is also the one thing that divides us from our fellow creatures. It was a bitter birthday present from evolution, cutting us off at both ends. I get in the car and drive home. * * *

TOTAL ECLIPSE

I

It had been like dying, that sliding down the mountain pass. It had been like the death of someone, irrational, that sliding down the mountain pass and into the region of dread. It was like slipping into fever, or falling down that hole in sleep from which you wake yourself whimpering. We had crossed the mountains that day, and now we were in a strange place—a hotel in central Washington, in a town near Yakima. The eclipse we had traveled here to see would occur early the next morning.

I lay in bed. My husband, Gary, was reading beside me. I lay in bed and looked at the painting on the hotel room wall. It was a print of a detailed and lifelike painting of a smiling clown's head, made out of vegetables. It was a painting of the sort which you do not intend to look at, and which, alas, you never forget. Some tasteless fate presses it upon you; it becomes part of the complex interior junk you carry with you wherever you go. Two years have passed since the total eclipse of which I write. During those years I have forgotten, I assume, a great many things I wanted to remember—but I have not forgotten that clown painting or its lunatic setting in the old hotel.

The clown was bald. Actually, he wore a clown's tight rubber wig,

Teaching a Stone to Talk: Expeditions and Encounters (New York: Harper & Row, 1982).

painted white; this stretched over the top of his skull, which was a cabbage. His hair was bunches of baby carrots. Inset in his white clown makeup, and in his cabbage skull, were his small and laughing human eyes. The clown's glance was like the glance of Rembrandt in some of the self-portraits: lively, knowing, deep, and loving. The crinkled shadows around his eyes were string beans. His eyebrows were parsley. Each of his ears was a broad bean. His thin, joyful lips were red chili peppers; between his lips were wet rows of human teeth and a suggestion of a real tongue. The clown print was framed in gilt and glassed.

To put ourselves in the path of the total eclipse, that day we had driven five hours inland from the Washington coast, where we lived. When we tried to cross the Cascades range, an avalanche had blocked the pass.

A slope's worth of snow blocked the road; traffic backed up. Had the avalanche buried any cars that morning? We could not learn. This highway was the only winter road over the mountains. We waited as highway crews bulldozed a passage through the avalanche. With two-by-fours and walls of plyboard, they erected a one-way, roofed tunnel through the avalanche. We drove through the avalanche tunnel, crossed the pass, and descended several thousand feet into central Washington and the broad Yakima valley, about which we knew only that it was orchard country. As we lost altitude, the snows disappeared; our ears popped; the trees changed, and in the trees were strange birds. I watched the landscape innocently, like a fool, like a diver in the rapture of the deep who plays on the bottom while his air runs out.

The hotel lobby was a dark, derelict room, narrow as a corridor, and seemingly without air. We waited on a couch while the manager vanished upstairs to do something unknown to our room. Beside us on an overstuffed chair, absolutely motionless, was a platinum-blond woman in her forties wearing a black silk dress and a strand of pearls. Her long legs were crossed; she supported her head on her fist. At the dim far end of the room, their backs toward us, sat six bald old men in their shirtsleeves, around a loud television. Two of them seemed asleep. They were drunks. "Number six!" cried the man on television, "Number six!"

On the broad lobby desk, lighted and bubbling, was a ten-gallon aquarium containing one large fish; the fish tilted up and down in its water. Against the long opposite wall sang a live canary in its cage. Beneath the cage, among spilled millet seeds on the carpet, were a decorated child's sand bucket and matching sand shovel.

Now the alarm was set for six. I lay awake remembering an article I had read downstairs in the lobby, in an engineering magazine. The article was about gold mining.

In South Africa, in India, and in South Dakota, the gold mines extend so deeply into the earth's crust that they are hot. The rock walls burn the miners' hands. The companies have to air-condition the mines; if the air conditioners break, the miners die. The elevators in the mine shafts run very slowly, down, and up, so the miners' ears will not pop in their skulls. When the miners return to the surface, their faces are deathly pale.

Early the next morning we checked out. It was February 26, 1979, a Monday morning. We would drive out of town, find a hilltop, watch the eclipse, and then drive back over the mountains and home to the coast. How familiar things are here; how adept we are; how smoothly and professionally we check out! I had forgotten the clown's smiling head and the hotel lobby as if they had never existed. Gary put the car in gear and off we went, as off we have gone to a hundred other adventures.

It was before dawn when we found a highway out of town and drove into the unfamiliar countryside. By the growing light we could see a band of cirrostratus clouds in the sky. Later the rising sun would clear these clouds before the eclipse began. We drove at random until we came to a range of unfenced hills. We pulled off the highway, bundled up, and climbed one of these hills.

II

The hill was five hundred feet high. Long winter-killed grass covered it, as high as our knees. We climbed and rested, sweating in the cold; we passed clumps of bundled people on the hillside who were setting up telescopes and fiddling with cameras. The top of the hill stuck up in the middle of the sky. We tightened our scarves and looked around.

East of us rose another hill like ours. Between the hills, far below, was the highway which threaded south into the valley. This was the Yakima valley; I had never seen it before. It is justly famous for its beauty, like every planted valley. It extended south into the horizon, a distant dream of a valley, a Shangri-la. All its hundreds of low, golden slopes bore orchards. Among the orchards were towns, and roads, and plowed and fallow fields. Through the valley wandered a thin, shining river; from the river extended fine, frozen irrigation ditches. Distance blurred and blued the sight, so that the whole valley looked like a thickness or sediment at the bottom of the sky. Directly behind us was more sky, and empty lowlands blued by distance, and Mount Adams. Mount Adams was an enormous, snow-covered volcanic cone rising flat, like so much scenery.

Now the sun was up. We could not see it; but the sky behind the band of clouds was yellow, and, far down the valley, some hillside orchards had lighted up. More people were parking near the highway and climbing the hills. It was the West. All of us rugged individualists were wearing knit caps and blue nylon parkas. People were climbing the nearby hills and setting up shop in clumps among the dead grasses. It looked as though we had all gathered on hilltops to pray for the world on its last day. It looked as though we had all crawled out of spaceships and were preparing to assault the valley below. It looked as though we were scattered on hilltops at dawn to sacrifice virgins, make rain, set stone stelae in a ring. There was no place out of the wind. The straw grasses banged our legs.

Up in the sky where we stood the air was lusterless yellow. To the west the sky was blue. Now the sun cleared the clouds. We cast rough shadows on the blowing grass; freezing, we waved our arms. Near the sun, the sky was bright and colorless. There was nothing to see.

It began with no ado. It was odd that such a well-advertised public event should have no starting gun, no overture, no introductory speaker. I should have known right then that I was out of my depth. Without pause or preamble, silent as orbits, a piece of the sun went away. We looked at it through welders' goggles. A piece of the sun was missing; in its place we saw empty sky.

I had seen a partial eclipse in 1970. A partial eclipse is very interesting. It bears almost no relation to a total eclipse. Seeing a partial eclipse bears the same relation to seeing a total eclipse as kissing a man does to marrying him, or as flying in an airplane does to falling out of an airplane. Although the one experience precedes the other, it in no way prepares you for it. During a partial eclipse the sky does not darken—not even when 94 percent of the sun is hidden. Nor does the sun, seen colorless through protective devices, seem terribly strange. We have all seen a sliver of light in the sky; we have all seen the crescent moon by day. However, during a partial eclipse the air does indeed get cold, precisely as if someone were standing between you and the fire. And blackbirds do fly back to their roosts. I had seen a partial eclipse before, and here was another.

What you see in an eclipse is entirely different from what you know. It is especially different for those of us whose grasp of astronomy is so frail that, given a flashlight, a grapefruit, two oranges, and fifteen years, we still could not figure out which way to set the clocks for Daylight Saving Time. Usually it is a bit of a trick to keep your knowledge from blinding you. But during an eclipse it is easy. What you see is much more convincing than any wild-eyed theory you may know.

You may read that the moon has something to do with eclipses. I have never seen the moon yet. You do not see the moon. So near the sun, it is as completely invisible as the stars are by day. What you see before your eyes is the sun going through phases. It gets narrower and narrower, as the waning moon does, and, like the ordinary moon, it travels alone in the simple sky. The sky is of course background. It does not appear to eat the sun; it is far behind the sun. The sun simply shaves away; gradually, you see less sun and more sky.

The sky's blue was deepening, but there was no darkness. The sun was a wide crescent, like a segment of tangerine. The wind freshened and blew steadily over the hill. The eastern hill across the highway grew dusky and sharp. The towns and orchards in the valley to the south were dissolving into the blue light. Only the thin river held a trickle of sun.

Now the sky to the west deepened to indigo, a color never seen. A dark sky usually loses color. This was a saturated, deep indigo, up in the air. Stuck up into that unwordly sky was the cone of Mount Adams, and the alpenglow was upon it. The alpenglow is that red light of sunset which holds out on snowy mountaintops long after the valleys and tablelands are dimmed. "Look at Mount Adams," I said, and that was the last sane moment I remember.

I turned back to the sun. It was going. The sun was going, and the world was wrong. The grasses were wrong; they were platinum. Their every detail of stem, head, and blade shone lightless and artificially distinct as an art photographer's platinum print. This color has never been seen on earth. The hues were metallic; their finish was matte. The hillside was a nineteenth-century tinted photograph from which the tints had faded. All the people you see in the photograph, distinct and detailed as their faces look, are now dead. The sky was navy blue. My hands were silver. All the distant hills' grasses were finespun metal which the wind laid down. I was watching a faded color print of a movie filmed in the Middle Ages; I was standing in it, by some mistake. I was standing in a movie of hillside grasses filmed in the Middle Ages. I missed my own century, the people I knew, and the real light of day.

I looked at Gary. He was in the film. Everything was lost. He was a platinum print, a dead artist's version of life. I saw on his skull the darkness of night mixed with the colors of day. My mind was going out; my eyes were receding the way galaxies recede to the rim of space. Gary was light-years away, gesturing inside a circle of darkness, down the wrong end of a telescope. He smiled as if he saw me; the stringy crinkles around his eyes moved. The sight of him, familiar and wrong, was something I was remembering from centuries hence, from the other side of death: yes, *that* is the way he used to look, when we were living. When it was our generation's turn to be alive. I could not hear him; the wind was too loud. Behind him the sun was going. We had all started down a chute of time. At first it was pleasant; now there was no stopping it. Gary was chuting away across space, moving and talking and catching my eye, chuting down the long corridor of separation. The skin on his face moved like thin bronze plating that would peel.

The grass at our feet was wild barley. It was the wild einkorn wheat which grew on the hilly flanks of the Zagros Mountains, above the Euphrates valley, above the valley of the river we called *River*. We harvested the grass with stone sickles, I remember. We found the grasses on the hillsides; we built our shelter beside them and cut them down. That is how he used to look then, that one, moving and living and catching my eye, with the sky so dark behind him, and the wind blowing. God save our life.

From all the hills came screams. A piece of sky beside the crescent sun was detaching. It was a loosened circle of evening sky, suddenly lighted from the back. It was an abrupt black body out of nowhere; it was a flat disk; it was almost over the sun. That is when there were screams. At once this disk of sky slid over the sun like a lid. The sky snapped over the sun like a lens cover. The hatch in the brain slammed. Abruptly it was dark night, on the land and in the sky. In the night sky was a tiny ring of light. The hole where the sun belongs is very small. A thin ring of light marked its place. There was no sound. The eyes dried, the arteries drained, the lungs hushed. There was no world. We were the world's dead people rotating and orbiting around and around, embedded in the planet's crust, while the earth rolled down. Our minds were light-years distant, forgetful of almost everything. Only an extraordinary act of will could recall to us our former, living selves and our contexts in matter and time. We had, it seems, loved the planet and loved our lives, but could no longer remember the way of them. We got the light wrong. In the sky was something that should not be there. In the black sky was a ring of light. It was a thin ring, an old, thin silver wedding band, an old, worn ring. It was an old wedding band in the sky, or a morsel of bone. There were stars. It was all over.

III

It is now that the temptation is strongest to leave these regions. We have seen enough; let's go. Why burn our hands any more than we have to? But two years have passed; the price of gold has risen. I return to the same buried alluvial beds and pick through the strata again.

I saw, early in the morning, the sun diminish against a backdrop of sky. I saw a circular piece of that sky appear, suddenly detached, blackened, and backlighted; from nowhere it came and overlapped the sun. It did not look like the moon. It was enormous and black. If I had not read that it was the moon, I could have seen the sight a hundred times and never thought of the moon once. (If, however, I had not read that it was the moon—if, like most of the world's people throughout time, I had simply glanced up and seen this thing—then I doubtless would not have speculated much, but would have, like Emperor Louis of Bavaria in 840, simply died of fright on the spot.) It did not look like a dragon, although it looked more like a dragon than the moon. It looked like a lens cover, or the lid of a pot. It materialized out of thin air—black, and flat, and sliding, outlined in flame.

Seeing this black body was like seeing a mushroom cloud. The heart screeched. The meaning of the sight overwhelmed its fascination. It obliterated meaning itself. If you were to glance out one day and see a row of mushroom clouds rising on the horizon, you would know at once that what you were seeing, remarkable as it was, was intrinsically not worth remarking. No use running to tell anyone. Significant as it was, it did not matter a whit. For what is significance? It is significance for people. No people, no significance. This is all I have to tell you.

In the deeps are the violence and terror of which psychology has warned us. But if you ride these monsters deeper down, if you drop with them farther over the world's rim, you find what our sciences cannot locate or name, the substrate, the ocean or matrix or ether which buoys the rest, which gives goodness its power for good, and evil its power for evil, the unified field: our complex and inexplicable caring for each other, and for our life together here. This is given. It is not learned.

The world which lay under darkness and stillness following the closing of the lid was not the world we know. The event was over. Its devastation lay round about us. The clamoring mind and heart stilled, almost indifferent, certainly disembodied, frail, and exhausted. The hills were hushed, obliterated. Up in the sky, like a crater from some distant cataclysm, was a hollow ring.

You have seen photographs of the sun taken during a total eclipse. The corona fills the print. All of those photographs were taken through telescopes. The lenses of telescopes and cameras can no more cover the breadth and scale of the visual array than language can cover the breadth and simultaneity of internal experience. Lenses enlarge the sight, omit its context, and make of it a pretty and sensible picture, like something on a Christmas card. I assure you, if you send any shepherds a Christmas card on which is printed a three-by-three photograph of the angel of the Lord, the glory of the Lord, and a multitude of the heavenly host, they will not be sore afraid. More fearsome things can come in envelopes. More moving photographs than those of the sun's corona can appear in magazines. But I pray you will never see anything more awful in the sky.

You see the wide world swaddled in darkness; you see a vast breadth of hilly land, and an enormous, distant, blackened valley; you see towns' lights, a river's path, and blurred portions of your hat and scarf; you see your husband's face looking like an early black-and-white film; and you see a sprawl of black sky and blue sky together, with unfamiliar stars in it, some barely visible bands of cloud, and over there, a small white ring. The ring is as small as one goose in a flock of migrating geese—if you happen to notice a flock of migrating geese. It is one 360th part of the visible sky. The sun we see is less than half the diameter of a dime held at arm's length.

The Crab Nebula, in the constellation Taurus, looks, through binoculars, like a smoke ring. It is a star in the process of exploding. Light from its explosion first reached the earth in 1054; it was a supernova then, and so bright it shone in the daytime. Now it is not so bright, but it is still exploding. It expands at the rate of seventy million miles a day. It is interesting to look through binoculars at something expanding seventy million miles a day. It does not budge. Its apparent size does not increase. Photographs of the Crab Nebula taken fifteen years ago seem identical to photographs of it taken yesterday. Some lichens are similar. Botanists have measured some ordinary lichens twice, at fifty-year intervals, without detecting any growth at all. And yet their cells divide; they live.

The small ring of light was like these things—like a ridiculous lichen up in the sky, like a perfectly still explosion 4,200 light-years away: it was interesting, and lovely, and in witless motion, and it had nothing to do with anything.

It had nothing to do with anything. The sun was too small, and too cold, and too far away, to keep the world alive. The white ring was not enough. It was feeble and worthless. It was as useless as a memory; it was as off kilter and hollow and wretched as a memory.

When you try your hardest to recall someone's face, or the look of a place, you see in your mind's eye some vague and terrible sight such as this. It is dark; it is insubstantial; it is all wrong.

The white ring and the saturated darkness made the earth and the sky look as they must look in the memories of the careless dead. What I saw, what I seemed to be standing in, was all the wrecked light that the memories of the dead could shed upon the living world. We had all died in our boots on the hilltops of Yakima, and were alone in eternity. Empty space stoppered our eyes and mouths; we cared for nothing. We remembered our living days wrong. With great effort we had remembered some sort of circular light in the sky—but only the outline. Oh, and then the orchard trees withered, the ground froze, the glaciers slid down the valleys and overlapped the towns. If there had ever been people on earth, nobody knew it. The dead had forgotten those they had loved. The dead were parted one from the other and could no longer remember the faces and lands they had loved in the light. They seemed to stand on darkened hilltops, looking down.

IV

We teach our children one thing only, as we were taught: to wake up. We teach our children to look alive there, to join by words and activities the life of human culture on the planet's crust. As adults we are almost all adept at waking up. We have so mastered the transition we have forgotten we ever learned it. Yet it is a transition we make a hundred times a day, as, like so many will-less dolphins, we plunge and surface, lapse and emerge. We live half our waking lives and all of our sleeping lives in some private, useless, and insensible waters we never mention or recall. Useless, I say. Valueless, I might add—until someone hauls their wealth up to the surface and into the wide-awake city, in a form that people can use.

I do not know how we got to the restaurant. Like Roethke, "I take my waking slow." Gradually I seemed more or less alive, and already forgetful. It was now almost nine in the morning. It was the day of a solar eclipse in central Washington, and a fine adventure for everyone. The sky was clear; there was a fresh breeze out of the north.

The restaurant was a roadside place with tables and booths. The other eclipse-watchers were there. From our booth we could see their cars' California license plates, their University of Washington parking stickers. Inside the restaurant we were all eating eggs or waffles; people were fairly shouting and exchanging enthusiasms, like fans after a World Series game. Did you see . . . ? Did you see . . . ? Then somebody said something which knocked me for a loop.

A college student, a boy in a blue parka who carried a Hasselblad, said to us, "Did you see that little white ring? It looked like a Life Saver. It looked like a Life Saver up in the sky."

And so it did. The boy spoke well. He was a walking alarm clock. I myself had at that time no access to such a word. He could write a sentence, and I could not. I grabbed that Life Saver and rode it to the surface. And I had to laugh. I had been dumbstruck on the Euphrates River, I had been dead and gone and grieving, all over the sight of something which, if you could claw your way up to that level, you would grant looked very much like a Life Saver. It was good to be back among people so clever; it was good to have all the world's words at the mind's disposal, so the mind could begin its task. All those things for which we have no words are lost. The mind—the culture—has two little tools, grammar and lexicon: a decorated sand bucket and a matching shovel. With these we bluster about the continents and do all the world's work. With these we try to save our very lives.

There are a few more things to tell from this level, the level of the restaurant. One is the old joke about breakfast. "It can never be satisfied, the mind, never." Wallace Stevens wrote that, and in the long run he was right. The mind wants to live forever, or to learn a very good reason why not. The mind wants the world to return its love, or its awareness; the mind wants to know all the world, and all eternity, and God. The mind's sidekick, however, will settle for two eggs over easy.

The dear, stupid body is as easily satisfied as a spaniel. And, incredibly, the simple spaniel can lure the brawling mind to its dish. It is everlastingly funny that the proud, metaphysically ambitious, clamoring mind will hush if you give it an egg.

Further: while the mind reels in deep space, while the mind grieves or fears or exults, the workaday senses, in ignorance or idiocy, like so many computer terminals printing out market prices while the world blows up, still transcribe their little data and transmit them to the warehouse in the skull. Later, under the tranquilizing influence of fried eggs, the mind can sort through this data. The restaurant was a halfway house, a decompression chamber. There I remembered a few things more.

The deepest, and most terrifying, was this: I have said that I heard screams. (I have since read that screaming, with hysteria, is a common reaction even to expected total eclipses.) People on all the hillsides, including, I think, myself, screamed when the black body of the moon detached from the sky and rolled over the sun. But something else was happening at that same instant, and it was this, I believe, which made us scream.

The second before the sun went out we saw a wall of dark shadow come speeding at us. We no sooner saw it than it was upon us, like thunder. It roared up the valley. It slammed our hill and knocked us out.

It was the monstrous swift shadow cone of the moon. I have since read that this wave of shadow moves 1,800 miles an hour. Language can give no sense of this sort of speed—1,800 miles an hour. It was 195 miles wide. No end was in sight—you saw only the edge. It rolled at you across the land at 1,800 miles an hour, hauling darkness like plague behind it. Seeing it, and knowing it was coming straight for you, was like feeling a slug of anesthetic shoot up your arm. If you think very fast, you may have time to think, "Soon it will hit my brain." You can feel the deadness race up your arm; you can feel the appalling, inhuman speed of your own blood. We saw the wall of shadow coming, and screamed before it hit.

This was the universe about which we have read so much and never before felt: the universe as a clockwork of loose spheres flung at stupefying, unauthorized speeds. How could anything moving so fast not crash, not veer from its orbit amok like a car out of control on a turn?

Less than two minutes later, when the sun emerged, the trailing edge of the shadow cone sped away. It coursed down our hill and raced eastward over the plain, faster than the eye could believe; it swept over the plain and dropped over the planet's rim in a twinkling. It had clobbered us, and now it roared away. We blinked in the light. It was as though an enormous, loping god in the sky had reached down and slapped the earth's face.

Something else, something more ordinary, came back to me along about the third cup of coffee. During the moments of totality, it was so dark that drivers on the highway below turned on their cars' headlights. We could see the highway's route as a strand of lights. It was bumper-to-bumper down there. It was eight-fifteen in the morning, Monday morning, and people were driving into Yakima to work. That it was as dark as night, and eerie as hell, an hour after dawn, apparently meant that in order to *see* to drive to work, people had to use their headlights. Four or five cars pulled off the road. The rest, in a line at least five miles long, drove to town. The highway ran between hills; the people could not have seen any of the eclipsed sun at all. Yakima will have another total eclipse in 2086. Perhaps, in 2086, businesses will give their employees an hour off.

From the restaurant we drove back to the coast. The highway crossing the Cascades range was open. We drove over the mountain like old pros. We joined our places on the planet's thin crust; it held. For the time being, we were home free.

Early that morning at six, when we had checked out, the six bald men were sitting on folding chairs in the dim hotel lobby. The television was on. Most of them were awake. You might drown in your own spittle, God knows, at any time; you might wake up dead in a small hotel, a cabbage head watching TV while snows pile up in the passes, watching TV while the chili peppers smile and the moon passes over the sun and nothing changes and nothing is learned because you have lost your bucket and shovel and no longer care. What if you regain the surface and open your sack and find, instead of treasure, a beast which jumps at you? Or you may not come back at all. The winches may jam, the scaffolding buckle, the air conditioning collapse. You may glance up one day and see by your headlamp the canary keeled over in its cage. You may reach into a cranny for pearls and touch a moray eel. You yank on your rope; it is too late.

Apparently people share a sense of these hazards, for when the total eclipse ended, an odd thing happened.

When the sun appeared as a blinding bead on the ring's side, the eclipse was over. The black lens cover appeared again, backlighted, and slid away. At once the yellow light made the sky blue again; the black lid dissolved and vanished. The real world began there. I remember now: we all hurried away. We were born and bored at a stroke. We rushed down the hill. We found our car; we saw the other people streaming down the hillsides; we joined the highway traffic and drove away.

We never looked back. It was a general vamoose, and an odd one, for when we left the hill, the sun was still partially eclipsed—a sight rare enough, and one which, in itself, we would probably have driven five hours to see. But enough is enough. One turns at last even from glory itself with a sigh of relief. From the depths of mystery, and even from the heights of splendor, we bounce back and hurry for the latitudes of home.

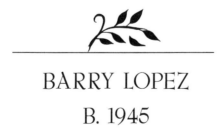

BARRY LOPEZ
B. 1945

*In his books Barry Lopez has looked long and hard at the uses, or misuses, to which the human mind has put its natural environment. His early collections of essays—*Desert Notes *(1976),* Giving Birth to Thunder *(1978) and* River Notes *(1979)—contain surrealistic fictional narratives and retellings of Western Indian myths, presenting non-Western, unconventional visions of landscape and animals.* Of Wolves and Men *(1978), winner of the John Burroughs Medal, is a definitive and fascinating exploration of how these social predators have been portrayed and treated by native American cultures, European myth, American folklore, and contemporary biologists.*

With the publication of Arctic Dreams: Imagination and Desire in A Northern Landscape *(1986), Lopez became a leading contemporary spokesman for an ethical revaluation of our ecological behavior. Based on several years of personal research, the book surveys Arctic landscape, wildlife, culture, exploration, and exploitation to demonstrate how we project our dreams and desires on the earth's natural areas, more often than not to our own as well as the environment's detriment. One pervasive theme of the book is how native folklore and myth generally reflect the reality of a landscape more accurately than the "history" and "science" of a culture bent on conquest. Yet Lopez does not believe we must abandon our own cultural heritage—a fact which separates him from more absolute critics of Western civilization. In fact the wide-ranging and penetrating intellect which informs his writing stems from a loyalty to the best traditions of Western ethics and philosophy. Rather he asserts that we have an urgent need to understand our past behavior towards animals and to "renegotiate the contracts" with them. Above all, his books are eloquent and informed appeals for tolerance and dignity in our dealings with all of the earth's inhabitants.*

From ARCTIC DREAMS

LANCASTER SOUND

* * * The first narwhals I ever saw lived far from here, in Bering Strait. The day I saw them I knew that no element of the earth's natural history had ever before brought me so far, so suddenly. It was as though something from a bestiary had taken shape, a creature strange as a giraffe. It was as if the testimony of someone I had no reason to doubt, yet could not quite believe, a story too farfetched, had been verified at a glance.

I was with a bowhead whale biologist named Don Ljungblad, flying

Arctic Dreams: Imagination and Desire in a Northern Landscape (New York: Scribners, 1986).

search transects over Bering Sea. It was May, and the first bowheads of spring were slowly working their way north through Bering Strait toward their summer feeding grounds in the Chukchi and Beaufort seas. Each day as we flew these transects we would pass over belukha whale and walrus, ringed, spotted, and ribbon seals, bearded seals, and flocks of birds migrating to Siberia. I know of no other region in North America where animals can be met with in such numbers. Bering Sea itself is probably the richest of all the northern seas, as rich as Chesapeake Bay or the Grand Banks at the time of their discovery. Its bounty of crabs, pollock, cod, sole, herring, clams, and salmon is set down in wild numbers, the rambling digits of guesswork. The numbers of birds and marine mammals feeding here, to a person familiar with anything but the Serengeti or life at the Antarctic convergence, are magical. At the height of migration in the spring, the testament of life in Bering Sea is absolutely stilling in its dimensions.

The two weeks I spent flying with Ljungblad, with so many thousands of creatures moving through the water and the air, were a heady experience. Herds of belukha whale glided in silent shoals beneath transparent sheets of young ice. Squadrons of fast-flying sea ducks flashed beneath us as they banked away. We passed ice floes stained red in a hundred places with the afterbirths of walrus. Staring all day into the bright light reflected from the ice and water, however, and the compression in time of these extraordinary events, left me dazed some evenings.

Aspects of the arctic landscape that had become salient for me—its real and temporal borders; a rare, rich oasis of life surrounded by vast stretches of deserted land; the upending of conventional kinds of time; biological vulnerability made poignant by the forgiving light of summer—all of this was evoked over Bering Sea.

The day we saw the narwhals we were flying south, low over Bering Strait. The ice in Chukchi Sea behind us was so close it did not seem possible that bowheads could have penetrated this far; but it is good to check, because they can make headway in ice as heavy as this and they are able to come a long way north undetected in lighter ice on the Russian side. I was daydreaming about two bowheads we had seen that morning. They had been floating side by side in a broad lane of unusually clear water between a shelf of shorefast ice and the pack ice—the flaw lead. As we passed over, they made a single movement together, a slow, rolling turn and graceful glide, like figure skaters pushing off, these 50-ton leviathans. Ljungblad shouted in my earphones: "Waiting." They were waiting for the ice in the strait to open up. Ljungblad saw nearly 300 bowheads waiting calmly like this one year, some on their backs, some with their chins resting on the ice.

The narwhals appeared in the middle of this reverie. Two males, with ivory tusks spiraling out of their foreheads, the image of the unicorn with which history has confused them. They were close to the same size and light-colored, and were lying parallel and motionless in a long, straight lead in the ice. My eye was drawn to them before my conscious mind, let alone my voice, could catch up. I stared dumbfounded while someone else shouted. Not just to see the narwhals, but *here,* a few miles northwest of King Island in Bering Sea. In all the years scientists have kept records for these waters, no one had ever seen a narwhal alive in Bering Sea. Judging from the heaviness of the ice around them, they must have spent the winter here.* They were either residents, a wondrous thought, or they had come from the nearest population centers the previous fall, from waters north of Siberia or from northeastern Canada.

The appearance of these animals was highly provocative. We made circle after circle above them, until they swam away under the ice and were gone. Then we looked at each other. Who could say what this was, really?

Because you have seen something doesn't mean you can explain it. Differing interpretations will always abound, even when good minds come to bear. The kernel of indisputable information is a dot in space; interpretations grow out of the desire to make this point a line, to give it a direction. The directions in which it can be sent, the uses to which it can be put by a culturally, professionally, and geographically diverse society, are almost without limit. The possibilities make good scientists chary. In a region like the Arctic, tense with a hunger for wealth, with fears of plunder, interpretation can quickly get beyond a scientist's control. When asked to assess the meaning of a biological event—What were those animals doing out there? Where do they belong?—they hedge. They are sometimes reluctant to elaborate on what they saw, because they cannot say what it means, and they are suspicious of those who say they know. Some even distrust the motives behind the questions.

I think along these lines in this instance because of the animal. No large mammal in the Northern Hemisphere comes as close as the narwhal to having its very existence doubted. For some, the possibility that this creature might actually live in the threatened waters of Bering Sea is portentous, a significant apparition on the eve of an era of disruptive oil exploration there. For others, those with the leases to search for oil and

*The narwhal is not nearly as forceful in the ice as the bowhead. It can break through only about 6 inches of ice with its head. A bowhead, using its brow or on occasion its more formidable chin, can break through as much as 18 inches of sea ice. [Lopez's note]

gas in Navarin and Norton basins, the possibility that narwhals may live there is a complicating environmental nuisance. Hardly anyone marvels solely at the fact that on the afternoon of April 16, 1982, five people saw two narwhals in a place so unexpected that they were flabbergasted. They remained speechless, circling over the animals in a state of wonder. In those moments the animals did not have to mean anything at all. * * *

MIGRATION

* * * I visited Anaktuvuk Pass in 1978 with a friend, a wolf biologist who had made a temporary home there and who was warmly regarded for his tact, his penchant for listening, and his help during an epidemic of flu in the village. We spent several days watching wolves and caribou in nearby valleys and visiting at several homes. The men talked a lot about hunting. The evenings were full of stories. There were moments of silence when someone said something very true, peals of laughter when a man told a story expertly at his own expense. One afternoon we left and traveled far to the west to the headwaters of the Utukok River.

The Alaska Department of Fish and Game had a small field camp on the Utukok, at the edge of a gravel-bar landing strip. Among the biologists there were men and women studying caribou, moose, tundra grizzly, wolverine, and, now that my companion had arrived, wolves. The country around the Utukok and the headwaters of the Kokolik River is a wild and serene landscape in summer. Parts of the Western Arctic caribou herd are drifting over the hills, returning from the calving grounds. The sun is always shining, somewhere in the sky. For a week or more we had very fine, clear weather. Golden eagles circled high over the tundra, hunting. Snowy owls regarded us from a distance from their tussock perches. Short-eared owls, a gyrfalcon. Familiar faces.

A few days after we arrived, my companion and I went south six or seven miles and established a camp from which we could watch a distant wolf den. In that open, rolling country without trees, I had the feeling, sometimes, that nothing was hidden. It was during those days that I went for walks along Ilingnorak Ridge and started visiting ground-nesting birds, and developed the habit of bowing to them out of regard for what was wonderful and mysterious in their lives.

The individual animals we watched tested their surroundings, tried things they had not done before, or that possibly no animal like them had ever done before—revealing their capacity for the new. The preservation of this capacity to adapt is one of the central mysteries of evolution.

We watched wolves hunting caribou, and owls hunting lemmings. Arctic ground squirrel eating *irok,* the mountain sorrel. I thought a great deal about hunting. In 1949, Robert Flaherty told an amazing story, which Edmund Carpenter was later successful in getting published. It was about a man named Comock. In 1902, when he and his family were facing starvation, Comock decided to travel over the sea ice to an island he knew about, where he expected they would be able to find food (a small island off Cape Wolstenholme, at the northern tip of Quebec's Ungava Peninsula). On the journey across, they lost nearly all their belongings—all of Comock's knives, spears, and harpoons, all their skins, their stone lamps, and most of their dogs—when the sea ice suddenly opened one night underneath their camp. They were without hunting implements, without a stone lamp to melt water to drink, without food or extra clothing. Comock had left only one sled, several dogs, his snow knife, with which he could cut snow blocks to build a snow house, and stones to make sparks for a fire.

They ate their dogs. The dogs they kept ate the other dogs, which were killed for them. Comock got his family to the island. He fashioned, from inappropriate materials, new hunting weapons. He created shelter and warmth. He hunted successfully. He reconstructed his entire material culture, almost from scratch, by improvising and, where necessary, inventing. He survived. His family survived. His dogs survived and multiplied.

Over the years they carefully collected rare bits of driftwood and bone until Comock had enough to build the frame for an umiak. They saved bearded-seal skins, from which Comock's wife made a waterproof hull. And one summer day they sailed away, back toward Ungava Peninsula. Robert Flaherty, exploring along the coast, spotted Comock and his family and dogs approaching across the water. When they came close, Flaherty, recognizing the form of an umiak and the cut of Eskimo clothing but, seeing that the materials were strange and improvised, asked the Eskimo who he was. He said his name was Comock. "Where in the world have you come from?" asked Flaherty. "From far away, from big island, from far over there," answered Comock, pointing. Then he smiled and made a joke about how poor the umiak must appear, and his family burst into laughter.

I think of this story because at its heart is the industry and competence, the determination and inventiveness of a human family. And because it is about people who lived resolutely in the heart of every moment they found themselves in, disastrous and sublime.

During those days I spent on Ilingnorak Ridge, I did not know what I know now about hunting; but I had begun to sense the outline of what I would learn in the years ahead with Eskimos and from being introduced, by various people, to situations I could not have easily found my way to alone. The insights I felt during those days had to do with the nature of hunting, with the movement of human beings over the land, and with fear. The thoughts grew out of watching the animals.

The evidence is good that among all northern aboriginal hunting peoples, the hunter saw himself bound up in a sacred relationship with the larger animals he hunted. The relationship was full of responsibilities—to the animals, to himself, and to his family. Among the great and, at this point, perhaps tragic lapses in the study of aboriginal hunting peoples is a lack of comprehension about the role women played in hunting. We can presume, I think, that in the same way the hunter felt bound to the animals he hunted, he felt the contract incomplete and somehow even inappropriate if his wife was not part of it. In no hunting society could a man hunt successfully alone. He depended upon his wife for obvious reasons—for the preparation of food and clothing, companionship, humor, subtle encouragement—and for things we can only speculate about, things of a religious nature, bearing on the mutual obligations and courtesies with which he approached the animals he hunted.

Hunting in my experience—and by hunting I simply mean being out on the land—is a state of mind. All of one's faculties are brought to bear in an effort to become fully incorporated into the landscape. It is more than listening for animals or watching for hoofprints or a shift in the weather. It is more than an analysis of what one *senses*. To hunt means to have the land around you like clothing. To engage in a wordless dialogue with it, one so absorbing that you cease to talk with your human companions. It means to release yourself from rational images of what something "means" and to be concerned only that it "is." And then to recognize that things exist only insofar as they can be related to other things. These relationships—fresh drops of moisture on top of rocks at a river crossing and a raven's distant voice—become patterns. The patterns are always in motion. Suddenly the pattern—which includes physical hunger, a memory of your family, and memories of the valley you are walking through, these particular plants and smells—takes in the caribou. There is a caribou standing in front of you. The release of the arrow or bullet is like a word spoken out loud. It occurs at the periphery of your concentration.

The mind we know in dreaming, a nonrational, nonlinear comprehension of events in which slips in time and space are normal, is, I believe, the conscious working mind of an aboriginal hunter. It is a frame of mind that redefines patience, endurance, and expectation.

The focus of a hunter in a hunting society was not killing animals but attending to the myriad relationships he understood bound him into the world he occupied with them. He tended to those duties carefully because he perceived in them everything he understood about survival. This does not mean, certainly, that every man did this, or that good men did not starve. Or that shamans whose duty it was to intercede with the forces that empowered these relationships weren't occasionally thinking of personal gain or subterfuge. It only means that most men understood how to behave.

A fundamental difference between our culture and Eskimo culture, which can be felt even today in certain situations, is that we have irrevocably separated ourselves from the world that animals occupy. We have turned all animals and elements of the natural world into objects. We manipulate them to serve the complicated ends of our destiny. Eskimos do not grasp this separation easily, and have difficulty imagining themselves entirely removed from the world of animals. For many of them, to make this separation is analogous to cutting oneself off from light or water. It is hard to imagine how to do it.

A second difference is that, because we have objectified animals, we are able to treat them impersonally. This means not only the animals that live around us but animals that live in distant lands. For Eskimos, most relationships with animals are local and personal. The animals one encounters are part of one's community, and one has obligations to them. A most confusing aspect of Western culture for Eskimos to grasp is our depersonalization of relationships with the human and animal members of our communities. And it is compounded, rather than simplified, by their attempting to learn how to objectify animals.

Eskimos do not maintain this intimacy with nature without paying a certain price. When I have thought about the ways in which they differ from people in my own culture, I have realized that they are more afraid than we are. On a day-to-day basis, they have more fear. Not of being dumped into cold water from an umiak, not a debilitating fear. They are afraid because they accept fully what is violent and tragic in nature. It is a fear tied to their knowledge that sudden, cataclysmic events are as much a part of life, of really living, as are the moments when one pauses to look at something beautiful. A Central Eskimo shaman named Aua, queried by Knud Rasmussen about Eskimo beliefs, answered, "We do not believe. We fear."

To extend these thoughts, it is wrong to think of hunting cultures like the Eskimo's as living in perfect harmony or balance with nature. Their regard for animals and their attentiveness to nuance in the landscape were not rigorous or complete enough to approach an idealized harmony. No one knew that much. No one would say they knew that much. They faced nature with fear, with *ilira* (nervous awe) and *kappia* (apprehension). And with enthusiasm. They accepted hunting as a way of life—its violence, too, though they did not seek that out. They were unsentimental, so much so that most outsiders thought them cruel, especially in their treatment of dogs. Nor were they innocent. There is murder and warfare and tribal vendetta in their history; and today, in the same villages I walked out of to hunt, are families shattered by alcohol, drugs, and ambition. While one cannot dismiss culpability in these things, any more than one can hold to romantic notions about hunting, it is good to recall what a *struggle* it is to live with dignity and understanding, with perspicacity or grace, in circumstances far better than these. And it is helpful to imagine how the forces of life must be construed by people who live in a world where swift and fatal violence, like *ivu*, the suddenly leaping shore ice, is inherent in the land. The land, in a certain, very real way, compels the minds of the people.

A good reason to travel with Eskimo hunters in modern times is that, beyond nettlesome details—foods that are not to one's liking, a loss of intellectual conversation, a consistent lack of formal planning—in spite of these things, one feels the constant presence of people who know something about surviving. At their best they are resilient, practical, and enthusiastic. They pay close attention in realms where they feel a capacity for understanding. They have a quality of *nuannaarpoq*, of taking extravagant pleasure in being alive; and they delight in finding it in other people. Facing as we do our various Armageddons, they are a good people to know.

In the time I was in the field with Eskimos I wondered at the basis for my admiration. I admired an awareness in the men of providing for others, and the soft tone of voice they used around bloodshed. I never thought I could understand, from their point of view, that moment of preternaturally heightened awareness, and the peril inherent in taking a life; but I accepted it out of respect for their seriousness toward it. In moments when I felt perplexed, that I was dealing with an order outside my own, I discovered and put to use a part of my own culture's wisdom, the formal divisions of Western philosophy—metaphysics, epistemology, ethics, aesthetics, and logic—which pose, in order, the following questions. What is real? What can we understand? How should we behave? What is beautiful? What are the patterns we can rely upon?

As I traveled, I would say to myself, What do my companions see where I see death? Is the sunlight beautiful to them, the way it sparkles on the water? Which for the Eskimo hunter are the patterns to be trusted? The patterns, I know, could be different from ones I imagined were before us. There could be other, remarkably different insights.

Those days on Ilingnorak Ridge, when I saw tundra grizzly tearing up the earth looking for ground squirrels, and watched wolves hunting, and horned lark sitting so resolutely on her nest, and caribou crossing the river and shaking off the spray like diamonds before the evening sun, I was satisfied only to watch. This was the great drift and pause of life. These were the arrangements that made the land ring with integrity. Somewhere downriver, I remembered, a scientist named Edward Sable had paused on a trek in 1947 to stare at a Folsom spear point, a perfectly fluted object of black chert resting on a sandstone ledge. People, moving over the land. *   *   *

ICE AND LIGHT

*   *   * During the sea-lift passage of the *Soodoc* north through Davis Strait, en route to Little Cornwallis Island, I got in the habit of spending afternoons in the cab of a large front-loader that was chained down on the deck alongside other pieces of heavy machinery. I could sit there out of the wind and occasional rain, looking out through its spacious windows at the sea and ice. Sometimes I would read in the *Pilot of Arctic Canada.* Or I would read arctic history with a map spread out in my lap.

The days among the icebergs passed slowly. I sat in my makeshift catbird seat on the deck, or stood watching in the bows, or up on the bridge with my binoculars and sketchbook.

The icebergs were like pieces of Montana floating past. A different geography, I thought, from the one I grew up knowing.

Icebergs create an unfamiliar sense of space because the horizon retreats from them and the sky rises without any lines of compression behind them. It is this perspective that frightened pioneer families on the treeless North American prairies. Too much space, anchored only now and then by a stretch of bur oak savanna. Landscape painting of the T'ang and Sung dynasties (seventh to twelfth centuries) used this arrangement of space to create the sense of a large presence beyond. Indeed, the subject of such paintings was often their apparent emptiness.

American landscape painting in the nineteenth century, to return to an earlier thought, reveals a struggle with light and space that eventually set it apart from a contemporary European tradition of pastoral landscapes framed by trees, the world viewed from a carriage window. American painters meant to locate an actual spiritual presence in the North American landscape. Their paintings, according to art historians of the period, were the inspirations of men and women who "saw the face of God" in the prairies and mountains and along the river bottoms. One of the clearest expressions of this recasting of an understanding of what a landscape is were the almost austere compositions of the luminists. The atmosphere of these paintings is silent and contemplative. They suggest a private rather than a public encounter with the land. Several critics, among them Barbara Novak in her study of this period in American art, *Nature and Culture,* have described as well a peculiar "loss of ego" in the paintings. The artist disappears. The authority of the work lies, instead, with the land. And the light in them is like a creature, a living, integral part of the scene. The landscape is numinous, imposing, real. It ceases to be, as it was in Europe, merely symbolic.

At the height of his critical and popular acclaim in 1859, Frederic Edwin Church, one of the most prominent of the luminists, set sail for waters off the Newfoundland coast. He wanted to sketch the icebergs there. They seemed to him the very embodiment of light in nature. Following a three-week cruise, he returned to his studio in New York to execute a large painting.

The small field sketches he made—some are no larger than the palm of your hand—have a wonderful, working intimacy about them. He captures both the monolithic inscrutability of icebergs and the weathered, beaten look they have by the time they arrive that far south in the Labrador Sea. Looking closely at one drawing, made on July 1, I noticed that Church had penciled underneath it the words "strange supernatural."

The oil painting he produced from these sketches came to be called *The Icebergs.* It is so imposing—6 feet by 10 feet wide—a viewer feels he can almost step into it, which was Church's intent. In the foreground is a shelf of ice, part of an iceberg that fills most of the painting and which rises abruptly in the left foreground. On the right, the flooded ice shelf becomes part of a wave-carved grotto. In the central middle ground is a becalmed embayment, opening onto darker ocean waters to the left, which continue to a stormy horizon and other, distant icebergs. Dominating the background on the far side of the embayment is a high wall of ice and snow that carries all the way to the right of the painting. In the ocean air above is a rolling mist. The shading and forms of the icebergs are expertly limned—Church was an avid naturalist, and conscientious about such accuracy—and the colors, though slightly embellished, are true.

There are two oddities about this now very famous American landscape painting. When it was undraped at Gaupil's Gallery in New York on April 24, 1861, the reaction was more reserved than the lionized Church had anticipated. But *The Icebergs* differed from the rest of Church's work in one, crucial aspect: there was no trace of man in it. Convinced that he had perhaps made a mistake, Church took the work back to his studio and inserted in the foreground a bit of flotsam from a shipwreck, a portion of the main-topmast with the crow's nest. The painting was then exhibited in Boston, where it was no better received than it had been in New York. Only when it arrived in London did critics and audiences marvel. "A most weird and beautiful picture," wrote a reviewer in the *Manchester Guardian.* England, with its longer history of arctic exploration and whaling and but a few years removed from the tragedy of Sir John Franklin, was certainly more appreciative, at least, of its subject matter.

The second oddity is that Church's painting "disappeared" for 116 years. It was purchased in 1863 by a Sir Edward Watkin, after the London showing, to hang at his estate outside Manchester, called Rose Hill. It then passed by inheritance through Watkins' son to a purchaser of the estate; and then, by donation, to Saint Wilfred's Church nearby (which returned it to Rose Hill with regrets about its size). By 1979 Rose Hill had become the Rose Hill Remand Home for Boys, and *The Icebergs,* hanging without a frame in a stairwell, had been signed by one of the boys. Unaware of its value and seeking funds for the reform school's operation, the owners offered it for sale. The painting was brought back to New York and sold at auction on October 25, 1979, for $2.5 million, the highest price paid to that time for a painting in America. It now hangs in the Dallas Museum of Fine Arts, in Texas.

CHURCH's decision to add the broken mast to *The Icebergs* speaks, certainly, to his commercial instincts, but the addition, I think, is more complex than this; and such a judgment is both too cynical and too simple.

Try as we might, we ultimately can make very little sense at all of nature without resorting to such devices. Whether they are such bald assertions of human presence as Church's cruciform mast or the intangible, metaphorical tools of the mind—contrast, remembrance, analogy—we bring our own worlds to bear in foreign landscapes in order to clarify them for ourselves. It is hard to imagine that we could do otherwise. The risk we take is of finding our final authority in the metaphors rather than in the land. To inquire into the intricacies of a distant landscape, then, is to provoke thoughts about one's own interior landscape, and the familiar landscapes of memory. The land urges us to come around to an understanding of ourselves.

A comparison with cathedrals has come to many Western minds in searching for a metaphor for icebergs, and I think the reasons for it are deeper than the obvious appropriateness of line and scale. It has to do with our passion for light.

Cathedral architecture signaled a quantum leap forward in European civilization. The gothic cathedral churches, with their broad bays of sunshine, flying buttresses that let windows rise where once there had been stone in the walls, and harmonious interiors—this "architecture of light" was a monument to a newly created theology. "God is light," writes a French cultural historian of the era, Georges Duby, and "every creature stems from that initial, uncreated, creative light." Robert Grosseteste, the twelfth-century founder of Oxford University, wrote that "physical light is the best, the most delectable, the most beautiful of all the bodies that exist."

Intellectually, the eleventh and twelfth centuries were an age of careful dialectics, a working out of relationships that eventually became so refined they could be expressed in the mathematics of cathedrals. Not only was God light but the *relationship* between God and man was light. The cathedrals, by the very way they snared the sun's energy, were an expression of God and of the human connection with God as well. The aesthetics of this age, writes Duby, was "based on light, logic, lucidity, and yearning for a God in a human form." Both the scholastic monks in their exegetical disquisitions and the illiterate people who built these churches, who sent these structures soaring into the sky—157 feet at Beauvais before it fell over on them—both, writes Duby, were "people trying to rise above their poverty through dreams of light."

It was an age of mystics. When Heinrich Suso, a Dominican monk, prayed at night in church, "it often seemed as if he were floating on air or sailing between time and eternity, on the deep tide of the unsoundable marvels of God." And it was an age of visionaries who spoke of the New Jerusalem of the Apocalypse, where there would be no darkness.

The erection of these monuments to spiritual awareness signaled a revival of cities, without which these edifices could not have survived. (The money to build them came largely from an emerging class of merchants and tradesmen, not royalty.) In time, however, the cathedrals became more and more esoteric, so heavily intellectualized an enterprise that, today, the raw, spiritual desire that was their original impetus seems lost. To the modern visitor, familiar with an architecture more facile and clever with light, the cathedrals now seem dark. Their stone has been eaten away by the acids and corrosives of industrial air. The age of mystics that bore them gave way rather too quickly to an age of rational intellects, of vast, baroque theological abstraction.

A final, ironic point: the mathematics that made the building of the cathedrals possible was carefully preserved by Arabs and Moors, by so-called infidels.

By the thirteenth century, Europe was starting to feel the vastness of Asia, the authority of other cultures. "The dissemination of knowledge," writes Duby, "and the strides made in the cultural sphere had opened [European] eyes and forced them to face facts: the world was infinitely larger, more various, and less docile than it had seemed to their forefathers; it was full of men who had not received the word of God, who refused to hear it, and who would not be easily conquered by arms. In Europe the days of holy war were over. The days of the explorers, traders, and missionaries had begun. After all, why persist in struggling against all those infidels, those expert warriors, when it was more advantageous to negotiate and attempt to insinuate oneself in those invincible kingdoms by business transactions and peaceful preaching?"

This was the philosophy that carried the Portuguese to India, the Spaniards to Peru, and the French and British into the hinterlands of northern North America. Hundreds of years later, a refinement on this philosophy of acquisition propelled Americans, Canadians, and Russians into the Arctic.

The conventional wisdom of our time is that European man has advanced by enormous strides since the age of cathedrals. He has landed on the moon. He has cured smallpox. He has harnessed the power in the atom. Another argument, however, might be made in the opposite direction, that all European man has accomplished in 900 years is a more complicated manipulation of materials, a more astounding display of his grasp of the physical principles of matter. That we are dazzled by mere styles of expression. That ours is not an age of mystics but of singular adepts, of performers. That the erection of the cathedrals was the last wild stride European man made before falling back into the confines of his intellect.

Of the sciences today, quantum physics alone seems to have found its way back to an equitable relationship with metaphors, those fundamental tools of the imagination. The other sciences are occasionally so bound by rational analysis, or so wary of metaphor, that they recognize and denounce anthropomorphism as a kind of intellectual cancer, instead of employing it as a tool of comparative inquiry, which is perhaps the only way the mind works, that parallelism we finally call narrative.

There is a word from the time of the cathedrals: agape, an expression of intense spiritual affinity with the mystery that is "to be sharing life with other life." Agape is love, and it can mean "the love of another for the sake of God." More broadly and essentially it is a humble, impassioned embrace of something outside the self, in the name of that which we refer to as *God,* but which also includes the self and *is* God. We are clearly indebted as a species to the play of our intelligence; we trust our future to it; but we do not know whether intelligence is reason or whether intelligence is this desire to embrace and be embraced in the pattern that both theologians and physicists call God. Whether intelligence, in other words, is love.

One day, sitting in my accustomed spot on the cargo deck of the *Soodoc,* I turned to see the second engineer, who had brought two cups of coffee. He was from Guyana. We talked about Guyana, and about the icebergs, some forty or fifty of which were then around us. He raised his chin to indicate and said, "How would you like to live up there? A fellow could camp up there, sail all the way to Newfoundland. Get off at Saint John's How about it?" He laughed.

We laughed together. We searched the horizon for mirages with the binoculars, but we were not successful. When his break was over, the engineer went back below decks. I hung over the bow, staring into the bow wave at the extraordinary fluidity of that geometry on the calm waters of Melville Bay. I looked up at the icebergs. They so embodied the land. Austere. Implacable. Harsh but not antagonistic. Creatures of pale light. Once, camped in the Anaktiktoak Valley of the central Brooks Range in Alaska, a friend had said, gazing off across that broad glacial valley of soft greens and straw browns, with sunlight lambent on Tulugak Lake and the Anaktuvuk River in the distance, that it was so beautiful it made you cry.

I looked out at the icebergs. They were so beautiful they also made you afraid.

THE RAVEN

I am going to have to start at the other end by telling you this: there are no crows in the desert. What appear to be crows are ravens. You must examine the crow, however, before you can understand the raven. To forget the crow completely, as some have tried to do, would be like trying to understand the one who stayed without talking to the one who left. It is important to make note of who has left the desert.

To begin with, the crow does nothing alone. He cannot abide silence

Desert Notes: Reflections in the Eye of a Raven (Kansas City, Mo.: Andrews and McMeel, 1976).

and he is prone to stealing things, twigs and bits of straw, from the nests of his neighbors. It is a game with him. He enjoys tricks. If he cannot make up his mind the crow will take two or three wives, but this is not a game. The crow is very accommodating and he admires compulsiveness.

Crows will live in street trees in the residential areas of great cities. They will walk at night on the roofs of parked cars and peck at the grit; they will scrape the pinpoints of their talons across the steel and, with their necks outthrust, watch for frightened children listening in their beds.

Put all this to the raven: he will open his mouth as if to say something. Then he will look the other way and say nothing. Later, when you have forgotten, he will tell you he admires the crow.

The raven is larger than the crow and has a beard of black feathers at his throat. He is careful to kill only what he needs. Crows, on the other hand, will search out the great horned owl, kick and punch him awake, and then, for roosting too close to their nests, they will kill him. They will come out of the sky on a fat, hot afternoon and slam into the head of a dozing rabbit and go away laughing. They will tear out a whole row of planted corn and eat only a few kernels. They will defecate on scarecrows and go home and sleep with 200,000 of their friends in an atmosphere of congratulation. Again, it is only a game; this should not be taken to mean that they are evil.

There is however this: when too many crows come together on a roost there is a lot of shoving and noise and a white film begins to descend over the crows' eyes and they go blind. They fall from their perches and lie on the ground and starve to death. When confronted with this information, crows will look past you and warn you vacantly that it is easy to be misled.

The crow flies like a pigeon. The raven flies like a hawk. He is seen only at a great distance and then not very clearly. This is true of the crow too, but if you are very clever you can trap the crow. The only way to be sure what you have seen is a raven is to follow him until he dies of old age, and then examine the body.

Once there were many crows in the desert. I am told it was like this: you could sit back in the rocks and watch a pack of crows working over the carcass of a coyote. Some would eat, the others would try to squeeze out the vultures. The raven would never be seen. He would be at a distance, alone, perhaps eating a scorpion.

There was, at this time, a small alkaline water hole at the desert's edge. Its waters were bitter. No one but crows would drink there, although they drank sparingly, just one or two sips at a time. One day a raven warned someone about the dangers of drinking the bitter water and was overheard by a crow. When word of this passed among the crows they felt insulted. They jeered and raised insulting gestures to the ravens. They bullied each other into drinking the alkaline water until they had drunk the hole dry and gone blind.

The crows flew into canyon walls and dove straight into the ground at forty miles an hour and broke their necks. The worst of it was their cartwheeling across the desert floor, stiff wings outstretched, beaks agape, white eyes ballooning, surprising rattlesnakes hidden under sage bushes out of the noonday sun. The snakes awoke, struck and held. The wheeling birds strew them across the desert like sprung traps.

When all the crows were finally dead, the desert bacteria and fungi bored into them, burrowed through bone and muscle, through aqueous humor and feathers until they had reduced the stiff limbs of soft black to blue dust.

After that, there were no more crows in the desert. The few who watched from a distance took it as a sign and moved away.

Finally there is this: one morning four ravens sat at the edge of the desert waiting for the sun to rise. They had been there all night and the dew was like beads of quicksilver on their wings. Their eyes were closed and they were as still as the cracks in the desert floor.

The wind came off the snow-capped peaks to the north and ruffled their breath feathers. Their talons arched in the white earth and they smoothed their wings with sleek, dark bills. At first light their bodies swelled and their eyes flashed purple. When the dew dried on their wings they lifted off from the desert floor and flew away in four directions. Crows would never have had the patience for this.

If you want to know more about the raven: bury yourself in the desert so that you have a commanding view of the high basalt cliffs where he lives. Let only your eyes protrude. Do not blink—the movement will alert the raven to your continued presence. Wait until a generation of ravens has passed away. Of the new generation there will be at least one bird who will find you. He will see your eyes staring up out of the desert floor. The raven is cautious, but he is thorough. He will sense your peaceful intentions. Let him have the first word. Be careful: he will tell you he knows nothing.

If you do not have the time for this, scour the weathered desert shacks for some sign of the raven's body. Look under old mattresses and beneath loose floorboards. Look behind the walls. Sooner or later you will find a severed foot. It will be his and it will be well preserved.

Take it out in the sunlight and examine it closely. Notice that there are three fingers that face forward, and a fourth, the longest and like a thumb, that faces to the rear. The instrument will be black but no longer shiny, the back of it sheathed in armor plate and the underside padded like a wolf's foot.

At the end of each digit you will find a black, curved talon. You will see that the talons are not as sharp as you might have suspected. They are made to grasp and hold fast, not to puncture. They are more like the jaws of a trap than a fistful of ice picks. The subtle difference serves the raven well in the desert. He can weather a storm on a barren juniper limb; he can pick up and examine the crow's eye without breaking it.

DAVID RAINS WALLACE
B. 1945

David Rains Wallace calls evolution "the great myth of modern times." Like all myths, it is double edged: a potential source of self-delusion, but also a means of liberating us from obsolete and destructive notions about ourselves and our place in the world. In his John Burroughs Medal-winning book, The Klamath Knot *(1984), Wallace explores an unusual tract of wilderness on the California-Oregon border in order to consider not only the complexities of current evolutionary theory, but also the way in which evolutionary ideas, by recognizing the uniformity of all life, have the capacity to change human behavior for the better. In this he follows writers like John Burroughs, Aldo Leopold, and Lewis Thomas who see in evolution's very lack of a clear ethical code a useful model, for "In a world where such ambiguities reign, the idea that there can be no predetermined future may be a salutary one." By looking at evolution in the light of older myths—such as medieval alchemy and the legends of Bigfoot—he articulates one of the major aims of contemporary nature writers: to refashion the parables of our race in the light of new scientific understanding.*

From THE KLAMATH KNOT

THE HUMAN ELEMENT

There were giants in the earth in those days;
and also after that.

Genesis 6:4

Humanity has always been hard to define, and evolution hasn't made it easier. Older myths generally placed humans on a scale midway between animals and gods. This position had a comfortable stability. It gave people something to look down on and something to look up to. Some evolutionary myths have repeated this formula, with the idea that humans, having evolved from animals, will presently evolve into superintelligent beings somewhat like the gods of earlier myth. This is understandably the most popular kind of evolutionary myth. It takes dozens of forms, from Teilhard de Chardin's noosphere to Nazi superman eugenics.

A godlike future for the human race may be possible, indeed desirable, assuming our future godlike omnipotence and immortality are accompanied by better behavior than that of, say, the Olympian gods. Evolution's four billion years on this planet do not foreshadow such a future, however. The symmetry of transformation from animal to god is not reflected in evolutionary evidence. Humans have not evolved from animals; we *are* animals, no less dependent on plant photosynthesis and bacterial decomposition for our survival than the lowliest flatworm. The ancient thinkers who developed the animal-human-god hierarchy were not aware of what we *have* evolved from. Like all animals, we have evolved from an intricate, fortuitous symbiosis of single-celled organisms. If there *is* symmetry to evolution, the future will not see us dominating all other life as gods. It will see us become part of a greater organism which we cannot imagine.

Evolutionary humanity is a truer microcosm of nature than medieval philosophers dreamed. The human body does not merely resemble nature in its parts, it recapitulates the history of life, as much a living reenactment of evolutionary dramas as the Klamath Mountains. Corpuscles float in a primal nutrient bath of blood; intestines crawl about absorbing food in the manner of primitive worms; lungs absorb and excrete gases as do gills and leaves. No human organ would look out of place if planted in some Paleozoic sponge bed or coral reef. Even our brain is an evolutionary onion, the core we share with fish and reptiles, the secondary layer we share with other mammals, and the outer layer we share with other primates.

Humanity can't be defined apart from the intricacies of natural selection, mutation, symbiosis, preadaptation, and neoteny that formed it. It can't be defined apart from the millions of other species on the earth. Our evolutionary myths have been greatly oversimplified in our attempts to follow the thread of humanity into the past (and the future) while we ignore its entanglements with the threads of grasses, trees, snakes, and

The Klamath Knot (San Francisco: Sierra Club, 1983).

other beings. Such myths make a falsely passive background of an actively evolving world. To say that humanity descended from the trees,
adopted a grassland hunting life, then invented agriculture and civilization, is racial solipsism. It would be quite as accurate to say that the
forest abandoned the hominids, that the grasslands adopted them, that
the first domestic plants and animals chose to live with our Neolithic
ancestors. I could write an evolutionary history of the human species in
which its main significance is not as an inventor of language or builder of
cities but as an ally of grasslands in their thirty-million-year struggle with
forests. An extraterrestrial observer of the human colonization of North
America would have seen more of spreading grasslands than of spreading
cities, grasslands spread first by Indians with fire, then by whites with
axes and plows.

It is possible to look upon humans and their civilization as a biological
and geological force not qualitatively different from the volcanic eruptions, glaciations, and other catastrophes that have disturbed organic
evolution. Nuclear war and wholesale industrial pollution may do life on
earth more damage than a billion years of exploding volcanoes, but anthropoid greed and convection currents in the earth's mantle seem about
equally random and senseless. Molecules simmering in the skull of a
primate or sixty miles underground—what's the difference? Both explode when pressures get critical.

Such a view falls into the error of seeing evolution as a predetermined
phenomenon, though. A humanity destined for demonic holocaust by
its manipulative cleverness is a mirror image of the more popular evolutionary myth of a humanity destined for godlike triumph. If the four
billion years of evolution demonstrate one thing, it is that humanity is
not *destined* for anything. Evolution has always been open to new possibilities, which is why it has been so chaotic and devious. Every organism
continually confronts a galaxy of evolutionary choices.

The difference between humans and other organisms is that humans,
having discerned something of how evolution works, are now able to
confront their choices consciously. This is not the same as saying that we
now can *control* evolution. I don't know how much of a difference it is in
effect: we may be able to perceive our choices and still be unable to
choose and act. By overpopulating the planet as we are now doing, for
example, we are making an evolutionary choice just as unplanned as that
of our hominid ancestors when they began cracking antelope and other
hominids over the head with sticks. Nevertheless, we do differ from the
first hominids in our having some notion of the implications of our
behavior. In Biblical terms we have heeded the serpent, eaten of the tree

of knowledge, and lost our innocence. We now must face the possibility of choosing between good and evil, or, in evolutionary terms, between survival and extinction.

In other words humans have some degree of free will. As two millennia of theologians have been telling us, this is a perilous position. Pride is the great danger to the soul consciously seeking salvation. I think it is the great danger to the species consciously seeking survival too. In both cases pride can transform the best of virtues into the worst of vices. It can transform an individual's high intelligence into arrogance, and it can transform a species' considerable understanding of nature into stupid plundering.

The King of Phrygia tied the Gordian Knot in the temple of Apollo and prophesied that whoever untied it would become Lord of Asia. Alexander, proud young conqueror, cleverly cut the knot with his sword, became Lord of Asia, and died at age thirty-three of alcoholism, disease, or poison. Apollo was a god of the serpent as well as of the lyre. Conquering civilization could cut the Klamath knot, and that of every other wilderness: dam every river, log every forest, plow every meadow, until the last gasp of splendor subsides from the earth. "What now?" the serpent might whisper, as it perhaps whispered to Alexander on the banks of the Ganges.

The mythic resonance that evolution has given the natural world expresses a multitude of choices that humans have not consciously faced before. In old myths wherein nature remained the same from the world's creation until its end, our relationship with nature was much less laden with choices. Men couldn't change what the gods had made: "saving the planet" would have seemed an impertinence. But evolution, wherein a bear is not simply a black, shaggy animal but a wave of animals surging up through abysses of time from the original one-celled beings, raises troubling questions. Should we follow its competitive trend, manifested in natural selection, and try to survive by destroying everything that seems to get in our way? Should we follow its cooperative trend, manifested in symbiosis, and try to coexist with our parasites and our hosts (whoever *they* may be) in hope of some new synthesis? Should we try to do both? After all, that is what evolution does.

Much of the disquiet that has beset our thinking in the past two centuries seems related to evolution's burden of new choices. If life has taken such different shapes in the past, who can feel any assurance about the future? Entire realms of confident human activity begin to seem absurd. This is not necessarily a bad thing, of course. Some of the worst atrocities have been committed in pursuit of assurance, in flight from anxiety. If the future is essentially unknowable, at least good ends can no longer justify evil means. If it dispels our dreams of heaven, a world without destiny also wakens us from nightmares of hell.

The giants who left their tracks near Bluff Creek are eloquent mythic expressions of evolutionary uncertainty. Are they competitive lords of the snow forest? Cooperative children of the ancestral forest? Are they human? Are they alive? In a sense the giants are the missing link that Victorian society demanded Darwin and Huxley produce before it would bow to the new version of genesis. (Newspaper articles of 1884 tell of a young giant captured in British Columbia and shipped to London alive. It never arrived, victim, perhaps, of some conspiracy of Anglican divines?) Giants express our familial relationship to the rest of life. If we found them, could we rightfully continue to clear cut the giants' forests, dam their rivers, and trample their meadows? Even giant-hunters who consider them "just animals" advocate creating large preserves for giants.

With their elusiveness to civilized knowledge, giants express a gap that has arisen between our thinking habits, which are expressed in everyday speech, and our very recent awareness of evolutionary evidence. We condemn "brutality" and scorn murderers as "animals." We fear the sight of a shaggy beast shaped like a human. Yet we know that no wild animal is remotely capable of the deliberate torture and mass extermination that have become common in this most civilized of centuries. Knowing how unprecedented these horrors are, we no longer can blame them on our "lower" animal instincts, or hope to escape them by "rising above" our animal nature. We will not rise above our animal nature until we begin to live without food, water, and air. We are more protected by the timidity of the wild animal that remains in us than we are threatened by its aggressiveness.

We are fortunate to have the self-consciousness that allows us the possibility of free will. But we no longer can assume that our consciousness imbues us with a predetermined destiny separate from the rest of life. The only way we can separate ourselves from our animal, plant, and fungus relatives is to stop living, a viable and popular evolutionary option (considering the millions of extinct species) but one we're self-consciously averse to. Yet as we develop from species-exterminating hunters to land-eroding farmers to biosphere-polluting industrialists, we increasingly separate ourselves.

Few organisms survive in rapidly changing environments, and the world is changing faster than ever before. The fact that we've set these changes in motion doesn't mean we can control them. *We* must change to survive. No biological change will be fast enough now, though; we can't evolve as fast as the insects or rodents or microorganisms we've "conquered" because we reproduce so much more slowly. We must depend on cultural evolution. If our behavior is to change, our myths will have to change.

Myths began as imaginative projections of human consciousness onto nature. Trees had language, birds had thoughts, spiders had technology. When science found that nature does not, in fact, have a human consciousness, some thinkers concluded that myth was dead, that there was no further need for imaginative views of a world which, they thought, had no consciousness at all. But they misunderstood science. That nonhuman life has no human consciousness doesn't mean it has no consciousness. Science has opened a potential for imaginative interpretation of nature that is enormously greater than the simple projection of human thoughts and feelings onto the nonhuman. It has allowed us to begin to imagine states of consciousness quite different from our own. We can begin to see trees, birds, and spiders not as masks concealing humanlike spirits but as beings in their own right, beings that are infinitely more mysterious and wonderful than the nymphs and sprites of the old myths.

Science has raised the possibility that there are as many different consciousnesses in the world as there are organisms capable of perception. It also has raised the possibility that consciousness may arise in ways that seem very alien to us. The symbiotic superconsciousness I vaguely sense in forests is not outside scientific possibility.

The age of myth is not dead; it is just beginning, if humans can survive to inhabit it. Only, instead of myths peopled with talking trees, we must begin to create the opposite. (The fact that such myths—inhabited by "treeing talks"—aren't fully expressible with our present syntax and vocabulary is one measure of the magnitude of the enterprise.) Instead of inflating our human consciousness to fill trees, we must let the trees into our minds. It is not a sentimental undertaking. When science found that we don't have thoughts and feelings in common with the nonhuman, it also found we do have something equally important in common—origins. We are very different from trees, but we also are like them. As we learn how they live, we learn a great deal of how *we* live.

Learning does not occur only in the mind. High towers of intellectual learning require deep foundations of emotional knowledge, or they lack stability. The more we know about trees, the more we need to feel about them. The human element has grown too large and powerful for petty or trivial feelings about the nonhuman. What we feel about pettily, we begin to destroy, as we are destroying forests to produce junk mail and other trivialities.

Future myths will be different from past myths, but their function will be the same—to sustain life. When the human element was small, when there were billions of trees and only thousands of people, it was sustaining to imagine that trees contained spirits humans could talk to, propitiate, befriend. It gave proportion to the world. Now, when there are billions of people, and not so many trees, it is sustaining to imagine what it might be like to open one's flowers on a spring afternoon, or to stand silently, making food out of sunlight, for a thousand years. It gives proportion to the world.

Of course, imagination can only go so far. The incompleteness of scientific knowledge also limits emotional knowledge. We can't fully imagine a tree's existence because we don't know how, or if, a tree experiences its life. So something of the old mythological imagination probably will linger for a long time. We will continue to project our human feelings onto other organisms, as we try to imagine their nonhuman experience.

As with organisms, new myths don't appear fully formed, but evolve imprecisely out of old myths. Giants may be an example of such evolution. Giants seem to have originated as a way of giving human form to all that is titanic and inchoate in nature. In human form the awesomeness of rocks, waters, and tangled vegetation could be wrestled into submission, even befriended, by heroes and gods. Today's Klamath giants have something of this. In their dominance of the awesome snow forest, the giants affirm a desire for human power over wilderness, for a linkage with nature that is advantageous, albeit peaceable. If we found the Klamath giants, we would grasp some essence of the titanic knot of rocks, waters, and trees, as Beowulf and Gilgamesh grasped their ancient lands by defeating Grendel and Enkidu.

But the Klamath giants also have become more than shaggy, beetle-browed projections of human desire. We begin to see in them the possibility of a consciousness quite different from our own, of a being that may be very close to us in hominid origins, but that may have evolved in mysterious ways. We imagine an animal that somehow has understood the world more deeply than we have, and that thus inhabits it more comfortably and freely, while eluding our self-involved attempts to capture it.

Giants might be seen as a kind of preadapted myth that can help us to survive the world we've created. Giants have hovered for thousands of years in the backgrounds of our dreams of immortality and omniscience, large shadows humans cast behind them as they moved toward brilliant visions of limitless power. But now the visions are fading into a natural world that has proved much deeper than we ever had imagined. Giants can have a new function in an evolutionary myth. They link us to lakes, rivers, forests, and meadows that are our home as well as theirs. They lure us into the wilderness, as they lured me, not to devour us but to remind us where we are, on a living planet. If giants do not exist, to paraphase Voltaire, it is necessary to invent them.

GRETEL EHRLICH
B. 1946

When The Solace of Open Spaces *(1985) was published, Gretel Ehrlich immediately established herself as one of the outstanding nature writers of our day. It tells the story of how, as she says in the Preface, she "was able to take up residence on earth with no alibis, no self-promoting schemes." Her road back to the earth led her to the arduous work and invigorating life of a Wyoming rancher. As she narrates her passage into that role, she also paints the portrait of a land, and those of people who came into it along paths different from her own. Ehrlich brings out forcefully the fact that, where extremes of weather are so sudden and so great, no one, rancher or animals, can survive many mistakes. Such an awareness of Wyoming's basic demands for alertness lends an ironic quality to her writing that complements her lyrical quality. Reading about Ehrlich's Wyoming, like reading about Norman Maclean's Montana, is exciting for readers who have not lived in those sparsely settled, dramatic lands. Avidly, we turn the pages of lives we will not live, of landscapes we will not forget.*

From THE SOLACE OF OPEN SPACES

FRIENDS, FOES, AND WORKING ANIMALS

I used to walk in my sleep. On clear nights when the seals barked and played in phosphorescent waves, I climbed out the window and slept in a horse stall. Those "wild-child" stories never seemed odd to me; I had the

The Solace of Open Spaces (New York: Viking, 1985).

idea that I was one of them, refusing to talk, sleeping only on the floor. Having become a city dweller, the back-to-the-land fad left me cold and I had never thought of moving to Wyoming. But here I am, and unexpectedly, my noctambulist's world has returned. Not in the sense that I still walk in my sleep—such restlessness has left me—but rather, the intimacy with what is animal in me has returned. To live and work on a ranch implicates me in new ways: I have blood on my hands and noises in my throat that aren't human.

Animals give us their constant, unjaded faces and we burden them with our bodies and civilized ordeals. We're both humbled by and imperious with them. We're comrades who save each other's lives. The horse we pulled from a boghole this morning bucked someone off later in the day; one stock dog refuses to work sheep, while another brings back a calf we had overlooked while trailing cattle to another pasture; the heifer we doctored for pneumonia backed up to a wash and dropped her newborn calf over the edge; the horse that brings us home safely in the dark kicks us the next day. On and on it goes. What's stubborn, secretive, dumb, and keen in us bumps up against those same qualities in them. Their births and deaths are as jolting and random as ours, and because ranchers are food producers, we give ourselves as wholly to the sacrament of nurturing as to the communion of eating their flesh. What develops in this odd partnership is a stripped-down compassion, one that is made of frankness and respect and rigorously excludes sentimentality.

What makes westerners leery of "outsiders"—townspeople and city-slickers—is their patronizing attitude toward animals. "I don't know what in the hell makes those guys think they're smarter than my horse. Nothing I see them do would make me believe it," a cowboy told me. "They may like their steaks, but they sure don't want to help out when it comes to butchering. And their damned back-yard horses are spoiled. They make it hard for a horse to do something right and easy for him to do everything wrong. They're scared to get hot and tired and dirty out here like us; then they don't understand why a horse won't work for them."

On a ranch, a mother cow must produce calves, a bull has to perform, a stock dog and working horse should display ambition, savvy, and heart. If they don't, they're sold or shot. But these relationships of mutual dependency can't be dismissed so briskly. An animal's wordlessness takes on the cleansing qualities of space: we freefall through the beguiling operations of our own minds with which we calculate our miseries to responses that are immediate. Animals hold us to what is present: to who we are at the time, not who we've been or how our bank accounts describe us. What is obvious to an animal is not the embellishment that fattens our emotional résumés but what's bedrock and current in us: aggression, fear, insecurity, happiness, or equanimity. Because they have the ability to read our involuntary tics and scents, we're transparent to them and thus exposed—we're finally ourselves.

Living with animals makes us redefine our ideas about intelligence. Horses are as mischievous as they are dependable. Stupid enough to let us use them, they are cunning enough to catch us off guard. We pay for their loyalty: they can be willful, hard to catch, dangerous to shoe, and buck on frosty mornings. In turn, they'll work themselves into a lather cutting cows, not for the praise they'll get but for the simple glory of outdodging a calf or catching up with an errant steer. The outlaws in a horse herd earn their ominous names—the red roan called Bonecrusher, the sorrel gelding referred to as Widowmaker. Others are talented but insist on having things their own way. One horse used only for roping doesn't like to be tied up by the reins. As soon as you jump off he'll rub the headstall over his ears and let the bit drop from his mouth, then just stand there as if he were tied to the post. The horses that sheepherders use become chummy. They'll stick their heads into a wagon when you get the cookies out, and eat the dogfood. One sheepherder I knew, decked out in bedroom slippers and baggy pants, rode his gelding all summer with nothing but bailing string tied around the horse's neck. They picnicked together every day on the lunch the herder had fixed: two sandwiches and a can of beer for each of them.

A dog's reception of the jolts and currents of life comes in more clearly than a horse's. Ranchers use special breeds of dogs to work livestock—blue and red heelers, border collies, Australian shepherds, and kelpies. Heelers, favored by cattlemen, are small, muscular dogs with wide heads and short, blue-gray hair. Their wide and deep chests enable them—like the quarter horse—to run fast for a short distance and endow them with extra lung capacity to work at high altitudes. By instinct they move cows, not by barking at them but by nipping their heels. What's uncanny about all these breeds is their responsiveness to human beings: we don't shout commands, we whisper directions, and because of their unshakable desire to please us, they can be called back from chasing a cow instantaneously. Language is not an obstacle to these dogs; they learn words very quickly. I know several dogs who are bilingual: they understand Spanish and English. Others are whizzes with names. On a pack trip my dog learned the names of ten horses and remembered the horse and the sound of his name for years. One friend taught his cowdog to jump onto the saddle so he could see the herd ahead, wait for a command with his front feet riding the neck of the horse, then leap to the ground and bring a calf back or turn the whole herd.

My dog was born under a sheep wagon. He's a blue heeler–kelpie cross with a natural bobbed tail. Kelpies, developed in Australia in the nineteenth century, are also called dingoes, though they're part Scottish sheepdog too. While the instinct to work livestock is apparent from the time they are puppies, they benefit from further instruction, the way anyone with natural talent does. They're not sent to obedience school; these dogs learn from each other. A pup, like mine was, lives at sheep camp and is sent out with an older dog to learn his way around a band of sheep. They learn to turn the herd, to bring back strays, and to stay behind the horse when they're not needed.

Dogs who work sheep have to be gentler than cowdogs. Sheep are skittish and have a natural fear of dogs, whereas a mother cow will turn and fight a dog who gets near her calf. If kelpies, border collies, and Australian shepherds cower, they do so from timidness and because they've learned to stay low and out of sight of the sheep, With their pointed ears and handsome, wolfish faces, their resemblance to coyotes is eerie. But their instinct to work sheep is only a refinement of the desire to kill; they lick their chops as they approach the herd.

After a two-year apprenticeship at sheep camp, Rusty came home with me. He was carsick all the way, never having ridden in a vehicle, and, once home, there were more firsts: when I flushed the toilet, he ran out the door; he tried to lick the image on the screen of the television; when the phone rang he jumped on my lap, shoving his head under my arm. In April the ewes and lambs were trailed to spring range and Rusty rejoined them. By his second birthday he had walked two hundred miles behind a horse, returning to the mountain top where he had been born.

Dogs read minds and also maps. Henry III's greyhound tracked the king's coach from Switzerland to Paris, while another dog found his owner in the trenches during World War I. They anticipate comings and goings and seem to possess a prescient knowledge of danger. The night before a sheep foreman died, his usually well-behaved blue heeler acted strangely. All afternoon he scratched at the windows in an agony of panic, yet refused to go outside. The next day Keith was found dead on the kitchen floor, the dog standing over the man's chest as if shielding the defective heart that had killed his master.

While we cherish these personable working animals, we unfairly malign those that live in herds. Konrad Lorenz thinks of the anonymous flock as the first society, not unlike early medieval cities: the flock works as a wall of defense protecting the individual against aggressors. Herds are democratic, nonhierarchical. Wyoming's landscapes are so wide they can accommodate the generality of a herd. A band of fifteen hundred sheep moves across the range like a single body of water. To work them in a corral means opposing them: if you walk back through the middle of the herd, they will flow forward around you as if you were a rock in a stream. Sheep graze up a slope, not down the way cows do, as if they were curds of cream rising.

Cows are less herd-smart, less adhesive, less self-governing. On long treks, they travel single file, or in small, ambiguous crowds from which individuals veer off in a variety of directions. That's why cowboying is more arduous than herding sheep. On a long circle, cowboys are assigned positions and work like traffic cops directing the cattle. Those that "ride point" are the front men. They take charge of the herd's course, turning the lead down a draw, up a ridge line, down a creek, galloping ahead to chase off steers or bulls from someone else's herd, then quickly returning to check the speed of the long column. The cowboys at the back "ride drag." They push the cows along and pick up stragglers and defectors, inhaling the sweet and pungent perfume of the animals—a mixture of sage, sweet grass, milk, and hide, along with gulps of dust. What we may miss in human interaction here we make up for by rubbing elbows with wild animals. Their florid, temperamental lives parallel ours, as do their imperfect societies. They fight and bicker, show off, and make love. I watched a Big Horn ram in rut chase a ewe around a tree for an hour. When he caught and mounted her, his horns hit a low branch and he fell off. She ran away with a younger ram in pursuit. The last I saw of them, she was headed for a dense thicket of willows and the old ram was peering through the maze looking for her.

When winter comes there is a sudden population drop. Frogs, prairie dogs, rattlesnakes, and rabbits go underground, while the mallards and cinnamon teal, as well as scores of songbirds, fly south because they are smarter than we are. One winter day I saw a coyote take a fawn down on our frozen lake where in summer I row through fragrant flowers. He jumped her, grabbed her hind leg, and hung on as she ran. Halfway across the lake the fawn fell and the coyote went for her jugular. In a minute she was dead. Delighted with his catch, he dragged her here and there on the ice, then lay down next to her in a loving way and rubbed his silvery ruff in her hair before he ate her.

In late spring, which here, at six thousand feet, is June, the cow elk become proud mothers. They bring their day-old calves to a hill just above the ranch so we can see them. They're spotted like fawns but larger, and because they are so young, they wobble and fall when they try to play.

Hot summer weather brings the snakes and bugs. It's said that 80 percent of all animal species are insects, including six thousand kinds of ants and ten thousand bugs that sing. Like the wild ducks that use our lake as a flyaway, insects come and go seasonally. Mosquitoes come early and stay late, followed by black flies, gnats, Stendhalian red-and-black ants, then yellow jackets and wasps.

I know it does no good to ask historical questions—why so many insects exist—so I content myself with the cold ingenuity of their lives. In winter ants excavate below their hills and live snugly in subterranean chambers. Their heating system is unique. Worker ants go above ground and act as solar collectors, descending frequently to radiate heat below. They know when spring has come because the workers signal the change of seasons with the sudden increase of body heat: it's time to reinhabit the hill.

In a drought year rattlesnakes are epidemic. I sharpen my shovel before I irrigate the alfalfa fields and harvest vegetables carrying a shotgun. Rattlesnakes have heat sensors and move toward warm things. I tried nude sunbathing once: I fell asleep and woke just in time to see the grim, flat head of a snake angling toward me. Our new stock dog wasn't as lucky. A pup, he was bitten three times in one summer. After the first bite he staggered across the hayfield toward me, then keeled over, his eyes rolling back and his body shaking. The cure for snakebite is the same for animals as it is for humans: a costly antiserum must be injected as quickly as possible. I had to carry the dog half a mile to my pickup. By the time I had driven the thirty miles to town, his head and neck had swollen to a ghoulish size, but two days later he was heeling cows again.

Fall brings the wildlife down from the mountains. Elk and deer migrate through our front yard while in the steep draws above us, mountain lions and black bears settle in for the winter. Last night, while I was sleeping on the veranda, the sound of clattering dishes turned out to be two buck deer sparring in front of my bed. Later, a porcupine and her baby waddled past: "Meeee . . . meeee . . . meeee," the mother squeaked to keep the young one trundling along. From midnight until dawn I heard the bull elk bugle—a whistling, looping squeal that sounds porpoiselike at first, and then like a charging elephant. The screaming catlike sound that wakes us every few nights is a bobcat crouched in the apple tree.

Bobcats are small, weighing only twenty pounds or so, with short tails and long, rabbity back feet. They can nurse two small litters of kittens a year. "She's meaner than a cotton sack full of wildcats," I heard a cowboy say about a woman he'd met in the bar the night before. A famous riverman's boast from the paddlewheel days on the Mississippi goes this way: "I'm all man, save what's wildcat and extra lightning." *Les chats sauvages,* the French call them, but their savagery impresses me much less than their acrobatic skills. Bobcats will kill a doe by falling on her from a tree and riding her shoulders as she runs, reaching around and scratching her face until she falls. But just as I was falling asleep again, I thought I heard the bobcat purring.

ROBERT MICHAEL PYLE
B. 1947

Robert Pyle is probably best known as the author of six books on butterflies, including The Audubon Field Guide to North American Butterflies. *A Coloradan by birth, he now lives in southwestern Washington State.* Wintergreen: Listening to the Land's Heart *(1986), winner of the John Burroughs Medal, is an ecological and philosophical survey of the Willapa Hills region near his home, an area that has been heavily logged-over in recent decades. The book confronts a central question in contemporary nature writing, namely, how does one construct a viable environmental ethic in the face of apparently incorrigible human behavior and a nature which "doesn't care"? For Pyle, as for many other current writers, the answer lies in the adoption of what he calls "cosmic optimism," an evolutionary "frame of reference that does not encompass human fortunes alone." While not rejecting the idea of responsible stewardship towards the earth, Pyle takes heart in the view that, in the long run, the actions of human beings, for good or ill, matter little. Yet the author's own good humor and zest in natural experience make this attitude seem anything but cynical and nihilistic.*

From WINTERGREEN: LISTENING TO THE LAND'S HEART

AND THE COYOTES WILL LIFT A LEG

I wish I had said it first. Someone else did—who knows who?— and won't get credit for it. Spinners of clever quotations share the relative immortality of their words sometimes; platitude-makers, almost never. Even so, I still wish I'd said it first; "nature bats last."

Wintergreen: Listening to the Land's Heart (Boston: Houghton Mifflin, 1986).

On the other hand, maybe this isn't a platitude. The thing about a "good" platitude is that it should be self-evident. I'm not at all sure that "nature bats last" is self-evident to very many people at all. Perhaps it's just a platitude for pantheists, a byword for Earth Firsters and others who sometimes seem as willing to exclude humans from their concept of nature as most people are to neglect the other species. In which case, it misses the point altogether.

The point of a platitude, as I see it, is to preach a point to people who already know it but act as if they don't. I doubt that those who need to know that nature bats last have any clue at all as to what it means, even lack a cosmology in which it could make any sense. That renders it an esoteric idea, an impossibility for a platitude. I guess it isn't one after all.

An aphorism, then; a verbal balm, a tonic thought. It was meant, of course, as a warning, a shaken finger; but falling on mostly deaf ears as such, it recycles pretty well as a curse of revenge.

What does it mean? "Nature bats last." It means, we may be in the lead now, the natural world may seem the underdog and down in points as well. But when we've finished our act, hit the grand slam, or struck out (which may be the same thing), nature has an extra inning coming—all to herself, unopposed, unending. No one will be keeping score anymore, and guess who wins?

Let me be clear from the start. This is not a threat. I am not writing another admonishment to repent before the day of ecological reckoning. It is late in the day for us to clean up our environmental act, and I am assuming we will not. On the local scale (as in Willapa) and increasingly on the larger, the major decisions have already been made, and we can only live with them. But I'm not preaching doom—what a waste of time to preach the inevitable! We all die; all species die. The only question is, when will we pull ourselves off the respirator?

To me, nature's batting last is neither a warning nor a threat. It is a cheerfully flip recognition of a certainty. And a comforting certainty it is: imagine, the glory of the universe going on and on, free at last of the bad bet that was man on earth! When John Lennon wrote "Imagine," he could have added a verse: "Imagine there's no people." My humanism ends where we become so fond of ourselves that we cannot imagine the mortality of mankind.

But supposing, against all odds, we began to run the world right (a phrase that contains in its emphasis the seeds of its own defeat)? Couldn't we then change the batting order? Wouldn't I at least want to hope for the endlessness of the human race?

Sure. But that's vain. The best we could do would be to postpone our departure. Any time on for good behavior would just amount to a stay of execution. To think we could indefinitely put off the end of the age of man by acting right toward the earth for a change is like taking up running in dissipated middle age in the hope of cheating death: it might work for a while. You can't prolong life forever, not for an organism, not for a species. But you can sure as hell hasten its demise.

This is harsh stuff, and there has been some harshness in some of the previous essays. I have criticized and taken account of what I feel to have been mistakes. An ungenerous reader could mutter "Cynic!" and close the book, so near the end. But I am not cynical about humans and the rest of nature. When I insist upon the mortality of all species, including our own, it is not an unhappy thought. And when I invoke that aphorism of uncertain category and origin, "nature bats last," it is in good cheer that I do so. My outlook, ultimately, is not a pessimistic one. But then my frame of reference does not encompass human fortunes alone.

Let's look at outlook, for nature, humans, and otherwise. I have always been a short-term optimist, by nature. Whether that has a genetic element or comes from example, I cannot know. But I have always believed that more good things were likely to occur than bad. (This may have to do with my rather catholic tastes as to what constitutes "good.") It is a matter of being open to possibility and aware of serendipity's whisper. Everyone is invited to serendipity's picnic, but only a few bother to attend. Positive thinking? Are we headed toward platitudes? It's more than that. It's being willing to conspire with the physics of fate (chance, really) to harvest luck from happenstance.

Jung called coincidence "synchronicity" and it happens to us all if we are only aware. Co-incidence—happening with. You must be ready to see it and do more than say "wow" when you do. To pluck a plum when you pass beneath the bough, you've got to be looking up. To catch the glisten of the green snail beneath the plum tree, you must regard the ground. To capture more good than bad, you scan the whole and, mantislike, snatch the happy moment before it springs away, out of reach.

I am not a fatalist, and when some great coincidence brings me joy I try not to say it was "meant to happen." Strings of bad "luck" do sometimes befall people, even those who watch for the good. My brother has had a lifelong run of bad breaks, more than his share, while I feel I've had more than my fair share of good ones. Stochastically (a word I learned to toss around in graduate school that means "chances are") one is as likely to be felled by lightning as lifted by the lottery. Life *is* a lottery. But somehow, seekers after something often seem to get better breaks than others who fail to look around. Or do they simply find more compensations?

Of course, another reason for short-term optimism lies in our ability to apply will and thought and action to effect change in our time. We can create a nature reserve and enjoy it for the rest of our lives. We can vote the bums out. We can live selectively, choosing that which we wish to experience. And there are, after all, far too many pleasures available to be able to sample them all: too many wild and intriguing places to ever visit, people to meet, birds to watch, symphonies to hear, and so on. The riches embarrass our poor ability to enjoy them. Pessimism in the short-term is its own punishment, since it vitiates the will and makes one a pawn of circumstance.

Looking out toward the midterm, however, my attitude rotates. Beyond the here and now, a cautiously pessimistic outlook seems only reasonable and realistic. I suppose this means shifting out of my own life and into the many other lives on earth. Speaking of the world, there is no gravity; the earth sucks (whoever said this first probably wouldn't own to it). My, how it sucks these days. Admittedly the *Wahkiakum County Eagle* gives one a less jaundiced view than *The New York Times* might, but I also see the *Longview Daily News* occasionally, listen to *All Things Considered,* and watch what the cat brings in. How anyone can be honestly optimistic over the next century, regarding mankind, I cannot divine. I won't repeat the litany; it's there for all to see, who read any papers at all, or the walls, between the lines, tea leaves, sweaty palms, tarot cards, or the weather. Even the Bible seems to have it about right, somewhere toward the back (if not in the "to have dominion" part in the beginning).

Come to think of it, the Bible does get it right at both ends. Humans took dominion over the earth, now they face Armageddon. The story is rather circuitous from A to B and the cause-and-effect gets a bit mixed up, but it's all there. The sad part is that it gives people the idea that someone else is going to clean up after them. If they're not responsible for the outcome, if they're not culpable for their mess, how can people be expected to function with the future in mind?

The present and near future could get downright depressing if it weren't for nature. As John Hay more elegantly put it in his small classic, *In Defense of Nature,* "What is there to be optimistic about, especially in the face of enduring human perversity? Not a great deal that is pre-dictable; but if enough of us are willing to walk out and meet nature instead of bypassing it, then we will at last belong. And when all is said and done, real stature comes from an attachment to the unknown."

Yes. And this brings me to the long-term, where for me optimism swings round like a major moon to again eclipse the darker view. Un-reservedly, I am optimistic in the long run. Not necessarily for *Homo sapiens,* whose puny fate fails to concern the cosmos. But for nature, which is everything, the whole to which our greater allegiance belongs. And for the earth, which is all most of us shall ever directly know of the universe, finally to be freed from human bondage.

Here is where I differ from many deists. They see salvation from earthly dross in an afterlife for the soul. I see afterlife as salvation of earthly dross that is the soul. The perpetuation of my matter in crocus, coal, or comet is all I need know about the next act—that atoms continue in nature. We both see something coming that ratifies what has gone before and flenses the flesh of suffering. To them, however, heaven is full of personalities on permanent vacation; to me, heaven is a permanent vacation from personality.

This inability to face the extinction of personality serves as one of the main reasons for the rejection of evolution by some creationists. They are smart enough to see that, if life evolved, it will continue to do so, and that we (body and soul) may not survive the process. So they seek to preserve their cherished selves by pushing fairy tales—as if, by evangelizing hard enough, they could make it so!

The latest version of the creationist credo delivered to my door is a "textbook" that its makers, the Jehovah's Witnesses, hope to have placed in schools. Entitled *Life—How Did It Get Here? (By Evolution or Creation?)*, this heavily illustrated and simply written tract attempts to convince the reader that evolution is a "lie," claiming: "We should feel even stronger indignation toward the doctrine of evolution and its originator since the intent is to defraud us of eternal life."

The "marvelous new era" that this book promises for believers will have peace and plenty and endless health, youth and life for all. Apparently there will be room for endless population growth, because "mankind will have the enjoyable task of transforming the earth into a paradise." Man's "loving dominion of animals" *(sic)* will be a feature, and "the wilderness and waterless plain will exult." I am struck by the presence, in one of the pretty illustrations of paradise, of a bulldozer. Not my idea of heaven!

Nor is my purpose to make fun. The picture painted *is* a pretty one, and touching, in a way. But were such beliefs to gain many adherents, I would tremble for the stewardship of the earth. What incentive could there possibly be to maintain biological diversity if you didn't believe in its mortality? In the same way, millions trembled on hearing Ronald Reagan speak of biblical Armageddon during the 1984 campaign. If it is inevitable, as foretold, what incentive exists to keep the finger off the button?

Probabilities speak louder than prophecies, but they both speak of annihilation if we carry on the way we have been. I would rather it didn't happen and support peace- and nonnuclear activism for that reason. I see no inevitabilities as regards human behavior. However, should annihilation occur, I console myself that nature will persist.

I call this attitude a cosmic optimism. It simply suggests that nature, *sensu latu,* will carry on, having batted last in its minor-league game with us. We played catch for a brief while, dropped the ball, and threw a tantrum; whereupon nature took her big blue ball and went home to repair the scratches and scuffs we'd inflicted in its soft hide. We lost by default, and there were no more games in the season, for our season was finished. It mattered very much to us, but the rest of nature just didn't care, was rather tired of our company, thought perhaps we'd been a bad recruit to the league of species in the first place, and that she might not try that same experiment again.

That's supposed to make one optimistic? Let me put it another way, dropping the tired metaphor of a ball game like a high fly with the sun in my eyes (which was my first and last act in Little League). Imagine the sun in your eyes—your lizard eyes—through no smog. Imagine the lakes in your fish gills, fresh, pH 7. Conceive the cosmos untroubled by that spot of bother on earth, as all its peaceful, dumb species go back to their business of life and death and evolution, unperturbed by busy-busy men. I like these thoughts.

It would be dishonest to say that I feel no sadness at the prospect of the passing of humanity. Untellable sadness greets the very thought of it. When I consider the moldering of the last lost manuscript of Mozart; the combustion of the libraries when Fahrenheit 451 is reached early in the firestorms; the tumbling of towers and the crumbling of cottages, I could swoon (if I knew how) with earnest, dolorous regret. But think: all of the sadness in the world belongs to us. When we're gone, there will be no sadness, for it is a human conceit. So it would not matter, afterward.

The fact is, nature doesn't care. Only we care. And if we care so much, perhaps we should look for a few good platitudes to guide our critical actions in these days. T-shirts make a good source. "Extinction Is Forever" is a good one; "We All Live Downstream" is another; and "Share the Earth."

"Cosmic discipline," John Hay wrote, "will not allow too much ignorance of what it cherishes." It is that discipline, finally, that lies at the root of my so-called cosmic optimism (just as our mammoth ignorance of what it cherishes makes me dread what comes next). And the "real stature" Hay mentioned, that "comes from an attachment with the unknown," I take to mean a buckling-up of our seat belt for the universal ride. Attaching to the unknown can be acceptance of nature, a faith in the course of natural events, even if they entail our own eventual extinction.

Taking satisfaction from such ideas implies a nonanthropocentric viewpoint. Copernicus saw that we weren't in the middle; why can't we? The natural world does not revolve around us, it merely tolerates us for a spell. We are indulged, yet we continue to indulge our own earthly xenophobia. Biting the land that feeds us, behaving like bulls in nature's china shop, and casting clichés across the littered landscape, we run serious risks. I am told the Finns around here had a saying: "You shouldn't shit in your own house." Taking it literally, they built their johns outside long after others had brought them in. We not only foul our own nest, we do it in the living room.

I can't help but keep on quoting John Hay, who employs never a tired phase and whose phrases never tire: "We have been cutting ourselves off, and we are wise to be alarmed. We have not been meeting the earth, we have only been erasing its opportunities, missing its indefinite, healing associations. Suddenly there is a terrible need for a great cognizance of the unity and interdependence of the world, in the sense of both human and natural communities."

There is another need, among progressive people, to realize that humanism can only take us so far down the agenda of "what," to quote Lenin, "is to be done." Beyond that, speciesism takes over. Liberation doesn't mean a damn in the face of imminent extinction, if we can arrange a rain check on infinity, liberation means everything.

To return to heaven briefly, the popular idea of deferring it till later does nothing for our sense of obligation to the earth. The naturalist knows that heaven is here on earth (for those whose lives are neither too meager nor too glutted, too shackled or too free, to notice). The traditional view holds that there's more, and better, where this came from. I prefer to think that this is all we're gonna get, and it is more than enough, if we take time to experience it and care for it.

Beyond heaven and humanism, an evolutionary view is necessary. Evolution, we find, will adjust in rate and degree to the kinds of stresses imposed upon organisms. Extinctions will occur under stress, but so will resistance evolve, tolerances develop, and tactics adjust. Organic evolution will go on. As the only show in town, it must. Whether it goes without us is another matter entirely. Eventually, it will.

Leading conservation biologists believe that opportunities may have ended already for significant evolution among large mammals, under the management regimes, stresses, and rarity we impose. Otto Frankel and Michael Soule, in *Conservation and Evolution*, argue that this may be the case and that we bear the responsibility of preserving evolutionary potential for as many species as possible. Whether we give them a chance to get back on the world by getting off ourselves, or take them with us one way or the other, will soon be seen. We still have some limited powers to affect the outcome. What stands certain is that we shan't arrest evolution much more without arresting our own.

Whether we choose to remain is our concern, and ours alone. Nature doesn't care. We are but a drip of spittle on the whisker of a beast in a constellation we can't even see. Nature has a right to care, and a sagging sack of grievances against our tenancy, but she doesn't. Nature gets along. Which brings me around at last to Willapa.

In the ravaged land through which we have been rambling, rarities have been lost, common creatures rendered rare, and the productivity of a great forest diminished for ages. The big trees and the bears are nearly gone, and the humans, many of them, are following. But certain species are doing just fine. Natives like the salal and the coyote thrive in the logged-off land, finding opportunities for expansion that they never dreamed of in the old-growth forest. Aliens such as the gaudy foxglove and the dowdy opossum proliferate still more, covering the clearcuts and the roads with their magenta blossoms and gray hides, respectively. These organisms evolved under stress; they know adversity and eat it up.

The weeds do it even better. Farmers with their sprays and archaic weed boards with nefarious powers battle gamely the tansy ragwort, Canadian thistles, and Himalayan blackberry. They make inroads with their powerful poisons. But make no mistake: the weeds will win: nature bats last.

In a sense, all life in the ravaged land is a bunch of weeds—survivors, coping and adapting under adversity. That goes for tenacious families who find something else to do when the creameries go under and the timber companies pull out, as well as for abandoned cats foraging at the local dump, and for huckleberries that clothe the clearcuts as soon as anything can.

Whether or not the weedy, faithful humans choose to remain, nature will not be crowded out, even here. Tonight I watched a possum waddle across the yard and up the slope to the road; every night, it takes what it will from our compost. We look forward to the marsupial's visits and hope it never has a date with a Dodge. I appreciate possums in the same way I admire starlings and cabbage butterflies and reed canary grass— not as native species, but as tough, clever, evolutionarily and ecologically astute organisms—as survivors, against all we dish out.

Last night the coyotes called by the covered bridge: first one tight, metallic yip, then a tentative croon, followed by five minutes of falsetto chorus in many parts, all countertenor and tremolo. "We are here," they say; "we'll eat your apples, your voles, your cats, the afterbirth of your calves; we're here, we set your dogs to barking, we intend to multiply. We are here to stay." That's what they say. Then silence, as they go about their wise, tenacious hunt for whatever there is. No other animal is more systematically or aggressively persecuted across the West. The coyote: evolving, getting better all the time, under heavy pressure.

In his book *Giving Birth to Thunder Sleeping with His Daughter*, Barry Lopez recounts a wide array of North American Indian tales of coyote. Coyote as trickster and in many other incarnations emerges from the pages as from the ancient campfires. I suspect one of those storytellers originated the last aphorism I wish to use. Anyway, whether ancient or modern, it is a good one, and after publication someone will write to say they said it first. Watch for a credit in the second edition, should I be so fortunate. The saying: "When the last man takes to his grave, there will be a coyote on hand to lift his leg over the marker." The image should be struck on a new coin, with Charles Darwin on the other side; not negotiable, but a good-luck coin to remind us of change and evolution, and of creatures that will be happy to adapt if we ourselves cannot.

The land has been hurt. Misuse is not to be excused, and its ill effects will long be felt. But nature will not be eliminated, even here. Rain, moss, and time apply their healing bandage, and the injured land at last recovers.

Nature is evergreen, after all.

DAVID QUAMMEN
B. 1948

"Biology," asserts David Quammen, "has great potential for vulgar entertainment." As the natural history columnist for Outside *magazine, he has not only entertained his readers with his witty and provocative style, but also employed biological phenomena as a means of understanding human behavior—using, for instance, the structure of a chambered nautilus to discuss the nature of memory or the mating patterns of wild geese to examine marital fidelity. Born in Cincinnati, Quammen now*

lives in Montana, where he studied aquatic entomology at the state
university in Missoula. He is not, as he says, a scientist but "a follower of
science"—often for the purpose of catching the scientists themselves in
biased or untenable positions. In this essay from his book, Natural Acts
(1985), he addresses the question of animal rights, a growing ethical
issue among conservationists. By following some recent treatises on the
subject to their logical but absurd conclusions, he suggests that some of
our most thorny ecological questions may not be subject to conventional
argument, and that tolerance and forbearance may represent a more
valuable approach.

ANIMAL RIGHTS AND BEYOND

THE SEARCH FOR A NEW MORAL FRAMEWORK AND A RIGHTEOUS GUMBO

Do non-human animals have rights? Should we humans feel morally
bound to exercise consideration for the lives and well-being of individual
members of other animal species? If so, how much consideration, and by
what logic? Is it permissible to torture and kill? Is it permissible to kill
cleanly, without prolonged pain? To abuse or exploit without killing? For
a moment, don't think about whales or wolves or the California condor;
don't think about the cat or the golden retriever with whom you share
your house. Think about chickens. Think about laboratory monkeys and
then think about lab rats and then also think about lab frogs. Think
about scallops. Think about mosquitoes.

It's a Gordian question, by my lights, but one not very well suited to
Alexandrian answers. Some people would disagree, judging the matter
simply enough settled, one way or the other. *Of course they have rights.*
Of course they don't. I say beware any such snappy, steel-trap thinking.
Some folk would even—this late in the evolution of human sensibility—
call it a frivolous question, a time-filling diversion for emotional hemo-
philiacs and cranks. *Women's rights, gay rights, now for Christ sake they*
want ANIMAL rights. Notwithstanding the ridicule, the strong biases
toward each side, it is certainly a serious philosophical issue, important
and tricky, with almost endless implications for the way we humans live
and should live on this planet.

Philosophers of earlier ages, if they touched the subject at all, were
likely to be dismissive. Thomas Aquinas announced emphatically that
animals "are intended for man's use in the natural order. Hence it is no

Natural Acts: A Sidelong View of Science and Nature (New York: Schocken, 1985).

wrong for man to make use of them, either by killing or in any other way whatever." Descartes held that animals are merely machines. As late as 1901, a moral logician named Joseph Rickaby (who happened to be a Jesuit, but don't necessarily hold that against him) declared: "Brute beasts, not having understanding and therefore not being persons, cannot have any rights. The conclusion is clear." Maybe not quite so clear. Recently, just during the past decade, professional academic philosophers have at last begun to address the matter more open-mindedly.

Two thinkers in particular have been influential: an Australian named Peter Singer, an American named Tom Regan. In 1975 Singer published a book titled *Animal Liberation*, which stirred up the debate among his colleagues and is still treated as a landmark. Eight years later Tom Regan published *The Case for Animal Rights*, a more thorough and ponderous opus that stands now as a sort of companion piece to the Singer book. In between there came a number of other discussions of animal rights—including a collection of essays edited jointly by Singer and Regan. Despite the one-time collaboration, Peter Singer and Tom Regan represent two distinct schools of thought: They reach similar conclusions about the obligations of humans to other animals, but the moral logic is very different, and possibly also the implications. Both men have produced some formidable work and both, to my simple mind, show some shocking limitations of vision.

I've spent the past week amid these books, Singer's and Regan's and the rest. It has been an edifying experience, and now I'm more puzzled than ever. I keep thinking about monkeys and frogs and mosquitoes and—sorry, but I'm quite serious—carrots.

Peter Singer's view is grounded upon the work of Jeremy Bentham, that eighteenth-century British philosopher generally known as the founder of utilitarianism. "The greatest good for the greatest number" is a familiar cartoon version of what, according to Bentham, should be achieved by the ethical ordering of society and behavior. A more precise summary is offered by Singer: "In other words, the interests of every being affected by an action are to be taken into account and given the same weight as the like interests of any other being." If this much is granted, the crucial next point is deciding what things constitute *interests* and who or what qualifies as a *being*. Evidently Bentham did not have just humans in mind. Back in 1789, optimistically and perhaps presciently, he wrote: "The day *may* come when the rest of the animal creation may acquire those rights which never could have been withholden from them but by the hand of tyranny." Most philosophers of his day were inclined (as most in our day are still inclined) to extend moral coverage only to humans, because only humans (supposedly) are rational and communicative. Jeremy Bentham took exception: "The question is not, Can they *reason?* nor, Can they *talk?* but, Can they *suffer?*" On this crucial point, Peter Singer follows Bentham.

The capacity to suffer, says Singer, is what separates a being with legitimate interests from an entity without interests. A stone has no interests that must be respected, because it cannot suffer. A mouse can suffer; therefore it has interests and those interests must be weighed in the moral balance. Fine, that much seems simple enough. Certain people of sophistic or Skinnerian bent would argue that there is no proof a mouse can in fact suffer, that it's merely an anthropomorphic assumption; but since each of us has no proof that *anyone* else actually suffers besides ourselves, we are willing, most of us, to grant the assumption. More problematic is that very large gray area between stones and mice.

Peter Singer declares: "If a being suffers, there can be no moral justification for disregarding that suffering, or for refusing to count it equally with the like suffering of any other being. But the converse of this is also true. If a being is not capable of suffering, or of enjoyment, there is nothing to take into account." Where is the boundary? Where falls the line between creatures who suffer and those that are incapable? Singer's cold philosophic eye travels across the pageant of living species—chickens suffer, mice suffer, fish suffer, um, lobsters most likely suffer, *look alive, you other creatures!*—and his damning stare lands on the oyster.

No I'm not making this up. The oyster, by Singer's best guess, doesn't suffer. Its nervous system lacks the requisite complexity. Therefore, while lobsters and crawfish and shrimp possess inviolable moral status, the oyster has none. It is a difficult judgment, Singer admits, by no means an infallible one, but "somewhere between a shrimp and an oyster seems as good a place to draw the line as any, and better than most."

Moral philosophy, no one denies, is an imperfect science.

Tom Regan takes exception with Singer on two important points. First, he disavows the utilitarian framework, with its logic that abuse or killing of animals by humans is wrong because it yields a net *overall* decrease in welfare, among all beings who qualify for moral status. No, argues Regan, that logic is false and pernicious. The abuse or killing is wrong in its *essence*—however the balance comes out on overall welfare—because it violates the rights of those individual animals. Individual rights, in other words, take precedence over the maximizing of the common good. Second, in Regan's opinion the capacity to suffer is not what marks the elect. Mere suffering is not sufficient. Instead he posits the concept of *inherent value,* a complex and magical quality possessed by some living creatures but not others.

A large portion of Regan's book is devoted to arguing toward this concept. He is more uncompromisingly protective of certain creatures—those with rights—than Singer, but he is also more selective; the hull of his ark is sturdier, but the gangplank is narrower. According to Regan, individual beings possess inherent value (and therefore inviolable rights) if they "are able to perceive and remember; if they have beliefs, desires, and preferences; if they are able to act intentionally in pursuit of their desires or goals; if they are sentient and have an emotional life; if they have a sense of the future, including a sense of their own future; if they have a psychophysical identity over time; and if they have an individual experiential welfare that is logically independent of their utility for, and the interests of, others." So Tom Regan is not handing rights around profligately, to every cute little beast that crawls over his foot. In fact we all probably know a few humans who, at least on a bad night, might have trouble meeting those standards. But how would Regan himself apply them? Where does he see the line falling? Who qualifies for inherent value, and what doesn't?

Like Singer, Regan has thought this point through. Based on his grasp of biology and ethology, he is willing to grant rights to "mentally normal mammals of a year or more."

Also like Singer, he admits that the judgment is not infallible: "Because we are uncertain where the boundaries of consciousness lie, it is not unreasonable to advocate a policy that bespeaks moral caution." So chickens and frogs should be given the benefit of the doubt, as should all other animals that bear a certain degree of anatomical and physiological resemblance to us mentally normal mammals.

But Regan does not specify just what degree.

The books by Singer and Regan leave me with two very separate reactions. The first combines admiration and gratitude. These men are applying the methods of systematic philosophy to an important and much-neglected question. Furthermore, they don't content themselves with just understanding and describing a pattern of gross injustice; they also emphatically say *Let's stop it!* They are fighting a good fight. Peter Singer's book in particular has focused attention on the outrageous practices that are routine in American factory farms, in "psychological" experimentation, in research on the toxicity of cosmetics. Do you know how chickens are dealt with on the large poultry operations? How veal is produced? How the udders of dairy cows are kept flowing? Do you know the sorts of ingenious but pointless torment that thousands of monkeys and millions of rats endure, each year, to fill the time and the dissertations of uninspired graduate students? If you don't, by all means read Singer's *Animal Liberation.*

The second reaction is negative. Peter Singer and Tom Regan, it seems to me, share a breathtaking smugness and myopia not too dissimilar to the brand they so forcefully condemn. Theirs is a righteous and vigorous smugness, not a passive and unreflective one. But still.

Singer inveighs against a sin he labels *speciesism*—discrimination against certain creatures based solely upon the species to which they belong. Regan uses a slightly less confused and less clumsy phrase, *human chauvinism,* to indicate roughly the same thing. Both of them arrive (supposedly by sheer logic) at the position that vegetarianism is morally obligatory: To kill and eat a "higher" animal represents absolute violation of one being's rights; to kill and eat a plant evidently violates nothing at all. Both Singer and Regan claim to disparage the notion— pervasive in Western philosophy since Protagoras—that "Man is the measure of all things." Both argue elaborately against anthropocentrism, while creating new moral frameworks that are also decidedly anthropocentric. Make no mistake: Man is still the measure, for Singer and Regan. The test for inherent value has changed only slightly. Instead of asking *Is the creature a human?,* they simply ask *How similar to human is similar enough?*

Peter Singer explains that shrimp deserve brotherly treatment but oysters, so different from us, are fair game for the gumbo. In Tom Regan's vocabulary, the redwood tree is an "inanimate natural object," sharing that category with clouds and rocks. But some simple minds would say: Life is life.

LESLIE MARMON SILKO
B. 1948

Leslie Silko addresses the role of ritual and myth in lending order to contemporary life—in helping people both to survive and to grow. This theme is developed in her 1977 novel Ceremony, *which tells the story of a World War II veteran trying to make peace with himself and his world on a New Mexico reservation. Her poems and stories, too,* (Laguna Woman, *1974;* Storyteller, *1981) portray lives within which traditional beliefs and spirits can make sense of a fragmented social world. Silko's essay about naming as a traditional form of storytelling, making the landscape into a sustaining, holy text, brings a crucial element into the American literature of nature. For Indians and non-Indians alike, she suggests that naming may be a form of deep identification, rather than the analytical distancing from nature that other writers about wilderness sometimes assume it to be.*

LANDSCAPE, HISTORY, AND THE PUEBLO IMAGINATION

FROM A HIGH ARID PLATEAU IN NEW MEXICO

You see that after a thing is dead, it dries up. It might take weeks or years, but eventually if you touch the thing, it crumbles under your fingers. It goes back to dust. The soul of the thing has long since departed. With the plants and wild game the soul may have already been borne back into bones and blood or thick green stalk and leaves. Nothing is wasted. What cannot be eaten by people or in some way used must then be left where other living creatures may benefit. What domestic animals or wild scavengers can't eat will be fed to the plants. The plants feed on the dust of these few remains.

The ancient Pueblo people buried the dead in vacant rooms or partially collapsed rooms adjacent to the main living quarters. Sand and clay used to construct the roof make layers many inches deep once the roof has collapsed. The layers of sand and clay make for easy gravedigging. The vacant room fills with cast-off objects and debris. When a vacant room has filled deep enough, a shallow but adequate grave can be scooped in a far corner. Archaeologists have remarked over formal burials complete with elaborate funerary objects excavated in trash middens of abandoned rooms. But the rocks and adobe mortar of collapsed walls were valued by the ancient people. Because each rock had been carefully selected for size and shape, then chiseled to an even face. Even the pink clay adobe melting with each rainstorm had to be prayed over, then dug and carried some distance. Corn cobs and husks, the rinds and stalks and animal bones were not regarded by the ancient people as filth or garbage.

Antaeus, no. 57, Autumn 1986.

The remains were merely resting at a mid-point in their journey back to dust. Human remains are not so different. They should rest with the bones and rinds where they all may benefit living creatures—small rodents and insects—until their return is completed. The remains of things—animals and plants, the clay and the stones—were treated with respect. Because for the ancient people all these things had spirit and being. The antelope merely consents to return home with the hunter. All phases of the hunt are conducted with love. The love the hunter and the people have for the Antelope People. And the love of the antelope who agree to give up their meat and blood so that human beings will not starve. Waste of meat or even the thoughtless handling of bones cooked bare will offend the antelope spirits. Next year the hunters will vainly search the dry plains for antelope. Thus it is necessary to return carefully the bones and hair, and the stalks and leaves to the earth who first created them. The spirits remain close by. They do not leave us.

The dead become dust, and in this becoming they are once more joined with the Mother. The ancient Pueblo people called the earth the Mother Creator of all things in this world. Her sister, the Corn Mother, occasionally merges with her because all succulent green life rises out of the depths of the earth.

Rocks and clay are part of the Mother. They emerge in various forms, but at some time before, they were smaller particles or great boulders. At a later time they may again become what they once were. Dust.

A rock shares this fate with us and with animals and plants as well. A rock has being or spirit, although we may not understand it. The spirit may differ from the spirit we know in animals or plants or in ourselves. In the end we all originate from the depths of the earth. Perhaps this is how all beings share in the spirit of the Creator. We do not know.

FROM THE EMERGENCE PLACE

Pueblo potters, the creators of petroglyphs and oral narratives, never conceived of removing themselves from the earth and sky. So long as the human consciousness remains *within* the hills, canyons, cliffs, and the plants, clouds, and sky, the term *landscape,* as it has entered the English language, is misleading. "A portion of territory the eye can comprehend in a single view" does not correctly describe the relationship between the human being and his or her surroundings. This assumes the viewer is somehow *outside* or *separate from* the territory he or she surveys. Viewers are as much a part of the landscape as the boulders they stand on. There is no high mesa edge or mountain peak where one can stand and not immediately be part of all that surrounds. Human identity is linked with all the elements of Creation through the clan: you might belong to the Sun Clan or the Lizard Clan or the Corn Clan or the Clay Clan.[1] Standing deep within the natural world, the ancient Pueblo understood the thing as it was—the squash blossom, grasshopper, or rabbit itself could never be created by the human hand. Ancient Pueblos took the modest view that the thing itself (the landscape) could not be improved upon. The ancients did not presume to tamper with what had already been created. Thus *realism,* as we now recognize it in painting and sculpture, did not catch the imaginations of Pueblo people until recently.

The squash blossom itself is *one thing:* itself. So the ancient Pueblo potter abstracted what she saw to be the key elements of the squash blossom—the four symmetrical petals, with four symmetrical stamens in the center. These key elements, while suggesting the squash flower, also link it with the four cardinal directions. By representing only its intrinsic form, the squash flower is released from a limited meaning or restricted identity. Even in the most sophisticated abstract form, a squash flower or a cloud or a lightning bolt became intricately connected with a complex system of relationships which the ancient Pueblo people maintained with each other, and with the populous natural world they lived within. A bolt of lightning is itself, but at the same time it may mean much more. It may be a messenger of good fortune when summer rains are needed. It may deliver death, perhaps the result of manipulations by the Gunnadeyahs, destructive necromancers. Lightning may strike down an evil-doer. Or lightning may strike a person of good will. If the person survives, lightning endows him or her with heightened power.

Pictographs and petroglyphs of constellations or elk or antelope draw their magic in part from the process wherein the focus of all prayer and concentration is upon the thing itself, which, in its turn, guides the hunter's hand. Connection with the spirit dimensions requires a figure or form which is all-inclusive. A "lifelike" rendering of an elk is too restrictive. Only the elk *is* itself. A *realistic* rendering of an elk would be only one particular elk anyway. The purpose of the hunt rituals and magic is to make contact with *all* the spirits of the Elk.

The land, the sky, and all that is within them—the landscape—includes human beings. Interrelationships in the Pueblo landscape are

[1]Clan—*A social unit composed of families sharing common ancestors who trace their lineage back to the Emergence where their ancestors allied themselves with certain plants or animals or elements.* [Silko's note]

complex and fragile. The unpredictability of the weather, the aridity and harshness of much of the terrain in the high plateau country explain in large part the relentless attention the ancient Pueblo people gave the sky and the earth around them. Survival depended upon harmony and coop-eration not only among human beings, but among all things—the ani-mate and the less animate, since rocks and mountains were known to move, to travel occasionally.

The ancient Pueblos believed the Earth and the Sky were sisters (or sister and brother in the post-Christian version). As long as good family relations are maintained, then the Sky will continue to bless her sister, the Earth, with rain, and the Earth's children will continue to survive. But the old stories recall incidents in which troublesome spirits or beings threaten the earth. In one story, a malicious ka'tsina, called the Gam-bler, seizes the Shiwana, or Rainclouds, the Sun's beloved children.[2] The Shiwana are snared in magical power late one afternoon on a high moun-tain top. The Gambler takes the Rainclouds to his mountain stronghold where he locks them in the north room of his house. What was his idea? The Shiwana were beyond value. They brought life to all things on earth. The Gambler wanted a big stake to wager in his games of chance. But such greed, even on the part of only one being, had the effect of threatening the survival of all life on earth. Sun Youth, aided by old Grandmother Spider, outsmarts the Gambler and the rigged game, and the Rainclouds are set free. The drought ends, and once more life thrives on earth.

THROUGH THE STORIES WE HEAR WHO WE ARE

All summer the people watch the west horizon, scanning the sky from south to north for rain clouds. Corn must have moisture at the time the tassels form. Otherwise pollination will be incomplete, and the ears will be stunted and shriveled. An inadequate harvest may bring disaster. Stories told at Hopi, Zuni, and at Acoma and Laguna describe drought and starvation as recently as 1900. Precipitation in west-central New Mexico averages fourteen inches annually. The western pueblos are located at altitudes over 5,600 feet above sea level, where winter temper-atures at night fall below freezing. Yet evidence of their presence in the high desert plateau country goes back ten thousand years. The ancient Pueblo people not only survived in this environment, but many years they thrived. In A.D. 1100 the people at Chaco Canyon had built cities

[2]Ka'tsina—*Ka'tsinas are spirit beings who roam the earth and who inhabit kachina masks worn in Pueblo ceremonial dances.* [Silko's note]

with apartment buildings of stone five stories high. Their sophistication as sky-watchers was surpassed only by Mayan and Inca astronomers. Yet this vast complex of knowledge and belief, amassed for thousands of years, was never recorded in writing.

Instead, the ancient Pueblo people depended upon collective memory through successive generations to maintain and transmit an entire culture, a world view complete with proven strategies for survival. The oral narrative, or "story," became the medium in which the complex of Pueblo knowledge and belief was maintained. Whatever the event or the subject, the ancient people perceived the world and themselves within that world as part of an ancient continuous story composed of innumerable bundles of other stories.

The ancient Pueblo vision of the world was inclusive. The impulse was to leave nothing out. Pueblo oral tradition necessarily embraced all levels of human experience. Otherwise, the collective knowledge and beliefs comprising ancient Pueblo culture would have been incomplete. Thus stories about the Creation and Emergence of human beings and animals into this World continue to be retold each year for four days and four nights during the winter solstice. The "humma-hah" stories related events from the time long ago when human beings were still able to communicate with animals and other living things. But, beyond these two preceding categories, the Pueblo oral tradition knew no boundaries. Accounts of the appearance of the first Europeans in Pueblo country or of the tragic encounters between Pueblo people and Apache raiders were no more and no less important than stories about the biggest mule deer ever taken or adulterous couples surprised in cornfields and chicken coops. Whatever happened, the ancient people instinctively sorted events and details into a loose narrative structure. Everything became a story.

Traditionally everyone, from the youngest child to the oldest person, was expected to listen and to be able to recall or tell a portion, if only a small detail, from a narrative account or story. Thus the remembering and retelling were a communal process. Even if a key figure, an elder who knew much more than others, were to die unexpectedly, the system would remain intact. Through the efforts of a great many people, the community was able to piece together valuable accounts and crucial information that might otherwise have died with an individual.

Communal storytelling was a self-correcting process in which listeners were encouraged to speak up if they noted an important fact or detail omitted. The people were happy to listen to two or three different versions of the same event or the same humma-hah story. Even conflicting versions of an incident were welcomed for the entertainment they provided. Defenders of each version might joke and tease one another, but seldom were there any direct confrontations. Implicit in the Pueblo oral tradition was the awareness that loyalties, grudges, and kinship must always influence the narrator's choices as she emphasizes to listeners this is the way *she* has always heard the story told. The ancient Pueblo people sought a communal truth, not an absolute. For them this truth lived somewhere within the web of differing versions, disputes over minor points, outright contradictions tangling with old feuds and village rivalries.

A dinner-table conversation, recalling a deer hunt forty years ago when the largest mule deer ever was taken, inevitably stimulates similar memories in listeners. But hunting stories were not merely after-dinner entertainment. These accounts contained information of critical importance about behavior and migration patterns of mule deer. Hunting stories carefully described key landmarks and locations of fresh water. Thus a deer-hunt story might also serve as a "map." Lost travelers, and lost piñon-nut gathers, have been saved by sighting a rock formation they recognize only because they once heard a hunting story describing this rock formation.

The importance of cliff formations and water holes does not end with hunting stories. As offspring of the Mother Earth, the ancient Pueblo people could not conceive of themselves within a specific landscape. Location, or "place," nearly always plays a central role in the Pueblo oral narratives. Indeed, stories are most frequently recalled as people are passing by a specific geographical feature or the exact place where a story takes place. The precise date of the incident often is less important than the place or location of the happening. "Long, long ago," "a long time ago," "not too long ago," and "recently" are usually how stories are classified in terms of time. But the places where the stories occur are precisely located, and prominent geographical details recalled, even if the landscape is well-known to listeners. Often because the turning point in the narrative involved a peculiarity or special quality of a rock or tree or plant found only at that place. Thus, in the case of many of the Pueblo narratives, it is impossible to determine which came first: the incident or the geographical feature which begs to be brought alive in a story that features some unusual aspect of this location.

There is a giant sandstone boulder about a mile north of Old Laguna, on the road to Paguate. It is ten feet tall and twenty feet in circumference. When I was a child, and we would pass this boulder driving to Paguate village, someone usually made reference to the story about Kochininako, Yellow Woman, and the Estrucuyo, a monstrous giant who nearly ate her. The Twin Hero Brothers saved Kochininako, who had been out hunting rabbits to take home to feed her mother and sisters. The Hero Brothers had heard her cries just in time. The Estrucuyo had cornered her in a cave too small to fit its monstrous head. Kochininako had already thrown to the Estrucuyo all her rabbits, as well as her moccasins and most of her clothing. Still the creature had not been satisfied. After killing the Estrucuyo with their bows and arrows, the Twin Hero Brothers slit open the Estrucuyo and cut out its heart. They threw the heart as far as they could. The monster's heart landed there, beside the old trail to Paguate village, where the sandstone boulder rests now.

It may be argued that the existence of the boulder precipitated the creation of a story to explain it. But sandstone boulders and sandstone formations of strange shapes abound in the Laguna Pueblo area. Yet most of them do not have stories. Often the crucial element in a narrative is the terrain—some specific detail of the setting.

A high dark mesa rises dramatically from a grassy plain fifteen miles southeast of Laguna, in an area known as Swanee. On the grassy plain one hundred and forty years ago, my great-grandmother's uncle and his brother-in-law were grazing their herd of sheep. Because visibility on the plain extends for over twenty miles, it wasn't until the two sheepherders came near the high dark mesa that the Apaches were able to stalk them. Using the mesa to obscure their approach, the raiders swept around from both ends of the mesa. My great-grandmother's relatives were killed, and the herd lost. The high dark mesa played a critical role: the mesa had compromised the safety which the openness of the plains had seemed to assure. Pueblo and Apache alike relied upon the terrain, the very earth herself, to give them protection and aid. Human activities or needs were maneuvered to fit the existing surroundings and conditions. I imagine the last afternoon of my distant ancestors as warm and sunny for late September. They might have been traveling slowly, bringing the sheep closer to Laguna in preparation for the approach of colder weather. The grass was tall and only beginning to change from green to a yellow which matched the late-afternoon sun shining off it. There might have been comfort in the warmth and the sight of the sheep fattening on good pasture which lulled my ancestors into their fatal inattention. They might have had a rifle whereas the Apaches had only bows and arrows. But there would have been four or five Apache raiders, and the surprise attack would have canceled any advantage the rifles gave them.

Survival in any landscape comes down to making the best use of all available resources. On that particular September afternoon, the raiders made better use of the Swanee terrain than my poor ancestors did. Thus the high dark mesa and the story of the two lost Laguna herders became inextricably linked. The memory of them and their story resides in part with the high black mesa. For as long as the mesa stands, people within the family and clan will be reminded of the story of that afternoon long ago. Thus the continuity and accuracy of the oral narratives are reinforced by the landscape—and the Pueblo interpretation of that landscape is *maintained.*

THE MIGRATION STORY: AN INTERIOR JOURNEY

The Laguna Pueblo migration stories refer to specific places—mesas, springs, or cottonwood trees—not only locations which can be visited still, but also locations which lie directly on the state highway route linking Paguate village with Laguna village. In traveling this road as a child with older Laguna people I first heard a few of the stories from that much larger body of stories linked with the Emergence and Migration.[3] It may be coincidental that Laguna people continue to follow the same route which, according to the Migration story, the ancestors followed south from the Emergence Place. It may be that the route is merely the shortest and best route for car, horse, or foot traffic between Laguna and Paguate villages. But if the stories about boulders, springs, and hills are actually remnants from a ritual that retraces the creation and emergence of the Laguna Pueblo people as a culture, as the people they became, then continued use of that route creates a unique relationship between the ritual-mythic world and the actual, everyday world. A journey from Paguate to Laguna down the long incline of Paguate Hill retraces the original journey from the Emergence Place, which is located slightly north of the Paguate village. Thus the landscape between Paguate and Laguna takes on a deeper significance: the landscape resonates the spiritual or mythic dimension of the Pueblo world even today.

Although each Pueblo culture designates a specific Emergence Place—usually a small natural spring edged with mossy sandstone and full of cattails and wild watercress—it is clear that they do not agree on any single location or natural spring as the one and only true Emergence Place. Each Pueblo group recounts its own stories about Creation, Emergence, and Migration, although they all believe that all human

---

[3]The Emergence—*All the human beings, animals, and life which had been created emerged from the four worlds below when the earth became habitable.*

The Migration—*The Pueblo people emerged into the Fifth World, but they had already been warned they would have to travel and search before they found the place they were meant to live.* [Silko's note]

beings, with all the animals and plants, emerged at the same place and at the same time.[4]

Natural springs are crucial sources of water for all life in the high desert plateau country. So the small spring near Paguate village is literally the source and continuance of life for the people in the area. The spring also functions on a spiritual level, recalling the original Emergence Place and linking the people and the spring water to all other people and to that moment when the Pueblo people became aware of themselves as they are even now. The Emergence was an emergence into a precise cultural identity. Thus the Pueblo stories about the Emergence and Migration are not to be taken as literally as the anthropologists might wish. Prominent geographical features and landmarks which are mentioned in the narratives exist for ritual purposes, not because the Laguna people actually journeyed south for hundreds of years from Chaco Canyon or Mesa Verde, as the archaeologists say, or eight miles from the site of the natural springs at Paguate to the sandstone hilltop at Laguna.

The eight miles, marked with boulders, mesas, springs, and river crossings, are actually a ritual circuit or path which marks the interior journey the Laguna people made: a journey of awareness and imagination in which they emerged from being within the earth and from everything included in earth to the culture and people they became, differentiating themselves for the first time from all that had surrounded them, always aware that interior distances cannot be reckoned in physical miles or in calendar years.

The narratives linked with prominent features of the landscape between Paguate and Laguna delineate the complexities of the relationship which human beings must maintain with the surrounding natural world if they hope to survive in this place. Thus the journey was an interior process of the imagination, a growing awareness that being human is somehow different from all other life—animal, plant, and inanimate. Yet we are all from the same source: the awareness never deteriorated into Cartesian duality, cutting off the human from the natural world.

The people found the opening into the Fifth World too small to allow them or any of the animals to escape. They had sent a fly out through the small hole to tell them if it was the world which the Mother Creator had promised. It was, but there was the problem of getting out. The antelope

[4]Creation—*Tse'itsi'nako, Thought Woman, the Spider, thought about it, and everything she thought came into being. First she thought of three sisters for herself, and they helped her think of the rest of the Universe, including the Fifth World and the four worlds below. The Fifth World is the world we are living in today. There are four previous worlds below this world.* [Silko's note]

tried to butt the opening to enlarge it, but the antelope enlarged it only a little. It was necessary for the badger with her long claws to assist the antelope, and at last the opening was enlarged enough so that all the people and animals were able to emerge up into the Fifth World. The human beings could not have emerged without the aid of antelope and badger. The human beings depended upon the aid and charity of the animals. Only through interdependence could the human beings survive. Families belonged to clans, and it was by clan that the human being joined with the animal and plant world. Life on the high arid plateau became viable when the human beings were able to imagine themselves as sisters and brothers to the badger, antelope, clay, yucca, and sun. Not until they could find a viable relationship to the terrain, the landscape they found themselves in, could they *emerge.* Only at the moment the requisite balance between human and *other* was realized could the Pueblo people become a culture, a distinct group whose population and survival remained stable despite the vicissitudes of climate and terrain.

Landscape thus has similarities with dreams. Both have the power to seize terrifying feelings and deep instincts and translate them into images—visual, aural, tactile—into the concrete where human beings may more readily confront and channel the terrifying instincts or powerful emotions into rituals and narratives which reassure the individual while reaffirming cherished values of the group. The identity of the individual as a part of the group and the greater Whole is strengthened, and the terror of facing the world alone is extinguished.

Even now, the people at Laguna Pueblo spend the greater portion of social occasions recounting recent incidents or events which have occurred in the Laguna area. Nearly always, the discussion will precipitate the retelling of older stories about similar incidents or other stories connected with a specific place. The stories often contain disturbing or provocative material, but are nonetheless told in the presence of children and women. The effect of these inter-family or inter-clan exchanges is the reassurance for each person that she or he will never be separated or apart from the clan, no matter what might happen. Neither the worst blunders or disasters nor the greatest financial prosperity and joy will ever be permitted to isolate anyone from the rest of the group. In the ancient times, cohesiveness was all that stood between extinction and survival, and, while the individual certainly was recognized, it was always as an individual simultaneously bonded to family and clan by a complex bundle of custom and ritual. You are never the first to suffer a grave loss or profound humiliation. You are never the first, and you understand that you will probably not be the last to commit or be victimized by a repugnant act. Your family and clan are able to go on at length about others now passed on, others older or more experienced than you who suffered similar losses.

The wide deep arroyo near the Kings Bar (located across the reservation borderline) has over the years claimed many vehicles. A few years ago, when a Viet Nam veteran's new red Volkswagen rolled backwards into the arroyo while he was inside buying a six-pack of beer, the story of his loss joined the lively and large collection of stories already connected with that big arroyo. I do not know whether the Viet Nam veteran was consoled when he was told the stories about the other cars claimed by the ravenous arroyo. All his savings of combat pay had gone for the red Volkswagen. But this man could not have felt any worse than the man who, some years before, had left his children and mother-in-law in his station wagon with the engine running. When he came out of the liquor store his station wagon was gone. He found it and its passengers upside down in the big arroyo. Broken bones, cuts and bruises, and a total wreck of the car. The big arroyo has a wide mouth. Its existence needs no explanation. People in the area regard the arroyo much as they might regard a living being, which has a certain character and personality. I seldom drive past that wide deep arroyo without feeling a familiarity with and even a strange affection for this arroyo. Because as treacherous as it may be, the arroyo maintains a strong connection between human beings and the earth. The arroyo demands from us the caution and attention that constitute respect. It is this sort of respect the old believers have in mind when they tell us we must respect and love the earth.

Hopi Pueblo elders have said that the austere and, to some eyes, barren plains and hills surrounding their mesa-top villages actually help to nurture the spirituality of the Hopi *way*. The Hopi elders say the Hopi people might have settled in locations far more lush where daily life would not have been so grueling. But there on the high silent sandstone mesas that overlook the sandy arid expanses stretching to all horizons, the Hopi elders say the Hopi people must "live by their prayers" if they are to survive. The Hopi way cherishes the intangible: the riches realized from interaction and interrelationships with all beings above all else. Great abundances of material things, even food, the Hopi elders believe, tend to lure human attention away from what is most valuable and important. The views of the Hopi elders are not much different from those elders in all the Pueblos.

The bare vastness of the Hopi landscape emphasizes the visual impact of every plant, every rock, every arroyo. Nothing is overlooked or taken for granted. Each ant, each lizard, each lark is imbued with great value simply because the creature is there, simply because the creature is alive in a place where any life at all is precious. Stand on the mesa edge at

Walpai and look west over the bare distances toward the pale blue outlines of the San Francisco peaks where the ka'tsina spirits reside. So little
lies between you and the sky. So little lies between you and the earth.
One look and you know that simply to survive is a great triumph, that
every possible resource is needed, every possible ally—even the most
humble insect or reptile. You realize you will be speaking with all of
them if you intend to last out the year. Thus it is that the Hopi elders are
grateful to the landscape for aiding them in their quest as spiritual people.

VICKI HEARNE
B. 1952

*Vicki Hearne is a professional animal trainer and an assistant professor
of English at Yale. Born in Texas, she studied writing at Stanford University and has published two volumes of poetry,* Nervous Horses *(1980)*
and In the Absence of Horses *(1984).* Adam's Task *(1989) treats a
little-explored field of nature writing—the domestication of animals—
and explores Hearne's interest in the philosophical and ethical implications of her chosen profession.*

From ADAM'S TASK: CALLING ANIMALS BY NAME

CALLING ANIMALS BY NAME

> *And Adam gave names to all cattle, and to the fowl of the
> air, and to every beast of the field. . . .*
>
> Genesis 2:20

In the course of restoring Drummer Girl to herself, I obedience-
trained her, and in the course of doing this work with me, she learned
what her name was. In fact, although there are often problems even for
humans about learning their names, about knowing what one's own or

Adam's Task: Calling Animals by Name (New York: Knopf, 1986).

another's name is (as when I don't know whether to call you Freddie or Professor Jones), for us naming the animals is the original emblem of animal responsiveness to and interest in humans, in Genesis, our first text. An apocryphal expansion of the verse that forms the epigraph to this chapter says that not only did Adam name the animals but the moment he did, each recognized his or her name; the cow now knew she was Cow and came when called by name, and so it was like this, as John Hollander describes it:

> Every burrower, each flier,
>   Came for the name he had to give:
> Gay, first work, ever to be prior,
>   Not yet sunk to primitive.

Now it is the case, sadly, that many horses go through their whole lives without even knowing that they have a name, and this misleads some logicians into believing that they can't have names, and therefore can't have the mental faculties that go with knowing one's name. But in fact many horses learn their names, either informally around the barn or stable, just as most humans learn their names, or through formal obedience work of the sort I did with Salty and Drummer Girl.

I would like to take a little time here to consider the general implications of naming and acknowledging naming. I see us—meaning anyone possessed of that particular sort of literacy that makes him/her want to write and read books like this one—as not being in the enviable position Adam was when he named the animals—"not yet sunk to primitive." I don't mean that we are primitive in our consciousness but rather that we have gone on to a further distancing. We did this when we learned to write and thus to add to the possibilities of consciousness conceptions made possible by typography of various sorts. One example of this is the advance in mathematical thinking when numerals were devised and replaced the prose descriptions of arithmetic. It was typography that eventually made statistics possible and all of the errors as well as the epiphanies of statistical thinking.

Typography has also made possible further gaps between us and animals, because we have become able to give them labels without ever calling them by name. The registered names of most horses and dogs are primary examples. Champion Redheath Nimble Gunner, C.D., C.D.X., U.D., for example, is not a name but something halfway between labels (of the sort found on packing lists or in livestock inventories) and titles—not titles such as Sir, Madam or Your Highness, but titles like the titles of books. Such names are bookkeeping.

It is only when I am saying, "Gunner, Come!" that the dog has a name. His name becomes larger when we proceed to "Gunner, Fetch!" and eventually when he and his name become near enough to being the same size, he is as close to having a proper name as anyone ever gets. When Drummer Girl learned her name, one of the things it meant was that she became able to fit into her name properly; when I said in her story that "her soul was several sizes too large for her," I could as accurately have said that her soul was several sizes too large for the truncated version of a "name" she had so far had, not a name she could answer to. Without a name and someone to call her by name, she couldn't enter the moral life.

There are other things at stake. I knew a woman named Shelley Mason, who took a job running an animal shelter in a small desert town. She didn't do this because she thought that the activity of merely housing dogs and feeding them was an especially meaningful activity (especially as one of her duties was destroying unwanted animals) but because she understood the importance of training as a way of increasing the number of animals who were wanted and who would not be abandoned, thus reducing the piles of corpses. She figured that from that small shelter she could insist that anyone who adopted a dog learn at least the rudiments of training a dog to heel and sit before they were allowed to take the dog home, thereby of necessity naming the dog. And she usually had several dogs from the shelter at her house, teaching them more advanced work in order to increase their chances of placement.

One day when I was visiting her, she gestured at the dogs, most of them doomed, in the runs at the shelter and said, "Goddamit! Most of them wouldn't be here if only they knew their names!"

The grammar of the world we imagine when we call creatures by name is not the grammar of the world in which they have no names, is not the same form of life. But our grammar, or maybe I mean punctuation or typography, has given us the possibility of attenuations of naming, of names that are not invocative. Consider for example that

I am involved with a dog

does not indicate a world as fully as when we say

I am involved with a dog called "Annie"

or

I am involved with "Annie."

The last example gives the feel of a more committed and thoughtful relationship than the first two do, but it is still a disturbing (to me) convention of English punctuation to put what philosophers call scare quotes around animal names, to indicate that these aren't real names, in the way Vicki Hearne is, and even many animal lovers conventionally use the pronoun "it" rather than "he" or "she" to refer to an animal. I find this to be extraordinarily weird, evidence of the superstitions that control the institutionalization of thought. It is as weird, to me, as these examples:

> I am married to "Robert."
> Pass the butter, "Robert."
> Kiss me, "Robert."
> I wish "Robert" would return.

When I asked my husband, whose name in fact is not "Robert," but Robert, to look at those sentences, he reported feeling a slight jolt of uneasiness, as though what had been a name for a person—his person—had suddenly become something like a label, and the uneasiness—the dis-ease—is the uneasiness of someone the labeler won't and can't talk to.

Obedience-training horses creates a logic that demands not only the use of a call name, since the imperatives demand it, especially for the command "Dobbin, Come!" but also the removal of the quotes from the name, the making of the name into a real name rather than a label for a piece of property, which is what most racehorses' names are.

Which leads me to my final small point about the disciplines of naming, one of which is horse training. I believe that the disciplines come to us in the form they do because deep in human beings is the impulse to perform Adam's task, to name animals and people as well, and to name them in such a way that the grammar is flexible enough to do at least two things. One is to make names that give the soul room for expansion. My talk of the change from utterances such as "Belle, Sit!" to "Belle, Go find!" is an example of names projecting the creature named into more glorious contexts. Our awareness of the importance of this is indicated, at least partially, by the fact that we have occasions to say, "Well, Rosemary has really made a name for herself."

But I think our impulse is also conservative, an impulse to return to Adam's divine condition. I can't imagine how we would do that, or what it would be like, but linguistic anthropology has found out some things about illiterate peoples that suggest at least names that really call, language that is genuinely invocative and uncontaminated by writing and thus by the concept of names as labels rather than genuine invocations.

I once, for example, heard a linguist talking about the days when the interest in learning and especially recording illiterate languages revealed some surprises. One of his stories was about an eager linguist in some culturally remote corner trying to elicit from a peasant the nominative form of "cow" in the peasant's language.

The linguist met with frustrations. When he asked, "What do you call that animal?" pointing to the peasant's cow, he got, instead of the nominative of "cow," the vocative of "Bossie." When he tried again, asking, "Well, what do you call your neighbor's animal that moos and gives milk?" the peasant replied, "Why should I call my neighbor's animal?"

Since I am a creature born to writing, my horses are not born to their names but to their labels, and care and discipline are required. The dog trainer's knowledge of genuine names—"call name," in fact, is the technical term for a true name—is one of the reasons true trainers say, as I reported in my discussion of Salty, "Joe, Sit!" less frequently than most people and to fewer dogs. They know what the peasant in the linguist's story knew—there has to be a reason for a name or else there is no name.

I am not arguing against advances in culture, only pointing out that it is paradoxically the case that some advances create the need for other advances that will take us back to what we call the primitive, even if not all the way back to paradise, to that region of consciousness in which naming is "Gay, first work, ever to be prior, not yet sunk to primitive." But no advance will enable me to call Drummer Girl with anything less than her name, which is why obedience training is centrally a sacred and poetic rather than a philosophical or scientific discipline.

GARY PAUL NABHAN
B. 1952

Gary Nabhan is an ethnobiologist—one who studies the relationship between native cultures and traditionally used plants and animals. He is co-founder of Native Seeds—SEARCH, *a nonprofit organization that maintains seed banks of indigenous southwestern plants, and is assistant director of research at the Desert Botanical Garden in Phoenix. His books,* The Desert Smells Like Rain *(1982) and* Gathering the Desert *(1985), winner of the John Burroughs Medal, come from his work with the Papago Indians of southwestern Arizona. Nabhan's books show more than an ecologist's interest in their desert-adaptive traditions and the potential value of little known plant varieties. He writes with great appreciation of the Indians' sense of history and ritual interaction with the desert and convincingly of their seemingly paradoxical sense of the desert as a place of great fertility and vitality.*

From THE DESERT SMELLS LIKE RAIN: A NATURALIST IN PAPAGO INDIAN COUNTRY

AN OVERTURE

> With many dust storms, with many lightnings, with
> many thunders, with many rainbows, it started to go.
> From within wet mountains, more clouds came out
> and joined it.
> —Joseph Pancho, *Mockingbird Speech*

Last Saturday before dusk, the summer's 114-degree heat broke to 79 within an hour. A fury of wind whipped up, pelting houses with dust, debris, and gravel. Then a scatter of rain came, as a froth of purplish clouds charged across the skies. As the last of the sun's light dissipated, we could see Baboquivari Peak silhouetted on a red horizon, lightning dancing around its head.

The rains came that night—they changed the world.

Crusty dry since April, the desert floor softened under the rain's dance. Near the rain-pocked surface, hundreds of thousands of wild sprouts of bloodroot amaranth are popping off their seedcoats and diving toward light. Barren places will soon be shrouded in a veil of green.

Desert arroyos are running again, muddy water swirling after a head of suds, dung, and detritus. Where sheetfloods pool, buried animals awake, or new broods hatch. At dawn, dark egg-shaped clouds of flying ants hover over ground, excited in the early morning light.

In newly filled waterholes, spadefoot toads suddenly congregate. The males bellow. They seek out mates, then latch onto them with their

The Desert Smells Like Rain: A Naturalist in Papago Indian Country (San Francisco: North Point Press, 1982).

special nuptial pads. The females spew out egg masses into the hot murky water. For two nights, the toad ponds are wild with chanting while the Western spadefoot's burnt-peanut-like smell looms thick in the air.

A yellow mud turtle crawls out of the drenched bottom of an old adobe borrow pit where he had been buried through the hot dry spell. He plods a hundred yards over to a floodwater reservoir and dives in. He has no memory of how many days it's been since his last swim, but the pull of the water—*that* is somehow familiar.

This is the time when the Papago Indians of the Sonoran Desert celebrate the coming of the rainy season moons, the *Jujkiabig Mamsad,* and the beginning of a new year.

Fields lying fallow since the harvest of the winter crop are now ready for another planting. If sown within a month after summer solstice, they can produce a crop quick enough for harvest by the Feast of San Francisco, October 4.

When I went by the Madrugada home in Little Tucson on Monday, the family was eagerly talking about planting the flashflood field again. At the end of June, Julian wasn't even sure if he would plant this year— no rain yet, too hot to prepare the field, and hardly any water left in their *charco* catchment basin.

Now, a fortnight later, the pond is nearly filled up to the brim. Runoff has fed into it through four small washes. Sheetfloods have swept across the field surface. Julian imagines big yellow squash blossoms in his field, just another month or so away. It makes his mouth water.

Once I asked a Papago youngster what the desert smelled like to him. He answered with little hesitation:

"The desert smells like rain."

His reply is a contradiction in the minds of most people. How could the desert smell like rain, when deserts are, by definition, places which lack substantial rainfall?

The boy's response was a sort of Papago shorthand. Hearing Papago can be like tasting a delicious fruit, while sensing that the taste comes from a tree with roots too deep to fathom.

The question had triggered a scent—creosote bushes after a storm— their aromatic oils released by the rains. His nose remembered being out in the desert, overtaken: *the desert smells like rain.*

Most outsiders are struck by the apparent absence of rain in deserts, feeling that such places lack something vital. Papago, on the other hand,

are intrigued by the unpredictability rather than the paucity of rainfall—
theirs is a dynamic, lively world, responsive to stormy forces that may
come at any time.

A Sonoran Desert village may receive five inches of rain one year and
fifteen the next. A single storm may dump an inch and a half in the
matter of an hour on one field and entirely skip another a few miles away.
Dry spells lasting four months may be broken by a single torrential
cloudburst, then resume again for several more months. Unseasonal
storms, and droughts during the customary rainy seasons, are frequent
enough to reduce patterns to chaos.

The Papago have become so finely tuned to this unpredictability that
it shapes the way they speak of rain. It has also ingrained itself deeply in
the structure of their language.

Linguist William Pilcher has observed that the Papago discuss events
in terms of their probability of occurrence, avoiding any assumption that
an event will happen for sure:

> . . . it is my impression that the Papago abhor the idea of making definite
> statements. I am still in doubt as to how close a rain storm must be before
> one may properly say *t'o tju:* (It is going to rain on us), rather than *tki'o
> tju:ks* (something like: It looks like it may be going to rain on us).

Since few Papago are willing to confirm that something will happen
until it does, an element of surprise becomes part of almost everything.
Nothing is ever really cut and dried. When rains do come, they're a gift,
a windfall, a lucky break.

Elderly Papago have explained to me that rain is more than just water.
There are different ways that water comes to living things, and what it
brings with it affects how things grow.

Remedio Cruz was once explaining to me why he plants the old
White Sonora variety of wheat when he does. He had waited for some
early January rains to gently moisten his field before he planted.

"That Pap'go wheat—it's good to plant just in January or early February. It grows good on just the *rain* water from the sky. It would not do
good with water from the *ground,* so that's why we plant it when those
soft winter rains come to take care of it."

In the late 1950s, a Sonoran Desert ecologist tried to simulate the
gentle winter rains in an attempt to make the desert bloom. Lloyd Tevis
used untreated groundwater from a well, sprayed up through a sprinkler,
to encourage wildflower germination on an apparently lifeless patch of
desert. While Tevis did trigger germination of one kind of desert wildflower with a little less than two inches of fake rain, none germinated

with less than an inch. In general, production of other wildflowers required more than three or four inches of fake rain.

Tevis was then surprised to see what happened when less than an inch of real rain fell on his experimental site in January. He noticed in the previously sparse vegetation "a tremendous emergence of seedlings. Real rain demonstrated an extraordinary superiority over the artificial variety to bring about a high rate of germination." With one particular kind of desert wildflower, seedlings were fifty-six times more numerous after nearly an inch of real rain than they were after the more intense artificial watering.

The stimulating power of rain in the desert is simply more than moisture. Be it the nutrients released in a rainstorm, or the physical force of the water, there are other releasing mechanisms associated with rainwater. But even if someone worked up a better simulation of rain using *fortified* groundwater, would it be very useful in making the desert bloom?

Doubtful. Remedio himself wonders about the value of groundwater pumping for farming, for water is something he *sings* rather than pumps into his field. Every summer, Remedio and a few elderly companions sing to bring the waters from the earth and sky to meet each other. Remedio senses that only with this meeting will his summer beans, corn, and squash grow. A field relying solely on groundwater would not have what it takes. He has heard that well water has some kind of "medicine" (chemical) in it that is no good for crops. In addition, he believes that groundwater pumping as much as twenty miles away adversely affects the availability of moisture to his field.

I joined in a study with other scientists to compare the nutritive value of tepary beans grown in Papago flashflood fields with those grown in modern Anglo-American-style groundwater-irrigated fields nearby. The protein content of the teparies grown in the traditional flashflood environments tended to be higher than that of the same tepary bean varieties grown with water pumped from the ground. Production appeared to be more efficient in the Papago fields—more food energy was gained with less energy in labor and fuel spent. No wonder—it is a way of agriculture that has fine-tuned itself to local conditions over generations.

There they are, Julian and Remedio—growing food in a desert too harsh for most kinds of agriculture—using cues that few of us would ever notice. Their sense of how the desert works comes from decades of day-to-day observations. These perceptions have been filtered through a cultural tradition that has been refined, honed, and handed down over centuries of living in arid places.

If others wish to adapt to the Sonoran Desert's peculiarities, this ancient knowledge can serve as a guide. Yet the best guide will tell you: there are certain things you must learn on your own. The desert is unpredictable, enigmatic. One minute you will be smelling dust. The next, the desert can smell just like rain.

TERRY TEMPEST WILLIAMS
B. 1955

Terry Tempest Williams is Naturalist-in-Residence at the Utah Museum of Natural History in Salt Lake City. She says that she writes "through my biases of gender, geography, and culture, that I am a woman whose ideas have been shaped by the Colorado Plateau and the Great Basin, that these ideas are then sorted out through the prism of my culture—and my culture is Mormon. Those tenets of family and community that I see at the heart of that culture are then articulated through story." Her first book, Pieces of White Shell: A Journey to Navajoland *(1984), based on her experiences as a teacher among the Navajo, is a personal retelling and exploration of Native American myths. The strong link between story and landscape is further explored in* Coyote's Canyon *(1989), personal narratives of southern Utah's desert canyons in collaboration with photographer John Telford. The following essay records her first visit to the Serengeti Plains of Kenya two generations after another "outsider in Maasailand"—Isak Dinesen.*

IN THE COUNTRY OF GRASSES

Traveling, for a naturalist, into unfamiliar territory is like turning a kaleidoscope ninety degrees. Suddenly the colors and pieces of glass find a new arrangement. The light shifts, and you enter a new landscape in search of the order you know to be there.

As a naturalist who calls the Great Basin home, I entered the Seren-

VII Magazine, vol. 1, no. 1, October 1987.

geti Plains of Africa with beginner's eyes. The sky arched over me like a taut bow. George Schaller describes the Serengeti as "a boundless region with horizons so wide one can see clouds between the legs of an ostrich."

This is true. It is also true that the Serengeti ecosystem is defined by the hooves of migrating wildebeests. It covers the borders of Tanzania and Kenya like the stretched skin of an animal—25,000 square kilometers of open plains and wooded grasslands harbor one of the last refuges on earth where great herds of animals and their predators can wander at will.

I chose to wander in the northern appendage of these plains, in an area known as Maasai Mara.

The Mara is Kenya's most stunning reserve. It is wild, uninterrupted country capable of capturing one's spirit like cool water in a calabash. And it appears endless as its southern boundary is contiguous with Tanzania's Serengeti National Park.

The Mara belongs to the Maasai or the Maasai to the Mara. The umbilical cord between man and earth has not been severed here. They are a fierce and proud people who pasture their cattle next to leopard and lion. The Maasai are fearless. They know the songs of grasses and the script of snakes. They move like thin shadows across the savannah. A warrior with a red cloak draped over his shoulder stands silhouetted against the sun. Beef-eaters, blood-drinkers, the Maasai are one of the last strongholds of nomadic life.

Samuel Kiplangat was my guide in the Mara. He is Maasai. The stretched holes in the lobes of his ears are like small windows and a reminder of the traditional life he has left behind. But he has not abandoned his native intelligence. Samuel felt the presence of animals long before he saw them. I watched him pull animals out of crypsis with his eyes. I saw him penetrate stillness with his senses.

When traveling to new country, it is a gift to have a guide. They know the nuances of the world they live in. Samuel smells rain the night before it falls. I trust his instincts and borrow them until I uncover my own. But there is danger here. One can become lazy in the reliance of a guide. The burden of a newcomer is to pay attention.

The land rover slips into the savannah like a bird dog entering a marsh. We are fully present. I watch Samuel's eyes scan the horizon. He points south.

"Zebra," he says. "They are migrating north from Tanzania. Thousands more are on their way."

Hundreds of zebras walk the skyline. They become animated heat waves.

We drive closer. I have never seen such concentrations of animals. At one point I think I hear thunder. It is the hooves of wildebeests. Suddenly, the herd of zebra expands to include impalas, gazelles, and animals I do not recognize.

"Topi," Samuel says.

I flip through my field guide of African mammals and find it. An extraordinary creature, it is the color of mahogany with blue patches on its flanks and ocher legs. I look at the topi again, this time through binoculars. Its black linear face with spiraling horns creates the illusion of a primitive mask. The topi I watch stands motionless on a termite mound. Binoculars down, I look at Samuel. He says the topi resemble hartebeests. A small herd of topi runs in front of the vehicle in a rocking-horse gait and vanishes.

Samuel gives away his knowledge sparingly—in gentle, quiet doses. He is respectful of his teachers and those he is teaching. In this way, he is generous. He gives me the pleasure of discovery. Slowly, African riddles unravel themselves like a piece of cut linen.

The sweet hissing of grasses accompanies us as we move ahead. We pass the swishing tails of wildebeests. We are looking for lions.

Anticipation is another gift for travelers in unfamiliar territory. It quickens the spirit. The contemplation of the unseen world; imagination piqued in consideration of animals.

We stop. Samuel points. I see nothing. I look at Samuel for clues. He points again. I still see nothing but tall, tawny grasses around the base of a lone tree. He smiles and says, "Lions."

I look. I look so hard it becomes an embarrassment—and then I see eyes. Lion eyes. Two amber beads with a brown matrix. Circles of contentment until I stand; the lion's eyes change, and I am flushed with fear.

"Quiet," Samuel whispers. "We will watch for awhile."

As my eyes become acquainted with lion, I begin to distinguish fur from grass. I realize there are two lions, a male and female lying together under the stingy shade of a thorn tree. I can hear them breathe. The male is breathing hard and fast, his black mane in rhythm with the breeze. He puts his right paw on the female's shoulder. Ears twitch. We are no more than 10 feet away. He yawns. His yellow canines are as long as my index finger. His jowls look like well-worn leather. He stands. The grasses brush his belly. Veins protrude from his leg muscles. This lion is lean and strong. No wonder in the Maasi mind every aspect of a lion is embued with magic.

Acting oblivious to us, he moves to the other side of the tree. From the protection of the land rover, we spot a fresh kill. It is a wildebeest whose black flesh has been peeled back from a red scaffolding of bones.

The lion sits on his haunches and feeds. He separates the wildebeest's legs with his paws and slowly sinks his teeth into the groin. He pulls and tears large strips of meat. With his head tilted, his carnassials slice more muscle and viscera from the body cavity. His rasping tongue licks the blood from the bones. Ribs snap. His claws clamp down on the wildebeest as though escape was still possible.

The carcass is like a cave that the lion enters. He growls, and the female joins him. He nibbles her ear and then licks her face and neck. I am startled by his blood-stained muzzle. Side by side, two lions devour their prey.

The sensuality of predator-prey relations is riveting. My Great Basin eyes transfer lion and wildebeest to mountain lion and mule deer. The guffawing hyena on the periphery of the pride becomes a coyote squinting through sage.

The wildebeest is smothered by the lion's paw. Who knows how long they will stay. Night falls, and beyond the pride of lions, hyenas jockey for their place among bones. Beyond hyenas, jackals pace. Finally, white-backed vultures clean the kill as ravens do in the desert. There is no such thing as waste except in the world of man. The concentric circles which bind a healthy habitat include vulnerable and venerable species.

It is a familiar scenario, predator and prey, as though a shaft of light falls in the forgotten corner of an attic, and a precious possession is retrieved. We too are predators. A primal memory is struck like a match.

I hold on to a rope between two poles. I grip with both hands the life I live and the one I have forgotten. When in the presence of natural order, we remember a potentiality of life which has been overgrown by civilization.

Morning comes quickly near the equator. There is little delineation of dawn. On the Serengeti, it is either day or night. A peculiar lull occurs just before sunrise. The world is cool and still. Gradually, the sun climbs the ladder of clouds until the sky mirrors the nacreous hues of abalone.

Samuel tells us this morning we will look for rhinos. I dream of looking into the eyes of these creatures, but Samuel warns us our chances are few. There are only two rhinoceros in the region. Only two. Male and female.

No one speaks for some time. The isolation of endangered species is disquieting. Two rhinos. And in 10 years what will the count be?

We drive towards Rhino Ridge. It is broken country—rugged, pocked, and gnarled. Volcanic boulders lie on the land like corpses of stone. Even if we don't see rhino, I say to myself, it is good to know where they live.

Samuel points out a dung heap around a small bush. Tracks surrounding the mound indicate spreading of the dung. A well-trodden path is also apparent. I later learn from Samuel that because rhinos are solitary and nomadic, they have a complex olfactory system of communication. These "lavatories" are an indirect means of keeping in touch.

I am fascinated by what Samuel sees and what I am missing. In the Great Basin I can read the landscape well. I know the subtleties of place. Horned lizard buried in the sand cannot miss my eyes because I anticipate his. A kit fox at night streaks across the road. His identity is told by the beam of my headlights. And when great horned owl hoots above my head, I hoot too. Home is the range of one's instincts.

As a naturalist, I yearn to extend my range like the nomadic lion, rhino, or Maasai. But in remote and unfamiliar territory, I must learn to read the landscape inch by inch. The grasses become braille as I run my fingers through them.

Samuel is listening. I listen too. My attention is splayed between hoopoes and hyenas. Suddenly, there is a rumbling. Samuel nods. Elephants. A herd of a dozen or more, young and old, thunder through the underbrush. Trunks flaring, waving up and down, ears fanning back and forth, tusks on the front end, tails at the rear. These were animals I had never imagined wild. As they pass, I focus on their skin. It is a landscape unto itself. The folds and creases in the hide become basin and range topography.

In the scheme of the savannah, the elephant breaks into forests and opens wooded country to the vegetation and animals of the plains. The rhino depends on the elephant to create a transition zone from woodlands to grasslands. Under natural conditions, a new generation of elephants would migrate to another area and repeat the cycle of vegetative succession. But with man's encroachment there is not much space left for the emigration of elephants. The land becomes abused, and rhinos are left with less options for range. Even in Maasai Mara, whose appearance is primordial, natural equilibrium is shifting.

Samuel and I follow a bushfire. The smoke is a serpent winding down the Siria Escarpment. My eyes burn. Suddenly, Samuel freezes.

"Rhinos," he says. "Two rhinos."

Through the wildebeests, through the zebras, topi, and gazelles—I see two beasts the color of pewter moving quickly over the ridge. I guess them to be a mile away.

As we advance closer and closer, the anticipation of seeing rhinoceros is like crossing the threshold of a dream. The haze lifts and there they are—two rhinos, male and female, placidly eating grass with prehensile lips. Their prehistoric skin is reminiscent of another time. It is the spirit of the animal that stands. Two rhinos, their eyes hidden in the folds of their armor. Oxpeckers perch on crescent horns. I catch the female's eye. She does not waver.

My vision blurs. Who would kill a rhinoceros? It seems clear that the true aphrodisiac is not found in their horns but in simply knowing they exist.

Only a few minutes of daylight remain. We leave. I look back one more time. From a distance, they have become outcroppings of stone. Two rhinos on the Serengeti Plains.

In *Out of Africa,* Isak Dinesen writes about what it means to be an outsider in Maasailand. She says, "I feel that it might altogether be described as the existence of a person who had come from a rushed and noisy world into still country."

We have forgotten what we can count on. The natural world provides refuge. In the Great Basin, I know the sounds of strutting grouse and the season when sage blooms. A rattlesnake coiled around the base of greasewood is both a warning and a wonder. In Maasai Mara, marabou storks roost before sunset and baboons move in the morning. The dappled light on leaves may be leopard in a tree. These are the patterns that awaken us to our surroundings. Each of us harbors a homeland, a landscape we naturally comprehend. By understanding the dependability of place, we can anchor ourselves as trees.

One night, Jonas Ole Sademaki, a Maasai elder, and I sit around the fire telling stories. Sparks enter the ebony sky and find their places among stars.

"My people worship trees," he says. "It was the tree that gave birth to the Maasai. Grasses are also trustworthy. When a boy is beaten for an inappropriate act, the boy falls to the ground and clutches a handful of grass. His elder takes this gesture as a sign of humility. The child remembers where the source of his power lies."

As I walk back to my tent, I stop and look up at the southern cross. These are new constellations for me. I kneel in the grasses and hold tight.

SELECTED BIBLIOGRAPHY

In addition to the works cited in the headnotes and text and the general collections mentioned in the Acknowledgments, we list here some anthologies for further reading of individual authors:

Edward Abbey, *Slumgullion Stew: An Edward Abbey Reader* (New York: Dutton, 1984).

John James Audubon, *Audubon Reader: The Best Writings of John James Audubon*, Scott Russell Sanders, ed. (Bloomington, IN: Indiana University Press, 1986).

Henry Beston, *Especially Maine: The Natural World of Henry Beston, from Cape Cod to the St. Lawrence*, Elizabeth Coatsworth, ed. (Brattleboro, VT: Stephen Greene, 1970).

John Burroughs, *John Burroughs' America*, Farida A. Wiley, ed. (Greenwich, CT: Devin-Adair, 1951).

Samuel Clemens, *The Portable Mark Twain*, Bernard De Voto, ed. (New York: Penguin, 1977).

Samuel Taylor Coleridge, *The Portable Coleridge*, Ivor A. Richards, ed. (New York: Penguin, 1977).

Charles Darwin, *Darwin: A Norton Critical Edition*, Philip Appleman, ed. (New York: Norton, 1979).

Isak Dinesen, *Isak Dinesen's Africa: Images of the Wild Continent from the Writer's Life and Words* (San Francisco: Sierra Club, 1985).

Loren Eiseley, *The Star Thrower* (New York: Times Books, 1978).

Ralph Waldo Emerson, *Emerson in His Journals*, Joel Porte, ed. (Cambridge, MA: Belknap Press, 1982).

J. Henri Fabre, *The Insect World of J. Henri Fabre*, Edwin Way Teale, ed. (New York: Dodd, Mead, 1961).

Edward Hoagland, *Heart's Desire: The Best of Edward Hoagland* (New York: Simon & Schuster, 1988).

Gerard Manley Hopkins, *Gerard Manley Hopkins: Selected Prose*, Gerald Roberts, ed. (New York: Oxford University Press, 1980).

W.H. Hudson, *The Best of W.H. Hudson*, Odell Shepard, ed. (New York: Dutton, 1949).

Richard Jefferies, *Landscape with Figures: An Anthology of Richard Jefferies's Prose,* Richard Mabey, ed. (New York: Penguin, 1983).

Joseph Wood Krutch, *The Best Nature Writing of Joseph Wood Krutch* (New York: William Morrow, 1970).

D.H. Lawrence, *The Portable D.H. Lawrence,* Diana Trilling, ed. (New York: Penguin, 1977).

John McPhee, *The John McPhee Reader,* William L. Howarth, ed. (New York: Farrar, Straus & Giroux, 1976).

Farley Mowat, *The World of Farley Mowat: A Selection from His Work,* Peter Davison, ed. (Boston: Little, Brown, 1980).

John Muir, *The Wilderness World of John Muir,* Edwin Way Teale, ed. (Boston: Houghton Mifflin, 1954).

George Orwell, *The Orwell Reader: Fiction, Essays and Reportage* (New York: Harcourt, Brace, 1961).

Sigurd Olson, *Songs of the North: A Sigurd Olson Reader,* Howard Frank Mosher, ed. (New York: Penguin, 1987).

John Steinbeck, *The Portable Steinbeck,* Pascal Covici, ed. (New York: Penguin, 1976).

Henry David Thoreau, *Walden and Other Writings,* Brooks Atkinson, ed. (New York: Modern Library, 1981).

E.B. White, *Essays of E.B. White* (New York: Harper & Row, 1979).

Gilbert White, *The Essential Gilbert White of Selborne,* H. J. Massingham, ed. (Boston: David Godine, 1985).

PERMISSIONS

INDEX